THEORY OF FORMAL LANGUAGES WITH APPLICATIONS

THEORY OF FORMAL LANGUAGES WITH APPLICATIONS

Dan A Simovici
Richard L Tenney
Department of Mathematics and Computer Science,
University of Massachusetts at Boston

World Scientific
Singapore • New Jersey • London • Hong Kong

Published by

World Scientific Publishing Co. Pte. Ltd.

P O Box 128, Farrer Road, Singapore 912805

USA office: Suite 1B, 1060 Main Street, River Edge, NJ 07661

UK office: 57 Shelton Street, Covent Garden, London WC2H 9HE

British Library Cataloguing-in-Publication Data
A catalogue record for this book is available from the British Library.

THEORY OF FORMAL LANGUAGES WITH APPLICATIONS

ISBN 981-02-3729-4

Printed in Singapore by Uto-Print

Contents

Preface

The theory of formal languages has a long and dignified history. A major influence on the nascent theory, around 1960, were the attempts of the linguist Noam Chomsky to formulate a general theory of the syntax of natural languages. Chomsky's intellectual itinerary greatly influenced the field at a time when computers were starting to cope with increasingly complex tasks. A melting pot of ideas then developed, with a surprising convergence of thought between linguists, mathematicians, logicians, and newly born computer scientists.

At present, formal languages are part of the basic training of most computer scientists. They are everywhere to be found in the design and in the very operation of computer systems. A modem, like an interface manager, will have to respond to various external stimuli. Its design and its behavior are then best understood when it is viewed as a device reacting to external events while being governed by a finite set of rules—in short, a finite automaton. Next, the syntax of programming languages is best described by context-free grammars, themselves recognized by pushdown automata. We then have available one of the fundamental building blocks of the design of parsers and compilers. Finally, the last steps of the complexity ladder take us to languages of a higher structural complexity, which swiftly lead to (un)decidability questions. This brings us to the humbling realization that mathematically well-posed problems are far from being all decidable!

The theory of formal languages and their companion automata thus provides a powerful approach to the design of systems and to a variety of problems in computer science. Dan Simovici and Richard Tenney develop the core theory in a lucid manner. Their self-contained presentation combines mathematical rigor and intellectually stimulating applications. For instance, the reader will find in the book a perspective on algorithms for the processing of text files, lexical analysis, and parsing. A notably innovative aspect is the last part that offers two chapters on coding theory, data compression, as well as biological applications. It should be a pleasure for most to discover there formal models that describe the development of simple organisms or the splicing of nucleic acids.

To make a long story short, we have here a new book that offers new perspectives on an old subject. It contains a thorough treatment of a theory that is fundamental not only in computer science but in many other scientific endeavors. The authors have done a great job of exposition. I hope you will enjoy reading the book as much as I did.

Philippe Flajolet
Rocquencourt, February 28, 1999

Preface

Introduction

The theory of formal languages is an important part of the fundamental education of computer scientists and linguists. It is also becoming significant for biologists. This discipline blends algebraic techniques with abstract models of computing devices. Its origins can be traced to the work of Chomsky, Rabin, Scott, Nerode, Ginsburg, and Schützenberger, and this beautiful area of theoretical computer science remains active today. Along the way are such milestones as the theory of abstract families of languages and various applications of the theory of complexity in the study of formal languages.

This book combines algebraic and algorithmic methods with decidability results and explores applications both within and outside computer science.

Formal languages provide the theoretical underpinnings for the study of programming languages. They are also the foundation for compiler design, and they are important in such areas as data compression, computer networks, etc. Recently, formal languages have been applied in biology and economics.

The first part of the book presents mathematical preliminaries. It begins with a chapter that elucidates the mathematical background expected of the reader—elementary notions about sets, algebras, and graphs—as well as the notation that we use. It is intended to make this book as self-contained as practical. The second chapter deals with words and languages viewed as collections of words. These are basic ingredients in the discipline of formal languages, so this chapter presents the most important algebraic and combinatorial properties of words and languages in order to make later chapters more readable.

The second part is centered on regular and context-free languages. The class of regular languages is studied in the third chapter, starting with deterministic finite automata. We then consider various extensions of these devices, including nondeterministic automata and transition systems, as alternative ways of defining the same class of languages. We introduce regular expressions as notations for regular languages, and we conclude the chapter by examining several applications of the notions developed in the chapter.

The fourth chapter introduces the notions of semi-Thue system, and especially important, the notion of grammar. We study Chomsky's hierarchy, and we show the closure of each Chomsky class with respect to the regular operations.

We place particular emphasis on context-free languages due to their role in compiler design. This class of languages is introduced using the class of context-free grammars; the devices that provide an alternative characterization of this class, pushdown automata are discussed in the next chapter. To allow us to include topics that are usually not found in text books, we minimize our discussion of applications to compilers. There are excellent texts that cover this area.

The third part of the book focuses on the algorithmic aspects of formal languages.

We use labeled Markov algorithms and Turing machines as general abstract models of computation. We cover undecidability results starting with the halting problem for Turing machines and the Post correspondence problem and continuing with undecidability results for various classes of languages. Particular attention is paid in to the class of context-sensitive languages.

The last part of the book presents applications of formal language theory. We have chosen two distinct and representative areas: coding theory over free monoids, important for computer communications and applications of formal languages in biology. We believe that the presence of these applications motivates students to study formal languages.

The book is intended as a textbook for an upper-level undergraduate or a graduate course is formal languages.

Each chapter ends with suggestions for further reading. The book contains more than 600 exercises; they form an integral part of the material. Some of the exercises are in reality supplemental material. For these, we include solutions.

The authors are grateful for support received from the University of Massachusetts at Boston and extend special thanks to Professors Tatsuo Higuchi, Michitaka Kameyama, and Akira Maruoka from Tohoku University, who hosted Dan Simovici in 1998.

Part I

Introductory Notions

Chapter 1

Preliminaries

1.1 Introduction

In this chapter we present some mathematical preliminaries intended to provide a referrence for the reader. We discuss basic facts of set theory, universal algebra and the notion of cardinality of a set.

1.2 Sets, Relations, and Functions

In this section we review briefly some concepts from set theory.

1.2.1 Sets

Informally, a set is a collection of objects, called *elements*. For any set S and object a, either a is one of the objects in S or it is not. In the former case, we use any of the following phrases: "a is a member of S," "a is an element of S," or "a is in S," and we write $a \in S$.

The elements of a set $\mathcal{C}$ may be themselves sets; in such cases, we refer to $\mathcal{C}$ as a *collection* of sets.

We use the following notations for various subsets of the set $\mathbb{R}$ of real numbers:

$\mathbb{N}$ for the set of natural numbers
$\mathbb{P}$ for the set of positive integers
$\mathbb{Q}$ for the set of rational numbers
$\mathbb{Z}$ for the set of integers

Let S and T be two sets. The set S is *included* in T (or S is a *subset* of T) if every element of S is an element of T. In this case, we write $S \subseteq T$. If S is not a subset of T, we write $S \not\subseteq T$.

If S and T are sets such that $S \subseteq T$ and $S \neq T$, then we say that S is *strictly included* in T. We denote this by $S \subset T$. If S is not strictly included in T, we write $S \not\subset T$.

There exists a set with no members. This set is called the *empty set* and is denoted by $\emptyset$.

A *singleton* is a set $\{x\}$ that consists of a unique element.

If S is a set, then the *power set* of S is the set that consists of all the subsets of S. We denote the power set of S by $\mathcal{P}(S)$.

Note that for every set S, $\emptyset \in \mathcal{P}(S)$, so $\mathcal{P}(S)$ is never empty.

1.2.2 Ordered Pairs and Cartesian Products

Given two objects a and b, we can form the set $\{a, b\}$, which we refer to as an *unordered pair.*

Definition 1.2.1 Let a and b be two objects. The *ordered pair*, or simply, the *pair*, (a, b) is the collection of sets $\{\{a\}, \{a, b\}\}$. □

The pair (a, a) is the singleton $\{\{a\}\}$. Conversely, if (a, b) is a singleton then $\{a, b\} = \{a\}$, so $b \in \{a\}$, that is, $b = a$.

It is easy to see that if $(a, b) = (c, d)$, then $a = c$ and $b = d$. For the pair (a, b), we call a the *first component* and b its *second component.*

Definition 1.2.2 Let A and B be two sets. The *Cartesian product* of A and B, written $A \times B$, is the set of all pairs (a, b) such that $a \in A$ and $b \in B$. □

If either of the two sets A or B is empty, then so is their Cartesian product.

Definition 1.2.3 Let $\mathcal{C}$ be a collection of sets. The *union* of $\mathcal{C}$, denoted by $\bigcup \mathcal{C}$, is the set defined by

$$\bigcup \mathcal{C} = \{x \mid x \in A \text{ for some } A \in \mathcal{C}\}.$$

□

If $\mathcal{C} = \{A, B\}$, we have $x \in \bigcup \mathcal{C}$ if and only if $x \in A$ or $x \in B$. In this case, $\bigcup \mathcal{C}$ may be denoted $A \cup B$. We refer to the set $A \cup B$ as the *union of A and B*.

For any sets A, B, C, we have

1. $A \cup (B \cup C) = (A \cup B) \cup C = \bigcup\{A, B, C\}$ (associativity of union),
2. $A \cup B = B \cup A$ (commutativity of union),
3. $A \cup A = A$ (idempotency of union), and
4. $A \cup \emptyset = A$.

Let $\mathcal{C}$ be a nonempty collection of sets. The *intersection* of $\mathcal{C}$, denoted by $\bigcap \mathcal{C}$, is the set defined by

$$\bigcap \mathcal{C} = \{x \mid x \in A \text{ for every } A \in \mathcal{C}\}.$$

If $\mathcal{C} = \{A, B\}$, we may denote $\bigcap \mathcal{C}$ by $A \cap B$, and we refer to $A \cap B$ as the *intersection of A and B*. Then, $x \in A \cap B$ if and only if $x \in A$ and $x \in B$.

Definition 1.2.4 Two sets A, B are *disjoint* if $A \cap B = \emptyset$.

A collection of sets $\mathcal{C}$ is *pairwise disjoint* if for every A and B in $\mathcal{C}$, if $A \neq B$, then A and B are disjoint.

A *partition* of a set M is a collection $\mathcal{C} = \{B_i \mid i \in I\}$ of nonempty, pairwise disjoint sets such that $\bigcup \mathcal{C} = M$. We refer to the members of the partition as *blocks* and to I as the *index set*. □

Example 1.2.5 If E, O are the sets of even and odd natural numbers, respectively, then the collection $\{E, O\}$ is a partition of the set $\mathbb{N}$. This partition can be generalized as follows. Let $k \in \mathbb{N}$ be a natural number, $k > 0$. For every number $n \in \mathbb{N}$ there is a unique number $r \in \mathbb{N}$, $0 \leq r \leq k-1$, such that $n = kp + r$, namely the remainder of the division of n by k. Let $B_r = \{n \in \mathbb{N} \mid n = kp + r\}$ for $0 \leq r \leq k-1$. Since the remainder of the division of n by k is uniquely determined for every n, it follows that $\mathcal{C}_k = \{B_0, \ldots, B_{k-1}\}$ is a collection of pairwise disjoint sets. It is easy to see that

$$\bigcup_{0 \leq r \leq k-1} B_r = \mathbb{N},$$

so $\mathcal{C}_k$ is a partition. We refer to $\mathcal{C}_k$ as the *partition of the natural numbers modulo k*.

If $k = 2$, the partition $\{B_0, B_1\}$ is simply the partition $\{E, O\}$ discussed before. □

Definition 1.2.6 Let A, B be two sets. The *difference* of A and B is the set $A - B$ defined by

$$A - B = \{x \in A \mid x \notin B\}.$$

□

Sometimes, when the set A is understood from the context, we write $\overline{B}$ for $A - B$, and we refer to the set $\overline{B}$ as the *complement of B with respect to A* or simply the *complement of B*.

For every set A and nonempty collection $\mathcal{C}$ of sets, we have

$$\begin{aligned} A - \bigcup \mathcal{C} &= \bigcap \{A - C \mid C \in \mathcal{C}\}, \\ A - \bigcap \mathcal{C} &= \bigcup \{A - C \mid C \in \mathcal{C}\}. \end{aligned}$$

In the special case when $\mathcal{C} = \{B, C\}$ we have:

$$\begin{aligned} A - (B \cup C) &= (A - B) \cap (A - C), \\ A - (B \cap C) &= (A - B) \cup (A - C). \end{aligned}$$

If the set A is understood, $B, C \subseteq A$, and we denote $A - M$ by $\overline{M}$ for each $M \in \mathcal{P}(M)$, then we get the following equalities

$$\begin{aligned} \overline{B \cup C} &= \overline{B} \cap \overline{C} \\ \overline{B \cap C} &= \overline{B} \cup \overline{C}, \end{aligned}$$

known as the *DeMorgan's laws.*

The linkage between union and intersection is given by the distributivity properties. Namely, for any collection of sets $\mathcal{C}$ and set A, we have

$$\left(\bigcup \mathcal{C}\right) \cap A = \bigcup \{C \cap A \mid C \in \mathcal{C}\}.$$

If $\mathcal{C}$ is nonempty, we also have

$$\left(\bigcap \mathcal{C}\right) \cup A = \bigcap \{C \cup A \mid C \in \mathcal{C}\}.$$

1.2.3 Relations

Definition 1.2.7 A *relation* is a set of ordered pairs. If A and B are sets and ρ is a relation, then we call ρ a *relation from A to B* if $\rho \subseteq A \times B$. A relation from A to A is called a *relation on A.* □

The set $\mathcal{P}(A \times B)$ is the set of all relations from A to B. Among the relations from A to B, we distinguish the *empty relation*, $\emptyset$, and the *full relation*, $A \times B$.

If $(a, b) \in \rho$, we sometimes denote this fact by $a \, \rho \, b$, and we write $a \not\rho \, b$ to denote $(a, b) \notin \rho$.

Example 1.2.8 For any set A, we can consider the *identity relation* $\iota_A \subseteq A \times A$ defined by

$$\iota_A = \{(x, x) \mid x \in A\}.$$

□

Note that $A \subseteq B$ if and only if $\iota_A \subseteq \iota_B$.

Definition 1.2.9 The *domain* of a relation ρ is the set

$$\text{Dom}(\rho) = \{a \mid (a, b) \in \rho \text{ for some } b\}.$$

The *range* of ρ is the set

$$\text{Ran}(\rho) = \{b \mid (a, b) \in \rho \text{ for some } a\}.$$

□

It follows easily that if ρ is a relation and A and B are sets, then ρ is a relation from A to B if and only if $\text{Dom}(\rho) \subseteq A$ and $\text{Ran}(\rho) \subseteq B$. Naturally, ρ is always a relation from $\text{Dom}(\rho)$ to $\text{Ran}(\rho)$.

If ρ and σ are relations and $\rho \subseteq \sigma$, then we have $\text{Dom}(\rho) \subseteq \text{Dom}(\sigma)$ and $\text{Ran}(\rho) \subseteq \text{Ran}(\sigma)$. We also remark that $\text{Dom}(A \times B) = A$ unless $B = \emptyset$. In the latter case, we have $\text{Dom}(A \times \emptyset) = \emptyset$. Similarly, $\text{Ran}(A \times B) = B$ if $A \neq \emptyset$. For $A = \emptyset$, we have $\text{Ran}(\emptyset \times B) = \emptyset$.

Example 1.2.10 Let A be a subset of $\mathbb{N}$. The relation "less than" on A is given by

$$\{(x,y) \mid x,y \in A \text{ and } y = x+z \text{ for some positive integer } z\}.$$

□

Example 1.2.11 Consider the relation $\nu \subseteq \mathbb{Z} \times \mathbb{Q}$ given by

$$\nu = \{(n,q) \mid n \in \mathbb{Z},\ q \in \mathbb{Q}, \text{ and } n \leq q < n+1\}.$$

We have $(-3,-2.3) \in \nu$ and $(2,2.3) \in \nu$. Clearly, $(n,q) \in \nu$ if and only if n is the integral part of the rational number q. □

Example 1.2.12 We can define a relation $\delta_{\mathbb{Z}} \subseteq \mathbb{Z} \times \mathbb{Z}$, where $(m,n) \in \delta_{\mathbb{Z}}$ if there is $k \in \mathbb{Z}$ such that $n = mk$. In other words, $(m,n) \in \delta_{\mathbb{Z}}$ if m divides n evenly. □

Example 1.2.13 Let S be a set. Then, the relation from S to $\mathcal{P}(S)$ "is a member of" is given by

$$\{(x,X) \mid X \in \mathcal{P}(S) \text{ and } x \in X\}.$$

□

If ρ and σ are relations from A to B, then so are $\rho \cup \sigma$, $\rho \cap \sigma$, and $\rho - \sigma$.

Definition 1.2.14 Let ρ be a relation. The *inverse* of ρ is the relation ρ^{-1} given by

$$\rho^{-1} = \{(y,x) \mid (x,y) \in \rho\}.$$

□

Theorem 1.2.15 *Let ρ and σ be relations.*

1. $\mathrm{Dom}(\rho^{-1}) = \mathrm{Ran}(\rho)$.
2. $\mathrm{Ran}(\rho^{-1}) = \mathrm{Dom}(\rho)$.
3. *If ρ is a relation from A to B, then ρ^{-1} is a relation from B to A.*
4. $(\rho^{-1})^{-1} = \rho$.
5. *If $\rho \subseteq \sigma$, then $\rho^{-1} \subseteq \sigma^{-1}$ (montonicity of the inverse).*

Proof. We leave these arguments to the reader. ∎

Definition 1.2.16 Let ρ and σ be relations. The *product* of ρ and σ is the relation $\rho \circ \sigma$, where

$$\rho \circ \sigma = \{(x,z) \mid (x,y) \in \rho \text{ and } (y,z) \in \sigma \text{ for some } y\}.$$

□

The product of two relations ρ and σ is also called the *composition* of ρ and σ, and we also use the alternative notation $\sigma\rho$ for the relation product $\rho \circ \sigma$.

Definition 1.2.17 The powers of a relation $\rho \subseteq A \times A$ are relations denoted by $\rho^n \subseteq A \times A$, defined recursively as follows:

$$\begin{aligned} \rho^0 &= \iota_A \\ \rho^{n+1} &= \rho^n \circ \rho, \end{aligned}$$

for $n \in \mathbb{N}$. □

Example 1.2.18 If $\rho \subseteq A \times A$, then we have $(a_0, a_1) \in \rho^2$ if and only if there is $a \in A$ such that $(a_0, a) \in \rho$ and $(a, a_1) \in \rho$. □

Several properties of the relation product are listed below.

Let ρ, σ, and θ be relations.

1. $\mathrm{Dom}(\rho \circ \sigma) \subseteq \mathrm{Dom}(\rho)$.
2. $\mathrm{Ran}(\rho \circ \sigma) \subseteq \mathrm{Ran}(\sigma)$.
3. If ρ is a relation from A to B and σ is a relation from C to D, then $\rho \circ \sigma$ is a relation from A to D.
4. $\rho \circ (\sigma \circ \theta) = (\rho \circ \sigma) \circ \theta$ (associativity of relation product).
5. $$\begin{aligned} \rho \circ (\sigma \cup \theta) &= (\rho \circ \sigma) \cup (\rho \circ \theta), \\ (\rho \cup \sigma) \circ \theta &= (\rho \circ \theta) \cup (\sigma \circ \theta) \end{aligned}$$
   (distributivity of relation product over union).
6. $(\rho \circ \sigma)^{-1} = \sigma^{-1} \circ \rho^{-1}$.
7. If $\sigma \subseteq \theta$, then
   $$\begin{aligned} \rho \circ \sigma &\subseteq \rho \circ \theta, \\ \sigma \circ \rho &\subseteq \theta \circ \rho \end{aligned}$$
   (monotonicity of relation product).
8. If A and B are any sets, then $\iota_A \circ \rho \subseteq \rho$ and $\rho \circ \iota_B \subseteq \rho$. Furthermore, $\iota_A \circ \rho = \rho$ if and only if $\mathrm{Dom}(\rho) \subseteq A$, and $\rho \circ \iota_B = \rho$ if and only if $\mathrm{Ran}(\rho) \subseteq B$. (Thus, ρ is a relation from A to B if and only if $\iota_A \circ \rho = \rho = \rho \circ \iota_B$).

Definition 1.2.19 A relation ρ on a set M, $\rho \subseteq M \times M$ is

- *reflexive*, if $\iota_M \subseteq \rho$;
- *symmetric*, if $\rho = \rho^{-1}$;
- *antisymmetric*, if $\rho \cap \rho^{-1} = \emptyset$;
- *transitive*, if $\rho^2 \subseteq \rho$.

□

Let $\{\rho_i \mid i \in I\}$ be a collection of relations. If every relation in this collection is reflexive, then so is $\bigcap\{\rho_i \mid i \in I\}$. Similarly, if each ρ_i is transitive, then $\bigcap\{\rho_i \mid i \in I\}$ is transitive.

Theorem 1.2.20 *Let $\rho \subseteq M \times M$ be a relation. The relation ρ^+ defined by*

$$\rho^+ = \bigcup\{\rho^n \mid n \geq 1\}$$

is transitive. Moreover, if $\sigma \subseteq M \times M$ is a transitive relation such that $\rho \subseteq \sigma$, then $\rho^+ \subseteq \sigma$. In other words, ρ^+ is the least transitive relation that contains ρ.

Proof. Suppose that $(x, y), (y, z) \in \rho^+$. There exist $p, q \in \mathbb{N}$ such that $(x, y) \in \rho^p$ and $(y, z) \in \rho^q$. This implies $(x, z) \in \rho^{p+q} \subseteq \rho^+$. Therefore, ρ^+ is indeed transitive.

Suppose that σ is a transitive relation such that $\rho \subseteq \sigma$. We prove, by induction on n, that $\rho^n \subseteq \sigma$ for $n \geq 1$.

For $n = 1$, we have $\rho^1 = \rho \subseteq \sigma$.

Let $(x, y) \in \rho^{n+1}$. Since $\rho^{n+1} = \rho^n \circ \rho$, there is $t \in M$ such that $(x, t) \in \rho^n$ and $(t, y) \in \rho$. By the inductive hypothesis, we have $(x, t) \in \sigma$; also, $(t, y) \in \sigma$. The transitivity of σ implies $(x, y) \in \sigma$, so $\rho^+ \subseteq \sigma$. ∎

We refer to ρ^+ as *the transitive closure of* ρ.

A similar result involves the least reflexive and transitive relation that includes a relation $\rho \subseteq M \times M$.

Theorem 1.2.21 *Let* $\rho \subseteq M \times M$ *be a relation. The relation* ρ^* *defined by*

$$\rho^* = \bigcup\{\rho^n \mid n \geq 0\}$$

is reflexive and transitive. Moreover, if $\sigma \subseteq M \times M$ *is a reflexive and transitive relation such that* $\rho \subseteq \sigma$*, then* $\rho^* \subseteq \sigma$*. In other words,* ρ^* *is the least reflexive and transitive relation that contains* ρ.

Proof. The argument is similar to the one used in Theorem 1.2.20; we leave it to the reader. ∎

We refer to ρ^* as *the reflexive and transitive closure of* ρ.

1.2.4 Equivalence Relations

A special type of relations that play a very important role in formal language theory is introduced next.

Definition 1.2.22 An *equivalence relation* on a set M is a relation $\rho \subseteq M \times M$ that is reflexive, symmetric, and transitive. □

Example 1.2.23 Let $k \in \mathbb{N}$; define the relation $\mu_k \subseteq \mathbb{N} \times \mathbb{N}$ by

$$\mu_k = \{(p, q) \mid p, q \in \mathbb{N} \text{ and } p - q = kr \text{ for some } r \in \mathbb{Z}\}.$$

In other words, $(p, q) \in \mu_k$ if $p - q$ is a multiple of k.

The relation μ_k is reflexive because 0 is a multiple of k and symmetric, because if $p - q$ is a multiple of k, then so is $q - p$. Further, if $p - q = kr_1$ and $q - s = kr_2$, then $p - s = k(r_1 + r_2)$, which implies $(q, s) \in \mu_k$. Thus, μ_k is transitive, so it is an equivalence relation. □

Definition 1.2.24 Let M be a set, x be an element of M, and ρ be an equivalence relation on M. The *equivalence class of* x is the set $[x]_\rho$ given by

$$[x]_\rho = \{y \in M \mid (x, y) \in \rho\}$$

for $x \in M$.

The set of equivalence classes of ρ is the *quotient set of* ρ and is denoted by M/ρ. □

Example 1.2.25 Let $[n]_{\mu_k}$ be the equivalence class of an element $n \in \mathbb{N}$, where μ_k is the equivalence relation introduced in Example 1.2.23. There exists a unique number ℓ such that $n = kr + \ell$ and $0 \leq \ell \leq k - 1$. Clearly, $(n, \ell) \in \mu_k$, so $[n]_{\mu_k} = [\ell]_{\mu_k}$. Therefore, the quotient set $\mathbb{N}/\mu_k$ consists in exactly k equivalence classes. Namely, we have

$$\mathbb{N}/\mu_k = \{[0]_{\mu_k}, \ldots, [k-1]_{\mu_k}\}.$$

The elements of the set $\mathbb{N}/\mu_k$ are the *equivalence classes of the natural numbers modulo* k. □

Equivalence relations on a set M are related to partitions of M as the next theorem shows.

Theorem 1.2.26 *Let $\mathcal{C} = \{B_i \mid i \in I\}$ be a partition of a set M. The relation*

$$\rho_{\mathcal{C}} = \{(x,y) \in M \times M \mid \{x,y\} \subseteq B_i \text{ for some } B_i \in \mathcal{C}\}$$

is an equivalence relation on M.

Conversely, the collection $\{[x]_\rho \mid x \in M\}$ is a partition $\mathcal{C}_\rho$. Moreover, we have

$$\mathcal{C}_{(\rho_{\mathcal{C}})} = \mathcal{C} \text{ and } \rho_{(\mathcal{C}_\rho)} = \rho.$$

Proof. Let $\mathcal{C} = \{B_i \mid i \in I\}$ be a partition of a set M. Since $\bigcup \mathcal{C} = M$, each $x \in M$ belongs to a block of the partition. Therefore, $(x,x) \in \rho_{\mathcal{C}}$ for every $x \in M$, so $\iota_M \subseteq \rho_{\mathcal{C}}$, which shows that $\rho_{\mathcal{C}}$ is reflexive.

Since $(x,y) \in \rho_{\mathcal{C}}$ if and only if $\{x,y\} \subseteq B_i$ for some block B_i of $\mathcal{C}$, it is clear that this implies $(y,x) \in \rho_{\mathcal{C}}$, so $\rho_{\mathcal{C}}$ is symmetric.

Finally, suppose that $(x,y),(y,z) \in \rho_{\mathcal{C}}$. There are $B_i, B_j \in \mathcal{C}$ such that $\{x,y\} \subseteq B_i$ and $\{y,z\} \subseteq B_j$. Since $y \in B_i \cap B_j$, $B_i \cap B_j \neq \emptyset$. But for a partition, this implies $i = j$, so $x \in B_i$ and $z \in B_i$, which proves that $(x,z) \in \rho_{\mathcal{C}}$, so $\rho_{\mathcal{C}}$ is transitive.

Conversely, let ρ be an equivalence relation on the set M. Since ρ is reflexive, we have $x \in [x]_\rho$, so

$$\bigcup_{x \in M} [x]_\rho = M.$$

If $[x]_\rho \neq [y]_\rho$ it follows that $[x]_\rho \cap [y]_\rho = \emptyset$. Indeed, if $t \in [x]_\rho \cap [y]_\rho$ this would imply $(t,x),(t,y) \in \rho$. The symmetry and transitivity of ρ would imply $(x,y) \in \rho$ and this would contradict the fact that $[x]_\rho \neq [y]_\rho$. Thus, we conclude that the collection $\{[x]_\rho \mid x \in M\}$ is a partition of M.

We leave to the reader the proof of the last part of the theorem. ∎

Definition 1.2.27 Let ρ be an equivalence relation on a set M. A subset P of M is *saturated by* ρ, or ρ-saturated if $x \in P$ and $(x,y) \in \rho$ implies $y \in P$ for every $x, y \in M$. □

A characterization of sets saturated by equivalence relations is given next.

Theorem 1.2.28 *A subset P of a set M is saturated by an equivalence relation ρ on M if and only if P is the union of a collection of blocks of the quotient set M/ρ.*

Proof. Suppose that P is ρ-saturated and let $\mathcal{D}_P = \{[x]_\rho \mid x \in P\}$. By the reflexivity of equivalence relations we have $P \subseteq \bigcup \mathcal{D}_P$. Let $t \in \bigcup \mathcal{D}_P$. There exists a block $[x]_\rho$, where $x \in P$ such that $t \in [x]_\rho$. This means that $(x,t) \in \rho$, so $t \in P$ because P is ρ-saturated. This shows that $P = \bigcup \mathcal{D}_P$.

Conversely, suppose that $P = \bigcup \mathcal{D}_P$ and let $x \in P$ and $(x,y) \in \rho$. Since P is a union of blocks of $\mathcal{D}_P$ it follows that $[x]_\rho \subseteq P$, so $y \in P$ because $y \in [x]_\rho$. ∎

Theorem 1.2.29 *Let M be a set and let ρ, ρ' be equivalence relations on M. The following statements are equivalent:*

(i) $\rho \subseteq \rho'$;
(ii) *every ρ'-saturated set is ρ-saturated;*
(iii) *every block of the quotient set M/ρ' is ρ-saturated.*

Proof. `(1) implies (2):` Suppose that $\rho \subseteq \rho'$ and let P be a subset of M that is ρ'-saturated. Let $x \in M$ and assume that $(x, y) \in \rho$. Then $(x, y) \in \rho'$ and this implies $y \in P$. Therefore, P is ρ-saturated.

`(2) implies (3):` Suppose that every ρ'-saturated set is ρ-saturated. Since every block of M/ρ' is ρ'-saturated it follows that each such block is ρ-saturated.

`(3) implies (1):` Assume that every block of the quotient set M/ρ' is ρ-saturated and let $(x, y) \in \rho$, so $y \in [x]_\rho$. Note that $[x]_{\rho'}$ is ρ-saturated; therefore, $[x]_\rho \subseteq [x]_{\rho'}$ and this implies $y \in [x]_{\rho'}$. Therefore, $y \in [x]_{\rho'}$, so $(x, y) \in \rho'$. ∎

Corollary 1.2.30 *Let M be a set and let ρ, ρ' be equivalence relations on M such that $\rho \subseteq \rho'$. If M/ρ is a finite set, then so is M/ρ'.*

Proof. Since every block of the quotient set M/ρ' is the union of blocks of the quotient set M/ρ it is immediate that M/ρ' is finite. ∎

Theorem 1.2.31 *Let ρ be an equivalence on a set M. If $L, L' \subseteq M$ are two ρ-saturated sets, then $L \cup L'$, $L \cap L'$ and $M - L$ are ρ-saturated languages.*

Proof. We leave this straightforward argument to the reader. ∎

1.2.5 Partial Orders

Definition 1.2.32 A *partial order on a set M* is a relation $\rho \subseteq M \times M$ that is reflexive, antisymmetric and transitive. □

Example 1.2.33 Define the relation $\rho \subseteq \mathbb{N} \times \mathbb{N}$ by

$$\rho = \{(m, n) \in \mathbb{N} \times \mathbb{N} \mid n = mp \text{ for some } p \in \mathbb{N}\}.$$

It is easy to see that ρ is reflexive and transitive. Suppose that $(m, n) \in \rho$ and $(n, m) \in \rho$. Then, there are $p, q \in \mathbb{N}$ such that $n = mp$ and $m = nq$. Note that $n = 0$ if and only if $m = 0$; otherwise, we have $n = nqp$, so $pq = 1$ because $n \neq 0$. This implies $p = q = 1$,so $m = n$. □

Definition 1.2.34 A *partially ordered set* (or, in short a *poset*) is a pair (M, ρ), where M is a set and ρ is a partial order on M. □

Example 1.2.35 The pair $(\mathbb{N}, \rho)$ is a poset, where ρ is the partial order introduced in Example 1.2.33.

If S is a set, it is easy to verify that the pair $(\mathcal{P}(S), \subseteq)$ is a poset. □

In general, partial ordered relations are denoted using the symbol "$\leq$"; also, instead of writing $(a, b) \in \leq$ we use the more common notation $a \leq b$.

Definition 1.2.36 A partial order "$\leq$" on a set M is a *total order* if for every $x, y \in M$ we have either $x \leq y$, or $y \leq x$.

If "$\leq$" is a total order on M, then we refer to the pair $(M, \leq)$ as a *chain.* □

Example 1.2.37 Consider the poset $(\mathbb{N}, \leq)$, where $\leq$ consists of those pairs $(m, n) \in \mathbb{N} \times \mathbb{N}$ such that $n = m + \ell$ for some $\ell \in \mathbb{N}$. It is clear that "$\leq$" is a total order on $\mathbb{N}$. □

1.2.6 Functions

Functions are relations that satisfy a special condition given in the following definition.

Definition 1.2.38 A relation ρ is called a *function* if $(a, b_1) \in \rho$ and $(a, b_2) \in \rho$ imply $b_1 = b_2$ for all a, b_1,and b_2. □

Note that $\emptyset$ is a function (referred to in this context as the *empty function*). Indeed, if $\emptyset$ were not a function we should have $a \in \text{Dom}(\rho)$ and $b_1 \neq b_2$ such that both $(a, b_1) \in \emptyset$ and $(a, b_2) \in \emptyset$. Since no such elements can be found $\emptyset$ is indeed a function; $\emptyset$ satisfies vacuously the defining condition for being a function.

A related notion is given next.

Definition 1.2.39 A relation ρ is an *one-to-one relation* if for all a_1, a_2, and b, $(a_1, b) \in \rho$ and $(a_2, b) \in \rho$ imply $a_1 = a_2$. □

Example 1.2.40 For every set A, the relation ι_A is both a function and also a one-to-one relation. □

Definition 1.2.41 A relation ρ from A to B is called *total* if $\text{Dom}(\rho) = A$ and is called *onto* if $\text{Ran}(\rho) = B$. □

Any relation ρ is a total and onto relation from $\text{Dom}(\rho)$ to $\text{Ran}(\rho)$. If A and B are nonempty, than $A \times B$ is a total, onto relation from A to B.

If ρ is a relation, then one can determine whether or not ρ is a function or is one-to-one just by examining the ordered pairs of ρ. Whether ρ is a total or onto relation from A to B depends on what A and B are.

If ρ is a function, then, for each a in $\text{Dom}(\rho)$, we let $\rho(a)$ denote the unique b with $(a, b) \in \rho$, and we sometimes call $\rho(a)$ the *image of a under ρ* .

Definition 1.2.42 Let A and B be sets. A *partial function from A to B* is a relation from A to B that is a function.

A *total function from A to B* (also called a *function from A to B* or a *mapping from A to B*) is a partial function from A to B that is a total relation from A to B. □

When we say that ρ is a relation from A to B this does not necessarily mean that ρ is a total relation from A to B; however, when we say that ρ is a *function from A to B*, this automatically means that ρ is total in addition to being a relation from A to B that is a function.

The letters f, g, h, and k are used to denote functions, and we denote the identity relation ι_A, which we have already remarked is a function, by 1_A.

The *set of all partial functions from A to B* is denoted by $A \mapsto B$ and the set of all functions from A to B is denoted by $A \longrightarrow B$. For any sets A and B, we have $A \longrightarrow B \subseteq A \mapsto B$.

A function is usually defined by giving its domain and specifying for each domain element x the value that the function takes on x. A common way to give the value of a function f on a domain element x is to write $f(x) = \mathcal{E}$, where $\mathcal{E}$ is some expression that can be evaluated for each domain element x.

For any sets A and B, we have $\emptyset \in A \mapsto B$. If either A or B is empty, then $\emptyset$ is the only partial function from A to B. If $A = \emptyset$, then the empty function is a total function from A to any B. Thus, for any sets A and B, we have

$$\begin{aligned} A \mapsto \emptyset &= \{\emptyset\}, \\ \emptyset \mapsto B &= \{\emptyset\}, \\ \emptyset \longrightarrow B &= \{\emptyset\}. \end{aligned}$$

Furthermore, if A is nonempty, then there can be no (total) function from A to the empty set, so we have

$$A \longrightarrow \emptyset = \emptyset \text{ (if } A \neq \emptyset).$$

Definition 1.2.43 A one-to-one function is called an *injection.* A function $f : A \mapsto B$ is called a *surjection (from A to B)* if f is an onto relation from A to B.

A function $f : A \longrightarrow B$ is called a *bijection (from A to B)* if it is both an injection and a surjection. □

Using our notation for functions, we can restate the definition of injection as follows: f is an injection if for all $a_1, a_2 \in \text{Dom}(f)$, $f(a_1) = f(a_2)$ implies $a_1 = a_2$. Likewise, $f : A \mapsto B$ is a surjection if for every $b \in B$ there is an $a \in A$ with $f(a) = b$.

Example 1.2.44 Let A, B be two sets and assume that $A \subseteq B$. The *containment mapping* $c : A \longrightarrow B$ defined by $c(a) = a$ for $a \in A$ is an injection. □

Example 1.2.45 Let $m \in \mathbb{N}$ be a natural number, $m \geq 2$. Consider the function $r_m : \mathbb{N} \longrightarrow \{0, \ldots, m-1\}$, where $r_m(n)$ is the remainder when n is divided by m. Obviously, r_m is well defined since the remainder p when a natural number is divided by m is unique and satisfies $0 \leq p \leq m-1$. The function r_m is onto because for any $p \in \{0, \ldots, m-1\}$ we have $r_m(km+p) = p$ for any $k \in \mathbb{N}$.

For instance, if $m = 4$, we have $r_4(0) = r_4(4) = r_4(8) = \cdots = 0$, $r_4(1) = r_4(5) = r_4(9) = \cdots = 1$, $r_4(2) = r_4(6) = r_4(10) = \cdots = 2$ and $r_4(3) = r_4(7) = r_4(11) = \cdots = 3$. □

Another notation commonly used for the set of total functions from A to B is B^A. This notation is suggested by the following combinatorial result.

Theorem 1.2.46 *Let A and B be two finite sets. There exist $|B|^{|A|}$ functions from A to B.*

Proof. The argument is by induction on $|A|$. If $|A| = 0$, then $A = \emptyset$, and there is only one function from A to B, namely the empty function.

Suppose that the statement holds for sets that have n elements and let $A = \{a_0, \ldots, a_n\}$ be a set that contains $n+1$ elements. If $A' = A - \{a_n\}$, there are $|B|^n$ functions from A to B. Let $f : A' \longrightarrow B$ be such a function. We can extend f' to a function f from A to B in $|B|$ distinct ways, by defining $f(a_n)$ as one of the $|B|$ elements of the set B. Thus, there are $|B|^n \cdot |B| = |B|^{n+1}$ functions from A to B. ∎

The fact that f is a partial function from A to B is indicated by writing $f : A \mapsto B$, rather than $f \in A \mapsto B$. Similarly, instead of writing $f \in A \longrightarrow B$, we use the notation $f : A \longrightarrow B$.

Since a function is a relation, the ideas introduced in the previous section for relations in general can be applied equally well to functions. In particular, we can consider the inverse of a function and the product of two functions.

If f is a function, then, f^{-1} is a one-to-one relation; however, f^{-1} is not necessarily a function. In fact, if f is a function, then f^{-1} is a function if and only if f is an injection.

Suppose now that $f : A \mapsto B$ is an injection. Then, $f^{-1} : B \mapsto A$ is also an injection. Further, $f^{-1} : B \mapsto A$ is total if and only if $f : A \mapsto B$ is a surjection, and $f^{-1} : B \mapsto A$ is a surjection if and only if $f : A \mapsto B$ is total. It follows that $f : A \mapsto B$ is a bijection if and only if $f^{-1} : B \mapsto A$ is a bijection.

If f and g are functions, then we use, in general, the alternative notation gf for the product $f \circ g$, and we call gf *the composition of* f *and* g rather than the product.

It is easy to see that the composition of two functions is a function. Furthermore, it follows from the definition of composition that

$$\mathrm{Dom}(gf) = \{a \in \mathrm{Dom}(f) \mid f(a) \in \mathrm{Dom}(g)\},$$

and for all $a \in \mathrm{Dom}(gf)$,

$$gf(a) = g(f(a)).$$

This is why we use gf rather than $f \circ g$.

It is easy to verify that the composition of two injections is an injection. Also, let $f : A \mapsto B$ and $g : B \mapsto C$. Then, $gf : A \mapsto C$. If f and g are both total, then gf is total (i.e., if $f : A \longrightarrow B$ and $g : B \longrightarrow C$, then $gf : A \longrightarrow C$). If f and g are both surjections, then gf is also a surjection. Finally, if f and g are both bijections, then gf is also a bijection.

If $f : A \longrightarrow B$, then $f1_A = f = 1_B f$.

Definition 1.2.47 Let f be a function and let K be a set. The *restriction* of f to K, $f\rceil K$, is the set of all pairs in f whose first component is in K, that is,

$$f\rceil K = f \cap (K \times \mathrm{Ran}(f)).$$

□

It is easy to see that for any function f and set K, $f\rceil K = f1_K$. Hence, any restriction of a function is a function. In fact, the domain of $f\rceil K$ is $\mathrm{Dom}(f) \cap K$, and for each $a \in \mathrm{Dom}(f\rceil K)$, $f\rceil K(a) = f(a)$. If $f : A \mapsto B$, then $f\rceil K : A \cap K \mapsto B$. If $f : A \longrightarrow B$ and $K \subseteq A$, then $f\rceil K : K \longrightarrow B$. In addition, any restriction of an injection is an injection.

Example 1.2.48 Consider the function $f : \mathbb{N} \longrightarrow \mathbb{R}$ given by $f(n) = n/2$ for every $n \in \mathbb{N}$. Its restriction $f\rceil E : E \longrightarrow \mathbb{R}$ to the set E of even natural numbers maps every even natural number $2m$ to m. Note that we also have $f\rceil E : E \longrightarrow \mathbb{N}$. □

If f and g are functions such that $f \subseteq g$, then we call g an *extension* of f. Thus, g is an extension of f if and only if $\mathrm{Dom}(f) \subseteq \mathrm{Dom}(g)$ and $f(a) = g(a)$ for every $a \in \mathrm{Dom}(f)$. Observe that g is an extension of f if and only if f is the restriction of g to some set, i.e. $f = g\rceil \mathrm{Dom}(f)$.

The next definition provides another way of viewing a subset of a fixed set M.

Definition 1.2.49 Let M be a set. A *characteristic function over* M is a function $\chi : M \longrightarrow \{0,1\}$. If P is a subset of M, then the *characteristic function of* P (as a subset of M) is the function $\chi_P : M \longrightarrow \{0,1\}$ given by

$$\chi_P(x) = \begin{cases} 1 & \text{if } x \in P \\ 0 & \text{otherwise,} \end{cases}$$

for every $x \in M$. □

The next theorem captures the connection between subsets and characteristic functions.

Theorem 1.2.50 *There is a bijection* $\Psi : \mathcal{P}(M) \longrightarrow (M \longrightarrow \{0,1\})$ *between the set of subsets of* M *and the set of characteristic functions defined on* M.

Proof. For $P \in \mathcal{P}(M)$ define $\Psi(P) = \chi_P$. The mapping Ψ is one-to-one. Indeed, assume that $\chi_P = \chi_Q$, where $P, Q \in \mathcal{P}(M)$. We have $x \in P$ if and only if $\chi_P(x) = 1$, which is equivalent to $\chi_Q(x) = 1$. This happens if and only if $x \in Q$; hence, $P = Q$ so Ψ is one-to-one.

Let $f : M \longrightarrow \{0,1\}$ be an arbitrary function. Define the set $T_f = \{x \in M \mid f(x) = 1\}$. It is easy to see that f is the characteristic function of the set T_f; hence, $\Psi(T_f) = f$ which shows that the mapping Ψ is also onto; hence, it is a bijection. ■

If M is a finite set, $M = \{x_0, \ldots, x_{n-1}\}$, we can represent subsets using *characteristic vectors*. Namely, if $P \in \mathcal{P}(M)$, then its characteristic vector is $\mathbf{b}_P = (b_0, \ldots, b_{n-1})$, where $b_i = \chi_P(x_i)$ for $0 \leq i \leq n-1$.

Definition 1.2.51 Let M be a set and let $f : M \longrightarrow M$ be a function. The kth *iteration power of* f is the function $f^{(k)} : M \longrightarrow M$, defined recursively by:

$$\begin{aligned} f^{(0)} &= 1_M \\ f^{(k+1)} &= f f^{(k)}, \end{aligned}$$

for every $k \in \mathbb{N}$. □

Clearly, $f^{(1)} = f$. This definition is consistent with Definition 1.2.17.

Example 1.2.52 Let $f : \mathbb{N} \longrightarrow \mathbb{N}$ be the function given by $f(n) = an + b$ for $n \in \mathbb{N}$, where $a, b \in \mathbb{N}$. It is easy to verify by induction on $k > 0$ that

$$f^{(k)}(n) = a^k n + a^{k-1} b + \ldots + ab + b,$$

for every $n \in \mathbb{N}$. □

Starting from a function $f : A \longrightarrow B$, we define a function $F : \mathcal{P}(A) \longrightarrow \mathcal{P}(B)$ by

$$F(X) = \{y \in B \mid y = f(x) \text{ for some } x \in X\}$$

for every $X \in \mathcal{P}(A)$. Also, we define a function $G : \mathcal{P}(B) \longrightarrow \mathcal{P}(A)$ by

$$G(Y) = \{x \in A \mid f(x) \in Y\}.$$

Unless there is risk of confusion, we denote the sets $F(X)$ and $G(Y)$ by $f(X)$ and $f^{-1}(Y)$, respectively.

It is easy to verify that if $f : A \longrightarrow B$ is a function, then

$$\begin{aligned} f(X_0 \cup X_1) &= f(X_0) \cup f(X_1) \\ f(X_0 \cap X_1) &\subseteq f(X_0) \cap f(X_1) \\ f^{-1}(Y_0 \cup Y_1) &= f^{-1}(Y_0) \cup f^{-1}(Y_1) \\ f^{-1}(Y_0 \cap Y_1) &= f^{-1}(Y_0) \cap f^{-1}(Y_1), \end{aligned}$$

for every $X_0, X_1 \in \mathcal{P}(A)$ and $Y_0, Y_1 \in \mathcal{P}(B)$.

Every function $f : A \longrightarrow B$ generates an equivalence relation on A.

Definition 1.2.53 The kernel equivalence of f is the relation $\mathbf{ker}(f) \subseteq A \times A$ defined by

$$\mathbf{ker}(f) = \{(a, a') \in A \times A \mid f(a) = f(a')\}.$$

□

Example 1.2.54 Consider the mapping $f : \mathbb{N} \longrightarrow \mathbb{Z}$ defined by $f(n) = (-1)^n$. We have $(p, q) \in \mathbf{ker}(f)$ if and only if p, q have the same parity. Thus, the quotient set $\mathbb{N}/\mathbf{ker}(f)$ is the partition $\{O, E\}$ of $\mathbb{N}$, discussed in Example 1.2.5.

□

The notion of Cartesian product can be extended to arbitrary collection of sets.

Definition 1.2.55 Let $\mathcal{C} = \{A_i \mid i \in I\}$ be a collection of sets indexed by the set I. The *Cartesian product of* $\mathcal{C}$ is the set that consists of all functions $f : I \longrightarrow \bigcup \mathcal{C}$ such that $f(i) \in A_i$ for every $i \in I$.

The Cartesian product of $\mathcal{C}$ is denoted by $\Pi\mathcal{C}$. □

For $\mathcal{C} = \{A_i \mid i \in I\}$ we introduce the ith projection $P_i : \Pi\mathcal{C} \longrightarrow A_i$ given by $P_i(f) = f(i)$ for every $f \in \Pi\mathcal{C}$. If $\mathcal{C} = \{A_0, \ldots, A_{n-1}\}$ is a collection of n sets we denote the ith projection by P_i^n.

If $I = \{0, \ldots, n-1\}$, then we use the alternate notation $A_0 \times \cdots \times A_{n-1}$ for $\Pi\mathcal{C}$. In this case, we refer to the elements of $A_0 \times \cdots \times A_{n-1}$ as n-tuples.

For $n = 2$, $A_0 \times A_1$ consists of those functions $f : \{0, 1\}$ such that $f(0) \in A_0$ and $f(1) \in A_1$. Of course, f is completely and unequivocally described by the ordered pais $(f(0), f(1))$, so the current definition is consistent with Definition 1.2.2.

If $A_0 = \cdots = A_{n-1} = A$ and $n \geq 1$, then the set $A_0 \times \cdots \times A_{n-1}$ is denote by A^n; we refer to A^n as the nth Cartesian power of A. For the special case $n = 0$, A^0 is defined as $\{\emptyset\}$. Note that, in principle, the sets A^1 and A are different; however, in practice these sets are identified.

An n-ary relation on the sets $A_0, \ldots, A_{n-1}$ is a subset ρ of the Cartesian product $A_0 \times \cdots \times A_{n-1}$. If $A_0 = \cdots = A_{n-1} = A$, then we refer to ρ as an n-ary relation over A.

1.3 Operations and Algebras

The goal of this section is to introduce several algebraic structures that are commonly used by the theory of formal languages.

1.3.1 Operations

Definition 1.3.1 An *n-ary operation* on a set A is a mapping $f : A^n \longrightarrow A$. The number n is the *arity* of f. □

For $n = 1$, we obtain *a unary operation.* Such an operation $f : M \longrightarrow M$ is often called a *transformation* of the set M. When $n = 2$ or $n = 3$, we refer to the n-ary operations as *binary operations* and *ternary operations*, respectively.

Example 1.3.2 The function $f : \mathbb{N}^3 \longrightarrow \mathbb{N}$ defined by

$$f(p, q, r) = p + q + r$$

for $p, q, r \in \mathbb{N}$ is a ternary operation on $\mathbb{N}$. □

Taking $n = 0$ in Definition 1.3.1, we obtain the case of the *zero-ary* operation. Such an operation $f : M^0 \longrightarrow M$ singles out an element $f(\emptyset)$ of the set M. We denote both the operation and the selected element with the same symbol.

Example 1.3.3 Union is a binary operation $f_\cup : \mathcal{P}(M)^2 \longrightarrow \mathcal{P}(M)$, where

$$f_\cup(K, L) = K \cup L,$$

for $K, L \in \mathcal{P}(M)$. Similarly, intersection and the difference of sets are binary operations on $\mathcal{P}(M)$. □

Following standard mathematical practice, we use the notation xfy instead of $f(x, y)$ when dealing with binary operations. Also, these operations are usually designated by special symbols, such as

$$\vee, \wedge, +, \cdot, -, \star, \circ.$$

In keeping with the previous convention, we write $x \star y$ rather than $\star(x, y)$.

We reconsider here several properties of binary operations that we already have used informally.

Definition 1.3.4 A binary operation $\star$ on a set M is

1. *commutative* if $x \star y = y \star x$ for all $x, y \in M$;
2. *associative* if $x \star (y \star z) = (x \star y) \star z$ for all $x, y, z \in M$;
3. *idempotent* if $x \star x = x$ for every $x \in M$.

□

Example 1.3.5 Both set union and set intersection are commutative, associative, and idempotent. The relation product is associative; however, it is neither commutative nor idempotent. □

Example 1.3.6 Define the operation $*$ on $\mathbb{R}$ by

$$x * y = \frac{x + y}{2}.$$

This operation is commutative and idempotent but not associative since $x * (y * z) = 0.5x + 0.25y + 0.25z$ and $(x * y) * z = 0.25x + 0.25y + 0.5z$. □

Example 1.3.7 Consider the two-element set $\mathbf{B} = \{0, 1\}$. Define the operations $\vee$ and $\wedge$ on $\mathbf{B}$ by

$$0 \vee 0 = 0, \quad 0 \vee 1 = 1,$$
$$1 \vee 0 = 1, \quad 1 \vee 1 = 1,$$

and

$$0 \wedge 0 = 0, \quad 0 \wedge 1 = 0,$$
$$1 \wedge 0 = 0, \quad 1 \wedge 1 = 1.$$

Both these operations are associative, commutative, and idempotent (exercise). The operations $\vee$ and $\wedge$ are sometimes called "or" and "and," respectively. □

A binary operation defines certain special elements of a set on which it acts.

Definition 1.3.8 Let M be a set, and assume that $\star$ is a binary operation on M. An element u of the set M is

1. *a left identity for the operation* $\star$ on the set M if $u \star x = x$ for all $x \in M$;
2. *a right identity for the operation* $\star$ on the set M if $x \star u = x$ for all $x \in M$;
3. *an identity for the operation* $\star$ *on* M if it is both a left and a right identity for this operation.

□

Example 1.3.9 Addition on the set of integers $\mathbb{Z}$ has 0 as an identity; the identity of the multiplication is 1. The operation $*$ introduced in Example 1.3.6 has no left or right identity. □

Theorem 1.3.10 *An operation has at most one identity element.*

Proof. Suppose that both u and v are identities for the operation $\star$. Then,

$$\begin{aligned} u \star x &= x \star u = x, \\ v \star x &= x \star v = x, \end{aligned}$$

for all $x \in M$.

Taking $x = v$ in the first equality, we obtain $u \star v = v$; taking $x = u$ in the second, we have $u \star v = u$, which shows that $u = v$. ■

By repeatedly using binary operations, we can build expressions that involve more than two elements. If a binary operation is not associative, the result of the computation is dependent on the order in which the elements get involved with the operation, as can be seen from Example 1.3.6. For an associative operation $\star$ on a set M, the terms $x \star (y \star z)$ and $(x \star y) \star z$ refer to the same element. Therefore, it is natural to denote their common value by $x \star y \star z$ that is, to eliminate parentheses. An expression such as $(x \star y) \star (x \star (z \star v))$ yields the same element as $((x \star y) \star x) \star (z \star v)$. Applying associativity again, we obtain an equivalent expression $(((x \star y) \star x) \star z) \star v$. Clearly, the value of each of these expressions depends on the nature of the elements and on the order they appear in the expression. The order in which the operation itself is applied is immaterial, and we can use the notation $x \star t \star x \star z \star v$ to designate each of these expressions.

Definition 1.3.11 Let $*$ be a binary operation on the set M and let u be an identity for this operation.

A *left (right) inverse of the element* $x \in M$ is an element $x' \in M$ such that $x' * x = u$ $(x * x' = u)$.

The element x' is *inverse* for x if it is both a right and a left inverse □

Theorem 1.3.12 *If $*$ is an associative operation on a set M then, if x has a left inverse x_1 and a right inverse x_2, $x_1 = x_2$ and x has the inverse $x' = x_1 = x_2$. Furthermore, if x has an inverse y, then this inverse is unique.*

Proof. Indeed, we have $x_1 = x_1 * u = x_1 * (x * x_2) = (x_1 * x) * x_2 = u * x_2 = x_2$. For the second part of the theorem observe that if both y and z are inverses of x then y is a left inverse and z is a right inverse; hence, $y = z$. ∎

1.3.2 Algebras, Semigroups, and Monoids

The notion of an algebra, introduced next, is the central notion of this section. Semigroups and monoids are specific instances of algebras that satisfy additional conditions.

Definition 1.3.13 An *algebra* is a pair $\mathcal{A} = (M, O)$, where M is a set and O is a set of operations on M. The set M is the *carrier* of the algebra. We refer to the operations in O as *the operations of the algebra $\mathcal{A}$*. □

To simplify the notation, if $\mathcal{A} = (M, \{\star_0, \ldots, \star_{k-1}\})$ is an algebra that has a finite set of operations, then we write $\mathcal{A} = (M, \star_0, \ldots, \star_{k-1})$.

Example 1.3.14 A *semigroup* is an algebra $(M, \star)$, where $\star$ is an associative binary operation on M. If, in addition, $\star$ is commutative, then $(M, \star)$ is a *commutative semigroup*. □

Example 1.3.15 Both $(B, \vee)$ and $(B, \wedge)$ are commutative semigroups, where $\vee$ and $\wedge$ are the operations introduced in Example 1.3.7. □

Recall that the set of functions from A to B is denoted alternatively by B^A. In particular, M^M is the set of all functions from M to M.

Example 1.3.16 The pair $(\mathbb{Q}^{\mathbb{Q}}, \circ)$, where $\circ$ is the function composition operation is a semigroup, but not a commutative semigroup. □

Example 1.3.17 A *monoid* is an algebra $(M, \star, 1)$, where $\star$ is an associative binary operation on M and 1 is a zero-ary operation that is an identity for $\star$. If $\star$ is also commutative, then $(M, \star, 1)$ is a *commutative monoid.* □

Example 1.3.18 $(\mathbb{R}, +, 0)$ is a commutative monoid, and so is $(\mathbb{R}, \cdot, 1)$. □

Example 1.3.19 The algebra $\mathsf{T}(M) = (M^M, \circ, 1_M)$ is a monoid that is not commutative. We refer to $\mathsf{T}(M)$ as *the monoid of transformations of the set M*.

For the monoid $\mathsf{T}(M)$, we adopt a special notation that will be useful in Chapter 3. Namely, if $m \in M$ and $f \in F_M$ we may write mf instead of $f(m)$. Thus, $g(f(m))$ can be written as $(mf)g$, which is consistent with the order of application of the transformations f and g. This also suggests the use of the notation $f \circ g$; we adopt this notation whenever we deal with the monoid of transformations of a set; we have $(mf)g = m(f \circ g)$ for every $m \in M$, $f, g \in F_M$.

The associativity of the operation "$\circ$" makes possible to denote the element $m(f_0 \circ \cdots f_n)$ simply by $mf_0 \cdots f_n$, where $f_0, \ldots, f_n \in \mathsf{T}(M)$. □

Example 1.3.20 Let $M_{m\times n}$ be the set of $(m\times n)$-matrices having real numbers as its entries. The diagonal matrix $I_n \in M_{n\times n}$ is defined as

$$I_n = \begin{pmatrix} 1 & 0 & \cdots & 0 \\ 0 & 1 & \cdots & 0 \\ \vdots & \vdots & \vdots & \vdots \\ 0 & 0 & \cdots & 1 \end{pmatrix}$$

Since the matrix product is associative, and I_n is a unit element with respect to matrix multiplication, it follows that the triple $(M_{n\times n}, \cdot, I_n)$ is a monoid. We will refer to this monoid as *the monoid of* $(n \times n)$*-matrices over* $\mathbb{R}$. □

If $(S, \star)$ is a semigroup, then the operation "$\star$" can be extended to subsets of S as follows. For $X, Y \subseteq S$ define

$$X \star Y = \{x \star y \mid x \in X, y \in Y\}. \tag{1.1}$$

The reader can easily verify the following elementary properties of subset product:

$$X \star (Y \star Z) = (X \star Y) \star Z, \tag{1.2}$$

$$\emptyset \star X = X \star \emptyset = \emptyset, \tag{1.3}$$

for all subsets X, Y, Z of S. Equation (1.2) implies that $(\mathcal{P}(S), \star)$ is also a semigroup.

If $(S, \star, 1)$ is a monoid then, in addition, we have

$$\{1\} \star X = X \star \{1\} = X, \tag{1.4}$$

which shows that $(\mathcal{P}(S), \star, \{1\})$ is also a monoid.

The product $X \star Y$ of the subsets X, Y of S, where $(S, \star)$ is a semigroup, is written as XY; also, $\{x\}X$ is written as xX; likewise, we write Xx instead of $X\{x\}$. The product of subsets of S is distributive with respect to union as the following theorem shows.

Theorem 1.3.21 *Let* $(S, \star)$ *be a semigroup. We have*

$$X(Y \cup Z) = XY \cup XZ \text{ and } (X \cup Y)Z = XZ \cup YZ,$$

for all $X, Y, Z \subseteq S$.

Proof. We prove only the first equality; the proof of the second is similar.

Let $x \in X(Y \cup Z)$. We have $x = uv$, where $u \in X$ and $v \in Y \cup Z$. If $v \in Y$, then $x \in XY$; if $v \in Z$, then $x \in XZ$; in either case, $x \in XY \cup XZ$.

If $x \in XY \cup XZ$, then either $x \in XY$ or $x \in XZ$. In the first case, $x = uv$, where $u \in X$ and $v \in Y$. Therefore, $v \in Y \cup Z$, and this imples $x \in X(Y \cup Z)$. The case when $x \in XZ$ implies the same conclusion; hence, we obtain the first equality of the proposition. ∎

Corollary 1.3.22 *Let* $(S, \star)$ *be a semigroup and let* X, Y, Z *be three subsets of* S. *If* $X \subseteq Y$, *then*

$$XZ \subseteq YZ \text{ and } ZX \subseteq ZY.$$

This property is called the monotonicity of subset product.

Proof. If $X \subseteq Y$, then $X \cup Y = Y$; therefore, using the previous proposition, we have $XZ \cup YZ = YZ$, that is, $XZ \subseteq YZ$. The second inclusion of the Corollary can be proved similarly. ∎

1.3.3 Morphisms and Subalgebras

Whenever we consider functions from one algebra to another, we are mainly interested in those that are compatible with the operations of the algebras. Such functions, known as *morphisms*, exist between algebras whose sets of operations are similar.

Definition 1.3.23 The algebras $\mathcal{A} = (M, O)$ and $\mathcal{A}' = (M', O')$ are *similar* if there exists a bijection $\beta : O \longrightarrow O'$ between their sets of operations such that both f and $\beta(f)$ have the same arity for every operation $f \in O$.

We refer to $\beta(f)$ as the operation that corresponds to f. □

For instance, any two monoids $(M, \star, 1)$, $(M', \bullet, 1')$ are similar because the mapping $\beta : \{\star, 1\} \longrightarrow \{\bullet, 1'\}$ given by $\beta(\star) = \bullet$, and $\beta(1) = 1'$ is a bijection; likewise, any two semigroups are similar.

Definition 1.3.24 Let $\mathcal{A} = (M, O), \mathcal{A}' = (M', O')$ be two similar algebras. A function $h : M \longrightarrow M'$ is a *morphism* if for every n-ary operation $f \in O$ we have

$$h(f(a_0, \ldots, a_{n-1})) = g(h(a_0), \ldots, h(a_{n-1})), \tag{1.5}$$

for every $(a_0, \ldots, a_{n-1}) \in M^n$, where g is the n-ary operation in O' that corresponds to f.

If h is a bijection, then we refer to h as an *isomorphism* between the algebras $\mathcal{A}$ and $\mathcal{A}'$. If an isomorphism exists between two similar algebras, we say that the algebras are *isomorphic*. □

In the case of zero-ary operations, the Equation (1.5) becomes $h(u) = v$ if u is a zero-ary operation in $\mathcal{A}$ and v is the corresponding operation in $\mathcal{A}'$. Consequently, any identified constants are mapped into corresponding constants.

Next, we specialize Definition 1.3.24 to semigroups and monoids.

Definition 1.3.25 Let $(S, \star)$, $(P, \bullet)$ be two semigroups. A mapping $h : S \longrightarrow P$ is a semigroup morphism if $h(a_0 \star a_1) = h(a_0) \bullet h(a_1)$ for every $a_0, a_1 \in S$.

If $(S, \star, 1)$ and $(P, \bullet, 1')$ are monoids, a mapping $h : S \longrightarrow P$ is a monoid morphism if $h(1) = 1'$ and $h(a_0 \star a_1) = h(a_0) \bullet h(a_1)$ for every $a_0, a_1 \in S$. □

Example 1.3.26 Consider the semigroups $(\mathbb{N}, +), (\mathbb{N}, \cdot)$. The function $h : \mathbb{N} \longrightarrow \mathbb{N}$ defined by $h(n) = 2^n$ is a morphism because

$$h(n_0 + n_1) = 2^{n_0 + n_1} = 2^{n_0} \cdot 2^{n_1} = h(n_0) \cdot h(n_1),$$

for every $n_0, n_1 \in \mathbb{N}$. Similarly, the mapping $g : \mathbb{N} \longrightarrow \mathbb{R}$ between the semigroups $(\mathbb{N}, \cdot)$ and $(\mathbb{R}, +)$ given by $g(n) = \log n$ is a morphism because

$$g(n_0 \cdot n_1) = \log n_0 n_1 = \log n_0 + \log n_1 = g(n_0) + g(n_1)$$

for every $n_0, n_1 \in \mathbb{N}$. □

Definition 1.3.27 Let $\mathcal{A} = (M, O)$ be an algebra and let $f \in O$ be an n-ary operation of $\mathcal{A}$. A subset P of M is *f-closed* if $a_0, \ldots, a_{n-1} \in P$ imply $f(a_0, \ldots, a_{n-1}) \in P$.

P is a *closed subset* of $\mathcal{A}$ if P is f-closed for each operation f of $\mathcal{A}$. □

Note that if P is a closed subset of an algebra, then P contains the values of every zero-ary operation of $\mathcal{A}$. Therefore, algebras that have zero-ary operations cannot have an empty closed set. Further, if $\{P_i \mid i \in I\}$ is a nonempty collection of closed subsets of $\mathcal{A}$, then it is easy to see that $\bigcap\{P_i \mid i \in I\}$ is also a closed set.

If $L \subseteq M$, then

$$\hat{L} = \bigcap\{P \mid L \subseteq P \subseteq M \text{ and } P \text{ is closed}\}$$

is a closed set. We refer to $\hat{L}$ as *the closed set generated by* L; it is easy to see that this is the smallest closed set that contains L. If $K = \hat{L}$, then L is a *set of generators* for K.

Example 1.3.28 Let $(S, \star)$ be a semigroup. L is a set of generators for S if every element x of S can be written as a product $x = x_0 \star x_1 \star \cdots x_{n-1}$ of elements of L, for $n \geq 1$. □

Definition 1.3.29 A *subalgebra* of the algebra $\mathcal{A} = (M, O)$ is an algebra $\mathcal{A}' = (P, O_P)$, where $P \subseteq M$ is a closed subset of M and

$$O_P = \{f\rceil P^n \mid f \in O \text{ is an } n\text{-ary operation}\}.$$

□

For specific algebras we have specific terms to designate their subalgebras. For example, subalgebras of semigroups and monoids are referred to as *subsemigroups* and *submonoids*, respectively. If $\mathcal{S} = (S, \star)$ is a semigroup then $(T, \star)$ is a subsemigroup of $\mathcal{S}$ if $T \subseteq S$, and $x, y \in T$ imply $x \star y \in T$. The monoid $(P, \star, 1)$ is a submonoid of $(M, \star, 1)$ if $P \subseteq M$, $1 \in P$, and $x, y \in P$ imply $x \star y \in P$.

Theorem 1.3.30 *If P is a closed set of an algebra $\mathcal{A} = (M, O)$ and $h : M \longrightarrow M'$ is a morphism from $\mathcal{A}$ to $\mathcal{A}' = (M', O')$, then $h(P)$ is a closed subset of $\mathcal{A}'$.*

Proof. Let f' be an n-ary operation of $\mathcal{A}'$ and let $b_0, \ldots, b_{n-1}$ be n elements in $h(P)$. There exist $a_0, \ldots, a_{n-1} \in P$ such that $h(a_i) = b_i$ for $0 \leq i \leq n-1$, so

$$\begin{aligned} f'(b_0, \ldots, b_{n-1}) &= f'(h(a_0), \ldots, h(a_{n-1})) \\ &= h(f(a_0, \ldots, a_{n-1})) \in h(P). \end{aligned}$$

Thus $h(P)$ is closed. ■

Corollary 1.3.31 *If $h : M \longrightarrow M'$ is a morphism from the algebra $\mathcal{A} = (M, O)$ to the algebra $\mathcal{A}' = (M', O')$, then $(h(M), O'_{h(M)})$ is a subalgebra of $\mathcal{A}'$.*

Proof. This statement is an immediate consequence of Theorem 1.3.30. ■

1.3.4 Congruences

Congruences are equivalence relations defined on carriers of algebras that are compatible with the algebra operations. This is formalized in the next definition.

Definition 1.3.32 Let $\mathcal{A} = (M, O)$ be an algebra. A *congruence* is an equivalence relation $\rho \subseteq A \times A$ such that for every n-ary operation $f \in O$,

$$(a_0, b_0), \ldots, (a_{n-1}, b_{n-1}) \in \rho$$

imply $(f(a_0, \ldots, a_{n-1}), f(b_0, \ldots, b_{n-1})) \in \rho$. □

Note that zero-ary operations do not impose any special conditions on congruences.

In the case of semigroups the previous definition can be specialized as follows. If $(S, \star)$ is a semigroup, then the equivalence relation ρ on S is a congruence if $(a_0, a_1), (b_0, b_1) \in \rho$ imply $(a_0 \star b_0, a_1 \star b_1) \in \rho$. Exactly the same definition applies to the congruences on a monoid $(S, \star, 1)$.

Next, we give a characterization of congruences on semigroups and monoids.

Theorem 1.3.33 *Let $(S, \star)$ be a semigroup. An equivalence relation ρ on the set S is a congruence of $(S, \star)$ if and only if $(a, a') \in \rho$ implies $(b \star a, b \star a') \in \rho$ and $(a \star c, a' \star c) \in \rho$ for every $a, a', b, c \in S$.*

If $(S, \star, 1)$ is a monoid, the following statements are equivalent:

(i) *ρ is a congruence;*

(ii) *$(a, a') \in \rho$ implies $(b \star a, b \star a') \in \rho$ and $(a \star c, a' \star c) \in \rho$ for every $a, a', b, c \in S$;*

(iii) *$(a, a') \in \rho$ implies $(b \star a \star c, b \star a' \star c) \in \rho$ for every $a, a', b, c \in S$.*

Proof. Let ρ be a congruence of $(S, \star)$ and let $(a, a') \in \rho$. Since ρ is reflexive we have $(b, b), (c, c) \in \rho$. This implies $(b \star a, b \star a') \in \rho$, and $(a \star c, a' \star c) \in \rho$.

Conversely, let ρ be an equivalence relation on S such that $(a, a') \in \rho$ implies $(b \star a, b \star a') \in \rho$ and $(a \star c, a' \star c) \in \rho$ for every $a, a', b, c \in S$, and assume that $(a_0, a_1), (b_0, b_1) \in \rho$. We have $(a_0 \star b_0, a_1 \star b_0) \in \rho$ and $(a_1 \star b_0, a_1 \star b_1) \in \rho$. The transitivity of ρ implies $(a_0 \star b_0, a_1 \star b_1) \in \rho$.

The argument for the second part of the theorem is immediate and is left to the reader. ∎

An useful weaker notion is given next.

Definition 1.3.34 A *right-invariant equivalence relation* on a semigroup $(S, \star)$ is an equivalence relation ρ on S such that $(a, a') \in \rho$ implies $(a \star b, a' \star b) \in \rho$ for every $a, a', b \in S$.

Similarly, a *left-invariant equivalence relation* on a semigroup $(S, \star)$ is an equivalence relation ρ on S such that $(a, a') \in \rho$ implies $(b \star a, b \star a') \in \rho$ for every $a, a', b \in S$. □

It is clear that a relatiòn ρ over S is a congruence if and only if it is both a right-invariant and a left-invariant equivalence relation.

Example 1.3.35 Let $\mathsf{T}(M) = (M^M, \circ, 1_M)$ be the monoid of transformations of the set M. For $m \in M$ consider the equivalence relation $\rho_m = \{(f, g) \mid f, g \in M^M, f(m) = g(m)\}$. Then, ρ_m is a right-invariant equivalence relation because $mf = mg$ implies $m(fh) = m(gh)$ for every $h \in M^M$. It is easy to see that ρ_m is not left-invariant, in general, so ρ_m is not a congruence of $\mathsf{T}(M)$. □

Theorem 1.3.36 *Let $\mathcal{A} = (M, O)$ and $\mathcal{A}' = (M', O')$ be two similar algebras. For every morphism $h : M \longrightarrow M'$ the equivalence relation $\mathbf{ker}(h)$ is a congruence of the algebra $\mathcal{A}$.*

Proof. We already know that the relation $\mathbf{ker}(h)$ is an equivalence relation on M. Let $f \in O, g \in O'$ be two corresponding operations in $\mathcal{A}, \mathcal{A}'$ and assume that $(a_0, b_0), \ldots, (a_{n-1}, b_{n-1}) \in \mathbf{ker}(f)$. We have $h(a_i) = h(b_i)$ for $0 \leq i \leq n-1$, so

$$\begin{aligned} h(f(a_0, \ldots, a_{n-1})) &= g(h(a_0), \ldots, h(a_{n-1})) \\ &= g(h(b_0), \ldots, h(b_{n-1})) \\ &= h(f(b_0, \ldots, b_{n-1})), \end{aligned}$$

so $(f(a_0, \ldots, a_{n-1}), f(b_0, \ldots, b_{n-1})) \in \mathbf{ker}(f)$, which shows that $\mathbf{ker}(f)$ is a congruence of $\mathcal{A}$. ∎

In the case of monoids we can attach a congruence to every subset as shown in the next theorem. Let $(M, \star, 1)$ be a monoid and let L be a subset of M. Define the relation $\mu_L \subseteq M \times M$ by

$$\begin{aligned} \mu_L = \{(x, y) \in M \times M \mid & \ u \star x \star v \in L \text{ if and only if} \\ & u \star y \star v \in L \text{ for every } u, v \in M\}, \end{aligned}$$

Theorem 1.3.37 *The relation μ_L is a congruence of the monoid $(M, \star, u)$. Further, L is a μ_L-saturated set, and for every congruence μ that saturates L we have $\mu \subseteq \mu_L$.*

Proof. It is easy to see that μ_L is an equivalence relation on M. If $(x, y) \in \mu_L$, then we claim that $(s \star x \star t, s \star y \star t) \in \mu_L$ for every $s, t \in M$. Indeed, we have

$$\begin{aligned} u \star (s \star x \star t) \star v \in L & \text{ if and only if } (u \star s) \star x \star (t \star v) \in L \\ & \text{ if and only if } (u \star s) \star y \star (t \star v) \in L \\ & \text{ if and only if } u \star (s \star y \star t) \star v \in L \end{aligned}$$

for every $u, v \in M$, in view of the associativity of the operation $\star$. Now, from Theorem 1.3.33, it follows that μ_L is a congruence.

Suppose now that μ is a congruence that saturates L, and let $(x, y) \in \mu$. We have $(u \star x \star v, u \star y \star v) \in \mu$. Observe that we have $u \star x \star v \in L$ then $u \star y \star v \in L$ and vice versa, because μ saturates L. This shows that $(x, y) \in \mu_L$, so $\mu \subseteq \mu_L$. ∎

Definition 1.3.38 Let $(M, \star, 1)$ be a monoid and let L be a subset of M. The *syntactic congruence of* L is the congruence μ_L. □

Note that if L is a subset of M, where $(M, \star, 1)$ is a monoid, then both L and its complement $M - L$ have the same syntactic congruences. In particular, $\mu_\emptyset = \mu_M = M \times M$.

1.4 Sequences

In this section we focus on the properties of sequences, an important mathematical concept that is central to the theory of formal languages.

Definition 1.4.1 A *finite sequence of elements of a set D* is a function $s : \{0, \ldots, n-1\} \longrightarrow D$, for some $n \in \mathbb{N}$. The number n is called the *length* of s and is denoted by $|s|$; s is called a *sequence of length n*. The elements of the range of s are called the *components* of s. □

If s is a sequence of length n, then s is denoted by $(s_0, \ldots, s_{n-1})$, where $s_i = s(i)$, for $0 \leq i \leq n-1$.

If $d = s(i)$ we refer to the pair (d, i) as an *occurrence* of d in the sequence s.

For every element $d \in D$ we denote by $n_d(s)$ the number of occurrences of d in the sequence s; in other words,

$$n_d(s) = |\{i \mid 0 \leq i \leq n-1, s(i) = d\}|.$$

For a set D we use both $\mathbf{Seq}_n(D)$ and D^n to denote the set of all sequences of length n over D.

Example 1.4.2 Consider the sequence $s : \{0, 1, 2, 3\} \longrightarrow \mathbb{Z}$ given by $s(0) = -2$, $s(1) = 0$, $s(2) = -10$, and $s(3) = 4$. Using the convention just introduced, we denote s by $(-2, 0, -10, 4)$.

For the sequence $z : \{0, 1, 2, 3, 4\} \longrightarrow \{a, b, c\}$ given by $z = (b, a, a, c, a)$ we have $|z| = 5$ and $n_a(z) = 3$, $n_b(z) = 1$, and $n_c(z) = 1$. □

A sequence of length 0 is a function whose domain is the empty set. There is exactly one such function, namely, the empty function, so there is only one sequence of length 0. We call this sequence *the null sequence* or *the empty sequence*. According to the notation for sequences introduced previously, $()$ denotes the empty sequence. We prefer to use the notation λ for the empty sequence.

A sequence t of length 1 is completely determined by its value $t(0)$. Sometimes we find convenient to regard an object d as representing the sequence (d) of length 1 whose only entry is d, even though d and (d) are not in fact the same.

Definition 1.4.3 Let s be a sequence of length $n \in \mathbb{N}$.

A *prefix* of s is a restriction of s to $\{0, \ldots, m-1\}$, where $0 \leq m \leq n-1$.

An *infix* of s is a restriction of s to $\{p, \ldots, q-1\}$, where $0 \leq p < q \leq n$.

A *suffix* of s is a restriction of s to $\{p, \ldots, n-1\}$, where $0 \leq p \leq n-1$.

The sets of prefixes, infixes and suffixes of a sequence s are denoted by $\mathsf{PREF}(s)$, $\mathsf{INFIX}(s)$ and $\mathsf{SUFF}(s)$, respectively. □

Example 1.4.4 Let $s = (6, 1, 4)$ be a sequence of natural numbers. The set of its prefixes is

$$\mathsf{PREF}(s) = \{\lambda, (6), (6, 1), (6, 1, 4)\}.$$

The set of suffixes of s is

$$\mathsf{SUFF}(s) = \{\lambda, (4), (1, 4), (6, 1, 4)\}.$$

Clearly, (1) is the single infix of s that is neither a prefix nor a suffix of s. □

If $s = (a_0, \ldots, a_{n-1}) \in \mathbf{Seq}_n(A)$, then we denote by $s_{i,j}$ the infix $r \in \mathbf{Seq}_{j-i}(A)$ of s given by $r = (a_i, \ldots, a_{j-1})$ for $0 \leq i < j \leq n$. If $j \leq i$, we define $s_{i,j}$ to be the empty sequence. Thus, $s_{i,i} = \lambda$ for every i, $0 \leq i \leq n-1$, $s_{0,j} \in \mathsf{PREF}(s)$ for $0 \leq j \leq n$, and $s_{i,n} \in \mathsf{SUFF}(s)$ for $0 \leq i \leq n$.

Functions also allow us to formalize the notion of infinite sequence.

Definition 1.4.5 An *infinite sequence* is a function with domain $\mathbb{N}$. The elements of the range of an infinite sequence s are called the *entries* of s. If D is a set, then an *infinite sequence of elements of D* or an *infinite sequence over D* is an infinite sequence whose range is contained in D. □

An infinite sequence s is denoted by $(s_0, s_1, \ldots, s_n, \ldots)$, where $s_n = s(n)$ for $n \in \mathbb{N}$.

Example 1.4.6 Consider the infinite sequence $s : \mathbb{N} \longrightarrow \mathbb{P}$, where $s(n) = 2n + 1$, for every natural number n. Then, s is denoted by $(1, 3, 5, \ldots)$. The entries of this sequence are all the odd natural numbers. □

We denote the set of all finite sequences over D by $\mathbf{Seq}(D)$; the set of all finite, nonnull sequences over D is denoted by $\mathbf{Seq}^+(D)$, and $\mathbf{Seq}_\infty(D)$ denotes the set of all infinite sequences over D.

The following equalities are an immediate consequence of the previous notations.

$$\begin{aligned}
\mathbf{Seq}_n(D) &= \{0, \ldots, n-1\} \longrightarrow D, \\
\mathbf{Seq}(D) &= \bigcup_{n \geq 0} \mathbf{Seq}_n(D), \\
\mathbf{Seq}^+(D) &= \bigcup_{n \geq 1} \mathbf{Seq}_n(D), \\
\mathbf{Seq}_\infty(D) &= \mathbb{N} \longrightarrow D.
\end{aligned}$$

Observe that $D^0 = \{\lambda\}$, and, as discussed previously, D^1 can be identified with D and D^2 can be identified with $D \times D$. (More precisely, there are natural bijections between D^1 and D and between D^2 and $D \times D$. For instance, we have the bijection $\Psi : D^1 \longrightarrow D$ given by $\Psi((d)) = d$ for every $(d) \in D^1$.)

If $D = \emptyset$, then $D^0 = \{\lambda\}$, and for all $n > 0$, $D^n = \emptyset$; hence, $\mathbf{Seq}(D) = \{\lambda\}$.

1.4.1 The Monoid of Sequences

In the next definition we introduce the binary operation of adjoining one sequence to another.

Definition 1.4.7 Let s be a sequence of length n and let t be a sequence of length m. The *product* or *concatenation* of the sequences s, t is the sequence z of length $n + m$ defined by

$$z(i) = \begin{cases} s(i) & \text{if } 0 \leq i \leq n-1 \\ t(i-n) & \text{if } n \leq i \leq n+m-1. \end{cases}$$

□

The concatenation of the sequences s and t is denoted by st. If $s, t \in \mathbf{Seq}(D)$, then so is st.

Example 1.4.8 Let $A = \{a, b, c, d, e\}$ be a set and let $s \in \mathbf{Seq}_3(A)$ and $t \in \mathbf{Seq}_2(A)$ be the sequences $s = (b, e, a)$ and $t = (a, b)$. The concatenation st of these sequences is $z = (b, e, a, b, a) \in \mathbf{Seq}_5(A)$. □

The basic properties of concatenation are given in the next theorem.

Theorem 1.4.9 *Let u, v, w be finite sequences, $u, v, w \in \mathbf{Seq}(D)$. We have*

1. *$u(vw) = (uv)w$ (associativity of concatenation);*
2. *if $uv = uw$, then $v = w$ (left cancellation);*
3. *if $vu = wu$, then $v = w$ (right cancellation);*
4. *$\lambda u = u = u\lambda$.*

Proof. Let $|u| = n$, $|v| = m$, $|w| = p$. To prove the associativity, let $y = u(vw)$ and $z = (uv)w$. Clearly, we have $|vw| = m + p$ and $|uv| = n + m$. Applying Definition 1.4.7, we have

$$y(i) = \begin{cases} u(i) & \text{if } 0 \leq i \leq n-1 \\ v \cdot w(i-n) & \text{if } n \leq i \leq n+m+p-1, \end{cases}$$

and

$$(vw)(j) = \begin{cases} v(j) & \text{if } 0 \leq j \leq m-1 \\ w(j-m) & \text{if } m \leq j \leq m+p-1. \end{cases}$$

This, in turn, results in

$$y(i) = \begin{cases} u(i) & \text{if } 0 \leq i \leq n-1 \\ v(i-n) & \text{if } n \leq i \leq n+m-1 \\ w(i-n-m) & \text{if } n+m \leq i \leq n+m+p-1. \end{cases}$$

For the sequence uv, we have

$$(uv)(i) = \begin{cases} u(i) & \text{if } 0 \leq i \leq n-1 \\ v(i-n) & \text{if } n \leq i \leq n+m-1, \end{cases}$$

and therefore, we obtain $z(i) = y(i)$ for $0 \leq i \leq n+m+p-1$.

We leave to the reader the arguments for the remaining parts of this theorem. ∎

Theorem 1.4.9 shows that the triple $(\mathbf{Seq}(D), \cdot, \lambda)$ is a monoid, where "$\cdot$" denotes sequence concatenation. We refer to this monoid as *the free monoid generated by the set D*.

In general, free monoids are not commutative as shown by the next theorem.

Theorem 1.4.10 *Sequence concatenation is not commutative; in fact, we have $uv = vu$ for all $u, v \in \mathbf{Seq}(D)$ if and only if D is empty or a singleton.*

Proof. If $D = \emptyset$, then $\mathbf{Seq}(D) = \{\lambda\}$, and the commutativity of sequence concatenation for sequences in $\mathbf{Seq}(D)$ is trivial.

If $D = \{a\}$, $|u| = n$, and $|v| = m$, then we have $(uv)(i) = (vu)(i) = a$ for all i, $0 \leq i \leq n+m-1$, which implies $uv = vu$, showing that sequence concatenation is commutative for all sequences in $\mathbf{Seq}(D)$.

Conversely, assume that D is nonempty and is not a singleton. Then, D contains two distinct elements, say, a, b. Choosing $u = (a)$ and $v = (b)$, we obtain $uv = (a, b) \neq (b, a) = vu$, so we do not have commutativity of concatenation for all sequences in $\mathbf{Seq}(D)$. ∎

Example 1.4.11 Let $\mathbf{FSeq}(\mathbb{N}) \subseteq \mathbf{Seq}_\infty(\mathbb{N})$ be the set of all infinite sequences of natural numbers that have only a finite number of components different from 0. If $q, r \in \mathbf{FSeq}(\mathbb{N})$ define $q + r$ by $(q + r)(n) = q(n) + r(n)$ for $n \in \mathbb{N}$. It is easy to verify that $(\mathbf{FSeq}(\mathbb{N}), +, \lambda)$ is a monoid.

Let $p_0, p_1, \ldots$ be the increasing sequence of all the prime integers. Define the mapping $h : \mathbf{FSeq} \longrightarrow \mathbb{N}$ by

$$h(n_0, n_1, \ldots, n_k, \ldots) = p_0^{n_0} p_1^{n_1} \cdots p_k^{n_k} \cdots$$

for every $(n_0, n_1, \ldots, n_k, \ldots) \in \mathbf{FSeq}(\mathbb{N})$ and $h(\lambda) = 1$. Since every natural number can be expressed uniquely as a product of primes, h is an isomorphism between the monoids $(\mathbf{FSeq}, +, \lambda)$ and $(\mathbb{N}, \cdot, 1)$. □

Definition 1.4.12 Let x be a finite sequence, where $|x| = n$. The *reversal* of x, is the sequence x^R of length n such that $x^R(i) = x(n-i-1)$ for $0 \leq i \leq n-1$. □

Note that $\lambda^R = \lambda$.

Theorem 1.4.13 *For all finite sequences $x, y \in \mathbf{Seq}(D)$ we have*

1. $\left(x^R\right)^R = x$
2. $(x \cdot y)^R = y^R \cdot x^R$.

Proof. The argument is an immediate application of the definition and is left to the reader. ∎

We assume that the following statement holds for every alphabet A:

> **The Ordering Principle for Seq(D):** Every non-empty set of sequences $L \subseteq \mathbf{Seq}(D)$ contains one or more sequences of minimal length.

An important consequence of this statement is given next. Recall, we may write a one-element sequence (d) simply as d.

Theorem 1.4.14 (Induction Principle for Sequences) *Let L be a set of sequences, $L \subseteq \mathbf{Seq}(D)$, such that $\lambda \in L$, and $x \in L$ implies $xd \in L$ for every $d \in D$. Then, $L = \mathbf{Seq}(D)$.*

Proof. Suppose that $L \neq \mathbf{Seq}(D)$, and let w be a sequence of minimal length in $\mathbf{Seq}(D) - L$. Note that $w \neq \lambda$ since $\lambda \in L$. Therefore, $w = yd$ for some $d \in D$ and $y \in \mathbf{Seq}(D)$. Since w is of minimal length in $\mathbf{Seq}(D) - L$, it follows that $y \in L$, which implies $yd \in L$ by the definition of L; but $w = yd \notin L$. This contradiction implies that $L = \mathbf{Seq}(D)$. ∎

Theorem 1.4.15 *Let $(S, \star, u)$ be a monoid, and let D be a set. Every mapping $h : D \longrightarrow S$ has a unique extension to a morphism between the monoid $(\mathbf{Seq}(D), \cdot, \lambda)$ and $(S, \star, u)$.*

Proof. Define the mapping $h^* : \mathbf{Seq}(D) \longrightarrow S$ by

$$h^*(\lambda) = u \tag{1.6}$$

$$h^*(x(d)) = h^*(x) \star h(d), \tag{1.7}$$

for $x \in \mathbf{Seq}(D)$ and $d \in D$. Taking $x = \lambda$ in Equation (1.7) we obtain $h^*((d)) = h^*(\lambda) \star h(d) = u \star h(d) = h(d)$, so h^* is indeed an extension of h.

To prove that h^* is a monoid morphism we have to show that $h^*(xy) = h^*(x) \star h^*(y)$ for every $x, y \in \mathbf{Seq}(D)$. Let

$$L = \{y \in \mathbf{Seq}(D) \mid h^*(xy) = h^*(x) \star h^*(y) \text{ for every } x \in \mathbf{Seq}(D)\}.$$

Clearly, $\lambda \in L$. Suppose that $y \in L$ and $d \in D$. We have

$$\begin{aligned} h^*(x(y(d))) &= h^*((xy)(d)) \text{ (by associativity of concatenation)} \\ &= h^*(xy) \star h(d) \text{ (by Equation (1.7))} \\ &= h^*(x) \star h^*(y) \star h(d) \\ &= h^*(x) \star h^*(y(d)), \end{aligned}$$

so $y(d) \in L$. By Theorem 1.4.14 we have $L = \mathbf{Seq}(D)$ which means that $h^*(xy) = h^*(x) \star h^*(y)$ for every $x, y \in \mathbf{Seq}(D)$.

We show now that the extension of h to a morphism is unique. Suppose that $k : \mathbf{Seq}(D) \longrightarrow S$ is another monoid morphism such that $k((d)) = h(d)$, and let $K = \{x \in \mathbf{Seq}(D) \mid h^*(x) = k(x)\}$. Since both h^* and k are monoid morphisms we have $h^*(\lambda) = k(\lambda) = \lambda$, so $\lambda \in K$. If $x \in K$ and $d \in D$ we have

$$\begin{aligned} k(x(d)) &= k(x)k(d) \\ &= h^*(x)h(d) \text{ since } x \in K \\ &= h^*(x)h^*((d)) \\ &= h^*(x(d)) \end{aligned}$$

so $x(d) \in K$. Therefore, $K = \mathbf{Seq}(D)$, so $k = h^*$. ∎

1.4.2 Arithmetic Progressions

Definition 1.4.16 An *arithmetic progression* is a sequence $p \in \mathbf{Seq}_\infty(\mathbb{N})$ such that $p_n = p_0 + nr$ for every $n \in \mathbb{N}$. □

The set of values of an arithmetic progression p is completely determined by the numbers $b = p_0$ and r; we denote this set by $\mathsf{PROG}(b, r)$.

Example 1.4.17 Consider the arithmetic progression p where $p_n = 2n$. We have $b = 0$ and $r = 2$. The set $\mathsf{PROG}(0, 2)$ coincides with the set of even natural numbers.

Note that $\mathsf{PROG}(b, 0) = \{b\}$. □

Observe that if $\ell \geq b$, then $\ell \in \mathsf{PROG}(b, r)$ if and only if $\ell + r \in \mathsf{PROG}(b, r)$. This property of the set of values of an arithmetic progression is generalized in the next definition.

Definition 1.4.18 A set $S \subseteq \mathbb{N}$ is *ultimately periodic* if it is finite or if there exist $b, r \in \mathbb{N}$ such that if $\ell \geq b$, then $\ell \in S$ if and only if $\ell + r \in S$. □

Lemma 1.4.19 *Let S_i, $0 \leq i \leq k-1$, be k ultimately periodic sets. Their union $S = \bigcup\{S_i \mid 0 \leq i \leq k-1\}$ is an ultimately periodic set.*

Proof. Suppose that for the ultimately periodic set S_i the numbers introduced in Definition 1.4.18 are b_i and r_i for $0 \leq i \leq k-1$. Define $b = \max\{b_0, \ldots, b_{k-1}\}$ and let r be the least common multiple of the numbers $r_0, \ldots, r_{k-1}$. We claim that if $\ell \geq b$, then $\ell \in S$ if and only if $\ell + r \in S$.

Suppose that $\ell \in S$ and $\ell > b$. Then, there exists i, $0 \leq i \leq k-1$ such that $\ell \in S_i$. Therefore, $\ell + mr_i \in S_i \subseteq S$ for every $m \in \mathbb{N}$. Since $r = m_i r_i$ for some $m_i \in \mathbb{N}$, we obtain $\ell + r \in S$ by taking $m = m_i$.

Conversely, let $\ell + r \in S$, where $\ell > b$. Then, there exists S_i such that $\ell + r \in S_i$. Since S_i is ultimately periodic, $\ell + r \in S_i$ if and only if $\ell + r - mr_i \in S_i$ for $m \in \mathbb{N}$, provided that $\ell + r - mr_i > b_i$. Since r is the least common multiple of the numbers $r_0, \ldots, r_{k-1}$ there is a number m_i such that $r = m_i r_i$. Choosing $m = m_i$, we obtain $\ell \in S_i \subseteq S$. ∎

Example 1.4.20 The set $S = \{21, 22, 31, 32, 41, 42, \ldots\} = \{21 + 10 * i \mid i \in \mathbb{N}\} \cup \{22 + 10 * i \mid i \in \mathbb{N}\}$ is ultimately periodic. Indeed, if $\ell \geq 21$, then $\ell \in S$ if and only if $\ell + 10 \in S$. □

Theorem 1.4.21 *A set S of natural numbers is ultimately periodic if and only if there is a finite collection of sets of values of arithmetic progressions* $\mathsf{PROG}(b_i, r_i)$ *for* $0 \leq i \leq k-1$ *such that*

$$S = \bigcup \{\mathsf{PROG}(b_i, r_i) \mid 0 \leq i \leq k-1\}.$$

Proof. The sufficiency of the condition follows from Lemma 1.4.19 and from the fact that every set of the form $\mathsf{PROG}(b_i, r_i)$ is ultimately periodic.

To prove the necessity, observe that if S is a finite set then the statement holds because every finite set can be regarded as a union of one-element sets of the form $\mathsf{PROG}(b_i, 0)$. Therefore, let S be an infinite, ultimately periodic set, and let b, r be the numbers introduced in Definition 1.4.18 for the set S. Consider the finite sets

$$\begin{aligned} I_0 &= \{p \in S \mid 0 \leq p < b\} \\ I &= \{q \in S \mid b \leq q < b + r\}. \end{aligned}$$

If $\ell \in S$ and $\ell - r \geq b$, then $\ell - r \in S$. By repeating this argument, we obtain $\ell - mr \in S$ if $\ell - mr \geq b$. Let m_ℓ be the largest m such that $\ell - mr \geq b$. The definition of m_ℓ means that

$$\ell - (m_\ell + 1)r < b \leq \ell - m_\ell r.$$

This shows that $b \leq \ell - m_\ell r < b + r$, that is $\ell - m_\ell r \in I$. Therefore, for every element ℓ of S such that $\ell > b$, by repeated subtractions of r we reach $b_i = \ell - m_\ell r$, one of the members of the finite set I, so $\ell \in \mathsf{PROG}(b_i, r)$. Since S is ultimately periodic we have $\mathsf{PROG}(b_i, r) \subseteq S$. Thus, we have $S = I_0 \cup \bigcup_i \mathsf{PROG}(b_i, r)$ so S is the union of a finite number of sets of elements of arithmetic progressions. ∎

1.5 Graphs

We begin by introducing the notion of a system as a general framework for defining various types of graphs.

Definition 1.5.1 A *system* is a quadruple $G = (V, E, s, d)$, where V, E are two sets, referred to as the *set of vertices of* G and the *set of edges of* G, respectively, and $s, d : E \longrightarrow \mathcal{P}(V)$ are two functions, referred to as *the source function* and the *destination function of a system.* □

In this section we are concerned with several types of systems that can be defined by changing the properties of the functions s and d.

Definition 1.5.2 A *undirected graph* is a graph $G = (V, E, s, d)$ such that for every $e \in E$, $s(e) = d(e)$ and $|s(e)| = |d(e)| = 2$. □

Undirected graphs can be represented by diagrams that consist of points representing vertices. If e is an edge in the undirected graph G such that $s(e) = d(e) = \{u, v\}$, then we join the point that represents the vertex u to the point that represents the vertex v by a line that represents the edge e.

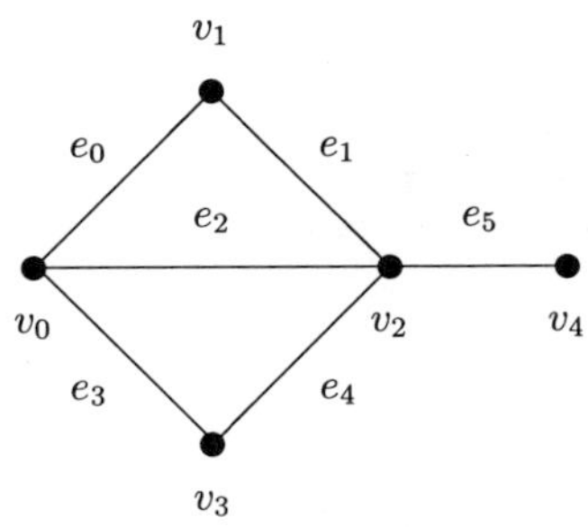

Figure 1.1: Representation of an Undirected Graph

Example 1.5.3 Consider the undirected graph $G = (\{v_i \mid 0 \leq i \leq 4\}, \{e_j \mid 0 \leq j \leq 5\}, s, d)$, where the values of $s(e)$ and $d(e)$ are given by

e	e_0	e_1	e_2	e_3	e_4	e_5
$s(e) = d(e)$	$\{v_0, v_1\}$	$\{v_1, v_2\}$	$\{v_0, v_2\}$	$\{v_0, v_3\}$	$\{v_2, v_3\}$	$\{v_2, v_4\}$

G is represented in Figure 1.1. □

Definition 1.5.4 A *directed multigraph* is a graph $G = (V, E, s, d)$, where both sets $s(e)$ and $d(e)$ are singletons. If $s(e) = \{v\}$ and $d(e) = \{v'\}$, then we refer to v and v' as the *source* and the *destination* of the edge e, respectively.

If $s(e) = \{u\}, d(e) = \{v\}$, then we write $s(e) = u$ and $d(e) = v$ in order to simplify the notation. Also, we say that *e is an edge that joins u to v.* □

Note that in a directed multigraph we may have several edges that join a vertex v to a vertex v'. Directed multigraphs can be represented by diagrams that consist of points representing vertices. If e is an edge in the directed multigraph G such that $s(e) = u$ and $d(e) = v$, then we join u to v by an arrow directed from u to v.

Example 1.5.5 Let $G = (\{v_i \mid 0 \leq i \leq 2\}, \{e_j \mid 0 \leq j \leq 3\}, s, d)$ be the directed multigraph defined by

e	e_0	e_1	e_2	e_3
$s(e)$	$\{v_0\}$	$\{v_0\}$	$\{v_0\}$	$\{v_1\}$
$d(e)$	$\{v_1\}$	$\{v_1\}$	$\{v_1\}$	$\{v_2\}$

This directed multigraph is represented in Figure 1.2. □

Definition 1.5.6 A multigraph $G = (V, E, s, d)$ is a *directed graph* (or a *digraph*) if for every two edges e, e' that have the same source and the same destination we have $e = e'$. □

In a digraph at most one edge may exist that joins a vertex u to another vertex v. Therefore, an edge e in a digraph can be identified with the ordered pair of its endpoints (u, v) and we shall refer to the edge e for which $s(e) = u$ and $d(e) = v$ either as $e_{u,v}$ or, simply, as (u, v).

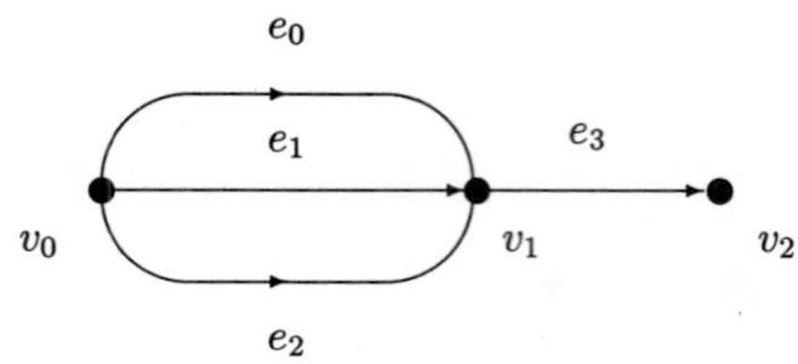

Figure 1.2: Representation of a Multigraph

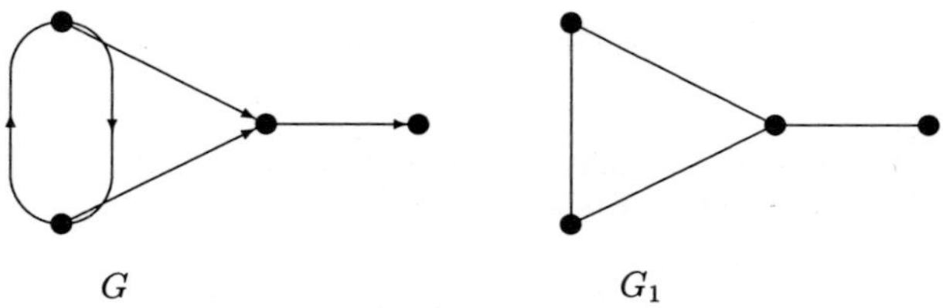

Figure 1.3: The digraph G and its underlying graph G_1

If $G = (V, E, s, d)$ is a digraph, then its *underlying graph* is the undirected graph $G_1 = (V, E_1, s_1, d_1)$, where an edge e' exists in E_1 with $s_1(e') = s_1(e') = \{u, v\}$ if and only if there is an edge $e \in E$ such that $s(e) = u, d(e) = v$, or $s(e) = v, d(e) = u$ with $u \neq v$.

Example 1.5.7 Consider the digraph G shown in the left side of Figure 1.3. The underlying graph G_1 is shown in the right side of the same figure.

□

Example 1.5.8 Directed graphs are a vehicle for representing relations. To represent a relation $\rho \subseteq A \times A$ by a digraph $G = (V, E, s, d)$, consider as vertices of the digraph the elements of the set A; an edge e exists between two vertices x and y if $(x, y) \in \rho$.

Consider the set $A = \{1, 2, 3, 4, 5, 6\}$ and the relation ρ that consists of those pairs $(p, q) \in A \times A$ such that $p \neq q$ and p divides q. The pair

$$\begin{aligned} G_1 &= (\{1,2,3,4,5,6\}, \{(1,2),(1,3),(1,4), \\ &\quad (1,5),(1,6),(2,4),(2,6),(3,6)\}). \end{aligned}$$

is the directed graph that represents the relation ρ. This graph is represented in Figure 1.4. □

Definition 1.5.9 Let $G = (V, E, s, d)$ be a directed multigraph. A *path* of length n is a sequence of $n + 1$ vertices $(v_0, \ldots, v_n)$ such that for every i, $1 \leq i \leq n$ there is an edge e_i such that $s(e_i) = v_{i-1}$ and $d(e_i) = v_i$. When convenient, we will refer to the sequence of edges $(e_1, \ldots, e_n)$ as a path of length n. Note that a path of length 0 comprises a single vertice.

The vertex $v_0 = s(e_1)$ is called *the source, the origin*, or *the beginning* of the

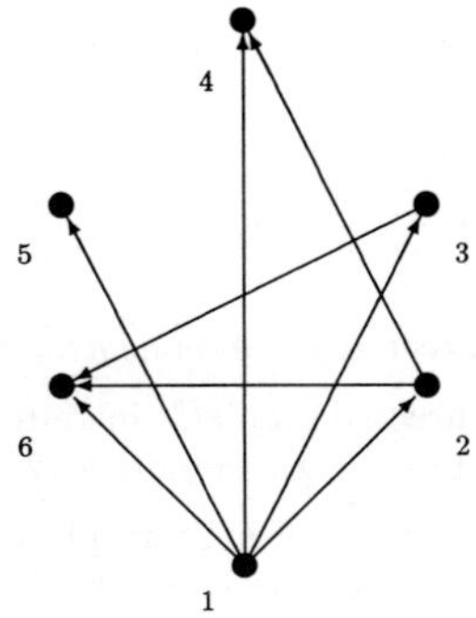

Figure 1.4: Directed graph G_1 of Relation ρ

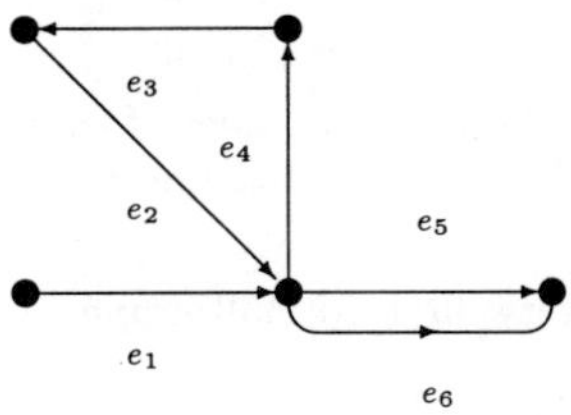

Figure 1.5: A Directed Multigraph

path; $v_n = d(e_n)$ is the *destination* or *the end.* If v_0 is the source of the path ϖ and v_n is its destination, then we say that ϖ joins v_0 to v_n. The vertices $v_0, \ldots, v_n$ are said to be *traversed* by ϖ.

If there exists a path whose source is u and destination is v we write $u \rightsquigarrow v$. □

Example 1.5.10 The sequence $(1, 3, 6)$ is a path of length 2 in the directed graph G_1 introduced in Example 1.5.8. The same path is designated by the sequence of edges $(e_{1,3}, e_{3,6})$. □

If $G = (V, E, s, d)$ is a digraph that represents a relation $\rho \subseteq V \times V$, then there exists a path of length n in the directed graph $G = (V, E)$ joining the vertex x with the vertex y if and only if $(x, y) \in \rho^n$ for $n \in \mathbb{N}$.

Definition 1.5.11 A path in a directed multigraph is *elementary* if no vertex appears twice on the path. A path is *simple* if no edge is traversed twice by the path. A *circuit* is a path of length at least 1 whose source and destination coincide. □

Example 1.5.12 Consider the directed multigraph shown in Figure 1.5.

The sequence (e_1, e_4, e_3) is an elementary path in G_2, while (e_4, e_3, e_2) is a circuit. The path $(e_1, e_4, e_3, e_2, e_5)$ is a simple but non-elementary path and the sequence

$$(e_1, e_4, e_3, e_2, e_4)$$

is a non-simple path. □

Definition 1.5.13 A directed graph is *acyclic* if it contains no circuits. □

Example 1.5.14 The directed graph G_1 introduced in Example 1.5.8 is acyclic, while the multigraph defined in Example 1.5.12 is not. □

If $G = (V, E, s, d)$ is a directed multigraph, consider the binary relation κ_G on V that contains all pairs of the form (x, x) for every $x \in V$ as well as all pairs $(x, y) \in V \times V$ such that $x \rightsquigarrow y$ and $y \rightsquigarrow x$. It is easy to verify that κ_G is an equivalence relation on V.

The κ_G-equivalence class of a vertex v is called the *connected component of* v. A directed multigraph is *connected* if all vertices have the same connected component.

Definition 1.5.15 Let $G = (V, E, s, d)$ be a directed multigraph. The *out-degree*, $\partial_{out}(v)$ of a vertex v is the number of edges that have v as their source. The *in-degree*, $\partial_{in}(v)$ of a vertex v is the number of edges that have v as their destination. □

It is clear that in every directed multigraph we have

$$\sum\{\partial_{out}(v) \mid v \in V\} = \sum\{\partial_{in}(v) \mid v \in V\}.$$

A directed multigraph $G = (V, E, s, d)$ is *balanced* if for every $v \in V$ we have $\partial_{out}(v) = \partial_{in}(v)$.

In formal languages we are sometimes interested in placing labels on the vertices and edges of directed graphs. This gives us the notion of labeled directed multigraph introduced next.

Definition 1.5.16 A *labeled directed multigraph* is a triple $\mathcal{G} = (G, M, \mathsf{m})$, where G is a directed multigraph, $G = (V, E, s, d)$, M is the *marking set* , and $\mathsf{m} : V \cup E \mapsto M$ is the *labelling function of* $\mathcal{G}$.

If $v \in \text{Dom}(\mathsf{m})$ or $e \in \text{Dom}(\mathsf{m})$ we say that the vertex v (or, respectively the edge e) is labeled by the symbol $\mathsf{m}(v)$ (by $\mathsf{m}(e)$). □

Trees, which are central to much of computer science – indeed, to many branches of mathematics – are a special case of digraphs.

Definition 1.5.17 A *tree* is a pair $\mathtt{T} = (G, v_0)$, where $G = (V, E, s, d)$ is a digraph and v_0 is a vertex in V such that for every vertex $v \in V$ there exists a unique path whose source is v_0 and whose end is v. The vertex v_0 is the *root* of the tree. □

If (G, v_0) is a tree then G is an acyclic graph.

Example 1.5.18 The directed graph given in Figure 1.4 fails to be a tree with root in 1 since both $e_{1,6}$ and $e_{1,2}, e_{2,6}$ are paths that join 1 to 6.

The directed graph given in Figure 1.6 is a tree with root 1. □

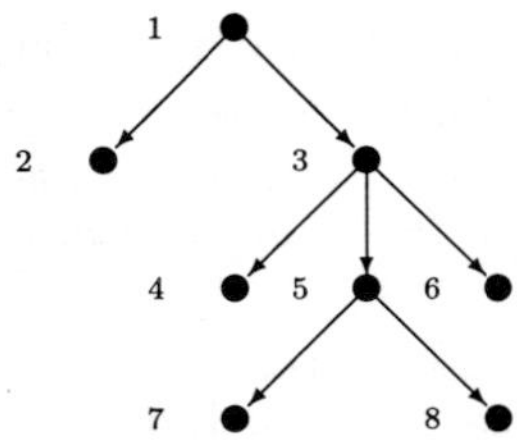

Figure 1.6: Tree whose root is 1

When drawing trees we will always place the initial vertex of an edge above the final vertex of the edge. Thus, we will be able to replace the arrows with simple lines.

Definition 1.5.19 Let $\mathtt{T} = (G, v_0)$ be a tree. If v and v' are vertices of G and there is a path ϖ from v to v', then we refer to v' as a *descendant* of v and to v as an *ancestor* of v'. If ϖ has length 1, then we call v' an *immediate descendant* or a *child* of v and v an *immediate ancestor* or *parent* of v'. The set of children of a vertex v is denoted by $\mathsf{CHILDREN}(v)$.

A *leaf* of T is a vertex of G with no immediate descendants. We write $\mathsf{LEAVES}(\mathtt{T})$ to denote the set of leaves of T.

An *interior vertex* of a tree is a vertex v that is not a leaf of T. The set of interior vertices of T will be denoted by $\mathsf{INTN}(\mathtt{T})$.

The *level* of a vertex v of a tree T is the length of the unique path that joins the root v_0 to v. The ith *level* of T is the set of vertices at level i of T.

The *height of a vertex* v is the length of the longest path that joins v to a leaf of T. For a finite tree T, we define $\mathsf{height}(\mathtt{T})$ to be the height of the root of T. □

A *branch* of a tree T is a path of T that is not properly contained in any other path of T. Then, it is easy to see that $\mathsf{height}(\mathtt{T})$ is the length of the longest branch of T.

Example 1.5.20 For the tree T shown in Figure 1.6 we have

$$\begin{aligned} \mathsf{LEAVES}(\mathtt{T}) &= \{2,4,6,7,8\} \\ \mathsf{INTN}(\mathtt{T}) &= \{1,3,5\} \end{aligned}$$

□

Definition 1.5.21 A *subgraph* of a directed multigraph $G = (V, E, s, d)$ is a directed multigraph $G' = (V', E', s', d')$ such that $V' \subseteq V$, $E' \subseteq E$, and $s'(e') = s(e')$, $d'(e') = d(e')$ for every $e' \in E'$.

Let $G = (V, E, s, d)$ be a directed multigraph, and let $A \subseteq V$ be a set of vertices of G. The *subgraph* of G generated by the set A is the directed multigraph $G_A = (A, E_A, s_A, d_A)$, where $E_A = \{e \in E \mid s(e) \cup d(e) \subseteq A\}$, $s_A(e) = s(e)$, and $d_A(e) = d(e)$ for every $e \in E$. □

In other words, the set of edges of the subgraph generated by the set of vertices A consists of those edges whose source and end both belong to A.

Theorem 1.5.22 *Let* $\mathtt{T} = (G, v_0)$ *be a tree, where* $G = (V, E, s, d)$*, and let* v *be a vertex,* $v \in V$*. If* $V_{[v]}$ *is the set of descendants of* v*, then* $\mathtt{T}_{[v]} = (G_{V_{[v]}}, v)$ *is a tree.*

Proof. It is clear that every vertex $v' \in V_{[v]}$ can be reached from v. Therefore, we need to show only that there is only one path leading from v to v'. Suppose that ϖ is the path that joins v_0 with v and that there are two paths ϖ_1 and ϖ_2 that join v to v'. Then, we would have the distinct paths $\varpi\varpi_1$ and $\varpi\varpi_2$ joining v_0 to v', and this would contradict that $\mathtt{T}$ is a tree. ∎

We refer to $\mathtt{T}_{[v]}$ as *the subtree rooted at the vertex* v *in* $\mathtt{T}$.

Note that if v is an ancestor of v' in the tree $\mathtt{T}$, then $\mathsf{LEAVES}(\mathtt{T}_{[v']}) \subseteq \mathsf{LEAVES}(\mathtt{T}_{[v]})$.

Theorem 1.5.23 *Let* $\mathtt{T}$ *be a tree and let* v, v' *be two vertices. If* $\mathsf{LEAVES}(\mathtt{T}_{[v]}) \cap \mathsf{LEAVES}(\mathtt{T}_{[v']}) \neq \emptyset$*, then* $\mathsf{LEAVES}(\mathtt{T}_{[v']}) \subseteq \mathsf{LEAVES}(\mathtt{T}_{[v]})$ *or* $\mathsf{LEAVES}(\mathtt{T}_{[v]}) \subseteq \mathsf{LEAVES}(\mathtt{T}_{[v']})$.

Proof. Suppose that v, v' are two vertices in $\mathtt{T}$ such that $\mathsf{LEAVES}(\mathtt{T}_{[v]}) \cap \mathsf{LEAVES}(\mathtt{T}_{[v']}) \neq \emptyset$. If w is a leaf in $\mathsf{LEAVES}(\mathtt{T}_{[v]}) \cap \mathsf{LEAVES}(\mathtt{T}_{[v']})$, then both v and v' are located on the path that joins the root with w, so either v is an ancestor of v', or v' is an ancestor of v. In the first case, $\mathsf{LEAVES}(\mathtt{T}_{[v']}) \subseteq \mathsf{LEAVES}(\mathtt{T}_{[v]})$ in the second, $\mathsf{LEAVES}(\mathtt{T}_{[v]}) \subseteq \mathsf{LEAVES}(\mathtt{T}_{[v']})$. ∎

We introduce now the notion of a labeled ordered tree, which plays a central role in the study of context-free grammars. Labeled ordered trees combine the notions of labeled digraph (cf. Definition 1.5.16) with the notion of tree (see Definition 1.5.17); in addition, labeled ordered trees impose an ordering on the children of each interior vertex.

Definition 1.5.24 An *A-labeled ordered tree* is a 4-tuple $\mathtt{T} = (G, v_0, M, \mathsf{m})$ such that (G, M, m) is a labeled digraph, (G, v_0) is a tree, the marking set is $M = \mathbb{N} \times A$ and, for every vertex v, if $|\mathsf{CHILDREN}(v)| = n > 0$, then $\mathsf{m}\rceil\mathsf{CHILDREN}(v)$ is a bijection between the sets $\mathsf{CHILDREN}(v)$ and the set $\{(0, a_{i_0}), \ldots, (n-1, a_{i_{n-1}})\}$, for some $a_{i_0}, \ldots, a_{i_{n-1}} \in A$.

Also, $\mathsf{m}(v_0) = (0, a)$ for some $a \in A$. □

Assume that $\mathtt{T} = (G, v_0, M, \mathsf{m})$ is a labeled ordered tree, and let $v \in V$. If the vertex v has n children, then we refer to the child u of v for which $\mathsf{m}(u) = (0, a_{i_0})$ as the *leftmost child of* v; the child w of v for which $\mathsf{m}(w) = (n-1, a_{i_{n-1}})$ is *the rightmost child* of v.

Example 1.5.25 Consider the labeled ordered tree

$$\mathtt{T} = (G, v_0, \mathbb{N} \times \{a, b, c\}, \mathsf{m})$$

represented in Figure 1.7, where $V = \{v_i \mid 0 \leq i \leq 10\}$. Note that the children of v_1, the vertices v_4, v_5, v_6 and v_7 are labeled by $(0, a), (1, a), (2, c)$ and $(3, b)$, respectively. □

Consider n labeled trees $\mathtt{T}_i = (G_i, v_{0i}, \mathbb{N} \times A_i, \mathsf{m}_i)$, where $0 \leq i \leq n-1$ and $V_i \cap V_j = \emptyset$ for $i \neq j$, where V_i is the set of vertices of G_i. If v is a

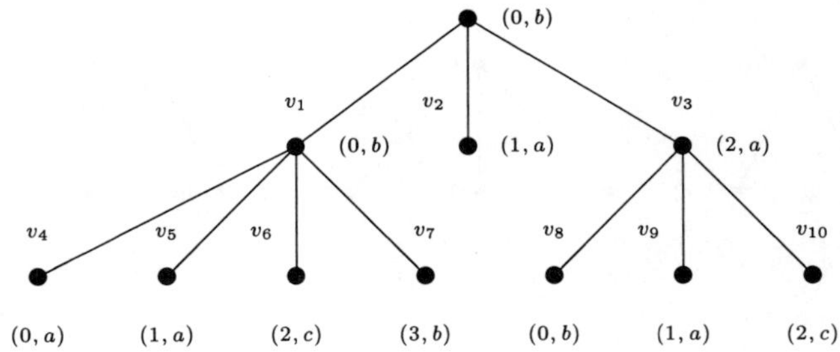

Figure 1.7: Labeled Ordered Tree

new vertex, $v \notin \cup\{V_i \mid 0 \leq i \leq n-1\}$, define a new labeled ordered tree $\mathtt{T} = \langle \mathtt{T}_0, \ldots, \mathtt{T}_{n-1}; a\rangle$ given by $\mathtt{T} = (V, \rho, v_0, \mathbb{N} \times A, \mathsf{m})$. Here $V = \bigcup\{V_i \mid 0 \leq i \leq n-1\}$, $E = \bigcup\{E_i \mid 0 \leq i \leq n-1\} \cup \{(v_0, v_{0i}) \mid 0 \leq i \leq n-1\}$, and $A = \bigcup\{A_i \mid 0 \leq i \leq n-1\}$. The marking function is

$$\mathsf{m}(v) = \begin{cases} \mathsf{m}_i(v) & \text{if } v \in V_i - \{v_{0i}\} \\ (i, a_i) & \text{if } v = v_{0i} \text{ and } \mathsf{m}(v) = (0, a_i) \\ (0, a) & \text{if } v = v_0, \end{cases}$$

for $v \in V$.

Example 1.5.26 Let $\mathtt{T}_0, \mathtt{T}_1$ and $\mathtt{T}_2$ be the labeled ordered trees shown in Figure 1.8(a),(b) and (c), respectively. The tree $\mathtt{T} = \langle \mathtt{T}_0, \mathtt{T}_1, \mathtt{T}_2; b\rangle$ is shown in Figure 1.8(d). □

Definition 1.5.27 Let $\mathtt{T} = (G, v_0, M, \mathsf{m})$ be a labeled ordered tree, where $G = (V, E, s, d)$, and let u be a vertex of this tree. Denote by V_u the set of all vertices in V such that there exists a path whose origin is u and whose end is v. The *v-labeled ordered subtree of* T is the labeled ordered tree $\mathtt{T}_v = (G_u, u, M, \mathsf{m}\rceil V_u)$, where G_u is the subgraph generated by the set V_u. □

Example 1.5.28 The v_1-labeled ordered subtree of the labeled ordered tree shown in Figure 1.7 is the labeled ordered tree shown in Figure 1.9. □

To simplify the representation of labeled ordered trees, from now on, we will show only the second component of the value of the labelling function for each vertex of the tree. Also, the names of the vertices will be omitted. For example, the tree represented in Figure 1.7 will be drawn as shown in Figure 1.10.

1.6 Cardinality

The purpose of this section is to present a formalization of the notion of size of a set.

Definition 1.6.1 Two sets, A, B have the same *cardinality*, written $A \sim B$, if there exists a bijection $f : A \longrightarrow B$. □

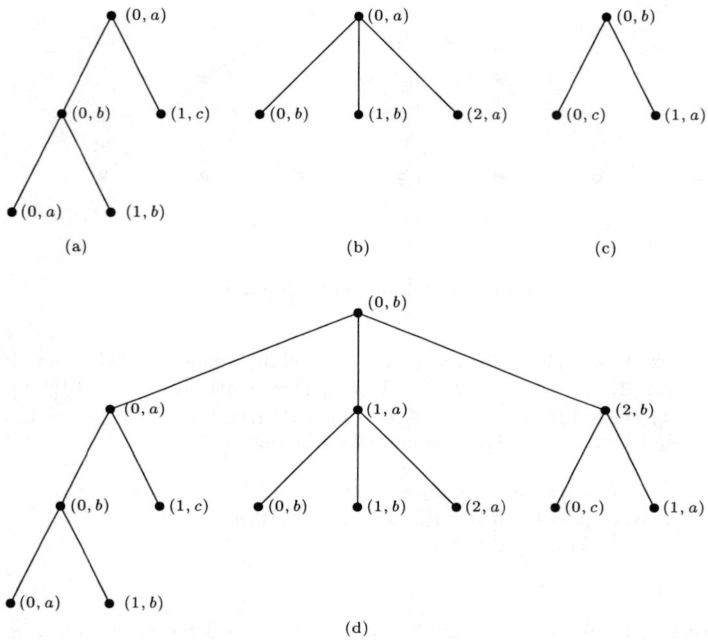

Figure 1.8: Construction of the tree $\langle T_0, T_1, T_2; b\rangle$

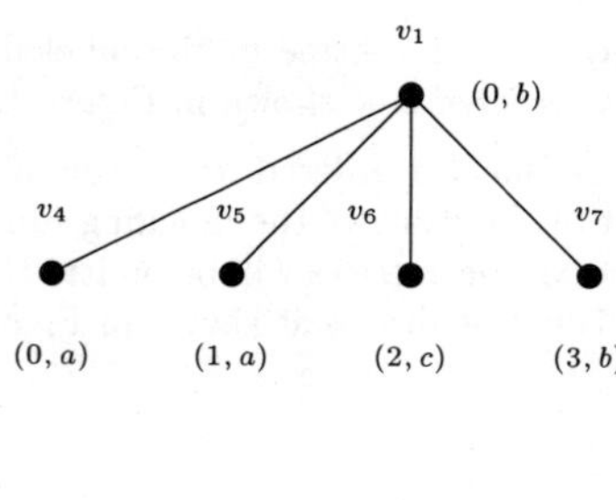

Figure 1.9: A Labeled Ordered Subtree of a Labeled Ordered Tree

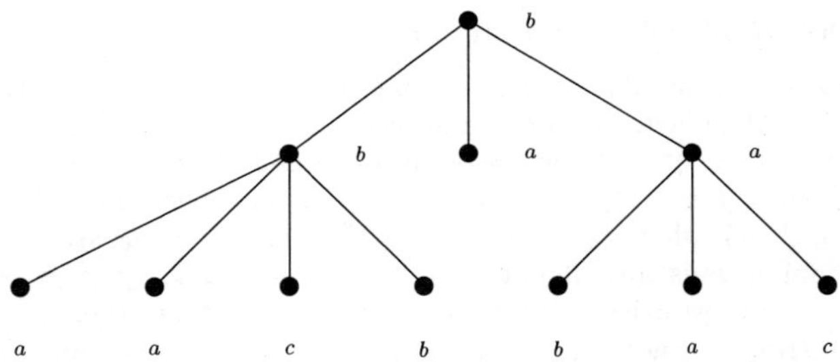

Figure 1.10: Labeled Ordered Tree

Example 1.6.2 The set of even numbers, $E = \{n \mid n = 2k, \text{ for some } k \in \mathbb{N}\}$ and the set $\mathbb{N}$ have the same cardinality, because $f : \mathbb{N} \longrightarrow E$ defined by $f(n) = 2n$ is a bijection. □

Theorem 1.6.3 *The relation* $\sim$ *is an equivalence relation.*

Proof. For every set A, $1_A : A \longrightarrow A$ is a bijection. Therefore, $A \sim A$ for every A, so $\sim$ is reflexive. If $f : A \longrightarrow B$ is a bijection, then $f^{-1} : A \longrightarrow A$ is a bijection, so $A \sim B$ implies $B \sim A$, which shows that $\sim$ is symmetric. Transitivity follows from the fact that the composition of two bijections is a bijection. ∎

Theorem 1.6.4 *If* $A \sim B$, *then* $\mathcal{P}(A) \sim \mathcal{P}(B)$.

Proof. Let $f : A \longrightarrow B$ be a bijection between A and B. Define the mapping $F : \mathcal{P}(A) \longrightarrow \mathcal{P}(B)$ by $F(L) = \{b \in B \mid b = f(a) \text{ for some } a \in L\}$ for every $L \in \mathcal{P}(A)$. It is easy to verify that F is a bijection. Thus, $\mathcal{P}(A) \sim \mathcal{P}(B)$. ∎

Definition 1.6.5 A set A is *countable* if it has the same cardinality as a subset of $\mathbb{N}$. A is *finite* if there is an integer $k \in \mathbb{N}$ such that A has the same cardinality as a subset of $\{0, 1, \ldots, k\}$. □

Note that any finite set is countable. The following theorem will help us enumerate finite sets.

Theorem 1.6.6 *If* A *is finite, then there is a unique* $k \in \mathbb{N}$ *for which* $A \sim \{0, 1, \ldots, k-1\}$. *In this case, we write* $|A| = k$ *and say that "A has k elements."*

Proof. Assume A is finite. Let $M = \{m \in \mathbb{N} \mid A \text{ has the same cardinality as some subset of } \{0, 1, \ldots, m-1\}\}$. Since A is finite, $M \neq \emptyset$, so M has a least element, k, which clearly satisfies the requirements of the theorem. ∎

Often it is desirable to be able explicitly to enumerate the elements of A. If A is finite, with $|A| = k$, then there is a bijection $f : \{0, 1, \ldots k-1\} \longrightarrow A$, and we can enumerate $A = \{a_0, a_1, \ldots, a_{k-1}\}$, where $a_i = f(i)$.

If A is infinite but countable, we write $|A| = \aleph_0$ and say "A is countably infinite." [1] The following theorem permits us to enumerate countably infinite sets.

[1] The symbol ℵ (pronounced "aleph") is the first letter of the Hebrew alphabet. This notation is standard in set theory.

Theorem 1.6.7 *If $|A| = \aleph_0$, then there is a bijection $f : \mathbb{N} \longrightarrow A$.*

Proof. Since A is countable, there is a bijection $g : A \longrightarrow S \subseteq \mathbb{N}$. To define $f : \mathbb{N} \longrightarrow A$ inductively, we simultaneously define both f and a subset of S. Let $f(0) = g^{-1}(s_0)$, where s_0 is the smallest element in S. Assume $\{f(0), f(1), \ldots f(k-1)\}$ and $\{s_0, s_1, \ldots s_{k-1}\}$ have been defined. Then define $f(k) = g^{-1}(s_k)$, where s_k is the smallest element in $S - \{s_0, s_1, \ldots s_{k-1}\}$. Since A is infinite, S is also infinite, so $S - \{s_0, s_1, \ldots s_{k-1}\} \neq \emptyset$, and a smallest element always exists. By construction, if $m_0 < m_1$ then $f(m_1) \notin \{f(0), f(1), \ldots f(m_0)\}$, since g is a bijection (and hence g^{-1} is, too.) So, if $f(m_0) = f(m_1)$ then clearly $m_0 = m_1$. We have to check that f is also onto. An easy induction shows that $s_k \geq k$, for all $k \in \mathbb{N}$. Let $a \in A$, with $g(a) = m$. Then, $m = s_j$ for some $j \leq m$, so $f(s_j) = a$. ∎

Corollary 1.6.8 *If $|A| = \aleph_0$, then there is a bijection $g : A \longrightarrow \mathbb{N}$.*

Proof. This follows from the fact that the inverse of a bijection is again a bijection. ∎

If A is countably infinite, then we can "enumerate" A using the the bijection of Theorem 1.6.7. Thus, we have $A = \{a_0, a_1, a_2, \ldots\}$, where, just as in the finite case, $a_i = f(i)$. On the other hand, Corollary 1.6.8 allows us to associate a natural number with each element of a countably infinite set.

Next we give a useful characterization of countable sets.

Theorem 1.6.9 *A set A is countable if and only if there exists an injection $f : A \longrightarrow \mathbb{N}$.*

Proof. The necessity of the condition is immediate since every bijection is also an injection. Suppose, therefore, that $f : A \longrightarrow \mathbb{N}$ is an injection. Then, the function $g : A \longrightarrow \text{Ran}(h)$ is obviously a bijection between A and $\text{Ran}(h)$, a subset of $\mathbb{N}$, so A is indeed countable. ∎

Theorem 1.6.10 *Let A, B be two countable sets. Then, $A \cup B$ is countable.*

Proof. Assume A, B are two countable sets, and let $f : A \longrightarrow \mathbb{N}$ and $g : B \longrightarrow \mathbb{N}$ be injections. Define $h : A \cup B \longrightarrow \mathbb{N}$ by

$$h(x) = \begin{cases} 2f(x) & \text{if } x \in A - B \\ 2g(x) + 1 & \text{if } x \in B. \end{cases}$$

The function $h : A \cup B \longrightarrow \mathbb{N}$ is easily seen to be an injection; hence, $A \cup B$ is countable. ∎

Corollary 1.6.11 *The union of any finite collection of countable sets is countable.*

Proof. Use proof by induction and Theorem 1.6.10. ∎

A stronger version of Corollary 1.6.11 is shown below (cf. Theorem 1.6.7). The following Theorem and its Corollary simplify the proofs of several theorems.

Theorem 1.6.12 *Let A, B, C be sets, where A is countable.*

(i) *If there is a surjection $f : A \longrightarrow B$, then B is countable.*

(ii) *If there is an injection $\ell : C \longrightarrow A$, then C is countable.*

Proof. For the first part of the theorem assume A is countable and $f : A \longrightarrow B$ is a surjection. Since A is countable, there is an injection $g : A \longrightarrow \mathbb{N}$. Define $h : B \longrightarrow \mathbb{N}$ by

$$h(b) = \min\{g(a) \mid f(a) = b\}.$$

We need to verify that h is an injection. Let $b_0, b_1 \in B$ such that $h(b_0) = h(b_1)$. Let $a_i \in A$ be the element such that $h(b_i) = g(a_i)$ for $i = 0, 1$. Then, $g(a_0) = g(a_1)$, and since g is an injection, $a_0 = a_1$, so $f(a_0) = f(a_1)$, and thus $b_0 = b_1$.

For the second part note that the function $g\ell : C \longrightarrow \mathbb{N}$ is an injection; this implies immediately the countability of C. ∎

Corollary 1.6.13 *Let A, B be two sets. If $f : A \longrightarrow B$ is a bijection, then A is countable if and only if B is countable.*

Proof. The statement is an immediate consequence of Theorem 1.6.12. ∎

Corollary 1.6.14 *Let A, B be two sets. If $f : A \longrightarrow B$ is an injection and A is not countable, then B is not countable.*

Proof. The statement is an immediate consequence of Theorem 1.6.12. ∎

Corollary 1.6.15 *Any subset of a countable set is countable.*

Proof. Assume $B \subseteq A$, where A is countable. If $B = \emptyset$, then it is clearly countable. If $B \neq \emptyset$, pick $b \in B$, and define $f : A \longrightarrow B$ by

$$f(x) = \begin{cases} x & \text{if } x \in B \\ b & \text{if } x \notin B. \end{cases}$$

The function f is clearly a surjection, so B is countable. ∎

Theorem 1.6.16 *Let $A_0, \ldots, A_{n-1}$ be n countable sets. The Cartesian product $A_0 \times \cdots \times A_{n-1}$ is countable.*

Proof. Since $A_0, \ldots, A_{n-1}$ are countable sets, by Corollary 1.6.8, there exist injections $f_i : A_i \longrightarrow \mathbb{N}$ for $0 \leq i \leq n-1$. For $(a_0, \ldots, a_{n-1}) \in A_0 \times \cdots \times A_{n-1}$, define

$$h(a_0, \ldots, a_{n-1}) = 2^{f_0(a_0)} \cdot 3^{f_1(a_1)} \cdot \cdots \cdot p_{n-1}^{a_{n-1}},$$

where p_{i-1} is the ith prime number for $0 \leq i \leq n-1$. By the Fundamental Theorem of Arithmetic[2], $h : A_0 \times \cdots \times A_{n-1} \longrightarrow \mathbb{N}$ is an injection, so $A_0 \times \cdots \times A_{n-1}$ is countable. ∎

Example 1.6.17 Let D be a countable set. The set $\mathbf{Seq}_n(D) = D^n$ is a countable set for every $n \in \mathbb{N}$. □

For the purposes of defining bijections, it is sometimes convenient to be able to force sets in a collection that might not be pairwise disjoint to be disjoint. We do this by making a copies of the sets, each "marked" with its index. Once they are marked, we may combine the sets and show the result is countable. Then we

[2] The Fundamental Theorem of Arithmetic states that each natural number larger than one can be written uniquely as a product powers of primes.

remove the markings with a projection function to obtain the desired, final set. Since the projection is a surjection from the set built with the marked sets onto this resultant set, Theorem 1.6.12 guarantees that the final set is countable. Corollary 1.6.19 gives an example of this technique.

Let P_0^2 and P_1^2 be the usual projection functions, so $P_i^2(x_0, x_1) = x_i$, for $i = 0, 1$.

Theorem 1.6.18 *The union of a countable collection of countable sets that are pairwise disjoint, is a countable set.*

Proof. Let K be a countable set, and let each $\{A_k \mid k \in K\}$ be countable. Then there are injections $f : K \longrightarrow \mathbb{N}$ and $g_k : A_k \longrightarrow \mathbb{N}$ for each $k \in K$. Assume that $A_i \cap A_j = \emptyset$ for $i \neq j \in K$. To show that

$$A = \bigcup_{k \in K} A_k \text{ is countable,}$$

we define an injection $h : A \longrightarrow \mathbb{N}$. Let $P = \{p_0, p_1, \dots\}$ be an enumeration of the prime numbers. Since the sets A_k are pairwise disjoint, given any $a \in A$, there is a unique k with $a \in A_k$. We use this fact to define

$$h(a) = p_{f(k)}^{g_k(a)}.$$

It follows from the Fundamental Theorem of Arithmetic that h is an injection, and thus A is countable. ∎

Corollary 1.6.19 *The union of a countable collection of countable sets is a countable set.*

Proof. Let K be a countable set, and let each $\{A_k \mid k \in K\}$ be countable. Form sets $A'_k = A_k \times \{k\}$. These are clearly pairwise disjoint, so

$$A' = \bigcup_{k \in K} A'_k \text{ is countable.}$$

Let

$$A = \bigcup_{k \in K} A_k.$$

The projection $P_0^2 : A' \longrightarrow A$ is a surjection, and thus by Theorem 1.6.12 A is countable. ∎

Example 1.6.20 We proved that if D is a countable set, $\mathbf{Seq}_n(D)$ is countable (cf. Example 1.6.17). Therefore, $\mathbf{Seq}(D) = \bigcup\{D^n \mid n \in \mathbb{N}\}$ is countable as a union of a countable collection of sets. □

Proofs related to that of Theorem 1.6.18 are important in the area of the theory of computation, so let us revisit it. The set $\mathbb{N} \times \mathbb{N}$ is countably infinite, so, by Corollary 1.6.8, there exists a bijection $\wp : \mathbb{N} \times \mathbb{N} \longrightarrow \mathbb{N}$.

Definition 1.6.21 A *pairing function* is a bijection $\wp : \mathbb{N} \times \mathbb{N} \longrightarrow \mathbb{N}$. □

Example 1.6.22 There are many possible pairing functions, but consider the one suggested by the following picture:

$\wp(i,j)$			j				
i	0	1	2	3	4	5	...
0	0	1	3	6	10	...	
1	2	4	7	11	...		
2	5	8	12	...			
3	9	13	...				
4	14	...					
	...						

Let D_m be the diagonal that contains all pairs (i,j) such that $i+j=m$. It is clear that D_m contains $m+1$ pairs. Note that the pair (i,j) is located on the diagonal D_{i+j} and that this diagonal is preceded by the diagonals $D_0,\ldots,D_{i+j-1}$ that have a total of $1+2+\cdots+(i+j)=(i+j)(i+j+1)/2$ elements. Thus, the pair (i,j) is enumerated on the place $(i+j)(i+j+1)/2+i$ and this shows that the mapping $h:\mathbb{N}\times\mathbb{N}\longrightarrow\mathbb{N}$ given by

$$\wp(i,j)=\frac{1}{2}[(i+j)^2+3i+j] \tag{1.8}$$

is a bijection. □

This is a way of counting a countably infinite collection of copies of $\mathbb{N}$. We can turn it into a way of counting many similar things, such as the sets A_k of Theorem 1.6.18. For our purposes here, we will assume that $K=\mathbb{N}$ and each of the sets A_k is infinite (that was not the case in the theorem).

In position (i,j), we place the jth element of the ith set. Technically, this is the element $g_i^{-1}(j)$ of the set A_i. If we tried to count the first set, A_0, all the way to the end, we would never get to the second set, so instead, we count one element from A_0. Then we count a second element from A_0 and one from the second set, A_1. Then we count a third from the first set, a second from the second, and one from the third, and so forth. This is called *"dovetailing."* In this way, we eventually count all possible elements in the set $\bigcup\{A_i \mid i\in\mathbb{N}\}$.

So, the proof relies on using such a counting as a way to navigate through a countably infinite collection of sets, each of which is countable. Dovetailing is an important proof technique in computability and we shall use it in Chapter 8.

It is important to realize that not all sets are countable. Consider $\mathcal{P}(\mathbb{N})$, the power set of $\mathbb{N}$. This certainly has at least as many elements as $\mathbb{N}$, since $\{k\}$ is in $\mathcal{P}(\mathbb{N})$ for each $k\in\mathbb{N}$. However, it has so many more sets that it is not possible to count them all.

Theorem 1.6.23 *The set $\mathcal{P}(\mathbb{N})$ is not countable.*

Proof. Assume that $\mathcal{P}(\mathbb{N})$ were countable. Then there would be an bijection $f:\mathbb{N}\longrightarrow\mathcal{P}(\mathbb{N})$; i.e., for each $n\in\mathbb{N}$, we would have a distinct subset $f(n)\subseteq\mathbb{N}$. We show that the existence of this bijection leads to a contradiction. Define the set $D=\{n \mid n\notin f(n)\}$. Clearly, $D\subseteq\mathbb{N}$, so we must have $D=f(k)$ for some $k\in\mathbb{N}$. We must now have one of two situations: either $k\in D$, or $k\notin D$. First, suppose that $k\in D$. Then, by the definition of D, $k\notin f(k)$, but $f(k)=D$, so we have that $k\in D$ implies that $k\notin D$; this cannot be. Suppose, on the other hand, that $k \notin D$. Then, by the definition of D, $k \in f(k)$, and since $f(k) = D$, we have $k \notin D$ implies $k \in D$. Again, this cannot be. Either way, we have a contradiction. From this, we necessarily conclude that the assumed bijection f cannot exist. ∎

An important way to regard this proof is the following. If there were a bijection $f : \mathbb{N} \longrightarrow \mathcal{P}(\mathbb{N})$, then we could have the following list:

$$\begin{array}{rl}
0: & a_{00}\ a_{01}\ a_{02}\ a_{03}\ a_{04} \dots \\
1: & a_{10}\ a_{11}\ a_{12}\ a_{13}\ a_{14} \dots \\
2: & a_{20}\ a_{21}\ a_{22}\ a_{23}\ a_{24} \dots \\
3: & a_{30}\ a_{31}\ a_{32}\ a_{33}\ a_{34} \dots \\
4: & a_{40}\ a_{41}\ a_{42}\ a_{43}\ a_{44} \dots \\
5: & a_{50}\ a_{51}\ a_{52}\ a_{53}\ a_{54} \dots \\
 & \vdots \\
k: & a_{k0}\ a_{k1}\ a_{k2}\ a_{k3}\ a_{k4} \dots a_{kk}
\end{array}$$

where

$$a_{ij} = \begin{cases} 0 & \text{if } j \notin f(i) \\ 1 & \text{if } j \in f(i). \end{cases}$$

In other words, the a_{ij}s correspond to the characteristic function of the set $f(i)$. The set D is formed by "going down the diagonal" and spoiling the possibility that $D = f(k)$, for each k. At row k, we look at a_{kk} in column k. If this is 1, i.e., if $k \in f(k)$, then we make sure that the corresponding position for the set D has a 0 in it by saying that $k \notin D$. On the other hand, if a_{kk} is a 0, i.e., $k \notin f(k)$, then we force the corresponding position for the set D to be a 1 by putting k into D. This guarantees that $D \neq f(k)$, because its characteristic functions differs from that of $f(k)$ in column k.

This proof technique, usually referred to as *diagonalization*, first appeared in an 1891 paper of Georg Cantor (1845–1918); it has found many applications in the theory of computation.

Corollary 1.6.24 *If A is a countably infinite set, then $\mathcal{P}(A)$ is not countable.*

Proof. Let A be a countably infinite set. Since $A \sim \mathbb{N}$, we have $\mathbb{N} \sim A$, so by Theorem 1.6.4, there is a bijection $F : \mathcal{P}(\mathbb{N}) \longrightarrow \mathcal{P}(A)$. If $\mathcal{P}(A)$ were countable (and, therefore, countably infinite), this would imply the existence of a bijection $G : \mathcal{P}(A) \longrightarrow \mathbb{N}$, so we would obtain a bijection between $\mathcal{P}(\mathbb{N})$ and $\mathbb{N}$, which contradicts Theorem 1.6.23. ∎

Corollary 1.6.14 allows us to show the uncountability of other sets.

Example 1.6.25 Let F_2 be the set of all functions of the form $f : \mathbb{N} \longrightarrow \{0, 1\}$. Define the mapping $\phi : F_2 \longrightarrow \mathcal{P}(\mathbb{N})$ by $\phi(f) = \{n \in \mathbb{N} \mid f(n) = 1\}$. It is not difficult to see that ϕ is a bijection. Indeed, suppose that $\phi(f) = \phi(g)$, that is $\{n \in \mathbb{N} \mid f(n) = 1\} = \{n \in \mathbb{N} \mid g(n) = 1\}$. This means that $f(n) = 1$ if and only if $g(n) = 1$ for $n \in \mathbb{N}$, so $f = g$, which means that ϕ is an injection. To prove that ϕ is a bijection consider an arbitrary subset K of $\mathbb{N}$. Then, for its characteristic function f_K (given by $f_K(n) = 1$ if $n \in K$ and $f_K(n) = 0$, otherwise) we have $\phi(f_K) = K$, so ϕ is also a surjection, and therefore, a bijection. Thus, we conclude that the set F_2 is not countable.

If F is the set of functions of the form $f : \mathbb{N} \longrightarrow \mathbb{N}$, then the uncountability of F_2 implies the uncountability of F. □

1.7 Exercises

Sets, Relations, and Functions

1. Let A be a set and let $x, y \in A$. Show that $(A - \{x\}) \cup (A - \{y\}) = A$ if and only if $x \neq y$.
2. Let S and T be two sets.
   (a) Prove that $S \subseteq T$ if and only if $\mathcal{P}(S) \subseteq \mathcal{P}(T)$.
   (b) Conclude that $S = T$ if and only if $\mathcal{P}(S) = \mathcal{P}(T)$.
3. For any x, y, z, define (x, y, z) to be the pair $((x, y), z)$. Prove that if $(x, y, z) = (x', y', z')$ then $x = x', y = y'$, and $z = z'$.
4. Consider the sets $A = \{1, 2, 3, 4\}$ and $B = \{2, 3\}$. List the pairs of the following sets: $A \times B, B \times A, (A \times B) \cap (B \times A), (A \times B) - (B \times A), (B \times A) - (A \times B)$.
5. Compute $\mathcal{P}(\mathcal{P}(\mathcal{P}(\emptyset)))$.
6. Prove the following equalities that show the distributivity of the Cartesian product over union, intersection, and difference, respectively.

$$\begin{aligned} (A \cup B) \times C &= (A \times C) \cup (B \times C) \\ C \times (A \cup B) &= (C \times A) \cup (C \times B) \\ (A \cap B) \times C &= (A \times C) \cap (B \times C) \\ C \times (A \cap B) &= (C \times A) \cap (C \times B) \\ (A - B) \times C &= (A \times C) - (B \times C) \\ C \times (A - B) &= (C \times A) - (C \times B) \end{aligned}$$

7. Let $\mathcal{C}$ be a nonempty collection of sets.
   (a) Show that for all $A \in \mathcal{C}$, $\bigcap \mathcal{C} \subseteq A$.
   (b) Show that for all sets B, if $B \subseteq A$ for every $A \in \mathcal{C}$, then $B \subseteq \bigcap \mathcal{C}$.
8. Let S and T be two sets. Show that $S - T$ is the largest subset of S which is disjoint from T; that is, $S - T \subseteq S$, $(S - T) \cap T = \emptyset$, and for every U such that $U \subseteq S$ and $U \cap T = \emptyset$, we have $U \subseteq S - T$.
9. Let $\mathcal{C}$ and $\mathcal{D}$ be collections of sets.
   (a) Show that if $\mathcal{C} \subseteq \mathcal{D}$, then $\bigcup \mathcal{C} \subseteq \bigcup \mathcal{D}$.
   (b) Show that if for every $C \in \mathcal{C}$ there is a $D \in \mathcal{D}$ such that if $C \subseteq D$, then $\bigcup \mathcal{C} \subseteq \bigcup \mathcal{D}$.
   (c) Show that if $\emptyset \subset \mathcal{C} \subseteq \mathcal{D}$, then $\bigcap \mathcal{D} \subseteq \bigcap \mathcal{C}$.
   (d) Show that if $\mathcal{C}$ and $\mathcal{D}$ are nonempty and for every $C \in \mathcal{C}$ there is a $D \in \mathcal{D}$ such that $D \subseteq C$, then $\bigcap \mathcal{D} \subseteq \bigcap \mathcal{C}$.
10. (a) Let $\mathcal{C}$ and $\mathcal{D}$ be two collections of sets. Prove the following identities:

$$\begin{aligned} \bigcup \mathcal{C} \cup \bigcup \mathcal{D} &= \bigcup (\mathcal{C} \cup \mathcal{D}), \\ \bigcup \mathcal{C} \cap \bigcup \mathcal{D} &= \bigcup \{C \cap D \mid C \in \mathcal{C} \text{ and } D \in \mathcal{D}\}. \end{aligned}$$

In addition, if $\mathcal{D}$ is nonempty, then for each $D \in \mathcal{D}$, define $F_D = \bigcup\{C - D \mid C \in \mathcal{C}\}$. Prove that

$$\bigcup \mathcal{C} - \bigcup \mathcal{D} = \bigcap \{F_D \mid D \in \mathcal{D}\}.$$

Finally, prove that if $\mathcal{C}$ and $\mathcal{D}$ are both nonempty, then

$$\bigcup \mathcal{C} \cup \bigcup \mathcal{D} = \bigcup \{C \cup D \mid C \in \mathcal{C} \text{ and } D \in \mathcal{D}\}.$$

(b) Find examples of collections $\mathcal{C}$ and $\mathcal{D}$ such that

$$\begin{aligned}\bigcup \mathcal{C} \cap \bigcup \mathcal{D} &\neq \bigcup (\mathcal{C} \cap \mathcal{D}),\\ \bigcup \mathcal{C} - \bigcup \mathcal{D} &\neq \bigcup (\mathcal{C} - \mathcal{D}).\end{aligned}$$

11. (a) Let $\mathcal{C}$ and $\mathcal{D}$ be two nonempty collections of sets. Prove the following identities:

$$\begin{aligned}\bigcap \mathcal{C} \cup \bigcap \mathcal{D} &= \bigcap \{C \cup D \mid C \in \mathcal{C} \text{ and } D \in \mathcal{D}\},\\ \bigcap \mathcal{C} \cap \bigcap \mathcal{D} &= \bigcap (\mathcal{C} \cup \mathcal{D})\\ &= \bigcap \{C \cap D \mid C \in \mathcal{C} \text{ and } D \in \mathcal{D}\}.\end{aligned}$$

For each $D \in \mathcal{D}$, define $G_D = \bigcap\{C - D \mid C \in \mathcal{C}\}$. Prove that

$$\bigcap \mathcal{C} - \bigcap \mathcal{D} = \bigcup \{G_D \mid D \in \mathcal{D}\}.$$

(b) Find examples of collections $\mathcal{C}$ and $\mathcal{D}$ such that

$$\begin{aligned}\bigcap \mathcal{C} \cup \bigcap \mathcal{D} &\neq \bigcap (\mathcal{C} \cup \mathcal{D}),\\ \bigcap \mathcal{C} \cap \bigcap \mathcal{D} &\neq \bigcap (\mathcal{C} \cap \mathcal{D}),\\ \bigcap \mathcal{C} - \bigcap \mathcal{D} &\neq \bigcap (\mathcal{C} - \mathcal{D}).\end{aligned}$$

12. Let A, B be two sets. Prove that if any two of the statements
    (a) A and B are disjoint,
    (b) $A \subseteq B$, and
    (c) $A = \emptyset$

    are true then the third one is also true.
13. Prove that for all sets A, B the following statements are equivalent:
    (a) $A \subseteq B$,
    (b) $A - B = \emptyset$,
    (c) $A \cup B = B$, and
    (d) $A \cap B = A$.
14. Prove that for all sets A, B, C we have

$$(A \cup C) - (B \cup C) \subseteq A - B.$$

Give conditions under which the above inclusion becomes an equality.

15. Let A, B, C, D be four sets.
    (a) Prove that if $C \neq \emptyset$ and $A \times C \subseteq B \times C$ then $A \subseteq B$; similarly, $C \neq \emptyset$ and $C \times A \subseteq C \times B$ implies $A \subseteq B$.

(b) Prove that

$$(A \times B) - (C \times D) = ((A - C) \times B) \cup (A \times (B - D)).$$

16. Let S be a set. Prove that for every a the following three statements are equivalent:
   (a) $a \in S$,
   (b) $\{a\} \subseteq S$, and
   (c) $\{a\} \cap S \neq \emptyset$.
   Conclude that for every set S, $S \in S$ if and only if $S \cap \{S\} \neq \emptyset$.
17. Let A, B be two sets. Prove that $A \times B \subseteq \mathcal{P}(\mathcal{P}(A \cup B))$.
18. (a) Let U be a set and let A and B be subsets of U. Prove that the equation $A \cap X = B$ has a solution $X \in \mathcal{P}(U)$ if and only if $B \subseteq A$. Show that, in this case, X is a solution if and only if there is a $P \subseteq U - A$ with $X = B \cup P$.
   (b) Prove that the equation $A \cup X = B$ has a solution in X if and only if $A \subseteq B$. In this case, show that X is a solution if and only if $B - A \subseteq X \subseteq B$.
   (c) Let U be a set and let A, B, and C be subsets of U. Find necessary and sufficient conditions for the equation $(A \cap X) \cup B = C$ to have a solution $X \in \mathcal{P}(U)$. Find the general form of the solution if solutions exist.
19. Prove that sets A, B, and C satisfy the equality

$$\bigcap\{A \cup B, B \cup C, C \cup A\} = \bigcup\{A, B, C\}$$

   if and only if there exist sets K, L, and M such that $A = K \cup L, B = L \cup M$, and $C = M \cup K$.
20. Show that for any sets A, B, and C, the following equalities are true (and hence various distributive laws hold).

$$\begin{aligned}
A \cup (B \cup C) &= (A \cup B) \cup (A \cup C),\\
A \cap (B \cap C) &= (A \cap B) \cap (A \cap C),\\
A \cap (B - C) &= (A \cap B) - (A \cap C),\\
(B \cup C) - A &= (B - A) \cup (C - A),\\
(B \cap C) - A &= (B - A) \cap (C - A),\\
(B - C) - A &= (B - A) - (C - A).
\end{aligned}$$

21. The *symmetric difference* of two sets A and B is the set $A \oplus B$ given by $(A - B) \cup (B - A)$.
   Prove that
   (a) $A \oplus B = (A \cup B) - (A \cap B)$;
   (b) if $B \subseteq A$, then $A \oplus B = A - B$;
   (c) if A and B are disjoint, then $A \oplus B = A \cup B$;
   (d) $A \oplus \emptyset = \emptyset \oplus A = A$;
   (e) $A \oplus B = \emptyset$ if and only if $A = B$;
   (f) $A \oplus B = B \oplus A$;
   (g) $A \oplus (B \oplus C) = (A \oplus B) \oplus C$;
   (h) $A \cap (B \oplus C) = (A \cap B) \oplus (A \cap C)$;

(i) $(B \oplus C) - A = (B - A) \oplus (C - A)$;
(j) $A \times (B \oplus C) = (A \times B) \oplus (A \times C)$;
(k) $(B \oplus C) \times A = (B \times A) \oplus (C \times A)$;
(l) $A \cup B = A \oplus (B \oplus (A \cap B))$;
(m) If $A - C = B - C$, then $A \oplus B \subseteq C$;
(n) If $A \oplus B = A \oplus C$, then $B = C$,

for all sets A, B, C.

22. Let A, B, W be three sets. If $A \cap W = B \cap W$ and $A \cup W = B \cup W$, prove that $A = B$.
23. Let ρ be a relation.
    (a) Prove that ρ is a function if and only if
    $$\rho^{-1} \circ \rho \subseteq \iota_{\text{Ran }(\rho)}.$$
    (b) Prove that ρ is a one-to-one relation if and only if
    $$\rho \circ \rho^{-1} \subseteq \iota_{\text{Dom }(\rho)}.$$
24. Let ρ be a relation from A to B.
    (a) Prove that ρ is a total relation from A to B if and only if
    $$\iota_A \subseteq \rho \circ \rho^{-1}.$$
    (b) Prove that ρ is an onto relation from A to B if and only if
    $$\iota_B \subseteq \rho^{-1} \circ \rho.$$
25. Let ρ and σ be relations.
    (a) Prove that if ρ and σ are functions, then $\rho \circ \sigma$ is also a function.
    (b) Prove that if ρ and σ are one-to-one relations, then $\rho \circ \sigma$ is also a one-to-one relation.
26. Let ρ be a relation from A to B and σ be a relation from B to C.
    (a) If ρ is a total relation from A to B and σ is a total relation from B to C, prove that $\rho \circ \sigma$ is a total relation from A to C.
    (b) If ρ is an onto relation from A to B and σ is an onto relation from B to C, prove that $\rho \circ \sigma$ is an onto relation from A to C.
27. Let $f : \{0, \ldots, n-1\} \times \{0, \ldots, m-1\} \longrightarrow \{0, \ldots, nm-1\}$ be the function defined by $f(i, j) = im + j$ for $0 \leq i \leq n-1$ and $0 \leq j \leq m-1$. Prove that f is a bijection.
28. Prove that if A and B are two finite sets such that $|A| = m$ and $|B| = n$, then there are n^m functions from A to B.

Let $f : A \longrightarrow B$. The function $g : B \longrightarrow A$ is a *right inverse of f* if $f(g(b)) = b$ for every $b \in B$. The function $h : B \longrightarrow A$ is a *left inverse of f* if $g(f(a)) = a$ for every $a \in A$.

29. Let $f : A \longrightarrow B$.
    (a) Prove that f is a surjection if and only if f has a right inverse.
    (b) If A is nonempty, then f is an injection if and only if f has a left inverse.

30. Let $f : A \longrightarrow B$. Prove that the following statements are equivalent.
    (a) f is a bijection.
    (b) There is a function $g : B \longrightarrow A$ that is both a left and a right inverse for f.
    (c) f has a left inverse and f has a right inverse.
31. Prove that if f is a bijection, then f^{-1} is the only left inverse that f has, and it is the only right inverse that f has.
32. Give an example of a function $f : A \longrightarrow B$ and two subsets X_0, X_1 of A such that the strict inclusion

$$f(X_0 \cap X_1) \subset f(X_0) \cap f(X_1)$$

holds.
Prove that if f is one-to-one, then we have the equality

$$f(X_0 \cap X_1) = f(X_0) \cap f(X_1)$$

for every $X_0, X_1 \in \mathcal{P}(A)$.

Operations and Algebras

33. Let $M = \{a_0, a_1, a_2, 1\}$ and let $\star$ be the binary operation defined by $a_i \star 1 = 1 \star a_i = a_i$ and $a_i \star a_j = a_j$ for $0 \leq i, j \leq 2$. Prove that $(M, \star, 1)$ is a monoid.
34. Let $(M, \star, 1)$ be a monoid. If $x \in M$ and $P \subseteq M$, define the binary relation $\Theta(x, P) \subseteq M \times M$ by

$$\Theta(x, P) = \{(u, v) \in M \times M \mid u \star x \star v \in P\}.$$

    (a) Prove that $(x, y) \in \mu_P$ if and only if $\theta(x, P) = \theta(y, P)$.
    (b) Prove that

$$\begin{aligned} \Theta(x, P \cup P') &= \Theta(x, P) \cup \Theta(x, P') \\ \Theta(x, P \cap P') &= \Theta(x, P) \cap \Theta(x, P') \\ \Theta(x, M) &= M \times M \\ \Theta(x, \emptyset) &= \emptyset, \end{aligned}$$

    for every $x \in M$ and $P \subseteq M$.
    (c) Compute the sets $\Theta(x, P)$ for the monoid defined in Exercise 33, where $x \in M$ and $P \subseteq M$.

Solution. We solve only the last part of the exercise. Note that

$$\begin{aligned} \Theta(1, \{a_i\}) &= \{(u, a_i) \mid u \in M\} \cup \{(a_i, 1)\} \\ \Theta(a_j, \{a_i\}) &= \{(u, a_i) \mid u \in M\} \\ \Theta(a_i, \{a_i\}) &= \{(u, a_i) \mid u \in M\} \cup \{(u, 1) \mid u \in M\}, \\ \Theta(x, \{1\}) &= \begin{cases} \emptyset & \text{if } x \neq 1 \\ \{(1, 1)\} & \text{if } x = 1 \end{cases} \end{aligned}$$

for $0 \leq i, j \leq 2$ and $i \neq j$. The computation of the remaining sets can be done using the second equality in Part (b) of the Exercise. For example, $\Theta(a_j, \{a_i, a_k\}) = \{(u, a_i) \mid u \in M\} \cup \{(u, a_k) \mid u \in M\}$ for i, j, k pairwise distinct, and $\Theta(a_i, \{a_i, a_k\}) = \{(u, a_i) \mid u \in M\} \cup \{(u, 1) \mid u \in M\} \cup \{(u, a_k) \mid u \in M\}$. Also, $\Theta(1, \{a_i, a_k\}) = \{(u, a_i) \mid u \in M\} \cup \{(a_i, 1)\} \cup \{(u, a_k) \mid u \in M\} \cup \{(a_k, 1)\}$. ■

35. Let $(M, \star, 1)$ be a monoid. A subset P of M is *disjunctive* if $\mu_P = \iota_M$. Prove that the monoid defined in Exercise 33 contains no disjunctive subset.
Solution. Suppose that P is a disjunctive subset of M. Clearly, we have $P \neq \emptyset$ and $P \neq M$. Then, by exhaustive search we can verify that for every proper subset P of M there are two distinct elements x, y such that $\Theta(x, P) = \Theta(y, P)$ (where Θ is the mapping introduced in Exercise 34), which implies that $\mu_P \neq \iota_M$. For example, if $P = \{a_i, a_k\}$, we have $\Theta(a_i, P) = \Theta(a_k, P)$. ■
36. $^\diamond$ Let $(M, \star, u)$ be a monoid and let $\{\rho_i \mid i \in I\}$ be a nonempty set of congruences of this monoid. Prove that $\bigcap\{\rho_i \mid i \in I\}$ is a congruence of this monoid.
37. $^\diamond$ Let $(M, \star, u)$ be a monoid and let $\sigma \subseteq M \times M$ be a relation on M.
    (a) Prove that there is at least one congruence ρ of M that contains σ.
    (b) Let $\hat{\sigma} = \bigcap\{\rho \mid \rho \text{ is a congruence of } M \text{ and } \sigma \subseteq \rho\}$. Prove that $\hat{\sigma}$ is a congruence of M and that for any congruence ρ' of M that contains σ we have $\hat{\sigma} \subseteq \rho'$. The congruence $\hat{\sigma}$ is referred to as *the congruence generated by* σ.
38. Let $(S, \star, 1)$ and $(P, \bullet, 1')$ be two monoids, $h : S \longrightarrow P$ be a surjective morphism of monoids and let L be a subset of S.
    (a) Prove that $L = h^{-1}(h(L))$ if and only if L is saturated by the congruence $\mathbf{ker}(h)$. Conclude that $\mathbf{ker}(h) \subseteq \mu_L$.
    (b) Let $h_L : M \longrightarrow M/\mu_L$ be the mapping defined by $h_L(m) = [m]_{\mu_L}$ for $m \in M$. Prove that there is a morphism $k : M/\mu_L \longrightarrow P$ such that $h(m) = k(h_L(m))$ for every $m \in M$.

A monoid $(M, \cdot, 1)$ is *aperiodic* if there exists $n \in \mathbb{P}$ such that $m^n = m^{n+1}$ for every $m \in M$. The number n is the index of aperiodicity of the monoid.

39. Prove that if $(M, \cdot, 1)$ is an aperiodic monoid and $p = mpq$, then $p = mp = pq$ for every $p, m, q \in M$ (the cancellation law for aperiodic monoids).
Solution. The equality $p = mpq$ implies $p = m^n p q^n$ for every $n \geq 1$. If n is the degree of aperiodicity of the monoid, then since $m^n = m^{n+1}$, we obtain $p = m^{n+1} p q^n = m m^n p q^n = mp$. The argument for $p = pq$ is similar. ■
40. Let $(M, \cdot, 1)$ be an aperiodic monoid. Prove that if $mp = 1$, then $m = p = 1$, for any $m, p \in M$.
41. Prove that if $(M, \cdot, 1)$ is an aperiodic monoid, then $(mM \cap Mm) - \{q \in M \mid m \notin MqM\} = \{m\}$.
Solution. Since $m = m1 = 1m = 1m1$, it is clear that $\{m\} \subseteq (mM \cap Mm) - \{q \in M \mid m \notin MqM\}$.
Conversely, let $z \in (mM \cap Mm) - \{q \in M \mid m \notin MqM\}$. Then $z = mr = r'm$ for some $r, r' \in M$ since $z \in (mM \cap Mm)$. Also, since $z \notin \{q \in M \mid m \notin MqM\}$, it follows that $m \in MzM$, so $m = pzp'$ for some $p, p' \in M$.

Consequently, we have $m = pzp' = pmrp' = pr'mp'$. By Supplement 39 we have $m = pm = mrp' = pr'm = mp'$ by the cancellation law for aperiodic monoids. Thus, $m = zp' = pz$. Therefore, $m = r'mp' = pmr$ and, by the cancellation law we obtain $m = r'm = mp' = pm = mr = z$. We conclude that $(mM \cap Mm) - \{q \in M \mid m \notin MqM\} \subseteq \{m\}$. ■

A monoid $(M, \vee, 0)$ is *idempotent* if $x \vee x = x$ for every $x \in M$. In other words, a monoid is idempotent if and only if it is aperiodic with index 1. The property of the operation $\vee$ is called *idempotency*.

42. Verify that the following monoids are idempotent:
    (a) $(\mathcal{P}(M), \cup, \emptyset)$ for every set M;
    (b) $(\mathcal{P}(M), \cap, M)$ for every set M;
    (c) $(\mathbb{N}, *, 0)$, where $n \star n'$ is the greatest common divisor of n and n';
    (d) $(\mathbb{N}, *, 1)$, where $n \star n'$ is the least common multiple of n and n'.
43. Let $(M, \cdot, 1)$ be an idempotent monoid. Define $m \leq p$ for $m, p \in M$ if $m \cdot p = m$. Verify that the relation $\leq$ is a partial order on M. Further, prove that if $m \leq p$, then $qm \leq qp$ and $mq \leq pq$.

A *semiring* is an algebra $(M, +, \cdot, 0, 1)$ such that $(M, +, 0)$ is a commutative and idempotent monoid, and $(M, \cdot, 1)$ is a monoid, $0 \cdot x = x \cdot 0 = 0$ for every $x \in M$ and we have the distributivity properties

$$\begin{aligned} x \cdot (y + z) &= xy + xz \\ (y + z) \cdot x &= yx + zx, \end{aligned}$$

for every $x, y, z \in M$.

If $(M, +, \cdot, 0, 1)$ is a semiring, we consider the order defined on M as the order generated by the commutative monoid $(M, +, 0)$.

44. Let M be a set. Verify that $(\mathcal{P}(M), \cup, \cap, \emptyset, M)$ is a semiring.

Sequences

45. Prove that if $x, y \in \mathsf{PREF}(z)$ and $|x| \leq |y|$, then $x \in \mathsf{PREF}(y)$. Formulate and prove a similar statement for $\mathsf{SUFF}(z)$.
46. Prove that if D is a finite set, then $|\mathbf{Seq}_n(D)| = |D|^n$ for $n \in \mathbb{N}$.
47. Show that if $\mathsf{PROG}(b, r) = \mathsf{PROG}(b', r')$, then $b = b'$ and $r = r'$.
48. Let $p = (p_0, \ldots, p_n, \ldots)$ be an arithmetic progression. Prove that

$$\sum \{p_i \mid 0 \leq i \leq n\} = (p_0 + p_n)(n + 1)/2.$$

Let $a, b \in \mathbb{N}$, where $0 < b \leq a$. Define the sequence $E(a,b) \in \mathbf{Seq}(\mathbb{N})$ given by $E(a,b) = (r_0, r_1, \ldots, r_k, r_{k+1})$ as:

$$\begin{aligned}
a &= bq + r_0 \\
b &= r_0 q_0 + r_1 \\
r_0 &= r_1 q_1 + r_2 \\
&\vdots \\
r_{i-1} &= r_i q_i + r_{i+1} \\
&\vdots \\
r_{k-1} &= r_k q_k + r_{k+1},
\end{aligned}$$

where r_0 is the remainder of the division of a by b, r_1 is the remainder of the division of b by r_0, and r_{i+1} is the remainder of the division of r_{i-1} by r_i. Also, $r_{k+1} = 0$. Since the remainders form a decreasing sequence of natural numbers such a sequence can always be constructed.

49. (a) Prove that for every i, $0 \leq i \leq k$, there are two integers ℓ_i, h_i such that $r_i = a\ell_i + bh_i$.
    (b) Prove that r_k, the last non-zero member of the sequence $E(a,b)$ is the greatest common divisor of a, b.
    (c) Prove that the equation $ax + by = c$ has integer solutions in x, y if and only if c is a multiple of the greatest common divisor of a and b.
    (d) Suppose that a, b are relatively prime natural numbers (that is, the greatest common divisor of a and b is 1). Let $(x_0, y_0) \in \mathbb{Z}^2$ be a solution of the equation $ax + by = c$. Prove that (x, y) is an arbitrary solution of $ax + by = c$ if and only if there is $k \in \mathbb{Z}$ such that $x = x_0 + kb$ and $y = y_0 - ka$. Formulate and prove a similar statement for the case when a and b are not relatively prime.
    (e) Let a, b be two relatively prime natural numbers. Prove that the distance between two consecutive solutions of the equation $ax + by = c$ on the line $ax + by = c$ is $\sqrt{a^2 + b^2}$. Conclude that if $c \geq \sqrt{ab}$ then the equation $ax + by = c$ has at least one solution x, y, where $x \geq 0$ and $y \geq 0$.
    (f) Let $a_0, \ldots, a_{m-1}$ be m natural numbers. Prove by induction on $m \geq 2$ that $a_0 x_0 + \ldots + a_{m-1} x_{m-1} = c$ has a solution in integers for $x_0, \ldots, x_{m-1}$ if and only if d, the greatest common divisor of $a_0, \ldots, a_{m-1}$ divides c. Further, prove that if c is sufficiently large, then the previous equation has a solution in natural numbers relative to $x_0, \ldots, x_{m-1}$.

Let L be a set of natural numbers. Denote by $\gcd L$ the greatest common divisor of all members of L.

50. Let S be an infinite subset of $\mathbb{N}$ and let $d = \gcd S$. Prove that there exists a finite subset U of S such that $d = \gcd U$.
    Solution. Let $d' = \min\{\gcd T \mid T \text{ is a finite subset of } S\}$, and let T' be a finite subset such that $d' = \gcd T'$. Certainly d divides d', since

$d = \gcd S$, so $d \leq d'$. If $d = d'$, we're done. Assume that $d < d'$. Then, there must be some natural number $n \in S$ such that d' does not divide n. But then $T' \cup \{n\}$ is also a finite set, but it has a smaller greatest common divisor than T', which contradicts the choice of d'. ■

The *Fibonacci sequence* is the sequence $(f_0, f_1, \dots) \in \mathbf{Seq}_\infty(\mathbb{N})$ defined by $f_0 = 0$, $f_1 = 1$ and $f_n = f_{n-1} + f_{n-2}$ for $n \geq 2$.

51. Prove that
$$\begin{pmatrix} f_{n+1} & f_n \\ f_n & f_{n-1} \end{pmatrix} = \begin{pmatrix} 1 & 1 \\ 1 & 0 \end{pmatrix}^n$$
for $n \geq 1$.
52. Prove that $f_0 + f_1 + \cdots + f_n = f_{n+2} - 1$ for $n \in \mathbb{N}$.
53. Prove that every positive number $n \in \mathbb{N}$ has a unique representation as a sum of non-consecutive Fibonacci numbers; in other words, prove that for every $n \in \mathbb{P}$ there is a unique set of numbers $\{i_0, i_1, \dots, i_\ell\} \subseteq \mathbb{N}$ such that $i_0 \geq 2$, $i_p > i_{p-1} + 1$ for $1 \leq p \leq \ell$ and $n = f_{i_0} + f_{i_1} + \cdots + f_{i_\ell}$.
Solution. The argument is by induction on n. For $n = 1$ it is clear that $n = f_2$, so the basis case is immediate. Suppose that f_k is the largest Fibonacci number that does not exceed n, that is, $f_k \leq n < f_{k+1}$. Then, $0 \leq n - f_k < f_{k-1}$. The number $n - f_k$ can be written uniquely as $n - f_k = f_{i_0} + f_{i_1} + \cdots + f_{i_\ell}$ by the inductive hypothesis and we have $i_\ell + 1 < k$. Thus, n can be uniquely written as $n = f_k + f_{i_0} + f_{i_1} + \cdots + f_{i_\ell}$. ■

A semiring $(M, +, \cdot, 0, 1)$ is *closed* if for every infinite sequence

$$(m_0, m_1, \dots, m_n, \dots) \in \mathbf{Seq}_\infty(M)$$

there is an element $m \in M$, denoted by $\sum_n m_n$ such that the following statements hold.

- For every $(m_0, m_1, \dots, m_n, \dots) \in \mathbf{Seq}_\infty(M)$ and $p \in M$ we have:
$$p \cdot \sum_n m_n = \sum_n p \cdot m_n$$
$$\sum_n m_n \cdot p = \sum_n m_n \cdot p$$
- Let $(p_0, p_1, \dots) \in \mathbf{Seq}_\infty(M)$ be the *sequence of partial sums* of the sequence $(m_0, m_1, \dots)$, where $p_n = m_0 + m_1 + \cdots + m_n$. We have $\sum_n p_n = \sum_n m_n$.
- Let $(m_0, m_1, \dots), (m'_0, m'_1, \dots)$ be two infinite sequences in $\mathbf{Seq}_\infty(M)$. If for every $n \in \mathbb{N}$ there exists $k \in \mathbb{N}$ such that $m_n \leq m'_k$, then $\sum_n m_n \leq \sum_n m'_n$.

If $m \in M$ define the powers m^n of m as $m^0 = 1$ and $m^{n+1} = m \cdot m^n$ for $n \in \mathbb{N}$. Define the *closure* m^* *of an element* $m \in M$ as $m^* = \sum_n m^n$.

54. Let $(M, +, \cdot, 0, 1)$ be a semiring. Prove that
$$\sum_n m_n \sum_r m'_r = \sum_n \left(\sum_r m_n m'_r \right)$$

for every infinite sequences

$$(m_0, m_1, \dots), (m'_0, m'_1, \dots) \in \mathbf{Seq}_\infty(M).$$

55. Prove that the algebra $(\mathbb{R}_{\geq 0} \cup \{\infty\}, \min, +, \infty, 0)$ is a closed semiring, where $\sum_n m_n$ is the greatest lower bound of the set $\{m_n \mid n \in \mathbb{N}\}$.
56. Prove that the algebra $(\{0,1\}, \max, \min, 0, 1)$ is a closed semiring, where $\sum_n m_n$ is 1 if and only if there is a member of the sequence $(m_0, m_1, \dots)$ that equals 1.
57. Let $(M, +, \cdot, 0, 1)$ be a closed semiring. Prove that for every infinite sequences $(m_0, m_1, \dots), (m'_0, m'_1, \dots) \in \mathbf{Seq}_\infty(M)$ we have

$$\left(\sum_r m_r\right)\left(\sum_n m'_n\right) = \sum_r \sum_n (m_r \cdot m'_n).$$

58. Let $(M, +, \cdot, 0, 1)$ be a closed semiring. Prove that:
    (a) $0^* = 1^* = 1$;
    (b) $m \leq m^*$;
    (c) $m_0 \leq m_1$ implies $m_0^* = m_1^*$;
    (d) $(m^*)^* = m^*$.

A *Kleene algebra* is an algebra $\mathcal{K} = (M, +, \cdot, *, 0, 1)$, where $(M, +, \cdot, 0, 1)$ is a semiring and $*$ is a unary operation. For a Kleene algebra $\mathcal{K} = (M, +, \cdot, 0, 1)$ the supremum of the set $\{m_0 m^n m_1 \mid n \in \mathbb{N}\}$ exists for $m_0, m_1, m_1 \in M$ (with respect to the partial order induced by the semiring) and is denoted by $m_0 m^* m_1$.

59. Prove that every closed semiring is a Kleene algebra.
60. Prove that $\mathcal{K}_2 = (\{0,1\}, \max, \min, *, 0, 1)$ is a Kleene algebra, where $x^* = 1$ for $x \in \{0,1\}$.
61. Let $\mathcal{R}(X)$ the set of all relations on a set X. Show that

$$\mathcal{K} = (\mathcal{R}(X), \cup, \circ, *, \emptyset, \iota_X)$$

is a Kleene algebra, where $\rho^* = \bigcup_n \rho^n$.

Graphs

62. Let $A = \{0, 1, \dots, m\}$ be a set. Define a *de Bruijn graph* as $G_{m,n} = (\mathbf{Seq}_{n-1}(A), \mathbf{Seq}_n(A), s, d)$, where $s(x) = x_{0,n-1}$ and $d(e) = x_{1,n}$ for $x \in \mathbf{Seq}_n$.
    Prove that $G_{m,n}$ has an Euler circuit for every $m, n \in \mathbb{P}$.

A *Hamiltonian circuit* in a digraph $G = (V, E, s, d)$ is a simple circuit on which every vertex of V appears exactly once.

63. Let $G = (V, E, s, d)$ be a digraph such that for every two vertices $u, v \in V$ we have $u \rightsquigarrow v$ or $v \rightsquigarrow v$. Prove that G contains a Hamiltonian circuit.

A *weighted digraph* is a labeled directed graph $\mathcal{G} = (G, M, \mathsf{m})$, where $\mathrm{Dom}(\mathsf{m}) = E$ and the range of values is the universe M of a closed semiring $(M, +, \cdot, 0, 1)$.

The number $\mathsf{m}(e)$ is referred to as *the weight of the edge e.* .

If $\varpi = (e_0, \ldots, e_{n-1})$ is a path with $n \geq 1$, then m is extended to ϖ by $\mathsf{m}(\varpi) = \mathsf{m}(e_0) \cdot \ldots \cdot \mathsf{m}(e_n)$. If $n = 0$, then $\mathsf{m}(\varpi) = 0$. We refer to $\mathsf{m}(\varpi)$ as *the label of the path* ϖ.

Let $L = \{\varpi_0, \varpi_1, \ldots\}$ be a set of paths in the graph. The cost of the set L is $\sum_n \mathsf{m}(\varpi_n)$. If $L_{x,y}$ is the set of paths that join x to y, then $\mathsf{cost}(x, y)$ is the cost of $L_{x,y}$.

64. Let $\mathcal{G} = (G, M, \mathsf{m})$ be a weighted graph, where $G = (V, E, s, d)$ is a digraph whose set of vertices is $V = \{v_0, \ldots, v_{n-1}\}$, and let $(M, +, \cdot, 0, 1)$ be a closed semiring.
Define the elements c_{ij}^k of the semiring as
$$c_{ij}^0 = \begin{cases} 1 + m(e) & \text{if } i = j \text{ and } s(e) = d(e) = v_i \\ m(e) & \text{if } i \neq j,\ s(e) = v_i \text{ and } d(e) = v_i \end{cases}$$
$$c_{ij}^k = c_{ij}^{k-1} + c_{ik-1}^{k-1} \cdot (c_{k-1k-1}^{k-1})^* \cdot c_{k-1j}^{k-1}.$$
Prove that c_{ij}^k is the cost of the set of paths that join v_i to v_j without passing through any vertex v_ℓ with $\ell \geq k$. In other words, the vertices that occur on these paths, except v_i and v_j, belong to the set $\{v_0, \ldots, v_{k-1}\}$.
65. Let $(\mathbb{R}_{\geq 0} \cup \{\infty\}, \min, +, \infty, 0)$ be the closed semiring considered in Exercise 55 and let $\mathcal{G} = (G, \mathbb{R}, \mathsf{m})$ be a weighted graph such that $|V| = n$. Prove that:
    (a) We have $c_{ij}^k = \min\{c_{ij}^{k-1}, c_{ik-1}^{k-1} + c_{k-1j}^{k-1}\}$ for $0 \leq i, j, k \leq n - 1$.
    (b) c_{ij}^n equals the minimal cost of a path that joins v_i to v_j in G.

1.8 Bibliographical Comments

See [Fejer and Simovici, 1991] for an introduction to set theory and related concepts. The notion of Kleene algebra originates in Kleene's work and was introduced in [Kozen, 1981].

Chapter 2

Words and Languages

2.1 Introduction

Words are mathematical abstractions of the every-day notion of a word on the printed page. The study of words and of sets of words, referred to as *languages*, plays a central role in computer science, since programs and the data they manipulate may be regarded as words over appropriate alphabets. In a very real sense, all data manipulation is simply operations on words.

We introduce words as sequences of elements of finite, nonempty sets, referred to as *alphabets*. We study algebraic operations on words and on languages. Then we present substitutions on languages and morphisms between free monoids.

The concluding section on polynomials is important for equational characterizations of classes of languages.

2.2 Words

An *alphabet* is a finite, nonempty set. We refer to the elements of an alphabet as the *symbols* of the alphabet.

Definition 2.2.1 A *word* of length n on an alphabet A is a sequence of length n of symbols of this alphabet (i.e., an element of $\mathbf{Seq}_n(A)$). □

We write $w(0) \cdots w(n-1)$ for the word $(w(0), \ldots, w(n-1))$.

Example 2.2.2 Let $A = \{a, b, c\}$ be an alphabet. The word (a, a, b, a, a, c) is written as *aabaac*. □

Example 2.2.3 Any C program is a word over the basic alphabet of this language that includes small and capital letters, as well as special symbols, such as parentheses, brackets, braces, spaces, new line characters, quotation marks, etc. Not all these characters are visible; in other words, some characters (such as spaces) appear on paper only as white spaces. For example, the famous C program

```
#include <stdio.h> main() { printf("hello, world\n"); }
```

can be looked at as a word. □

Under the notation previously introduced, a word w of length 1 is denoted by $w(0)$. Hence, we use the same notation for a symbol from the alphabet and the word of length one whose entry is the symbol.

Since words are sequences, each word w has a length $|w|$, and we have the *null word*, λ, of length 0. Also, Definition 1.4.12 can be applied to words. The reversal w^R of a word w is

$$w^R = \begin{cases} \lambda & \text{if } w = \lambda \\ a_{n-1} \cdots a_0 & \text{if } w = a_0 \cdots a_{n-1} \end{cases}$$

We can form the *concatenation* or *product* of two words over an alphabet to get another word over the alphabet. We write uv for the concatenation of the two words u and v rather than $u \cdot v$. This is consistent with the notation for words as a juxtaposition of the names of the individual symbols. Clearly, $|uv| = |u| + |v|$.

If A is an alphabet, then we write A^* for $\mathbf{Seq}(A)$, the set of all words over A, and we write A^+ for $\mathbf{Seq}^+(A)$, the set of all nonnull words over A. Note that $A^* = A^+ \cup \{\lambda\}$.

In Section 1.4, we defined the notions of prefix, suffix and infix of a sequence. Since words are sequences, these notions are, of course, applicable to words. Moreover, the same notions can be redefined for words using concatenation.

Definition 2.2.4 Let t be a word, $t \in A^*$. A *prefix* of t is a word u such that $t = uw$ for some $w \in A^*$. The prefix u is *proper* if $u \neq \lambda$ and $u \neq t$.

A *suffix* of t is a word y such that $t = xy$ for some $x \in A^*$. The suffix y is *proper* if $y \neq \lambda$ and $y \neq t$.

An *infix* of t is a word w such that $t = vwx$ for some $v, x \in A^*$. The infix w is *proper* if $w \neq \lambda$ and $w \neq t$.

The sets of prefixes, infixes and suffixes of a word t are denoted by $\mathsf{PREF}(t)$, $\mathsf{INFIX}(t)$, and $\mathsf{SUFF}(t)$, respectively. Also, the sets of proper prefixes, proper infixes and proper suffixes of a word t are denoted by $\mathsf{PREFpr}(t)$, $\mathsf{INFIXpr}(t)$, and $\mathsf{SUFFpr}(t)$, respectively. □

Example 2.2.5 Let $A = \{a, b, c\}$, and consider the word $t = accabac$. The word *acc* is a prefix of t, *abac* is a suffix of t, and *ccab* is an infix of t. □

Since $\lambda x = \lambda x \lambda = x \lambda = x$, every word x is a prefix, a suffix, and an infix of itself. Similarly, the null word is a prefix, an infix, and a suffix of every word.

Following the notation introduced in Section 1.4, we denote by $x_{i,j}$ the infix $y = a_i \cdots a_{j-1}$ of $x = a_0 \cdots a_{n-1}$ for $0 \leq i < j \leq n$. In other words, $x_{i,j}$ is the infix that begins with a_i and ends with a_{j-1}. We extend this notation by defining $x_{i,j} = \lambda$ when $j \leq i$. Thus, $x_{i,i} = \lambda$ for every i, $0 \leq i \leq n-1$; $x_{0,j} \in \mathsf{PREF}(x)$ for $0 \leq j \leq n$; and $x_{i,n} \in \mathsf{SUFF}(x)$ for $0 \leq i \leq n$. If $i \leq j$, we have $|x_{i,j}| = j - i$.

Definition 2.2.6 Let $x_{i,j}, x_{p,q}$ be two infixes of a word x. Then, $x_{i,j}, x_{p,q}$ are *disjoint* if $j \leq p$. □

Example 2.2.7 Let $x = abacbabbabaca$ be a word over the alphabet $\{a, b, c\}$. The infixes $x_{2,7} = acbab$ and $x_{7,10} = bab$ are disjoint. □

Let $A = \{a_0, \ldots, a_{n-1}\}$ be an alphabet containing n symbols. Words over A can be encoded as natural numbers; in other words, we can define a bijection $\phi_A : A^* \longrightarrow \mathbb{N}$ by

$$\phi_A(x) = \begin{cases} 0 & \text{if } x = \lambda \\ n\phi_A(y) + i + 1 & \text{if } x = ya_i \end{cases}$$

for every $x \in A^*$. It is easy to verify that

$$\begin{aligned} \phi_A(a_{i_0} \cdots a_{i_{k-1}}) &= n^{k-1}(i_0 + 1) + n^{k-2}(i_1 + 1) + \cdots \\ &\quad + n(i_{k-2} + 1) + i_{k-1} + 1. \end{aligned}$$

In Exercise 29 we show that ϕ_A is indeed a bijection.

Example 2.2.8 If $A = \{a_0, a_1, a_2\}$, $x = a_0 a_1 a_0 a_2$, and $y = a_2 a_2 a_2$, then

$$\begin{aligned} \phi_A(x) &= 3^3 \cdot 1 + 3^2 \cdot 2 + 3^1 \cdot 1 + 3 = 51 \\ \phi_A(y) &= 3^2 \cdot 2 + 3^1 \cdot 2 + 2 = 26. \end{aligned}$$

□

Note that $\phi_A(x)$ is not the representation of the number $i_0 \cdots i_{k-1}$ in base n, since we are using the "digits" $1, 2, \ldots, n$ rather than $0, 1, \ldots, n-1$. We leave it to the reader to verify that ϕ_A is indeed a bijection (cf. Exercise 29).

The existence of the bijection $\phi_A : A^* \longrightarrow \mathbb{N}$ shows that A^* is a countably infinite set for every alphabet A.

The function ϕ_A generates a total order on A^* as shown in the next definition.

Definition 2.2.9 Let A be an alphabet and let $x, y \in A^*$. We have $x \prec y$ if $\phi_A(x) < \phi_A(y)$. □

It is easy to see that $\prec$ is a strict partial order on A^*. The partial order induced by $\prec$ will be denoted by $\preceq$.

Example 2.2.10 We have $y \prec x$, where x, y are the words introduced in Example 2.2.8 because $\phi_A(y) < \phi_A(x)$. □

Another important partial order on A^* is the *lexicographic order*. Suppose that we have a total order "<" on A, say $a_0 < a_1 < \cdots < a_{n-1}$.

Definition 2.2.11 The *lexicographic order* on A^* is the relation $\ll$ on A^* defined by $u \ll v$ if either $ut = v$ for some $t \in A^+$ or $u = wa_iu'$, $v = wa_jv'$ for some $w, u', v' \in A^*$ and $i < j$. □

We leave it to the reader to prove that $u \ll v$ implies $zu \ll zv$ for every $z \in A^*$; also, if $u \ll v$ and u is not a prefix of v, then $uz \ll vz'$ for every $z, z' \in A^*$.

The link between the partial order $\prec$ and the lexicographic order $\ll$ is given in the next theorem.

Theorem 2.2.12 *Let $A = \{a_0, \ldots, a_{n-1}\}$ be an alphabet. For $x, y \in A^*$ we have $x \prec y$ if and only if $|x| < |y|$ or $|x| = |y|$ and $x \ll y$.*

Proof. Suppose that $x \prec y$. We have $\phi_A(x) < \phi_A(y)$, so $|x| \leq |y|$ by Exercise 29. If $|x| < |y|$ the first alternative of the statement is satisfied. Therefore, suppose that $|x| = |y|$. Let w be the longest common prefix of x and y (Observe that x and y have at least the null word as a common prefix). Then, we can write $x = wa_ix'$ and $y = wa_jy'$, where $|x'| = |y'| = \ell$. Since

$$\begin{aligned} \phi_A(x) &= \phi_A(w)|A|^{1+\ell} + \phi_A(a_i)|A|^\ell + \phi_A(x') \\ \phi_A(y) &= \phi_A(w)|A|^{1+\ell} + \phi_A(a_j)|A|^\ell + \phi_A(y'), \end{aligned}$$

we obtain

$$\phi_A(a_i)|A|^\ell + \phi_A(x') < \phi_A(a_j)|A|^\ell + \phi_A(y').$$

The inequalities

$$\frac{|A|^\ell - 1}{|A| - 1} \leq \phi_A(x') \text{ and } \phi_A(y') \leq \frac{|A|^{\ell+1} - |A|}{|A| - 1}$$

imply $\phi_A(a_i) < \phi_A(a_j) + \frac{|A|^\ell - 1}{|A|^\ell}$, so $\phi_A(a_i) < \phi_A(a_j)$, which amounts to $i < j$.

The converse implication is left to the reader. ∎

2.3 Languages

The main objects of study of the theory of formal languages are languages, which are defined as sets of certain sequences of symbols.

Definition 2.3.1 Let A be an alphabet. A *language over* A is a subset of A^*. □

In other words, a language over A is any set of words over this alphabet. For instance, $\{a, ab, abba\}$ is a finite language over the alphabet $\{a, b\}$. Similarly, $L = \{a^n \mid n \in \mathbb{N}\}$ is an infinite language over the same alphabet.

Since we identify words of length 1 with the symbols of A, the set A itself is a language over A. Also among the languages over A are the *empty language* $\emptyset$, the *full language* A^*, and the *null language* $\{\lambda\}$.

Since A^* is a countably infinite set, the set of languages over A, $\mathcal{P}(A^*)$ is not countable, as we saw in Corollary 1.6.24.

Observe that if L is a language over an alphabet A and $A \subseteq A'$, then L is also a language over the alphabet A'. Therefore, if $\{L_0, \ldots, L_{n-1}\}$ is a finite collection of languages over the alphabets $\{A_0, \ldots, A_{n-1}\}$, respectively, then for $0 \leq i \leq n-1$, each L_i is a language over $A = \bigcup_{1 \leq i \leq n} A_i$.

We denote by A_L the alphabet that consists of those symbols that occur in at least one word in L. If L is a language over A, then $A_L \subseteq A$.

Definition 2.3.2 A language L is λ-*free* if $\lambda \notin L$. □

The set of all prefixes of the words of a language L is denoted by $\mathsf{PREF}(L)$. Similarly, the sets of infixes and suffixes of the words of L are denoted by $\mathsf{INFIX}(L)$ and $\mathsf{SUFF}(L)$, respectively. Note that $L \subseteq L'$ implies $\Omega(L) \subseteq \Omega(L')$, where Ω is any of $\mathsf{PREF}, \mathsf{SUFF}$, or INFIX. Also, $\mathsf{INFIX}(L), \mathsf{PREF}(L), \mathsf{SUFF}(L)$ contain the null word and include L.

The sets of proper prefixes, proper suffixes and proper infixes of a language L are denoted by $\mathsf{PREFpr}(L)$, $\mathsf{INFIXpr}(L)$, and $\mathsf{SUFFpr}(L)$, respectively.

Since languages are sets of words, we can apply to them set-theoretical operations such as union, intersection, difference, etc. If $L \subseteq A^*$, the complement of L with respect to the alphabet A is $\overline{L}_A = A^* - L$. If A is understood from the context, we may denote the complement $\overline{L}_A$ simply by $\overline{L}$.

Definition 2.3.3 The *product* of two languages L and K over an alphabet A is the language LK defined by

$$LK = \{xy \mid x \in L \text{ and } y \in K\}.$$

□

The definition of language product is a special case of the subset product for subsets of semigroups previously introduced in Equation (1.1).

Properties of language products are derived from properties of subsets of semigroups discussed in Section 1.3 (see Equations (1.2), (1.3), and (1.4), as well as Theorem 1.3.21 and Corollary 1.3.22).

Definition 2.3.4 Let $L \subseteq A^*$ be a language over the alphabet A. The nth *power of* L is the language L^n given by

$$\begin{aligned} L^0 &= \{\lambda\} \\ L^{n+1} &= L^n L \end{aligned}$$

for every language L and natural number n. □

Note that $L^1 = L$. In general, L^n is the set of all words that can be written as products of n words of L. For $n = 0$, we regard λ as the product of zero words of L.

Example 2.3.5 Let $L = \{ab, a\}$ be a language over the alphabet $A = \{a, b\}$. We have

$$\begin{aligned} L^0 &= \{\lambda\} \\ L^1 &= \{ab, a\} \\ L^2 &= \{abab, aba, aab, aa\} \\ &\vdots \end{aligned}$$

□

Definition 2.3.6 Let L be a language. The language L^*, the *star closure* or *Kleene closure* of L, is the set

$$L^* = \bigcup \{L^n \mid n \in \mathbb{N}\}.$$

The language L^+, the *positive closure* of L, is the set of words

$$L^+ = \bigcup \{L^n \mid n \in \mathbb{P}\}.$$

□

In other words, L^* is the set of all words that can be written as a product of zero or more words of L; L^+ is the set of all words that can be written as a product of one or more words of L.

Since L^* includes the product of zero words of L, the null word λ is a member of L^* for any language L. On the other hand, the above definition also implies that $L \subseteq L^+ \subseteq L^*$ and $LL^* = L^*L = L^+$. Furthermore, if $u, v \in L^*$, then $uv \in L^*$. Also, note that $\lambda \in L^+$ if and only if $\lambda \in L$.

Example 2.3.7 Let $L = \{a, bab\}$ be a language over the alphabet $A = \{a, b\}$. L^* comprises the words λ, a, bab, $abab$, $baba$, $babbab$, aa, etc., and L^+ consists of the same words except for λ. □

In view of the definition of L^*, it is easy to see that we have the following properties for any language L:

$$\begin{array}{rclrcl} L^*L^* & = & L^*, & (L^*)^* & = & L^*, \\ L^*L & = & LL^*, & (L^+)^+ & = & L^+, \\ L^+L & = & LL^+ & & & \end{array}$$

Also, note that $L \subseteq H$ implies $L^* \subseteq H^*$. Further properties of language operations are given in the next theorem.

Theorem 2.3.8 *Let A be an alphabet. We have:*

(i) $L_0 \cup (L_1 \cup L_2) = (L_0 \cup L_1) \cup L_2$,
(ii) $L_0(L_1L_2) = (L_0L_1)L_2$,
(iii) $L_0 \cup L_1 = L_1 \cup L_0$,
(iv) $L_0(L_1 \cup L_2) = (L_0L_1) \cup (L_0L_2)$,
(v) $(L_0 \cup L_1)L_2 = (L_0L_2) \cup (L_1L_2)$,
(vi) $L \cup L = L$,
(vii) $\{\lambda\}L = L\{\lambda\} = L$,
(viii) $\emptyset L = L\emptyset = \emptyset$,
(ix) $L \cup \emptyset = \emptyset \cup L = L$,
(x) $L^* = \{\lambda\} \cup L^*L$,
(xi) $L^* = (\{\lambda\} \cup L)^*$,
(xii) $\emptyset^* = \{\lambda\}$,

for every $L, L_0, L_1, L_2 \in \mathcal{P}(A^*)$.

Proof. The argument is straightforward and is left to the reader. ∎

Theorem 2.3.9 *Let A be an alphabet and let L be a language over A. We have*

$$L^* = \{\lambda\} \cup L \cup L^2 \cup \cdots \cup L^k \cup L^{k+1}L^*,$$

for every $k \in \mathbb{N}$.

Proof. It is clear that

$$\{\lambda\} \cup L \cup L^2 \cup \cdots \cup L^k \cup L^{k+1}L^* \subseteq L^*,$$

for every $k \in \mathbb{N}$.

Conversely, let $x \in L^*$. We have either $x = \lambda$ or $x \in L^n$ for some $n \geq 1$. If $n \leq k$, then $x \in \{\lambda\} \cup L \cup L^2 \cup \cdots \cup L^k \cup L^{k+1}L^*$. If $n > k$, then $L^n = L^{k+1}L^{n-(k+1)} \subseteq L^{k+1}L^*$, so again $x \in \{\lambda\} \cup L \cup L^2 \cup \cdots \cup L^k \cup L^{k+1}L^*$. Thus, $\{\lambda\} \cup L \cup L^2 \cup \cdots \cup L^k \cup L^{k+1}L^* \subseteq L^*$. ∎

Corollary 2.3.10 *For every language L we have:*

$$L^* = \{\lambda\} \cup LL^*.$$

Proof. The equality of the corollary follows from Theorem 2.3.9 by taking $k = 0$. ∎

Definition 2.3.11 The *reversal of a language* $L \subseteq A^*$ is the language L^R given by

$$L^R = \{x^R \mid x \in L\}.$$

□

It is easy to see that $(L^R)^R = L$ for every language L.

Example 2.3.12 Let $A = \{a, b, c\}$ be an alphabet. The reversal of the language $L \subseteq A^*$, where $L = \{a, abb, aba, abac\}$ is the language $L^R = \{a, bba, aba, caba\}$. □

When A is considered as a language over itself, then A^* is $\mathbf{Seq}(A)$. In general, however, L^* is not the same thing as $\mathbf{Seq}(L)$ for a language L over A.

Definition 2.3.13 Let L, K be two languages over the alphabet A. The *right quotient* LK^{-1} and the *left quotient* $K^{-1}L$ are the languages:

$$\begin{aligned} LK^{-1} &= \{x \in A^* \mid xy \in L \text{ for some } y \in K\} \\ K^{-1}L &= \{x \in A^* \mid yx \in L \text{ for some } y \in K\}. \end{aligned}$$

□

Example 2.3.14 Let $A = \{a, b, c\}$ be an alphabet and $L = \{\lambda, a, ab, abc\}$ be a language over A. Consider the languages $K_0 = \{c\}$, $K_1 = \{b, c\}$, and $K_2 = \{b, c\}^*$ over the same alphabet. Then, we have

$$\begin{aligned} LK_0^{-1} &= \{ab\}, \\ LK_1^{-1} &= \{a, ab\}, \\ LK_2^{-1} &= \{\lambda, a, ab, abc\}. \end{aligned}$$

□

The left quotient of two languages can be expressed through the right quotient of related languages by the equality

$$K^{-1}L = \left(L^R(K^R)^{-1}\right)^R. \tag{2.1}$$

To prove this equality consider the following equivalent statements.

1. $x \in K^{-1}L$;
2. $yx \in L$ for some $y \in K$;
3. $x^R z \in L^R$ for some $z \in K^R$;
4. $x^R \in L^R(K^R)^{-1}$;
5. $x \in \left(L^R(K^R)^{-1}\right)^R$.

Similarly, we can write

$$LK^{-1} = \left((K^R)^{-1}L^R\right)^R. \tag{2.2}$$

Example 2.3.15 Let L be a language over an alphabet A. It is easy to see that the set $\mathsf{PREF}(L)$ of prefixes of a language L is $L(A^*)^{-1}$, while the set $\mathsf{SUFF}(L)$ of suffixes of L is $(A^*)^{-1}L$. □

Theorem 2.3.16 *Let L_0, L_1, K be languages over the alphabet A and let $a \in A$. We have*

$$(L_0 \cup L_1)K^{-1} = L_0K^{-1} \cup L_1K^{-1} \tag{2.3}$$
$$(L_0 \cup L_1)^{-1}K = L_0^{-1}K \cup L_1^{-1}K \tag{2.4}$$
$$(L_0 \cap L_1)K^{-1} \subseteq L_0K^{-1} \cap L_1K^{-1} \tag{2.5}$$
$$(L_0 \cap L_1)^{-1}K \subseteq L_0^{-1}K \cap L_1^{-1}K \tag{2.6}$$
$$L_0K^{-1} - L_1K^{-1} \subseteq (L_0 - L_1)K^{-1}. \tag{2.7}$$
$$K^{-1}(L_0 \cup L_1) = K^{-1}L_0 \cup K^{-1}L_1 \tag{2.8}$$
$$K^{-1}(L_0 \cap L_1) \subseteq K^{-1}L_0 \cap K^{-1}L_1 \tag{2.9}$$
$$K^{-1}L_0 - K^{-1}L_1 \subseteq K^{-1}(L_0 - L_1). \tag{2.10}$$
$$\{a\}^{-1}(L_0L_1) = \begin{cases} (\{a\}^{-1}L_0)L_1 & \text{if } \lambda \notin L_0 \\ (\{a\}^{-1}L_0)L_1 \cup \{a\}^{-1}L_1 & \text{if } \lambda \in L_0 \end{cases} \tag{2.11}$$
$$\{a\}^{-1}L_1^* = (\{a\}^{-1}L_1)L_1^* \tag{2.12}$$

Proof. We present only the argument for Equality 2.3. Let $x \in (L_0 \cup L_1)K^{-1}$. There is $y \in K$ such that $xy \in L_0 \cup L_1$, which means that $xy \in L_0$ or $xy \in L_1$. In other words, $x \in L_0K^{-1} \cup L_1K^{-1}$. Conversely, let $x \in L_0K^{-1} \cup L_1K^{-1}$. We have $xy \in L_0$ or $xy' \in L_1$ for some $y, y' \in K$. In either case, $x \in (L_0 \cup L_1)K^{-1}$, which proves the Equality 2.3. ∎

If K is a singleton, $K = \{u\}$, we denote the languages $\{u\}^{-1}L$ and $L\{u\}^{-1}$ by $u^{-1}L$ and Lu^{-1}, respectively. These languages are referred to as *the left derivative of L with respect to u* and *the right derivative of L with respect to u*, respectively.

The reader will easily verify the equalities:

$$(L_0 \cup L_1)u^{-1} = L_0u^{-1} \cup L_1u^{-1} \tag{2.13}$$
$$(L_0 \cap L_1)u^{-1} = L_0u^{-1} \cap L_1u^{-1} \tag{2.14}$$
$$L_0u^{-1} - L_1u^{-1} = (L_0 - L_1)u^{-1} \tag{2.15}$$
$$u^{-1}(L_0 \cup L_1) = u^{-1}L_0 \cup u^{-1}L_1 \tag{2.16}$$
$$u^{-1}(L_0 \cap L_1) = u^{-1}L_0 \cap u^{-1}L_1 \tag{2.17}$$
$$u^{-1}L_0 - u^{-1}L_1 = u^{-1}(L_0 - L_1) \tag{2.18}$$
$$u^{-1}(v^{-1}L) = (vu)^{-1}L \tag{2.19}$$
$$(Lu^{-1})v^{-1} = L(vu)^{-1}, \tag{2.20}$$

for all words u, v.

The next result is a specialization of the Induction Principle for Sequences (Theorem 1.4.14).

Theorem 2.3.17 (Induction Principle for Words) *Let $L \subseteq A^*$ be a set of words such that $\lambda \in L$, and $x \in L$ implies $xa \in L$ for every $a \in A$. Then, $L = A^*$.*

Proof. This statement follows immediately from Theorem 1.4.14. ∎

Example 2.3.18 Let A be an alphabet, $x \in A^*$, and $a \in A$. We prove, by applying the Induction Principle for Words, that for every $x \in A^*$, if $xa = ax$, then $x = a^m$ for some $m \in \mathbb{N}$. Let

$$L = \{x \in A^* \mid xa = ax \text{ implies } x = a^m \text{ for some } m \in \mathbb{N}\}.$$

Since $\lambda a = a\lambda = a$ and $\lambda = a^0$, we have $\lambda \in L$. Suppose that $x \in L$ and consider the word $y = xa$. If $ya \neq ay$, then the implication in the definition of L holds and $y \in L$. Therefore, assume that $ya = ay$. Thus, implies $xaa = axa$, so $xa = ax$, which implies $x = a^m$ because we assumed $x \in L$. Thus, $y = xa = a^{m+1}$, so $y \in L$. By the Induction Principle for Words we have $L = A^*$, which concludes our argument. This result is expanded in Supplement 5. □

2.4 Substitutions and Morphisms

Definition 2.4.1 Let A, B be two alphabets. A *substitution* from A to B is a mapping $s : A \longrightarrow \mathcal{P}(B^*)$. □

In other words, a substitution from A to B maps every symbol of A to a language over B.

A substitution s from A to B is extended inductively to the mapping $s^* : A^* \longrightarrow \mathcal{P}(B^*)$ by

$$\begin{aligned} s^*(\lambda) &= \{\lambda\} \\ s^*(xa) &= s^*(x)s(a) \end{aligned}$$

for every word $x \in A^*$.

By taking $x = \lambda$, the second equality gives $s^*(a) = s(a)$, so s^* is indeed an extension of s. Further, it is easy to verify by induction on the length of the word y that $s^*(xy) = s^*(x)s^*(y)$ for all words $x, y \in A^*$.

Example 2.4.2 Let $A = \{a_0, a_1\}$, $B = \{b_0, b_1, b_2\}$. Define the substitution s by $s(a_0) = \{b_1\}^+$ and $s(a_1) = b_0\{b_2\}^+b_0$. The image of the word $a_0a_1a_0$ under s^* is the language $\{b_1\}^+b_0\{b_2\}^+b_0\{b_1\}^+$. □

When there is no risk of confusion, we frequently denote the extension of a substitution s simply by s rather than s^*.

A substitution $s : A \longrightarrow \mathcal{P}(B^*)$ can be further extended to a mapping between languages over A and B by taking

$$s(L) = \{s(x) \mid x \in L\}$$

for every language $L \subseteq A^*$. Then, we have the following result.

Theorem 2.4.3 *For any languages L_1, L_2*

$$\begin{aligned} s(L_1 \cup L_2) &= s(L_1) \cup s(L_2) \\ s(L_1L_2) &= s(L_1)s(L_2) \\ s(L_1^*) &= (s(L_1))^* \end{aligned}$$

Proof. The arguments are simple applications of the definition of the value of a substitution, and they are left for the reader. ∎

Definition 2.4.4 A *morphism* between A^* and B^* is a mapping $h : A^* \longrightarrow B^*$ such that $h(xy) = h(x)h(y)$ for every $x, y \in A^*$. □

If $h : A^* \longrightarrow B^*$ is a morphism, then $h(\lambda) = \lambda$. Indeed, since $h(x) = h(x\lambda) = h(x)h(\lambda)$ the equality $h(\lambda) = \lambda$ follows immediately.

The following definition introduces certain classes of morphisms.

Definition 2.4.5 A morphism $h : A^* \longrightarrow B^*$ is

(i) *λ-free* if $h(x) = \lambda$ implies $x = \lambda$;
(ii) *fine* if $h(a) \in B \cup \{\lambda\}$ for every $a \in A$;
(iii) *very fine* if $h(a) \in B$ for every $a \in A$.

□

If a morphism h is one-to-one, then h is λ-free since $h(x) = \lambda$ means that $h(x) = h(\lambda)$ which implies $x = \lambda$.

Morphisms will be denoted, in general, by $h, k, l, \ldots$ with or without subscripts.

If $h : A^* \longrightarrow B^*$ is a morphism and $K \subseteq B^*$, we denote by $h^{-1}(K)$ the set $\{x \in A^* \mid h(x) \in K\}$. We refer to $h^{-1}(K)$ as *the inverse image of K under h*.

Example 2.4.6 Suppose, for instance, that $A = \{a_0, a_1\}$ and $B = \{b\}$ are two disjoint alphabets and $h : (A \cup B)^* \longrightarrow A^*$ is a morphism such that $h(a) = a$ for every $a \in A$ and $h(b) = \lambda$. Then, we have

$$h^{-1}(\{a_0^n a_1^n \mid n \in \mathbb{N}\}) \cap \{ba_0\}^*\{a_1 b\}^* = \{(ba_0)^n (a_1 b)^n \mid n \in \mathbb{N}\}$$

□

It is easy to show by induction that a morphism $h : A^* \longrightarrow B^*$ is completely and uniquely defined by its values on the symbols of A. Consequently, morphisms may be regarded as a special case of substitutions, where for each letter in A the corresponding language has only one element.

We introduce an operation on languages that is best expresed using morphisms.

Definition 2.4.7 Let A be an alphabet and let G, K be two languages over A. The *shuffle* of G and K is the language

$$\mathsf{shuffle}(G, K) = \{x_0 y_0 x_1 y_1 \cdots x_{n-1} y_{n-1} \mid x_0 x_1 \cdots x_{n-1} \in G \text{ and } y_0 y_1 \cdots y_{n-1} \in K\}.$$

□

Theorem 2.4.8 *There is an alphabet B and there exist three morphisms g, k, h from B^* to A^* such that h is a very fine morphism, g, k are fine morphisms and* $\mathsf{shuffle}(G, K) = h(g^{-1}(G) \cap k^{-1}(K))$.

Proof. Let $B = A \cup A'$, where $A' = \{a' \mid a \in A\}$. Define the morphisms h, g, k by $h(a) = h(a') = a$, $g(a) = a$, $g(a') = \lambda$, $k(a) = \lambda$, and $k(a') = a$.

Let $w \in h(g^{-1}(G) \cap k^{-1}(K))$. There is $y \in g^{-1}(G) \cap k^{-1}(K)$ such that $h(y) = w$. In addition, $g(y) \in G$ and $k(y) \in K$. Note that g erases all primed symbols in y while k erases all non-primed symbols in y. Since y is a mix of primed and non-primed symbols we can write $y = u_0v'_0u_1v'_1 \ldots u_{n-1}v'_{n-1}$, where $u_0, u_1, \ldots, u_{n-1}$ are the non-primed infixes of y and $v'_0, v'_1, \ldots, v'_{n-1}$ are the primed infixes of y. Therefore, $g(y) = u_0u_1 \cdots u_{n-1} \in G$, $k(y) = v_0v_1 \cdots v_{n-1} \in K$, and $w = h(y) = u_0v_0u_1v_1 \cdots u_{n-1}v_{n-1}$. Thus, $w \in \mathsf{shuffle}(G, K)$.

Conversely, if $w \in \mathsf{shuffle}(G, K)$ we can write $w = u_0v_0u_1v_1 \cdots u_{n-1}v_{n-1}$, where $u_0u_1 \cdots u_{n-1} \in G$ and $v_0v_1 \cdots v_{n-1} \in K$. Let y be the word $y = u_0v'_0u_1v'_1 \cdots u_{n-1}v'_{n-1}$, where v'_i is the primed version of v_i for $0 \leq i \leq n-1$. It is easy to see that $h(y) = w$ and that

$$\begin{aligned} g(y) &= u_0u_1 \cdots u_{n-1} \in G \\ k(y) &= v_0v_1 \cdots v_{n-1} \in K. \end{aligned}$$

Therefore, $y \in g^{-1}(G) \cap k^{-1}(K)$, so $w \in h(g^{-1}(G) \cap k^{-1}(K))$, which concludes our argument. ∎

2.5 Matrices and Languages

As in linear algebra, vectors and matrices help organize the concepts and simplify the notation for certain classes of functions.

Definition 2.5.1 An $m \times n$*-matrix of languages over* A is a mapping $\boldsymbol{M} : \{0, \ldots, m-1\} \times \{0, \ldots, n-1\} \longrightarrow \mathcal{P}(A^*)$.

If $m = n$ we say that M is a *square matrix* of languages. □

The set of all $m \times n$-matrices over A is denoted by $\mathsf{MATR}_{m,n}(A)$.

Unless there is risk of confusion, we may refer to a matrix of languages simply as a matrix.

If $\boldsymbol{M}$ is an $m \times n$-matrix, we say that $\boldsymbol{M}$ has m rows and n columns. The values $\boldsymbol{M}_{ij} = \boldsymbol{M}(i, j)$ are usually arranged in a rectangular, two-dimensional array, where $\boldsymbol{M}_{ij}$ is the entry at row i and column j. When $m = 1$, we call $\boldsymbol{M}$ a *row*; when $n = 1$, we refer to $\boldsymbol{M}$ as a *column*.

If $\boldsymbol{M}, \boldsymbol{P}$ are two $m \times n$-matrices, we write $\boldsymbol{M} \subseteq \boldsymbol{P}$ if $\boldsymbol{M}_{ij} \subseteq \boldsymbol{P}_{ij}$ for every i, j, where $0 \leq i \leq m-1$ and $0 \leq j \leq n-1$.

Definition 2.5.2 Let $\{\boldsymbol{M}^\ell \mid \ell \in I\}$ be a collection of $m \times n$-matrices. The *union* of this collection is the $m \times n$-matrix $\boldsymbol{M}$ given by

$$\boldsymbol{M}_{ij} = \bigcup \{\boldsymbol{M}^\ell_{ij} \mid \ell \in I\}$$

for every i, j, where $0 \leq i \leq m-1$ and $0 \leq j \leq n-1$. □

Since the underlying set operation of union is associative, commutative and idempotent, it is easy to see that matrix union is associative, commutative and idempotent. In other words, if $\boldsymbol{M}, \boldsymbol{P}$, and $\boldsymbol{Q}$ are $m \times n$-matrices, then

$$\begin{aligned} (\boldsymbol{M} \cup \boldsymbol{P}) \cup \boldsymbol{Q} &= \boldsymbol{M} \cup (\boldsymbol{P} \cup \boldsymbol{Q}) \\ (\boldsymbol{M} \cup \boldsymbol{P}) &= (\boldsymbol{P} \cup \boldsymbol{M}) \\ (\boldsymbol{M} \cup \boldsymbol{M}) &= \boldsymbol{M}. \end{aligned}$$

The product of matrices is defined by analogy with the usual matrix product between matrices that have numerical entries: addition is replaced with union, while the product is replaced with language product.

Definition 2.5.3 Let $\boldsymbol{M}$ be an $m \times n$-matrix, and let $\boldsymbol{P}$ be an $n \times p$-matrix of languages over A. Their *product* $\boldsymbol{MP}$ is a $m \times p$-matrix defined by

$$(\boldsymbol{MP})_{ik} = \bigcup\{\boldsymbol{M}_{ij}\boldsymbol{P}_{jk} \mid 0 \leq j \leq n-1\},$$

for $0 \leq i \leq m-1$ and $0 \leq k \leq p-1$. □

Example 2.5.4 Consider the matrices $\boldsymbol{M}$ and $\boldsymbol{P}$ of languages over $\{a, b\}$:

$$\boldsymbol{M} = \begin{pmatrix} \{a\}^* & \emptyset \\ \{\lambda\} & \{b\} \\ \{a, b\} & \emptyset \end{pmatrix} \text{ and } \boldsymbol{P} = \begin{pmatrix} \{a, b\} & \{b\} \\ \{a\} & \emptyset \end{pmatrix}$$

Their product is the matrix

$$\boldsymbol{MP} = \begin{pmatrix} \{a\}^*\{a, b\} & \{a\}^*b \\ \{a, b, ba\} & \{b\} \\ \{a, b\}^2 & \{a, b\}b \end{pmatrix}$$

□

The matrix product is associative. Let $\boldsymbol{M}$ be an $m \times n$-matrix, $\boldsymbol{P}$ be an $n \times p$-matrix, and let $\boldsymbol{Q}$ be a $p \times q$-matrix. It is clear that both $\boldsymbol{S} = (\boldsymbol{MP})\boldsymbol{Q}$ and $\boldsymbol{T} = \boldsymbol{M}(\boldsymbol{PQ})$ are $m \times q$-matrices. We have

$$\begin{aligned}
\boldsymbol{S}_{i\ell} &= \bigcup_{0 \leq k \leq p-1} \left(\bigcup_{0 \leq j \leq n-1} \boldsymbol{M}_{ij}\boldsymbol{P}_{jk} \right) \boldsymbol{Q}_{k\ell} \\
&= \bigcup_{0 \leq k \leq p-1} \bigcup_{0 \leq j \leq n-1} \boldsymbol{M}_{ij}\boldsymbol{P}_{jk}\boldsymbol{Q}_{k\ell} \\
&= \bigcup_{0 \leq j \leq n-1} \bigcup_{0 \leq k \leq p-1} \boldsymbol{M}_{ij}\boldsymbol{P}_{jk}\boldsymbol{Q}_{k\ell} \\
&= \bigcup_{0 \leq j \leq n-1} \boldsymbol{M}_{ij} \left(\bigcup_{0 \leq k \leq p-1} \boldsymbol{P}_{jk}\boldsymbol{Q}_{k\ell} \right) \\
&= \bigcup_{0 \leq j \leq n-1} \boldsymbol{M}_{ij}(\boldsymbol{PQ})_{j\ell} \\
&= \boldsymbol{T}_{i\ell}
\end{aligned}$$

for $0 \leq i \leq m-1$ and $0 \leq \ell \leq q-1$, which proves the associativity of matrix product.

The diagonal $n \times n$-matrix I_n defined by

$$\boldsymbol{I}_n = \begin{pmatrix} \{\lambda\} & \emptyset & \cdots & \emptyset \\ \emptyset & \{\lambda\} & \cdots & \emptyset \\ \vdots & \vdots & \vdots & \vdots \\ \emptyset & \emptyset & \cdots & \{\lambda\} \end{pmatrix}$$

is a unit element with respect to matrix multiplication. In other words, if $\boldsymbol{U}$ is a $n \times r$-matrix and $\boldsymbol{V}$ is an $s \times n$-matrix, then

$$\boldsymbol{I}_n\boldsymbol{U} = \boldsymbol{U} \text{ and } \boldsymbol{VI}_n = \boldsymbol{V},$$

as the reader can easily verify.

Matrix powers can be defined for square matrices. If $\boldsymbol{M}$ is an $n \times n$-matrix, then

$$\begin{aligned} \boldsymbol{M}^0 &= \boldsymbol{I}_n \\ \boldsymbol{M}^{i+1} &= \boldsymbol{M}\boldsymbol{M}^i \end{aligned}$$

for $i \in \mathbb{N}$.

Example 2.5.5 Let L, K be two languages over A and consider the 2×2-matrix:

$$\boldsymbol{M} = \begin{pmatrix} L & \{\lambda\} \\ \emptyset & K \end{pmatrix}.$$

We have $\boldsymbol{M}^0 = \boldsymbol{I}_2$, $\boldsymbol{M}^1 = \boldsymbol{M}$, and

$$\boldsymbol{M}^2 = \begin{pmatrix} L & \{\lambda\} \\ \emptyset & K \end{pmatrix} \begin{pmatrix} L & \{\lambda\} \\ \emptyset & K \end{pmatrix} = \begin{pmatrix} L^2 & L \cup K \\ \emptyset & K^2 \end{pmatrix}$$

□

It is easy to verify by induction on $n \in \mathbb{N}$ that

$$\boldsymbol{M}^n = \begin{pmatrix} L^n & \bigcup_{i+j=n-1} L^i K^j \\ \emptyset & K^n \end{pmatrix}$$

If $\boldsymbol{M} \in \mathsf{MATR}_{n,n}(A)$, then

$$(\boldsymbol{M}^{(p)})_{ij} = \bigcup_{(i_1,\ldots,i_{p-1})} \boldsymbol{M}_{ii_1}\boldsymbol{M}_{i_1 i_2}\cdots\boldsymbol{M}_{i_{p-1}j},$$

where the union involves all $(p-1)$-tuples

$$(i_1, \ldots, i_{p-1}) \in \mathbf{Seq}_{p-1}(\{0, \ldots, n-1\})$$

and $0 \leq i, j \leq n-1$.

We will refer to a product of the form $\boldsymbol{M}_{ii_1}\boldsymbol{M}_{i_1 i_2}\cdots\boldsymbol{M}_{i_{p-1}j}$ as a *monomial of* $\boldsymbol{M}$.

Definition 2.5.6 Let

$$\boldsymbol{M}_{ii_1}\boldsymbol{M}_{i_1 i_2}\cdots\boldsymbol{M}_{i_{p-1}j}$$

be a monomial of a matrix $\boldsymbol{M} \in \mathsf{MATR}_{nn}(A)$. This monomial is is

- *strictly cyclic*, if the subscripts $i, i_1, \ldots, i_{p-1}$ are pairwise distinct and $j = i$;
- *k-cyclic*, if it contains k strictly cyclic monomials;
- *cyclic*, if it is k-cyclic for some $k \geq 1$.

□

Example 2.5.7 Let $\boldsymbol{L} \in \mathsf{MATR}_{n,n}(A)$. The monomial $\boldsymbol{L}_{ii}$ is strictly cyclic for every i, $0 \leq i \leq n-1$; also, the monomial $\boldsymbol{L}_{13}\boldsymbol{L}_{32}\boldsymbol{L}_{21}$ is strictly cyclic.

On the other hand, the monomial

$$L_{43}L_{32}L_{24}L_{44}L_{42}L_{25}L_{57}L_{74}L_{45}$$

is a 3-cyclic monomial because it contains the three strictly cyclic monomials $L_{43}L_{32}L_{24}$, L_{44}, and $L_{42}L_{25}L_{57}L_{74}$. □

Theorem 2.5.8 *A monomial $M_{ii_1}M_{i_1i_2}\cdots M_{i_{p-1}j}$ of an $n \times n$ matrix $M \in \mathsf{MATR}_{nn}(A)$ is at least $\lfloor p/n \rfloor$-cyclic.*

Proof. If $p < n$, then $\lfloor p/n \rfloor = 0$ and the statement follows trivially.

Suppose that $p \geq n$, and let $\ell = \lfloor p/n \rfloor$. The argument is by induction on $\ell \geq 1$.

If $\ell = 1$, we have $n \leq p < 2n$, and the set $\{i, i_1, \ldots, i_{p-1}, j\}$ contains $p+1$ elements. At most n of those elements are distinct, and so, at least one index appears twice. Therefore, this monomial contains at least one stricly cyclic monomial.

Suppose that the statement holds for $\ell \leq m$, and let p be such that $(m+1)n \leq p < (m+2)n$.

By the inductive hypothesis, the monomial that consists of the first mn factors contains at least m strictly cyclic monomials. The remaining $p - mn$ factors contain at least one strictly cyclic monomial because $n \leq p - mn < 2n$. Therefore, the entire monomial contains at least $m+1$ strictly cyclic monomials. ∎

Definition 2.5.9 A matrix $L \in \mathsf{MATR}_{n,n}(A)$ is *singular* if there exists a strictly cyclic monomial of L that contains the null word. □

Example 2.5.10 If $M \in \mathsf{MATR}_{n,n}(A)$ such that λ belongs to a diagonal entry M_{ii} is singular. □

Example 2.5.11 Let $L \in \mathsf{MATR}_{3,3}(A)$ be the matrix given by

$$M = \begin{pmatrix} \{a,b\} & \{a\} & \{\lambda\} \\ \{\lambda,a\} & \{bb,a\} & \{ab\} \\ \{a\} & \{\lambda,b\} & \{b\} \end{pmatrix}$$

The matrix M is singular because the strictly cyclic monomial

$$M_{13}M_{32}M_{21} = \{\lambda\}\{\lambda,b\}\{\lambda,a\} = \{\lambda,a,b,ba\},$$

contains λ. □

Theorem 2.5.12 *Let $L \in \mathsf{MATR}_{n,n}(A)$ be a non-singular matrix. If $r \in \mathbb{N}$ is such that $r = mn$ for some $m \geq 1$, then*

$$\min\{|x| \mid x \in (M^{(r)})_{ij}, 0 \leq i,j \leq n-1\} \geq m.$$

Proof. Note that $M^{(r)}_{ij}$ is the union of monomials that contain r factors and each monomial is at least $\lceil m \rceil$-cyclic, by Theorem 2.5.8. Since M is non-singular, the length of the words that belong to the strictly cyclic monomials have length at least 1. Therefore, the length of the words that belong to a language $M^{(r)}_{ij}$ is at least m. ∎

Let $\boldsymbol{M}$ be an $n \times n$-matrix. The $n \times n$-matrix $\boldsymbol{M}^*$ is defined by:

$$\boldsymbol{M}^* = \bigcup\{M^i \mid i \in \mathbb{N}\}.$$

Example 2.5.13 For the 2×2-matrix considered in Example 2.5.5,

$$\boldsymbol{M}^* = \begin{pmatrix} L^* & L^*K^* \\ \emptyset & K^* \end{pmatrix}$$

□

2.6 Polynomial Functions

In this section we present polynomial functions, a class of functions defined on the set of languages over an alphabet A. These functions help us present important algebraic results in Chapters 3 and 5.

Let $\boldsymbol{L} = (L_0, \ldots, L_{n-1}), \boldsymbol{K} = (K_0, \ldots, K_{n-1}) \in (\mathcal{P}(A^*))^n$ be two finite sequences of languages over A. We write $\boldsymbol{L} \subseteq \boldsymbol{K}$ if $L_i \subseteq K_i$, for $0 \leq i \leq n-1$. Define $\boldsymbol{\emptyset}_n = \underbrace{(\emptyset, \ldots, \emptyset)}_{n}$; then, $\boldsymbol{\emptyset}_n \subseteq \boldsymbol{H}$ for every $\boldsymbol{H} \in (\mathcal{P}(A^*))^n$.

For a function $f : (\mathcal{P}(A^*))^n \longrightarrow \mathcal{P}(A^*)$ we use the alternative notation $f(\boldsymbol{L})$ for $f(L_0, \ldots, L_{n-1})$, where $\boldsymbol{L} = (L_0, \ldots, L_{n-1})$.

Let $f, g : (\mathcal{P}(A^*))^n \longrightarrow \mathcal{P}(A^*)$ be two functions of n arguments. Their union $(f \cup g) : (\mathcal{P}(A^*))^n \longrightarrow \mathcal{P}(A^*)$ and product $(f \cdot g) : (\mathcal{P}(A^*))^n \longrightarrow \mathcal{P}(A^*)$ are defined by

$$\begin{aligned} (f \cup g)(\boldsymbol{X}) &= f(\boldsymbol{X}) \cup g(\boldsymbol{X}) \\ (f \cdot g)(\boldsymbol{X}) &= f(\boldsymbol{X})g(\boldsymbol{X}) \end{aligned}$$

for every $\boldsymbol{X} \in (\mathcal{P}(A^*))^n$.

It is easy to verify that if $f, g, h : (\mathcal{P}(A^*))^n \longrightarrow \mathcal{P}(A^*)$ then

$$\begin{aligned} f \cup (g \cup h) &= (f \cup g) \cup h \\ f \cdot (g \cdot h) &= (f \cdot g) \cdot h. \end{aligned}$$

In other words, both the union and the product of functions with n arguments are associative operations. When there is no risk of confusion, we may denote the union and the product of the functions f and g simply by $f \cup g$ and fg, respectively.

Operations involving functions are extended to sequences of functions as follows.

Let $(f_0, \ldots, f_{m-1})$ be a sequence of functions, where $f_i : (\mathcal{P}(A^*))^n \longrightarrow \mathcal{P}(A^*)$ for $0 \leq i \leq m-1$ and $m > 0$.

Define the union $\bigcup_{0 \leq i \leq m-1} f_i$ by

$$\left(\bigcup_{0 \leq i \leq m-1} f_i\right)(\boldsymbol{L}) = \bigcup_{0 \leq i \leq m-1} f_i(\boldsymbol{L})$$

for every $\boldsymbol{L} \in (\mathcal{P}(A^*))^n$.

Similarly, the product $\prod_{0\leq i\leq m-1} f_i$ is given by

$$\left(\prod_{0\leq i\leq m-1} f_i\right) \boldsymbol{L} = f_0(\boldsymbol{L})\cdots f_{m-1}(\boldsymbol{L}),$$

for every $\boldsymbol{L} \in (\mathcal{P}(A^*))^n$ and $m > 0$.

A sequence of functions $(f_0, \ldots, f_{m-1})$, where $f_i : (\mathcal{P}(A^*))^n \longrightarrow \mathcal{P}(A^*)$ for $0 \leq i \leq m-1$ and $m > 0$, defines a function $\vec{f} : (\mathcal{P}(A^*))^n \longrightarrow (\mathcal{P}(A^*)^m$, where

$$\vec{f}(\boldsymbol{L}) = (f_0(\boldsymbol{L}), \ldots, f_{m-1}(\boldsymbol{L}))$$

for every $\boldsymbol{L} = (\boldsymbol{L}) \in \mathcal{P}(A^*)$. We refer to $f_0, \ldots, f_{m-1}$ as the *components* of f.

We define the class of polynomial functions starting from the following basic functions:

Definition 2.6.1 Let $L \subseteq A^*$ be a language over the alphabet A. The n-ary *constant function* $C_L : (\mathcal{P}(A^*))^n \longrightarrow \mathcal{P}(A^*)$ is given by:

$$C_L(X_0, \ldots, X_{n-1}) = L$$

for every $X_0, \ldots, X_{n-1} \in \mathcal{P}(A^*)$ and $n \in \mathbb{N}$.

The n-ary *projections* $P_i^n : (\mathcal{P}(A^*))^n \longrightarrow \mathcal{P}(A^*)$ are given by

$$P_i^n(X_0, \ldots, X_{n-1}) = X_i$$

for $0 \leq i \leq n-1$, $X_0, \ldots, X_{n-1} \in \mathcal{P}(A^*)$ and $n \in \mathbb{N}$. □

Now we can define the class of n-ary polynomial functions.

Definition 2.6.2 The class of n-ary polynomial functions consists of the following functions:

(i) Every n-ary constant function and every n-ary projection is a polynomial function.

(ii) If $f, g : (\mathcal{P}(A^*))^n \longrightarrow \mathcal{P}(A^*)$ are n-ary polynomial functions, then $f \cup g$ and fg are n-ary polynomial functions.

A function is *polynomial* if it is an n-ary polynomial function for some $n \in \mathbb{N}$. □

Example 2.6.3 Let $A = \{a, b\}$ be an alphabet. Consider the binary function $f : (\mathcal{P}(A^*))^2 \longrightarrow \mathcal{P}(A^*)$, where $f(X_0, X_1) = \{a, bb\} \cup aX_0X_1 \cup X_1$ for $(X_0, X_1) \in (\mathcal{P}(A^*))^2$. We claim that f is a binary polynomial function. Indeed, consider the languages $L = \{a, bb\}$ and $L' = \{a\}$. The constant functions

$$\begin{aligned} C_L(X_0, X_1) &= \{a, bb\}, \\ C_{L'}(X_0, X_1) &= \{a\} \end{aligned}$$

are binary polynomial functions, and so are the projections P_0^2 and P_1^2 given by

$$\begin{aligned} P_0^2(X_0, X_1) &= X_0, \\ P_1^2(X_0, X_1) &= X_1. \end{aligned}$$

Consequently, the function $g : (\mathcal{P}(A^*))^2 \longrightarrow \mathcal{P}(A^*)$ given by $g = C_{L'} \cdot P_0^2 \cdot P_1^2$ is a binary polynomial function, and we have $g(X_0, X_1) = C_{L'}(X_0, X_1) \cdot P_0^2(X_0, X_1) \cdot P_1^2(X_0, X_1) = aX_0X_1$. Now, we can conclude that f is a binary polynomial function because $f = C_L \cup g \cup P_1^2$. This is indeed the case, because $(C_L \cup g \cup P_1^2)(X_0, X_1) = L \cup aX_0X_1 \cup X_1 = f(X_0, X_1)$ for every $(X_0, X_1) \in (\mathcal{P}(A^*))^2$. Thus, f is a binary polynomial function. □

The notion of polynomial function is extended to sequences of functions.

Definition 2.6.4 Let $\vec{f} : (\mathcal{P}(A^*))^n \longrightarrow (\mathcal{P}(A^*)^m$ be a function, where $\vec{f} = (f_0, \ldots, f_{m-1})$. If each component $f_i : (\mathcal{P}(A^*))^n \longrightarrow \mathcal{P}(A^*)$ is an n-ary polynomial function, then we also refer to $\vec{f}$ as an *n-ary polynomial function.* □

Lemma 2.6.5 (Monotonicity of Polynomial Functions) *If $\boldsymbol{K} \subseteq \boldsymbol{L}$ for $\boldsymbol{K}, \boldsymbol{L} \in (\mathcal{P}(A^*))^n$, then $f(\boldsymbol{K}) \subseteq f(\boldsymbol{L})$, for every polynomial function f.*

Proof. The argument is by induction on the definition of n-ary polynomial functions. It is immediate that the property holds for every n-ary constant function and every n-ary projection.

Suppose that the property holds for $f, g : (\mathcal{P}(A^*))^n \longrightarrow \mathcal{P}(A^*)$ and let $\boldsymbol{K} \subseteq \boldsymbol{L}$ for $\boldsymbol{K}, \boldsymbol{L} \in (\mathcal{P}(A^*))^n$. Then,

$$f(\boldsymbol{K}) \subseteq f(\boldsymbol{L}), g(\boldsymbol{K}) \subseteq g(\boldsymbol{L}),$$

which implies

$$\begin{aligned} f(\boldsymbol{K}) \cup g(\boldsymbol{K}) &\subseteq f(\boldsymbol{L}) \cup g(\boldsymbol{L}), \\ f(\boldsymbol{K})g(\boldsymbol{K}) &\subseteq f(\boldsymbol{L})g(\boldsymbol{L}), \end{aligned}$$

due to the monotonicity of language union and product. ■

Let $\boldsymbol{L}_0, \ldots, \boldsymbol{L}_i, \ldots$ be a sequence of n-tuples from $(\mathcal{P}(A^*))^n$, where $\boldsymbol{L}_i = (L_{i0}, \ldots, L_{i\,n-1})$ for $i \in \mathbb{N}$. Define $\bigcup\{\boldsymbol{L}_i \mid i \in \mathbb{N}\}$ as the n-tuple $\boldsymbol{L} = (L_0, \ldots, L_{n-1})$ given by

$$L_\ell = \bigcup\{L_{i\ell} \mid i \in \mathbb{N}\}.$$

Theorem 2.6.6 (Continuity Theorem for Polynomial Functions) *For every increasing sequence of n-tuples $\boldsymbol{L}_0, \ldots, \boldsymbol{L}_m, \ldots$ (that is, $\boldsymbol{L}_\ell \subseteq \boldsymbol{L}_j$ for $\ell \leq j$), and for every n-ary polynomial function f we have*

$$f\left(\bigcup\{\boldsymbol{L}_\ell \mid \ell \in \mathbb{N}\}\right) = \bigcup\{f(\boldsymbol{L}_\ell) \mid \ell \in \mathbb{N}\}.$$

Proof. By Lemma 2.6.5, we have $f(\boldsymbol{L}_\ell) \subseteq f\left(\bigcup\{\boldsymbol{L}_\ell \mid \ell \in \mathbb{N}\}\right)$, so

$$\bigcup\{f(\boldsymbol{L}_\ell) \mid \ell \in \mathbb{N}\} \subseteq f\left(\bigcup\{\boldsymbol{L}_\ell \mid \ell \in \mathbb{N}\}\right).$$

Therefore, we need prove only the reverse inclusion

$$f\left(\bigcup\{\boldsymbol{L}_\ell \mid \ell \in \mathbb{N}\}\right) \subseteq \bigcup\{f(\boldsymbol{L}_\ell) \mid \ell \in \mathbb{N}\}.$$

We use an argument by induction on the definition of polynomial functions. The basis case (when f is a constant function or a projection) is immediate.

Suppose now that the statement holds for the n-ary polynomial functions f and g and consider the polynomial functions $f' = f \cup g$ and $f'' = fg$. We present here the slightly more complicated argument for f'' and leave the argument for f' to the reader.

Applying the inductive hypothesis, we can write:

$$\begin{aligned} &f''\left(\bigcup\{\boldsymbol{L}_i \mid i \in \mathbb{N}\}\right) \\ &= fg\left(\bigcup\{\boldsymbol{L}_i \mid i \in \mathbb{N}\}\right) \\ &= \left(f(\bigcup\{\boldsymbol{L}_i \mid i \in \mathbb{N}\})\right)\left(g(\bigcup\{\boldsymbol{L}_i \mid i \in \mathbb{N}\})\right) \\ &= \left(\bigcup\{f(\boldsymbol{L}_i) \mid i \in \mathbb{N}\}\right)\left(\bigcup\{g(\boldsymbol{L}_i) \mid i \in \mathbb{N}\}\right)\end{aligned}$$

For any $x \in f''(\bigcup\{\boldsymbol{L}_i \mid i \in \mathbb{N}\})$ we can write $x = uv$, where $u \in \bigcup\{f(\boldsymbol{L}_i) \mid i \in \mathbb{N}\}$ and $v \in \bigcup\{g(\boldsymbol{L}_i) \mid i \in \mathbb{N}\}$. In other words, there are $j, k \in \mathbb{N}$ such that $u \in f(\boldsymbol{L}_j)$ and $v \in g(\boldsymbol{L}_k)$. Since the sequence $\boldsymbol{L}_0, \ldots, \boldsymbol{L}_m, \ldots$ is increasing, if $\ell = \max\{j, k\}$, we have $x = uv \in f(\boldsymbol{L}_\ell)g(\boldsymbol{L}_\ell) = f''(\boldsymbol{L}_\ell)$, so $x \in \bigcup\{f''(\boldsymbol{L}_i) \mid i \in \mathbb{N}\}$. ∎

Let $f : (\mathcal{P}(A^*))^m \longrightarrow \mathcal{P}(A^*)$ and $g_i : (\mathcal{P}(A^*))^n \longrightarrow \mathcal{P}(A^*)$ for $0 \leq i \leq m-1$. The function $f(g_0, \ldots, g_{m-1}) : (\mathcal{P}(A^*))^m \longrightarrow \mathcal{P}(A^*)$ is defined by

$$f(g_0, \ldots, g_{m-1})(\boldsymbol{L}) = f(g_0(\boldsymbol{L}), \ldots, g_{m-1}(\boldsymbol{L}))$$

for every $\boldsymbol{L} \in (\mathcal{P}(A^*))^n$.

Example 2.6.7 Recall that we denote the nth iteration of a function $f : M \longrightarrow M$ by $f^{(n)}$ (cf. Definition 1.2.51).

Let f be a unary polynomial function $f(X) = H \cup XL$, where H, L are languages over the alphabet A. Its second iteration is $f^{(2)}(X) = H \cup (H \cup XL)L = H \cup HL \cup XL^2$. It is not difficult to prove (by induction on i) that

$$f^{(i)}(X) = H \cup HL \cup \cdots HL^{i-1} \cup XL^i$$

for every $X \in \mathcal{P}(A^*)$ and $i > 0$. □

Theorem 2.6.8 *If f is an m-ary polynomial function and $g_0, \ldots, g_{m-1}$ are n-ary polynomial functions, then $f(g_0, \ldots, g_{m-1})$ is an n-ary polynomial function.*

Let $\vec{f} : (\mathcal{P}(A^*))^n \longrightarrow (\mathcal{P}(A^*))^n$ be a polynomial function. For every $i \in \mathbb{N}$, $\vec{f}^{(i)}$ of $\vec{f}$ is a polynomial function.

Proof. The argument is left to the reader. ∎

Note that if $\vec{f} : (\mathcal{P}(A^*))^n \longrightarrow (\mathcal{P}(A^*))^n$ is a polynomial function, then the sequence

$$(\emptyset, \vec{f}(\emptyset), \vec{f}^{(2)}(\emptyset), \ldots)$$

is an increasing sequence of n-tuples of languages over A. This observation is useful in the proof of Theorem 2.6.10.

Recall that $\mathsf{MATR}_{1,n}(A)$ is the set of $1 \times n$ matrices over the alphabet A.

Let $\vec{f} = (f_0, \ldots, f_{n-1})$ be a sequence of functions, where $f_i : \mathcal{P}(A^*)^n \longrightarrow \mathcal{P}(A^*)$. We can regard $\vec{f}$ as a function $\vec{f} : \mathsf{MATR}_{1,n}(A) \longrightarrow \mathsf{MATR}_{1,n}(A)$ given by

$$\vec{f}(\boldsymbol{L}) = (f_0(\boldsymbol{L}), \ldots, f_{n-1}(\boldsymbol{L})),$$

for every $\boldsymbol{L} \in \mathcal{P}(A^*)$.

Definition 2.6.9 An n-tuple $\boldsymbol{L} \in (\mathcal{P}(A^*))^n$ is a *fixed point* of $\vec{f}$ if $\boldsymbol{L} = \vec{f}(\boldsymbol{L})$. □

We refer to finding the fixed points of a function $\vec{f}$ as *solving the system of equations* $\boldsymbol{L} = \vec{f}(\boldsymbol{L})$.

Theorem 2.6.10 *If $f_0, \dots, f_{n-1}$ are n-ary polynomial functions over $\mathcal{P}(A^*)$, then $\vec{f} = (f_0, \dots, f_{n-1})$ has a fixed point. Moreover, the n-tuple $\mu(\vec{f})$ given by*

$$\mu(\vec{f}) = \bigcup_{i \in \mathbb{N}} \vec{f}^{(i)}(\emptyset)$$

is the least such fixed point.

Proof. Note that

$$\begin{aligned}
&\vec{f}(\mu(\vec{f})) \\
&= (f_0(\mu(\vec{f})), \dots, f_{n-1}(\mu(\vec{f}))) \\
&= (f_0(\bigcup_{i_0 \in \mathbb{N}} \vec{f}^{(i_0)}(\emptyset)), \dots, f_{n-1}(\bigcup_{i_{n-1} \in \mathbb{N}} \vec{f}^{(i_{n-1})}(\emptyset))) \\
&= (\bigcup_{i_0 \in \mathbb{N}} f_0(\vec{f}^{(i_0)}(\emptyset)), \dots, \bigcup_{i_{n-1} \in \mathbb{N}} f_{n-1}(\vec{f}^{(i)}(\emptyset))) \\
&= \bigcup_{i \in \mathbb{N}} (f_0(\vec{f}^{(i)}(\emptyset)), \dots, f_{n-1}(\vec{f}^{(i)}(\emptyset))) \\
&= \bigcup_{i \in \mathbb{N}} \vec{f}^{(i+1)}(\emptyset),
\end{aligned}$$

by the definition of $\vec{f}$ and the continuity of polynomial functions. Since

$$\vec{f}^{(0)}(\emptyset) = (\emptyset),$$

we have

$$\bigcup_{i \in \mathbb{N}} \vec{f}^{(i+1)}(\emptyset) = \bigcup_{i \in \mathbb{N}} \vec{f}^{(i)}(\emptyset) = \mu(\vec{f}),$$

so $\vec{f}(\mu(\vec{f})) = \mu(\vec{f}))$, which shows that $\mu(\vec{f})$ is a fixed point of $\vec{f}$.

Let $\boldsymbol{Z}$ be a fixed point of $\vec{f}$. We show that $\mu\vec{f}$ is the least fixed point of $\vec{f}$; that is,

$$\mu\vec{f} \subseteq \boldsymbol{Z}.$$

We claim that

$$\vec{f}^{(i)}(\emptyset) \subseteq \boldsymbol{Z}$$

for every $i \in \mathbb{N}$. The argument is by induction on i. The basis case, $i = 0$ is immediate because

$$\vec{f}^{(0)}(\emptyset) = (\emptyset) \subseteq \boldsymbol{Z}.$$

Suppose that

$$\vec{f}^{(i)}(\emptyset) \subseteq \boldsymbol{Z}.$$

By Lemma 2.6.5, we have

$$f_j(\vec{f}^{(i)}(\emptyset)) \subseteq f_j(\boldsymbol{Z}) = Z_j,$$

so $\vec{f}^{(i+1)} \subseteq \boldsymbol{Z}$. Therefore, $\mu(f) \subseteq \boldsymbol{Z}$. ∎

We denote the least fixed point of a function $\vec{f}$ by $\mathtt{lfp}(\vec{f})$. The tuple $\vec{f}^{(i)}(\emptyset)$ is the ith *approximation of the least fixed point.*

A technical result that is useful in Chapter 5 is given next.

Theorem 2.6.11 *Let $f_0, \ldots, f_{n-1}$ be n-ary polynomial functions over $\mathcal{P}(A^*)$, and let $\vec{f} = (f_0, \ldots, f_{n-1})$. We have $\mathtt{lfp}(\vec{f}) = \mathtt{lfp}(\vec{f}^{(k)})$ for every $k \geq 1$.*

Proof. Since

$$\begin{aligned} \mathtt{lfp}(\vec{f}^k) &= \bigcup_{i \in \mathbb{N}} \vec{f}^{(ik)}(\emptyset) \\ &\subseteq \bigcup_{i \in \mathbb{N}} \vec{f}^{(i)}(\emptyset) = \mathtt{lfp}(\vec{f}), \end{aligned}$$

it follows that $\mathtt{lfp}(\vec{f}^k) \subseteq \mathtt{lfp}(\vec{f})$. On the other hand, since

$$(\emptyset, \vec{f}(\emptyset), \vec{f}^{(2)}(\emptyset), \ldots)$$

is an increasing sequence, we have

$$\vec{f}^{(i)}(\emptyset) \subseteq \vec{f}^{(ik)}(\emptyset),$$

for every $i \in \mathbb{N}$, so $\mathtt{lfp}(\vec{f}) \subseteq \mathtt{lfp}(\vec{f}^k)$. Therefore, $\mathtt{lfp}(\vec{f}) = \mathtt{lfp}(\vec{f}^{(k)})$. ∎

Example 2.6.12 Consider the polynomial function $f(X) = H \cup XL$ introduced in Example 2.6.7. The least fixed point of f is

$$\begin{aligned} \mathtt{lfp}(f) &= \bigcup_{i \in \mathbb{N}} f^{(i)}(\emptyset) = \bigcup_{i \in \mathbb{N}} (H \cup HL \cup \cdots \cup HL^{i-1}) \\ &= H \left(\bigcup_{i \in \mathbb{N}} L^i \right) = HL^*. \end{aligned}$$

□

Definition 2.6.13 An n-ary *left linear polynomial function* is an n-ary polynomial function f given by

$$f(X_0, \ldots, X_{n-1}) = L \cup X_0 L_0 \cup \cdots \cup X_{n-1} L_{n-1}$$

for every $X_0, \ldots, X_{n-1} \in \mathcal{P}(A^*)$, where $L, L_0, \ldots, L_{n-1}$ are languages from $\mathcal{P}(A^*)$ called the *coefficients* of f. Similarly, an n-ary *right linear polynomial function* is an n-ary polynomial function f given by

$$f(X_0, \ldots, X_{n-1}) = L \cup L_0 X_0 \cup \cdots L_{n-1} X_{n-1},$$

for every $X_0, \ldots, X_{n-1} \in \mathcal{P}(A^*)$. □

The simplest equation we are interested in solving (for reasons that will become apparent in Chapter 3) involves a unary left-linear polynomial function. In Example 2.6.12, we noted that the least fixed point of the polynomial function $f = H \cup XL$ is HL^*; in other words, the least solution of the equation $X = f(X)$ is HL^*.

Theorem 2.6.14 *Let H, L be two languages over the alphabet A. If $\lambda \notin L$, then the equation $X = H \cup XL$ has the language $X = HL^*$ as its unique solution.*

Proof. From the remarks above, $X = HL^*$ is a solution of $X = H \cup XL$. Suppose that $Y = H \cup YL$ is another solution of the same equation and $X \neq Y$. Then, at least one of the sets $X - Y$ or $Y - X$ is nonempty. Suppose that $X - Y \neq \emptyset$, and let w be a word in $X - Y$ having minimal length. Clearly, $w \notin H$, because this would imply $w \in Y$. Therefore, $w \in XL$, so $w = xz$, where $x \in X$ and $z \in L$. Since $\lambda \notin L$, we have $z \neq \lambda$, so $|x| < |w|$. Then, $x \notin Y$ because, otherwise, we would have $w = xz \in YL \subseteq Y$. Consequently, $x \in X - Y$, and this contradicts the minimality of w. The case when $Y - X \neq \emptyset$ is symmetric. ∎

An entirely similar argument allows us to prove

Theorem 2.6.15 *Let H, L be two languages over the alphabet A. If $\lambda \notin L$, then the equation $X = H \cup LX$ has the language $X = L^*H$ as its unique solution.*

Proof. The argument is left to the reader. ∎

Theorem 2.6.16 *Let H, L be two languages over the alphabet A. If $\lambda \in L$, then for every language T, $X_T = (H \cup T)L^*$ is a solution of the equation $X = H \cup XL$, and every solution of the equation has this form.*

Proof. For $X_T = (H \cup T)L^*$ we can write:

$$\begin{aligned} H \cup X_T L &= H \cup (H \cup T)L^*L \\ &= H \cup HL^+ \cup TL^+ \\ &= H(\{\lambda\} \cup L^+) \cup TL^+ \\ &= HL^* \cup TL^+ \\ &= HL^* \cup TL^* (\text{ since } \lambda \in L) \\ &= (H \cup T)L^* = X_T, \end{aligned}$$

which shows that X_T is indeed a solution.

Conversely, let X be an arbitrary solution of the equation. Since HL^* is the least solution of the equation, there exists a language T such that $X = HL^* \cup T$. We prove by induction on n that $X = HL^* \cup TL^n$ for every $n \in \mathbb{N}$. The basis case is immediate for $L^0 = \{\lambda\}$. Suppose this is true for n. Since X is a solution of $X = H \cup XL$ we can write

$$X = H \cup (HL^* \cup TL^n)L = H \cup HL^+ \cup TL^{n+1} = HL^* \cup TL^{n+1},$$

which proves the previous equality. Therefore,

$$X = HL^* \cup \bigcup \{TL^n \mid n \in \mathbb{N}\} = HL^* \cup TL^* = (H \cup T)L^*.$$

∎

Example 2.6.17 Consider the function $\vec{f} = (f_0, f_1, f_2)$, where

$$\begin{aligned} f_0(X_0, X_1, X_2) &= aX_2 \cup bX_1 \\ f_1(X_0, X_1, X_2) &= \{a\} \cup aX_0 \cup bX_1X_1 \\ f_2(X_0, X_1, X_2) &= \{b\} \cup bX_0 \cup aX_2X_2. \end{aligned}$$

We have

$$\begin{aligned} \vec{f}^{(1)}(\emptyset) &= (\emptyset, \{a\}, \{b\}) \\ \vec{f}^{(2)}(\emptyset) &= (\{ab, ba\}, \{a, baa\}, \{b, abb\}) \\ \vec{f}^{(3)}(\emptyset) &= (\{ab, aabb, ba, bbaa\}, \\ &\quad \{a, aab, aba, baa, babaa, bbaaa, bbaabaa\} \\ &\quad \{b, bab, bba, abb, ababb, aabbb, aabbabb\}) \\ &\vdots \end{aligned}$$

If $\texttt{lfp}(\vec{f}) = (L_0, L_1, L_2)$, L_0 contains words in $\{a, b\}^*$ that have the same number of as and bs, L_1 contains words that have one more a than b, while L_2 contains words that have one more b than a. □

When studying certain classes of languages we encounter more general linear equations, such as

$$\begin{aligned} X_0 &= H_0 \cup X_0L_{00} \cup \cdots \cup X_{n-1}L_{n-1\,0} \\ X_1 &= H_1 \cup X_0L_{01} \cup \cdots \cup X_{n-1}L_{n-1\,1} \\ &\vdots \\ X_{n-1} &= H_{n-1} \cup X_0L_{0n-1} \cup \cdots \cup X_{n-1}L_{n-1\,n-1} \end{aligned}$$

Solving this system of equations amounts to finding the fixed points of function

$$\vec{f} = (f_0, \ldots, f_{n-1}),$$

where

$$\begin{aligned} f_0(\boldsymbol{X}) &= H_0 \cup X_0L_{00} \cup \cdots \cup X_{n-1}L_{n-1\,0} \\ f_1(\boldsymbol{X}) &= H_1 \cup X_0L_{01} \cup \cdots \cup X_{n-1}L_{n-1\,1} \\ &\vdots \\ f_{n-1}(\boldsymbol{X}) &= H_{n-1} \cup X_0L_{0n-1} \cup \cdots \cup X_{n-1}L_{n-1\,n-1} \end{aligned}$$

Using matrices, the previous system can be written as

$$\boldsymbol{X} = \boldsymbol{H} \cup \boldsymbol{X}\boldsymbol{L}, \tag{2.21}$$

where $\boldsymbol{X} = (X_0, \ldots, X_{n-1})$, $\boldsymbol{H} = (H_0, \ldots, H_{n-1})$ and

$$\boldsymbol{L} = \begin{pmatrix} L_{00} & \cdots & L_{0\,n-1} \\ \vdots & \vdots & \vdots \\ L_{n-1\,0} & \cdots & L_{n-1\,n-1} \end{pmatrix}$$

Now, the iterations of the function $\vec{f}$ are very easy to write. Namely,

$$\begin{aligned}\vec{f}(\emptyset) &= \boldsymbol{H}\\ \vec{f}^{(2)}(\emptyset) &= \boldsymbol{H}\cup\boldsymbol{HL}\\ \vec{f}^{(3)}(\emptyset) &= \boldsymbol{H}\cup\boldsymbol{HL}\cup\boldsymbol{HL}^2\\ &\vdots\end{aligned}$$

By Theorem 2.6.10, the least fixed point of $\vec{f}$ is

$$\begin{aligned}\mathtt{lfp}(\vec{f}) &= \boldsymbol{H}(\boldsymbol{I}_n\cup\boldsymbol{L}\cup\boldsymbol{L}^2\cup\cdots\cup\boldsymbol{L}^n\cup\cdots)\\ &= \boldsymbol{HL}^*\end{aligned}$$

A similar system of equations, involving right linear polynomial functions, is

$$\begin{aligned}Z_0 &= K_0\cup L_{00}Z_0\cup\cdots\cup L_{0\,n-1}Z_{n-1}\\ Z_1 &= K_1\cup L_{10}Z_0\cup\cdots\cup L_{1\,n-1}Z_{n-1}\\ &\vdots\\ Z_{n-1} &= K_{n-1}\cup L_{n-1\,0}Z_0\cup\cdots\cup L_{n-1\,n-1}Z_{n-1}\end{aligned}$$

If we define the polynomial functions $g_0,\ldots,g_{n-1}$ as

$$\begin{aligned}g_0(Z_0,\ldots,Z_{n-1}) &= K_0\cup L_{00}Z_0\cup\cdots\cup L_{0\,n-1}Z_{n-1}\\ g_1(Z_0,\ldots,Z_{n-1}) &= K_1\cup L_{10}Z_0\cup\cdots\cup L_{1\,n-1}Z_{n-1}\\ &\vdots\\ g_{n-1}(Z_0,\ldots,Z_{n-1}) &= K_{n-1}\cup L_{n-1\,0}Z_0\cup\cdots\cup L_{n-1\,n-1}Z_{n-1}\end{aligned}$$

and the function $\vec{g}:\mathsf{MATR}_{n,1}(A)\longrightarrow\mathsf{MATR}_{n,1}(A)$ by

$$\vec{g}=\begin{pmatrix}Q_0\\ \vdots\\ Q_{n-1}\end{pmatrix},$$

the above system can be written as

$$\vec{g}(\boldsymbol{Z})=\boldsymbol{K}\cup\boldsymbol{LZ},$$

where

$$\boldsymbol{Z}=\begin{pmatrix}Z_0\\ \vdots\\ Z_{n-1}\end{pmatrix}\text{ and }\boldsymbol{K}=\begin{pmatrix}K_0\\ \vdots\\ K_{n-1}\end{pmatrix}.$$

The least fixed point of $\vec{g}$ is

$$\begin{aligned}\mathtt{lfp}(\vec{g}) &= (\boldsymbol{I}_n\cup\boldsymbol{L}\cup\boldsymbol{L}^2\cup\cdots\cup\boldsymbol{L}^n\cup\cdots)\boldsymbol{K}\\ &= \boldsymbol{L}^*\boldsymbol{K}\end{aligned}$$

The uniqueness result of Theorem 2.6.14 can be extended to more general systems.

Theorem 2.6.18 *If the matrix $\boldsymbol{L}\in\mathsf{MATR}_{n,n}(A)$ is non-singular, then the system (2.21) has a unique solution.*

Proof. Let $\boldsymbol{L} \in \mathsf{MATR}_{n,n}(A)$ be a non-singular matrix, and let $\boldsymbol{Y}$ be a solution of the system $\boldsymbol{X} = \vec{f}(\boldsymbol{X})$, where $\vec{f}(\boldsymbol{X}) = \boldsymbol{H} \cup \boldsymbol{XL}$. Clearly, we have $\mathtt{lfp}(\vec{f}) \subseteq \boldsymbol{Y}$. Therefore, to prove the uniqueness of the solution of the system (2.21) we need to show that, under the hypothesis of the theorem, we have $\boldsymbol{Y} \subseteq \mathtt{lfp}(\vec{f})$.

By applying substitution repeatedly we obtain

$$\begin{aligned} \boldsymbol{Y} &= \boldsymbol{H} \cup \boldsymbol{YL}, \\ \boldsymbol{Y} &= \boldsymbol{H} \cup \boldsymbol{HL} \cup \boldsymbol{YL}^2 \\ &\vdots \\ \boldsymbol{Y} &= \boldsymbol{H} \cup \boldsymbol{HL} \cup \cdots \cup \boldsymbol{HL}^k \cup \boldsymbol{YL}^{k+1}, \end{aligned}$$

for every $k \in \mathbb{N}$.

Let $x \in Y_i$ be a word, where $0 \leq i \leq n-1$. Since $\boldsymbol{L}$ is nonsingular, by choosing $k = (|x|+1)n$, every word in $\boldsymbol{YL}^{k+1}$ has length at least $|x|+1$, according to Theorem 2.5.12. Therefore, $x \in (\boldsymbol{H} \cup \boldsymbol{HL} \cup \cdots \cup \boldsymbol{HL}^k)_i \subseteq (\boldsymbol{HL}^*)_i = (\mathtt{lfp}(\vec{f}))_i$, so $Y_i \subseteq (\mathtt{lfp}(\vec{f}))_i$ for $0 \leq i \leq n-1$. This allows us to conclude that $\boldsymbol{Y} \subseteq \mathtt{lfp}(\vec{f})$. ∎

We introduce a subclass of the class of polynomial functions that can be denoted using a finitary notation.

Definition 2.6.19 The class of n-ary *finitary polynomial functions* consists of the following functions:

(i) every n-ary constant function C_L, where L is a finite language;
(ii) every n-ary projection;
(iii) If f, g are n-ary finitary polynomial functions, then $f \cup g$ and fg are both n-ary finitary polynomial functions.

□

A function is a *finitary polynomial function* if it is an n-ary finitary polynomial function for some $n \in \mathbb{N}$.

Definition 2.6.20 Let A be an alphabet and let $A_X = \{X_0, \ldots, X_{n-1}\}$ be a set such that $A_X \cap A = \emptyset$. An *n-ary (A_X, A)-term* is a word $u \in (A_X \cup A)^*$. The variables of the term u are the symbols from A_X that occur in u. □

Example 2.6.21 Let $A = \{a, b\}$ and $A_X = \{X_0, X_1, X_2\}$. The words

$$\begin{aligned} u_0 &= abX_1baaX_0, \\ u_1 &= \lambda, \\ u_2 &= X_0X_1 \end{aligned}$$

are ternary (A_X, A)-terms. □

Definition 2.6.22 Let u be an n-ary (A_X, A)-term. The function defined by the (A_X, A)-term $u = u_0X_{i_0}u_1 \cdots u_{k-1}X_{i_{k-1}}u_k$, $f_u : (\mathcal{P}(A^*))^n \longrightarrow \mathcal{P}(A^*)$ is given by

$$f_u(\boldsymbol{L}) = u_0L_{i_0}u_1 \cdots u_{k-1}L_{i_{k-1}}u_k,$$

for every $\boldsymbol{L} = (L_0, \ldots, L_{n-1}) \in (\mathcal{P}(A^*))^n$. □

The function generated by an (A_X, A)-term is a finitary function. This can be easily shown by induction on k, the number of variables that occur in the right member of the definition of f. Functions generated by the (A_X, A)-terms are also called terms whenever there is no risk of confusion. Also, we denote the function f_u by the term u.

Example 2.6.23 By the previous notational convention we can write $X_i(\boldsymbol{L}) = L_i$ for $\boldsymbol{L} = (L_0, \ldots, L_{n-1})$. Therefore, the function generated by the n-ary term X_i is the projection P_i^n.

The function generated by a term u that contains no variables is the constant function $C_{\{u\}}$. □

Theorem 2.6.24 *If $f : (\mathcal{P}(A^*))^n \longrightarrow \mathcal{P}(A^*)$ is a finitary polynomial function, then*

$$f(\boldsymbol{X}) = \bigcup_{i=0}^{m-1} g_i(\boldsymbol{X}), \tag{2.22}$$

for every $(\boldsymbol{X}) \in (\mathcal{P}(A^*))^n$, where $g_0, \ldots, g_{m-1}$ are n-ary terms.

Proof. The argument is by induction on the finitary polynomial functions. If $f = C_L$, where $L = \{w_0, \ldots, w_\ell\}$, then

$$C_L(\boldsymbol{X}) = \bigcup_{i=0}^{\ell-1} g_i(\boldsymbol{X}),$$

where each g_i is a constant term, $g_i = w_i$ for $0 \leq i \leq \ell - 1$.

If $f = P_i^n$, then f equals the term n-ary term X_i for $0 \leq i \leq \ell - 1$.

Suppose that the statement holds for the finitary polynomial functions f', f'', that is

$$\begin{aligned} f'(\boldsymbol{X}) &= \bigcup_{i=0}^{m'-1} g_i'(\boldsymbol{X}), \\ f''(\boldsymbol{X}) &= \bigcup_{i=0}^{m''-1} g_i''(\boldsymbol{X}), \end{aligned}$$

for every $(\boldsymbol{X}) \in (\mathcal{P}(A^*))^n$, where $g_0', \ldots, g_{m'-1}', g_0'', \ldots, g_{m''-1}''$ are n-ary terms. Then

$$\begin{aligned} &(f' \cup f'')(\boldsymbol{X}) \\ &= \bigcup_{i=0}^{m'-1} g_i'(\boldsymbol{X}) \cup \bigcup_{i=0}^{m''-1} g_i''(\boldsymbol{X}), \end{aligned}$$

which shows that $f' \cup f''$ has the desired form. Similarly, we have

$$\begin{aligned} &(f'f'')(\boldsymbol{X}) \\ &= \left(\bigcup_{i=0}^{m'-1} g_i'(\boldsymbol{X})\right)\left(\bigcup_{i=0}^{m''-1} g_i''(\boldsymbol{X})\right). \end{aligned}$$

By applying the distributivity of language product with respect to the union we obtain

$$(f'f'')(\boldsymbol{X}) = \bigcup_{i=0}^{m'-1} \bigcup_{j=0}^{m''-1} (g_i'g_j'')(\boldsymbol{X})$$

Since the product of two terms is clearly a term we obtain the desired result. ∎

We refer to the equality (2.22) as the *term expression* of f.

The notion of finitary polynomial function is extended to functions of the form $f : (\mathcal{P}(A^*))^n \longrightarrow (\mathcal{P}(A^*))^m$. Namely, $\vec{f}$ is a finitary polynomial function if all its components $f_0, \dots, f_{m-1}$ are finitary polynomial functions.

2.7 Exercises

Words

1. Let x, y, u, v be words in A^+ such that $xy = uv$ and $|x| \leq |u|$. Show that there exists $z \in A^*$ such that $u = xz$ and $y = zv$.
2. $^\diamond$ Let x, y, z be three words from A^* such that $xy = yz$ and $x \neq \lambda$. Prove that there exist $u, v \in A^*$ such that $x = uv$, $y = (uv)^n u$ and $z = vu$ for some $n \in \mathbb{N}$.
3. Define the mapping $f : A^* \longrightarrow A^*$ by
$$\begin{aligned} f(\lambda) &= \lambda \\ f(ax) &= xa, \end{aligned}$$
for every $x \in A^*$ and $a \in A$. Prove that f is a bijection.
4. Let A be an alphabet. If $x \in A^*$ and $k \in \mathbb{N}$ define $k : x$ as
$$k : x = \begin{cases} x_{0,k-1} & \text{if } |x| \geq k, \\ x & \text{otherwise.} \end{cases}$$
   (a) Prove that if $u' = k : u$ and $v' = k : v$, then $k : (uv) = k : (u'v')$ for $k \in \mathbb{N}$.
   (b) Prove that the operation $x \odot_k y$ given by $x \odot_k y = k : (xy)$ for $x, y \in A^*$ is associative, that is, $x \odot_k (y \odot_k z) = (x \odot_k y) \odot_k z$ for $x, y, z \in A^*$.
5. $^{\diamond\diamond}$ Let x, y be two words in A^*. Prove that the following statements are equivalent:
   (a) there exist $m, n \in \mathbb{N}$ such that the words x^m and y^n have a common prefix of length $|x| + |y|$.
   (b) $xy = yx$;
   (c) there exist $z \in A^*$ and $p, q \in \mathbb{N}$ such that $x = z^p$ and $y = z^q$;

   Solution. `(a) implies (b)` Suppose that there exist $m, n \in \mathbb{N}$ such that the words x^m and y^n have a common prefix of length $|x| + |y|$. Then, the words yx^m and y^{n+1} have a common prefix of length $|x| + 2|y|$. Therefore, yx^m and y^n have a common prefix of length $|x| + |y|$. In a similar manner, xy^n and x^m have a common prefix of length $|x| + |y|$. This implies that xy^n and yx^m have a common prefix of length $|x| + |y|$, so $xy = yx$.
   `(b) implies (c)` The argument is by induction on $k = |x| + |y|$. If $k = 0$, then $x = y = \lambda$ and the conclusion follows immediately. Suppose that the statement holds for $k < n$ and let $x, y \in A^*$ be such that $xy = yx$. We need to consider three cases: $|x| = |y|$, $|x| < |y|$, and $|x| > |y|$. In the first case, $xy = yx$ implies $x = y$, so the statement obviously holds. Suppose now that $|x| < |y|$. Then, there exists $t \in A^*$ such that $y = xt$, which implies

$xxt = xtx$. This, in turn, implies $xt = tx$. By the inductive hypothesis, there exists a word $z \in A^*$ such that $x = z^k$ and $t = z^\ell$. Consequently, $y = xt = z^{k+\ell}$, which concludes the argument for the second case. The third case is entirely similar to the second.

(c) implies (a) This implication is immediate and it is left to the reader. ∎

6. $^{\diamond\diamond}$ If $x^m = y^n$ for $m, n > 0$, then both x and y are powers of the same word z.

   Solution. If $m = 1$ or $n = 1$ the conclusion follows immediately. Suppose that $m \geq 2$ and $n \geq 2$. It is easy to see that $m|x| = n|y| > |x| + |y|$, so x^m and y^n have a common prefix of length at least $|x| + |y|$. Therefore, the conclusion follows immediately from Exercise 5. ∎

7. Let $A = \{a, b\}$. Prove that there are no words x, y in A^* such that $xay = ybx$.
8. Prove that there is no word $x \in \{a, b\}^*$ such that $ax = xb$.

A word $x \in A^+$ is *primitive* if $x = y^n$ for some $y \in A^+$ implies $n = 1$ and $y = x$. The set of all primitive words over A is denoted by $\mathsf{PRIM}(A)$.

Two words $u, v \in A^*$ are *conjugate* if we can write $u = xy$ and $v = yx$ for some words $x, y \in A^*$.

9. $^{\diamond}$ Let $f : A^* \longrightarrow A^*$ be the mapping introduced in Exercise 3.
   (a) Prove that $f^{|x|}(xy) = yx$ for every $x, y \in A^*$. Conclude that $f^{|x|}(x) = x$ for every $x \in A^*$.
   (b) Prove that $x, y \in A^*$ are conjugate words if and only if $x = f^n(y)$ for some $n \in \mathbb{N}$.
10. $^{\diamond}$ Define the binary relation κ, where $(x, y) \in \kappa$ if they are conjugate. Prove that κ is an equivalence relation on A^*.
11. $^{\diamond\diamond}$ Prove that if $x \in A^+$ then there exists a unique primitive word $y \in A^+$ and a unique integer n such that $x = y^n$.

    Solution. The argument is by induction on $\ell = |x| > 0$. For $\ell = 1$ the conclusion is immediate. Suppose that the statement holds for words shorter than ℓ and let x be a word of length ℓ that is not primitive. Then, $x = w^p$ for some word $w \in A^+$ and $p > 1$. Therefore, $|w| < |x|$ and, by the inductive hypothesis, there exists a primitive word y such that $w = y^q$. Therefore, $x = y^{pq}$. The uniqueness follows from Exercise 5. ∎
12. $^{\diamond}$ Let u, v be two conjugate words in A^*. Prove that if u is a primitive word, then so is v.

    Solution. Suppose that $u = xy$ is a primitive word but $v = yx$ is not primitive. Then, $yx = z^j$, where $z \in \mathsf{PRIM}(A)$ and $j \geq 2$. Thus, $y = z^p z_1$ and $x = z_2 z^q$, where $z = z_1 z_2$ and $p, q \geq 0$. This implies $x = z_2(z_1 z_2)^q$ and $y = (z_1 z_2)^p z_1$, so $xy = z_2(z_1 z_2)^q (z_1 z_2)^p z_1 = (z_2 z_1)^j$ which contradicts the fact that xy is primitive. ∎
13. $^{\diamond}$ Let u, v be two conjugate words from A^+. If $u = w^i$, where $w \in \mathsf{PRIM}(A)$ and $i > 0$, then there is $z \in \mathsf{PRIM}(A)$ such that $v = z^i$ and w, z are conjugate words.

    Solution. If $u = xy$ is a primitive word the conclusion follows immediately from Exercise 12. Suppose, therefore, that $xy = w^i$. Then, there are $p, q \in \mathbb{N}$ such that $x = w^p w_1$, $y = w_2 w^q$, where $w = w_1 w_2$ and $p+q = i-1$. Note that by Exercise 12 the word $z = w_2 w_1$ is primitive and we have

$$v = yx = w_2(w_1w_2)^q(w_1w_2)^p w_1 = (w_2w_1)^{(p+q+1)} = (w_2w_1)^i.$$

■

14. $^{\circ\circ}$ Let $x \in A^*$ and let $f : A^* \longrightarrow A^*$ be the mapping introduced in Exercise 3. If x is a power of the primitive word z, prove that $j = |z|$ is the least member of the set $\{\ell \in \mathbb{N} \mid f^\ell(x) = x\}$.
Solution. If x is a power of the primitive word z, then it is immediate that $f^{|z|}(x) = x$. Suppose that $f^\ell(x) = x$ for some ℓ, where $0 < \ell < |z|$. Clearly, $\ell \leq |x|$. Let w be the prefix of length ℓ of x, so $x = wv$. We have $f^\ell(x) = f^{|w|}(wv) = vw$, so $wv = vw$. The words w and v must be powers of the primitive word z (since, otherwise, the uniqueness of the primitive word for x would be contradicted) and this is impossible because the length of w is less than the length of z. ■
15. $^{\circ\circ}$ Exercise 13 shows that all words in a class C of the equivalence of the relation κ defined in Exercise 10 are the same power i of some primitive words of length m. Prove that C contains m words.
Solution. Note that an equivalence class C can be written as $C = \{x, f(x), \ldots, f^{m-1}(x)\}$, where $m = |C|$ and $f^m(x) = x$. If $x = z^i$, where $z \in \mathsf{PRIM}(A)$, then $|z|$ is the least integer ℓ such that $f^\ell(x) = x$. Thus, $m = |z|$. ■
16. $^{\circ\circ}$ Let x be a word over the alphabet A such that $x \in A^* - \{a\}^*$. Then, either x or xa is a primitive word.
Solution. Suppose that neither x nor xa are primitive words. Then, $x = u^m$ and $xa = v^n$, where $u, v \in \mathsf{PRIM}(A)$ and $m, n \geq 2$. Note that

$$|u| + |v| = \frac{|x|}{m} + \frac{|x|+1}{n} = |x|(\frac{1}{m} + \frac{1}{n}) + \frac{1}{n} < |x| + 1.$$

Since u^m and v^n have x as a common factor, by Exercise 5a, it follows that u and v are powers of a word w. Since u and v are primitive it follows that $u = v$. Thus, $x = u^m$ and $xa = u^n$, which is impossible. ■
17. $^{\circ\circ}$ Let $x, z \in \mathsf{PRIM}(A)$ be two words such that $x^2 = z^k u$, where u is a prefix of z and $k \geq 2$. Show that $x = y$.
Solution. Suppose that $x \neq y$. Then, $x^2 = z^k u$ implies $x = z^n z_1$, where $z_1 \in A^+$ and $n > 0$. This, in turn, gives $x = z_2 z^{k-n-1} u$, where $z = z_1 z_2$. If $k - n - 1 > 0$, then $x = z^n z_1 = z_2 z^{k-n-1} u$, so $z_1 z_2 = z_2 z_1$. If $k - n - 1 = 0$, we have $x = z z_1 = z_2 u$, so $z_1 z_2 z_1 = z_2 u$, which implies $|z_1| < |u|$. Since u is a prefix of z this means that $u = z_1 u'$ and these equalities give $z_1 z_2 = z_2 z_1$. Therefore, by Exercise 5, z_1 and z_2 are powers of the same word w, so z is a power of w and this contradicts the fact that z is primitive. ■
18. $^{\circ\circ\circ}$ If $x^m y^n = z^p$, where $x, y, z \in A^*$, $m, n \geq 2$, and $p \geq 4$, then there exists a word $w \in A^*$ such that x, y, and z are powers of w.
19. $^{\circ}$ A word on an alphabet A is *square-free* if it contains no infix of the form xx, where $x \in A^+$.

(a) List all square-free words of length three over the alphabet $\{a, b\}$.
(b) Show that for the alphabet $\{a, b\}$ there are no square-free words of length at least equal to 4.
(c) Let $f : A \longrightarrow A$ be a one-to-one mapping. Prove that if x is square-free then so is $f(x)$.

20. $\diamond$ Prove that

$$\lambda^{-1}L = L\lambda^{-1} = L$$
$$x^{-1}\emptyset = \emptyset x^{-1} = \emptyset$$
$$(x^{-1}L)y^{-1} = x^{-1}(Ly^{-1})$$

21. $\diamond$ Let A be an alphabet and let $a \in A$.
(a) Prove that $a^{-1}A^* = a^{-1}A^+ = A^*$.
(b) Prove that $a^{-1}A^n = A^{n-1}$.

22. $\diamond\diamond$ Let $A = \{0, 1\}$ be an alphabet and let $L = A^*1A^n$. Prove that the collection of languages $\{x^{-1}L \mid x \in A^*\}$ consists of 2^{n+1} distinct languages.

23. $\diamond$ Let L be a language on the alphabet A. Prove that $(A^*)^{-1}L = \mathsf{SUFF}(L)$ and $L(A^*)^{-1} = \mathsf{PREF}(L)$.

24. $\diamond$ Let A be an alphabet. If $a \in A$, denote by $L_{A,a}$ the language that consists of all words that end in a and contain no other occurrence of a; in other words, $L_{A,a} = (A - \{a\})^*a$.
(a) Prove that if $a \neq a'$, then $L_{A,a} \cap L_{A,a'} = \emptyset$.
(b) Prove that

$$b^{-1}L_{A,a} = \begin{cases} \{\lambda\} & \text{if } b = a \\ L_{A,a} & \text{otherwise,} \end{cases}$$

for every $a, b \in A$.
(c) Let $L_A = \bigcup\{L_{A,a} \mid a \in A\}$. Show that

$$x^{-1}L_A = L_A - \bigcup\{L_{A,a} \mid a \text{ occurs in } x\} \cup Z$$

for every word $x \in A^+$, where $Z \in \{\{\lambda\}, \emptyset\}$.

25. $\diamond\diamond$ Let $u = a_0 \ldots a_{k-1} \in A^*$, where A is a finite alphabet. If v is a word in A^*, denote by $\binom{v}{u}$ the number of distinct factorizations of v as $v = v_0a_0v_1 \cdots v_{k-1}a_{k-2}v_k$. Prove the following identities:

$$\binom{a^n}{a^m} = \binom{n}{m} = \frac{n!}{m!(n-m)!}$$
$$\binom{a}{u} = \begin{cases} 1 & \text{if } u \in \{a, \lambda\} \\ 0 & \text{otherwise} \end{cases}$$
$$\binom{vv'}{u} = \sum\left\{\binom{v}{x}\binom{v'}{y} \mid xy = u\right\}$$
$$\binom{va}{ua'} = \binom{v}{ua'} + d_{aa'}\binom{v}{u},$$

$$\text{where } d_{aa'} = \begin{cases} 1 & \text{if } a = a' \\ 0 & \text{otherwise} \end{cases}$$

A word $u \in A^*$ is a *subword of a word* $v \in A^*$ if there are

$$u_0, \ldots, u_{n-1}, v_0, v_1, \ldots, v_n \in A^*$$

such that $u = u_0 \cdots u_{n-1}$ and $v = v_0 u_0 v_1 u_1 \cdots v_{n-1} u_{n-1} v_n$. In this case we also say that u *divides* v.

26. Define the relation "$\leq_{\mathrm{sub}}$" by $u \leq_{\mathrm{sub}} v$ if u is a subword of v. Prove that $\leq_{\mathrm{sub}}$ is a partial order on A^*. Further prove that for every $v \in A^*$ the set $\{x \in A^* \mid x \leq_{\mathrm{sub}} v\}$ is finite.
27. $^{\circ\circ}$ Let $L \subseteq A^*$ be a language whose words are pairwise incomparable words (with respect to the relation $\leq_{\mathrm{sub}}$). Prove that there is a word $x \in A^*$ such that $x \not\leq_{\mathrm{sub}} y$ for all $y \in L$.
Solution. Suppose that the statement is false; then, for each $x \in A^*$ there exists $y \in L$ such that $x \leq_{\mathrm{sub}} y$. Consider the word $x = za$ for some $z \in L$. Then, since $x \not\leq_{\mathrm{sub}} z$, there exists $y \in L$ such that $x \leq_{\mathrm{sub}} z$. This implies $z \leq_{\mathrm{sub}} x \leq_{\mathrm{sub}} y$ which contradicts the definition of the set L. ■
28. $^{\circ\circ}$ Prove that every set L of pairwise incompatible words in $(A^*, \leq_{\mathrm{sub}})$ is finite.
Solution. Suppose that the statement is false. Then, there exists an infinite set of pairwise incomparable words in $(A^*, \leq_{\mathrm{sub}})$; we may assume that there exists an infinite sequence of words in A^*, $s = (x_0, x_1, \ldots, x_n, \ldots)$ such that if $i, j \in \mathbb{N}$ and $i < j$, then x_i is not a subword of x_j. We refer to such a sequence as a *division-free sequence.* Using the Axiom of Choice (see [Fejer and Simovici, 1991], Chapter 3), we define a special division-free sequence s_0 called the *earliest sequence* as follows. Let z_0 be the shortest word that starts a division-free sequence; next, let z_1 be the shortest word such that the finite sequence (z_0, z_1) is the prefix of a division-free sequence; next, let z_2 be the shortest word such that the finite sequence (z_0, z_1, z_2) is the prefix of a division-free sequence, etc. Then, $s_0 = (z_0, z_1, z_2, \ldots)$. Since A is a finite alphabet, there is an infinite set of words $\{z_{i_0}, z_{i_1}, \ldots\}$ that begin with the same symbol a. In other words, we have $z_{i_p} = aw_p$ for $p \in \mathbb{N}$. Note that if $p < q$, then w_p is not a subword of w_q since, otherwise, z_{i_p} would be a subword of z_{i_q}. Therefore, the sequence $(z_0, \ldots, z_{i_0 - 1}, w_0, w_1, \ldots)$ is a division-free sequence and this contradicts the definition of s_0 as the earliest sequence because w_0 is shorter that z_{i_0}. ■
29. $^{\circ}$ Let $A = \{a_0, \ldots, a_{n-1}\}$ be an alphabet containing n symbols and let $\phi_A : A^* \longrightarrow \mathbb{N}$ be the function introduced in Section 2.2, defined by

$$\phi_A(x) = \begin{cases} 0 & \text{if } x = \lambda \\ n\phi_A(y) + i + 1 & \text{if } x = ya_i \end{cases}$$

for every $x \in A^*$.
(a) Prove that for every word $x \in A^*$ we have $|x| = k$ if and only if

$$\frac{n^k - 1}{n - 1} \leq \phi_A(x) \leq \frac{n^{k+1} - n}{n - 1}.$$

(b) Prove that the function $\phi_A : A^* \longrightarrow \mathbb{N}$ is injective.
(c) Let $x, y \in A^*$. Prove that if $|x| < |y|$, then $\phi_A(x) < \phi_A(y)$; also, $|x| \leq |y|$ implies $\phi_A(x) \leq |A|\phi_A(y)$.
(d) Prove that the restriction of ϕ_A to the set $A^k = \{x \in A^* \mid |x| = k\}$ is a bijection between A^k and the set $\{p \in \mathbb{N} \mid \frac{n^k-1}{n-1} \leq p \leq \frac{n^{k+1}-n}{n-1}\}$. Also, show that if $x, y \in A^*$ and $|x| = |y| = \ell$, then $|\phi_A(x) - \phi_A(y)| \leq |A|^\ell$.
(e) Prove that the function ϕ_A is a surjection between A^* and $\mathbb{N}$ and therefore, it is a bijection between these sets.
(f) Prove that if $\phi_A(x) < \phi_A(y)$, then $|x| \leq |y|$ for every $x, y \in A^*$.
(g) Prove that

$$\begin{aligned}&\phi_A(u_0 u_1 \cdots u_{k-1})\\&= \phi_A(u_0)|A|^{|u_1 \cdots u_{k-1}|} + \phi_A(u_1)|A|^{|u_2 \cdots u_{k-1}|} + \cdots +\\&\quad \phi_A(u_{k-2})|A|^{|u_{k-1}|} + \phi_A(u_{k-1})\end{aligned}$$

for $u_0, \cdots, u_{k-1} \in A^*$.
(h) Prove that if $|A| \geq 2$, then for every $w \in A^*$ we have

$$|A|^\ell \phi_A(w) \geq \phi_A(w^\ell) \geq |A|^{\ell-1}\phi_A(w)$$

for $\ell \in \mathbb{N}$.

30. Let $A = \{a_0, \dots, a_{n-1}\}$ be an alphabet. Prove that $x \ll u \ll xy$ if and only if $u = xt$ for some $t \in A^*$ such that $t \ll y$ for every $x, y, u \in A^*$.

A word $x \in A^*$ is *unbordered* if $\mathsf{PREFpr}(x) \cap \mathsf{SUFFpr}(x) = \emptyset$.

31. $^\diamond$ Prove that if x is an unbordered word, then $xA^* \cap A^*x = xA^*x \cup \{x\}$.
32. $^{\diamond\diamond}$ Let A be an alphabet such that $|A| \geq 2$. Prove that for each word $u \in A^+$, there is $v \in A^*$ such that uv is an unbordered word.
Solution. We claim that if a is the first letter of u, $|u| = k$ and $b \neq a$, then the word $w = uab^k$ is unbordered. Suppose that w is not unbordered. Then, there exists a proper prefix t of w that is also a proper suffix of w. Note that the first symbol of t must be a. Therefore, t can be a proper suffix of w only if $|t| > k$, which means that $t = t'ab^k$ for some $t' \in A^*$. Since $|t| > |u|$ and t is a prefix of w we also have $t = uab^{|t'|}$. Therefore, $|t'| = |u|$, which implies $t = w$, which contradicts the definition of t.

Languages

33. Prove that for every language L, $L^* = L^+ \cup \{\lambda\}$. Under which conditions do we have $L^+ = L^* - \{\lambda\}$?
34. Let L be a language. Prove that $L^+ = L$ if and only if there exists a language K such that $L = K^+$. Similarly, prove that $L^* = L$ if and only if $L = K^*$ for some language K.
35. Show that if at least one of the languages L, L' is λ-free, then $L \cap L'$ and LL' are λ-free.
36. $^\diamond$ Prove that for any language L over an alphabet A the following statements are equivalent:
(a) $L \cap LA^+ = \emptyset$;

(b) $L \cap \mathsf{PREFpr}(L) = \emptyset$;

(c) the sets L, $\mathsf{PREFpr}(L)$ and LA^+ are pairwise disjoint;

(d) if $x, xy \in L$, then $y = \lambda$;

(e) for every $u, v, s, t \in A^*$, if $uv = st$ and $u, s \in L$, then $u = s$ and $v = t$.

37. Prove each of the following identities:

$$\begin{aligned}
\emptyset^* &= \{\lambda\}, \\
\{\lambda\}^* &= \{\lambda\}, \\
\emptyset^+ &= \emptyset, \\
\{\lambda\}^+ &= \{\lambda\}, \\
\overline{\emptyset}_A &= A^*, \\
\overline{\{\lambda\}}_A &= A^+.
\end{aligned}$$

38. ◇ Let A be an alphabet and let L and K be languages over A. Prove that the following identities hold.

$$\begin{aligned}
(L^*)^+ &= L^*, \\
(L^+)^* &= L^*, \\
(L^+)^+ &= L^+, \\
(L \cup K)^* &= (L^*K^*)^* = (K^*L^*)^*.
\end{aligned}$$

39. ◇ Prove that for any languages L, K, and H the following inclusions hold (assume that complementation is with respect to A^*):

$$\begin{aligned}
(L \cap K)H &\subseteq LH \cap KH, \\
H(L \cap K) &\subseteq HL \cap HK, \\
(L - K)H &\supseteq LH - KH, \\
H(L - K) &\supseteq HL - HK, \\
(L \cup K)^* &\supseteq L^* \cup K^*, \\
(L \cap K)^* &\subseteq L^* \cap K^*, \\
(L \cup K)^+ &\supseteq L^+ \cup K^+, \\
(L \cap K)^+ &\subseteq L^+ \cap K^+, \\
\overline{L^*} &\subseteq (\overline{L})^*, \\
\overline{L^+} &\subseteq (\overline{L})^+, \\
(LH)^* &\subseteq (L \cup H)^*.
\end{aligned}$$

Give examples of languages for which these inclusions are strict.

40. Prove the following identities involving reversal of languages, where L and K can be any languages and complementation is with respect to some

alphabet A.

$$\begin{aligned}
\emptyset^R &= \emptyset, \\
\{\lambda\}^R &= \{\lambda\}, \\
(LK)^R &= K^R L^R, \\
(L \cup K)^R &= L^R \cup K^R, \\
(L \cap K)^R &= L^R \cap K^R, \\
(L - K)^R &= L^R - K^R, \\
(L^*)^R &= (L^R)^*, \\
(L^+)^R &= (L^R)^+, \\
(\overline{L})^R &= \overline{L^R} \\
\mathsf{PREF}(L^R) &= \mathsf{SUFF}(L)^R \\
\mathsf{SUFF}(L^R) &= \mathsf{PREF}(L)^R \\
\mathsf{INFIX}(L^R) &= \mathsf{INFIX}(L)^R
\end{aligned}$$

41. Let L and K be two languages over an alphabet A. Define $f : L \times K \longrightarrow LK$ by $f(u, v) = uv$ for all $(u, v) \in L \times K$. Show that f is surjective. Give examples to show that f can be, but is not necessarily, a bijection.
42. Let A be an alphabet. Prove that the 5-tuple $(\mathcal{P}(A^*), \cup, \cdot, \emptyset, A^*)$ is a closed semiring, where the closure of any $L \in \mathcal{P}(A^*)$ is L^*.
43. Verify that if Ω, Ω' range over the set $\{\mathsf{PREF}, \mathsf{SUFF}, \mathsf{INFIX}\}$, then the composition $\Omega\Omega'$ is given by the following table:

	Ω'		
Ω	SUFF	PREF	INFIX
SUFF	SUFF	INFIX	INFIX
PREF	INFIX	PREF	INFIX
INFIX	INFIX	INFIX	INFIX

Let A be an alphabet. A language $L \subseteq A^*$ is *k-bounded* if there exist k nonempty words, $w_0, \ldots, w_{k-1}$ in A^+ such that $L \subseteq \{w_0\}^* \cdots \{w_{k-1}\}^*$. L is *bounded* if it is k-bounded for some $k \in \mathbb{N}$. If L is not bounded, we say that L is *unbounded.*

44. $\diamond$ Show that the product and the union of two bounded languages is a bounded language.
45. Prove that A^* is bounded if and only if $|A| = 1$.
46. Prove that any subset of a bounded language is bounded.
47. $\diamond$ Prove that L is 1-bounded if and only if $uv = vu$ for every $u, v \in L$.
48. $\diamond$ Prove that L is k-bounded if and only if L^R is k-bounded.
49. $\diamond$ Prove that if L is a bounded language, then $\mathsf{INFIX}(L)$ is a bounded language.
50. $\diamond\diamond$ Let $A = \{a, b\}$ and let $x, y \in A^*$. Prove that the language $L = \{ax, by\}^*$ is unbounded.

    Solution. Suppose L is bounded, that is

$$\{ax, by\}^* \subseteq \{w_0\}^* \cdots \{w_{k-1}\}^*$$

for some $w_0, \ldots, w_{k-1} \in A^*$. Let m be the least common multiple of the numbers $|w_0|, \ldots, |w_{k-1}|$. Then, $((ax)^m(by)^m)^k = w_0^{i_0} \cdots w_{k-1}^{i_{k-1}}$. Note that it is not possible to have $(ax)^m(by)^m = w_i^p$ for $p \in \mathbb{N}$. Indeed, if this were the case, then since both $|(ax)^m|$ and $|(by)^m|$ are multiples of $|w_i|$, this would imply that $(ax)^m = w^q$ and $(by)^m = w^r$, where $p = q + r$. The first equality would mean that the first symbol of w_i is a, while the second would imply that the first symbol is b. Therefore, $(ax)^m(by)^m$ must contain at least two distinct words w_i, w_j. Note however that this leads to another contradiction, since the word $((ax)^m(by)^m)^k$ consists of k words of the form $(ax)^m(by)^m$, and this would imply

$$((ax)^m(by)^m)^k = (w_{i_0}w_{i_1})(w_{i_2}w_{i_3}) \cdots (w_{i_{2k-2}}w_{i_{2k-1}}),$$

with $i_0 \neq i_1$, $i_2 \neq i_3, \ldots, i_{2k-2} \neq i_{2k-1}$. The least number of words we could use is obtained by taking $i_2 = i_1$, $i_4 = i_3, \ldots, i_{2k-2} = i_{2k-1}$ and this would still require $k + 1$ distinct words, more than we have available. ■

51. °° Prove that the language L over $\{a, b\}$ given by $L = \{abab^2a \cdots ab^na \mid n \in N\}$ is not bounded.

Substitutions and Morphisms

52. Let $A = \{a, b\}$ and $B = \{0, 1\}$ be two alphabets and let $h : A^* \longrightarrow B^*$ be the morphism defined by $h(a) = 10101$ and $h(b) = 010$.
    (a) If $L = \{(ab)^n \mid n \in \mathbb{N}\}$, what is $h(L)$?
    (b) Let $K = \{x \in \{0, 1\}^* \mid n_0(x) = n_1(x)\}$. What is $h^{-1}(K)$?
53. Let $A = \{a, b\}$ be an alphabet. Prove that the mapping $h : A^* \longrightarrow \mathbb{Z}$ given by $h(x) = n_a(x) - n_b(x)$ for every $x \in A^*$ is a morphism between the monoids $(A^*, \cdot, \lambda)$ and $(\mathbb{Z}, +, 0)$.
54. Prove that the composition of two fine morphisms is a fine morphism; prove that the composition of a fine morphism and a very fine morphism is a fine morphism.
55. ° Let $A = \{a, a', a''\}$ and $B = \{b, b'\}$ be two alphabets. Define the morphisms $h : A^* \longrightarrow A^*$ and $k : A^* \longrightarrow B^*$ given by $h(a) = h(a'') = a$, $h(a') = a'a$, $k(a) = b$, and $k(a') = k(a'') = b'$. Prove that

$$k(h^{-1}(\{a^n a' a^n \mid n \geq 1\}) \cap \{a\}^* a' \{a''\}^*) = \{b^n b'^n \mid n \geq 1\}.$$

56. ° Let $h : A^* \longrightarrow A^*$ be a morphism and let $x \in A^*$. The language $L_{h,x}$ is given by

$$L_{h,x} = \{h^{(i)}(x) \mid i \in \mathbb{N}\}.$$

Prove that if x is a prefix of $h(x)$, then for any distinct words $u, v \in L_{h,x}$ either u is a prefix of v, or v is a prefix of u.
57. °° Let A, B be two disjoint alphabets and let $s : A \longrightarrow \mathcal{P}(B^*)$ be a substitution. Define the language L_s over $A \cup B$ by $L_s = \bigcup\{as(a) \mid a \in A\}$. If $h : (A \cup B)^* \longrightarrow A^*$ and $k : (A \cup B)^* \longrightarrow B^*$ are two morphisms

such that $h(a) = a$, $h(b) = \lambda$, $k(b) = b$ and $k(a) = \lambda$ for every $a \in A$ and $b \in B$, prove that

$$s(L) = k(h^{-1}(L) \cap L_s).$$

58. $^{\circ\circ}$ Let $h : A^* \longrightarrow M$ be a morphism between the monoids $(A^*, \cdot, \lambda)$ and $(M, \cdot, 1)$. For $m \in M$ define the languages

$$\begin{aligned} U_m &= \bigcup \{h^{-1}(p)a \mid p \in M, a \in A, ph(a)M = mM \\ &\qquad \text{and } p \notin mM\} \\ V_m &= \bigcup \{ah^{-1}(p) \mid p \in M, a \in A, Mh(a)p = Mm \\ &\qquad \text{and } p \notin Mm\} \\ W_m &= \bigcup \{ah^{-1}(p)b \mid p \in M, m \in Mh(a)pM \cap Mph(a)M \\ &\qquad \text{and } m \notin Mh(a)ph(b)M\} \\ T_m &= \{a \mid m \notin Mh(a)M\}. \end{aligned}$$

Prove that if M is aperiodic monoid, then for every $m \in M - \{1\}$ we have $h^{-1}(m) = (U_m A^* \cap A^* V_m) - A^*(W_m \cup T_m)A^*$.

Solution. Let $w \in h^{-1}(m)$ for some $m \in M$ such that $m \neq 1$. We have $h(w) = m$, so $mM = h(w)M$. Let u be the shortest prefix of w such that $mM = h(u)M$. Note that $u \neq \lambda$ since $h(\lambda) = 1$ and $mM = M$ would imply $mp = 1$, thus giving $m = 1$ (cf. Exercise 40). If $u = va$ and $p = h(v)$, then $ph(a)M = h(v)h(a)M = h(va)M = mM$, but $p \notin mM$ since otherwise the minimality of u would be contradicted. Thus, $w \in U_m A^*$. Similarly, $w \in A^* V_m$. Observe that $w \notin A^*(W_m \cup T_m)A^*$ since $m \notin Mh(t)M$ for every $t \in W_m \cup T_m$.

Let now a word $x \in (U_m A^* \cap A^* V_m) - A^*(W_m \cup T_m)A^*$ and let $q = h(x)$. Since $x \in U_m A^*$ we have $q \in mM$. Similarly, $q \in Mm$. We claim that $m \in MqM$. Suppose that $m \notin MqM = Mh(x)M$ and let $x = uwv$ with $m \notin Mh(w)M$ and w of minimal length. Note that $w \neq \lambda$. Also, $|w| > 1$ since otherwise we would have $w = a$ for some $a \in A$ and this would imply $w \in T_m$.

Let now $w = atb$, with $a, b \in A$. Then, $m \in Mh(at)M = Mh(a)h(t)$ since w was chosen of minimal length such that $m \notin Mh(w)M$ and $|at| = |w| - 1$. Similarly, $m \in Mh(tb)M = Mh(t)h(b)M$, so $w \in W_m$, which conflicts with $m \notin A^*(W_m \cup T_m)A^*$.

Thus, $q \in (mM \cap Mm) - \{r \in M \mid m \notin MrM\} = \{m\}$ (by Supplement 41 of Chapter 1), which gives $q = m$. Consequently, $x \in h^{-1}(m)$. ∎

Matrices

59. Let $\boldsymbol{M}, \boldsymbol{P}$ be the 2×2 matrices over the alphabet A given by

$$\boldsymbol{M} = \begin{pmatrix} \emptyset & L \\ L & L^* \end{pmatrix} \text{ and } \boldsymbol{P} = \begin{pmatrix} \emptyset & K \\ K & K^* \end{pmatrix},$$

where L and K are languages over the same alphabet A. Compute the matrices $\boldsymbol{Q} = \boldsymbol{MP}$ and $\boldsymbol{Q}' = \boldsymbol{PM}$.

60. $^{\circ\circ}$ An $n \times n$-matrix $\boldsymbol{M}$ is *idempotent* if $M^{(2)} = M$. Prove that if $\boldsymbol{P}$ is a $n \times n$-matrix, then P^* is the least idempotent matrix such that $P \subseteq P^*$. In other words, prove that P^* is idempotent and for any idempotent $n \times n$-matrix $\boldsymbol{Q}$ such that $P \subseteq Q$, we have $P^* \subseteq Q$.
61. $^{\circ}$ Prove that a matrix $\boldsymbol{L} \in \mathsf{MATR}_{n,n}(A)$ has the e.w.p. if and only if there exists $k \in \mathbb{N}$ such that $\lambda \in (\boldsymbol{L}^{(k)})_{ii}$ for some i, where $0 \leq i \leq n-1$.

Polynomial Functions

62. $^{\circ}$ Let $f(X) = K \cup LX$ be a unary polynomial function on $\mathcal{P}(A^*)$. Prove that for every $X, Y \in \mathcal{P}(A^*)$ we have $f(X) - f(Y) \subseteq L(X - Y)$.
63. $^{\circ}$ Let K, L, H be languages over the alphabet A. Find the least fixed point of the polynomial function f, where $f(X) = K \cup LXH$ for $X \in \mathcal{P}(A^*)$.
64. $^{\circ}$ Define the partial order "$\leq$" on the set of polynomial functions over the alphabet A by $f \leq g$ if $f(X) \subseteq g(X)$ for every $X \in \mathcal{P}(A^*)$. Show that if $f \leq g$, then $\mathtt{lfp}(f) \subseteq \mathtt{lfp}(g)$.
65. $^{\circ}$ Theorem 2.6.14 can be generalized as follows. Let $f(X)$ be a unary polynomial function such that $\lambda \notin f(\emptyset)$. Show that there is a unique fixed point of f.
66. $^{\circ}$ Consider the polynomial function $\vec{f} = (f_0, f_1)$, where

$$\begin{aligned} f_0(X_0, X_1) &= aX_1X_0b \cup X_1X_0 \cup \{ba\} \\ f_1(X_0, X_1) &= \{ab\} \cup bX_1X_1 \end{aligned}$$

Compute the first three approximations of the $\mathtt{lfp}(\vec{P})$.

Let A be an alphabet. Define the function $\vec{f} : (\mathcal{P}(A^*))^n \longrightarrow (\mathcal{P}(A^*))^n$ whose components $f_0, \ldots, f_{n-1})$ are n-ary polynomial functions on $\mathcal{P}(A^*)$. A tuple of languages $\vec{L} = (\boldsymbol{L}) \in \mathcal{P}(A^*)$ is *$\vec{f}$-contractable* if

$$\vec{f}((\boldsymbol{L})) \subseteq (\boldsymbol{L}).$$

67. $^{\circ\circ}$ Let $\vec{f} : (\mathcal{P}(A^*))^n \longrightarrow (\mathcal{P}(A^*))^n$ be a function whose components are n-ary polynomial functions on $\mathcal{P}(A^*)$.
    (a) Show that the set $\mathcal{C}_f$ of $\vec{f}$-contractable tuples is nonempty for every polynomial function $\vec{f}$.
    (b) Prove that $\bigcap \mathcal{C}_f$ is a $\vec{f}$-contractable tuple of languages. Further, show that $\bigcap \mathcal{C}_f$, the least $\vec{f}$-contractable tuple of languages coincides with $\mathtt{lfp}(\vec{f})$, the least fixed point of $\vec{f}$.
68. $^{\circ}$ Let $f : \mathcal{P}(A^*) \longrightarrow \mathcal{P}(A^*)$ be a unary polynomial function. If $f(X) = g(X) \cup g'(X)$, where g, g' are unary polynomials, prove that $\mathcal{C}_f = \mathcal{C}_g \cap \mathcal{C}_{g'}$.

2.8 Bibliographical Comments

An encyclopedic source for combinatorial properties of words is [Lothaire, 1983]. Another rich source is [Shyr, 1979]. Exercise 36 is from [Berstel and Perrin,

1985]. Exercise 50 is from [Harrison, 1978]. The source of the exercises 31 and 32 is [Berstel and Perrin, 1985]. Exercise 30 is from [Lothaire, 1983]. A variety of research results and open problems is discussed in [Cummings, 1983].

Part II

Regular and Context-Free Languages

Chapter 3

Regular Languages

3.1 Introduction

This chapter presents the class of regular languages. This class is the smallest class of languages that contains all finite languages and is closed with respect to union, product, and Kleene closure. These properties lead to *regular expressions*, a notation for languages in the class.

Regular languages are recognized by the abstract computing devices known as *deterministic finite automata*. This class of languages is very robust: several enhanced automata that one might expect to recognize a larger class of languages actually recognize exactly the same class of languages. We discuss three of these variants: nondeterministic finite automata, transition systems, and two-way automata.

We consider several additional closure properties of this class, including closure under complement, under quotient, and morphisms. This leads naturally to considering the general algebraic properties of these languages, which we use to discuss minimal automata and syntactic monoids.

Not all languages are regular, of course. Closure properties and automata help show which languages are regular, while it is also useful to be able to tell which languages are not regular. One of the most powerful tools to accomplish this is the *pumping lemma.*

The chapter conludes by examining some applications of regular languages, both in computer science, where they are used to characterize portions of computer languages, to select text for processing, etc., and in areas like molecular biology, where detection of patterns in strings is used to study DNA and protein sequences.

3.2 Finite Automata

The study of formal languages is intimately bound to the study of automata. An *automaton* is a mathematical abstraction of a machine. It is thought of as having "states". At any moment in time, the automaton's state completely describes all the information about the machine that is relevant for whatever is being considered. The automaton's functioning consists of changing from one state to another in response to outside inputs. The change from one state to another, called a "transition", is generally regarded as atomic, meaning that it cannot be interrupted: once it begins, it always completes. It is also often regarded as instantaneous.

For instance, if the machine were a model of a simple traffic light, its states would be "red" and "green". Some outside event, such as a pedestrian pushing a button, provides the input that effects the change from one state to another. This is clearly an abstraction of what happens: it ignores the situation (that occurs in the actual traffic light during the transition from one state to the other) when neither the red nor the green lamp is lighted, and it ignores the possibility that the traffic light malfunctions and lights both the red and the green lamps simultaneously. If these situations were relevant to the system under study, these states would be added.

When we consider automata in relation to formal languages, the inputs are words of letters from an alphabet. They are written on a tape marked off in cells, one letter to a cell. States are simply named and gathered into a set.

Automata are classified by the complexity of their model. The simplest are the deterministic finite automata (dfa), and we study these first.

3.2.1 Deterministic Automata

Informally, a deterministic finite automaton consists of:

- an *input tape* divided into *cells*;
- a *control device* equipped with a *reading head* that scans the input tape one cell at a time.

Each cell of the input tape contains a symbol $a \in A$, where A is an alphabet, called the *input alphabet.* The tape can accommodate words of arbitrary finite length. Thus, although the tape is thought of as being infinitely long, only a finite initial segment of it contains input symbols.

A dfa works discretely. Consider a clock that advances in discrete units; at any time on the clock, the automaton is resting in one of its states. Between

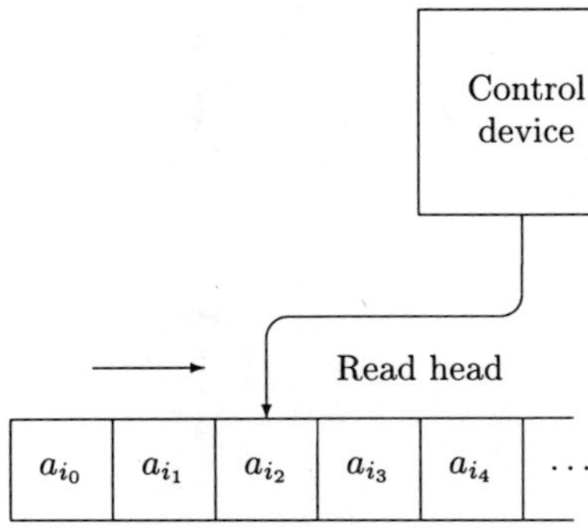

Figure 3.1: Main Components of a Finite Automaton

two successive clock times, the automaton consumes its next available input and goes into a new state (which may happen to be the same state it was in at the previous time). Since the act of consuming one of its inputs, selecting the next state, and changing state is atomic, it cannot be interrupted, and just as in the case of the traffic light above, we cannot see any intermediate conditions, when, e.g., the automaton is not in any of its defined states or when the input is only partially consumed. This means that we may regard the time scale of the automaton to be the set $\mathbb{N}$ of natural numbers. We represent the *internal states* of the control device as a set Q. If $q \in Q$ is the state of the device at time n, then q', the state at time $n+1$, is determined by the symbol a read by the reading head from the input tape and by q. After reading the symbol from the input tape at time n, the reading head moves one position to the right (see Figure 3.1). Since the reading head moves in only one direction, the character read at time n has effectively been consumed; it will never be revisited. When the automaton has consumed the last input character its reading head is on an empty cell. At this point, the automaton can no longer change state, i.e. it has come to a stop. We can now examine the state of the automaton. If it is in a preselected subset F of Q, we say that the automaton has *accepted* the input word; otherwise, it has rejected the input.

More formally, we have the following definition.

Definition 3.2.1 A *deterministic finite automaton* (dfa) is a quintuple

$$\mathcal{M} = (A, Q, \delta, q_0, F),$$

where A and Q are two finite, disjoint sets called the *input alphabet* of $\mathcal{M}$, and the *set of states* of $\mathcal{M}$, respectively, $\delta : Q \times A \longrightarrow Q$ is the *transition function*, q_0 is the *initial state* of $\mathcal{M}$, and $F \subseteq Q$ is the *set of final states* of $\mathcal{M}$. □

Example 3.2.2 Let $\mathcal{M} = (\{a,b\}, \{q_0, q_1, q_2, q_3\}, \delta, q_0, \{q_3\})$ be the dfa defined

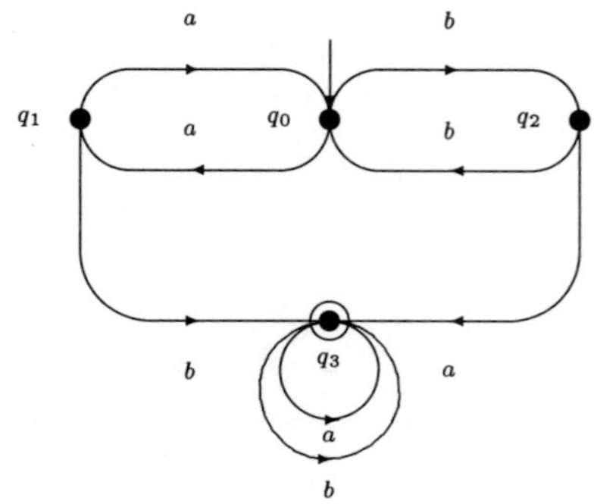

Figure 3.2: The Graph of the Automaton $\mathcal{M}$

by the following table:

Input	State			
	q_0	q_1	q_2	q_3
a	q_1	q_0	q_3	q_3
b	q_2	q_3	q_0	q_3

The entry that corresponds to the input line labeled i and the state column labeled q gives the value of $\delta(q, i)$. □

Alternatively, deterministic finite automata can be represented by labeled directed multigraphs. The *graph of the deterministic finite automaton* $\mathcal{M} = (A, Q, \delta, q_0, F)$ is the marked, directed multigraph $\mathcal{G}(\mathcal{M})$, whose set of vertices is the set of states Q. The set of edges of $\mathcal{G}(\mathcal{M})$ consists of all pairs (q, q') such that there is a transition from q to q'; an edge (q, q') is labeled by the symbol a if $\delta(q, a) = q'$. The initial state q_0 is denoted by an incoming arrow with no source, and the final states are circled.

Example 3.2.3 The graph of the automaton defined in Example 3.2.2 is given in Figure 3.2.

□

Deterministic finite automata are used for processing words over certain alphabets, that is sequences of symbols over these alphabets; the symbols of a word $x = a_{i_0} \cdots a_{i_{n-1}}$ are read by the automaton one at a time. To compute the state reached by the dfa after the application of this sequence of symbols, the function δ must be extended from single symbols to a function δ^* defined for words. Starting from a function δ we define the function $\delta^* : Q \times A^* \longrightarrow Q$ by

$$\delta^*(q, \lambda) = q \quad (3.1)$$
$$\delta^*(q, xa) = \delta(\delta^*(q, x), a), \quad (3.2)$$

for every $x \in A^*$ and $a \in A$. Note that for single character words, e.g., $y = a$, where $a \in A$, $\delta^*(q, y) = \delta(q, a)$. This follows from Equation (3.2), by setting

$x = \lambda$ and noticing that $y = \lambda a$. Thus, we may write $\delta^*(q, a) = \delta(q, a)$ for all $q \in Q$ and $a \in A$, justifying our observation that δ^* extends δ.

This next theorem shows that the only information a dfa can remember about the portion of the word it has processed must be captured in its state. In other words, when the word $w = xy$ is processed by a dfa $\mathcal{M}$ beginning with the state q, the effect of the first part of the computation, that is, the effect caused by x, is remembered by $\mathcal{M}$ in the state $\delta^*(q, x)$.

Theorem 3.2.4 *Let $\delta : Q \times A \longrightarrow Q$ be a function, and let δ^* be its extension to $Q \times A^*$. Then*

$$\delta^*(q, xy) = \delta^*(\delta^*(q, x), y)$$

for every $x, y \in A^*$.

Proof. The argument is by induction on $|y|$. The basis step, $|y| = 0$, is immediate since the equality of the theorem amounts to

$$\delta^*(q, x\lambda) = \delta^*(\delta^*(q, x), \lambda) = \delta^*(q, x),$$

by Equality (3.1).

For the induction step, suppose that the equality holds for words of length less or equal to n, and let y be a word of length $n + 1$, $y = za$, where $z \in A^*$ and $a \in A$. We have

$$\begin{aligned}
\delta^*(q, xy) &= \delta^*(q, xza) \\
&= \delta(\delta^*(q, xz), a) \text{ (since } \delta^* \text{ extends } \delta) \\
&= \delta(\delta^*(\delta^*(q, x), z), a) \text{ (ind. hyp.)} \\
&= \delta^*(\delta^*(q, x), za) \text{ (since } \delta^* \text{ extends } \delta) \\
&= \delta^*(\delta^*(q, x), y).
\end{aligned}$$

∎

Finite automata are used in various ways. The two most common in computer science are as language acceptors and as translators between the sets of words over two alphabets, that is as transducers. We first study the simpler and more common of these two: language acceptors.

If an automaton begins in its start state q_0 and ends up in a state q that is in the set F of final states as a result of reading a word x, the automaton is said to *accept the word* x. Clearly, the set of words that the automaton accepts is a subset of A^*, the set of words over the input alphabet of the automaton, and thus forms a language. Any set that comprises exactly the words accepted by some finite automaton is called a *regular* language. This is formalized in the following definition.

Definition 3.2.5 The *language accepted by the dfa* $\mathcal{M} = (A, Q, \delta, q_0, F)$ is the set

$$L(\mathcal{M}) = \{x \in A^* \mid \delta^*(q_0, x) \in F\}.$$

A language $L \subseteq A^*$ is *regular* if it is accepted by some finite automaton $\mathcal{M}$ whose input alphabet is A. □

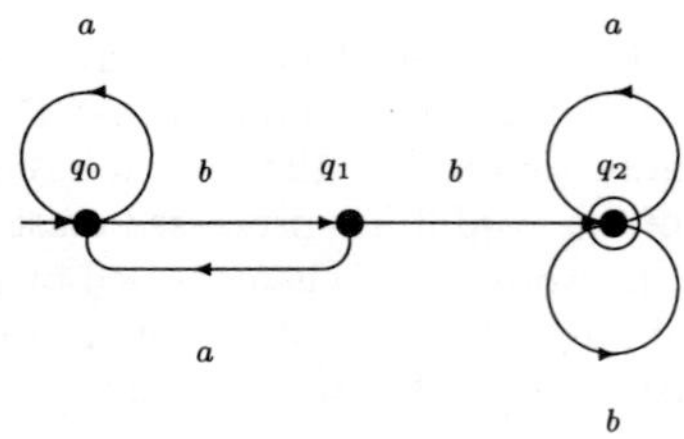

Figure 3.3: Graph of a dfa that accepts A^*bbA^*

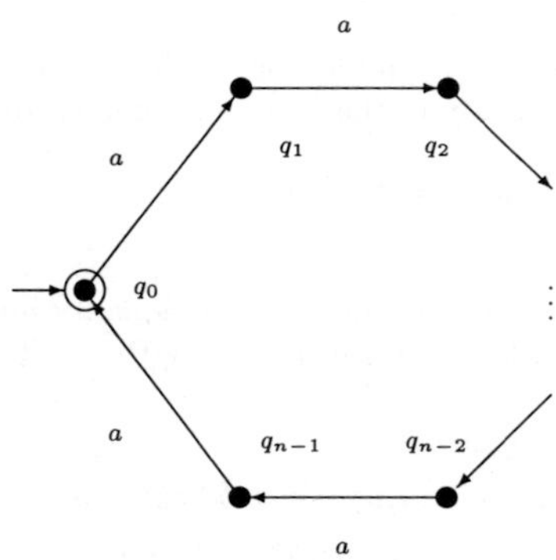

Figure 3.4: Dfa that accepts $\{x \in \{a\}^* \mid |x| \equiv 0 \pmod{n}\}$

Example 3.2.6 Let $\mathcal{M} = (A, Q, \delta, q_0, F)$ be the dfa whose graph is given in Figure 3.3, where $A = \{a, b\}$ and $Q = \{q_0, q_1, q_2\}$. The language accepted by $\mathcal{M}$ consists of all words over A that contain at least two consecutive b symbols; in other words, $L(\mathcal{M}) = A^*bbA^*$.

It is easy to verify that if $x \in L(\mathcal{M})$, then x contains two consecutive b symbols since q_2 cannot be reached otherwise from q_0 using the symbols of x. Conversely, suppose that x contains two consecutive b symbols. We can decompose $x = ubbv$, where bb is the leftmost occurrence of bb in x. The definition of $\mathcal{M}$ implies that $\delta^*(q_0, u) = q_0$, $\delta^*(q_0, bb) = q_2$ and $\delta^*(q_2, v) = q_2$. Thus, $\delta^*(q_0, x) = q_2$, and this implies $x \in L(\mathcal{M})$. We conclude that $L(\mathcal{M}) = A^*bbA^*$. □

Example 3.2.7 One of the things that finite automata can do is count modulo a number. For instance, a dfa with n states such as that shown in Figure 3.4 accepts only inputs whose length is $0 (\bmod\ n)$, that is, an integral multiple of n.

Similarly, the dfa in Figure 3.5 accepts those words in $\{a, b\}^*$ that have 0

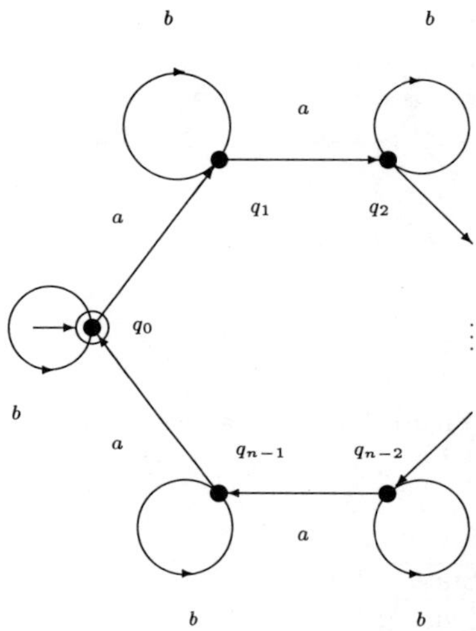

Figure 3.5: Dfa that accepts $\{x \in \{a, b\}^* \mid n_a(x) \equiv 0 \pmod{n}\}$

(mod n) a's, regardless of how many b's are in the input. □

The following example describes a more sophisticated dfa that accepts words over the alphabet $\{0, 1\}$ only when their binary equivalents are multiples of a fixed integer, say $m \in \mathbb{N}$.

Example 3.2.8 Let $B = \{0, 1\}$. A word $x \in B^*$ can be regarded as a binary number as follows. Define the function $f : B^* \longrightarrow \mathbb{N}$ by

$$f(\lambda) = 0$$

$$f(xb) = \begin{cases} 2f(x) + 0 & \text{if } b = 0 \\ 2f(x) + 1 & \text{if } b = 1, \end{cases}$$

for every $x \in B^*$ and $b \in B$. Note that $f(x)$ is the value represented by x regarded as a binary number.

Let $m \in \mathbb{N}$ be a number such that $m > 1$. Note that for every $x \in B^*$, there exists a number k, $0 \leq k \leq m - 1$, such that $f(x) \equiv k(\text{mod } m)$. Of course, if $f(x) \equiv 0(\text{mod } m)$, then $f(x)$ is a multiple of m, so x will be accepted by the automaton that we intend to define.

We design an automaton $\mathcal{M}_m$ that accepts the set of words x such that $f(x)$ is a multiple of a fixed number m. The states of $\mathcal{M}_m$ are defined such that $\delta^*(q_0, x) = q_h$ if and only if $f(x) \equiv h(\text{mod } m)$. In other words, if $\mathcal{M}_m$ reaches the state q_h after reading the symbols of x, then $f(x)$ is congruent to h modulo m. Therefore, after reading the symbol b, $\mathcal{M}$ enters the state q_ℓ, where $2h + b \equiv \ell$ (mod m). This allows us to define the transition function by $\delta(q_h, b) = q_\ell$. For instance, the automaton $\mathcal{M}_3 = (B, \{q_0, q_1, q_2\}, \delta, q_0, \{q_0\})$ that recognizes the set of multiples of 3 is defined by the table:

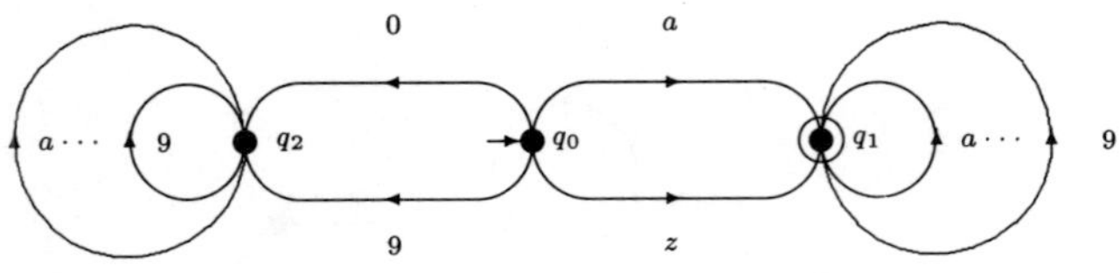

Figure 3.6: Dfa that accepts $\{a, \ldots, z\}A^*$

Input	State		
	q_0	q_1	q_2
0	q_0	q_2	q_1
1	q_1	q_0	q_2

Therefore, the language $L = \{x \in B^* \mid f(x) \equiv 0 (\text{mod } 3)\}$ is regular. □

Example 3.2.9 Let $A = \{a, b, \ldots, z, 0, \ldots, 9\}$. The automaton

$$\mathcal{M} = \{A, \{q_0, q_1, q_2\}, \delta, q_0, \{q_1\}\}$$

whose graph is given in Figure 3.6 accepts those words in A^* that begin with a letter and contain a sequence of letters and digits. In other words, $L(\mathcal{M}) = \{a, \ldots, z\}A^*$. Thus, this, or a similar automaton, can be used to recognize identifiers in most computer languages. □

Example 3.2.10 To determine the language accepted by the automaton

$$\mathcal{M} = (\{a, b\}, \{q_0, q_1, q_2, q_3\}, \delta, q_0, \{q_3\})$$

introduced in Example 3.2.2, note that the final state q_3 can be reached from q_0 either through q_1 or through q_2. In turn, the state q_1 can be reached from q_0 by any word in the language $\{a^2\{b^2\}^*\}^*a$, and q_2 can be reached from q_0 by any word in the language $\{b^2\{a^2\}^*\}^*b$. Thus, we have

$$\begin{aligned} L(\mathcal{M}) &= \{a^2\{b^2\}^*\}^*ab\{a, b\}^* \cup \\ & \quad \{b^2\{a^2\}^*\}^*ba\{a, b\}^*. \end{aligned}$$

□

The finiteness of the set of states Q of a dfa $\mathcal{M} = (A, Q, \delta, q_0, F)$ is essential for the definition of regular languages. If this assumption is dropped we obtain a more general notion, defined below.

Definition 3.2.11 A *deterministic automaton* (da) is a quintuple

$$\mathcal{M} = (A, Q, \delta, q_0, F),$$

where A is an alphabet, called the *input alphabet*; Q is a set that is disjoint from A, called the *set of states* of $\mathcal{M}$; $\delta : Q \times A \longrightarrow Q$ is the *transition function of the da*; q_0 is the *initial state* of $\mathcal{M}$; and $F \subseteq Q$ is the *set of final states* of $\mathcal{M}$. □
The transition function δ can be extended to $Q \times A^*$ in exactly the same way as for the deterministic finite automata. Again, we denote this extension by δ^*.

The role of the finiteness of the set of states of a dfa is highlighted by the next theorem.

Theorem 3.2.12 *For every language $L \subseteq A^*$, there is a deterministic automaton $\mathcal{M} = (A, Q, \delta, q_0, F)$ such that $L = L(\mathcal{M})$.*

Proof. Consider the da $\mathcal{M} = (A, Q, \delta, q_\lambda, \{q_u \mid u \in L\})$, where $Q = \{q_x \mid x \in A^*\}$ and $\delta(q_x, a) = q_{xa}$ for every $x \in A^*$ and $a \in A$. It is easy to verify that $\delta^*(q_x, y) = q_{xy}$ for every $x, y \in A^*$. Therefore, $L(\mathcal{M}) = \{y \in A^* \mid \delta^*(q_\lambda, y) = q_y \text{ and } y \in L\} = L$, which means that L is the language accepted by $\mathcal{M}$. ∎

In other words, Theorem 3.2.12 shows that every language is accepted by some deterministic automaton. One way of interpreting this result is that the notion of a da is too general to be interesting. Of course, our main interest in this chapter is in languages acceped by deterministic finite automata, that is, in regular languages.

Definition 3.2.13 Let $\mathcal{M} = (A, Q, \delta, q_0, F)$ be an automaton. The *set of accessible states* is the set

$$\mathsf{acc}(\mathcal{M}) = \{q \in Q \mid \delta^*(q_0, x) = q \text{ for some } x \in A^*\}.$$

The automaton $\mathcal{M}$ is *accessible* if $\mathsf{acc}(\mathcal{M}) = Q$. □

Only the set of accessible states plays a role in defining the language accepted by the automaton. If δ' is the restriction of δ to $\mathsf{acc}(\mathcal{M}) \times A$, then the automata $\mathcal{M}$ and $\mathcal{M}' = (A, \mathsf{acc}(\mathcal{M}), \delta', q_0, F \cap \mathsf{acc}(\mathcal{M}))$ accept the same language. Indeed, let $x \in L(\mathcal{M})$, then $\delta^*(q_0, x) \in F$ and $\delta^*(q_0, y) \in \mathsf{acc}(\mathcal{M})$ for every prefix y of x (including x). Therefore, $(\delta')^*(q_0, x) = \delta^*(q_0, x) \in F$, so $x \in L(\mathcal{M}')$. Conversely, it is immediate that $x \in L(\mathcal{M}')$ implies $x \in L(\mathcal{M})$, so $L(\mathcal{M}) = L(\mathcal{M}')$. We denote the automaton $\mathcal{M}'$ by $\mathsf{ACC}(\mathcal{M})$ and we refer to it as *the accessible component of* $\mathcal{M}$.

Example 3.2.14 Consider an automaton $\mathcal{M} = (\{a\}, Q, \delta, q_0, F)$ having a one-symbol input alphabet. We have $\mathsf{acc}(\mathcal{M}) = \{\delta(q_0, a^n) \mid n \in \mathbb{N}\}$. Therefore, the subgraph of the accessible states in the graph of $\mathcal{M}$ consists of a path attached to a circuit, as shown in Figure 3.7. □

Theorem 3.2.15 *Let $\mathcal{M} = (A, Q, \delta, q_0, F)$ be an accessible automaton. For every state $q \in Q$ there is a word $x \in A^*$ such that $|x| < |Q|$ and $\delta^*(q_0, x) = q$.*

Proof. Since $\mathcal{M}$ is an accessible automaton, for every state $q \in Q$ there is a word y such that $\delta^*(q_0, y) = q$. Let x be a word of minimal length that allows $\mathcal{M}$ to reach the state q. We claim that $|x| < |Q|$. Let $x = a_{i_0} \cdots a_{i_p}$, and let $q_1, \ldots, q_{p+1}$ be the sequence of states reached while processing x, i.e.,

$$\begin{aligned} q_1 &= \delta(q_0, a_{i_0}) \\ &\vdots \\ q_{p+1} &= \delta(q_p, a_{i_p}) = q, \end{aligned}$$

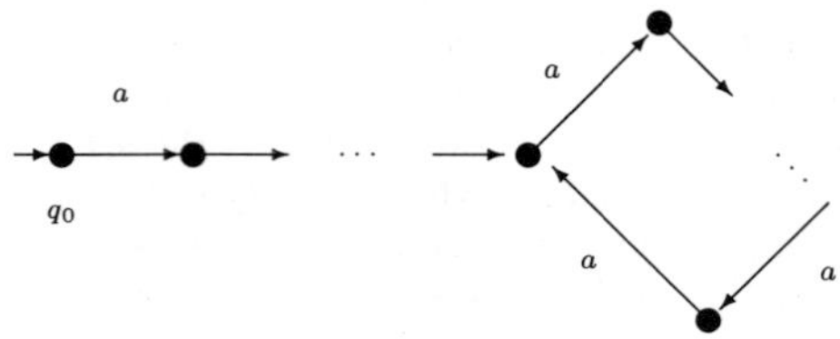

Figure 3.7: Subgraph of Accessible States for One-Symbol Input Alphabets

that is, the sequence of states assumed by $\mathcal{M}$ when the symbols of x are applied starting from the state q_0.

If $p+1 \geq |Q|$, then the sequence $(q_0, q_1, \ldots, q_{p+1})$ must contain two equal states because its length exceeds the number of elements of Q. If, say, $q_c = q_d$, we can write $x = uvw$, where $\delta^*(q_0, u) = q_c$, $\delta^*(q_c, v) = q_d$, $\delta^*(q_d, w) = q_{p+1}$ and $|v| > 0$. Since $q_d = q_c$, we have $\delta^*(q_0, uw) = q_{p+1} = q$, and this contradicts the minimality of x. Therefore, $|x| < |Q|$. ∎

To compute the set of accessible states of a dfa $\mathcal{M} = (A, Q, \delta, q_0, F)$ we can use the following algorithm.

Algorithm 3.2.16 (Computation of Accessible States)
Input: A dfa $\mathcal{M} = (A, Q, \delta, q_0, F)$.
Output: The set $\mathsf{acc}(\mathcal{M})$.
Method: Define the sequence $Q_0, Q_1, \ldots, Q_n, \ldots$ by $Q_0 = \{q_0\}$ and

$$Q_{i+1} = Q_i \cup \{s = \delta(q, a) \mid q \in Q_i \text{ and } a \in A\}.$$

Then, $\mathsf{acc}(\mathcal{M}) = Q_k$, where k is the least number such that $Q_k = Q_{k+1}$.

Proof of Correctness: Since $Q_0, \ldots, Q_i, \ldots$ is an increasing sequence and all sets Q_i are subsets of the finite set Q, there is a number k such that $Q_0 \subset Q_1 \subset \cdots \subset Q_k = Q_{k+1} = \cdots$.

We claim that

$$Q_i = \{q \in Q \mid \delta^*(q_0, x) = q, \text{ for some } x \in A^*, |x| \leq i\},$$

for every $i \in \mathbb{N}$. The argument is by induction on i and is left to the reader. Thus, every state in Q_k belongs to $\mathsf{acc}(\mathcal{M})$. Conversely, if $q \in \mathsf{acc}(\mathcal{M})$, then, by Theorem 3.2.15, there is a word x such that $|x| < |Q|$ and $\delta^*(q_0, x) = q$. Therefore, $q \in Q_{|x|} \subseteq Q_k$. We conclude that $\mathsf{acc}(\mathcal{M}) = Q_k$. ∎

Example 3.2.17 Let $\mathcal{M} = (\{a, b\}, \{q_i \mid 0 \leq i \leq 7\}, \delta, q_0, \{q_5, q_6\})$ be the dfa whose graph is shown in Figure 3.8. We have

$$\begin{aligned} Q_0 &= \{q_0\} \\ Q_1 &= \{q_0, q_1, q_2\} \\ Q_2 &= \{q_0, q_1, q_2, q_4, q_5\} \\ Q_3 &= \{q_0, q_1, q_2, q_4, q_5\} \end{aligned}$$

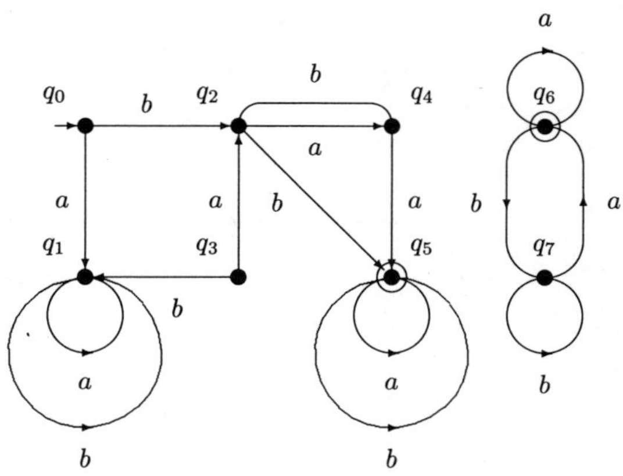

Figure 3.8: Graph of a dfa

Thus, $\mathsf{ACC}(\mathcal{M})$ is the dfa $\mathcal{M}' = (\{a, b\}, \{q_0, q_1, q_2, q_4, q_5\}, \delta', q_0, \{q_5\})$ whose graph is given in Figure 3.9.

□

3.2.2 Nondeterministic Automata

A deterministic finite automaton is a quite simple machine, and for many purposes we wish that it could be more powerful. One way we might try to accomplish this might be to allow the automaton in state q, when it consumes input a, to "guess" what state to go into from among a specified collection of states. We could then say that this automaton accepts an input x if it can make a series of guesses as it consumes x that results in the automaton's ending in a final state. Such a machine is called a nondeterministic finite automaton, because choices are offered for the next state, and consequently the behavior of the machine is not deterministic.

Definition 3.2.18 A *nondeterministic finite automaton* (ndfa) is a quintuple $\mathcal{M} = (A, Q, \delta, q_0, F)$, where A is the input alphabet of $\mathcal{M}$, Q is a finite *set of states*, $\delta : Q \times A \longrightarrow \mathcal{P}(Q)$ is the transition function, $q_0 \in Q$ is the initial state, and $F \subseteq Q$ is the set of final states of $\mathcal{M}$. We assume $A \cap Q = \emptyset$. □

Example 3.2.19 Consider the ndfa

$$\mathcal{M} = (\{a, b\}, \{q_0, q_1, q_2, q_2, q_4\}, \delta, q_0, \{q_1, q_3\}),$$

whose transition function is defined by the table:

	State				
Input	q_0	q_1	q_2	q_3	q_4
a	$\{q_1, q_2\}$	$\emptyset$	$\{q_3\}$	$\emptyset$	$\emptyset$
b	$\{q_0\}$	$\{q_3\}$	$\{q_4\}$	$\emptyset$	$\emptyset$

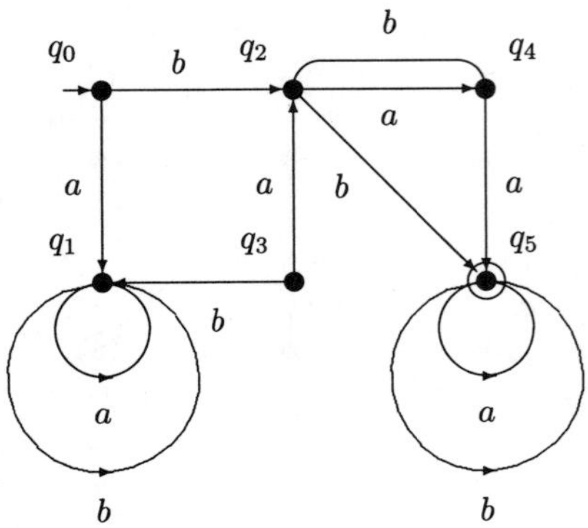

Figure 3.9: Accessible Component of a dfa

Note the presence of pairs (q, a) such that $\delta(q, a) = \emptyset$. We refer to such pairs as *blocking situations* of $\mathcal{M}$. For instance, (q_1, a) is a blocking situation of $\mathcal{M}$. □

As in the case of the dfa, we can extend the ndfa's transition function δ, defined on single characters, to δ^*, defined on words.

Starting from the transition function δ, we define the function $\delta^* : Q \times A^* \longrightarrow \mathcal{P}(Q)$ as follows:

$$\begin{aligned} \delta^*(q, \lambda) &= \{q\} \\ \delta^*(q, xa) &= \bigcup_{q' \in \delta^*(q,x)} \delta(q', a) \end{aligned}$$

Graphs of nondeterministic finite automata are defined in a manner that is similar to the deterministic case. Namely, if $\mathcal{M} = (A, Q, \delta, q_0, F)$ is an ndfa, then the *graph* of $\mathcal{M}$ is the marked, directed multigraph $\mathcal{G}(\mathcal{M})$, whose set of vertices is the set of states Q. The set of edges of $\mathcal{G}(\mathcal{M})$ consists of all pairs (q, q') such that $q' \in \delta(q, a)$ for some $a \in A$; an edge (q, q') is labeled by the input symbol a, where $q' \in \delta(q, a)$. The initial state q_0 is denoted by an incoming arrow with no source, and the final states are circled.

It is easy to see that if $q' \in \delta^*(q, x)$, then there is a path in the graph $\mathcal{G}(\mathcal{M})$ labeled by x that leads from q to q'.

Example 3.2.20 The graph of the ndfa $\mathcal{M}$ defined in Example 3.2.19 is shown in Figure 3.10. Note that two edges emerge from q_0, leading to q_1 and q_2, since $\delta(q_0, a) = \{q_1, q_2\}$. Since $\delta(q_1, a) = \emptyset$, no edge labeled a begins at q_1. □

Definition 3.2.21 The *language accepted by the ndfa* $\mathcal{M} = (A, Q, \delta, q_0, F)$ is

$$L(\mathcal{M}) = \{x \in A^* \mid \delta^*(q_0, x) \cap F \neq \emptyset\}.$$

□

In other words, $x \in L(\mathcal{M})$ if there exists a path in the graph of $\mathcal{M}$ labeled by x that leads from the initial state into one of the final states. Note that it is not

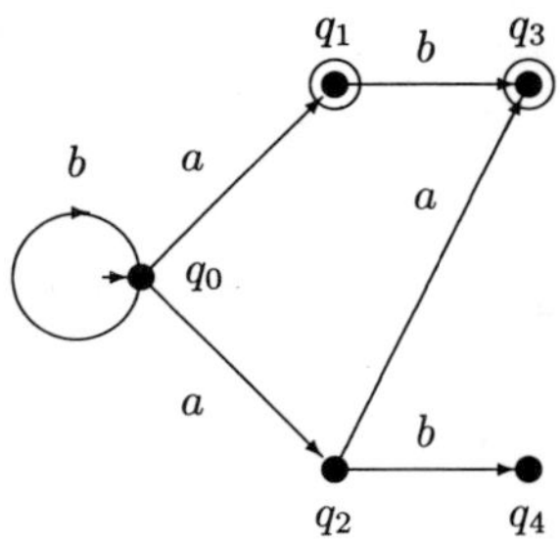

Figure 3.10: Graph of an ndfa

necessary that all paths labeled by x lead to a final state; the existence of one such path suffices to put x into the language $L(\mathcal{M})$.

Example 3.2.22 Let $\mathcal{M}$ be the ndfa introduced in Example 3.2.19. Note that $ab \in L(\mathcal{M})$ because of the existence of the path (q_0, q_1, q_3) labeled by this word and the fact that q_3 is a final state. On the other hand, (q_0, q_2, q_4) is another path labeled by x but $q_4 \notin F$.

This ndfa is simple enough to allow an easy identification of all types of words in $L(\mathcal{M})$:

1. The final state q_1 can be reached by applying an arbitrary number of bs followed by an a.
2. The final state q_3 can be reached by a path of the form $(q_0, \dots, q_0, q_1, q_3)$, that is by a word of the form $b^k ab$ for $k \in \mathbb{N}$.
3. The same final state q_3 can be reached via q_2. Input words that allow this transition have the form $b^k aa$ for $k \in \mathbb{N}$.

Thus, we have

$$L(\mathcal{M}) = \{b\}^* a \cup \{b\}^* ab \cup \{b\}^* aa = \{b\}^* \{a, ab, aa\}.$$

□

Example 3.2.23 Consider an alphabet $A = \{a_0, \dots, a_{n-1}\}$ and a binary relation $\rho \subseteq A \times A$. The language

$$L_\rho = \{a_{i_0} \cdots a_{i_p} \mid p \in \mathbb{N}, (a_{i_j}, a_{i_{j+1}}) \in \rho \text{ for } 0 \leq j \leq p-1\}$$

is accepted by the ndfa $\mathcal{M}_\rho = (A, Q, \delta, q, F)$, where $Q = \{q, q_0, \dots, q_{n-1}\}$, $F = \{q_0, \dots, q_{n-1}\}$, and δ is given by

- $\delta(q, a_i) = \{q_i\}$ for $0 \leq i \leq n-1$;
- for every i, j such that $0 \leq i, j \leq n-1$,

$$\delta(q_i, a_j) = \{q_j \in Q \mid (a_i, a_j) \in \rho\}.$$

The graph of $\mathcal{M}_\rho$ is given in Figure 3.11. Note that if $(a_i, a_j) \notin \rho$, then (q_i, a_j) is a blocking situation. The existence of these blocking situations is precisely what

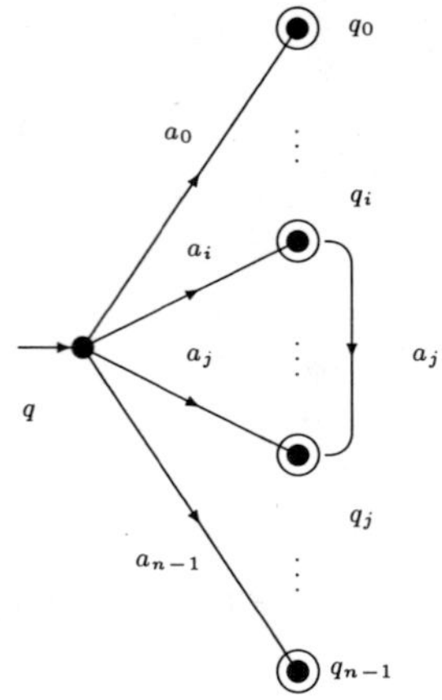

Figure 3.11: Graph of the ndfa $\mathcal{M}_\rho$.

makes this device a nondeterministic automaton. We show that $L_\rho = L(\mathcal{M}_\rho)$. Let $x = a_{i_0} \cdots a_{i_p}$ be a word in L_ρ with $p \geq 0$. We prove by induction on $p = |x| - 1$ that $x \in L(\mathcal{M}_\rho)$ and that $\delta^*(q, x) = \{q_{i_p}\}$. The base case, $p = 0$, is immediate, since the condition $(a_{i_j}, a_{i_{j+1}}) \in \rho$ for $0 \leq j \leq p - 1$ is vacuous.

Suppose that the statement holds for words in L_ρ of length at most p and let $x = a_{i_0} \cdots a_{i_p}$ be a word in L_ρ of length $p + 1$. It is clear that the word $y = a_{i_0} \cdots a_{i_{p-1}}$ belongs to L_ρ. By the inductive hypothesis, $y \in L(\mathcal{M}_\rho)$ and $\delta^*(q, y) = \{q_{i_{p-1}}\}$. Since $(a_{i_{p-1}}, a_{i_p}) \in \rho$ (by the definition of L_ρ), we have $\delta(q_{i_{p-1}}, a_{i_p}) = \{q_{i_p}\}$, so

$$q_{i_p} \in \bigcup_{q' \in \delta(q,y)} \delta(q', a_{i_p}) = \delta^*(q, ya_{i_p}) = \delta^*(q, x).$$

Therefore, $x \in L(\mathcal{M}_\rho)$.

To prove the converse inclusion $L(\mathcal{M}_\rho) \subseteq L_\rho$ we use an argument by induction on $|x| \geq 1$, where x is a word from $L(\mathcal{M}_\rho)$, to show that if $x = a_{i_0} \cdots a_{i_p} \in L(\mathcal{M}_\rho)$, then $\delta^*(q, x) = \{q_{i_p}\}$ and $x \in L_\rho$. Again, the base case is immediate.

Suppose that the statement holds for words in $L(\mathcal{M}_\rho)$ of length less than $p+1$ that belong to L_ρ, and let $x = a_{i_0} \cdots a_{i_p}$ be a word in $L(\mathcal{M}_\rho)$ of length $p+1$. If $y = a_{i_0} \ldots a_{i_{p-1}}$, it is easy to see that $y \in L(\mathcal{M}_\rho)$ because no blocking situation may arise in $\mathcal{M}_\rho$ while the symbols of y are read. Therefore, by the inductive hypothesis, $y \in L_\rho$ and $\delta^*(q, y) = \{q_{i_{p-1}}\}$. Further, since $\delta(q_{i_{p-1}}, a_{i_p}) \neq \emptyset$, it follows that $(a_{i_{p-1}}, a_{i_p}) \in \rho$, so $x \in L_\rho$, and $\delta^*(q, x) = q_{i_p}$.

Thus, L_ρ is accepted by the ndfa $\mathcal{M}_\rho$. □

Let $\mathcal{M} = (A, Q, \delta, q_0, F)$ be a nondeterministic automaton, and let $\Delta : \mathcal{P}(Q) \times A \longrightarrow \mathcal{P}(Q)$ be defined by

$$\Delta(S, a) = \bigcup_{q \in S} \delta(q, a) \tag{3.3}$$

for every $S \subseteq Q$ and $a \in A$. Starting from Δ, we define $\Delta^* : \mathcal{P}(Q) \times A^* \longrightarrow \mathcal{P}(Q)$ in the manner used for the transition functions of deterministic automata. Namely, we define

$$\Delta^*(S, \lambda) = S \tag{3.4}$$

$$\Delta^*(S, xa) = \Delta(\Delta^*(S, x), a) \tag{3.5}$$

for every $S \subseteq Q$ and $a \in A$.

Lemma 3.2.24 *The functions Δ and Δ^* defined above satisfy the following properties:*

(i) *For every family of sets $\{S_0, \ldots, S_{n-1}\}$ and every $a \in A$, we have:*

$$\Delta\left(\bigcup_{0 \leq i \leq n-1} S_i, a\right) = \bigcup_{0 \leq i \leq n-1} \Delta(S_i, a).$$

(ii) *For every set $S \subseteq Q$ and $x \in A^*$ we have*

$$\Delta^*(S, x) = \bigcup_{q \in S} \delta^*(q, x).$$

Proof. The first part of the lemma is immediate, because

$$\begin{aligned}\Delta(\textstyle\bigcup_{0 \leq i \leq n-1} S_i, a) &= \textstyle\bigcup\{\delta(q, a) \mid q \in \bigcup_{0 \leq i \leq n-1} S_i\}\\ &= \textstyle\bigcup_{0 \leq i \leq n-1}\{\delta(q, a) \mid q \in S_i\}\\ &= \textstyle\bigcup_{0 \leq i \leq n-1} \Delta(S_i, a).\end{aligned}$$

The argument of the second part of the lemma is by induction on $|x|$. For the basis step, we have $|x| = 0$, so $x = \lambda$, and $\Delta^*(S, \lambda) = S$, $\bigcup_{q \in S} \delta^*(q, \lambda) = \bigcup_{q \in S}\{q\} = S$.

Suppose that the argument holds for words of length n, and let $x = za$ be a word of length $n + 1$. We have

$$\begin{aligned}\Delta^*(S, x) &= \Delta^*(S, za)\\ &= \Delta(\Delta^*(S, z), a)\\ &= \Delta(\bigcup_{q \in S} \delta^*(q, z), a) \text{(by ind. hyp.)}\\ &= \bigcup_{q \in S} \Delta(\delta^*(q, z), a)\\ &= \bigcup_{q \in S} \bigcup_{r \in \delta^*(q, z)} \delta(r, a)\\ &= \bigcup_{q \in S} \delta^*(q, za)\\ &= \bigcup_{q \in S} \delta^*(q, x)\end{aligned}$$

∎

Nondeterministic automata can be regarded as generalizations of deterministic automata in the following sense. If $\mathcal{M} = (A, Q, \delta, q_0, F)$ is a deterministic automaton, consider a nondeterministic automaton $\mathcal{M}' = (A, Q, \delta', q_0, F)$, where $\delta'(q,a) = \{\delta(q,a)\}$. It is easy to verify that for every $q \in Q$ and $x \in A^*$ we have $\delta'^*(q,x) = \{\delta^*(q,x)\}$. Therefore,

$$\begin{aligned} L(\mathcal{M}') &= \{x \in A^* \mid \delta'^*(q_0,x) \cap F \neq \emptyset\} \\ &= \{x \in A^* \mid \{\delta^*(q_0,x)\} \cap F \neq \emptyset\} \\ &= \{x \in A^* \mid \delta^*(q_0,x) \in F\} \\ &= L(\mathcal{M}). \end{aligned}$$

(In other words, for every deterministic finite automaton there exists a nondeterministic one that recognizes the same language.)

It is surprising that the reverse is also true, as shown by the next theorem.

Theorem 3.2.25 *For every nondeterministic automaton, there exists a deterministic automaton that accepts the same language.*

Proof. Let $\mathcal{M} = (A, Q, \delta, q_0, F)$ be a nondeterministic automaton. Define the function Δ as in the equality (3.3), and consider the deterministic automaton $\mathcal{M}' = (A, \mathcal{P}(Q), \Delta, \{q_0\}, \{S \mid S \subseteq Q \text{ and } S \cap F \neq \emptyset\})$. For every $x \in A^*$ we have the following equivalent statements:

1. $x \in L(\mathcal{M})$;
2. $\delta^*(q_0,x) \cap F \neq \emptyset$;
3. $\Delta^*(\{q_0\},x) \cap F \neq \emptyset$;
4. $x \in L(\mathcal{M}')$.

This proves that $L(\mathcal{M}) = L(\mathcal{M}')$. ∎

It is sometimes helpful to think of the action of a nondeterministic finite automaton in terms of markers (e.g., poker chips, stones, or tiddlywinks) placed on states. If there is a marker on the state q and the input is a, then the marker is removed from q, and new markers are placed on all states in $\delta(q,a)$. If there are markers on several states, then this process is performed in parallel for each of these states. Since there need never be more than one marker on any state, a supply of $|Q|$ markers suffices to carry out this process. The word x is accepted by $\mathcal{M}$ if, beginning from a marker on q_0, any marker ends up on a state in F after processing x. If one begins with an ndfa and then regards each possible pattern of markers on the set of states as a state in a second automaton in which the transitions are those just described, then this second automation is a dfa that accepts the same language as the ndfa.

Example 3.2.26 Consider the nondeterministic finite automaton

$$\mathcal{M} = (\{a,b\}, \{q_0,q_1,q_2\}, \delta, q_0, \{q_2\})$$

whose graph is given in Figure 3.12. It is easy to see that the language accepted by this automaton is A^*bbA^*, that is the language that consists of all words that contain two consecutive b symbols. This language coincides with the language accepted by the dfa given in Example 3.2.6. Note that the graph of the nondeterministic automaton given in Figure 3.12 is simpler than the graph of the deterministic automaton given in Figure 3.3; this simplification is made possible by the nondeterminism.

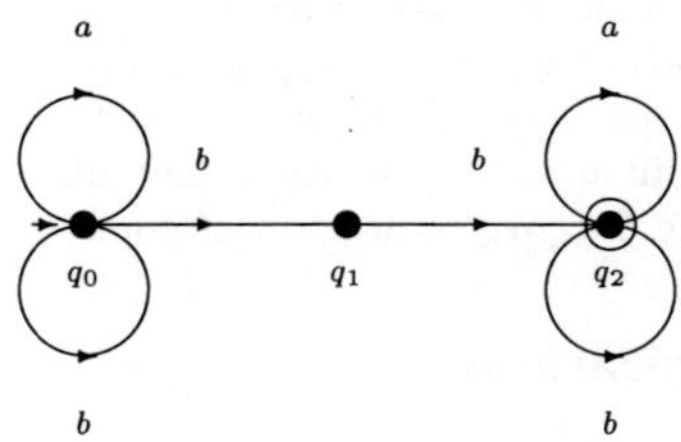

Figure 3.12: Graph of the Nondeterministic Finite Automaton $\mathcal{M}$

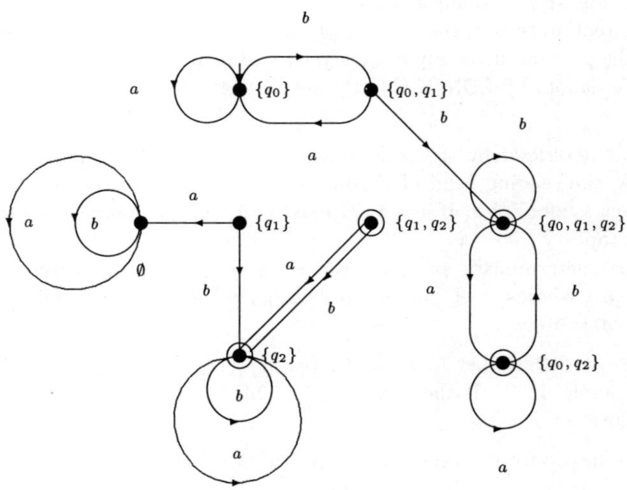

Figure 3.13: Graph of the Equivalent dfa

The deterministic automaton obtained through the construction described in Theorem 3.2.25 has $\mathcal{P}(\{q_0, q_1, q_2\})$ as its set of states. Its graph is given in Figure 3.13. Note how inefficient this construction is; we obtained a dfa that has eight states; we know from Example 3.2.6 that the language A^*bbA^* can be accepted by a dfa that has only three states. There are algorithmic techniques for calculating minimal automata that would allow us to reduce the eight-state dfa to a three-state dfa. We return to this topic in Section 3.6. □

3.2.3 Configurations

The complete description of an automaton at any moment in time comprises the input word, the state of the automaton, and the position of its read head. This can be captured in a *configuration* of the form uqv, where u is the portion of the word already processed, v is the portion remaining to be processed, and q is the state of the automaton. Since $A \cap Q = \emptyset$, we can always parse such a string unambiguously. When we wish to consider the next action of the automaton, we can explicitly identify the first symbol of v and write the configuration as $uqav'$, where $v = av'$. Of course, this requires that $v \neq \lambda$. If $v = \lambda$, then the automaton halts, as it has exhausted its input.

Definition 3.2.27 Let $\mathcal{M} = (A, Q, \delta, q_0, F)$ be a nondeterministic automaton. A *configuration* of an automaton $\mathcal{M}$ is a word $\mathsf{c} = uqv \in A^*QA^*$, where $q \in Q$ and $u, v \in A^*$. The automaton $\mathcal{M}$ is *described by the configuration* $\mathsf{c} = uqv$ if its current state is q, the portion of tape already scanned contains the word u, and the portion of the input tape yet to be read contains the word $v \in A^*$.

We denote by $\mathsf{CONFIG}(\mathcal{M})$ the set A^*QA^* of all possible configurations of $\mathcal{M}$. □

If $\mathcal{M}$ is described by the configuration $\mathsf{c} = uqv$, we distinguish two cases. If $v \neq \lambda$, the reading head of the automaton is scanning the cell containing the leftmost symbol of v. If $v = \lambda$, $\mathcal{M}$ must halt, since it has reached the end of its input tape.

For a deterministic automaton $\mathcal{M} = (A, Q, \delta, q_0, F)$, the current configuration $\mathsf{c} = uqav$, where $v \in A^*$, determines uniquely the next configuration $\mathsf{c}' = uaq'v$, where $q' = \delta(q, a)$.

Example 3.2.28 Let $\mathcal{M} = (\{a, b\}, \{q_0, q_1, q_2, q_3\}, \delta, q_0, \{q_3\})$ be the dfa defined in Example 3.2.2. If the input tape of $\mathcal{M}$ contains the word $abac$, its initial configuration is q_0abac. □

We introduce the relation $\underset{\mathcal{M}}{\vdash}$ on the set $\mathsf{CONFIG}(\mathcal{M})$ by defining $\mathsf{c} \underset{\mathcal{M}}{\vdash} \mathsf{c}'$ if and only if $\mathsf{c} = uqav$, $\mathsf{c}' = uaq'v$, and $q' \in \delta(q, a)$. In other words, $\mathcal{M}$ may change its configuration from $uqav$ to $uaq'v$, precisely when $\mathcal{M}$ may switch its state from q to q' by reading the symbol a. When $\mathcal{M}$ is clear from context we may simply write $\mathsf{c} \vdash \mathsf{c}'$.

Definition 3.2.29 Let $\mathcal{M} = (A, Q, \delta, q_0, F)$ be a nondeterministic finite automaton. A *run* is a sequence of configurations $\mathsf{r} = (\mathsf{c}_0, \dots, \mathsf{c}_{n-1})$ such that $\mathsf{c}_i \underset{\mathcal{M}}{\vdash} \mathsf{c}_{i+1}$ for $0 \leq i \leq n-2$ and $n \geq 1$. □

Starting from the relation " $\underset{\mathcal{M}}{\vdash}$ " we denote its nth power by $\overset{n}{\underset{\mathcal{M}}{\vdash}}$, its transitive closure by $\overset{+}{\underset{\mathcal{M}}{\vdash}}$, and its reflexive and transitive closure by $\overset{*}{\underset{\mathcal{M}}{\vdash}}$. Thus, if $\mathsf{c}, \mathsf{c}' \in \mathsf{CONFIG}(\mathcal{M})$ we have $\mathsf{c} \overset{+}{\underset{\mathcal{M}}{\vdash}} \mathsf{c}'$ if and only if there is an $n \geq 1$ such that $\mathsf{c} \overset{n}{\underset{\mathcal{M}}{\vdash}} \mathsf{c}'$, that is, if and only if there exists a run in $\mathcal{M}$ that begins with c and ends with c'. Also, $\mathsf{c} \overset{*}{\underset{\mathcal{M}}{\vdash}} \mathsf{c}'$ if and only if there is an $n \geq 0$ such that $\mathsf{c} \overset{n}{\underset{\mathcal{M}}{\vdash}} \mathsf{c}'$, that is if and only if $\mathsf{c} = \mathsf{c}'$, or there exists a run that begins with c and ends with c'.

Example 3.2.30 Let $\mathcal{M}$ be the nondeterministic finite automaton introduced in Example 3.2.26. We have $q_0aabba \overset{*}{\underset{\mathcal{M}}{\vdash}} aabbaq_2$ because

$$\begin{array}{llll} q_0aabba & \underset{\mathcal{M}}{\vdash} & aq_0abba & (\text{since } q_0 \in \delta(q_0, a)) \\ & \underset{\mathcal{M}}{\vdash} & aaq_0bba & (\text{since } q_0 \in \delta(q_0, a)) \\ & \underset{\mathcal{M}}{\vdash} & aabq_1bba & (\text{since } q_1 \in \delta(q_0, b)) \\ & \underset{\mathcal{M}}{\vdash} & aabbq_2a & (\text{since } q_2 \in \delta(q_1, b)) \\ & \underset{\mathcal{M}}{\vdash} & aabbaq_2 & (\text{since } q_2 \in \delta(q_2, a)) \end{array}$$

□

Theorem 3.2.31 *Let $\mathcal{M} = (A, Q, \delta, q_0, F)$ be an ndfa. For each $u, v, x \in A^*$ and $q, q' \in Q$ we have $uqxv \overset{*}{\underset{\mathcal{M}}{\vdash}} uxq'v$ if and only if $q' \in \delta^*(q, x)$.*

Proof. Let $\mathsf{c} = uqxv$ and $\mathsf{c}' = uxq'v$, where $u, v, x \in A^*$ and $q, q' \in Q$.

First, suppose that $\mathsf{c} \overset{*}{\underset{\mathcal{M}}{\vdash}} \mathsf{c}'$. Then, there is $n \in \mathbb{N}$ such that $\mathsf{c} \overset{n}{\underset{\mathcal{M}}{\vdash}} \mathsf{c}'$. We prove by induction on n, that if $\mathsf{c} \overset{n}{\underset{\mathcal{M}}{\vdash}} \mathsf{c}'$, then $q' \in \delta^*(q, x)$.

For $n = 0$ we have $\mathsf{c} = \mathsf{c}'$, so $x = \lambda$ and $q = q'$. The statement holds because $\delta^*(q, \lambda) = \{q\} = \{q'\}$.

Suppose the statement holds for n and that $\mathsf{c} \overset{n+1}{\underset{\mathcal{M}}{\vdash}} \mathsf{c}'$. Let $\bar{\mathsf{c}}$ be the penultimate configuration; i.e., $\mathsf{c} \overset{n}{\underset{\mathcal{M}}{\vdash}} \bar{\mathsf{c}} \underset{\mathcal{M}}{\vdash} \mathsf{c}'$. Then, $\bar{\mathsf{c}}$ must be $u\bar{x}\bar{q}av$, where $\bar{x}a = x$ and, by the induction hypothesis, $\bar{q} \in \delta^*(q, \bar{x})$. From the definition of $\Rightarrow$ it now follows that $q' \in \delta(\bar{q}, a)$, so $\mathsf{c}' = u\bar{x}aq'v = uxq'v$, as required.

Conversely, suppose that $q' \in \delta^*(q, x)$, for some word $x \in A^*$. We claim that $\mathsf{c} \overset{*}{\underset{\mathcal{M}}{\vdash}} \mathsf{c}'$. We leave the argument (by induction on $|x|$) to the reader. ∎

Corollary 3.2.32 *Let $\mathcal{M} = (A, Q, \delta, q_0, F)$ be an ndfa. We have $x \in L(\mathcal{M})$ if and only if there is a final state $q' \in F$ such that $q_0x \overset{*}{\underset{\mathcal{M}}{\vdash}} xq'$.*

Proof. This statement is an immediate consequence of Theorem 3.2.31. ∎

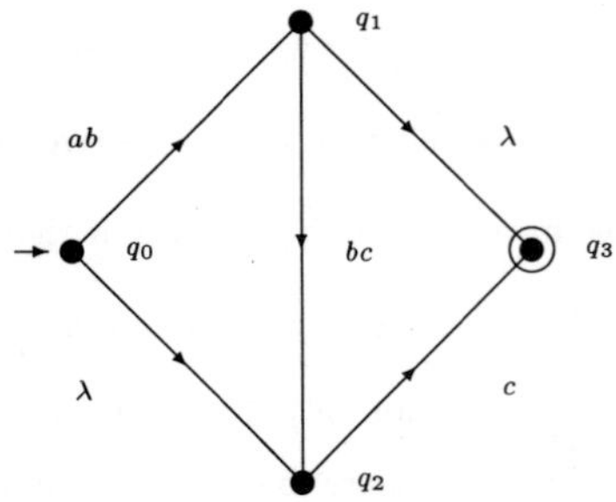

Figure 3.14: The Graph of the Transition System $\mathcal{T}_1$

3.3 Transition Systems

Nondeterministic finite automata can be further generalized by allowing transitions between states without reading any input symbol. To formalize this notion consider the following definition.

Definition 3.3.1 A *transition system* (ts) is a 5-tuple $\mathcal{T} = (A, Q, \theta, Q_0, F)$, where A, Q, and F are as in a finite automaton, θ is a finite relation, $\theta \subseteq Q \times A^* \times Q$, called the *transition relation of* $\mathcal{T}$, and Q_0 is a nonempty subset of Q called the *set of initial states.*

A *transition* in $\mathcal{T}$ is a triple $(q, x, q') \in \theta$. We refer to transitions of the form (q, λ, q') as *null transitions.* □

Transition systems are conveniently represented by labeled directed multigraphs. Namely, if $\mathcal{T} = (A, Q, \theta, Q_0, F)$ is a transition system, then its graph is a labeled directed multigraph $G(\mathcal{T}) = (G, A^*, \mathsf{m})$ that has Q as its set of vertices. Each directed edge e with $s(e) = q$, $d(e) = q'$, and $\mathsf{m}(e) = x$ corresponds to a triple $(q, x, q') \in \theta$, and every such triple is represented by an edge in G.

Observe that, unlike the graph of a dfa or an ndfa, the edges of the directed graph of a ts can be labelled with words, including the null word.

Example 3.3.2 Consider the transition system

$$\mathcal{T}_1 = (\{a, b, c\}, \{q_0, q_1, q_2, q_3\}, \theta, \{q_0\}, \{q_3\}),$$

where θ is given by

$$\theta = \{(q_0, ab, q_1), (q_0, \lambda, q_2), (q_1, bc, q_2), (q_1, \lambda, q_3), (q_2, c, q_3)\}.$$

Its directed graph is shown in Figure 3.14. □

As we did with the transition functions of dfas and ndfas, we wish to extend the transition relation θ of a transition system $\mathcal{T}$ to the set $Q \times A^* \times Q$. The extension $\theta^* \subseteq Q \times A^* \times Q$ is given next.

1. For every $q \in Q$ define $(q, \lambda, q) \in \theta^*$.

2. Every triple $(q, x, q') \in \theta$ belongs to θ^*.
3. If $(q, x, q'), (q', y, q'') \in \theta^*$, then $(q, xy, q'') \in \theta^*$.

Note that $(q, w, q') \in \theta^*$ if and only if there is a path in $G(\mathcal{T})$ that begins with q and ends with q' such that the concatenated labels of the directed edges of this path form the word w.

Example 3.3.3 If $\mathcal{T}$ is the transition system introduced in Example 3.3.2, then $(q_0, abbcc, q_3) \in \theta^*$ because $(q_0, ab, q_1), (q_1, bc, q_2), (q_2, c, q_3) \in \theta$. Similarly, $(q_0, c, q_3) \in \theta$ because $(q_0, \lambda, q_2), (q_2, c, q_3) \in \theta$. □

Definition 3.3.4 Let $\mathcal{T} = (A, Q, \theta, Q_0, F)$ be a transition system. The *language accepted by* $\mathcal{T}$ is

$$L(\mathcal{T}) = \{x \in A^* \mid (q_0, x, q) \in \theta^* \text{ for some } q_0 \in Q_0, q \in F\}.$$

□

Thus, a word x belongs to $L(\mathcal{T})$ if there is a path in $G(\mathcal{T})$ that begins in an initial state $q_0 \in Q_0$, labeled by x, such that the path ends in one of the states of F, the set of final states.

Transition systems generalize nondeterministic automata in the following sense. If $\mathcal{M} = (A, Q, \delta, q_0, F)$ is a nondeterministic automaton, define the transition system $\mathcal{T}_{\mathcal{M}} = (A, Q, \theta, \{q_0\}, F)$, where

$$\theta = \{(q, a, q') \mid q, q' \in Q, a \in A \text{ and } q' \in \delta(q, a)\}.$$

It is easy to verify by induction on $|x|$ that $(q, x, q') \in \theta^*$ if and only if $q' \in \delta^*(q, x)$. This implies that $L(\mathcal{T}_{\mathcal{M}}) = L(\mathcal{M})$. Therefore, every regular language can be accepted by a transition system. Furthermore, any language that can be accepted by a transition system is regular. Showing this is the goal of the next theorem. We prove a technical lemma that shows that transition systems can be restricted to transitions that consume at most one input symbol without affecting the class of languages they accept.

Lemma 3.3.5 *For every transition system $\mathcal{T} = (A, Q, \theta, Q_0, F)$ there exists a transition system $\mathcal{T}' = (A, Q', \theta', Q_0, F)$ such that $(q, x, q_1) \in \theta'$ implies $|x| \leq 1$ and $L(\mathcal{T}') = L(\mathcal{T})$.*

Proof. Define the relation θ' and the set Q' as follows:

1. Every state $q \in Q$ also belongs to Q'.
2. Every triple $(q, x, q') \in \theta$ such that $|x| \leq 1$ also belongs to θ'.
3. If $t = (q, x, q') \in \theta$ such that $x = a_0 \dots a_{n-1}$ and $n \geq 2$, add $n - 1$ new states $q_0^t, \dots q_{n-2}^t$ to Q' and the triples

$$(q, a_0, q_0^t), (q_0^t, a_1, q_1^t), \dots, (q_{n-2}^t, a_{n-1}, q')$$

to θ'.

The ts $\mathcal{T}'$ clearly satisfies the conditions of the lemma, since $(q, x, q') \in \theta^*$ if and only if $(q, x, q') \in \theta'^*$. ∎

Theorem 3.3.6 *For every transition system $\mathcal{T} = (A, Q, \theta, Q_0, F)$ there exists a deterministic finite automaton $\mathcal{M}$ such that $L(\mathcal{T}) = L(\mathcal{M})$.*

Proof. The argument is similar to the one used in Theorem 3.2.25. By Lemma 3.3.5, we can assume that $(q, x, q') \in \theta$ implies $|x| \leq 1$. Define the deterministic finite automaton $\mathcal{M} = (A, \mathcal{P}(Q), \Delta, Q'_0, F')$, where the initial state of $\mathcal{M}$ is

$$Q'_0 = \{q \in Q \mid (q_0, \lambda, q) \in \theta^* \text{ for some } q_0 \in Q_0\},$$

the set of final states is $F' = \{S \mid S \subseteq Q, S \cap F \neq \emptyset\}$, and the function Δ is defined by

$$\Delta(S, a) = \{q' \in Q \mid (q, a, q') \in \theta^* \text{ for some } q \in S\},$$

for every $S \subseteq Q$ and $a \in A$.

It is not difficult to verify, by induction on $|x|$, that

$$\Delta^*(Q'_0, x) = \{q' \in Q \mid (q_0, x, q') \in \theta^* \text{ for some } q_0 \in Q_0\}, \tag{3.6}$$

for $x \in A^*$. For the basis case, $|x| = 0$, so the above equality becomes

$$Q'_0 = \{q' \in Q \mid (q_0, \lambda, q') \in \theta^* \text{ for some } q_0 \in Q_0\},$$

which holds by the definition of Q'_0.

Suppose that the equality holds for words of length n, and let y be a word of length $n+1$. We can write $y = xa$, so

$$\begin{aligned}
\Delta^*(Q'_0, y) &= \Delta^*(Q'_0, xa)\\
&= \Delta(\Delta^*(Q'_0, x), a)\\
&= \Delta(\{q' \in Q \mid (q_0, x, q') \in \theta^* \text{ for some } q_0 \in Q_0\}, a)\\
&\quad \text{(by the inductive hypothesis)}\\
&= \{r \in Q \mid (q', a, r) \in \theta^*, \text{ for some } q' \text{ such that}\\
&\quad (q_0, x, q') \in \theta^* \text{ for some } q_0 \in Q_0\}\\
&\quad \text{(by the definition of } \Delta)\\
&= \{r \in Q \mid (q_0, xa, r) \in \theta^* \text{ for some } q_0 \in Q_0\}\\
&\quad \text{(by the definition of } \theta^*)\\
&= \{r \in Q \mid (q_0, y, r) \in \theta^* \text{ for some } q_0 \in Q_0\},
\end{aligned}$$

which concludes our inductive argument.

From this it follows that $L(\mathcal{M}) = L(\mathcal{T})$. By definition, $x \in L(\mathcal{M})$ if and only if $\Delta^*(Q'_0, x) \in F'$. This is equivalent to $\Delta^*(Q'_0, x) \cap F \neq \emptyset$. By Equality (3.6) this is equivalent to the existence of a state $q' \in F'$ such that $(q_0, x, q') \in \theta^*$ for some $q_0 \in Q_0$, and this is equivalent to $x \in L(\mathcal{T})$. ∎

Corollary 3.3.7 *The class of languages that are accepted by transition systems is the class $\mathcal{R}$ of regular languages.*

Proof. The statement follows immediately from Theorem 3.3.6. ∎

Next, we discuss an algorithm for computing a dfa that accepts the same language as a transition system.

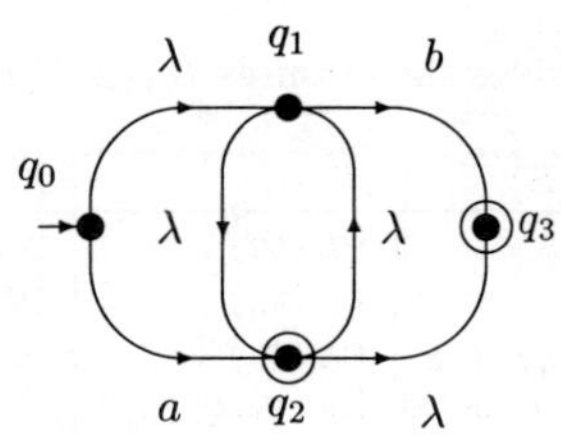

Figure 3.15: Graph of Transition System

Definition 3.3.8 Let $\mathcal{T} = (A, Q, \theta, Q_0, F)$ be a transition system. The λ-*closure* is the mapping $K_{\mathcal{T}} : \mathcal{P}(Q) \longrightarrow \mathcal{P}(Q)$ given by

$$K_{\mathcal{T}}(S) = \{q \in Q \mid (s, \lambda, q) \in \theta^* \text{ for some } s \in S\}.$$

□

The set $K_{\mathcal{T}}(S)$ comprises the states in S plus all the states that can be reached from a state in S using a series of λ-transitions.

Theorem 3.3.9 *Let $\mathcal{T} = (A, Q, \theta, Q_0, F)$ be a transition system. The λ-closure of $\mathcal{T}$ has the following properties.*

(i) $S \subseteq K_{\mathcal{T}}(S)$;

(ii) $S \subseteq S'$ *implies* $K_{\mathcal{T}}(S) \subseteq K_{\mathcal{T}}(S')$;

(iii) $K_{\mathcal{T}}(K_{\mathcal{T}}(S)) = K_{\mathcal{T}}(S)$,

for every $S, S' \in \mathcal{P}(Q)$.

Proof. Since $(s, \lambda, s) \in \theta^*$ it is immediate that $S \subseteq K_{\mathcal{T}}(S)$ for every $S \in \mathcal{P}(Q)$. The second part of the theorem is a direct consequence of the definition of $K_{\mathcal{T}}$. Note that Parts (i) and (ii) imply $K_{\mathcal{T}}(S) \subseteq K_{\mathcal{T}}(K_{\mathcal{T}}(S))$. Let $q \in K_{\mathcal{T}}(K_{\mathcal{T}}(S))$. There is a state $s \in S$ and a state $r \in K_{\mathcal{T}}(S)$ such that $(s, \lambda, r) \in \theta^*$ and $(r, \lambda, q) \in \theta^*$. By the definition of θ^* we obtain $(s, \lambda, q) \in \theta^*$, so $q \in K_{\mathcal{T}}(S)$. This implies $K_{\mathcal{T}}(K_{\mathcal{T}}(S)) \subseteq K_{\mathcal{T}}(S)$, which gives the last part of the theorem. ∎

Definition 3.3.10 Let $\mathcal{T} = (A, Q, \theta, Q_0, F)$ be a transition system. A $K_{\mathcal{T}}$-closed subset of Q is a set S such that $S \subseteq Q$ and $K_{\mathcal{T}}(S) = S$. □

Example 3.3.11 Consider the transition system

$$\mathcal{T} = (\{a, b\}, \{q_0, q_1, q_2, q_3\}, \theta, \{q_0\}, \{q_2, q_3\})$$

whose graph is shown in Figure 3.15.

The following table gives the closures $K_{\mathcal{T}}(S)$ for every $S \subseteq Q = \{q_0, q_1, q_2, q_3\}$.

S	$K_{\mathcal{T}}(S)$	S	$K_{\mathcal{T}}(S)$
$\emptyset$	$\emptyset$	$\{q_1, q_2\}$	$\{q_1, q_2, q_3\}$
$\{q_0\}$	Q	$\{q_1, q_3\}$	$\{q_1, q_2, q_3\}$
$\{q_1\}$	$\{q_1, q_2, q_3\}$	$\{q_2, q_3\}$	$\{q_1, q_2, q_3\}$
$\{q_2\}$	$\{q_1, q_2, q_3\}$	$\{q_0, q_1, q_2\}$	Q
$\{q_3\}$	$\{q_3\}$	$\{q_0, q_1, q_3\}$	Q
$\{q_0, q_1\}$	Q	$\{q_0, q_2, q_3\}$	Q
$\{q_0, q_2\}$	Q	$\{q_1, q_2, q_3\}$	$\{q_1, q_2, q_3\}$
$\{q_0, q_3\}$	Q	$\{q_0, q_1, q_2, q_3\}$	Q

The closed subsets of Q are $\emptyset$, $\{q_3\}$, $\{q_1, q_2, q_3\}$, and Q itself. □

Theorem 3.3.12 *Let $\mathcal{T} = (A, Q, \theta, Q_0, F)$ be a transition system and let $\mathcal{M} = (A, \mathcal{P}(Q), \Delta, Q_0', F')$ be the dfa constructed in Theorem 3.3.6. The set $\Delta(S, a)$ is a $K_{\mathcal{T}}$-closed set of states for every subset S of Q and $a \in A$.*

Proof. To prove the theorem it suffices to show that $K_{\mathcal{T}}(\Delta(S, a)) \subseteq \Delta(S, a)$. Let $p \in K_{\mathcal{T}}(\Delta(S, a))$. There is $p_1 \in \Delta(S, a)$ such that $(p_1, \lambda, p) \in \theta^*$. The definition of $\Delta(S, a)$ implies the existence of $q \in S$ such that $(q, a, p_1) \in \theta^*$. Thus, $(q, a, p) \in \theta^*$, so $p \in \Delta(q, a)$. ∎

Corollary 3.3.13 *Let $\mathcal{T} = (A, Q, \theta, Q_0, F)$ be a transition system, and let $\mathcal{M} = (A, \mathcal{P}(Q), \Delta, Q_0', F')$ be the dfa constructed in Theorem 3.3.6. The accessible states of the dfa $\mathcal{M}$ are $K_{\mathcal{T}}$-closed subsets of Q.*

Proof. The initial state Q_0' of $\mathcal{M}$ is obviously closed. If Q' is an accessible state of $\mathcal{M}$, then $Q' = \Delta(S, a)$ for some $S \subseteq Q$. Theorem 3.3.12 implies that Q' is closed. ∎

Theorem 3.3.14 *Let $\mathcal{T} = (A, Q, \theta, Q_0, F)$ be a transition system, and let $\mathcal{M} = (A, \mathcal{P}(Q), \Delta, Q_0', F')$ be the dfa constructed in Theorem 3.3.6. Then, $\Delta(S, a) = K_{\mathcal{T}}(\{q \in Q \mid (s, a, q) \in \theta$ for some $s \in S\})$, where S is an accessible state of $\mathcal{M}$.*

Proof. Let $s \in S$. Note that if $(s, a, q) \in \theta$ and $(q, \lambda, q_1) \in \theta^*$, then by the definition of θ^* we have $(s, a, q_1) \in \theta^*$. Therefore, $K_{\mathcal{T}}(\{q \in Q \mid (s, a, q) \in \theta\} \subseteq \Delta(S, a)$.

To prove the converse inclusion, $\Delta(S, a) \subseteq K_{\mathcal{T}}(\{q \in Q \mid (s, a, q) \in \theta\}$, let $(s, a, q_1) \in \theta^*$. Then, there is a path in $G(\mathcal{T})$ that begins with s and ends with q_1 such that the concatenated labels of the directed edges of this path form the word a. This implies the existence of the states $p, p' \in Q$ such that $(s, \lambda, p) \in \theta^*$, $(p, a, p_1) \in \theta$, and $(p_1, \lambda, q_1) \in \theta^*$. Since S is $K_{\mathcal{T}}$-closed it follows that $p \in S$ and this gives the desired conclusion. ∎

Informally, the automaton's actions may be described by saying that each time an input is consumed, the resultant state takes both that input and then all possible subsequent λ-transitions into account.

By combining Algorithm 3.2.16 with Theorem 3.3.14, it is possible to formulate an algorithm for constructing the dfa that accepts the same language as a transition system.

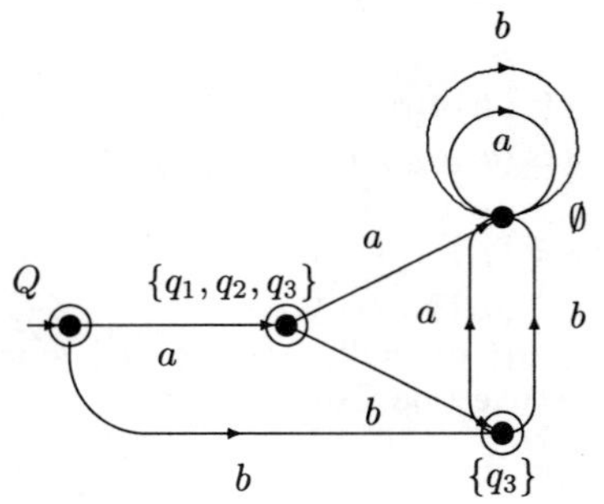

Figure 3.16: Graph of Deterministic Finite Automaton

Algorithm 3.3.15 (Construction of a dfa Corresponding to a ts)
Input: A transition system $\mathcal{T} = (A, Q, \theta, Q_0, F)$.
Output: An accessible dfa $\mathcal{M}_1$ such that $L(\mathcal{M}_1) = L(\mathcal{T})$.
Method: Compute the increasing sequence of collections of subsets of Q, $\mathcal{Q}_0, \ldots, \mathcal{Q}_i, \ldots$, where

$$\begin{aligned} \mathcal{Q}_0 &= \{Q'_0\} \\ \mathcal{Q}_{i+1} &= \mathcal{Q}_i \cup \{U \in \mathcal{P}(Q) \mid U = \Delta(S, a) \text{ for some } S \in \mathcal{Q}_i \text{ and } a \in A\}. \end{aligned}$$

By Theorem 3.3.14, the computation of $U = \Delta(S, a)$ can be done by computing first the set $W = \{q \in Q \mid (s, a, q) \in \theta \text{ for some } s \in S\}$ and then $U = K_{\mathcal{T}}(W)$. Stop when $\mathcal{Q}_{i+1} = \mathcal{Q}_i$. The set $\mathcal{Q}_i$ is the set of accessible states of $\mathcal{M}$, the dfa constructed in Theorem 3.3.6. Ouput $\mathcal{M}' = \mathsf{ACC}(\mathcal{M})$, the accessible component of $\mathcal{M}$.

Proof of Correctness: The correctness of the algorithm follows from the correctness of Algorithm 3.2.16 and from Theorem 3.3.14. ∎

Example 3.3.16 The dfa that accepts the language accepted by the ts $\mathcal{T}$ defined in Example 3.3.11 is given in Figure 3.16.

Note that $\mathcal{Q}_0 = \{Q'_0\} = K_{\mathcal{T}}(\{q_0\}) = \{Q\}$. Next, we have

$$\begin{aligned} \{q \mid (s, a, q) \in \theta \text{ for some } s \in Q\} &= \{q_2\} \\ \{q \mid (s, b, q) \in \theta \text{ for some } s \in Q\} &= \{q_3\} \end{aligned}$$

Since

$$K_{\mathcal{T}}(\{q_2\}) = \{q_1, q_2, q_3\} \text{ and } K_{\mathcal{T}}(\{q_3\}) = \{q_3\}$$

we have

$$\Delta(Q, a) = \{q_1, q_2, q_3\} \text{ and } \Delta(Q, b) = \{q_3\},$$

and $\mathcal{Q}_1 = \{Q, \{q_1, q_2, q_3\}, \{q_3\}\}$.

Next,

$$\{q \mid (s, a, q) \in \theta \text{ for some } s \in \{q_1, q_2, q_3\}\} = \emptyset$$
$$\{q \mid (s, b, q) \in \theta \text{ for some } s \in \{q_1, q_2, q_3\}\} = \{q_3\}$$

and

$$\{q \mid (s, a, q) \in \theta \text{ for some } s \in \{q_3\}\} = \emptyset$$
$$\{q \mid (s, b, q) \in \theta \text{ for some } s \in \{q_3\}\} = \emptyset.$$

These equalities imply $\Delta(\{q_1, q_2, q_3\}, a) = \emptyset$, $\Delta(\{q_1, q_2, q_3\}, b) = \{q_3\}$, and $\Delta(\{q_3\}, a) = \Delta(\{q_3\}, b) = \emptyset$. The collection $\mathcal{Q}_2$ is

$$\mathcal{Q}_1 = \{Q, \{q_1, q_2, q_3\}, \{q_3\}, \emptyset\}.$$

Clearly, $\Delta(\emptyset, a) = \Delta(\emptyset, b) = \emptyset$. □

3.4 Closure Properties

In this section we discuss the behavior of the class of regular languages with respect to several operations previously defined. We prove that this class is the smallest class of languages that contains all finite languages and is closed with respect to union, product, and Kleene closure. This is an important result, as it permits us to develop a notation for regular languages.

The class of regular languages is closed with respect to the complement operations as shown by the next theorem.

Theorem 3.4.1 *Let A be an alphabet. If $L \subseteq A^*$ is a regular language, then its complement $\bar{L} = A^* - L$ is also a regular language.*

Proof. Suppose that $\mathcal{M} = (A, Q, \delta, q_0, F)$ is an automaton such that $L = L(\mathcal{M})$. Define the automaton $\mathcal{M}' = (A, Q, \delta, q_0, Q - F)$; thus, only the set of final states of $\mathcal{M}'$ differs from the corresponding set for $\mathcal{M}$. We have $x \in L(\mathcal{M}')$ if and only if $\delta^*(q_0, x) \in Q - F$, or, equivalently, if and only if $\delta^*(q_0, x) \notin F$. Therefore $L(\mathcal{M}') = A^* - L$, which proves that $A^* - L$ is regular. ∎

Transition systems are very convenient for proving closure properties of the class $\mathcal{R}$. To make use of these devices we use the following technical result.

Lemma 3.4.2 *For every nonempty regular language $L \subseteq A^*$ there exists a transition system that accepts L and has a single initial state q_0 and a single final state q_f.*

Proof. Since L is a nonempty regular language, there exists a transition system $\mathcal{T} = (A, Q, \theta, Q_0, F)$ such that $L(\mathcal{T}) = L$ and $F \neq \emptyset$. Define the transition system $\mathcal{T}' = (A, Q \cup \{q_0, q_f\}, \theta', \{q_0\}, \{q_f\})$, where $q_0, q_f \notin Q$. The relation θ' is given by:

$$\theta' = \theta \cup \{(q_0, \lambda, q) \mid q \in Q_0\} \cup \{(q, \lambda, q_f) \mid q \in F\}.$$

The graph of $\mathcal{T}'$ is represented in Figure 3.17. Clearly, $(q, x, q') \in \theta^*$ for some $q \in Q_0$ and $q' \in F$ if and only if $(q_0, \lambda x \lambda, q_f) = (q_0, x, q_f) \in \theta'^*$. Therefore, $L(\mathcal{T}) = L(\mathcal{T}')$. ∎

Theorem 3.4.3 *If L is a regular language, then L^R is also regular.*

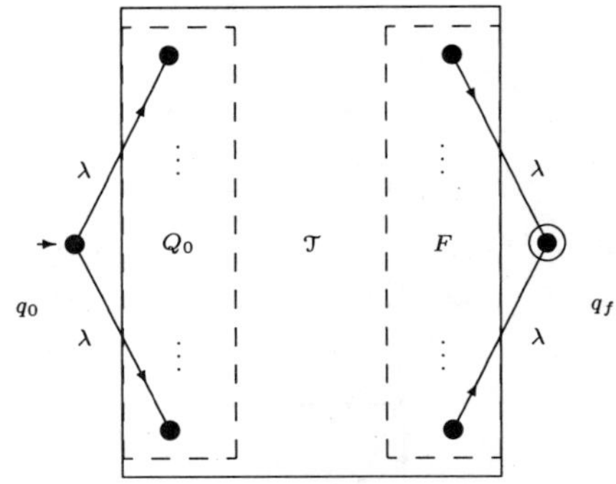

Figure 3.17: Graph of the Transition System $\mathcal{T}'$

Proof. Let A be an alphabet such that $L \subseteq A^*$ and let $\mathcal{T} = (A, Q, \theta, \{q_0\}, \{q_f\})$ be a transition system such that $L = L(\mathcal{T})$.

Define a new transition system $\mathcal{T}' = (A, Q, \theta', \{q_f\}, \{q_0\})$, where

$$\theta' = \{(q_2, w, q_1) \mid (q_1, w, q_2) \in \theta\}.$$

We have $(q, x^R, q') \in \theta'^*$ if and only if $(q', x, q) \in \theta^*$. Therefore, $x \in L(\mathcal{T})$ if and only if $x^R \in L(\mathcal{T}')$, so $L(\mathcal{T}') = (L(\mathcal{T}))^R$. ∎

Next, we show that the class of regular languages is closed under union.

Theorem 3.4.4 *If L_0, L_1 are regular languages, then $L_0 \cup L_1$ is regular.*

Proof. Without loss of generality, assume that both L_0 and L_1 are regular languages over the same alphabet A. Suppose that $L_i = L(\mathcal{T}_i)$, where $\mathcal{T}_i$, $i = 0, 1$, are two transition systems. By Lemma 3.4.2 we can assume that each $\mathcal{T}_i$ has a single initial and a single final state, $\mathcal{T}_i = (A, Q_i, \theta_i, \{q_{0i}\}, \{q_{fi}\})$ for $i = 0, 1$; also, assume that $Q_0 \cap Q_1 = \emptyset$.

Define a new transition system $\mathcal{T}' = (A, Q', \theta', \{q_0\}, \{q_f\})$ (see Figure 3.18) given by $Q' = Q_0 \cup Q_1 \cup \{q_0, q_f\}$, and

$$\theta = \theta_0 \cup \theta_1 \cup \{(q_0, \lambda, q_{00}), (q_0, \lambda, q_{01}), (q_{f0}, \lambda, q_f), (q_{f1}, \lambda, q_f)\}.$$

In other words, $\mathcal{T}'$ is obtained from $\mathcal{T}_0$ and $\mathcal{T}_1$ by adding a new initial state q_0, a new final state q_f, and null transitions from q_0 to q_{00} and q_{01}, and from q_{f0} and q_{f1} to q_f. Since $Q_0 \cap Q_1 = \emptyset$, a path ϖ in $\mathcal{T}$ that joins q_0 to q_f exists in $\mathcal{T}$ if and only if that path passes through q_{00} and q_{f0}, or through q_{01} and q_{f1}. If x is the label of the path ϖ, then x belongs to $L(\mathcal{T}_0)$ or $L(\mathcal{T}_1)$, respectively. This amounts to $L(\mathcal{T}) = L(\mathcal{T}_0) \cup L(\mathcal{T}_1) = L_0 \cup L_1$, which implies that $L_0 \cup L_1$ is regular. ∎

Corollary 3.4.5 *The class of regular languages is closed under intersection. In other words, if L_0, L_1 are regular languages, then $L_0 \cap L_1$ is regular.*

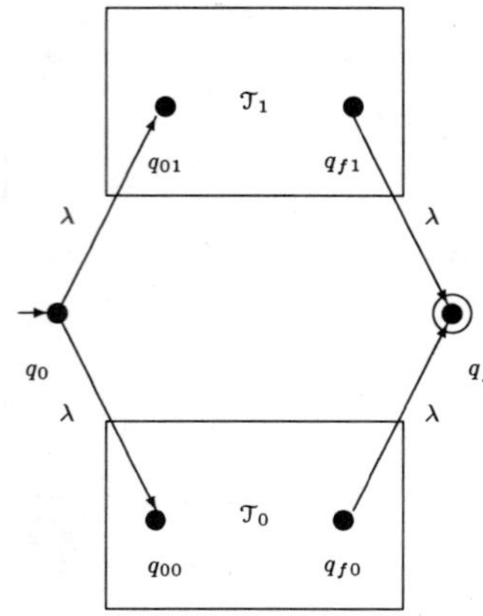

Figure 3.18: Transition System Accepting $L_0 \cup L_1$

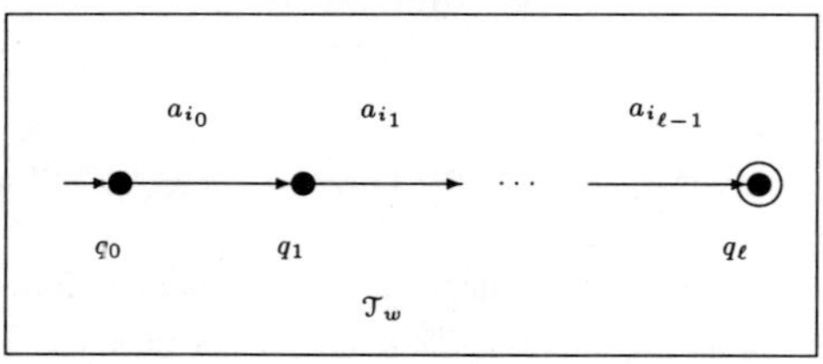

Figure 3.19: The Transition System $\mathcal{T}_w$

Proof. This statement follows immediately by Theorems 3.4.4, 3.4.1 and by De Morgan's law. Specifically, $L_0 \cap L_1 = \overline{\overline{L_0} \cup \overline{L_1}}$, and each subexpression of the right hand side is regular if L_0 and L_1 are. ∎

Corollary 3.4.6 *Every finite language over an alphabet A is regular.*

Proof. The empty language is clearly regular. Then, by Theorem 3.4.4, it suffices to show that one-word languages are regular. It is easy to see that if $L = \{w\}$, where $w = a_{i_0} \ldots a_{i_{\ell-1}}$, then L is accepted by the transition system $\mathcal{T}_w$ given in Figure 3.19, which implies the regularity of L. ∎

Theorem 3.4.7 *If L_0, L_1 are regular languages, then L_0L_1 is regular.*

Proof. Assume that both L_0 and L_1 are regular languages over the same alphabet A such that $L_i = L(\mathcal{T}_i)$, where $\mathcal{T}_i$, $i = 0, 1$, are two transition systems. We assume that each $\mathcal{T}_i$ has a single initial and a single final state, $\mathcal{T}_i = (A, Q_i, \theta_i, \{q_{0i}\}, \{q_{fi}\})$ for $i = 0, 1$; also, assume that $Q_0 \cap Q_1 = \emptyset$. Define

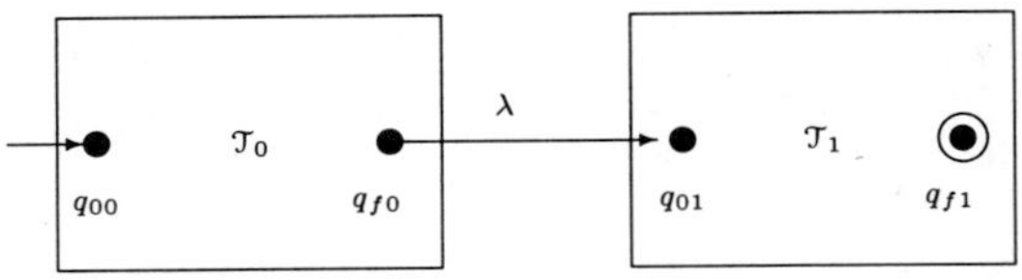

Figure 3.20: Transition System Accepting L_0L_1

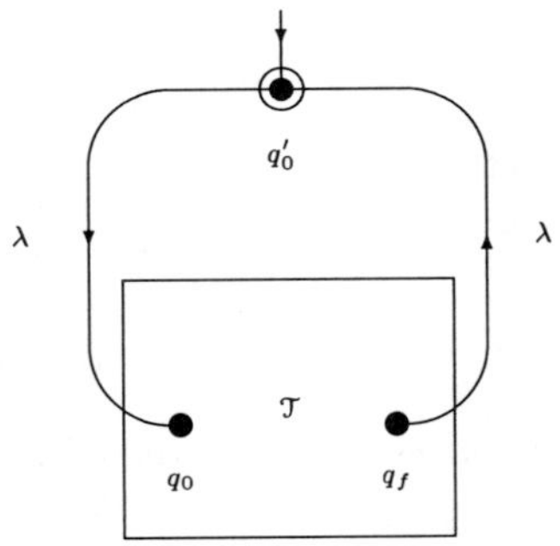

Figure 3.21: Transition System that Accepts L_1^*

the transition system $\mathcal{T} = (A, Q_0 \cup Q_1, \theta, \{q_{00}\}, \{q_{f1}\})$, where $\theta = \theta_0 \cup \theta_1 \cup \{(q_{f0}, \lambda, q_{01})\}$ (see Figure 3.20).

Since $Q_0 \cap Q_1 = \emptyset$, to reach the state q_{f1} from the initial state q_{00} reading the symbols of the word x, the transition system $\mathcal{T}$ must pass through the states q_{f0} and q_{01} (via the null transition $(q_{f0}, \lambda, q_{01})$). This happens if and only if $x = uv$, where $(q_{00}, u, q_{f0}) \in \theta_0^*$ and $(q_{01}, v, q_{f1}) \in \theta_1^*$, so $L(\mathcal{T}) = L(\mathcal{T}_0)L(\mathcal{T}_1) = L_0L_1$. Hence, L_0L_1 is a regular language. ∎

Theorem 3.4.8 *If L is a regular language, then L^* is regular.*

Proof. Let $\mathcal{T} = (A, Q, \theta, \{q_0\}, \{q_f\})$ be a transition system such that $L = L(\mathcal{T})$. Define the transition system $\mathcal{T}' = (A, Q \cup \{q_0'\}, \theta', \{q_0'\}, \{q_0'\})$, where $\theta' = \theta \cup \{(q_f, \lambda, q_0'), (q_0', \lambda, q_0)\}$ and q_0' is a new state (see Figure 3.21).

We have $\lambda \in L(\mathcal{T}')$ because q_0' is both the initial and the final state of $\mathcal{T}'$. Further, if $w \in L(\mathcal{T})$, we have $(q_0, w, q_f) \in \theta^*$. Since both triples (q_0', λ, q_0) and (q_f, λ, q_0') belong to θ, we obtain $(q_0', w^k, q_0') \in \theta^*$ for every $k \in \mathbb{N}$, $k \geq 1$. Therefore, $L^k \subseteq L(\mathcal{T}')$ for $k \in \mathbb{N}$, so $L^* \subseteq L(\mathcal{T}')$.

Conversely, if $u \in L(\mathcal{T}')$, the transition system $\mathcal{T}'$ starts in q_0' and finishes in q_0' while reading the symbols of u. Let m be the number of times the transition system $\mathcal{T}'$ leaves the state q_0' while processing the word u.

If $m = 0$, then $u = \lambda$. Otherwise, $m \geq 1$ and $\mathcal{T}'$ passes through the sequence of states: $q_0, \ldots, q_f, q_0', q_0, \ldots, q_f, q_0', \ldots, q_f$, where q_0' occurs m times. Here "passes through" means "enters and then leaves." This implies that we can write $u = u_0 \cdots u_{m+1}$, where $(q_0, u_i, q_f) \in \theta^*$ for $0 \leq i \leq m+1$. Thus, $w \in L^{m+1}$, so $L(\mathcal{T}') \subseteq L^*$. Hence, $L(\mathcal{T}') = L^*$. ∎

Theorem 3.4.9 *Let L be a regular language over the alphabet A. For every language K, both the right and the left quotients LK^{-1} and $K^{-1}L$ are regular.*

Proof. We first deal with the left quotient. Let $\mathcal{T} = (A, Q, \theta, Q_0, F)$ be a transition system such that $L = L(\mathcal{T})$. Let $Q_K = \{q \in Q \mid (q_0, x, q) \in \theta^*$ for some $q_0 \in Q_0$ and $x \in K\}$ and let $\mathcal{T}_K$ be the transition system $\mathcal{T}_K = (A, Q, \theta, Q_K, F)$. The following statements are easily seen to be equivalent:

1. $y \in K^{-1}L$;
2. $xy \in L$ for some $x \in K$;
3. $(q_0, xy, q') \in \theta^*$ for some $q_0 \in Q_0$ and $q' \in F$;
4. there is $q \in Q_K$ such that $(q_0, x, q) \in \theta^*$ and $(q, y, q') \in \theta^*$ for some $q_0 \in Q_0$ and $q' \in F$;
5. $y \in L(\mathcal{T}_K)$.

From these equivalences it follows that $K^{-1}L = L(\mathcal{T}_K)$, and thus $K^{-1}L$ is regular.

To make the argument for the right quotient, let P_K be the set $P_K = \{q \in Q \mid (q, z, q') \in \theta^*$ for some $q' \in F$ and $z \in K\}$. Define the transition system $\mathcal{T}^K$ as $\mathcal{T}^K = (A, Q, \theta, Q_0, P_K)$. We have the following equivalent statements:

1. $y \in L(\mathcal{T}^K)$;
2. $(q_0, y, q) \in \theta^*$ for some $q_0 \in Q_0$ and some $q \in P_K$;
3. $(q_0, y, q) \in \theta^*$ and $(q, z, q') \in \theta^*$ for some $q_0 \in Q_0$ and some $q' \in F$;
4. $(q_0, yz, q') \in \theta^*$ for some $q_0 \in Q_0$ and some $q' \in F$ and $z \in K$;
5. $yz \in L$ for some $z \in K$;
6. $y \in LK^{-1}$.

Therefore, $LK^{-1} = L(\mathcal{T}^K)$. This proves that the language LK^{-1} is regular. Note that this property of closure under quotients does not depend on the regularity of K. ∎

Corollary 3.4.10 *If $L \subseteq A^*$ is a regular language, then there exists a finite number of distinct left (right) quotients of the form $K^{-1}L$ (of the form LK^{-1}), where $K \subseteq A^*$.*

Proof. Suppose that $L = L(\mathcal{T})$, where $\mathcal{T} = (A, Q, \theta, Q_0, F)$. Using the notations introduced in the proof of Theorem 3.4.9, note that if K, H are two languages such that $Q_K = Q_H$, then $K^{-1}L = H^{-1}L$. In other words, there are no more distinct left quotients than subsets of Q, which implies that the number of distinct left quotients of L is finite. ∎

An important special case of Corollary 3.4.10 is given next.

Corollary 3.4.11 *If $L \subseteq A^*$ is a regular language, then there exists a finite number of distinct left (right) derivatives of L.*

Proof. The statement follows immediately from Corollary 3.4.10 by considering the quotients of L and singleton languages $K = \{x\}$ for $x \in A^*$. ∎

Corollary 3.4.12 *If L is a regular language, then* $\mathsf{PREF}(L)$, $\mathsf{SUFF}(L)$, *and* $\mathsf{INFIX}(L)$ *are all regular languages.*

Proof. The statement follows from Example 2.3.15 and Theorem 3.4.9. ∎

Theorem 3.4.13 *The language $L(\mathcal{M})$ accepted by a dfa $\mathcal{M}$ can be constructed starting from finite languages by using union, product, and Kleene closure.*

Proof. Let $\mathcal{M} = (A, \{q_0, \ldots, q_{n-1}\}, \delta, q_0, F)$ be a dfa that has n states. Define the language R^k_{ij} to be those words $x \in A^*$ that take $\mathcal{M}$ from state q_i to state q_j without passing through any state q_ℓ with $\ell \geq k$. Since $\mathcal{M}$ does not pass through the starting and the ending states q_i and q_j, i, j may exceed k. Thus, R^k_{ij} comprises those words $x \in A^*$ such that $\delta^*(q_i, x) = q_j$, and for every proper prefix u of x, the automaton is in an intermediate state $\delta^*(q_i, u) \in \{q_0, \ldots, q_{k-1}\}$. For $k = 0$, no intermediate state is possible. Therefore, R^0_{ij} is the finite language

$$R^0_{ij} = \begin{cases} \{a \in A \mid \delta(q_i, a) = q_j\} & \text{if } i \neq j, \\ \{\lambda\} \cup \{a \in A \mid \delta(q_i, a) = q_i\} & \text{if } i = j. \end{cases}$$

To reach the state q_j starting from the state q_i, allowing only $q_0, \ldots, q_{k-1}$ as intermediate states presents two choices: either the automaton avoids q_{k-1} entirely (which corresponds to a word in R^{k-1}_{ij}), or the automaton goes from q_i to the first use of q_{k-1} (along a string in R^{k-1}_{ik-1}); it then may revisit q_{k-1} zero or more times (each time along a string in R^{k-1}_{k-1k-1}), and finally, it goes from the last use of q_{k-1} to q_j (along a string in R^{k-1}_{k-1j}). From this we see that

$$R^k_{ij} = R^{k-1}_{ij} \cup R^{k-1}_{ik-1}(R^{k-1}_{k-1k-1})^* R^{k-1}_{k-1j}. \tag{3.7}$$

This can be regarded as a recursive definition of the set R^k_{ij}. If the set of final states is $F = \{q_{i_0}, \ldots, q_{i_{m-1}}\}$, then the language accepted by $\mathcal{M}$ is

$$L(\mathcal{M}) = R^n_{0i_0} \cup \cdots \cup R^n_{0i_{m-1}},$$

since every state is allowed as an intermediate state. Thus, $L(\mathcal{M})$ can be indeed constructed starting from the finite languages R^0_{ij}, using union, product and Kleene closure. ∎

Theorem 3.4.14 (Kleene's Theorem) *The class $\mathcal{R}$ of regular languages is the least class of languages that contains the class of finite languages and is closed with respect to union, product and Kleene closure.*

Proof. Corollary 3.4.6 and Theorems 3.4.4, 3.4.7, and 3.4.8 imply that the class $\mathcal{R}$ contains the class of finite languages and is closed with respect to union, product, and Kleene closure, respectively.

Let $\mathcal{R}'$ be an arbitrary class of languages that contains the class of finite languages and is closed with respect to union, product and Kleene closure. If $L \in \mathcal{R}$, Theorem 3.4.13 implies that $L \in \mathcal{R}'$, so $\mathcal{R} \subseteq \mathcal{R}'$. ∎

Example 3.4.15 Using closure properties, it is easy to verify that if $\rho \subseteq A \times A$, then the language $L_\rho \subseteq A^*$ of Example 3.2.23 is regular. Indeed, we can write

$$A^* - L_\rho = \bigcup \{A^* a a' A^* \mid (a, a') \in (A \times A) - \rho\}.$$

Note that each language of the form $A^*aa'A^*$ is regular by Corollary 3.4.6, Theorems 3.4.8, and 3.4.7. Furthermore, since A is a finite set, the right member of the equality is the union of a finite number of regular languages. Therefore, by Theorem 3.4.4, $A^* - L_\rho$ is regular. Theorem 3.4.1 implies that L_ρ is regular. □

Next, we prove a representation result for regular languages that highlights the special role played by languages of the form L_ρ. This theorem is the first of several such results.

Theorem 3.4.16 (Representation of Regular Languages) *For every regular λ-free language L over an alphabet A there is an alphabet C, a relation $\rho \subseteq C \times C$ and two subsets C_0, C_1 of C such that*

$$L = h(L_\rho \cap C_0C^* \cap C^*C_1),$$

where $h : C^* \longrightarrow A^*$ is a morphism.

Proof. Suppose that $L = L(\mathcal{M})$, where $\mathcal{M} = (A, Q, \delta, q_0, F)$ is a dfa. Define the alphabet C to be of symbols of the form $\langle q, a, q' \rangle$, where $\delta(q, a) = q'$. Note that C is a finite set and $|C| \leq |Q|^2|A|$.

Let C_0, C_1 be the subsets of C defined by

$$\begin{aligned} C_0 &= \{\langle q_0, a, q \rangle \mid q \in Q\} \\ C_1 &= \{\langle q, a, q_1 \rangle \mid q_1 \in F\}. \end{aligned}$$

If ρ is the relation given by

$$\rho = \{(\langle q, a, q' \rangle, \langle q', a_1, q'' \rangle) \mid a, a_1 \in A, q, q', q'' \in Q\},$$

we claim that

$$L = h(L_\rho \cap C_0C^* \cap C^*C_1),$$

where $h : C^* \longrightarrow A^*$ is given by $h(\langle q, a, q' \rangle) = a$ for every $\langle q, a, q' \rangle \in C$. Indeed, let $x = a_0 \ldots a_{n-1} \in L$, where $n \geq 1$. Consider the sequence of states $q_0, \ldots, q_n$ of the dfa $\mathcal{M}$ such that $\delta(q_i, a_i) = q_{i+1}$ for $0 \leq i \leq n-1$. The definitions of C and ρ imply that

$$w = \langle q_0, a_0, q_1 \rangle \langle q_1, a_1, q_2 \rangle \cdots \langle q_{n-1}, a_{n-1}, q_n \rangle \in L_\rho.$$

It is clear that $w \in C_0C^*$. On the other hand, $q_n \in F$, so $w \in C^*C_1$. Thus, $w \in L_\rho \cap C_0C^* \cap C^*C_1$. Since

$$\begin{aligned} h(w) &= h(\langle q_0, a_0, q_1 \rangle) h(\langle q_1, a_1, q_2 \rangle) \cdots h(\langle q_{n-1}, a_{n-1}, q_n \rangle) \\ &= a_0 a_1 \cdots a_{n-1} = x \end{aligned}$$

it follows that $L \subseteq h(L_\rho \cap C_0C^* \cap C^*C_1)$.

We leave to the reader the straightforward reverse inclusion. ∎

3.5 The Pumping Lemma

The main focus of this section is a powerful tool for proving that certain languages are not regular. Although traditionally named the *Pumping Lemma*, we state it as a theorem to reflect its importance.

Theorem 3.5.1 (Pumping Lemma) *If L is a regular language, then there exists a number $n_0 \in \mathbb{P}$ such that if $x \in L$ and $|x| \geq n_0$, then x can be written as $x = uvw$ such that $v \neq \lambda$, $|uv| \leq n_0$, and $uv^n w \in L$ for every $n \in \mathbb{N}$.*

Proof. Since L is a regular language there exists a deterministic finite automaton $\mathcal{M} = (A, Q, \delta, q_0, F)$ such that $L = L(\mathcal{M})$. Choose $n_0 = |Q|$, and let $x = a_0 \ldots a_{\ell-1}$ be a word of length ℓ, where $\ell \geq n_0$.

Consider the sequence of states $(q_0, q_1, \ldots, q_\ell)$, where $q_i = \delta(q_{i-1}, a_{i-1})$ for $1 \leq i \leq \ell$. This sequence is of length $\ell + 1 > n_0$, so at least two of these states must coincide. Pick k to be the position of the first repeated state and let q_j be its first occurence.

Let $u = a_0 a_1 \cdots a_{j-1}$, $v = a_j \cdots a_{k-1}$, and $w = a_k \cdots a_{\ell-1}$. Then, $q_j = \delta^*(q_0, u) = \delta^*(q_0, uv) = q_k$. Consequently, $\delta^*(q_j, v) = q_k = q_j$. Since $\delta^*(q_k, w) = q_\ell \in F$, we have $\delta^*(q_j, w) = q_\ell \in F$, so $\delta^*(q_0, uw) = q_\ell \in F$, and $uw \in L$.

By a simple induction, we can prove that $\delta^*(q_j, v^n) = q_j$ for all $n \in \mathbb{N}$, so $\delta^*(q_0, uv^n w) = \delta^*(q_j, v^n w) = \delta^*(q_j, w) = q_\ell \in F$. Hence, $uv^n w \in L$ for all $n \in \mathbb{N}$.

By the selection of k, $0 \leq j < k \leq n_0$, which implies $|v| = k - j > 0$, that is $v \neq \lambda$, and also that $|uv| \leq n_0$. ∎

We refer to a number n_0 whose existence is established by the Pumping Lemma as a *pumping threshold* for the language L.

One of most interesting areas of study of twentieth century mathematics is the area of "decidability". In this section, we approach decidability informally. Specifically, we say that a question is decidable when there is an effective procedure that always accurately answers the question, either yes or no. The notion of "effective procedure" may be made explicit using computer programs with unlimited resources or other computing models.

The results we prove are formal, but we do not show how to go from them to a formal proof of decidability. This would entail showing the program that decided the question. For the questions in this section, these programs could be written quite easily in almost any programming language, and we trust that the reader could do so without great difficulty.

Note that if A is an alphabet, $L \subseteq A^*$ is a regular language, and $x \in A^*$ is a word, then it is decidable whether $x \in L$. Indeed, in order to decide this problem it suffices to write the word x on the input tape of a dfa $\mathcal{M}$ that accepts L and determine if the state q of $\mathcal{M}$ is a final state. If this is the case, $x \in L$; otherwise $x \notin L$.

The next two decidability results are a direct consequence of the Pumping Lemma.

Corollary 3.5.2 *It is decidable whether a regular language is empty.*

Proof. Let L be a regular language, and let n_0 be a pumping threshold for L. We claim that if $L \neq \emptyset$, then there is a word z in L such that $|z| < n_0$. Clearly, if such a word exists in L, then $L \neq \emptyset$. Suppose that $L \neq \emptyset$. Then, let x be a word in L having minimal length. If $|x| \geq n_0$, then, by the Pumping Lemma, we can write $x = uvw$ with $|v| > 0$ and $uv^n w \in L$ for every $n \in \mathbb{N}$. Taking $n = 0$, we obtain that $uw \in L$. The inequality $|uw| < |x|$, contradicts the minimality of x. Therefore, L must contain a word shorter than n_0.

The previous argument shows that in order to decide whether a regular language L is empty it is sufficient to test whether any word $x \in A^*$ with $|x| < n_0$ belongs to L. This implies the decidability result. ∎

Corollary 3.5.3 *It is decidable whether a regular language is infinite.*

Proof. Let L be a regular language. We prove that L is infinite if and only if it contains a word x such that $n_0 \leq |x| < 2n_0$, where n_0 a pumping threshold for L.

Suppose that the language L is infinite. Then, there exists a word $y \in L$ such that $|y| \geq 2n_0$. Suppose that y is one of the shortest such words. By the Pumping Lemma we can write $y = uvw$ with $v \neq \lambda$, $|v| \leq n_0$ and $uv^n w \in L$ for every $n \in \mathbb{N}$. Therefore, taking $n = 0$, we obtain $y' = uw \in L$. Note that $n_0 \leq |y'| = |y| - |v| < |y|$. Since y was supposed to be a shortest word in L such that $|y| \geq 2n_0$ we obtain $n_0 \leq |y'| < 2n_0$. Conversely, if L contains a word y with $n_0 \leq |y| < 2n_0$ it is obvious, by the Pumping Lemma, that L is infinite. Therefore, in order to determine if L is infinite it is sufficient to examine the finite set $L_f = \{x \in L \mid n_0 \leq |x| < 2n_0\}$. L is infinite if and only if $L_f \neq \emptyset$. ∎

Example 3.5.4 The language $L = \{a^m b^m \mid m \in \mathbb{N}\}$ is not regular. To justify this claim, suppose that L is regular, and let n_0 be a pumping threshold for L. Choose $m \in \mathbb{N}$ such that $m \geq n_0$. Then, $x = a^m b^m$ can be factored as $x = uvw$ such that $1 \leq |uv| \leq n_0$ and $uv^n w \in L$ for every $n \in \mathbb{N}$. This implies that every symbol of v is equal to a, since uv is a prefix of a^m. So, $u = a^k$, $v = a^\ell$, and $w = a^h b^m$, where $k + \ell + h = m$, and $\ell \geq 1$. By "pumping" v we obtain $uv^2 w = a^k a^{2\ell} a^h b^m = a^{m+\ell} b^m \in L$, which contradicts the definition of L. □

Example 3.5.5 The language $L = \{a^p \mid p \text{ is prime }\}$ is not regular. Suppose that L were regular and that n_0 is a pumping threshold for L. If $x \in L$ and $|x| \geq n_0$, then x can be written as $x = uvw$ such that $v \neq \lambda$, $|uv| \leq n_0$, and $uv^n w \in L$ for every $n \in \mathbb{N}$. Let $k = |v| \geq 1$. We have $p = h + k$ such that $h + nk$ is prime for every value of $n \in \mathbb{N}$. If $h = 0$ this is a clear contradiction. If $h = 1$ choose, for example, $n = 6k + 5$. This would imply $h + nk = 1 + (6k + 5)k = (3k + 1)(2k + 1)$, which is not prime. Otherwise, if $h > 1$, choose $n = h$. This implies $a^{h(1+k)} \in L$, which contradicts the definition of L since $h(1 + k)$ is never a prime. □

Example 3.5.6 The language $L = \{a^p b^q \mid p, q \in \mathbb{N} \text{ and } p \leq q\}$ is not regular. Suppose that L were regular, and let n_0 be a pumping threshold for L. Choose $p > n_0$. Then, if $x = a^p b^q \in L$ with $p \leq q$, x can be factored as $x = uvw$ with $|uv| \leq n_0$ such that $uv^n w \in L$ for every $n \in \mathbb{N}$. By the choice for p, the words u and v consist only of as, so we can write $u = a^k$, $v = a^\ell$ and $w = a^h b^q$, where $k + \ell + h = p$, and $\ell \geq 1$. Thus, $uv^n w = a^{k+n\ell+h} b^q = a^{p+(n-1)\ell} b^q \in L$ for every $n \in \mathbb{N}$. By choosing n such that $p + (n-1)\ell > q$, that is $n > \frac{q-p}{\ell} + 1$ we obtain a word that violates the definition of L, which requires every word to contain more bs than as. □

Example 3.5.7 Consider the language $L = \{a^p b^{2q} a^p \mid p, q \in \mathbb{N}, q \geq 1\}$. We claim that L is not regular. Suppose that L were regular and let $x = a^p b^{2q} a^p \in L$ such that $p \geq n_0$, where n_0 is a pumping threshold for L. Consider the factorization $x = uvw$ whose existence follows from the Pumping Lemma, where

$|uv| \leq n_0$, such that $uv^n w \in L$ for every $n \in \mathbb{N}$. Both u and v consist of a symbols, so any kind of pumping of v alters the balance between the p a symbols located at the beginning of the word and the last p a symbols. Therefore, L is not regular.

The nonregularity of L implies that the language $K = \{xx^R \mid x \in \{a,b\}^*\}$ is not regular. Indeed, note that $K \cap \{a\}^*\{b\}^+\{a\}^* = L$, so the regularity of K would imply the regularity of L. □

Example 3.5.8 The language $L = \{a^p b^q a^p b^q \mid p, q \in \mathbb{P}\}$ is not regular. This can be easily shown using an argument similar to the one used in Example 3.5.7. Hence, since

$$\{xx \mid x \in \{a,b\}^*\} \cap \{a\}^*\{b\}^*\{a\}^*\{b\}^* = L$$

we can conclude that the language $\{xx \mid x \in \{a,b\}^*\}$ is not regular. □

A positive consequence of the Pumping Lemma is a characterization of regular languages over alphabets that contain only one symbol. We need to strengthen the formulation of the Pumping Lemma in order to take advantage of the fact that the alphabet consists of one symbol.

Theorem 3.5.9 *Let $L \subseteq \{a\}^*$ be a regular language over a one-symbol alphabet. There is a number $n_0 \in \mathbb{N}$ such that $L = K \cup L_0 \cup L_1 \cup \cdots \cup L_{m-1}$ for some $m \in \mathbb{N}$, $m \leq n_0$, where K is a finite language, and there exists a word v with $0 < |v| \leq n_0$, such that $L_i = \{a^{k_i} v^n \mid n \in \mathbb{N}\}$ for some $k_i \in \mathbb{N}$, $k_i \leq n_0$ for $0 \leq i \leq m-1$.*

Proof. If L is a finite, then setting $K = L$ and $m = 0$ satisfies the theorem. So, assume that L is not finite.

Suppose that L is a language over the alphabet $\{a\}$ accepted by the dfa $\mathcal{M} = (\{a\}, Q, \delta, q_0, F)$. Without loss of generality, we may assume that $\mathcal{M}$ is accessible. Let $n_0 = |Q_0|$. Then, its graph consists of a path ϖ (possibly empty) joining the initial state q_0 to a cycle of length ℓ, where $\ell \geq 0$ (cf. Example 3.2.14). Let ϖ' be the set of states of ϖ excluding the state situated on the cycle.

Define the language $L_q = \{x \in \{a\}^* \mid \delta^*(q_0, x) = q\}$. Clearly, we have $L = \bigcup\{L_q \mid q \in F\}$. If $q \in \varpi'$, then L_q consists of one word a^{m_q} such that $\delta^*(q_0, a^{m_q}) = q$; therefore, the language

$$K = \bigcup\{L_q \mid q \in \varpi' \text{ and } q \in F\}$$

is finite.

If q_i belongs to the cycle of the graph of $\mathcal{M}$, let $t = a^{k_i}$ be the shortest word such that $\delta^*(q_0, t) = q_i$. Clearly, we have $k_i < n_0$. We claim that

$$L_{q_i} = \{a^{k_i} v^n \mid n \in \mathbb{N}\}, \tag{3.8}$$

where $v = a^\ell$. Note that

$$\delta^*(q_0, a^{k_i} v^n) = \delta^*(q_i, v^n) = \delta^*(q_i, v^{n-1}) = \cdots = \delta^*(q_i, v) = q_i,$$

because q_i is located on the cycle. Thus, $a^{k_i}v^n \in L_{q_i}$ for every $n \in \mathbb{N}$. Conversely, if $x \in L_{q_i}$, we have $\delta^*(q_0, x) = q_i$. The definition of k_i implies that a^{k_i} is a prefix of x and that $\delta^*(q_0, a^{k_i}) = q_i$. If $x = a^{k_i}y$, then $\delta^*(q_i, y) = q_i$. The structure of the graph of $\mathcal{M}$ implies that $y = v^n$ for some $n \in \mathbb{N}$, where $v = a^\ell$. This completes the proof of equality (3.8).

Let $q_{i_0}, q_{i_1}, \ldots, q_{i_{m-1}}$ be those states of the cycle of $\mathcal{M}$ that are in F. Then, clearly, $L(\mathcal{M}) = K \cup \{L_{q_{i_j}} \mid 0 \leq j \leq m-1\}$. ∎

Theorem 3.5.10 *Let S be a set of natural numbers. The language $L_S = \{a^n \mid n \in S\}$ over the alphabet $A = \{a\}$ is regular if and only if S is an ultimately periodic set.*

Proof. The language $L_{n_0,r} = \{a^n \mid n \in \mathsf{PROG}(n_0, r)\}$ is regular for any $\mathsf{PROG}(n_0, r)$ because $L_{n_0,r} = \{a^{n_0}\}\{a^r\}^*$. Therefore, if S is an ultimately periodic set, by Theorem 1.4.21, L_S is the union of a finite number of langauges of the form L_{n_i,r_i}, so L_S is regular.

Conversely, let L_S be a regular language over the alphabet $\{a\}$. If L_S is finite, then S is ultimately periodic. Therefore, assume that L_S is infinite. By Theorem 3.5.9, L can be written as $L = K \cup L_0 \cup L_1 \cup \cdots \cup L_{m-1}$ where $m \in \mathbb{N}$, $m \leq n_0$, K is a finite language, and there exists a word v with $0 < |v| \leq n_0$, such that $L_i = \{a^{k_i}v^n | n \in \mathbb{N}\}$ for some $k_i \in \mathbb{N}$, $k_i \leq n_0$ for $0 \leq i \leq m-1$. Since for every language L_i we have $L_i = \{a^n \mid n \in \mathsf{PROG}(k_i, \ell)\}$, it follows that S is the union of a finite collection of sets of values of arithmetic progressions. By Theorem 1.4.21, S is an ultimately periodic set. ∎

Example 3.5.11 The set $L_S = \{a^{n^2} \mid n \in \mathbb{N}\}$ is not a regular language because the set $S = \{n^2 \mid n \in \mathbb{N}\}$ is not ultimately periodic. Indeed, suppose that S were ultimately periodic, so $n_0, r \in \mathbb{N}$ exist such that if $p > n_0$, then $p \in S$ if and only if $p + r \in S$. Choose n such that $2n + 1 > r$. Then, $n^2 \in S$ but $n^2 + r \notin S$ because the next member of S is $n^2 + 2n + 1 = (n+1)^2$. □

3.6 Minimal Automata

For any regular language L there are several automata that are capable of recognizing it. Naturally, we are interested in finding among these automata the ones that have the smallest number of states. This is the main goal of this section.

Definition 3.6.1 The *Nerode equivalence* of a language $L \subseteq A^*$ is the relation

$$\nu_L = \{(x, y) \in A^* \times A^* \mid xw \in L \text{ if and only if } yw \in L \text{ for every } w \in A^*\}.$$

□

The relation ν_L is a right-invariant equivalence relation. In other words, if $(x, y) \in \nu_L$, then $(xu, yu) \in \nu_L$ for every $u \in A^*$. In terms of equivalence classes, $[x]_{\nu_L} = [y]_{\nu_L}$ implies $[xu]_{\nu_L} = [yu]_{\nu_L}$ for every $u \in A^*$.

Recall that $[x]_{\nu_L}$ denotes the ν_L-equivalence class of the word x. The set of all equivalence classes of ν_L will be denoted by A^*/ν_L.

Lemma 3.6.2 *Let $L \subseteq A^*$ be a language over an alphabet A. We have $(x, y) \in \nu_L$ if and only if $x^{-1}L = y^{-1}L$.*

Proof. Let $x, y \in A^*$ such that $(x, y) \in \nu_L$, and let $t \in x^{-1}L$. This means that $xt \in L$, which implies $yt \in L$ because of the definition of ν_L. Therefore, $t \in y^{-1}L$, so $x^{-1}L \subseteq y^{-1}L$. The reverse inclusion can be obtained in the same manner, so $x^{-1}L = y^{-1}L$.

Conversely, if $x^{-1}L = y^{-1}L$, then $xt \in L$ if and only if $yt \in L$ for every $t \in A^*$, which means that $(x, y) \in \nu_L$. ∎

Definition 3.6.3 Let $L \subseteq A^*$ be a language over the alphabet A. The *set of left derivatives of* L is the set $\mathcal{Q}_L = \{t^{-1}L \mid t \in A^*\}$. □

Lemma 3.6.4 *Let $L \subseteq A^*$ be a language over an alphabet A. The set of left derivatives of L is finite if and only if A^*/ν_L is finite.*

Proof. Lemma 3.6.2 shows that the function $h_L : A^*/\nu_L \longrightarrow \mathcal{Q}_L$ defined by $h_L([x]_{\nu_L}) = x^{-1}L$ is a bijection. The desired conclusion follows immediately. ∎

The importance of the Nerode equivalence is highlighted by the following lemma, which (by Theorem 1.2.28) is equivalent to stating that any language is the union of equivalence classes of a Nerode equivalence.

Lemma 3.6.5 *Any language $L \subseteq A^*$ is a ν_L-saturated set.*

Proof. In order to prove that L is ν_L-saturated, it suffices to show that the ν_L-equivalence class of every $x \in L$ is included in L. Let $x \in L$. If $(x, y) \in \nu_L$, then $yz \in L$ whenever $xz \in L$ for any $z \in A^*$. Selecting $z = \lambda$ gives the required result. ∎

Note that Lemma 3.6.5 is equivalent to saying that for all words $x, y \in A^*$, if $x \in L$ and $x^{-1}L = y^{-1}L$, then $y \in L$. No assumption is made about the language L; in particular, L need not be regular.

Definition 3.6.6 Let $L \subseteq A^*$ be a language over the alphabet A. The *automaton of the language* L is the deterministic automaton $\mathcal{M}_L = (A, \mathcal{Q}_L, \delta_L, L, F_L)$ is defined by $\delta_L(t^{-1}L, a) = (ta)^{-1}L$ for $t \in A^*$ and $a \in A$, and $F_L = \{x^{-1}L \mid x \in L\}$. □

Note that the mapping δ_L is well defined; that is, $t^{-1}L = y^{-1}L$ implies $(ta)^{-1}L = (ya)^{-1}L$. Indeed, let $w \in (ta)^{-1}L$. We have $taw \in L$ which implies $aw \in t^{-1}L = y^{-1}L$. Consequently, $yaw \in L$, so $w \in (ya)^{-1}L$. Thus, $(ta)^{-1}L \subseteq (ya)^{-1}L$. The reverse inclusion can be shown similarly, so $(ta)^{-1}L = (ya)^{-1}L$.

Also, note that $\delta(t^{-1}L, a) = a^{-1}(t^{-1}L)$ for every $t \in A^*$ and $a \in A$. This remark is very important for the algorithm 3.6.10 discussed below.

We claim that we have $\delta_L^*(x^{-1}L, y) = (xy)^{-1}L$ for every $x, y \in A^*$. The argument is by induction on $\ell = |y|$. The basis case, $\ell = 0$, is immediate. Suppose that the equality holds for words of length less than ℓ, and let y be a word of length ℓ. We have $y = za$, where $z \in A^*$, $a \in A$ and $|z| = \ell - 1$. This gives:

$$\begin{aligned}
&\delta_L^*(x^{-1}L, y) \\
&\quad = \delta_L^*(x^{-1}L, za) = \delta_L(\delta_L^*(x^{-1}L, z), a) \\
&\quad = \delta_L((xz)^{-1}L, a) = (xza)^{-1}L = (xy)^{-1}L
\end{aligned}$$

which justifies our claim.

The set of final states of $\mathcal{M}_L$ can now be written as

$$F_L = \{\delta^*(L, x) \mid x \in L\},$$

which allows us to compute the set F_L, once we have computed the transition function.

Theorem 3.6.7 (Nerode's Theorem) *The language L is regular if and only if the set $\mathcal{Q}_L$ is finite.*

Proof. Suppose that the set $\mathcal{Q}_L$ is finite. In this case $\mathcal{M}_L$ is a dfa and we have

$$\begin{aligned} L(\mathcal{M}_L) &= \{x \in A^* \mid \delta_L^*(L, x) \in F_L\} \\ &= \{x \in A^* \mid x^{-1}L \in F_L\}. \end{aligned}$$

From the definition of F_L it follows that $x \in L(\mathcal{M}_L)$ implies that $x^{-1}L = z^{-1}L$ for some word $z \in L$, which shows that $(x, z) \in \nu_L$. Since L is a ν_L-saturated set, this implies $x \in L$. The reverse inclusion, $L \subseteq L(\mathcal{M}_L)$ is immediate, and it is left to the reader. Therefore, L is accepted by the dfa $\mathcal{M}_L$, so L is regular.

Conversely, suppose that L is a regular language. The finiteness of the set $\mathcal{Q}_L$ follows from Corollary 3.4.11. ∎

Corollary 3.6.8 *A language $L \subseteq A^*$ is regular if and only if the set A^*/ν_L is finite.*

Proof. This statement is an immediate consequence of the existence of a bijection between the sets A^*/ν_L and $\mathcal{Q}_L$. ∎

The dfa $\mathcal{M}_L$ plays a special role among the automata that accept the language L, as shown by the next theorem.

Theorem 3.6.9 *Let L be a regular language. The automaton $\mathcal{M}_L$ has the least number of states among all dfas that accept L.*

Proof. Let $\mathcal{M} = (A, Q, \delta, q_0, F)$ be a dfa such that $L = L(\mathcal{M})$. We intend to show that $|\mathcal{Q}_L| \leq |Q|$. Clearly, if $\mathcal{M}$ is to be minimal, it must be accessible, otherwise the automaton resulting from removing inaccessible states accepts the same language but has fewer states. In other words, we assume that for every state $q \in Q$ there exists a word $t \in A^*$ such that $\delta^*(q_0, t) = q$.

Define the mapping $f : Q \longrightarrow \mathcal{Q}_L$ by $f(q) = t^{-1}L$ if $\delta^*(q_0, t) = q$.

We need to verify that f is well-defined, that is, that $\delta^*(q_0, u) = \delta^*(q_0, v)$ implies $u^{-1}L = v^{-1}L$. If $x \in u^{-1}L$, then $ux \in L$, that is, $\delta^*(q_0, ux) \in F$. Since $\delta^*(q_0, ux) = \delta^*(\delta^*(q_0, u), x)$ and $\delta^*(q_0, u) = \delta^*(q_0, v)$, it follows that $\delta^*(\delta^*(q_0, v), x) = \delta^*(q_0, vx) \in F$, so $vx \in L$ and $x \in v^{-1}L$. The reverse implication can be obtained by exchanging u and v, so f is indeed well-defined.

It is clear that the mapping f is surjective, so $|\mathcal{Q}_L| \leq |Q|$, which shows that $\mathcal{M}_L$ has the least number of states among all dfas that accept the language L. ∎

We refer to $\mathcal{M}_L$ as the *minimal automaton of* L. Of course, several automata exist that have the same number of states as $\mathcal{M}_L$ and accept the language L. Nevertheless, the term *minimal automaton* is reserved for $\mathcal{M}_L$. The number of states of $\mathcal{M}_L$, that is, the number of distinct languages of the form $t^{-1}L$, is the *weight of* L and is denoted by $w(L)$.

The core of the construction of the minimal automaton is the computation of the set $\mathcal{Q}_L$. This can be done using the following algorithm.

Algorithm 3.6.10 (Computation of the States of the Minimal Automaton)
Input: A regular language L over an alphabet A.
Output: The set $\mathcal{Q}_L$ of left derivatives of L.
Method: Construct an increasing chain $\mathcal{Q}_0, \ldots, \mathcal{Q}_k, \ldots$ of finite subsets of $\mathcal{Q}_L$ as follows:

$$\begin{aligned}\mathcal{Q}_0 &= \{L\}\\ \mathcal{Q}_{k+1} &= \mathcal{Q}_k \cup \{a^{-1}K \mid a \in A \text{ and } K \in \mathcal{Q}_k\}\end{aligned}$$

Continue until $\mathcal{Q}_{k+1} = \mathcal{Q}_k$; then stop and output $\mathcal{Q}_k$.

Proof of Correctness: The algorithm must stop, since $\mathcal{Q}_L$ is a finite set. It is easy to see that $K \in \mathcal{Q}_p$ if and only if the set K (considered as a state of the automaton $\mathcal{M}_L$) can be reached by a word of length less than or equal to p in $\mathcal{M}_L$. By Theorem 3.2.15, every state of the automaton $\mathcal{M}_L$ can be reached through a word of length less than $|\mathcal{Q}_L|$. Therefore, when the algorithm stops, all members of $\mathcal{Q}_L$ have been computed. ∎

We remind the reader several equalities shown in Chapter 2 that are useful in the computation of left derivatives of languages. Namely, if L, K are two languages over the alphabet A and $a \in A$, then we have:

$$\begin{aligned}a^{-1}(L \cup K) &= a^{-1}L \cup a^{-1}K\\ a^{-1}(LK) &= (a^{-1}L)K \cup (L \cap \{\lambda\})a^{-1}K\\ a^{-1}L^* &= (a^{-1}L)L^*\end{aligned}$$

Example 3.6.11 Let $A = \{a, b\}$. Consider the regular language L that consists of all words from A^* that contain the infix aba. In other words, $L = A^*abaA^*$. We have $\mathcal{Q}_0 = \{L\}$ and $\mathcal{Q}_1 = \mathcal{Q}_0 \cup \{a^{-1}L, b^{-1}L\}$. Note that

$$\begin{aligned}a^{-1}L &= a^{-1}(A^*abaA^*)\\ &= (a^{-1}A^*)(abaA^*) \cup (A^* \cap \{\lambda\})a^{-1}(abaA^*)\\ &= A^*abaA^* \cup baA^*\\ &= L \cup baA^*\end{aligned}$$

and

$$\begin{aligned}b^{-1}L &= b^{-1}(A^*abaA^*)\\ &= (b^{-1}A^*)(abaA^*) \cup (A^* \cap \{\lambda\})b^{-1}(abaA^*)\\ &= A^*abaA^*\\ &= L,\end{aligned}$$

because $b^{-1}(abaA^*) = \emptyset$, $(A^* \cap \{\lambda\})b^{-1}(abaA^*) = \emptyset$, and $b^{-1}A^* = A^*$.

Thus,

$$\mathcal{Q}_1 = \{L, L \cup baA^*\}.$$

Next, in order to compute $\mathcal{Q}_2$, observe that

$$\begin{aligned}a^{-1}baA^* &= \emptyset\\ b^{-1}baA^* &= aA^*.\end{aligned}$$

Using Theorem 2.3.16 we obtain:

$$\begin{aligned}a^{-1}(L \cup baA^*) &= a^{-1}L = L \cup baA^*\\ b^{-1}(L \cup baA^*) &= b^{-1}L \cup aA^* = L \cup aA^*,\end{aligned}$$

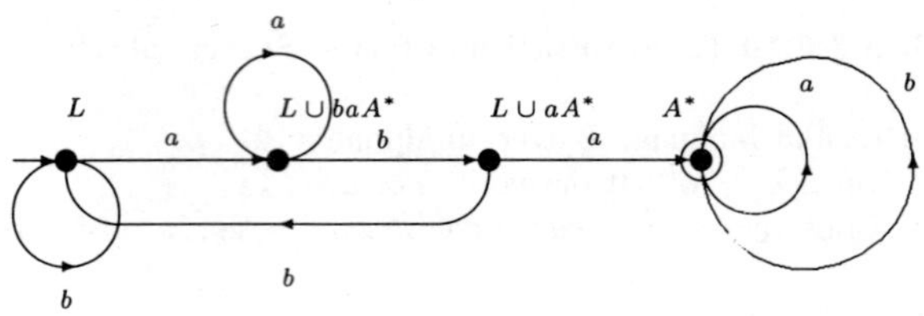

Figure 3.22: Directed Graph of the Automaton $\mathcal{M}_L$

The collection $\mathcal{Q}_2$ is

$$\mathcal{Q}_2 = \{L, L \cup baA^*, L \cup aA^*\}$$

Now we have

$$\begin{aligned} a^{-1}aA^* &= A^* \\ b^{-1}aA^* &= \emptyset, \end{aligned}$$

which allows us to write:

$$\begin{aligned} a^{-1}(L \cup aA^*) &= a^{-1}L \cup A^* = A^* \\ b^{-1}(L \cup aA^*) &= b^{-1}L = L. \end{aligned}$$

The collection $\mathcal{Q}_3$ is given by

$$\mathcal{Q}_3 = \{L, L \cup baA^*, L \cup aA^*, A^*\}.$$

Since $a^{-1}A^* = b^{-1}A^* = A^*$, it follows that $\mathcal{Q}_4 = \mathcal{Q}_3$, so

$$\mathcal{Q}_L = \{L, L \cup baA^*, L \cup aA^*, A^*\}.$$

The automaton $\mathcal{M}_L$ is defined by the following table:

Input	State			
	L	$L \cup baA^*$	$L \cup aA^*$	A^*
a	$L \cup baA^*$	$L \cup baA^*$	A^*	A^*
b	L	$L \cup aA^*$	L	A^*

Since $F_L = \{\delta^*(L, x) \mid x \in L\}$ we can compute F_L by determining those members of $\mathcal{Q}_L$ that can be reached from the initial state L using words from L of length not greater than 3 (cf. Theorem 3.2.15). The language L contains only one word of length 3, namely aba, so $F_L = \{\delta^*(L, aba)\} = \{A^*\}$. The graph of $\mathcal{M}_L$ is given in Figure 3.22.

□

3.7 Syntactic Monoids

In this section we associate a monoid to every language, and we show that a language is regular if and only if this monoid is finite. Syntactic monoids were introduced by Rabin and Scott in [1959], where they are attributed to J. Myhill. The importance of these algebraic structures is that they allow the characterization of certain classes of languages (see Exercises 87– 92).

3.7.1 Automata and Monoids

We begin by defining the monoid of a deterministic finite automaton.

Let $\mathcal{M} = (A, Q, \delta, q_0, F)$ be a dfa. If $x \in A^*$, then x defines a transformation $t_x : Q \longrightarrow Q$ given by $t_x(q) = \delta^*(q, x)$ for $q \in Q$. Observe that $\{t_x \mid x \in A^*\}$ is a closed subset of the monoid of transformations $\mathsf{T}(Q) = (Q^Q, \circ, 1_Q)$ of the set Q. Indeed, if t_x, t_y are two transformations associated with the words x and y respectively, then

$$qt_xt_y = \delta^*(\delta^*(q, x), y) = \delta^*(q, xy) = qt_{xy}$$

for $q \in Q$, which shows that $t_xt_y = t_{xy}$.

Definition 3.7.1 Let $\mathcal{M} = (A, Q, \delta, q_0, F)$ be a dfa. The *transition monoid of* $\mathcal{M}$ is the submonoid $\mathsf{TRANS}(\mathcal{M}) = \{t_x \mid x \in A^*\}$ of $\mathsf{T}(Q)$. □

Note that $\mathsf{T}(Q)$ is a finite monoid, because there are n^n transformations of the set Q, where $|Q| = n$. Therefore, $\mathsf{TRANS}(\mathcal{M})$ is a finite monoid for every automaton $\mathcal{M}$. The identity of $\mathsf{T}(Q)$ is the function $t_\lambda = 1_Q$. Therefore, 1_Q is also the identity of $\mathsf{TRANS}(\mathcal{M})$

Definition 3.7.2 Let A be an alphabet and let $\mathcal{M} = (A, Q, \delta, q_0, F)$ be a dfa. The words $x, y \in A^*$ are $\mathcal{M}$-*congruent* if $t_x = t_y$. □

We remind the reader that compositions of transformations of sets are denoted using the convention introduced in Example 1.3.19.

If x, y are $\mathcal{M}$-congruent we write $x \equiv_{\mathcal{M}} y$.

It is easy to verify that $\equiv_{\mathcal{M}}$ is an equivalence. To prove that $\equiv_{\mathcal{M}}$ is a congruence we must check that it is compatible with the word concatenation. Suppose that $x \equiv_{\mathcal{M}} y$. Then, $t_{uxv} = t_ut_xt_v = t_ut_yt_v = t_{uyv}$, so $uxv \equiv_{\mathcal{M}} uyv$, for every $u, v \in A^*$.

Theorem 3.7.3 *The transition monoid of a dfa $\mathcal{M}$ is isomorphic to the quotient monoid $A^*/\equiv_{\mathcal{M}}$.*

Proof. Define the mapping $\phi : A^*/\equiv_{\mathcal{M}} \longrightarrow \mathsf{TRANS}(\mathcal{M})$ by $\phi([x]_{\equiv_{\mathcal{M}}}) = t_x$. Note that ϕ is well-defined, for if $x' \in [x]_{\equiv_{\mathcal{M}}}$, then $t_x = t_{x'}$. The mapping ϕ is clearly onto. If $\phi([x]_{\equiv_{\mathcal{M}}}) = \phi([y]_{\equiv_{\mathcal{M}}})$, then $t_x = t_y$, so $x \equiv_{\mathcal{M}} y$ which gives $[x]_{\equiv_{\mathcal{M}}} = [y]_{\equiv_{\mathcal{M}}}$. Thus, ϕ is a bijection. Further, $\phi([x]_{\equiv_{\mathcal{M}}}[y]_{\equiv_{\mathcal{M}}}) = \phi([xy]_{\equiv_{\mathcal{M}}}) = t_{xy} = t_x \circ t_y$, so ϕ is indeed an isomorphism. ∎

To compute the transition monoid of a dfa we apply the following algorithm.

Algorithm 3.7.4 (Computation of the Transition Monoid)
Input: A dfa $\mathcal{M} = (A, Q, \delta, q_0, F)$.
Output: The transition monoid $\mathsf{TRANS}(\mathcal{M})$.
Method: Construct an increasing chain $T_0, \ldots, T_k, \ldots$ of finite subsets of Q^Q as follows:

$$\begin{aligned} T_0 &= \{1_Q\} \\ T_{k+1} &= T_k \cup \{t \circ t_a \mid a \in A \text{ and } t \in T_k\} \end{aligned}$$

Continue until $T_{k+1} = T_k$; then stop and output T_k.

Proof of Correctness: Since the sequence $T_0, \ldots, T_k, \ldots$ of subsets of the finite set Q^Q is increasing it is easy to see that the algorithm must stop.

We claim that if $w \in A^*$ and $|w| \leq k$, then $t_w \in T_k$. This is clearly the case for $k = 0$. Suppose that this statement holds for k, and let w be a word such that $|w| \leq k+1$. If $|w| \leq k$, then $w \in T_k \subseteq T_{k+1}$. Therefore, we need to consider only the case when $|w| = k+1$. We can write $w = va$, where $|v| = k$ and $t_w = t_v \circ t_a$. By the inductive hypothesis, $t_v \in T_k$, so $t_w \in T_{k+1}$ by the definition of T_k. Therefore, when the algorithm stops, we have $t_w \in T_k$ for every $w \in A^*$. ∎

Example 3.7.5 Let $\mathcal{M} = (\{a,b\}, \{q_0, q_1\}, \delta, q_0, \{q_1\})$ be the dfa defined by

Input	State	
	q_0	q_1
a	q_1	q_1
b	q_1	q_0

We have $T_0 = \{1_Q\}$, $T_1 = \{t_a, t_b, 1_Q\}$, and

$$T_2 = \{1_Q, t_a, t_b, t_{aa}, t_{ab}, t_{ba}, t_{bb}\},$$

where the mappings $t_{aa}, t_{ab}, t_{ba}, t_{bb}$ are given by

	State		Equal to
	q_0	q_1	
t_{aa}	q_1	q_1	t_a
t_{ab}	q_0	q_0	
t_{ba}	q_1	q_1	t_a
t_{bb}	q_0	q_1	1_Q

We have $T_1 \subset T_2$ because $t_{ab} \in T_2 - T_1$. Also, from the table we see that $aa \equiv_{\mathcal{M}} a$, $ba \equiv_{\mathcal{M}} a$, $bb \equiv_{\mathcal{M}} \lambda$.

Next, in order to compute T_3 we need to compute the mappings $t_v t_a$ and $t_v t_b$ with $v \in \{1_Q, t_a, t_b, t_{ab}\}$.

We have

$$\begin{array}{ll} aaa \equiv_{\mathcal{M}} aa \equiv_{\mathcal{M}} a & baa \equiv_{\mathcal{M}} aa \equiv_{\mathcal{M}} a \\ aab \equiv_{\mathcal{M}} ab & bab \equiv_{\mathcal{M}} ab \\ aba \equiv_{\mathcal{M}} aa \equiv_{\mathcal{M}} a & bba \equiv_{\mathcal{M}} a \\ abb \equiv_{\mathcal{M}} a & bbb \equiv_{\mathcal{M}} b \end{array}$$

which shows that no new mappings occur in T_3, so the algorithm stops. The transition monoid of $\mathcal{M}$ consists of $\{t_a, t_b, t_{ab}, 1_Q\}$ and is defined by the multiplication table:

$\circ$	1_Q	t_a	t_b	t_{ab}
1_Q	1_Q	t_a	t_b	t_{ab}
t_a	t_a	t_a	t_{ab}	t_{ab}
t_b	t_b	t_a	1_Q	t_{ab}
t_{ab}	t_{ab}	t_a	t_a	t_{ab}

□

3.7.2 The Syntactic Monoid of a Language

To define the syntactic monoid of a language we need to introduce a congruence defined by a language.

Definition 3.7.6 The *Myhill congruence* of a language $L \subseteq A^*$ is the relation $\mu_L \subseteq A^* \times A^*$ given by

$$\mu_L = \{(x,y) \in A^* \times A^* \mid uxv \in L \text{ if and only if } uyv \in L \text{ for every } u,v \in A^*\}.$$

□

We verified in Theorem 1.3.37 that μ_L is a congruence on A^*.

Note that if $(x,y) \in \mu_L$, then $(x,y) \in \nu_L$. Therefore, every equivalence class of ν_L is a union of equivalence classes of μ_L. By Lemma 3.6.5, L is a μ_L-saturated set. Theorem 1.3.37 shows that μ_L is the largest congruence of the free monoid $(A^*, \cdot, \lambda)$ that saturates the language L.

Definition 3.7.7 The *syntactic monoid of a language* $L \subseteq A^*$, is the quotient monoid A^*/μ_L. □

Theorem 3.7.8 *The syntactic monoid of a language L is isomorphic to the transition monoid of its minimal automaton $\mathcal{M}_L$.*

Proof. It is sufficient to verify that $(x,y) \in \mu_L$ if and only if $x \equiv_{\mathcal{M}_L} y$. Let $\mathcal{M}_L = (A, A^*/\nu_L, \delta_L, [\lambda]_{\nu_L}, F)$. The theorem follows immediately from the following equivalent statements:

1. $x \equiv_{\mathcal{M}_L} y$;
2. $\delta_L^*([z]_{\nu_L}, x) = \delta_L^*([z]_{\nu_L}, y)$ for every $z \in A^*$;
3. $[zx]_{\nu_L} = [zy]_{\nu_L}$ for every $z \in A^*$;
4. $(zx, zy) \in \nu_L$ for every $z \in A^*$;
5. $zxv \in L$ if and only if $zyv \in L$ for every $z, v \in A^*$;
6. $(x,y) \in \mu_L$.

■

Theorem 3.7.8 combined with Algoritm 3.7.4 allows us to compute the syntactic monoid of a language L by computing the transition monoid of the minimal automaton $\mathcal{M}_L$.

Example 3.7.9 Starting from the computation of the minimal automaton of the language A^*abaA^* given in Example 3.6.11, let us compute its syntactic monoid. To simplify the presentation we denote the states of the automaton $\mathcal{M}_L$ as follows

$$\begin{aligned} q_0 &= L \\ q_1 &= L \cup baA^* \\ q_2 &= L \cup aA^* \\ q_3 &= A^* \end{aligned}$$

With this notation the transition function of the automaton is specified by the

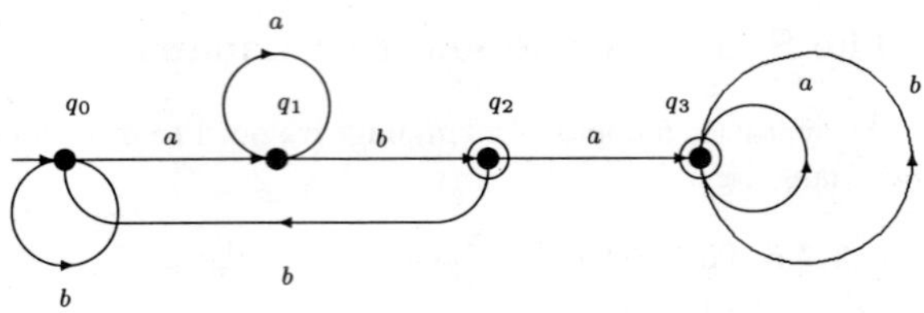

Figure 3.23: Directed Graph of the Automaton $\mathcal{M}_L$

following table:

Input	State			
	q_0	q_1	q_2	q_3
a	q_1	q_1	q_3	q_3
b	q_0	q_2	q_0	q_3

The digraph of the automaton is reproduced in Figure 3.23 for the convenience of the reader.

We have $T_0 = \{1_Q\}$ and $T_1 = \{1_Q, t_a, t_b\}$. The mappings $t_{aa}, t_{ab}, t_{ba}, t_{bb}$ are defined by:

	State				Equal to
	q_0	q_1	q_2	q_3	
t_{aa}	q_1	q_1	q_3	q_3	t_a
t_{ab}	q_2	q_2	q_3	q_3	
t_{ba}	q_1	q_3	q_1	q_3	
t_{bb}	q_0	q_0	q_0	q_3	

This shows that $aa \equiv_{\mathcal{M}_L} a$ and

$$T_2 = \{1_Q, t_a, t_b, t_{ab}, t_{ba}, t_{bb}\}.$$

Next, we compute T_3. We need to compute the mappings t_w for $|w| = 3$, taking into account the previous results. In other words, we start the computation knowing that

$$\begin{aligned} &aaa \equiv_{\mathcal{M}_L} aa \equiv_{\mathcal{M}_L} a \\ &aab \equiv_{\mathcal{M}_L} ab \\ &baa \equiv_{\mathcal{M}_L} ba \end{aligned}$$

This leaves us the mappings

	State				Equal to
	q_0	q_1	q_2	q_3	
t_{aba}	q_3	q_3	q_3	q_3	
t_{abb}	q_0	q_0	q_3	q_3	
t_{bab}	q_2	q_3	q_2	q_3	
t_{bba}	q_1	q_1	q_1	q_3	
t_{bbb}	q_0	q_0	q_0	q_3	t_{bb}

This gives $bbb \equiv_{\mathcal{M}_L} bb$. Thus,

$$T_3 = \{1_Q, t_a, t_b, t_{ab}, t_{ba}, t_{bb}, t_{aba}, t_{abb}, t_{bab}, t_{bba}\}.$$

Next, there are 16 words of length 4 to consider in the computation of T_4. Using the fact that $aa \equiv_{\mathcal{M}_L} a$ and $bbb \equiv_{\mathcal{M}_L} bb$, we can eliminate some computations. Namely, we have:

$$\begin{array}{ll} aaaa \equiv_{\mathcal{M}_L} aa & baaa \equiv_{\mathcal{M}_L} ba \\ aaab \equiv_{\mathcal{M}_L} ab & baab \equiv_{\mathcal{M}_L} bab \\ aaba \equiv_{\mathcal{M}_L} aba & bbaa \equiv_{\mathcal{M}_L} bba \\ aabb \equiv_{\mathcal{M}_L} abb & bbba \equiv_{\mathcal{M}_L} bba \\ abaa \equiv_{\mathcal{M}_L} aba & bbbb \equiv_{\mathcal{M}_L} bb \\ abbb \equiv_{\mathcal{M}_L} abb & \end{array}$$

This leaves the mappings

	State				Equal to
	q_0	q_1	q_2	q_3	
t_{abab}	q_3	q_3	q_3	q_3	t_{aba}
t_{abba}	q_1	q_1	q_3	q_3	t_a
t_{baba}	q_3	q_3	q_3	q_3	t_{aba}
t_{babb}	q_0	q_3	q_0	q_3	
t_{bbab}	q_2	q_2	q_2	q_3	

So,

$$T_4 = \{1_Q, t_a, t_b, t_{ab}, t_{ba}, t_{bb}, t_{aba}, t_{abb}, t_{bab}, t_{bba}, t_{babb}, t_{bbab}\},$$

and we have the equivalences

$$\begin{aligned} abab &\equiv_{\mathcal{M}_L} aba \\ abba &\equiv_{\mathcal{M}_L} a \\ baba &\equiv_{\mathcal{M}_L} aba \end{aligned}$$

It is straightforward to verify that words of length five to not produce any further distinct transformations of Q, so the computation of the carrier of the syntactic monoid stops with T_4. □

3.8 Fixed Points and Regular Languages

We present now a characterization of regular languages as components of fixed points of right-linear polynomial functions. We will present similar characterizations for context-free languages in Section 5.3.

Definition 3.8.1 Let $\mathcal{M} = (A, Q, \delta, q_0, F)$ be a dfa, where $|Q| = n$. The *matrix of* $\mathcal{M}$ is an $n \times n$-matrix of languages over A, $\boldsymbol{L}_{\mathcal{M}}$ defined by

$$(\boldsymbol{L}_{\mathcal{M}})_{ij} = \{a \in A \mid \delta(q_i, a) = q_j\}$$

for $0 \leq i, j \leq n - 1$. □

Example 3.8.2 The matrix of the dfa $\mathcal{M}$ discussed in Example 3.2.2 is

$$\boldsymbol{L}_{\mathcal{M}} = \begin{pmatrix} \emptyset & \{a\} & \{b\} & \emptyset \\ \{a\} & \emptyset & \emptyset & \{b\} \\ \{b\} & \emptyset & \emptyset & \{a\} \\ \emptyset & \emptyset & \emptyset & \{a,b\} \end{pmatrix}$$

□

Theorem 3.8.3 *Let $\mathcal{M} = (A, Q, \delta, q_0, F)$ be a dfa, where $|Q| = n$, and let $\boldsymbol{L}_{\mathcal{M}}$ be the matrix of this dfa. We have $x \in (\boldsymbol{L}_{\mathcal{M}}^{(k)})_{ij}$ if and only if $|x| = k$ and $\delta^*(q_i, x) = q_j$, for $0 \leq i, j \leq n-1$.*

Proof. The argument is by induction on $k \geq 0$. For $k = 0$, we have $\boldsymbol{L}_{\mathcal{M}}^{(0)} = \boldsymbol{I}_n$. For $i = j$, we have $x \in (\boldsymbol{L}_{\mathcal{M}}^{(0)})_{ij}$ if and only if $x = \lambda$; in this case $\delta^*(q_i, \lambda) = q_i = q_j$. For $i \neq j$, we have $(\boldsymbol{L}_{\mathcal{M}}^{(0)})_{ij} = \emptyset$, and the statement holds vacuously.

Suppose that the statement holds for $k \geq 0$. The following statements are equivalent:

1. $x \in A^*$, $|x| = k+1$, and $\delta^*(q_i, x) = q_j$;
2. $x = ya$, for $|y| = k$, $\delta^*(q_i, y) = q_h$, and $\delta(q_h, a) = q_j$ for some h where $0 \leq h \leq n-1$;
3. $x = ya$, for $|y| = k$, $y \in (\boldsymbol{L}_{\mathcal{M}}^{(k)})_{ih}$, $a \in (\boldsymbol{L}_{\mathcal{M}})_{hj}$ for some h, $0 \leq h \leq n-1$;
4. $x \in (\boldsymbol{L}_{\mathcal{M}}^{(k)})_{ih}(\boldsymbol{L}_{\mathcal{M}})_{hj}$ for some h, $0 \leq h \leq n-1$;
5. $x \in (\boldsymbol{L}_{\mathcal{M}}^{(k+1)})_{ij}$,

which proves the theorem. ∎

Define $\vec{K}_{\mathcal{M}} = \begin{pmatrix} K_0 \\ \vdots \\ K_{n-1} \end{pmatrix}$ by $K_i = \begin{cases} \{\lambda\} & \text{if } q_i \in F \\ \emptyset & \text{otherwise,} \end{cases}$ for $0 \leq i \leq n$.

Theorem 3.8.4 *Let $\mathcal{M} = (A, Q, \delta, q_0, F)$ be a dfa, where $|Q| = n$, and let $\vec{Q}_{\mathcal{M}} : \mathsf{MATR}_{n,1}(A) \longrightarrow \mathsf{MATR}_{n,1}(A)$ be the function defined by $\vec{Q}_{\mathcal{M}}(\vec{Z}) = \vec{K}_{\mathcal{M}} \cup \boldsymbol{L}_{\mathcal{M}}\vec{Z}$ for $\vec{Z} \in \mathsf{MATR}_{n,1}(A)$. The least fixed point $\mathtt{lfp}(\vec{Q}_{\mathcal{M}})$ of the function $\vec{Q}_{\mathcal{M}}$ is the n-tuple of languages*

$$\begin{pmatrix} H_0 \\ \vdots \\ H_{n-1} \end{pmatrix},$$

where $H_i = \{x \in A^* \mid \delta^*(q_i, x) \in F\}$ for $0 \leq i \leq n-1$.

Proof. In Section 2.6, we saw that the least fixed point of the function $\vec{Q}_{\mathcal{M}}$ is

$$\mathtt{lfp}(\vec{Q}_{\mathcal{M}}) = \boldsymbol{L}_{\mathcal{M}}^* \vec{K}_{\mathcal{M}}.$$

Therefore, the ith component of this fixed point is

$$\mathtt{lfp}(\vec{Q}_{\mathcal{M}})_i = \bigcup_{j=0}^{n-1} (\boldsymbol{L}_{\mathcal{M}}^*)_{ij} K_j.$$

Taking into account the definition of $\boldsymbol{L}^*_{\mathcal{M}}$ we have

$$\begin{aligned}
\mathtt{lfp}(\vec{Q}_{\mathcal{M}})_i &= \bigcup_{j=0}^{n-1}\Big(\bigcup_{n\geq 0}\boldsymbol{L}^{(n)}_{\mathcal{M}}\Big)_{ij}K_j \\
&= \bigcup_{n\geq 0}\bigcup_{j=0}^{n-1}(\boldsymbol{L}^{(n)}_{\mathcal{M}})_{ij}K_j \\
&= \bigcup_{n\geq 0}\bigcup_{j=0}^{n-1}\{x \in A^* \mid \delta^*(q_i,x) = q_j \text{ and } |x| = n\}K_j,
\end{aligned}$$

by Theorem 3.8.3. The definition of $\vec{K}_{\mathcal{M}}$ implies

$$\mathtt{lfp}(\vec{Q}_{\mathcal{M}})_i = \bigcup_{n\geq 0}\bigcup_{j=0}^{n-1}\{x \in A^* \mid \delta^*(q_i,x) = q_j, |x| = n \text{ and } q_j \in F\},$$

so $\mathtt{lfp}(\vec{Q}_{\mathcal{M}})_i = \{x \in A^* \mid \delta^*(q_i,x) \in F\}$ for $0 \leq i \leq n$. ∎

Corollary 3.8.5 *Every regular language is a component of the least fixed point of a function whose components are right linear polynomial functions.*

Proof. The statement follows immediately from Theorem 3.8.4. ∎

Example 3.8.6 Let

$$\mathcal{M} = (\{a,b\}, \{q_0,q_1,q_2,q_3\}, \delta, q_0, \{q_3\})$$

be the dfa considered in Example 3.8.2. We have

$$\vec{K}_{\mathcal{M}} = \begin{pmatrix} \emptyset \\ \emptyset \\ \emptyset \\ \{\lambda\} \end{pmatrix}$$

and the languages $L_i = \{x \in A^* \mid \delta^*(q_i,x) \in F\}$ (for $0 \leq i \leq 3$) are components of the least fixed point of the function $\vec{Q}_{\mathcal{M}}$ given by:

$$\vec{Q}_{\mathcal{M}}\begin{pmatrix} Z_0 \\ Z_1 \\ Z_2 \\ Z_3 \end{pmatrix} = \begin{pmatrix} \emptyset \\ \emptyset \\ \emptyset \\ \{\lambda\} \end{pmatrix} \cup \begin{pmatrix} \emptyset & \{a\} & \{b\} & \emptyset \\ \{a\} & \emptyset & \emptyset & \{b\} \\ \{b\} & \emptyset & \emptyset & \{a\} \\ \emptyset & \emptyset & \emptyset & \{a,b\} \end{pmatrix}\begin{pmatrix} Z_0 \\ Z_1 \\ Z_2 \\ Z_3 \end{pmatrix}.$$

Therefore, the function $\vec{Q}_{\mathcal{M}}$ can be written as

$$\vec{Q}_{\mathcal{M}}\begin{pmatrix} Z_0 \\ Z_1 \\ Z_2 \\ Z_3 \end{pmatrix} = \begin{pmatrix} aZ_1 \cup bZ_2 \\ aZ_0 \cup bZ_3 \\ bZ_0 \cup aZ_3 \\ \{a,b\}Z_3 \cup \{\lambda\} \end{pmatrix}.$$

Equivalently, the languages L_i are the components of the least solution of the system of equations:

$$\begin{aligned} Z_0 &= aZ_1 \cup bZ_2 \\ Z_1 &= aZ_0 \cup bZ_3 \\ Z_2 &= bZ_0 \cup aZ_3 \\ Z_3 &= \{a,b\}Z_3 \cup \{\lambda\} \end{aligned}$$

The approximations $\vec{Q}_{\mathcal{M}}^{(n)} \begin{pmatrix} \emptyset \\ \emptyset \\ \emptyset \\ \emptyset \end{pmatrix}$ for $0 \leq n \leq 3$ are given by

$$\begin{pmatrix} \emptyset \\ \emptyset \\ \emptyset \\ \emptyset \end{pmatrix}, \begin{pmatrix} \emptyset \\ \emptyset \\ \emptyset \\ \{\lambda\} \end{pmatrix}, \begin{pmatrix} \emptyset \\ \{b\} \\ \{a\} \\ \{a,b\} \end{pmatrix}, \begin{pmatrix} \{ab,ba\} \\ \{ba,bb\} \\ \{aa,ab\} \\ \{aa,ab,ba,bb,\lambda\} \end{pmatrix},$$

respectively. □

Example 3.8.6 shows the importance of finding the least solution of systems of right-linear equations of the form

$$\begin{aligned} Z_0 &= K_0 \cup L_{00}Z_0 \cup \cdots \cup L_{0\,n-1}Z_{n-1} \\ Z_1 &= K_1 \cup L_{10}Z_0 \cup \cdots \cup L_{1\,n-1}Z_{n-1} \\ &\vdots \\ Z_{n-1} &= K_{n-1} \cup L_{n-1\,0}Z_0 \cup \cdots \cup L_{n-1\,n-1}Z_{n-1} \end{aligned}$$

If we concentrate on the last equation of this system and we regard the languages $Z_0, \ldots, Z_{n-2}$ as parameters of this equation, then, for any fixed values of $Z_0, \ldots, Z_{n-2}$, the language $\hat{Z}_{n-1}(Z_0, \ldots, Z_{n-2})$ given by

$$\begin{aligned} &\hat{Z}_{n-1}(Z_0, \ldots, Z_{n-2}) \\ &\quad = L^*_{n-1\,n-1}(K_{n-1} \cup L_{n-1\,0}Z_0 \cup \cdots \cup L_{n-1\,n-2}Z_{n-2}) \end{aligned}$$

is the least solution of this equation. Since the least solution of the system $(\bar{Z}_0, \ldots, \bar{Z}_{n-1})$ is also a solution of the last equation of the system we have:

$$\hat{Z}_{n-1}(\bar{Z}_0, \ldots, \bar{Z}_{n-2}) \subseteq \bar{Z}_{n-1}. \tag{3.9}$$

If we substitute $\hat{Z}_{n-1}(Z_0, \ldots, Z_{n-2})$ for Z_{n-1} in the first $n-1$ equations of the system, we obtain a system of $n-1$ equations in $Z_0, \ldots, Z_{n-2}$; the process can now be repeated for $\hat{Z}_{n-2}(Z_0, \ldots, Z_{n-3})$ and we have

$$\hat{Z}_{n-2}(\bar{Z}_0, \ldots, \bar{Z}_{n-3}) \subseteq \bar{Z}_{n-2}. \tag{3.10}$$

Eventually, we obtain $\hat{Z}_0 = \bar{Z}_0$. This shows that the sequence

$$\begin{aligned} &\hat{Z}_{n-1}(\bar{Z}_0, \ldots, \bar{Z}_{n-2}) \\ &\hat{Z}_{n-2}(\bar{Z}_0, \ldots, \bar{Z}_{n-3}) \\ &\vdots \\ &\hat{Z}_0 \end{aligned}$$

is a solution of the system. This implies

$$\begin{aligned}\bar{Z}_{n-1} &\subseteq \hat{Z}_{n-1}(\bar{Z}_0,\ldots,\bar{Z}_{n-2})\\ \bar{Z}_{n-2} &\subseteq \hat{Z}_{n-2}(\bar{Z}_0,\ldots,\bar{Z}_{n-3})\\ &\vdots\\ \bar{Z}_0 &\subseteq \hat{Z}_0,\end{aligned}$$

so

$$\bar{Z}_{n-1} = \hat{Z}_{n-1},\ldots,\bar{Z}_0 = \hat{Z}_0.$$

These considerations lead to the following recursive algorithm for solving systems of right-linear equations:

Algorithm 3.8.7 (Solving Systems of Right-Linear Equations)
Input: A system of n right-linear equations.
Output: The least solution of the system.
Method: If $n = 1$, the system consists of the unique equation $Z_0 = K_0 \cup L_{00}Z_0$; the least solution of this equation is L^*K.

Suppose that $n > 1$. Extract $\hat{Z}_{n-1}(Z_0,\ldots,Z_{n-2})$ from the last equation and substitute for Z_{n-1} in the first $n-1$ equations. Solve the system that consists of the first $n-1$ equations. If $Z_0,\ldots,Z_{n-2}$ is the solution of this system, then the solution of the entire system is $(Z_0,\ldots,Z_{n-2},Z_{n-1})$, where Z_{n-1} is given by

$$Z_{n-1} = L^*_{n-1\,n-1}(K_{n-1} \cup L_{n-1\,0}Z_0 \cup \cdots \cup L_{n-1\,n-2}Z_{n-2})$$

■

Example 3.8.8 To solve the system

$$\begin{aligned}Z_0 &= aZ_1 \cup bZ_2\\ Z_1 &= aZ_0 \cup bZ_3\\ Z_2 &= bZ_0 \cup aZ_3\\ Z_3 &= \{a,b\}Z_3 \cup \{\lambda\}\end{aligned}$$

considered in Example 3.8.6 we start with the last equality which yields $Z_3 = \{a,b\}^*$. By substituting this value in the first three equations we have

$$\begin{aligned}Z_0 &= aZ_1 \cup bZ_2\\ Z_1 &= aZ_0 \cup b\{a,b\}^*\\ Z_2 &= bZ_0 \cup a\{a,b\}^*\end{aligned}$$

Next, we eliminate Z_2:

$$\begin{aligned}Z_0 &= aZ_1 \cup b(bZ_0 \cup a\{a,b\}^*)\\ Z_1 &= aZ_0 \cup b\{a,b\}^*\end{aligned}$$

This is followed by eliminating Z_1:

$$Z_0 = a(aZ_0 \cup b\{a,b\}^*) \cup b(bZ_0 \cup a\{a,b\}^*)$$

The last equality can also be written as

$$Z_0 = (a^2 \cup b^2)Z_0 \cup (ab \cup ba)\{a,b\}^*,$$

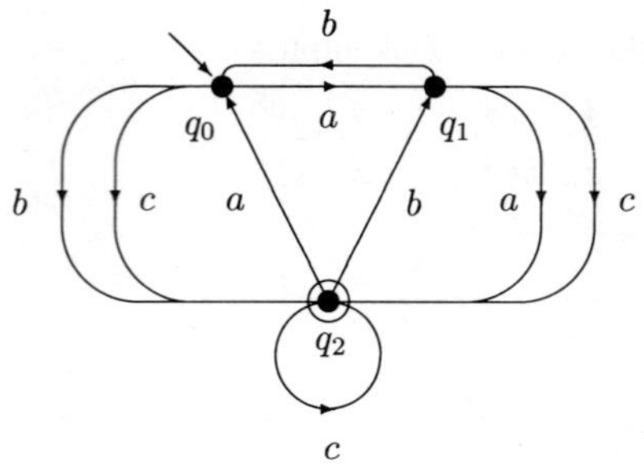

Figure 3.24: Transition Graph of $\mathcal{M}$

which allows us to write

$$Z_0 = (a^2 \cup b^2)^*(ab \cup ba)\{a,b\}^*.$$

□

Example 3.8.9 Let $\mathcal{M} = (\{a,b,c\},\{q_0,q_1,q_2\},\delta,q_0,\{q_2\})$ be the automaton whose transition digraph is shown in Figure 3.24. The system that describes this automaton is

$$\begin{aligned} Z_0 &= aZ_1 \cup \{b,c\}Z_2 \\ Z_1 &= bZ_0 \cup \{a,c\}Z_2 \\ Z_2 &= \{\lambda\} \cup aZ_0 \cup bZ_1 \cup cZ_2 \end{aligned}$$

The last equation implies

$$\begin{aligned} Z_2 &= \{c\}^*(\{\lambda\} \cup aZ_0 \cup bZ_1) \\ &= \{c\}^* \cup \{c\}^*aZ_0 \cup \{c\}^*bZ_1 \end{aligned}$$

Substituting Z_2 in the first two equation gives

$$\begin{aligned} Z_0 &= aZ_1 \cup \{b,c\}(\{c\}^* \cup \{c\}^*aZ_0 \cup \{c\}^*bZ_1) \\ Z_1 &= bZ_0 \cup \{a,c\}(\{c\}^* \cup \{c\}^*aZ_0 \cup \{c\}^*bZ_1) \end{aligned}$$

After regrouping the right hand members, we obtain

$$\begin{aligned} Z_0 &= \{b,c\}\{c\}^* \cup \{b,c\}\{c\}^*aZ_0 \cup (\{a\} \cup \{b,c\}\{c\}^*b)Z_1 \\ Z_1 &= \{a,c\}\{c\}^* \cup (\{b\} \cup \{a,c\}\{c\}^*a)Z_0 \cup \{a,c\}\{c\}^*bZ_1 \end{aligned}$$

Now we can extract Z_1 from the last equality as

$$\begin{aligned} Z_1 &= (\{a,c\}\{c\}^*b)^*(\{a,c\}\{c\}^* \cup (\{b\} \cup \{a,c\}\{c\}^*a)Z_0) \\ &= (\{a,c\}\{c\}^*b)^*\{a,c\}\{c\}^* \cup (\{a,c\}\{c\}^*b)^*(\{b\} \cup \{a,c\}\{c\}^*a)Z_0 \end{aligned}$$

Finally, we obtain the equation that involves only Z_0 as

$$\begin{aligned} Z_0 = &\{b,c\}\{c\}^* \cup \{b,c\}\{c\}^*aZ_0 \\ &\cup(\{a\} \cup \{b,c\}\{c\}^*b)((\{a,c\}\{c\}^*b)^*\{a,c\}\{c\}^* \\ &\cup(\{a,c\}\{c\}^*b)^*(\{b\} \cup \{a,c\}\{c\}^*a)Z_0) \end{aligned}$$

If K, L are the languages defined by

$$\begin{aligned} K &= \{b,c\}\{c\}^* \cup (\{a\} \cup \{b,c\}\{c\}^*b)(\{a,c\}\{c\}^*b)^*\{a,c\}\{c\}^* \\ L &= \{b,c\}\{c\}^*a \\ &\quad \cup(\{a\} \cup \{b,c\}\{c\}^*b)(\{a,c\}\{c\}^*b)^*(\{b\} \cup \{a,c\}\{c\}^*a), \end{aligned}$$

then $Z_0 = L^*K$ is the language accepted by $\mathcal{M}$. □

3.9 Regular Expressions

Regular expressions are notations for regular languages. In order to describe languages over an alphabet A we introduce a new alphabet $\boldsymbol{A}$, called a *meta-alphabet*, that has symbols that correspond to each symbol of A as well as other symbols used to form regular expressions. Namely, if $A = \{a_0, \dots, a_{n-1}\}$, then

$$\boldsymbol{A} = \{\boldsymbol{a}_0, \dots, \boldsymbol{a}_{n-1}, (,), \Lambda, \emptyset, \cup, *\}$$

Definition 3.9.1 The set of *regular expressions over an alphabet* A is the set of all words over the meta-alphabet $\boldsymbol{A}$ defined inductively as follows:

The basis:

1. $\boldsymbol{a}_0, \dots, \boldsymbol{a}_{n-1}$ are regular expressions.
2. Λ is a regular expression.
3. $\emptyset$ is a regular expression.

Inductive steps:

4. If E_0, E_1 are regular expressions, then $(E_0 \cup E_1)$ is a regular expression.
5. If E_0, E_1 are regular expressions, then $(E_0 \cdot E_1)$ is a regular expression.
6. If E is a regular expression, then (E^*) is a regular expression.

□

Let $\mathsf{REXP}(A)$ be the set of regular expressions over an alphabet A.

Example 3.9.2 Let $A = \{a, b\}$. The word $((\boldsymbol{a} \cdot (\boldsymbol{b}^*)) \cup \Lambda)$ is a regular expression over A because:

1. $\boldsymbol{a}$ is a regular expression by Rule 1;
2. $\boldsymbol{b}$ is a regular expression by Rule 1;
3. $(\boldsymbol{b}^*)$ is a regular expression because of Step 2 and Rule 6;
4. $(\boldsymbol{a} \cdot (\boldsymbol{b}^*))$ is a regular expression due to Steps 1 and 3, and Rule 5;
5. Λ is a regular expression by Rule 2;
6. $((\boldsymbol{a} \cdot (\boldsymbol{b}^*)) \cup \Lambda)$ is a regular expression due to Steps 4 and 5, and Rule 4.

□

3.9.1 The Unique Readability of Regular Expressions

The definition of regular expressions satisfies the *unique readability condition.* This means that for each regular expression E there is only one rule that puts E into $\mathsf{REXP}(A)$, and if this rule is an inductive rule, then there is only one sequence of hypotheses that can be used with the rule to put the string into $\mathsf{REXP}(A)$. This is necessary because it guarantees that inductive definitions of functions of regular expressions based on Definition 3.9.1 are correct, i.e. that such functions are well-defined (see Chapter 4 of [Fejer and Simovici, 1991]).

This may seem tedious, but if a regular expression could be constructed in two essentially different ways, an inductively defined function based on the regular expression could have two different values and thus not be a function at all. There is a tendency to ignore this possibility, trusting to luck and experience rather than proofs.

Recall that $n_a(w)$ is the number of occurrences of the symbol a in the sequence w. Thus, $n_((E)$ is the number of left parentheses in the regular expression E.

Lemma 3.9.3 *Let A be an alphabet. The following statements hold for every regular expression $E \in \mathsf{REXP}(A)$:*

(i) *We have $n_((E) = n_)(E)$.*

(ii) *If w is a proper prefix of a regular expression, then $n_((w) > n_)(w)$.*

(iii) *If w is a proper suffix of a regular expression, then $n_((w) < n_)(w)$.*

Proof. To prove the Part (i) of the lemma, we use induction on E. If $E = \mathbf{a}$ or $E = \Lambda$ or $E = \mathbf{\emptyset}$, then $n_((E) = n_)(E) = 0$.

Suppose now that $E = (F^*)$, where $n_((F) = n_)(F)$. Clearly, we can write

$$n_((E) = 1 + n_((F) = 1 + n_)(F) = n_)(E).$$

Assume that $E = (F \omega G)$, where ω is either $\cup$ or $\cdot$ and that $n_((F) = n_)(F)$, $n_((G) = n_)(G)$. By the inductive hypothesis, we have

$$n_((E) = 1 + n_((F) + n_((G) = 1 + n_)(F) + n_)(G) = n_)(E),$$

which concludes the argument for the Part (i).

The argument for the Part (ii) of the lemma is also by induction on E. If $E = \mathbf{a}$, or $E = \Lambda$, or $E = \mathbf{\emptyset}$, then E has no proper prefixes, and the statement is vacuously true.

Consider a regular expression $E = (F^*)$, where $n_((w) > n_)(w)$ for every proper prefix w of F. If u is a proper prefix of E, then one of the cases shown below must hold, where w represents a proper prefix of F:

Proper prefix u	$n_((u)$	$n_)(u)$
$($	1	0
$(w$	$1 + n_((w)$	$n_)(w)$
$(F$	$1 + n_((F)$	$n_)(F)$
$(F^*$	$1 + n_((F)$	$n_)(F)$

By the inductive hypothesis and the first part of the lemma we obtain $n_((u) > n_)(u)$ in all cases.

Let now E be $E = (F\,\omega\,G)$, where F, G are regular expressions such that for every proper prefix v of F and for every proper prefix w of G, we have $n_((v) > n_)(v)$ and $n_((w) > n_)(w)$, respectively, and ω is $\cup$ or $\cdot$. If u is a proper prefix of E, one of the following cases must hold, where v is a proper prefix of F and w is a prefix of G:

Proper prefix u	$n_($(u)$	$n_)(u)$
(	1	0
$(v$	$1+n_((v)$	$n_)(v)$
$(F$	$1+n_((F)$	$n_)(F)$
$(F\,\omega$	$1+n_((F)$	$n_)(F)$
$(F\,\omega\,w$	$1+n_((F)+n_((w)$	$n_)(F)+n_)(w)$
$(F\,\omega\,G$	$1+n_((F)+n_((G)$	$n_)(F)+n_)(G)$

By the inductive hypothesis and the first part of the lemma, we have in each case $n_((u) > n_)(u)$.

If w is a proper suffix of a regular expression E, then we have $E = uw$, where u is a proper prefix of E. Using the first two parts of the theorem, we can write $n_)(w) = n_)(E) - n_)(u) > n_((E) - n_((u) = n_((w)$. ∎

Theorem 3.9.4 *No proper prefix of a regular expression is a suffix of a regular expression, and therefore, no proper prefix of a regular expression is a regular expression.*

Proof. The proof is an immediate consequence of Lemma 3.9.3. ∎

Theorem 3.9.5 *Definition 3.9.1 of the set* $\mathsf{REXP}(A)$ *satisfies the unique readability condition.*

Proof. The proof is by induction on the construction of the regular expression E. If E enters the set $\mathsf{REXP}(A)$ by Rule 1 of Definition 3.9.1, then $E = \boldsymbol{a}_i$ for some i, $0 \leq i < n-1$. Similarly, if E enters $\mathsf{REXP}(A)$ by Rules 2 or 3, then we have $E = \Lambda$, or $E = \boldsymbol{\emptyset}$, respectively. On the other hand, if E enters $\mathsf{REXP}(A)$ by Rules 4, 5, or 6, then E begins with a left parenthesis. Thus, a regular expression that enters $\mathsf{REXP}(A)$ by Rule 1, 2, or 3, may not be put there by any other rule.

Let E be a regular expression that enters $\mathsf{REXP}(A)$ by Rule 6. We have $E = (F^*)$ for some regular expression F, where F is uniquely readable by the inductive hypothesis. Note that E may not be put in $\mathsf{REXP}(A)$ by either Rule 4 or Rule 5. Indeed, if E enters $\mathsf{REXP}(A)$ due to Rule 4 or 5, then $(F^*) = (F\,\omega G)$, so by character-by-character matching of the words, we obtain $* = \omega$, which is impossible.

Consider now a regular expression E that enters $\mathsf{REXP}(A)$ because of Rule 4; that is, $E = (F \cup G)$, where F and G are uniquely readable by the inductive hypothesis. Suppose that E can also be obtained by applying Rule 5. This implies $E = (F\,\omega G) = (F' \cdot G')$. If $F \neq F'$ then either F is a proper prefix of F' or F' is a proper prefix of F. Neither case is possible because of Theorem 3.9.4, so $F = F'$. Again, matching the strings character-by-character, this implies $\cup = \cdot$, which is a contradiction. The case for Rule 5, where $E = (F \cdot G)$ is similar and is left for the reader.

We conclude that the unique readability condition is satisfied. ∎

Each regular expression $E \in \mathsf{REXP}(A)$ denotes a language $\| E \|$ over A as follows:

1. (a) The language $\| \boldsymbol{a}_i \|$ defined by the regular expression $\boldsymbol{a}_i$ is $\{a_i\}$.
   (b) We have $\| \Lambda \| = \{\lambda\}$ and $\| \boldsymbol{\emptyset} \| = \emptyset$.

2. Let E_0, E_1 be regular expressions. We have

$$\begin{aligned} \| (E_0 \cup E_1) \| &= \| E_0 \| \cup \| E_1 \| \\ \| (E_0 \cdot E_1) \| &= \| E_0 \| \cdot \| E_1 \| \\ \| (E_0^*) \| &= \| E_0 \|^*. \end{aligned}$$

To simplify the writing of regular expressions, we may use the following conventions:

- Regular expressions are written imposing a precedence of operations: in decreasing order we have $*, \cdot, \cup$.
- Parentheses may be omitted whenever there is no risk of confusion.
- The symbol "$\cdot$" may be omitted.
- We associate repeated use of $\cup$ or $\cdot$ to the left. This means that $E_0 \cup E_1 \cup E_2 \cup \cdots \cup E_{n-1}$ stands for $(\cdots((E_0 \cup E_1) \cup E_2) \cdots \cup E_{n-1})$ and $E_0 \cdot E_1 \cdot E_2 \cdot \cdots \cdot E_{n-1}$ stands for $(\cdots((E_0 \cdot E_1) \cdot E_2) \cdot \cdots \cdot E_{n-1})$.

For example, we write $E \cup E'$ rather than $(E \cup E')$, E^* instead of (E^*), and EF for $(E \cdot F)$. Consequently, $E \cup FG^*$ should be interpreted as $(E \cup (F \cdot (G^*)))$.

3.9.2 Regular Expressions as Notations for Regular Languages

Theorem 3.9.6 *Let A be an alphabet. A language $L \subseteq A^*$ is regular if and only if $L = \| E \|$ for some regular expression $E \in \mathsf{REXP}(A)$.*

Proof. Let $L \subseteq A^*$ be a language such that $L = \| E \|$ for some regular expression $E \in \mathsf{REXP}(A)$. To prove that L is regular we use an inductive argument on the definition of regular expressions.

The basis case, when $E = \boldsymbol{a}_i$, is immediate since $L = \{a_i\}$, and every finite language is regular (cf. Corollary 3.4.6). Similarly, the languages $\| \Lambda \| = \{\lambda\}$ and $\| \boldsymbol{\emptyset} \| = \emptyset$ are regular.

For the inductive step, let $E_0, E_1 \in \mathsf{REXP}(A)$, and assume that both $L_1 = \| E_0 \|$ and $L_2 = \| E_1 \|$ are regular. Then, $\| E_0 \cup E_1 \| = L_1 \cup L_2$ is regular (cf. Theorem 3.4.4), $\| E_0 \cdot E_1 \| = L_1 L_2$ is regular (cf. Theorem 3.4.7), and $\| E_1^* \| = L_1^*$ is regular (cf. Theorem 3.4.8).

Conversely, let $L \subseteq A^*$ be a regular language. Suppose initially that L consists of one word, $L = \{x\}$. We prove by induction on $\ell = |x|$ that there is a regular expression $E \in \mathsf{REXP}(A)$ such that $L = \| E \|$. For the basis step, $\ell = 0$, we have $x = \lambda$ and $L = \| \Lambda \|$. For the induction step, suppose that the statement holds for words of length ℓ and let y be a word of length $\ell + 1$. We can write $y = xa$, where $|x| = \ell$ and $a \in A$, hence $\{y\} = \{x\}\{a\}$. By the inductive hypothesis, there is a regular expression $E \in \mathsf{REXP}(A)$ such that $\{x\} = \| E \|$; therefore, $\{y\} = \| E\boldsymbol{a} \|$.

Suppose now that L is a finite language. In this case, we show the existence of a regular expression E such that $L = \| E \|$ by induction on $n = |L|$. The basis case, $n = 0$, is immediate since $L = \emptyset$ and $L = \| \boldsymbol{\emptyset} \|$. Suppose that the statement holds for languages that contain no more than n words, and let L be a language that contains $n + 1$ words. We can write $L = L_1 \cup \{x\}$, where $|L_1| = n$. By the inductive hypothesis, there is a regular expression $E_0 \in \mathsf{REXP}(A)$ such that $L_1 = \| E_0 \|$. Therefore, $L = \| E_0 \cup E_x \|$, where E_x is the regular

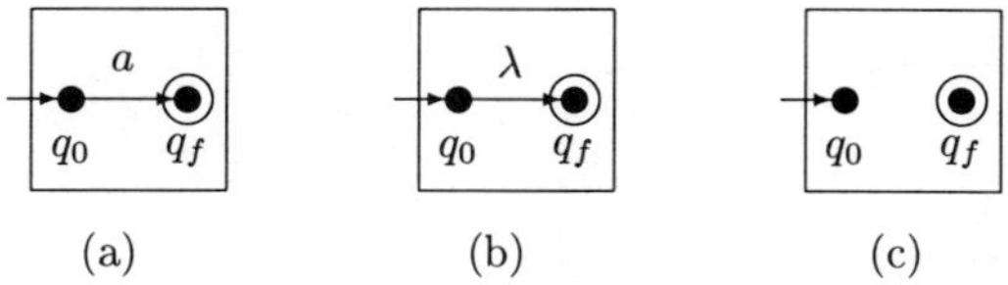

Figure 3.25: Transition Systems for Simple Regular Expressions

expression that denotes the one-word language $\{x\}$. We conclude that for every finite language L there is a regular expression E such that $L = \| E \|$.

Theorem 3.4.13 shows that every regular language can be constructed from finite languages using union, product, and Kleene closure. We use an induction argument on the number of steps m of this construction to show that for every regular language L there exists a regular expression $E \in \mathsf{REXP}(A)$ such that $L = \| E \|$.

The basis step $m = 0$ is immediate, since in this case L is a finite language.

Suppose that the statement holds for at most m steps, each applying union, product, or Kleene closure, and let L be a regular language obtained from finite languages in $m + 1$ steps. Then, one of the following cases occurs

1. $L = K \cup H$,
2. $L = KH$, or
3. $L = K^*$,

where each of H, K is obtained from finite languages through at most m steps. By the inductive hypothesis, there are regular expression $E_H, E_K \in \mathsf{REXP}(A)$ such that $H = \| E_H \|$ and $K = \| E_K \|$. The language L is thus denoted by $E_K \cup E_H$, $E_K \cdot E_H$, or E_K^*, respectively. ∎

Starting from regular expressions it is easy to construct transition systems that accept the languages denote by these expressions; we can use the following algorithm:

Algorithm 3.9.7 (Thompson's Algorithm)
Input: An alphabet A and a regular expression $E \in \mathsf{REXP}(A)$.
Output: A transition system $\mathcal{T}$ such that $L(\mathcal{T}) = \| E \|$.
Method: If $E = \boldsymbol{a}$, $E = \Lambda$, or $E = \emptyset$, then the corresponding transition systems are shown in Figure 3.25a, b and c, respectively.

If $E \in \mathsf{REXP}(A)$ and $E \notin \{\boldsymbol{a} \mid a \in A\} \cup \{\Lambda, \emptyset\}$, then, by Theorem 3.9.5, there is a unique way of parsing E as $E = (E_0 \cup E_1)$, $E = (E_0 \cdot E_1)$, or as $E = (E_0^*)$. If $\mathcal{T}_1$ and $\mathcal{T}_2$ are transition systems such that $L(\mathcal{T}_i) = \| E_i \|$ for $i = 0, 1$, then $\mathcal{T}$ is the transition system shown in Figures 3.18, 3.20, and 3.21, respectively.

Proof of Correctness: The correctness of the algorithm follows from Theorems 3.9.5, 3.4.4, 3.4.7, and 3.4.8. ∎

Example 3.9.8 Let $A = \{a, b\}$ and let $E \in \mathsf{REXP}(A)$ be given by $E = ((\Lambda \cup \boldsymbol{a})\boldsymbol{b})^*$. E can be written as $E = E_0^*$, where $E_0 = (\Lambda \cup \boldsymbol{a})\boldsymbol{b}$; in turn, $E_0 = E_1 E_2$, where $E_1 = \Lambda \cup \boldsymbol{a}$ and $E_2 = \boldsymbol{b}$; finally, $E_1 = E_3 \cup E_4$, where $E_3 = \Lambda$ and $E_4 = \boldsymbol{a}$. The transition systems for E_2, E_3, E_4 are immediate. Using the construction of

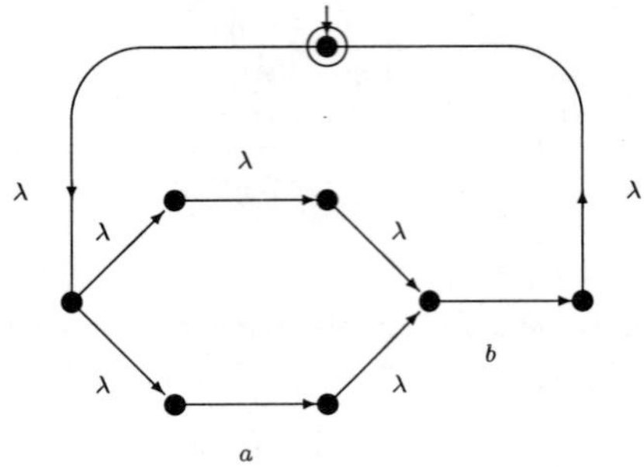

Figure 3.26: Transition System for $E = ((\mathbf{\Lambda} \cup \boldsymbol{a})\boldsymbol{b})^*$

Thompson's algorithm we obtain the transition system given in Figure 3.26. □

3.9.3 Closure Properties and Regular Expressions

Regular expressions facilitate proving several closure properties of regular languages.

Definition 3.9.9 Let A, B be two alphabets. A *regular substitution* from A to B is a substitution $s : A \longrightarrow \mathcal{P}(B^*)$ such that $s(a)$ is a regular language for each $a \in A$. □

The closure of regular languages under regular substitutions is fundamental to showing the closure of the family of regular languages under morphisms and inverse morphisms. These lead to powerful techniques for proving that certain languages are regular.

Theorem 3.9.10 *The class of regular languages is closed under regular substitutions.*

Proof. Let A, B be two alphabets, and let $\boldsymbol{A}, \boldsymbol{B}$ be the corresponding meta-alphabets. Consider a regular substitution $s : A \longrightarrow \mathcal{P}(B^*)$, and let E_a be the regular expression in $\mathsf{REXP}(B)$ that denotes the regular language $s(a)$; that is, $s(a) = \parallel E_a \parallel$ for each $a \in A$.

Define the morphism $h : \boldsymbol{A}^* \longrightarrow \boldsymbol{B}^*$ by $h(\boldsymbol{a}) = E_a$ for each $a \in A$, and $h(\sigma) = \sigma$ for every other symbol of the meta-alphabet $\boldsymbol{A}$. We prove that if E is a regular expression, then $h(E)$ is a regular expression that denotes the language $s(\parallel E \parallel)$. In other words, we prove that $\parallel h(E) \parallel = s(\parallel E \parallel)$.

The argument is by induction on the definition of the regular expressions.

For the basis case, there are three kinds of regular expressions, $\boldsymbol{a}_i$, Λ, and $\boldsymbol{\emptyset}$. If $E = \boldsymbol{a}_i$, the equality $\parallel h(E) \parallel = s(\parallel E \parallel)$ amounts to $\parallel E_{a_i} \parallel = s(a_i)$, which follows immediately from the definition of E_{a_i}. If $E = \Lambda$, the required equality is satisfied since $\parallel \Lambda \parallel = \{\lambda\} = s(\lambda)$. Also, if $E = \boldsymbol{\emptyset}$, $\parallel \boldsymbol{\emptyset} \parallel = \emptyset = s(\emptyset)$.

For the inductive step, suppose that

$$\begin{aligned} \parallel h(E_0) \parallel &= s(\parallel E_0 \parallel) \\ \parallel h(E_1) \parallel &= s(\parallel E_1 \parallel). \end{aligned}$$

Note that

$$h((E_0 \cup E_1)) = h(()h(E_0)h(\cup)h(E_1)h()) = (h(E_0) \cup h(E_1))$$
$$h((E_0 \cdot E_1)) = h(()h(E_0)h(\cdot)h(E_1)h()) = (h(E_0) \cdot h(E_1))$$
$$h((E_0^*)) = h(()h(E_0)h(^*)h()) = (h(E_0))^*$$

because h is a morphism. For the case $E = (E_0 \cup E_1)$, we have

$$\begin{aligned}
\| h(E_0 \cup E_1) \| &= \| h(E_0) \cup h(E_1) \| \\
&= \| h(E_0) \| \cup \| h(E_1) \| \\
&\quad \text{(by the definition of } \| \cdot \|) \\
&= s(\| E_0 \|) \cup s(\| E_1 \|) \\
&\quad \text{(by the inductive hypothesis)} \\
&= s(\| E_0 \cup E_1 \|) \\
&\quad \text{(by Theorem 2.4.3)}
\end{aligned}$$

Similar arguments hold for the two remaining subcases of the inductive step.

Since the language $s(\| E \|)$ is denoted by the regular expression $h(E)$, it follows that $s(\| E \|)$ is regular. ∎

Corollary 3.9.11 *If h is a morphism and $L \subseteq A^*$ is a regular language, then $h(L)$ is a regular language.*

Proof. This statement follows immediately from the fact that every morphism can be regarded as a special case of a regular substitution and from the fact that for every symbol $a \in A$, the language $\{h(a)\}$ is finite and, therefore, regular. ∎

Theorem 3.9.12 *Let A, B be two alphabets, and let $K \subseteq B^*$ be a regular language. If $h : A^* \longrightarrow B^*$ is a morphism, then $h^{-1}(K)$ is a regular language on A.*

Proof. Let $\mathcal{M}' = (B, Q, \delta', q_0, F)$ be an automaton such that $K = L(\mathcal{M}')$. Define the automaton $\mathcal{M} = (A, Q, \delta, q_0, F)$ by $\delta(q, a) = \delta'^*(q, h(a))$ for every $q \in Q$ and $a \in A$. We claim that $L(\mathcal{M}) = h^{-1}(K)$; that is,

$$L(\mathcal{M}) = \{x \in A^* \mid h(x) \in K\}.$$

To justify this claim we need to show that $\delta^*(q, x) = \delta'^*(q, h(x))$ for every $x \in A^*$. The argument is by induction on $|x|$.

For the basis case, the equality holds since $\delta^*(q, \lambda) = q = \delta'^*(q, \lambda)$. Suppose it holds for words of length n, and let $x = ya$ be a word of length $n + 1$, where $|y| = n$. This gives

$$\begin{aligned}
\delta^*(q, x) &= \delta^*(q, ya) \\
&= \delta(\delta^*(q, y), a) \\
&= \delta'^*(\delta'^*(q, h(y)), h(a)) \\
&= \delta'^*(q, h(y)h(a)) \\
&= \delta'^*(q, h(ya)) \\
&= \delta'^*(q, h(x))
\end{aligned}$$

The following statements are easily seen to be equivalent:

1. $x \in L(\mathcal{M})$;

2. $\delta^*(q_0, x) \in F$;
3. $\delta'^*(q_0, h(x)) \in F$;
4. $h(x) \in K$;
5. $x \in h^{-1}(K)$.

This proves that $L(\mathcal{M}) = h^{-1}(K)$, so $h^{-1}(K)$ is regular. ∎

Theorem 3.9.13 *If L_0, L_1 are two regular languages, then* $\mathsf{shuffle}(L_0, L_1)$ *is a regular language.*

Proof. This result follows immediately from Theorem 2.4.8, Corollary 3.9.11 and Theorem 3.9.12. ∎

Example 3.9.14 Theorems 3.9.10 and 3.9.12 can be used to prove regularity or non-regularity of languages. Consider, for example, the alphabet $A_k = \{a_0, \ldots, a_{k-1}\}$ with $k \geq 3$ and the morphism $h : A_k^* \longrightarrow \{a, b\}^*$ defined by $h(a_0) = a$, $h(a_1) = b$ and $h(a_i) = \lambda$ for $i \geq 2$. The language $K = \{a_0^n a_1^n \cdots a_{k-1}^n \mid n \in \mathbb{N}\}$ is not regular because $h(K) = \{a^n b^n \mid n \in \mathbb{N}\}$. If K were regular, this would imply that $L = \{a^n b^n \mid n \in \mathbb{N}\}$ is regular. Since we know (from Example 3.5.4) that L is not regular, it follows that K is not regular. □

We saw that every regular language over an alphabet A is denoted by a regular expression, which is a word over the meta-alphabet $\boldsymbol{A}$ (cf. Theorem 3.9.6). In general, a regular language can be denoted by many different regular expressions.

Example 3.9.15 Consider the alphabet $A = \{a\}$ and the regular expressions $E, E' \in \mathsf{REXP}(A)$ given by $E = \boldsymbol{a}^*$ and $E' = \Lambda \cup \boldsymbol{aa}^*$. We have $\| E \| = \{a\}^*$ and $\| E' \| = \| \Lambda \| \cup \| \boldsymbol{aa}^* \|$.

For $\| \boldsymbol{aa}^* \|$ we have

$$\begin{aligned} \| \boldsymbol{aa}^* \| &= \| \boldsymbol{a} \| \| \boldsymbol{a}^* \| \\ &= \{a\}\{a\}^* \\ &= \{a\}^+, \end{aligned}$$

so $\| E' \| = \{\lambda\} \cup \{a\}^+ = \{a\}^*$. Therefore, both E and E' denote the same language $\{a\}^*$. □

Definition 3.9.16 Let E, E' be two regular expressions from $\mathsf{REXP}(A)$. E is *equivalent* to E' if $\| E \| = \| E' \|$. We denote the equivalence of E and E' by $E \equiv E'$. □

It is easy to see that the relation $\equiv$ is an equivalence relation on $\mathsf{REXP}(A)$.

In transforming regular expressions, we often want to replace one part of an expression by another expression. However, we must do this in a controlled way, since we cannot replace arbitrary portions of a regular expression. To make this precise, we have to know what portions can be replaced and by what. To this end, we now define subexpressions.

Definition 3.9.17 Let E be a regular expression over the alphabet A. The set $\mathsf{SUBEXP}(E)$ of subexpressions of E is defined as follows.

(i) If $E \in \{\boldsymbol{a}_0, \ldots, \boldsymbol{a}_{n-1}, \Lambda, \emptyset\}$, then $\mathsf{SUBEXP}(E) = \{E\}$.

(ii) If $E = (E_0 \, \omega \, E_1)$, where ω is one of $\cup, \cdot$, then $\mathsf{SUBEXP}(E) = \{E\} \cup \mathsf{SUBEXP}(E_0) \cup \mathsf{SUBEXP}(E_1)$.

(iii) If $E = (E_0^*)$, then $\mathsf{SUBEXP}(E) = \{E\} \cup \mathsf{SUBEXP}(E_0)$.

□

Applying Definition 3.9.17, we can see that any regular expression is always a subexpression of itself. This follows by structural induction on regular expressions.

Example 3.9.18 Let $E = ((((\boldsymbol{a}^*)(\boldsymbol{b}^*)) \cup (\boldsymbol{a}^*))(\boldsymbol{ab}))$ be a regular expression. The set of subexpressions of E consists of E iself, $\mathsf{SUBEXP}((((\boldsymbol{a}^*)(\boldsymbol{b}^*)) \cup (\boldsymbol{a}^*)))$, and $\mathsf{SUBEXP}((\boldsymbol{ab}))$.

In turn, we have

$$\begin{aligned} &\mathsf{SUBEXP}((((\boldsymbol{a}^*)(\boldsymbol{b}^*)) \cup (\boldsymbol{a}^*))) = \{(((\boldsymbol{a}^*)(\boldsymbol{b}^*)) \cup (\boldsymbol{a}^*))\} \\ &\cup \quad \mathsf{SUBEXP}(((\boldsymbol{a}^*)(\boldsymbol{b}^*))) \cup \mathsf{SUBEXP}((\boldsymbol{a}^*)) \\ &= \quad \{(((\boldsymbol{a}^*)(\boldsymbol{b}^*)) \cup (\boldsymbol{a}^*)), ((\boldsymbol{a}^*)(\boldsymbol{b}^*)), (\boldsymbol{a}^*)\} \\ &\cup \quad \mathsf{SUBEXP}((\boldsymbol{a}^*)) \cup \mathsf{SUBEXP}((\boldsymbol{b}^*)) \\ &= \quad \{(((\boldsymbol{a}^*)(\boldsymbol{b}^*)) \cup (\boldsymbol{a}^*)), ((\boldsymbol{a}^*)(\boldsymbol{b}^*)), (\boldsymbol{a}^*), \boldsymbol{a}, \boldsymbol{b}\}. \end{aligned}$$

Finally, this gives

$$\begin{aligned} &\mathsf{SUBEXP}(E) \\ &= \quad \{(((\boldsymbol{a}^*)(\boldsymbol{b}^*)) \cup (\boldsymbol{a}^*)), ((\boldsymbol{a}^*)(\boldsymbol{b}^*)), (\boldsymbol{a}^*), \boldsymbol{a}, \boldsymbol{b}, (\boldsymbol{ab})\}. \end{aligned}$$

□

Definition 3.9.19 Let $E_0 = s_{i_0} s_{i_1} \cdots s_{i_{m-1}} \in \mathsf{REXP}(A)$. If E is a subexpression of E_0, where $E = s_{i_k} \cdots s_{i_{k+\ell-1}}$, then we refer to the pair (E, k) as *an occurrence* of E in E_0. □

Theorem 3.9.20 *Let $E_0 = s_{i_0} s_{i_1} \cdots s_{i_{m-1}}$ be a regular expression in $\mathsf{REXP}(A)$, and let (E, k) be an occurrence of the regular expression $E = s_{i_k} \cdots s_{i_{k+\ell-1}}$ in E_0. Denote by $\mathsf{replace}(E_0, (E, k), E')$ the word*

$$s_{i_0} s_{i_1} \cdots s_{i_{k-1}} z_{j_0} z_{j_1} \cdots z_{j_{p-1}} s_{k+\ell} \cdots s_{i_{m-1}}$$

obtained by replacing E in E_0 by $E' = z_{j_0} z_{j_1} \cdots z_{j_{p-1}}$. Then, we have

$$\mathsf{replace}(E_0, (E, k), E') \in \mathsf{REXP}(A).$$

Proof. The argument is by induction on the expression E_0. For the basis case, if $E_0 = \boldsymbol{\emptyset}$, or $E_0 = \Lambda$, or $E_0 = \boldsymbol{a}_i$, then $E = E_0$, $k = 0$, and $\mathsf{replace}(E_0, (E, 0), E') = E' \in \mathsf{REXP}(A)$.

Suppose that $E_0 = (E_1^*)$ and the statement holds for E_1. If (E, k) is an occurrence of E in E_0, then we have $E = E_1$ and $k = 1$, or E is a subexpression of E_1 and there is an occurrence $(E, k-1)$ of E in E_1. In the first case we have $\mathsf{replace}(E_0, (E, k), E') = (E'^*) \in \mathsf{REXP}(A)$. In the second case, we have $\mathsf{replace}(E_0, (E, k), E') = (\mathsf{replace}(E_1, (E, k-1), E')^*)$. By the inductive hypothesis, $\mathsf{replace}(E_1, (E, k-1), E') \in \mathsf{REXP}(A)$, so $\mathsf{replace}(E_0, (E, k), E') \in \mathsf{REXP}(A)$. We leave to the reader the remaining inductive cases, all of which are similar. ∎

Theorem 3.9.21 (The Replacement Theorem) *Consider the regular expressions E_0, E_1, E, E' over the alphabet A such that E_0 is a subexpression of E and $E' = \mathsf{replace}(E, (E_0, k), E_1)$. If $E_0 \equiv E_1$, then $E \equiv E'$.*

Proof. As in the case of Theorem 3.9.20, the argument is by structural induction on E_0. We leave it to the reader. ∎

Theorem 3.9.22 *Let A be an alphabet. We have the following equivalent regular expressions:*

(i) $E_0 \cup (E_1 \cup E_2) \equiv (E_0 \cup E_1) \cup E_2$ (union associativity),
(ii) $E_0(E_1E_2) \equiv (E_0E_1)E_2$ (product associativity),
(iii) $E_0 \cup E_1 \equiv E_1 \cup E_0$ (union commutativity),
(iv) $E_0(E_1 \cup E_2) \equiv (E_0E_1) \cup (E_0E_2)$ (left distributivity),
(v) $(E_0 \cup E_1)E_2 \equiv (E_0E_2) \cup (E_1E_2)$ (right distributivity),
(vi) $E \cup E \equiv E$ (union idempotency),
(vii) $E\Lambda \equiv E$,
(viii) $E\boldsymbol{\emptyset} \equiv \boldsymbol{\emptyset}$,
(ix) $E \cup \boldsymbol{\emptyset} \equiv E$,
(x) $E^* \equiv EE^* \cup \Lambda$,
(xi) $E^* \equiv (\Lambda \cup E)^*$,
(xii) $\boldsymbol{\emptyset}^* \equiv \Lambda$,

for every $E, E_0, E_1, E_2 \in \mathsf{REXP}(A)$.

Proof. We prove only the last equivalence; the remaining equivalences have similar, simple proofs that use elementary properties of languages.

Note that

$$\| \boldsymbol{\emptyset}^* \| = \| \boldsymbol{\emptyset} \|^* = \bigcup_{n\in\mathbb{N}} \emptyset^n,$$

according to the definition of the function $\| \cdot \|$. Since $\emptyset^0 = \{\lambda\}$ and $\emptyset^n = \emptyset$ for $n \geq 1$, it follows that $\bigcup_{n\in\mathbb{N}} \emptyset^n = \{\lambda\} = \| \Lambda \|$, which implies the equivalence $\boldsymbol{\emptyset}^* \equiv \Lambda$. ∎

Definition 3.9.23 Let A, B be two alphabets. An *h-substitution instance* of a regular expression $E \in \mathsf{REXP}(A)$ is a regular expression $E' \in \mathsf{REXP}(B)$ such that $E' = h(E)$, where $h : \boldsymbol{A}^* \longrightarrow \boldsymbol{B}^*$ is a morphism such that $h(\boldsymbol{a}) \in \mathsf{REXP}(B)$ for each $a \in A$.

A regular expression $E' \in \mathsf{REXP}(B)$ is a *substitution instance* of an expression $E \in \mathsf{REXP}(A)$ if it is an h-substitution instance for a morphism $h : \boldsymbol{A}^* \longrightarrow \boldsymbol{B}^*$. □

If $E_0, E_1 \in \mathsf{REXP}(A)$ and $E_0', E_1' \in \mathsf{REXP}(B)$ are two h-substitution instances of E_0, E_1, respectively, then $E_0 \equiv E_1$ implies $E_0' \equiv E_1'$ by Theorem 3.9.10.

Definition 3.9.24 A regular expression $E \in \mathsf{REXP}(A)$ has the *empty word property* (ewp) if one of the following cases occur:

(i) $E = \Lambda$;
(ii) $E = F^*$ for some $F \in \mathsf{REXP}(A)$;
(iii) $E = E_0E_1$, where $E_0, E_1 \in \mathsf{REXP}(A)$ and both E_0 and E_1 have the ewp;
(iv) $E = E_0 \cup E_1$, where $E_0, E_1 \in \mathsf{REXP}(A)$ and at least one of E_0 or E_1 has the ewp.

□

Theorem 3.9.25 *The regular expression $E \in \mathsf{REXP}(A)$ has the ewp if and only if $\lambda \in \| E \|$.*

Proof. Suppose that $\lambda \in \| E \|$. We prove by structural induction on E that E has the ewp.

For the basis case we must have $E = \Lambda$, as otherwise $\lambda \notin \| E \|$, so E has the ewp.

Suppose now that the statement holds for the regular expressions F and G, and let E be a regular expression built from F and G. We need to consider three cases:

1. If $E = F^*$ for some $F \in \mathsf{REXP}(A)$, then E has the ewp by Definition 3.9.24.
2. If $E = FG$, then, since $\| E \| = \| F \| \| G \|$ we have both $\lambda \in \| F \|$ and $\lambda \in \| G \|$, so both F and G have the ewp by the inductive hypothesis. Therefore, E has the ewp by Definition 3.9.24.
3. If $E = F \cup G$, then, since $\| E \| = \| F \| \cup \| G \|$ we have $\lambda \in \| F \|$ or $\lambda \in \| G \|$. By the inductive hypothesis, at least one of F or G has the ewp. Therefore, E has the ewp, by Definition 3.9.24.

Conversely, suppose that E has the ewp. An inductive argument based on the Definition 3.9.24 shows that $\lambda \in \| E \|$. We leave this argument to the reader. ∎

Theorem 3.9.26 *If $E \equiv G \cup (FE)$, where F does not have the ewp, then $E \equiv (F^*)G$.*

Proof. Let $\| E \| = X$, $\| G \| = H$ and $\| F \| = L$. Note that the equivalence $E \equiv G \cup (FE)$ implies that the equation $X = H \cup LX$ has a solution. By Theorem 3.9.25, $\lambda \notin L$, so $X = L^*H$ by the uniqueness of this solution (cf. Theorem 2.6.15). This implies the desired equivalence. ∎

Definition 3.9.27 Let $E \in \mathsf{REXP}(A)$. The regular expression $\varepsilon(E)$ is given by

$$\begin{aligned} \varepsilon(\mathbf{a}) &= \emptyset \\ \varepsilon(\Lambda) &= \Lambda \\ \varepsilon(\emptyset) &= \emptyset, \end{aligned}$$

and

$$\begin{aligned} \varepsilon(E \cup F) &= \varepsilon(E) \cup \varepsilon(F) \\ \varepsilon(EF) &= \varepsilon(E)\varepsilon(F) \\ \varepsilon(E^*) &= \Lambda \end{aligned}$$

□

Theorem 3.9.28 *We have $\| \varepsilon(E) \| = \| E \| \cap \{\lambda\}$ for every regular expression E.*

Proof. The argument is by induction on the definition of regular expressions and is left to the reader. ∎

Corollary 3.9.29 *We have*

$$\| \varepsilon(E) \| = \begin{cases} \{\lambda\} & \text{if } E \text{ has the ewp} \\ \emptyset & \text{otherwise} \end{cases}$$

Proof. The statement follows immediately from Theorem 3.9.28 ∎

Using an inductive approach it is possible to build regular expressions that define the left derivatives of a regular language. Namely, if E is a regular expression, $E \in \mathsf{REXP}(A)$ and $\boldsymbol{a} \in \boldsymbol{A}$ define the regular expression $\boldsymbol{a}^{-1}E$ as follows:

$$\begin{aligned} \boldsymbol{a}^{-1}\boldsymbol{b} &= \begin{cases} \Lambda & \text{if } \boldsymbol{a} = \boldsymbol{b} \\ \emptyset & \text{otherwise} \end{cases} \\ \boldsymbol{a}^{-1}\Lambda &= \emptyset \\ \boldsymbol{a}^{-1}\emptyset &= \emptyset \end{aligned}$$

and

$$\begin{aligned} \boldsymbol{a}^{-1}(E \cup F) &= \boldsymbol{a}^{-1}(E) \cup \boldsymbol{a}^{-1}(F) \\ \boldsymbol{a}^{-1}(EF) &= (\boldsymbol{a}^{-1}E)F \cup \varepsilon(E)(\boldsymbol{a}^{-1}F) \\ \boldsymbol{a}^{-1}(E^*) &= (\boldsymbol{a}^{-1}E)E^* \end{aligned}$$

Theorem 3.9.30 *We have* $\| \boldsymbol{a}^{-1}E \| = a^{-1}\| E \|$ *for every regular expression* $E \in \mathsf{REXP}(A)$ *and every* $a \in A$.

Proof. Again, the argument is by induction on the definition of regular expressions and is left to the reader. ∎

3.9.4 A Formal System for Regular Expressions

We discuss an axiomatic approach to the equivalence of regular expressions. To this end, we present a formal system that consists of a list of axioms and two inference rules. The objects of this system are strings of symbols of the form $E \sim F$, where E, F are regular expressions. We prove that this system is sound and complete with respect to the equivalence between regular expressions. In other words, we prove that if $E \sim F$ has a proof in the system, then $E \equiv F$ (the soundness property), and that for every pair (E, F) such that $E \equiv F$ there is a proof in the formal system of $E \sim F$ (the completeness property). This formal system was introduced by A. Salomaa in [1966].

Definition 3.9.31 Let E, F be two regular expressions. If E' and F' are substitution instances of the regular expressions E and F, respectively, then $E' \sim F'$ is a *substitution instance* of $E \sim F$. □

The axioms of the formal system correspond to the equivalences introduced in Theorem 3.9.22. Namely, we have the following axioms:

1. $E_0 \cup (E_1 \cup E_2) \sim (E_0 \cup E_1) \cup E_2$ (union associativity axiom),
2. $E_0(E_1E_2) \sim (E_0E_1)E_2$ (product associativity axiom),
3. $E_0 \cup E_1 \sim E_1 \cup E_0$ (union commutativity axiom),
4. $E_0(E_1 \cup E_2) \sim (E_0E_1) \cup (E_0E_2)$ (left distributivity axiom),
5. $(E_0 \cup E_1)E_2 \sim (E_0E_2) \cup (E_1E_2)$ (right distributivity axiom),
6. $E \cup E \sim E$ (union idempotency axiom),
7. $E\Lambda \sim E$
8. $E\emptyset \sim \emptyset$
9. $E \cup \emptyset \sim E$,
10. $E^* \sim EE^* \cup \Lambda$,
11. $E^* \sim (\Lambda \cup E)^*$,
12. $\emptyset^* \sim \Lambda$,

13. $E \sim E$ (reflexivity axiom)

for every $E, E_0, E_1, E_2 \in \mathsf{REXP}(A)$.

The inference rules are:

- **The Replacement Rule (RR):** Let E_0, E_1, E, E' be regular expressions over the alphabet A such that E_0 is a subexpression of E and $E' = \mathsf{replace}(E, (E_0, k), E_1)$. From $E_0 \sim E_1$ we may infer $E \sim E'$.
- **Solutions of Equations (SE):** Let $E, U, W \in \mathsf{REXP}(A)$. From $E \sim (UE) \cup W$, where U does not have the ewp, we may infer $E \sim (U^*)W$.
- **The Symmetry Rule:** From $E \sim F$ we may infer $F \sim E$ for every $E, F \in \mathsf{REXP}(A)$.
- **The Transitivity Rule:** From $E \sim F$ and $F \sim G$ we may infer $E \sim G$.

Definition 3.9.32 A *proof of* $E \sim F$ is a sequence of pairs

$$E_0 \sim F_0, \dots, E_{n-1} \sim F_{n-1}$$

such that $E_{n-1} = E$, $F_{n-1} = F$, and for each i, $0 \leq i \leq n-1$, one of the following cases occurs:

(i) $E_i \sim F_i$ is a substitution instance of an axiom;

(ii) there is j such that $0 \leq j < i$, and $E_i \sim F_i$ is obtained from $E_j \sim F_j$ by the Replacement Rule, the **SE** Rule, or the Symmetry Rule;

(iii) there are j, j' such that $0 \leq j, j' < i$, and $E_i \sim F_i$ is obtained from $E_j \sim F_j, E_{j'} \sim F_{j'}$ by the Transitivity Rule.

The number n is the *length of the proof.* □

If a proof $E_0 \sim F_0, \dots, E_{n-1} \sim F_{n-1}$ exists for $E \sim F$, we may write $\vdash E \sim F$.

Theorem 3.9.33 *The formal system for regular expressions is sound.*

Proof. We need to prove that if $\vdash E \sim F$, then $E \equiv F$. The argument is by induction on the length of the proof $\vdash E \sim F$ and is left to the reader. ∎

Theorem 3.9.34 *Let E, F, G, H be regular expressions. If $\vdash E \sim F$ and $\vdash G \sim H$, then $\vdash E \cup G \sim F \cup H$, $\vdash EG \sim FH$, and $\vdash E^* \sim F^*$.*

Proof. We provide the proof only for the last part of the theorem and leave the remaining, similar proofs for the reader.

By the Reflexivity Axiom, we have $\vdash E^* \sim E^*$. Then, since $\vdash E \sim F$, by applying the Replacement Rule we obtain $\vdash F^* \sim E^*$. An application of the Symmetry Rule yields $\vdash E^* \sim F^*$. ∎

Example 3.9.35 We show how to prove that $\vdash \emptyset E \sim \emptyset$, and $\vdash \Lambda E \sim E$. Note that these equivalences are obtained from the axioms (8) and (7) respectively, by reversing the order of the factors of the left members.

The proof of $\emptyset E \sim \emptyset$ consists of the following steps:

1. $\emptyset\emptyset \sim \emptyset$ by Axiom 8;
2. $\emptyset \sim \emptyset\emptyset$ by the Symmetry Rule and Step 1;
3. $\emptyset E \sim (\emptyset\emptyset)E$ by the Replacement Rule and Step 2;
4. $(\emptyset\emptyset)E \sim \emptyset(\emptyset E)$ by Axiom 2;
5. $\emptyset E \sim \emptyset(\emptyset E)$ by the Transitivity Rule and Steps 3 and 4;
6. $\emptyset(\emptyset E) \sim \emptyset(\emptyset E) \cup \emptyset$ by Axiom 9;

7. $\emptyset E \sim \emptyset(\emptyset E) \cup \emptyset$ by the Transitivity Rule and Steps 5 and 6;
8. $\emptyset E \sim (\emptyset^*)\emptyset$ by the **SE** Rule and Step 7;
9. $(\emptyset^*)\emptyset \sim \emptyset$ by Axiom 8;
10. $\emptyset E \sim \emptyset$ by the Transitivity Rule and Steps 8 and 9.

The proof for $\vdash \Lambda E \sim E$ consists of the following steps:

1. $E \sim E \cup \emptyset$ by Axiom 9;
2. $\emptyset E \sim \emptyset$ by the first part of this example;
3. $\emptyset \sim \emptyset E$ by Step 2 and the Symmetry Rule;
4. $E \cup \emptyset \sim E \cup (\emptyset E)$by Step 3 and the Replacement Rule;
5. $E \sim E \cup (\emptyset E)$ by Steps 1, 4, and the Transitivity Rule;
6. $E \cup (\emptyset E) \sim (\emptyset E) \cup E$ by Axiom 3;
7. $E \sim (\emptyset E) \cup E$ by Steps 5, 6, and the Transitivity Rule;
8. $E \sim (\emptyset^*)E$ by Step 7 and the **SE** Rule;
9. $\emptyset^* \sim \Lambda$ by Axiom 12;
10. $(\emptyset^*)E \sim \Lambda E$ by Step 9 and the Replacement Rule;
11. $E \sim \Lambda E$ by Steps 8, 10, and the Transitivity Rule.

□

To prove the completeness of the formal system, we begin by developing a method of dealing with systems of pairs of regular expressions. We use these to define the notion of equational characterizability, a property that we prove applies to every regular expression. We then show completeness by showing that every pair of equivalent equationally characterizable expressions can be proven equivalent.

We deal with pairs of regular expressions as follows. If both (E_0, F_0) and (E_1, F_1) are pairs of regular expressions over A, then we define $(E_0, F_0) \cup (E_1, F_1)$ and $(E_0, F_0)(E_1, F_1)$ by

$$\begin{aligned}(E_0, F_0) \cup (E_1, F_1) &= (E_0 \cup E_1, F_0 \cup F_1)\\ (E_0, F_0)(E_1, F_1) &= (E_0E_1, F_0F_1).\end{aligned}$$

Also, if E is a regular expression, then $E(E_0, F_0)$ is the pair (EE_0, EF_0). Further, we write $\vdash (E_0, F_0) \sim (E_1, F_1)$ if and only if we have both $\vdash E_0 \sim E_1$ and $\vdash F_0 \sim F_1$.

The following theorem is a counterpart of the uniqueness result contained in Theorem 2.6.18:

Theorem 3.9.36 *Let U_{ij} be regular expressions from* $\mathsf{REXP}(A)$ *such that none of them has the ewp, and let $W_i \in \mathsf{REXP}(A)$ for $0 \leq i, j \leq n-1$, where $n \geq 1$. If*

$$\vdash (E_i, F_i) \sim U_{i0}(E_0, F_0) \cup \cdots \cup U_{i\,n-1}(E_{n-1}, F_{n-1}) \cup (W_i, W_i) \tag{3.11}$$

for $0 \leq i \leq n-1$, then $\vdash E_i \sim F_i$ for $0 \leq i \leq n-1$.

Proof. The argument is by strong induction on n. In the basis case ($n = 1$) we have $\vdash E_0 \sim U_{00}E_0 \cup W_0$ and $\vdash F_0 \sim U_{00}F_0 \cup W_0$. By the Rule **SE**, we have $\vdash E_0 \sim (U_{00}^*)W_0$ and $\vdash F_0 \sim (U_{00}^*)W_0$, so $\vdash E_0 \sim F_0$ by the Symmetry and Transitivity Rules.

Suppose that the statement holds for $1, 2, \ldots, n-2$. The equation

$$\begin{aligned}\vdash (E_{n-1}, F_{n-1}) \sim\ & U_{n-1\,0}(E_0, F_0) \cup \cdots \cup U_{n-1\,n-1}(E_{n-1}, F_{n-1})\\ & \cup (W_{n-1}, W_{n-1})\end{aligned}$$

can now be separated into two equations as

$$\begin{aligned} \vdash E_{n-1} &\sim U_{n-1\,0}E_0 \cup \cdots \cup U_{n-1\,n-2}E_{n-2} \cup U_{n-1\,n-1}E_{n-1} \\ &\quad \cup W_{n-1} \\ \vdash F_{n-1} &\sim U_{n-1\,0}F_0 \cup \cdots \cup U_{n-1\,n-2}F_{n-2} \cup U_{n-1\,n-1}F_{n-1} \\ &\quad \cup W_{n-1}. \end{aligned}$$

By applying the Commutativity Axiom (3) and then the **SE** Rule we obtain

$$\vdash E_{n-1} \sim (U^*_{n-1\,n-1})\left(\bigcup_{j=0}^{n-2} U_{n-1\,j}E_j \cup W_{n-1}\right) \qquad (3.12)$$

$$\vdash F_{n-1} \sim (U^*_{n-1\,n-1})\left(\bigcup_{j=0}^{n-2} U_{n-1\,j}F_j \cup W_{n-1}\right) \qquad (3.13)$$

Applying the Replacement and Transitivity Rules and the Commutative and Distributive axioms, we eliminate the pair (E_n, F_n) from the equivalences 3.11 using the last equivalences:

$$\begin{aligned} \vdash (E_i, F_i) &\sim (U_{i0} \cup U_{i\,n-1}(U^*_{n-1\,n-1})U_{n-1\,0})(E_0, F_0) \cup \cdots \\ &\cup (U_{i\,n-2} \cup U_{i\,n-1}(U^*_{n-1\,n-1})U_{n-1\,n-2})(E_{n-2}, F_{n-2}) \\ &\cup (Y_i, Y_i), \end{aligned}$$

where $Y_i = W_i \cup U_{i\,n-1}(U^*_{n-1\,n-1})W_{n-1}$ for $0 \le i \le n-2$.

Since none of the regular expressions $U_{ij} \cup U_{i\,n-1}(U^*_{n-1\,n-1})U_{n-1\,j}$ has the ewp, by the inductive hypothesis we have $\vdash E_i \sim F_i$ for $0 \le i \le n-2$. Therefore, by the equivalences (3.12) and (3.13), we have $E_{n-1} \sim F_{n-1}$. ∎

Definition 3.9.37 Let $A = \{a_0, \ldots, a_{n-1}\}$ be an alphabet. A regular expression $E \in \mathsf{REXP}(A)$ is *equationally characterizable* if there exist m regular expressions $E_0, \ldots, E_{m-1}$ such that $E = E_0$ and

$$\vdash E_i \sim \bigcup_{j=0}^{n-1} \boldsymbol{a}_j E_i^j \cup \varepsilon(E_i),$$

where $E_i^j \in \{E_0, \ldots, E_{m-1}\}$, for $0 \le i \le m-1$ and $0 \le j \le n-1$. □

Note that if

$$E \equiv \bigcup_{j=0}^{n-1} \boldsymbol{a}_j E^j \cup \varepsilon(E),$$

then $\| E^j \| = a_j^{-1} \| E \|$, for $0 \le j \le n-1$.

Theorem 3.9.38 *Let* $E_0, \ldots, E_{n-1}, F_0, \ldots, F_{n-1} \in \mathsf{REXP}(A)$.

If $P_0, \ldots, P_{n-1}$ *are regular expressions,* R_{ij} *are regular expressions that do not have the ewp property, for* $0 \le i, j \le n-1$, *and*

$$\vdash (E_i, F_i) \sim R_{i0}(E_0, F_0) \cup \cdots \cup R_{i\,n-1}(E_{n-1}, F_{n-1}) \cup (P_i, P_i)$$

for $0 \le i \le n-1$, *then* $\vdash (E_i, F_i)$ *for* $0 \le i \le n-1$.

Proof. The argument is by induction on n. For $n = 0$ we have

$$\vdash (E_0, F_0) \sim R_{i0}(E_0, F_0) \cup (P_0, P_0),$$

which amounts to $\vdash E_0 \sim R_{00}E_0 \cup P_0$ and $\vdash F_0 \sim R_{00}F_0 \cup P_0$. Since F_{00} does not have the ewp property, by the **SE** Rule, $\vdash E_0 \sim R_{00}^* P_0$ and $\vdash F_0 \sim R_{00}^* P_0$. Next, by the Symmetry and Transitivity Rules we obtain $\vdash E_0 \sim F_0$.

Suppose now that the statement holds for n. Consider the regular expressions $E_0, \ldots, E_{n-1}, E_n, F_0, \ldots, F_{n-1}, F_n \in \mathsf{REXP}(A)$ such that

$$\vdash (E_i, F_i) \sim R_{i0}(E_0, F_0) \cup \cdots \cup R_{i\,n}(E_n, F_n) \cup (P_i, P_i),$$

for $0 \leq i \leq n$, where R_{ij} are regular expressions such that $\lambda \notin \| R_{ij} \|$ for $0 \leq i, j \leq n$.

Since $\vdash E_n \sim R_{n0}E_0 \cup \cdots \cup R_{nn}E_n \cup P_n$ and $\vdash F_n \sim R_{n0}F_0 \cup \cdots \cup R_{nn}F_n \cup P_n$, by the **SE** Rule,

$$\vdash E_n \sim R_{nn}^*(R_{n0}E_0 \cup \cdots \cup R_{n\,n-1}E_{n-1} \cup P_n)$$

and

$$\vdash F_n \sim R_{nn}^*(R_{n0}F_0 \cup \cdots \cup R_{n\,n-1}F_{n-1} \cup P_n).$$

Thus, we have

$$\begin{aligned} \vdash (E_n, F_n) \quad \sim \quad & R_{nn}^* R_{n0}(E_0, F_0) \cup \cdots \cup R_{nn}^* R_{n\,n-1}(E_{n-1}, F_{n-1}) \\ & \cup (R_{nn}^* P_n, R_{nn}^* P_n). \end{aligned}$$

By the Replacement Rule and other rules that facilitate algebraic manipulations we obtain:

$$\begin{aligned} \vdash (E_i, F_i) \quad \sim \quad & (R_{i0} \cup R_{nn}^* R_{n0})(E_0, F_0) \cup \cdots \\ & \cup (R_{i\,n-1} \cup R_{nn}^* R_{n\,n-1})(E_{n-1}, F_{n-1}) \\ & \cup (P_i \cup R_{nn}^* P_n, P_i \cup R_{nn}^* P_n) \end{aligned}$$

for $0 \leq i \leq n - 1$.

Clearly, $\lambda \notin \| R_{ij} \cup R_{nn}^* R_{nj} \|$, so, by the inductive hypothesis, $\vdash (E_i, F_i)$ for $0 \leq i \leq n - 1$, which in turn, imply $\vdash (E_n, F_n)$. ∎

Theorem 3.9.39 *Every regular expression is equationally characterizable.*

Proof. Let $E \in \mathsf{REXP}(A)$, where $A = \{a_0, \ldots, a_{n-1}\}$. The argument is by induction on regular expressions. The basic step has the following three substeps:

1. If $E = \emptyset$, then

$$\vdash \emptyset \sim \boldsymbol{a}_0\emptyset \cup \cdots \cup \boldsymbol{a}_{n-1}\emptyset \cup \emptyset,$$

by repeatedly applying Axiom 8, Axiom 6 and the Replacement, Symmetry and Transitivity Rules, so $\emptyset$ is equationally characterizable.

2. When $E = \boldsymbol{a}_i$ we have

$$\vdash \boldsymbol{a}_i \sim \boldsymbol{a}_0\emptyset \cup \cdots \cup \boldsymbol{a}_i\Lambda \cup \cdots \cup \boldsymbol{a}_{n-1}\emptyset \cup \emptyset,$$

using Axioms 7,8,9 and the Replacement, Symmetry and Transitivity Rules.

3. If $E = \Lambda$, we obtain

$$\vdash \Lambda \sim \boldsymbol{a}_0\emptyset \cup \cdots \cup \boldsymbol{a}_{n-1}\emptyset \cup \Lambda.$$

Assume that the regular expressions E, F are equationally characterizable, that is there are regular expressions $E_0, \ldots, E_{m-1}$ and $F_0, \ldots, F_{p-1}$ such that $E = E_0$, $F = F_0$,

$$\vdash E_i \sim \bigcup_{j=0}^{n-1} \boldsymbol{a}_j E_i^j \cup \varepsilon(E_i), \tag{3.14}$$

and

$$\vdash F_k \sim \bigcup_{j=0}^{n-1} \boldsymbol{a}_j F_k^j \cup \varepsilon(F_k), \tag{3.15}$$

where $E_i^j \in \{E_0, \ldots, E_{m-1}\}$, $F_k^j \in \{F_0, \ldots, F_{p-1}\}$, for $0 \leq j \leq n-1$, $0 \leq i \leq m-1$, and $0 \leq k \leq p-1$.

We need to show that $E \cup F$, EF and E^* are equationally characterizable.

Let $\xi(i, k)$ be the regular expression $E_i \cup F_k$ for $0 \leq i \leq m-1$ and $0 \leq k \leq p-1$. It is easy to see that $\vdash \emptyset \cup \emptyset \sim \emptyset$, $\vdash \emptyset \cup \Lambda \sim \Lambda$, $\vdash \Lambda \cup \emptyset \sim \Lambda$, and $\vdash \Lambda \cup \Lambda \sim \Lambda$. From these, Equations 3.14 and 3.15, and the appropriate distributivity and commutativity axioms we obtain

$$\vdash \xi(i,k) = \bigcup_{j=0}^{n-1} \boldsymbol{a}_j (E_i^j \cup F_k^j) \cup \varepsilon(i,k),$$

for $0 \leq i \leq m-1$ and $0 \leq k \leq p-1$, where $\varepsilon(i,k) = \varepsilon(E_i \cup F_k)$. Since $\xi(0,0) = E \cup F$, $E \cup F$ is equationally characterizable.

Consider now the regular expression

$$\eta(i, k_0, \ldots, k_{h-1}) = (E_i F) \cup F_{k_0} \cup \cdots \cup F_{k_{h-1}},$$

where $0 \leq i \leq m-1$, $h \geq 0$, and $0 \leq k_0 < k_1 < \cdots < k_{h-1} \leq p-1$. Note that there are $m \cdot 2^p$ such expressions.

If $\varepsilon(E_i) = \emptyset$, we have

$$\vdash \eta(i, k_0, \ldots, k_{h-1}) \sim \left(\bigcup_{j=0}^{n-1} \boldsymbol{a}_j E_i^j \right) F \cup \bigcup_{\ell=0}^{h-1} \left(\bigcup_{j=0}^{n-1} \boldsymbol{a}_j F_{k_\ell}^j \cup \varepsilon(F_{k_\ell}) \right)$$

This implies

$$\vdash \eta(i, k_0, \ldots, k_{h-1}) \sim \bigcup_{j=0}^{n-1} \boldsymbol{a}_j \left(E_i^j F \cup \bigcup_{\ell=0}^{h-1} F_{k_\ell}^j \right) \cup \bigcup_{\ell=0}^{h-1} \varepsilon(F_{k_\ell}).$$

If $\varepsilon(E_i) = \Lambda$, then

$$\vdash \eta(i, k_0, \ldots, k_{h-1}) \sim \bigcup_{j=0}^{n-1} \boldsymbol{a}_j \left(E_i^j F \cup F_0^j \cup \bigcup_{\ell=0}^{h-1} F_{k_\ell}^j \right) \cup \bigcup_{\ell=0}^{h-1} \varepsilon(F_{k_\ell}).$$

Note that the expressions $E_i^j F \cup \bigcup_{\ell=0}^{h-1} F_{k_\ell}^j$, or $E_i^j F \cup F_0^j \cup \bigcup_{\ell=0}^{h-1} F_{k_\ell}^j$ are among the regular expressions of the form $\eta(i, k_0, \ldots, k_{h-1})$, in view of the assumptions that concern the expressions E_i^j. Thus, $\eta(i, k_0, \ldots, k_{h-1})$ are equationally characterizable. Since $\eta(0) = EF$, we conclude that EF is equationally characterizable.

Now let $\zeta(0) = E^*$ and $\zeta(i_0, \ldots, i_{h-1}) = (E_{i_0} \cup \cdots \cup E_{i_{h-1}})E^*$, where $h \geq 1$ and $0 \leq i_0 < i_1 < \cdots < i_{h-1} \leq m$. Note that there are 2^m such regular expressions.

Since

$$\vdash E_i \sim \bigcup_{j=0}^{n-1} \boldsymbol{a}_j E_i^j \cup \varepsilon(E_i),$$

for $0 \leq i \leq m-1$, where $E = E_0$, using either Axiom (9) or Axiom (11) (depending on the value of $\varepsilon(E_0)$), we can write

$$\vdash E^* \sim \left(\bigcup \boldsymbol{a}_j E_0^j\right)^*.$$

By Axiom (10) we obtain

$$\vdash E^* \sim \bigcup \boldsymbol{a}_j E_0^j E^* \cup \Lambda,$$

so

$$\vdash \zeta(0) \sim \bigcup \boldsymbol{a}_j E_0^j E^* \cup \Lambda.$$

If $E_{i_0} \cup \cdots \cup E_{i_{h-1}}$ does not have the ewp, we can write

$$\vdash \zeta(i_0, \ldots, i_{h-1}) \sim \bigcup_{j=0}^{n-1} \boldsymbol{a}_j (E_{i_0}^j \cup \cdots \cup E_{i_{h-1}}^j) E^* \cup \emptyset.$$

Otherwise, that is, if $E_{i_0} \cup \cdots \cup E_{i_{h-1}}$ has the ewp we have

$$\vdash \zeta(i_0, \ldots, i_{h-1}) \sim \bigcup_{j=0}^{n-1} \boldsymbol{a}_j (E_0^j \cup E_{i_0}^j \cup \cdots \cup E_{i_{h-1}}^j) E^* \cup \Lambda,$$

In either case, the coefficients of $\boldsymbol{a}_j$ have the form $\zeta(\cdots)$, so the expressions $\zeta(i_0, \ldots, i_{h-1})$ are equationally characterizable. In particular, E^* is equationally characterizable. ∎

Theorem 3.9.40 (Completeness Theorem) *Let E, F be two regular expressions. If $E \equiv F$, then $\vdash E \sim F$.*

Proof. Suppose that $E \equiv F$. By Theorem 3.9.39, both E and F are equationally characterizable. Therefore, we have the regular expressions $E_0, \ldots, E_{m-1}$ and $F_0, \ldots, F_{p-1}$ such that $E = E_0$, $F = F_0$,

$$\vdash E_i \sim \bigcup_{j=0}^{n-1} \boldsymbol{a}_j E_{ij} \cup \varepsilon(E_i), \tag{3.16}$$

and

$$\vdash F_k \sim \bigcup_{j=0}^{n-1} \boldsymbol{a}_j F_{kj} \cup \varepsilon(F_k), \tag{3.17}$$

where $\varepsilon(E_i) = \varepsilon(F_k)$, $E_{ij} \in \{E_0, \ldots, E_{m-1}\}$, $F_{kj} \in \{F_0, \ldots, F_{p-1}\}$, for $0 \leq j \leq n-1$, $0 \leq i \leq m-1$, and $0 \leq k \leq p-1$. Therefore,

$$\vdash (E, F) = (E_0, F_0) \sim \bigcup_{j=0}^{n-1} \boldsymbol{a}_j (E_{0j}, F_{0j}) \cup (\varepsilon(E), \varepsilon(E)).$$

By Theorem 3.9.38, we obtain

$$\vdash (E_{0j}, F_{0j}) \sim \bigcup_{j'=0}^{n-1} \boldsymbol{a}_{j'} (E'_{0j'}, F'_{0j'}) \cup (\varepsilon(E_{0j}), \varepsilon(E_{0j})),$$

where the pairs $(E'_{0j'}, F'_{0j'})$ are among the pairs (E_i, F_k). This is carried on until no new pairs appear and the process generates a set of pairs of regular expressions $\{(E^{[0]}, F^{[0]}), (E^{[1]}, F^{[1]}), \ldots, (E^{[r-1]}, F^{[r-1]})\}$, where $r \leq mp$ and

$$\vdash (E^{[i]}, F^{[i]}) \sim \bigcup_{j=0}^{n-1} \boldsymbol{a}_j (E_i^{[j]}, F_i^{[j]}) \cup (D_i, D_i),$$

where every pair $(E_i^{[j]}, F_i^{[j]})$ is among the pairs

$$(E^{[0]}, F^{[0]}), (E^{[1]}, F^{[1]}), \ldots, (E^{[r-1]}, F^{[r-1]}).$$

By regrouping the regular expressions involved we obtain

$$\vdash (E^{[i]}, F^{[i]}) \sim \bigcup_{k=0}^{r-1} C_{ij} (E_i^{[k]}, F_i^{[k]}) \cup (D_i, D_i),$$

where $C_{ij} = \emptyset$, or $C_{ij} = \boldsymbol{a}_{\ell_1} \cup \cdots \cup \boldsymbol{a}_{\ell_h}$. Since none of the expressions C_{ij} has the ewp we obtain, by Theorem 3.9.36, that $\vdash E^{[i]} \sim F^{[i]}$. In particular, for $i = 0$, we obtain $\vdash E \sim F$. ∎

3.10 Transducers

Transducers are extensions of automata that are capable of transforming words over one alphabet into words over another alphabet.

Definition 3.10.1 A *transducer* is a 6-tuple $\mathcal{T} = (A, Q, B, \theta, q_0, F)$, where A is the *input alphabet*, B is the *output alphabet*, Q is a finite set called the *set of states*, θ is a finite relation, $\theta \subseteq Q \times A^* \times B^* \times Q$, called the *transition relation*, q_0 is the *initial state of the transducer*, and F is the set of final states, where $F \subseteq Q$. The set Q is disjoint from the set $A \cup B$. □

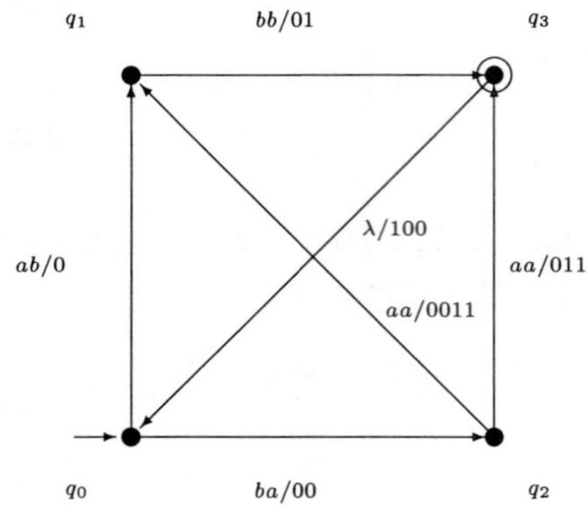

Figure 3.27: Graph of the Transducer $\mathcal{T}$

If $(q, x, y, q') \in \theta$, then applying the input word x to the transducer $\mathcal{T}$ in state q results in the output word y and places $\mathcal{T}$ into the state q', usually called the *next state* of $\mathcal{T}$. The activity of $\mathcal{T}$ begins in the state q_0.

Note that θ may contain several quadruples having q, x as their first two components, and thus, $\mathcal{T}$ is a nondeterministic device. Also, θ may contain a quadruple of the form (q, λ, y, q'), sometimes called a *null transition*, which means that $\mathcal{T}$ may produce an output word y without consuming an input symbol.

A transducer $\mathcal{T} = (A, Q, B, \theta, q_0, F)$ is:

- *λ-free* if $(q, x, y, q') \in \theta$ implies $y \neq \lambda$;
- *k-bounded* if $(q, x, y, q') \in \theta$ implies $|x| \leq k$ and $|y| \leq k$;
- *k-output* if $(q, x, y, q') \in \theta$ implies $|y| = k$.

Transducers can be represented by labeled directed multigraphs. Let $/$ be a symbol such that $/ \notin A \cup B$. The *graph of a transducer* $\mathcal{T} = (A, Q, B, \theta, q_0)$ is the labeled directed multigraph $G(\mathcal{T}) = (G, A^*/B^*, \mathsf{m})$ where $G = (Q, E, s, d)$ is a directed multigraph whose set of vertices is the set of states Q of $\mathcal{T}$ and whose set of edges E contains an edge e with $s(e) = q$, $d(e) = q'$, and $\mathsf{m}(e) = x/y$ for every quadruple $(q, x, y, q') \in \theta$. Following the convention introduced for automata, the initial state q_0 is denoted by an incoming arrow, and the final states are circled.

Example 3.10.2 Let $Q = \{q_0, q_1, q_2, q_3\}$, $A = \{a, b\}$ and $B = \{0, 1\}$. If θ is the relation

$$\begin{aligned} \theta &= \{(q_0, ab, 0, q_1), (q_1, bb, 01, q_3), (q_0, ba, 00, q_2), \\ &\quad (q_2, aa, 011, q_3), (q_3, \lambda, 100, q_0), (q_2, aa, 0011, q_1)\}. \end{aligned}$$

and $F = \{q_3\}$, then the graph of the transducer $\mathcal{T} = (A, Q, B, \theta, q_0, F)$ is given in Figure 3.27

□

Example 3.10.3 A morphism $h : A^* \longrightarrow B^*$ defines a one-state transducer $\mathcal{T}_h = (A, \{q_0\}, B, \theta_h, q_0, \{q_0\})$, where $\theta_h = \{(q_0, a, h(a), q_0) \mid a \in A\}$.

T_h produces the word $h(a)$ when the symbol a is applied at the input of the transducer $\mathcal{T}_h$. □

Definition 3.10.4 Let $\mathcal{T} = (A, Q, B, \theta, q_0, F)$ be a transducer. The set $\mathcal{I}(\mathcal{T})$ of *instantaneous descriptions of* $\mathcal{T}$ is the set $Q \times A^* \times B^*$.

A transducer $\mathcal{T}$ is *described* by $(q, u, v) \in \mathcal{I}(\mathcal{T})$ if $\mathcal{T}$ is in the state q, u is the portion of input that is still to be read, and v is the output word already generated by the transducer.

Any instantaneous description of the form (q_0, u, λ) is an *initial instantaneous description of* $\mathcal{T}$ *on input* u. □

Let $\mathcal{T} = (A, Q, B, \theta, q_0, F)$ be a transducer. The binary relation $\underset{\mathcal{T}}{\vdash}$ on the set $\mathcal{I}(\mathcal{T})$ is defined as follows: if $(q, u, v, q') \in \theta$, then $(q, uw, t) \underset{\mathcal{T}}{\vdash} (q', w, tv)$ for every $w \in A^*$.

The reflexive and transitive closure of $\underset{\mathcal{T}}{\vdash}$ is denoted, as usual, by $\overset{*}{\underset{\mathcal{T}}{\vdash}}$.

Note that if $(q, u, t) \overset{*}{\underset{\mathcal{T}}{\vdash}} (q', u', t')$, then $|u| \geq |u'|$ and $|t| \leq |t'|$.

Example 3.10.5 Let $\mathcal{T}$ be the transducer defined in Example 3.10.2. We have

$$(q_0, abbb, \lambda) \underset{\mathcal{T}}{\vdash} (q_1, bb, 0)$$

and

$$(q_1, bb, 0) \underset{\mathcal{T}}{\vdash} (q_3, \lambda, 001).$$

Therefore, $(q_0, abbb, \lambda) \overset{*}{\underset{\mathcal{T}}{\vdash}} (q_3, \lambda, 001)$. □

Definition 3.10.6 Let $\mathcal{T} = (A, Q, B, \theta, q_0, F)$ be a transducer. If $u \in A^*$, let $\mathcal{T}(u) \subseteq B^*$ be the set

$$\mathcal{T}(u) = \{v \in B^* \mid (q_0, u, \lambda) \overset{*}{\underset{\mathcal{T}}{\vdash}} (q, \lambda, v) \text{ for some } q \in F\}.$$

If $L \subseteq A^*$, we denote by $\mathcal{T}(L)$ the language

$$\mathcal{T}(L) = \{v \in B^* \mid v \in \mathcal{T}(u) \text{ for some } u \in L\}.$$

For $K \subseteq B^*$, let $\mathcal{T}^{-1}(K)$ be the language

$$\mathcal{T}^{-1}(K) = \{u \in A^* \mid \mathcal{T}(u) \subseteq K\}.$$

□

Note that if θ contains no quadruple (q, λ, y, q'), then $\mathcal{T}$ produces no output for the null word, that is $\mathcal{T}(\lambda) = \emptyset$.

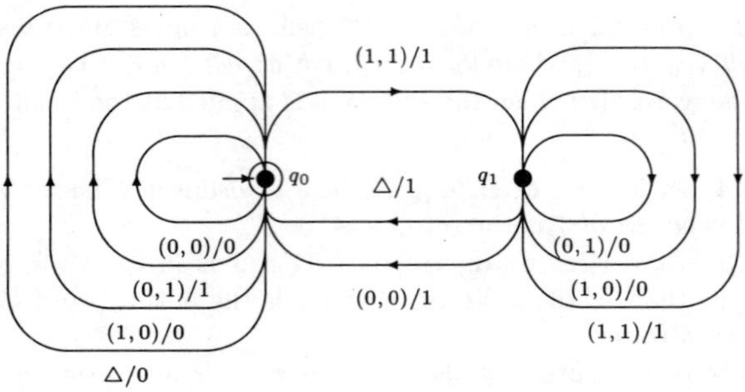

Figure 3.28: Graph of the Transducer $\mathcal{T}_2$

Example 3.10.7 In this example, we construct a transducer that adds two binary numbers, p and r. It works much as do people in that it starts from the least significant bit; thus for our purposes, the numbers are written from right to left. The lengths of the two representations are made equal by padding the shorter with zeros, and the end of the input is marked with a $\triangle$.

Let $p, r \in \mathbb{N}$ and let

$$\begin{aligned} p &= b_{n-1} \cdots b_1 b_0 \\ r &= b'_{n-1} \cdots b'_1 b'_0 \end{aligned}$$

be their binary representations.

Consider the transducer

$$\mathcal{T}_2 = ((B \times B) \cup \{\triangle\}, \{q_0, q_1\}, B, \theta, q_0, \{q_0\}),$$

where $B = \{0, 1\}$ and θ consists of the following quadruples:

$$\begin{array}{ll} (q_0, (0,0), 0, q_0) & (q_1, (0,0), 1, q_0) \\ (q_0, (0,1), 1, q_0) & (q_1, (0,1), 0, q_1) \\ (q_0, (1,0), 0, q_0) & (q_1, (1,0), 0, q_1) \\ (q_0, (1,1), 1, q_1) & (q_1, (1,1), 1, q_1) \\ (q_0, \triangle, 0, q_0) & (q_1, \triangle, 1, q_0) \end{array}$$

Its graph is given in Figure 3.28. If the sequence $(b_0, b'_0) \cdots (b_{n-1}, b'_{n-1})\triangle \in (B^2 \cup \{\triangle\})^*$ is entered in the transducer, then $\mathcal{T}_2$ yields at the output a word in B^* that represents the reverse of the binary equivalent of the sum $p + r$ of the numbers p, r.

By examining the tuples of θ, the role of the states of $\mathcal{T}_2$ is clear: they remember the carry resulting from adding the component of a pair (a_i, b_i) and any carry resulting from the previous additions. For example, the binary representations of $p = 7$ and $r = 12$ are 0111 and 1100, so the binary representation of the pair (p, r) is $(0,1)(0,1)(1,1),(1,0)\triangle$. The binary representation of 7 was padded with leading zeros to equalize the length of the two words. The transducer yields 11001 as its output, which is the binary representation of 19. In general, we have

$$\mathcal{T}_2((b_0, b'_0) \cdots (b_{n-1}, b'_{n-1})\triangle) = \{c_0 \cdots c_m\}$$

if the binary representation of the sum of p and r is $c_m \cdots c_0$. □

The following is an algebraic description of the image of an arbitrary language under the mapping induced by a transducer. Special cases of this theorem facilitate proving that certain families of languages are closed under transducer mappings. The first example is Corollary 3.10.9.

Theorem 3.10.8 *Let $\mathcal{T} = (A, Q, B, \theta, q_0, F)$ be a transducer. There exist an alphabet C, a morphism $h : C^* \longrightarrow A^*$, a morphism $g : C^* \longrightarrow B^*$ and a regular languages $R \subseteq C^*$ such that for every language $L \subseteq A^*$ we have $\mathcal{T}(L) = g(h^{-1}(L) \cap R)$. Moreover, if $\mathcal{T}$ is λ-free, then g is a λ-free morphism.*

Proof. Define the alphabet $C = \{\langle q, u, v, q'\rangle \mid (q, u, v, q') \in \theta\}$ and the morphisms h, g by

$$\begin{aligned} h(\langle q, u, v, q'\rangle) &= u \\ g(\langle q, u, v, q'\rangle) &= v, \end{aligned}$$

for every $\langle q, u, v, q'\rangle \in C$. If $\mathcal{T}$ is λ-free, then so is the morphism g.

Let ρ be the binary relation on C defined by

$$\rho = \{(\langle q, u, v, q'\rangle, \langle q', t, s, q''\rangle \mid \langle q, u, v, q'\rangle \in C, \langle q', t, s, q''\rangle \in C\}.$$

In Example 3.4.15 we saw that L_ρ is a regular language. Therefore, the language $H = C \cup L_\rho$ is also regular. This implies the regularity of the language

$$\begin{aligned} K = \; & H \cap \{\langle q_0, u, v, q\rangle \mid \langle q_0, u, v, q\rangle \in C\}C^* \\ & \cap\, C^*\{\langle q, t, s, q'\rangle \mid \langle q, t, s, q'\rangle \in C \text{ and } q' \in F\}. \end{aligned}$$

Observe that

$$\begin{aligned} K = \; & \{\langle q_{i_0}, u_{i_1}, v_{i_1}, q_{i_1}\rangle \cdots \langle q_{i_{n-1}}, u_{i_n}, v_{i_n}, q_{i_n}\rangle \mid \\ & \langle q_{i_{p-1}}, u_{i_p}, v_{i_p}, q_{i_p}\rangle \in C \text{ for } 1 \leq p \leq n \text{ and } n \geq 1\}. \end{aligned}$$

We assume that $i_0 = 0$.

Define R to be the regular language

$$R = \begin{cases} K & \text{if } q_0 \notin F \\ K \cup \{\lambda\} & \text{otherwise} \end{cases}$$

We claim that $\mathcal{T}(L) = g(h^{-1}(L) \cap R)$. Indeed, let $v \in \mathcal{T}(L)$. There exists a word $u \in L$ such that $v = \mathcal{T}(u)$. By the definition of $\mathcal{T}(u)$, $u = u_0 \cdots u_{n-1}$ and $v = v_0 \cdots v_{n-1}$ such that

$$\begin{aligned} (q_{i_0}, u_0 \cdots u_{n-1}, \lambda) & \vdash_{\mathcal{T}} (q_{i_1}, u_1 \cdots u_{n-1}, v_0) \\ & \vdash_{\mathcal{T}} (q_{i_2}, u_2 \cdots u_{n-1}, v_0 v_1) \\ & \vdots \\ & \vdash_{\mathcal{T}} (q_{i_{n-1}}, u_{n-1}, v_0 v_1 \cdots v_{n-2}) \\ & \vdash_{\mathcal{T}} (q_{i_n}, \lambda, v_0 v_1 \cdots v_{n-2} v_{n-1}), \end{aligned}$$

where $i_0 = 0$ and $q_{i_n} \in F$. This implies the existence of the quadruples $(q_{i_p}, u_p, v_p, q_{i_{p+1}}) \in \theta$ for $0 \leq p \leq n-1$. Consequently, the word $r \in C^*$ given by

$$r = \langle q_{i_0}, u_0, v_0, q_{i_1} \rangle \cdots \langle q_{i_{n-1}}, u_{n-1}, v_{n-1}, q_{i_n} \rangle$$

belongs to R. Note that $h(r) = u$ and $g(r) = v$. Therefore, $r \in h^{-1}(L) \cap L$, so $v \in g(h^{-1}(L) \cap R)$. We leave to the reader the proof of the reverse inclusion. ∎

Corollary 3.10.9 *If $\mathcal{T} = (A, Q, B, \theta, q_0, F)$ is a transducer and $L \subseteq A^*$ is a regular language, then $\mathcal{T}(L)$ is regular.*

Proof. Let L be a regular language, $L \subseteq A^*$. Theorem 3.10.8 allows us to write $\mathcal{T}(L) = g(h^{-1}(L) \cap R)$, where g, h are morphisms, and R is a regular language, $R \subseteq C^*$.

By applying Theorems 3.9.12, and Corollaries 3.9.11 and 3.4.5 it follows that $\mathcal{T}(L)$ is regular. ∎

Next, we examine transducers that have certain restrictions imposed on their transition relations.

Definition 3.10.10 A *generalized sequential machine* (gsm) is a transducer $\mathcal{T} = (A, Q, B, \theta, q_0, F)$ such that there are two functions $\delta : Q \times A \longrightarrow Q$ and $\gamma : Q \times A \longrightarrow B^*$ that allow us to write

$$\begin{aligned} \theta &= \{(q, a, \gamma(q, a), \delta(q, a)) \mid q \in Q, a \in A\} \\ &\cup \{(q, \lambda, \lambda, q) \mid q \in Q\}. \end{aligned}$$

The functions δ, γ are *the transition function* and *the output function*, respectively. □

Example 3.10.11 The transducer $\mathcal{T}_2$ introduced in Example 3.10.7 is actually a gsm. The transition function and the output functions are given by the following tables:

$\delta(q,a)$	$(0,0)$	$(0,1)$	$(1,0)$	$(1,1)$	$\triangle$
q_0	q_0	q_0	q_0	q_1	q_0
q_1	q_1	q_1	q_1	q_1	q_0

$\gamma(q,a)$	$(0,0)$	$(0,1)$	$(1,0)$	$(1,1)$	$\triangle$
q_0	0	1	1	0	0
q_1	1	0	0	1	1

□

If $\mathcal{T} = (A, Q, B, \theta, q_0)$ is a gsm whose transition relation is defined by the functions $\delta : Q \times A \longrightarrow Q$ and $\gamma : Q \times A \longrightarrow B^*$, then we shall denote $\mathcal{T}$ by the 7-tuple $\mathcal{T} = (A, Q, B, \delta, \gamma, q_0, F)$. If $\gamma(q, a) \neq \lambda$, we refer to $\mathcal{T}$ as a *λ-free gsm.*

A popular special case of generalized sequential machines are the *Mealy automata.*

Definition 3.10.12 A *Mealy automaton* is a gsm $\mathcal{T} = (A, Q, B, \delta, \gamma, q_0, Q)$ such that $|\gamma(q, a)| = 1$ for every $q \in Q$ and $a \in A$. □

Note that all states are final states. Therefore, we can denote a Mealy automaton as a 6-tuple $\mathcal{T} = (A, Q, B, \delta, \gamma, q_0)$.

Let $\mathcal{T} = (A, Q, B, \delta, \gamma, q_0)$ be a Mealy automaton. Both δ and γ can be extended to $Q \times A^*$. For δ^*, the extension of δ we use the definition contained in Section 3.2, namely

$$\begin{aligned}\delta^*(q, \lambda) &= q\\ \delta^*(q, xa) &= \delta(\delta^*(q, x), a),\end{aligned}$$

for every $x \in A^*$ and $a \in A$. The extension $\gamma^* : Q \times A^* \longrightarrow B^*$ is given by

$$\begin{aligned}\gamma^*(q, \lambda) &= \lambda\\ \gamma^*(q, xa) &= \gamma^*(q, x)\gamma(\delta^*(q, x), a)\end{aligned}$$

for every $x \in A^*$ and $a \in A$. Thus, for a Mealy automaton $\mathcal{T}$ we have:

$$\mathcal{T}(u) = \{v\}, \text{ where } v = \gamma^*(q_0, u).$$

3.11 Automata and String Patterns

The task of identifying string patterns that occur in longer strings of symbols is important in many diverse areas, ranging from text editing programs to molecular biology to the study of bird songs (see [Smith, 1994; Sankoff and Kruskal, 1983]). This topic is of such significance that there is a major body of work in the area. We begin with an obvious approach to the problem and then show more recent, elegant solutions.

Here is a simple C program that identifies the leftmost occurrence of a pattern `p` in a string `s` using a brute force approach. For each position in the string `s`, the function `patinstr` verifies whether the pattern `p` occurs in `s` by comparing the infix of the string `s` that begins at that position with the pattern. If the pattern exists in the string, its beginning index is returned, where, consistent with the usual C convention and our notation, 0 is the position of the first character in the string; if not, `-1` is returned.[1] The purpose of the main program is simply to try `patinstr` as a simple example.

```
#include <stdio.h>
#include <string.h>

int patinstr(char *p, char *s);

void main()
{
    char *str1 = "United States of America",
         *str2 = "of";
    int pos;

    if ((pos = patinstr(str2, str1)) >= 0)
        printf("Pattern '%s' occurs in string '%s "
               "at position %d.\n", str2, str1, pos);
```

[1]The C library `string.h` contains a similar function, called `strstr`, which returns a pointer to the leftmost occurrence of the pattern, or a null pointer, if the pattern is not in the string.

```
    else
        printf("Pattern '%s' does not occur in string "
               "'%s'.\n", str2, str1);
}

int patinstr(char *p, char *s)
/*****************************************
* return index of pattern p in string s,  *
*        or -1 if p not in s.             *
*****************************************/
{
    char *pp,        /* pointer to current place in pattern */
         *sp,        /* pointer to current place in string  */
         *s0p = s;   /* pointer to original string          */

    for( ; *s; s++) {
        for(sp = s, pp = p; *pp && (*sp == *pp); pp++)
            sp++;
        if (!*pp)
            return s-s0p;    /* index of p in s  */
    }
    return -1;               /* p not found in s */
}
```

The time required by this algorithm is proportional to the product of the length of the pattern and the length of the analyzed string. A more efficient method for finding patterns in strings is given by the *Rabin-Karp algorithm* that we describe below.

Let A be an alphabet, where $|A| = n$. To determine whether a pattern $u = a_{i_0} \dots a_{i_{k-1}} \in A^*$ occurs in a word $w \in A^*$, we compute the number $f_A(u)$ given by

$$f_A(a_{i_0} \dots a_{i_k}) = n^{k-1}(i_0+1) + n^{k-2}(i_1+1) + \cdots + n(i_{k-2}+1) + i_{k-1} + 1,$$

where f_A is the bijection introduced in Section 2.2. Observe that

$$f_A(a_{i_0} \dots a_{i_k}) = (\cdots(((i_0+1)\cdot n + i_1 + 1)\cdot n + i_2 + 1)\cdots + i_{k-2} + 1)\cdot n + i_{k-1} + 1.$$

This shows that we can compute $f_A(a_{i_0} \dots a_{i_k})$ in $O(k)$ time.

Suppose now that $w = a_{j_0} a_{j_1} \cdots a_{j_{m-1}}$. Recall that we use the notation $w_{p,r}$ to represent the infix $a_{j_p} \cdots a_{j_{r-1}}$. We can compute the values $f_A(w_{\ell,\ell+k})$ for all infixes $w_{\ell,\ell+k}$ of length k of the word w for $0 \leq \ell \leq m-k$. It is easy to see that

$$f_A(w_{\ell+1,\ell+k+1}) = n \cdot f_A(w_{\ell,\ell+k}) - n^k \cdot (j_\ell + 1) + j_{\ell+k} + 1.$$

The value n^k can be precomputed, so $f_A(w_{\ell+1,\ell+k+1})$ can be computed from $f_A(w_{\ell,\ell+k})$ in constant time. Therefore, the computation of all values $f_A(w_{\ell,\ell+k})$ for all infixes $w_{\ell,\ell+k}$ of length k of the word w for $0 \leq \ell \leq m-k$ requires

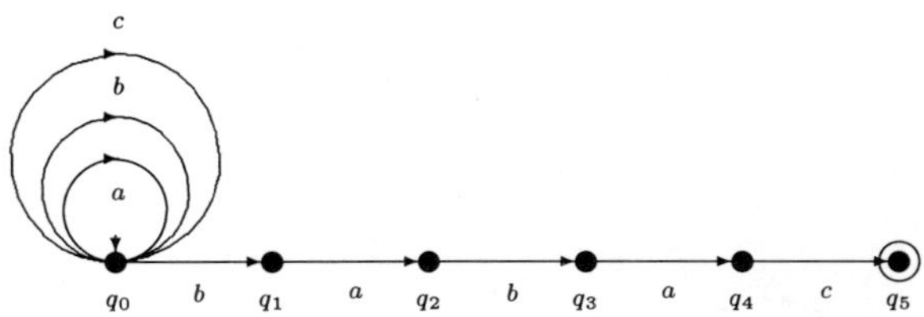

Figure 3.29: Graph of the ndfa $\mathcal{M}^{nd}_{babac}$

$O(k) + (m - k)b$ operations, where $b \in \mathbb{N}$ is a constant number; in other words, we can determine the values $f_A(w_{\ell,\ell+k})$ for $0 \leq \ell \leq m - k$ in $O(m + k)$ time. The word w contains the pattern u if and only if there exists an infix $w_{\ell,\ell+k}$ such that $f_A(u) = f_A(w_{\ell,\ell+k})$ (which implies $u = w_{\ell,\ell+k}$). Thus, we can determine in $O(k + m)$ time if w contains the pattern u.

This approach to the problem has the disadvantage that it involves very large numbers that exceed by far the largest integers ordinarily represented in computers. For example, if $A = \{a_0, \ldots , a_{25}\}$ is the set of capital letters of the latin alphabet, the code of a relatively small pattern like `PATTERN` is

$$\begin{aligned} & 16 \cdot 26^6 + 1 \cdot 26^5 + 20 \cdot 26^4 + 20 \cdot 26^3 + 5 \cdot 26^2 + 18 \cdot 26 + 14 \\ = \;& 3,338,254,409,494. \end{aligned}$$

The Rabin-Karp algorithm replaces the computation of the value of $f_A(x)$ with a *fingerprint* of the string x, defined as $f_A(x) \bmod q$, where q is a prime number. The function $f_{A,q} : A^* \longrightarrow \mathbb{N}$ defined by $f_{A,q}(x) = f_A(x) \bmod q$ is, of course, not a bijection any longer. In other words, even if $f_{A,q}(u) = f_{A,q}(v)$, we cannot conclude that $u = v$; however, if $f_{A,q}(u) \neq f_{A,q}(v)$, then $u \neq v$. Thus, if $f_{A,q}(u) = f_{A,q}(v)$, we need to examine the strings u, v character by character to make sure that we do not falsely match u and v. Thus, in the best case, this algorithm takes $O(k + m)$ operations; in the worst case, it takes $O(km)$ operations.

Next, we discuss an algorithm that makes use of deterministic finite automata. Let A be an alphabet, and let $u = a_{i_0} \cdots a_{i_{n-1}} \in A^*$ be a pattern that we need to identify in words from A^*. If $t \in A^*$ contains the infix u, there is a prefix x of t that ends in u. Thus, we need to design a dfa that accepts the language A^*u. Using the techniques discussed in Section 3.9, it is easy to design a nondeterministic finite automaton $\mathcal{M}^{nd}_u$ that accepts this language. It is clear that $\mathcal{M}^{nd}_u$ enters a final state q' when reading a prefix x of a word t if and only if $x = vu$ for some $v \in A^*$; that is, if and only if $t = vuz$ for some $v, z \in A^*$.

Example 3.11.1 Consider the alphabet $A = \{a, b, c\}$ and the pattern $u = babac$. The graph of the ndfa $\mathcal{M}^{nd}_u$ is shown in Figure 3.29.

Since $\mathcal{M}^{nd}_{babac}$ has six states, the usual construction of the deterministic automaton that accepts the same language (discussed in Section 3.2) yields a device that has $2^6 = 64$ states. Actually, we need consider only the accessible

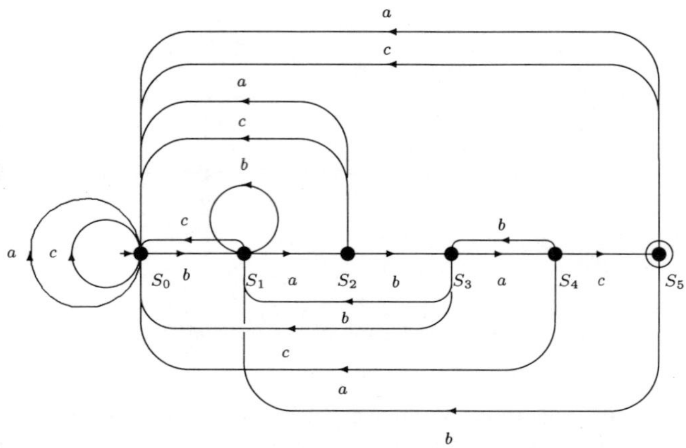

Figure 3.30: Graph of the dfa $\mathcal{M}_{babac}$

part $\mathcal{M}_{babac}$ of the state diagram of this dfa; its graph is shown in Figure 3.30. The sets of states of $\mathcal{M}^{nd}_{babac}$ that are the states of $\mathcal{M}_{babac}$ are denoted as shown in the following table:

$\{q_0\}$	$\{q_0, q_1\}$	$\{q_0, q_2\}$	$\{q_0, q_1, q_3\}$	$\{q_0, q_2, q_4\}$	$\{q_0, q_5\}$
S_0	S_1	S_2	S_3	S_4	S_5

Note that the number of states of $\mathcal{M}_{babac}$ is also six. □

Much of the rest of this section is devoted to showing that this is no accident. The "combinatorial explosion" that occurs in the usual construction of the deterministic automaton that accepts the same language as a nondeterministic automaton can be avoided in this special case. The argument is detailed and rather complex, but the result is worth the effort both because it yields a surprisingly fast algorithm for pattern matching and because it is a beautiful and clever theoretical result.

The graph of the ndfa $\mathcal{M}^{nd}_u$ for $u = a_{i_0} \cdots a_{i_{n-1}}$ is given in Figure 3.31. Note that the transition function δ is defined by

$$\delta(q_0, a) = \begin{cases} \{q_0\} & \text{if } a \neq a_{i_0} \\ \{q_0, q_1\} & \text{if } a = a_{i_0} \end{cases}$$

and

$$\delta(q_\ell, a) = \begin{cases} \emptyset & \text{if } a \neq a_{i_\ell} \\ \{q_{\ell+1}\} & \text{if } a = a_{i_\ell}, \end{cases}$$

for $1 \leq \ell \leq n - 1$. Also, $\delta(q_n, a) = \emptyset$ for every $a \in A$.

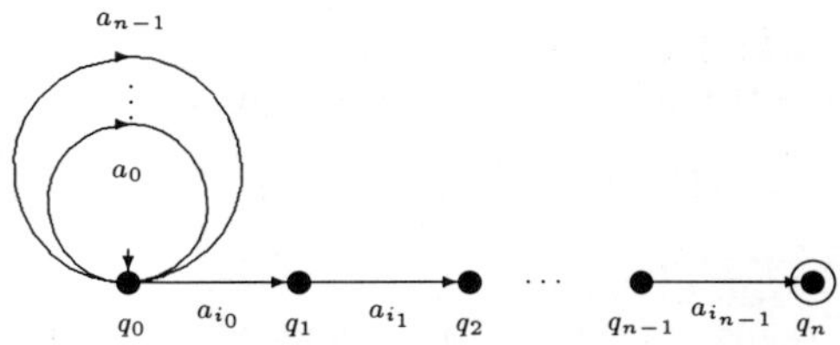

Figure 3.31: Graph of the ndfa $\mathcal{M}_u^{nd}$

Theorem 3.11.2 *Let A be an alphabet, $u = a_{i_0} \cdots a_{i_{n-1}} \in A^*$ be a word of length n, and let $\mathcal{M}_u^{nd} = (A, \{q_0, \ldots, q_n\}, \delta, q_0, \{q_n\})$ be the ndfa that accepts the language A^*u (shown in Figure 3.31). If $\Delta : \mathcal{P}(\{q_0, \ldots, q_n\}) \times A \longrightarrow \mathcal{P}(\{q_0, \ldots, q_n\})$ is the transition function of the equivalent dfa given by*

$$\Delta(S, a) = \bigcup_{q \in S} \delta(q, a),$$

for every $S \subseteq Q$ and $a \in A$, then $\Delta^*(\{q_0\}, x) = \{q_\ell \mid u_{0,\ell} \in \mathsf{SUFF}(x)\}$ for every $x \in A^*$.

Proof. The argument is by induction on $|x|$. If $|x| = 0$, then $x = \lambda$ and the result follows immediately.

Suppose that the equality holds for words of length n, and let y be a word of length $n + 1$. We can write $y = xa$, where $|x| = n$ and $a \in A$, and we have

$$\begin{aligned}\Delta^*(\{q_0\}, xa) &= \Delta(\Delta^*(\{q_0\}, x), a)\\ &= \Delta(\{q_\ell \mid u_{0,\ell} \in \mathsf{SUFF}(x)\}, a)\\ &= \bigcup\{\delta(q_\ell, a) \mid u_{0,\ell} \in \mathsf{SUFF}(x)\}.\end{aligned}$$

Observe now that the state q_ℓ has a successor state q_m (with $m > 0$) in $\mathcal{M}_u^{nd}$ when a is read as the input symbol if and only if $m = \ell + 1$ and $a = a_{i_\ell}$. This is equivalent to $u_{0,m} = u_{0,\ell+1} \in \mathsf{SUFF}(xa)$. Thus,

$$\Delta^*(\{q_0\}, xa) = \{q_m \mid u_{0,m} \in \mathsf{SUFF}(xa)\}.$$

∎

Corollary 3.11.3 *The state q_0 belongs to $\Delta^*(\{q_0\}, x)$ for every $x \in A^*$.*

Proof. Since $u_{0,0} = \lambda \in \mathsf{SUFF}(x)$, the conclusion follows immediately from Theorem 3.11.2. ∎

Theorem 3.11.2 shows that the accessible part of the dfa $\mathcal{M}'$ that accepts the same language as $\mathcal{M}_u^{nd}$ consists of subsets of $\mathcal{P}(\{q_0, \ldots, q_n\})$ that have the form $\{q_\ell \mid u_{0,\ell} \in \mathsf{SUFF}(x)\}$ for some $x \in A^*$. We denote the corresponding dfa $\mathsf{ACC}(\mathcal{M}')$ by $\mathcal{M}_u$.

To achieve our goal of showing that $\mathcal{M}_u$ has no more states than $\mathcal{M}_u^{nd}$ we need to introduce two important functions: the suffix function and the failure function.

Definition 3.11.4 Let A be an alphabet and let $u \in A^*$. The *suffix function* defined by u is the function $\mathbf{s}_u : A^* \longrightarrow \mathbb{N}$ given by

$$\mathbf{s}_u(x) = \max\{k \in \mathbb{N} \mid u_{0,k} \in \mathsf{SUFF}(x)\}$$

for every $x \in A^*$. □

In other words, $\mathbf{s}_u(x)$ is the length of the longest prefix of the word u that is a suffix of the word x. To show that $\mathbf{s}_u(x)$ is well-defined, we note that $\max P$ is defined whenever the finite set P is not empty. Since $\lambda \in \mathsf{PREF}(u) \cap \mathsf{SUFF}(x)$, and since the set $\mathsf{PREF}(u) \cap \mathsf{SUFF}(x)$ is finite, $\mathbf{s}_u(x)$ is indeed well-defined for each $x \in A^*$.

Example 3.11.5 Let $A = \{a, b, c\}$ and $u = acaba$. For $x = babaca \in A^*$ we have $\mathbf{s}_u(x) = 3$, since the longest prefix of u that is a suffix of x is aca. □

For every $x \in A^*$, $\mathbf{s}_u(x) = |u|$ if and only if $u \in \mathsf{SUFF}(x)$. Thus, $\mathbf{s}_u(u_{0,j}) = j$ for $0 \leq j \leq |u|$.

Lemma 3.11.6 *For all $x, y \in A^*$, if $x \in \mathsf{SUFF}(y)$, then $\mathbf{s}_u(x) \leq \mathbf{s}_u(y)$.*

Proof. Suppose that $x \in \mathsf{SUFF}(y)$, that is, $y = wx$. Let z be the longest prefix of u that is a suffix of x, so $\mathbf{s}_u(x) = |z|$. Since z is a suffix of x, there is $v \in A^*$ such that $x = vz$, so $y = wvz$. Therefore, z is both a prefix of u and a suffix of y, so $|z|$ is not greater than $\mathbf{s}_u(y)$. ■

Lemma 3.11.7 *For every $x \in A^*$ and $a \in A$ we have $\mathbf{s}_u(xa) \leq \mathbf{s}_u(x) + 1$.*

Proof. Suppose that z is the longest prefix of u that is a suffix of the word xa. This means that z has the form $z = va$, where v is a suffix of x. It is clear that v is a prefix of u since z is a prefix of u, so $\mathbf{s}_u(x)$ is at least $|v| = |z| - 1 = \mathbf{s}_u(xa) - 1$. ■

Theorem 3.11.8 *If $\mathbf{s}_u(x) = \ell$, then $\mathbf{s}_u(xa) = \mathbf{s}_u(u_{0,\ell}a)$ for every $x \in A^*$ and $a \in A$.*

Proof. The hypothesis implies that $u_{0,\ell}a$ is a suffix of xa since $u_{0,\ell}$ is a suffix of x. Therefore, by Lemma 3.11.6, we obtain $\mathbf{s}_u(u_{0,\ell}a) \leq \mathbf{s}_u(xa)$.

Let $r = \mathbf{s}_u(xa)$. By Lemma 3.11.7, we have $r \leq \ell + 1$. Since both $u_{0,\ell}$ and $u_{0,r}$ are suffixes of xa, the last inequality implies that $u_{0,r}$ is a suffix of $u_{0,\ell}a$. Therefore, $r \leq \mathbf{s}_u(u_{0,\ell}a)$, so $\mathbf{s}_u(xa) \leq s_u(u_{0,\ell}a)$. Combining this inequality with the inequality of the previous paragraph yields the desired equality. ■

By Theorem 3.11.2, the states of the dfa $\mathcal{M}_u$ have the form

$$\Delta^*(\{q_0\}, x) = \{q_\ell \mid u_{0,\ell} \in \mathsf{SUFF}(x)\}$$

for some $x \in A^*$. In order to clarify the structure of these sets we need the notion introduced next.

Definition 3.11.9 Let A be an alphabet. The *failure function* of a non-null word u is the function $\varphi_u : \{1, \ldots, |u|\} \longrightarrow \{0, \ldots, |u| - 1\}$ defined by

$$\varphi_u(j) = \max\{k \mid k < j \text{ and } u_{0,k} \in \mathsf{SUFF}(u_{0,j})\}$$

for $1 \leq j \leq |u|$. □

In other words, if $u_{0,j}$ is a nonempty prefix of u, then $k = \varphi_u(j)$ if k is the length of the longest suffix of $u_{0,j}$ that is a prefix of u and is shorter than $u_{0,j}$. Note that $\varphi_u(j) < j$ for $0 \leq j \leq |u|$.

The term *failure function* is explained later, after Theorem 3.11.17.

Lemma 3.11.10 *Let $p = \mathbf{s}_u(x)$. We have $u_{0,\ell} \in \mathsf{SUFF}(x)$ if and only if $u_{0,\ell} \in \mathsf{SUFF}(u_{0,p})$.*

Proof. Suppose that $u_{0,\ell} \in \mathsf{SUFF}(x)$; then, $x = wu_{0,\ell}$. The definition of p implies that there is $v \in A^*$ such that $x = vu_{0,p}$ and $\ell \leq p$. Therefore, $u_{0,\ell}$ is a suffix of $u_{0,p}$.

Conversely, suppose that $u_{0,\ell} \in \mathsf{SUFF}(u_{0,p})$, that is $u_{0,p} = tu_{0,\ell}$ for some $t \in A^*$. Since $x = vu_{0,p}$ it follows that $x = vtu_{0,\ell}$ which means that $u_{0,\ell}$ is a suffix of $u_{0,p}$. ∎

Theorem 3.11.11 *In the dfa $\mathcal{M}_u$ we have*

$$\Delta^*(\{q_0\}, x) = \{q_\ell \mid u_{0,\ell} \in \mathsf{SUFF}(u_{0,p})\},$$

where $p = \mathbf{s}_u(x)$.

Proof. The statement follows immediately from Lemma 3.11.10. ∎

Theorem 3.11.11 shows that the states of $\mathcal{M}_u$ have the form $\{q_\ell \mid u_{0,\ell} \in \mathsf{SUFF}(u_{0,p})\}$. Using the failure function we obtain the more precise description given in the next theorem. The import of this theorem is that any state S_r of the dfa $\mathcal{M}_u$ is determined by the state q_r of $\mathcal{M}_u^{nd}$. Therefore, there are no more states in $\mathcal{M}_u$ than there are states in $\mathcal{M}_u^{nd}$.

Theorem 3.11.12 *Let $S_r = \{q_\ell \mid u_{0,\ell} \in \mathsf{SUFF}(u_{0,r})\}$ be a state of the dfa $\mathcal{M}_u$. We have $S_r = \{q_{\varphi_u^{(i)}(r)} \mid i \in \mathbb{N}$ and $\varphi_u^{(i)}(r) \geq 0\}$.*

Proof. We begin by showing, by induction on i, that

$$u_{0,\varphi_u^{(i)}(r)} \in \mathsf{SUFF}(u_{0,r}).$$

The basis case, $i = 0$, is immediate since $\varphi_u^{(0)}(r) = r$.

Suppose that $u_{0,\varphi_u^{(i)}(r)} \in \mathsf{SUFF}(u_{0,r})$. If $m = \varphi_u^{(i+1)}(r)$, then $m = \varphi_u(k) = \max\{j \mid j < k \text{ and } u_{0,j} \in \mathsf{SUFF}(u_{0,k})\}$, where $k = \varphi_u^i(r)$. By the inductive hypothesis, $u_{0,k} \in \mathsf{SUFF}(u_{0,r})$. Thus, $u_{0,m} \in \mathsf{SUFF}(u_{0,r})$. This gives the inclusion

$$\{q_{\varphi_u^{(i)}(r)} \mid i \in \mathbb{N} \text{ and } \varphi_u^{(i)}(r) \geq 0\} \subseteq S_r.$$

To prove the converse inclusion we need to show that $u_{0,\ell} \in \mathsf{SUFF}(u_{0,r})$ implies the existence of an $i \in \mathbb{N}$ such that $\ell = \varphi_u^{(i)}(r)$.

The argument is by strong induction on $d = r - \ell$. The basis, $d = 0$, is immediate.

Suppose that the statement holds for all $d < n$, and let ℓ be a number such that $r - \ell = n > 0$ and $u_{0,\ell} \in \mathsf{SUFF}(u_{0,r})$. If ℓ is the largest number such that $u_{0,\ell} \in \mathsf{SUFF}(u_{0,r})$, then $\ell = \varphi_u(r)$ and the conclusion is immediate. Otherwise, there exists a smallest number ℓ' such that $\ell < \ell' \leq r$ and $u_{0,\ell'} \in \mathsf{SUFF}(u_{0,r})$.

Since $0 < r - \ell' < r - \ell = n$, by the inductive hypothesis, $\ell' = \varphi_u^{(i)}(r)$ for some $i \in \mathbb{N}$.

It is easy to see that $u_{0,\ell}$ is a suffix of $u_{0,\ell'}$ because both words are suffixes of $u_{0,r}$ and $\ell < \ell'$. Moreover, ℓ is the largest number such that $u_{0,\ell} \in \mathsf{SUFF}(u_{0,\ell'})$. Indeed, the existence of a number ℓ_1 such that $\ell < \ell_1 < \ell'$ with $u_{0,\ell_1} \in \mathsf{SUFF}(u_{0,\ell'})$, would contradict the definition of ℓ'. Hence, $\ell = \varphi_u(\ell')$, so $\ell = \varphi_u^{(i+1)}(r)$. ∎

To obtain a more condensed definition of the dfa $\mathcal{M}_u$ we need the following technical result.

Theorem 3.11.13 *Let $u = a_{i_0} \cdots a_{i_{n-1}} \in A^*$. In the dfa*

$$\mathcal{M}_u = (A, \{S_0, \ldots, S_n\}, \Delta, S_0, \{S_n\})$$

we have $\Delta(S_r, a) = S_{\mathbf{s}_u(u_{0,r}a)}$ for $0 \leq r \leq n$ and $a \in A^*$.

Proof. The definition of the function Δ implies that we need to prove that

$$\bigcup_{q \in S_r} \delta(q, a) = S_{\mathbf{s}_u(u_{0,r}a)},$$

for $0 \leq r \leq n$ and $a \in A^*$.

Let $q_h \in \delta(q_\ell, a)$, where $u_{0,\ell} \in \mathsf{SUFF}(u_{0,r})$. If $h = 0$, then it is clear that $q_0 \in S_{\mathbf{s}_u(u_{0,r}a)}$. Suppose therefore that $h > 0$. The definition of δ implies that $h = \ell + 1$ and $a = a_{i_\ell}$. In order to prove that $q_h \in S_{\mathbf{s}_u(u_{0,r}a)}$, we need to show that $u_{0,\ell+1} \in \mathsf{SUFF}(u_{0,\mathbf{s}_u(u_{0,r}a)})$. Since $u_{0,\mathbf{s}_u(u_{0,r}a)}$ is the longest prefix of u that is a suffix of $u_{0,r}a$ (by the definition of $\mathbf{s}_u$), $u_{0,\ell}$ is a suffix of $u_{0,r}$ and $a = a_{i_\ell}$, it follows that $u_{0,\ell+1}$ is indeed a suffix of $u_{0,\mathbf{s}_u(u_{0,r}a)}$, so $q_h \in S_{\mathbf{s}_u(u_{0,r}a)}$.

Conversely, suppose that $q_h \in S_{\mathbf{s}_u(u_{0,r}a)}$, so $u_{0,h} \in \mathsf{SUFF}(u_{0,\mathbf{s}_u(u_{0,r}a)})$. Since $\mathbf{s}_u(u_{0,r}a)$ gives the length of the longest prefix of u that is a suffix of $u_{0,r}a$, it follows that $w = u_{0,\mathbf{s}_u(u_{0,r}a)}$ is itself this prefix of u and that $u_{0,h}$ is a suffix of w. Therefore, $u_{0,h}$ ends in a which means that $a = a_{i_h}$ and $u_{0,\,h-1}$ is a suffix of $u_{0,r}$. Consequently, $q_{h-1} \in S_r$ and $q_h \in \delta(q_{h-1}, a) \subseteq \bigcup_{q \in S_r} \delta(q, a)$. ∎

Theorem 3.11.13 allows us to compute the transition function of the dfa $\mathcal{M}_u$. Once we construct the transition function Δ_u for a pattern u we have a simple algorithm for determining in linear time (that is, in time proportional to $|x|$) whether x contains the pattern u. The algorithm consists of reading the symbols of x from left to right in the automaton and stoping when the automaton enters the final state n. Therefore, the main issue is the computation of the function $\mathbf{s}_u(u_{0,r}a)$ for $0 \leq r \leq |u| - 1$ and $a \in A$, which defines the function Δ_u.

Example 3.11.14 Consider the pattern $u = babac$. The transition function of the automaton $\mathcal{M}_u$ is given by the following table:

Input	State					
	S_0	S_1	S_2	S_3	S_4	S_5
a	S_0	S_2	S_0	S_4	S_0	S_0
b	S_1	S_1	S_3	S_1	S_3	S_1
c	S_0	S_0	S_0	S_0	S_5	S_0

The transition function was computed by using the following simple C program.

```
#include <stdio.h>
#include <string.h>
#define PATTERN_SIZE 5
#define ALPHABET_SIZE 3

char *pref(char *, char *, int);
char *suff(char *, char *, int);

char alphabet[ALPHABET_SIZE] = "abc";
char u[PATTERN_SIZE] = "babac";

void main()
{
    int l,j,p;
    static char v[PATTERN_SIZE+1],
                sb[PATTERN_SIZE+1];
    char t0[PATTERN_SIZE+2],
         t1[PATTERN_SIZE+2];    /* temporary storage */

    for (l = 0; l <= PATTERN_SIZE; l++)
        for (p = 0; p < ALPHABET_SIZE; p++) {
            sb[0]=alphabet[p];sb[1]='\0';
            pref(v,u,l);
            strcat(v,sb);
            printf("\n state: %d input symb.: %s ",l,sb);
            j = l + 1;
            while(strcmp(suff(t0, v, j),pref(t1, u, j))!=0)
                  j--;
            printf("next state: %d\n",j);
        }
}

char *pref(char * r, char *s, int n)
{
    strncpy(r, s, n);
    *(r+n) = '\0';
    return r;
}

char *suff(char *r, char *s, int n)
{
    strncpy(r, s+strlen(s)-n, n);
    *(r+n) = '\0';
    return r;
}
```

We saw that if $|u| = n$, the dfa $\mathcal{M}_u$ has $n+1$ states; namely, the set of states will be $\{S_0, \ldots, S_n\}$. The basic idea of the design is store in the current state the length of the longest prefix of the pattern u that is a suffix of the portion of the input string that was read at the current moment. This is clearly the case at the beginning of the activity of the dfa. Suppose that at a certain moment the length of the longest prefix of the pattern u that is a suffix of the portion x of the input string that was read is r, that is, $\mathbf{s}_u(x) = r$, and the symbol $a \in A$ is read. The length of the longest prefix of u that is a suffix of xa is $\mathbf{s}_u(xa)$. By Theorem 3.11.8, $\mathbf{s}_u(xa) = \mathbf{s}_u(u_{0,r}a)$, which justifies our claim.

If the state of $\mathcal{M}_u$ equals q_n this obviously means that the pattern u occurs in x.

Example 3.11.15 Using the pattern $u = babac$, the dfa $\mathcal{M}_u$ has the set of states $Q = \{S_0, S_1, S_2, S_3, S_4, S_5\}$. Let $x = abababac$. Then, if the initial state of $\mathcal{M}_u$ is S_0, $\mathcal{M}_u$ should go through the states shown in Figure 3.32. □

Using the failure function it is possible to avoid the construction of the transition function of the dfa $\mathcal{M}_u$. To this end, we need the following result.

Lemma 3.11.16 *Let $u = a_{i_0} \cdots a_{i_{n-1}} \in A^*$. If $a \in A$ and $a \neq a_{i_r}$, then*

$$\mathbf{s}_u(u_{0,r}a) = \mathbf{s}_u(u_{0,\varphi_u(r)}a),$$

for $0 \leq r \leq |u| - 1$.

Proof. We will prove the set equality

$$\{k \mid u_{0,k} \in \mathsf{SUFF}(u_{0,r}a)\} = \{k \mid u_{0,k} \in \mathsf{SUFF}(u_{0,\varphi_u(r)}a)\}$$

Since $\mathbf{s}_u(u_{0,r}a)$ and $\mathbf{s}_u(u_{0,\varphi_u(r)}a)$ are the maxima of the above sets, respectively, the statement will follow immediately.

It is clear that 0 belongs to both sets. Suppose that $u_{0,k} \in \mathsf{SUFF}(u_{0,r}a)$ and $k > 0$. This implies $u_{0,k-1} \in \mathsf{SUFF}(u_{0,r})$ and $a = a_{i_{k-1}}$. The definition of $\varphi_u(r)$ implies $k - 1 \leq \varphi_u(r)$. Since both $u_{0,k-1}$ and $u_{0,\varphi(r)}$ are suffixes of $u_{0,r}$, $u_{0,k-1}$ is a suffix of $u_{0,\varphi_u(r)}$ and $u_{0,k}$ is a suffix of $u_{0,\varphi_u(r)}a$.

To prove the converse inclusion, let $k > 0$ be such that $u_{0,k}$ is a suffix of $u_{0,\varphi_u(r)}a$. As before, $u_{0,k-1} \in \mathsf{SUFF}(u_{0,\varphi(r)})$ and $a = a_{i_{k-1}}$. Since $u_{0,\varphi(r)}$ is a suffix of $u_{0,r}$ it follows that $u_{0,k-1}$ is a suffix of $u_{0,r}$ and, so $u_{0,k} \in \mathsf{SUFF}(u_{0,r}a)$. ∎

Theorem 3.11.17 *Let $u = a_{i_0} \cdots a_{i_{n-1}} \in A^*$. In the dfa*

$$\mathcal{M}_u = (A, \{S_0, \ldots, S_n\}, \Delta, S_0, \{S_n\})$$

we have

$$\Delta(S_r, a) = \begin{cases} S_{r+1} & \textit{if } u_{0,r}a \in \mathsf{PREF}(u) \\ \Delta(S_{\varphi_u(r)}, a) & \textit{otherwise.} \end{cases}$$

Proof. From Theorem 3.11.13 we know that $\Delta(S_r, a) = S_{\mathbf{s}_u(u_{0,r}a)}$ for $0 \leq r \leq n$ and $a \in A^*$. If $u_{0,r}a \in \mathsf{PREF}(u)$, then $a = a_{i_r}$, or, equivalently, $u_{0,r}a = u_{0,r+1}$. This implies $\mathbf{s}_u(u_{0,r}a) = \mathbf{s}_u(u_{0,r+1}) = r + 1$, which gives $\Delta(S_r, a) = S_{r+1}$.

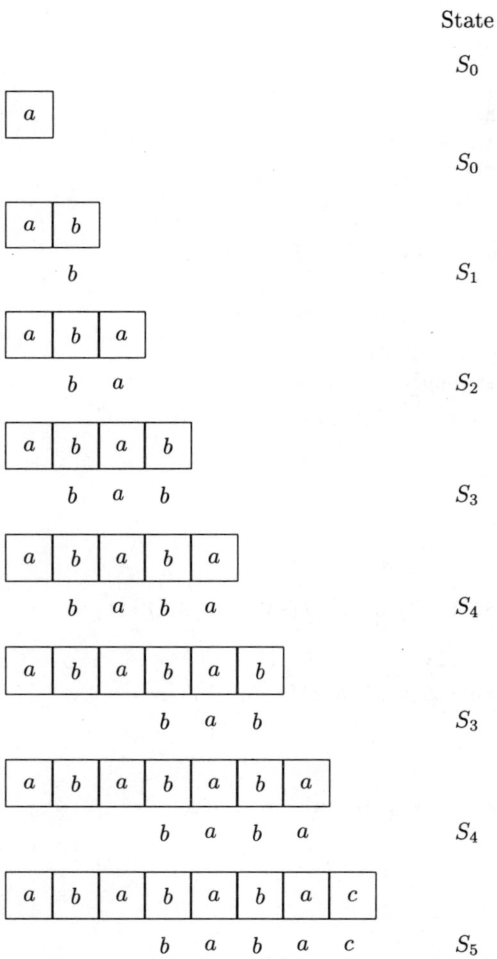

Figure 3.32: The evolution of the dfa $\mathcal{M}_u$

The second part of the statement, follows from Lemma 3.11.16. ∎

A C program that computes the failure function of the pattern $u = babac$ is given next. The failure function was denoted by `fail`.

```
#include <stdio.h>
#include <string.h>
#define PATTERN_SIZE 5

char *pref(char *, char *, int);
char *suff(char *, char *, int);
int isasuff(char *, char *);
int failf(int );

char u[PATTERN_SIZE] = "babac";

void main()
{
    int j;
    for(j = 1;j <= PATTERN_SIZE;j++)
printf("Value of failure function for j = %d is %d\n",
       j,failf(j));
}

int failf(int j)
{
    int k, res;
    char t0[PATTERN_SIZE+1]; char t1[PATTERN_SIZE+1];
    res = 0;
    for(k = 0; k < j; k++)
        if(isasuff(pref(t0,u,k),pref(t1,u,j))) res = k;
    return res;
}

char *pref(char * r, char *s, int n)
{
    strncpy(r, s, n);
    *(r+n) = '\0';
    return r;
}

char *suff(char *r, char *s, int n)
{
    strncpy(r, s+strlen(s)-n, n);
    *(r+n) = '\0';
    return r;
}

int isasuff(char *s, char *t)
```

```
{
    char temp[PATTERN_SIZE+1];
    return(strcmp(s,suff(temp,t,strlen(s)))==0);
}
```

This program yields the function specified below.

j	1	2	3	4	5
$\varphi_u(j)$	0	0	1	2	0

Theorem 3.11.17 explains the term *failure function.* If the current state of the automaton $\mathcal{M}_u$ is S_r and the input symbol a fails to match the $(r+1)$-st character a_{i_r} of the pattern, then the next state is $\Delta(S_{\varphi_u(r)}, a)$. The essence of the *Knuth-Morris-Pratt algorithm* is to apply replace the computation of the next state by using the transition function with the computation that makes use of the failure function, according to Theorem 3.11.17.

The Knuth-Morris-Pratt algorithm is presented below as a C program.

```
#include <stdio.h>
#include <string.h>
#define PATTERN_SIZE 5
#define STRING_SIZE 15
char *pref(char *, char *, int);
char *suff(char *, char *, int);
int isasuff(char *, char *);
int failf(int );

char u[PATTERN_SIZE] = "babac";
char s[STRING_SIZE] = "acbabacaababacb";


void main()
{
    int i,q,occ;
    q = 0; occ = 0;
    for(i = 0;i < STRING_SIZE;i++){
        while((q > 0) && (s[i] != u[q])) q = failf(q);
        if (s[i] == u[q]) q++;
        if (q == PATTERN_SIZE){
            printf("Pattern occurs at position %d\n",
                   i - PATTERN_SIZE + 1);
                occ = 1;
        }
    }
    if(occ == 0) printf("Pattern does not occur!\n");
}
```

3.12 Applications of Regular Expressions

Regular languages and regular expressions are useful for many programs that process text files; also, they play an essential role in compiler design.

3.12.1 Regular Expressions and UNIX

There are several text handling programs commonly available on UNIX systems that make use of regular expressions to specify portions of text for processing. These include editors such as `ed`, `sed`, and `vi`, programming languages such as `aux` and `perl`, and text searching programs such as `grep` and `egrep`. On any one UNIX system, these programs share a common definition of what a simple regular expression is. However, some of them extend the definition in various ways. Furthermore, different versions of UNIX have slightly different versions of regular expressions. To guide our discussion, we focus on regular expressions as defined for `aux`.

UNIX regular expressions are extensions of ordinary regular expressions (see Definition 3.9.1). The meta-alphabet used by the UNIX regular expressions coincides with the ASCII alphabet. If x is a word[2], E a regular expression, and $x \in \| E \|$, then we say that E *matches* x.

The UNIX operating system treats character files as unstructured sequences of ASCII characters, terminated by an ASCII EOT ("End of Transmission") character (numeric code 4). The programs that use regular expressions impose a line structure on the files they process, where a line is terminated by the single ASCII character LF ("Line Feed", numerically a 10), which is usually called a "newline" character in this context. If x is matched by a regular expression, then x must be within a single line of text. In other words, the semantics of regular expressions limits them to specifying words within a line; they generally cannot specify words that span multiple lines. However, the special sequence `\n` can be used in regular expressions in `aux` to match the newline character and thus create an expression that is matched by a word that spans more than one line.

In UNIX regular expressions, most ASCII characters represent themselves, but certain ASCII characters are defined to be *metacharacters*, and they have special meanings. Some of these always carry this meaning; others are defined only in specific circumstances. The metacharacters are are summarized in table 3.1.

Extended regular expressions are defined inductively as follows: ()

- `c` matches the set $\{c\}$, where c is a single character; thus, for example, `D` matches $\{D\}$.
- The metacharacter `.` matches any single character except a newline.
- The metacharacter `^`, when used at the beginning of a subexpression, matches the beginning of a text line. Its other use is discussed below.
- The metacharacter `$`, when used at the end of a subexpression, matches the end of a text line.

[2]Recall that we use *word* in a technical sense, meaning any string of characters in a specified alphabet; in a text file, it may correspond to several words of English text.

<table>
<tr><td>.</td><td>matches any single character except newline.</td></tr>
<tr><td>^</td><td>used at the beginning of a subexpression, matches the beginning of the line; used as the first character of a character expression, it negates the sense of the character expression.</td></tr>
<tr><td>$</td><td>used at the end of a subexpression, matches the end of the line.</td></tr>
<tr><td>\</td><td>either removes the special meaning of the following metacharacter or begins a sequence to define a character not easily represented with printing ASCII.</td></tr>
<tr><td>[</td><td>begins a character expression.</td></tr>
<tr><td>]</td><td>ends a character expression.</td></tr>
<tr><td>|</td><td>union operator; $E_0 \mid E_1$ represents $E_0 \cup E_1$.</td></tr>
<tr><td>*</td><td>Kleene closure operator (see definition 2.3.6).</td></tr>
<tr><td>+</td><td>positive closure operator (see definition 2.3.6).</td></tr>
<tr><td>?</td><td>an operator defined such that $E? = \lambda \cup E$.</td></tr>
<tr><td>(</td><td>begins a grouped expression.</td></tr>
<tr><td>)</td><td>ends a grouped expression.</td></tr>
<tr><td>-</td><td>within a character expression, c_0-c_1 represents the characters from c_0 to c_1 (inclusive).</td></tr>
</table>

Table 3.1: Regular Expression Metacharacters Used in `aux`.

- The character \ is used in three different ways. When followed by one of the symbols in Table 3.2, it is matched by the character indicated in the table. This enables a regular expression to match such non-printing characters as tabs. When followed by a three octal digit sequence, \ matches the character with the corresponding octal value. Thus the regular expression `\033` matches $\{<\text{esc}>\}$. When followed by any other character `c`, the effect of the \ is to force `c` to match $\{c\}$. Thus, if c were a metacharacter, the effect of \ is to remove its special meaning. For example, `\.` matches only {.} and not any character, while `\$` matches {$} and not the end of the line.
- A character expression is indicated by square brackets. It represents a single character taken from the set specified in the brackets. Within the brackets, any character matches itself, except as follows. A range of characters is expressed by placing a hyphen between two characters; it represents all the characters between the character to its left and the one to its right, inclusive. For example, `[a-m]` matches any letter in the first half of the alphabet.. If the hyphen does not have a character in both sides, it matches itself. Thus, `[-+*/]` matches any of the common arithmetic operators. At the beginning of the character expression, the caret ^ serves to compliment the remainder of the expression. So, `[^a-m]` matches any character except one from the first half of the alphabet. Note that within a character expression, all characters represent themselves except the \, the ^ when it appears at the beginning of the expression, and the - when it appears between two characters. In particular, the usual aux metacharacters such as $ or . match themselves and have no special meaning.

Expression	Matches
\b	<BS> (backspace)
\f	<FF> (form feed)
\n	<LF> (line feed, used as a newline character in UNIX)
\r	<CR> (carriage return)
\t	<HT> (horizontal tab)

Table 3.2: Special characters for `aux`.

We now come to operators on expressions. Let `|E|` and `|F|` be UNIX regular expressions matching sets E and F, respectively.

- `|E||F|` denotes $E \cup F$.
- `|E||F|` denotes $E \cdot F$.
- `|E|*` denotes E^*.
- `|E|+` denotes $E \cdot E^*$.
- `|E|?` denotes $E \cup \{\lambda\}$.
- `(|E|)` denotes E. Parentheses serve merely to group operations.

Example 3.12.1 The regular expression `^A.*Z$` matches lines that begin with A and end with Z.

The regular expression `^[A-Z]*$` matches lines that contain only upper-case letters.

The regular expression `^([a-zA-Z]+␣)*[a-zA-Z]+\.$` (where ␣ is used here to represent a space, which you might otherwise not notice) matches lines that contain only nonempty groups of lower- and upper-case case letters, each group separated from the next by a single space, and the last one followed by a period. □

3.12.2 The `grep` utility and its relatives

One of the extremely useful utilities that comes with UNIX is the `grep` program. It is used to search through files for a word that matches a pattern specified as a simplified regular expression. Unconfirmed rumor suggests that `grep` stands for "generalized regular expression parser". Two common variants of `grep` are `egrep`, which uses extended regular expressions to specifv the pattern, and `fgrep`, which simply matches the specified pattern as a fixed string and uses no metacharacters. For dealing with compressed files, some systems also include `zgrep`, `zegrep`, and `zfgrep`, written by Charles Levert. The most commonly used flag is `i`, to ignore the case of the characters when matching. Another useful flag is `w`, which causes `grep` to search for whole words.

When invoked `grep pattern file1 file2···fileN`, the output is a series of lines, each of the form `fileI:matchline`, where `fileI` is the name of the file in which a line that contains a word matching `pattern` is found, and `matchline` is the line with the matching word in it.

Example 3.12.2 Assume you keep your electronic mail archives in a series of files named `mail.jan97`, `mail.feb97`, etc., and that you want to find mail from

1997 that deals with computer science courses, all of which are designated `CS` followed by three digits. You could use the following command:

```
grep CS[0-9][0-9][0-9] mail.*97
```

The `.` and the `*` used in this command are processed by the command interpreter and should not be confused with the metacharacters used in regular expressions. The `.` is interpreted literally as representing a dot, and the `*` is the equivalent of the regular expression `[^␣\t]*`, meaning any number of non-blank, non-tab characters. □

3.12.3 The aux text processing program

An `aux`[3] program is a sequence of statements of the form

pattern {*action*}
pattern {*action*}
⋮

The input to an `aux` program is regarded as a series of records. Since `aux`'s default record separator is the newline character, these records usually correspond to lines. For convenience, we will simply refer to the records as lines.

Each line of the input file is matched against each pattern in the program. If the line contains a substring that matches one of the patterns, the actions corresponding to each of the patterns it matches are executed. Thus `aux` contains implicit looping constructs: the outer one cycles over all lines of its input file, and for each input line, the inner loop cycles over all the patterns. If the input line matches more than one pattern, more than one action will be executed. Either the pattern or the action can be omitted in each line of an `aux` program, but not both. If no action is present the matching line is simply printed to the output. If there is no pattern for an action, then the action is performed for each line.

Patterns have several forms, but the one that interests us most here are those that match strings. These are indicated by placing a regular expression between slash marks, e.g., `/[oO]wl/`, which matches lines containing the word "owl" whether capitalized or not. Care must be taken, because it also matches lines with the word "fowl" and many others as well.

`aux` recognizes two pre-defined patterns, `BEGIN` and `END`. The actions corresponding to `BEGIN` are performed before any input is processed; those corresponding to `END` are performed after all the input is processed.

Actions are expressed in a language that closely resembles the C programming language. Action statements may be separated by newlines or semicolons. Comments are introduced by `#` and continue to the end of the line. `aux` has built-in variables, including those given in Table 3.3. Two slightly unusual features of `aux` are the ~ operator and associate arrays. The boolean ~ operator compares a regular expression to a string. A construct of the form *expression*~*/regular-expression/* is *true* if a substring of the *expression* on the left-hand side of ~

[3] `aux` is an acronym of the names of its creators, A. V. Aho, P. J. Weinberger, and B. W. Kernigan

Variable	Meaning
FNR	number of current record within current file.
FS	character that separates fields.
NF	number of fields in current record.
NR	overall number of records processed so far.
RS	character that separates records.

Table 3.3: Some aux built-in variables.

matches the *regular-expression* on the right-hand side. The boolean operator $! \sim$ is the negation of $\sim$.

`aux` supports one-dimensional arrays. Like all variables, arrays may be used without being declared. They are called *associative arrays* because their subscripts may be strings. Thus, one could write,

```
daysin["Jan"] = 31;
daysin["Feb"] = 28;
      ⋮
```

Since `aux` frequently is concerned with strings, it is no surprise that it has several built-in string functions. These run from the usual, like `length(`*str*`)`, which returns the length of *str*, to the more exotic, like `split(`*str*, *arr*, *delim*`)`. This function splits the string *str* into fields, where the fields are separated by the character *delim*. It places the fields into the array *arr*, such that the first field is *arr[1]*.

As input lines are processed, they are separated into fields. By default, fields are separated by blanks and tabs, but this can be changed assigning a different character to the built-in variable `FS`. The variable `$1` refers to the first field, `$2`, to the second, etc. `$NF` refers to the last field, and `$0` refers to the entire line.

Example 3.12.3 Assume you have a data file that records payments made to people, one to a line, with the name of the person, the amount, the date, and the reason. A few typical lines might look like this.

```
Ben      174.87  3-Mar-97 air fare
Karen    487.22  3-Mar-97 hotel
Karl      38.00  4-Mar-97 meals
Ben      185.72  4-Mar-97 per diem
Karen     29.95  4-Mar-97 meals
```

To print out and total the payments to Ben, you could write

```
BEGIN  { total = 0.0; }
/^Ben/ {total += $2; print ;}
END    {print "Total = $", total;}
```

The first line creates the variable `total` and zeroes it. The second selects only those input lines that begin with `Ben`. For those, it increments `total` by the second field (the amount paid). The `print` statement prints its arguments with a default format; if it has no arguments, it prints the current input line. The third line labels and prints the total amount paid.

To print out those payments for meals, simply change the pattern of the second line from `/^Ben/` to `/meals$/`. □

3.12.4 The lex Lexical Analyzer Generator

The two programs `lex` and `yacc` were designed to work together to produce compilers; indeed, `yacc` stands for "yet another compiler compiler". The inputs to these programs are instructions on how the resulting compiler should process its input; the outputs from these programs are portions of a compiler that work together. In the usual configuration, the compiler developer uses `yacc` to produce the main portion of the compiler and uses `lex` to produce its front end, that portion of the program that simplifies the task of parsing the input by converting it into a series of *tokens*. For example, the front end of the compiler might aid the parsing task by identifying the input line

```
VariableOne := VariableTwo + 123
```

as

Identifier AssignmentOp Identifier AddOp Integer

where the terms *Identifier*, *AssignmentOp*, etc., are tokens.

Because of their history, `lex` and `yacc` conform in many particulars to C. For example, comments begin with `/*` and end with `*/`; identifiers are strings of letters and digits, beginning with a letter (where the underscore, _, is regarded as a letter), and except in string expressions, all white space is equivalent to a single space. We will revisit the construction of compilers again, but for now we concentrate on `lex`'s task of producing the tokenizer.

The output of `lex` is the code for a C function named `yylex()`, usually placed in the file `lex.yy.c`. This function reads from the input stream `yyin`, which defaults to the standard input (`stdin`). In the usual course of events, `yylex()` finds a token that matches a pattern in one of its rules, and the corresponding action returns an `int` that is used to identify the type of token it found. If `yylex()` encounters an end-of-file, it returns `0`. By convention, it also assigns the actual token to the external string `yytext`[4] and the length of the token to the external integer `yyleng`. If there is a value associated to the token, it is usually returned in the external named `yylval`, which defaults to an integer.

A `lex` program comprises three parts, separated by lines that contain only two percent signs `%%`: definitions, rules, and function code.

Definitions provide names for regular expressions to make their subsequent use easier to read and write. They are of the form *name expression*, where *name* is an identifier that conforms to the C syntax for identifiers, and *expression* is a regular expression that has a somewhat more complex syntax than those introduced to this point. The *expression* can be referenced by enclosing the associated *name* in braces.

Example 3.12.4 The following definitions serve to define C identifiers:

```
digit  [0-9]
uc     [A-Z]                  /* upper case */
lc     [a-z]                  /* lower case */
```

[4]Technically, `yytext` is an array of `char`, not a pointer to `char`.

```
us      _                    /* underscore */
letter {uc}|{lc}|{us}
ident  {letter}({letter}|{digit})*
```

□

Rules are of the form *expression action.* The first whitespace character that is not escaped with a \ or part of a string (between quotes) terminates the pattern; the rest of the line is interpreted as the action. An action may be a single C statement, contained entirely on the one line, or, more commonly, a collection of C statements, surrounded by braces, that may span more than one line. `yylex()` continues to process its input until it encounters a `return` statement in an action or an end-of-file in its input.

C code may be placed in both the definitions and rules sections of a `lex` program simply by placing a line with `%{` before the code and a line with `%}` after the code. The lines between these two are copied to the output. Typically, this facility is used for declarations. Those that occur in the definitions section are external to `yylex()`; those in the rules section are local to `yylex()`.

Example 3.12.5 A common example that shows some of the capabilities of `lex` is a program to count letters, words, and lines.

```
    %{
int nchars = 0;
int nlines = 0;
    int nwords = 0;
    %}
    %%
    \n {
    nchars++;
    nlines++;
}
    [ \t]+ {
    nchars += yyleng;
}
    [^ \t\n]+ {
nchars += yyleng;
                    nwords++;
}

    %%
    main()
{
yylex();
printf( "%d lines; %d words; %d characters\n",
                    nlines, nwords, nchars );
}
```

The three lines in the definitions section serve to declare and initialize variables. The `\n` pattern matches a newline and increases the count of characters and lines. The `[ \t]+` pattern matches a sequence of whitespace characters (note the blank at the beginning of the character class) and adds the number found to the character count. The `[^ \t\n]+` pattern matches any sequence of non-whitespace characters. It increments the number of words found and adds the length of the token to the character count. For historical reasons, in `lex`, unlike other UNIX programs that use regular expressions, the complement of a character class matches a newline character unless `\n` or some equivalent escape sequence is explicitly mentioned. The main program merely calls the function `yylex()` that `lex` produces and then prints out the three values it has calculated. □

Many `lex` programs have ambiguous rules: more than one pattern may match the input. To resolve this situation, all rules that match the input are tried. Where a pattern may match the input in several ways, the longest possible match is used. If more than one pattern matches the input, the one that matches the longest portion of the input is used. If there is a tie, then the one that occurs first in the rules section is used. For example, if the pattern were `a+` and the input were `aaa`, the pattern matches 1, 2, and 3 `a`s; but `lex` always selects the longest match. If there were two rules, with patterns `aaa` and `[a-z]*`, the input `aaa` would match both, so the action associated with the rule that occurs first in the input will be selected.

Example 3.12.6 These rules make it easy to match keywords in a language. If `const` is a keyword in the language, then rules

```
const                  action for const
[a-zA-Z][a-zA-Z0-9]*   action for identifier
```

have the effect of matching the input `const` as the keyword, because while both rules match five characters, the keyword rule comes first. However, `con` and `constant` are matched as identifiers. The former, because the first rule simply does not apply; the latter, because the first rule matches only five characters, while the second rule matches eight. □

`lex` supports many additions to the usual UNIX regular expression syntax. Strings surrounded by quote marks " are treated literally: none of the characters has any special meaning, except that the sequence \" represents a ". A particularly unexpected addition is the ability to recognize a match only in context. The expression `x/y` matches the input `x` only if it is followed by `y`. This is a generalization of the defintion of the `$`, where `x$` matches `x` only at the end of a line.

Rules with empty actions implicitly copy the matching input to the output. Likewise, input that matches no rules is copied to the output. The C function `printf()` can be used to print the token by including `printf("%s",yytext);` in the action of a rule.

3.13 Exercises

Finite Automata

1. Determine the language accepted by each of the dfa $\mathcal{M}_0, \mathcal{M}_1, \mathcal{M}_2$ shown in Figure 3.33.

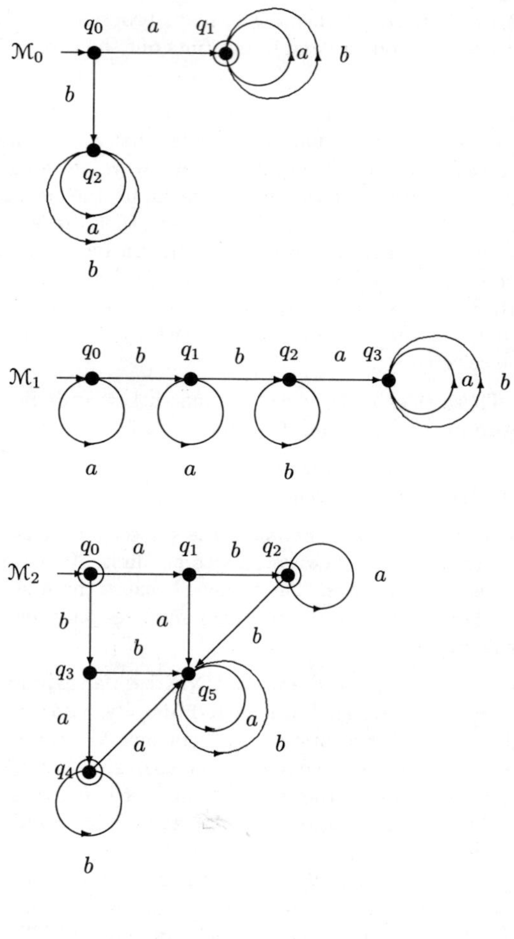

Figure 3.33: Graphs of Deterministic Finite Automata $\mathcal{M}_0, \mathcal{M}_1$ and $\mathcal{M}_2$

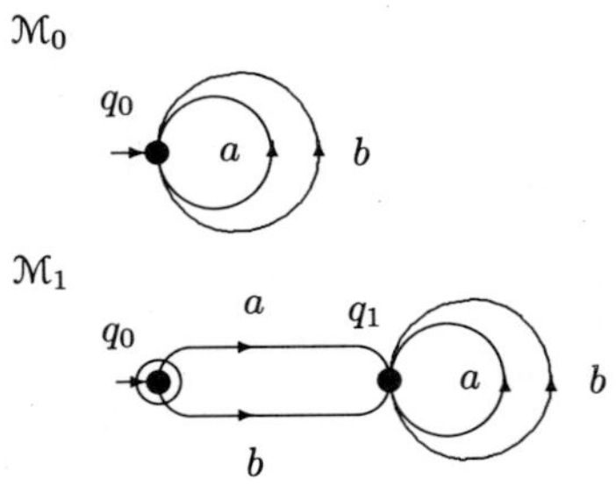

Figure 3.34: Graphs of Deterministic Finite Automata $\mathcal{M}_0$ and $\mathcal{M}_1$

2. Determine the languages accepted by the automata $\mathcal{M}_0$ and $\mathcal{M}_1$ shown in Figure 3.34.
3. Consider the dfa $\mathcal{M} = (\{a, b\}, \{q_0, q_1, q_2\}, \delta, q_0, \{q_1\})$ whose graph is given in Figure 3.35. Determine the language accepted by the automaton $\mathcal{M}$.
4. Construct deterministic finite automata that accept the following languages over the alphabet $A = \{a, b, c\}$:
   (a) The set of all words that begin with ab and end with ba.
   (b) The set $\{bab\}$.
   (c) The set $A^* - \{bab\}$.
   (d) The set of all words $x \in A^*$ that contain at least three as.
5. $^\diamond$ Let $\mathcal{M} = (A, Q, \delta, q_0, F)$ be a dfa and let P be a subset of Q. Prove that there exists a subset B_P of A such that $\delta^*(p, x) \in P$ for every $p \in P$ and $x \in B_P^*$.
6. Each of these is a regular language over the alphabet $A = \{0, 1\}$. Draw the transition diagram of a deterministic finite automaton that accepts it.
   (a) A^*.
   (b) $\{\lambda\}$.
   (c) $\emptyset$.
7. Let A be an alphabet. If b is a symbol such that $b \notin A$, construct a nondeterministic finite automaton that accepts the language A^*b.
8. Draw a transition diagram for a nondeterministic finite automaton $\mathcal{M}$ that accepts all strings over the alphabet $A = \{0, 1\}$ that begin in 10 and end in 00. Construct the dfa that accepts the same language as $\mathcal{M}$.
9. $^\diamond$ Let A be an alphabet and let $a \in A$ be a symbol. If k is a natural number, construct a nondeterministic finite automaton that accepts the language $L_{k,a} = \{uav \mid u, v \in A^* \text{ and } |v| = k\}$.
10. $^\diamond$ A *nonrestarting dfa* is an automaton whose initial state is not in the range of its transition function. Prove that for every regular language L there is an effective way to construct a nonrestarting dfa that accepts L.
11. Construct nondeterministic finite automata that accept the following languages over $A = \{a, b\}$:

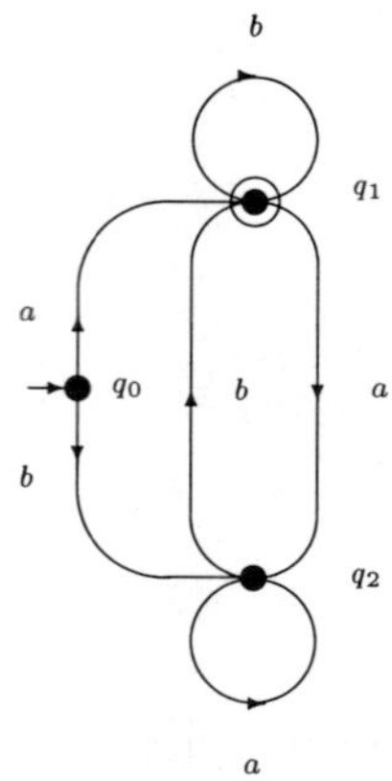

Figure 3.35: Graph of the Deterministic Finite Automaton $\mathcal{M}$

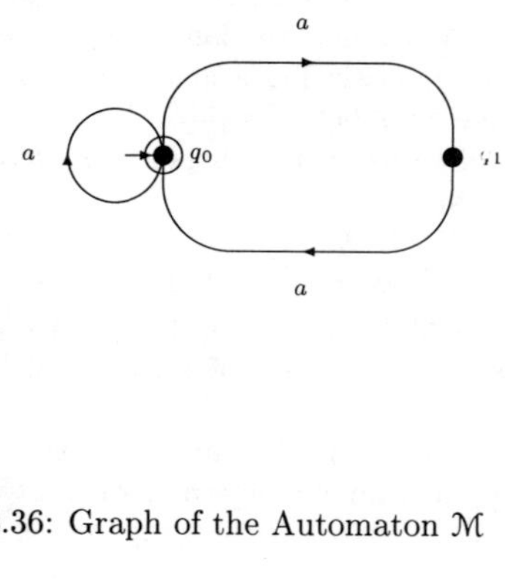

Figure 3.36: Graph of the Automaton $\mathcal{M}$

(a) The set of words that begin with an a or begin and end with a b.

(b) The set $\{a\}^* \cup \{b\}^*$.

(c) The set of words that contain bab as an infix.

12. $^\diamond$ Let $\mathcal{M} = (A, Q, \delta, q_0, F)$ be a ndfa. Define $\phi(q, w, q')$ as the number of paths in the graph of $\mathcal{M}$ from the state q to the state q' with label w. Prove that for the automaton $\mathcal{M} = (\{a, b\}, \{q_0, q_1\}, \delta, q_0, \{q_0\})$ whose graph is given in Figure 3.36 we have $\phi(q_0, a^n, q_0) = f_{n+1}$, where f_n is the nth Fibonacci number and $n \geq 0$.

13. Construct the deterministic finite automata that accept the same languages as the nondeterministic automata constructed in Exercise 11.

14. $^\diamond$ Let A be an alphabet, and let $L = \{w_0, \ldots, w_{n-1}\}$ be a finite nonempty language on A. Consider the ndfa $\mathcal{M} = (A, Q_L, \delta_L, q_\lambda, F)$, where $Q_L =$

$\{q_u \mid u \in \mathsf{PREF}(L)\}$, $F = \{q_x \mid x \in L\}$, and δ_L is given by

$$\delta_L(q_u, a) = \begin{cases} \{q_{ua}\} & \text{if } ua \in \mathsf{PREF}(L) \\ \emptyset & \text{otherwise.} \end{cases}$$

Prove that L is accepted by the automaton $\mathcal{M}$.

15. $^\diamond$ Prove or disprove the following statements. Proving requires an argument; disproving requires a counterexample.
    (a) Every language is contained in a regular language.
    (b) Every nonempty language contains a nonempty regular language.
    (c) The union of a collection of regular languages is a regular language.
    (d) If L_0, L_1 are regular languages and $L_0 \subseteq L \subseteq L_1$, then L is a regular language.
16. $^\diamond$ Let A be an alphabet and let Q be a finite set, where $|A| = p$ and $|Q| = n$.
    (a) Prove that if $n > 1$, then there are $n^{np+1+\frac{n}{\log_2 n}}$ distinct deterministic finite automata having the input alphabet A and the set of states Q.
    (b) Calculate the number of nondeterministic automata having the input alphabet A and the set of states Q.
17. $^{\diamond\diamond}$ Let $\mathcal{M} = (A, Q, \delta, q_0, F)$ be a dfa. Let $\mathsf{back} : \mathcal{P}(Q) \longrightarrow \mathcal{P}(Q)$ be the function given by

$$\mathsf{back}(S) = \{q \in Q \mid \delta(q, a) \in S \text{ for some } a \in A\}$$

for $S \in \mathcal{P}(Q)$.
    (a) Prove that

$$\mathsf{back}^{(n)}(S) = \{q \in Q \mid \delta^*(q, x) \in S \text{ for some } x \in A^*, |x| = n\}.$$

    (b) Prove that $L(\mathcal{M}) \neq \emptyset$ if and only if $q_0 \in \bigcup_{0 \leq j \leq |Q|-1} \mathsf{back}^{(j)}(F)$.
    (c) Define the function $\mathsf{forw} : \mathcal{P}(Q) \longrightarrow \mathcal{P}(Q)$ by $\mathsf{forw}(S) = \{q \in Q \mid \delta(q', a) = q \text{ for some } q' \in S \text{ and } a \in A\}$ for $S \in \mathcal{P}(Q)$. Show that $\mathsf{forw}^{(n)}(S) = \{q \in Q \mid \delta(q', x) = q \text{ for some } q' \in S \text{ and } x \in A^* \text{ such that } |x| = n\}$ for $S \in \mathcal{P}(Q)$.
18. $^{\diamond\diamond}$ Let L be a regular language, $L \subseteq A^*$. For $k \in \mathbb{N}$, $k > 0$, define the language $L_{|1/k}$ by

$$L_{|1/k} = \left\{x \in A^* \mid w = xy \in L \text{ and } |x| = \left\lfloor \frac{|w|}{k} \right\rfloor\right\}$$

Prove that $L_{|1/k}$ is a regular language for every $k > 0$.

Solution. Suppose that the language L is recognized by the dfa $\mathcal{M} = (A, Q, \delta, q_0, F)$. Consider the automaton

$$\mathcal{M}_k = (A, Q \times \mathcal{P}(Q), \delta_k, (q_0, F), F'),$$

where the set of final states is $F' = \{(q, P) \in Q \times \mathcal{P}(Q) \mid q \in P\}$, and $\delta_k((q, P), a) = (\delta(q, a), \mathsf{back}^{(k)}(P))$. It is easy to verify that $\delta_k^*((q, P), t) = (\delta(q, t), \mathsf{back}^{((k-1)|t|)}(P))$ for every $t \in A^*$. Therefore, the following statements are equivalent:

- $x \in L(\mathcal{M}_k)$;
- $\delta_k^*((q_0, F), x) \in F'$;
- $(\delta(q_0, x), \mathsf{back}^{((k-1)|x|)}(F)) \in F'$;
- $\delta(q_0, x) \in \mathsf{back}^{((k-1)|x|)}(F)) \in F'$;
- $\delta(\delta(q_0, x), y) \in F$ for some $y \in A^*$ such that $|y| = (k-1)|x|$;
- $xy \in L(\mathcal{M})$ for some $y \in A^*$ such that $|y| = (k-1)|x|$;
- $x \in L_{|1/k}$,

which shows that $L_{|1/k} = L(\mathcal{M}_k)$, so $L_{|1/k}$ is regular. Here back is the function defined in Exercise 17. ■

19. °° Let L be a regular language, $L \subseteq A^*$. For $k \in \mathbb{N}$, $k > 0$, define the language $L_{1/k|}$ by

$$L_{1/k|} = \left\{ x \in A^* \mid w = yx \in L \text{ and } |x| = \left\lfloor \frac{|w|}{k} \right\rfloor \right\}$$

Prove that $L_{1/k|}$ is a regular language for every $k > 0$.
Hint. Apply Theorem 3.4.3 and Exercise 18.

20. °° Let L be a regular language, $L \subseteq A^*$. For $k, h \in \mathbb{N}$, $k, h > 0$, define the language $L_{k,h}$ by

$$L_{k,h} = \{x \in A^* \mid w = uxv \in L \text{ and } |u| = k|x| \text{ and } |v| = h|x|\}.$$

Prove that $L_{k,h}$ is a regular language for every $k, h > 0$.
Solution. Suppose that $L = L(\mathcal{M})$, where $\mathcal{M} = (A, Q, \delta, q_0, F)$ is a dfa. Let $n = |Q|$, and assume that $Q = \{q_0, \ldots, q_{n-1}\}$. Consider the dfa $\mathcal{M}_{k,h} = (A, Q^n \times \mathcal{P}(Q)^2, \gamma, (q_0, \ldots, q_{n-1}, \{q_0\}, F), F')$, where

$$\begin{aligned} &\gamma((q_{i_0}, \ldots, q_{i_{n-1}}, P, R), a) \\ &= (\delta(q_{i_0}, a), \ldots, \delta(q_{i_{n-1}}, a), \mathsf{forw}^{(k)}(P), \mathsf{back}^{(h)}(R)), \end{aligned}$$

for every state $(q_{i_0}, \ldots, q_{i_{n-1}}, P, R)$ and $a \in A$. The set of final states is

$$\begin{aligned} F' = \{ &(q_{i_0}, \ldots, q_{i_{n-1}}, P, R) \in Q^n \times (\mathcal{P}(Q))^2 \mid \\ &q_j \in P, q_{i_j} \in R \text{ for some } j, 0 \le j \le n-1\} \end{aligned}$$

It is easy to verify that

$$\begin{aligned} &\gamma^*((q_{i_0}, \ldots, q_{i_{n-1}}, P, R), x) \\ &= (\delta(q_{i_0}, x), \ldots, \delta(q_{i_{n-1}}, x), \mathsf{forw}^{(k|x|)}(P), \mathsf{back}^{(h|x|)}(R)), \end{aligned}$$

for every state $(q_{i_0}, \ldots, q_{i_{n-1}}, P, R)$ and every $a \in A^*$. Therefore, $x \in L(\mathcal{M}')$ if and only if there is j, $0 \le j \le n-1$ such that $q_j \in \mathsf{forw}^{(k|x|)}(\{q_0\})$ and $q_{i_j} = \delta^*(q_j, x)$ belongs to $\mathsf{back}^{(h|x|)}(F)$. This happens only if there is $w \in L$ such that $w = uxv$, $|u| = k|x|$, and $|v| = h|x|$, that is, if and only if $x \in L_{k,h}$.
Note that if $k = h = 1$, then $L_{1,1}$ consists of the "middle thirds" of the words of L. ■

21. °° Let $B = \{0, 1\}$ be a two-symbol alphabet. For $a \in \mathbb{R}$, $0 \le a < 1$, define the language L_a as consisting of all words $x = b_0 \cdots b_{n-1} \in B^+$ such that the binary number $0.b_0 \cdots b_{n-1}$ is greater than a. Prove that the language L_a is regular if and only if a is a rational number.

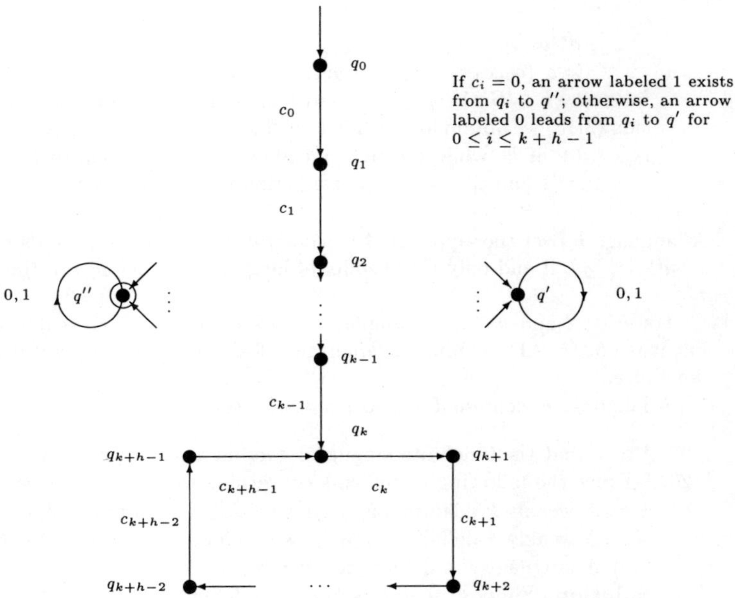

Figure 3.37: The Graph of the dfa $\mathcal{M}_a$

Solution. Let a be a rational number. This implies the existence of a binary representation of a given by

$$a = c_0 \cdots c_{k-1} c_k \cdots c_{k+h-1} c_k \cdots c_{k+h-1} \cdots$$

We can assume that this expansion does not end with an infinite sequence of 1s. It is easy to see that the language L_a is accepted by the dfa $\mathcal{M}_a = (B, \{q_0, q_1, q_{k+h-1}, q', q''\}, \delta, q_0, \{q''\})$, whose graph is given in Figure 3.37. Conversely, suppose that $a = c_0 \cdots c_{k-1} c_k \cdots$ is irrational and that L_a is a regular language. Let $\mathcal{M} = (B, Q, \delta, q_0, F)$ be a dfa such that $L = L(\mathcal{M})$. There exist $k, l \in \mathbb{N}$ such that $k < l$ and $\delta^*(q_0, c_0 \cdots c_k) = \delta^*(q_0, c_0 \cdots c_k c_{k+1} \cdots c_l)$ because Q is a finite set. Since a is not a rational number, for any such $k, l \in \mathbb{N}$ there are numbers m such that $c_{k+m} \neq c_{l+m}$. Let h be the least such number. We have $c_{k+j} = c_{l+j}$ for $0 \leq j \leq h-1$, so

$$\begin{aligned}&\delta^*(q_0, c_0 \cdots c_k c_{k+1} \cdots c_{k+h-1} b)\\ &= \delta^*(q_0, c_0 \cdots c_k c_{k+1} \cdots c_l c_{l+1} \cdots c_{l+h-1} b)\end{aligned} \tag{3.18}$$

for every $b \in B$. If $c_{k+h} = 0$ and $c_{l+h} = 1$, by choosing $b = 1$ in Equation (3.18) we obtain a contradiction since the left member of this equation is a state in F, while the right member does not belong to F. Similarly, if $c_{k+h} = 1$ and $c_{l+h} = 0$ a contradiction is obtained by taking $b = 0$. ■

A language L over the alphabet A is *weakly k-definite* if $x \in L$ holds for a word x with $|x| \geq k$ if and only if the suffix of length k of x belongs to the language L.

For $k \in \mathbb{N}$ and $k \geq 1$, a language L is k-definite if L is weakly k-definite but it is not $(k-1)$-definite. A language is 0-definite if and only if it is weakly 0-definite.

A language is *definite* if it is k-definite for some $k \in \mathbb{N}$.

22. Prove that the 0-definite languages over an alphabet A are $\emptyset$ and A^*.
23. $^\diamond$ Prove the following statements concerning weakly definite languages:
    (a) A weakly k-definite language is weakly ℓ-definite for all $\ell \geq k$.
    (b) A weakly k-definite language is h-definite for some h, $0 \leq h \leq k$.
    (c) A language is k-definite for at most one k.

    Solution. Suppose that L is k-weakly definite and that $\ell \geq k$. If $x \in L$ and $|x| \geq \ell$, let z be the suffix of x having length ℓ. Note that the suffix w of x of length k coincides with the suffix of length k of z. Therefore, $w \in L$ and this implies $z \in L$.
    Conversely, let $y \in A^*$ and assume that u, the suffix of y of length ℓ belongs to L. Since $\ell \geq k$, v, the suffix of length k of u belongs to L. The word v coincides with the suffix of length k of y and this implies $y \in L$, which shows that L is weakly ℓ-definite, which concludes the proof of Part (a).
    We leave the arguments for the last two parts to the reader. ■

Part (c) of Exercise 23 allows us to define the *degree* of a definite language as the number $k \in \mathbb{N}$ such that L is k-definite. This number is denoted by $d(L)$.

24. $^\diamond$ Prove that every finite language over an alphabet A is k-definite for some $k \in \mathbb{N}$. Prove that every k-definite language is regular.
25. $^{\diamond\diamond}$ Prove that a language L over A is definite if and only if $L = K \cup A^*H$, where K, H are finite languages over A.

    Solution. Suppose that $L = K \cup A^*H$, where K, H are finite languages and let $k = \max\{1 + \max\{|x| \mid x \in K\}, \max\{|y| \mid y \in H\}\}$. Let $w \in A^*$ such that $|w| \geq k$ and let u be the suffix of length k of x. Note that $w \notin K$ since no word in K is longer than $k-1$; therefore, $w \in A^*H$ which means that $w = tv$, where $t \in A^*$ and $v \in H$. Since $|u| = k$ we have $u = zv$ for some $z \in A^*$, so $u \in A^*H \subseteq L$. Conversely, if w is a word from A^* such that $y \in L$, where $|w| \geq k$ and y is the suffix of length k of w we have $y \in A^*H$ which implies $x \in A^*H \subseteq L$. This shows that L is weakly k-definite, so it is h-definite for some h, $0 \leq h \leq k$ (by Part (b) of Exercise 23.)

Conversely, suppose that L is definite and, therefore, it is k-definite for some $k \in \mathbb{N}$. If $k = 0$, we have either $L = \emptyset$ or $L = A^*$. In the first case, we can write $L = \emptyset \cup A^*\emptyset$; in the second, $L = \emptyset \cup A^*\{\lambda\}$, so L has the prescribed form.

Suppose now that L is k-definite for $k \geq 1$. If L is finite, we can take $K = L$ and $H = \emptyset$; otherwise, if L is infinite define

$$\begin{aligned} K &= \{x \in L \mid |x| < k\} \\ H &= \{x \in L \mid |x| = k\} \end{aligned}$$

It is easy to see that since L is k-definite, we have $L = K \cup A^*H$; we leave this straightforward argument to the reader. ■

26. ◦ Let L be a definite language over the alphabet A such that $L = K \cup A^*H$, where K, H are two finite languages. Prove that the length of the longest word in $K \cup H$ is less or equal than $d(L)$.

A dfa $\mathcal{M} = (A, Q, \delta, q_0, F)$ is *weakly k-definite* for $k \in \mathbb{N}$ if $|x| \geq k$ implies $\delta^*(q, x) = \delta^*(q', x)$ for all $q, q' \in Q$.

$\mathcal{M}$ is 0-definite if it is weakly 0-definite, and is k-definite if it is weakly k-definite but not weakly $(k-1)$-definite. If $\mathcal{M}$ is a k-definite dfa, we refer to k as the degree of $\mathcal{M}$. The degree of $\mathcal{M}$ is denoted by $d(\mathcal{M})$.

$\mathcal{M}$ is definite if it is k-definite for some $k \in \mathbb{N}$.

27. ◦◦ Prove that if $\mathcal{M} = (A, Q, \delta, q_0, F)$ is a definite dfa, then $L(\mathcal{M})$ is a definite language. Further, show that $d(L) \leq d(\mathcal{M})$.

Solution. Suppose that $\mathcal{M}$ is a definite dfa and that $d(\mathcal{M}) = k$. Consider the words $u = yx$ and $v = zx$, where $|x| = k$. Let $\delta^*(q_0, y) = q'$ and $\delta^*(q_0, v) = q''$. Since $\mathcal{M}$ is k-definite we have $\delta^*(q', x) = \delta^*(q'', x)$, so

$$\begin{aligned} \delta^*(q_0, u) &= \delta^*(\delta^*(q_0, y), x) = \delta^*(q', x) \\ &= \delta^*(q'', x) = \delta^*(\delta^*(q_0, z), x) = \delta^*(q_0, v) \end{aligned}$$

Thus, if $u \in A^*$ and $|u| \geq k$, then $u \in L$ if and only if the suffix of length k of u belongs to L. So, L is weakly k-definite which implies that it is h-definite for some h, $h \leq k$. ■

28. ◦◦ Let $\mathcal{M} = (A, Q, \delta, q_0, F)$ be a dfa. Prove that either $L(\mathcal{M})$ is bounded, or there exist $a, b \in A$, $a \neq b, u, v, w, z \in A^*$ and a state $q \in Q$ such that $\delta^*(q_0, u) = q$, $\delta^*(q, av) = q$, $\delta^*(q, bw) = q$, and $\delta^*(q, z) \in F$.

Solution. Without restricting the generality we can assume that $\mathcal{M}$ contains a state $\hat{q}$ such that for no $t \in A^*$ we have $\delta^*(\hat{q}, t) \in F$.

The argument is by induction on $k = |Q| \geq 1$. The basis case, when $k = 1$ is immediate since we can have either $L(\mathcal{M}) = \emptyset$, or $L(\mathcal{M}) = A^*$. In the first case, $L(\mathcal{M})$ is bounded; in the latter case, $q_0 \in F$ and $v = w = z = \lambda$ satisfy the second alternative.

Suppose that the statement holds for dfas with at most k states, and let $\mathcal{M}$ be a dfa with $k+1$ states that accepts a nonempty language.

Assume that the second condition is not satisfied. This means that for all $a, b \in A$, $a \neq b$, $u, v, w, z \in A^*$, and $q \in Q$ at least one of $\delta^*(q_0, u) = q$, $\delta^*(q, av) = q$, $\delta^*(q, bw) = q$, and $\delta^*(q, z) \in F$ does not hold. Choose $q = q_0$ and z such that $\delta^*(q_0, z) \in F$. This is possible because $L(\mathcal{M})$ is supposed to be nonempty. Further, choose $v = w$. Then, for at most one

$a \in A$ does there exist $v \in A^*$ such that $\delta^*(q_0, av) = q_0$.
Let $c \in A$ be such that for no $t \in A^*$ we have $\delta^*(\delta(q_0, c), t) = q_0$. Define the dfa $\mathcal{M}_c = (A, Q_c, \delta(q_0, c), \delta_c, F - \{q_0\})$, where Q_c is the set of all states accessible from $\delta(q_0, c)$ and δ_c is the restriction of δ to $Q_c \times A$. Since $q_0 \notin Q_c$, we have $|Q_c| \leq k$, so by the inductive hypothesis, $L(\mathcal{M}_c)$ is bounded.
If no a exists in A such that $\delta^*(q_0, av) = q_0$, then $L(\mathcal{M}) = \bigcup\{cL(\mathcal{M}_c) \mid c \in A\}$, so $L(\mathcal{M})$ is bounded by the closure properties of bounded languages (cf. Exercise 44 of Chapter 2).
Suppose now that there is $a \in A$ such that $\delta^*(q_0, av) = q_0$; we can assume that v is the shortest word such that this equality is satisfied. Define the dfa $\mathcal{M}_a = (A, Q - \{q_0\}, \delta(q_0, a), \delta_a, F - \{q_0\})$, where $\delta_a(q, b) = \delta(q, b)$ if $\delta(q, b) \neq q_0$, $\delta_a(q, b) = \hat{q}$ if $\delta(q, b) \neq q_0$. Since $\mathcal{M}_a$ has k states, $L(\mathcal{M}_a)$ is bounded. Then,

$$L(\mathcal{M}) = \begin{cases} (av) * \bigcup_{b \in A} L(\mathcal{M}_b) & \text{if } q_0 \notin F \\ (av) * \bigcup_{b \in A} L(\mathcal{M}_b) \cup (av)^* & \text{if } q_0 \in F. \end{cases}$$

Thus, $L(\mathcal{M})$ is bounded. ∎

29. °° Let $L \subseteq \{a, b\}^*$ be a regular language. Then, the following are equivalent:
   (a) L is unbounded;
   (b) there exist $u, v, w, z \in \{a, b\}^*$ such that $u\{av, bw\}^*z \subseteq L$;
   (c) there exist $u, v, w, z \in \{a, b\}^*$ such that $u\{va, wb\}^*z \subseteq L$.

   Solution. Part (a) implies Part (b) by Exercise 28. We prove now that Part (b) implies Part (a). Suppose that there exist $u, v, w, z \in \{a, b\}^*$ such that $u\{av, bw\}^*z \subseteq L$. Since the language $\{av, bw\}^*$ is unbounded (by Exercise 50 from Chapter 2), it follows that $u\{av, bw\}^*z$ is also unbounded. If L were bounded, this would imply that $u\{av, bw\}^*z$ is bounded, which gives a contradiction. Thus, L is unbounded.
   The equivalence between Parts (b) and (c) follows from Exercise 48 of Chapter 2. ∎

30. ° Prove that if $L = L(\mathcal{M})$, where $\mathcal{M} = (A, Q, \delta, q_0, F)$ is a dfa, then $|Q| > \min\{|p| \mid p \in A^* - L\}$.

31. °° Let L be a regular language, $L \subseteq A^*$. Prove that if there exists a set of pairs of words, $P = \{(x_i, y_i) \mid 0 \leq i \leq n-1\}$ such that $x_i y_i \in L$ for $0 \leq i \leq n-1$ and $x_i y_j \notin L$ for $0 \leq i, j \leq n-1$ and $i \neq j$, then any ndfa that accepts L has at least n states.

   Solution. Let $\mathcal{M} = (A, Q, \delta, q_0, F)$ be an ndfa that accepts L and let $S_k = \delta^*(q_0, x_k)$ for $0 \leq k \leq n-1$. Since $x_i y_i \in L$, there is a state $p_i \in S_i$ such that $\delta^*(p_i, y_i) \cap F \neq \emptyset$, that is, there exists a state $r_i \in F$ such that $r_i \in \delta^*(p_i, y_i)$ for $0 \leq i \leq n-1$.
   We claim that $p_i \notin S_j$ for $j \neq i$. Indeed, if $p_i \in S_j$, then $r_i \in \delta^*(p_i, y_i) \subseteq \delta^*(q_0, x_j y_i)$, so $x_i y_j \in L$, which contradicts the hypothesis. Thus, each set S_i contains a state p_i that is not contained in any other set S_j with $j \neq i$. So, $\mathcal{M}$ has at least n states. ∎

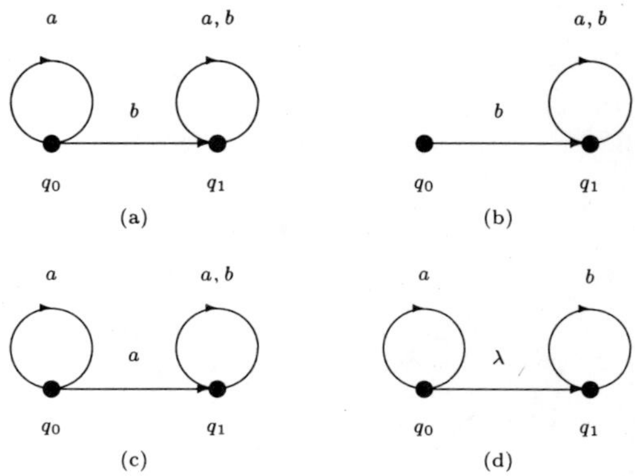

Figure 3.38: Graphs to be Identified

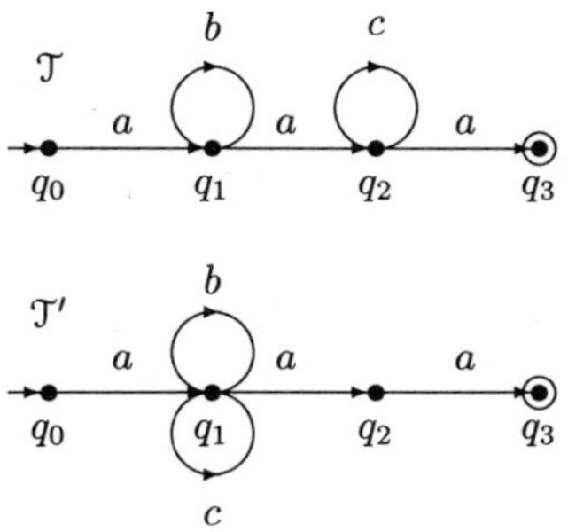

Figure 3.39: Graphs of Transition Systems $\mathcal{T}$ and $\mathcal{T}'$

Transition Systems

32. Examine the graphs shown in Figure 3.38. Determine whether they represent deterministic automata, nondeterministic automata, or transition systems over the alphabet $A = \{a, b\}$?
33. $^\diamond$ Consider the transition systems $\mathcal{T}, \mathcal{T}'$ on the input alphabet $A = \{a, b, c\}$, whose graphs are shown in Figure 3.39.
    (a) Determine the languages $L(\mathcal{T})$ and $L(\mathcal{T}')$.
    (b) How many words of length n exist in $L(\mathcal{T})$ and in $L(\mathcal{T}')$ for $n \in \mathbb{N}$?
34. Let $\mathcal{T}_i$ be transition systems that accept the languages L_i for $1 \leq i \leq 5$, respectively. What is the language accepted by the transition system $\mathcal{T}$ given in Figure 3.40?
35. Construct the deterministic finite automaton equivalent to the transition system $\mathcal{T}$ shown in Figure 3.41.
36. $^{\diamond\diamond}$ Let $A = \{a_0, \ldots, a_{n-1}\}$ be an alphabet and let L_A be the language on

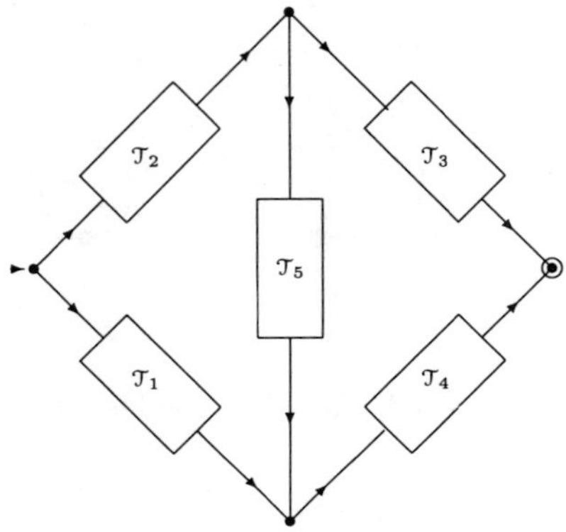

Figure 3.40: Transition System $\mathcal{T}$

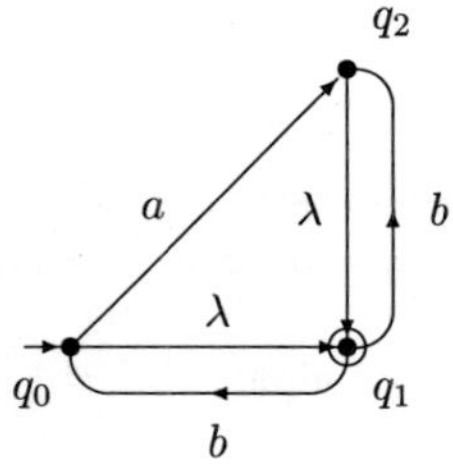

Figure 3.41: Graph of the Transition System $\mathcal{T}$

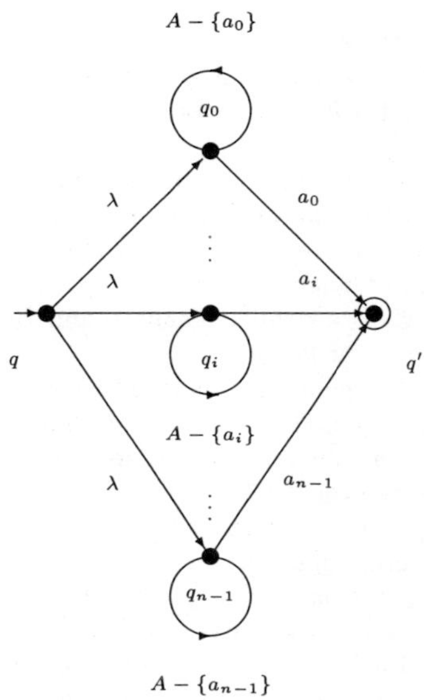

Figure 3.42: Transition System that Accepts the Language L_A

A that consists of all words $x \in A^+$ such that the last symbol of x never occurs in any other position in x. Recall that we discussed this language in Exercise 24 of Chapter 2. Prove that there exists a transition system having $n+2$ states that accepts the language L_A.

Solution. It is not difficult to see that L is accepted by the transition system given in Figure 3.42. ■

37. $^\diamond$ Let $\mathcal{T}$ be a transition system that accepts the regular language L. Give an algorithm that accepts $\mathcal{T}$ as input and yields a transition system that accepts the language L^R.
38. $^\diamond$ Let $\mathcal{T}$ be a transition system. Prove that for every sets of states S, S' of $\mathcal{T}$ we have $K_{\mathcal{T}}(S \cup S') = K_{\mathcal{T}}(S) \cup K_{\mathcal{T}}(S')$.
39. Construct transition systems that accept the following languages over the alphabet $A = \{a, b\}$:
    (a) The set of all words that contain *bab* as an infix.
    (b) The set $\{a\}^*\{b\}^*\{a\}^*$.

    Construct the corresponding finite state automata that accept the languages listed above.

Closure Properties

40. Let A be an alphabet. Define the binary relation $\sim$ on $\mathcal{P}(A^*)$ by $L \sim L'$

if $L \oplus L'$ is a finite language.

(a) Prove that $\sim$ is an equivalence on $\mathcal{P}(A^*)$.

(b) Prove that if L is a regular language and $L \sim L'$, then L' is a regular language.

41. $^\diamond$ Prove or disprove the following statements. Proving requires an argument; disproving requires a counterexample.

(a) If $L_0 \cup L_1$ is a regular language and L_1 is a finite language, then L_0 is a regular language.

(b) If $L_0 \cup L_1$ is a regular language and L_1 is a regular language, then L_0 is a regular language.

(c) If $L_0 L_1$ is regular and L_1 is finite, then L_0 is regular.

(d) If $L_0 L_1$ is regular and L_1 is finite but not empty, then L_0 is regular.

(e) If $L_0 L_1$ is a regular language and L_1 is a regular, non-empty language, then L_0 is a regular language.

(f) If $L_0 L_1$ is a regular language and L_1 is a regular language, then L_0 is a regular language.

(g) If L^* is a regular language, then L is regular.

42. $^\diamond$ Corollary 3.4.12 shows that if L is a regular language, then $\mathsf{PREF}(L)$, $\mathsf{SUFF}(L)$, and $\mathsf{INFIX}(L)$ are all regular language. Prove that the converse statement is not true. In other words, give an example of a non-regular language such that $\mathsf{PREF}(L)$, $\mathsf{SUFF}(L)$, and $\mathsf{INFIX}(L)$ are all regular languages.

Hint. Consider the non-regular language $\{a^{2^n} \mid n \in \mathbb{N}\}$.

43. $^\diamond$ Let L be a language over an alphabet A. Define the languages

$$\begin{aligned} \max(L) &= \{x \in L \mid xy \in L \text{ implies } y = \lambda\} \\ \min(L) &= \{x \in L \mid y \in \mathsf{PREF}(x) \text{ and } y \neq x \text{ implies } y \notin L\} \end{aligned}$$

Prove that if L is a regular language, then so are $\max(L)$ and $\min(L)$.

Fixed Points and Regular Languages

44. Let

$$\mathcal{M} = (\{0,1\}, \{q_0, q_1, q_2\}, \delta, q_0, \{q_1, q_2\})$$

be the dfa shown in Figure 3.43. Write and then solve the system of right-linear equations attached to this automaton.

45. $^\diamond$ Let $\mathcal{M} = (A, Q, \delta, q_0, F)$ be a dfa. Prove that if the language $L(\mathcal{M})$ is infinite, then at least one component of the first line of the matrix $\bigcup_{|Q| \leq k < 2|Q|} \boldsymbol{L}^{(k)}$ is not empty.

46. $^{\diamond\diamond}$ Prove that a dfa is k-definite if and only if for every $m \in \mathbb{N}$ such that $m \geq k$ all rows of the matrix $\boldsymbol{L}_{\mathcal{M}}^{(k)}$ are equal.

Regular Expressions

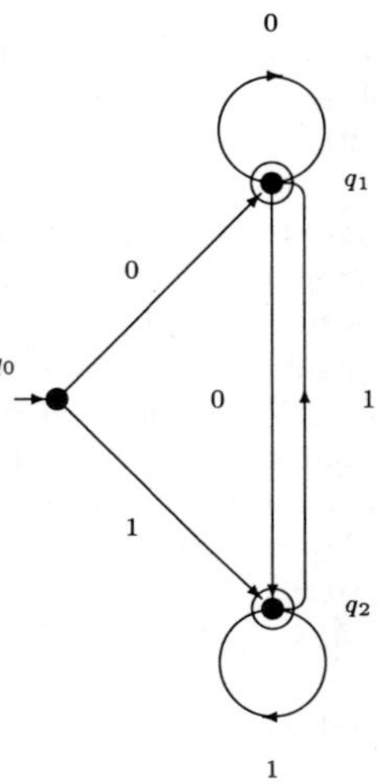

Figure 3.43: Transition System that Accepts the Language L_A

47. For each language L mentioned in Exercise 4 construct a regular expression E such that $\| E \| = L$.
48. $^\diamond$ Let $A = \{a, b, c\}$. Write regular expressions that denote the following languages over A:
    (a) the set of words that contain no infix aa;
    (b) the set of words that contain no more than three as or bs;
    (c) the set of words that contain the infixes abc and bca;
    (d) the set of words that contain exactly two as;
    (e) the set of words that contain a number of cs divisible by three.
49. $^\diamond$ Prove that the following regular expressions are equivalent:
    (a)
    $$(\boldsymbol{a} \cup \boldsymbol{b})^* \equiv (\boldsymbol{a} \cup \boldsymbol{b})^* \boldsymbol{a}^*$$
    (b)
    $$(\boldsymbol{a} \cup \boldsymbol{b})^* \equiv \boldsymbol{a}^* (\boldsymbol{a} \cup \boldsymbol{b})^*$$
    (c)
    $$(\boldsymbol{a} \cup \boldsymbol{b})^* \equiv (\boldsymbol{a}^* (\boldsymbol{b} \cup \Lambda) \boldsymbol{a}^*)^*$$
50. $^{\diamond\diamond}$ Let A be an alphabet and let $\boldsymbol{A}$ be its corresponding regular expression alphabet. Prove that if E is a regular expression over $\boldsymbol{A}$, then there exists a transition system $\mathcal{T}$ having no more than $2|E|$ states that accepts the language $\| E \|$.

Solution. The argument is by induction on regular expressions. Note that if E is one of $\boldsymbol{a}_0, \ldots, \boldsymbol{a}_{n-1}, \Lambda, \emptyset$, their corresponding languages are accepted by transition systems that have two states, so the basis case holds.

Suppose that E_1, E_2 are two regular expressions such that the languages $\| E_1 \|, \| E_2 \|$ are accepted by transition systems having n_1 and n_2 states, respectively, where $n_1 \leq 2|E_1|$ and $n_2 \leq 2|E_2|$. The transition system whose graph is given in Figure 3.18 accepts the language $\| E_1 \| \cup \| E_2 \|$ and has $n_1 + n_2 + 2$ states. Note that $n_1 + n_2 + 2 \leq 2(|E_1| + |E_2| + 3) = 2|(E_1 \cup E_2)|$. Similarly, the transition system given in Figure 3.20 has $n_1 + n_2$ states and $n_1 + n_2 \leq |E_1| + |E_2| + 2 = |(E_1 E_2)|$. Finally, the transition system shown in Figure 3.21 that accepts the language $\| (E_1^*) \|$ has $n_1 + 1$ states, so $n_1 + 1 \leq 2|E| < 2(|E| + 3) = 2|(E_1^*)|$. ∎

51. °° Let $\mathcal{M} = (A, Q, \delta, q_0, F)$ be a finite automaton and let R_{ij}^k be the language that consists of those words $x \in A^*$ such that $\delta(q_i, x) = q_j$ and for every proper prefix u of x, the automaton is in an intermediate state $\delta^*(q_i, u) \in \{q_0, \ldots, q_{k-1}\}$ (as introduced in Theorem 3.4.13).
    (a) Prove that there exist regular expressions E_{ij}^k such that $\| E_{ij}^k \| = R_{ij}^k$ and $|E_{ij}^k| \leq 3^k(|A| + 1.5) - 1.5$ for every $i, j, k \in \{0, \ldots, |Q|\}$.
    (b) Prove that there exists a regular expression E such that $\| E \| = L(\mathcal{M})$ and $|E| \leq |F|((3^{|Q|} + 1.5) - 1.5)$.
52. ° Prove that if L, L' are two regular languages, then $\mathsf{shuffle}(L, L')$ is a regular language.

Let A be an alphabet. The *star height* of regular expressions over A is a mapping $\mathsf{sth} : \mathsf{REXP}(A) \longrightarrow \mathbb{N}$ given by

$$\begin{aligned} &\mathsf{sth}(\boldsymbol{a}_i) = \mathsf{sth}(\Lambda) = \mathsf{sth}(\emptyset) = 0, \\ &\mathsf{sth}(E_1 \cup E_2) = \mathsf{sth}(E_1 E_2) = \max\{\mathsf{sth}(E_1), \mathsf{sth}(E_2)\}, \end{aligned}$$

and

$$\mathsf{sth}(E_1^*) = 1 + \mathsf{sth}(E_1).$$

53. ° Prove that there are equivalent regular expressions that have different star hights.
    Hint. Consider the regular expressions $E = (\boldsymbol{a}_0)^*$ and $E' = ((\boldsymbol{a}_0)^*)^*$.
54. ° Prove that for every regular expression E over the alphabet $A = \{a\}$ there is an equivalent regular expression of star height at most 1.
55. ° A regular expression E is *simple* if $E = \emptyset$ or E does not contain $\emptyset$ as a subexpression. Prove that for every regular expression $F \in \mathsf{REXP}(A)$ there exists an equivalent simple expression.
    Hint. Use an argument by induction on regular expressions.

Let $G = (V, E, s, d)$ be a directed graph. A *path expression of type* (v, w), where $v, w \in V$ is a simple regular expression $P \in \mathsf{REXP}(E)$ such that $\| P \|$ consists of paths joining v to w.

56. $^\diamond$ Prove that every subexpression of a path expression of a graph is a path expression of that graph whose type can be determined as follows. If P is a path expression of type (v, w), then
    - if $P = P_0 \cup P_1$, then P_0 and P_1 are path expressions of type (v, w);
    - if $P = P_0P_1$, then there is a unique $u \in V$ such that P_0 is a path expression of type (v, u) and P_1 is a path expression of type (u, w);
    - if $P = (P_0)^*$, then $v = w$ and P_0 is a path expression of type (v, v).
57. $^\diamond$ Let A be an alphabet. Define the function $f : \mathsf{REXP}(A) \longrightarrow \mathbb{N} \cup \{\infty\}$ by $f(\boldsymbol{a}) = 1$, $f(\Lambda) = 0$, $f(\boldsymbol{\emptyset}) = \infty$ and
$$\begin{aligned} f(E_0 \cup E_1) &= \min\{f(E_0), f(E_1)\} \\ f(E_0 \cdot E_1) &= f(E_0) + f(E_1) \\ f(E^*) &= 0. \end{aligned}$$
We make the "natural" assumptions $n+\infty = \infty+n = \infty$ and $\min\{n, \infty\} = n$ for every $n \in \mathbb{N}$. Prove that if $\| E \| \neq \emptyset$, then $f(E)$ is the length of the shortest word in the language $\| E \|$.
58. $^\diamond$ Show that Algorithm 3.8.7 can be used to generate a regular expression that denotes the language accepted by a dfa. Illustrate the application of this technique for the language $L(\mathcal{M})$, where $\mathcal{M}$ is the dfa whose graph is given in Figure 3.43.

The Pumping Lemma

59. $^\diamond$ Let $A = \{0, 1\}$ be an alphabet. Define the language L as follows:
    - $\lambda \in L$.
    - if $x \in L$, then $0x1 \in L$.
    - if $x \in L$ and $y \in L$, then $xy \in L$.

    (a) Show that if $x \in L$, then x is a word that has exactly as many 0's as 1's.
    (b) Show that L is not regular.
60. $^\diamond$ Let $f : \mathbb{N} \longrightarrow \mathbb{N}$ be a monotonic function such that for every $k \in \mathbb{N}$, there exists $n \in \mathbb{N}$ such that $f(n) < k$ and $f(n + 1) \geq 2k$. Prove that the language $\{a^{f(n)} \mid n \in \mathbb{N}\}$ is not regular.
61. $^{\diamond\diamond}$
    (a) Prove that if $f : \mathbb{N} \longrightarrow \mathbb{P}$ is a one-to-one function, the language $L_f = \{a^n b^{f(n)} \mid n \in \mathbb{N}\}$ is not regular.
    (b) Consider the alphabet $A_k = \{a, b_1, \ldots, b_k\}$. Prove that if $f_i : \mathbb{N} \longrightarrow \mathbb{P}$, $1 \leq i \leq k$ are k one-to-one functions, then the language
$$L_{f_1,\ldots,f_k} = \{x \in A_k^* \mid x = a^n b_1^{f_1(n)} \cdots b_k^{f_k(n)}\}$$
    is not regular.

Solution. Part (a) is a generalization of Example 3.5.4. Suppose that L_f is regular. Then, there is $n_0 \in \mathbb{N}$ such that if $x \in L$ and $|x| > n_0$, then x can be written as $x = uvw$ with $1 \leq |uv| \leq n_0$, and $|v| \geq 1$ such that $uv^n w \in L_f$ for every $n \in \mathbb{N}$. Let $x = a_p b^{f(p)}$, where $p > n_0$. Both u and v

consists only of as, say $u = a^k, v = a^\ell$ and $w = a^h b^{f(p)}$, where $k+\ell+h = p$. Therefore, $a^k a^{n\ell} a^h b^{f(p)} \in L$ for $n \in \mathbb{N}$. This implies $a^{p+(n-1)\ell} b^{f(p)} \in L$ for $n \geq 1$ and this contradicts the fact that f is one-to-one.

Part (b) generalizes Part (a); the argument is left to the reader. ■

62. $^\diamond$ Prove that the language $\{x \in \{a,b\}^* \mid n_a(x) \leq n_b(x)\}$ is not regular.
Hint. Note that $H \cap \{a\}^*\{b\}^* = L$, where L is the language introduced in Example 3.5.6.
63. Prove that the language $\{x \in \{a,b\}^* \mid n_a(x) | n_b(x)\}$ is not regular.
64. $^\diamond$ Prove that for every language L such that $L \subseteq \{a\}^*$, the language L^* is regular.
Hint. See Exercise 50 of Chapter 1.
65. $^{\diamond\diamond}$ Prove that the language $L = \{a\}^*\{b^n c^n \mid n \in \mathbb{N}\} \cup \{b\}^*\{c\}^*$ is not regular using closure properties of the class of regular functions. Can you prove that this language is not regular using the Pumping Lemma?

Minimal Automata

66. Let $\chi_L : A^* \longrightarrow \{0,1\}$ be the characteristic function of the language L given by

$$\chi_L(z) = \begin{cases} 1 & \text{if } z \in L \\ 0 & \text{if } z \notin L \end{cases}$$

Prove that $(x,y) \in \nu_L$ if and only if $\chi_L(xw) = \chi_L(yw)$ for every $w \in A^*$,
67. $^{\diamond\diamond}$ Let L be a language, $L \subseteq A^*$.
(a) Prove that if ν is a right-invariant equivalence on A^* that saturates L, then $\nu \subseteq \nu_L$; in other words, prove that ν_L is the largest right-invariant congruence that saturates L.
(b) Prove that if L is saturated by a right-invariant congruence ν on A^* such that the quotient set A^*/ν is finite, then L is regular.
Solution. Let $(x,y) \in \nu$ and suppose that $xu \in L$. Since ν is right-invariant, we have $(xu, yu) \in \nu$. The fact that L is saturated by ν implies $yu \in L$. This shows that for every $u \in A^*$ we have $xu \in L$ if and only if $yu \in L$, so $(x,y) \in \nu_L$. Part (b) follows immediately. ■

A *unitary language* is a nonempty regular language that is accepted by a dfa whose set of final states is a singleton.

If $L \subseteq A^*$ is unitary and a submonoid of the monoid $(A^*, \lambda, \cdot)$ (that is if $\lambda \in L$ and $x, y \in L$ implies $xy \in L$) we refer to L as a *unitary monoid.*

68. $^\diamond$ Let L be a regular language over the alphabet A. Prove that L is a unitary language if and only if $u, uv, w \in L$ imply $wv \in L$.
Hint. The necessity of the condition is immediate. To prove that the condition is sufficient the reader can show that $x, y \in L$ imply $(x,y) \in \nu_L$. Then, the dfa $\mathcal{M}_L$ constructed in the proof of Theorem 3.6.7 has a unique final state.

69. $\diamond$ Let A be an alphabet. For $x, y \in A^*$ such that $x = a_0 \cdots a_{n-1}$ and $y = a'_0 \cdots a'_{n-1}$ define $d(x, y) = \{i \mid 0 \leq i \leq n-1 \text{ and } a_i \neq a'_i\}$. Let $C(L)$ be the language $C(L) = \{y \in A^* \mid d(x, y) \leq 1 \text{ for some } x \in L\}$. Prove that if L is regular, then $C(L)$ is regular.
70. $\diamond$ Let L be a nonempty, regular language. Prove that L can be written as a finite union of disjoint unitary regular languages.
71. $\diamond$ A *prefix language* is a language L such that $L \cap \mathsf{PREF}(L) = \emptyset$. Prove that every regular prefix language is a unitary language.
72. $\diamond\diamond$ If L is a unitary language, then prove that $L^{-1}L$ is a unitary monoid.
Solution. Suppose that $L = L(\mathcal{M})$, where $\mathcal{M} = (A, Q, \delta, q_0, \{q_1\}$. We claim that $L^{-1}L = L(\mathcal{M}_1)$, where $\mathcal{M}_1 = (A, Q, \delta, q_1, \{q_1\}$. Indeed, let $x \in L(\mathcal{M}_1)$. We have $\delta^*(q_1, x) = q_1$. Since L is nonempty, there exists a word $u \in L$ such that $\delta^*(q_0, u) = q_1$. Therefore, $\delta^*(q_0, ux) = \delta^*(\delta^*(q_0, u), x)) = q_1$, so both u and ux belong to L; we may conclude that $x \in L^{-1}L$. Conversely, if $y \in L^{-1}L$, there exist $u, v \in L$ such that $u = vy$. This means that $\delta^*(q_0, v) = q_1$, $\delta^*(q_0, u) = \delta^*(q_0, vy) = q_1$, so $\delta^*(q_1, y) = q_1$, which implies $y \in L(\mathcal{M}_1)$. Since $L^{-1}L = L(\mathcal{M}_1)$, it follows that $L^{-1}L$ is unitary. We leave to the reader to verify that $\lambda \in L(\mathcal{M}_1)$ and that $x, y \in L(\mathcal{M}_1)$ implies $xy \in L(\mathcal{M}_1)$. ∎
73. $\diamond$ Prove that every regular language L is a finite union of products of unitary languages and unitary monoids. In other words, show that if L is a regular language, then there exist the unitary languages $U_0, \ldots, U_{k-1}$ and the unitary monoids $W_0, \ldots, W_{k-1}$ such that

$$L = \bigcup_{0 \leq j \leq k-1} U_j W_j.$$

74. $\diamond$ Decompose the language $L(\mathcal{M})$, where $\mathcal{M}$ is the dfa whose graph is represented in Figure 3.43 into a finite union of products of unitary languages and unitary monoids.
75. Compute the minimal automata of the following languages over the alphabet $A = \{a, b\}$:
    (a) $L_k = A^* a^k A^*$, where $k > 1$;
    (b) $L = \{a\}^* \{b\}^*$;
    (c) $L = \{a\}^+ \{b\}^+$;
    (d) $L = \{a\}^* ba \cup ab\{a\}^*$.

The next Exercise shows that there is a regular language that requires a deterministic automaton having a number of states exponential in the number of states of a corresponding nondeterministic automaton that accepts the same language.

76. $\diamond\diamond$ Let $A = \{a_0, \ldots, a_{n-1}\}$ be an alphabet containing n symbols and let L_A be the language discussed in Exercise 24 of Chapter 2 and in Exercise 36. Prove that if $\mathcal{M}$ is a dfa that accepts L, then $\mathcal{M}$ has at least $2^{n+1} + 1$ states.
77. $\diamond$ Starting from the transition function δ of an ndfa $\mathcal{M} = (A, Q, \delta, q_0, F)$ we defined the function $\Delta : \mathcal{P}(Q) \times A \longrightarrow \mathcal{P}(Q)$ using Equalities (3.3),

(3.4) and (3.5). Prove that if Equality (3.5) is replaced by

$$\Delta^*(S, ax) = \Delta^*(\Delta(S, a), x)$$

for all $a \in A$ and $x \in A^*$, then we obtain the same function.

To generalize the notion of ndfa define an *alternating finite automaton* (afn) as a 5-tuple $\mathcal{M} = (A, Q, g, q_0, F)$, where A, Q, q_0, F are as in the definition of ndfa, and $g : Q \times A \times \mathbf{B}^k \longrightarrow \mathbf{B}$, where $\mathbf{B} = \{0, 1\}$ and $k = |Q|$.

If $q_i \in Q$, the function $g_i : A \times \mathbf{B}^k \longrightarrow \mathbf{B}$ is given by:

$$g_i(a, (b_0, \ldots, b_{k-1}) = g(q_i, a, (b_0, \ldots, b_{k-1}))$$

for every $a \in A$ and $(b_0, \ldots, b_{k-1}) \in \mathbf{B}$.

Let $P_i : \mathbf{B}^k \longrightarrow \mathbf{B}$ be the ith projection for $0 \leq i \leq k-1$, where $Q = \{q_0, \ldots, q_{k-1}\}$. Define the mapping $H_i : A^* \longrightarrow (\mathbf{B}^k \longrightarrow \mathbf{B})$ recursively by

$$H_i(\lambda) = P_i \tag{3.19}$$

$$H_i(ax)(\mathbf{b}) = g_i(a, H_0(x)(\mathbf{b}), \ldots, H_{k-1}(x)(\mathbf{b})) \tag{3.20}$$

for $a \in A$, $x \in A^*$ and $\mathbf{b} \in \mathbf{B}^k$.

Note that $H_i(\lambda)(\mathbf{b}_F) = 1$ if and only if $q_i \in F$. The language accepted by $\mathcal{M}$ is

$$L(\mathcal{M}) = \{x \in A^* \mid H_0(x)(\mathbf{b}) = 1\}.$$

78. $^{\circ\circ}$ Let $\mathcal{M} = (A, Q, g, q_0, F)$ be an alternating automaton, whose set of states is $Q = \{q_0, \ldots, q_{k-1}\}$. Define the functions $G_i : A^* \longrightarrow (\mathbf{B}^k \longrightarrow \mathbf{B})$ recursively by
$$G_i(\lambda) = P_i$$
$$G_i(xa)(\mathbf{b}) = G_i(x)(g_0(a, \mathbf{b}), \ldots, g_{k-1}(a, \mathbf{b}))$$
for $0 \leq i \leq k-1$, $a \in A$, $x \in A^*$ and $\mathbf{b} \in \mathbf{B}^k$.
Prove that $G_i = H_i$ for $0 \leq i \leq k-1$.
79. $^{\circ}$ The purpose of this exercise is to explain why afns generalize ndfas. We show that a ndfa $\mathcal{M} = (A, Q, \delta, q_0, F)$ can be regarded as a afn where all states are "existential"; in other words, an afn accepts a word ax when started in an existential state q if at least one of the states in $\delta(q, a)$ leads to acceptance.
Define the afn $\mathcal{M}' = (A, Q, g, q_0, F)$ by $g(q, a, \mathbf{b}) = 1$ if and only if $\delta(q, a) \cap S_{\mathbf{b}} \neq \emptyset$, where $\mathbf{b} = (b_0, \ldots, b_{k-1})$ and $S_{\mathbf{b}} = \{q_i \in Q \mid b_i = 1\}$. Prove that $L(\mathcal{M}) = L(\mathcal{M}')$.
Hint. Prove that $H_i(x, \mathbf{b}) = 1$ if and only if $\delta^*(q_j, x) \cap S_{\mathbf{b}} \neq \emptyset$.
80. $^{\circ\circ}$ Prove that if $\mathcal{M}$ is an alternating automaton, then $L(\mathcal{M})$ is a regular language.
Solution. Define the equivalence $\rho_{\mathcal{M}}$ on A^* by $(x, y) \in \rho_{\mathcal{M}}$ if $G_0(x) = G_0(y)$. The quotient set $A^*/\rho_{\mathcal{M}}$ may contain at most 2^{2^k} classes because this is the number of elements of the set $\mathbf{B}^k \longrightarrow \mathbf{B}$. Moreover, $\rho_{\mathcal{M}}$ is a

right congruence since $G_0(x) = G_0(y)$ implies

$$\begin{aligned} G_0(xa)(\mathbf{b}) &= G_i(x)(g_0(a,\mathbf{b}),\ldots,g_{k-1}(a,\mathbf{b})) \\ &= G_i(y)(g_0(a,\mathbf{b}),\ldots,g_{k-1}(a,\mathbf{b})) \\ &= G_0(ya). \end{aligned}$$

The language $L = L(\mathcal{M})$ is $\rho_{\mathcal{M}}$-saturated. Indeed, suppose that $(x,y) \in \rho_{\mathcal{M}}$ and $x \in L$. We have $H_0(x)(\mathbf{b}) = 1$, so $H_0(y)(\mathbf{b}) = G_0(y)(\mathbf{b}) = G_0(x)(\mathbf{b}) = H_0(x)(\mathbf{b}) = 1$, by Exercise 78. Thus, $y \in L$, which shows that L is $\rho_{\mathcal{M}}$-saturated. By Exercise 67, L is regular. ∎

81. $^{\circ\circ}$ A language $L \subseteq A^*$ is ***strongly accepted*** by a nondeterministic finite automaton $\mathcal{M} = (A, Q, \delta, q_0, F)$ if $L = \{x \in A^* \mid \delta^*(q_0, x) \subseteq F\}$. In other words, L is strongly accepted by a ndfa $\mathcal{M}$ if L consists of those words $x \in A^*$ such that every sequence of states generated in $\mathcal{M}$ by a x ends in a final state. Prove that the class of languages strongly recognized by nondeterministic automata coincides with the class of regular languages.
82. $^{\circ\circ}$ Let L be a k-definite language such that $L = L(\mathcal{M})$, where $\mathcal{M}$ is a dfa. If $|Q| = w(L)$, then $\mathcal{M}$ is k-definite.
Solution. Since $\mathcal{M}$ has the least number of states of a dfa that accepts $\mathcal{M}$ it follows that every state $q \in Q$ is accessible from q_0. Consider the states $q', q'' \in Q$, where $q' = \delta^*(q_0, u)$ and $q'' = \delta^*(q_0, v)$. Let $x \in A^*$ be a word such that $|x| \geq k$.
Suppose that $\delta^*(q', x) = q_1$ and $\delta^*(q'', x) = q_2$. Since L is k-definite, $uxw \in L$ if and only if $vxw \in L$ for all words $w \in A^*$. Thus, $\delta^*(q_1, w) \in F$ if and only if $\delta^*(q_2, w) \in F$ for every $w \in A^*$. The minimality of $\mathcal{M}$ implies $q_1 = q_2$ since, otherwise, by identifying q_1 and q_2 we would contradict the minimality of $\mathcal{M}$. Therefore, $\mathcal{M}$ is indeed, weakly k-definite.
Since L is not $(k-1)$-definite, there are $x, y, z \in A^*$ such that $|z| = k-1$, $xz \in L$ and $yz \notin L$ which implies $\delta^*(\delta^*(q_0, x), z) \in F$ and $\delta^*(\delta^*(q_0, y), z) \notin F$. Therefore, $\delta^*(\delta^*(q_0, x), z) \neq \delta^*(\delta^*(q_0, y), z)$ and this shows that $\mathcal{M}$ is not weakly $(k-1)$-definite. We conclude that $\mathcal{M}$ is k-definite. ∎

Syntactic Monoids

83. $^{\circ}$ A *spanning set for a language L*, $L \subseteq A^*$, is a finite language over A such that for every $x \in A^*$ there is a word $y \in S$ such that $(x, y) \in \nu_L$.
Prove that a language L is regular if and only if it has a spanning set.
84. $^{\circ\circ}$ Let A be an alphabet. Show that a language $L \subseteq A^*$ is regular if and only if there is a finite monoid $(M, \cdot, 1)$, a subset P of M and a morphism of monoids $h : A^* \longrightarrow M$ such that $L = h^{-1}(P)$.
Solution. Suppose that $L \subseteq A^*$ is such that $L = h^{-1}(P)$, where $h : A^* \longrightarrow M$ is a monoid morphism, and $P \subseteq M$. Let $\mathcal{M} = (A, M, \delta, u, P)$ be the automaton defined by $\delta(m, a) = m \star h(a)$ for $m \in M$ and $a \in A$. It is easy to verify that $\delta^*(m, x) = m \star h(x)$ for every $m \in M$ and $x \in A^*$. Therefore, $L(\mathcal{M}) = \{x \in A^* \mid u \star h(x) \in P\} = \{x \in A^* \mid h(x) \in P\} = h^{-1}(P) = L$.
Conversely, let L be a regular language and let A^*/μ_L be its finite syntactic

monoid. Define the morphism $h : A^* \longrightarrow A^*/\mu_L$ by $h(x) = [x]_{\mu_L}$ for $x \in A^*$, where $[x]_{\mu_L}$ is the μ_L-equivalence class of x. Since L is μ_L-saturated, we have $L = \bigcup\{[x]_{\mu_L} \mid x \in L\}$, so $L = h^{-1}(\{[x]_{\mu_L} \mid x \in L\})$. ■

85. $^{\circ\circ}$ Let L be a language, $L \subseteq A^*$. Prove that the quotient monoid A^*/μ_L contains a disjunctive set.
Solution. Let $P = \{[w]_{\mu_L} \mid w \in L\}$. Suppose that $[x]_{\mu_L}$ and $[y]_{\mu_L}$ are such that $[u]_{\mu_L}[x]_{\mu_L}[v]_{\mu_L} \in P$ if and only if $[u]_{\mu_L}[y]_{\mu_L}[v]_{\mu_L} \in P$ for every $[u]_{\mu_L}, [v]_{\mu_L} \in A^*/\mu_L$. Note that this means that for every $u, v \in A^*$ $(uxv, w) \in \mu_L$ for some $w \in L$ if and only if $(uyv, w') \in \mu_L$ for some $w' \in L$. Since L is μ_L-saturated, this means that $uxv \in L$ if and only if $uyv \in L$, so $(x, y) \in \mu_L$, which implies $[x]_{\mu_L} = [y]_{\mu_L}$. This proves that P is disjunctive. ■
86. $^{\circ\circ}$ Show that not every finite monoid is isomorphic to a syntactic monoid.
Hint. See Exercise 35 of Chapter 1.

A language $L \subseteq A^*$ is *aperiodic* if there is a number $n \in \mathbb{P}$ such that $(x^n, x^{n+1}) \in \mu_L$, where μ_L is the Myhill congruence introduced in Definition 3.7.6. The least number n with this property is the *index* of L and is denoted by $\mathsf{index}(L)$.

87. $^{\circ\circ}$ Prove that a language $L \subseteq A^*$ is aperiodic if and only there exists an aperiodic monoid $(M, \cdot, 1)$ and a morphism of monoids $h : A^* \longrightarrow M$ such that $L = h^{-1}(P)$ for some subset P of M.
88. $^{\circ}$ Show that every finite language is aperiodic.
89. $^{\circ\circ}$ Prove that if K, L are aperiodic languages, then $K \cup L$ and KL are aperiodic languages. Also, the complement of an aperiodic language is aperiodic. Further, show that

$$\begin{aligned} \mathsf{index}(K \cup L) &\leq \max\{\mathsf{index}(K), \mathsf{index}(L)\} \\ \mathsf{index}(KL) &\leq \mathsf{index}(K) + \mathsf{index}(L) \\ \mathsf{index}(\overline{K}) &= \mathsf{index}(K). \end{aligned}$$

Solution. We discuss only the argument for the second statement. Suppose that $\mathsf{index}(K) = n$ and $\mathsf{index}(L) = m$ and let $ux^pv \in KL$ for some $p \geq \mathsf{index}(K) + \mathsf{index}(L)$. We can write $x = rs$ such that $ux^kr \in K$ and $sx^\ell v \in L$, where $k + \ell + 1 = p$. Then, at least one of $k \geq \mathsf{index}(K)$ or $\ell \geq \mathsf{index}(L)$ holds. In the first case, $ux^{k+1}r \in K$, so $ux^{k+1}rsx^\ell v = ux^{k+\ell+2}v = ux^{p+1}v \in KL$. A similar conclusion can be obtained if the second inequality holds. So, in either case, $ux^pv \in KL$ implies $ux^{p+1}v \in KL$. This shows that KL is aperiodic and that $\mathsf{index}(KL) \leq \mathsf{index}(K) + \mathsf{index}(L)$. ■

Let A be an alphabet. The collection of *star-free languages* is defined by:

1. Every finite language is star-free.
2. If K, L are two star-free languages over A, then $K \cup L$, KL and $\overline{K} = A^* - K$ are star-free languages.

90. $^{\circ}$ Prove that:
(a) every star-free language is regular;

(b) the intersection of two star-free languages is a star-free language.

91. $^\diamond$ Let $A = \{a, b\}$. Prove that the following languages are star-free:
(a) the language A^*;
(b) the language $(ab)^*$.
Hint. For the second part observe that $(ab)^* = (aA^* \cap A^*b) - (A^*aaA^* \cup A * bbA^*) \cup \{\lambda\}$.

92. $^{\diamond\diamond\diamond}$ Prove that a language is star-free if and only if is aperiodic.
Solution. The argument to prove that a star-free language is aperiodic is by induction on the definition of star-free languages, and makes use of the closure properties of the class of aperiodic languages. We leave this part of the proof to the reader.
Conversely, if $L \subseteq A^*$ is aperiodic, then there exists a morphism $h : A^* \longrightarrow M$, where $(M, \cdot, 1)$ is a finite aperiodic monoid and $L = h^{-1}(P)$ for some subset P of M (see Exercise 87). Since $L = \bigcup_{m \in P} h^{-1}(m)$ it suffices to show that every language $h^{-1}(m)$ is star-free. We prove this by induction on the number $n_m = |M - MmM|$. Note that $n_1 = 0$; also, if $m \neq 1$, then $n_m > 0$. Indeed, in this case, we have $1 \in M - MmM$ because $1 = pmr$ would imply $p = r = m = 1$ by Exercise 39 of Chapter 1. Thus, the basis step $n_m = 0$ involves only $m = 1$. In this case, we claim that $h^{-1}(1) = A^* - A^*\{a \in A \mid h(a) \neq 1\}A^*$. Indeed, if $u \in A^* - A^*\{a \in A \mid h(a) \neq 1\}A^*$, than every symbol that occurs in u is mapped by h into 1, so $h(u) = 1$. Conversely, if $h(u) = 1$, then for every symbol a that occurs in u we have $h(a) = 1$ due to the cancellation property of aperiodic monoids (see Exercise 40. This proves the equality from the previous claim, so $h^{-1}(1)$ is star-free.
For the inductive step, suppose that the for every $p \in M$ such that $n_p < n_m$, the language $h^{-1}(n_p)$ is star-free. By Exercise 58 we have $h^{-1}(m) = (U_mA^* \cap A^*V_m) - A^*(W_m \cup T_m)A^*$. We claim that the languages U_m, V_m, W_m, and T_m are star-free. Recall that

$$U_m = \bigcup\{h^{-1}(p)a \mid p \in M, a \in A, ph(a)M = mM \text{ and } p \notin mM\}$$

If $ph(a)M = mM$ and $p \notin mM$, then $n_p < n_m$. Indeed, if $q \in MmM$, then $q = q'mq''$ for some $q', q'' \in M$. On the other hand, $mq'' \in mM = ph(a)M$, so $mq'' = ph(a)r$ for some $r \in M$ and this implies $q = q'ph(a)r \in MpM$; thus, $MmM \subseteq MpM$, so $n_p \leq n_m$. Suppose that $n_p = n_m$. Then, we would have $MpM = MmM$ and that would imply $p = p'mp''$ for some $p', p'' \in M$. Since $m \in ph(a)M$ we would also have $m = pm'$ for some $m' \in M$ and this would give $p = p'pm'p''$. By Exercise 39, we would obtain $p = p'm$ and $p = pm'p'' = mp''$ and this would contradict the fact that $p \notin mM$. Therefore, we have $n_p < n_m$ for every $p \in U_m$. By the inductive hypothesis, every language $h^{-1}(p)$ is star-free, so U_m is star free. A similar argument shows that V_m is star-free.
To prove that

$$W_m = \bigcup\{ah^{-1}(p)b \mid p \in M, m \in Mh(a)pM \cap Mph(a)M \text{ and } m \notin Mh(a)ph(b)M\}$$

is star-free let $p \in M$ be such that $m \in Mh(a)pM \cap Mph(a)M$ and

$m \notin Mh(a)ph(b)M$. It is clear that $n_p \leq n_m$. Suppose that $n_p = n_m$. Then, $p = p'mp''$ and $m = m_0h(a)pm_1 = m_2ph(b)m_3$ for some $m_i \in M$ and $0 \leq i \leq 3$. Thus, $p = p'm_0h(a)pm_1p''$ and this gives $p = p'm_0h(a)p$ by the cancellation law. Consequently, $m = m_2p'm_0h(a)ph(b)m_3$ which means that $m \in MpM$. This contradicts the definition of the set W_m, so the $n_p < n_m$. It is easy to see now that W_m is star-free. The fact that T_m is star-free is immediate. This concludes the argument. ∎

Let A be an alphabet. The set of *locally testable languages* is defined as follows.

- Every language of the form KA^*, A^*K, or A^*KA^* is locally testable, where K is a subset of A.
- If L, H are locally testable languages, then $L \cup H$, $L \cap H$ and $\overline{L} = A^* - L$ are locally testable languages.

93. $^\diamond$ Prove that every locally testable language is aperiodic.
94. $^{\diamond\diamond}$ Prove that a language L is locally testable if and only if there exists an integer $n \geq 1$ such that if two words $u, v \in A^*$ with $|u| \geq n$ and $|v| \geq n$ have the same prefix of length n, the same suffix of length n and the same set of infixes of length $n+1$, then $u \in L$ if and only if $v \in L$.

The notion of regular language can be extended to arbitrary monoids as follows. Let $(M, \cdot, e)$ be a monoid. A subset L of M is *recognizable* if there exist a finite monoid $(P, \cdot, u)$, a morphism $h : M \longrightarrow P$ and a subset Q of P such that $L = h^{-1}(Q)$. Note that Exercise 84 implies that if M is a free monoid A^* for some alphabet A, then L is recognizable if and only if it is regular. The set of recognizable subsets of the monoid M will be denoted by $\mathsf{RS}(M)$.

95. $^{\diamond\diamond}$ Let $(M, \cdot, e)$ be a monoid. Prove that $\emptyset$ and M belong to $\mathsf{RS}(M)$. Further, prove that $\mathsf{RS}(M)$ is closed with respect to union, intersection, and complementation.
Solution. Let $U = (\{1\}, \cdot, 1)$ be the monoid defined by $1 \cdot 1 = 1$. Note that the mapping $h : M \longrightarrow \{1\}$ given by $h(m) = 1$ for every $m \in M$ is a morphism and that $\emptyset = h^{-1}(\emptyset)$ and $M = h^{-1}(1)$.
If $L = h^{-1}(Q)$, where $L \subseteq M$, $Q \subseteq P$ and h is a morphism between the monoid $(M, \cdot, e)$ and the finite monoid $(P, \cdot, u)$, then $M - L = h^{-1}(P - Q)$; this proves that $\mathsf{RS}(M)$ is closed with respect to complementation.
Suppose that $L, L' \in \mathsf{RS}(M)$. Then, there exist two finite monoids $(P, \cdot, u)$ and $(P', \cdot, u')$ and two morphisms $h : M \longrightarrow P$ and $h' : M \longrightarrow P'$ such that $L = h^{-1}(Q)$ and $L' = h^{-1}(Q')$. Define the morphism $\ell : M \longrightarrow P \times P'$ by $\ell(x) = (h(x), h'(x))$ for $x \in M$. It is easy to see that $L \cap L' = h^{-1}(Q \times Q')$, which proves that $\mathsf{RS}(M)$ is closed with respect to intersection. The closure of $\mathsf{RS}(M)$ with respect to union follows immediately. ∎
96. $^{\diamond\diamond}$ Let $h : M \longrightarrow M'$ be a morphism between the monoids $(M, \cdot, e)$ and $(M', \cdot, e')$. If $L' \in \mathsf{RS}(M')$, then prove that $h^{-1}(L') \in \mathsf{RS}(L)$.
97. $^{\diamond\diamond}$ Let $(M, \cdot, e), (M', \cdot, e')$ be two monoids. Prove that $L \in \mathsf{RS}(M_1 \times M_2)$ if and only if L is a finite union of sets of the form $K \times K'$, where $K \in \mathsf{RS}(M)$

and $K' \in \mathsf{RS}(M')$.

Solution. Consider the projections $\pi : M \times M' \longrightarrow M$ and $\pi' : M \times M' \longrightarrow M'$ given by $\pi(x, y) = x$ and $\pi'(x, y) = y$ for every $(x, y) \in M \times M'$. Clearly, both π and π' are monoid morphisms. Note that if $K \in \mathsf{RS}(M)$ and $K' \in \mathsf{RS}(M')$, then $K \times K' = (K \times M') \cap (M \times K) = \pi^{-1}(K) \cap \pi^{-1}(K')$. Therefore, by Exercise 96, and by Exercise 95, we have $K \times K' \in \mathsf{RS}(M \times M')$. Consequently, every finite union of sets of the form $K \times K'$ belongs to $\mathsf{RS}(M \times M')$.

Conversely, let $H \in \mathsf{RS}(M \times M')$. There exists a finite monoid $(P, \cdot, u)$, a monoid morphism $h : M \times M' \longrightarrow P$, and a subset Q of P such that $H = h^{-1}(Q)$.

Define the morphisms $k : M \longrightarrow P$ and $k' : M' \longrightarrow P$ by $k(x) = h(x, e')$ and $k'(y) = h(e, y)$. Also, define the morphism $\ell : M \times M' \longrightarrow P \times P$ by $\ell(x, y) = (k(x), k'(y))$ for every $(x, y) \in M \times M'$. Observe that $k(x) \cdot k'(y) = h(x, e') \cdot h(e, y) = h(x \cdot e, e' \cdot y) = h(x, y)$ for every $(x, y) \in M \times M'$ and that $\ell^{-1}(p, p') = k^{-1}(p) \times k'^{-1}(p')$ for $(p, p') \in P \times P$.

If $R = \{(p, p') \mid p \cdot p' \in Q\}$, then $\ell(x, y) \in R$ if and only if $k(x) \cdot k'(y) = h(x, y) \in Q$. Thus, $H = h^{-1}(Q) = \ell^{-1}(R) = \bigcup_{(p,p') \in R} k^{-1}(p) \times k'^{-1}(p')$.

The statement follws from the fact that the sets $k^{-1}(p)$ and $k'^{-1}(p')$ are recognizable in M and M', respectively. ■

The notion of automaton can be generalized to monoids as follows. An automaton on a monoid $(M, \cdot, e)$ is a 5-tuple $\mathcal{M} = (M, Q, \delta, q_0, F)$, where $\delta : Q \times M \longrightarrow Q$ satisfies the following conditions:

$$\begin{aligned} \delta(q, e) &= q \\ \delta(q, x \cdot y) &= \delta(\delta(q, x), y) \end{aligned}$$

for every $q \in Q$ and $x, y \in M$.

The set accepted by $\mathcal{M}$ is $L(\mathcal{M}) = \{x \in M \mid \delta(q_0, x) \in F\}$.

98. $^\diamond$ Let $(M, \cdot, e)$ be a monoid. Prove that $L \in \mathsf{RS}(M)$ if and only if there exists an automaton $\mathcal{M}$ on the monoid M such that $L = L(\mathcal{M})$.

Transducers

99. Let

$$\mathcal{T} = (\{a, b, c\}, \{q_0, \}, \{0, 1\}, \theta, q_0, F)$$

be the transducer whose graph is given in Figure 3.44.
Compute $\mathcal{T}(abc), \mathcal{T}(abca)$ and $\mathcal{T}(bca)$.

100. $^\diamond$ Let $\mathcal{T} = (A, Q, B, \theta, q_0, F)$ be a transducer. Show that $\mathcal{T}$ is λ-free if and only if $\mathcal{T}(u)$ is a λ-free language for every $u \in A^+$ and $\lambda \in \mathcal{T}(\lambda)$ if and only if $q_0 \in F$.

101. $^{\diamond\diamond}$ Let A be an alphabet and let R be a regular language over A. Prove that there is a gsm $\mathcal{T}_R$ such that $\mathcal{T}_R(L) = L \cap R$ for every language L over A.

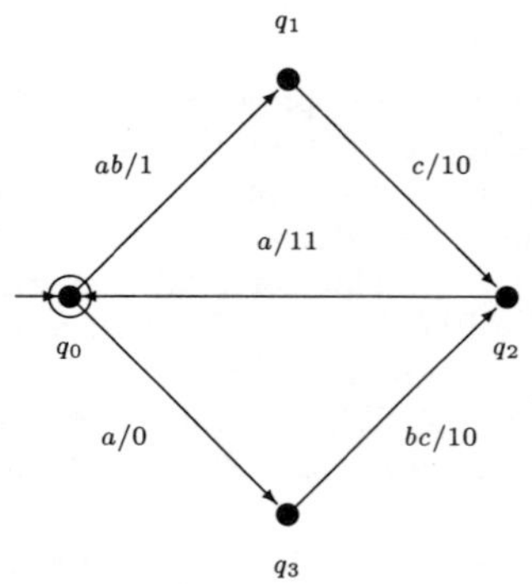

Figure 3.44: Graph of the transducer $\mathcal{T}$

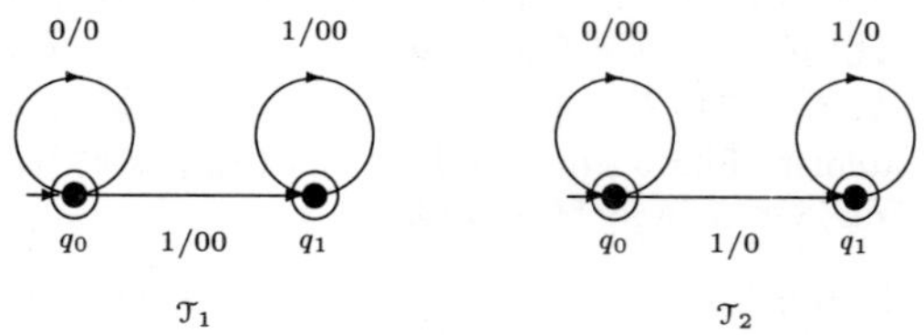

Figure 3.45: Graphs of the transducers $\mathcal{T}_1$ and $\mathcal{T}_2$

Solution. Let $\mathcal{M} = (A, Q, \delta, q_0, F)$ be a dfa such that $R = L(\mathcal{M})$. Define the gsm $\mathcal{T}_R = (A, Q, A, \delta, \gamma, q_0, F)$ by $\gamma(q, a) = a$ for every $q \in Q, a \in A$. Since the input symbols are reproduced at the output, if $w \in \mathcal{T}_R(L)$, then $\delta^*(q_0, u) = q' \in F$ and $\gamma^*(q_0, u) = u = w$. Therefore, $u \in L(\mathcal{M}) = R$, so $u \in L \cap R$. The converse inclusion is left to the reader. ∎

102. $^\diamond$ Let $h : A^* \longrightarrow B^*$ be a morphism. Prove that there exists an λ-free transducer $\mathcal{T}$ such that $\mathcal{T}(L) = h^{-1}(L)$ for every language $L \subseteq B^*$.

103. $^{\diamond\diamond}$ Let $\mathcal{T} = (A, Q, B, \theta, q_0, F)$ be a transducer. The relation $\rho(\mathcal{T})$ defined by $\mathcal{T}$ consists of the pairs $(u, v) \in A^* \times B^*$ such that $v \in \mathcal{T}(u)$. Prove that $\text{Dom}(\rho)$ is a regular language over A.

104. $^\diamond$ Consider the transducers $\mathcal{T}_1$ and $\mathcal{T}_2$ whose graphs are given in Figure 3.45.

 (a) Prove that
$$\begin{aligned} \rho(\mathcal{T}_1) &= \{(0^n 1^m, 0^{n+2m} \mid n, m \in \mathbb{N}\} \\ \rho(\mathcal{T}_2) &= \{(0^p 1^q, 0^{2p+q} \mid p, q \in \mathbb{N}\} \end{aligned}$$
 (b) Prove that there is no transducer $\mathcal{T}$ such that $\rho(\mathcal{T}) = \rho(\mathcal{T}_1) \cap \rho(\mathcal{T}_2)$.

Hint. : For Part (b) use exercise 103.

105. $^{\diamond\diamond}$ Let $\mathcal{T} = (A, Q, B, \theta, q_0, F)$ be a transducer. Prove that there is an 1-bounded transducer $\mathcal{T}' = (A, Q', B, \theta', q_0, F)$ such that $\mathcal{T}(L) = \mathcal{T}'(L)$ for

every language L over A.

Solution. To define the transducer $\mathcal{T}'$ set initially $Q' = Q$ and $\theta' = \theta$. Let $d = (q, u, v, q')$ be a quadruple from θ'. If both $|u| \leq 1$ and $|v| \leq 1$ then include d in θ'. Otherwise, write $u = u_0 \ldots u_{\ell(d)-1}$ and $v = v_0 \ldots v_{\ell(d)-1}$, where $u_i \in A \cup \{\lambda\}$, $v_i \in B \cup \{\lambda\}$, and $\ell(d) \geq 2$. Add the new states $p_0^d, \ldots, p_{\ell(d)-2}^d$ to Q' and replace the quadruple $d \in \theta'$ by the quadruples

$$(q, u_0, v_0, p_0^d), (p_0^d, u_1, v_1, p_1^d), \ldots, (p_{\ell(d)-2}^d, u_{\ell(d)-1}, v_{\ell(d)-1}, q')$$

to θ'. Note that $(q, uw, t) \underset{\mathcal{T}}{\vdash} (q', w, tv)$ if and only if

$$\begin{aligned}
(q, uw, t) &= (q, u_0 \ldots u_{\ell(d)-1} w, t) \underset{\mathcal{T}'}{\vdash} \\
&\quad (p_0^d, u_1 \ldots u_{\ell(d)-1} w, tv_0) \underset{\mathcal{T}'}{\vdash} \\
&\quad \vdots \\
&\quad (p_{\ell(d)-2}^d, u_{\ell(d)-1} w, tv_0 \cdots v_{\ell(d)-2}) \underset{\mathcal{T}'}{\vdash} \\
&\quad (q', w, tv_0 \cdots v_{\ell(d)-1}) = (q', w, tv).
\end{aligned}$$

Clearly, $\mathcal{T}'$ is 1-bounded. It is immediate that $\mathcal{T}(L) = \mathcal{T}'(L)$ for every language L over A. ■

106. °° Let $\mathcal{T} = (A, Q, B, \theta, q_0, F)$ be a λ-free transducer. Prove that there is an 1-output transducer $\mathcal{T}' = (A, Q', B, \theta', q_0, F)$ such that $\mathcal{T}(L) = \mathcal{T}'(L)$ for every language L over A.

Solution. Set initially $Q' = Q$ and $\theta' = \theta$. For every quadruple $d = (q, u, v, q') \in \theta$ we can write $v = b_0^d \cdots b_{|v|-1}^d$, where $b_j^d \in B$ for $0 \leq j \leq |v| - 1$ and $|v| \geq 1$.

If $|v| = 1$, do nothing. Otherwise, add the new states $p_0^d, \ldots, p_{|v|-2}^d$ to Q' and replace the quadruple d in θ' by the quadruples

$$(q, u, b_0^d, p_0^d), (p_0^d, \lambda, b_1^d, p_1^d), \ldots, (p_{|v|-2}^d, \lambda, b_{|v|-1}^d, q').$$

It is easy to see that $\mathcal{T}'(L) = \mathcal{T}(L)$ and that $\mathcal{T}'$ is an 1-output transducer. ■

107. °° Let $\mathcal{T} = (A, Q, B, \theta, q_0, F)$ and $\mathcal{T}' = (B, Q', C, \theta', q_0', F')$ be two transducers. Prove that there is a transducer $\overline{\mathcal{T}}$ such that $\mathcal{T}_1(L) = \mathcal{T}'(\mathcal{T}(L))$ for every $L \subseteq A^*$. Further, if both $\mathcal{T}$ and $\mathcal{T}'$ are λ-free, then there is an λ-free transducer $\overline{\mathcal{T}}$ with the above property.

Solution. We give the solution for the first statement of this exercise. By Exercise 106 we can assume that both $\mathcal{T}$ and $\mathcal{T}'$ are 1-output. Consider the sets of quadruples

$$\begin{aligned}
\theta_1 &= \theta \cup \{(q, \lambda, \lambda, q) \mid q \in Q\} \\
\theta_1' &= \theta' \cup \{(q, \lambda, \lambda, q) \mid q \in Q'\}.
\end{aligned}$$

Thus, we obtain the 1-bounded transducers

$$\mathcal{T}_1 = (A, Q, B, \theta_1, q_0, F) \text{ and } \mathcal{T}_1' = (B, Q', C, \theta_1', q_0', F'),$$

where $\mathcal{T}_1(L) = \mathcal{T}(L)$ for every $L \subseteq A^*$ and $\mathcal{T}_1'(K) = \mathcal{T}(K)$ for every $K \subseteq B^*$.

Define $\overline{\mathcal{T}} = (A, Q\times Q', C, \overline{\theta}, (q_0, q_0'), F\times F')$, where $\overline{\theta}$ consists of all quadruples $((q,q'), u, w, (p,p'))$, such that $(q,u,z,p) \in \theta_1$ and $(q', z, w, p') \in \theta_1'$. We claim that $\overline{\mathcal{T}}(L) = \mathcal{T}_1'(\mathcal{T}_1(L))$ for every $L \subseteq A^*$.
Suppose that $u \in L$ and that $w \in \overline{\mathcal{T}}(u)$. Then, we can write $u = u_0 \dots u_{n-1}$ and $w = w_0 \dots w_{n-1}$ such that the quadruples

$$((q_{i_0}, q'_{i_0}), u_0, w_0, (q_{i_1}, q'_{i_1})),$$
$$\vdots,$$
$$((q_{i_{n-1}}, q'_{i_{n-1}}), u_{n-1}, w_{n-1}, (q_{i_n}, q'_{i_n})),$$

exist in $\overline{\theta}$, where $i_0 = 0$, $q_{i_n} \in F$, and $q'_{i_n} \in F'$. The definition of $\overline{\theta}$ implies that the quadruples

$$(q_{i_0}, u_0, z_0, q_{i_1}), \dots, (q_{i_{n-1}}, u_{n-1}, z_{n-1}, q_{i_n}),$$

exist in θ_1, and the quadruples

$$(q'_{i_0}, z_0, w_0, q'_{i_1}), \dots, (q'_{i_{n-1}}, z_{n-1}, w_{n-1}, q'_{i_n}),$$

exist in θ_1'. This implies

$$z = z_0 \cdots z_{n-1} \in \mathcal{T}_1(u) \text{ and } w = w_0 \cdots w_{n-1} \in \mathcal{T}_1'(z),$$

so $w \in \mathcal{T}_1'(\mathcal{T}_1(u))$. Thus, $\overline{\mathcal{T}}(L) \subseteq \mathcal{T}_1'(\mathcal{T}_1(L))$ for every $L \subseteq A^*$. We leave to the reader the argument for the inverse inclusion. ∎

108. Let $\mathcal{T} = (A, Q, B, \delta, \gamma, q_0)$ be a Mealy automaton. Define $\mathsf{last}_{\mathcal{T}} : A^+ \longrightarrow B$ by

$$\begin{aligned} \mathsf{last}_{\mathcal{T}}(a) &= \gamma(q_0, a) \\ \mathsf{last}_{\mathcal{T}}(xa) &= \gamma(\delta^*(q_0, x), a). \end{aligned}$$

Prove that $\mathsf{last}_{\mathcal{T}}(x)$ equals the last output symbol emitted when the word x is applied to the input of $\mathcal{T}$.

Let A, B be two alphabets. A *sequential function* is a mapping $\phi : A^* \longrightarrow B^*$ that satisfies the following conditions:

1. $|f(x)| = |x|$ for every $x \in A^*$;
2. for every $x, y \in A^*$ we have $f(xy) = f(x)z$ for some $z \in B^*$.

109. $^\diamond$ Let $f : A^* \longrightarrow B^*$ be a sequential function. The *state of* f in t (where $t \in A^*$) is the mapping $f_t : A^* \longrightarrow B^*$ defined by $f_t(x) = r$, where $f(tx) = f(t)r$. Prove that every state of a sequential function is also a sequential function.
110. $^\diamond$ Let $\mathcal{T} = (A, Q, B, \delta, \gamma, q_0)$ be a Mealy automaton. Prove that the mapping $f : A^* \longrightarrow B^*$ given by $f_{\mathcal{T}}(x) = \gamma^*(q_0, x)$ is a sequential mapping. Furthermore, show that for the state of $f_{\mathcal{T}}$ in the word $t \in A*$ we have $f_{\mathcal{T},t}(x) = \gamma^*(\delta^*(q_0, t), x)$ for every $x \in A^*$.
111. $^\diamond$ Let $f : A^* \longrightarrow B^*$ be a sequential function. Prove that there is a Mealy automaton $\mathcal{T}$ such that $f = f_{\mathcal{T}}$ if and only if the set of states of f is is finite.

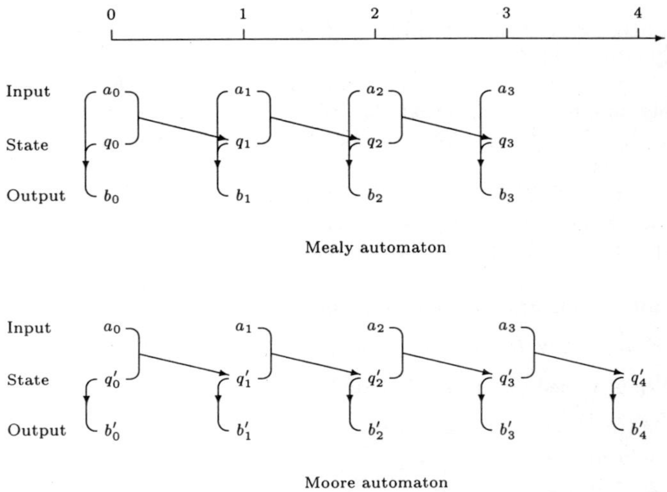

Figure 3.46: Timeline for Mealy vs. Moore automata

A *Moore automaton* is a 6-tuple $\mathcal{M} = (A, Q, B, \delta, \omega, q_0)$, where A, Q, B, δ, q_0 are as in the definition of Mealy automata and $\omega : Q \longrightarrow B$ is a mapping that associates an output symbol with each state of $\mathcal{M}$. This differs from a Mealy machine in that the output depends only on the state and is independent of the input.

The input-output mapping defined by $\mathcal{M}$, $\Omega_{\mathcal{M}} : A^* \longrightarrow B^*$ is given by

$$\begin{aligned} \Omega_{\mathcal{M}}(\lambda) &= \omega(q_0) \\ \Omega_{\mathcal{M}}(xa) &= \Omega_{\mathcal{M}}(x)\omega(\delta^*(q_0, xa)) \end{aligned}$$

Visually, this looks something like this.

The diagram 3.46 shows that at time i, the output of the Mealy machine depends on input a_i and on the state q_i, while the output of a Moore machine depends merely on the state q_i. For both machines, the state at time $i+1$ depends on the input a_i and the state q_i. Consider the last input, a_{n-1}. In the case of the Mealy machine, its effect is seen at time $n-1$, but for the Moore machine, its effect is not seen until time n, where its effect was to affect the chosen state. Thus, the Moore machine's outputs trail the Mealy machine's by one time unit.

112. $\diamond$ Show that for every regular language $L \subseteq A^*$ there is a Moore automaton $\mathcal{M} = (A, Q, \{0,1\}, \delta, \omega, q_0)$ such that $L = \Omega^{-1}(\{0,1\}^*1)$.
Solution. If L is a regular language, then $L = L(\mathcal{M}_1)$, where $\mathcal{M}_1 = (A, Q, \delta, q_0, F)$ is a dfa. Starting from $\mathcal{M}$, define the Moore automaton as $\mathcal{M} = (A, Q, \{0,1\}, \delta, \omega, q_0)$, where $\omega(q) = 1$ if and only if $q \in F$.

Then, $\delta^*(q_0, x) \in F$ if and only if $\omega(\delta^*(q_0, x)) = 1$, which is equivalent to $\Omega_{\mathcal{M}}(x) \in \{0,1\}^*1$. ■

113. ° Let $\mathcal{M} = (A, Q, B, \delta, \omega, q_0)$ be a Moore automaton. Prove that there is a Mealy automaton $\mathcal{T}$ such that $\Omega_{\mathcal{M}}(x) = \omega(q_0)\mathcal{T}(x)$ for every $x \in A^*$.
Hint. Let $\mathcal{T} = (A, Q, B, \delta, \gamma, q_0)$ be the Mealy automaton defined by $\gamma(q, a) = \omega(\delta(q, a))$.

114. ° Let $\mathcal{T} = (A, Q, B, \delta, \gamma, q_0)$ be a Mealy automaton. Prove that there exists a Moore automaton $\mathcal{M}$ such that $\Omega_{\mathcal{M}}(x) = \omega(q_0)\mathcal{T}(x)$, where ω is the output function and $\Omega_{\mathcal{M}}$ is the input-output function of the Moore automaton.
Solution. Define the Moore automaton

$$\mathcal{M} = (A, Q \times B, B, \delta', \omega, (q_0, b_0)),$$

where b_0 is a fixed output symbol, and

$$\begin{aligned} &\delta'((q, b), a) = (\delta(q, a), \gamma(q, a)) \\ &\omega(q, b) = b \end{aligned}$$

for every $q \in Q, a \in A, b \in B$.
We leave to the reader to verify that

$$\delta'^*((q_0, b_0), x) = (\delta^*(q_0, x), \mathsf{last}_{\mathcal{T}}(x))$$

for every $x \in A^+$, where $\mathsf{last}_{\mathcal{T}}$ is the function introduced in Exercise 108. As a consequence, we can show that

$$\gamma(\delta^*(q_0, x), a) = \omega(\delta'^*((q_0, b_0), xa)) \tag{3.21}$$

Indeed, we have

$$\begin{aligned} \omega(\delta'^*((q_0, b_0), xa)) &= \omega(\delta'(\delta'^*((q_0, b_0), x), a)) \\ &= \omega(\delta'((\delta^*(q_0, x), \mathsf{last}_{\mathcal{T}}(x)), a)) \\ &= \omega(\delta^*(q_0, xa), \gamma(\delta^*(q_0, x), a)) \\ &= \gamma(\delta^*(q_0, x), a), \end{aligned}$$

which gives the equality (3.21).
We prove by induction on x that $\Omega_{\mathcal{M}}(x) = \omega(q_0, b_0)\gamma^*(q_0, x)$. For $x = \lambda$ the equality follows immediately since $\gamma^*(q_0, \lambda) = \lambda$.
Suppose that the equality holds for x. We have

$$\begin{aligned} \Omega_{\mathcal{M}}(xa) &= \Omega_{\mathcal{M}}(x)\omega(\delta'^*((q_0, b_0), xa)) \\ &= \omega(q_0, b_0)\gamma^*(q_0, x)\omega(\delta'^*((q_0, b_0), xa)) \\ &= \omega(q_0, b_0)\gamma^*(q_0, x)\gamma(\delta^*(q_0, x), a) \\ &= \omega(q_0, b_0)\gamma^*(q_0, xa), \end{aligned}$$

because of equality (3.21). ■

115. ° A Mealy automaton can be regarded as a language acceptor. This is the most commonly done by choosing the output alphabet of a Mealy automaton $\mathcal{T} = (A, Q, B, \delta, \gamma, q_0)$ as $B = \{0, 1\}$, and accepting precisely those words $x \in A^*$ such that $\mathsf{last}_{\mathcal{T}}(x) = 1$. Prove that the class of languages accepted by Mealy automata with the binary output alphabet B coincides with the class of regular languages.

Applications of Regular Expressions

116. (a) Write an `aux` program to remove all lines consisting of only uppercase letters from its input.
  (b) Write a `lex` program to do the same thing.
117. (a) Write an `aux` program to convert dates from the form *mm/dd/yyyy* to the form *dd-MMM-yyyy*; e.g., thus `04/03/1898` should become `03-APR-1898`.
  (b) Write a `lex` program to do the same thing.
118. ◇ Designing a regular expression to describe C comments is not so simple as it might seem. C now admits two different types of comments. Traditional ones begin with the two-character sequence `/*` and end with the two-character sequence `*/`, perhaps spanning several lines. Those that come from C++ begin with the two-character sequence `//` and end with the end of the input line.
  (a) Write a `lex` program to remove C++ comments from a program.
  (b) Write a `lex` program to remove one-line traditional C comments from a program. Be careful: `/*/` is not a comment, but it can begin a comment. On the other hand, `/***/` is a comment.
  (c) Write a `lex` program to remove all traditional C comments from a program.
  (d) For each of the above, write a `lex` program the leaves only the corresponding comments, removing all the code.

3.14 Bibliographical Comments

The beginning papers on finite automata were [Huffman, 1954; Mealy, 1955] and [Moore, 1956]. A systematic study of their properties as well as the study of regular languages was initiated in [Kleene, 1956] and in [Rabin and Scott, 1959]. The last paper, together with [Sheperdson, 1959] initiated the study of two-way automata.

Nerode's Theorem appeared in [Nerode, 1958]. The related Myhill congruence was studied in [Myhill, 1957b]. The Pumping Lemma was obtained in [Bar-Hillel *et al.*, 1961]. Various closure properties of regular languages were obtained in [Ginsburg and Rose, 1963; Ginsburg and Spanier, 1963] and [Ginsburg and Rose, 1966].

The notion of sequential function was introduced in [Raney, 1958]. The study of transducers began with [Ginsburg, 1962]. Our presentation of transducers follows [Ginsburg, 1975].

Thompson's Algorithm was proposed in [Thompson, 1968]. The source of the Exercises 17– 20 is the paper [Stearns and Hartmanis, 1963]. Exercise 68 is a result obtained in [Salomaa, 1964]. The result shown in Supplement 21 originates in [Even, 1964].

Supplements 28 and 29 originate in [Hopcroft, 1969]. See also [Hunt and Rosencrantz, 1978]. The result from Supplement 92 is from [Schützenberger, 1965] and has received a significant amount of attention in the literature. The proof given in the solution belongs to D. Perrin (see [1990]). The result contained in Supplement 31 was obtained in [Glaister and Shallit, 1996]. The notion of simple regular expression was introduced in [Tarjan, 1981a]; the same author introduced path expressions in graphs and their associated types (in [Tarjan, 1981b]). Exercise 57 is given in [Floyd and Beigel, 1994]. Exercises 70- 73 follow the treatment of unitary languages given in [Holcombe, 1982].

The treatment of alternating automata (Exercise 78 and Supplement 80) follows the original paper [Chandra *et al.*, 1981].

An useful reference to the application of regular expressions to various utility programs are [Gardner *et al.*, 1988; Johnson and Lesk, 1978].

Chapter 4

Rewriting Systems and Grammars

4.1 Introduction

As we have seen, language classes can be defined using abstract models of computation, such as dfas, transition systems, etc. In this chapter we are concerned with an alternative approach that uses certain transformers of words called rewriting systems. These systems can analyze or generate words and, therefore, can be used to recognize or generate languages.

4.2 Semi-Thue and Thue Systems

Semi-Thue systems consist essentially of transformation rules for words called productions, introduced in the next definitions.

Definition 4.2.1 Let A be an alphabet such that the symbol "$\rightarrow$" is not a member of A. A *production over* A is a pair of words $(\alpha, \beta) \in A^* \times A^*$.

A production (α, β) is denoted by $\alpha \rightarrow \beta$. We refer to α and β as the *left* and the *right member* of the production, respectively. □

Words on the alphabets of semi-Thue systems are denoted using lower case letters at the beginning of the Greek alphabet. We denote individual productions by the letter π with or without various adornments. If $\pi = \alpha \rightarrow \beta$, then we denote the production $\beta \to \alpha$ by π^{-1}; in this case, we refer to π^{-1} as *the inverse production* of π.

Example 4.2.2 Let $A = \{a, b\}$. The pairs $ab \to ba$ and $ba \to \lambda$ are productions over A. □

Example 4.2.3 Let $A = \{X, Y, Z, a, b\}$. The following are productions over A:

$$\pi_0 : aaX \to abXYa, \pi_1 : XaY \to \lambda, \pi_2 : Z \to bba.$$

□

Productions over A are used for transforming words from A^* as follows.

Definition 4.2.4 If π is the production $\gamma \to \gamma'$, and $\alpha, \beta \in A^*$ such that $\alpha = \alpha_1\gamma\alpha_2$ and $\beta = \alpha_1\gamma'\alpha_2$, we say that α *generates* β *by applying the production* $\gamma \to \gamma'$. This is denoted by $\alpha \underset{\pi}{\Rightarrow} \beta$. □

Example 4.2.5 Let π_i, $0 \le i \le 2$ be the productions introduced in Example 4.2.3. We have:

$$\begin{aligned} XYaaXZ &\underset{\pi_0}{\Rightarrow} XYabXYaZ \\ ZZXaYX &\underset{\pi_1}{\Rightarrow} ZZX \\ ZY &\underset{\pi_2}{\Rightarrow} bbaY \end{aligned}$$

□

Given a word γ, a production of the form $\lambda \to \beta$ applied to γ has the effect of inserting β at one point in γ.

Example 4.2.6 If $\gamma = a_0a_1a_2$, the application of the production $\lambda \to b_0b_1$ yields any of the words $b_0b_1a_0a_1a_2$, $a_0b_0b_1a_1a_2$, $a_0a_1b_0b_1a_2$, or $a_0a_1a_2b_0b_1$. □

Definition 4.2.7 A *semi-Thue system* is a triple $T = (A, M, P)$, where A is an alphabet, P is a finite set of productions over A, and M is a finite subset of A^* called the *set of axioms of* T.

The *inverse of a semi-Thue system* $T = (A, M, P)$ is the semi-Thue system $T^{-1} = (A, M, P^{-1})$, where $P^{-1} = \{\pi^{-1} \mid \pi \in P\}$.

If $P = P^{-1}$, then the triple $T = (A, M, P)$ is called a *Thue system.* □

Example 4.2.8 Let $A = \{a, b, c\}$ be an alphabet. The triple

$$T = (A, \{abac\}, \{ab \to aa, ba \to aa, ac \to aa, ca \to aa\})$$

is a the semi-Thue system; the triple

$$\begin{aligned} T' = (A, \{abac\}, \{&ab \to aa, ba \to aa, ac \to aa, ca \to aa, \\ &aa \to ab, aa \to ba, aa \to ac, aa \to ca\}) \end{aligned}$$

is a Thue system. □

Definition 4.2.9 Let $T = (A, M, P)$ be a semi-Thue system. We write $\alpha \underset{T}{\Rightarrow} \beta$ if $\alpha, \beta \in A^*$ and $\alpha \underset{\pi}{\Rightarrow} \beta$ for some production $\pi \in P$.

A word $\alpha \in A^*$ *produces* a word $\beta \in A^*$ in the semi-Thue system $T = (A, M, P)$ if there is a finite sequence $d = (\gamma_0, \gamma_1, \dots, \gamma_n)$ of words over A such that $\gamma_0 = \alpha$, $\gamma_n = \beta$, and $\gamma_k \underset{T}{\Rightarrow} \gamma_{k+1}$ for $0 \le k \le n - 1$.

The sequence $d = (\gamma_0, \gamma_1, \ldots, \gamma_n)$ is referred to as a *derivation of* β *from* α *in* T, where n is the *length of the derivation.*

The set of derivations of a semi-Thue system T will be denoted by $\mathsf{DER}(T)$.

An alternative notation for a derivation $d = (\gamma_0, \gamma_1, \ldots, \gamma_n)$ is

$$\gamma_0 \underset{T}{\Rightarrow} \gamma_1 \underset{T}{\Rightarrow} \cdots \underset{T}{\Rightarrow} \gamma_n.$$

When the semi-Thue system is understood from the context, we may omit the subscript T.

If $(\pi_0, \ldots, \pi_{n-1})$ is the sequence of productions used in the derivation d:

$$\gamma_0 \underset{T}{\Rightarrow} \gamma_1 \underset{T}{\Rightarrow} \cdots \underset{T}{\Rightarrow} \gamma_n,$$

then we refer to the word $\pi_0 \cdots \pi_{n-1}$ over the alphabet P as the *control word of the derivation d.* □

The existence of a derivation

$$\gamma_0 \underset{T}{\Rightarrow} \gamma_1 \underset{T}{\Rightarrow} \cdots \underset{T}{\Rightarrow} \gamma_n$$

that makes use of the productions $\pi_0, \pi_1, \ldots, \pi_{n-1}$ will be denoted by:

$$\gamma_0 \underset{\pi_0}{\Rightarrow} \gamma_1 \underset{\pi_1}{\Rightarrow} \cdots \underset{\pi_{n-1}}{\Rightarrow} \gamma_n,$$

where $\pi_0\pi_1 \cdots \pi_{n-1}$ is a control word of this derivation.

Example 4.2.10 Let $T = (A, \{aXX\}, P)$ be the semi-Thue system defined by $A = \{X, Y, a, b, c\}$, and $P = \{\pi_0 : aX \to abY, \pi_1 : bY \to Ya, \pi_2 : YaY \to c\}$.

The sequence $(aXX, abYX, aYaX, aYabY, aYaYa, aca)$ is a derivation of length 5 in the semi-Thue system T. A control word of this derivation is $\pi_0\pi_1\pi_0\pi_1\pi_2$. □

Given a derivation in a semi-Thue system, it is possible to have several control words that correspond to this derivation, as we show in the next example.

Example 4.2.11 Let

$$\begin{aligned} T &= (\{S, X, a\}, \{S\}, \{\pi_0 : S \to XX, \pi_1 : XX \to XX, \\ &\quad \pi_2 : X \to X, \pi_3 : XX \to a\}) \end{aligned}$$

be a semi-Thue system. The derivation

$$S \underset{T}{\Rightarrow} XX \underset{T}{\Rightarrow} XX \underset{T}{\Rightarrow} a$$

has both $\pi_0\pi_1\pi_3$ and $\pi_0\pi_2\pi_3$ as control words. □

We write $\overset{n}{\underset{T}{\Rightarrow}}$ for the nth power of $\underset{T}{\Rightarrow}$, $\overset{+}{\underset{T}{\Rightarrow}}$ for the transitive closure of $\underset{T}{\Rightarrow}$, and $\overset{*}{\underset{T}{\Rightarrow}}$ for the reflexive and transitive closure of $\underset{T}{\Rightarrow}$. Hence, $\alpha \overset{+}{\underset{T}{\Rightarrow}} \beta$ if and only if there is an $n \geq 1$ such that $\alpha \overset{n}{\underset{T}{\Rightarrow}} \beta$, and $\alpha \overset{*}{\underset{T}{\Rightarrow}} \beta$

if and only if there is an $n \geq 0$ such that $\alpha \overset{n}{\underset{T}{\Rightarrow}} \beta$. Clearly, we have $\gamma \overset{*}{\underset{T}{\Rightarrow}} \gamma'$ if and only if there is a derivation of length n of γ' from γ for some $n \in \mathbb{N}$.

If there is no risk of confusion, we may drop the subscript T in these notations. By the definition of the nth power of a relation, there is a derivation of length n of β from α in the semi-Thue system T if and only if $\alpha \overset{n}{\underset{T}{\Rightarrow}} \beta$.

If $\gamma \overset{n}{\underset{T}{\Rightarrow}} \gamma'$ and $\pi_0 \cdots \pi_{n-1}$ is a control word of this derivation, then we may write $\gamma \overset{n}{\underset{\pi_0 \cdots \pi_{n-1}}{\Rightarrow}} \gamma'$.

Semi-Thue systems are used in two main ways: as *analytic devices*, for recognizing the words of a language, and as *generative devices*, for producing the set of words of a language.

Definition 4.2.12 Let $T = (A, M, P)$ be a semi-Thue system, and let B be an alphabet that is a subset of A.

A word $x \in B^*$ is *recognized by* T if $x \overset{*}{\underset{T}{\Rightarrow}} \alpha$ for some $\alpha \in M$. *The language recognized by the semi-Thue system* T *relative to the alphabet* B is the set:

$$L_r(T|B) = \{x \in B^* \mid x \overset{*}{\underset{T}{\Rightarrow}} \alpha \text{ for some } \alpha \in M\}.$$

The word x is *generated by* T if $\alpha \overset{*}{\underset{T}{\Rightarrow}} x$ for some $\alpha \in M$. *The language generated by* T *relative to the alphabet* B is the set:

$$L_g(T|B) = \{x \in B^* \mid \alpha \overset{*}{\underset{T}{\Rightarrow}} x \text{ for some } \alpha \in M\}.$$

□

Theorem 4.2.13 *Let* $T = (A, M, P)$ *be a semi-Thue system. We have*

$$L_g(T|B) = L_r(T^{-1}|B)$$

for every alphabet B *such that* $B \subseteq A$.

Proof. It is easy to prove that $\alpha \overset{*}{\underset{T}{\Rightarrow}} x$ if and only if $x \overset{*}{\underset{T^{-1}}{\Rightarrow}} \alpha$ for every $\alpha \in A^*$ and $x \in B^*$. Therefore, the following statements are equivalent:

1. $x \in L_g(T|B)$ for $x \in B^*$;
2. $\alpha \overset{*}{\underset{T}{\Rightarrow}} x$ for some $\alpha \in M$;
3. $x \overset{*}{\underset{T^{-1}}{\Rightarrow}} \alpha$ for some $\alpha \in M$;
4. $x \in L_r(T^{-1}|B)$,

and this gives the desired equality. ∎

For any dfa, there is a natural, corresponding semi-Thue system, as shown by the next theorem.

Theorem 4.2.14 *Let* $\mathcal{M} = (A, Q, \delta, q_0, F)$ *be a dfa. Consider the semi-Thue system* $T_{\mathcal{M}} = (A \cup Q, \{q_0\}, P)$, *where* P *consists of the following productions:*

$$\begin{array}{ll} q \to aq' & \textit{for each } q, q', a \textit{ with } q' = \delta(q, a) \\ q \to \lambda & \textit{for each } q \in F. \end{array}$$

We have $L_g(T_{\mathcal{M}}|A) = L(\mathcal{M})$.

Proof. We need to show that $q_0 \overset{*}{\underset{T_{\mathcal{M}}}{\Rightarrow}} x$ if and only if $x \in L(\mathcal{M})$ for every $x \in A^*$. Actually, we prove a stronger statement, namely, that $\delta^*(q, x) = q'$, if and only if $q \overset{*}{\underset{T_{\mathcal{M}}}{\Rightarrow}} xq'$ for every $x \in A^*$ and $q, q' \in Q$. The argument is by induction on $|x|$.

Suppose that $|x| = 0$, that is $x = \lambda$. If $\delta^*(q, \lambda) = q'$, then $q = q'$, and we have $q \overset{*}{\underset{T_{\mathcal{M}}}{\Rightarrow}} q'$ because the relation $\overset{*}{\underset{T_{\mathcal{M}}}{\Rightarrow}}$ is reflexive.

Conversely, if $q \overset{*}{\underset{T_{\mathcal{M}}}{\Rightarrow}} q'$ we have $q = q'$ because no rule of $T_{\mathcal{M}}$ can be applied in this derivation. Since $\delta^*(q, \lambda) = q'$, we have the result for $|x| = 0$.

Suppose that our claim holds for words of length n, and let $y \in A^*$ be a word of length $n+1$. There exists a word $x \in A^*$ and a symbol $a \in A$ such that $y = xa$.

If $\delta^*(q, y) = q'$, let $\bar{q} = \delta^*(q, x)$. Clearly, we have $\delta(\bar{q}, a) = q'$. By the inductive hypothesis, $q \overset{*}{\underset{T_{\mathcal{M}}}{\Rightarrow}} x\bar{q}$; by the definition of $T_{\mathcal{M}}$ we have $\bar{q} \underset{T_{\mathcal{M}}}{\Rightarrow} aq'$, so

$$q \overset{*}{\underset{T_{\mathcal{M}}}{\Rightarrow}} x\bar{q} \overset{1}{\underset{T_{\mathcal{M}}}{\Rightarrow}} xaq' = yq'.$$

Conversely, suppose that $q \overset{*}{\underset{T_{\mathcal{M}}}{\Rightarrow}} xq'$ implies $\delta^*(q, x) = q'$ for every word x of length n and every $q, q' \in Q$, and let $y \in A^*$ be a word of length $n + 1$ such that $q \overset{*}{\underset{T_{\mathcal{M}}}{\Rightarrow}} yq' = xaq'$, where a is the last symbol of y. The definition of the productions of $T_{\mathcal{M}}$ imply that the derivation $q \overset{*}{\underset{T_{\mathcal{M}}}{\Rightarrow}} yq'$ can be written as

$$q \overset{*}{\underset{T_{\mathcal{M}}}{\Rightarrow}} x\bar{q} \underset{T_{\mathcal{M}}}{\Rightarrow} xaq'$$

for some $\bar{q} \in Q$. This means that $q \overset{*}{\underset{T_{\mathcal{M}}}{\Rightarrow}} x\bar{q}$ and that $\bar{q} \underset{T_{\mathcal{M}}}{\Rightarrow} aq'$, so $\delta^*(q, x) = \bar{q}$ (by the inductive hypothesis) and $\delta(\bar{q}, a) = q'$ by the definition of $T_{\mathcal{M}}$. We conclude that $\delta^*(q, y) = \delta^*(q, xa) = q'$.

Now, the following statements are immediately seen to be equivalent:

- $x \in L(\mathcal{M})$;
- $\delta^*(q_0, x) = q'$ from some $q' \in F$;
- $q_0 \overset{*}{\underset{T_{\mathcal{M}}}{\Rightarrow}} xq'$ from some $q' \in F$;
- $q_0 \overset{*}{\underset{T_{\mathcal{M}}}{\Rightarrow}} x$ (because we have the production $q' \to \lambda$ in $T_{\mathcal{M}}$ if and only if $q' \in F$;
- $q_0 x \in L_g(T_{\mathcal{M}})$.

∎

Theorems 4.2.13 and 4.2.14 are stated in terms of generative semi-Thue systems. However, it is easy to convert these results to equivalent theorems about an analytic semi-Thue system that recognizes a regular language. Using the same notations as in Theorem 4.2.14, we have $L = L_r(T^{-1}|A)$, where $T^{-1} =$

$(A \cup Q, \{q_0\}, P^{-1})$ has productions of the form $aq' \to q$ when $q' = \delta(q, a)$, and $\lambda \to q$ for $q \in F$.

We shall see that several other abstract devices can also be described by analytic semi-Thue systems.

Definition 4.2.15 Let $T = (A, M, P)$ be a semi-Thue system. A production $\alpha \to \beta \in P$ is *length-increasing* if $|\alpha| \leq |\beta|$.

T is a *length-increasing semi-Thue system* if every production in P is length-increasing. □

A more accurate term for length-increasing productions would be nondecreasing-length productions. Nevertheless, we shall continue to use the term "length-increasing," due to its preponderence in the formal languages literature.

Example 4.2.16 The semi-Thue system $T = (\{a, b, c\}, \{abc, cab\}, P)$ having the set of productions $P = \{ab \to bc, cc \to bbb\}$ is length-increasing. □

Length-increasing semi-Thue systems enjoy an important decidability property.

Theorem 4.2.17 *Let $T = (A, M, P)$ be a length-increasing semi-Thue system. It is decidable whether a word $\alpha \in A^*$ belongs to $L_g(T|A)$.*

Proof. A word $x \in A^*$ belongs to $L_g(T|A)$ if and only if there exists a derivation $\alpha_0 \Rightarrow \cdots \Rightarrow \alpha_{n-1} = x$ in T such that the words $\alpha_0, \ldots, \alpha_{n-1}$ are distinct, $\alpha \in M$, and we have $|\alpha_0| \leq \cdots \leq |\alpha_{n-1}| = |\alpha|$. We can decide whether a sequence $(\alpha_0, \ldots, \alpha_{n-1})$ is a derivation in T, by checking if $\alpha_i \underset{T}{\Rightarrow} \alpha_{i+1}$ for $0 \leq i \leq n-2$. Note that the number of such derivations is finite because there are $1 + |A| + \cdots + |A|^\ell$ words of length at most ℓ, where $\ell = |x|$, so it suffices to check a finite set in order to decide whether $x \in L_g(T|A)$. ∎

A related, more specific result is presented later, in Theorem 7.8.11.

4.3 Grammars and Chomsky Hierarchy

Grammars are devices that generate or analyze words. They represent multiple and mutually recursive definitions of certain finite collections of languages.

Definition 4.3.1 A *grammar* is a semi-Thue system $G = (A, M, P)$ such that the alphabet A is partitioned in two sets A_N and A_T, referred as the *nonterminal* and the *terminal* alphabet, respectively, and $M = \{S\}$ consists of a unique symbol, $S \in A_N$.

We refer to the symbols in A_N and A_T as *nonterminal symbols* and *terminal symbols*, respectively.

The set of derivations of a grammar G will be denoted by $\mathsf{DER}(G)$.

If $G = (A, M, P)$ is a grammar, where $A = A_N \cup A_T$, $A_N \cap A_T = \emptyset$, and $M = \{S\}$, then we abuse the notation and denote G by the quadruple (A_N, A_T, S, P). The symbol S is *the start symbol of* G. □

Definition 4.3.2 Let $G = (A_N, A_T, S, P)$ be a grammar. A production $\pi = \alpha \to \beta \in P$ is *generative* if α contains at least one nonterminal symbol; π is *analytic* if β contains at least one such symbol. □

It is clear that π is a generative production if and only if π^{-1} is an analytic production.

Example 4.3.3 The productions introduced in Example 4.2.3 can be regarded as productions of the grammar

$$G = (\{X, Y, Z\}, \{a, b\}, X, \{aaX \to abXYa, XaY \to \lambda, Z \to bba\}).$$

They are classified as follows:

π_0	:	$aaX \to abXYa$	analytic and generative
π_1	:	$XaY \to \lambda$	generative
π_2	:	$Z \to bba$	generative

□

Definition 4.3.4 A grammar G is *generative* if all its productions are generative. G is *analytic* if all its productions are analytic.

If G is a generative grammar, then the language generated by G relative to its terminal alphabet

$$L_g(G|A_T) = \{x \in A_T^* \mid S \overset{*}{\underset{G}{\Rightarrow}} x\}$$

will be referred to *the language generated by G*.

If G is an analytic grammar, then the language recognized by G relative to its terminal alphabet

$$L_r(G|A_T) = \{x \in A_T^* \mid x \overset{*}{\underset{G}{\Rightarrow}} S\}$$

will be referred to as the language recognized by G. □

If there is no risk of confusion, we may denote both the language generated by a generative grammar G, or the language recognized by an analytic grammar G, by $L(G)$.

From now on, we focus predominantly on generative grammars. They are classified according to the form of their productions. The term *grammar* will be used for generative grammars in order to simplify the exposition.

Definition 4.3.5 A derivation $\alpha_0 \underset{G}{\Rightarrow} \alpha_1 \underset{G}{\Rightarrow} \cdots \underset{G}{\Rightarrow} \alpha_n$ in a generative grammar $G = (A_N, A_T, S, P)$ is *complete* if $\alpha_n \in A_T^*$.

If $S \overset{*}{\underset{G}{\Rightarrow}} \alpha$, we refer to α as a *sentential form* of G. □

Clearly, every word in $L(G)$ is a sentential form of G that contains no nonterminal symbols.

Definition 4.3.6 Let A_N, A_T be two disjoint alphabets. A production $\alpha \to \beta$ is

(i) a *context-free production* on A_N, A_T if α consists of one nonterminal symbol X and $\beta \in (A_N \cup A_T)^*$;

(ii) a *context-sensitive production* if $\alpha = \alpha' X \alpha''$ and $\beta = \alpha' \gamma \alpha''$, where $X \in A_N$, $\alpha', \alpha'', \gamma \in (A_N \cup A_T)^*$ and $\gamma \neq \lambda$.

□

Example 4.3.7 Let $A_N = \{X, Y, Z\}$ and let $A_T = \{a, b\}$. The following pairs are context-free productions over A_N, A_T:

$$\pi_0 \;:\; X \to abXYa$$

$$\pi_1 \;:\; Y \to \lambda$$

$$\pi_2 \;:\; Z \to bba$$

The production $\pi_3 : aYXb \to abXZXb$ is context-sensitive; note that π_3 involves replacing Y by bXZ when Y is surrounded by a at left and by Xb at the right, that is, Y occurs in the context of a and Xb. □

Context-free productions of the form $X \to \lambda$ are called *null productions* or *erasure productions*. The effect of $X \to \lambda$ is to erase the symbol X.

A grammar without erasure productions is said to be λ*-free*.

The classes of generative grammars that correspond to the restrictions on productions described in Definition 4.3.6 are introduced next. This classification is known as the *Chomsky hierarchy*.

Definition 4.3.8 Let $G = (A_N, A_T, S, P)$ be a grammar.

- Every grammar is a grammar of type 0.
- G is of *type* 1 (or, is *context-sensitive*) if all its productions are context-sensitive with the possible exception of a production $S \to \lambda$; if P contains $S \to \lambda$, then S does not occur in the right member of any production of G.
- G is of *type* 2 (or, is *context-free*) if all its productions are context-free.
- G is of *type* 3 (or, is *regular*) if every production has the form $X \to uY$ or $X \to u$, where $X, Y \in A_N$ and $u \in A_T^*$.

In addition, we shall say that G is a *length-increasing grammar* if all its productions are length-increasing with the possible exception of a production $S \to \lambda$; if P contains $S \to \lambda$, then S does not occur in the right member of any production of G. □

It is clear that every grammar of type 3 is also of type 2, every grammar of type 1 is also of type 0 and every context-sensitive grammar is also length-increasing.

For type 3 grammars, productions may include those of the form $X \to Y$, or $X \to \lambda$.

If $G = (A_N, A_T, S, P)$ is a grammar, then we use capital roman letters with or without subscripts, to denote single nonterminals, lower case roman letters late in the alphabet (u, v, w, x, y, z) to denote words in A_T^*, and lower case Greek letters to denote words in $(A_N \cup A_T)^*$. With this convention, the language generated by G is the set of words $L(G)$ given by:

$$L(G) = \{x \in A_T^* \mid S \overset{*}{\underset{G}{\Rightarrow}} x\}.$$

Definition 4.3.9 Let $\mathcal{G}$ be a class of grammars. A language L is a $\mathcal{G}$*-language* if there is a grammar G in $\mathcal{G}$ such that $L(G) = L$. □

For example, L is a context-free language if there exists a context-free grammar G such that $L = L(G)$. Similarly, K is a length-increasing language if there is a grammar G_1 such that $K = L(G_1)$, etc. We denote by $\mathcal{L}_i$ the class of languages generated by grammars of type i for $0 \leq i \leq 3$. Clearly, we have $\mathcal{L}_3 \subseteq \mathcal{L}_2 \subseteq \mathcal{L}_0$ and $\mathcal{L}_1 \subseteq \mathcal{L}_0$. Actually, as we shall see later, in Corollary 4.5.7, we also have the inclusion $\mathcal{L}_2 \subseteq \mathcal{L}_1$, so

$$\mathcal{L}_3 \subseteq \mathcal{L}_2 \subseteq \mathcal{L}_1 \subseteq \mathcal{L}_0.$$

As with the grammars, so also the corresponding classes $\mathcal{L}_i$ of languages are referred to as the Chomsky hierarchy. All these inclusions will be shown to be strict. Also, it is clear that every language in $\mathcal{L}_1$ is length-increasing. Actually, we shall prove that $\mathcal{L}_1$ coincides with the class of length-increasing languages.

Example 4.3.10 The language generated by the context-free grammar

$$G = (\{S\}, \{a, b\}, S, \{S \to \lambda, S \to aSb\})$$

is $\{a^n b^n \mid n \in \mathbb{N}\}$.

We prove by induction on $n \geq 0$ that $a^n b^n \in L(G)$ for every $n \in \mathbb{N}$.

The case $n = 0$ follows from the existence of the production $\pi_0 : S \to \lambda$ in G.

Suppose now that $a^n b^n \in L(G)$, so $S \overset{*}{\underset{G}{\Rightarrow}} a^n b^n$. Using the production $S \to aSb$ we obtain the derivation

$$S \underset{G}{\Rightarrow} aSb \overset{*}{\underset{G}{\Rightarrow}} aa^n b^n b = a^{n+1} b^{n+1},$$

which shows that $a^{n+1} b^{n+1} \in L(G)$.

Conversely, we prove by induction on the length $m \geq 1$ of the derivation $S \overset{*}{\underset{G}{\Rightarrow}} x$ that x has the form $x = a^n b^n$ for some $n \in \mathbb{N}$.

If $m = 1$, $S \overset{*}{\underset{G}{\Rightarrow}} x$ implies $x = \lambda$ since $S \to \lambda$ is the single production that erases S. Therefore, $x = a^n b^n$ for $n = 0$.

Suppose that the statement holds for derivations of length m and let $S \overset{*}{\underset{G}{\Rightarrow}} x$ be a derivation of length $m + 1$. If we write the first step of this derivation explicitly we have

$$S \underset{G}{\Rightarrow} aSb \overset{*}{\underset{G}{\Rightarrow}} x,$$

so $x = ayb$, where $S \overset{*}{\underset{G}{\Rightarrow}} y$ is a derivation of length m. By the inductive hypothesis, $y = a^n b^n$ for some $n \in \mathbb{N}$, so $x = a^{n+1} b^{n+1}$, which concludes our argument. Thus, $\{a^n b^n \mid n \in \mathbb{N}\}$ is a context-free language. □

Example 4.3.11 Consider the length-increasing grammar

$$G = (\{S, X, Y\}, \{a, b, c\}, S, P),$$

where P consists of the following productions:

$$\begin{array}{lll} \pi_0 : S \to abc, & \pi_1 : S \to aXbc, \\ \pi_2 : Xb \to bX, & \pi_3 : Xc \to Ybcc, \\ \pi_4 : bY \to Yb, & \pi_5 : aY \to aaX, \\ \pi_6 : aY \to aa & \end{array}$$

We claim that $L(G) = \{a^n b^n c^n \mid n \in \mathbb{P}\}$.

Note that any word $\alpha \in \{S, X, Y, a, b, c\}^*$ that occurs in a derivation, $S \overset{*}{\Rightarrow} \alpha$ contains at most one nonterminal symbol. Further, a derivation must end either by applying the production $S \to abc$ or the production $aY \to aa$ because only these productions allow us to eliminate a nonterminal symbol. If the last production applied is $S \to abc$, then the derivation is $S \Rightarrow abc$, and the derived word has the form prescribed. Otherwise, the symbol Y must be generated starting from S, and the first production applied is $S \to aXbc$.

Note that for every $i \geq 1$ we have $a^i X b^i c^i \overset{*}{\Rightarrow} a^{i+1} X b^{i+1} c^{i+1}$. Indeed, we can write:

$$\begin{array}{lclcl} a^i X b^i c^i & \underset{\pi_2}{\overset{i}{\Rightarrow}} & a^i b^i X c^i & \underset{\pi_3}{\overset{1}{\Rightarrow}} & a^i b^i Y b c^{i+1} \\ & \underset{\pi_4}{\overset{i}{\Rightarrow}} & a^i Y b^{i+1} c^{i+1} & \underset{\pi_5}{\overset{1}{\Rightarrow}} & a^{i+1} X b^{i+1} c^{i+1} \end{array}$$

We claim that a word α contains the infix aY (which allows us to apply the production π_5) and $S \overset{*}{\Rightarrow} \alpha$ if and only if α has the form $\alpha = a^i Y b^{i+1} c^{i+1}$ for some $i \geq 1$.

An easy argument by induction on $i \geq 1$ allows us to show that if $\alpha = a^i Y b^{i+1} c^{i+1}$ then $S \overset{*}{\Rightarrow} \alpha$. We need to prove only the inverse implication. This can be done by strong induction on the length $n \geq 3$ of the derivation $S \overset{*}{\Rightarrow} \alpha$.

The shortest derivation that allows us to generate the word containing the infix aY is

$$S \Rightarrow aXbc \Rightarrow abXc \Rightarrow abYbcc \Rightarrow aYb^2c^2,$$

and this word has the prescribed form. Suppose now that for derivations shorter than n the condition is satisfied, and let $S \underset{G}{\overset{*}{\Rightarrow}} \alpha$ be a derivation of length n such that α contains the infix aY. By the inductive hypothesis the previous word in this derivation that contains the infix aY has the form $\alpha' = a^j Y b^{j+1} c^{j+1}$. To proceed from α' we must apply the production π_5 and replace Y by X. Thus, we have

$$S \underset{G}{\overset{*}{\Rightarrow}} a^j Y b^{j+1} c^{j+1} \underset{G}{\Rightarrow} a^{j+1} X b^{j+1} c^{j+1}.$$

Next, the symbol X must "travel" to the right using the production π_2, transform itself into an Y (when in touch with the cs) and Y must "travel" to the left to create the infix aY. This can happen only through the application of the productions π_3 and π_4, as follows:

$$\begin{array}{lcl} a^{j+1} X b^{j+1} c^{j+1} & \underset{\pi_2}{\overset{j+1}{\Rightarrow}} & a^{j+1} b^{j+1} X c^{j+1} \\ & \underset{\pi_3}{\overset{1}{\Rightarrow}} & a^{j+1} b^{j+1} Y b c^{j+2} \\ & \underset{\pi_4}{\overset{i}{\Rightarrow}} & a^{j+1} Y b^{j+2} c^{j+2}, \end{array}$$

which proves that α has the desired form. Therefore, all the words in the language $L(G)$ have the form $a^n b^n c^n$.

Although this grammar is not context-sensitive (only productions π_0, π_1, π_5 and π_6 are context-sensitive), we will exhibit a context-sensitive grammar for this language (cf. Example 4.3.17). Moreover, we will show (in Section 5.5) that this language is not context-free, so it will serve to show that $\mathcal{L}_2 \subset \mathcal{L}_1$. □

4.3.1 Equivalent Grammars

There are certainly an infinite number of grammars for any language $L \in \mathcal{L}_0$ (cf. Exercise 9). We will define two grammars to be equivalent if they generate the same language. There are many benefits to examining equivalent grammars that generate a language. For example, we may be given a context-sensitive grammar for a language for which there exists a context-free grammar or even a regular grammar. The simpler grammar leads to easier recognition of words in the language and provides more information about the structure of the language. Perhaps more important, however, is the fact that by selecting specific characteristics of the form of the productions of a grammar, we may prove interesting facts about the language it generates.

Definition 4.3.12 Two grammars G, G' are *equivalent* if $L(G) = L(G')$. □

Theorem 4.3.13 *Let $G = (A_N, A_T, S, P)$ be a length-increasing grammar or a grammar of type i, where $i \in \{0, 1, 2\}$. There exists an equivalent grammar $G' = (A'_N, A_T, S, P')$ of the same type as G such that every production of P' that contains a terminal symbol is of the form $X \to a$.*

Proof. Consider the alphabet $A' = \{X_a \mid a \in A_T\}$ that contains a symbol X_a for every terminal symbol a, where $A_N \cap A' = \emptyset$, and define A'_N as $A'_N = A_N \cup A'$. The productions of P' are obtained by replacing each terminal symbol a by the corresponding nonterminal X_a and by adding the productions $X_a \to a$ for $a \in A_T$. The set of productions P' satisfies the requirements of the theorem, and the resulting grammar is clearly of the same type as G.

Let $u = a_{i_0} \cdots a_{i_{n-1}} \in L(G)$. The definition of the grammar G' implies that $S \xRightarrow[G']{*} X_{a_{i_0}} \cdots X_{a_{i_{n-1}}}$. By using the productions $X_a \to a$ we obtain

$$S \xRightarrow[G']{*} a_{i_0} \cdots a_{i_{n-1}},$$

so $a_{i_0} \cdots a_{i_{n-1}} \in L(G')$. Thus, $L(G) \subseteq L(G')$.

To prove the converse inclusion, $L(G') \subseteq L(G)$, consider a morphism $h : (A'_N \cup A_T)^* \longrightarrow (A_N \cup A_T)^*$ defined by $h(X_a) = a$ for $a \in A_T$ and $h(Y) = Y$ for every $Y \in A_N \cup A_T$. We claim that if $\alpha \xRightarrow[G']{} \beta$ for some $\alpha, \beta \in (A'_N \cup A_T)^*$, then $h(\alpha) \xRightarrow[G]{*} h(\beta)$. Indeed, if a production of the form $X \to a$ was used in $\alpha \xRightarrow[G']{} \beta$, then $h(\alpha) = h(\beta)$. If another kind of production was used, then $h(\alpha) \xRightarrow[G]{} h(\beta)$, so in any case, $h(\alpha) \xRightarrow[G']{*} h(\beta)$. Let now $v \in L(G')$. We have $S \xRightarrow[G']{*} v$, so $S = h(S) \xRightarrow[G]{*} h(v) = v$, which implies $v \in L(G)$. Therefore, $L(G) = L(G')$. ∎

Example 4.3.14 Let $G = (\{S, X, Y\}, \{a, b, c\}, S, P)$ be the length-increasing grammar considered in Example 4.3.11. The grammar G' defined below is length-increasing, equivalent to G, and every production of this grammar that contains a terminal symbol is of the form $X \to a$.

Specifically, the set of productions P' of the grammar

$$G' = (\{S, X, Y, X_a, X_b, X_c\}, \{a, b, c\}, S, P')$$

consists of the following productions:

$$\begin{array}{llll} \pi'_0 & : & S \to X_a X_b X_c, & \pi'_1 & : & S \to X_a X X_b X_c, \\ \pi'_2 & : & X X_b \to X_b X, & \pi'_3 & : & X X_c \to Y X_b X_c X_c, \\ \pi'_4 & : & X_b Y \to Y X_b, & \pi'_5 & : & X_a Y \to X_a X_a X, \\ \pi'_6 & : & X_a Y \to X_a X_a & \pi'_7 & : & X_a \to a \\ \pi'_8 & : & X_b \to b & \pi'_9 & : & X_c \to c \end{array}$$

□

A more general result is given next.

Corollary 4.3.15 *Let $G = (A_N, A_T, S, P)$ be a grammar of type i. There exists an equivalent grammar $G' = (A'_N, A_T, S, P')$ of the same type i such that no production of P' contains a terminal symbol in its left member.*

Proof. For type-2 or type-3 grammars the statement is immediate. For $i \in \{0, 1\}$, this is a direct consequence of Theorem 4.3.13. ∎

Theorem 4.3.16 *The class $\mathcal{L}_1$ equals the class of length-increasing languages.*

Proof. Clearly, every type-1 grammar is length-increasing. Therefore, as we observed earlier, $\mathcal{L}_1$ is included in the class of length-increasing languages.

To prove the converse inclusion, consider a length-increasing grammar $G = (A_N, A_T, S, P)$. By Theorem 4.3.13, we can assume that every production of P that contains a terminal symbol is of the form $X \to a$.

Let $\pi : \alpha \to \beta \in P$ be a production such that $\alpha = X_0 \cdots X_{n-1}$, $\beta = Y_0 \cdots Y_{m-1}$. If $n = 1$, then π is already a context-sensitive production. Therefore, suppose that $2 \leq n \leq m$. By hypothesis, $X_0, \ldots, X_{n-1}, Y_0, \ldots, Y_{m-1}$ are nonterminals. Consider n new nonterminals $Z_0^\pi, \ldots, Z_{n-1}^\pi$ and the set of productions P_π that consists of:

$$\begin{array}{l} X_0 \cdots X_{n-1} \to Z_0^\pi X_1 \cdots X_{n-1} \\ Z_0^\pi X_1 \cdots X_{n-1} \to Z_0^\pi Z_1^\pi X_2 \cdots X_{n-1} \\ \vdots \\ Z_0^\pi Z_1^\pi \cdots Z_{n-2}^\pi X_{n-1} \to Z_0^\pi Z_1^\pi \cdots Z_{n-1}^\pi Y_n \cdots Y_{m-1} \\ Z_0^\pi Z_1^\pi \cdots Z_{n-1}^\pi Y_n \cdots Y_{m-1} \to Y_0 Z_1^\pi \cdots Z_{n-1}^\pi Y_n \cdots Y_{m-1} \\ Y_0 Z_1^\pi \cdots Z_{n-1}^\pi Y_n \cdots Y_{m-1} \to Y_0 Y_1 \cdots Z_{n-1}^\pi Y_n \cdots Y_{m-1} \\ \vdots \\ Y_0 Y_1 \cdots Z_{n-1}^\pi Y_n \cdots Y_{m-1} \to Y_0 Y_1 \cdots Y_{n-1} Y_n \cdots Y_{m-1}. \end{array}$$

The set P_π obviously consists of context-sensitive productions.

Let P_1 be the set of productions that consists of $\bigcup\{P_{\alpha\to\beta} \mid 2 \leq |\alpha| \leq |\beta|\}$ and the productions of the form $X \to \beta$ or $S \to \lambda$ (whenever such productions belong to P). Consider the context-sensitive grammar $G_1 = (A_N \cup A, A_T, S, P_1)$, where A consists of all new nonterminal symbols introduced when the production sets P_π were constructed. Note that a derivation step in G that consists of the application of a production $\pi : \alpha \to \beta$ with $2 \leq |\alpha| \leq |\beta|$ corresponds to the successive application of the productions of P_π in G_1; conversely, the productions of P_π can be applied only in this order in a derivation in G_1, and they simulate a step in a derivation in G that makes use of the production π. A step that uses a production $X \to \beta$ or $S \to \lambda$ is the same in both G and G_1. Thus, $S \overset{*}{\underset{G}{\Rightarrow}} x$ if and only if $S \overset{*}{\underset{G_1}{\Rightarrow}} x$, so $L(G) = L(G_1)$. This shows that the class of length-increasing languages is included in $\mathcal{L}_1$. ∎

Example 4.3.17 Let

$$G' = (\{S, X, Y, X_a, X_b, X_c\}, \{a, b, c\}, S, P')$$

be the length-increasing grammar constructed in Example 4.3.14. The set of productions P_1 consists of the following:

- The context-sensitive productions in P', namely:

$$\begin{array}{lllllll} \pi'_0 & : & S \to X_a X_b X_c, & \pi'_1 & : & S \to X_a X X_b X_c, \\ \pi'_7 & : & X_a \to a, & \pi'_8 & : & X_b \to b \\ \pi'_9 & : & X_c \to c \end{array}$$

- Each remaining production in P' generates the following productions:
  - For $\pi'_2 : XX_b \to X_b X$, include the productions:

$$\begin{array}{lll} \pi'_{10} & : & XX_b \to Z_0 X_b \\ \pi'_{11} & : & Z_0 X_b \to Z_0 Z_1 \\ \pi'_{12} & : & Z_0 Z_1 \to X_b Z_1 \\ \pi'_{13} & : & X_b Z_1 \to X_b X \end{array}$$

  - For $\pi'_3 : XX_c \to YX_bX_cX_c$, include the productions:

$$\begin{array}{lll} \pi'_{14} & : & XX_c \to Z_2 X_c \\ \pi'_{15} & : & Z_2 X_c \to Z_2 Z_3 X_c X_c \\ \pi'_{16} & : & Z_2 Z_3 X_c X_c \to Y Z_3 X_c X_c \\ \pi'_{17} & : & Y Z_3 X_c X_c \to Y X_b X_c X_c \end{array}$$

  - For $\pi'_4 : X_b Y \to Y X_b$, include the productions:

$$\begin{array}{lll} \pi'_{18} & : & X_b Y \to Z_4 Y \\ \pi'_{19} & : & Z_4 Y \to Z_4 Z_5 \\ \pi'_{20} & : & Z_4 Z_5 \to Y Z_5 \\ \pi'_{21} & : & Y Z_5 \to Y X_b \end{array}$$

  - For $\pi'_5 : X_a Y \to X_a X_a X$, include the productions:

$$\begin{array}{lll} \pi'_{22} & : & X_a Y \to Z_6 Y \\ \pi'_{23} & : & Z_6 Y \to Z_6 Z_7 X \\ \pi'_{24} & : & Z_6 Z_7 X \to X_a Z_7 X \\ \pi'_{25} & : & X_a Z_7 X \to X_a X_a X \end{array}$$

– Finally, for $\pi'_6 : X_aY \to X_aX_a$, include the productions:

$$\begin{aligned}
\pi'_{26} &: X_aY \to Z_8Y \\
\pi'_{27} &: Z_8Y \to Z_8Z_9 \\
\pi'_{28} &: Z_8Z_9 \to X_aZ_9 \\
\pi'_{29} &: X_aZ_9 \to X_aX_a
\end{aligned}$$

This gives the context-sensitive grammar:

$$\begin{aligned}
G_1 = &(\{S, X, Y, X_a, X_b, X_c\} \cup \{Z_i \mid 0 \le i \le 10\}, \{a, b, c\}, S, \\
&\{\pi'_0, \pi'_1, \pi'_7, \pi'_8, \pi'_9\} \cup \{\pi'_j \mid 10 \le j \le 29\}.
\end{aligned}$$

that generates the language $L = \{a^nb^nc^n \mid n \in \mathbb{N}\}$. This implies that L is a context-sensitive language. □

In the next section we shall examine closure properties of Chomsky classes with respect to several fundamental operations. As a prelude to this kind of results, we give the following theorem.

Theorem 4.3.18 *The classes $\mathcal{L}_0, \mathcal{L}_1, \mathcal{L}_2$ are closed with respect to the reversal operation; in other words, if $L \in \mathcal{L}_i$, then $L^R \in \mathcal{L}_i$ for $i \in \{0, 1, 2\}$.*

Proof. Let $G = (A_N, A_T, S, P)$ be a grammar, and let $P^R = \{\alpha^R \to \beta^R \mid \alpha \to \beta \in P\}$. Consider the grammar $G^R = (A_N, A_T, S, P^R)$. It is easy to see that if G is of type i, then so is G^R for $i \in \{0, 1, 2\}$. Further, we have $\gamma \overset{*}{\underset{G}{\Rightarrow}} \gamma'$ if and only if $\gamma^R \overset{*}{\underset{G^R}{\Rightarrow}} \gamma'^R$, as the reader can prove easily (by induction on the length of the two derivations). Thus, $S \overset{*}{\underset{G}{\Rightarrow}} w$ if and only if $S = S^R \overset{*}{\underset{G^R}{\Rightarrow}} w^R$. This shows that $L(G^R) = L(G)^R$, so $L(G)^R$ has the same type as the language $L(G)$. ∎

The notion of a control word of a derivation introduced for semi-Thue systems is applicable to grammars.

Definition 4.3.19 Let $G = (A_N, A_T, S, P)$ be a grammar. The *Szilard language* of G is the language that consists of all control words for complete derivations in G. We denote the Szilard language of G by $\mathsf{Sz}(G)$. □

Example 4.3.20 Let $G = (\{S, X, Y\}, \{a, b, c\}, S, P)$ be the length-increasing grammar considered in Example 4.3.11. The Szilard language of this grammar consists of all words having the form π_0 or

$$\pi_1(\pi_2\pi_3\pi_4\pi_5)(\pi_2^2\pi_3\pi_4^2\pi_5)\cdots(\pi_2^{n-2}\pi_3\pi_4^{n-2}\pi_5)(\pi_2^{n-1}\pi_3\pi_4^{n-1}\pi_6),$$

for $n \ge 2$. □

Leftmost derivations are particularly important for context-free grammars, but we first consider them in a more general setting.

Definition 4.3.21 Let $G = (A_N, A_T, S, P)$ be a grammar. A *leftmost derivation* is a derivation $\gamma_0 \Rightarrow \cdots \Rightarrow \gamma_n$ in G such that, if the production applied in deriving γ_{k+1} from γ_k is $\alpha_k \to \beta_k$, then $\gamma_k = \gamma'_k\alpha_k\gamma''_k$, $\gamma_{k+1} = \gamma'_k\beta_k\gamma''_k$ and $|\gamma'_k| < |\gamma'_{k+1}\alpha_{k+1}|$. □

In each step of a leftmost derivation, the rewriting takes place at the right of, or overlaps with, that part of the word that was rewritten in the previous step.

A leftmost derivation of length n, $\gamma_0 \underset{G}{\Rightarrow} \gamma_1 \underset{G}{\Rightarrow} \cdots \underset{G}{\Rightarrow} \gamma_n$ will be denoted by

$$\gamma_0 \underset{G,\text{left}}{\Rightarrow} \gamma_1 \underset{G,\text{left}}{\Rightarrow} \cdots \underset{G,\text{left}}{\Rightarrow} \gamma_n.$$

We will also use the relations $\overset{n}{\underset{G,\text{left}}{\Rightarrow}}$ and $\overset{*}{\underset{G,\text{left}}{\Rightarrow}}$, representing the nth power and the transitive and reflexive closure of the relation $\underset{G,\text{left}}{\Rightarrow}$, respectively.

Example 4.3.22 Let $G = (\{X,Y\},\{a,b,c\},X,\{\pi_0 : X \rightarrow aXX, \pi_1 : aX \rightarrow aabY, \pi_2 : bY \rightarrow Ya, \pi_3 : aYa \rightarrow c, \pi_4 : acX \rightarrow b\})$ be a grammar.

The derivation

$$X \underset{G}{\Rightarrow} aXX \underset{G}{\Rightarrow} aabYX \underset{G}{\Rightarrow} aaYaX \underset{G}{\Rightarrow} acX \underset{G}{\Rightarrow} b$$

is a leftmost derivation in G. □

Theorem 4.3.23 *For every derivation $\gamma \overset{n}{\underset{G}{\Rightarrow}} \theta$ in a grammar G there exists a leftmost derivation $\gamma \overset{n}{\underset{G,\text{left}}{\Rightarrow}} \theta$ of the same length.*

Proof. Let $\gamma = \gamma_0 \underset{G}{\Rightarrow} \gamma_1 \underset{G}{\Rightarrow} \cdots \underset{G}{\Rightarrow} \gamma_n = \theta$ be a derivation that is not leftmost. Let k be the first step that does not satisfy the definition of leftmost derivations. We have $\gamma_k = \gamma_k'\alpha_k\gamma_k''$, $\gamma_{k+1} = \gamma_k'\beta_k\gamma_k'' = \gamma_{k+1}'\alpha_{k+1}\gamma_{k+1}''$, and $|\gamma_k'| \geq |\gamma_{k+1}\alpha_{k+1}|$. Also, $\gamma_{k+2} = \gamma_{k+1}'\beta_{k+1}\gamma_{k+1}''$. The productions applied are $\alpha_k \rightarrow \beta_k$ and $\alpha_{k+1} \rightarrow \beta_{k+1}$. Note that at step k the rewriting takes place "inside" the word γ_k', so $\gamma_k' = \gamma_{k+1}'\alpha_{k+1}\gamma$, for some word $\gamma \in (A_N \cup A_T)^*$. Thus, we can write $\gamma_k = \gamma_{k+1}'\alpha_{k+1}\gamma\alpha_k\gamma_k''$.

By reversing the order of the application of the productions we can replace the sequence $\gamma_k \Rightarrow \gamma_{k+1} \Rightarrow \gamma_{k+2}$ by

$$\begin{aligned}\gamma_k &= \gamma_{k+1}'\alpha_{k+1}\gamma\alpha_k\gamma_k'' \Rightarrow \gamma_{k+1}'\beta_{k+1}\gamma\alpha_k\gamma_k'' = \bar{\gamma}_{k+1} \\ &\Rightarrow \gamma_{k+1}'\beta_{k+1}\gamma\beta_k\gamma_k'' = \gamma_{k+2}.\end{aligned}$$

In the new derivation,

$$\gamma_0 \Rightarrow \cdots \Rightarrow \gamma_k \Rightarrow \bar{\gamma}_{k+1} \Rightarrow \gamma_{k+2} \Rightarrow \cdots \Rightarrow \gamma_n,$$

the first $k+1$ steps constitute a leftmost derivation. By repeating this transformation of the derivations, we obtain a leftmost derivation that has the same number of steps as the original one. ∎

Theorem 4.3.23 shows that whenever it is convenient, we may assume that a derivation is a leftmost derivation.

4.4 Regular Operations

A family of languages $\mathcal{L}$ is closed with respect to an operation if every application of that operation to languages in $\mathcal{L}$ results in a language in $\mathcal{L}$. In this section we focus on three operations: union, product, and Kleene closure, known collectively as *regular operations,* and we prove that every class $\mathcal{L}_i$ of Chomsky's hierarchy contains all finite languages and is closed with respect to each regular operation. Further closure properties are discussed in later chapters.

Theorem 4.4.1 *Each of the classes $\mathcal{L}_i$ of Chomsky's hierarchy contains the class of finite languages, for $i \in \{0, 1, 2\}$.*

Proof. Let $L = \{u_0, \ldots, u_{n-1}\}$ be a finite, nonempty language over an alphabet A. The grammar $G = (\{S\}, A, S, \{S \to u_0, \ldots, S \to u_{n-1}\})$ is of type 3 and, therefore, of type 2, 1, and 0. If $L = \emptyset$, then L is generated by the grammar $G = (\{S\}, A, S, \{S \to S\})$ that is, again, of type 3. ∎

Theorem 4.4.2 *If L is a language of type i, where $i \in \{0, 1\}$, then so is the language K, where $K = L - \{\lambda\}$.*

Proof. If L is a type-1 language, then there exists a type-1 grammar $G = (A_N, A_T, S, P)$ such that $L(G) = L$. If $\lambda \in L$, the production $S \to \lambda$ belongs to P, and S does not occur in the right member of any production. The language K is generated by the type-1 grammar $G' = (A_N, A_T, S, P - \{S \to \lambda\})$. If $\lambda \notin L$, we have $K = L$.

Assume now that L is of type 0 and that $\lambda \in L$. Let P' be the set of productions obtained from P by replacing all erasure productions $\alpha \to \lambda$ with $Y\alpha \to Y$ and $\alpha Y \to Y$ for every $Y \in A_N \cup A_T$. The grammar (A_N, A_T, S, P') generates the language K, so K is a type-0 language. ∎

Theorem 4.4.3 *$\mathcal{L}_i$ is closed with respect to union, for $i \in \{0, 1, 2, 3\}$.*

Proof. Suppose that L, L' are two languages of type i that are generated by the grammars $G = (A_N, A_T, S, P)$ and $G' = (A'_N, A_T, S', P')$, respectively, where $A_N \cap A'_N = \emptyset$.

Consider the grammar $G_\cup = (A_N \cup A'_N \cup \{S_0\}, A_T, S, P \cup P' \cup \{S_0 \to S, S_0 \to S'\})$, where S_0 is a new nonterminal symbol such that $S_0 \notin A_N \cup A'_N$. Note that the grammar $G_\cup$ is of the same type i as the grammars G and G'. To complete the proof, we need to show that $L \cup L' = L(G_\cup)$.

Let $x \in L \cup L'$. If $x \in L$, then $S \overset{*}{\underset{G}{\Rightarrow}} x$, so $S_0 \underset{G_\cup}{\Rightarrow} S \overset{*}{\underset{G_\cup}{\Rightarrow}} x$ which shows that $x \in L(G)$. The case when $x \in L'$ is entirely similar and is left to the reader. Thus, $L \cup L' \subseteq L(G_\cup)$.

Conversely, suppose that $x \in L(G_\cup)$. We have $S_0 \overset{*}{\underset{G_\cup}{\Rightarrow}} x$. If the first production applied in this derivation is $S_0 \to S$, then the derivation can be written as $S_0 \underset{G_\cup}{\Rightarrow} S \overset{*}{\underset{G_\cup}{\Rightarrow}} x$. The last part of this derivation $S \overset{*}{\underset{G_\cup}{\Rightarrow}} x$ uses only productions from P since $A_N \cap A'_N = \emptyset$ implies $P \cap P' = \emptyset$. Therefore, we have $S \overset{*}{\underset{G}{\Rightarrow}} x$, so $x \in L(G)$. Similarly, if the first production applied is $S_0 \to S'$, then $x \in L(G')$. Therefore, $L(G_\cup) \subseteq L(G) \cup L(G')$, hence $L(G_\cup) = L(G) \cup L(G')$. ∎

We now embark on showing that each class in the Chomsky hierarchy is closed with respect to the $*$ operation.

Lemma 4.4.4 *The classes $\mathcal{L}_0$ and $\mathcal{L}_1$ are closed with respect to the $*$ operation.*

Proof. We must prove that if $L \in \mathcal{L}_i$, then $L^* \in \mathcal{L}_i$ for $i \in \{0, 1\}$. Let us assume initially that $\lambda \notin L$.

Let $G = (A_N, A_T, S, P)$ be a grammar of type 0 or type 1 that generates the language L. By Corollary 4.3.15, we can assume that terminal symbols do not occur in the left member of any production of P.

Let S_0, S_1 be new symbols such that $S_0, S_1 \notin A_N$, and let $G_* = (A_N \cup \{S_0, S_1\}, A_T, S_0, P_*)$ be the grammar whose set of productions is

$$\begin{aligned} P_* &= P \cup \{S_0 \to \lambda, S_0 \to S, S_0 \to S_1 S\} \cup \\ &\quad \{S_1 a \to S_1 S a \mid a \in A_T\} \cup \{S_1 a \to S a \mid a \in A_T\}. \end{aligned}$$

It is easy to see that if G is of type 1, then so is G_*.

We begin by showing that $L^n \subseteq L(G_*)$ for $n \in \mathbb{N}$. Let $x \in L^n$. If $n = 0$ we have $x = \lambda$, and $x \in L(G_*)$ because $S_0 \to \lambda$ is in P_*. Suppose now that $x = x_0 x_1 \ldots x_{n-1}$, where $x_0, \ldots, x_{n-1} \in L$ for $n \geq 1$. We have $S \overset{*}{\underset{G}{\Rightarrow}} x_j$ for $0 \leq j \leq n-1$, and the same derivations are valid in G_* because $P \subset P_*$. Thus, we can put together the following derivation in the grammar G_*:

$$\begin{aligned} S_0 &\underset{G_*}{\Rightarrow} S_1 S \overset{*}{\underset{G_*}{\Rightarrow}} S_1 x_{n-1} \\ &\underset{G_*}{\Rightarrow} S_1 S x_{n-1} \overset{*}{\underset{G_*}{\Rightarrow}} S_1 x_{n-2} x_{n-1} \\ &\vdots \\ &\underset{G_*}{\Rightarrow} S_1 S x_2 \cdots x_{n-1} \overset{*}{\underset{G_*}{\Rightarrow}} S_1 x_1 \cdots x_{n-1} \\ &\underset{G_*}{\Rightarrow} S x_1 \cdots x_{n-1} \overset{*}{\underset{G_*}{\Rightarrow}} x_0 x_1 \cdots x_{n-1} = x \end{aligned}$$

which proves that $x \in L(G_*)$. Thus, $L^* = \bigcup_{n \in \mathbb{N}} L^n \subseteq L(G_*)$. Observe that the "regeneration" of the symbol S is made possible in the above derivation by the fact that the words x_j are not null (which puts S_1 adjacent with terminal symbols, thereby allowing the application of the productions $S_1 a \to S_1 S a$).

Conversely, let $x \in L(G_*)$. There exists a derivation $S_0 \overset{*}{\underset{G_*}{\Rightarrow}} x$. If we write this derivation explicitly,

$$S_0 \underset{G_*}{\Rightarrow} \alpha_1 \underset{G_*}{\Rightarrow} \cdots \underset{G_*}{\Rightarrow} \alpha_{n-1} = x,$$

we have to consider three cases:

`Case 1`: If the first production applied in this derivation is $S_0 \to \lambda$, then $x = \lambda$, so $x \in L^*$.

`Case 2`: If the first production applied is $S_0 \to S$, then we have $S \overset{*}{\underset{G_*}{\Rightarrow}} x$, and the same derivation is valid in G, which shows that $x \in L(G) = L$.

`Case 3`: If the first production applied is $S_0 \to S_1 S$, then each word α_ℓ in the above derivation falls into one of the following two cases:

`Case 3a`: α_ℓ is of the form $S_1 \beta_1 \cdots \beta_k$, where $k \geq 1$, $S \overset{*}{\underset{G}{\Rightarrow}} \beta_q$ for $1 \leq q \leq k$, and the first symbol of each of the words $\beta_2, \ldots, \beta_k$ is a terminal.

`Case 3b`: α_ℓ is of the form $\beta_0 \beta_1 \cdots \beta_k$, where $k \geq 1$, the first symbol of each β_p is a terminal for $p \geq 1$, and $S \overset{*}{\underset{G}{\Rightarrow}} \beta_p$ for $0 \leq p \leq k$.

We can make this argument by induction on $\ell \geq 1$. It is clear that α_1 falls in Case 3a.

Suppose that α_h satisfies the conditions of either Case 3a or Case 3b. Since the productions of P do not have terminal symbols in their left members, their application may involve only one word β_i. This guarantees that if α_{h+1} was obtained through the application of a production in P, then α_{h+1} satisfies one of the conditions of the previous cases. The same conclusion can be reached if α_{h+1} was obtained by applying a production of the form $S_1 a \longrightarrow S_1 S a$ or $S_1 a \longrightarrow S a$.

The existence of the derivation $S_0 \overset{*}{\underset{G_*}{\Rightarrow}} x \in A_T^*$ implies that x is a word of the form 3b. Therefore x can be written as a product, $x = \beta_0 \cdots \beta_k$, where $k \geq 1$, and $S \overset{*}{\underset{G}{\Rightarrow}} \beta_p$ for $0 \leq p \leq k$. Since every word $\beta_0, \beta_1, \ldots, \beta_k \in A_T^*$ it follows that $\beta_0, \beta_1, \ldots, \beta_k \in L(G)$. Thus, $x \in (L(G))^{k+1} \subseteq L(G)^*$ which implies $L(G_*) \subseteq L(G)^*$.

If $\lambda \in L$, then consider the language $K = L - \{\lambda\}$. By Theorem 4.4.2, the language K is of the same type as L and, by the above argument, so is K^*. Since $K^* = L^*$ we obtain the desired closure property. ∎

Lemma 4.4.5 *The class $\mathcal{L}_2$ is closed with respect to the $*$ operation.*

Proof. Let L be a context-free language generated by the type-2 grammar $G = (A_N, A_T, S, P)$. Suppose that S_0 is a new nonterminal symbol and consider the type-2 grammar $G_* = (A_N \cup \{S_0\}, A_T, S_0, P \cup \{S_0 \to \lambda, S_0 \to S_0 S\})$. It is easy to verify that $L(G_*) = L^*$, so $L^* \in \mathcal{L}_2$. ∎

Lemma 4.4.6 *The class $\mathcal{L}_3$ is closed with respect to the $*$ operation.*

Proof. Let $L \in \mathcal{L}_3$ such that $L = L(G)$, where $G = (A_N, A_T, S, P)$ is a type-3 grammar. Define the set of productions $P_1 = \{X \to uS \mid X \to u \in P\}$.

Consider the type-3 grammar

$$G_* = (A_N \cup \{S_0\}, A_T, S_0, P \cup P_1 \cup \{S_0 \to \lambda, S_0 \to S\}),$$

where S_0 be a new nonterminal symbol, $S_0 \notin A_N$. It is easy to verify that $L(G_*) = L^*$, so $L^* \in \mathcal{L}_3$. ∎

Theorem 4.4.7 *The classes $\mathcal{L}_i$ are closed with respect to the $*$ operation for $i \in \{0, 1, 2, 3\}$.*

Proof. This statement follows immediately from Lemmas 4.4.4, 4.4.5, and 4.4.6. ∎

Corollary 4.4.8 *The classes $\mathcal{L}_i$ are closed with respect to the $+$ operation for $i \in \{0, 1, 2, 3\}$.*

Proof. Let $\mathcal{L}_i$ be one of the classes of Chomsky's hierarchy, and let $L \in \mathcal{L}_i$. Note that

$$L^+ = \begin{cases} L^* & \text{if } \lambda \in L \\ L^* - \{\lambda\} & \text{if } \lambda \notin L. \end{cases}$$

In the first case, $L^+ \in \mathcal{L}_i$ by Theorem 4.4.7; in the second case, we reach the same conclusion using Theorem 4.4.2 and Theorem 4.4.7. ∎

Lemma 4.4.9 *The classes $\mathcal{L}_0$ and $\mathcal{L}_2$ are closed with respect to the product operation.*

Proof. Let L, L' be two languages of type i, and let $G = (A_N, A_T, S, P)$, $G' = (A'_N, A_T, S', P')$ be two grammars of type i such that $L(G) = L$ and $L(G') = L'$, where $i \in \{0, 2\}$. Without any loss of generality, we can assume that $A_N \cap A'_N = \emptyset$.

If S_0 is a new symbol, $S_0 \notin A_N \cup A'_N$, then the grammar $G_p = (A_N \cup A'_N \cup \{S_0\}, A_T, S_0, P \cup P' \cup \{S_0 \to SS'\})$ is also of type i. We claim that $L(G_p) = LL'$.

Let $x \in LL'$. We can write $x = uv$ for some $u \in L$ and $v \in L'$. By hypothesis, $S \overset{*}{\underset{G}{\Rightarrow}} u$ and $S' \overset{*}{\underset{G'}{\Rightarrow}} v$, so

$$S_0 \underset{G_p}{\Rightarrow} SS' \overset{*}{\underset{G_p}{\Rightarrow}} uS' \overset{*}{\underset{G_p}{\Rightarrow}} uv = x.$$

Thus, $x \in L(G_p)$.

Conversely, suppose that $x \in L_p$. There is a derivation

$$S_0 \underset{G_p}{\Rightarrow} SS' \overset{*}{\underset{G_p}{\Rightarrow}} x.$$

Since A_N and A'_N are disjoint sets, the sets of productions P and P' are disjoint. Therefore, the productions of G_p used to transform S into a word over A_T belong to P, while the ones used to rewrite S' belong to P'. Thus, we can write $x = uv$, where $S \overset{*}{\underset{G}{\Rightarrow}} u$ and $S' \overset{*}{\underset{G'}{\Rightarrow}} v$, which implies $x \in LL'$. ∎

Lemma 4.4.10 *The class $\mathcal{L}_1$ is closed with respect to the product operation.*

Proof. Let L, L' be two languages in $\mathcal{L}_1$. If neither L nor L' contains the null word, we may assume that both languages are generated by type-1 grammars that have no erasure rules. It is easy to see that, in this case, the construction of the grammar G_p given in the proof of Lemma 4.4.9 yields a type-1 grammar, so LL' belongs to $\mathcal{L}_1$.

Suppose now that $\lambda \in L$ or $\lambda \in L'$. By Theorem 4.4.2, the languages $L_1 = L - \{\lambda\}$ and $L'_1 = L' - \{\lambda\}$ also belong to $\mathcal{L}_1$ and, by the previous argument $L_1 L'_1 \in \mathcal{L}_1$. We need to consider the cases summarized in the next table.

Case	$\lambda \in L$	$\lambda \in L'$	L	L'	LL'
1	yes	no	$L_1 \cup \{\lambda\}$	L'_1	$L_1 L'_1 \cup L'_1$
2	no	yes	L_1	$L'_1 \cup \{\lambda\}$	$L_1 L'_1 \cup L_1$
3	yes	yes	$L_1 \cup \{\lambda\}$	$L'_1 \cup \{\lambda\}$	$L_1 L'_1 \cup L_1 \cup L'_1$

In each case, we have $LL' \in \mathcal{L}_1$ from Theorem 4.4.3. ∎

Lemma 4.4.11 *The class $\mathcal{L}_3$ is closed with respect to the product operation.*

Proof. Let L, L' be two languages in $\mathcal{L}_3$ and assume that L, L' are generated by the grammars $G = (A_N, A_T, S, P)$ and $G' = (A'_N, A'_T, S', P')$, respectively. Without loss of generality, we may assume that $A_N \cap A'_N = \emptyset$; this also implies $P \cap P' = \emptyset$. Consider the set of productions $P_1 = \{X \to uY \mid X \to uY \in P\} \cup \{X \to uS' \mid X \to u \in P\}$, which is obtained from P by replacing every production $X \to u$ by a production $X \to uS'$.

The type-3 grammar $G_1 = (A_N \cup A'_N, A_T \cup A'_T, S, P_1 \cup P')$ generates the language LL'. Indeed, if $x \in L(G)$ and $y \in L(G')$, then $S \overset{*}{\underset{G}{\Rightarrow}} x$ and $S' \overset{*}{\underset{G'}{\Rightarrow}} y$. Since P was replaced by P_1 in G_1, we have $S \overset{*}{\underset{G_1}{\Rightarrow}} xS'$. Note that we also have $S' \overset{*}{\underset{G_1}{\Rightarrow}} y$. Combining the last two derivations we can write $S \overset{*}{\underset{G_1}{\Rightarrow}} xy$, so $LL' \subseteq L(G_1)$.

Conversely, let $z \in L(G_1)$. We have $S \overset{*}{\underset{G_1}{\Rightarrow}} z$. This derivation begins with a symbol from A_N and must eventually use a production from P' since, otherwise, nonterminal symbols cannot be erased. Therefore, the last derivation can be written as

$$S \overset{*}{\underset{G_1}{\Rightarrow}} uS' \overset{*}{\underset{G_1}{\Rightarrow}} uv = z,$$

where $u \in A_T^*$ and $v \in {A'_T}^*$. This implies the existence of the derivations $S \overset{*}{\underset{G_1}{\Rightarrow}} uS'$ and $S' \overset{*}{\underset{G_1}{\Rightarrow}} v$. Note that the first derivation corresponds to $S \overset{*}{\underset{G}{\Rightarrow}} u$; the second corresponds to $S' \overset{*}{\underset{G'}{\Rightarrow}} v$. Thus, $u \in L(G)$, $v \in L(G')$, and this implies $z = uv \in LL'$. Therefore, $L(G_1) \subseteq LL'$. ∎

4.5 Properties of Type-2 Grammars

In this section we discuss several elementary properties of context-free languages. We focus on the constriction of "simpler" context-free grammars equivalent to a given context-free grammar. In particular, we examine the possibility of using fewer nonterminal symbols and fewer productions without altering the generative capability of such grammars.

The next theorem shows that certain derivations in context-free grammars can be decomposed into simpler ones.

Theorem 4.5.1 *Let $G = (A_N, A_T, S, P)$ be a context-free grammar. If*

$$X_0 \cdots X_{k-1} \overset{n}{\underset{G}{\Rightarrow}} \alpha,$$

where $X_0, \ldots, X_{k-1} \in A_N \cup A_T$ and $\alpha \in (A_N \cup A_T)^*$, then we can write $\alpha = \alpha_0 \cdots \alpha_{k-1}$, where $X_i \overset{n_i}{\underset{G}{\Rightarrow}} \alpha_i$ for $0 \leq i \leq k-1$ and $\sum_{0 \leq i \leq k-1} n_i = n$.

Proof. We use an argument by induction on n, $n \geq 0$. For $n = 0$, we have $\alpha_i = X_i$ for $0 \leq i \leq k-1$, and the statement is obviously true; in this case, $n_0 = \cdots = n_{k-1} = 0$.

Assume that the statement is true for derivations of length n, and let

$$X_0 \cdots X_{k-1} \overset{n+1}{\underset{G}{\Rightarrow}} \alpha.$$

If $X_0 \cdots X_{k-1} \overset{n}{\underset{G}{\Rightarrow}} \gamma \underset{G}{\Rightarrow} \alpha$, by the inductive hypothesis, we have $\gamma = \gamma_0 \cdots \gamma_{k-1}$, where $X_i \overset{n_i}{\underset{G}{\Rightarrow}} \gamma_i$ for $0 \leq i \leq k-1$ and $\sum\{n_i \mid 0 \leq i \leq k-1\} = n$.

Let $Y \rightarrow \beta$ be the production applied in the last step $\gamma \underset{G}{\Rightarrow} \alpha$. Y occurs in one of the words $\gamma_0, \ldots, \gamma_{k-1}$, say, γ_j. In this case, we can write $\gamma_j = \gamma_j' Y \gamma_j''$ and α can be written as $\alpha = \alpha_0 \cdots \alpha_{k-1}$, where $\alpha_i = \gamma_i$ for $0 \leq i \leq j-1$, and $j+1 \leq i \leq k-1$, $X_j \overset{n_j}{\underset{G}{\Rightarrow}} \gamma_j \underset{G}{\Rightarrow} \gamma_j' \beta \gamma_j'' = \alpha_j$, which proves the statement. ∎

Definition 4.5.2 A derivation $\gamma_0 \underset{G}{\Rightarrow} \gamma_1 \underset{G}{\Rightarrow} \cdots \underset{G}{\Rightarrow} \gamma_n$ in a context-free grammar $G = (A_N, A_T, S, P)$ is *complete* if $\gamma_n \in A_T^*$. □

Note that if $X_0 \cdots X_{k-1} \underset{G}{\Rightarrow} \cdots \underset{G}{\Rightarrow} \alpha$ is a complete derivation in G, then every derivation that results from "splitting" this derivation according to Theorem 4.5.1 is also complete.

Consider the following example, which makes use of Theorem 4.5.1.

Example 4.5.3 Let $G = (A_N, A_T, S_0, P)$ be a context-free grammar, where $A_N = \{S_0, S_1, S_2\}$, $A_T = \{a, b\}$, and P contains the following productions:

$$S_0 \rightarrow aS_2, S_0 \rightarrow bS_1, S_1 \rightarrow a, S_1 \rightarrow aS_0,$$
$$S_1 \rightarrow bS_1S_1, S_2 \rightarrow b, S_2 \rightarrow bS_0, S_2 \rightarrow aS_2S_2.$$

We prove that $L(G)$ consists of all nonnull words over $\{a, b\}$ that contain an equal number of a's and b's. Recall that $n_X(\alpha)$ is the number of occurrences of symbol X in the word α.

We will show by strong induction on p, $p \geq 1$, that

1. if $n_a(u) = n_b(u) = p$, then $S_0 \overset{*}{\underset{G}{\Rightarrow}} u$;
2. if $n_a(u) = n_b(u) + 1 = p$, then $S_1 \overset{*}{\underset{G}{\Rightarrow}} u$;
3. if $n_b(u) = n_a(u) + 1 = p$, then $S_2 \overset{*}{\underset{G}{\Rightarrow}} u$.

In the first case, for $p = 1$, we have either $u = ab$ or $u = ba$; hence, we have either $S_0 \underset{G}{\Rightarrow} aS_2 \underset{G}{\Rightarrow} ab$ or $S_0 \underset{G}{\Rightarrow} bS_1 \underset{G}{\Rightarrow} ba$.

For the second case, $u = a$, and we have $S_1 \underset{G}{\Rightarrow} a$; the third case, for $u = b$, is similar.

Suppose that the statement holds for $p \leq n$. Again, we consider three cases for the word u:

1. $n_a(u) = n_b(u) = n + 1$;
2. if $n_a(u) = n_b(u) + 1 = n + 1$;
3. if $n_b(u) = n_a(u) + 1 = n + 1$.

In the first case, we may have four situations:

1_1. $u = abt$, where $t \in \{a, b\}^*$ and $n_a(t) = n_b(t) = n$,
1_2. $u = bat$, where $t \in \{a, b\}^*$ and $n_a(t) = n_b(t) = n$,
1_3. $u = aav$ with $n_b(v) = n + 1$ and $n_a(v) = n - 1$, or
1_4. $u = bbw$ with $n_a(w) = n + 1$ and $n_b(w) = n - 1$.

By the inductive hypothesis, we have $S_0 \overset{*}{\underset{G}{\Rightarrow}} t$, and therefore, we obtain one of the following derivations:

$$S_0 \underset{G}{\Rightarrow} aS_2 \underset{G}{\Rightarrow} abS_0 \overset{*}{\underset{G}{\Rightarrow}} abt = u,$$
$$S_0 \underset{G}{\Rightarrow} bS_1 \underset{G}{\Rightarrow} baS_0 \overset{*}{\underset{G}{\Rightarrow}} bat = u,$$

for the cases (1_1) and (1_2), respectively.

On the other hand, if $u = aav$, we can write $v = v'v''$, where v' is the shortest prefix of v, where the number of bs exceeds the number of as. Clearly, we must have $n_b(v') = n_a(v') + 1 = n'$, and therefore, $n_b(v'') = n_a(v'') + 1 = n''$, where $n' + n'' = n + 1$. By the inductive hypothesis, we have $S_2 \overset{*}{\underset{G}{\Rightarrow}} v'$, $S_2 \overset{*}{\underset{G}{\Rightarrow}} v''$; hence,

$$S_0 \underset{G}{\Rightarrow} aS_2 \underset{G}{\Rightarrow} aaS_2S_2 \overset{*}{\underset{G}{\Rightarrow}} aav'v'' = u,$$

which concludes the argument for (1_3). We leave to the reader the similar arguments for the remaining cases. This allows us to conclude that every word that contains an equal number of a's and b's belongs to $L(G)$.

To prove the reverse inclusion, we justify the following implications:

1. If $S_0 \overset{n}{\underset{G}{\Rightarrow}} \alpha$, then $n_a(\alpha) + n_{S_1}(\alpha) = n_b(\alpha) + n_{S_2}(\alpha)$.
2. If $S_1 \overset{n}{\underset{G}{\Rightarrow}} \alpha$, then $n_a(\alpha) + n_{S_1}(\alpha) = n_b(\alpha) + n_{S_2}(\alpha) + 1$.
3. If $S_2 \overset{n}{\underset{G}{\Rightarrow}} \alpha$, then $n_a(\alpha) + n_{S_1}(\alpha) + 1 = n_b(\alpha) + n_{S_2}(\alpha)$.

The proof is by strong induction on n, where $n \geq 1$. For $n = 1$, the verification is immediate. For instance, if $S_1 \underset{G}{\Rightarrow} \alpha$, we have $\alpha = a$, $\alpha = aS_0$, or $\alpha = bS_1S_1$; in every case, the equality is satisfied.

Suppose that the implications hold for derivations no longer than n.

If $S_0 \overset{n+1}{\underset{G}{\Rightarrow}} \alpha$, the first production applied in the derivation is $S_0 \to aS_2$ or $S_0 \to bS_1$. In the first case, by Theorem 4.5.1, we have $\alpha = a\beta$, where $S_2 \overset{n}{\underset{G}{\Rightarrow}} \beta$, and by the inductive hypothesis, we have $n_a(\beta) + n_{S_1}(\beta) + 1 = n_b(\beta) + n_{S_2}(\beta)$, so

$$\begin{aligned} n_a(\alpha) + n_{S_1}(\alpha) &= n_a(\beta) + 1 + n_{S_1}(\beta) \\ &= n_b(\beta) + n_{S_2}(\beta) \\ &= n_b(\alpha) + n_{S_2}(\alpha). \end{aligned}$$

The second case has a similar treatment.

If $S_1 \overset{n+1}{\underset{G}{\Rightarrow}} \alpha$, we have three possibilities.

(a) If the first production of the derivation is $S_1 \to a$, then $\alpha = a$ and the equality corresponding to this case is obviously satisfied.

(b) If the first production is $S_1 \to aS_0$, we can write $\alpha = a\beta$, where $S_0 \overset{n}{\underset{G}{\Rightarrow}} \beta$; hence, $n_a(\beta) + n_{S_1}(\beta) = n_b(\beta) + n_{S_2}(\beta)$, so

$$\begin{aligned} n_a(\alpha) + n_{S_1}(\alpha) &= n_a(\beta) + 1 + n_{S_1}(\beta) \\ &= n_b(\beta) + n_{S_2}(\beta) + 1 \\ &= n_b(\alpha) + n_{S_2}(\alpha) + 1. \end{aligned}$$

(c) If the derivation begins with $S_1 \to bS_1S_1$, then, by Theorem 4.5.1 we can write $\alpha = b\beta\gamma$, where $S_1 \overset{p}{\underset{G}{\Rightarrow}} \beta$ and $S_1 \overset{q}{\underset{G}{\Rightarrow}} \gamma$, where $p, q \leq n$. By the inductive hypothesis, $n_a(\beta) + n_{S_1}(\beta) = n_b(\beta) + n_{S_2}(\beta) + 1$, and $n_a(\gamma) + n_{S_1}(\gamma) =$

$n_b(\gamma) + n_{S_2}(\gamma) + 1$. Consequently,

$$\begin{aligned} n_a(\alpha) + n_{S_1}(\alpha) &= n_a(\beta) + n_a(\gamma) + n_{S_1}(\beta) + n_{S_1}(\gamma) \\ &= n_b(\beta) + n_{S_2}(\beta) + 1 + n_b(\gamma) + n_{S_2}(\gamma) + 1 \\ &= n_b(\alpha) + n_{S_2}(\alpha) + 1. \end{aligned}$$

The case of the derivation $S_2 \overset{*}{\underset{G}{\Rightarrow}} \alpha$ can be treated in a similar manner, and it is left to the reader.

Let $u \in L(G)$. From the existence of the derivation $S_0 \overset{*}{\underset{G}{\Rightarrow}} u$ we obtain $n_a(u) = n_b(u)$, which shows that $L(G) \subseteq \{x \in \{a,b\}^* \mid n_a(x) = n_b(x)\}$. □

Theorem 4.4.2 deals with the elimination of the null word from type-0 and type-1 languages. Its counterpart for context-free languages is considered next.

Theorem 4.5.4 *For every context-free grammar G, there is a context-free, λ-free grammar G' such that $L(G') = L(G) - \{\lambda\}$.*

Proof. Let $G = (A_N, A_T, S_0, P)$ be a context-free grammar. Consider the sequence $U_0, \ldots, U_m, \ldots$ of subsets of A_N defined by

$$\begin{aligned} U_0 &= \{X \mid X \in A_N \text{ and } X \rightarrow \lambda \in P\}, \\ U_{m+1} &= U_m \cup \{X \in A_N \mid X \rightarrow \alpha \in P \text{ for some } \alpha \in U_m^*\}, \end{aligned}$$

for $m \in \mathbb{N}$.

Since $U_0 \subseteq U_1 \subseteq \cdots \subseteq A_N$, there is $k \in \mathbb{N}$ such that $U_k = U_{k+1}$. A simple argument (by induction on $h \geq 1$) shows that $U_k = U_{k+h}$ for every $h \geq 1$. The base step is immediate. Suppose that $U_k = U_{k+h}$ and let $X \in U_{k+h+1}$. If $X \in U_{k+h}$, then $X \in U_k$ by the inductive hypothesis. Otherwise, there is a production $X \rightarrow \alpha \in P$ such that $\alpha \in U_{k+h}^*$. By the inductive hypothesis, $\alpha \in U_k^*$, so $X \in U_{k+1} = U_k$. Therefore, $U_{k+h+1} = U_k$.

We claim that $X \overset{+}{\underset{G}{\Rightarrow}} \lambda$ if and only if $X \in U_k$.

We prove by strong induction on $p \geq 1$ that if $X \overset{p}{\underset{G}{\Rightarrow}} \lambda$, then $X \in U_k$. For $p = 1$, if $X \underset{G}{\Rightarrow} \lambda$, then $X \in U_0$ and $U_0 \subseteq U_k$.

Suppose that the statement is true for derivations $X \overset{+}{\underset{G}{\Rightarrow}} \lambda$ of length no greater than p and let $X \overset{p+1}{\underset{G}{\Rightarrow}} \lambda$. The first production applied in this derivation must have the form $X \rightarrow X_{i_1} \cdots X_{i_q}$; therefore, we have

$$X_{i_1} \cdots X_{i_q} \overset{p}{\underset{G}{\Rightarrow}} \lambda.$$

Hence, $X_{i_\ell} \overset{p_\ell}{\underset{G}{\Rightarrow}} \lambda$, where $p_\ell \leq p$ for $1 \leq \ell \leq q$, by Theorem 4.5.1. By the inductive hypothesis, we have $X_{i_\ell} \in U_k$, so $X_{i_1} \cdots X_{i_q} \in (U_k)^*$, which implies $X \in U_{k+1} = U_k$.

Conversely, it is easy to prove (by induction on n) that for every $X \in U_n$ we have $X \overset{+}{\underset{G}{\Rightarrow}} \lambda$. We leave this argument to the reader. From this it follows that if $\theta \in U_k^*$, then $\theta \overset{*}{\underset{G}{\Rightarrow}} \lambda$.

Consider now the set of productions P', where

$$P' = \{X \to \alpha' \mid \alpha' \neq \lambda, \text{ there is } X \to \alpha \in P \text{ and } \alpha' \text{ is obtained from } \alpha \text{ by erasing 0 or more symbols from } U_k\}.$$

If G' is the context-free grammar $G' = (A_N, A_T, S_0, P')$, then $L(G') = L(G) - \{\lambda\}$. Indeed, suppose that $X \overset{p}{\underset{G'}{\Rightarrow}} \gamma$. Clearly, $\gamma \neq \lambda$ since G' has no erasure productions. We prove, by strong induction on p, that we have $X \overset{*}{\underset{G}{\Rightarrow}} \gamma$.

For $p = 0$, the statement is trivially true. Assume that it holds for derivations of length less than or equal to p, and let $X \overset{p+1}{\underset{G'}{\Rightarrow}} \gamma$. If the first production applied in this derivation is $X \to X_{i_0} \cdots X_{i_{h-1}}$, then, by Theorem 4.5.1, we can write $\gamma = \gamma_0 \ldots \gamma_{h-1}$, where $X_{i_j} \overset{p_j}{\underset{G'}{\Rightarrow}} \gamma_j$, $p_j \leq p$, for $0 \leq j \leq h-1$. By the inductive hypothesis we have $X_{i_j} \overset{*}{\underset{G}{\Rightarrow}} \gamma_j$ for $0 \leq j \leq h-1$. Furthermore, assume that the production $X \to X_{j_0} \cdots X_{j_{h-1}}$ was obtained from the production $X \to \theta_0 X_{j_0} \theta_1 \cdots X_{j_{h-1}} \theta_h$ from P, where $\theta_0, \ldots, \theta_h \in (U_k)^*$. Our previous discussion allows us to infer the existence of the derivations $\theta_q \overset{*}{\underset{G}{\Rightarrow}} \lambda$ for $0 \leq q \leq h$. By combining the derivations obtained above, we have

$$\begin{aligned} X &\underset{G}{\Rightarrow} \theta_0 X_{j_0} \theta_1 \cdots X_{i_{h-1}} \theta_h \\ &\overset{*}{\underset{G}{\Rightarrow}} X_{j_0} \cdots X_{j_{h-1}} \\ &\overset{*}{\underset{G}{\Rightarrow}} \gamma_0 \cdots \gamma_{h-1} = \gamma. \end{aligned}$$

This implies $L(G') \subseteq L(G) - \{\lambda\}$.

To prove the converse inclusion, consider a derivation $X \overset{p}{\underset{G}{\Rightarrow}} \gamma$, where $\gamma \neq \lambda$. We claim that $X \overset{*}{\underset{G'}{\Rightarrow}} \gamma$. Again, the argument is by strong induction on $p \geq 0$.

The case $p = 0$ is trivially true. Assume that the statement holds for derivations of length of no more than p, and let $X \overset{p+1}{\underset{G}{\Rightarrow}} \gamma$, where $\gamma \neq \lambda$. Let $\beta = X_{j_0} \cdots X_{j_{l-1}}$ be the word that follows X in the previous derivation, that is, $X \underset{G}{\Rightarrow} \beta \overset{p}{\underset{G}{\Rightarrow}} \gamma$.

By Theorem 4.5.1, we can write $\gamma = \gamma_0 \cdots \gamma_{l-1}$, where $X_{j_m} \overset{p_m}{\underset{G}{\Rightarrow}} \gamma_m$ and $p_m \leq p$ for $0 \leq m \leq l-1$. If $\gamma_m \neq \lambda$, by the inductive hypothesis, we have $X_{j_m} \overset{*}{\underset{G'}{\Rightarrow}} \gamma_m$. On the other hand, if $\gamma_m = \lambda$, we have $X_{j_m} \in U_k$. Let

$$\{h_0, \ldots, h_{q-1}\} = \{h \mid 0 \leq h \leq l-1 \text{ and } \gamma_h \neq \lambda\}.$$

The definition of P' implies that we have the production $X \to X_{j_{h_0}} \cdots X_{j_{h_{q-1}}}$ in P'. Therefore, we can write

$$X \underset{G'}{\Rightarrow} X_{j_{h_0}} \cdots X_{j_{h_{q-1}}} \overset{*}{\underset{G'}{\Rightarrow}} \gamma_{h_0} \cdots \gamma_{h_{q-1}} = \gamma.$$

This implies $L(G) - \{\lambda\} \subseteq L(G')$. ∎

Theorem 4.5.5 *If G is a context-free grammar, then there is an equivalent context-free grammar G' such that one of the following two cases occurs:*

1. *if $\lambda \notin L(G)$, then G' is λ-free;*
2. *if $\lambda \in L(G)$, then G' contains a unique erasure production $S' \to \lambda$, where S' is the start symbol of G', and S' does not occur in any right member of any production of G'.*

Proof. Theorem 4.5.4 implies that for every context-free grammar G there is a context-free, λ-free grammar G_1 such that $L(G_1) = L(G) - \{\lambda\}$. If $\lambda \notin L(G)$, then the grammars G and G_1 are equivalent, and we can define G' as G_1. This proves the first case of this theorem.

If $\lambda \in L(G)$, by the same theorem, we have the context-free, λ-free grammar $G_1 = (A_N, A_T, S_1, P)$ such that $L(G_1) = L(G) - \{\lambda\}$. Define the grammar G' by

$$G' = (A_N \cup \{S'\}, A_T, S', \{S' \to S_1, S' \to \lambda\} \cup P),$$

where S' is a new nonterminal symbol (i.e., that $S' \notin A_N$). It is immediate that G' satisfies the conditions of the second case of this Theorem and that $L(G') = L(G_1) \cup \{\lambda\} = L(G)$. ∎

Example 4.5.6 Let $G = (\{S, X, Y, Z\}, \{a, b\}, S, \{S \to XYZ, X \to YZ, X \to aYb, X \to a, Y \to \lambda, Y \to b, Z \to \lambda, Z \to c\})$ be a context-free grammar that contains erasure productions. The sequence of subsets of $\{S, X, Y, Z\}$ constructed in Theorem 4.5.4 is

$$U_0 = \{Y, Z\}, U_1 = \{Y, Z, X\}, U_2 = \{Y, Z, X, S\}, U_3 = U_2.$$

Therefore, the set of productions P' constructed in Theorem 4.5.4 is given by

$$\begin{aligned} P' \ = \ & \{S \to XYZ, S \to YZ, S \to XZ, S \to XY, S \to X, S \to Y, \\ & S \to Z, X \to YZ, X \to Y, X \to Z, X \to aYb, X \to ab, \\ & X \to a, Y \to b, Z \to c\} \end{aligned}$$

Observe that the productions of P' are obtained by erasing zero, one, or more of the symbols X, Y, Z from the rules of P. □

Theorem 4.5.5 shows that it is possible to limit the erasure productions in context-free grammars that generate a language L to a single production that has the start symbol as its left member, without restricting the generality. Thus, we obtain the following corollary.

Corollary 4.5.7 *Every context-free language is a context-sensitive language; in other words, $\mathcal{L}_2 \subseteq \mathcal{L}_1$.*

Proof. This is an immediate consequence of Theorem 4.5.5 and the definitions of $\mathcal{L}_1$ and $\mathcal{L}_2$. ∎

Definition 4.5.8 Let $G = (A_N, A_T, S, P)$ be a context-free grammar. A *chain production* is a production $X \to Y$, where $X, Y \in A_N$. □

It is possible to eliminate chain productions from context-free grammars.

Theorem 4.5.9 *Let $G = (A_N, A_T, S, P)$ be a context-free grammar. There is a context-free grammar G_1 such that G_1 is equivalent to G and G_1 does not contain chain productions.*

Proof. We assume initially that G is λ-free. Let X be a nonterminal symbol. To eliminate productions of the form $X \rightarrow Y$ consider the following sequence of sets:

$$\begin{aligned} U_0^X &= \{X\} \\ U_{n+1}^X &= U_n^X \cup \{Z \in A_N \mid Y \rightarrow Z \in P \text{ for some } Y \in U_n^X\} \end{aligned}$$

It is clear that the sequence $U_0^X, \ldots, U_n^X, \ldots$ is an increasing sequence of subsets of A_N. The finiteness of A_N implies the existence of a number i such that $U_i^X = U_{i+1}^X$. Then, by induction on $\ell \geq 1$, we can easily prove that $U_i^X = U_{i+\ell}^X$ for $\ell \geq 1$.

We shall prove that $U_i^X = \{Z \in A_N \mid X \overset{*}{\underset{G}{\Rightarrow}} Z\}$.

A straightforward argument by induction on n shows that $U_n^X \subseteq \{Z \in A_N \mid X \overset{*}{\underset{G}{\Rightarrow}} Z\}$ for $n \in \mathbb{N}$. In particular, $U_i^X \subseteq \{Z \in A_N \mid X \overset{*}{\underset{G}{\Rightarrow}} Z\}$.

To prove the converse inclusion, we prove that if a derivation $X \overset{k}{\underset{G}{\Rightarrow}} Z$, then $Z \in U_i^X$. The argument is by induction on k. For $k = 0$, $Z = X$, and $Z \in U_0^X \subseteq U_i^X$, so the conclusion follows. Suppose that the statement holds for derivations of length k, and let $X \overset{k+1}{\underset{G}{\Rightarrow}} Z'$. Since the grammar has no erasure rules, we can write $X \overset{k}{\underset{G}{\Rightarrow}} Z \underset{G}{\Rightarrow} Z'$. By the inductive hypothesis, $Z \in U_i^X$; the existence of the production $Z \rightarrow Z'$ implies that $Z \in U_{i+1}^X = U_i^X$. Thus, $\{Z \in A_N \mid X \overset{*}{\underset{G}{\Rightarrow}} Z\} \subseteq U_i^X$.

Denote the set $\{Z \in A_N \mid X \overset{*}{\underset{G}{\Rightarrow}} Z\}$ by U_*^X. The context-free grammar $G_1 = (A_N, A_T, S, P_1)$ is defined by

$$P_1 = \{X \rightarrow \alpha \mid Z \rightarrow \alpha \in P \text{ for some } Z \in U_*^X \text{ and } \alpha \notin A_N\}.$$

It is clear that the grammar G_1 has no chain productions and is equivalent to G.

If G is not λ-free, then, by Theorem 4.5.5, there exists an equivalent context-free grammar $G' = (A_N \cup \{S'\}, A_T, S', P' \cup \{S' \rightarrow \lambda\})$ where $S' \rightarrow \lambda$ is the unique erasure production of G', and S' does not occur in any right member of any production of G'. The grammar $G'' = (A_N \cup \{S'\}, A_T, S', P')$ generates the language $L(G) - \{\lambda\}$. By applying the previous construction to G'' we obtain the grammar $G_1'' = (A_N \cup \{S'\}, A_T, S', P_1'')$ that has no chain rules and for which $L(G_1'') = L(G) - \{\lambda\}$. Then, the desired grammar G_1 is given by

$$G_1 = (A_N \cup \{S'\}, A_T, S', P_1'' \cup \{S' \rightarrow \lambda\}),$$

where S_1 is a new start symbol. ∎

Example 4.5.10 The grammar

$$\begin{aligned} G = \; & (\{S, X, Y\}, \{a, b, c\}, S, \{S \rightarrow X, S \rightarrow aX, X \rightarrow Y, \\ & X \rightarrow bY, S \rightarrow a, X \rightarrow b, Y \rightarrow c\}) \end{aligned}$$

is λ-free and contains some chain productions.

We have $U_0^S = \{S\}$, $U_1^S = \{S, X\}$, $U_2^S = \{S, X, Y\}$, and $U_2^S = U_3^S = \cdots$, so $U_*^S = \{S, X, Y\}$. Similar computations give $U_*^X = \{X, Y\}$ and $U_*^Y = \{Y\}$. The grammar

$$\begin{aligned} G_1 &= (\{S, X, Y\}, \{a, b, c\}, S, \{S \to aX, S \to bY, S \to a, S \to b, \\ &\quad S \to c, X \to c, X \to bY, X \to b, Y \to c\}). \end{aligned}$$

is equivalent to G and has no chain productions. □

Let $G = (A_N, A_T, S, P)$ be a context-free grammar, and let X be a nonterminal symbol. Denote by $L(G, X)$ the set of terminal words that can be generated from X in the grammar G,, that is,

$$L(G, X) = \{x \in A_T^* \mid X \overset{*}{\underset{G}{\Rightarrow}} x\}.$$

Clearly, we have $L(G, S) = L(G)$.

Definition 4.5.11 Let $G = (A_N, A_T, S, P)$ be a context-free grammar. A symbol $s \in A_N \cup A_T$ is *accessible* if it occurs in a word $\alpha \in (A_N \cup A_T)^*$ such that $S \overset{*}{\underset{G}{\Rightarrow}} \alpha$.

A symbol $X \in A_N$ is *productive* if $L(G, X) \neq \emptyset$. □

Theorem 4.5.12 *Let $G = (A_N, A_T, S, P)$ be a context-free grammar. There is a construction of an equivalent grammar $G' = (A'_N, A_T, S, P')$ such that $P' = \emptyset$ if $L(G) = \emptyset$, and if $L(G) \neq \emptyset$, then every symbol in A'_N is productive.*

Proof. Define the sequence $U_0, \ldots, U_n, \ldots$ of subsets of A_N by

$$\begin{aligned} U_0 &= \{X \in A_N \mid X \to u \in P \text{ for some } u \in A_T^*\} \\ U_{n+1} &= U_n \cup \{X \in A_N \mid X \to \alpha \in P \text{ for some } \alpha \in (U_n \cup A_T)^*\} \end{aligned}$$

Note that $U_0 \subseteq U_1 \subseteq \cdots \subseteq U_n \subseteq \cdots \subseteq A_N$. Therefore, there is i such that $U_i = U_{i+1}$. An easy argument by induction on k shows that $U_i = U_{i+k}$ for $k \geq 1$. This part of the proof is left to the reader.

We claim that

$$\{X \in A_N \mid L(G, X) \neq \emptyset\} = U_i.$$

We show first that $U_n \subseteq \{X \in A_N \mid L(G, X) \neq \emptyset\}$. The argument is by induction on n.

If $n = 0$, the conclusion follows from the definition of U_0. Suppose that the inclusion holds for U_n and let $Y \in U_{n+1}$. If $Y \in U_n$ the conclusion is immediate. Otherwise, there is a production $Y \to \alpha$, where $\alpha = w_0 Z_0 w_1 Z_1 \cdots w_{p-1} Z_{p-1} w_p$, where $w_i \in A_T^*$ for $0 \leq i \leq p$ and $Z_j \in U_n$ for $0 \leq j \leq p-1$. By the inductive hypothesis, we have the derivations $Z_j \overset{*}{\underset{G}{\Rightarrow}} z_j$, where $z_j \in A_T^*$ for $0 \leq j \leq p-1$. Thus, we obtain the derivation

$$Y \underset{G}{\Rightarrow} w_0 Z_0 w_1 Z_1 \cdots w_{p-1} Z_{p-1} w_p \overset{*}{\underset{G}{\Rightarrow}} w_0 z_0 w_1 z_1 \cdots w_{p-1} z_{p-1} w_p \in A_T^*,$$

which gives the desired conclusion. In particular,

$$U_i \subseteq \{X \in A_N \mid X \overset{*}{\underset{G}{\Rightarrow}} u \text{ for some } u \in A_T^*\}.$$

To prove the converse inclusion we prove by strong induction on $m \geq 1$ that $X \overset{m}{\underset{G}{\Rightarrow}} u$ for $u \in A_T^*$ implies $X \in U_{m-1}$. The basis case, $m = 1$, is immediate.

Suppose that the statement holds for derivations of length less than or equal to m and consider a derivation $X \overset{m+1}{\underset{G}{\Rightarrow}} u$ for $u \in A_T^*$. If we write the first step of this derivation, we obtain

$$X \underset{G}{\Rightarrow} w_0 Z_0 w_1 Z_1 \cdots w_{p-1} Z_{p-1} w_p \overset{m}{\underset{G}{\Rightarrow}} u,$$

where $w_0, \ldots, w_{p-1}, u \in A_T^*$, and $Z_0, \ldots, Z_{p-1} \in A_N$. By Theorem 4.5.1, the word u can be written as $u = w_0 z_0 w_1 z_1 \cdots w_{p-1} z_{p-1} w_p$, where $Z_j \overset{\ell_j}{\underset{G}{\Rightarrow}} z_j, \ell_j \le m$ for $0 \le j \le p-1$. By the inductive hypothesis, we have $Z_j \in U_{\ell_j - 1} \subseteq U_{m-1}$, so $w_0 Z_0 w_1 Z_1 \cdots w_{p-1} Z_{p-1} w_p \in (U_{m-1} \cup A_T)^*$. Thus, $X \in U_m$.

Since $U_m \subseteq U_i$ for every $m \in \mathbb{N}$ and $m \ge 1$, we obtain the converse inclusion and, therefore, the desired equality.

Note that $S \in U_i$ if and only if $L(G) \ne \emptyset$. Define the set of productions P' by

$$P' = \begin{cases} \emptyset \text{ if } S \notin U_i \\ \{X \to \alpha \mid \alpha \in (U_i \cup A_T)^* \text{ and } X \to \alpha \in P\} \text{ otherwise.} \end{cases}$$

Since $P' \subseteq P$ it follows that $L(G') \subseteq L(G)$. Conversely, if $u \in L(G)$, then $S \overset{*}{\underset{G}{\Rightarrow}} u$. Let $X \to \alpha$ be a production that occurs in this derivation. We have

$$S \overset{*}{\underset{G}{\Rightarrow}} \beta X \gamma \overset{*}{\underset{G}{\Rightarrow}} \beta \alpha \gamma \overset{*}{\underset{G}{\Rightarrow}} u.$$

Therefore, every nonterminal symbol that occurs in α must be productive. This allows us to conclude that $\alpha \in (U_i \cup A_T)^*$, hence $X \to \alpha \in P'$. Since every production used in the derivation $S \overset{*}{\underset{G}{\Rightarrow}} u$ belongs to P', it follows that $u \in L(G')$, so $L(G) \subseteq L(G')$. ∎

Corollary 4.5.13 *The emptiness of the language $L(G)$ generated by a context-free grammar $G = (A_N, A_T, S, P)$ is decidable.*

Proof. Note that the start symbol S of a context-free grammar G is productive if and only if $L(G) \ne \emptyset$. Therefore, in order to decide if $L(G) = \emptyset$, it suffices to compute the set U_i as in the proof of Theorem 4.5.12. Then, $L(G) = \emptyset$ if and only if $S \notin U_i$. ∎

Example 4.5.14 Let $G = (\{S, X, Y, Z\}, \{a, b\}, S, \{S \to YZ, S \to XY, S \to XZ, Z \to ab, Y \to bc\})$ be a context-free grammar. The sequence $U_0, U_1, \ldots$ is given by $U_0 = \{Y, Z\}$, $U_1 = \{S, Y, Z\}$, $U_1 = U_2 = \cdots$. Therefore, the grammar $G' = (\{S, Y, Z\}, \{a, b\}, S, \{S \to YZ, Z \to ab, Y \to bc\})$ has only productive symbols and is equivalent to G. □

A similar technique can be used for eliminating inaccessible symbols from a context-free grammar.

Theorem 4.5.15 *Let $G = (A_N, A_T, S, P)$ be a context-free grammar. There is a construction of an equivalent grammar $G' = (A'_N, A'_T, S, P')$ such that every symbol in $A'_N \cup A'_T$ is accessible.*

Proof. Define the increasing sequence $U_0, U_1, \ldots$ of subsets of $A_N \cup A_T$ by

$$\begin{aligned} U_0 &= \{S\} \\ U_{n+1} &= U_n \cup \{X \in A_N \cup A_T \mid Y \to \alpha X \beta \in P \text{ and } Y \in U_n\} \end{aligned}$$

We leave to the reader to show that there exists $i \in \mathbb{N}$ such that $U_0 \subseteq U_1 \subseteq \cdots \subseteq U_i = U_{i+1} = \cdots \subseteq A_N \cup A_T$. The argument is similar to the one used in Theorem 4.5.4.

We shall prove that U_ℓ consists of those symbols in $A_N \cup A_T$ that can be reached from S through a derivation of length not greater than ℓ. The base case, $\ell = 0$, is immediate. Suppose that the statement holds for sets U_k with $k < \ell$. If $X \in U_\ell$, then there exists a production $Y \to \alpha X \beta$ in P, where $Y \in U_{\ell-1}$. By the inductive hypothesis, there exists a derivation of length no greater than $\ell - 1$ such that $S \overset{*}{\underset{G}{\Rightarrow}} \gamma Y \gamma'$. Therefore, we have $S \overset{*}{\underset{G}{\Rightarrow}} \gamma Y \gamma' \underset{G}{\Rightarrow} \gamma \alpha X \beta \gamma'$, so X can be accessed from S through a derivation of length not greater than ℓ. In particular, U_i consists of the symbols that can be reached from S through derivations of any length.

Conversely, let Z is a symbol that is accessible from S and let $S \overset{m}{\underset{G}{\Rightarrow}} \gamma Z \gamma'$ be a derivation of that produces a word in $(A_N \cup A_T)^*$ that contains Z. We show by strong induction on m that $Z \in U_m$.

The basis case, $m = 0$, is immediate. Suppose that the statement holds for derivation of length at most m and that $S \overset{m+1}{\underset{G}{\Rightarrow}} \alpha Z \beta$ is a derivation that generates a word that contains Z. Then, we can write:

$$S \overset{p}{\underset{G}{\Rightarrow}} \gamma_0 Y \gamma_1 \underset{G}{\Rightarrow} \gamma_0 \alpha Z \beta \gamma_1 \overset{*}{\underset{G}{\Rightarrow}} \gamma Z \gamma',$$

where $\gamma_0 \alpha Z \beta \gamma_1$ is the first word in the above derivation where Z occurs and $p \leq m$. Since $S \overset{p}{\underset{G}{\Rightarrow}} \gamma_0 Y \gamma_1$, by the inductive hypothesis, we have $Y \in U_p$. Thus, $Z \in U_{p+1} \subseteq U_{m+1}$ due to the existence of the production $Y \to \alpha Z \beta$. This shows that all accessible symbols are contained in $\bigcup_{m \in \mathbb{N}} U_m = U_i$.

Define the grammar $G' = (A_N \cap U_i, A_T \cap U_i, S, P')$, where $P' = \{X \to \alpha \mid X \to \alpha \in P \text{ and } X \in U_i\}$. Since $P' \subseteq P$ it is clear that $L(G') \subseteq L(G)$. Conversely, if $x \in L(G)$ we have the derivation $S \overset{*}{\underset{G}{\Rightarrow}} x$ that makes use only of accessible symbols. Therefore, every production used in this derivation belongs to P', so we also have $S \overset{*}{\underset{G'}{\Rightarrow}} x$. This shows that the grammars G and G' are equivalent and all symbols in G' are accessible. ∎

Example 4.5.16 Let

$$\begin{aligned} G = \; & (\{S, X, Y, Z\}, \{a, b, c\}, S, \{S \to XS, X \to SX, \\ & X \to Ybb, Z \to aXc, X \to ab, Y \to ba\}) \end{aligned}$$

be a context-free grammar. We have the sequence

$$\begin{aligned} U_0 &= \{S\}, \\ U_1 &= \{S, X\}, \\ U_2 &= \{S, X, Y, a, b\}, \\ U_3 &= \{S, X, Y, a, b\}, \end{aligned}$$

constructed as in the proof of Theorem 4.5.15. Since the set of accessible symbols is $\{S, X, Y, a, b\}$, we obtain the equivalent grammar G':

$$\begin{aligned} G' &= (\{S, X, Y\}, \{a, b\}, S, \{S \to XS, X \to SX, \\ &\quad X \to Ybb, X \to ab, Y \to ba\}) \end{aligned}$$

that has only accessible symbols. □

Definition 4.5.17 A context-free grammar G is *reduced* if its set of productions is empty or if all its symbols are both accessible and productive. □

By combining the Theorems 4.5.12 and 4.5.15 it is possible to prove the existence of a equivalent reduced grammar for every context-free grammar. Namely, we have:

Corollary 4.5.18 *For every context-free grammar G there exists an equivalent reduced context-free grammar.*

Proof. Let $G = (A_N, A_T, S, P)$ be a context-free grammar. Using the algorithm contained in the proof of Theorem 4.5.12, we construct a grammar G' that contains only productive symbols. If the start symbol S is not productive then $L(G) = \emptyset$, and we can take G'', the reduced grammar, as $G'' = (A_N, A_T, S, \emptyset)$. Otherwise, that is, if S is productive, using the algorithm of Theorem 4.5.15, we eliminate from G' those symbols that are not accessible and the productions where they occur. Note that all symbols remain productive, so we obtain a reduced grammar G'' equivalent to G' and, therefore, equivalent to G. ∎

The order of the application of the algorithms for eliminating unproductive and, then, inaccessible symbols is important. Consider, for example the context-free grammar

$$G = (\{S, X, Y\}, \{a\}, S, \{S \to XY, S \to a, X \to a\}).$$

The set of productive symbols is $\{S, X\}$. Thus, if we eliminate unproductive symbols we obtain the grammar

$$G' = (\{S, X\}, \{a\}, S, \{S \to a, X \to a\}).$$

S is the unique accessible nonterminal symbol of this grammar, so we obtain the reduced grammar

$$G'' = (\{S\}, \{a\}, S, \{S \to a\}).$$

Note that all symbols of G are accessible. Therefore, the grammar G_1 obtained from G by applying the algorithm that eliminates inaccessible symbols coincides with G. Now, if we apply the algorithm to eliminate the unproductive symbols we end up with the grammar G_2 given by:

$$G_2 = (\{S, X, Y\}, \{a\}, S, \{S \to a, X \to a\}),$$

which has an inaccessible symbol, namely X. In other words, while the elimination of inaccessible symbols does not affect the set of productive symbols, the elimination of unproductive symbols may affect the set of accessible symbols.

Nonterminal symbols that generate finite sets of words can be eliminated from context-free grammars, as shown by the next theorem.

Theorem 4.5.19 *Let $G = (A_N, A_T, S, P)$ be a context-free grammar. There is an equivalent context-free grammar $G' = (A_N, A_T, S, P')$ such that if $X \in A_N - \{S\}$, then $L(G', X)$ is an infinite set.*

Proof. Let $Y \in A_N - \{S\}$ be such that $L(G, Y)$ is finite, namely $L(G, Y) = \{u_0, \ldots, u_{k-1}\}$.

Define the context-free grammar $G_1 = (A_N - \{Y\}, A_T, S, P_1)$, where P_1 consists of

1. those productions in P with no occurrence of Y, and
2. productions of the form $Z \to \alpha_0 w_0 \cdots \alpha_{n-1} w_{n-1} \alpha_n$, where P contains $Z \to \alpha_0 Y \cdots \alpha_{n-1} Y \alpha_n$, $Z \neq Y$, Y does not occur in any α_i for $0 \leq i \leq n$, and $w_j \in L(G, Y)$ for $0 \leq j \leq n-1$.

We have $L(G_1) \subseteq L(G)$. Indeed, in a derivation $S \overset{*}{\underset{G_1}{\Rightarrow}} x$ we can use productions of the first type (which belong to P), or productions of the second type. If

$$\gamma Z \gamma' \underset{G_1}{\Rightarrow} \gamma \alpha_0 w_0 \cdots \alpha_{n-1} w_{n-1} \alpha_n \gamma'$$

is a step in the above derivation that makes use of a production of the second type, then we have the derivation

$$\gamma Z \gamma' \underset{G}{\Rightarrow} \gamma \alpha_0 Y \cdots \alpha_{n-1} Y \alpha_n \gamma' \overset{*}{\underset{G}{\Rightarrow}} \gamma \alpha_0 w_0 \cdots \alpha_{n-1} w_{n-1} \alpha_n \gamma'.$$

Thus, we also have $S \overset{*}{\underset{G}{\Rightarrow}} x$, which gives $L(G_1) \subseteq L(G)$.

Conversely, to prove that $L(G) \subseteq L(G_1)$, it suffices to show that if $\theta \overset{*}{\underset{G}{\Rightarrow}} x$, where Y does not occur in θ, then $\theta \overset{*}{\underset{G_1}{\Rightarrow}} x$ (because we can take $\theta = S$). Suppose that this does not hold. Then, let

$$\theta = \theta_0 \underset{G}{\Rightarrow} \theta_1 \underset{G}{\Rightarrow} \cdots \underset{G}{\Rightarrow} \theta_m = x \tag{4.1}$$

be the shortest derivation in G such that $\theta \overset{*}{\underset{G_1}{\Rightarrow}} x$ does not hold. Note that in this derivation we can must use some production that contains Y, otherwise these productions are also in P_1, and this would imply that $\theta \overset{*}{\underset{G_1}{\Rightarrow}} x$. By the minimality of this derivation, Y occurs in θ_1. The step $\theta_0 \underset{G}{\Rightarrow} \theta_1$ is achieved using a production of the form $Z \to \alpha_0 Y \cdots \alpha_{n-1} Y \alpha_n$, so $\theta_0 = \gamma Z \gamma'$ and $\theta_1 = \gamma \alpha_0 Y \cdots \alpha_{n-1} Y \alpha_n \gamma'$, where none of α_i contains Y. By Theorem 4.5.1, x can be written as $x = u_0 y_0 \cdots y_{n-1} u_n$ such that

$$\begin{aligned}
\gamma \alpha_0 &\overset{*}{\underset{G}{\Rightarrow}} u_0 \\
\alpha_1 &\overset{*}{\underset{G}{\Rightarrow}} u_1 \\
&\vdots \\
\alpha_{n-1} &\overset{*}{\underset{G}{\Rightarrow}} u_{n-1} \\
\alpha_n \gamma' &\overset{*}{\underset{G}{\Rightarrow}} u_n,
\end{aligned}$$

and $Y \stackrel{*}{\underset{G}{\Rightarrow}} y_j$ for $0 \leq j \leq n-1$. Thus, $y_j \in L(G,Y)$ for $0 \leq j \leq n-1$. By the minimality of the derivation (4.1), we also have

$$\begin{aligned} \gamma\alpha_0 &\stackrel{*}{\underset{G_1}{\Rightarrow}} u_0 \\ \alpha_1 &\stackrel{*}{\underset{G_1}{\Rightarrow}} u_1 \\ &\vdots \\ \alpha_{n-1} &\stackrel{*}{\underset{G_1}{\Rightarrow}} u_{n-1} \\ \alpha_n\gamma' &\stackrel{*}{\underset{G_1}{\Rightarrow}} u_n. \end{aligned}$$

Since $Z \rightarrow \alpha_0 y_0 \cdots \alpha_{n-1} y_{n-1} \alpha_n$ is a production in P_1 it follows that

$$\theta = \gamma Z \gamma' \underset{G_1}{\Rightarrow} \gamma\alpha_0 y_0 \cdots \alpha_{n-1} y_{n-1} \alpha_n \gamma' \stackrel{*}{\underset{G_1}{\Rightarrow}} u_0 y_0 \cdots u_{n-1} y_{n-1} u_n = x,$$

which contradicts the assumption that $\theta \stackrel{*}{\underset{G_1}{\Rightarrow}} x$ does not hold. This shows that G and G_1 are equivalent grammars.

By applying this procedure again for all nonterminal symbols Y_1 for which $L(G_1, Y_1)$ is finite, we obtain a context-free grammar G_2 with fewer nonterminal symbols that is equivalent to G_1, etc. Eventually, after a finite number of applications of this procedure, we achieve with a context-free grammar G' that is equivalent to G such that $L(G', X)$ is infinite for every $X \in A_N - \{S\}$. ∎

4.6 Regular Languages and Type-3 Grammars

The main result of this section is a proof that the class $\mathcal{R}$ of regular languages coincides with $\mathcal{L}_3$.

Theorem 4.6.1 *Let G be a type-3 grammar, and let L be the language generated by G. There is a transition system $\mathcal{T}$ such that $L = L(\mathcal{T})$.*

Proof. Suppose that $G = (A_N, A_T, S, P)$ is a type-3 grammar. Define the transition system $\mathcal{T} = (A_T, A_N \cup \{Z\}, \theta, S, \{Z\})$, where Z is a new symbol, $Z \notin A_N \cup A_T$, and

$$\begin{aligned} \theta &= \{(X, u, Y) \mid X \rightarrow uY \in P\} \\ &\quad \cup \{(X, u, Z) \mid X \rightarrow u \in P\}. \end{aligned}$$

Let $w \in L(G)$. There exists a derivation

$$\begin{aligned} &S \underset{G}{\Rightarrow} u_0 X_{i_0} \underset{G}{\Rightarrow} u_0 u_1 X_{i_1} \cdots \underset{G}{\Rightarrow} \\ &u_0 u_1 \cdots u_{n-1} X_{i_{n-1}} \underset{G}{\Rightarrow} u_0 u_1 \cdots u_{n-1} u_n, \end{aligned}$$

where $w = u_0 \cdots u_{n-1} u_n$. The productions used in this derivation are $S \rightarrow u_0 X_{i_0}$, $X_{i_{p-1}} \rightarrow u_p X_{i_p}$ for $1 \leq p \leq n-1$, and $X_{i_{n-1}} \rightarrow u_n$. Therefore, the triples

$$(S, u_0, X_{i_0}), (X_{i_0}, u_1, X_{i_1}), \ldots, (X_{i_{n-2}}, u_{n-1}, X_{i_{n-1}}), (X_{i_{n-1}}, u_n, Z)$$

must all be in θ, which implies that $(S, u_0 \cdots u_n, Z) \in \theta^*$. Since Z is a final state of $\mathcal{T}$, we have $u \in L(\mathcal{T})$, so $L(G) \subseteq L(\mathcal{T})$.

Conversely, if $u \in L(\mathcal{T})$, then $(S, u, Z) \in \theta^*$. Taking into account the definition of θ, there are n intermediate states in $\mathcal{T}$, $X_{i_0}, \ldots, X_{i_{n-1}}$ such that $u = u_0 \cdots u_n$ and the triples

$$(S, u_0, X_{i_0}), (X_{i_0}, u_1, X_{i_1}), \ldots, (X_{i_{n-2}}, u_{n-1}, X_{i_{n-1}}), (X_{i_{n-1}}, u_n, Z)$$

exist in θ. This implies the existence in P of the productions

$$S \to u_0 X_{i_0}, X_{i_0} \to u_1 X_{i_1}, \ldots, X_{i_{n-2}} \to u_{n-1} X_{i_{n-1}}, X_{i_{n-1}} \to u_n$$

Using these productions we obtain the derivation

$$\begin{aligned} S &\underset{G}{\Rightarrow} u_0 X_{i_0} \underset{G}{\Rightarrow} u_0 u_1 X_{i_1} \cdots \underset{G}{\Rightarrow} \\ u_0 u_1 &\cdots u_{n-1} X_{i_{n-1}} \underset{G}{\Rightarrow} u_0 u_1 \cdots u_{n-1} u_n, \end{aligned}$$

which implies that $x \in L(\mathcal{T})$. This proves the inclusion $L(\mathcal{T}) \subseteq L(G)$. ∎

Theorem 4.6.2 *For every regular language L there is a type-3 grammar G such that $L(G) = L$.*

Proof. Let $\mathcal{M} = (A, Q, \delta, q_0, F)$ be a dfa such that $L = L(\mathcal{M})$. The semi-Thue system $T_{\mathcal{M}}$ defined in Theorem 4.2.14 is actually a type-3 grammar $G = (Q, A, q_0, F)$ since its productions (which have the form $q \to aq'$ or $q \to \lambda$) satisfy the defining restrictions of this type of grammars. ∎

Corollary 4.6.3 *The class $\mathcal{L}_3$ coincides with the class $\mathcal{R}$ of regular languages.*

Proof. This statement follows immediately from Theorems 4.6.1 and 4.6.2. ∎

Corollary 4.6.3 allows us to conclude that $\mathcal{L}_3$ is closed with respect to all regular operations. This also implies that $\mathcal{L}_3$ is closed with respect to complementation (cf. Theorem 3.4.1), reversal, left and right quotients with arbitrary languages (cf. Theorem 3.4.9), substitution, morphic images and inverse images, and the shuffle operation. We can also conclude that the class $\mathcal{L}_3$ is the least class of languages that contains the class of finite languages and is closed with respect to union, product and Kleene closure (cf. Theorem 3.4.14).

Definition 4.6.4 Let $G = (A_N, A_T, S, P)$ be a context-free grammar. G is *linear* if all its productions have the form $X \to uYv$ or $X \to u$, where $X, Y \in A_N$ and $u, v \in A_T^*$.

G is *left-linear* (*right-linear*) if its productions have the form $X \to Yv$ or $X \to v$ ($X \to uY$ or $X \to u$, respectively).

G is *strongly left-linear* if its productions have the form $X \to Ya$ or $X \to \lambda$. Similarly, G is *strongly right-linear* if its productions have the form $X \to aY$ or $X \to \lambda$.

If G is a linear, left- or right-linear, or strongly left-linear or strongly right-linear, and $L(G) = L$, then we will refer to L as a *linear*, *left-*, *right-linear*, *strongly left-linear*, or *strongly right-linear language*, respectively. □

Clearly, a type-3 grammar is right-linear, so a type-3 language is a right-linear language.

Theorem 4.6.5 *The class of linear languages is closed with respect to reversal.*

Proof. The statement follows immediately from Theorem 4.3.18 by observing that if G is a linear grammar, then the grammar G^R constructed in the proof of that theorem is a linear grammar. ∎

Note that $\mathcal{L}_3$ is a proper subset of the class of linear languages. Indeed, by Example 4.3.10, the language $\{a^n b^n \mid n \in \mathbb{N}\}$ is linear. On the other hand, this language is not regular (cf. Example 3.5.4).

Theorem 4.6.6 *Let L be a language. The following statements are equivalent:*

(i) *L is a regular language (or a right-linear language);*
(ii) *L is a strongly right-linear language;*
(iii) *L is a left-linear language;*
(iv) *L is a strongly left-linear language.*

Proof. It is immediate that (ii) implies (i). The argument of Theorem 4.6.2 shows that (i) implies (ii), so (i) and (ii) are equivalent.

`(iii) implies (i).` Let L be a left-linear language. There is a left-linear grammar G such that $L(G) = L$. Let G^R be the grammar constructed from G as in the proof of Theorem 4.3.18. Clearly, G^R is a type-3 grammar, so L^R is a regular language because $L^R = L(G^R)$. Since the class of regular languages is closed with respect to reversal it follows that $L = (L^R)^R$ is a regular language.

`(iv) implies (ii).` The argument is exactly the same as for the fact that (i) implies (iii).

`(i) implies (iii).` Let L be a regular, or a right-linear language. Since the class of regular languages is closed with respect to reversal, the language L^R is regular and, therefore, there exists a type-3 grammar G such that $L^R = L(G)$. Since G is right-linear, the grammar G^R is left-linear, and the statement follows from the fact that $L = L(G^R)$.

`(ii) implies (iv).` If G is a strongly right-linear grammar, then G^R is a strongly left-linear grammar. The remaining argument is similar to the one we used to prove that (i) implies (iii).

Thus, all four statements are equivalent. ∎

We conclude this section with a characterization of $\mathcal{L}_3$ as a subclass of $\mathcal{L}_2$.

Definition 4.6.7 Let $G = (A_N, A_T, S, P)$ be a context-free grammar. G is *self-embedding* if there is an $X \in A_N$ such that $X \overset{+}{\underset{G}{\Rightarrow}} \alpha X \beta$ for some $\alpha, \beta \in (A_N \cup A_T)^*$ such that $\alpha \neq \lambda$ and $\beta \neq \lambda$.

A context-free language L is *self-embedding* if every context-free grammar G that generates L is self-embedding. □

Theorem 4.6.8 *A context-free language L is regular if and only if it is not self-embedding.*

Proof. Since no type-3 grammar is self-embedding, it is clear that a regular language is not self-embedding.

Conversely, let L be a context-free language that is not self-embedding. There exists a reduced type-2 grammar $G = (A_N, A_T, S, P)$ without chain rules such that $L(G) = L$. Then, G must satisfy one of the following two conditions:

1. for every $X \in A_N$, there exists a derivation $X \overset{*}{\underset{G}{\Rightarrow}} \gamma S \gamma'$, or

2. there is a nonterminal symbol $X \in A_N$ such that no derivation $X \overset{*}{\underset{G}{\Rightarrow}} \gamma S \gamma'$ exists.

We consider first the case when G satisfies condition 1. Since G is a reduced grammar, the productions of G that contain a nonterminal symbol in their right member have one of the following three forms: $Y \to \alpha Z \beta$, $Y \to \alpha Z$, $Y \to Z\beta$, where $Y, Z \in A_N$ and $\alpha, \beta \in (A_N \cup A_T)^+$.

We claim that P may not contain productions of the form $Y \to \alpha Z \beta$. Indeed, if this were the case, then we would have the derivation

$$Y \underset{G}{\Rightarrow} \alpha Z \beta \overset{*}{\underset{G}{\Rightarrow}} \alpha \gamma S \gamma' \beta,$$

since condition 1 is satisfied. Then, since Y is an accessible symbol, we have $S \overset{*}{\underset{G}{\Rightarrow}} \theta Y \theta'$, which implies

$$Y \overset{*}{\underset{G}{\Rightarrow}} \alpha \gamma \theta Y \theta' \gamma' \beta.$$

Since both $\alpha\gamma\theta$ and $\theta'\gamma'\beta$ are nonnull words, this contradicts the fact that G is not self-embedding.

Further, P may not contain both productions of the form $Y \to \alpha Z$ and productions of the form $Y \to Z\beta$. Indeed, if P did contain both $Y \to \alpha Z$ and $Y' \to Z'\beta'$, then by the first condition and the accessibility of all symbols, we would have the derivation:

$$\begin{aligned} Y & \underset{G}{\Rightarrow} \alpha Z \\ & \overset{*}{\underset{G}{\Rightarrow}} \alpha \gamma S \gamma' \\ & \overset{*}{\underset{G}{\Rightarrow}} \alpha \gamma \theta Y' \theta' \gamma' \\ & \underset{G}{\Rightarrow} \alpha \gamma \theta Z' \beta' \theta' \gamma' \\ & \overset{*}{\underset{G}{\Rightarrow}} \alpha \gamma \theta \gamma_0 S \gamma_0' \beta' \theta' \gamma' \\ & \overset{*}{\underset{G}{\Rightarrow}} \alpha \gamma \theta \gamma_0 \theta_0 Y \theta_0' \gamma_0' \beta' \theta' \gamma', \end{aligned}$$

which contradicts the assumption that G is not self-embedding.

Thus, if P contains a production of the form $Y \to \alpha Z$, then for all productions in P of this form α contains only terminal symbols (in order to avoid the existence of productions of the form $Y \to \alpha Z \beta$) which means that all productions of P are right-linear and G is a type-3 grammar. Similarly, if P contains a production of the form $Y \to Z\beta$, G must be left-linear, so $L(G)$ is regular, by Theorem 4.6.6.

In the second case, we proceed by induction on A_N. If $|A_N| = 1$, the grammar G has only one nonterminal symbol, and since it is not self-embedding, it may not contain a derivation of the form $S \overset{+}{\underset{G}{\Rightarrow}} \alpha S \beta$ for some $\alpha, \beta \in (A_N \cup A_T)^*$ such that $\alpha\beta \neq \lambda$. This means that every completed derivation in this grammar consists of applying one production of the form $S \to u$ for some $u \in A_T^*$, which means that $L(G)$ is finite.

Suppose that the statement holds for grammars that have at most n nonterminal symbols and let $G = (A_N, A_T, S, P)$ be a grammar such that $|A_N| = n+1$ and there is a nonterminal symbol $X \in A_N$ such that no derivation $X \overset{*}{\underset{G}{\Rightarrow}} \gamma S \gamma'$ exists.

Consider the type-2 grammars $G' = (A_N - \{S\}, A_T, X, F')$ and $G'' = (A_N - \{X\}, A_T \cup \{X\}, S, F'')$, where F' is obtained from F by removing all productions that involve the start symbol S, and F'' is obtained from F by removing all productions of the form $X \to \cdots$. Both $L(G')$ and $L(G'')$ are regular languages, either by Case 1, or by the inductive hypothesis and $L(G)$ is obtained by substituting $L(G')$ in $L(G'')$ for X. Theorem 3.9.10 implies that $L(G)$ is regular. ∎

4.7 Exercises

Semi-Thue and Thue Systems

1. Let $T = (A, M, P)$ be a semi-Thue system. Can both relations $\overset{*}{\underset{T}{\Rightarrow}}$ and $\overset{+}{\underset{T}{\Rightarrow}}$ be empty? Explain.
2. Let $T = (A, M, P)$ be a semi-Thue system. Prove that the triple $T' = (A, M, P \cup P^{-1})$ is a Thue system.
3. Let $T = (A, M, P)$ be a semi-Thue system. Prove that $M \cap B^* \subseteq L_g(T|B)$ and $M \cap B^* \subseteq L_r(T|B)$.
4. $^\diamond$ Let A, A' be two alphabets and let $h : A^* \longrightarrow A'^*$ be an injective morphism. If $T = (A, M, P)$ is a semi-Thue system, define the semi-Thue system $T_h = (A', h(M), h(P))$, where $h(M) = \{h(\alpha) \mid \alpha \in M\}$ and $h(P) = \{h(\alpha) \to h(\beta) \mid \alpha \to \beta \in P\}$. Prove that $\gamma \overset{*}{\underset{T}{\Rightarrow}} \gamma'$ if and only if $h(\gamma) \overset{*}{\underset{T_h}{\Rightarrow}} h(\gamma')$.
5. $^\diamond$ Let $T = (A, M, P)$ be a semi-Thue system, where $A = \{0, 1, a, b\}$, and let $B = \{0, 1\}$. Determine the language $L_g(T|B)$, where the set of axioms M and the set of productions P are given below:
   (a) $M = \{\lambda\}$, $P = \{\lambda \to ab, ab \to 01\}$;
   (b) $M = \{a, b\}$, $P = \{a \to bab, b \to aba, ab \to 00, ba \to 11\}$;
   (c) $M = \{a0b1, a^2 0 b^2 1, \ldots, a^k 0 b^k 1\}$, $P = \{0b \to b0, ab \to \lambda\}$.
6. $^{\diamond\diamond}$ Let $T = (A, M, P)$ be a semi-Thue system. If $x, y \in A^*$ and $x \overset{k}{\underset{T}{\Rightarrow}} y$ determine an upper bound on $|y|$ in terms of $|x|$ and of T.
7. $^\diamond$ Construct a semi-Thue system $T = (A, M, P)$ such that $\{0,1\} \cup (\{0,1\} \times \{0,1\}) \subseteq A$ and there exists a derivation

   $$(a_0, b_0)(a_1, b_1) \cdots (a_{n-1}, b_{n-1}) \overset{*}{\underset{T}{\Rightarrow}} w,$$

   if and only if $w \in \{0,1\}^*$ and the sum of the binary numbers $a_0 a_1 \cdots a_{n-1}$ and $b_0 b_1 \cdots b_{n-1}$ equals the number whose binary representation is w.
8. $^\diamond$ Let $T = (A, M, P)$ be a semi-Thue system such that the symbol $\Rightarrow$ does not belong to $A = \{a_0, \ldots, a_{k-1}\}$, and let $B = A \cup \{\Rightarrow\}$.

(a) Prove that if $v = w_0 \Rightarrow w_1 \Rightarrow \cdots \Rightarrow w_{n-1}$ is a derivation in T, then

$$\phi_B(v) = \sum_{j=0}^{n-1} \phi_B(w_j)|B|^{n-j-1+|w_{j+1}\cdots w_{n-1}|} + (k+1)\sum_{j=1}^{n-1} |B|^{j-1+|w_{n-j}\cdots w_{n-1}|},$$

where $\phi_B(\Rightarrow) = k+1$.

(b) If T is a length-increasing semi-Thue system, then prove that for every derivation v as above, we have $\phi_B(w_i) \leq |B|^{j-i}\phi_B(w_j)$ for $0 \leq i \leq j \leq n-1$.

(c) If T is a length-increasing semi-Thue system, then show that

$$\phi_B(v) \leq |B|^{n(2+|w_{n-1}|)}(\phi_B(w_{n-1}) + k + 1)$$

for every derivation v of the form $w_0 \Rightarrow \cdots \Rightarrow w_{n-1}$. Further, prove that for every word $w \in L_g(T|A)$ there is a derivation v such that

$$\phi_B(v) \leq |B|^{(2+|w|)|A|^{|w|+1}}(\phi_B(w) + k + 1), \tag{4.2}$$

where $\phi_B(\Rightarrow) = k+1$.

(d) Let $h : \mathbb{N} \to \mathbb{N}$ be the function defined by

$$h(m) = (2+m)|B|^{m+1}(k+2)$$

for $m \in \mathbb{N}$. Starting from the inequality (4.2) and the inequality from Part (f) of Exercise 29 of Chapter 2, prove that if T is a length-increasing semi-Thue system, then for every word $w \in L_g(T|A)$ there is a derivation v such that $\phi_B(v) \leq \phi_B(w^{h(|w|)})$.

Grammars and the Chomsky Hierarchy

9. $\diamond$ Let $L \in \mathcal{L}_0$ be a language. Prove that there is an infinite set of grammars that generate the language L.
10. $\diamond$ Prove that for every grammar $G = (A_N, A_T, S, P)$, there exists an equivalent grammar $G' = (A'_N, A_T, S', P')$ such that if $\alpha \to \beta \in P'$ and $|\beta| < |\alpha|$, then $\alpha = X \in A_N$, and $\beta = \lambda$.

    Solution. Define $A'_N = A_N \cup \{Y\}$ and

    $$P' = \{\alpha \to \beta \mid \alpha \to \beta \in P \text{ and } |\alpha| \leq \beta\} \cup\{\alpha \to Y^{|\alpha|-|\beta|}\beta \mid \alpha \to \beta \in P \text{ and } |\alpha| > \beta\} \cup \{Y \to \lambda\}$$

    It is easy to see that G' is equivalent to G and it satisfies the condition imposed by the exercise. ■
11. $\diamond\diamond\diamond$ Prove that if every non-context-free production of a grammar $G = (A_N, A_T, S, P)$ has the form $uXv \to u\alpha v$ for $X \in A_N$, $u, v \in A_T^*$ and $\alpha \in (A_N \cup A_T)^*$, then $L(G)$ is a context-free language.
12. $\diamond$ Let $\mathcal{L}'_0$ be the class of languages generated by grammars that may contain both context-sensitive productions and erasure productions. Prove that $\mathcal{L}'_0 = \mathcal{L}_0$.

13. $^{\circ\circ}$ Consider the following modification of the proof of Theorem 4.3.16. In the construction of the context-sensitive grammar that is equivalent to a length-increasing grammar G, replace a length-increasing production $\pi : X_0 \cdots X_{n-1} \to Y_0 \cdots Y_{m-1}$ with the set of productions P'_π given by

$$
\begin{array}{l}
X_0 \cdots X_{n-1} \to Z_0^\pi X_1 \cdots X_{n-1} \\
Z_0^\pi X_1 \cdots X_{n-1} \to Z_0^\pi Z_1^\pi X_2 \cdots X_{n-1} \\
\vdots \\
Z_0^\pi Z_1^\pi \cdots Z_{n-2}^\pi X_{n-1} \to Z_0^\pi Z_1^\pi \cdots Z_{n-1}^\pi Y_n \cdots Y_{m-1} \\
Z_0^\pi Z_1^\pi \cdots Z_{n-1}^\pi Y_n \cdots Y_{m-1} \to Z_0^\pi Z_1^\pi \cdots Y_{n-1} Y_n \cdots Y_{m-1} \\
Z_0^\pi Z_1^\pi \cdots Y_{n-1} Y_n \cdots Y_{m-1} \to Z_0^\pi Z_1^\pi \cdots Z_{n-3}^\pi Y_{n-2} Y_{n-1} Y_n \cdots Y_{m-1} \\
\vdots \\
Z_0^\pi Y_1 \cdots Y_n \cdots Y_{m-1} \to Y_0 Y_1 \cdots Y_{n-1} Y_n \cdots Y_{m-1},
\end{array}
$$

Prove that the context-sensitive grammar obtained in this manner is not necessarily equivalent to G.

Solution. Let $G = (\{S, X, Y, U, W\}, \{a, b, c\}, S, P)$ be a length-increasing grammar, where $P = \{S \to XY, XY \to UYW, X \to a, Y \to b, U \to c, W \to c\}$. The language generated by this grammar is $L(G) = \{ab, cbc\}$. On the other hand, the context-sensitive grammar obtained by applying the previous construction is $G' = (\{S, X, Y, U, W\}, \{a, b, c\}, S, P')$, where

$$
\begin{aligned}
P' \;=\; & \{S \to XY, XY \to Z_0 Y, Z_0 Y \to Z_0 Z_1 W, \\
& Z_0 Z_1 W \to Z_0 Y W, Z_0 Y W \to U Y W, X \to a, \\
& Y \to b, U \to c, W \to c\}.
\end{aligned}
$$

In this new grammar we have the derivation

$$
\begin{aligned}
S & \underset{G'}{\Rightarrow} XY \underset{G'}{\Rightarrow} Z_0 Y \underset{G'}{\Rightarrow} Z_0 Z_1 W \\
& \underset{G'}{\Rightarrow} Z_0 Y W \underset{G'}{\Rightarrow} Z_0 Z_1 W W \underset{G'}{\Rightarrow} Z_0 Y W W \\
& \underset{G'}{\Rightarrow} U Y W W \underset{G'}{\Rightarrow} c Y W W \underset{G'}{\Rightarrow} c b W W \\
& \underset{G'}{\Rightarrow} c b c W \underset{G'}{\Rightarrow} c b c c,
\end{aligned}
$$

which shows that $cbcc \in L(G')$. ∎

14. $^{\circ\circ}$ In order to prove that the classes $\mathcal{L}_0$ and $\mathcal{L}_1$ are closed with respect to the $*$ operation we constructed the grammar G_* in Lemma 4.4.4. The similar construction for the class $\mathcal{L}_2$ was given in Lemma 4.4.5.
Give an example of a type-0 grammar for whch the construction given in Lemma 4.4.5 does not work. In other words, if G'_* is the grammar obtained from G by applying the construction of Lemma 4.4.5, then $L(G'_*) \neq (L(G_*))^*$.
Hint. Consider the type-0 grammar $G = (\{S\}, \{a, b\}, S, \{S \to a, SS \to b\})$.

15. Construct a length-increasing grammar G such that $L(G) = \{xx \mid x \in \{a, b\}^*\}$. Starting from G construct a context-sensitive grammar G_1 equivalent to G.

16. $\diamond$ Construct a grammar G_k such that $L(G_k) = \{a^{k^n} \mid n \in \mathbb{N}\}$, where k is a fixed number, $k \in \mathbb{N}$ and $k > 0$.
Hint. Consider the grammar $G_k = (\{S, X, Y, T, A\}, \{a\}, S, P)$, where $P = \{S \to XAY, X \to XT, TA \to A^kT, TY \to Y, X \to \lambda, Y \to \lambda, A \to a\}$.
17. $\diamond$ Let A be an alphabet. Prove that $\mathsf{REXP}(A)$, the set of regular expressions over A is a context-free language over the meta-alphabet $\boldsymbol{A}$.
18. $\diamond\diamond$ Let $m, m', n, j, i \in \mathbb{N}$, where $\lfloor \frac{i}{n} \rfloor = k > 1$.
 (a) Prove that if $\frac{m}{n} \leq \frac{j}{i} \leq \frac{m'}{n}$, then there are $p, q \in \mathbb{N}$ such that $p + q = k - 1$ and

$$\frac{m}{n} \leq \frac{j - pm - qm'}{i - (k-1)n} \leq \frac{m'}{n}.$$

 (b) Using Part (a) prove that the for any m, m', n such that $0 \leq m \leq m'$ and $n > 0$, the language

$$L = \{a^i b^j \mid \frac{m}{n} \leq \frac{j}{i} \leq \frac{m'}{n}\}$$

 is context-free.
 (c) Construct the context-free grammar that corresponds to $m = 1, m' = 4$, and $n = 5$.

Solution. The argument is by induction on k. For $k = 2$ we have to show that if $i \geq 2n$ and $\frac{m}{n} \leq \frac{j}{i} \leq \frac{m'}{n}$, then we have either

$$\frac{m}{n} \leq \frac{j - m}{i - n} \leq \frac{m'}{n} \text{ or } \frac{m}{n} \leq \frac{j - m'}{i - n} \leq \frac{m'}{n}.$$

By hypothesis, we have

$$m \leq \frac{jn}{i} \leq m'.$$

Then, $\frac{jn}{i}$ belongs either to the left half of the interval $[m, m']$, that is

$$m \leq \frac{jn}{i} \leq m' - \frac{m' - m}{2},$$

or to the right half of the same interval, that is

$$m + \frac{m' - m}{2} \leq \frac{jn}{i} \leq m'.$$

Since $\frac{n}{i} \leq \frac{1}{2}$, the first inequality implies

$$m \leq \frac{jn}{i} \leq m' - \frac{(m' - m)n}{i},$$

while the second one implies

$$m + \frac{(m' - m)n}{i} \leq \frac{jn}{i} \leq m'.$$

It is easy to see that these inequalities are equivalent to the ones we need to show.
Suppose now that the statement holds for $k-1$ and assume that $\frac{m}{n} \leq \frac{j}{i} \leq \frac{m'}{n}$ and $\lfloor \frac{i}{n} \rfloor = k > 1$. Then, by the initial step we have

$$\frac{m}{n} \leq \frac{j-m}{i-n} \leq \frac{m'}{n}$$

or

$$\frac{m}{n} \leq \frac{j-m'}{i-n} \leq \frac{m'}{n}.$$

In the first case, since $i-n \geq (k-1)n$, by the inductive hypothesis, there are $r, s \in \mathbb{N}$ such that $r+s = k-2$ and

$$\frac{m}{n} \leq \frac{j-m-rm-sm'}{i-n-(k-2)n} \leq \frac{m'}{n},$$

or, equivalently

$$\frac{m}{n} \leq \frac{j-(1+r)m-sm'}{i-(k-1)n} \leq \frac{m'}{n},$$

By taking $p = 1+r$ and $q = s$ we obtain the desired inequality. The second case can be treated in a similar manner.
For the second part note that, by Part (a), if $\frac{m}{n} \leq \frac{j}{i} \leq \frac{m'}{n}$ and $\lfloor \frac{i}{n} \rfloor = k > 1$, this implies the existence of a sequence of rational numbers

$$\frac{i-p_1m-q_1m'}{i-n}, \frac{i-p_2m-q_2m'}{i-2n}, \ldots, \frac{i-p_{k-1}m-q_{k-1}m'}{i-(k-1)n},$$

such that $p_j + q_j = j$ for $1 \leq j \leq k-1$, and all these numbers are included in the interval $\left[\frac{m}{n}, \frac{m'}{n}\right]$. Correspondingly, we have in L the sequence of words

$$a^{i-p_1m-q_1m'}b^{i-n}, a^{i-p_2m-q_2m'}b^{i-2n}, \ldots, a^{i-p_{k-1}m-q_{k-1}m'}b^{i-(k-1)n}.$$

Observe that for the last word of this sequence $n \leq i-(k-1)n < 2n$. Also, we have either $p_l = 1+p_{l-1}, q_l = q_{l-1}$, or $p_l = p_{l-1}, q_l = 1+q_{l-1}$ for $2 \leq l \leq k-1$.
There are only a finite number of rational numbers of the form $\frac{j}{i}$ in the interval $\left[\frac{m}{n}, \frac{m'}{n}\right]$ such that $n \leq i-(k-1)n < 2n$. For each such number consider a production $S \rightarrow a^iSb^j$. Then, any word of the form $a^{i'}Sb^{j'}$, where $\frac{m}{n} \leq \frac{j'}{i'} \leq \frac{m'}{n}$ can be derived from a word a^iSb^j by applying either the production $S \rightarrow a^mSb^n$, or the production $S \rightarrow a^{m'}b^n$. If we add to these productions $S \rightarrow \lambda$ we obtain a context-free grammar that generates the desired language. ∎

A *simple contextual grammar* is a triple $G = (A, B, C)$, where A is an alphabet, $B \subseteq A^*$ is a finite language, and $C \subseteq A^* \times A^*$ is a finite relation on A^*. The language B is the *base of the grammar* ; the pairs in C are referred to as the *contexts* of the grammar.

The language generated by a simple contextual grammar G is the language $L(G) = B \cup \{u_{n-1} \cdots u_0 x v_0 \cdots v_{n-1} \mid (u_i, v_i) \in C \text{ for } 0 \leq i \leq n-1\}$. A language $L \subseteq A^*$ is a *simple contextual language* if $L = L(G)$ for some simple contextual grammar. The class of simple contextual languages will be denote by $\mathcal{C}$.

19. Let $G = (A, B, C)$ be a simple contextual grammar. Prove that $L(G)$ is the least language on A that contains B such that $x \in L(G)$ and $(u, v) \in C$ implies $uxv \in L(G)$.
20. Let A be an alphabet. Prove that the empty language, A^*, and any finite language on A are simple contextual languages.
21. $\diamond$ Prove that the language $\{a^n b^n \mid n \in \mathbb{N}\}$ is a simple contextual language.
22. $\diamond$ Prove that for every simple contextual language $L \subseteq A^*$ there are three finite languages $H, K, M \subseteq A^*$ such that $L \subseteq H^* K^* M^*$; furthermore, for every $u \in H^*$ there is $v \in M^*$ such that $uLv \subseteq L$.

A *generalized contextual grammar* is a 4-tuple $G = (A, B, B', C)$, where A, C are as in the definition of contextual grammars and B, B' are finite languages on A. The language generated by a generalized contextual grammar is

$$\begin{aligned} L(G) &= B \cup \{u_{n-1} \cdots u_0 x y^n v_0 \cdots v_{n-1} \mid x \in B, y \in B', \\ &\quad (u_i, v_i) \in C \text{ for } 0 \leq i \leq n-1\}. \end{aligned}$$

A language $L \subseteq A^*$ is a generalized contextual language if $L = L(G)$ for some generalized contextual grammar. The class of generalized contextual languages will be denoted by $\mathcal{G}$.

23. Prove that any simple contextual language is a generalized contextual language.
24. $\diamond$ Prove that the language $\{a^n b^n c^n \mid n \in \mathbb{N}\}$ is a generalized contextual language.
25. $\diamond$ Let $L \in \mathcal{G}$ and $L \subseteq A^*$. Prove that if A_0 is a subset of A such that there is a number $p \in \mathbb{N}$ such that $x \in L$ implies $n_a(x) \leq p$, then the language

$$K_0(L) = \{x \in A^* \mid x = ayb, a, b \in A_0 \text{ and } x \in \mathsf{INFIX}(L)\}$$

is finite.
26. $\diamond$ Prove that if L is an infinite generalized contextual language, then the set $\{|x| \mid x \in L\}$ contains an infinite arithmetic progression.
27. $\diamond$ Prove that the language $\{ab^n a \mid n \in \mathbb{N}\} \cup \{ab^n \mid n \in \mathbb{N}\}$ is not a generalized contextual language.
28. $\diamond$ Prove that for every grammar $G = (A_N, A_T, S, P)$, there exists an equivalent grammar $G' = (A'_N, A_T, S', P')$ that satisfies the following conditions:
(i) if $\alpha \to \beta \in P'$ and $|\beta| < |\alpha|$, then $\alpha = X \in A_N$, and $\beta = \lambda$;
(ii) for every production $\alpha \to \beta \in P'$ we have $|\beta| \leq 2$.

Solution. Starting from G construct an equivalent grammar $G_1 = (A_N \cup \{Y\}, A_T, S, P_1)$ such that if π is a length-decreasing production of G_1, then π has the form $X \to \lambda$ by applying the method discussed in Exercise 10. If $\alpha \to \beta \in P_1$ and $|\beta| \geq 3$, then we have $|\alpha| \leq |\beta|$. There are two cases to consider:

(A) if $|\alpha| < |\beta|$, replace the production $\pi : \alpha \to \beta$ by $\alpha \to \beta_{0,|\alpha|}X_\pi$ and $X_\pi \to \beta_{|\alpha|,|\beta|}$, where X_π is a new nonterminal symbol;

(B) If $\alpha = X_0 \cdots X_{m-1}$ and $\beta = Z_0 \cdots Z_{m-1}$, then replace the production π by the following m productions: $X_0X_1 \to Z_0U_{\pi 0}$, $U_{\pi,i}X_{i+2} \to Z_{i+1}U_{\pi,i+1}$ for $0 \leq i \leq m-2$, and $U_{\pi,m-2}X_m \to Z_{m-2}Z_{m-1}$.

The process is repeated until we obtain a grammar that satisfies the conditions of the exercise. ■

29. $G = (A_N, A_T, S, P)$ is a *context-sensitive grammar with erasing* if its productions have the form $\alpha' X \alpha'' \to \alpha' \gamma \alpha''$, where $X \in A_N$ and $\alpha', \alpha'', \gamma \in (A_N \cup A_T)^*$. Prove that for every grammar there exists an equivalent context-sensitive grammar G' with erasing.

Solution. By Exercise 28 we may assume, without loss of generality, that G contains only productions of the form $\alpha \to \beta$ with $|\alpha| \leq |\beta| \leq 2$ or $X \to \lambda$, where $X \in A_N$. Let P' be the set of productions of G'. Include in P' every production $\alpha \to \beta$, where $|\alpha| = 1$; further, for every production $\pi : XY \to UV \in P$ with $X \neq U$ and $Y \neq V$ include in P' the context-sensitive productions $XY \to X_\pi Y$, $X_\pi Y \to X_\pi Y_\pi$, $X_\pi Y_\pi \to UY_\pi$, and $UY_\pi \to UV$, where X_π, Y_π are new nonterminal symbols. We leave to the reader to prove that G' is equivalent to G. ■

A *nonterminal rewriting grammar* is a grammar $G = (A_N, A_T, S, P)$ such that every production of P has the form

$$u_0X_0u_1 \cdots u_{n-1}X_{n-1}u_n \to u_0\alpha_0u_1 \cdots u_{n-1}\alpha_{n-1}u_n,$$

where $n > 0$, $u_i \in A_T^*$ for $0 \leq i \leq n$, and $\alpha_i \in (A_N \cup A_T)^*, X_i \in A_N$ for $0 \leq i \leq n-1$.

A nonterminal rewriting grammar is *terminal bounded* if each production has the form

$$u_0X_0u_1 \cdots u_{n-1}X_{n-1}u_n \to v_0Y_0v_1 \cdots v_{m-1}Y_{m-1}v_m,$$

where $u_0, \ldots, u_{n-1}, v_0, \ldots, v_{m-1} \in A_T^*$ and either $n = 1$, or there exists j such that $0 \leq j \leq m-1$ and $|v_j| > |u_i|$ for $0 \leq i \leq n-1$.

30. $^{\circ\circ\circ}$ Define the context-free index of a terminal bounded grammar $G = (A_N, A_T, S, P)$ as the number $N(G) = \sum\{|\alpha| - 1 \mid \alpha \to \beta \in P\}$. Prove that if G is a terminal bounded grammar with $N(G) > 0$, then there exists a terminal bounded grammar G_1, a regular language R and a gsm $\mathfrak{T}$ such that $L(G_1) = \mathfrak{T}(L(G) \cap R)$ and $N(G_1) < N(G)$.

A *g-system* is a 4-tuple $GS = (A_N, A_T, S, \mathfrak{T})$, where A_N, A_T, S are as in the definition of grammars and $\mathfrak{T}$ is a transducer $\mathfrak{T} = (A, Q, A, \theta, q_0, F)$, where $A = A_N \cup A_T$. It is assumed that if $(q, x, y, q') \in \theta$, then $|x| = 1$.

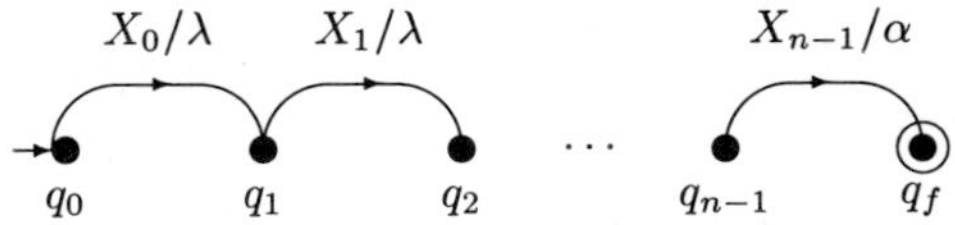

Figure 4.1: Transitions that correspond to $X_0 \cdots X_{n-1} \to \alpha$

For $u \in A^+$ and $v \in A^*$ we have $u \underset{GS}{\Rightarrow} v$ if and only if $(q_0, u, \lambda) \overset{*}{\underset{\mathcal{T}}{\vdash}} (q, \lambda, v)$ for some $q \in F$. The relations $\overset{*}{\underset{GS}{\Rightarrow}}$ and $\overset{+}{\underset{GS}{\Rightarrow}}$ are the reflexive and transitive closure, and the transitive closure, respectively of the relation $\underset{GS}{\Rightarrow}$. The *language generated by a g-system GS* is $L(GS) = \{x \in A_T^* \mid S \overset{*}{\underset{GS}{\Rightarrow}} x\}$.

31. $\diamond$ Prove that for every grammar G there exists a g-system GS whose transducer has exactly one final state, distinct from its initial state, such that $L(G) = L(GS)$.
Hint. If $X_0 \ldots X_{n-1} \to \alpha$ is a production of the grammar, the subgraph of $\mathcal{T}$ that corresponds to this production is shown in Figure 4.1.

Elementary Properties of Context-Free Grammars

32. $\diamond$ Consider the context-free grammar

$$G = (\{S\}, \{a, b\}, S, \{S \to aS, S \to aSbS, S \to \lambda\})$$

Prove that $L(G)$ is the set of all words $x \in \{a, b\}^*$ such that for every prefix y of x, $n_a(y) \geq n_b(y)$.

33. $\diamond$ Prove that the context-free grammar
$$\begin{aligned} G &= (\{S\}, \{a, b, c\}, S, \{S \to SS, S \to \lambda, \\ &\quad S \to aSb, S \to bSa, S \to aSc, S \to cSa\}) \end{aligned}$$
generates the language $L = \{x \in \{a, b, c\}^* \mid n_a(x) = n_b(x) + n_c(x)\}$.
Hint. To prove that $L \subseteq L(G)$ one should examine the first and the last symbol of x.

34. $\diamond$ Let $A = \{a, b\}$ and let L be the language defined inductively as follows:
    - $ab \in L$ and $ba \in L$;
    - if $x \in L$, then both $axb \in L$ and $bxa \in L$;
    - if $x, y \in L$, then $xy \in L$.

    (a) Prove that

    $$L = \{x \in A^+ \mid n_a(x) = n_b(x)\}.$$

    In other words, show that the language defined in Example 4.5.3 can be defined inductively as above.

(b) Prove that $L = L(G)$, where $G = (\{S\}, A, S, P)$ is the context-free grammar defined by

$$P = \{S \to ab, S \to ba, S \to aSb, S \to bSa, S \to SS\}.$$

Note the correspondence between the productions of P and various parts of the inductive definition.

35. $\diamond$ Let $G = (A_N, A_T, S, P)$ be a context-free grammar and let $\alpha, \beta \in (A_N \cup A_T)^*$ be two words such that $|\alpha| > |\beta|$ and $\alpha \overset{*}{\underset{G}{\Rightarrow}} \beta$. Prove that α contains at least one nonterminal symbol X such that $X \overset{*}{\underset{G}{\Rightarrow}} \lambda$.
36. $\diamond$ Let $U_0^X, \ldots, U_n^X, \ldots$ be the sequence of sets of nonterminal symbols constructed in the proof of Theorem 4.5.9. Prove that there exists $i \in \mathbb{N}$ such that $U_i^X = U_{i+\ell}^X$ for $\ell \geq 1$.
37. Using the algorithm given in proof of Theorem 4.5.4 construct a context-free grammar G' such that $L(G') = L(G) - \{\lambda\}$, where G is one of the following context-free grammars:
    (a) $G = (\{S, X, Y, Z\}, \{a\}, S, \{S \to XYZ, X \to a, Y \to a, Z \to a, X \to \lambda, Y \to \lambda, Z \to \lambda\})$;
    (b) $G = (\{S, X\}, \{a, b\}, S, \{S \to aX, S \to bX, S \to a, X \to aX, X \to bXb, X \to \lambda\})$;
    (c) $G = (\{S, X, Y\}, \{a, b\}, S, \{S \to a, S \to aX, S \to Y, X \to aY, X \to \lambda, Y \to Xa\})$.
38. $\diamond$ Prove that for every context-free grammar $G = (A_N, A_T, S, P)$ and every integer $k \in \mathbb{N}$ there exists a grammar $G_k = (A_N, A_T, S, P_k)$ such that $L(G_k) = L(G) - \{x \in A_T^* \mid |x| \leq k\}$ and $X \to \alpha \in P_k$ implies $|\alpha| > k$.
39. $\diamond$ Using the algorithm given in proof of Theorem 4.5.9 construct a context-free grammar that contains no chain productions and is equivalent to the context free grammar G given by:
    (a) $G = (\{S, X, Y, Z\}, \{a\}, S, \{S \to X, X \to Y, Y \to Z, Z \to S, Y \to aa\})$;
    (b) $G = (\{S, X, Y\}, \{a, b\}, S, \{S \to Xa, S \to Ya, S \to Y, X \to Aa, X \to \lambda, Y \to YY, Y \to \lambda\})$;
    (c) $G = (\{S, X, Y, Z\}, \{a, b\}, S, \{S \to XY, S \to YZ, X \to YZ, X \to Y, Z \to X, X \to a, Y \to b\})$.
40. For each of the following context-free grammars find an equivalent reduced context-free grammar:
    (a) $G = (\{S, X, Y, Z\}, \{a, b, c\}, S, \{S \to SX, S \to YZ, X \to aa, Y \to b\})$;
    (b) $G = (\{S, X, Y, Z\}, \{a, b\}, S, \{S \to XX, X \to YY, Z \to XY, Y \to XX, Y \to a, Z \to b\})$;
    (c) $G = (\{S, X, Y, Z\}, \{a, b\}, S, \{S \to YY, S \to XX, S \to XY, X \to aY, Y \to a, Z \to b\})$.

Regular Languages and Type-3 Grammars

41. $^{\circ\circ}$ Let A be an alphabet and let $L \subseteq A^*$. Prove that L is a linear language if and only if there exist an alphabet B, a regular language $R \subseteq B^*$ and two morphisms $h, h' : B^* \longrightarrow A^*$ such that $L = \{h(w)h'(w^R) \mid w \in R\}$.
42. $^{\circ}$ Let A be an alphabet and let c be a symbol such that $c \notin A$. Prove that if L is a regular language, then the set $\{xcx^R \mid x \in L\}$ is a linear context-free language.
Hint. Let $\mathcal{M} = (A, Q, \delta, q_0, F)$ be a dfa such that $L(\mathcal{M}) = L$. Prove that $L = L(G)$, where $G = (Q, A \cup \{c\}, q_0, P)$ is a grammar whose productions have either the form $q \to a\delta(q,a)a$ for $q \in Q$ and $a \in A$, or $q \to c$ if $q \in F$.

A context-free grammar $G = (A_N, A_T, S, P)$ is *k-linear* if each production in P is of one of forms: $X \to uYv$, $X \to w$, or $S \to \alpha$, where $u, v, w \in A_T^*$, $\alpha \in (A_N \cup A_T)^*$ and α contains at most k nonterminal symbols. In addition, there is no production in P of the form $X \to \gamma S \gamma'$.

A language is *k-linear* if it is generated by a k-linear grammar. L is a *metalinear language* if it is a k-linear language for some $k \in \mathbb{P}$.

Clearly, every 1-linear grammar is linear.

43. Prove that a language is linear if and only if it is an 1-linear language.
44. $^{\circ}$ Let $A = \{a, b\}$ be an alphabet. Prove that the language
$$L = \{a^{i_0}b^{i_0}a^{i_1}b^{i_1}\cdots a^{i_{k-1}}b^{i_{k-1}} \mid i_0, i_1, \ldots, i_{k-1} \in \mathbb{N}\}$$
is k-linear.
45. $^{\circ}$ Prove that the class of metalinear languages is closed with respect to union and product.
46. $^{\circ\circ}$ Prove that L is a metalinear language if and only if $L = L_0 \cup \cdots \cup L_{m-1}$, where L_i is a product of linear languages.
47. $^{\circ}$ Prove that the class of linear languages coincides with the class of languages that can be generated by simple contextual grammars.
48. Show that the Szilard language of the context-free grammar
$$G = (\{S\}, \{a, b\}, S, \{S \to \lambda, S \to aSb\})$$
introduced in Example 4.3.10 is regular.
49. $^{\circ}$ Let $G = (\{S, X, Y\}, \{a\}, S, P)$ be a context-free grammar having the set of productions:
$$\pi_0 \ : \ S \to XSY$$
$$\pi_1 \ : \ S \to a$$
$$\pi_2 \ : \ X \to \lambda$$
$$\pi_3 \ : \ Y \to \lambda$$
Show that the Szilard language $\mathsf{Sz}(G)$ is not context-free.
50. $^{\circ\circ}$ Prove that the Szilard language of any type-3 grammar is regular.

4.8 Bibliographical Comments

Chomsky's hierarchy was introduced in [Chomsky, 1956] and [Chomsky, 1959].

Supplement 13 appears in [Salomaa, 1973]. Exercises 38 and 42 appear in [Ginsburg, 1966]. Exercise 41 originates in [Chomsky and Schützenberger, 1963], while Exercise 7 is a modification of a similar problem in [Davis *et al.*, 1994]. Leftmost derivations for type 0 grammars are treated in [Révész, 1983]. Exercise 18 is a generalization of an exercise from [McNaughton, 1982]. The result contained by Exercise 11 belongs to [Book, 1972].

Contextual grammars were introduced in [Marcus, 1969] in relation to the study of natural languages. Detailed studies of these grammars can be found in [Păun, 1982] and [Ehrenfeucht *et al.*, 1997].

The result contained in Exercise 30 was obtained in [Baker, 1972]. An excellent and detailed presentation can be found in [Harrison, 1978].

Szilard languages are studied in [Moriya, 1973] and in [Igarashi, 1977]. The notion of g-system was introduced by B. Rovan in [1981].

Chapter 5

Context-Free Languages

5.1 Introduction

The context-free languages were initially introduced to provide a model of natural languages. They have proven equally useful in the area of programming languages. The most popular definition mechanism for the syntax of programming languages, namely the Backus-Naur definitions, are in essence, context-free grammars.

In this chapter we discuss derivation trees as tools for describing generation of words in context-free grammars. We then show that context-free grammars can be regarded as systems of equations whose unknowns range over languages, a point of view that helps relate these grammars to Backus-Naur definitions of syntactic notions in programming languages. This point of view is used in presenting the Greibach normal form for context-free grammars.

We discuss specific closure and non-closure properties for the class $\mathcal{L}_2$ of context-free languages, as well as the relationship between regular and context-free languages. A section of special interest for programming languages is dedicated to ambiguity phenomenon. We conclude this chapter with a study of the symbol distribution in context-free languages and with a well-known representation result for context-free languages known as the Chomsky-Schützenberger

Theorem.

5.2 Derivations and Derivation Trees

Leftmost derivations introduced for arbitrary grammars in Definition 4.3.21 are especially important for context-free grammars. As we shall see in this section, in the case of context-free grammars, for every completed derivation there exists a leftmost completed derivation that generates the same terminal word.

For context-free grammars, the definition of leftmost derivations is formulated in a form that is stronger than for general grammars.

Definition 5.2.1 Let $G = (A_N, A_T, S, P)$ be a context-free grammar. A *leftmost derivation* is a derivation $\gamma_0 \Rightarrow \cdots \Rightarrow \gamma_n$ in G such that, if the production applied in deriving γ_{k+1} from γ_k is $X_k \rightarrow \beta_k$, then $\gamma_k = \gamma'_k X_k \gamma''_k$, $\gamma_{k+1} = \gamma'_k \beta_k \gamma''_k$ and $\gamma'_k \in A_T^*$.

The words γ_k (for $0 \leq k \leq n$) are referred to as *left sentential forms.* If $\gamma_k = \gamma'_k X_k \gamma''_k$, where $\gamma'_k \in A_T^*$, then γ'_k is the *closed part* of γ_k, while $X_k \gamma''_k$ is the *open part* of γ_k. □

Note that no rewriting can take place in γ'_k since this word does not contain a nonterminal symbol. Therefore, $|\gamma'_k| < |\gamma_{k+1} X_{k+1}|$, and this implies that every leftmost derivation in a context-free grammar is a leftmost derivation in the sense of Definition 4.3.21. Thus, in a context-free grammar G,

$$\gamma_0 \Rightarrow \gamma_1 \Rightarrow \ldots \Rightarrow \gamma_n$$

is a leftmost derivation if, at every step of this derivation, we always rewrite the leftmost nonterminal symbol.

As in arbitrary grammars, the existence of a leftmost derivation of length n in the context-free grammar G, $\gamma_0 \Rightarrow \gamma_1 \Rightarrow \ldots \Rightarrow \gamma_n$, will be denoted by $\gamma_0 \overset{n}{\underset{G,\text{left}}{\Rightarrow}} \gamma_n$. The existence of a leftmost derivation of any length of γ' from γ in the same grammar will be denoted by $\gamma \overset{*}{\underset{G,\text{left}}{\Rightarrow}} \gamma'$. The existence of a leftmost derivation of positive length of γ' from γ will be denoted by $\gamma \overset{+}{\underset{G,\text{left}}{\Rightarrow}} \gamma'$.

Example 5.2.2 Let G be the grammar introduced in Example 4.5.3. The derivation

$$\begin{array}{llll} S_0 & \Rightarrow bS_1 & \Rightarrow bbS_1S_1 & \Rightarrow bbS_1aS_0 \\ & \Rightarrow bbS_1aaS_2 & \Rightarrow bbaaaS_2 & \Rightarrow bbaaab \end{array}$$

is not leftmost since in deriving bbS_1aaS_2 from bbS_1aS_0 we do not replace the leftmost nonterminal S_1. It is not difficult to see that we can transform this derivation into a leftmost derivation by changing the order in which nonterminals are replaced. Namely, in grammar G, we have the leftmost derivation

$$\begin{array}{ll} S_0 & \Rightarrow bS_1 \Rightarrow bbS_1S_1 \Rightarrow bbaS_1 \\ & \Rightarrow bbaaS_0 \Rightarrow bbaaaS_2 \Rightarrow bbaaab. \end{array}$$

□

Rightmost derivations in context-free grammars are defined in a similar manner.

Definition 5.2.3 Let $G = (A_N, A_T, S, P)$ be a context-free grammar. A *rightmost derivation* is a derivation $\gamma_0 \Rightarrow \cdots \Rightarrow \gamma_n$ in G such that, if the production applied in deriving γ_{k+1} from γ_k is $X_k \rightarrow \beta_k$, then $\gamma_k = \gamma'_k X_k \gamma''_k$, $\gamma_{k+1} = \gamma'_k \beta_k \gamma''_k$ and $\gamma''_k \in A_T^*$.

The words γ_k (for $0 \leq k \leq n$) are referred to as *right sentential forms.* If $\gamma_k = \gamma'_k X_k \gamma''_k$ is a right sentential form and $\gamma''_k \in A_T^*$ as above, then we refer to γ''_k as the *closed part* of γ_k; the word $\gamma'_k X_k$ is the *open part* of γ_k. □

The existence of a leftmost derivation of length n in the context-free grammar G, $\gamma_0 \Rightarrow \gamma_1 \Rightarrow \ldots \Rightarrow \gamma_n$, will be denoted by $\gamma_0 \overset{n}{\underset{G,\text{right}}{\Rightarrow}} \gamma_n$. The existence of a leftmost derivation of any length of γ' from γ in the same grammar will be denoted by $\gamma \overset{*}{\underset{G,\text{right}}{\Rightarrow}} \gamma'$. The existence of a leftmost derivation of positive length of γ' from γ will be denoted by $\gamma \overset{+}{\underset{G,\text{right}}{\Rightarrow}} \gamma'$.

Example 5.2.4 A rightmost derivation for the word $x = bbaaab$ in the grammar considered in Examples 4.5.3 and 5.2.2 is:

$$\begin{aligned} S_0 &\Rightarrow bS_1 \Rightarrow bbS_1S_1 \Rightarrow bbS_1aS_0 \\ &\Rightarrow bbS_1aaS_2 \Rightarrow bbS_1aab \Rightarrow bbaaab. \end{aligned}$$

□

Theorem 5.2.5 *Let $G = (A_N, A_T, S, P)$ be a context-free grammar. For every complete derivation d of length n in G, $X \Rightarrow \gamma_1 \Rightarrow \cdots \Rightarrow \gamma_n$, where $\gamma_n = u \in A_T^*$, there is a complete leftmost (rightmost) derivation of length n, using the same productions as d, that allows us to derive γ_n from X.*

Proof. The argument is by strong induction on $n \geq 1$ for leftmost derivations. The discussion for rightmost derivation is entirely similar and is left to the reader.

For $n = 1$, the statement is trivially true, since any derivation $X \Rightarrow w_1$ is a leftmost derivation.

Suppose that the statement holds for derivations whose length is no more than n, and let d

$$X \Rightarrow \gamma_1 \Rightarrow \cdots \Rightarrow \gamma_{n+1}$$

be a derivation of length $n + 1$. If the first production used in this derivation is $X \rightarrow w_0 X_{i_1} w_1 \cdots X_{i_k} w_k$, where $w_i \in A_T^*$ for $0 \leq i \leq k$, then we can write $\gamma_{n+1} = w_0 u_1 w_1 \cdots u_k w_k$, where d_j is a complete derivation $X_{i_j} \overset{*}{\underset{G}{\Rightarrow}} u_j$ of length no greater than n, for $1 \leq j \leq k$. By the inductive hypothesis, for each of these derivations d_j, we obtain the existence of the leftmost derivation d'_j: $X_{i_j} \overset{*}{\underset{G,\text{left}}{\Rightarrow}} u_j$ for $1 \leq j \leq k$, which uses the same set of productions as d_j. Now, we obtain the existence of the leftmost derivation d':

$$\begin{array}{lll} X & \Rightarrow & w_0 X_{i_1} w_1 X_{i_2} \ldots X_{i_k} w_k \\ & \stackrel{*}{\Rightarrow} & w_0 u_1 w_1 X_{i_2} \ldots X_{i_k} w_k \text{ (using derivation } d'_1) \\ & \stackrel{*}{\Rightarrow} & w_0 u_1 w_1 u_2 \ldots X_{i_k} w_k \text{ (using derivation } d'_2) \\ & \vdots & \\ & \stackrel{*}{\Rightarrow} & w_0 u_1 w_1 u_2 \ldots u_k w_k \text{ (using derivation } d'_k), \end{array}$$

which concludes our argument. ∎

The next example shows that Theorem 5.2.5 may fail if the derivation is not complete, that is, the final word is not in A_T^*.

Example 5.2.6 Let

$$\begin{array}{rcl} G & = & (\{S, X, Y, U, V\}, \{a, b\}, S, \{S \rightarrow XY, Y \rightarrow UV, \\ & & X \rightarrow a, U \rightarrow b, V \rightarrow b\}) \end{array}$$

be a context-free grammar. Consider the derivation

$$S \Rightarrow XY \Rightarrow XUV$$

This derivation is not leftmost, and there is no leftmost derivation in G such that $S \stackrel{*}{\underset{G}{\Rightarrow}} XUV$. □

Corollary 5.2.7 *Let $G = (A_N, A_T, S, P)$ be a context-free grammar. For every complete derivation d of length n in G, $\gamma_0 \Rightarrow \gamma_1 \Rightarrow \cdots \Rightarrow \gamma_n$, where $\gamma_0 \in (A_N \cup A_T)^+$ and $\gamma_n \in A_T^*$, there is a complete leftmost (rightmost) derivation of length n, using the same productions as d, that allows us to derive γ_n from γ_0.*

Proof. Suppose that $\gamma_0 = s_0 \ldots s_{k-1}$, where $s_i \in A_N \cup A_T$ for $0 \leq i \leq k-1$. By Theorem 4.5.1 we can write $\gamma_n = u_0 \cdots u_{k-1}$ such that $s_i \stackrel{*}{\underset{G}{\Rightarrow}} u_i \in A_T^*$ for $0 \leq i \leq k-1$. Theorem 5.2.5 implies the existence of the leftmost derivations $s_i \stackrel{*}{\underset{G,left}{\Rightarrow}} u_i$ for $0 \leq i \leq k-1$ that use the same productions as the corresponding previous derivations. Starting from these derivations we obtain the leftmost derivation:

$$\begin{array}{ll} \gamma_0 = s_0 s_1 \cdots s_{k-1} & \\ \stackrel{*}{\underset{G,left}{\Rightarrow}} & u_0 s_1 \cdots s_{k-1} \\ \stackrel{*}{\underset{G,left}{\Rightarrow}} & u_0 u_1 \cdots s_{k-1} \\ \vdots & \\ \stackrel{*}{\underset{G,left}{\Rightarrow}} & u_0 u_1 \cdots u_{k-1} = \gamma_n. \end{array}$$

The case of the rightmost derivations can be dealt with in a similar manner. ∎

Definition 5.2.8 A context-free grammar $G = (A_N, A_T, S, P)$ is *ambiguous* if there exists a word $w \in A_T^*$ such that there are at least two leftmost derivations from S to w in G. Otherwise, G is *unambiguous*. □

A context-free language can be generated by both ambiguous and unambiguous grammars, as the next Example shows.

Example 5.2.9 Consider the context-free grammars

$$G_1 = (\{S\}, \{a\}, S, \{S \to SS, S \to a\})$$

and

$$G_2 = (\{S\}, \{a\}, S, \{S \to aS, S \to a\}).$$

They both generate the language $\{a^n \mid n \geq 1\}$. Note that in G_1 we have distinct leftmost derivations:

$$\begin{array}{llll} S & \underset{G_1}{\Rightarrow} SS & \underset{G_1}{\Rightarrow} SSS & \underset{G_1}{\Rightarrow} aSS \\ & \underset{G_1}{\Rightarrow} aaS & \underset{G_1}{\Rightarrow} aaa & \end{array}$$

and

$$\begin{array}{llll} S & \underset{G_1}{\Rightarrow} SS & \underset{G_1}{\Rightarrow} aS & \underset{G_1}{\Rightarrow} aSS \\ & \underset{G_1}{\Rightarrow} aaS & \underset{G_1}{\Rightarrow} aaa. & \end{array}$$

Thus, G_1 is an ambiguous grammar.

On other hand, the equivalent grammar G_2 is unambiguous, since for every a^n, $n \leq 1$, we have exactly one derivation:

$$S \underset{G_2}{\Rightarrow} aS \underset{G_2}{\Rightarrow} a^2S \cdots \underset{G_2}{\Rightarrow} a^n.$$

□

Since a language may have both an ambiguous and an unambiguous grammar, it may not be sufficient to to examine one grammar to determine whether or not a language is ambiguous. This suggests the following definition.

Definition 5.2.10 Let L be a context-free language. L is *unambiguous* if there is an unambiguous context-free grammar G such that $L = L(G)$.

L is *inherently ambiguous* if every context-free grammar G such that $L(G) = L$ is ambiguous. □

Example 5.2.9 shows that the language $\{a^n \mid n \geq 1\}$ is unambiguous. We will show (in Theorem 5.8.1) the existence of inherently ambiguous context-free languages.

As an alternative to writing a sequence of derivation steps as we have done up to this point, we may describe context-free derivations using labeled ordered trees, so-called derivation trees.

The labels of the leaves of an A-labeled ordered tree, when read from left-to-right, spell out a word in A^*. This is made precise in the following definition. In this definition, we make use of the projection functions P_0 and P_1 to select the position as a child and the label of a node in the tree.

Definition 5.2.11 Let $\mathtt{T} = (G, v_0, M, \mathsf{m})$ be an A-labeled ordered tree. The *word spelled by* $\mathtt{T}$, written $\mathsf{word}(\mathtt{T})$, is defined by strong induction on the height of $\mathtt{T}$.

If $\text{height}(\mathtt{T}) = 0$, then $\text{word}(\mathtt{T}) = P_1(\text{m}(v_0))$.

Assume that for each A-labeled ordered tree T of height at most n, word(T) is defined. Assume that T has height $n+1$. Let $u_0, u_1, \ldots, u_{k-1}$ be the children of v_0, where $P_0(\text{m}(u_j)) = j$, for $0 \leq j \leq k-1$. Let $\mathtt{T}_j$ be the subtree of T rooted at u_j. Since $\text{height}(\mathtt{T}_j) < n+1$ for each $0 \leq j \leq k-1$, by the inductive hypothesis, $\text{word}(\mathtt{T}_j)$ is defined. Now, define $\text{word}(\mathtt{T}) = \text{word}(\mathtt{T}_0) \cdots \text{word}(\mathtt{T}_{k-1})$. □

Example 5.2.12 The tree T in Figure 1.7 spells the word $\text{word}(\mathtt{T}) = aacbabac$. □

Definition 5.2.13 Let $G = (A_N, A_T, S, P)$ be a λ-free context-free grammar, and let $d = (\gamma_0, \ldots, \gamma_m)$ be a derivation in G, where $\gamma_0 = X \in A_N$ and $\gamma_i \in (A_N \cup A_T)^*$ for $0 \leq i \leq m$. Let $A = A_N \cup A_T$.

The *derivation tree of the derivation* d is an A-labeled, ordered tree $\mathtt{T}_d$ defined inductively as follows:

(i) If $m = 0$, then $\mathtt{T}_d$ consists of only one node labeled by $(0, X)$.

(ii) Suppose that $m \geq 1$ and that $\gamma_1 = X_0 \ldots X_{n-1}$, where $X_0 \ldots X_{n-1} \in (A_N \cup A_T)^*$. Let $\mathtt{T}_i$ be the A-labeled ordered tree that corresponds to the derivation $(X_i, \ldots, \alpha_i)$ for $0 \leq i \leq n-1$, where $\alpha = \alpha_0 \cdots \alpha_{n-1}$. Then, $\mathtt{T}_d$ is $\langle \mathtt{T}_0, \ldots, \mathtt{T}_{n-1}; X \rangle$.

The *set of derivation trees of* G is the set

$$\text{TREES}(G) = \{\mathtt{T}_d \mid d \text{ is a derivation in } G\}.$$

A derivation tree $\mathtt{T}_d \in \text{TREES}(G)$ is *complete* if $\text{word}(\mathtt{T}_d) \in A_T^*$, i.e. if all its leaves are labeled by terminal symbols of the grammar. The set of complete derivation trees of G is denoted by $\text{TREES}_c(G)$. □

Example 5.2.14 Let

$$\begin{aligned} G &= (\{S, X, Y\}, \{a, b\}, S, \{S \rightarrow XY, S \rightarrow a, X \rightarrow YS, \\ &\qquad Y \rightarrow XS, X \rightarrow b, Y \rightarrow b\}) \end{aligned}$$

be a context-free grammar in Chomsky normal form. The derivation tree of

$$S \Rightarrow XY \Rightarrow YSY \Rightarrow YSXS \Rightarrow bSXS \Rightarrow baXS \Rightarrow babS \Rightarrow baba$$

is given in Figure 5.1.

□

Definition 5.2.13 shows that every derivation in a context-free grammar $G = (A_N, A_T, S, P)$ is described by a derivation tree. Conversely, if T is a derivation tree such that $\text{word}(\mathtt{T}) = x \in A_T^*$ then, in general, several distinct derivations exist for the word x.

Example 5.2.15 Consider the grammar

$$\begin{aligned} G &= (\{S, X, Y\}, \{a, b\}, S, \{S \rightarrow XY, S \rightarrow a, X \rightarrow YS, \\ &\qquad Y \rightarrow XS, X \rightarrow b, Y \rightarrow b\}) \end{aligned}$$

introduced in Example 5.2.14. In addition to the derivation given in Example 5.2.14, the derivation tree given in Figure 5.1 also describes the derivation

$$S \Rightarrow XY \Rightarrow XXS \Rightarrow XXa \Rightarrow YSXa \Rightarrow bSXa \Rightarrow baXa \Rightarrow baba$$

□

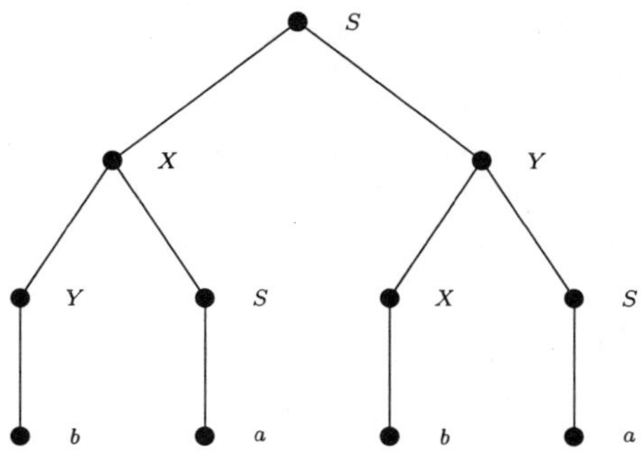

Figure 5.1: Derivation Tree

Theorem 5.2.16 *Let $G = (A_N, A_T, S, P)$ be a context-free grammar, and let $\mathtt{T} \in \mathsf{TREES}_c(G)$ be a complete derivation tree whose root is labeled by X, where the word spelled by $\mathtt{T}$, $\mathsf{word}(\mathtt{T}) = u \in A_T^*$. There is a unique leftmost (rightmost) derivation $X \overset{*}{\underset{G,left}{\Rightarrow}} u$. Moreover, the lengths of the leftmost and the rightmost derivations equal the number of internal nodes of $\mathtt{T}$.*

Proof. The argument for leftmost derivations is by induction on the height of $\mathtt{T}$. We leave to the reader the argument for rightmost derivations.

If $\mathsf{height}(\mathtt{T}) = 1$, then the derivation that corresponds to $\mathtt{T}$ is (X, u), which is an one-step leftmost derivation.

Suppose that the statement holds for complete derivation trees of height less than n, and let $\mathtt{T}$ be a complete derivation tree in G such that $\mathsf{height}(\mathtt{T}) = n$. Then, $\mathtt{T} = \langle \mathtt{T}_0, \ldots, \mathtt{T}_{k-1}; X\rangle$, where $\mathsf{height}(\mathtt{T}_i) < n$ for $0 \leq i \leq k-1$. Also, the root of $\mathtt{T}_i$ is labeled by the symbol $X_i \in A_N \cup A_T$ and its leaves are labeled by the terminal word u_i for $0 \leq i \leq k-1$, where $u_0 \cdots u_{k-1} = u$.

By the inductive hypothesis, for each of the trees $\mathtt{T}_i$, there is a unique leftmost derivation d_i:

$$X_i \Rightarrow w_{i0} \Rightarrow \cdots \Rightarrow w_{i\ell_i-1} = u_i$$

and the length of d_i is equal to the number of internal nodes of $\mathtt{T}_i$ for $0 \leq i \leq k-1$.

Then, we obtain the following leftmost derivation that corresponds to $\mathtt{T}$:

$$\begin{aligned}
X & \Rightarrow X_0 X_1 \cdots X_{k-1} \\
& \Rightarrow w_{00} X_1 \cdots X_{k-1} \Rightarrow \cdots \Rightarrow u_0 X_1 \cdots X_{k-1} \\
& \Rightarrow u_0 w_{10} \cdots X_{k-1} \Rightarrow \cdots \Rightarrow u_0 u_1 \cdots X_{k-1} \\
& \ \ \vdots \\
& \Rightarrow u_0 u_1 \cdots w_{k-1\,0} \Rightarrow \cdots \Rightarrow u_0 u_1 \cdots u_{k-1}.
\end{aligned}$$

If d is a leftmost derivation for T, then it must expand the nonterminals symbol $X_{i_0}, \ldots, X_{i_p}$ that occur in $X_0 \cdots X_{k-1}$. Thus, the derivation d must use the productions that occur in the leftmost derivations $d_{i_0}, \ldots, d_{i_{k-1}}$, respectively, in that order. This shows that the lefmost derivation is unique and the length of this derivation equals the number of internal nodes of T. ∎

Example 5.2.17 For the derivation tree considered in Figure 5.1 the derivations

$$\begin{aligned} S &\Rightarrow XY \Rightarrow YSY \Rightarrow bSY \Rightarrow \\ &baY \Rightarrow baXS \Rightarrow babS \Rightarrow baba \end{aligned}$$

and

$$\begin{aligned} &S \Rightarrow XY \Rightarrow XXS \Rightarrow XXa \Rightarrow Xba \\ &\Rightarrow YSba \Rightarrow Yaba \Rightarrow baba \end{aligned}$$

are the leftmost and the rightmost derivations, respectively. □

Representations of derivation trees for words generated by context-free grammars are built by compilers during that phase of the compilation process called *parsing* that determines the syntactic correctness of programs. These representations are introduced next.

Definition 5.2.18 Let $G = (A_N, A_T, S, P)$ be a context-free grammar and let $w \in L(G)$. A control word $\omega \in P^*$ is a *left parse* of w if $S \overset{*}{\underset{\omega}{\Rightarrow}} w$ is a leftmost derivation.

A control word $\omega \in P^*$ is a *right parse* of w if $S \overset{*}{\underset{\omega^R}{\Rightarrow}} w$ is a rightmost derivation. □

A left parse of a word w is associated with the construction of a derivation tree for w in a top-down manner, while a right parse is associated with the construction of a derivation tree for w in a bottom-up manner.

Example 5.2.19 Let

$$G_{ae} = (\{X_e, X_t, X_f\}, \{+, -, *, /, (,), \boldsymbol{v}, \boldsymbol{n}\}, X_e, P)$$

be the context-free grammar whose set of productions consists of

$$\begin{array}{ll} \pi_0 : X_e \to X_e + X_t & \pi_1 : X_e \to X_e - X_t \\ \pi_2 : X_e \to X_t & \pi_3 : X_t \to X_t * X_f \\ \pi_4 : X_t \to X_t / X_f & \pi_5 : X_t \to X_f \\ \pi_6 : X_f \to \boldsymbol{v} & \pi_7 : X_f \to \boldsymbol{n} \\ \pi_8 : X_f \to (X_e) & \end{array}$$

The control word $\omega_l = \pi_0\pi_2\pi_5\pi_7\pi_3\pi_5\pi_7\pi_7$ is a left parse of the word $w = \boldsymbol{n}+\boldsymbol{n}*\boldsymbol{n}$ since

$$\begin{aligned} X_e \underset{\pi_0}{\Rightarrow} & X_e + X_t \underset{\pi_2}{\Rightarrow} X_t + X_t \underset{\pi_5}{\Rightarrow} X_f + X_t \underset{\pi_7}{\Rightarrow} \boldsymbol{n} + X_t \\ & \underset{\pi_3}{\Rightarrow} \boldsymbol{n} + X_t * X_f \underset{\pi_5}{\Rightarrow} \boldsymbol{n} + X_f * X_f \underset{\pi_7}{\Rightarrow} \boldsymbol{n} + \boldsymbol{n} * X_f \\ & \underset{\pi_7}{\Rightarrow} \boldsymbol{n} + \boldsymbol{n} * \boldsymbol{n} \end{aligned}$$

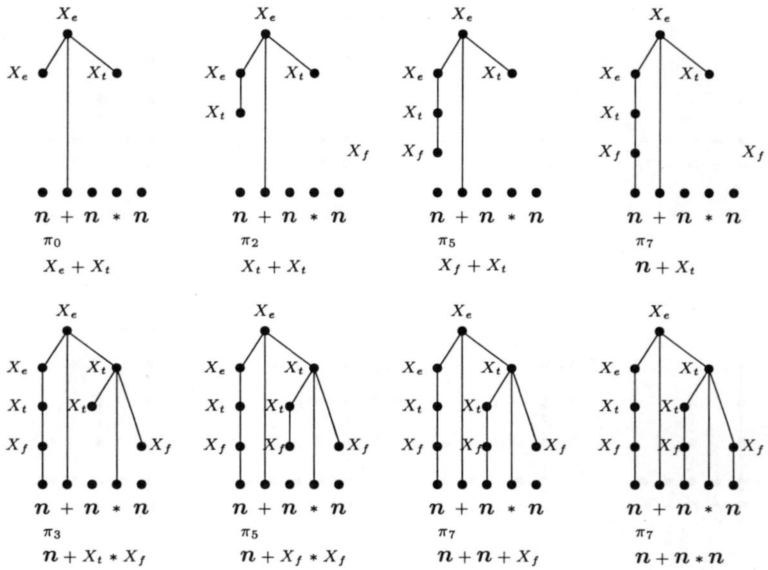

Figure 5.2: Top-down Construction of a Derivation Tree

is a leftmost derivation of w. The phases of the top-down construction of the derivation tree for w are shown in Figure 5.2.

The control word $\omega_r = \pi_7\pi_5\pi_2\pi_7\pi_5\pi_7\pi_3\pi_0$ is a right parse of the word $w = \boldsymbol{n} + \boldsymbol{n} * \boldsymbol{n}$ since

$$\begin{aligned} X_e \underset{\pi_0}{\Rightarrow} \; & X_e + X_t \underset{\pi_3}{\Rightarrow} X_e + X_t * X_f \underset{\pi_7}{\Rightarrow} X_e + X_t * \boldsymbol{n} \\ & \underset{\pi_5}{\Rightarrow} X_e + X_f * \boldsymbol{n} \underset{\pi_7}{\Rightarrow} X_e + \boldsymbol{n} * \boldsymbol{n} \underset{\pi_2}{\Rightarrow} X_t + \boldsymbol{n} * \boldsymbol{n} \\ & \underset{\pi_5}{\Rightarrow} X_f + \boldsymbol{n} * \boldsymbol{n} \underset{\pi_7}{\Rightarrow} \boldsymbol{n} + \boldsymbol{n} * \boldsymbol{n} \end{aligned}$$

is a rightmost derivation for w. The phases of the bottom-up construction of the derivation tree for w are shown in Figure 5.3. □

In general, if G is a context-free grammar and $x \in L(G)$, several distinct derivation trees may exist for x. In some cases, a considerable number of such distinct trees may exist. Using some elementary considerations, the next example shows a grammar that provides an exponential number of derivation trees for the words in its language.

Example 5.2.20 Let $G = (\{S\}, \{a\}, S, \{S \to SS, S \to a\})$ be a context-free grammar. It is not difficult to see that the language generated by G is $D(G) = \{a^m \mid m \geq 1\}$. Denote by $C(n)$ the number of derivation trees that describe

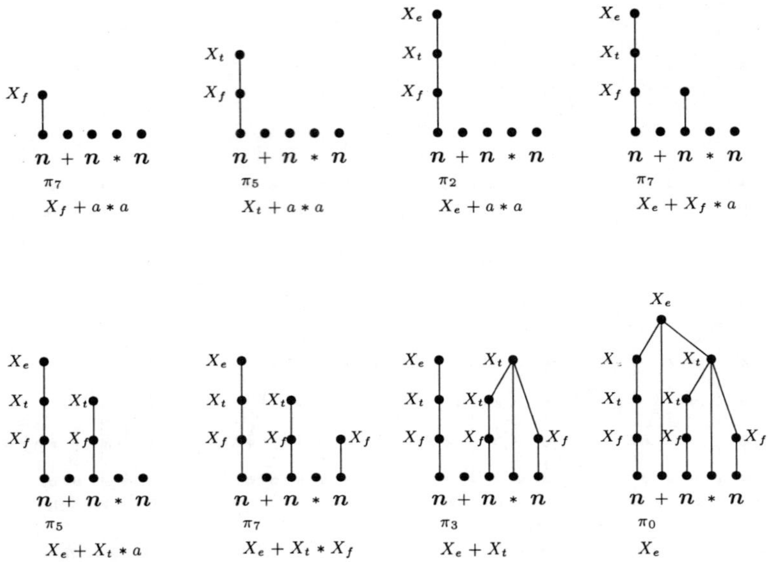

Figure 5.3: Bottom-up Construction of a Derivation Tree

derivations of the form $S \overset{*}{\underset{G}{\Rightarrow}} a^{n+1}$. We have $C(0) = 1$, and

$$C(n) = \sum_{j=0}^{n-1} C(j)C(n-1-j), \tag{5.1}$$

for $n \geq 1$. Indeed, if $n = 0$, there is only one derivation tree for the derivation $S \Rightarrow a$. For $n > 0$, the word a^{n+1} can be derived in two parts as shown in Figure 5.4.

Suppose that there exist $C(k)$ derivation trees that describe derivations of the form $S \overset{*}{\underset{G}{\Rightarrow}} a^{k+1}$ for $k < n$. Consider the derivation trees T and T′ that describe the derivations $S \overset{*}{\underset{G}{\Rightarrow}} a^{j+1}$ and $S \overset{*}{\underset{G}{\Rightarrow}} a^{n-j}$, respectively. Combining the trees T and T′ as shown in Figure 5.4 we obtain a derivation tree that describes a derivation $S \overset{*}{\underset{G}{\Rightarrow}} a^{n+1}$. This justifies the recurrence (5.1). The following analysis uses this recurrence to show that there are an exponential number of derivation trees in this grammar for a word a^n.

Consider the formal series $f(z) = C(0) + C(1)z + \cdots + C(n)z^n + \cdots$. We

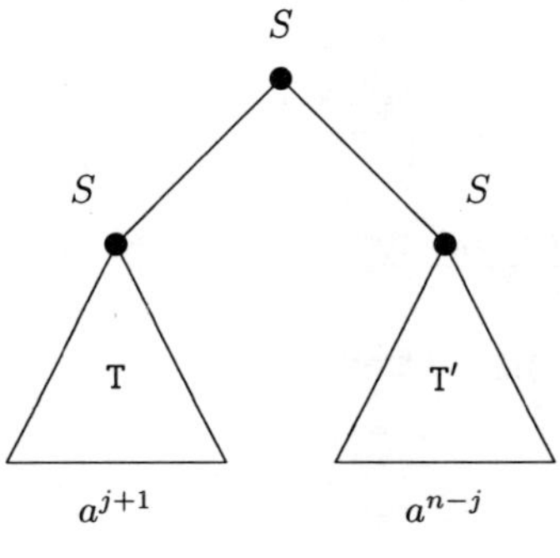

Figure 5.4: Derivation Tree Obtained from T and T'

have

$$\begin{aligned}
1 + zf^2(z) &= 1 + z\left(\sum_{j\geq 0} C(j)z^j\right)\left(\sum_{k\geq 0} C(k)z^k\right) \\
&= 1 + z\sum_{n\geq 1}\left(\sum_{\ell=0}^{n-1} C(\ell)C(n-1-\ell)\right) z^{n-1} \\
&= 1 + \sum_{n\geq 1}\left(\sum_{\ell=0}^{n-1} C(\ell)C(n-1-\ell)\right) z^{n} \\
&= C(0) + \sum_{n\geq 1} C(n)z^n \\
&= f(z).
\end{aligned}$$

Solving the quadratic equation $zf^2(z) - f(z) + 1 = 0$, we have:

$$2zf(z) = 1 \pm \sqrt{1-4z}$$

Note that $\lim_{z\to 0} 2zf(z) = 0$. This means that we need to take the solution with a minus sign, so

$$f(z) = \frac{1-\sqrt{1-4z}}{2z}$$

Using the binomial expansion with exponent $\frac{1}{2}$ we expand $\sqrt{1-4z}$ and we obtain:

$$\begin{aligned}
f(z) &= \frac{1}{2z}\left(1 - \sum_{k\geq 0} \frac{\frac{1}{2}(\frac{1}{2}-1)\cdots(\frac{1}{2}-k+1)}{k!}(-4z)^k\right) \\
&= \frac{1}{2z}\sum_{k\geq 1} \frac{1\cdot 3\cdots(2k-3)2^k z^k}{k!} \\
&= \sum_{k\geq 1} \frac{1\cdot 3\cdots(2k-3)2^{k-1} z^{k-1}}{k!} \\
&= \sum_{n\geq 0} \frac{1\cdot 3\cdots(2n-1)2^n z^n}{(n+1)!} \\
&= \sum_{n\geq 0} \frac{1}{n+1}\frac{1\cdot 2\cdots 2n}{(n!)^2} z^n \\
&= \frac{1}{n+1}\binom{2n}{n} z^n.
\end{aligned}$$

Therefore, $C(n) = \frac{1}{n+1}\binom{2n}{n}$ for $n \geq 0$. Using Stirling's formula,

$$n! = \sqrt{2\pi n}\left(\frac{n}{e}\right)^n O(1 + \frac{1}{n})$$

we obtain

$$C(n) = \Theta\left(\frac{4^n}{n^{1.5}}\right),$$

which shows that the number of derivation trees for a^{n+1} grows exponentially with n.[1] □

Another useful notion related to derivations in context-free grammars is introduced next.

Definition 5.2.21 Let $G = (A_N, A_T, S, P)$ be a context-free grammar and let $x \in L(G)$. A *phrase of x in G* is a word $v \in A_T^*$ such that

$$S \overset{*}{\underset{G}{\Rightarrow}} uXw \overset{*}{\underset{G}{\Rightarrow}} uvw = x.$$

The set of phrases of a word x in a context-free grammar G is denoted by $\mathsf{PHRASES}(x, G)$. □

Theorem 5.2.22 *If $G = (A_N, A_T, S, P)$ is an unambiguous context-free grammar, $x \in L(G)$, and $x_{i,j}, x_{p,q} \in \mathsf{PHRASES}(x, G)$, one of the following four cases must occur:*

(i) $i \leq j \leq p \leq q$,
(ii) $i \leq p \leq q \leq j$,
(iii) $p \leq i \leq j \leq q$, *or*

[1] For a function $f : \mathbb{N} \longrightarrow \mathbb{N}$ we denote by $\Theta(f(n))$ the set of functions g for which there exist $c, c' \in \mathbb{R}$ and $n_0 \in \mathbb{N}$ such that $n \geq n_0$ implies $cg(n) \leq f(n) \leq c'g(n)$.

(iv) $p \leq q \leq i \leq j$.

Proof. Since G is unambiguous, there is a unique leftmost derivation for x:

$$S \underset{G}{\Rightarrow} \alpha_1 \underset{G}{\Rightarrow} \cdots \underset{G}{\Rightarrow} \alpha_{n-1} \underset{G}{\Rightarrow} x.$$

Then, since $x_{i,j} \in \mathsf{PHRASES}(x, G)$, there is $k \in \mathbb{N}$ such that $S \overset{*}{\underset{G,\text{left}}{\Rightarrow}} \alpha_k = t_k X \beta_k$ and $X \overset{*}{\underset{G,\text{left}}{\Rightarrow}} x_{i,j}$, where $1 \leq k \leq n-1$, and $t_k \in A_T^*$. Similarly, there exists $\ell \in \mathbb{N}$, $1 \leq \ell \leq n-1$, such that $S \overset{*}{\underset{G,\text{left}}{\Rightarrow}} \alpha_\ell = t_\ell Y \beta_\ell$ and $Y \overset{*}{\underset{G,\text{left}}{\Rightarrow}} x_{p,q}$.

If $k = \ell$, we have $X = Y$ and $i = p$, $j = q$, which fits in the second or third case. Suppose, therefore, that $k < \ell$. Since $\alpha_k = t_k X \beta_k \overset{*}{\underset{G,\text{left}}{\Rightarrow}} t_\ell Y \beta_\ell = \alpha_\ell$ is a leftmost derivation, it follows that one of the following two cases may occur:

1. $X \overset{*}{\underset{G,\text{left}}{\Rightarrow}} wY\gamma$ for some $w \in A_T^*$ and $\gamma \in (A_N \cup A_T)^*$, or
2. $\beta_k \overset{*}{\underset{G,\text{left}}{\Rightarrow}} w'Y\gamma'$ for some $w' \in A_T^*$ and $\gamma' \in (A_N \cup A_T)^*$.

In the first case we have

$$X \overset{*}{\underset{G,\text{left}}{\Rightarrow}} wY\gamma \overset{*}{\underset{G,\text{left}}{\Rightarrow}} wx_{p,q}\gamma \overset{*}{\underset{G,\text{left}}{\Rightarrow}} x_{i,j},$$

so $i \leq p \leq q \leq j$. In the second case,

$$\begin{aligned} S &\overset{*}{\underset{G,\text{left}}{\Rightarrow}} t_k X \beta_k \overset{*}{\underset{G,\text{left}}{\Rightarrow}} t_k x_{i,j} \beta_k \\ &\overset{*}{\underset{G,\text{left}}{\Rightarrow}} t_k x_{i,j} w' Y \gamma' \overset{*}{\underset{G,\text{left}}{\Rightarrow}} t_k x_{i,j} w' x_{p,q} \gamma' \overset{*}{\underset{G,\text{left}}{\Rightarrow}} x, \end{aligned}$$

which shows that $i \leq j \leq p \leq q$.

If $\ell < k$ the argument is entirely similar to the case when $k < \ell$ but with the roles of (i, j) and (p, q) reversed. ∎

Using Definition 2.2.6, we can reformulate Theorem 5.2.22 as follows. If $x \in L(G)$, where G is an unambiguous context-free grammar, and $x_{i,j}, x_{p,q} \in \mathsf{PHRASES}(x, G)$, then either $x_{i,j}$ is an infix of $x_{p,q}$, or $x_{p,q}$ is an infix of $x_{i,j}$, or $x_{i,j}$ and $x_{p,q}$ are disjoint infixes of x. In other words, in an unambiguous grammar G, no word in $L(G)$ may contain overlapping phrases.

5.3 Fixed-Points and Context-Free Languages

In this section we present the link between fixed points of finitary polynomial functions (introduced in Section 2.6) and context-free languages. We show that a language is context-free if and only if it is a component of a fixed point of a finitary polynomial function. This classic result is due to Ginsburg and Rice [1962].

Consider a definition of arithmetic expressions (written in Backus-Naur style) that is shared by many programming languages:

⟨arith-expression⟩	=	⟨arith-expression⟩ + ⟨term⟩ |
		⟨arith-expression⟩ − ⟨term⟩ | ⟨term⟩
⟨term⟩	=	⟨term⟩ ∗ ⟨factor⟩ | ⟨term⟩ / ⟨factor⟩ | ⟨factor⟩
⟨factor⟩	=	⟨variable⟩ | ⟨number⟩ | (⟨arith-expression⟩)

Let $L_{ae}, L_{term}, L_{factor}$ be the language of arithmetic expressions, the language of terms, and the language of factors, respectively. If L_v is the language of variables and L_n is the language of constants[2], then the Backus-Naur definition of arithmetic expressions can be written as:

$$\begin{aligned} L_{ae} &= L_{ae} + L_{term} \cup L_{ae} - L_{term} \cup L_{term} \\ L_{term} &= L_{term} * L_{factor} \cup L_{term}/L_{factor} \cup L_{factor} \\ L_{factor} &= L_v \cup L_n \cup (L_{ae}) \end{aligned}$$

The previous equalities can be regarded as a system of equations:

$$\begin{aligned} L_{ae} &= f_0(L_{ae}, L_{term}, L_{factor}) \\ L_{term} &= f_1(L_{ae}, L_{term}, L_{factor}) \\ L_{factor} &= f_2(L_{ae}, L_{term}, L_{factor}), \end{aligned}$$

where f_0, f_1, f_2 are the components of $\vec{f} : (\mathcal{P}(A^*))^3 \longrightarrow (\mathcal{P}(A^*))^3$ which is a finitary polynomial function. These components are given by:

$$\begin{aligned} f_0(L_{ae}, L_{term}, L_{factor}) &= L_{ae} + L_{term} \cup L_{ae} - L_{term} \cup L_{term} \\ f_1(L_{ae}, L_{term}, L_{factor}) &= L_{term} * L_{factor} \cup L_{term}/L_{factor} \cup L_{factor} \\ f_2(L_{ae}, L_{term}, L_{factor}) &= L_v \cup L_n \cup (L_{ae}). \end{aligned}$$

By Theorem 2.6.10 the least fixed point of $\vec{f}$ is obtained as $\bigcup_{i\in\mathbb{N}} \vec{f}^{(i)}(\emptyset)$. The initial approximations are given by:

$$\begin{aligned} L_0^0 &= f_0(\emptyset, \emptyset, \emptyset) = \emptyset \\ L_1^0 &= f_1(\emptyset, \emptyset, \emptyset) = \emptyset \\ L_2^0 &= f_2(\emptyset, \emptyset, \emptyset) = L_v \cup L_n \\ L_0^1 &= f_0(L_0^0, L_1^0, L_2^0) = \emptyset \\ L_1^1 &= f_1(L_0^0, L_1^0, L_2^0) = L_v \cup L_n \\ L_2^1 &= f_2(L_0^0, L_1^0, L_2^0) = L_v \cup L_n \\ L_0^2 &= f_0(L_0^1, L_1^1, L_2^1) = L_v \cup L_n \\ L_1^2 &= f_1(L_0^1, L_1^1, L_2^1) \\ &= (L_v \cup L_n) * (L_v \cup L_n) \cup (L_v \cup L_n)/(L_v \cup L_n) \cup L_v \cup L_n \\ L_2^2 &= f_2(L_0^1, L_1^1, L_2^1) = L_v \cup L_n \\ &\vdots \end{aligned}$$

To relate the least fixed points of finitary polynomial functions to context-free grammars we need the next defintion.

Definition 5.3.1 Let $\vec{f} : (\mathcal{P}(A^*))^n \longrightarrow (\mathcal{P}(A^*))^n$ be a finitary polynomial function and let

$$f_i(\boldsymbol{X}) = \bigcup_{j=0}^{\ell_i - 1} t_{ij}(\boldsymbol{X})$$

be the term expressions of each of its components $f_0, \ldots, f_{n-1}$. Here ℓ_i is the number of terms of the f_i component of f for $0 \le i \le n-1$.

[2] L_v and L_n are usually expressed as regular languages, but because of implementation restrictions they are actually finite. For our purposes here, this latter characterization is more convenient; it simplifies and focuses the discussion.

The *context-free grammars associated with the finitary polynomial function* $\vec{f}$ are the grammars $G_j = (A_X, A, X_j, P)$, where the set of productions P consists of all productions of the form $X_j \to t_{ij}$ for $0 \leq j \leq \ell_i - 1$ and $0 \leq i \leq n-1$. □

Note that we use the notion of term in two ways: as an n-ary finitary polynomial function, and also as a word over $A_X \cup A$, where $A_X = \{X_0, \ldots, X_{n-1}\}$ is an alphabet disjoint from A called the *alphabet of the variables.*

Example 5.3.2 In order to simplify this example suppose that $L_v = \{\boldsymbol{v}\}$ and $L_n = \{\boldsymbol{n}\}$. Consider the finitary polynomial function $\vec{f} : (\mathcal{P}(A^*))^3 \longrightarrow (\mathcal{P}(A^*))^3$ introduced above. We prefer to write the components of this function as

$$\begin{aligned} f_0(X_e, X_t, X_f) &= X_e + X_t \cup X_e - X_t \cup X_t \\ f_1(X_e, X_t, X_f) &= X_t * X_f \cup X_t / X_f \cup X_f \\ f_2(X_e, X_t, X_f) &= \{\boldsymbol{v}, \boldsymbol{n}\} \cup (X_e). \end{aligned}$$

in order to be closer to the notations used in Definition 5.3.1. The grammars associate with the components of the function $\vec{f}$ share the set of productions P that consists of the following:

$$\begin{aligned} &\pi_0 : X_e \to X_e + X_t, \pi_1 : X_e \to X_e - X_t, \pi_2 : X_e \to X_t, \\ &\pi_3 : X_t \to X_t * X_f, \pi_4 : X_t \to X_t / X_f, \pi_5 : X_t \to X_f \\ &\pi_6 : X_f \to \boldsymbol{v}, \pi_7 : X_f \to \boldsymbol{n}, \pi_8 : X_f \to (X_e). \end{aligned}$$

The three grammars are:

$$\begin{aligned} G_0 &= (\{X_e, X_t, X_f\}, \{+, -, *, /, (,), \boldsymbol{v}, \boldsymbol{n}\}, X_e, P) \\ G_1 &= (\{X_e, X_t, X_f\}, \{+, -, *, /, (,), \boldsymbol{v}, \boldsymbol{n}\}, X_t, P) \\ G_2 &= (\{X_e, X_t, X_f\}, \{+, -, *, /, (,), \boldsymbol{v}, \boldsymbol{n}\}, X_f, P) \end{aligned}$$

In the sequel we refer to G_0 as the grammar of arithmetic expressions; this grammar was denoted by G_{ae} in Example 5.2.19. □

We discuss the connection between the least fixed point of $\vec{f}$ and the languages generated by the grammars G_i, where $0 \leq i \leq n-1$.

Theorem 5.3.3 (Ginsburg-Rice Theorem) *The least fixed point of* $\vec{f}$ *is the* n*-tuple of context-free languages* $\boldsymbol{L}$*, where* $L_j = L(G_j)$ *for* $0 \leq j \leq n-1$.

Proof. We begin by proving that $\mathtt{lfp}(\vec{f}) \subseteq \boldsymbol{L}$, that is, $(\mathtt{lfp}(\vec{f}))_j \subseteq L(G_j)$. Since $(\mathtt{lfp}(\vec{f}))_j = \bigcup_{i \in \mathbb{N}} (\vec{f}^{(i)}(\emptyset))_j$, it suffices to show that

$$(\vec{f}^{(i)}(\emptyset))_j \subseteq L(G_j)$$

for every $i \in \mathbb{N}$ and j, $0 \leq j \leq n-1$. The argument is by induction on i.

The basis step, $i = 0$, is immediate since $(\vec{f}^{(0)}(\emptyset))_j = \emptyset$. For the induction step, suppose that $(\vec{f}^{(i)}(\emptyset))_j \subseteq L(G_j)$ for every j, $0 \leq j \leq n-1$, and let $u \in (\vec{f}^{(i+1)}(\emptyset))_j$. This means that

$$u \in f_j((\vec{f}^{(i)}(\emptyset))_0, \ldots, (\vec{f}^{(i)}(\emptyset))_{n-1}).$$

There exists a term $t_{jk} = w_0 X_{q_0} w_1 \cdots w_{\ell-1} X_{q_{\ell-1}} w_\ell$, such that $w_0, \ldots, w_\ell \in A^*$, $u = w_0 u_0 w_1 \cdots w_{\ell-1} u_{\ell-1} w_\ell$, and

$$u_i \in (\vec{f}^{(i)}(\emptyset))_{q_i}$$

for $0 \leq i \leq \ell - 1$. Also, P contains the production

$$X_j \rightarrow w_0 X_{q_0} w_1 \cdots w_{\ell-1} X_{q_{\ell-1}} w_\ell.$$

By the inductive hypothesis, $u_i \in L(G_{q_i})$, so we have the derivations $X_{q_i} \overset{*}{\underset{G_{q_i}}{\Rightarrow}} u_i$ for $0 \leq i \leq \ell - 1$. This allows us to construct the derivation

$$\begin{aligned} X_j &\underset{G_j}{\Rightarrow} w_0 X_{q_0} w_1 \cdots w_{\ell-1} X_{q_{\ell-1}} w_\ell \\ &\overset{*}{\underset{G_j}{\Rightarrow}} w_0 u_0 w_1 \cdots w_{\ell-1} X_{q_{\ell-1}} w_\ell \\ &\vdots \\ &\overset{*}{\underset{G_j}{\Rightarrow}} w_0 u_0 w_1 \cdots w_{\ell-1} u_{\ell-1} w_\ell = u, \end{aligned}$$

so $u \in L(G_j)$, which gives the desired inclusion.

To prove the converse inclusion, $L(G_j) \subseteq (\mathtt{lfp}(\vec{f}))_j$, it suffices to show that if t, t' are two terms such that $t \overset{*}{\Rightarrow} t'$, then $t'(\mathtt{lfp}(\vec{f})) \subseteq t(\mathtt{lfp}(\vec{f}))$. Indeed, if this is the case, then $u \in L(G_j)$ implies $X_j \overset{*}{\Rightarrow} u$, so $u = u(\mathtt{lfp}(\vec{f})) \subseteq X_j(\mathtt{lfp}(\vec{f})) = (\mathtt{lfp}(\vec{f}))_j$.

So, suppose that we have $t \overset{n}{\Rightarrow} t'$. The argument is by induction on n. The basis step, $n = 0$ is immediate. Suppose that the statement holds for derivations of length less than n and that $t \overset{n}{\Rightarrow} t'$. If t'' is the next to the last term that appears in this derivation, then we can write

$$t'' = t_0 X_j t_1, t' = t_0 w t_1,$$

where the production $X_j \rightarrow w$ from R was applied in the last step of the derivation. Therefore,

$$\begin{aligned} f_{t''}(\mathtt{lfp}(\vec{f})) &= f_{t_0}(\mathtt{lfp}(\vec{f}))\,(\mathtt{lfp}(\vec{f}))_j\, f_{t_1}(\mathtt{lfp}(\vec{f})) \\ f_{t'}(\mathtt{lfp}(\vec{f})) &= f_{t_0}(\mathtt{lfp}(\vec{f}))\, f_w(\mathtt{lfp}(\vec{f}))\, f_{t_1}(\mathtt{lfp}(\vec{f})). \end{aligned}$$

Note that w is a term that enters the polynomial function f_j, so $f_j(\mathtt{lfp}(\vec{f})) \subseteq f_w(\mathtt{lfp}(\vec{f}))$. The definition of $\mathtt{lfp}(\vec{f})$ implies that $f_j(\mathtt{lfp}(\vec{f})) = (\mathtt{lfp}(\vec{f}))_j$, so $(\mathtt{lfp}(\vec{f}))_j \subseteq f_w(\mathtt{lfp}(\vec{f}))$. This, in turn, implies $f_{t''}(\mathtt{lfp}(\vec{f}) \subseteq f_{t'}(\mathtt{lfp}(\vec{f})$. The inductive hypothesis shows that $t(\mathtt{lfp}(\vec{f})) \subseteq t''(\mathtt{lfp}(\vec{f}))$, so $t(\mathtt{lfp}(\vec{f})) \subseteq t'(\mathtt{lfp}(\vec{f}))$. ∎

Conversely, starting from a context-free grammar $G = (A_N, A_T, S, P)$ we introduce a finitary polynomial function $\vec{f_G} : (\mathcal{P}(A^*))^n \longrightarrow (\mathcal{P}(A^*))^n$. Without loss of generality we can assume that $A_N = \{X_0, \ldots, X_{n-1}\}$ and that the productions of P that have X_i in their left member are $X_i \rightarrow t_{i\,0}, \ldots, X_i \rightarrow t_{i\,\ell_i - 1}$.

Definition 5.3.4 The polynomial function $\vec{f_G} : (\mathcal{P}(A^*))^n \longrightarrow (\mathcal{P}(A^*))^n$ generated by the context-free grammar G is the finitary polynomial function whose components are

$$f_i(\boldsymbol{X}) = t_{i0}(\boldsymbol{X}) \cup \cdots \cup t_{i\,\ell_i - 1}(\boldsymbol{X})$$

for $0 \leq i \leq n - 1$. □

If $G = (\{X_0, \ldots, X_{n-1}\}, A, X_0, P)$ is a context-free grammar, $\vec{f}_G$ is the finitary polynomial function associated with this grammar, then G coincides with the first grammar G_0 of the sequence of grammars associated to $\vec{f}_G$.

If $\vec{f}$ is an n-ary finitary polynomial function, and $G_0, \ldots, G_{n-1}$ are the associated context-free grammars, then the finitary polynomial function associated to the grammar G_0 coincides with $\vec{f}$

Theorem 5.3.5 *Every context-free language is a component of the least fixed point of a finitary polynomial function.*

Proof. Let L be a context-free language, and let $G = (A_N, A_T, X_0, P)$ be a context-free grammar such that $L(G) = L$. Let $\vec{f}_G$ be polynomial function associated with this grammar. Since X_0 is the start symbol of G, Theorem 5.3.3 implies that the first component of the least fixed point of the function $\vec{f}_G$ coincides with the language generated by the grammar G_0, the first in the sequence of grammars associated to $\vec{f}_G$. Since G coincides with G_0, it follows that L is the first component of the least fixed point of $\vec{f}_G$. ∎

Corollary 5.3.6 *The class of context-free languages coincides with the class of languages that are components of the least fixed point of a finitary polynomial function.*

Proof. This result follows immediately from Theorems 5.3.3 and 5.3.5. ∎

Example 5.3.7 Let $G = (\{S_0, S_1, S_2\}, \{a, b\}, S, P)$ be the context-free grammar defined in Example 4.5.3. The polynomial function $\vec{f}_G : (\mathcal{P}(\{a,b\}^*))^3 \longrightarrow (\mathcal{P}(\{a,b\}^*))^3$ defined by G is given by

$$\vec{f}(\boldsymbol{L}) = (aL_2 \cup bL_1, \{a\} \cup aL_0 \cup bL_1L_1, \{b\} \cup bL_0 \cup aL_2L_2).$$

We give a few approximations of the least fixed point of $\vec{f}$:

$$\begin{aligned}
\vec{f}(\emptyset,\emptyset,\emptyset) &= (\emptyset, \{a\}, \{b\}) \\
\vec{f}^{(2)}(\emptyset,\emptyset,\emptyset) &= (\{ab, ba\}, \{a, baa\}, \{b, abb\}) \\
\vec{f}^{(3)}(\emptyset,\emptyset,\emptyset) &= (\{ab, ba, aabb, bbaa\}, \{a, aab, aba, baa, bbaaa, babaa, \\
&\qquad bbaabaa\}, \{b, bab, bba, abb, aabbb, ababb, aabbabb\}) \\
&\vdots
\end{aligned}$$

□

Example 5.3.8 The first approximation of the least fixed point of $\vec{f}$, the polynomial function introduced in Example 5.3.2, are

$$\begin{aligned}
f_0^{(1)}(\emptyset,\emptyset,\emptyset) &= \emptyset \\
f_1^{(1)}(\emptyset,\emptyset,\emptyset) &= \emptyset \\
f_2^{(1)}(\emptyset,\emptyset,\emptyset) &= \{v,n\} \\
f_0^{(2)}(\emptyset,\emptyset,\emptyset) &= \emptyset \\
f_1^{(2)}(\emptyset,\emptyset,\emptyset) &= \{v,n\} \\
f_2^{(2)}(\emptyset,\emptyset,\emptyset) &= \{v,n\} \\
f_0^{(3)}(\emptyset,\emptyset,\emptyset) &= \{v,n\} \\
f_1^{(3)}(\emptyset,\emptyset,\emptyset) &= \{v,n\} * \{v,n\} \cup \{v,n\}/\{v,n\} \cup \{v,n\} \\
f_2^{(3)}(\emptyset,\emptyset,\emptyset) &= \{v,n\} \\
f_0^{(4)}(\emptyset,\emptyset,\emptyset) &= \{v,n\} + \{v,n\} * \{v,n\} \\
&\quad \cup\{v,n\} + \{v,n\}/\{v,n\} \cup \{v,n\} + \{v,n\} \\
&\quad \cup\{v,n\} - \{v,n\} * \{v,n\} \cup \{v,n\} - \{v,n\}/\{v,n\} \\
&\quad \cup\{v,n\} - \{v,n\} \cup \{v,n\} * \{v,n\} \\
&\quad \cup\{v,n\}/\{v,n\} \cup \{v,n\} \\
&\vdots
\end{aligned}$$

□

5.4 Normal Forms

Normal forms of context-free grammars are classes of context-free grammars whose productions satisfy certain restrictions. If $\mathcal{N}$ is a normal form for context-free grammars and $G \in \mathcal{N}$, we say that G is in the normal form $\mathcal{N}$. We are especially interested in those normal forms $\mathcal{N}$ such that for every context-free language L there is a grammar $G \in \mathcal{N}$ such that $L = L(G)$.

5.4.1 Chomsky Normal Form

Definition 5.4.1 A context-free grammar $G = (A_N, A_T, S, P)$ is in *Chomsky normal form* if all productions are either of the form $X \to YZ$ or of the form $X \to a$, where $X, Y, Z \in A_N$ and $a \in A_T$. □

If G is in Chomsky normal form, then G is λ-free, so $\lambda \notin L(G)$.

Theorem 5.4.2 *For every context-free grammar G such that $\lambda \notin L(G)$ there is an equivalent grammar in Chomsky normal form.*

Proof. By Theorem 4.5.4 we can assume that G is a λ-free grammar. Further, by Theorems 4.5.9 and 4.3.13, we can assume that G has no chain productions and that every production that contains a terminal symbol is of the form $X \to a$. The productions of G have either the form $X \to a$ or the form $X \to X_{i_0} \cdots X_{i_{k-1}}$ with $k \geq 2$.

Productions of the form $X \to a$ or $X \to X_{i_0}X_{i_1}$ already conform to Chomsky normal form. If $\pi : X \to X_{i_0} \cdots X_{i_{k-1}}$ is a production of P with $k \geq 3$, consider $k-2$ new nonterminals $Z_0^\pi, \ldots, Z_{k-3}^\pi$ and the productions

$$X \to X_{i_0}Z_0^\pi, Z_0^\pi \to X_{i_1}Z_1^\pi, \cdots, Z_{k-3}^\pi \to X_{i_{k-2}}X_{i_{k-1}}$$

Define the grammar $G' = (A_N \cup A', A_T, S, P')$, where A' consists of all symbols Z_ℓ^π, and P' consists of all productions of the form $X \to a$ or $X \to X_{i_0}X_{i_1}$, and of productions obtained from productions of P having the form $X \to X_{i_0} \cdots X_{i_{k-1}}$ with $k \geq 3$, by applying the method described above. It is easy to see that G' is equivalent to G and that G' is in Chomsky normal form. ∎

Example 5.4.3 Let $G = (\{S_0, S_1, S_2\}, \{a, b\}, S_0, P)$ be the context-free grammar defined in Example 4.5.3, where P contains the following productions:

$$S_0 \to aS_2, S_0 \to bS_1, S_1 \to a, S_1 \to aS_0, S_1 \to bS_1S_1,$$
$$S_2 \to b, S_2 \to bS_0, S_2 \to aS_2S_2.$$

By introducing the new nonterminal symbols X_a, X_b we obtain the grammar $G_1 = (\{S_0, S_1, S_2, X_a, X_b\}, \{a, b\}, S_0, P_1)$, where P_1 consists of

$$S_0 \to X_aS_2, S_0 \to X_bS_1, S_1 \to a, S_1 \to X_aS_0, S_1 \to X_bS_1S_1,$$
$$S_2 \to b, S_2 \to X_bS_0, S_2 \to X_aS_2S_2, X_a \to a, X_b \to b.$$

Note that G_1 is equivalent to G, has no chain productions and every production that contains a terminal symbol is of the form $X \to a$. This grammar has two productions, $S_1 \to X_bS_1S_1$ and $S_2 \to X_aS_2S_2$, that violate Chomsky normal form, so we introduce the new nonterminals Z_0, Z_1. Applying the technique of Theorem 5.4.2 to these productions results in the set of productions P' given by:

$$S_0 \to X_aS_2,\ S_0 \to X_bS_1,\ S_1 \to a,\ S_1 \to X_aS_0,$$
$$S_1 \to X_bZ_0,\ Z_0 \to S_1S_1,\ S_2 \to b,\ S_2 \to X_bS_0,$$
$$S_2 \to X_aZ_1,\ Z_1 \to S_2S_2,\ X_a \to a,\ X_b \to b.$$

The resulting grammar $G' = (\{S_0, S_1, S_2, X_a, X_b, Z_0, Z_1\}, \{a, b\}, S_0, P')$ is in Chomsky normal form and is equivalent to G. □

Using Chomsky normal form we can prove an important decidability result for the class $\mathcal{L}_2$. To this end, we need the following technical result relating the length of a word to the length of its derivation.

Lemma 5.4.4 *Let $G = (A_N, A_T, S, P)$ be a context-free grammar in Chomsky normal form. Then, if $S \overset{*}{\underset{\alpha}{\Rightarrow}} x$ we have $|\alpha| \leq 2|x| - 1$.*

Proof. We prove a slightly stronger statement, namely that if $X \overset{*}{\underset{\alpha}{\Rightarrow}} x$ for some $X \in A_N$, then $|\alpha| \leq 2|x| - 1$.

The argument is by induction on $n = |x| \geq 1$. If $n = 1$, we have $x = a$ for $a \in A_T$ and the derivation $X \overset{*}{\underset{\alpha}{\Rightarrow}} x$ consists in the application of the production $\pi : X \to a$. Therefore, $|\alpha| = 1$ and the inequality is satisfied.

Suppose that the statement holds for words of length less than n, and let $x \in L(G)$ be a word such that $|x| = n$, where $n > 1$. Let the first production applied be $X \to YZ$; then we can write $x = uv$, there $Y \overset{*}{\underset{\beta}{\Rightarrow}} u$ and $Z \overset{*}{\underset{\gamma}{\Rightarrow}} v$ and $|\alpha| = |\beta| + |\gamma| + 1$, because the productions used in the last two derivations are exactly the ones used in $X \overset{*}{\underset{\alpha}{\Rightarrow}} x$. Applying the inductive hypothesis we obtain

$$|\alpha| = |\beta| + |\gamma| + 1 \leq 2|u| - 1 + 2|v| - 1 + 1 = 2(|u| + |v|) - 1 = 2|x| - 1.$$

∎

Theorem 5.4.5 *There is an algorithm to determine for a context-free grammar* $G = (A_N, A_T, S, P)$ *and a word* $x \in A_T^*$ *whether or not* $x \in L(G)$.

Proof. Using the algorithm from the proof of Theorem 4.5.4 and Theorem 4.5.5, construct a grammar G' equivalent to G such that one of the following two cases occurs:

1. if $\lambda \notin L(G)$ then G' is λ-free;
2. if $\lambda \in L(G)$ then G' contains a unique erasure production $S' \to \lambda$, where S' is the start symbol of G' and S' does not occur in any right member of any production of G'.

If $x = \lambda$, then $x \in L(G)$ if and only if $S \to \lambda$ is a production in G'. Suppose, therefore, that $x \neq \lambda$. Let G_1 be a context-free grammar in Chomsky normal form such that $L(G_1) = L(G') - \{\lambda\} = L(G) - \{\lambda\}$. We have $x \in L(G_1)$ if and only if $x \in L(G)$. By Lemma 5.4.4, if $S \overset{*}{\underset{\alpha}{\Rightarrow}} x$, then $|\alpha| \leq 2|x| - 1$, so we can decide if $x \in L(G)$ by listing all derivations of length at most $2|x| - 1$. ∎

Grammars in Chomsky normal form correspond to finitary polynomial functions that have a very useful and simple form, as shown by the next examples.

Example 5.4.6 Let $G = (\{X_0, \ldots, X_{n-1}\}, A, X_0, P)$ be a context-free grammar in Chomsky normal form such that the productions in P that have X_i in their left member are

$$X_i \to a_{j_0}, \ldots, X_i \to a_{j_{r-1}}, X_i \to X_m X_k, \ldots$$

The ith component f_i of $\vec{f}_G$ is given by

$$f_i(\boldsymbol{X}) = \{a_{j_0}, \ldots, a_{j_{r-1}}\} \cup \{X_m X_k \mid X_i \to X_m X_k \in P\},$$

for $\boldsymbol{X} = (X_0, \ldots, X_{n-1}) \in (\mathcal{P}(A_T^*))^n$.

For instance, if $G = (\{X_0, X_1, X_2\}, \{a, b\}, X_0, P)$ is a grammar in Chomsky normal form such that P consists of the productions

$$\begin{array}{lll} X_0 \to a, & X_0 \to X_1X_2, & X_0 \to X_0X_1, \\ X_1 \to b, & X_1 \to X_1X_1, & X_1 \to X_0X_2, \\ X_2 \to X_0X_1, & & \end{array}$$

then the finitary polynomial function $f_G : (\mathcal{P}(\{a,b\}^*))^3 \longrightarrow (\mathcal{P}(\{a,b\}^*))^3$ has the components

$$\begin{aligned} f_0(X_0, X_1, X_2) &= \{a\} \cup X_1X_2 \cup X_0X_1, \\ f_1(X_0, X_1, X_2) &= \{b\} \cup X_1X_1 \cup X_0X_2, \\ f_2(X_0, X_1, X_2) &= X_0X_1. \end{aligned}$$

□

Theorem 5.4.7 *If $G = (\{X_0, \ldots, X_{n-1}\}, A_T, X_0, P)$ is a context-free grammar in Chomsky normal form and $\vec{f}_G = (f_0, \cdots, f_{n-1})$, then we can write $\vec{f}_G$ in matrix form as*

$$\vec{f}_G(\boldsymbol{X}) = \boldsymbol{b} \cup \boldsymbol{XD},$$

where $\boldsymbol{b}$ is a row whose components are subsets of A_T and $\boldsymbol{D}$ is a matrix whose entries are subsets of $\{X_0, \ldots, X_{n-1}\}$. Further, $L(G)$ is the first component of the least fixed point of the function $\vec{f}_G$.

Proof. We leave to the reader the simple verification of this statement. ∎

Example 5.4.8 Let $G = (\{X_0, X_1, X_2\}, \{a, b\}, X_0, \{X_0 \rightarrow a, X_0 \rightarrow b, X_0 \rightarrow X_1X_2, X_1 \rightarrow b, X_1 \rightarrow X_1X_1, X_1 \rightarrow X_1X_2, X_1 \rightarrow X_2X_0, X_2 \rightarrow X_1X_1\})$ be a grammar in Chomsky normal form. The finitary polynomial function $f_G : (A_T^*)^3 \longrightarrow (A_T^*)^3$ is given by

$$\begin{aligned} \vec{f}_G(X_0, X_1, X_2) &= (\{a, b\}, \{b\}, \emptyset) \\ &\cup \ (X_0, X_1, X_2) \begin{pmatrix} \emptyset & \emptyset & \emptyset \\ X_2 & X_1 \cup X_2 & X_1 \\ \emptyset & X_0 & \emptyset \end{pmatrix} \end{aligned}$$

□

Observe that for every word $w \in (\boldsymbol{D}^k)_{ij}$ we have $|w| = k$ (cf. Exercise 10).

5.4.2 Greibach Normal Form

Definition 5.4.9 A context-free grammar $G = (A_N, A_T, S, P)$ is in *Greibach normal form* if all its productions are of the form $X \rightarrow a\alpha$, where $X \in A_N$, $a \in A_T$, and $\alpha \in A_N^*$. □

If G is in Greibach normal form, then G is λ-free, so $\lambda \notin L(G)$.

We discuss two approaches to proving that every λ-free context-free grammar has an equivalent grammar in Greibach normal form.

Elimination of Left-Recursive Symbols

This technique for obtaining the Greibach normal form of a context-free grammar is important in itself due to its applications in compiler design.

Definition 5.4.10 Let $G = (A_N, A_T, S, P)$ be a context-free grammar. A nonterminal symbol X is *left-recursive* (*right-recursive*) if there exists a derivation $X \overset{+}{\underset{G}{\Rightarrow}} X\alpha$ ($X \overset{+}{\underset{G}{\Rightarrow}} \alpha X$) for some $\alpha \in (A_N \cup A_T)^*$.

A context-free grammar G is *immediately left-recursive* (*immediately right-recursive*) if it contains a production $X \rightarrow X\alpha$ ($X \rightarrow \alpha X$).

G is *left-recursive* (*right-recursive*) if it contains a left-recursive nonterminal (right-recursive nonterminal). □

We present now some preliminary technical results.

Lemma 5.4.11 *Let $G = (A_N, A_T, S, P)$ be a context-free grammar, and let X, Y be two nonterminal symbols. Suppose that $X \to \alpha Y \beta \in P$, and let*

$$Y \to \gamma_0, \ldots, Y \to \gamma_{n-1}$$

be the list of all productions in P whose left member is Y. Then G is equivalent to the grammar $G' = (A_N, A_T, S, P')$, where

$$P' = (P - \{X \to \alpha Y \beta\}) \cup \{X \to \alpha \gamma_i \beta \mid 0 \leq i \leq n-1\}.$$

Proof. We have $L(G') \subseteq L(G)$. Indeed if a production $X \to \alpha\gamma_i\beta$ is used in a derivation step

$$\gamma' X \gamma'' \underset{G'}{\Rightarrow} \gamma' \alpha \gamma_i \beta \gamma'',$$

then, we can write in G:

$$\gamma' X \gamma'' \underset{G}{\Rightarrow} \gamma' \alpha Y \beta \gamma'' \underset{G}{\Rightarrow} \gamma' \alpha \gamma_i \beta \gamma''.$$

To prove the converse inclusion, $L(G) \subseteq L(G')$, we prove by induction on n, the length of a derivation $\theta \overset{*}{\underset{G}{\Rightarrow}} u$, that we have $\theta \overset{*}{\underset{G'}{\Rightarrow}} u$, where $\theta \in (A_N \cup A_T)^*$ and $u \in A_T^*$.

The base case, $n = 1$, is immediate. Suppose that this statement holds for derivations of length less than n and let $\theta \overset{n}{\underset{G}{\Rightarrow}} u$. If the production $X \to \alpha Y \beta$ is not used in this derivation, then we obviously have $\theta \overset{*}{\underset{G'}{\Rightarrow}} u$. Otherwise, this derivation can be written as

$$\theta \overset{*}{\underset{G}{\Rightarrow}} \theta' X \theta'' \underset{G}{\Rightarrow} \theta' \alpha Y \beta \theta'' \overset{*}{\underset{G}{\Rightarrow}} u.$$

Thus, u can be written as a product, $u = u' u_\alpha u_Y u_\beta u''$, where

$$\theta' \overset{*}{\underset{G}{\Rightarrow}} u', \alpha \overset{*}{\underset{G}{\Rightarrow}} u_\alpha, Y \overset{*}{\underset{G}{\Rightarrow}} u_Y, \beta \overset{*}{\underset{G}{\Rightarrow}} u_\beta, \theta'' \overset{*}{\underset{G}{\Rightarrow}} u''.$$

are derivations that are shorter than n. By the inductive hypothesis, we have the derivations

$$\begin{array}{cccccc} \theta' & \overset{*}{\underset{G'}{\Rightarrow}} & u', & \alpha & \overset{*}{\underset{G'}{\Rightarrow}} & u_\alpha, \\ \beta & \overset{*}{\underset{G'}{\Rightarrow}} & u_\beta, & \theta'' & \overset{*}{\underset{G'}{\Rightarrow}} & u'' \end{array}$$

Also, the existence of the derivation $Y \overset{*}{\underset{G}{\Rightarrow}} u_Y$ entails the existence of a derivation $\gamma_i \overset{*}{\underset{G}{\Rightarrow}} u_Y$; by the inductive hypothesis, we obtain the derivation $\gamma_i \overset{*}{\underset{G'}{\Rightarrow}} u_Y$. Thus, we obtain the derivation

$$\theta = \theta' \alpha X \beta \theta'' \underset{G'}{\Rightarrow} \theta' \alpha \gamma_i \beta \theta'' \overset{*}{\underset{G'}{\Rightarrow}} u' u_\alpha u_Y u_\beta u'' = u.$$

By taking $\theta = S$, we obtain the desired conclusion. ∎

The next theorem shows that it is possible to eliminate immediate left-recursiveness in context-free grammars.

Theorem 5.4.12 *Let $G = (A_N, A_T, S, P)$ be a context-free grammar that contains no erasure productions. Denote by P_X the set of productions in P having X as their left members.*

If $X \in A_N$ is a left recursive symbol, let P_X be the set that consists of productions that have X as their left member. The set P_X comprises two classes of productions:

(i) *the productions of P_X whose right members begin with X:*

$$X \to X\alpha_0, \ldots, X \to X\alpha_{k-1},$$

where $\alpha_i \neq \lambda$ for $0 \leq i \leq k-1$;

(ii) *the remaining productions in P_X:*

$$X \to \beta_0, \ldots, X \to \beta_{\ell-1},$$

where no β_j begins with X, $0 \leq j \leq \ell - 1$.

Let Y be a new nonterminal symbol, and let $G' = (A_N \cup \{Y\}, A_N, S, P')$ be the context-free grammar whose set of productions is given by

$$\begin{aligned} P' &= (P - P_X) \cup \{X \to \beta_j Y, X \to \beta_j \mid 0 \leq j \leq \ell - 1\} \\ &\cup \ \{Y \to \alpha_i Y, Y \to \alpha_i \mid 0 \leq i \leq k-1\}. \end{aligned}$$

The grammars G' and G are equivalent.

Proof. Note that we replaced the productions that make X a left-recursive symbol by productions that make the new symbol Y a right-recursive symbol; also, since $\alpha_j \neq \lambda$ for $0 \leq j \leq k-1$, Y is not left-recursive.

Let $x \in L(G)$ and let

$$S \underset{G,\text{left}}{\Rightarrow} \gamma_1 \underset{G,\text{left}}{\Rightarrow} \cdots \underset{G,\text{left}}{\Rightarrow} \gamma_n = x$$

be a leftmost derivation of x. If X does not occur in this derivation, then the same derivation can take place in G', and we have $x \in L(G')$. Otherwise, suppose that $X \overset{*}{\underset{G,\text{left}}{\Rightarrow}} w$ is a derivation that allows us to generate an infix w of x from X and is part of the previous derivation. The last derivation necessarily has the form

$$\begin{aligned} X &\underset{G,\text{left}}{\Rightarrow} X\alpha_{i_0} \underset{G,\text{left}}{\Rightarrow} X\alpha_{i_1}\alpha_{i_0} \underset{G,\text{left}}{\Rightarrow} \cdots \\ &\underset{G,\text{left}}{\Rightarrow} X\alpha_{i_{\ell-1}} \cdots \alpha_{i_1}\alpha_{i_0} \underset{G,\text{left}}{\Rightarrow} \beta_j \alpha_{i_{\ell-1}} \cdots \alpha_{i_1}\alpha_{i_0} \end{aligned}$$

The word $\beta_j \alpha_{i_{\ell-1}} \cdots \alpha_{i_1}\alpha_{i_0}$ can be derived in G' from X using the derivation

$$\begin{aligned} X &\underset{G',\text{right}}{\Rightarrow} \beta_j Y \underset{G',\text{right}}{\Rightarrow} \beta_j \alpha_{i_{\ell-1}} \underset{G',\text{right}}{\Rightarrow} \cdots \\ &\underset{G',\text{right}}{\Rightarrow} \beta_j \alpha i_{\ell-1} \cdots \alpha_{i_1} Y \underset{G',\text{right}}{\Rightarrow} \beta_j \alpha_{i_{\ell-1}} \cdots \alpha_{i_1}\alpha_{i_0}. \end{aligned}$$

Thus, for every leftmost derivation $S \overset{*}{\underset{G,\text{left}}{\Rightarrow}} x$ corresponds a rightmost derivation $S \overset{*}{\underset{G',\text{right}}{\Rightarrow}} x$, so $L(G) \subseteq L(G')$.

The reverse implication can be argued in a completely similar manner, so we have $L(G) = L(G')$. ∎

Example 5.4.13 Let G_{ae} be the grammar introduced in Example 5.3.2. The grammar G'_{ae} obtained from G_{ae} by applying the transformation mentioned in Theorem 5.4.12 is

$$G'_{ae} = (\{X_e, X_t, X_f, Y_e, Y_t\}, \{+, -, *, /, (,), \boldsymbol{v}, \boldsymbol{n}\}, X_e, P').$$

Its set of productions consists of the following:

$$\begin{aligned}
&X_e \to X_tY_e, X_e \to X_t,\\
&Y_e \to +X_tY_e, Y_e \to +X_t,\\
&Y_e \to -X_tY_e, Y_e \to -X_t,\\
&X_t \to X_fY_t, X_t \to X_f,\\
&Y_t \to *X_fY_t, Y_t \to *X_f,\\
&Y_t \to /X_fY_t, Y_t \to /X_f,\\
&X_f \to \boldsymbol{v}, X_f \to \boldsymbol{n}, X_f \to (X_e)
\end{aligned}$$

It is easy to verify that we eliminated not only the immediate left-recursiveness from $G_{ae'}$; this grammar is not left-recursive. □

To derive a Greibach normal form grammar for a λ-free context-free language L we start from a grammar G in Chomsky normal form such that $L(G) = L$.

Lemma 5.4.14 *Let* $G = (\{X_0, \ldots, X_n\}, A_T, X_0, P)$ *be a context-free grammar in Chomsky normal form. There exists an equivalent grammar* $G' = (A'_N, A_T, X_0, P')$ *that satisfies the following conditions:*

1. $\{X_0, \ldots, X_n\} \subseteq A'_N$;
2. *the productions that have* X_i *as their left members have the form* $X_i \to a\alpha$ *or* $X_i \to X_j\alpha \in P'$, *where* $a \in A_T$, $\alpha \in (A'_N)^*$ *and* $i < j$;
3. *if* $Y \in A'_N - \{X_0, \ldots, X_{n-1}\}$, *then for every production* $Y \to \gamma \in P'$, $\gamma \neq \lambda$, *all symbols in* γ *except the first symbol are nonterminals, and the first symbol of* γ *belongs to* $\{X_0, \ldots, X_{n-1}\} \cup A_T$.

Proof. Suppose that k is a number such that $0 \leq k \leq n$. Starting with $k = 0$, we consider an inductive process such that modifies the productions of the form $X_i \to X_j\alpha$, where $0 \leq i < k$ to produce an equivalent grammar G_k with the property that for any production in G_k of the form $X_i \to X_j\alpha$, where $0 \leq i < k$, we have $i < j$.

For $k = 0$, we have nothing to do, since there are no productions $X_i \to X_j\alpha$ with $i < 0$. Suppose that we have built the grammar G_k, that is, for every production $X_i \to X_j\alpha$ (with $0 \leq i < k$) we have $i < j$. Let $X_k \to X_j\alpha$ be a production such that $j \leq k$. Using Lemma 5.4.11, if $X_j \to \gamma_0, \ldots, X_j \to \gamma_{m-1}$ are the productions that have X_j in their left members, then we can replace $X_k \to X_j\alpha$ by $X_k \to \gamma_0\alpha, \ldots, X_k \to \gamma_{m-1}\alpha$.

By the inductive hypothesis, if $X_k \to X_\ell\beta$ is one of these new productions, then $k - \ell < k - j$. By repeating this operations at most $k - 1$ times we obtain productions of the form $X_k \to X_p\beta$ with $k \leq p$. At this point, the productions that have X_k in their left members are either of the form $X_k \to X_k\alpha$, or $X_k \to \beta$, such that β does not begin with X_k. If the grammar contains productions of the form $X_k \to X_k\alpha$, then these productions are eliminated using the technique outlined in Theorem 5.4.12, that is, by introducing a new symbol

Y_k and replacing these productions by productions of the form $X_k \to \beta Y_k$, $X_k \to \beta$, $Y_k \to \alpha Y_k Y$, and $Y_k \to \alpha$, with $\alpha, \beta \neq \lambda$. It is clear that these productions satisfy the requirements of the lemma. ∎

Example 5.4.15 Let $G = (\{X_0, X_1, X_2\}, \{a, b\}, X_0, P)$ be a context-free grammar whose set of productions is

$$P = \{X_0 \to X_1X_2, X_1 \to X_0X_1, X_1 \to a, X_2 \to X_0X_2, X_2 \to b\}.$$

We see by inspection that G is in Chomsky normal form. Note that X_0 is a left-recursive symbol since we have

$$X_0 \underset{G}{\Rightarrow} X_1X_2 \underset{G}{\Rightarrow} X_0X_1X_2.$$

Also, X_1 is left-recursive due to the derivation

$$X_1 \underset{G}{\Rightarrow} X_0X_1 \underset{G}{\Rightarrow} X_1X_2X_1.$$

We replace the production $X_1 \to X_0X_1$ with $X_1 \to X_1X_2X_1$. At this point, the set of productions that have X_1 as their left member is

$$X_1 \to X_1X_2X_1, X_1 \to a.$$

Then, to eliminate the left-recursiveness of X_1 we introduce a new nonterminal symbol Y_1 and replace the productions $X_1 \to X_1X_2X_1$ and $X_1 \to a$ with $X_1 \to aY_1$, $X_1 \to a$, $Y_1 \to X_2X_1Y_1$, and $Y_1 \to X_2X_1$. The current set of productions is

$$X_0 \to X_1X_2,\ X_1 \to aY_1,\ X_1 \to a,\ Y_1 \to X_2X_1Y_1,$$
$$Y_1 \to X_2X_1,\ X_2 \to X_0X_2,\ X_2 \to b.$$

We focus our attention now on productions that involve X_2. Initially, we replace $X_2 \to X_0X_2$ by $X_2 \to X_1X_2X_2$. Next, we replace this production with $X_2 \to aY_1X_2X_2, X_2 \to aX_2X_2$, and obtain the set of productions:

$$X_0 \to X_1X_2,\ X_1 \to aY_1,\ X_1 \to a,\ Y_1 \to X_2X_1Y_1,$$
$$Y_1 \to X_2X_1,\ X_2 \to aY_1X_2X_2,\ X_2 \to aX_2X_2, X_2 \to b$$

of the grammar $G' = (\{X_0, X_1, X_2, Y_1\}, \{a, b\}, X_0, P')$. □

Theorem 5.4.16 *For every context-free grammar G such that $\lambda \notin L(G)$, there is an equivalent grammar in Greibach normal form.*

Proof. Without restricting generality, we can assume that G is in Chomsky normal form and has the form $G = (\{X_0, \ldots, X_n\}, A_T, X_0, P)$. By applying Lemma 5.4.14, we obtain a context-free grammar $G' = (A'_N, A_T, X_0, P')$ that is equivalent to G, such that

1. $\{X_0, \ldots, X_n\} \subseteq A'_N$;
2. the productions that have X_i as their left members have the form $X_i \to a\alpha$ or $X_i \to X_j\alpha \in P'$, where $a \in A_T$, $\alpha \in (A'_N)^*$ and $i < j$;

3. if $Y \in A'_N - \{X_0, \ldots, X_{n-1}\}$, then for every production $Y \to \gamma \in P'$, $\gamma \neq \lambda$, all symbols in γ except the first symbol are nonterminals, and the first symbol of γ belongs to $\{X_0, \ldots, X_{n-1}\} \cup A_T$.

Note that the productions that rewrite the symbol X_n are necessarily of the form $X_n \to a\alpha$, where a is a terminal symbol and α contains only nonterminal symbols.

The right member of a production of the form $X_{n-1} \to \cdots$ begins with a terminal symbol or with X_n. Then, applying Lemma 5.4.11, we replace X_n in all productions $X_{n-1} \to X_n \cdots$ with the right members of the productions $X_n \to \cdots$. Thus, all productions $X_{n-1} \to \cdots$ have the form $X_{n-1} \to a\gamma$, where $\gamma \in (A'_N)^*$. This process is repeated for $X_{n-2}, \ldots, X_0$.

Finally, since the first symbol of γ in $Y \to \gamma$ is a terminal or a symbol X_i, a last application of Lemma 5.4.11, allows us to replace the productions $Y \to X_i \cdots$ with productions whose right member begins with a terminal, thereby obtaining a grammar in Greibach normal form equivalent to the initial grammar. ∎

Example 5.4.17 In Example 5.4.15 we began with a context-free grammar G and obtained an equivalent grammar

$$G' = (\{X_0, X_1, X_2, Y_1\}, \{a, b\}, X_0, P').$$

The set P' consists of the following productions:

$$X_0 \to X_1X_2,\ X_1 \to aY_1,\ X_1 \to a,\ Y_1 \to X_2X_1Y_1,$$
$$Y_1 \to X_2X_1,\ X_2 \to aY_1X_2X_2,\ X_2 \to aX_2X_2, X_2 \to b.$$

By inspection, we see that to obtain a grammar in Greibach normal, form we need to deal with the production $X_0 \to X_1X_2$ and with productions of the form $Y_1 \to \cdots$. This yields the grammar

$$G_1 = (\{X_0, X_1, X_2\}, \{a, b\}, X_0, P_1)$$

whose set of productions is

$$X_0 \to aY_1X_2,\ X_0 \to aX_2,\ X_1 \to aY_1,\ X_1 \to a,$$
$$Y_1 \to aY_1X_2X_2X_1Y_1,\ Y_1 \to aX_2X_2X_1Y_1,\ Y_1 \to bX_1Y_1,$$
$$Y_1 \to aY_1X_2X_2X_2X_1,\ Y_1 \to aX_2X_2X_2X_1,\ Y_1 \to bX_2X_1,$$
$$X_2 \to aY_1X_2X_2,\ X_2 \to aX_2X_2,\ X_2 \to b.$$

□

Fixed-Points and Greibach Normal Forms

In this section we discuss an effective approach to obtaining the Greibach normal form that is based on the characterization of context-free languages as components of fixed-points of finitary polynomial functions.

We first give a mathematical explanation of the result and then a worked example. Some readers may find it helpful to work through the example as they read the explanation.

Let $G = (A_N, A_T, S, P)$ be a context-free grammar such that $\lambda \notin L(G)$. By Theorem 5.4.2, we can assume that G is in Chomsky normal form. Then, by Theorem 5.3.3, L is the first component of $\mathtt{lfp}(\vec{f}_G)$, where $\vec{f}_G$ is given by

$$\vec{f}_G(\boldsymbol{X}) = \boldsymbol{b} \cup \boldsymbol{XD},$$

by Theorem 5.4.7.

Theorem 2.6.11 implies that $\mathtt{lfp}(\vec{f}_G) = \mathtt{lfp}(\vec{f}_G^{(i)})$ for every $i \in \mathbb{P}$. Note that

$$\begin{aligned}
\vec{f}_G^{(1)}(\boldsymbol{X}) &= \boldsymbol{b} \cup \boldsymbol{XD},\\
\vec{f}_G^{(2)}(\boldsymbol{X}) &= \boldsymbol{b} \cup \boldsymbol{bD} \cup \boldsymbol{XD}^2,\\
&\vdots\\
\vec{f}_G^{(i)}(\boldsymbol{X}) &= \boldsymbol{b} \cup \boldsymbol{bD} \cup \cdots \cup \boldsymbol{bD}^{i-1} \cup \boldsymbol{XD}^i,\\
&\vdots
\end{aligned}$$

Let G^k be the context-free grammar associated with the first component of the function $\vec{f}_G^{(2^k)}$. Clearly, $L(G^k) = L(G)$ and

$$\vec{f}_G^{(2^k)}(\boldsymbol{X}) = \boldsymbol{b} \cup \boldsymbol{bD} \cup \cdots \cup \boldsymbol{bD}^{2^k-1} \cup \boldsymbol{XD}^{2^k}.$$

Let $\vec{g}_k : (\mathcal{P}(A_T^*))^n \longrightarrow (\mathcal{P}(A_T^*))^n$ be the constant function given by

$$\vec{g}_k(\boldsymbol{X}) = \boldsymbol{b} \cup \boldsymbol{bD} \cup \cdots \cup \boldsymbol{bD}^{2^k-1},$$

for $\boldsymbol{X} \in (\mathcal{P}(A_T^*))^n$. Since $\vec{f}_G^{(2^k)}(\boldsymbol{X}) = \vec{g}_k(\boldsymbol{X}) \cup \boldsymbol{XD}^{2^k}$, we have $\vec{g}_k \subseteq \vec{f}_G^{(2^k)}$, so $\mathtt{lfp}(\vec{g}_k) \subseteq \mathtt{lfp}(\vec{f}_G^{(2^k)})$. This implies

$$\boldsymbol{b} \cup \boldsymbol{bD} \cup \cdots \cup \boldsymbol{bD}^{2^k-1} \subseteq \mathtt{lfp}(\vec{f}_G^{(2^k)}).$$

Observe that for every production in G_k that corresponds to $\boldsymbol{XD}^{2^k}$ the length of the right member is $1 + 2^k$ (cf. Exercise 10). Therefore, no such production can be used for generating a word of length less or equal to 2^k in $L(G^k) = L(G)$.

Denote by G'^k the context-free grammar associated with the first component of the function $\vec{g}_k$. We have $L(G'^k) \subseteq L(G^k) = L(G)$. Moreover, if $x \in L(G)$ and $|x| \leq 2^k$, then x must be generated by G^k using a production that corresponds to an entry of the matrix $\boldsymbol{b} \cup \boldsymbol{bD} \cup \cdots \cup \boldsymbol{bD}^{2^k-1}$. Thus,

$$L(G) \cap \{x \in A_T^* \mid |x| \leq 2^k\} = L(G'^k),$$

for $k \in \mathbb{N}$.

Now consider n^2 new variables $\{Y_{ij} \mid 0 \leq i, j \leq n-1\}$ and the $n \times n$-matrix $\boldsymbol{Y}$ is the matrix whose (i,j) entry is $\{Y_{ij}\}$. The finitary polynomial function $h : (\mathcal{P}(A_T^*))^{n+n^2} \longrightarrow (\mathcal{P}(A_T^*))^{n+n^2}$ is defined by

$$\vec{h}(\boldsymbol{X}, \boldsymbol{Y}) = (\boldsymbol{b} \cup \boldsymbol{bY}, \boldsymbol{D} \cup \boldsymbol{DY}),$$

where Let H be the context-free grammar associated with the first component of $\vec{h}$.

The least fixed point of $\vec{h}$ is the same as the least fixed point of $\vec{h}^{(i)}$. Since

$$\begin{aligned}\vec{h}^{(i)}(\boldsymbol{X},\boldsymbol{Y}) &= (\boldsymbol{b}\cup\boldsymbol{bD}\cup\cdots\cup\boldsymbol{bD}^{i-1}\cup\boldsymbol{bD}^{i-1}\boldsymbol{Y},\\ &\quad \boldsymbol{D}\cup\boldsymbol{DY}\cup\cdots\cup\boldsymbol{D}^{i}\boldsymbol{Y}),\end{aligned}$$

Let H^k be the grammar associated with the first component of $\vec{h}^{(2^k)}$. By Theorem 2.6.11, $L(H) = L(H^k)$. Since all productions of G'^k are also productions of H^k it follows that $L(G'^k) \subseteq L(H^k) = L(H)$.

The entries of the matrix $\boldsymbol{bD}^{2^k-1}\boldsymbol{Y}$ are words of length 2^k+1. Therefore, they correspond to productions in the grammar G'^{2^k} that cannot be used in deriving a word of length less or equal to 2^k in this grammar. Consequently, if w is a word in $L(G)$ or $L(H)$ such that $1 \leq |w| \leq 2^k$, then $w \in L(G'^k)$. In other words, both $L(G)$ and $L(H)$ equal $\bigcup\{L(G'^k) \mid k \in \mathbb{N}\}$, so G and H are equivalent.

If $\boldsymbol{Y}^{[i]}$ is the ith row of the matrix $\boldsymbol{Y}$ and $\boldsymbol{D}^{[i]}$ is the ith row of the matrix $\boldsymbol{D}$, then

$$\boldsymbol{Y}^{[i]} = \boldsymbol{D}^{[i]} \cup \boldsymbol{D}^{[i]}\boldsymbol{Y}.$$

Note that $\boldsymbol{D}^{[i]} = \boldsymbol{XT}_i$, where $\boldsymbol{T}_i$ is a matrix whose entries are either $\{\lambda\}$ or $\emptyset$, so

$$\begin{aligned}\boldsymbol{Y}^{[i]} &= \boldsymbol{XT}_i\cup\boldsymbol{XT}_i\boldsymbol{Y}\\ &= (\boldsymbol{b}\cup\boldsymbol{bY})\boldsymbol{T}_i\cup(\boldsymbol{b}\cup\boldsymbol{bY})\boldsymbol{T}_i\boldsymbol{Y}\\ &= \boldsymbol{bT}_i\cup\boldsymbol{bYT}_i\cup\boldsymbol{bT}_i\boldsymbol{Y}\cup\boldsymbol{bYT}_i\boldsymbol{Y}\end{aligned}$$

Thus, the least fixed point of the function $\vec{h}$ is defined by the system of equations

$$\begin{aligned}\boldsymbol{X} &= \boldsymbol{b}\cup\boldsymbol{bY}\\ \boldsymbol{Y}^{[0]} &= \boldsymbol{b}(\boldsymbol{T}_0\cup\boldsymbol{YT}_0\cup\boldsymbol{T}_0\boldsymbol{Y}\cup\boldsymbol{YT}_0\boldsymbol{Y})\\ &\ \vdots\\ \boldsymbol{Y}^{[n-1]} &= \boldsymbol{b}(\boldsymbol{T}_{n-1}\cup\boldsymbol{YT}_{n-1}\cup\boldsymbol{T}_{n-1}\boldsymbol{Y}\cup\boldsymbol{YT}_{n-1}\boldsymbol{Y}).\end{aligned}$$

The grammar that corresponds to these equations has rules of the form $X \to b$, $X \to bY$, $Y \to b$, $Y \to bY$, and $Y \to bY'Y''$, where $X \in \{X_i \mid 0 \leq i \leq n-1\}$ and $Y, Y', Y'' \in \{Y_{ij} \mid 0 \leq i,j \leq n-1\}$ and, therefore, it is in Greibach normal form.

Example 5.4.18 Let $G = (\{X_0, X_1\}, \{a,b\}, X_0, P)$ be a context-free grammar, where

$$\begin{aligned}P &= \{X_0 \to a, X_0 \to X_1X_0, X_0 \to X_1X_1,\\ &\quad X_1 \to a, X_1 \to b, X_1 \to X_0X_1\}).\end{aligned}$$

G is clearly in Chomsky normal form. The function $\vec{f_G}$ is given by

$$\vec{f_G}(X_0, X_1) = (\{a\}, \{a,b\}) \cup (X_0, X_1)\begin{pmatrix}\emptyset & \{X_1\}\\ \{X_0, X_1\} & \emptyset\end{pmatrix}.$$

Therefore, the matrices $\boldsymbol{b}$ and $\boldsymbol{D}$ are given by

$$\begin{aligned}\boldsymbol{b} &= (\{a\}, \{a,b\})\\ \boldsymbol{D} &= \begin{pmatrix}\emptyset & \{X_1\}\\ \{X_0, X_1\} & \emptyset\end{pmatrix}\end{aligned}$$

We have

$$\begin{aligned} \boldsymbol{D}^{[0]} &= (X_0, X_1)\begin{pmatrix} \emptyset & \emptyset \\ \emptyset & \{\lambda\} \end{pmatrix} \\ \boldsymbol{D}^{[1]} &= (X_0, X_1)\begin{pmatrix} \{\lambda\} & \emptyset \\ \{\lambda\} & \emptyset \end{pmatrix}, \end{aligned}$$

which defines the matrices $\boldsymbol{T}_0, \boldsymbol{T}_1$ as

$$\begin{aligned} \boldsymbol{T}_0 &= \begin{pmatrix} \emptyset & \emptyset \\ \emptyset & \{\lambda\} \end{pmatrix} \\ \boldsymbol{T}_1 &= \begin{pmatrix} \{\lambda\} & \emptyset \\ \{\lambda\} & \emptyset \end{pmatrix}. \end{aligned}$$

Let

$$\boldsymbol{Y} = \begin{pmatrix} Y_{00} & Y_{01} \\ Y_{10} & Y_{11} \end{pmatrix}$$

be the matrix of new nonterminal symbols. If $\boldsymbol{Y}^{[0]}, \boldsymbol{Y}^{[1]}$ are the rows of this matrix, then the equations that define the context-free grammar in Greibach normal form are:

$$\boldsymbol{X} = \boldsymbol{b} \cup \boldsymbol{bY} \tag{5.2}$$

$$\boldsymbol{Y}^{[0]} = \boldsymbol{bT}_0 \cup \boldsymbol{bYT}_0 \cup \boldsymbol{bT}_0\boldsymbol{Y} \cup \boldsymbol{bYT}_0\boldsymbol{Y} \tag{5.3}$$

$$\boldsymbol{Y}^{[1]} = \boldsymbol{bT}_1 \cup \boldsymbol{bYT}_1 \cup \boldsymbol{bT}_1\boldsymbol{Y} \cup \boldsymbol{bYT}_1\boldsymbol{Y}. \tag{5.4}$$

By replacing the corresponding matrices we obtain

$$\begin{aligned} (X_0, X_1) &= (\{a\}, \{a, b\}) \cup (\{a\}, \{a, b\})\boldsymbol{Y} \\ (Y_{00}, Y_{01}) &= (\{a\}, \{a, b\})(\boldsymbol{T}_0 \cup \boldsymbol{YT}_0 \cup \boldsymbol{T}_0\boldsymbol{Y} \cup \boldsymbol{YT}_0\boldsymbol{Y}) \\ (Y_{10}, Y_{11}) &= (\{a\}, \{a, b\})(\boldsymbol{T}_1 \cup \boldsymbol{YT}_1 \cup \boldsymbol{T}_1\boldsymbol{Y} \cup \boldsymbol{YT}_1\boldsymbol{Y}). \end{aligned}$$

A straightforward computation gives

$$\begin{aligned} &\boldsymbol{T}_0 \cup \boldsymbol{YT}_0 \cup \boldsymbol{T}_0\boldsymbol{Y} \cup \boldsymbol{YT}_0\boldsymbol{Y} \\ &= \begin{pmatrix} \{Y_{01}Y_{10}\} & \{Y_{01}, Y_{01}Y_{11}\} \\ \{Y_{10}, Y_{11}Y_{10}\} & \{\lambda, Y_{11}\} \end{pmatrix}, \end{aligned}$$

and

$$\begin{aligned} &\boldsymbol{T}_1 \cup \boldsymbol{YT}_1 \cup \boldsymbol{T}_1\boldsymbol{Y} \cup \boldsymbol{YT}_1\boldsymbol{Y} \\ &= \begin{pmatrix} \{\lambda, Y_{00}, Y_{01}, Y_{00}Y_{00}, Y_{01}Y_{00}\} & \{Y_{01}, Y_{00}Y_{01}, Y_{01}Y_{01}\} \\ \{\lambda, Y_{10}, Y_{11}, Y_{00}, Y_{10}Y_{00}, Y_{11}Y_{00}\} & \{Y_{01}, Y_{10}Y_{01}, Y_{11}Y_{01}\} \end{pmatrix}. \end{aligned}$$

The set of productions of the grammar in Greibach normal form contains the following groups of rules that correspond to the three equalities (5.2)–(5.4):

The first group is

$$\begin{aligned} &X_0 \to a,\ X_1 \to a,\ X_1 \to b \\ &X_0 \to aY_{00},\ X_0 \to aY_{10},\ X_0 \to bY_{10} \\ &X_1 \to aY_{01},\ X_1 \to aY_{11},\ X_1 \to bY_{11} \end{aligned}$$

The group that corresponds to the equality (5.3) is:

$$\begin{aligned} &Y_{00} \to aY_{01}Y_{10},\ Y_{00} \to aY_{10},\ Y_{00} \to bY_{10}, \\ &Y_{00} \to aY_{11}Y_{10},\ Y_{00} \to bY_{11}Y_{10}, \\ &Y_{01} \to aY_{01},\ Y_{01} \to aY_{01}Y_{11},\ Y_{01} \to a, \\ &Y_{01} \to b,\ Y_{01} \to aY_{11},\ Y_{01} \to bY_{11}, \end{aligned}$$

Finally, the group that translates the third equality (5.4) is:

$$\begin{aligned}
&Y_{10} \to a,\ Y_{10} \to aY_{00},\ Y_{10} \to aY_{01},\\
&Y_{10} \to aY_{00}Y_{00},\ Y_{10} \to aY_{01}Y_{00},\\
&Y_{10} \to a,\ Y_{10} \to aY_{10},\ Y_{10} \to aY_{11},\\
&Y_{10} \to aY_{00},\ Y_{10} \to aY_{10}Y_{00},\ Y_{10} \to aY_{11}Y_{00},\\
&Y_{10} \to b,\ Y_{10} \to bY_{10},\ Y_{10} \to bY_{11},\\
&Y_{10} \to bY_{00},\ Y_{10} \to bY_{10}Y_{00},\ Y_{10} \to bY_{11}Y_{00},\\
&Y_{11} \to aY_{01},\ Y_{11} \to aY_{00}Y_{01},\ Y_{11} \to aY_{01}Y_{01},\\
&Y_{11} \to aY_{01},\ Y_{11} \to aY_{10}Y_{01},\ Y_{11} \to aY_{11}Y_{01},\\
&Y_{11} \to bY_{01},\ Y_{11} \to bY_{10}Y_{01},\ Y_{11} \to bY_{11}Y_{01}.
\end{aligned}$$

□

5.5 The Pumping Lemmas

In this section we discuss several related results whose main application is to show that certain languages do not belong to $\mathcal{L}_2$. As in the case of regular languages, these results are traditionally named *pumping lemmas* but are referred to below as theorems to reflect their importance.

For this discussion, we need to identify subsequences of symbols of words that occur in certain positions. This is done by identifying a subset M of $\mathbb{N}$ called a *marking set.* As no further assumptions are made about this set below, the results hold for all marking sets.

Definition 5.5.1 Let A be an alphabet, and let $w = a_{i_0} \cdots a_{i_{|w|-1}}$ be a word in A^*. The *set of marked occurrences in* w is the set $\{0, \ldots, |w|-1\} \cap M$, and the M-weight of w is the number $\| w \|_M = |\{0, \ldots, |w|-1\} \cap M|$. □

If the marking set is clear from the context, we may denote $\| w \|_M$ simply by $\| w \|$.

Theorem 5.5.2 (Ogden Lemma) *Let G be a context-free grammar, and let M be a marking set. There exists a number $n_G \in \mathbb{N}$ such that if $w \in L(G)$ and $\| w \|_M \geq n_G$, then we can write $w = xyzut$ such that $\| y \|_M \geq 1$ or $\| u \|_M \geq 1$, $\| yzu \|_M \leq n_G$ and $xy^n zu^n t \in L(G)$ for all $n \in \mathbb{N}$.*

Proof. Let $G = (A_N, A_T, S, P)$, and let $\ell(G) = \max\{|\alpha| \mid X \to \alpha \in P\}$. We can assume that $\ell(G) \geq 2$ since, otherwise, $L(G) \subseteq A_T \cup \{\lambda\}$, and by choosing $n_G \geq 2$, the theorem obviously holds. Define the number n_G by $n_G = \ell(G)^{|A_N|+1}$, and suppose that $w \in L(G)$ such that $\| w \|_M \geq n_G$.

Let $\mathtt{T}$ be a derivation tree of a derivation $S \overset{*}{\underset{G}{\Rightarrow}} w$. Suppose that an internal node v of $\mathtt{T}$ is labeled by the symbol nonterminal symbol X and that $\mathsf{word}(\mathtt{T}_{[v]}) = s$. Then, the weight of v is defined as $\mathsf{weight}(v) = \| s \|_M$. Clearly, we have $\mathsf{weight}(v) = \sum\{\mathsf{weight}(v') \mid v' \in \mathsf{CHILDREN}(v)\}$.

Let V be the set of vertices of $\mathtt{T}$. Define the function $h : V \longrightarrow \mathbb{N}$ by

$$h(v) = \begin{cases} 0 \text{ if } v \in \mathsf{LEAVES}(\mathtt{T}), \\ 1 + \max\{h(v') \mid v' \in \mathsf{CHILDREN}(v)\} \\ \qquad \text{if } |\{v' \mid v' \in \mathsf{CHILDREN}(v), \mathsf{weight}(v') > 0\}| > 1, \\ \max\{h(v') \mid v' \in \mathsf{CHILDREN}(v)\}, \text{ otherwise,} \end{cases}$$

for every $v \in V$.

Let v be an internal node of T. If $h(v) = h(v_1)$, where $v_1 \in \mathsf{CHILDREN}(v)$, then the third case of the above definition applies. In this case there is at most one child of v that has positive weight (namely, the node v_1), hence $\mathsf{weight}(v) = \mathsf{weight}(v_1)$. Conversely, suppose that v has a child v_1 such that $\mathsf{weight}(v) = \mathsf{weight}(v_1)$. Since $\mathsf{weight}(v) = \sum\{\mathsf{weight}(v') \mid v' \in \mathsf{CHILDREN}(v)\}$, it follows that every other child of v has a zero weight. Therefore, $h(v) = h(v_1)$, by the definition of h. This allows us to conclude that, for an internal node v, there exists a child v_1 of v such that $h(v) = h(v_1)$ if and only if a child exists such that $\mathsf{weight}(v) = \mathsf{weight}(v_1)$.

We claim that for each node v of T we have $\mathsf{weight}(v) \leq \ell(G)^{h(v)}$. The argument is by induction on $\mathsf{height}(v)$.

If $\mathsf{height}(v) = 0$, v is a leaf, $h(v) = 0$ and $\mathsf{weight}(v) \leq 1$, so $\mathsf{weight}(v) \leq \ell(G)^{h(v)}$. Suppose that the inequality holds for vertices of height less than n, and let v be a vertex of height n. The following two cases may occur.

1. If $h(v) = h(v_1)$, where $v_1 \in \mathsf{CHILDREN}(v)$, then $\mathsf{weight}(v) = \mathsf{weight}(v_1) \leq \ell(G)^{h(v_1)}$, by the inductive hypothesis. Thus, $\mathsf{weight}(v) \leq \ell(G)^{h(v)}$.
2. If $h(v) > h(v_1)$, for every $v_1 \in \mathsf{CHILDREN}(v)$, then $h(v) = 1+\max\{h(v') \mid v' \in \mathsf{CHILDREN}(v)\}$ and v has more than one child with positive weight. Let $v_{i_0}, \ldots, v_{i_{k-1}}$ be the set of all such children of v, where $k > 1$. Note that we have $k \leq \ell(G)$, by the definition of derivation trees. We have:

$$\begin{aligned}\mathsf{weight}(v) &= \mathsf{weight}(v_{i_0}) + \cdots + \mathsf{weight}(v_{i_{k-1}})\\ &\leq \ell(G)^{h(v_{i_0})} + \cdots + \ell(G)^{h(v_{i_{k-1}})}\\ &\quad \text{(by the inductive hypothesis)}\\ &\leq \ell(G) \cdot \ell(G)^{\max\{h(v_{i_0}),\ldots,h(v_{i_{k-1}})\}}\\ &= \ell(G)^{1+\max\{h(v_{i_0}),\ldots,h(v_{i_{k-1}})\}}\\ &= \ell(G)^{h(v)}.\end{aligned}$$

Since $\| w \|_M$ equals the weight of the root v_{root} of the tree T and $\| w \|_M \geq n_G$ it follows that $\ell(G)^{|A_N|+1} = n_G \leq \mathsf{weight}(v_{\text{root}}) \leq \ell(G)^{h(v_{\text{root}})}$. Thus, $h(v_{\text{root}}) \geq |A_N| + 1$. Consequently, T contains a branch B such that each node v in B with $h(v) > 0$ has a child v' such that $h(v) = 1 + h(v')$. Thus, we have a sequence of nodes $(v_0, v_1, \ldots)$ along B such that

$$h(v_0) = |A_N| + 1, h(v_1) = |A_N|, \ldots, h(v_i) = |A_N| - (i-1), \ldots$$

Since there are more than $|A_N|$ nodes in this sequence, there must be two nodes v_i, v_j with $i < j$, that are labeled with the same nonterminal symbol X (cf. Figure 5.5). Let z be the word over A_T given by $z = \mathsf{word}(\mathtt{T}_{[v_j]})$. Then, $\mathsf{word}(\mathtt{T}_{[v_i]})$ includes z, and so, it must have the form yzu for some $y, u \in A_T^*$. Further, yzu is an infix of w, so $w = xyzut$ for some $x, t \in A_T^*$ and we have the derivations in G:

$$S \underset{\omega_0}{\overset{*}{\Rightarrow}} xXt, X \underset{\omega_1}{\overset{*}{\Rightarrow}} yXu, X \underset{\omega_2}{\overset{*}{\Rightarrow}} z.$$

By repeated application of the second derivation, we obtain:

$$S \underset{\omega_0}{\overset{*}{\Rightarrow}} xXt \underset{\omega_1}{\overset{*}{\Rightarrow}} xyXut \underset{\omega_1}{\overset{*}{\Rightarrow}} xy^2Xu^2t \underset{\omega_1}{\overset{*}{\Rightarrow}} \cdots \underset{\omega_1}{\overset{*}{\Rightarrow}} xy^nXu^nt \underset{\omega_2}{\overset{*}{\Rightarrow}} xy^nzu^nt,$$

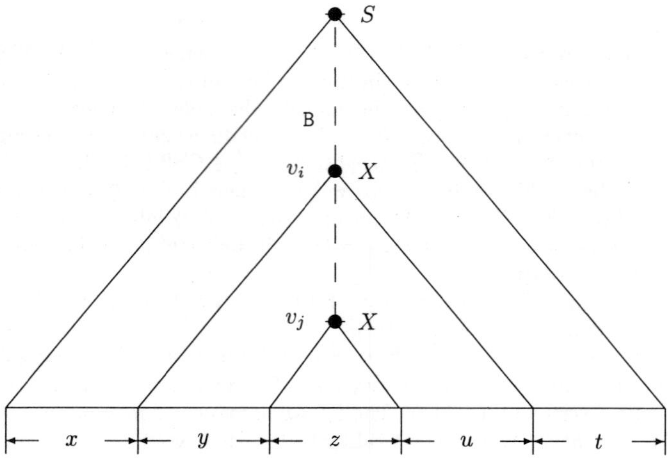

Figure 5.5: Derivation Tree T

so $xy^nzu^nt \in L(G)$ for $n \in \mathbb{N}$.

Since $h(v_i) > h(v_j)$, we must have $\| yzu \|_M > \| z \|_M$, so either $\| y \|_M \geq 1$, or $\| u \|_M \geq 1$. Also, since $h(v_i) \leq |A_N| + 1$, it follows that $\| yzu \|_M \leq \ell(G)^{|A_N|+1} = n_G$. ∎

The argument of Ogden's Lemma gives the next statement, which tells us something about certain phrases of words in the language generated by the grammar.

Corollary 5.5.3 *For every context-free grammar G and marking set M, there exists a number n_G such that if $w \in L(G)$ and $\| w \|_M \geq n_G$, then w can be written as $w = xyzut$ such that $\| y \|_M \geq 1$, $\| u \|_M \geq 1$, $\| yzu \|_M \leq n_G$ and $y^izu^i \in \mathsf{PHRASES}(w_i, G)$, where $w_i = xy^izu^it \in L(G)$ for every $i \in \mathbb{N}$.*

Proof. The argument is contained in the proof of Theorem 5.5.2. ∎

A special case of Ogden's Lemma is obtained when the marking set M coincides with $\mathbb{N}$:

Theorem 5.5.4 (Pumping Lemma of Bar-Hillel, Perles, and Shamir) *Let G be a context-free grammar. There exists a number $n_G \in \mathbb{N}$ such that if $w \in L(G)$ and $|w| \geq n_G$, then we can write $w = xyzut$ such that $|y| \geq 1$ or $|u| \geq 1$, $|yzu| \leq n_G$ and $xy^nzu^nt \in L(G)$ for all $n \in \mathbb{N}$.*

Proof. This statement follows immediately from Ogden's Lemma, by observing that $\| w \|_M = |w|$ if $M = \mathbb{N}$. ∎

Example 5.5.5 Let $A = \{a, b, c\}$ and let $L = \{a^nb^nc^n \mid n \in \mathbb{N}\}$. The language L is not context-free. Initially, we prove this statement by using the Pumping Lemma of Bar-Hillel, Perles, and Shamir.

Suppose that L were a context-free language. Then, there is $n_G \in \mathbb{N}$ satisfying the property stated in Theorem 5.5.4. Let $w = a^{n_G}b^{n_G}c^{n_G}$. Clearly, $|w| = 3n_G > n_G$, so $w = xyzut$ for some x, y, z, u, t such that $|y| \geq 1$ or $|u| \geq 1$, $|yzu| \leq n_G$ and $xy^nzu^nt \in L(G)$ for all $n \in \mathbb{N}$.

Note that neither y nor u may contain more than one type of symbol; indeed, if y contained both as and bs, then we could write $y = y'a \cdots ab \cdots by''$. Since

$$xy^2zu^2t = xy'a \cdots ab \cdots by''y'a \cdots ab \cdots by''zu^2t$$

we obtain a contradiction, since no b symbol may precede an a symbol in any word of $L(G)$. A similar argument works for u. Thus, each y and u may contain only one kind of symbol. Consequently, pumping y and u would violate the condition $n_a(w) = n_b(w) = n_c(w)$ satisfied by all words $w \in L(G)$. This shows that $L(G)$ does not satisfy the conditions of Theorem 5.5.4, hence $L(G)$ is not context-free.

One could make the same argument using Ogden's Lemma. Now let n_G be the number whose existence is guaranteed by this lemma, and assume that we mark all positions that contain b in the word $a^{n_G}b^{n_G}c^{n_G}$. Clearly, $|w| = 3n_G > n_G$, so $w = xyzut$ such that $\| y \|_M \geq 1$ or $\| u \|_M \geq 1$, $\| yzu \|_M \leq n_G$ and $xy^nzu^nt \in L(G)$ for all $n \in \mathbb{N}$. Then, at least one of y and z must contain a b. Moreover, by the same argument as above, they may consists only of one type of symbol, so they must both be infixes of b^{n_G}. Thus, pumping y and u increases the number of bs, which violates the condition $n_a(w) = n_b(w) = n_c(w)$. □

Ogden's Lemma allows us to show that certain languages are not context-free in situations when Theorem 5.5.4 would not allow us to make this argument.

Example 5.5.6 Consider the language $L = \{a^nb^nc^j \mid 0 \leq j \leq n\}$. We shall prove that this language is not context-free. Note, however, that Theorem 5.5.4 is not usable here, since L satisfies the conditions of this theorem. Indeed, let $w = a^nb^nc^j$ for some $n \geq n_G$, and let $j < n_G$. By choosing $y = a^p$ and $u = b^p$ with $p \geq 1$ we can write $w = xyzut$ such that $|y| \geq 1$ or $|u| \geq 1$, $|yzu| \leq n_G$ and $xy^nzu^nt \in L(G)$ for all $n \in \mathbb{N}$, since the pumping will increase the number of as and bs without violating the definition of the language.

To prove now that L is not context-free, assume, for the sake of obtaining a contradiction, that L is a context-free language, and let n_G be the number defined in Ogden's Lemma. Let $w = a^{n_G}b^{n_G}c^j$ for some $j < n_G$ and mark all positions that contain c. Since $|w| = 2n_G + j > n_G$, it follows that $w = xyzut$ such that $\| y \|_M \geq 1$ or $\| u \|_M \geq 1$, $\| yzu \|_M \leq n_G$ and $xy^nzu^nt \in L(G)$ for all $n \in \mathbb{N}$. Note that y and u must be infixes of a^{n_G}, b^{n_G}, or c^j. Since only positions that contain cs are marked, at least one of these words must contain a c, so at least one of them is an infix of c^j. Note that if they were both infixes of c^j, then, by pumping, we could obtain a word in $L(G)$ such that the number of cs would exceed the numbers of as or bs. If y is an infix of b^{n_G}, the pumping will increase the number of bs while the number of as will remain constant and thus the definition of L would be violated. A similar contradiction occurs when y is an infix of a^{n_G}. □

5.6 Closure Properties

We know that the class of context-free languages is closed with respect to union, product and Kleene closure. In this section we examine closure (and non-closure) properties of this class of languages with respect to other operations. We begin with two negative results.

Theorem 5.6.1 *The class $\mathcal{L}_2$ is not closed with respect to intersection.*

Proof. Consider the context-free grammars

$$\begin{aligned} G_0 &= (\{S,X,Y\},\{a,b,c\},S,\{S \to XY, X \to aXb, X \to \lambda,\\ &\quad Y \to cY, Y \to \lambda\})\\ G_1 &= (\{S,X,Y\},\{a,b,c\},S,\{S \to XY, X \to aX, X \to \lambda,\\ &\quad Y \to bYc, Y \to \lambda\}). \end{aligned}$$

It is easy to see that

$$\begin{aligned} L(G_0) &= \{a^m b^m c^p \mid m,p \in \mathbb{N}\}\\ L(G_1) &= \{a^m b^p c^p \mid m,p \in \mathbb{N}\}. \end{aligned}$$

Therefore, both $L_0 = \{a^m b^m c^p \mid m,p \in \mathbb{N}\}$ and $L_1 = \{a^m b^p c^p \mid m,p \in \mathbb{N}\}$ are context-free languages. On the other hand, since $L_0 \cap L_1 = \{a^n b^n c^n \mid n \in \mathbb{N}\}$, $L_0 \cap L_1$ does not belong to $\mathcal{L}_2$. ∎

Corollary 5.6.2 *The class $\mathcal{L}_2$ is not closed with respect to complement.*

Proof. Indeed, suppose that $\mathcal{L}_2$ were closed with respect to complement. Since $\mathcal{L}_2$ is closed with respect to union, and intersection can be expressed through union and complement (using De Morgan's equalities) this would imply that $\mathcal{L}_2$ is closed with respect to intersection. ∎

We have just seen that if L_0, L_1 are two context-free languages, then $L_0 \cap L_1$ is not necessarily a context-free language. However, if one of these languages is regular, their intersection is context-free.

Theorem 5.6.3 *If L is a context-free language and R is a regular language, then $L \cap R$ is a context-free language.*

Proof. Without loss of generality, we may assume that both L and R are languages over the same alphabet A_T. Initially, we also assume that neither L nor R contains the null word.

Suppose that $L = L(G)$, where $G = (A_N, A_T, S_0, P)$ is a λ-free context-free grammar and $R = L(\mathcal{M})$, where $\mathcal{M}$ is a deterministic finite automaton $\mathcal{M} = (A_T, Q, \delta, q_0, F)$. Define the context-free grammar $G' = (A'_N, A_T, S', P')$ as follows. The nonterminal alphabet A'_N consists of the new initial symbol S' together with $(|A_N| + |A_T|)|Q|^2$ new symbols of the form $s^{qq'}$ for every symbol $s \in A_N \cup A_T$ and every pair of states (q, q') of the automaton $\mathcal{M}$. The set P' consists of the following productions:

- $S' \to S^{q_0 q}$ for every final state q of $\mathcal{M}$;
- $X^{qq'} \to s_0^{qq_1} s_1^{q_1 q_2} \cdots s_{n-1}^{q_{n-1} q'}$ for every production $X \to s_0 \ldots s_{n-1}$ in P and every sequence of states $(q_1, \ldots, q_{n-1})$;
- $a^{qq'} \to a$ for every terminal symbol a of G such that $\delta(q, a) = q'$ in $\mathcal{M}$.

We claim that if $s^{qq'} \overset{n}{\underset{G'}{\Rightarrow}} x$ for some $x \in A_T^*$, then $\delta^*(q,x) = q'$ in $\mathcal{M}$ and that, if $s \in A_N \cup A_T$, then $s \overset{*}{\underset{G}{\Rightarrow}} x$. The argument is by induction on $n \geq 1$.

If $n = 1$ we have $s = x = a$ for some $a \in A_T$ and $\delta(q,a) = q'$ and the claim is clearly satisfied.

Suppose that the claim holds for derivations of length less than n, and let $s^{qq'} \overset{n}{\underset{G'}{\Rightarrow}} x$ be a derivation of length n. If we write the first step of this derivation explicitly, we obtain

$$s^{qq'} \underset{G'}{\Rightarrow} s_0^{qq_1} s_1^{q_1 q_2} \cdots s_{n-1}^{q_{n-1}q'} \overset{*}{\underset{G'}{\Rightarrow}} x.$$

Therefore, we have the production $s \to s_0 \ldots s_{n-1}$ in P, and we can write x as $x = x_0 \cdots x_{n-1}$, such that we have the derivations

$$\begin{array}{lll} s_0^{qq_1} & \overset{*}{\underset{G}{\Rightarrow}} & x_0 \\ s_1^{q_1 q_2} & \overset{*}{\underset{G}{\Rightarrow}} & x_1 \\ & \vdots & \\ s_{i-1}^{q_{i-1} q_i} & \overset{*}{\underset{G}{\Rightarrow}} & x_{i-1} \\ & \vdots & \\ s_{n-1}^{q_{n-1} q'} & \overset{*}{\underset{G}{\Rightarrow}} & x_{n-1} \end{array}$$

that are all shorter than n. By the inductive hypothesis we have

$$\delta^*(q, x_0) = q_1, \delta^*(q_1, x_1) = q_2, \ldots, \delta^*(q_{n-1}, x_{n-1}) = q',$$

so $\delta^*(q, x_0 \cdots x_{n-1}) = \delta^*(q,x) = q'$. Also, if s_i is a nonterminal, then $s_i \overset{*}{\underset{G}{\Rightarrow}} x_i$; otherwise, that is, if $s_i \in A_T$, we have $s_i = x_i$, so $s_i \overset{*}{\underset{G}{\Rightarrow}} x_i$ for $0 \leq i \leq n-1$. This allows us to construct the derivation

$$s \underset{G}{\Rightarrow} s_0 \ldots s_{n-1} \overset{*}{\underset{G}{\Rightarrow}} x_0 \ldots x_{n-1},$$

which justifies our claim.

We prove the theorem by showing that $L(G') = L \cap R$. Suppose that $x \in L(G')$. We have the derivation $S' \overset{*}{\underset{G'}{\Rightarrow}} x$, that is $S' \underset{G'}{\Rightarrow} S^{q_0 q} \overset{*}{\underset{G'}{\Rightarrow}} x$. By the previous claim this implies both $S \overset{*}{\underset{G}{\Rightarrow}} x$ and $\delta^*(q_0, x) = q$. Thus, $x \in L \cap R$.

Conversely, suppose that $x = a_0 \cdots a_{n-1} \in L \cap R$. We have the derivation $S \overset{*}{\underset{G}{\Rightarrow}} x$, so in G' we can write

$$S' \underset{G}{\Rightarrow} S^{q_0 q} \overset{*}{\underset{G}{\Rightarrow}} a_0^{q_0 q_1} a_1^{q_1 q_2} \cdots a_{n-1}^{q_{n-1} q},$$

for some final state q and any states $q_1, \ldots, q_{n-1}$. We can select these intermediate states such that $\delta(q_i, a_i) = q_{i+1}$ for $0 \leq i \leq n-2$ and $\delta(q_{n-1}, a_{n-1}) = q'$.

Therefore, we have the productions in P':

$$a_0^{q_0 q_1} \to a_0, a_1^{q_1 q_2} \to a_1, \ldots, a_{n-1}^{q_{n-1} q'} \to a_{n-1}$$

This implies the existence of the derivation $S' \overset{*}{\underset{G}{\Rightarrow}} a_0 a_1 \cdots a_{n-1}$, so $x \in L(G')$.

If $\lambda \in R$ or $\lambda \in L$ we consider the regular language $R' = R - \{\lambda\}$ and the context-free language $L' = L - \{\lambda\}$. By the previous argument we can construct a λ-free context-free grammar G' such that $L(G') = L' \cap R'$. If $\lambda \notin L \cap R$, then $L \cap R = L' \cap R'$ and this shows that $L \cap R$ is context-free. If $\lambda \in L \cap R$, we have $L \cap R = (L' \cap R') \cup \{\lambda\}$. Then, starting from $G' = (A'_N, A_T, S', P')$ we construct the context-free grammar

$$G'' = (A'_N \cup \{S''\}, A_T, S'', P' \cup \{S'' \to S', S'' \to \lambda\})$$

and we have $L \cap R = L(G'')$. ∎

Theorem 5.6.4 *Let $s : A^* \longrightarrow B^*$ be a substitution. If $s(a)$ is a context-free language for every $a \in A$ and $L \subseteq A^*$ is a context-free language, then $s(L)$ is a context-free language.*

Proof. Suppose that $L = L(G)$, where $G = (A_N, A, S, P)$ is a context-free grammar and let $s(a)$ is generated by the context-free grammar $G_a = (A_N^a, B, S_a, P_a)$ for $a \in A$. We may assume that the sets of nonterminal symbols A_N^a are pairwise disjoint. Let P' be the set of productions obtained from P as follows. In each production of P replace every letter $a \in A$ by the nonterminal S_a. We claim that the language $s(L)$ is generated by the grammar $G' = (A_N \cup \bigcup_{a \in A} A_N^a, B, S, P' \cup \bigcup_{a \in A} P_a)$.

Let $y \in s(L)$. There exists a word $x = a_{i_0} \ldots a_{i_{n-1}} \in L$ such that $y \in s(x)$. This means that $y = y_0 \ldots y_{n-1}$, where $y_k \in s(a_{i_k}) = L(G_{a_{i_k}})$ for $0 \leq k \leq n-1$. Thus, we have the derivations $S_{a_{i_k}} \overset{*}{\underset{G_{a_{i_k}}}{\Rightarrow}} y_k$ for $0 \leq k \leq n-1$, and the same derivations can be done in G'. Consequently, we obtain the derivation

$$S \overset{*}{\underset{G'}{\Rightarrow}} S_{a_{i_0}} \ldots S_{a_{i_{n-1}}} \overset{*}{\underset{G'}{\Rightarrow}} y_0 \ldots y_{n-1} = y, \tag{5.5}$$

which implies $y \in L(G')$, so $s(L) \subseteq L(G')$.

Conversely, if $y \in L(G')$, then any derivation $S \overset{*}{\underset{G'}{\Rightarrow}} y$ is of the form (5.5). By Theorem 4.5.1, y can be written as $y = y_0 \ldots y_{n-1}$, where $S_{a_{i_k}} \overset{*}{\underset{G'}{\Rightarrow}} y_k$ for $0 \leq k \leq n-1$, so $y_k \in L(G_{a_{i_k}}) = s(a_{i_k})$ for $0 \leq k \leq n-1$. This implies $y = y_0 \cdots y_{n-1} \in s(a_{i_0} \cdots s(a_{i_{n-1}}) = s(x) \in s(L)$, so $L(G') \subseteq s(L)$.

Since $s(L) = L(G')$, it follows that $s(L)$ is a context-free language. ∎

Corollary 5.6.5 *If $h : A^* \longrightarrow B^*$ is a morphism and $L \subseteq A^*$ is a context-free language, then $h(L)$ is a context-free language.*

Proof. This statement follows immediately from Theorem 5.6.4 since morphisms can be regarded as special cases of substitutions.

Theorem 5.6.6 *The class $\mathcal{L}_2$ is closed with respect to inverse morphic images. In other words, if $h : B^* \longrightarrow A^*$ is a morphism, and $L \subseteq A^*$ is a context-free language, then $h^{-1}(L)$ is a context-free language.*

Proof. Suppose that $B = \{b_0, \ldots , b_{m-1}\}$ and that $h(b_i) = x_i$ for $0 \leq i \leq m-1$. Let $B' = \{b'_0, \ldots , b'_{m-1}\}$, and let s be the substitution given by $s(a) = B'^*aB'^*$ for $a \in A$. Consider the finite language $H = \{b'_i x_i \mid 0 \leq i \leq m-1\}$ and the mapping $g : \mathcal{P}(A^*) \longrightarrow \mathcal{P}((A \cup B')^*)$ given by $g(L) = s(L) \cap H^*$.

Define the morphisms $h_1 : (A \cup B')^* \longrightarrow (\{c\} \cup B)^*$ and $h_2 : (\{c\} \cup B)^* \longrightarrow B^*$ by $h_1(a) = c$ for $a \in A$, $h_1(b') = b$ for all $b' \in B'$, and $h_2(c) = \lambda$, $h_2(b) = b$ for $b \in B$. We claim that for every language $L \in \mathcal{P}(A)$ such that $\lambda \notin L$, $h^{-1}(L) = g(h_2(h_1(L)))$ and hence, by three applications of Corollary 5.6.5, $h^{-1}(L)$ is context-free. This follows from the following equivalent statements:

1. $u = b_{i_0} \cdots b_{i_{k-1}} \in h^{-1}(L)$;
2. $h(u) = x_{i_0} \cdots x_{i_{k-1}} \in L$;
3. $b'_{i_0} x_{i_0} \cdots b'_{i_{k-1}} x_{i_{k-1}} \in g(L)$;
4. $h_1(b'_{i_0} x_{i_0} \cdots b'_{i_{k-1}} x_{i_{k-1}}) = b_{i_0} c \cdots c \cdots b_{i_{k-1}} c \cdots c \in h_1(g(L))$;
5. $h_2(b_{i_0} c \cdots c \cdots b_{i_{k-1}} c \cdots c) = b_{i_0} \cdots b_{i_{k-1}} = u \in h_2(h_1(g(L)))$.

If $\lambda \in L$, the language $L - \{\lambda\}$ is context-free, so $h^{-1}(L - \{\lambda\})$ is also context-free. Note that $h^{-1}(L) = h^{-1}(L - \{\lambda\}) \cup h^{-1}(\{\lambda\})$ and that $h^{-1}(\{\lambda\}) = \{a \in A \mid h(a) = \lambda\}^*$. Since $h^{-1}(\{\lambda\})$ is regular it follows that $h^{-1}(L)$ is context-free. ∎

Corollary 5.6.7 *Let $L \subseteq A^*$ be a context-free language and let $R \subseteq A^*$ be a regular language. Then,* shuffle(L, R) *is a context-free language.*

Proof. By Theorem 2.4.8, we have

$$\mathsf{shuffle}(L, R) = h(g^{-1}(L) \cap k^{-1}(R)),$$

where B is an appropriate alphabet and h, g, k are morphisms from B^* to A^*. Since $k^{-1}(R)$ is a regular language (by Theorem 3.9.12), the statement follows from Theorem 5.6.6 and Corollary 5.6.5. ∎

The relationship between context-free languages and transducers is given in the next theorem.

Theorem 5.6.8 *Let $\mathcal{T} = (A, Q, B, \theta, q_0, F)$ be a transducer. If $L \subseteq A^*$ is a context-free language, then $\mathcal{T}(L)$ is a context-free language over B.*

Proof. We saw in Theorem 3.10.8 that if $\mathcal{T} = (A, Q, B, \theta, q_0, F)$ is a transducer, then there exist an alphabet C, a morphism $h : C^* \longrightarrow A^*$, a morphism $g : C^* \longrightarrow B^*$ and a regular language $R \subseteq C^*$ such that for every language $L \subseteq A^*$ we have $\mathcal{T}(L) = g(h^{-1}(L) \cap R)$. Since the class of context-free languages is closed with respect to inverse morphic images (Theorem 5.6.6), intersection with regular languages (Theorem 5.6.3) and morphic images (Corollary 5.6.5) it follows that $\mathcal{T}(L)$ is a context-free language. ∎

Next, we discuss the closure of $\mathcal{L}_2$ with respect to quotients with regular languages.

Theorem 5.6.9 *If L is a context-free language and R is a regular language, then LR^{-1} and $R^{-1}L$ are both context-free languages.*

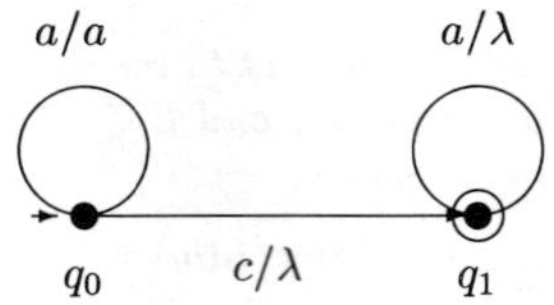

Figure 5.6: Graph of the transducer $\mathcal{T}$

Proof. Let A be an alphabet, and let c be a symbol such that $c \notin A$. Define the morphism $h : (A \cup \{c\})^* \longrightarrow A^*$ by $h(a) = a$ for $a \in A$ and $h(c) = \lambda$. Then, by Theorems 5.6.6 and 5.6.3, the language $h^{-1}(L) \cap A^*cR$ is context-free. Note that $w \in h^{-1}(L) \cap A^*cR$ if and only if $w = ucv$, where $uv \in L$ and $v \in R$ which is equivalent to $u \in LR^{-1}$. Now consider the transducer $\mathcal{T}$ whose graph is given in Figure 5.6. $\mathcal{T}$ will process a word $w = ucv$ with $u, v \in A^*$ as follows: all symbols in A are sent to the output intact until c is read. From that point on, the transducer produces only the null word at its output. Under the previous assumptions, $\mathcal{T}(w) = u$.

To summarize, the following statements are equivalent:

1. $u \in LR^{-1}$;
2. $uv \in L$ for some $v \in R$;
3. $ucv \in h^{-1}(L) \cap A^*cR$;
4. $u = \mathcal{T}(h^{-1}(L) \cap A^*cR)$.

Thus, $LR^{-1} = \mathcal{T}(h^{-1}(L) \cap A^*cR)$, which implies that $LR^{-1} \in \mathcal{L}_2$. The second part of the theorem follows from the equality (2.1) of Chapter 2 and from Theorem 4.3.18. ∎

5.7 Regular and Context-Free Languages

In this section we discuss relationships between the class of regular languages and the class of context-free languages.

Theorem 5.7.1 *Each context-free language over a one-letter alphabet is regular.*

Proof. Let $L \subseteq \{a\}^*$ be a context-free language over the alphabet $A = \{a\}$. Suppose initially that $\lambda \notin L$, and let $G = (A_N, A_T, S_0, P)$ be context-free grammar such that $L(G) = L$. By Theorem 5.5.4 there exists a number n_G such that, if $x \in L(G)$ and $|x| > n_G$, then x can be written as $x = uvwyz$ such that $vy \neq \lambda$, $|vwy| \leq n_G$ and $uv^iwy^iz \in L(G)$ for $i \in \mathbb{N}$.

We claim that if $x \in L$ and $|x| \geq n_G$, then $xa^{n_G!} \in L$. Indeed, since the concatenation of words over a one-letter alphabet is commutative, we can write $x = uwza^j$, where $vy = a^j$, $j \leq n_G$, and $uwz(a^j)^i \in L$ for $i \in \mathbb{N}$. In particular, taking $i = \frac{n_G!}{j} + 1$, this implies that

$$uwz(a^j)^{\frac{n_G!}{j}+1} = uwza^{j+n_G!} = uwza^j a^{n_G!} = xa^{n_G!} \in L,$$

for every word $x \in L$ such that $|x| \geq n_G$.

Consider the finite collection of languages $L_0, \ldots, L_{n_G!-1}$, where

$$L_i = a^{n_G+i}(a^{n_G!})^* \cap L$$

for $0 \leq i \leq n_G! - 1$. If $L_i \neq \emptyset$, let x_i be the shortest word in L_i. Then,

$$x \in \bigcup \{x_i(a^{n_G!})^* \mid 0 \leq i \leq n_G! - 1 \text{ and } L_i \neq \emptyset\}$$

for each $x \in L$ such that $|x| \geq n_G$. Indeed, if $x \in L$, $|x| \geq n_G$, and $|x| - n_G \equiv \ell$ (mod $n_G!$), where $0 \leq \ell \leq n_G! - 1$, then $|x| \in L_\ell$. Consequently, if x_ℓ is the shortest word from L_ℓ it follows that $x \in x_\ell(a^{n_G!})^*$. Therefore L can be written as a finite union of regular languages

$$L = \{x \mid x \in L \text{ and } |x| < n_G\} \cup \{x_i(a^{n_G!})^* \mid L_i \neq \emptyset, 0 \leq i \leq n_G! - 1\}.$$

This implies that L is regular.

When $\lambda \in L$ the same argument can be applied for the context-free language $L' = L - \{\lambda\}$. Since L' is regular, the regularity of L follows immediately. ∎

The class of regular languages can be characterized as a subclass of the class of context-free languages.

Definition 5.7.2 Let $G = (A_N, A_T, S, P)$ be a context-free grammar. We refer to G as *self-embedding* if there is $X \in A_N$ and $\alpha, \beta \in (A_N \cup A_T)^+$ such that $X \overset{*}{\underset{G}{\Rightarrow}} \alpha X \beta$. □

Theorem 5.7.3 *A context-free language L is regular if and only if there exists a context-free grammar G such that $L(G) = L$ and G is not self-embedding.*

Proof. If L is a regular language, then L can be generated by a right-linear grammar; since any such grammar is not self-embedding the necessity of the condition is immediate.

Conversely, assume that $L = L(G)$, where G is a context-free, non self-embedding grammar. Without loss of generality we may assume that all nonterminal symbols are accessible.

Two cases may occur:

1. There exists a derivation of the form $X \overset{*}{\underset{G}{\Rightarrow}} \gamma S \gamma'$ for some $\gamma, \gamma' \in (A_N \cup A_T)^*$ for each nonterminal X.
2. There exists a nonterminal X such that for no words $\gamma, \gamma' \in (A_N \cup A_T)^*$ does there exist a derivation of the form $X \overset{*}{\underset{G}{\Rightarrow}} \gamma S \gamma'$.

In the first case, we show that G must be either left- or right-linear. Any production that contains nonterminals in its right member has one of the forms: $X \rightarrow \alpha Y \beta$, $X \rightarrow \alpha Y$, $X \rightarrow Y \beta$, or $X \rightarrow Y$, where $\alpha, \beta \in (A_N \cup A_T)^+$. If P contains a production $X \rightarrow \alpha Y \beta$ we have the derivation:

$$X \underset{G}{\Rightarrow} \alpha Y \beta \overset{*}{\underset{G}{\Rightarrow}} \alpha \gamma S \gamma' \beta \overset{*}{\underset{G}{\Rightarrow}} \alpha \gamma \delta X \delta' \gamma \beta,$$

which contradicts the fact that G is not self-embedding (because both $\alpha \neq \lambda$ and $\beta \neq \lambda$).

Similarly, it is immediate (for the same reason) that G may not simultaneously contain both productions of the form $X \to \alpha Y$ and of the form $X \to Y\beta$. Therefore, G can be either right-linear or left-linear, so $L(G)$ is regular.

In the second case, suppose that there exists a nonterminal Z such that for no words $\gamma, \gamma' \in (A_N \cup A_T)^*$ does there exist a derivation of the form $Z \overset{*}{\underset{G}{\Rightarrow}} \gamma S \gamma'$. We can prove by induction on $n = |A_N|$ that $L(G)$ is regular.

The base case $n = 1$ is vacuous since in this case we have $A_N = \{S\}$ and $S \overset{*}{\underset{G}{\Rightarrow}} S$.

Suppose that the statement holds for context-free grammars with fewer than n nonterminals and let $G' = (A_N - \{Z\}, A_T \cup \{Z\}, S, P')$ be the grammar obtained from G by moving the symbol Z from the nonterminal alphabet into the terminal alphabet and by eliminating all productions that have Z in their left member. Note that G' is still non-self embedding, so by the inductive hypothesis, the language $L(G')$ is regular. Also, consider the grammar $G'' = (A_N - \{S\}, A_T, Z, P'')$ obtained by removing the start symbol from the nonterminal alphabet, replacing S with the new start symbol Z, and removing from P all productions that contain S. Both $L(G')$ and $L(G'')$ are regular, by the inductive hypothesis. Since S was inaccessible from Z we have $L(G'') = \{u \in A_T^* \mid Z \overset{*}{\underset{G}{\Rightarrow}} u\}$, and $L(G)$ can be obtained from $L(G')$ by substituting $L(G'')$ for Z. Since the class of regular languages is closed with respect to substitutions (see Theorem 3.9.10), it follows that $L(G)$ is regular. ∎

5.8 Ambiguity

We defined unambiguous and inherently ambiguous context-free languages in Section 5.2. The goal of this section is to prove the existence of inherently ambiguous languages and to examine several important cases of unambiguous languages.

In the proof of Theorem 5.6.1, we introduced the context-free grammars

$$\begin{aligned} G_0 &= (\{S, X, Y\}, \{a, b, c\}, S, \{S \to XY, X \to aXb, X \to \lambda, \\ &\quad\; Y \to cY, Y \to \lambda\}) \\ G_1 &= (\{S, X, Y\}, \{a, b, c\}, S, \{S \to XY, X \to aX, X \to \lambda, \\ &\quad\; Y \to bYc, Y \to \lambda\}), \end{aligned}$$

where

$$\begin{aligned} L_0 &= L(G_0) = \{a^m b^m c^p \mid m, p \in \mathbb{N}\} \\ L_1 &= L(G_1) = \{a^m b^p c^p \mid m, p \in \mathbb{N}\}. \end{aligned}$$

While $L(G_0) \cap L(G_1)$ is not a context-free language, $L(G_0) \cup L(G_1)$ is context-free and has the interesting property discussed in the next theorem.

Theorem 5.8.1 *The language $L = L(G_0) \cup L(G_1)$ is inherently ambiguous.*

Proof. We need to show that any context-free grammar that generates the language L is ambiguous. Suppose that G is a unambiguous context-free grammar such that $L(G) = L_0 \cup L_1$. Let n_G be the number given by Ogden Lemma for G and consider the words w_0, w_1 given by:

$$\begin{aligned} w_0 &= a^{n_G} b^{n_G} c^{n_G + n_G!} \in L_0 - L_1 \\ w_1 &= a^{n_G + n_G!} b^{n_G} c^{n_G} \in L_1 - L_0 \end{aligned}$$

We shall prove that w_0 and w_1 can both be "pumped" into a word w that has overlapping phrases, thus contradicting the fact that G is unambiguous (cf. Theorem 5.2.22).

Note that the part of a word that is pumped (using Ogden Lemma) is always a phrase in the grammar G. Suppose that we mark all positions occupied by bs in both w_0 and w_1. Since $\| w_0 \| = n_G$ we can write $w_0 = x_0 y_0 z_0 u_0 t_0$ such that at least one of the words y_0, u_0 contains a symbol b, $y_0^i z u_0^i \in \mathsf{PHRASES}(s_i, G)$, and $s_i = x_0 y_0^i z_0 u_0^i t \in L(G)$ for every $i \in L(G)$ due to Corollary 5.5.3. It is clear that neither y_0 nor u_0 may contain two distinct types of symbols, because, by pumping those words, we would obtain words that violate the definition of the language $L(G)$, where the as precede the bs and the bs precede the cs. Therefore, several cases may occur.

1. Suppose that both y_0 and u_0 contain only b symbols. In this case, by pumping y_0 and u_0 a sufficient number of times we could exceed both the number of as and the number of cs, which would violate the definition of $L(G)$. Therefore, this case may be excluded.
2. Assume that y_0 contains b symbols and z_0 contains c symbols, say $y_0 = b^k$ and $u_0 = c^j$ and $k \geq 1$. Further, assume that

   $$s_i = a^{n_G} b^{n_G - k + ki} c^{n_G + n_G! - j + ji} \in L(G)$$

   for every $i \in \mathbb{N}$. If $i \geq 1$, then $s_i \notin L_0$ because the number of bs in s_i is different from the number of as. Then, we must have $s_i \in L_1$, that is, $n_G - k + ki = n_G + n_G! - j + ji$. This gives $k \neq j$ and $i = \frac{n_G!}{k-j} + 1$. Since this must hold for every $i \in \mathbb{N}$ we have a contradiction. Thus, we can exclude this case.
3. Finally, suppose y_0 contains a symbols and z_0 contains b symbols, say $y_0 = a^k$ and $u_0 = b^j$. The pumping affects only the as and the bs, and we must have $k = j$ since, otherwise, the number of as and bs in the pumped words will differ and, after enough pumping, the number of bs will exceed the number of cs. This is the single acceptable situation.

The above discussion implies that $s_i = a^{n_G - k + ki} b^{n_G - k + ki} c^{n_G + n_G!} \in L(G)$ and $a^{ki} b^{\ell + ki} \in \mathsf{PHRASES}(s_i, G)$ for $i \in \mathbb{N}$ and some $\ell \in \mathbb{N}$. By choosing i such that $n_G - k + ki = n_G + n_G!$, that is, $i = \frac{n_G!}{k} + 1$, we obtain $s_i = a^{n_G + n_G!} b^{n_G + n_G!} b^{n_G + n_G!} \in L(G)$ and $a^{n_G! + k} b^{\ell + n_G! + k} \in \mathsf{PHRASES}(s_i, G)$.

In a similar manner, by using the word w_1 we can prove that s_i can be obtained by pumping infixes of w_1 and that $b^{\ell' + n_G! + k'} c^{n_G! + k'} \in \mathsf{PHRASES}(s_i, G)$. Note, however, that the phrases $a^{n_G! + k} b^{\ell + n_G! + k}$ and $b^{\ell' + n_G! + k'} c^{n_G! + k'}$ are not disjoint (since $n_G! \geq 1$), and this contradicts our assumption regarding the unambiguity of the grammar G. ∎

Theorem 5.8.2 *Every regular language is unambiguous.*

Proof. Let $L \subseteq A^*$ be a regular language and let $\mathcal{M} = (A, Q, \delta, q_0, F)$ be a dfa such that $L = L(\mathcal{M})$. If G is the type-3 grammar attached to $\mathcal{M}$ (as shown in the proofs of Theorems 4.2.14 and 4.6.2), then G is a unambiguous grammar. Indeed, if $x = a_{i_0} \cdots a_{i_{n-1}} \in L(G)$, then there exists a unique leftmost derivation:

$$q_0 \underset{G}{\Rightarrow} a_{i_0} q_1 \underset{G}{\Rightarrow} a_{i_0} a_{i_1} q_2 \underset{G}{\Rightarrow} \cdots \underset{G}{\Rightarrow} a_{i_0} \cdots a_{i_{n-1}} q_n \underset{G}{\Rightarrow} a_{i_0} \cdots a_{i_{n-1}},$$

where $q_{k+1} = \delta(q_k, a_k)$ for $0 \leq k \leq n-1$ and $q_n \in F$. ∎

Note that $\mathcal{L}_3$ is a proper subclass of the class of unambiguous context-free languages since the context-free language $\{a^n b^n \mid n \in \mathbb{N}\}$ is unambiguous but not regular. Indeed, let $G = (\{S\}, \{a, b\}, S, \{S \to aSb, S \to \lambda\}$ be a context-free grammar. It is easy to see that $L(G) = \{a^n b^n \mid n \in \mathbb{N}\}$. A word $a^n b^n$ from L has a unique derivation in this grammar:

$$S \underset{G}{\Rightarrow} aSb \cdots \underset{G}{\Rightarrow} a^n S b^n \underset{G}{\Rightarrow} a^n b^n,$$

so G is unambiguous, and therefore, L is unambiguous.

Example 5.8.3 In this example we show that the language L_{ae} of parenthesized arithmetic expressions that can be written using the operation symbols $+, -, *$ and $/$ is unambiguous. To simplify our discussion we use two place holder symbols $\boldsymbol{v}$ and $\boldsymbol{n}$ for variables and integers, respectively.

Let

$$G_{ae} = (\{X_e, X_t, X_f\}, \{+, -, *, /, (,), \boldsymbol{v}, \boldsymbol{n}\}, X_e, P)$$

the context-free grammar introduced in Example 5.3.2 whose set of productions consists of

$$\begin{array}{l} \pi_0 : X_e \to X_e + X_t, \pi_1 : X_e \to X_e - X_t, \pi_2 : X_e \to X_t, \\ \pi_3 : X_t \to X_t * X_f, \pi_4 : X_t \to X_t / X_f, \pi_5 : X_t \to X_f \\ \pi_6 : X_f \to \boldsymbol{v}, \pi_7 : X_f \to \boldsymbol{n}, \pi_8 : X_f \to (X_e). \end{array}$$

We saw that this context-free grammar is essentially identical to the Backus-Naur definition of arithmetic expressions given at the beginning of Section 5.3. We define L_{ae} as $L(G_{ae})$. For example, since

$$\begin{array}{l} X_e \underset{G_{ae}}{\Rightarrow} X_t \underset{G_{ae}}{\Rightarrow} X_t * X_f \\ \underset{G_{ae}}{\Rightarrow} X_f * X_f \underset{G_{ae}}{\Rightarrow} \boldsymbol{v} * X_f \\ \underset{G_{ae}}{\Rightarrow} \boldsymbol{v} * (X_e) \underset{G_{ae}}{\Rightarrow} \boldsymbol{v} * (X_e + X_t) \\ \underset{G_{ae}}{\Rightarrow} \boldsymbol{v} * (X_t + X_t) \underset{G_{ae}}{\Rightarrow} \boldsymbol{v} * (X_f + X_t) \\ \underset{G_{ae}}{\Rightarrow} \boldsymbol{v} * (\boldsymbol{n} + X_t) \underset{G_{ae}}{\Rightarrow} \boldsymbol{v} * (\boldsymbol{n} + X_f) \\ \underset{G_{ae}}{\Rightarrow} \boldsymbol{v} * (\boldsymbol{n} + \boldsymbol{v}), \end{array}$$

it follows that $\boldsymbol{v} * (\boldsymbol{n} + \boldsymbol{v})$ is an arithmetic expression.

To prove that G_{ae} is an unambiguous grammar, we show that for every nonterminal symbol X and every terminal word w, if $X \overset{*}{\underset{G_{ae}}{\Rightarrow}} w$, then there exists a unique leftmost derivation of w from X in G_{ae}.

Claim I. If $X \overset{m}{\underset{G_{ae}}{\Rightarrow}} w$, where $X \in \{X_e, X_t, X_f\}$ and w is a terminal word, then $n_((w) = n_)(w)$.

The argument is by induction on $m \geq 1$. For $m = 1$, we have either $w = \boldsymbol{v}$ or $w = \boldsymbol{n}$. In either case, $n_((w) = n_)(w) = 0$, so the claim holds for the basis case.

Assume now that $m > 1$ and that the claim holds for derivations with fewer than m steps. We have three cases to consider, one for each of X_e, X_t and X_f.

Case I.1: If $X = X_e$, we need to consider three subcases, one for each possible first production.

Case I.1.1: If $X_e \underset{G_{ae}}{\Rightarrow} X_e + X_t \overset{m-1}{\underset{G_{ae}}{\Rightarrow}} w$, then we can write $w = x + y$ such that $X_e \overset{p}{\underset{G_{ae}}{\Rightarrow}} x$ and $X_t \overset{q}{\underset{G_{ae}}{\Rightarrow}} y$, where $p, q < m - 1$. By the inductive hypothesis, $n_((x) = n_)(x)$ and $n_((y) = n_)(y)$, so $n_((w) = n_((x) + n_((y) = n_)(x) + n_)(y) = n_)(w)$.

Case I.1.2: If $X_e \underset{G_{ae}}{\Rightarrow} X_e - X_t \overset{m-1}{\underset{G_{ae}}{\Rightarrow}} w$, then the argument is identical to the previous one.

Case I.1.3: If $X_e \underset{G_{ae}}{\Rightarrow} X_t \overset{m-1}{\underset{G_{ae}}{\Rightarrow}} w$, then by the inductive hypothesis we obtain $n_((w) = n_)(w)$.

Case I.2: $X = X_t$ mirrors Case I.1 and is left to the reader.

Case I.3: In this case $X = X_f$. Since $m > 1$, we must have

$$X \Rightarrow (X_e) \overset{m-1}{\Rightarrow} w,$$

so the result follows immediately from the inductive hypothesis.

This concludes the argument for Claim I.

Let (ξ, i) be the occurrence of ξ in a word $x \in \{+, -, *, /, (,), \boldsymbol{v}, \boldsymbol{n}\}^*$, where ξ is one of the symbols $+, -, *, /$. The *level of this occurrence in* x is defined as $\ell_x(\xi, i) = n_((x_{0,i-1}) - n_)(x_{0,i-1})$, that is, the difference between the number of left parentheses located to the left of the occurrence (ξ, i) and the number of right parentheses located to the left of the same occurrence. Note that if y is a prefix of x that includes the occurrence (ξ, i), then $\ell_y(\xi, i) = \ell_x(\xi, i)$.

Claim II. If (ξ, i) is an occurrence of $\xi \in \{+, -, *, /\}$ in x, then

- $X_e \overset{m}{\underset{G_{ae}}{\Rightarrow}} x$ implies $\ell_x(\xi, i) \geq 0$;
- $X_t \overset{m}{\underset{G_{ae}}{\Rightarrow}} x$ implies $\ell_x(\xi, i) \geq 0$, and $\ell_x(\xi, i) = 0$ implies $\xi = *$ or $\xi = /$.
- $X_f \overset{m}{\underset{G_{ae}}{\Rightarrow}} x$ implies $\ell_x(\xi, i) > 0$.

Again, the argument is by induction on $m \geq 1$. If $m = 1$, then x does not contain any occurrence of ξ, so the statement holds vacuously.

Assume now that $m > 1$ and that this triple statement holds for derivations shorter than m. Let (ξ, i) be an occurrence of ξ in x, where $X \overset{m}{\underset{G_{ae}}{\Rightarrow}} x$. There are again three cases, one for each of X_e, X_t, and X_f.

Case II.1: If $X = X_e$, we have three subcases, depending on the first production applied in the derivation.

Case II.1.1: If $X_e \underset{G_{ae}}{\Rightarrow} X_e{+}X_t \overset{m-1}{\underset{G_{ae}}{\Rightarrow}} w$, then $w = x{+}y$, where $X_e \overset{p}{\underset{G_{ae}}{\Rightarrow}} x$ and $X_t \overset{q}{\underset{G_{ae}}{\Rightarrow}} y$, for some $p, q < m-1$. If $i \leq |x|$, then (ξ, i) is an occurrence in x and, by the inductive hypothesis, $\ell_w(\xi, i) = \ell_x(\xi, i) \geq 0$. If $i = |x| + 1$, Claim I implies $\ell_w(\xi, i) = 0$ because the number of occurrences of left and right parentheses in x are equal. Finally, if $i > |x| + 1$, the occurrence (ξ, i) in x corresponds to the occurrence $(\xi, i - |x| - 1)$ in y. By the inductive hypothesis we have $\ell_y(\xi, i - |x| - 1) \geq 0$, so $\ell_w(\xi, i) \geq 0$.

Case II.1.2: The subcase $X_e \underset{G_{ae}}{\Rightarrow} X_e - X_t \overset{m-1}{\underset{G_{ae}}{\Rightarrow}} w$ is entirely similar to the previous one.

Case II.1.3: If

$$X_e \underset{G_{ae}}{\Rightarrow} X_t \overset{m-1}{\underset{G_{ae}}{\Rightarrow}} w,$$

the inductive hypothesis implies $\ell_w(\xi, i) \geq 0$.

Case II.2: If $X = X_t$, we need to consider three subcases:

Case II.2.1: If the first production applied was $X_t \rightarrow X_t * X_f$, then $X_t \underset{G_{ae}}{\Rightarrow} X_t{*}X_f \overset{m-1}{\underset{G_{ae}}{\Rightarrow}} w$, so $w = u{*}v$, where $X_t \overset{p}{\underset{G_{ae}}{\Rightarrow}} u$ and $X_f \overset{q}{\underset{G_{ae}}{\Rightarrow}} v$. Any occurrence (ξ, i) with $i < |u| - 1$ is actually an occurrence in u and, by the inductive hypothesis we have $\ell_w(\xi, i) = \ell_u(\xi, i) \geq 0$. Moreover, by the inductive hypothesis, if $\ell_u(\xi, i) = 0$, then $\xi = *$ or $\xi = /$. If $i = |u|$, then $\xi = *$ and $\ell_w(*, i) = 0$ because in u we have an equal number of left and right parentheses. If $i > |u|$, then the occurrence (ξ, i) in w corresponds to the occurrence $(\xi, i - |u| - 1)$ in v, so $\ell_w(\xi, i) > 0$, again by the inductive hypothesis.

Case II.2.2: The subcase when the first production applied was $X_t \rightarrow X_t / X_f$ is similar to the previous subcase and is left to the reader.

Case II.2.3: If the first production applied was $X_t \rightarrow X_f$, then we have $X_f \overset{*}{\underset{m-1}{\Rightarrow}} w$, and the result follows from the inductive hypothesis.

Case II.3: If $X_f \overset{m}{\underset{G_{ae}}{\Rightarrow}} w$ and $m > 1$, then this derivation can be written as

$$X_f \underset{G_{ae}}{\Rightarrow} (X_e) \overset{m-1}{\underset{G_{ae}}{\Rightarrow}} w.$$

The word w can be written as $w = (u)$, where $X_e \overset{m-1}{\underset{G_{ae}}{\Rightarrow}} u$. Then, $\ell_w(\xi, i) = 1 + \ell_u(\xi, i) > 0$.

This concludes the argument for Claim II.

Having now established some necessary preliminaries, we proceed with the main part of the proof. Suppose that $X \overset{*}{\underset{G_{ae}}{\Rightarrow}} x$ and $|x| = n \geq 1$. We prove that there is a unique leftmost derivation of x starting from X, where $X \in \{X_e, X_f, X_t\}$. The argument is by induction on n.

In the basis case, $n = 1$, we have either $x = \boldsymbol{v}$ or $x = \boldsymbol{n}$. If $X_e \overset{*}{\underset{G_{ae}}{\Rightarrow}} \boldsymbol{v}$ the leftmost derivation is

$$X_e \underset{G_{ae}}{\Rightarrow} X_t \underset{G_{ae}}{\Rightarrow} X_f \underset{G_{ae}}{\Rightarrow} \boldsymbol{v}.$$

The unique leftmost derivations when $X = X_t$ or $X = X_f$ are included in the derivation above. The case $x = \boldsymbol{n}$ is entirely similar.

Suppose that unique leftmost derivations exists for any word of length less than n that is derivable from X, where $X \in \{X_e, X_t, X_f\}$, and $n > 1$.

Let x be a word such that $|x| = n$ and $X_f \overset{*}{\underset{G_{ae}}{\Rightarrow}} x$. Since $n > 1$, the first symbol of x is a left parenthesis. Therefore, the first production used is $X_f \to (X_e)$ and x can be written as $x = (y)$, where $|y| = n - 2$. By the inductive hypothesis, there exists a unique leftmost derivation $X_e \overset{*}{\underset{G_{ae},\text{left}}{\Rightarrow}} y$. This implies the existence of a unique leftmost derivation

$$X_f \underset{G_{ae},\text{left}}{\Rightarrow} (X_e) \overset{*}{\underset{G_{ae},\text{left}}{\Rightarrow}} (y) = x.$$

Now let x be a word such that $X_t \overset{*}{\underset{G}{\Rightarrow}} x$. Depending on the symbols that occur in x we have the following cases:

Case tA: If no occurrences (ξ, i) with $\ell_x(\xi, i) = 0$ exist in x, then the first production applied is $X_t \to X_f$. Therefore, the uniqueness of the leftmost derivation $X_t \overset{*}{\underset{G_{ae},\text{left}}{\Rightarrow}} x$ follows from uniqueness of the leftmost derivation $X_f \overset{*}{\underset{G_{ae},\text{left}}{\Rightarrow}} x$.

Case tB: Suppose that x contains occurrences (ξ, k) such that $\ell_x(\xi, k) = 0$. Then, ξ can be $*$ or $/$. Let (ξ, h) be the rightmost occurrence in x of ξ such that $\ell_x(\xi, h) = 0$. We claim that the first production applied in a derivation $X_t \overset{*}{\underset{G_{ae}}{\Rightarrow}} x$ is $X_t \to X_t \xi X_f$.

Note that a derivation of x cannot start with the application of the production $X_t \to X_f$, because this would imply $X_f \overset{*}{\underset{G}{\Rightarrow}} x$, and, by Claim II, we would have $\ell(\xi, k) > 0$. Therefore, the first production of any derivation must have the form $X_t \to X_t \xi' X_f$.

By Theorem 4.5.1, $X_t \overset{*}{\underset{G_{ae}}{\Rightarrow}} x_{0,p}$, $\xi' = x_{p,p+1}$, and $X_f \overset{*}{\underset{G_{ae}}{\Rightarrow}} x_{p+1,n-1}$. Since, by Claim I, $n_{(}(x_{0,p}) = n_{)}(x_{0,p})$, we have $\ell_x(\xi', p) = 0$. Therefore, (ξ', p) coincides with, or is located at the left of the occurrence (ξ, k). Suppose that $p < k$. Then, (ξ, k) corresponds to an occurrence (ξ, q) of ξ in $x_{p+1\,n}$ and, by Claim II, we would have $\ell_z(\xi, q) > 0$, where $z = x_{p+1\,n}$. Since the left and right parentheses balance in $x_{0,p}$, it follows that $\ell_x(\xi, k) = \ell_z(\xi, q) > 0$. This contradiction shows that $p = k$, and $\xi' = \xi$. From the inductive hypothesis, we have the unique leftmost derivations:

$$X_t \overset{*}{\underset{G_{ae},\text{left}}{\Rightarrow}} x_{0,p} \text{ and } X_f \overset{*}{\underset{G_{ae},\text{left}}{\Rightarrow}} x_{p+1\,n}.$$

Thus, we have the leftmost derivation:

$$X_t \underset{G_{ae},\text{left}}{\Rightarrow} X_t\xi X_f \underset{G_{ae},\text{left}}{\overset{*}{\Rightarrow}} x_{0,p}\xi X_f \underset{G_{ae},\text{left}}{\overset{*}{\Rightarrow}} x_{0,p}\xi x_{p+1\ n} = x.$$

Suppose now that $X_e \underset{G_{ae}}{\overset{*}{\Rightarrow}} x$.

Case eA: If the word x contains no level-0 occurrences of the symbols $+$ or $-$, then the first production applied in the derivation was $X_e \to X_t$, since otherwise, the application of $X_e \to X_e + X_t$ or $X_e \to X_e - X_t$ would create such occurrences. Therefore, the derivation can be written as

$$X_e \underset{G_{ae}}{\Rightarrow} X_t \underset{G_{ae}}{\overset{*}{\Rightarrow}} x,$$

and, by the previous argument, there exists a unique leftmost derivation $X_t \underset{G_{ae},\text{left}}{\overset{*}{\Rightarrow}} x$. This implies the uniqueness of the leftmost derivation $X_e \underset{G_{ae},\text{left}}{\overset{*}{\Rightarrow}} x$.

Case eB: Now suppose that x contains some level-0 occurrences of $\xi \in \{+, -\}$, and let (ξ, i) be the rightmost such occurrence. The first production applied has the form $X_e \to X_e\xi' X_t$, so we have $X_e \underset{G_{ae}}{\overset{*}{\Rightarrow}} x_{0,p}\xi' x_{p+1\ n} = x$, where $X_e \underset{G_{ae}}{\overset{*}{\Rightarrow}} x_{0,p}$, and $X_t \underset{G_{ae}}{\overset{*}{\Rightarrow}} x_{p+1\ n}$. The definition of (ξ, i) implies that $p \leq i$. Suppose that $p < i$. Then, (ξ, i) corresponds to an occurrence (ξ, k) in $z = x_{p+1\ n}$ and, by the second part of Claim II, $\ell_z(\xi, k) > 0$ because $\xi \notin \{*, /\}$. Since, by Claim I, the number of left parentheses in $x_{0,p}$ equals the number of right parentheses in the same word, we have $\ell_z(\xi, k) = \ell_x(\xi, i)$. This contradicts the definition of (ξ, i), so we have $p = i$. Thus, $\xi' = \xi$. The inductive hypothesis implies the existence of the unique leftmost derivations $X_e \underset{G_{ae},\text{left}}{\overset{*}{\Rightarrow}} x_{0,p}$, and $X_t \underset{G_{ae},\text{left}}{\overset{*}{\Rightarrow}} x_{p+1\ n}$, so we have a unique leftmost derivation:

$$X_e \underset{G_{ae},\text{left}}{\Rightarrow} X_e\xi X_t \underset{G_{ae},\text{left}}{\overset{*}{\Rightarrow}} x_{0,i}\xi X_t \underset{G_{ae},\text{left}}{\overset{*}{\Rightarrow}} x_{0,i}\xi x_{i+1\ n}.$$

Since G_{ae} is unambiguous grammar, it follows that L_{ae} is a unambiguous language. □

5.9 Parikh Theorem

Parikh Theorem describes the number of occurrences of various symbols in words that may appear in a context-free language.

Definition 5.9.1 Let $A = \{a_0, \ldots, a_{k-1}\}$ be an alphabet. The *Parikh mapping* $\mathsf{pk} : A^* \longrightarrow \mathbb{N}^k$ is given by $\mathsf{pk}(w) = (n_{a_0}(w), \ldots, n_{a_{k-1}}(w))$ for $w \in A^*$. □

Addition of k-tuples in $\mathbb{N}^k$ and multiplication of a k-tuple by a number are defined componentwise. Namely,

$$(p_0, \ldots, p_{k-1}) + (q_0, \ldots, q_{k-1}) = (p_0 + q_0, \ldots, p_{k-1} + q_{k-1})$$

and

$$r(p_0, \ldots, p_{k-1}) = (rp_0, \ldots, rp_{k-1}),$$

for every $r \in \mathbb{N}$ and $(p_0, \ldots, p_{k-1}), (q_0, \ldots, q_{k-1}) \in \mathbb{N}^k$.

Note that $\mathsf{pk}(ww') = \mathsf{pk}(w) + \mathsf{pk}(w')$. Also, if $\mathsf{pk}(L) = \{\mathsf{pk}(w) \mid w \in L\}$, then $\mathsf{pk}(L_0L_1) = \{\vec{v}_0 + \vec{v}_1 \mid \vec{v}_0 \in \mathsf{pk}(L_0) \text{ and } \vec{v}_1 \in \mathsf{pk}(L_1)\}$.

Example 5.9.2 Let $A = \{a_0, a_1, a_2\}$ be an alphabet. If $w = a_1a_2a_1a_0a_2a_0a_1 \in A^*$, then $\mathsf{pk}(w) = (2, 3, 2)$. □

Definition 5.9.3 A set $\boldsymbol{L} \subseteq \mathbb{N}^k$ is a *linear set* if there exist $\vec{v}_0, \vec{v}_1, \ldots, \vec{v}_n \in \mathbb{N}^k$ such that

$$\boldsymbol{L} = \{\vec{v} \in \mathbb{N}^k \mid \vec{v} = \vec{v}_0 + m_1\vec{v}_1 + \cdots + m_n\vec{v}_n\}.$$

Any finite union of linear sets is referred to as a *semilinear set.* □

It is clear that the union of a finite family of semilinear sets is a semilinear set.

Theorem 5.9.4 (Parikh Theorem) *Let $A = \{a_0, \ldots, a_{k-1}\}$ be an alphabet. If $L \subseteq A^*$ is a context-free language, then $\mathsf{pk}(L)$ is a semilinear subset of $\mathbb{N}^k$.*

Proof. Suppose initially that $\lambda \notin L$. Then, by Theorem 5.4.2, there is a grammar $G = (A_N, A_T, S, P)$ in Chomsky normal form such that $L = L(G)$.

Let B be a subset of A_N and let L_B be the set of all words w in $L(G)$ such that there exists a derivation $S \overset{*}{\underset{G}{\Rightarrow}} w$ such that the set of nonterminal symbols that occur in this derivation coincides with $B \cup \{S\}$. Clearly, we have

$$L(G) = \bigcup\{L_B \mid B \in \mathcal{P}(A_N)\}.$$

To prove the theorem it suffices to show that $\mathsf{pk}(L_B)$ is a semilinear set because there exist only a finite number of sets L_B.

Define a (B, X)-tree to be a derivation tree $\mathtt{T}$ with its root labeled by X, having $B \cup \{X\}$ as the set of labels of its interior nodes, and satisfying the constraint that no path contains more than $|B| + 1$ nodes labeled with the same nonterminal symbol. The finite languages D_B and $E_{B,X}$ are given by

$$\begin{aligned} D_B &= \{x \in L(G) \mid x = \mathsf{word}(\mathtt{T}) \text{ for some } (B, S)\text{-tree } \mathtt{T}\} \\ E_{B,X} &= \{u'Xu'' \in A_T^*A_NA_T^* \mid u'Xu'' = \mathsf{word}(\mathtt{T}) \\ &\qquad \text{for some } (B, X)\text{-tree } \mathtt{T}\}. \end{aligned}$$

Since D_B is a finite set, the set $\boldsymbol{V}_B = \{\mathsf{pk}(w) \mid w \in D_B\}$ can be enumerated as $\boldsymbol{V}_B = \{\vec{v}_0, \ldots, \vec{v}_{p-1}\}$.

Let $h : (A_N \cup A_T)^* \longrightarrow A_T^*$ be the morphism defined by $h(X) = \lambda$ for $X \in A_N$ and $h(a) = a$ for $a \in A_T$. The effect of h on a word in $(A_N \cup A_T)^*$ is to erase all its nonterminal symbols. Define the set $\boldsymbol{U}_B$ to be

$$\boldsymbol{U}_B = \bigcup_{X \in B \cup \{S\}} \{\mathsf{pk}(h(w)) \mid w \in E_{B,X}\} = \{\vec{u}_0, \ldots, \vec{u}_{q-1}\}.$$

Let $\boldsymbol{F}_{B,i}$ be the linear set

$$\boldsymbol{F}_{B,i} = \{\vec{v}_i + \sum_{0 \le j \le q-1} k_j\vec{u}_j \mid k_0, \ldots, k_{q-1} \in \mathbb{N}\},$$

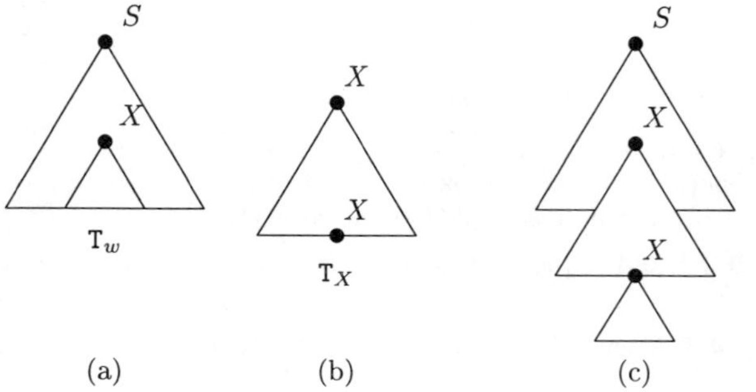

Figure 5.7: Construction of a New Derivation Tree

for $0 \leq i \leq p-1$, and let $\boldsymbol{F}_B = \bigcup_{0 \leq i \leq p} \boldsymbol{F}_{B,i}$. Clearly, $\boldsymbol{F}_B$ is a semilinear set. Note that $\boldsymbol{V}_B \subseteq \boldsymbol{F}_B$.

We claim that $\mathsf{pk}(L_B) = \boldsymbol{F}_B$. To prove that $\boldsymbol{F}_B \subseteq \mathsf{pk}(L_B)$, let $\vec{z} \in \boldsymbol{F}_B$. We have

$$\vec{z} = \vec{v}_i + \sum_{0 \leq j \leq q-1} k_j \vec{u}_j$$

for some i. We shall prove by induction on $k = \sum_{0 \leq j \leq q-1} k_j$ that $\vec{v} \in \mathsf{pk}(L_B)$.

If $k = 0$, we have $\vec{z} = \vec{v}_i$, hence

$$\vec{z} \in \boldsymbol{V}_B = \mathsf{pk}(D_B) \subseteq \mathsf{pk}(L_B).$$

Suppose that the statement holds for $\vec{z} = \vec{v}_i + \sum_{0 \leq j \leq q-1} k_j \vec{u}_j$. In other words, suppose that $\vec{z} \in \boldsymbol{F}_B \cap \mathsf{pk}(L_B)$. This means that there is a word $w \in L_B$ and a derivation tree $\mathtt{T}_w$ for the derivation $S \overset{*}{\underset{G}{\Rightarrow}} w$ such that the set of nonterminals that label the internal nodes of $\mathtt{T}_w$ equals $B \cup \{S\}$ (see Figure 5.7(a)).

Let $\vec{z}' = \vec{z} + \vec{u}_\ell$ for some ℓ, where $0 \leq \ell \leq q-1$. The definition of the set $\boldsymbol{U}_B$ implies that there is a nonterminal symbol X such that $\vec{u}_\ell = \mathsf{pk}(h(u))$, where $u = u'Xu''$, u is obtained through a derivation $X \overset{*}{\underset{G}{\Rightarrow}} u'Xu''$. Let $\mathtt{T}_X$ be the derivation tree that corresponds to this derivation, shown in Figure 5.7(b). Since $\mathtt{T}_w$ contains an internal node labeled X, we can insert $\mathtt{T}_X$ into $\mathtt{T}_w$ as shown in Figure 5.7(c). Let w' be the word generated by the new derivation tree. We have $w' \in L_B$ and $\mathsf{pk}(w') = \mathsf{pk}(w) + \mathsf{pk}(h(u)) = \vec{z} + \vec{u}_\ell$, so $\vec{z} + \vec{u}_\ell \in \mathsf{pk}(L_B)$. Thus, we conclude that $\boldsymbol{F}_B \subseteq \mathsf{pk}(L_B)$.

Conversely, to prove that $\mathsf{pk}(L_B) \subseteq \boldsymbol{F}_B$, let $\vec{w} \in \mathsf{pk}(L_B)$.

There is a word $w \in L_B$ such that $\vec{w} = \mathsf{pk}(w)$. The definition of L_B means that there exists a derivation tree $\mathtt{T}$ for a derivation $S \overset{*}{\underset{G}{\Rightarrow}} w$ whose internal nodes are labeled by the symbols of $B \cup \{S\}$. If $\mathtt{T}$ has no path that contains more than $|B| + 1$ nodes labeled with the same nonterminal, then $w \in D_B$, so $\vec{w} \in \mathsf{V}_B \subseteq \boldsymbol{F}_B$.

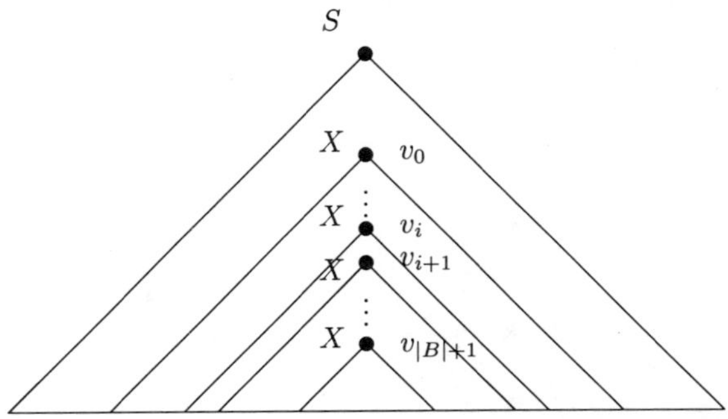

Figure 5.8: Derivation Tree T

Suppose that T contains a path ϖ that contains at least $|B|+2$ nodes labeled with the same nonterminal X, as shown in Figure 5.8.

Let nodes $v_0, v_1, \ldots, v_{|B|+1}$ be the first $|B|+2$ nodes in ϖ starting from the leaves of T labeled by X, and let $\mathtt{T}_j$ be the subtree of T whose root is v_j for $0 \leq j \leq |B|+1$.

There is no path in $\mathtt{T}_1$ that contains more than $|B|+1$ nodes labeled with the same terminal. Since at most $|B|$ nonterminal symbols occur as labels of internal nodes in $\mathtt{T}_1$, and at least one nonterminal symbol occurs as a label of the internal nodes of $\mathtt{T}_{|B|+1}$, there is a j such that the set of nonterminal symbols that occur in $\mathtt{T}_j$ is the same as the set of nonterminal symbols that occur in $\mathtt{T}_{j+1}$.

The tree $\mathtt{T}'_0$ is obtained from T by replacing $\mathtt{T}_j$ by $\mathtt{T}_{j+1}$ (cf. Figure 5.9). Denote by w'_0 the word generated by $\mathtt{T}'_0$. The tree $\mathtt{T}''$ is obtained from $\mathtt{T}_j$ by eliminating the descendants of v_{j+1} (cf. Figure 5.10). The word w'' generated by $\mathtt{T}''$ belongs to $E_{B,X}$ since no path in this tree contains more than $|B|+1$ vertices labeled by the same nonterminal symbol. Thus, $\mathsf{pk}(w'') = \vec{\boldsymbol{u}}_{j_0}$ for some j_0, $0 \leq j_0 \leq q-1$, and we have $\mathsf{pk}(w) = \mathsf{pk}(w'_0) + \vec{\boldsymbol{v}}_{j_0}$. The tree $\mathtt{T}'$ has fewer nodes than T. If $\mathtt{T}'$ contains a path with more than $|B|+1$ nodes labeled by the same nonterminal, then this process is repeated and we obtain a tree $\mathtt{T}'_1$ that generates a word w'_1 such that $\mathsf{pk}(w'_0) = \mathsf{pk}(w'_1) + \vec{\boldsymbol{v}}_{j_1}$. Thus, $\mathsf{pk}(w) = \mathsf{pk}(w'_1) + \vec{\boldsymbol{v}}_{j_0} + \vec{\boldsymbol{v}}_{j_1}$. Eventually, we will obtain a tree $\mathtt{T}'_m$ such that no path in this tree has more than $|B|+1$ nodes labeled by the same nonterminal. At that point, w'_m the word generated by $\mathtt{T}'_m$ belongs to D_B and we will be able to write $\mathsf{pk}(w'_m) = \vec{\boldsymbol{u}}_i$ for some i, $0 \leq i \leq p$. This implies

$$\mathsf{pk}(w) = \vec{\boldsymbol{u}}_i + \vec{\boldsymbol{v}}_{j_0} + \vec{\boldsymbol{v}}_{j_1} + \cdots + \vec{\boldsymbol{v}}_{j_m},$$

so $\mathsf{pk}(w) \in \boldsymbol{F}_B$, which gives the desired reverse inclusion $\mathsf{pk}(L_B) \subseteq \boldsymbol{F}_B$.

If $\lambda \in L$, then let $L' = L - \{\lambda\}$. Since L' is a λ-free context-free language $\mathsf{pk}(L')$ is a semilinear set by the previous argument. Thus, $\mathsf{pk}(L) = \mathsf{pk}(L') \cup$

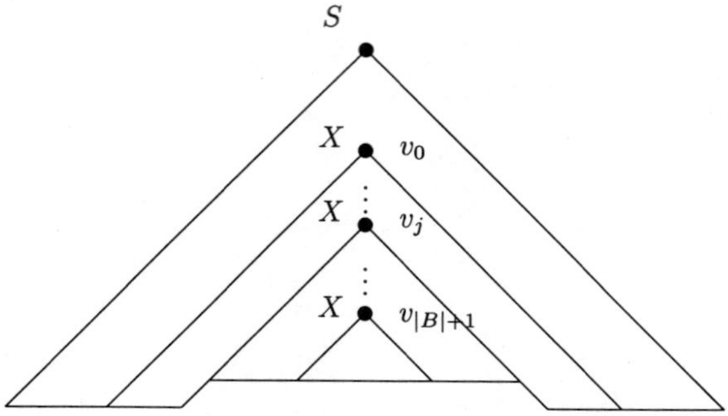

Figure 5.9: The Tree T'_0

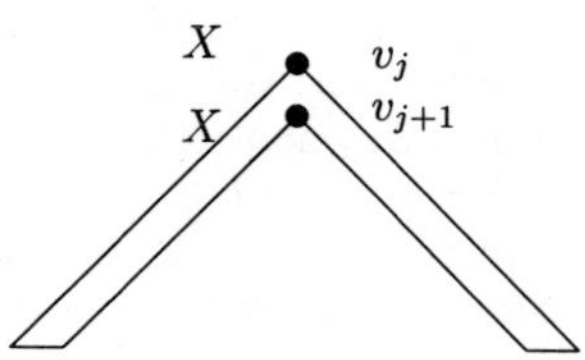

Figure 5.10: Tree T''

$\{(0, \ldots, 0)\}$ which implies that $\mathsf{pk}(L)$ is also semilinear. ∎

The semilinearity of $\mathsf{pk}(L)$ is necessary for L to be context-free but not sufficient. Indeed, consider the language $L = \{a^n b^n c^n \mid n \in \mathbb{N}\}$, known to be outside $\mathcal{L}_2$. We have $\mathsf{pk}(L) = \{n(1,1,1) \mid n \in \mathbb{N}\}$, so $\mathsf{pk}(L)$ is clearly linear, and therefore, semilinear. Similarly, for the language $L' = \{a^i b^j c^k \mid i = j \text{ or } j = k\}$ we have $\mathsf{pk}(L') = \{i(1,1,0) + k(0,0,1) \mid i, k \in \mathbb{N}\} \cup \{i(1,0,0) + k(0,1,1)\}$, so $\mathsf{pk}(L')$ is the union of two linear sets, and therefore, is a semilinear set.

Parikh's Theorem implies that, as far as the frequency of symbol occurrences is concerned, there is no difference between context-free languages and regular languages. To make this idea more precise we need the following definition.

Definition 5.9.5 Let A be an alphabet. Two languages L, L' over A are *letter-equivalent* if $\mathsf{pk}(L) = \mathsf{pk}(L')$. □

Note that if $L, L' \subseteq \{a\}^*$ and L, L' are letter-equivalent, then $L = L'$.

Theorem 5.9.6 *Let L be a context-free language over the alphabet A. There exists a regular language L' over the same alphabet that is letter-equivalent to L.*

Proof. Let

$$\boldsymbol{L} = \{\vec{v} \in \mathbb{N}^k \mid \vec{v} = \vec{v}_0 + m_1\vec{v}_1 + \cdots + m_n\vec{v}_n\}.$$

be a linear subset of $\mathbb{N}^k$ and let $w_0, w_1, \ldots, w_n$ be $n+1$ words in A^* such that $\mathsf{pk}(w_0) = \vec{v}_0$ and $\mathsf{pk}(w_i) = \vec{v}_i$ for $1 \leq i \leq n$. Then, $\boldsymbol{L} = \mathsf{pk}(R)$, where R is the regular language $L = \{w_0\}\{w_1\}^* \cdots \{w_n\}^*$.

Suppose that $\mathsf{pk}(L) = \boldsymbol{L}_0 \cup \cdots \cup \boldsymbol{L}_{k-1}$, where $\boldsymbol{L}_0, \ldots, \boldsymbol{L}_{k-1}$ are linear sets. Let R_i be a regular language such that $\mathsf{pk}(R_i) = \boldsymbol{L}_i$ for $0 \leq i \leq k-1$. Then, $\mathsf{pk}(L) = \mathsf{pk}(R_0) \cup \cdots \cup \mathsf{pk}(R_{k-1}) = \mathsf{pk}(R_0 \cup \cdots \cup R_{k-1})$, which shows that L is letter-equivalent to the regular language $R_0 \cup \cdots \cup R_{k-1}$. ∎

Theorem 5.9.6 allows another argument for the result contained in Theorem 5.7.1.

Corollary 5.9.7 *A language L over an one-symbol alphabet $A = \{a\}$ is context-free if and only if it is regular.*

Proof. If L is regular, then it is clearly context-free. Conversely, suppose that L is context-free. By Theorem 5.9.6, there exists a regular language R such that $\mathsf{pk}(L) = \mathsf{pk}(R)$. Since both L and R are languages over $\{a\}$ we obtain $L = R$, so L is regular. ∎

5.10 The Chomsky-Schützenberger Theorem

The theorem presented in this section shows that every context-free language is the morphic image of the intersection of a special language called a *parenthetic language* and a regular language.

Definition 5.10.1 Let n be a positive natural number. The *parenthetic alphabet of order n* is the set

$$A_n = \{(_0, \ldots, (_{n-1},)_0, \ldots,)_{n-1}\}$$

The *parenthetic language* of order n is the context-free language PAR_n generated by the grammar $G_n = (\{S\}, A_n, S, P)$ whose set of productions is

$$P = \{S \to SS, S \to \lambda, S \to (_0 S)_0, \ldots, S \to (_{n-1} S)_{n-1}\}.$$

□

The next result lists some elementary properties of parenthetic languages.

Lemma 5.10.2 *The following statements concerning the language* PAR_n *hold:*

(i) *if* $u, v \in \mathsf{PAR}_n$, *then* $uv \in \mathsf{PAR}_n$;

(ii) *if* $u \in \mathsf{PAR}_n$, *then* $(_i u)_i \in \mathsf{PAR}_n$ *for* $0 \leq i \leq n-1$;

(iii) *if* $(_i)_i u \in \mathsf{PAR}_n$ *for some* i, $0 \leq i \leq n-1$, *then* $u \in \mathsf{PAR}_n$;

(iv) *for every word* $w \in \mathsf{PAR}_n - \{\lambda\}$ *there are* $u, v \in \mathsf{PAR}_n$ *such that* $w = (_i u)_i v$ *for some* i, $0 \leq i \leq n-1$.

Proof. The arguments are straightforward and are left to the reader. ∎

Theorem 5.10.3 (The Chomsky-Schützenberger Theorem)
Every context-free language is the image through a morphism of the intersection of a parenthetic language and a regular language.

Proof. Let L be a context-free language on the alphabet $A = \{a_0, \ldots, a_{n-1}\}$; assume initially that $\lambda \notin L$ and that L is generated by the context-free grammar

$$G = (A_N, A, S, \{\pi_0, \ldots, \pi_{m-1}\})$$

in Chomsky normal form. We prove the existence of a regular language $R \subseteq (A_{n+m})^*$ such that $L = h(\mathsf{PAR}_{n+m} \cap R)$, where $h : (A_{n+m})^* \longrightarrow A^*$ is a morphism.

Consider the context-free grammar $G_1 = (A_N, A_{n+m}, S, P_1)$ whose set of productions P_1 consists of the following:

1. if $X \to a_i \in P$, then include the production $X \to (_i)_i$ in P_1 for $0 \leq i \leq n-1$;
2. if π_j is the production $X_j \to Y_j Z_j \in P$, then include $X_j \to (_{j+n-1} Y_j$ in P_1; include $X \to (_i)_i)_{j+n-1} Z_j$ for every production $X \to a_i \in P$.

Note that G_1 is a right-linear grammar, so $L(G_1)$ is a regular language by Theorem 4.6.6.

Let $h : (A_{n+m})^* \longrightarrow A^*$ be the morphism defined by the table

Symbol s	$0 \leq i \leq n-1$		$n \leq i \leq n+m-1$	
	$(_i$	$)_i$	$(_i$	$)_i$
$h(s)$	a_i	λ	λ	λ

We begin by proving the inclusion $L \subseteq h(\mathsf{PAR}_{n+m} \cap R)$. To this end, we show that if $X \overset{k}{\underset{G}{\Rightarrow}} w$, then there is a word $x \in \mathsf{PAR}_{n+m}$ such that $X \overset{*}{\underset{G_1}{\Rightarrow}} x$ and $h(x) = w$. The argument is by induction on $k \geq 1$.

For the basis step, $k = 1$, we have $w = a_i$ and $X \to a_i \in P$. Thus, $X \to (_i)_i \in P_1$, so we can take $x = (_i)_i$ because $x \in \mathsf{PAR}_{m+n}$ and $h(x) = a_i$.

Suppose that the statement holds for derivations of length less than k and that $X \overset{k}{\underset{G}{\Rightarrow}} w$. Since G is in Chomsky normal form there is a production $X_j \longrightarrow$

Y_jZ_j such that $X = X_j \underset{G}{\Rightarrow} Y_jZ_j \overset{k-1}{\underset{G}{\Rightarrow}} w$. Therefore, w can be written as $w = w'w''$, where $Y_j \overset{k'}{\underset{G}{\Rightarrow}} w'$, $Z_j \overset{k''}{\underset{G}{\Rightarrow}} w''$ and $k', k'' < k$. By the inductive hypothesis, there are $x', x'' \in \mathsf{PAR}_{m+n}$ such that $Y_j \overset{*}{\underset{G_1}{\Rightarrow}} x'$, $Z_j \overset{*}{\underset{G_1}{\Rightarrow}} x''$, $h(x') = w'$, and $h(x'') = w''$.

The definition of P_1 implies the existence of the production $X \rightarrow (_{j+n-1}Y_j$ in P_1; thus, $X \underset{G_1}{\Rightarrow} (_{j+n-1}Y_j \overset{*}{\underset{G_1}{\Rightarrow}} (_{j+n-1}x'$. The last production applied in this derivation must have the form $U \rightarrow (_l)_l$ for some nonterminal symbol U. The definition of P_1 implies the existence of the production $U \rightarrow (_l)_l)_{j+n-1}Z_j$ in this set. Therefore, by replacing the production $U \rightarrow (_l)_l$ by $U \rightarrow (_l)_l)_{j+n-1}Z_j$ in the last step of the derivation we obtain the derivation

$$X \underset{G_1}{\Rightarrow} (_{j+n-1}Y_j \overset{*}{\underset{G_1}{\Rightarrow}} (_{j+n-1}x')_{j+n-1}Z_j \overset{*}{\underset{G_1}{\Rightarrow}} (_{j+n-1}x')_{j+n-1}x''.$$

Consequently, by taking $X = S$, $S \overset{*}{\underset{G}{\Rightarrow}} w$ implies that there is a word $x \in \mathsf{PAR}_{n+m}$ such that $S \overset{*}{\underset{G_1}{\Rightarrow}} w$ and $h(x) = w$. In other words, we obtain the inclusion $L \subseteq h(\mathsf{PAR}_{n+m} \cap R)$.

Conversely, let $w \in h(\mathsf{PAR}_{n+m} \cap R)$. There is $x \in \mathsf{PAR}_{n+m} \cap R$ such that $w = h(x)$. Since $x \in R$ there is a derivation $S \overset{k}{\underset{G_1}{\Rightarrow}} x$. To obtain the reverse inclusion we need to prove that $S \overset{*}{\underset{G}{\Rightarrow}} h(x) = w$. Actually, we prove a stronger statement. Namely, we will show by induction on k that if $X \overset{k}{\underset{G_1}{\Rightarrow}} x$ and $x \in \mathsf{PAR}_{n+m}$, then $X \overset{*}{\underset{G}{\Rightarrow}} h(x)$.

For $k = 1$ we have $X \underset{G_1}{\Rightarrow} x$, so $x = (_i)_i$ by the definition of G_1. Therefore, we have the production $X \rightarrow a_i$ in P, so $X \underset{G}{\Rightarrow} a_i = h((_i)_i)$.

Suppose now that the statement holds for derivations of length less than $k \geq 2$ and let $X \overset{k}{\underset{G_1}{\Rightarrow}} x$, where $x \in \mathsf{PAR}_{n+m}$. The production used in the first step of the above derivation has either the form $X_j \rightarrow (_{j+n-1}Y_j$ or the form $X \rightarrow (_i)_i)_{j+n-1}Z_j$.

The second case can be excluded since this would imply $x = (_i)_i)_{j+n-1}z \in \mathsf{PAR}_{n+m}$, which, in turn, would imply $)_{j+n-1}z \in \mathsf{PAR}_{n+m}$ by Part (iii) of Lemma 5.10.2. Since no word in PAR_{n+m} can begin with a "right parenthesis," the second case cannot occur. Thus, the above derivation has the form $X_j \underset{G_1}{\Rightarrow} (_{j+n-1}Y_j \overset{*}{\underset{G_1}{\Rightarrow}} x$. This means that $x = (_{j+n-1}y$, where $Y_j \overset{*}{\underset{G_1}{\Rightarrow}} y$. Part (iv) of Lemma 5.10.2 implies that x can be written as $x = (_{j+n-1}u)_{j+n-1}v$ for $u, v \in \mathsf{PAR}_{n+m}$, so $y = u)_{j+n-1}v$.

Suppose that in the derivation $Y_j \overset{*}{\underset{G_1}{\Rightarrow}} u)_{j+n-1}v$ the symbol $)_{j+n-1}$ occurs at the ℓth step through the application of the production $U \rightarrow (_i)_i)_{j+n-1}Z_j$. This means that the production $U \rightarrow a_i$ exists in P, which, in turn, implies that the production $U \rightarrow (_i)_i$ belongs to P_1. By replacing the application of the production $U \to (_i)_i)_{j+n-1}Z$ by the production $U \to (_i)_i$ we obtain the derivation $Y_j \overset{\ell'}{\underset{G_1}{\Rightarrow}} u$.

Also, we obtain the existence of the derivation $Z_j \overset{\ell''}{\underset{G_1}{\Rightarrow}} v$, and we have both $\ell' < k$ and $\ell'' < k$. By the inductive hypothesis we obtain $Y_j \overset{*}{\underset{G}{\Rightarrow}} h(u)$ and $Z_j \overset{*}{\underset{G}{\Rightarrow}} h(v)$, which yield

$$X_j \underset{G}{\Rightarrow} Y_j Z_j \overset{*}{\underset{G}{\Rightarrow}} h(u)h(v) = h((_{j+n-1}u)_{j+n-1}v) = h(x).$$

Thus, $h(\mathsf{PAR}_{n+m} \cap R) \subseteq L$.

If $\lambda \in L$, by applying the previous argument to the context-free language $L - \{\lambda\}$ we obtain the existence of a regular language R such that $L - \{\lambda\} = h(\mathsf{PAR}_{n+m} \cap R)$. Then, $L = h(\mathsf{PAR}_{n+m} \cap (R \cup \{\lambda\}))$. ∎

5.11 Exercises

Derivation Trees

1. Let G be the context-free grammar

$$G = (\{S\}, \{+, -, *, /, (,), \boldsymbol{v}, \boldsymbol{n}\}, S, P)$$

the context-free grammar whose set of productions consists of

$$S \to S + S, S \to S - S, S \to S,$$
$$S \to S * S, S \to S/S, S \to \boldsymbol{v}, S \to \boldsymbol{n}, S \to (S).$$

Construct at least one derivation tree for the following words in $L(G)$:
   (a) $\boldsymbol{v}/\boldsymbol{v} + \boldsymbol{v}$
   (b) $\boldsymbol{v} + \boldsymbol{v} * \boldsymbol{n} + \boldsymbol{n} * \boldsymbol{v}$
   (c) $\boldsymbol{v} * (\boldsymbol{v} + \boldsymbol{n})$

2. ◇ Let $G = (\{S\}, \{a, b\}, S, P)$ be a context-free grammar, where $P = \{S \to \lambda, S \to aSb, S \to aSbb\}$.
   (a) Prove that $L(G) = \{a^n b^m \mid n \leq m \leq 2n\}$.
   (b) Determine the number of derivation trees of a word $a^n b^m$, where $n \leq m \leq 2n$.

3. Consider the context-free grammar $G = (\{S, X, Y\}, \{a, b\}, S, P)$, where the set of productions P is given by

$$P = \{S \to aXb, S \to Yb, X \to YaS, X \to b, Y \to bX, Y \to a\}.$$

   (a) Prove that the word $x = abbaabb$ belongs to $L(G)$ by constructing a derivation d for x. Construct the derivation tree $\mathtt{T}$ that corresponds to d.
   (b) Give the leftmost and the rightmost derivations that corresponds to $\mathtt{T}$.

4. Let G be a λ-free context-free grammar. Prove that every derivation tree for a word $w \in L(G)$ has at most $2|w| - 1$ internal nodes.
5. Consider the context-free grammar

$$G = (\{S, X, Y\}, \{a, b\}, S, \{S \to XY, X \to aX, X \to \lambda, Y \to bY, Y \to \lambda\}).$$

   (a) Prove that $L(G)$ is a regular language.
   (b) Prove that there is no leftmost derivation for the word X even though $S \overset{*}{\underset{G}{\Rightarrow}} X$.
6. $^\diamond$ A word $x \in A^*$ is a *palindrome* if $w = w^R$. Let $L_{A,pal}$ be the language of all palindromes on A.
   Prove that both $L_{A,pal}$ and $A^* - L_{A,pal}$ are context-free, non-regular languages.

Fixed-Points and Context-Free Languages

7. $^\diamond$ Let $\vec{f} : \mathcal{P}(A^*) \longrightarrow \mathcal{P}(A^*)$ be the polynomial function defined by $\vec{f}(X_0) = \{\lambda\} \cup aX_0 \cup aX_0bX_0$, for $X_0 \in \mathcal{P}(A^*)$, where $A = \{a, b\}$. Determine the least fixed point of $\vec{f}$.
8. $^\diamond$ Give the polynomial functions that correspond to context-free grammars that generate the following languages:
   (a) $\{a^nb^{2n} \mid n \in \mathbb{N}\}$;
   (b) $\{a^nb^m \mid m, n \in \mathbb{N} \text{ and } n \leq m\}$;
   (c) $\{a^nb^m \mid m, n \in \mathbb{N} \text{ and } n \neq m\}$.
9. $^\diamond$ Let $\vec{f} : (\mathcal{P}(A^*))^n \longrightarrow (\mathcal{P}(A^*))^n$, $\vec{g} : (\mathcal{P}(A^*))^m \longrightarrow (\mathcal{P}(A^*))^m$ be two polynomial functions. Construct two polynomial functions $\vec{h}$ and $\vec{k}$ such that the language $(\mathtt{lfp}(\vec{f}))_{n-1} \cup (\mathtt{lfp}(\vec{g}))_{m-1}$ is a component of $\mathtt{lfp}(\vec{h})$ and the language $(\mathtt{lfp}(\vec{f}))_{n-1}(\mathtt{lfp}(\vec{g}))_{m-1}$ is a component of $\mathtt{lfp}(\vec{k})$.
10. Let $A = \{X_0, \ldots, X_{n-1}\}$ be an alphabet and let $\boldsymbol{D}$ be an $n \times n$-matrix such that $(\boldsymbol{D})_{ij} \subseteq A$. Prove that if $w \in (\boldsymbol{D}^k)_{ij}$, then $|w| = k$ for $k \in \mathbb{N}$.

Normal Forms

11. Find an equivalent context-free grammar G' in Chomsky normal form for the following context-free grammars:
    (a) $G = (\{S\}, \{a, b\}, S, \{S \to a, S \to aS, S \to aSbS\}$;
    (b) $G = (\{S, X, Y\}, \{a, b\}, S, \{S \to XYX, S \to ab, X \to SYS, X \to ba, Y \to XSX, Y \to b\}$;
    (c) $G = (\{S\}, \{+, *, (,), a\}, S, \{S \to S + S, S \to S * S, S \to a, S \to (S)\})$.
12. Find an equivalent context-free grammar in Greibach normal form for the grammars listed in Exercise 11.
13. Construct equivalent grammars in Chomsky and Greibach normal forms for the context-free grammar

$$(\{S\}, \{a, b\}, S, \{S \to aSa, S \to bSb, S \to aa, S \to bb\}.$$

14. $^{\diamond\diamond}$ Let $G = (A_N, A_T, S, P)$ be a grammar in Chomsky normal form.

(a) Prove that $L_{G,X,a} = \{\alpha \in A_N^* \mid X \underset{G,\text{left}}{\overset{*}{\Rightarrow}} a\alpha\}$ is a regular language over the nonterminal alphabet A_N.

(b) Compute the languages $L(G, X_i, a), L(G, X_i, b)$ for the context-free grammar $G = (\{X_0, X_1, X_2\}, \{a, b\}, X_0, P)$ in Chomsky normal form considered in Example 5.4.15.

Solution. Let $A'_N = \{X' \mid X \in A_N\}$ be an alphabet that contains the primed versions of the symbols of A_N. Consider the strongly left-linear grammar $G'_{X,a} = (A'_N, A_N, X', P_{A,a})$ whose set of productions is

$$P' = \{X' \to Y'Z \mid X \to YZ \in P\} \cup \{X' \to \lambda \mid X \to a \in P\}.$$

The language $L_{G,X,a}$ is regular because it can be generated by $G'_{X,a}$ (cf. Theorem 4.6.6).

Suppose that $\alpha \in L_{G,X,a}$. In the derivation $X \underset{G,\text{left}}{\overset{*}{\Rightarrow}} a\alpha$ the rewriting affects only the first symbol at any time. Therefore, the productions applied have the form

$$X \to X_{i_0}Y_0, X_{i_0} \to X_{i_1}Y_1, \ldots, X_{i_{p-2}} \to X_{i_{p-1}}Y_{p-1}, X_{i_{p-1}} \to a,$$

and the previous leftmost derivation can be written as

$$\begin{aligned} X &\underset{G,\text{left}}{\Rightarrow} X_{i_0}Y_{i_0} \underset{G,\text{left}}{\Rightarrow} X_{i_1}Y_1Y_0 \underset{G,\text{left}}{\Rightarrow} \cdots \\ &\underset{G,\text{left}}{\Rightarrow} X_{i_{p-1}}Y_{p-1}\cdots Y_1Y_0 \underset{G,\text{left}}{\Rightarrow} aY_{p-1}\cdots Y_1Y_0, \end{aligned} \tag{5.6}$$

where $\alpha = Y_{p-1}\cdots Y_1Y_0$. Correspondingly, we have

$$\begin{aligned} X' &\underset{G'_{X,a}}{\Rightarrow} X'_{i_0}Y_{i_0} \underset{G'_{X,a},\text{left}}{\Rightarrow} X'_{i_1}Y_1Y_0 \underset{G'_{X,a}}{\Rightarrow} \cdots \\ &\underset{G'_{X,a}}{\Rightarrow} X'_{i_{p-1}}Y_{p-1}\cdots Y_1Y_0 \underset{G'_{X,a}}{\Rightarrow} Y_{p-1}\cdots Y_1Y_0, \end{aligned} \tag{5.7}$$

so $\alpha \in L(G'_{X,a})$.

To prove the converse implication let $\alpha \in L(G'_{X,a})$. Since $G'_{X,a}$ is a strongly left-linear grammar, there exists a derivation for α that is necessarily of the form (5.7). This, in turn implies the existence of a leftmost derivation of the form (5.6), so $\alpha \in L(G, X, a)$.

We have

$$\begin{aligned} L_{G,X_0,a} &= X_2(X_2X_1)^* \\ L_{G,X_0,b} &= \emptyset \\ L_{G,X_1,a} &= (X_2X_1)^* \\ L_{G,X_1,b} &= \emptyset \\ L_{G,X_2,a} &= (X_2X_1)^*X_2X_2 \\ L_{G,X_2,b} &= \{\lambda\}, \end{aligned}$$

as the reader can easily verify. ∎

15. °° Prove that for every λ-free context-free grammar G there is an equivalent grammar G' whose productions have either the form $X \to a$, or $X \to a\alpha b$, where a, b are terminal symbols and α is a word that contains nonterminal symbols.

16. $^{\diamond\diamond}$ Can every λ-free, context-free language L be generated by a context-free grammar whose productions are of the form $X \to YZU$ or $X \to a$? Here, X, Y, Z, U are nonterminal symbols and a is a terminal symoool of the grammar.
17. $^{\diamond}$ Let $G = (A_N, A_T, S, P)$ be a context-free grammar in Chomsky normal form. Prove that $L(G)$ is infinite if and only if there exists $w \in A_T^*$ such that $S \overset{m}{\underset{G}{\Rightarrow}} w$, where $m > |A_N|$.
18. $^{\diamond}$ Show that for every context-free grammar G there is an equivalent context-free grammar whose productions are of one of the following forms: $X \to a$, $X \to aY$, or $X \to Ya$, where X, Y are nonterminal symbols and a is a terminal symbol.
19. $^{\diamond\diamond}$ Show that every context-free language can be generated by a grammar whose productions have the form $X \to a$, where a is a terminal symbol, or $X \to X_{i_0} \cdots X_{i_{n-1}}$, where $X_{i_0}, \ldots, X_{i_{n-1}}$ are distinct nonterminal symbols.

The Pumping Lemma

20. $^{\diamond}$ Prove that the following languages are not context-free:
   (a) $\{a^p \mid p \text{ is prime }\}$;
   (b) $\{a^n b^{n^2} \mid n \in \mathbb{N}\}$;
   (c) $\{a^n b^{2n} c^n \mid n \in \mathbb{N}\}$.
21. $^{\diamond}$ Let $G = (\{S\}, \{a, b, c\}, S, P)$ and $G' = (\{S'\}, \{a, b, c\}, S', P')$ be two linear grammars given by

$$\begin{aligned} P &= \{S \to aaSc, S \to bSc, S \to bc\} \\ P' &= \{S \to aScc, S \to aSb, S \to ab\}. \end{aligned}$$

   (a) Determine $L(G)$ and $L(G')$.
   (b) Prove that $L(G) \cap L(G')$ is not context-free.
22. $^{\diamond\diamond}$ Prove that for every context-free grammar G there exists a number $n_G \in \mathbb{N}$ such that if $w \in L(G)$ and $|w| \geq n_G$, then we can write $w = xyzut$ such that $|y| \geq 1$, $|u| \geq 1$, $|yzu| \leq n_G$ and $xy^n zu^n t \in L(G)$ for all $n \in \mathbb{N}$. Note that this statement is stronger than Theorem 5.5.4, since we require both $y \neq \lambda$ and $u \neq \lambda$.
23. $^{\diamond}$ Prove that the languages

$$\begin{aligned} K &= \{a^i b^j c^k \mid i, j, k \in \mathbb{N} \text{ and } k = \min\{i, j\}\} \\ H &= \{a^i b^j c^k \mid i, j, k \in \mathbb{N} \text{ and } k = \max\{i, j\}\}. \end{aligned}$$

   are not context-free.

   Solution. Suppose that H were context-free. Then, by Theorem 5.5.4 there is $n_H \in \mathbb{N}$ such that if $w = a^i b^j c^k \in H$ and $|w| \geq n_H$, then $w = xyzut$ such that $|y| \geq 1$ or $|u| \geq 1$, $|yzu| \leq n_H$ and $xy^n zu^n t \in H$ for $n \in \mathbb{N}$. Choose $i = j = n_H$. If c does not occur in yu pumping will increase the number of as or bs without affecting the number of cs and we would obtain a contradiction. Therefore, c must occur in yzu. Since $|yzu| \leq n_H$, it follows that the word yzu cannot contain an a. By the pumping lemma the word xzt contains n_H as and there are fewer than n_H symbols b or c in xzt. Thus, $xzt \notin H$. ∎

24. $\diamond$ Show that the following languages are not context-free by applying Ogden Lemma:
    (a) $\{a^n b^n c^m \mid n \neq m\}$;
    (b) $\{a^n b^m c^p d^q \mid n = 0 \text{ or } m = p = q\}$;
    (c) $\{a^n b^n a^m b^m \mid n \neq m\}$.

    Examine the possibility of proving that these languages are not context-free using the standard pumping lemma (that is, Theorem 5.5.4).
25. $\diamond$ Let $f : \mathbb{N} \times \mathbb{N} \longrightarrow \mathbb{N}$ be an injective function such that for every $m, n, p, q \in \mathbb{N}$ such that $p \leq n$ and $q \leq f(m,n)$, there exists $i \in \mathbb{N}$ such that $f(m, n + ip) \neq f(m,n) + iq$.
    (a) Give an example of a function f that satisfies the conditions mentioned above.
    (b) Prove that the language $L = \{a^m b^n c^{f(m,n)} \mid m,n \in \mathbb{N}\}$ is not context-free.
26. $\diamond$ Show that the language $L_k = \{a^n b^m a^{n+k} b^{m+k} \mid m,n \geq 1\}$ is not context-free for any $k \in \mathbb{N}$.
    Hint. Use the Pumping Lemma of Bar-Hillel, Perles, and Shamir; make sure that you require that $|yzu| \leq n_G$.
27. $\diamond$ Let G be a linear context-free grammar such that $L(G)$ is an infinite language. Prove that there exists a number $n_G \in \mathbb{N}$ such that if $w \in L(G)$ and $|w| \geq n_G$, then we can write $w = xyzut$ such that $|xyut| \leq n_G$, $|yu| \geq 1$ and $xy^i zu^i t \in L(G)$ for every $i \in \mathbb{N}$.
28. $\diamond$ Prove that the language $L = \{w \in \{a,b\}^* \mid n_a(w) = n_b(w)\}$ introduced in Example 4.5.3 is not a linear context-free language.
29. $\diamond$ Give a direct proof of Theorem 5.5.4 using derivation trees.
30. $\diamond$ Prove the following Pumping Lemma for linear languages. Let G be a linear context-free grammar. There exists a number $n_G \in \mathbb{N}$ such that if $w \in L(G)$ and $|w| \geq n_G$, then we can write $w = xyzut$ such that $|y| \geq 1$ or $|u| \geq 1$, $|xyut| \leq n_G$ and $xy^n zu^n t \in L(G)$ for all $n \in \mathbb{N}$.
    Hint. A derivation tree in a linear grammar may contain at most one path of length at least two whose interior vertices are labeled by nonterminal symbols. Choose a constant n_G that assures that there would be repeated nonterminal symbols on this path in a derivation tree for a word $w \in L(G)$ and focus on the two topmost vertices labeled by a nonterminal that is repeated along the path.
31. Prove that the language $\{a^n b^n a^m b^m \mid n,m \in \mathbb{N}\}$ is a context-free, nonlinear language.
32. $\diamond$ Determine whether the following languages are
    (i) regular,
    (ii) context-free, but not regular,
    (iii) not context-free.

    (a) $\{a^m b^n \mid m,n \in \mathbb{N} \text{ and } \gcd(m,n) = 1\}$;
    (b) $\{xyx \mid x,y \in \{a,b\}^*\}$;
    (c) $\{xyx \mid x,y \in \{a,b\}^* \text{ and } |x| = 5\}$;
    (d) $\{xyx^R \mid x,y \in \{a,b\}^*\}$;
    (e) $\{xyx^R \mid x,y \in \{a,b\}^* \text{ and } |x| = 5\}$.

33. ◇ Construct a grammar G such that
   (a) G is not a context-free grammar but $L(G)$ is a context-free language;
   (b) G is not a type-3 grammar but $L(G)$ is a regular language.

Closure Properties

34. ◇ Let A be an alphabet and let $c \notin A$.
   (a) Prove that the languages
$$\begin{aligned} L_0 &= \{ucvcwct \mid u,v,w,t \in A^*, u = t^R \text{ and } v = w^R\} \\ L_1 &= \{ucvcwct \mid u,v,w,t \in A^* \text{ and } v \neq w^R\} \\ L_2 &= \{ucvcwct \mid u,v,w,t \in A^* \text{ and } u \neq t^R\} \end{aligned}$$
   are context-free.
   (b) Using Part (a) prove that the language $L = (A \cup \{c\})^* - L_0$ is a context-free language.
35. Let $A_k = \{a_0, \ldots, a_{k-1}\}$ be an alphabet that contains $k > 2$ symbols. Prove that the language $L \subseteq A^*$ given by
$$L = \{a_0^{p_0} a_1^{p_0+p_1} a_2^{p_1+p_2} \cdots a_{k-2}^{p_{k-3}+p_{k-2}} a_{k-1}^{p_{k-2}} \mid p_0, \ldots, p_{k-2} \in \mathbb{N}\}$$
   is context-free.
36. ◇ Let $A = \{a, b\}$. Prove that the languages
$$H = \{ww \mid w \in A^+\} \text{ and } K = \{ww \mid w \in A^*\}$$
   are not context-free.
   Hint. Use Exercise 26 for $k = 0$.
37. ◇◇ Let $L_{sc} \subseteq B^+$ be the language of all semantically correct programs in C, where B is the basic alphabet of an implementation of the C language. Prove that L_{sc} is not a context-free language.
   Solution. Suppose that L_{sc} is a context-free language. Then, by Theorem 5.6.3, the language
$$L = L_{sc} \cap \textbf{main()}\{\textbf{int}\ A^+; A^+ = 1;\}$$
   is context-free, where $A = \{c, d\}$. Define the morphism $h : B^* \longrightarrow A^*$ by $h(c) = c$, $h(d) = d$, and $h(s) = \lambda$ for every $s \in B - A$. Since every variable in a semantically correct program in C must be predeclared we have $w \in L$ if and only if
$$w = \textbf{main()}\{\textbf{int}\ x;\ x = 1;\}$$
   for some $x \in A^+$. Thus, $h(L) = \{xx \mid x \in A^+\}$, which is not a context-free language. ■
38. ◇◇ Prove that if $K = \{xx \mid x \in \{a,b\}^*\}$, then $\{a,b\}^* - K$ is context-free.
   Solution. Consider the regular languages
$$\begin{aligned} D &= \{x \in \{a,b\}^* \mid |x| \text{ is odd }\} \\ E &= \{x \in \{a,b\}^* \mid |x| \text{ is even }\} \end{aligned}$$

Note that $\{a,b\}^* - K = D \cup (E - K)$.
Since any word $x \in E - K$ can be split into two words of equal length, $x = x'x''$, such that there is j, $1 \leq j \leq |x'| = |x''|$, such that $x'(j) \neq x''(j)$, we have

$$\begin{aligned} E - K &= \{uawbv \mid u,v,w \in \{a,b\}^* \text{ and } |u| + |v| = |w|\} \\ &\cup \{ubwav \mid u,v,w \in \{a,b\}^* \text{ and } |u| + |v| = |w|\}. \end{aligned}$$

Then, it is easy to show that $E - K$ is context-free. ∎

39. $^\diamond$ Prove that the language $\{a^n b^m \mid n \neq m\}$ is context-free.
Hint. Prove first that the languages $\{a^n b^m \mid m,n \in \mathbb{N} \text{ and } n < m\}$ and $\{a^n b^m \mid m,n \in \mathbb{N} \text{ and } n > m\}$ are context-free.

40. $^\diamond$ Prove that the language $L = \{a^n b^m c^p \mid n,m,p \in \mathbb{N} \text{ and } n \neq m \text{ or } m \neq p\}$ is context-free.
Hint. Prove first that the languages $\{a^n b^m c^p \mid m,n,p \in \mathbb{N} \text{ and } n \neq m\}$ and $\{a^n b^m c^p \mid m,n,p \in \mathbb{N} \text{ and } m \neq p\}$ are context-free.

41. $^\diamond$ Prove that the languages

$$\begin{aligned} L_0 &= \{a^i b^j c^k \mid i,j,k \in \mathbb{N} \text{ and } i \leq k\}, \\ L_1 &= \{a^i b^j c^k \mid i,j,k \in \mathbb{N} \text{ and } j \leq k\}, \\ L_2 &= \{a^i b^j c^k \mid i,j,k \in \mathbb{N} \text{ and } i \geq k\}, \\ L_3 &= \{a^i b^j c^k \mid i,j,k \in \mathbb{N} \text{ and } j \geq k\} \end{aligned}$$

are context free. Conclude that the languages

$$\begin{aligned} L &= \{a^i b^j c^k \mid i,j,k \in \mathbb{N} \text{ and } k \geq \min\{i,j\}\}, \\ L' &= \{a^i b^j c^k \mid i,j,k \in \mathbb{N} \text{ and } k \leq \max\{i,j\}\} \end{aligned}$$

are context-free.

42. $^{\diamond\diamond}$ Recall that in Exercise 43 of Chapter 3 we defined the operations max and min. Prove that the class $\mathcal{L}_2$ is not closed with respect to these operations.
Hint. Observe that for the languages L, L' of Exercise 41 we have

$$\begin{aligned} \min(L) &= \{a^i b^j c^k \mid i,j,k \in \mathbb{N} \text{ and } k = \min\{i,j\}\} \\ \max(L') &= \{a^i b^j c^k \mid i,j,k \in \mathbb{N} \text{ and } k = \max\{i,j\}\}. \end{aligned}$$

Then, apply Exercise 23.

43. $^{\diamond\diamond}$ Prove that $\mathcal{L}_2$ is not closed with respect to quotient. In other words, give two context-free languages L and K such that LK^{-1} is not a context-free language.

44. $^\diamond$ Prove or disprove the following statements:
    (a) If L is a context-free language and $K \subseteq L$, then K is a context-free language.
    (b) If both L and L' are context-free languages on an alphabet A, then $L - L'$ is a context-free language.
    (c) If L is a context-free language, then LL^R is a context-free language.
    (d) If LL^R is a context-free language, then L is a context-free language.

45. $^{\diamond\diamond}$ Prove that if L, L' are context-free languages, then $\mathsf{shuffle}(L, L')$ is not necessarily a context-free language.

46. $^\diamond$ Let A be and alphabet and let $a, b \in A$ be two symbols. Prove that the language $\{x \in A^* \mid n_a(x) = n_b(x)\}$ is context-free.

47. $^{\diamond\diamond}$ Suppose that $L, K \subseteq A^*$ are generated by the type-3 grammars $G = (A_N, A, S, P)$ and $G' = (A'_N, A, S', P')$, respectively, where the productions in both P and P' have the form $X \to uY$ and $X \to u$ with $u \in A^*$, and $|u| \leq 1$. Let a, b be new symbols not in $A_N \cup A'_N \cup A$. Consider the type-3 grammar $G_1 = (A_N \times A'_N, A \cup \{a, b\}, (S, S'), P_1)$ whose set of productions is defined by the following table:

Production in P	Production in P'	Production in P_1
$X \to cY$	$X' \to cY'$	$(X, X') \to c(Y, Y')$ for $c \in A$
$X \to cY$	$X' \to c$	$(X, X') \to cb(Y, S')$ for $c \in A$
$X \to c$	$X' \to cY'$	$(X, X') \to ca(S, Y')$ for $c \in A$
$X \to c$	$X' \to c$	$(X, X') \to cab$ $(X, X') \to cab(S, S')$ for $c \in A$
$X \to \lambda$		$(X, X') \to a(S, X')$ for $X' \in A'_N$
	$X' \to \lambda$	$(X, X') \to b(X, S')$ for $X \in A_N$
$X \to Y$		$(X, X') \to (Y, Y')$ for $X', Y' \in A'_N$
	$X' \to Y'$	$(X, X') \to (Y, Y')$ for $X, Y \in A_N$

(a) Define the morphism $h : (A \cup \{a, b\})^* \longrightarrow A^*$ by $h(c) = c$ for $c \in A$ and $h(a) = h(b) = \lambda$. Prove that $h(L(G_1)) - \{\lambda\} = (L^* \cap K^*) - \{\lambda\}$.

(b) Prove that for $x \in L(G_1)$ we have $n_a(x) = p$ and $n_b(x) = q$ if and only if $h(x) \in L^p \cap K^q$ for $p, q \in \mathbb{N}$.

(c) Let $H = \bigcap\{L^n \cap K^n \mid n \in \mathbb{N}, n \geq 1\}$. Prove that

$$H = h(L(G_1) \cap \{x \in (A \cup \{a, b\})^* \mid n_a(x) = n_b(x)\}).$$

Conclude that L is a context-free language.

48. $^{\diamond}$ Starting from the result of Exercise 30 of Chapter 4 prove that if G is a terminal bounded grammar, then $L(G)$ is a context-free language.

49. $^{\diamond}$ Prove that if $G = (A_N, A_T, S, P)$ is a grammar such that each production is of the form $\alpha \to \beta$ with $\alpha \in A_N^+$ and $\beta \in (A_N \cup A_T)^* A_T (A_N \cup A_T)^*$, then $L(G)$ is a context-free language.

50. $^{\diamond}$ Prove that if $G = (A_N, A_T, S, P)$ is a grammar such that each production is of the form $\alpha \to \beta$ with $\alpha \in A_T^* A_N A_T^*$, then $L(G)$ is a context-free language.

51. $^{\diamond}$ Prove that if $G = (A_N, A_T, S, P)$ is a grammar such that each production is of the form $xX\beta \to x\gamma\beta$ with $x \in A_T^*$ and $|x| \geq |\beta$, then $L(G)$ is a context-free language.

52. $^{\diamond}$ Let $G = (A_N, A_T, S, P)$ is a grammar such that each production is of the form $\alpha X\beta \to \alpha\gamma\beta$ where either $\alpha \in A_T^*$ and $|\alpha| \geq |\beta|$ or $\beta \in A_T^*$ and $|\beta| \geq |\alpha|$. Prove that $L(G)$ is a context-free language.

53. °° Let $G = (A_N, A_T, S, P)$ be a grammar and assume that there exists a total order $<$ on the alphabet $A = A_N \cup A_T$ such that each production is of the form $X_0 \cdots X_{n-1} \to Y_1 \cdots Y_{m-1}$, where $X_i \in A_N$, and for some k, $0 \leq k \leq m-1$, and all i, $0 \leq i \leq n-1$, $X_i < Y_k$. Prove that $L(G)$ is context-free.
Solution. Let $n(Z)$ be the place occupied by the symbol $Z \in A$ in the total order on A. Suppose that c is a new terminal symbol and let G_1 be the grammar $G_1 = (A_N, A_T \cup \{c\}, S, P_1)$, where each production $X_0 \cdots X_{n-1} \to Y_0 \cdots Y_{m-1}$ is replaced by the production
$$X_0 c^{n(X_0)} \cdots X_{n-1} c^{n(X_{n-1})} \to Y_0 c^{n(Y_0)} \cdots Y_{m-1} c^{n(Y_{m-1})},$$
respectively. The grammar G_1 is a terminal-bounded grammar, so $L(G)$ is context-free. If h is a morphims that erases c and leaves unchanged every other symbol, then $h(L(G_1)) = L(G)$, which implies that $L(G)$ is context-free. ∎

Regular and Context-Free Languages

54. ° Prove that the language $L = \{w \in \{a,b,c\} \mid n_a(w) = n_b(w) = n_c(w)\}$ is not context-free.
Hint. Consider the intersection of L with $\{a\}^+\{b\}^+\{c\}^+$.
55. ° Let $G = (\{S,X,Y\}, \{a\}, \{\pi_0 : S \to XY, \pi_1 : X \to XX, \pi_2 : Y \to YY, \pi_3 : X \to a, \pi_4 : Y \to a\})$ be a context-free grammar. Prove that $\mathsf{Sz}(G)$ is not a context-free language.
Solution. Suppose that $\mathsf{Sz}(G)$ were a context-free language. Then, since $\mathsf{Sz}(G) \cup \{\pi_0\}\{\pi_1\}^*\{\pi_2\}^*\{\pi_3\}^*\{\pi_4\}^* = \{\pi_0\pi_1^i\pi_2^j\pi_3^{i+1}\pi_4^{j+1} \mid i,j \geq 0\}$ we obtain a contradiction, by Theorem 5.6.3 and Exercise 26. ∎
56. °° Prove that the language $K = \{xx \mid x \in \{a,b\}^*\}$ is not context-free.
Hint. Note that $K \cap \{a\}^+\{b\}^+\{a\}^+\{b\}^+ = L_0$, where L_0 is the language introduced in Exercise 26.
57. ° Prove or disprove the following statements:
    (a) If L is a context-free language and R is a regular language, then $L - R$ is a context-free language.
    (b) If L is a context-free language and R is a regular language, then $R - L$ is a context-free language.
    (c) Let L be a context-free language and R be a regular language. If $L \cup R$ is a regular language, then $R - L$ is a context-free language.

Ambiguity

58. ° Prove that if G is a λ-free, unambiguous context-free grammar and G' is the context-free grammar in Chomsky normal form equivalent to G, constructed by the algorithm contained in the proof of Theorem 5.4.2, then G' is unambiguous.
59. ° Let A be an alphabet. We saw in Exercise 17 of Chapter 4 that $\mathsf{REXP}(A)$ is a context-free language on the meta-alphabet $\boldsymbol{A}$. Prove that the context-free language $\mathsf{REXP}(A)$ is unambiguous.

60. $^\diamond$ Consider the context-free grammar intended to model conditional statements in programming languages:

$$G = (\{S\}, \{b, i, \textbf{if}, \textbf{ then}, \textbf{ else}\}, S, P),$$

where P consists of the productions:

$$S \to \textbf{if } b \textbf{ then } S \textbf{ else } S, \quad S \to \textbf{if } b \textbf{ then } S \ , \quad S \to i$$

Prove that G is ambiguous.

61. $^\diamond$ Prove that the context-free grammar

$$G = (\{S, S'\}, \{b, i, \textbf{if}, \textbf{ then}, \textbf{ else}\}, S, P'),$$

where P' is consists of the productions:

$$S \to \textbf{if } b \textbf{ then } S, \quad S \to \textbf{if } b \textbf{ then } S' \textbf{ else } S, \quad S \to i$$
$$S' \to \textbf{if } b \textbf{ then } S' \textbf{ else } S', \quad S' \to i$$

is equivalent to the grammar introduced in Exercise 60 and is unambiguous.

62. $^\diamond$ Consider the grammars

$$\begin{aligned} G &= (\{S\}, A, S, \{S \to SS, S \to (S), S \to \lambda\} \\ G' &= (\{S\}, A, S, \{S \to S(S), S \to \lambda\}. \end{aligned}$$

(a) Prove that G and G' are equivalent.
(b) Determine whether or not G and G' are ambiguous.

63. $^\diamond$ Consider the context-free grammar

$$G = (\{S\}, \{a\}, S, \{S \longrightarrow a^p S, S \to a^q S, S \to \lambda\}.$$

(a) Prove that G is an ambiguous grammar and that $L(G) = \{a^p\}^*\{a^q\}^*$.
(b) Construct a nonambiguous grammar equivalent to G.

64. $^{\diamond\diamond}$ Prove that the language $L \subseteq \{a, b, c, d\}$ given by

$$L = \{a^m b^m c^n d^n \mid m, n \in \mathbb{N}\} \cup \{a^m b^n c^n d^m \mid m, n \in \mathbb{N}\}$$

is inherently ambiguous.

Parikh Theorem

65. Let A be an alphabet with $|A| = n$ and let $h : A^* \longrightarrow A^*$ be a morphism. Define the $n \times n$-matrix $\boldsymbol{M}(h)$ as $(\boldsymbol{M}(h))_{ij} = p$ if $n_{a_j}(h(a_i)) = p$, that is, if a_j occurs p times in $h(a_i)$ for $0 \leq i, j \leq n - 1$.
(a) If $h, h' : A^* \longrightarrow A^*$ are two morphisms, then show that $\boldsymbol{M}(h'h) = \boldsymbol{M}(h)\boldsymbol{M}(h')$.
(b) Prove that $\mathsf{pk}(h(x)) = \mathsf{pk}(x)\boldsymbol{M}(h)$ for every word $x \in A^*$. Conclude that $\mathsf{pk}(h^{(p)}(x)) = \mathsf{pk}(x)(\boldsymbol{M}(h))^p$ for every word $x \in A^*$ and $p \in \mathbb{N}$.

66. $^{\diamond\diamond}$ Using Kleene Theorem, prove directly (without using Parikh Theorem) that the set $\mathsf{pk}(L)$ is semilinear, for every regular language L.

67. $^\diamond$ Prove that the following languages are not context-free:

(a) $\{a^p \mid p \text{ is a prime number}\}$;
(b) $\{a^{n^2} \mid n \in \mathbb{N}\}$;
(c) $\{a^{2^n} \mid n \in \mathbb{N}\}$

For $\boldsymbol{M}, \boldsymbol{P} \subseteq \mathbb{N}^k$, define $\boldsymbol{M} + \boldsymbol{P}$ as the set $\{\vec{u} + \vec{v} \mid \vec{u} \in \boldsymbol{M} \text{ and } \vec{v} \in \boldsymbol{P}\}$.

68. $^\diamond$ Let A be an alphabet. If $L, L' \subseteq A^*$, then prove that $\mathsf{pk}(L \cup L') = \mathsf{pk}(L) \cup \mathsf{pk}(L')$ and $\mathsf{pk}(LL') = \mathsf{pk}(L) + \mathsf{pk}(L')$.
69. $^\diamond$ Prove that if $\mathsf{pk}(L)$ is a semilinear set, then so is $\mathsf{pk}(L^*)$.
Hint. Show first that if $\mathsf{pk}(L)$ is a linear set, then $\mathsf{pk}(L^*)$ is a semilinear set.
70. $^\diamond$ Let $G = (\{S\}, \{a, b\}, S, \{S \to a^p S b^q S, S \to a^r, S \to b^s\}$. Determine the set $\mathsf{pk}(L(G))$.
71. Let $A = \{a_0, \ldots, a_{m-1}\}$ be an alphabet and let $\boldsymbol{w} = (w_0, \ldots, w_{k-1}) \in (A^*)^k$. Define the mapping $f_{\boldsymbol{w}} : \mathbb{N}^k \longrightarrow A^*$ by

$$f_{\boldsymbol{w}}(n_0, \ldots, n_{k-1}) = w_0^{n_0} \cdots w_{k-1}^{n_{k-1}}$$

for $(n_0, \ldots, n_{k-1}) \in \mathbb{N}^k$.
(a) If $L \subseteq \{a_0\}^* \{a_1\}^* \cdots \{a_{m-1}\}^*$, then show that $f_{(a_0, \ldots, a_{m-1})}(\mathsf{pk}(L)) = L$.
(b) Prove that if $\boldsymbol{w} = (w_0, \ldots, w_{k-1})$, where no word w_i is a prefix of another word w_j, for $0 \leq i, j \leq k-1$, then $f_{\boldsymbol{w}}$ is an one-to-one mapping.

Let $L_0, \ldots, L_{n-1}, K_0, \ldots, K_{n-1}, H$ be languages on the alphabet A. Define the language $(L_0, K_0) \cdots (L_{n-1}, K_{n-1}) \otimes H$ as

$$(L_0, K_0) \cdots (L_{n-1}, K_{n-1}) \otimes H =$$
$$\bigcup \{L_0^{m_0} \cdots L_{n-1}^{m_{n-1}} H K_{n-1}^{m_{n-1}} \cdots K_0^{m_0} | (m_0, \ldots, m_{n-1}) \in \mathbb{N}^n\}.$$

72. $^{\diamond\diamond}$ Prove that every context-free language $L \subseteq \{a\}^*\{b\}^*$ can be written as a finite union of sets of the form

$$(\{x_0\}, \{y_0\}) \cdots (\{x_{m-1}\}, \{y_{m-1}\}) \otimes \{z\},$$

where $x_0, \ldots, x_{m-1} \in \{a\}^*$, $y_0, \ldots, y_{m-1} \in \{b\}^*$, and $z \in \{a\}^*\{b\}^*$.
Solution. Let $\boldsymbol{L} \subseteq \mathbb{N}^2$ be a linear set. We have $\boldsymbol{L} = \{(p_0, q_0) + \sum m_i(p_i, q_i) \mid m_i \in \mathbb{N} \text{ for } 1 \leq i \leq n\}$, hence

$$f_{(a,b)}(\boldsymbol{L}) =$$
$$\{a^{p_0 + m_1 p_1 + \ldots + m_n p_n} b^{q_0 + m_1 q_1 + \ldots + m_n q_n} \mid m_1, \ldots, m_n \in \mathbb{N}\} =$$
$$(\{a^{p_1}\}, \{b^{q_1}\}) \cdots (\{a^{p_n}\}, \{b^{q_n}\}) \otimes \{a^{p_0} b^{q_0}\}$$

By Theorem 5.9.4 we have $\mathsf{pk}(L) = \boldsymbol{L}_0 \cup \cdots \boldsymbol{L}_{p-1}$, where $\boldsymbol{L}_0, \ldots, \boldsymbol{L}_{p-1}$ are linear sets. Consequently, $L = f_{(a,b)}(\mathsf{pk}(L)) = f_{a,b}(\boldsymbol{L}_0) \cup \cdots \cup f_{(a,b)}(\boldsymbol{L}_{p-1})$, which shows that L has the desired form. The converse implication is immediate since every set of the form

$$(\{x_0\}, \{y_0\}) \cdots (\{x_{m-1}\}, \{y_{m-1}\}) \otimes \{z\}^*$$

can be generated by the linear grammar $G = (\{S\}, A, S, \{S \to z, S \to x_0 S y_0, \ldots, S \to x_{m-1} S y_{m-1}\})$. ■

73. $^\diamond$ Prove that a language $L \subseteq \{a\}^*\{b\}^*$ is context-free if and only if $\mathsf{pk}(L)$ is semilinear.

Chomsky-Schützenberger Theorem

74. $^\diamond$ Prove Lemma 5.10.2.
75. $^\diamond$ Prove that if $w \in \mathsf{PAR}_n$, then $n_{(_i}(u) < n_{)_i}(u)$ for every proper prefix of w and $0 \leq i \leq n-1$.
76. $^\diamond$ Show that the grammar G_n that generates the parenthetic language of order n (cf. Definition 5.10.1) is ambiguous.
77. $^\diamond$ The parenthetic language PAR_{n+m} constructed in the proof of Theorem 5.10.3 depends both on n, the number of symbols of the terminal alphabet of the grammar G, and on m, the number of productions of this grammar. Prove that it is possible to select a parenthetic language that depends only on n.
Hint. Replace the alphabet A_{n+m} with the alphabet $A_n \cup \{[,], \langle, \rangle\}$. Then, replace each parenthesis $(_{n-1+k}$ by $[\langle^k]$, and each parenthesis $)_{n-1+k}$ by $[\rangle^k]$ for $0 \leq k \leq m-1$.
78. $^\diamond$ Consider the pairs of words $((_i)_i, \lambda)$ in $A_n^* \times A_n^*$ and the congruence ρ on the monoid A_n^* generated by these pairs (cf. Exercise 37 of Chapter 1). Prove that PAR_n equals $[\lambda]_\rho$, the equivalence class of λ relative to the congruence ρ.

Let $A = \{a_0, \ldots, a_{n-1}\}$ be an alphabet. The notion of parenthetic language can be extended to arbitrary alphabets as follows. Consider the alphabet $\bar{A} = \{\bar{a}_0, \ldots, \bar{a}_{n-1}\}$. The *parenthetic language* PAR_A is the language generated by the grammar $G_A = (\{S\}, A \cup \bar{A}, S, P)$ whose set of productions is

$$P = \{S \to SS, S \to \lambda, S \to a_0 S \bar{a}_0, \ldots, S \to a_{n-1} S \bar{a}_{n-1}\}.$$

79. Extend the statement contained by Exercise 78 to PAR_A.
80. Extend Lemma 5.10.2 to PAR_A. In other words prove the following statements concerning the language PAR_A.
    (a) if $u, v \in \mathsf{PAR}_A$, then $uv \in \mathsf{PAR}_A$;
    (b) if $u \in \mathsf{PAR}_A$, then $au\bar{a} \in \mathsf{PAR}_A$ for every $a \in A$;
    (c) if $a\bar{a}u \in \mathsf{PAR}_n$ for some $a \in A$, then $u \in \mathsf{PAR}_A$;
    (d) for every word $w \in \mathsf{PAR}_A - \{\lambda\}$ there are $u, v \in \mathsf{PAR}_A$ such that $w = au\bar{a}v$ for some $a \in A$.
81. $^{\diamond\diamond}$ Let L be a λ-free context-free language generated by a context-free grammar $G = (A_N, A_T, S, P)$ in Greibach normal form and let $A = A_N \cup A_T$. Define the morphism $h : A_T^* \longrightarrow \mathcal{P}((A \cup \bar{A})^*)$ by

$$h(a) = \{\bar{X}\alpha^R \mid X \to a\alpha \in P\}a\bar{a}$$

for $a \in A_T$. Prove that for every $x \in A_T^*$ we have $X \xRightarrow[G,left]{*} x$ if and only if there is $w \in h(x)$ such that $Xw \in \mathsf{PAR}_A$.

Solution. Suppose that $X \overset{m}{\underset{G,left}{\Rightarrow}} x$. We prove, by induction on $m \geq 1$, that there is $w \in h(x)$ such that $Xw \in \mathsf{PAR}_A$. For $m = 1$ we have $|x| = 1$, so $x = a \in A_T$, and the production $X \rightarrow a$ belongs to P. Therefore, $h(a) = \bar{X}aa\bar{a}$. If $w = \bar{X}aa\bar{a}$, then Xw clearly belongs to PAR_A.

Suppose that the statement is true for derivations of length less than m and that $X \overset{m}{\underset{G,left}{\Rightarrow}} x$. Since G is in Greibach normal form we have

$$X \underset{G,left}{\Rightarrow} aX_{i_0} \cdots X_{i_{p-1}} \overset{m}{\underset{G,left}{\Rightarrow}} ax_0 \cdots x_{p-1},$$

which implies the existence of the derivations $X_{i_l} \overset{m_l}{\underset{G,left}{\Rightarrow}} x_l$ for $0 \leq l \leq p-1$. By the inductive hypothesis, we have the words $w_0, \ldots, w_{p-1}$ such that $w_j \in h(x_j)$ and $X_{i_l}w_l \in \mathsf{PAR}_A$ for $0 \leq l \leq p-1$. Since $X \rightarrow aX_{i_0} \cdots X_{i_{p-1}} \in P$ we have $\bar{X}X_{i_{p-1}} \cdots X_{i_0}a\bar{a} \in h(a)$. Therefore, by defining

$$w = \bar{X}X_{i_{p-1}} \cdots X_{i_0}a\bar{a}w_0 \cdots w_{p-1}$$

we have $Xw \in \mathsf{PAR}_A$ and $w \in h(ax_0 \cdots x_{p-1}) = h(x)$.

Conversely, suppose that there is a word $w \in h(x)$ such that $Xw \in \mathsf{PAR}_A$. We prove, by induction on $n = |x| \geq 1$, that $X \overset{m}{\underset{G,left}{\Rightarrow}} x$.

For the basis case, $n = 1$, $x = a \in A_T$. The definition of h implies that $w = \bar{X}\alpha^R a\bar{a}$, where $X \rightarrow a\alpha \in P$. Since $Xw = X\bar{X}\alpha^R a\bar{a} \in \mathsf{PAR}_A$ we must have $\alpha = \lambda$ because otherwise the symbols of α would not be matched by suitable barred symbols. Thus, $X \rightarrow a \in P$ and this shows that $X \underset{G,left}{\Rightarrow} a = x$.

Suppose that the statement holds for words shorter than n, and let x be a word in A_T^* such that $|x| = n$, and there is $w \in h(x)$ such that $Xw \in \mathsf{PAR}_A$. Let a be the first symbol of x; we have $x = ay$. The definition of h implies that w must begin with a barred symbol. Since $Xw \in \mathsf{PAR}_L$ the initial symbol of w must be $\bar{X}$ since, otherwise, the initial symbol of w could not be matched by a previous non-barred symbol. Thus, we can write $w = \bar{X}\alpha^R a\bar{a}u$, where $X \rightarrow a\alpha \in P$, and $u \in h(y)$.

Since $Xw \in \mathsf{PAR}_A$, we have $X\bar{X}\alpha^R a\bar{a}u \in \mathsf{PAR}_A$, which implies $\alpha^R a\bar{a}u \in \mathsf{PAR}_A$. The symbols of $\alpha = X_{i_0} \cdots X_{i_{m-1}} \in A_N^*$ are matched by barred symbols that occur in u. By applying Part (d) of Exercise 80 repeatedly we can write $u = u_0 \cdots u_{m-1}$, where $X_{i_j}u_j \in \mathsf{PAR}_A$ and u_j begins with the symbol $\bar{X}_{i_j}$ for $0 \leq j \leq m-1$. Therefore, y can be factored as $y = y_0 \cdots y_{m-1}$ such that $u_j \in h(y_j)$ and $X_{i_j}u_j \in \mathsf{PAR}_A$ for $0 \leq j \leq m-1$. Since $|y_j| < n$, by the inductive hypothesis we have the derivations

$$X_{i_0} \overset{*}{\underset{G,left}{\Rightarrow}} y_0, \ldots, X_{i_{m-1}} \overset{*}{\underset{G,left}{\Rightarrow}} y_{m-1},$$

which can be combined in the derivation

$$\begin{aligned} X & \underset{G}{\Rightarrow} aX_{i_0}\cdots X_{i_{m-1}} \\ & \overset{*}{\underset{G}{\Rightarrow}} ay_0\cdots X_{i_{m-1}} \\ & \vdots \\ & \overset{*}{\underset{G}{\Rightarrow}} ay_0\cdots y_{m-1} = x. \end{aligned}$$

■

82. $\diamond$ Give a proof of Theorem 5.10.3 starting from the result contained by Exercise 81.

Solution. Let $L \subseteq A^*$ be a context-free language generated by the context-free grammar $G = (A_N, A, S, P)$. Without loss of generality we assume that G is in Greibach normal form. Let B be the alphabet $B = A_N \cup A$. Define the morphism $g : (B \cup \bar{B})^* \longrightarrow A^*$ by $g(X) = g(\bar{X}) = g(\bar{a}) = \lambda$, for $X \in A_N$, $a \in A$, and $g(a) = a$ for $a \in A$.
Let $h : A^* \longrightarrow \mathcal{P}((B \cup \bar{B})^*)$ be the morphism introduced in Exercise 81. It is easy to verify that $w \in h(x)$ if and only if $g(w) = x$ for $w \in h(A^*)$. Exercise 81 implies that $X \overset{*}{\underset{G,left}{\Rightarrow}} x$ if and only if $g(Xw) = x$ and $Xw \in \mathsf{PAR}_A$. If R is the regular language $R = Xh(A^*)$, then we have $X \overset{*}{\underset{G}{\Rightarrow}} x$ if and only if $g(Xw) = x$ and $Xw \in \mathsf{PAR}_A \cap R$, which implies immediately Theorem 5.10.3. ■

5.12 Bibliographical Comments

In section 5.4.2 we presented Greibach Normal Form using the approach presented in [Kozen, 1997]; an alternative approach that makes use of Ginsburg-Rice Theorem, presented in [Rosencrantz, 1967], is presented in section 5.4.2. The operation $\otimes$ defined in Exercise 72 was introduced in [Ginsburg, 1966]; this last title remains an unsurpassed reference for the study of context-free languages.

The inherent ambiguity of the language from Theorem 5.8.1 is mentioned in [Chomsky and Schützenberger, 1963]. Exercise 47 is from [Greibach, 1965].

Parikh's Theorem was published in [Parikh, 1966] (the original publication containing this result was [Parikh, 1961]). Exercise 14 appears in [Kozen, 1997].

Exercise 48 is an immediate application of the result contained by Exercise 30 of Chapter 4 and, at is is shown in [Baker, 1972], allows rather simple proofs of the results contained in Exercises 49–exer:dec3098f. These results belong to [Ginsburg and Greibach, 1966] (Exercise 49), [Book, 1972](Exercises 50–52) and [Hibbard, 1966] (Exercise 53). The result contained by Exercise 81 belongs to E. Shamir [1967]. The alternative proof of Chomsky-Schützenberger theorem is discussed in [J. Autebert, 1997].

Chapter 6

Pushdown Automata

6.1 Introduction

Like finite automata, pushdown automata provide abstract models of computation. They play the same role for the class of context-free languages that finite automata play for regular languages: the class of languages accepted by pushdown automata is precisely the class $\mathcal{L}_2$ of context-free languages. However, unlike finite automata, deterministic pushdown automata are weaker than non-deterministic ones; i.e., they accept only languages belonging to a strict subclass of $\mathcal{L}_2$.

6.2 Nondeterministic Pushdown Automata

Just like a finite automaton, a *pushdown automaton* (pda) has a finite set of states and a one-way, read-only input tape, divided into cells each of which contains a symbol of an alphabet A, referred to as the input alphabet. To this, the pushdown model adds a pushdown store, that can be conceptualized as a tape that has a beginning but is infinitely long. It, too, is divided into cells, and each cell that is in use contains a symbol from an alphabet Z, referred to as the pushdown alphabet. The tape is thought of as being oriented vertically, with the used portion at the top. The automaton can read and write only the top-most cell, referred to as the top of the pushdown store. The pushdown store is often described as similar to a stack of trays in a cafeteria, where a mechanical server offers the customer the top tray to take, and anyone who wants may put one or more trays onto the stack. Many computer scientists will be familiar with a storage mechanism known as a *stack* onto which one may push data that are later recovered by a pop operation. This is exactly a pushdown store.

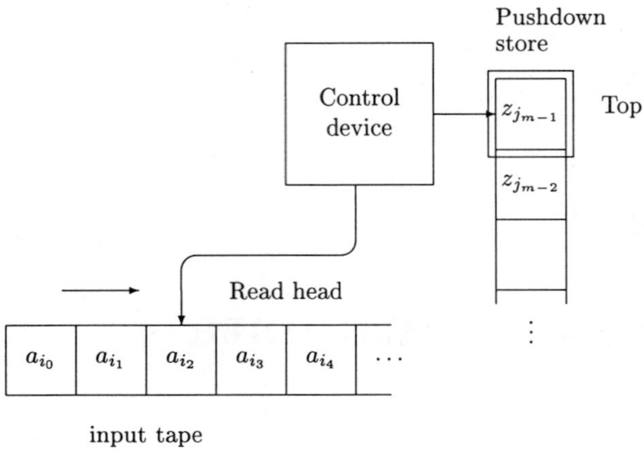

Figure 6.1: Components of a Pushdown Automaton

The pda's actions are determined by its internal state, its input tape, and its pushdown store. At each step, the pda bases its actions on its current state, the symbol at the top of the pushdown store, and, optionally, the result of reading the next input symbol. Its actions consist of writing zero or more symbols on its pushdown store and going into its next state. If the pda reads the input tape, the read head advances to the next cell of the input tape and cannot ever again return to the cell it just read. Also, the top symbol of the pushdown store is removed at each step and must be written back if it is to remain at the top. Since pdas are nondeterministic, there may be several options to choose from at each step.

As in the case of nondeterministic finite automata, a pda accepts a word if there is a sequence of choices that allows the suitably initialized pda to consume the word and end in a state that is an element of a specified set of accepting states. The set of words accepted by a pda is referred to as the language accepted by that pda. We shall show an exact correspondence between the class of languages accepted by pdas and the class of context-free languages.

The notion of pushdown automaton is formalized next. Let $\mathcal{P}_f(M)$ be the set of all finite subsets of a set M.

Definition 6.2.1 A *pushdown automaton* (pda) is a 7-tuple

$$\mathcal{M} = (A, Z, Q, \delta, q_0, z_0, F),$$

where A is the *input alphabet*, Z is the *alphabet of the pushdown store*,

$$\delta : Z \times Q \times (A \cup \{\lambda\}) \longrightarrow \mathcal{P}_f(Z^* \times Q)$$

is the *transition function*, q_0 is the *initial state*, z_0 is the *start symbol*, and F is the *set of final states*. We assume that $Q \cap A = Q \cap Z = \emptyset$.

We refer to the pairs $(q, w) \in \delta(z, q, a)$ as the *transitions of the triple* (z, q, a). The transitions of a triple (z, q, λ) are referred to as (z, q)-*null transitions*. $\square$

When scanning the input symbol a in the state q and reading the symbol z from the top of the pushdown store, the automaton selects a pair $(w, q') \in Z^* \times Q$ from the set $\delta(z, q, a)$; after that, the state changes to q' and the top symbol of the pushdown store is replaced by the word w. If $w = \lambda$, this amounts to popping the top symbol out of the top cell; if $|w| > 1$, the replacement of z by w causes the symbols located below the top cell to be pushed downwards by $|w| - 1$ cells in order to accommodate the symbols of the word w. Specifically, if the state of the pda is q, the the content of the pushdown store is $w'z$, where z is the symbol at the top, and the pda chooses the pair $(z_{j_0} \cdots z_{j_{m-1}}, q')$ from $\delta(z, q, a)$, then the new content of the pushdown store will be $w'z_{j_0} \cdots z_{j_{m-1}}$ and the new state will be q'. The symbol at the top of the stack will then be $z_{j_{m-1}}$.

Note that a pda is a nondeterministic device, because at any given moment a pda may chose one among several transitions (z, q') for its next step.

Example 6.2.2 Consider the pushdown automaton

$$\mathcal{M} = (\{a, b\}, \{z_0, z_1, z_2, z_3\}, \{q_0, q_1, q_2\}, \delta, q_0, z_0, \{q_2\}),$$

where δ is defined by the table

Top z	State q	Input a	Transition Function $\delta(z, q, a)$
z_0	q_0	λ	$\{(z_3z_0), q_1\}$
z_0	q_1	λ	$\{(\lambda, q_1), (z_1z_0z_1, q_1), (z_2z_0z_2, q_1)\}$
z_1	q_1	a	$\{(\lambda, q_1)\}$
z_2	q_1	b	$\{(\lambda, q_1)\}$
z_3	q_1	λ	$\{(z_3, q_2)\}$

For triples (z, q, a) that do not appear in this table we assume that $\delta(z, q, a) = \emptyset$.

It may help the reader visualize the intended functioning of this pda if we describe its actions in English. It begins by writing z_3z_0 onto the stack. Thus, z_3 is placed at the bottom of the stack. After reading through the entire input, the pda will have to find z_3 at the top of the stack in order to go into state q_2, which is the only accepting state.

When z_0 is at the top of the stack, the pda guesses whether the next symbol is a or b. If it guesses a, it pushes $z_1z_0z_1$ onto the stack. If it guesses b, it pushes $z_2z_0z_2$ onto the stack. It then verifies its guess by examining the next symbol. If it made the "wrong guess", it cannot proceed. If it made the "right guess", then it has left a trace of what that symbol was on the stack. Over time, this records the symbols read from the input with the most recent nearest the top. In other words, reading the stack from top to bottom would allow one to reconstruct the input word in reverse order.

This process continues until the pda guesses that it has reached the midpoint of the input word. At that time, it simply pops the z_0 off the stack. Now it reads through the remaining portion of the input, checking that what is there is the reverse of what was encountered in the first half, as only that input will match the trace left in the stack; i.e., if the word x was read from the input tape before the pda guessed it had reached the middle, only x^R will allow it to pop each symbol off the stack as the pda processes the remaining input word.

When it exhausts the input, z_3 should be at the top of the stack, allowing the pda to accept the word.

There are many places where the pda must make guesses, but if it is possible to make a sequence of guesses that allows the pda to read through the word on its input tape and end up in an accepting state, then the pda accepts the word. Only if no possible sequence of guesses permits the pda to accept the word does it reject the word. In this case, as we shall show in detail in Example 6.2.10, the language accepted by the pda is $\{xx^R \mid x \in \{a,b\}^*\}$. □

Definition 6.2.3 Let $\mathcal{M} = (A, Z, Q, \delta, q_0, z_0, F)$ be a pda. The set $\mathcal{I}(\mathcal{M})$ of *instantaneous descriptions of* $\mathcal{M}$ is the set $Z^* \times Q \times A^*$.

A pda $\mathcal{M}$ *is described by* $(w, q, u) \in \mathcal{I}(\mathcal{M})$ if $\mathcal{M}$ is in the state q, u is the portion of input that is still to be read, and w is the content of the pushdown store, with the rightmost symbol of w at the top of the pushdown store.

Any instantaneous description of the form (z_0, q_0, u) is an *initial instantaneous description of* $\mathcal{M}$. □

Definition 6.2.4 Let $\mathcal{M} = (A, Z, Q, \delta, q_0, z_0, F)$ be a pda. The binary relation $\underset{\mathcal{M}}{\vdash}$ on the set $\mathcal{I}(\mathcal{M})$ is given by $(w'z, q, au) \underset{\mathcal{M}}{\vdash} (w'w, p, u)$ if $(w, p) \in \delta(z, q, a)$, for $z \in Z$, $q \in Q$, and $a \in A \cup \{\lambda\}$.

When $\mathcal{M}$ is obvious from context we may simply write $\vdash$ for $\underset{\mathcal{M}}{\vdash}$.

The n-th power of $\underset{\mathcal{M}}{\vdash}$ is denoted, as usual, by $\overset{n}{\underset{\mathcal{M}}{\vdash}}$ for $n \in \mathbb{N}$; also, the transitive closure of $\underset{\mathcal{M}}{\vdash}$ is denoted by $\overset{+}{\underset{\mathcal{M}}{\vdash}}$ and the reflexive and transitive closure of the same relation is denoted by $\overset{*}{\underset{\mathcal{M}}{\vdash}}$. □

A pda may have instantaneous descriptions (w, q, u) such that there are no instantaneous descriptions (w_1, q_1, u_1) such that $(w, q, u) \underset{\mathcal{M}}{\vdash} (w_1, q_1, u_1)$. In this case we refer to (w, q, u) as a *blocking instantaneous description*. For instance, such instantaneous descriptions occur when the pushdown store is empty.

Definition 6.2.5 A *computation* in a pda $\mathcal{M}$ is a sequence $(\mathsf{c}_0, \ldots, \mathsf{c}_n)$ of instantaneous descriptions of $\mathcal{M}$ such that $\mathsf{c}_i \underset{\mathcal{M}}{\vdash} \mathsf{c}_{i+1}$ for $0 \le i \le n-1$.

We will denote the above computation by $\mathsf{c}_0 \underset{\mathcal{M}}{\vdash} \cdots \underset{\mathcal{M}}{\vdash} \mathsf{c}_n$. □

Example 6.2.6 Let $\mathcal{M}$ be the pda introduced in Example 6.2.2. We have

$$
\begin{aligned}
&(z_0, q_0, abbbba) \vdash (z_3 z_0, q_1, abbbba) \vdash (z_3 z_1 z_0 z_1, q_1, abbbba) \\
&\vdash (z_3 z_1 z_0, q_1, bbbba) \vdash (z_3 z_1 z_2 z_0 z_2, q_1, bbbba) \vdash (z_3 z_1 z_2 z_0, q_1, bbba) \\
&\vdash (z_3 z_1 z_2 z_2 z_0 z_2, q_1, bbba) \vdash (z_3 z_1 z_2 z_2 z_0, q_1, bba) \\
&\vdash (z_3 z_1 z_2 z_2, q_1, bba) \vdash (z_3 z_1 z_2, q_1, ba) \\
&\vdash (z_3 z_1, q_1, a) \vdash (z_3, q_1, \lambda) \vdash (z_3, q_2, \lambda).
\end{aligned}
$$

Therefore, we can write $(z_0, q_0, abbbba) \overset{*}{\underset{\mathcal{M}}{\vdash}} (z_3, q_2, \lambda)$.

When $\mathcal{M}$ reaches the state q_1 and z_0 is at the top of the pushdown store, there are three possible moves, namely (λ, q_1), $(z_1 z_0 z_1, q_1)$, or $(z_2 z_0 z_2, q_1)$. None of these involves reading an input symbol. If $\mathcal{M}$ makes the "wrong guess" when the instantaneous description $(z_3z_1z_2z_0, q_1, bbba)$ is reached and makes use of the pair $(z_1z_0z_1, q_1)$ instead of $(z_2z_0z_2, q_1)$, the next instantaneous description will be $(z_3z_1z_2z_1z_0z_1, q_1, bbba)$. Note that a symbol z_1 cannot be popped out of the pushdown store unless $\mathcal{M}$ reads a from the input. Since only one symbol a remains in the input, at most one z_1 can be popped off, and thus it would be impossible to get z_3 at the top of the pushdown store. This would prevent $\mathcal{M}$ from reaching the final state q_2. □

The next theorem contains a few technical results.

Theorem 6.2.7 *Let* $\mathcal{M} = (A, Z, Q, \delta, q_0, z_0, F)$ *be a pda.*

(i) *If* $(z_{i_0} \cdots z_{i_{n-1}}, p, t) \vdash^* (\lambda, p', \lambda)$, *then we can write* t *as a product of* n *words* $t = t_{n-1} \cdots t_0$ *such that*

$$\begin{array}{lcl}(z_{i_{n-1}}, p_0, t_{n-1}) & \vdash^* & (\lambda, p_1, \lambda)\\ (z_{i_{n-2}}, p_1, t_{n-2}) & \vdash^* & (\lambda, p_2, \lambda)\\ & \cdots & \\ (z_{i_0}, p_{n-1}, t_0) & \vdash^* & (\lambda, p_n, \lambda),\end{array}$$

where $p = p_0, p_1, \ldots, p_n = p'$ *is a sequence of states in* Q.

(ii) $(w, q, x) \vdash^* (w', q', \lambda)$ *for some* $q, q' \in Q$, $w, w' \in Z^*$, *and* $x \in A^*$ *if and only if* $(w, q, xy) \vdash^* (w', q', y)$ *for every* $y \in A^*$.

(iii) *If* $(w, q, xy) \vdash^* (w', q', y)$, *then* $(w_1w, q, xy) \vdash^* (w_1w', q', y)$ *for each* $w_1 \in Z^*$.

Proof. The argument for the first part of the theorem is by induction on the length n of the initial content of the pushdown store $w = z_{i_0} \cdots z_{i_{n-1}}$, where $n \geq 1$. The base case, $n = 1$ is immediate.

Suppose that the statement holds for $|w| \leq n - 1$, and let $w = z_{i_0} \cdots z_{i_{n-1}}$ be a word of length n. The symbol $z_{i_{n-1}}$ at the top of the pushdown store must eventually be erased. If t_{n-1} is the prefix of input word t that causes the erasure of $z_{i_{n-1}}$, then we can write $t = t_{n-1}t'$, where

$$\begin{array}{lcl}(z_{i_{n-1}}, p_0, t_{n-1}) & \vdash^* & (\lambda, p_1, \lambda)\\ (z_{i_0} \cdots z_{i_{n-2}}, p_1, t') & \vdash^* & (\lambda, p', \lambda)\end{array}$$

for some state $p_1 \in Q$. The inductive hypothesis implies that t' can be written as a product of $n - 1$ words $t' = t_{n-2} \ldots t_0$ such that

$$\begin{array}{lcl}(z_{i_{n-2}}, p_1, t_{n-2}) & \vdash^* & (\lambda, p_2, \lambda)\\ & \cdots & \\ (z_{i_0}, p_{n-1}, t_0) & \vdash^* & (\lambda, p_n, \lambda),\end{array}$$

where $p_1, p_2, \ldots, p_{n-1} = p'$ is a sequence of states of $\mathcal{M}$. Combining this fact with the previous observation gives the desired conclusion.

We leave the arguments for the second and third parts to the reader. ∎

As in the case of nondeterministic finite automata, pdas accept languages by reading through their input words, making guesses as necessary along the way, and ending in a final, accepting state. This is formalized in the next definition. Alternative definitions of language acceptance exist, such as accepting those words that cause the pda to empty its pushdown store. These will be shown to be equivalent to the definition below.

Definition 6.2.8 The *language accepted by the pda* $\mathcal{M} = (A, Z, Q, \delta, q_0, z_0, F)$

is the language

$$L(\mathcal{M}) = \{x \in A^* \mid (z_0, q_0, x) \overset{*}{\underset{\mathcal{M}}{\vdash}} (w, q, \lambda) \text{ for some } q \in F \text{ and } w \in Z^*\}$$

□

Definition 6.2.9 The pda $\mathcal{M}, \mathcal{M}'$ are said to be *equivalent* if $L(\mathcal{M}) = L(\mathcal{M}')$. □

Example 6.2.10 Here we show that the language accepted by $\mathcal{M}$, the pda introduced in Example 6.2.2, is $L(\mathcal{M}) = \{xx^R \mid x \in \{a,b\}^*\}$.

We begin by showing that for every $x \in \{a,b\}^*$ we have $xx^R \in L(\mathcal{M})$. To this end, we prove that $(z_0, q_1, xx^R) \overset{*}{\underset{\mathcal{M}}{\vdash}} (\lambda, q_1, \lambda)$. The argument is by induction on the length of x.

For $|x| = 0$, we have $xx^R = \lambda$ and $(z_0, q_1, \lambda) \overset{*}{\underset{\mathcal{M}}{\vdash}} (\lambda, q_1, \lambda)$ in view of the fact that $(q_1, \lambda) \in \delta(z_0, q_1, \lambda)$.

Suppose that our claim holds for words of length n, and let $y \in A^*$ be a word of length $n+1$. We can write either $y = au$, or $y = bv$ for some $u, v \in A^*$ with $|u| = |v| = n$, depending on the first symbol of y. In the first case we can write:

$$\begin{array}{lll} (z_0, q_1, yy^R) = (z_0, q_1, auu^Ra) & & \\ \quad \vdash & (z_1 z_0 z_1, q_1, auu^Ra) & (\text{since } (z_1 z_0 z_1, q_1) \in \delta(z_0, q_1, \lambda)) \\ \quad \vdash & (z_1 z_0, q_1, uu^Ra) & (\text{since } (\lambda, q_1) \in \delta(z_1, q_1, a)) \\ \quad \vdash^* & (z_1, q_1, a) & (\text{by the inductive hypothesis}) \\ \quad \vdash & (\lambda, q_1, \lambda) & (\text{since } (\lambda, q_1) \in \delta(z_1, q_1, a)). \end{array}$$

The case $y = bv$ can be treated similarly and is left to the reader.

Since $(z_3 z_0, q_1) \in \delta(z_0, q_0, \lambda)$ we have

$$(z_0, q_0, xx^R) \vdash (z_3 z_0, q_1, xx^R),$$

for every $x \in \{a,b\}^*$.

Therefore, by the previous claim, we obtain the computation:

$$\begin{array}{lll} (z_0, q_0, xx^R) & \vdash & (z_3 z_0, q_1, xx^R) \\ & \vdash^* & (z_3, q_1, \lambda) \\ & \vdash & (z_3, q_2, \lambda), \end{array}$$

so $xx^R \in L(\mathcal{M})$ because q_2 is a final state of $\mathcal{M}$.

Conversely, suppose that $t \in L(\mathcal{M})$. We have

$$(z_0, q_0, t) \vdash^* (w, q_2, \lambda),$$

for some $w \in Z^*$. The definition of $\mathcal{M}$ implies that this computation must be written as

$$(z_0, q_0, t) \vdash (z_3 z_0, q_1, t) \vdash^* (w, q_2, \lambda),$$

since this is the single means of switching from the state q_0 into the state q_1, which, in turn, is the unique state of $\mathcal{M}$ that precedes the final state q_2. In order to reach the final state q_2, the pda must have the symbol z_3 at the top of the pushdown store. Thus, the instantaneous description that precedes (w, q_2, λ) in the previous computation necessarily has the form (z_3, q_1, λ). This implies that $w = z_3$, so we have

$$(z_0, q_0, t) \vdash (z_3 z_0, q_1, t) \overset{*}{\vdash} (z_3, q_1, \lambda) \vdash (z_3, q_2, \lambda).$$

In turn, this means that we have the computation

$$(z_0, q_1, t) \overset{*}{\vdash} (\lambda, q_1, \lambda),$$

during which $\mathcal{M}$ remains in the state q_1. We prove by induction on $k = |t|$ that $t = xx^R$ for some $x \in \{a, b\}^*$.

If $k = 0$, then $t = \lambda$, so $t = \lambda\lambda^R$. In this case, $\mathcal{M}$ chooses the pair $(\lambda, q_1) \in \delta(z_0, q_1, \lambda)$, and we have

$$(z_0, q_1, t) \vdash (\lambda, q_1, t);$$

thus, the statement holds.

Suppose that the statement holds for words t of length less than k, and let $t \in A^*$ be a word of length k. If $\mathcal{M}$ chooses the pair $(z_1 z_0 z_1, q_1) \in \delta(z_0, q_1, \lambda)$, then

$$(z_0, q_1, t) \vdash (z_1 z_0 z_1, q_1, t) \overset{*}{\vdash} (\lambda, q_1, \lambda).$$

By the first part of Theorem 6.2.7, $t = t'ut''$, where

$$\begin{aligned} (z_1, q_1, t') &\overset{*}{\vdash} (\lambda, q_1, \lambda), \\ (z_0, q_1, u) &\overset{*}{\vdash} (\lambda, q_1, \lambda), \\ (z_1, q_1, t'') &\overset{*}{\vdash} (\lambda, q_1, \lambda). \end{aligned}$$

Note that if z_1 is at the top of the pushdown store, then the single way to eliminate this symbol is to have $t' = a$; similarly, $t'' = a$. By the inductive hypothesis, $u = zz^R$, so $t = azz^R a = az(az)^R$. A similar argument can be made when $\mathcal{M}$ chooses the pair $(z_2 z_0 z_2, q_1) \in \delta(z_0, q_1, \lambda)$. Thus, $L(\mathcal{M}) = \{xx^R \mid x \in \{a, b\}^*\}$. □

Another method for associating a language with a pda is to consider the language that consists of those input words for which there is a computation that leads to the emptying of the pushdown store. This is captured by the following definition.

Definition 6.2.11 Let $\mathcal{M} = (A, Z, Q, \delta, q_0, z_0, F)$ be a pda. The *language accepted by* $\mathcal{M}$ *with an empty store* is given by

$$N(\mathcal{M}) = \{x \in A^* \mid (z_0, q_0, x) \overset{*}{\underset{\mathcal{M}}{\vdash}} (\lambda, q, \lambda) \text{ for some } q \in Q\}.$$

□

The set F plays no role in the definition of $N(\mathcal{M})$.

As mentioned above, this definition can be shown equivalent to Definition 6.2.8. We begin this process with the next theorem.

Theorem 6.2.12 *For every pda* $\mathcal{M}$ *there is a pda* $\mathcal{M}'$ *such that* $L(\mathcal{M}) = N(\mathcal{M}')$.

Proof. Let $\mathcal{M} = (A, Z, Q, \delta, q_0, z_0, F)$. We have

$$L(\mathcal{M}) = \{x \in A^* \mid (z_0, q_0, x) \overset{*}{\underset{\mathcal{M}}{\vdash}} (w, q, \lambda) \text{ for some } w \in Z^* \text{ and } q \in F\}.$$

Define the pda $\mathcal{M}' = (A, Z \cup \{z'\}, Q \cup \{q', q_0'\}, \delta', q_0', z', \emptyset)$, where q', q_0' are two new states, and z' is a new initial pushdown symbol, where $z' \notin Z$.

The transition function δ' is given by

$$\delta'(z, q, a) = \begin{cases} \{(z'z_0, q_0)\} & \text{if } (z, q, a) = (z', q_0', \lambda), \\ \delta(z, q, a) & \text{if } q \in Q - F, a \in A \cup \{\lambda\}, z \in Z, \\ \delta(z, q, a) \cup \{(\lambda, q')\} & \text{if } q \in F, z \in Z \cup \{z'\}, a \in A \cup \{\lambda\}, \\ \{(\lambda, q')\} & \text{if } q = q', z \in Z \cup \{z'\}, a = \lambda, \\ \emptyset & \text{in any other case.} \end{cases}$$

The symbol z' was introduced for the pda $\mathcal{M}'$ since some words in $A^* - L(\mathcal{M})$ may empty the pushdown store of $\mathcal{M}$. The presence of z' at the bottom of the pushdown store makes this impossible in $\mathcal{M}'$.

Since $\delta(z', q_0', \lambda) = \{(z'z_0, q_0)\}$, $\mathcal{M}'$ begins its work by entering the state q_0 and by placing z_0 at the top of the pushdown store. If $x \in L(\mathcal{M})$, then $(z_0, q_0, x) \overset{*}{\underset{\mathcal{M}}{\vdash}} (w, q, \lambda)$ for some $w \in Z^*$ and $q \in F$. Correspondingly, in $\mathcal{M}'$ we have

$$(z', q_0', x) \underset{\mathcal{M}'}{\vdash} (z'z_0, q_0, x) \overset{*}{\underset{\mathcal{M}'}{\vdash}} (z'w, q, \lambda) \overset{*}{\underset{\mathcal{M}'}{\vdash}} (\lambda, q', \lambda),$$

by the definition of δ'. This implies $L(\mathcal{M}) \subseteq N(\mathcal{M}')$.

To prove the converse inclusion, let $x \in N(\mathcal{M}')$, so $(z', q_0', x) \overset{*}{\underset{\mathcal{M}'}{\vdash}} (\lambda, q, \lambda)$ for some state $q \in Q \cup \{q', q_0'\}$. The definition of δ' implies that this computation necessarily has the form

$$(z', q_0', x) \underset{\mathcal{M}'}{\vdash} (z'z_0, q_0, x) \overset{*}{\underset{\mathcal{M}'}{\vdash}} (\lambda, q, \lambda),$$

since there exists only one transition for the triple (z', q', λ), namely $(z'z_0, q_0)$. Note that the symbol z' can be erased by $\mathcal{M}'$ only if this pda reaches a state $q \in F \cup \{q'\}$. Let u be the suffix of x that remains to be read when $\mathcal{M}'$ reached the state q' for the first time. Since $\mathcal{M}'$ enters q' only from a final state q_1 of $\mathcal{M}$ we have:

$$(z', q_0', x) \underset{\mathcal{M}'}{\vdash} (z'z_0, q_0, x) \overset{*}{\underset{\mathcal{M}'}{\vdash}} (w, q_1, u) \underset{\mathcal{M}'}{\vdash} (w', q', u) \overset{*}{\underset{\mathcal{M}'}{\vdash}} (\lambda, q, \lambda),$$

Once $\mathcal{M}'$ enters the state q' no symbol is read from the input, so we have $u = \lambda$. This allows us to write the previous computation as

$$(z', q_0', x) \underset{\mathcal{M}'}{\vdash} (z'z_0, q_0, x) \overset{*}{\underset{\mathcal{M}'}{\vdash}} (w, q_1, \lambda) \underset{\mathcal{M}'}{\vdash} (w', q', \lambda) \overset{*}{\underset{\mathcal{M}'}{\vdash}} (\lambda, q, \lambda),$$

and this implies the existence of the computation

$$(z_0, q_0, x) \overset{*}{\underset{\mathcal{M}}{\vdash}} (w, q_1, \lambda),$$

which, in turn, implies $x \in L(\mathcal{M})$. This proves the needed inclusion $N(\mathcal{M}') \subseteq L(\mathcal{M})$. ∎

Theorem 6.2.13 *For every context-free grammar G there is a one-state pda $\mathcal{M}$ such that $L = N(\mathcal{M})$.*

Proof. Suppose that $L = L(G)$, where $G = (A_N, A_T, S, P)$ is a context-free grammar. Let $\mathcal{M} = (A_T, A_N \cup A_T, \{q_0\}, \delta, q_0, S, \emptyset)$ be a pda whose transition function is given by

$$\begin{aligned} \delta(X, q_0, \lambda) &= \{(\alpha^R, q_0) \mid X \to \alpha \in P\}, \\ \delta(a, q_0, a) &= \{(\lambda, q_0)\}, \end{aligned}$$

for every $a \in A_T$, $X \in A_N$, and $\delta(s, q_0, a) = \emptyset$ in all other cases.

Let

$$S = \gamma_0 \underset{G}{\Rightarrow} \gamma_1 \underset{G}{\Rightarrow} \cdots \underset{G}{\Rightarrow} \gamma_n = u\alpha$$

be a leftmost derivation of $u\alpha$ in G, where $u \in A_T^*$ and $\alpha \in (A_N \cup A_T)^*$ is either the null word or a word that begins with a nonterminal symbol. We claim that $(S, q_0, uw) \overset{*}{\underset{\mathcal{M}}{\vdash}} (\alpha^R, q_0, w)$ for every $w \in A_T^*$. The argument is by induction on n.

For $n = 0$, we have $u = \lambda$ and $\alpha = S$. Thus, the claim is simply

$$(S, q_0, w) \overset{*}{\underset{\mathcal{M}}{\vdash}} (S, q_0, w),$$

which follows from the definition of $\overset{*}{\underset{\mathcal{M}}{\vdash}}$.

For the induction step suppose that

$$S = \gamma_0 \underset{G}{\Rightarrow} \cdots \underset{G}{\Rightarrow} \gamma_n \underset{G}{\Rightarrow} \gamma_{n+1} = u\alpha$$

is a leftmost derivation, where $\gamma_n = u'X\theta$ and $\gamma_{n+1} = u'u''\beta\theta$. In other words, the last step of the derivation uses the production $X \to u''\beta$, where $u'' \in A_T^*$ and $\beta \in (A_N \cup A_T)^*$ is either the null word or a word that begins with a nonterminal symbol. Thus, the derivation above may be written

$$S \overset{n}{\underset{G}{\Rightarrow}} u'X\theta \underset{G}{\Rightarrow} u'u''\beta\theta,$$

and we have the following computation of $\mathcal{M}$:

$$\begin{aligned} (S, q_0, u'u''w) &\overset{*}{\vdash} ((X\theta)^R, q_0, u''w) = (\theta^R X, u''w) \\ &\qquad \text{(by the inductive hypothesis)} \\ &\vdash (\theta^R \beta^R u''^R, q_0, u''w) \\ &\qquad \text{(since } (\beta^R u''^R, q_0) \in \delta(X, q_0, \lambda)\text{)} \\ &\overset{*}{\vdash} (\theta^R \beta^R, q_0, w). \end{aligned}$$

The last line follows from the observation that $\delta(a, q_0, a) = \{(\lambda, q_0)\}$ for each $a \in A_T$ implies that $(x^R, q_0, x) \overset{*}{\vdash} (\lambda, q_0, \lambda)$ for every $x \in A_T^*$. Since $\theta^R \beta^R = (\beta\theta)^R$, we have completed the induction step. Therefore, if $u \in L(G)$ we have $S \overset{*}{\underset{G}{\Rightarrow}} u$, and this implies $(S, q_0, u) \overset{*}{\vdash} (\lambda, q_0, \lambda)$, which shows that $u \in N(\mathcal{M})$, hence $L(G) \subseteq N(\mathcal{M})$.

To prove that $N(\mathcal{M}) \subseteq L(G)$, we show that $(X, q_0, u) \overset{*}{\underset{\mathcal{M}}{\vdash}} (\lambda, q_0, \lambda)$ implies $X \overset{*}{\underset{G}{\Rightarrow}} u$ for $X \in A_N$ and $u \in A_T^*$.

We factor the input word u into a series of subwords $u = u_0 u_1 \cdots u_{k-1}$, each corresponding to a certain change in the pushdown store. Specifically, the top symbol of the pushdown store of each step of the computation can be either a terminal or a nonterminal symbol. Any step at which a nonterminal is at the top determines the boundary between a u_i and its successor u_{i+1} in the input. Thus, u_i could be empty (when a nonterminal at the top is replaced by a nonterminal) or could contain several symbols (when there are terminal symbols at the top that are popped off by transitions of the form $(\lambda, q_0) \in \delta(a, q_0, a)$). Thus, we can write $u = u_0 u_1 \cdots u_{k-1}$, where $u_i \in A_T^*$ for $0 \leq i \leq k-1$, and

$$\begin{aligned}
(X, q_0, u) &= (\gamma_0, q_0, u_0 u_1 \cdots u_{k-1}) \\
&\overset{*}{\vdash} (\gamma_1, q_0, u_1 \cdots u_{k-1}) \\
&\vdots \\
&\overset{*}{\vdash} (\gamma_{k-1}, q_0, u_{k-1}) \\
&\overset{*}{\vdash} (\lambda, q_0, \lambda),
\end{aligned}$$

where each γ_i has the form $\gamma_i' X$ for $\gamma_i' \in (A_T \cup A_N)^*$ and $X \in A_N$.

The definition of $\mathcal{M}$ implies that the computation

$$(\gamma_i, q_0, u_i \cdots u_{k-1}) \overset{*}{\underset{\mathcal{M}}{\vdash}} (\gamma_{i+1}, q_0, u_{i+1} \cdots u_{k-1})$$

can be written as

$$\begin{aligned}
(\gamma_i, q_0, u_i \cdots u_{k-1}) &= (\gamma_i' X_{p_i}, q_0, u_i \cdots u_{k-1}) \\
&\vdash (\gamma_i' {\alpha_{p_i}}^R, q_0, u_i \cdots u_{k-1}) \\
&\overset{*}{\vdash} (\gamma_{i+1}, q_0, u_{i+1} \cdots u_{k-1}),
\end{aligned}$$

where $X_{p_i} \rightarrow \alpha_{p_i} = u_i \beta_{p_i}$ is a production of G such that $\beta_{p_i} \in (A_N \cup A_T)^*$ is the null word or a word that begins with a nonterminal symbol, and $\gamma_{i+1} = \gamma_i' {\beta_{p_i}}^R$ for $0 \leq i \leq k-1$.

We prove by induction on ℓ that we have the leftmost derivation

$${\gamma_{k-1-\ell}}^R \overset{*}{\underset{G}{\Rightarrow}} u_{k-1-\ell} \cdots u_{k-1}.$$

For $\ell = 0$ we have

$$(\gamma_{k-1}, q_0, u_{k-1}) \underset{\mathcal{M}}{\vdash} ({u_{k-1}}^R, q_0, u_{k-1}) \overset{*}{\underset{\mathcal{M}}{\vdash}} (\lambda, q_0, \lambda),$$

because γ_{k-1} is the last content of the pushdown store that may contain a nonterminal, which means that $\gamma_{k-1} = X \in A_N$ and $X \rightarrow u_{k-1} \in P$. Therefore, ${\gamma_{k-1}}^R = X \overset{*}{\underset{G}{\Rightarrow}} u_{k-1}$.

Suppose that ${\gamma_{i+1}}^R \overset{*}{\underset{G}{\Rightarrow}} u_{i+1}\cdots u_{k-1}$; that is, $\beta_{p_i}{\gamma'_i}^R \overset{*}{\underset{G}{\Rightarrow}} u_{i+1}\cdots u_{k-1}$. This implies $u_i\beta_{p_i}{\gamma'_i}^R \overset{*}{\underset{G}{\Rightarrow}} u_iu_{i+1}\cdots u_{k-1}$, so $\alpha_{p_i}{\gamma'_i}^R \overset{*}{\underset{G}{\Rightarrow}} u_iu_{i+1}\cdots u_{k-1}$. The existence of the production $X_i \to \alpha_{p_i}$ allows us to write

$$X_i{\gamma'_i}^R \underset{G}{\Rightarrow} \alpha_{p_i}{\gamma'_i}^R \overset{*}{\underset{G}{\Rightarrow}} u_iu_{i+1}\cdots u_{k-1},$$

and $X_i{\gamma'_i}^R = (\gamma'_iX_i)^R = {\gamma_i}^R$.

Choosing $X = S$ we conclude that $x \in N(\mathcal{M})$ implies $(S, q_0, u) \overset{*}{\underset{\mathcal{M}}{\vdash}} (\lambda, q_0, \lambda)$, which in turn, implies $S \overset{*}{\underset{G}{\Rightarrow}} u$ and $u \in L(G)$. ∎

Note that a computation of the pda $\mathcal{M}$ that leads to the acceptance of a word u uniquely defines a leftmost derivation in the grammar G.

Example 6.2.14 Consider the nonambiguous context-free grammar

$$G_{ae} = (\{X_e, X_t, X_f\}, \{+, -, *, /, (,), \boldsymbol{v}, \boldsymbol{n}\}, X_e, P)$$

introduced in Example 5.8.3 which generates the language of parenthesized arithmetic expressions. The pda that accepts the language $L(G_{ae})$ with an empty pushdown store is

$$\begin{aligned}\mathcal{M} &= (\{+, -, *, /, (,), \boldsymbol{v}, \boldsymbol{n}\}, \{X_e, X_t, X_f, +, -, *, /, (,), \boldsymbol{v}, \boldsymbol{n}\},\\ &\quad \{q_0\}, \delta, q_0, X_e, \emptyset),\end{aligned}$$

where δ is specified by the following table:

Top	State	Input	Transition Function
z	q	a	$\delta(z, q, a)$
X_e	q_0	λ	$\{(X_t + X_e, q_0), (X_t - X_e, q_0), (X_t, q_0)\}$
X_t	q_0	λ	$\{(X_f * X_t, q_0), (X_f / X_t, q_0), (X_f, q_0)\}$
X_f	q_0	λ	$\{(\boldsymbol{v}, q_0), (\boldsymbol{n}, q_0), ()X_e(, q_0)\}$
a	q_0	a	$\{(\lambda, q_0)\}$

The last line of the table applies to every symbol $a \in \{+, -, *, /, (,), \boldsymbol{v}, \boldsymbol{n}\}$. If $\delta(z, q_0, a)$ is not mentioned in the table, then $\delta(z, q_0, a) = \emptyset$.

The word $(\boldsymbol{n} + \boldsymbol{n}) * \boldsymbol{n}$ can be generated in G_{ae} using the leftmost derivation

$$\begin{aligned} X_e &\underset{\pi_2}{\Rightarrow} X_t \underset{\pi_3}{\Rightarrow} X_t * X_f \underset{\pi_5}{\Rightarrow} X_f * X_f\\ &\underset{\pi_8}{\Rightarrow} (X_e) * X_f \underset{\pi_0}{\Rightarrow} (X_e + X_t) * X_f\\ &\underset{\pi_2}{\Rightarrow} (X_t + X_t) * X_f \underset{\pi_5}{\Rightarrow} (X_f + X_t) * X_f \underset{\pi_7}{\Rightarrow} (\boldsymbol{n} + X_t) * X_f\\ &\underset{\pi_5}{\Rightarrow} (\boldsymbol{n} + X_f) * X_f \underset{\pi_7}{\Rightarrow} (\boldsymbol{n} + \boldsymbol{n}) * X_f \underset{\pi_7}{\Rightarrow} (\boldsymbol{n} + \boldsymbol{n}) * \boldsymbol{n}.\end{aligned}$$

that corresponds to the derivation tree shown in Figure 6.2. The computation

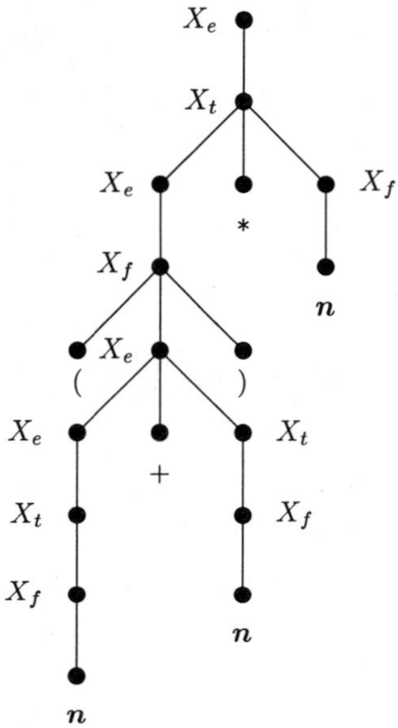

Figure 6.2: Derivation Tree for $(\boldsymbol{n}+\boldsymbol{n})*\boldsymbol{n}$ in G_{ae}

that leads to the acceptance of the word $(\boldsymbol{n}+\boldsymbol{n})*\boldsymbol{n}$ in $\mathcal{M}$ is

$$
\begin{aligned}
&(X_e, q_0, (\boldsymbol{n}+\boldsymbol{n})*\boldsymbol{n}) \vdash_{\mathcal{M}} (X_t, q_0, (\boldsymbol{n}+\boldsymbol{n})*\boldsymbol{n})\\
&\vdash_{\mathcal{M}} (X_f * X_t, q_0, (\boldsymbol{n}+\boldsymbol{n})*\boldsymbol{n}) \vdash_{\mathcal{M}} (X_f * X_f, q_0, (\boldsymbol{n}+\boldsymbol{n})*\boldsymbol{n})\\
&\vdash_{\mathcal{M}} (X_f*)X_e(, q_0, (\boldsymbol{n}+\boldsymbol{n})*\boldsymbol{n}) \vdash_{\mathcal{M}} (X_f*)X_e, q_0, \boldsymbol{n}+\boldsymbol{n})*\boldsymbol{n})\\
&\vdash_{\mathcal{M}} (X_f*)X_t + X_e, q_0, \boldsymbol{n}+\boldsymbol{n})*\boldsymbol{n}) \vdash_{\mathcal{M}} (X_f*)X_t + X_t, q_0, \boldsymbol{n}+\boldsymbol{n})*\boldsymbol{n})\\
&\vdash_{\mathcal{M}} (X_f*)X_t + X_f, q_0, \boldsymbol{n}+\boldsymbol{n})*\boldsymbol{n}) \vdash_{\mathcal{M}} (X_f*)X_t + \boldsymbol{n}, q_0, \boldsymbol{n}+\boldsymbol{n})*\boldsymbol{n})\\
&\vdash_{\mathcal{M}} (X_f*)X_t+, q_0, +\boldsymbol{n})*\boldsymbol{n}) \vdash_{\mathcal{M}} (X_f*)X_t, q_0, \boldsymbol{n})*\boldsymbol{n})\\
&\vdash_{\mathcal{M}} (X_f*)X_f, q_0, \boldsymbol{n})*\boldsymbol{n}) \vdash_{\mathcal{M}} (X_f*)\boldsymbol{n}, q_0, \boldsymbol{n})*\boldsymbol{n}) \vdash_{\mathcal{M}} (X_f*), q_0,)*\boldsymbol{n})\\
&\vdash_{\mathcal{M}} (X_f*, q_0, *\boldsymbol{n}) \vdash_{\mathcal{M}} (X_f, q_0, \boldsymbol{n}) \vdash_{\mathcal{M}} (\boldsymbol{n}, q_0, \boldsymbol{n}) \vdash_{\mathcal{M}} (\lambda, q_0, \lambda)
\end{aligned}
$$

□

We prove next that for every pda $\mathcal{M}$ the language $N(\mathcal{M})$ is context-free. To this end we need the following technical result showing that whenever there is a pda that accepts a language with an empty store, then there is a way to construct a pda that accepts the same language both with an empty store and by entering a final accepting state.

Theorem 6.2.15 *For every pda* $\mathcal{M} = (A, Z, Q, \delta, q_0, z_0, F)$ *there exists a pda*

$\mathcal{M}' = (A, Z', Q', \delta', q_0', z_0', \{q'\})$ *such that* $(z_0', q_0', x) \overset{*}{\underset{\mathcal{M}'}{\vdash}} (\lambda, q_1, \lambda)$ *implies* $q_1 = q'$ *and* $N(\mathcal{M}) = N(\mathcal{M}') = L(\mathcal{M}')$.

Proof. Pick $q_0', q' \notin Q$ and $z_0' \notin Z$. Define the pda

$$\mathcal{M}' = (A, Z', Q', \delta', q_0', z_0', \{q'\})$$

as $Q' = Q \cup \{q_0', q'\}$, $Z' = Z \cup \{z'\}$, $\delta'(z_0', q_0', \lambda) = \{(z_0' z_0, q_0)\}$, $\delta'(z_0', q, \lambda) = \{(\lambda, q')\}$ for every $q \in Q$, and $\delta'(z, q, a) = \delta(z, q, a)$ in every other case. In other words, $\mathcal{M}'$ begins by putting a marker, z_0', onto the pushdown store and then simulating $\mathcal{M}$ until $\mathcal{M}$ would have emptied its pushdown store. At this time $\mathcal{M}'$ removes the marker, thus emptying its store, and goes into a final state.

Let $x \in N(\mathcal{M})$. We have $(z_0, q_0, x) \overset{*}{\underset{\mathcal{M}}{\vdash}} (\lambda, q, \lambda)$ for some $q \in Q$. Therefore, in $\mathcal{M}'$ we have the computation

$$(z_0', q_0', x) \underset{\mathcal{M}'}{\vdash} (z_0' z_0, q_0, x) \overset{*}{\underset{\mathcal{M}'}{\vdash}} (z_0', q, \lambda) \underset{\mathcal{M}'}{\vdash} (\lambda, q', \lambda),$$

so $x \in N(\mathcal{M}')$ and $x \in L(\mathcal{M}')$, which shows that $N(\mathcal{M}) \subseteq N(\mathcal{M}')$ and $N(\mathcal{M}) \subseteq L(\mathcal{M}')$.

Conversely, suppose that $x \in N(\mathcal{M}')$ or that $x \in L(\mathcal{M}')$.

In the first case, $(z_0', q_0', x) \overset{*}{\underset{\mathcal{M}'}{\vdash}} (\lambda, \bar{q}, \lambda)$ for some state $\bar{q} \in Q'$. The definition of $\mathcal{M}'$ implies that this computation can be written as

$$(z_0', q_0', x) \underset{\mathcal{M}'}{\vdash} (z_0' z_0, q_0, x) \overset{*}{\underset{\mathcal{M}'}{\vdash}} (\lambda, \bar{q}, \lambda).$$

Note that in $\mathcal{M}'$ the symbol z_0' cannot be erased unless $\mathcal{M}'$ switches to the state q'. Therefore, in the previous computation we have $\bar{q} = q'$, and this computation can be written as

$$(z_0', q_0', x) \underset{\mathcal{M}'}{\vdash} (z_0' z_0, q_0, x) \overset{*}{\underset{\mathcal{M}'}{\vdash}} (z_0', q, \lambda) \underset{\mathcal{M}'}{\vdash} (\lambda, q', \lambda)$$

for some $q \in Q$. Thus, we must have $(z_0, q_0, x) \overset{*}{\underset{\mathcal{M}}{\vdash}} (\lambda, q, \lambda)$, that is $x \in N(\mathcal{M})$.

In the second case, $x \in L(\mathcal{M}')$ implies $(z_0', q_0', x) \overset{*}{\underset{\mathcal{M}'}{\vdash}} (w, q', \lambda)$. Observe that $\mathcal{M}'$ may enter its final state q' only by erasing the symbol z_0' located at the bottom of the pushdown store. This implies that the above computation has the form

$$(z_0', q_0', x) \underset{\mathcal{M}}{\vdash} (z_0' z_0, q_0, x) \overset{*}{\underset{\mathcal{M}'}{\vdash}} (z_0', q, \lambda) \underset{\mathcal{M}'}{\vdash} (\lambda, q', \lambda).$$

As before, this implies the existence of the computation $(z_0, q_0, x) \overset{*}{\underset{\mathcal{M}}{\vdash}} (\lambda, q, \lambda)$, so $x \in N(\mathcal{M})$.

We proved that $N(\mathcal{M}') \subseteq N(\mathcal{M})$ and $L(\mathcal{M}') \subseteq N(\mathcal{M})$. Thus, $N(\mathcal{M}) = N(\mathcal{M}') = L(\mathcal{M}')$, which is the desired conclusion. ∎

Theorem 6.2.16 *If L is a language such that $L = N(\mathcal{M})$ for some pda $\mathcal{M}$, then L is a context-free language.*

Proof. Suppose that $L = N(\mathcal{M})$, where $\mathcal{M} = (A, Z, Q, \delta, q_0, F)$ is a pda. By Theorem 6.2.15 we can assume without loss of generality that $F = \{q_f\}$ and that $L = \{x \in A^* \mid (z_0, q_0, x) \overset{*}{\underset{\mathcal{M}}{\vdash}} (\lambda, q_f, \lambda)\}$.

Consider the alphabet $\hat{Z} = \{z^{q_i q_j} \mid z \in Z, q_i, q_j \in Q\}$ and the context-free grammar $G = (\hat{Z}, A, z_0^{q_0 q_f}, P)$, whose set of productions P is constructed as follows:

1. If $(z_{i_k} \cdots z_{i_0}, p) \in \delta(z, q, a)$, then place the following productions into P:

$$z^{q q_{i_k}} \to a z_{i_0}^{p q_{i_0}} z_{i_1}^{q_{i_0} q_{i_1}} \cdots z_{i_k}^{q_{i_{k-1}} q_{i_k}},$$

   for every $q_{i_0}, \cdots, q_{i_k} \in Q$.
2. If $(\lambda, p) \in \delta(z, q, a)$, then place the production $z^{qp} \to a$ into P.

Define the relation $\rho \subseteq \hat{Z} \times \hat{Z}$ by $(z_m^{q_i q_j}, z_n^{q_k q_h}) \in \rho$ if and only if $q_j = q_k$ and consider the regular language $H = L_\rho$ (cf. Example 3.2.23). Let $d : \hat{Z}^* \longrightarrow Z^*$ be the morphism defined by $d(z^{q_i q_j}) = z$ for every $z^{q_i q_j} \in \hat{Z}$.

We prove that for $n \geq 1$, we have the leftmost derivation $z^{q_i q_j} \overset{n}{\underset{G}{\Rightarrow}} w\alpha$ (where $w \in A^*$ and $\alpha \in \hat{Z}^*$) if and only if $(z, q_i, wy) \overset{n}{\underset{\mathcal{M}}{\vdash}} (d(\alpha)^R, p, y)$ and one of the following conditions is satisfied:

1. $\alpha \in H$, the first symbol of α has the form z^{pq}, and the last symbol of α has the form $z^{q q_j}$, or
2. $\alpha = \lambda$ and $p = q_j$.

The argument is by induction on n. For the basis step, $n = 1$, suppose that $z^{q_i q_j} \underset{G}{\Rightarrow} w\alpha$. The production applied for this one-step derivation is either $z^{q_i q_j} \to a z_{i_0}^{p q_{i_0}} z_{i_1}^{q_{i_0} q_{i_1}} \cdots z_{i_k}^{q_{i_{k-1}} q_j}$ which implies

$$w = a \text{ and } \alpha = z_{i_0}^{p q_{i_0}} z_{i_1}^{q_{i_0} q_{i_1}} \cdots z_{i_k}^{q_{i_{k-1}} q_j},$$

or is $z^{qp} \to a$, which implies

$$w = a \text{ and } \alpha = \lambda,$$

respectively.

The first case may occur if and only if $(z_{i_k} \cdots z_{i_0}, p) \in \delta(z, q_i, a)$. Therefore, we have

$$(z, q_i, ay) \underset{\mathcal{M}}{\vdash} (z_{i_k} \cdots z_{i_0}, p, y) = (d(\alpha)^R, p, y)$$

Also, the second case takes place if and only if $(\lambda, p) \in \delta(z, q_i, a)$ which is equivalent to

$$(z, q_i, ay) \underset{\mathcal{M}}{\vdash} (\lambda, p, y).$$

This concludes the basis step.

For the inductive step assume that the statement holds for n and consider a leftmost derivation of length $n+1$: $z^{q_i q_j} \overset{n+1}{\underset{G}{\Rightarrow}} w'\alpha'$. Two cases may occur depending on form of the production applied in the last step of this derivation:

1. If the production applied in the last step was

$$z^{qq_{j_\ell}} \rightarrow a z_{j_0}^{rq_{j_0}} z_{j_1}^{q_{j_0}q_{j_1}} \cdots z_{j_\ell}^{q_{j_{\ell-1}}q_{j_\ell}},$$

then the derivation can be written as

$$z^{q_i q_j} \overset{n}{\underset{G}{\Rightarrow}} w z^{qq_{j_\ell}} \alpha \underset{G}{\Rightarrow} w a z_{j_0}^{rq_{j_0}} z_{j_1}^{q_{j_0}q_{j_1}} \cdots z_{j_\ell}^{q_{j_{k-1}}q_{j_\ell}} \alpha. \tag{6.1}$$

This takes place if and only if $w' = wa$, $\alpha' = z_{j_0}^{rq_{j_0}} z_{j_1}^{q_{j_0}q_{j_1}} \cdots z_{j_\ell}^{q_{j_{\ell-1}}q_{j_\ell}} \alpha$. By the inductive hypothesis, the first part of the derivation takes place if and only if $z^{qq_{j_\ell}}\alpha \in H$ and

$$(z, q_i, way) \overset{n}{\underset{\mathcal{M}}{\vdash}} (d(z^{qq_{j_\ell}}\alpha)^R, q, y) = (d(\alpha)^R z, q, ay).$$

The last step of the derivation can be executed if and only if

$$(z_{j_\ell} \cdots z_{j_0}, r) \in \delta(z, q, a),$$

by the definition of the grammar G. Thus, the derivation (6.1) takes place if and only if

$$\begin{aligned}
&(z, q_i, w'y) = (z, q_i, way) \overset{n}{\underset{\mathcal{M}}{\vdash}} (d(\alpha)^R z, q, ay) \\
&\underset{\mathcal{M}}{\vdash} (d(\alpha)^R z_{j_\ell} \cdots z_{j_0}, r, y) \\
&= (d(z_{j_0}^{rq_{j_0}} z_{j_1}^{q_{j_0}q_{j_1}} \cdots z_{j_\ell}^{q_{j_{\ell-1}}q_{j_\ell}} \alpha)^R, r, y) \\
&= (d(\alpha')^R, r, y).
\end{aligned}$$

2. If the production applied in the last step of the derivation was $z^{qq_{j_\ell}} \rightarrow a$, the derivation can be written

$$z^{q_i q_j} \overset{n}{\underset{G}{\Rightarrow}} w z^{qq_{j_\ell}} \alpha \underset{G}{\Rightarrow} wa\alpha. \tag{6.2}$$

Thus $w' = wa$ and $\alpha' = \alpha$. By the inductive hypothesis we have:

$$(z, q_i, w'y) = (z, q_i, way) \overset{n}{\underset{\mathcal{M}}{\vdash}} (d(z^{qq_{j_\ell}}\alpha)^R, q, ay) = (d(\alpha)^R z, q, ay).$$

In addition, the existence of the production $z^{qq_{j_\ell}} \rightarrow a$ is equivalent to $(\lambda, q_{j_\ell}) \in \delta(z, q, a)$, so the existence of the derivation (6.2) is equivalent to the existence of the computation

$$(z, q_0, w'y) \overset{n}{\underset{\mathcal{M}}{\vdash}} (d(\alpha)^R z, q, ay) \underset{\mathcal{M}}{\vdash} (d(\alpha)^R, q_{j_\ell}, y) = (d(\alpha')^R, q_{j_\ell}, y).$$

By taking $q_i = q_0$, $\alpha = \lambda$, $z = z_0$, $y = \lambda$, and $p = q_f$ in the initial claim, we conclude that a leftmost derivation $z^{q_0 q_f} \overset{n}{\underset{G}{\Rightarrow}} w$ exists if and only if

$$(z_0, q_i, w) \overset{n}{\underset{\mathcal{M}}{\vdash}} (\lambda, q_f, \lambda).$$

This shows that $L(G) = N(\mathcal{M})$, so $N(\mathcal{M})$ is indeed a context-free language. ∎

We now summarize the results presented in this section.

Theorem 6.2.17 *Let $L \subseteq A^*$ be a language over the alphabet A. The following statements are equivalent:*

(i) *There is a pda $\mathcal{M}$ such that $L = L(\mathcal{M})$.*
(ii) *There is a pda $\mathcal{M}$ such that $L = N(\mathcal{M})$.*
(iii) *There is a pda $\mathcal{M}$ (having a single final state) such that $L = N(\mathcal{M}) = L(\mathcal{M})$.*
(iv) *There is an one-state pda $\mathcal{M}$ such that $L = N(\mathcal{M})$.*
(v) *L is a context-free language.*

Proof. Statement (i) implies (ii) by Theorem 6.2.12. Also, statement (ii) implies (iii) by Theorem 6.2.15. Clearly, (iii) implies (i), so (i), (ii) and (iii) are equivalent.

On the other hand, (v) implies (iv) by Theorem 6.2.13, and (iv) clearly implies (ii); finally, (ii) implies (v) by Theorem 6.2.16, so (ii), (iv) and (v) are equivalent. This shows that all five statements are equivalent. ∎

Definition 6.2.18 A pda $\mathcal{M} = (A, Z, Q, \delta, q_0, z_0, F)$ is *λ-free* if $\delta(z, q, \lambda) = \emptyset$ for every $z \in Z$ and $q \in Q$. □

Theorem 6.2.19 *For every λ-free, context-free language L there exists a λ-free pda $\mathcal{M}$ such that $L = N(\mathcal{M})$.*

Proof. Let $G = (A_N, A_T, S, P)$ be a grammar in Greibach normal form that generates L. By analogy with the proof of Theorem 6.2.13, define the pda $\mathcal{M} = (A_T, A_N, \{q_0\}, \delta, q_0, S, \emptyset)$, where $\delta(X, q_0, a) = \{(\alpha^R, q_0) \mid X \to a\alpha \in P\}$ for every $X \in A_N$. An argument by induction on n shows that a leftmost derivation $X \overset{n}{\underset{G}{\Rightarrow}} u\alpha$ exists if and only if $(S, q_0, u) \overset{n}{\underset{\mathcal{M}}{\vdash}} (\alpha^R, q_0, \lambda)$. Thus, by taking $\alpha = \lambda$, we obtain that $X \overset{n}{\underset{G}{\Rightarrow}} u$ if and only if $(X, q_0, u) \overset{n}{\underset{\mathcal{M}}{\vdash}} (\lambda, q_0, \lambda)$. Thus, $L(G) = N(\mathcal{M})$. ∎

6.3 Deterministic Context-Free Languages

In this section we discuss a class of context-free languages that is important in compiler design. To this end we use deterministic pushdown automata defined below.

Definition 6.3.1 A *deterministic pushdown automaton* (dpda) is a pda $\mathcal{M} = (A, Z, Q, \delta, q_0, z_0, F)$ that satisfies the following conditions:

(i) For every $z \in Z$, $q \in Q$ and $a \in A \cup \{\lambda\}$ we have $|\delta(z, q, a)| \leq 1$.
(ii) If $\delta(z, q, \lambda) \neq \emptyset$, then $\delta(z, q, a) = \emptyset$ for every $a \in A$.

Top	State	Input	$\delta(z,q,a)$
z_0	q_0	λ	(z_0, q_2)
z_0	q_2	a	(z_0a, q_1)
a	q_1	a	(aa, q_1)
a	q_1	b	(λ, q_1)
z_0	q_1	λ	(z_0, q_2)

Figure 6.3: Definition of the dpda $\mathcal{M}$ of Example 6.3.2

A language L is *deterministic context-free* (dcfl) if there is some dpda $\mathcal{M}$ such that $L = L(\mathcal{M})$. □

The second condition of Definition 6.3.1 means that if a null transition exists when the dpda $\mathcal{M}$ sees z at the top of the pushdown store and its internal state is q, then no symbol can be read from the input tape of the automaton.

Clearly, every deterministic context-free language is also a context-free language.

Example 6.3.2 Here we show that $L = \{a^n b^n \mid n \in \mathbb{N}\}$ is a deterministic context-free language. Indeed, consider the dpda

$$\mathcal{M} = (\{a,b\}, \{z_0, a\}, \{q_0, q_1, q_2\}, \delta, q_0, z_0, \{q_2\}),$$

where δ is defined by the table shown in Figure 6.3. For triples (z,q,a) that do not occur in that table we have $\delta(z,q,a) = \emptyset$. For the word $aaabbb \in L$ we have the computation:

$$\begin{aligned}
&(z_0, q_0, aaabbb) \vdash (z_0, q_2, aaabbb) \vdash (z_0a, q_1, aabbb)\\
&\vdash (z_0aa, q_1, abbb) \vdash (z_0aaa, q_1, bbb) \vdash (z_0aa, q_1, bb)\\
&(z_0a, q_1, b) \vdash (z_0, q_1, \lambda) \vdash (z_0, q_2, \lambda),
\end{aligned}$$

which shows that $aaabbb \in L(\mathcal{M})$. Similarly, $\lambda \in L(\mathcal{M})$ because

$$(z_0, q_0, \lambda) \vdash (z_0, q_2, \lambda).$$

Note that $aab \notin L$. The computation that begins with the word bab on the input tape is

$$\begin{aligned}
&(z_0, q_0, aab) \vdash (z_0, q_2, aab) \vdash (z_0a, q_1, ab)\\
&(z_0aa, q_1, b) \vdash (z_0a, q_1, \lambda),
\end{aligned}$$

and no further move is possible. Therefore, the final state q_2 cannot be reached and we may conclude that $aab \notin L(\mathcal{M})$. For other input words, such as bab, the dpda is unable to read its input; indeed, in this case, we have a two-step computation

$$(z_0, q_0, bab) \vdash (z_0, q_2, bab),$$

and the impossibility of reading the input word implies $bab \notin L(\mathcal{M})$.

We leave it to the reader to prove that $L(\mathcal{M}) = \{a^n b^n \mid n \in \mathbb{N}\}$. □

Top	State	Input	$\delta(z, q, a)$
z_0	q_0	a	(z_0a, q_0)
z_0	q_0	b	(z_0b, q_0)
z_0	q_0	c	(z_0, q_1)
a	q_0	a	(aa, q_0)
a	q_0	b	(ab, q_0)
a	q_0	c	(a, q_1)
b	q_0	a	(ba, q_0)
b	q_0	b	(bb, q_0)
b	q_0	c	(b, q_1)
a	q_1	a	(λ, q_1)
b	q_1	b	(λ, q_1)
z_0	q_1	λ	(λ, q_2)

Figure 6.4: Definition of the dpda $\mathcal{M}$ of Example 6.3.3

Example 6.3.3 The language $L = \{xcx^R \mid x \in \{a,b\}^*\}$ is deterministic. To prove this statement consider the dpda

$$\mathcal{M} = (\{a,b,c\}, \{z_0, a, b\}, \{q_0, q_1, q_2\}, \delta, q_0, z_0, \{q_2\})$$

whose transition function is specified by the table shown in Figure 6.4. Transition sets not mentioned in the table are empty. Let $x = abbcbba$ be a word in L. The computation that leads $\mathcal{M}$ to accept w is

$$\begin{aligned}&(z_0, q_0, abbcbba) \underset{\mathcal{M}}{\vdash} (z_0a, q_0, bbcbba) \underset{\mathcal{M}}{\vdash} (z_0ab, q_0, bcbba)\\ &\underset{\mathcal{M}}{\vdash} (z_0abb, q_0, cbba) \underset{\mathcal{M}}{\vdash} (z_0abb, q_1, bba) \underset{\mathcal{M}}{\vdash} (z_0ab, q_1, ba)\\ &\underset{\mathcal{M}}{\vdash} (z_0a, q_1, a) \underset{\mathcal{M}}{\vdash} (z_0, q_1, \lambda) \underset{\mathcal{M}}{\vdash} (\lambda, q_2, \lambda).\end{aligned}$$

We leave to the reader to prove that $L(\mathcal{M}) = L$. □

Example 6.3.4 Let $A_n = \{(_0, \ldots, (_{n-1},)_0, \ldots,)_{n-1}\}$. The parenthetic language PAR_n on the alphabet A_n, introduced in Definition 5.10.1, is a deterministic context-free language. It is easy to verify that the dpda

$$\mathcal{M} = (A_n, \{z_0\} \cup A_n, \{q_0, q_1\}, \delta, q_0, z_0, \{q_0\}),$$

whose transition function is given by the table contained by Figure 6.5 (where $0 \leq i, j \leq n-1$) accepts the language PAR_n. □

For a dpda, we may write $\delta(z, q, a) = (w, p)$ instead of $\delta(z, q, a) = \{(w, p)\}$ in order to simplify the notation.

A dpda does not always have a next move. This may happen because for some pair $(z, q) \in Z \times Q$, such that $\delta(z, q, a) = \emptyset$ for every $a \in A \cup \{\lambda\}$, or because the pushdown store is empty. However, it is possible to insure that for each dpda there is an equivalent dpda that always has a next move. To do this,

Top	State	Input	Transition Function
z_0	q_0	$(_i$	$(z_0(_i, q_1)$
$(_j$	q_1	$(_i$	$((_j(_i, q_1)$
$(_i$	q_1	$)_i$	(λ, q_1)
z_0	q_1	λ	(z_0, q_0)

Figure 6.5: Definition of the dpda $\mathcal{M}$ for Example 6.3.4

we create $\mathcal{M}'$ by adding a marker symbol z_0', at the bottom of the pushdown store and a "sink" state $\bar{q}$, one that can never be left. Any computation of $\mathcal{M}$ that would have emptied the stack results in $\mathcal{M}'$ having z_0' at the top of the stack. This forces $\mathcal{M}'$ into state $\bar{q}$. Also, any pair (z, q) that could block a computation is augmented to allow a transition to $\bar{q}$ for each input symbol such that $\delta(z, q, a) = \emptyset$.

Theorem 6.3.5 *For every dpda $\mathcal{M} = (A, Z, Q, \delta, q_0, z_0, F)$ there exists a dpda $\mathcal{M}' = (A, Z', Q', \delta', q_0', z_0', F')$ that is equivalent to $\mathcal{M}$ and satisfies the following conditions:*

(i) *For every $z' \in Z'$, $q' \in Q'$ exactly one of the following cases may occur:*
   (a) $|\delta'(z', q', a)| = 1$ for every $a \in A$ and $\delta'(z', q', \lambda) = \emptyset$, or
   (b) $|\delta'(z', q', \lambda)| = 1$, and $\delta'(z', q', a) = \emptyset$ for every $a \in A$.

(ii) *For every $q', q'' \in Q$, if $\delta'(z_0', q', a) = (w, q'')$ for some $a \in A \cup \{\lambda\}$, then $w = z_0'u$ for some $u \in Z^*$.*

Proof. Let $Z' = Z \cup \{z_0'\}$, $Q' = Q \cup \{q_0', \bar{q}\}$, where $z_0' \notin Z$ and $q_0', \bar{q} \notin Q$, $F' = F$, and let δ' be defined as follows.

- $\delta'(z_0', q_0', \lambda) = (z_0'z_0, q_0)$;
- $\delta(z_0', q, a) = (z_0', \bar{q})$ for $q \in Q$ and $a \in A$;
- if $\delta(z, q, a) \neq \emptyset$, then $\delta'(z, q, a) = \delta(z, q, a)$ for $z \in Z$, $q \in Q$, and $a \in A \cup \{\lambda\}$;
- if $\delta(z, q, \lambda) = \emptyset$ and there is $a \in A$ such that $\delta(z, q, a) = \emptyset$, then $\delta'(z, q, a) = (z, \bar{q})$;
- $\delta'(z, \bar{q}, a) = (z, \bar{q})$ for every $z \in Z$ and $a \in A$.

It is easy to see, by inspecting the definition of δ', that the conditions of the theorem are satisfied. Furthermore, we have $(z_0, q_0, x) \overset{*}{\underset{\mathcal{M}}{\vdash}} (w, q, \lambda)$ if and only if

$$(z_0', q_0', x) \underset{\mathcal{M}'}{\vdash} (z_0'z_0, q_0, x) \overset{*}{\underset{\mathcal{M}}{\vdash}} (z_0'w, q, \lambda),$$

which implies $L(\mathcal{M}) = L(\mathcal{M}')$. ∎

Note that the dpda $\mathcal{M}'$ defined above never empties its stack (because its initial stack symbol z_0' always remains at the bottom of the stack); also, $\mathcal{M}'$ always has a next move, so Theorem 6.3.5 allows us to assume that for every dcfl L there exists a dpda $\mathcal{M}$ such that $\mathcal{M}$ always has a next move and $L = L(\mathcal{M})$.

Top	State	Input i	$\delta(z,q,i)$
z_0'	q_0'	λ	$(z_0'z_0, q_0)$
z_0'	$q \in \{q_0, q_1, q_2\}$	$i \in \{a,b\}$	$(z_0', \bar{q})$
z_0	q_0	λ	(z_0, q_2)
z_0	q_2	a	$(z_0 a, q_1)$
a	q_1	a	(aa, q_1)
a	q_1	b	(λ, q_1)
z_0	q_1	λ	(z_0, q_2)
$z \in \{a, z_0'\}$	q_0	$i \in \{a,b\}$	$(z, \bar{q})$
z_0'	q_2	$i \in \{a,b\}$	$(z, \bar{q})$
z_0	q_2	b	$(z_0, \bar{q})$
z_0'	q_1	$i \in \{a,b\}$	$(z, \bar{q})$
$z \in \{z_0, a, z_0'\}$	$\bar{q}$	$i \in \{a,b\}$	$(z, \bar{q})$

Figure 6.6: Definition of the dpda $\mathcal{M}'$ of Example 6.3.6

Example 6.3.6 The dpda $\mathcal{M}'$ obtained from the dpda introduced in Example 6.3.2 is

$$\mathcal{M}' = (\{a,b\}, \{z_0', z_0, a\}, \{q_0, q_1, q_2, q_0', \bar{q}\}, \delta', q_0', z_0', \{q_2\}),$$

where the transition function is defined by the table shown in Figure 6.6. Triples of the form (z,q,i) such that $i \in A \cup \{\lambda\}$ and $\delta(z,q,i) = \emptyset$ are omitted from this table. The dpda $\mathcal{M}'$ can read any input word. For example, we have the computation

$$\begin{aligned}&(z_0', q_0', bab) \vdash (z_0'z_0, q_0, bab) \vdash (z_0'z_0, q_2, bab)\\ &\vdash (z_0'z_0, \bar{q}, ab) \vdash (z_0'z_0, \bar{q}, b) \vdash (z_0'z_0, \bar{q}, \lambda).\end{aligned}$$

□

Definition 6.3.7 Let $\mathcal{M} = (A, Z, Q, \delta, q_0, z_0, F)$ be a dpda. An instantaneous description (w,q,x) of $\mathcal{M}$ is *looping* if for every $n \in \mathbb{N}$, $n > 0$, there exists an instantaneous description (w_n, q_n, x) such that $|w_n| \geq |w|$ for $n > 0$, and

$$(w,q,x) \underset{\mathcal{M}}{\vdash} (w_1, q_1, x) \underset{\mathcal{M}}{\vdash} \cdots \underset{\mathcal{M}}{\vdash} (w_n, q_n, x) \underset{\mathcal{M}}{\vdash} \cdots$$

The set of looping instantaneous descriptions of the dpda $\mathcal{M}$ will be denoted by $\mathsf{LOOP}(\mathcal{M})$. □

If $\mathsf{c} = (w,q,x) \in \mathsf{LOOP}(\mathcal{M})$, then the dpda can make an arbitrarily large number of moves starting from c without ever decreasing the length of the content of the pushdown store and without reading any input symbol. If $\mathcal{M}$ enters a looping instantaneous description while processing an input word, then the symbols that remain to be read will never be processed. Note than an instantaneous description (w,q,x) is looping if and only if (z,q,λ) is a looping instantaneous description, where $w = w'z$ for some $w' \in Z^*$.

Let $n(\mathcal{M})$ be the number defined by

$$n(\mathcal{M}) = \begin{cases} \frac{|Q|(|Z|^{|Q||Z|\ell(\mathcal{M})+1} - |Z|)}{|Z|-1} & \text{if } |Z| > 1 \\ |Q| & \text{if } |Z| = 1, \end{cases}$$

where

$$\ell(\mathcal{M}) = \max\{|v| \mid \delta(z, q, a) = (v, q') \text{ for some } z \in Z, q \in Q, a \in A \cup \{\lambda\}\}$$

is the length of the longest word written on the pushdown store in one step.

Theorem 6.3.8 *Let $\mathcal{M} = (A, Z, Q, \delta, q_0, z_0, F)$ be a dpda. We have $(z, q, \lambda) \in$ LOOP$(\mathcal{M})$ if and only if there is an instantaneous description (w, p, λ) such that $(z, q, \lambda) \overset{n(\mathcal{M})}{\underset{\mathcal{M}}{\vdash}} (w, p, \lambda)$.*

Proof. If $(z, q, \lambda) \in$ LOOP$(\mathcal{M})$, then it is clear that $(z, q, \lambda) \overset{n(\mathcal{M})}{\underset{\mathcal{M}}{\vdash}} (w, p, \lambda)$.

Conversely, suppose that $(z, q, \lambda) \overset{n(\mathcal{M})}{\underset{\mathcal{M}}{\vdash}} (w, p, \lambda)$. We need to consider two cases.

1. If there is $u \in Z^*$ such that $|u| > |Q||Z|\ell(\mathcal{M})$ and

$$(z, q, \lambda) \overset{*}{\underset{\mathcal{M}}{\vdash}} (u, r, \lambda) \overset{*}{\underset{\mathcal{M}}{\vdash}} (w, p, \lambda)$$

for some $r \in Q$, then, since there are be more than $|Q||Z|$ steps in the computation $(z, q, \lambda) \overset{*}{\underset{\mathcal{M}}{\vdash}} (u, r, \lambda)$, there are two instantaneous descriptions that have the same state and the same symbol at the top of the pushdown store. In other words, we have

$$(z, q, \lambda) \overset{*}{\underset{\mathcal{M}}{\vdash}} (vz', q', \lambda) \overset{*}{\underset{\mathcal{M}}{\vdash}} (vtz', q', \lambda) \overset{*}{\underset{\mathcal{M}}{\vdash}} (u, r, \lambda),$$

for some $u, v \in Z^*$. Because $(vz', q', \lambda) \overset{n}{\underset{\mathcal{M}}{\vdash}} (vtz', q', \lambda)$ we can write

$$(z, q, \lambda) \overset{*}{\underset{\mathcal{M}}{\vdash}} (vz', q', \lambda) \overset{nj}{\underset{\mathcal{M}}{\vdash}} (vt^j z', q', \lambda)$$

for any $j \in \mathbb{N}$, so $(z, q, \lambda) \in$ LOOP$(\mathcal{M})$.

2. Suppose now that for every $u \in Z^*$ such that

$$(z, q, \lambda) \overset{*}{\underset{\mathcal{M}}{\vdash}} (u, r, \lambda) \overset{*}{\underset{\mathcal{M}}{\vdash}} (w, p, \lambda) \tag{6.3}$$

we have $|u| \leq |Q||Z|\ell(\mathcal{M})$. Note that there are $\frac{|Z|^{|Q||Z|\ell(\mathcal{M})+1} - |Z|}{|Z|-1}$ non-null words of length less or equal to $|Q||Z|\ell(\mathcal{M})$ on the alphabet Z, and, therefore, there are no more than $n(\mathcal{M})$ distinct instantaneous descriptions (u, r, λ) of the dpda $\mathcal{M}$ that can be reached from (z, q, λ). Consequently, in the computation (6.3) there are some repeated instantaneous descriptions and this implies $(z, q, \lambda) \in$ LOOP$(\mathcal{M})$.

∎

Theorem 6.3.9 *Let $\mathcal{M} = (A, Z, Q, \delta, q_0, z_0, F)$ be a dpda. Then,*

$$(z, q, \lambda) \overset{*}{\underset{\mathcal{M}}{\vdash}} (w, p, \lambda),$$

where p is a final state if and only if there is a computation

$$(z, q, \lambda) \overset{m}{\underset{\mathcal{M}}{\vdash}} (w, p, \lambda),$$

where $m \leq n(\mathcal{M})$.

Proof. Suppose that $(z, q, \lambda) \overset{*}{\underset{\mathcal{M}}{\vdash}} (w, p, \lambda)$ is the shortest computation that leads to an instantaneous description (w, p, λ) where p is a final state. By the argument presented in Theorem 6.3.8, it follows that for every instantaneous description (u, r, λ) such that

$$(z, q, \lambda) \overset{*}{\underset{\mathcal{M}}{\vdash}} (u, r, \lambda) \overset{*}{\underset{\mathcal{M}}{\vdash}} (w, p, \lambda),$$

we have $|u| \leq |Q||Z|\ell(\mathcal{M})$. Since there are $n(\mathcal{M})$ distinct instantaneous descriptions of the form (u, r, λ) it follows that the length of the computation $(z, q, \lambda) \overset{*}{\underset{\mathcal{M}}{\vdash}} (w, p, \lambda)$ may not exceed $n(\mathcal{M})$ to avoid the presence of repeating instantaneous descriptions (which would contradict the definition of the computation $(z, q, \lambda) \overset{*}{\underset{\mathcal{M}}{\vdash}} (w, p, \lambda)$). Thus, we obtain $(z, q, \lambda) \overset{m}{\underset{\mathcal{M}}{\vdash}} (w, p, \lambda)$, where $m \leq n(\mathcal{M})$. The converse implication is obvious. ∎

Consider the sets

$$\begin{aligned} I(\mathcal{M}) &= \{(z,q) \in Z \times Q \mid (z,q,\lambda) \in \mathsf{LOOP}(\mathcal{M}) \\ &\qquad \text{and } (z,q,\lambda) \overset{*}{\underset{\mathcal{M}}{\vdash}} (w,p,\lambda) \text{ for some } p \in F \text{ and } w \in Z^*\} \\ I'(\mathcal{M}) &= \{(z,q) \in Z \times Q \mid (z,q,\lambda) \in \mathsf{LOOP}(\mathcal{M}) \text{ and there is} \\ &\qquad \text{no } p \in F \text{ such that } (z,q,\lambda) \overset{*}{\underset{\mathcal{M}}{\vdash}} (w,p,\lambda)\} \text{ for any } w \in Z^*. \end{aligned}$$

Theorem 6.3.8 suggests the following algorithm for computing the sets $I(\mathcal{M})$ and $I(\mathcal{M}')$.

Algorithm 6.3.10 (Computation of $I(\mathcal{M})$ and $I'(\mathcal{M})$)
Input: A dpda $\mathcal{M} = (A, Z, Q, \delta, q_0, z_0, F)$.
Output: The sets $I(\mathcal{M})$ and $I'(\mathcal{M})$.
Method: For an instantaneous description (z, q, λ) determine whether there exists an instantaneous description (w, p, λ) such that $(z, q, \lambda) \overset{n(\mathcal{M})}{\underset{\mathcal{M}}{\vdash}} (w, p, \lambda)$. If such an instantaneous description exists, then (z, q, λ) is a looping instantaneous description, so $(z, q) \in I(\mathcal{M}) \cup I'(\mathcal{M})$.

Next, for (z, q, λ) determine whether it is possible to reach an instantaneous description (w, p, λ), where p is a final state in no more than $n(\mathcal{M})$ steps. If this is the case, then $(z, q) \in I(\mathcal{M})$; otherwise, $(z, q) \in I(\mathcal{M}')$.

Proof of Correctness: the correctness of the algorithm follows from Theorems 6.3.8 and 6.3.9. ∎

A major result that we prove in this section is that the class of deterministic context-free languages is closed with respect to the complement operation. A natural idea would be to adapt here the argument used in Theorem 3.4.1 by constructing a dpda $\mathcal{M}'$ starting from a dpda $\mathcal{M}$ by replacing the set of final states of $\mathcal{M}$ by its complement. Unfortunately, this will not work in the case of dpdas for the following reasons:

- A dpda may not read its input tape in its entirety if it enters a looping instantaneous description. Thus, it could happen that there is an input word x such that x is neither in $L(\mathcal{M})$ nor in $L(\mathcal{M}')$.
- Even if no looping instantaneous descriptions exist, after reading its input and entering a final instantaneous descriptions a dpda may continue its computation using null transitions and go through some states that are final and through some states that are non-final; correspondingly, $\mathcal{M}'$ will reach non-final and final states. This implies the existence of input words that belong to both $L(\mathcal{M})$ and $L(\mathcal{M}')$.

To overcome these difficulties, we need the following result.

Theorem 6.3.11 *Let $\mathcal{M} = (A, Z, Q, \delta, q_0, z_0, F)$ be a dpda. There is a dpda $\mathcal{M}_1$ such that $L(\mathcal{M}) = L(\mathcal{M}_1)$, and for every $x \in A^*$ there is $q \in Q$ such that*

$$(z_0, q_0, x) \overset{*}{\underset{\mathcal{M}}{\vdash}} (w, q, \lambda),$$

for some $w \in Z^*$.

Proof. Starting from the dpda $\mathcal{M}$ define the dpda

$$\mathcal{M}_1 = (A, Z, Q \cup \{p, r\}, \delta_1, q_0, z_0, F \cup \{p\}),$$

where p, r are two new states. The transition function δ_1 is defined as follows.

- for $z \in Z$, $q \in Q$ and $a \in A$, $\delta_1(z, q, a) = \delta(z, q, a)$;
- if $(z, q\lambda)$ is not a looping instantaneous description in $\mathcal{M}$, that is, $(z, q) \notin I(\mathcal{M}) \cup I(\mathcal{M}')$, define $\delta_1(z, q, \lambda) = \delta(z, q, \lambda)$;
- if $(z, q) \in I(\mathcal{M})$, then $\delta_1(z, q, \lambda) = (z, p)$;
- if $(z, q) \in I'(\mathcal{M})$, then $\delta_1(z, q, \lambda) = (z, r)$;
- $\delta_1(z, p, a) = (z, r)$ and $\delta_1(z, r, a) = (z, r)$ for every $a \in A$ and $z \in Z$.

The dpda $\mathcal{M}_1$ always reads its input in its entirety. Indeed, $\mathcal{M}_1$ simulates the activity of $\mathcal{M}$. If no looping instantaneous description is encountered in the computation of $\mathcal{M}$, then $\mathcal{M}$ will read its entire input, and $\mathcal{M}_1$ will do the same. Otherwise, when $\mathcal{M}$ enters a looping instantaneous description, then $\mathcal{M}_1$ enters either the state p or the state r and the entire input word is read.

The definition of $\mathcal{M}_1$ implies that $L(\mathcal{M}) \subseteq L(\mathcal{M}_1)$ since every accepting computation in $\mathcal{M}$ can be simulated in $\mathcal{M}_1$. Suppose now that $x \in L(\mathcal{M}_1)$. There exists a computation in $\mathcal{M}_1$ that ends in a state in F or in the state p. In the first case it is clear that $x \in L(\mathcal{M})$; in the second, $\mathcal{M}$ reaches a looping instantaneous description (tz, q, y), that is, $(z_0, q_0, x) \overset{*}{\underset{\mathcal{M}}{\vdash}} (tz, q, y)$ and $(z, q) \in I(\mathcal{M})$. The definition of $I(\mathcal{M})$ implies that there exists a final state q' such that $(tz, q, y) \overset{*}{\underset{\mathcal{M}}{\vdash}} (w, q', y)$, so $x \in L(\mathcal{M})$. ∎

Theorem 6.3.12 *Let A be an alphabet and let $L \subseteq A^*$ be a dcfl. Then, the language $\bar{L} = A^* - L$ is a dcfl.*

Proof. Since L is a dcfl there exists a dpda $\mathcal{M} = (A, Z, Q, \delta, q_0, z_0, F)$ such that $L = L(\mathcal{M})$. By Theorem 6.3.11 we can assume that $\mathcal{M}$ reads every input word completely. Define the pda $\mathcal{M}' = (A, Z, Q', \delta', q', z_0, F')$, where $Q' = Q \times \{0, 1, 2\}$. The transition function δ' is defined by:

- For $z \in Z$, $q \in Q$, and $a \in A$, if $\delta(z, q, a) = (w, p)$, then
$$\delta'(z, (q, 0), a) = \delta'(z, (q, 2), a) = \begin{cases} (w, (p, 0)) & \text{if } p \in F \\ (w, (p, 1)) & \text{if } p \notin F. \end{cases}$$
and $\delta'(z, (q, 1), \lambda) = (z, (q, 2))$.
- For $z \in Z$ and $q \in Q$, if $\delta(z, q, \lambda) = (w, p)$, then $\delta'(z, (q, 0), \lambda) = (w, (p, 0))$, and
$$\delta'(z, (q, 1), \lambda) = \begin{cases} (w, (p, 0)) & \text{if } p \in F \\ (w, (p, 1)) & \text{if } p \notin F. \end{cases}$$

The initial state q_0' is
$$q_0' = \begin{cases} (q_0, 0) & \text{if } q_0 \in F \\ (q_0, 1) & \text{if } q_0 \notin F, \end{cases}$$
and the set of final states is $F' = \{(q, 2) \mid q \in Q\}$. Note that once $\mathcal{M}'$ enters a final state $(q, 2)$, then no null transition is possible. Also, $\mathcal{M}'$ can reach a final state $(q, 2)$ only by using a null transition from a state $(q, 1)$.

The role of the second component of a state of $\mathcal{M}'$ is to record whether $\mathcal{M}$ has entered a final state after its last non-null transition.

Suppose that $x \in L(\mathcal{M})$, that is, $(z_0, q_0, x) \overset{*}{\underset{\mathcal{M}}{\vdash}} (w, q, \lambda)$, where $q \in F$. If (q_0, i) is the initial state of $\mathcal{M}'$, the previous computation yields
$$(z_0, (q_0, i), x) \overset{*}{\underset{\mathcal{M}'}{\vdash}} (w, (q, 0), \lambda),$$
and $\mathcal{M}'$ cannot reach a final state. Thus, $x \notin L(\mathcal{M}')$. This shows that $L(\mathcal{M}') \subseteq A^* - L(\mathcal{M})$.

Conversely, suppose that $x \in A^* - L(\mathcal{M})$. Since $\mathcal{M}$ reads its entire input, we have $(z_0, q_0, x) \overset{*}{\underset{\mathcal{M}}{\vdash}} (wz, q, \lambda)$, where $q \notin F$ and q is the state entered by $\mathcal{M}$ after reading the last symbol of x. This implies the existence of the computation $(z_0, (q_0, i), x) \overset{*}{\underset{\mathcal{M}'}{\vdash}} (wz, (q, 1), \lambda)$. The definition of δ' implies $\delta'((q, 1), \lambda) = (z, (q, 2))$, so
$$(z_0, (q_0, i), x) \overset{*}{\underset{\mathcal{M}'}{\vdash}} (wz, (q, 1), \lambda) \overset{*}{\underset{\mathcal{M}'}{\vdash}} (wz, (q, 2), \lambda),$$
which shows that $x \in L(\mathcal{M}')$. Thus, we conclude that $L(\mathcal{M}') = A^* - L(\mathcal{M})$, so $A^* - L(\mathcal{M})$ is indeed a dcfl. ∎

The reader could follow the details of the construction presented in the proof of Theorem 6.3.12 in the next example.

Transition in $\mathcal{M}'$	Instantaneous description of $\mathcal{M}''$ and transition in $\mathcal{M}''$
	$(z_0', (q_0', 1), bab)$ (initial i.d.)
$\delta'(z_0', q_0', \lambda) = (z_0' z_0, q_0)$	$\delta''(z_0', (q_0', 1), \lambda) = (z_0' z_0, (q_0, 1))$
	$(z_0' z_0, (q_0, 1), bab)$
$\delta'(z_0, q_0, \lambda) = (z_0, q_2)$	$\delta''(z_0, (q_0, 1), \lambda) = (z_0, (q_2, 0))$ (since $q_2 \in F$)
	$(z_0' z_0, (q_2, 0), bab)$
$\delta'(z_0, q_2, b) = (z_0, \bar{q})$	$\delta''(z_0, (q_2, 0), b) = (z_0, (\bar{q}, 1))$ (since $\bar{q} \notin F$)
	$(z_0' z_0, (\bar{q}, 1), ab)$
$\delta'(z_0, \bar{q}, a) = (z_0, \bar{q})$	$\delta''(z_0, (\bar{q}, 1), \lambda) = (z_0, (\bar{q}, 2))$ $\delta''(z_0, (\bar{q}, 2), a) = (z_0, (\bar{q}, 1))$ (since $\bar{q} \notin F$)
	$(z_0' z_0, (\bar{q}, 2), ab)$ $(z_0' z_0, (\bar{q}, 1), b)$
$\delta'(z_0, \bar{q}, b) = (z_0, \bar{q})$	$\delta''(z_0, (\bar{q}, 1), \lambda) = (z_0, (\bar{q}, 2))$ $\delta''(z_0, (\bar{q}, 2), b) = (z_0, (\bar{q}, 1))$ (since $\bar{q} \notin F$)
	$(z_0' z_0, (\bar{q}, 2), b)$ $(z_0' z_0, (\bar{q}, 1), \lambda)$
	$\delta''(z_0, (\bar{q}, 1), \lambda) = (z_0, (\bar{q}, 2))$
	$(z_0' z_0, (\bar{q}, 2), \lambda)$

Figure 6.7: Computation in the dpda $\mathcal{M}''$ defined in Example 6.3.13

Example 6.3.13 Consider the dpda $\mathcal{M}'$ defined in Example 6.3.6 that accepts the language $\{a^n b^n \mid n \in \mathbb{N}\}$ and is capable of reading any input word $x \in \{a, b\}^*$. The dpda

$$\mathcal{M}'' = (\{a, b\}, \{z_0', z_0, a\}, Q' \times \{0, 1, 2\}\}, \delta'', (q_0', 1), z_0', Q' \times \{2\}),$$

constructed according to the algorithm contained in the proof of Theorem 6.3.12, accepts the language $\{a, b\}^* - \{a^n b^n \mid n \in \mathbb{N}\}$. Here $Q' = \{q_0, q_1, q_2, q_0', \bar{q}\}$. Since q_0 is not a final state of $\mathcal{M}'$, the initial state of $\mathcal{M}''$ is $(q_0', 1)$. The word *bab* is accepted by $\mathcal{M}''$ using the computation given in Figure 6.7. □

Corollary 6.3.14 *For every dcfl L there exists a dpda that accepts L and has no null transitions from its final states.*

Proof. The argument is contained in the proof of Theorem 6.3.12. ∎

Example 6.3.15 Theorem 6.3.12 allows us to give an example of a context-free language that is not deterministic.

In Theorem 5.8.1, we saw that

$$L = \{a^n b^m c^p \mid m, n, p \in \mathbb{N} \text{ and } n = m \text{ or } m = p\}$$

is a context-free language that is inherently ambiguous. If L were a deterministic context-free language, the language $\{a, b, c\}^* - L$ would be a deterministic context-free language, and therefore, the language

$$\begin{aligned} K &= (\{a,b,c\}^* - L) \cap \{a\}^*\{b\}^*\{c\}^* \\ &= \{a^n b^m c^p \mid n,m,p \in \mathbb{N}, n \neq m \text{ and } m \neq p\} \end{aligned}$$

would be a context-free language. However, we prove that K is not context-free. Indeed, suppose that K were a context-free language generated by a context-free grammar G. Let n_G be the number that corresponds to G by Ogden's Lemma. Then, we have $w = a^{n_G+n_G!}b^{n_G}c^{n_G+n_G!} \in K$. Suppose that the set of marked positions are the n_G positions in w occupied by the bs. Then, we can write $w = xyzut$ such that at least one of y or u contains a marked position, yzu no more than n_G marked positions, and $xy^nzu^nt \in L(G)$ for all $n \in \mathbb{N}$. In other words, at least one of y or u must contain a b.

Observe that neither y nor u may contain two distinct symbols. For example, if y were to contain both as and bs then, by pumping, b could precede as and this would conflict with the definition of K. Let $|y| = k$ and $|u| = \ell$. We need to consider the following cases:

1. $y \in \{b\}^*$ and $u \in \{b\}^*$;
2. $y \in \{a\}^*$ and $u \in \{b\}^*$;
3. $y \in \{b\}^*$ and $u \in \{c\}^*$.

In the first case, note that $k + \ell \leq n_G$ and that there are $n_G - (k+\ell)$ symbols b that do not occur in y or u. The effect of the pumping of y and u is to increase the number of bs to $n_G - (k+\ell) + (k+\ell)i = n_G + (k+\ell)(i-1)$. Note that there is an $i \in \mathbb{N}$ such that

$$n_G + n_G! = n_G + (k+\ell)(i-1)$$

because $k + \ell \leq n_G$. By pumping y and u a number of $i = n_G!/(k+\ell) + 1$ times we obtain a word that has the same number of as and bs and cs; this contradicts the definition of K.

In the second case, $\ell \leq n_G$. The effect of the pumping is to increase the number of as and bs while the number of cs remains constant. The word $w_i = xy^izu^it$ will contain $ki + n_G + n_G! - k$ as, and $\ell i + n_G - \ell = n_G + \ell(i-1)$ bs. By choosing $i = n_G!/\ell + 1$, the number of bs equals the number of cs, which contradicts the definition of K. The third case can be treated in a similar manner. □

To prove other closure properties of deterministic context-free languages we introduce a normal form for dpdas.

Lemma 6.3.16 *For every dpda $\mathcal{M} = (A, Z, Q, \delta, q_0, z_0, F)$ there exists an equivalent dpda $\mathcal{M}_1 = (A, Z, Q_1, \delta_1, q_0, z_0, F)$ such that if $\delta_1(z, q_1, a) = \{(w, p_1)\}$ for some $q_1, p_1 \in Q_1$, then $|w| \leq 2$.*

Proof. For each transition $\delta(z, q, a) = \{(u, p)\}$ such that $u = z_0 \cdots z_{k-1}$ and $k > 2$ we introduce $k - 2$ new states $r_0, \ldots, r_{k-3}$ and define

$$\begin{aligned}
\delta_1(z, q, a) &= \{(z_0 z_1, r_0)\} \\
\delta_1(z_1, r_0, \lambda) &= \{(z_1 z_2, r_1)\} \\
&\vdots \\
\delta_1(z_{k-3}, r_{k-4}, \lambda) &= \{(z_{k-3} z_{k-2}, r_{k-3})\} \\
\delta_1(z_{k-2}, r_{k-3}, \lambda) &= \{(z_{k-2} z_{k-1}, p)\}.
\end{aligned}$$

For every other transitions $\delta_1(z, q, a) = \delta(z, q, a)$. If

$$(uz, q, ax) \underset{\mathcal{M}}{\vdash} (uz_0 \cdots z_{k-1}, p, x),$$

then we have the computation

$$\begin{aligned}
(uz, q, ax) &\underset{\mathcal{M}_1}{\vdash} (uz_0 z_1, r_0, x) \\
&\underset{\mathcal{M}_1}{\vdash} (uz_0 z_1 z_1, r_1, x) \\
&\vdots \\
&\underset{\mathcal{M}_1}{\vdash} (uz_0 z_1 z_1 \cdots z_{k-3}, r_{k-4}, x) \\
&\underset{\mathcal{M}_1}{\vdash} (uz_0 z_1 z_1 \cdots z_{k-3} z_{k-2}, r_{k-3}, x) \\
&\underset{\mathcal{M}_1}{\vdash} (uz_0 z_1 z_1 \cdots z_{k-3} z_{k-2} z_{k-1}, p, x).
\end{aligned}$$

Thus, the dpda are easily seen to be equivalent and $\mathcal{M}_1$ is a dpda that satisfies the condition of the lemma. ∎

Theorem 6.3.17 (Normal Form Theorem for Pushdown Automata) *For every dpda $\mathcal{M} = (A, Z, Q, \delta, q_0, z_0, F)$ there exists an equivalent dpda $\mathcal{M}' = (A, Z, Q', \delta, q_0', z_0', F')$ such that if $\delta'(z, q, a) = \{(w, p)\}$, then*

$$w \in \{\lambda, z\} \cup \{zz' \mid z' \in Z\}.$$

Proof. By Lemma 6.3.16 we can assume without loss of generality that if $\delta(z, q, a) = (w, p)$, then $|w| \leq 2$. Define $Q' = Z \times Q$, $q_0' = (z_0, q_0)$, $Z' = Z \cup \{z_0'\}$, and $F' = Z' \times F$, where z_0' is a new symbol, $z_0 \notin Z$. The transition function δ' is given by:

1. if $\delta(z, q, a) = (\lambda, p)$, then $\delta'(z', (z, q), a) = (\lambda, (z', p))$;
2. if $\delta(z, q, a) = (y, p)$, then $\delta'(z', (z, q), a) = (z', (y, p))$;
3. if $\delta(z, q, a) = (yy_1, p)$, then $\delta'(z', (z, q), a) = (z'y, (y_1, p))$,

for every $z, z' \in Z$, $q \in Q$ and $a \in A \cup \{\lambda\}$. In addition, $\delta'(z_0', (z_0, q_0), \lambda) = (z_0' z_0, (z_0, q_0))$. The actions of $\mathcal{M}$ and $\mathcal{M}'$ are described succinctly in the following table:

Action of $\mathcal{M}$	Action of $\mathcal{M}'$
$\mathcal{M}$ pops the stack.	$\mathcal{M}'$ pops the stack and stores the popped symbol in its state.
$\mathcal{M}$ alters the top of the stack to y.	$\mathcal{M}'$ leaves the top of the stack intact and stores y in its state.
$\mathcal{M}$ pushes yy_1 on the stack.	$\mathcal{M}'$ stores y_1 in its state and pushes y on the stack.

We claim that $(z_0, q_0, x) \overset{*}{\underset{\mathcal{M}}{\vdash}} (z_{i_0} \cdots z_{i_{m-1}}, q, \lambda)$ if and only if

$$(z'_0, (z_0, q_0), x) \overset{*}{\underset{\mathcal{M}'}{\vdash}} (z'_0 z_{i_0} \cdots z_{i_{m-2}}, (z_{i_{m-1}}, q), \lambda).$$

Suppose that

$$(z_0, q_0, x) \overset{n}{\underset{\mathcal{M}}{\vdash}} (z_{i_0} \cdots z_{i_{m-1}}, q, \lambda) \tag{6.4}$$

We prove by induction on n that

$$(z'_0, (z_0, q_0), x) \overset{*}{\underset{\mathcal{M}'}{\vdash}} (z'_0 z_{i_0} \cdots z_{i_{m-2}}, (z_{i_{m-1}}, q), \lambda).$$

In the base case, $n = 0$, we have $m = 1$ and $z_{i_0} = z_0$ and the implication follows immediately. Suppose that the statement holds for computations of length less than n and that we have the computation (6.4). We need to consider three cases, depending on the action of $\mathcal{M}$ during the last step of the computation.

1. If $\mathcal{M}$ popped the stack, then the computation (6.4) has the form:

$$\begin{aligned} (z_0, q_0, x) & \overset{n-1}{\underset{\mathcal{M}}{\vdash}} (z_{i_0} \cdots z_{i_{m-1}} z, q', a) \\ & \underset{\mathcal{M}}{\vdash} (z_{i_0} \cdots z_{i_{m-1}}, q, \lambda), \end{aligned}$$

   where $\delta(z, q', a) = (\lambda, q)$, $x = x'a$, and $a \in A \cup \{\lambda\}$. Consequently, $\delta'(z_1, (z, q'), a) = (\lambda, (z_1, q))$ for every $z_1 \in Z$. By the inductive hypothesis, we have the computation:

$$\begin{aligned} (z'_0, (z_0, q_0), x) & \overset{*}{\underset{\mathcal{M}'}{\vdash}} (z'_0 z_{i_0} \cdots z_{i_{m-1}}, (z, q'), a) \\ & \underset{\mathcal{M}'}{\vdash} (z'_0 z_{i_0} \cdots z_{i_{m-2}}, (z_{i_{m-1}}, q), \lambda), \end{aligned}$$

   which completes the proof of the implication.

2. If $\mathcal{M}$ alters only the top of the stack by changing it to y, the computation (6.4) can be written as

$$\begin{aligned} (z_0, q_0, x) & \overset{n-1}{\underset{\mathcal{M}}{\vdash}} (z_{i_0} \cdots z_{i_{m-1}} z, q', a) \\ & \underset{\mathcal{M}}{\vdash} (z_{i_0} \cdots z_{i_{m-1}} y, q, \lambda) \end{aligned}$$

   and we have $\delta(z, q', a) = (y, q)$. Thus, $\delta'(z_1, (z, q'), a) = (z_1, (y, q))$ for every $z_1 \in Z$. By the inductive hypothesis, we have the computation:

$$\begin{aligned} (z'_0, (z_0, q_0), x) & \overset{*}{\underset{\mathcal{M}'}{\vdash}} (z'_0 z_{i_0} \cdots z_{i_{m-1}}, (z, q'), a) \\ & \underset{\mathcal{M}'}{\vdash} (z'_0 z_{i_0} \cdots z_{i_{m-1}}, (y, q), \lambda). \end{aligned}$$

3. Finally, suppose that $\mathcal{M}$ pushes yy_1 on the stack using the transition $\delta(z, q', a) = (yy_1, p)$. In this case, the computation (6.4) can be written as:
$$\begin{aligned}(z_0, q_0, x) &\overset{n-1}{\underset{\mathcal{M}}{\vdash}} (z_{i_0} \cdots z_{i_{m-1}} z, q', a)\\ &\underset{\mathcal{M}}{\vdash} (z_{i_0} \cdots z_{i_{m-1}} yy_1, p, \lambda),\end{aligned}$$
where $x = x'a$. We have $\delta'(z_1, (z, q'), a) = (z_1 y, (y_1, p))$ for every $z_1 \in Z$. Combining this fact with the inductive hypothesis yields the computation:
$$\begin{aligned}(z'_0, (z_0, q_0), x) &\overset{*}{\underset{\mathcal{M}'}{\vdash}} (z'_0 z_{i_0} \cdots z_{i_{m-1}}, (z, q'), a)\\ &\underset{\mathcal{M}'}{\vdash} (z'_0 z_{i_0} \cdots z_{i_{m-1}} y, (y_1, p), \lambda).\end{aligned}$$

Conversely, we can prove by induction of n that

$$(z'_0, (z_0, q_0), x) \overset{n}{\underset{\mathcal{M}'}{\vdash}} (z'_0 z_{i_0} \cdots z_{i_{m-2}}, (z_{i_{m-1}}, q), \lambda).$$

implies

$$(z_0, q_0, x) \overset{*}{\underset{\mathcal{M}}{\vdash}} (z_{i_0} \cdots z_{i_{m-1}}, q, \lambda).$$

The argument is similar to the one presented above and is left to the reader. ∎

Example 6.3.18 Let $Z' = \{z_0, a, b, z'_0\}$, $Q' = \{z_0, a, b\} \times \{q_0, q_1, q_2\}$, and let $\mathcal{M}'$ be the dpda

$$\mathcal{M}' = (\{a, b, c\}, Z', Q', \delta', (z_0, q_0), z'_0, Z' \times \{q_2\})$$

whose transition function δ' is shown in Figure 6.8 is in normal form and is equivalent to the dpda considered in Example 6.3.3. The transitions shown in the figure are valid for every $z' \in Z'$; we also have $\delta'(z'_0, (z_0, q_0), \lambda) = (z'_0 z_0, (z_0, q_0))$.

The counterpart of the computation presented in Example 6.3.3 that leads to the acceptance of the word $x = abbcbba$ is:
$$\begin{aligned}(z'_0, (z_0, q_0), abbcbba) &\vdash (z'_0 z_0, (z_0, q_0), abbcbba)\\ &\vdash (z'_0 z_0, (a, q_0), bbcbba)\\ &\vdash (z'_0 z_0 a, (b, q_0), bcbba)\\ &\vdash (z'_0 z_0 ab, (b, q_0), cbba)\\ &\vdash (z'_0 z_0 ab, (b, q_1), bba)\\ &\vdash (z'_0 z_0 a, (b, q_1), ba)\\ &\vdash (z'_0 z_0, (a, q_1), a)\\ &\vdash (z'_0, (z_0, q_1), \lambda)\\ &\vdash (\lambda, (z'_0, q_2)).\end{aligned}$$

□

Theorem 6.3.19 *If L is a deterministic context-free language and R is a regular language, then $L \cap R$ is a deterministic context-free language.*

z	q	a	$\delta(z,q,a)$	$\delta(z',(z,q),a)$
z_0	q_0	a	(z_0a, q_0)	$(z'z_0, (a, q_0))$
z_0	q_0	b	(z_0b, q_0)	$(z'z_0, (b, q_0))$
z_0	q_0	c	(z_0, q_1)	$(z', (z_0, q_1))$
a	q_0	a	(aa, q_0)	$(z'a, (a, q_0))$
a	q_0	b	(ab, q_0)	$(z'a, (b, q_0))$
a	q_0	c	(a, q_1)	$(z', (a, q_1))$
b	q_0	a	(ba, q_0)	$(z'b, (a, q_0))$
b	q_0	b	(bb, q_0)	$(z'b, (b, q_0))$
b	q_0	c	(b, q_1)	$(z', (b, q_1))$
a	q_1	a	(λ, q_1)	$(\lambda, (z', q_1))$
b	q_1	b	(λ, q_1)	$(\lambda, (z', q_1))$
z_0	q_1	λ	(λ, q_2)	$(\lambda, (z', q_2))$

Figure 6.8: Normal form of the dpda of Example 6.3.3

Proof. Suppose that $L = L(\mathcal{M})$, where $\mathcal{M} = (A, Z, Q, \delta, q_0, z_0, F)$ is a dpda that reads its entire input, and $R = L(\mathcal{M}')$, where $\mathcal{M}' = (A, Q', \delta', q_0', F')$ is a dfa. Define the dpda $\mathcal{M}_1 = (A, Z, Q \times Q', \delta_1, (q_0, q_0'), z_0, F \times F')$ by

$$\delta_1(z,(q,q'),a) = \begin{cases} (v,(q_1,q')) & \text{if } a = \lambda \text{ and} \\ & \delta(z,q,\lambda) = (v,q_1) \\ (v,(q_1,\delta'(q',a))) & \text{if } a \in A \text{ and} \\ & \delta(z,q,a) = \{(q_1,v)\}, \end{cases}$$

for $z \in Z, (q,q') \in Q \times Q'$ and $a \in A \cup \{\lambda\}$.

We claim that $(z_0,(q_0,q_0'),x) \overset{*}{\underset{\mathcal{M}_1}{\vdash}} (w,(q,q'),\lambda)$ if and only if

$$(z_0, q_0, x) \overset{*}{\underset{\mathcal{M}}{\vdash}} (w, q, \lambda) \text{ and } \delta'^*(q_0', x) = q'.$$

We prove, by induction on n, that if

$$(z_0,(q_0,q_0'),x) \overset{n}{\underset{\mathcal{M}_1}{\vdash}} (w,(q,q'),\lambda),$$

then $(z_0, q_0, x) \overset{n}{\underset{\mathcal{M}}{\vdash}} (w, q, \lambda)$ and $\delta'^*(q_0', x) = q'$. The base case, $n = 0$, is immediate since we have $q = q_0$, $q' = q_0'$, $w = z_0$, and $x = \lambda$.

Suppose that the implication holds for computations of length n and that $(z_0,(q_0,q_0'),x) \overset{n+1}{\underset{\mathcal{M}_1}{\vdash}} (w,(q,q'),\lambda)$. This computation can be written as

$$(z_0,(q_0,q_0'),x) \overset{n}{\underset{\mathcal{M}_1}{\vdash}} (w_1,(q_1,q_1'),a) \underset{\mathcal{M}_1}{\vdash} (w,(q,q'),\lambda),$$

where $x = ya$ and $a \in A \cup \{\lambda\}$. By the inductive hypothesis, we have

$$(z_0, q_0, y) \overset{n}{\underset{\mathcal{M}}{\vdash}} (w_1, q_1, \lambda) \text{ and } \delta'^*(q_0', y) = q_1'.$$

Also, $(w_1, q_1, a) \underset{\mathcal{M}}{\vdash} (w, q, \lambda)$ and $\delta'(q_1', a) = q'$. Therefore, we have

$$(z_0, q_0, x) = (z_0, q_0, ya) \overset{n}{\underset{\mathcal{M}}{\vdash}} (w_1, q_1, a) \underset{\mathcal{M}}{\vdash} (w, q, \lambda),$$

and

$$\delta'^*(q_0', x) = \delta'(\delta'^*(q_0', y), a) = \delta'(q_1', a) = q'.$$

We leave to the reader the proof of the reverse implication. ∎

Next, we introduce a method for constructing a so-called *predicting automaton*, $\mathsf{Pred}(\mathcal{M}, \mathcal{M}')$ from a dpda $\mathcal{M}$ and a dfa $\mathcal{M}'$. This automaton pushes symbols onto its stack that, in a sense, predict how $\mathcal{M}$ and $\mathcal{M}'$ may react while reading the remainder of the input. The formalization of this idea is given below in Definition 6.3.20. Using this construction, we show that the class of dcfls is closed under right quotient with regular languages.

Let $\mathcal{M} = (A, Z, Q, \delta, q_0, z_0, F)$ be a dpda in normal form and let $\mathcal{M}' = (A, Q', \delta', q_0', F')$ be a dfa. To begin, we introduce several notions that are needed for defining the transition function of the predicting automaton.

- Let $\mathcal{M}_{q,z}$ be the dpda $(A, Z, Q, \delta, q, z, F)$ obtained from $\mathcal{M}$ by selecting z as the initial symbol in the pushdown store and q as the initial state. It is clear that $L(\mathcal{M}_{q,z})$ is a dcfl.
- Let $\mathcal{M}'_{q'} = (A, Q', \delta', q, F')$ be the dfa obtained from $\mathcal{M}'$ by choosing q' as the initial state. The language $L(\mathcal{M}'_{q'})$ is regular.
- It is easy to see that the language

$$N_r(\mathcal{M}_{q,z}) = \{x \in A^* \mid (z, q, x) \overset{*}{\underset{\mathcal{M}_{q,z}}{\vdash}} (\lambda, r, \lambda\}$$

  of all words that empty the pushdown store of $\mathcal{M}$ is also a dcfl by Theorem 6.2.15.
- Finally, let $L_{r'}(\mathcal{M}'_{q'})$ be the regular language defined by

$$L_{r'}(\mathcal{M}'_{q'}) = \{x \in A^* \mid \delta'^*(q', x) = r'\}.$$

The pushdown alphabet of $\mathsf{Pred}(\mathcal{M}, \mathcal{M}')$ is

$$\bar{Z} = \{z_\rho \mid z \in Z \text{ and } \rho \in \mathcal{P}(Q \times Q')\}.$$

Define the morphism $h : \bar{Z}^* \longrightarrow Z^*$ by $h(z_\rho) = z$ for every $\rho \in \mathcal{P}(Q \times Q')$. The predicting automaton is a dpda that designed in such a way that if its instantaneous description is (wz_ρ, r, x), then the relation ρ (which is the subscript of the symbol at the top of the pushdown store) consists of those pairs (q, q') such that $(h(w)z, q, x) \overset{*}{\underset{\mathcal{M}}{\vdash}} (v, q_1, \lambda)$ for some $q_1 \in F$ and $v \in Z^*$, and $\delta'^*(q', x) \in F'$.

Recall that $\mathcal{M}$ is in the normal form defined by Theorem 6.3.17. The transition function $\bar{\delta}$ of $\mathsf{Pred}(\mathcal{M}, \mathcal{M}')$ is defined as follows.

1. If $\delta(z, q, a) = (\lambda, p)$, then $\bar{\delta}(z_\rho, q, a) = (\lambda, p)$.
2. If $\delta(z, q, a) = (z, p)$, then $\bar{\delta}(z_\rho, q, a) = (z_\rho, p)$.

3. If $\delta(z, q, a) = (zy, p)$, then $\bar{\delta}(z_\rho, q, a) = (z_\rho y_\sigma, p)$, where
$$\begin{aligned}\sigma &= \{(r, r') \mid r \in Q, r' \in Q' \text{ and } L(\mathcal{M}_{r,y}) \cap L(\mathcal{M}'_{r'}) \neq \emptyset \\ &\quad \text{or } N_s(\mathcal{M}_{r,y}) \cap L_{s'}(\mathcal{M}'_{r'}) \neq \emptyset \text{ for some } (s, s') \in \rho\}.\end{aligned}$$
The initial pushdown symbol of $\mathsf{Pred}(\mathcal{M}, \mathcal{M}')$ is z_{0,ρ_0}, where ρ_0 is the relation
$$\rho_0 = \{(q, q') \in Q \times Q' \mid L(\mathcal{M}_{q,z_0}) \cap L(\mathcal{M}'_{q'}) \neq \emptyset\}.$$

Note that the languages
$$L(\mathcal{M}_{r,y}) \cap L(\mathcal{M}'_{r'}), N_s(\mathcal{M}_{r,y}) \cap L_{s'}(\mathcal{M}'_{r'}), L(\mathcal{M}_{q,z_0}) \cap L(\mathcal{M}'_{q'})$$
are context-free by Theorem 5.6.3. Since the emptyness of context-free languages is decidable, it follows that we can effectively compute the transition function $\bar{\delta}$ and the initial state of the predicting automaton.

Definition 6.3.20 Let $\mathcal{M} = (A, Z, Q, \delta, q_0, z_0, F)$ be a dpda in normal form and let $\mathcal{M}' = (A, Q', \delta', q'_0, F')$ be a dfa. The *predicting automaton* of $\mathcal{M}$ and $\mathcal{M}'$ is the dpda
$$\mathsf{Pred}(\mathcal{M}, \mathcal{M}') = (A, \bar{Z}, Q, \bar{\delta}, q_0, z_{0,\rho_0}, F).$$
□

Theorem 6.3.21 *Let $\mathcal{M} = (A, Z, Q, \delta, q_0, z_0, F)$ be a dpda in normal form and let $\mathcal{M}' = (A, Q', \delta', q'_0, F')$ be a dfa. We have*
$$(z_{0,\rho_0}, q_0, x) \overset{*}{\underset{\mathsf{Pred}(\mathcal{M},\mathcal{M}')}{\vdash}} (z_{0,\rho_0} \cdots z_{n-1,\rho_{n-1}}, r, y) \tag{6.5}$$
if and only if
$$(z_0, q_0, x) \overset{*}{\underset{\mathcal{M}}{\vdash}} (z_0 \cdots z_{n-1}, r, y) \tag{6.6}$$
and
$$\begin{aligned}\rho_i &= \{(q, q') \in Q \times Q' \mid (z_0 \cdots z_i, q, u) \overset{*}{\underset{\mathcal{M}}{\vdash}} (w, r, \lambda) \\ &\quad \textit{where } r \in F \textit{ and } \delta'^*(q', u) \in F' \textit{ for some } u \in A^*\},\end{aligned} \tag{6.7}$$
for $0 \leq i \leq n-1$.

Proof. Observe that the equality (6.6) holds since the subscripts of the pushdown symbols in $\bar{Z}$ does not affect the symbols themselves.

The argument for (6.7) is by induction on i. In the base case, $i = 0$, the statement holds because of the definition of ρ_0 and the fact that $\mathcal{M}$ is in normal form.

Suppose that the equality (6.7) holds for $i - 1$. A new symbol z_{i,ρ_i} is pushed on the pushdown store of $\mathsf{Pred}(\mathcal{M}, \mathcal{M}')$ if $\delta(z_{i-1}, q, a) = (z_{i-1}z_i, p)$. We have $\bar{\delta}(z_{i-1,\rho_{i-1}}, q, a) = (z_{i-1,\rho_{i-1}} z_{i,\rho_i}, p)$, where
$$\begin{aligned}\rho_i &= \{(q, q') \mid q \in Q, q' \in Q' \text{ and } L(\mathcal{M}_{q,z_i}) \cap L(\mathcal{M}'_{q'}) \neq \emptyset \\ &\quad \text{or } N_s(\mathcal{M}_{q,z_i}) \cap L_{s'}(\mathcal{M}'_{q'}) \neq \emptyset \text{ for some } (s, s') \in \rho_{i-1}\}.\end{aligned}$$
Suppose that $(q, q') \in \rho_i$. We need to consider two cases:

1. If $L(\mathcal{M}_{q,z_i}) \cap L(\mathcal{M}'_{q'}) \neq \emptyset$, then $(z_i, q, y) \overset{*}{\underset{\mathcal{M}}{\vdash}} (w, s, \lambda)$ and $\delta'^*(q', y) \in F'$ for some $y \in A^*$. Consequently,

$$(z_0 \cdots z_{i-1} z_i, q, y) \overset{*}{\underset{\mathcal{M}}{\vdash}} (z_0 \cdots z_{i-1}, s, \lambda),$$

2. If $N_s(\mathcal{M}_{q,z_i}) \cap L_{s'}(\mathcal{M}'_{q'}) \neq \emptyset$ for some $(s, s') \in \rho_{i-1}$ we have

$$(z_i, q, u) \overset{*}{\underset{\mathcal{M}}{\vdash}} (\lambda, s, \lambda) \text{ and } \delta'^*(q, u) = s'$$

for some $u \in A^*$. By the inductive hypothesis, there is a word v such that $(z_0 \cdots z_{i-1}, s, v) \overset{*}{\underset{\mathcal{M}}{\vdash}} (\lambda, r, \lambda)$ for some $r \in F$ and $\delta'^*(s', v) \in F'$. Consequently, we can write

$$(z_0 \cdots z_{i-1} z_i, q, uv) \overset{*}{\underset{\mathcal{M}}{\vdash}} (z_0 \cdots z_{i-1}, s, v) \overset{*}{\underset{\mathcal{M}}{\vdash}} (\lambda, r, \lambda),$$

and

$$\delta'^*(q', uv) = \delta'^*(\delta'^*(q', u), v) = \delta'^*(s', v) \in F.$$

Conversely, let $(q, q') \in Q \times Q'$ be such that $(z_0 \cdots z_{i-1} z_i, q, y) \overset{*}{\underset{\mathcal{M}}{\vdash}} (w, r, \lambda)$ for some $r \in F$ and $\delta'^*(q', y) \in F'$.

If z_i was never popped we have $y \in L(\mathcal{M}_{q,z_i}) \cap L(\mathcal{M}'_{q'})$, so $(q, q') \in \rho_i$.

If z_i was popped we can write $y = uv$, where u is the input word that erased z_i. Thus, we have $(z_i, q, u) \overset{*}{\underset{\mathcal{M}}{\vdash}} (\lambda, t, \lambda)$ and $(z_0 \cdots z_{i-1}, t, v) \overset{*}{\underset{\mathcal{M}}{\vdash}} (w, r, \lambda)$. Let $t' = \delta'^*(q', u)$ and $\delta'^*(t', v) \in F$. Then, $u \in N_t(\mathcal{M}_{q,z_i}) \cap L_{t'}(\mathcal{M}'_{q'})$. By the inductive hypothesis, $(t, t') \in \rho_{i-1}$, so $(q, q') \in \rho_i$. ∎

Lemma 6.3.22 *Let $\mathcal{M} = (A, Z, Q, \delta, q_0, z_0, F)$ be a dpda. If $B \subseteq Z \times Q$, then the language*

$$L_B(\mathcal{M}) = \{x \in A^* \mid (z_0, q_0, x) \overset{*}{\underset{\mathcal{M}}{\vdash}} (wz, q, \lambda) \textit{ for some } (z, q) \in B\}$$

is a deterministic context-free language.

Proof. Define the pda $\mathcal{M}_B = (A, Z, \bar{Q}, \hat{\delta}, q_0, z_0, Q'')$, where $\bar{Q} = Q \cup Q' \cup Q''$, $Q' = \{q' \mid q \in Q\}$, and $Q'' = \{q'' \mid q \in Q\}$. The transition function is given by

$$\begin{aligned} \hat{\delta}(z, q, a) &= \{(w, p')\} \text{ if } \delta(z, q, a) = (w, p) \\ \hat{\delta}(z, q', \lambda) &= \begin{cases} \{(z, q)\} \text{ if } (z, q) \notin B \\ \{(z, q'')\} \text{ if } (z, q) \in B, \end{cases} \end{aligned}$$

for every $z \in Z$, $q \in Q$, and $q' \in Q''$. It is clear that $\mathcal{M}_B$ is a deterministic pushdown automaton.

For every step $(uz, q, ax) \underset{\mathcal{M}}{\vdash} (u_1 z_1, p, x)$ there is either a computation

$$(uz, q, ax) \underset{\mathcal{M}_B}{\vdash} (u_1 z_1, p', x) \underset{\mathcal{M}_B}{\vdash} (u_1 z_1, p, x)$$

if $(z_1, p) \notin B$, or a computation

$$(uz, q, ax) \underset{\mathcal{M}_B}{\vdash} (u_1 z_1, p', x) \underset{\mathcal{M}_B}{\vdash} (u_1 z_1, p'', x)$$

if $(z_1, p) \in B$. In other words, after simulating a move of $\mathcal{M}$, the dpda $\mathcal{M}_B$ tests whether the new pair (z_1, p') corresponds to a pair (z_1, p) in B; if it does not, the state reverts back to a non-primed version. If $(z_1, p) \in B$, then $\mathcal{M}_B$ enters a final state q''. Therefore, we have

$$\begin{aligned} & L(\mathcal{M}_B) \\ = \quad & \{x \in A^* \mid (z_0, q_0, x) \overset{*}{\underset{\mathcal{M}_B}{\vdash}} (v, q'', \lambda) \text{ for } q'' \in Q''\} \\ = \quad & \{x \in A^* \mid (z_0, q_0, x) \overset{*}{\underset{\mathcal{M}_B}{\vdash}} (wz, q', \lambda) \underset{\mathcal{M}_B}{\vdash} (v, q'', \lambda) \text{ for } (z, q) \in B\} \\ = \quad & \{x \in A^* \mid (z_0, q_0, x) \overset{*}{\underset{\mathcal{M}}{\vdash}} (wz, q, \lambda) \text{ for } (z, q) \in B\}. \end{aligned}$$

∎

Theorem 6.3.23 *If L is a deterministic context-free language and R is a regular language, then LR^{-1} is a deterministic context-free language.*

Proof. Suppose that $L = L(\mathcal{M})$, where $\mathcal{M} = (A, Z, Q, \delta, q_0, z_0, F)$ is a deterministic pushdown automaton in normal form that reads its entire input, and that $R = L(\mathcal{M}')$, where $\mathcal{M}' = (A, Q', \delta', q_0', F')$ is a dfa. Consider the predicting automaton $\mathsf{Pred}(\mathcal{M}, \mathcal{M}') = (A, \bar{Z}, Q, \bar{\delta}, q_0, z_{0,\rho_0}, F)$. Define $B = \{(z_\rho, q) \mid (q, q_0') \in \rho\}$. By Lemma 6.3.22, the language $L_B(\mathsf{Pred}(\mathcal{M}, \mathcal{M}'))$ is a deterministic context-free language. We have the following equivalent statements:

1. $x \in L_B(\mathsf{Pred}(\mathcal{M}, \mathcal{M}'))$;
2. $(z_{0,\rho_0}, q_0, x) \overset{*}{\underset{\mathsf{Pred}(\mathcal{M},\mathcal{M}')}{\vdash}} (wz_\rho, q, \lambda)$ and $(q, q_0') \in \rho$;
3. $$\begin{aligned} & (z_0, q_0, x) \overset{*}{\underset{\mathcal{M}}{\vdash}} (h(w)z, q, \lambda), \\ & (z, q, u) \overset{*}{\underset{\mathcal{M}}{\vdash}} (v, r, \lambda), \\ & \delta'^*(q_0', u) \in F' \end{aligned}$$

   for some $u \in A^*$ (by Theorem 6.3.21);
4. $(z_0, q_0, xu) \overset{*}{\underset{\mathcal{M}}{\vdash}} (h(w)z, q, u) \overset{*}{\underset{\mathcal{M}}{\vdash}} (h(w)v, r, \lambda)$, $r \in F$ and $\delta'^*(q_0', u) \in F'$ for some $u \in A^*$;
5. $xu \in L$ and $u \in R$;
6. $x \in LR^{-1}$.

Thus, LR^{-1} is a deterministic context-free language. ∎

6.4 Exercises

1. Prove that the following languages over the alphabet $A = \{a, b, c\}$ are context free by constructing the corresponding pushdown automaton:

(a) $L_0 = \{a^n b^m c^p \mid n, m, p \in \mathbb{N}, n < m\}$ and $L_1 = \{a^n b^m c^p \mid n, m, p \in \mathbb{N}, n > m\}$;
(b) $L_2 = \{a^n b^m c^p \mid n, m, p \in \mathbb{N}, n \neq m\}$;
(c) $L_3 = \{a^n b^m c^p \mid n, m, p \in \mathbb{N}, n \neq m \text{ or } m \neq p\}$

Prove that $L' = \{a, b, c\}^* - L_3$ is not context-free.

2. Let $L = \{x \in \{a, b\}^* \mid n_a(x) = n_b(x)\}$.
   (a) Construct a pushdown automaton $\mathcal{M}$ such that $N(\mathcal{M}) = L$.
   (b) Construct a pushdown automaton $\mathcal{M}$ such that $L(\mathcal{M}) = L$.
3. Let $G = (\{X_e\}, \{\boldsymbol{n}, +, *, (,)\}, X_e, P)$ be a context-free grammar, where P is the set of productions
$$P = \{X_e \to X_e + X_e, X_e \to X_e * X_e, X_e \to (X_e), X_e \to \boldsymbol{n}\}.$$
Construct a pda $\mathcal{M}$ such that $L(G) = N(\mathcal{M})$.
4. Let $\mathcal{M}$ be a pda and let $L \subseteq A^*$ be a language such that $L = L(\mathcal{M})$. Prove that if the length of the stack never exceeds a fixed number $k \in \mathbb{N}$, then L is a regular language.
5. $^{\circ\circ}$ For $n \in \mathbb{N}$ let $\langle n \rangle$ be the word in $\{0, 1\}^*$ that denotes the binary equivalent of n without leading zeros. For example, $\langle 9 \rangle = 1001$.
   (a) Prove that the language $\{\langle n \rangle \langle n+1 \rangle \mid n \in \mathbb{N}\}$ is not a context-free language.
   (b) Prove that the language $\{\langle n \rangle \langle n+1 \rangle^R \mid n \in \mathbb{N}\}$ is a context-free language.
6. $^{\circ}$ Let L be a language over the alphabet $A = \{a, b\}$ that consists of all words $x \in \{a, b\}$ that satisfy the following conditions:
   - $n_a(x) = n_b(x)$,
   - x does not contain the infix $baba$, and
   - aaa is a prefix or a suffix of x.

   Prove that L is a context-free language by constructing the corresponding pushdown automaton.
7. $^{\circ\circ}$ Let L, K be two regular languages. Prove that the language $H = \bigcup\{L^n \cap K^n \mid n \in \mathbb{N}\}$ is a context-free language by constructing a pushdown automaton $\mathcal{M}$ such that $H = L(\mathcal{M})$.
8. $^{\circ}$ Let $\mathcal{M} = (A, Z, Q, \delta, q_0, z_0, F)$ be a pushdown automaton. Define the semi-Thue system $T = (A \cup Q \cup Z, M, P)$, where $P = \{zqa \to wp \mid \delta(z, q, a) = (w, p)\}$. Prove that $x \in L(\mathcal{M})$ if and only if $z_0 q_0 x \overset{*}{\underset{T}{\Rightarrow}} wp$, where $w \in Z^*$ and $p \in F$.
9. $^{\circ}$ Let $\mathcal{M} = (A, Z, Q, \delta, q_0, z_0, F)$ be a pushdown automaton for which there is a number $k \in \mathbb{N}$ such that for every computation $(z_0, q_0, x) \vdash^* (w, q, y)$ we have $|w| \leq k$. Prove that $L(\mathcal{M})$ is a regular language.
10. Let $\mathcal{M} = (A, Q, \delta, q_0, F)$ be an ndfa. Prove that there is an one-state pushdown automaton having Q as the pushdown alphabet such that $L(\mathcal{M}) = L(\mathcal{M}')$.
11. Construct a pushdown automaton that accepts the following languages over the alphabet $A = \{a, b\}$:
    (a)
$$K = A^* - \{ww \mid w \in A^*\};$$

(b)

$$L = A^* - \{a^n b^n a^n \mid n \in \mathbb{N}\}.$$

12. ◦◦ Let $G = (A_N, A_T, S, P)$ be a grammar having the set of productions $P = \{\alpha_0 \to \beta_0, \ldots, \alpha_{m-1} \to \beta_{m-1}\}$, $A = A_N \cup A_T$, and let $\#$ be a symbol such that $\# \notin A$.
    (a) Prove that the languages
    $$R(G) = \{\alpha\#\beta^R \mid \alpha \underset{G}{\Rightarrow} \beta\},$$
    $$R'(G) = \{\alpha^R\#\beta \mid \alpha \underset{G}{\Rightarrow} \beta\}$$
    are context-free languages on $A \cup \{\#\}$.
    (b) Using pushdown automata prove that the complements $\overline{R(G)}$ and $\overline{R'(G)}$ of $R(G)$ and $R(G')$, respectively, are also context-free languages.

    Solution. It is easy to see that $R(G)$ is generated by the context-free grammar $G' = (\{S, Z\}, A_T \cup \{\#\}, S, P')$, where P' includes the following productions:
    - $S \to aSa$ for $a \in A_T$;
    - $S \to \alpha_i Z \beta_i^R$ for $0 \leq i \leq m-1$;
    - $Z \to aZa$ for $a \in A_T$, and
    - $Z \to \#$.

    The argument for $R'(G)$ is similar.
    To prove that complement of $R(G)$ note that $\theta \in (A \cup \{\#\})^* - R(G)$ if it satisfies one of the following conditions:
    - θ contains no $\#$ or at least two $\#$ occurrences;
    - $\theta = \theta'\#\theta''$ and $\theta' \notin A^*\{\alpha_0, \ldots, \alpha_{m-1}\}A^*$, for some $\theta', \theta'' \in A^*$;
    - $\theta = \theta'\#\theta''$, $\theta' \in \gamma\alpha_i\gamma'$ and $\theta'' \neq (\gamma')^R(\beta_i)^R\gamma^R$ for some $\gamma, \gamma' \in A^*$ and $0 \leq i \leq m-1$.

    The first two conditions describe regular languages. To prove that the language described by the third condition is context-free let K_i be the set of words on $A \cup \{\#\}$ that have the form $\theta = \theta'\#\theta''$, $\theta' \in \gamma\alpha_i\gamma'$ and $\theta'' \neq (\gamma')^R(\beta_i)^R\gamma^R$, where $0 \leq i \leq m-1$. We describe a dpa $\mathcal{M}_i$ that accepts the language K_i. $\mathcal{M}_i$ starts by writing in the pushdown store the symbols it reads from the input. At a certain moment $\mathcal{M}'$ switches nondeterministically to a state such that while reading α_i on the input tape it writes β_i on the pushdown store; after that it reverts to its previous mode of actions until it reaches the symbol $\#$. If no symbol $\#$ is found on the tape $\mathcal{M}_i$ does not reach a final state. When $\#$ is found, the pushdown store contains $\gamma\beta_i\gamma'$. Now, $\mathcal{M}_i$ compares the content of its store with its tape. $\mathcal{M}_i$ accepts if the content of the store is different from the content of the remaining input word. We have $K = \bigcup\{K_i \mid 0 \leq i \leq m-1\}$, so K is a context-free language and this shows that the complement of $R(G)$ is context-free (as the union of two regular and one context-free language). The argument for the complement of $R(G')$ is similar. ∎

13. ◦◦ Let θ be a word over an alphabet A. Define $\theta^{[n]}$ as

$$\theta^{[n]} = \begin{cases} \theta & \text{if } n \text{ is even} \\ \theta^R & \text{if } n \text{ is odd,} \end{cases}$$

for $n \in \mathbb{N}$.

(a) Prove that for any grammar G the language

$$D(G) = \{\theta_0\#\theta_1^{[1]}\#\cdots\#\theta_n^{[n]} \mid S = \theta_0 \underset{G}{\Rightarrow} \theta_1 \underset{G}{\Rightarrow} \cdots \underset{G}{\Rightarrow} \theta_n \in A_T^*\}$$

is the intersection of two context-free languages.

(b) Prove that $\overline{D(G)} = (A \cup \{\#\})^* - D(G)$, the complement of $D(G)$, is also a context-free language.

Solution. We use the results established in Exercise 12 For the first part, consider the context-free languages

$$L_0 = (R(G)\#)^*(\{\lambda\} \cup A_T^*\#)$$
$$L_1 = S\#(R'(G)\#)^* A_T^*\#.$$

Note that $\theta \in L_0 \cap L_1$ if and only if $\theta = \gamma_0\#\gamma_1\#\cdots\gamma_{n-1}\#$, where $\gamma_0 = S$, $\gamma_{n-1} \in A_T^*$, $\gamma_{2i}\#\gamma_{2i+1} \in R(G)$ for $0 \leq i \leq \lfloor n/2 \rfloor$ and $\gamma_{2i-1}\#\gamma_{2i} \in R'(G)$ for $1 \leq i \leq \lfloor n/2 \rfloor$. These are exactly the conditions required for $\theta \in D(G)$, so $D(G) = L_0 \cap L_1$.

For the second part observe that $\overline{D(G)}$ consists of those words in $(A_N \cup A_T \cup \{\#\})^*$ that satisfy one the following conditions:

(i) $\theta \notin ((A_N \cup A_T)^*\#)^*$;

(ii) $\theta_0 \neq S$, or equivalently, $\theta \notin S\#((A_N \cup A_T)^*\#)^*$;

(iii) $\theta_n \notin A_T^*$, or equivalently, $\theta \notin ((A_N \cup A_T)^*\#)^* A_T^*\#$;

(iv) $\theta \notin ((A_N \cup A_T)^*\#)^*$, $\theta = \theta_0\#\theta_1^{[1]}\#\cdots\#\theta_n^{[n]}$ and $\theta_i \not\underset{G}{\Rightarrow} \theta_{i+1}$ for some i, $0 \leq i \leq n-1$.

In the first three cases, the language described is regular. The last case describes the language $(A \cup \{\#\}) * (\overline{R(G)} \cup \overline{R'(G)})(A \cup \{\#\})*$, which is context-free by the second part. Thus, $\overline{D(G)}$ is context-free. ■

Deterministic Context-Free Languages

14. Let $L = \{a^{3n}b^{5n} \mid n \in \mathbb{N}\}$.
    (a) Prove that the language L is a deterministic context-free language by constructing a dpda $\mathcal{M}$ such that $L = L(\mathcal{M})$.
    (b) Construct a dpda $\mathcal{M}'$ in normal form equivalent to $\mathcal{M}$.
15. Prove that the language $L \subseteq \{a, b\}$ defined by $L = \{a\}^* \cup \{a^n b^n \mid n \in \mathbb{N}\}$ is deterministic context-free.
16. $^\diamond$ Prove that every regular language is a deterministic context-free language.
17. Prove that if L is a deterministic context-free language, then $\mathsf{PREF}(L)$ is also deterministic context-free.
18. Let R be a regular language. Prove that if L is a deterministic context-free language, then so are the languages $R - L$ and $L - R$.
19. Starting from the fact that

$$\{x \in \{a, b\}^* \mid n_a(x) = n_b(x)\}$$

is a is a deterministic context-free language prove that the languages

$$L_0 = \{a^n b^m \mid n, m \in \mathbb{N} \text{ and } n \neq m\}$$
$$L_1 = \{a^n b^{n+p} a^p \mid n, p \in \mathbb{N}\}$$

are deterministic context-free.

20. $^\diamond$ Let $A = \{a, b, c\}$.
    (a) Prove that the languages $L = \{x \in A^* \mid x = a^n b^n c^p, n, p \in \mathbb{N}\}$ and $L' = \{x \in A^* \mid x = a^n b^p c^p, n, p \in \mathbb{N}\}$ are deterministic context-free languages.
    (b) Prove that the class of deterministic context-free languages is not closed with respect to union.
21. $^\diamond$ Let A be an alphabet and let d be a symbol such that $d \notin A$. Prove that if L, L' are two deterministic context-free languages over the alphabet A, then the language $dL \cup L'$ is a deterministic context-free language over the alphabet $A \cup \{d\}$.
22. $^\diamond$ Prove that the class of deterministic context-free languages is not closed with respect to morphisms.
    Hint. Consider the languages L, L' introduced in Exercise 20, the deterministic context-free language $dL \cup L'$ (cf. Exercise 21) and the fine morphism $h : (A \cup \{d\})^* \longrightarrow A^*$ given by $h(d) = \lambda$ and $h(s) = s$ for $s \in A$.
23. $^\diamond$ Let A be an alphabet and let d be a symbol such that $d \notin A$.
    (a) Prove that $L \subseteq A^*$, then L is a dcfl if and only if dL is a dcfl.
    (b) Prove that $L \subseteq A^*$, then L is a dcfl if and only if $\{d\} \cup L$ is a dcfl.
24. $^{\diamond\diamond}$ Prove that the class of dcfls is not closed with respect to product.
    Solution. Let L, L' be the languages introduced in Exercise 20; we know that $H = L \cup L'$ is not a dcfl (see Example 6.3.15). On the other hand, $dL \cup L'$ is a dcfl. If the class of dcfls were closed with respect to product, the language $\{d\}^*(dL \cup L')$ would be a dcfl. This would imply that $K = \{d\}^*(dL \cup L') \cap \{d\}A^*$ is a dcfl. Since $K = dL \cup dL' = d(L \cup L')$ this would imply that $L \cup L'$ is a dcfl, which we know that is not the case. ■
25. $^{\diamond\diamond}$ Prove that the class of dcfls is not closed with respect to Kleene closure.
    Solution. Starting from the languages L, L' introduced in Exercise 20 consider the dcfl $K = \{d\} \cup dL \cup L'$. If the class of dcfls would be closed to Kleene closure, the language K^* would be a dcfl, which would imply that $K^* \cap dA^* = dL \cup dL' = d(L \cup L')$ would be a dcfl. ■
26. Let $\mathcal{M}$ be the dpda defined in Example 6.3.2. Prove that $L(\mathcal{M}) = \{a^n b^n \mid n \in \mathbb{N}\}$.
27. Let $\mathcal{M}$ be the dpda defined in Example 6.3.3. Prove that $L(\mathcal{M}) = \{xcx^R \mid x \in \{a, b\}^*\}$.

A language $L \subseteq A^*$ is accepted by a pushdown automaton with an empty store if there is a dpda Let $\mathcal{M} = (A, Z, Q, \delta, q_0, z_0, F)$ such that $L = N(\mathcal{M})$, where

$$N(\mathcal{M}) = \{x \in A^* \mid (z_0, q_0, x) \overset{*}{\underset{\mathcal{M}}{\vdash}} (\lambda, q, \lambda) \text{ for some } q \in Q\}.$$

28. Acceptance by a pushdown automaton with an empty store is not equivalent to acceptance by final states for dpdas. To justify this observation prove that the language L defined in Exercise 15 cannot be accepted by a dpda with an empty store.

Let $\mathcal{M} = (A, Z, Q, \delta, q_0, z_0, F)$ be a dpda, where $Q = \{q_0, \ldots, q_{n-1}\}$. For each word $w \in Z^*$ define an $n \times n$-matrix $\boldsymbol{M}_{\mathcal{M}}(w)$ by

$$(\boldsymbol{M}_{\mathcal{M}}(w))_{ij} = \begin{cases} 1 & \text{if } (w, q_i, x) \overset{*}{\underset{\mathcal{M}}{\vdash}} (\lambda, q_j, \lambda) \text{ for some } x \in A^*, \\ 0 & \text{otherwise.} \end{cases}$$

If the dpda $\mathcal{M}$ is clear from context we shall write $\boldsymbol{M}(w)$ instead of $\boldsymbol{M}_{\mathcal{M}}(w)$.

Since $\boldsymbol{M}(w)$ has n^2 entries, there are at most 2^{n^2} such distinct matrices. The matrix $M(\lambda)$ is the diagonal matrix.

29. $\diamond$ Let $\mathcal{M} = (A, Z, Q, \delta, q_0, z_0, F)$ be a dpda. Prove that it is possible to compute effectively $M(w)$ for every $w \in Z^*$.
Solution. Consider the language

$$L(\mathcal{M}, q_i, w, q_j) = \{x \in A^* \mid (w, q_i, x) \overset{*}{\underset{\mathcal{M}}{\vdash}} (\lambda, q_j, \lambda)\}.$$

It is clear that $(\boldsymbol{M}(w))_{ij} = 1$ if and only if $L(\mathcal{M}, q_i, w, q_j) \neq \emptyset$. We shall prove that $L(\mathcal{M}, q_i, x, q_j)$ is a context-free language. By Corollary 4.5.13 the problem "$L(\mathcal{M}, q_i, w, q_j) = \emptyset$?" is decidable, and we have an effective way of constructing the matrix $\boldsymbol{M}(w)$.
Starting from the dpda $\mathcal{M}$ define the dpda

$$\mathcal{M}_{w,i,j} = (A, Z, Q \cup \{q'_0\}, \delta', z'_0, \{q_j\})$$

by $\delta'(z'_0, q'_0, \lambda) = (w, q_i)$, and $\delta'(z, q, a) = \delta(z, q, a)$ for every $(z, q, a) \in Z \times Q \times (A \cup \{\lambda\})$. Then, $x \in N(\mathcal{M}_{w,i,j})$ if and only if

$$(z'_0, q'_0, x) \overset{*}{\underset{\mathcal{M}_{w,i,j}}{\vdash}} (\lambda, q_j, \lambda).$$

Writing explicitly the first step of this computation we have

$$(z'_0, q'_0, x) \underset{\mathcal{M}_{w,i,j}}{\vdash} (w, q_i, x) \overset{*}{\underset{\mathcal{M}_{w,i,j}}{\vdash}} (\lambda, q_j, \lambda).$$

This takes place if and only if $(w, q_i, x) \overset{*}{\underset{\mathcal{M}}{\vdash}} (\lambda, q_j, \lambda)$, that is, if and only if $x \in L(\mathcal{M}, q_i, w, q_j)$. Thus, $L(\mathcal{M}, q_i, w, q_j)$ is a context-free language. ∎

30. $\diamond$ Let $M(w)$ be the matrix associated to a dpda $\mathcal{M}$ and a word w on the alphabet of the pushdown store. Prove that the relation $\epsilon_{\mathcal{M}} = \{(w, w') \in Z^* \times Z^* \mid \boldsymbol{M}(w) = \boldsymbol{M}(w')\}$ is a right-invariant equivalence relation on Z^* and the set $Z^*/\epsilon_{\mathcal{M}}$ is finite.
Solution. It is easy to see that $\epsilon_{\mathcal{M}}$ is an equivalence relation on Z^*. Therefore, we need to show only that if $\boldsymbol{M}(w) = \boldsymbol{M}(w')$, then $\boldsymbol{M}(wu) = \boldsymbol{M}(w'u)$ for every $u \in Z^*$.
We have $(\boldsymbol{M}(wu))_{ij} = 1$ if and only if $(wu, q_i, x) \overset{*}{\underset{\mathcal{M}}{\vdash}} (\lambda, q_j, \lambda)$ for some $x \in A^*$. Let q_k be the state of $\mathcal{M}$ encountered during this computation

when the rightmost symbol of w occurs at the top of the pushdown store for the first time. Then, we have

$$(wu, q_i, x) \overset{*}{\underset{\mathcal{M}}{\vdash}} (w, q_k, t) \overset{*}{\underset{\mathcal{M}}{\vdash}} (\lambda, q_j, \lambda),$$

and, in addition $(u, q_i, z) \overset{*}{\underset{\mathcal{M}}{\vdash}} (\lambda, q_k, \lambda)$, where $x = zt$. Thus, $(\boldsymbol{M}(w))_{kj} = 1$, and this implies $(\boldsymbol{M}(w'))_{kj} = 1$, so $(w', q_k, t) \overset{*}{\underset{\mathcal{M}}{\vdash}} (\lambda, q_j, \lambda)$. Consequently, we have the computation

$$(w'u, q_i, x) \overset{*}{\underset{\mathcal{M}}{\vdash}} (w', q_k, t) \overset{*}{\underset{\mathcal{M}}{\vdash}} (\lambda, q_j, \lambda),$$

which implies $(\boldsymbol{M}(w'u))_{ij} = 1$. The converse implication can be shown in exactly the same manner.

Note that each equivalence class of the set $Z^*/\epsilon_{\mathcal{M}}$ corresponds to a matrix $\boldsymbol{M}(w)$. Since there are only a finite number of such distinct matrices, the set $Z^*/\epsilon_{\mathcal{M}}$ is finite. ■

31. ◇ Let $\mathcal{M} = (A, Z, Q, \delta, q_0, z_0, F)$ be a dpda. Prove that the language

$$L_{q_i q_j} = \{w \in Z^* \mid (w, q_i, x) \overset{*}{\underset{\mathcal{M}}{\vdash}} (\lambda, q_j, \lambda) \text{ for some } x \in A^*\}$$

is regular for every $q_i, q_j \in Q$.

Solution. We prove the regularity of $L_{q_i q_j}$ by showing that $L_{q_i q_j}$ is an $\epsilon_{\mathcal{M}}$-saturated language. Since $Z^*/\epsilon_{\mathcal{M}}$ is finite, by Supplement 67 of Chapter 3, this implies that $L_{q_i q_j}$ is regular.

Suppose that $(w, w') \in \epsilon_{\mathcal{M}}$ and that $w \in L_{q_i q_j}$. Then, there is $x \in A^*$ such that $(w, q_i, x) \overset{*}{\underset{\mathcal{M}}{\vdash}} (\lambda, q_j, \lambda)$ and $\boldsymbol{M}(w) = \boldsymbol{M}(w')$. The definition of the matrices $\boldsymbol{M}(w)$ and $\boldsymbol{M}(w')$ implies that $(\boldsymbol{M}(w))_{ij} = 1$ and $(\boldsymbol{M}(w'))_{ij} = (\boldsymbol{M}(w))_{ij} = 1$. Therefore, $(w', q_i, x) \overset{*}{\underset{\mathcal{M}}{\vdash}} (\lambda, q_j, \lambda)$, so $w' \in L_{q_i q_j}$, which shows that $L_{q_i q_j}$ is $\epsilon_{\mathcal{M}}$-saturated. ■

6.5 Bibliographical Comments

Pushdown automata were introduced in [Oettinger, 1961] and [Schützenberger, 1963]. Exercise 7 is extracted from [Greibach, 1965]. The treatment of the closure of dcfls under quotients with regular languages follows [Hopcroft and Ullman, 1979], where the notion of predicting automaton was introduced. Exercises 29–31 originate in [Harrison, 1978]. Extended pushdown automata were introduced in the first volume of [Aho and Ullman, 1972]. Exercises 12 and 13 are variants of results included in [Hopcroft and Ullman, 1979].

Part III

Algorithmic Aspects

Chapter 7

Partial Recursive Functions

7.1 Computable Functions

This chapter is concerned with functions that can be computed in an effective manner. We stress that the notion of "effective manner" is a non-mathematical one, but it will serve as a heuristic basis of our presentation. We will discuss ways of capturing its meaning through the formal, mathematical concept of partial recursive function. As a part of this discussion, we will introduce fundamental ideas of computability theory that are relevant for the study of formal languages.

Effective computability of functions is an issue of major importance for formal languages. Indeed, if $L \subseteq A^*$ is a language on the alphabet A such that $a_0 \in A$ and the function p_L defined by

$$p_L(x) = \begin{cases} a_0 & \text{if } x \in L \\ \lambda & \text{otherwise} \end{cases}$$

is effectively computable, then we can decide effectively whether $x \in L$ simply by computing $p_L(x)$ and determining whether or not $p_L(x) = a_0$. In other cases, p_L may not be effectively computable; instead, the partial function $\iota_L : A^* \leadsto A^*$ is effectively computable, where $\iota_L(x) = x$ for $x \in L$ and $\text{Dom}(\iota_L) = L$. Then, we can decide only "half" of the problem. More exactly, an affirmative answer to the problem $x \in L$ can be effectively reached; however, no answer is effectively available when $x \notin L$.

We will develop two models of effectively computable functions. The first of these is the class of primitive recursive functions. This class includes almost all functions encountered in current mathematical practice. This class is then extended to the class of partial recursive functions, which according to a generally accepted principle referred to as *Church's thesis*, coincides with the class of effectively computable functions. A detailed discussion of these ideas is presented in Chapter 8.

7.2 Primitive Recursive Functions

Let $A = \{a_0, \dots, a_{n-1}\}$ be an alphabet containing n symbols. We begin the definition of the class of *primitive recursive functions on* A by listing the basic primitive recursive functions.

Definition 7.2.1 The *basic primitive recursive functions* are:

- the *null function* $e : A^* \longrightarrow A^*$ defined by $e(x) = \lambda$ for every $x \in A^*$;
- the *successor functions* $s_i : A^* \longrightarrow A^*$ defined by $s_i(x) = xa_i$ for every $x \in A^*$ and $0 \leq i \leq n-1$;
- the *projection functions* $P_i^k : (A^*)^k \longrightarrow A^*$ given by $P_i^k(x_0, \dots, x_{k-1}) = x_i$ for $x_0, \dots, x_{k-1} \in A^*$, $0 \leq i \leq k-1$ and $k \geq 1$.

□

It is clear that every basic primitive recursive function is computable in an intuitive sense; it is equally clear that not every intuitively computable function is a basic primitive recursive one. For example, the concatenation function $\mathsf{conc} : (A^*)^2 \longrightarrow A^*$, where $\mathsf{conc}(x, y) = xy$ for $x, y \in A^*$, is not a basic primitive recursive function. Therefore, we expand the class of basic primitive recursive functions to the class of primitive recursive functions. To this end, we need the following definitions:

Definition 7.2.2 Let $m, p \in \mathbb{N}$, let $h_i : (A^*)^p \longrightarrow A^*$ for $0 \leq i \leq m-1$ be m functions of p arguments, and let $g : (A^*)^m \longrightarrow A^*$ be a function of m arguments. The function $f : (A^*)^p \longrightarrow A^*$ is obtained by *composition from the functions* $h_0, \dots, h_{m-1}$ *using the function* g if

$$f(x_0, \dots, x_{p-1}) = g(h_0(x_0, \dots, x_{p-1}), \dots, h_{m-1}(x_0, \dots, x_{p-1}))$$

for every $x_0, \dots, x_{p-1} \in A^*$. □

Example 7.2.3 Let A be an alphabet. To show the use of composition, assume that conc is available. The function $f : (A^*)^3 \longrightarrow A^*$ given by $f(x_0, x_1, x_2) = x_2x_0$ for $x_0, x_1, x_2 \in A^*$ may be obtained by composition from the projection functions P_2^3, P_0^3 using conc because

$$\mathsf{conc}(P_2^3(x_0, x_1, x_2), P_0^3(x_0, x_1, x_2)) = \mathsf{conc}(x_2, x_0) = x_2x_0,$$

for every $x_0, x_1, x_2 \in A^*$. □

Definition 7.2.4 Let $A = \{a_0, \ldots, a_{n-1}\}$ be an alphabet, $g : (A^*)^{m-1} \longrightarrow A^*$, and let $h_i : (A^*)^{m+1} \longrightarrow A^*$ for $0 \leq i \leq n-1$ be n functions of $m+1$ arguments, where $m > 1$.

The function $f : (A^*)^m \longrightarrow A^*$ is obtained from g and $h_0, \ldots, h_{n-1}$ by *primitive recursion* if $f(\lambda, x_1, \ldots, x_{m-1}) = g(x_1, \ldots, x_{m-1})$ and

$$\begin{aligned} f(xa_0, x_1, \ldots, x_{m-1}) &= h_0(x, x_1, \ldots, x_{m-1}, f(x, x_1, \ldots, x_{m-1})) \\ f(xa_1, x_1, \ldots, x_{m-1}) &= h_1(x, x_1, \ldots, x_{m-1}, f(x, x_1, \ldots, x_{m-1})) \\ &\vdots \\ f(xa_{n-1}, x_1, \ldots, x_{m-1}) &= h_{n-1}(x, x_1, \ldots, x_{m-1}, f(x, x_1, \ldots, x_{m-1})), \end{aligned}$$

for every $x, x_1, \ldots, x_{m-1} \in A^*$. □

Observe that if $m = 1$, then $f : A^* \longrightarrow A^*$ is defined by primitive recursion from $h_0, \ldots, h_{n-1}$ by

$$\begin{aligned} f(\lambda) &= u_0 \\ f(xa_i) &= h_i(x, f(x)), \end{aligned}$$

for every $x \in A^*$; here u_0 is a word in A^*.

The first argument of f is used to carry the definition of f to all of A^*. We say that f is *defined by primitive recursion on its first argument.* Below (in Theorem 7.2.6) we show that we could have used any argument.

Definition 7.2.5 The *set of primitive recursive functions on the alphabet* A, PRIMREC(A) consists of the following functions:

(i) every basic recursive function is a primitive recursive function;
(ii) if $f : (A^*)^p \longrightarrow A^*$ is obtained by composition from the primitive recursive functions $h_0, \ldots, h_{m-1}$ using the primitive recursive function g, then f is primitive recursive;
(iii) if f is obtained by primitive recursion from the primitive recursive functions g and $h_0, \ldots, h_{n-1}$, then f is primitive recursive.

□

An useful technical result is given next.

Theorem 7.2.6 *Let $(i_0, \ldots, i_{m-1})$ be a permutation of $(0, \ldots, m-1)$. If $f : (A^*)^m \longrightarrow A^*$ is a primitive recursive function, then the function $g : (A^*)^m \longrightarrow A^*$ given by $g(x_0, \ldots, x_{m-1}) = f(x_{i_0}, \ldots, x_{i_{m-1}})$, for $x_0, \ldots, x_{m-1} \in A^*$ is a primitive recursive function.*

Proof. The statement follows immediately from the equality

$$g(x_0, \ldots, x_{m-1}) = f(P^m_{i_0}(x_0, \ldots, x_{m-1}), \ldots, P^m_{i_{m-1}}(x_0, \ldots, x_{m-1}))$$

for every $x_0, \ldots, x_{m-1} \in A^*$. ■

Using Theorem 7.2.6 we gain more flexibility in the construction of primitive recursive functions. The definition of primitive recursion requires that the recursion be done on the first argument; thus, if $g : A^* \longrightarrow A^*$ and $h_i : (A^*)^3 \longrightarrow A^*$ for $0 \leq i \leq |A| - 1$ are primitive recursive functions, it does not follow directly from the definition of primitive recursive functions that the function $f : (A^*)^2 \longrightarrow A^*$ given by

$$\begin{aligned} f(x, \lambda) &= g(x) \\ f(x, ya_i) &= h_i(x, y, f(x, y)), \end{aligned}$$

for $x, y \in A^*$ and $a_i \in A$ is primitive recursive. Instead, consider the functions h'_i given by $h'_i(u, v, w) = h_i(v, u, w)$ for $u, v, w \in A^*$ and $0 \leq i \leq |A| - 1$. The function f' defined by primitive recursion from $g, h'_0, \ldots, h'_{n-1}$ (where $n = |A|$) is given by

$$\begin{aligned} f'(\lambda, v) &= g(v) \\ f'(ua_i, v) &= h'_i(u, v, f'(u, v)) \end{aligned}$$

for $u, v \in A^*$, and is primitive recursive. We claim that $f(x, y) = f'(y, x)$ for $x, y \in A^*$. The argument is by induction on y.

For the base case, $y = \lambda$, we have $f(x, \lambda) = f'(\lambda, x) = g(x)$, which corresponds to the definition of f. Suppose that $f(x, y) = f'(y, x)$. Then, we can write

$$\begin{aligned} f(x, ya_i) &= h_i(x, y, f(x, y)) \\ &= h'_i(y, x, f(x, y)) \\ &= h'_i(y, x, f'(y, x)) \\ &= f'(ya_i, x), \end{aligned}$$

which completes the proof of $f(x, y) = f'(y, x)$ for $x, y \in A^*$. By Theorem 7.2.6 we conclude that f is primitive recursive. This allows us to "liberalize" the primitive recursion construction scheme by allowing recursion on any argument, not necessarily the first.

We consider now a series of examples in order to build our collection of primitive recursive functions.

Example 7.2.7 Let $f : (A^*)^2 \longrightarrow A^*$ be the function defined by $f(x_0, x_1) = x_1 x_0$. Since $f(\lambda, x_1) = x_1$ and $f(xa_i, x_1) = x_1 x a_i = s_i(f(x, x_1))$, it follows that f is defined by primitive recursion from the functions $g, h_0, \ldots, h_{n-1}$, where $g = P^1_0$, and $h_i(x, x_1, y) = s_i(P^3_2(x, x_1, y))$ for $x, x_1, y \in A^*$ and $0 \leq i \leq n - 1$.

Then, $\mathsf{conc} : (A^*)^2 \longrightarrow A^*$ is primitive recursive (by Theorem 7.2.6) since $\mathsf{conc}(x_0, x_1) = f(x_1, x_0)$ for every $x_0, x_1 \in A^*$. □

Example 7.2.8 Let $l : A^* \longrightarrow A^*$ be the function that gives the length of its argument; $l(x) = a_0^{|x|}$ for $x \in A^*$. We define l by:

$$\begin{aligned} l(\lambda) &= \lambda \\ l(xa_i) &= h_i(x, l(x)), \end{aligned}$$

where $h_i(x, l(x)) = \mathsf{conc}(l(x), a_0)$ for $0 \leq i \leq n - 1$. Clearly, $l(x) = a_0^m$ if x is a word of length m over A. Thus, the function l that gives the length of its argument is primitive recursive. We denote, as usual, $l(x)$ by $|x|$. □

Example 7.2.9 For each word $w \in A^*$, the constant function $c_w : A^* \longrightarrow A^*$ defined by $c_w(x) = w$ for every $x \in A^*$ is primitive recursive. The argument is by induction on length of the word w.

For $|w| = 0$, $w = \lambda$, and we have $c_\lambda(x) = e(x)$ for $x \in A^*$. Thus, c_λ is primitive recursive.

Suppose that c_w is primitive recursive for words of length n. Then, $c_{wa_i}(x) = s_i(c_w(x))$ for every $a_i \in A$. This implies that c_{wa_i} is primitive recursive.

A generalization of this result is that the constant function $c^m_w : (A^*)^m \longrightarrow A^*$ given by $c^m_w(x_0, \ldots, x_{m-1}) = w$ for $x_0, \ldots, x_{m-1} \in A^*$ is primitive recursive for $m \in \mathbb{N}$. This can be easily seen by writing

$$c_w^m(x_0, \ldots, x_{m-1}) = c_w(P_1^m(x_0, \ldots, x_{m-1}),$$

for $x_0, \ldots, x_{m-1} \in A^*$. □

Example 7.2.10 The function $\mathsf{rev} : A^* \longrightarrow A^*$ given by $\mathsf{rev}(x) = x^R$ for $x \in A^*$ is primitive recursive. Indeed, note that

$$\begin{aligned} \mathsf{rev}(\lambda) &= \lambda \\ \mathsf{rev}(xa_i) &= h_i(x, \mathsf{rev}(x)), \end{aligned}$$

for $x \in A^*$ and $0 \leq i \leq n-1$, where $h_i(x,y) = \mathsf{conc}(c_{a_i}(P_0^2(x,y)), P_1^2(x,y))$ for $x, y \in A^*$. Note that the argument of c_{a_i} is irrelevant; however, the formal definition requires us to use the argument of this function. □

Example 7.2.11 Define the functions $\mathsf{trimlast} : A^* \longrightarrow A^*$, and $\mathsf{trimfirst} : A^* \longrightarrow A^*$ by

$$\begin{aligned} \mathsf{trimlast}(x) &= \begin{cases} y & \text{if } x = ya \text{ for some } y \in A^* \\ \lambda & \text{if } x = \lambda \end{cases} \\ \mathsf{trimfirst}(x) &= \begin{cases} y & \text{if } x = ay \text{ for some } y \in A^* \\ \lambda & \text{if } x = \lambda, \end{cases} \end{aligned}$$

for $x \in A^*$.

The primitive recursiveness of $\mathsf{trimlast}$ follows immediately from the equalities:

$$\begin{aligned} \mathsf{trimlast}(\lambda) &= \lambda \\ \mathsf{trimlast}(xa_i) &= h_i(x, \mathsf{trimlast}(x)), \end{aligned}$$

where $h_i(x,y) = P_0^2(x,y) = x$, for $x \in A^*$ and $0 \leq i \leq n-1$.

The primitive recursiveness of $\mathsf{trimfirst}$ follows from the equality:

$$\mathsf{trimfirst}(x) = \mathsf{rev}(\mathsf{trimlast}(\mathsf{rev}(x)),$$

for $x \in A^*$. □

Example 7.2.12 Define $x -_l y$ as the word obtained from x by erasing the leftmost $|y|$ symbols of x. To show that the function $f : (A^*)^2 \longrightarrow A^*$ given by $f(x,y) = x -_l y$ for $x, y \in A^*$ is primitive recursive, observe that f can be defined by primitive recursion as:

$$\begin{aligned} f(x, \lambda) &= x = P_0^1(x) \\ f(x, ya_i) &= h_i(x, y, f(x,y)) \end{aligned}$$

for $x, y \in A^*$ and $a_i \in A$. The functions h_i are given by

$$h_i(x,y,z) = \mathsf{trimlast}(z) = \mathsf{trimlast}(P_2^3(x,y,z))$$

for $0 \leq i \leq |A|-1$ and therefore are primitive recursive. This gives the primitive recursiveness of $x -_l y$. Similarly, if $x -_r y$ is the word obtained from x by erasing the $|y|$ rightmost symbols of x, the function defined by $g(x,y) = x -_r y$ for $x, y \in A^*$ can be proven to be primitive recursive. This is left to the reader (cf. Exercise 10). □

Example 7.2.13 The functions lastof : $A^* \longrightarrow A^*$ and firstof : $A^* \longrightarrow A^*$ are defined by

$$\mathsf{lastof}(x) = \begin{cases} a & \text{if } x = ya \text{ for some } y \in A^* \\ \lambda & \text{if } x = \lambda \end{cases}$$

$$\mathsf{firstof}(x) = \begin{cases} a & \text{if } x = ay \text{ for some } y \in A^* \\ \lambda & \text{if } x = \lambda, \end{cases}$$

for $x \in A^*$.

The function lastof can be obtained by primitive recursion by

$$\mathsf{lastof}(\lambda) = \lambda$$
$$\mathsf{lastof}(xa) = c_a(P_0^2(x, \mathsf{lastof}(x))),$$

for $x \in A^*$ and $a \in A$. This shows that lastof is primitive recursive.

The function firstof can be shown to be primitive recursive by using the functions rev and lastof; this is left as an exercise for the reader. □

Example 7.2.14 Let $A = \{a_0, \ldots, a_{n-1}\}$ be an alphabet, and let $h : A^* \longrightarrow A^*$ be any morphism. Define the primitive recursive functions $h_i : (A^*)^2 \longrightarrow A^*$ by $h_i(x, y) = \mathsf{conc}(y, c_{h(a_i)}(x))$ for $x, y \in A^*$ and $0 \leq i \leq n-1$. Then, h can be defined by primitive recursion as

$$h(\lambda) = \lambda$$
$$h(xa_i) = h_i(x, h(x)),$$

for $x \in A^*$, which proves that h is primitive recursive. □

The process of building a primitive recursive function can be captured as a sequence of sequences of words over a language. This can be thought of as a system for programming the primitive recursive functions.

Definition 7.2.15 Let $A = \{a_0, \ldots, a_{n-1}\}$ be an alphabet and let

$$B_A = \{\boldsymbol{e}, \boldsymbol{S}, \boldsymbol{R}\} \cup \{\boldsymbol{s}_i | 0 \leq i \leq n-1\} \cup \{\boldsymbol{p}_i^k | i, k \in \mathbb{N}, i < k\}$$

be a set of symbols. The set $\mathbf{PR}_A$ of *primitive recursive programs over the alphabet* A consists of the following sequences in $\mathbf{Seq}(B_A)$:

(i) The sequences $(\boldsymbol{e})$ and $(\boldsymbol{s}_i)$ are primitive recursive programs of arity 1.

(ii) The sequence $(\boldsymbol{p}_i^k)$ is a primitive recursive program of arity k for $k \in \mathbb{N}$ and $0 \leq i \leq k-1$.

(iii) If r is a primitive recursive program of arity m and $q_0, \ldots, q_{m-1}$ are m primitive recursive programs of arity $k \in \mathbb{N}$, then

$$(\boldsymbol{C}, r, q_0, \ldots, q_{m-1})$$

is a primitive recursive program of arity k.

(iv) If r is a primitive recursive program of arity $k-1$, $k \geq 1$, and $q_0, \ldots, q_{n-1}$ are n primitive recursive programs of arity $k+1$, then

$$(\boldsymbol{R}, r, q_0, \ldots, q_{n-1})$$

is a primitive recursive program of arity k.

□

Primitive recursive programs serve as notations for the definitions of primitive recursive functions. Namely, consider the function

$$\Phi : \mathbf{PR}_A \longrightarrow \bigcup_{k\in\mathbb{N}} ((A^*)^k \longrightarrow A^*)$$

given by

$$\begin{aligned}\Phi(\boldsymbol{e}) &= e,\\ \Phi(\boldsymbol{s}_i) &= s_i \text{ for } 0 \le i \le n-1,\\ \Phi(\boldsymbol{p}_i^k) &= P_i^k,\end{aligned}$$

and by

$$\begin{aligned}\Phi(\boldsymbol{C}, r, q_0, \dots, q_{m-1}) &= \Phi(r)(\Phi(q_0), \dots, \Phi(q_{n-1})),\\ \Phi(\boldsymbol{R}, r, q_0, \dots, q_{n-1}) &= f,\end{aligned}$$

where f is obtained from the functions $\Phi(r)$ and $\Phi(q_0), \dots, \Phi(q_{n-1})$ by primitive recursion.

Example 7.2.16 Consider the function $f : (A^*)^2 \longrightarrow A^*$ defined in Example 7.2.7. Recall that $f(x_0, x_1) = x_1x_0$ for $x_0, x_1 \in A^*$. The sequences $(\boldsymbol{p}_0^1)$, and $(\boldsymbol{C}, \boldsymbol{s}_i, \boldsymbol{p}_2^3)$ for $0 \le i \le n-1$ are primitive recursive programs for the functions $g = P_0^1$, and $h_i(x, x_1, y) = s_i(P_2^3(x, x_1, y))$, respectively. Therefore,

$$(\boldsymbol{R}, (\boldsymbol{p}_0^1), (\boldsymbol{C}, \boldsymbol{s}_0, \boldsymbol{p}_2^3), \dots, (\boldsymbol{C}, \boldsymbol{s}_{n-1}, \boldsymbol{p}_2^3))$$

is a primitive recursive program for f. □

It is clear that a function h is primitive recursive if and only if there exists a primitive recursive program $\boldsymbol{p}$ such that $\Phi(\boldsymbol{p}) = h$. Since primitive recursive programs can be listed effectively, it follows that we can list effectively the set of all primitive recursive functions. An interesting consequence of this fact is given in the next theorem.

Theorem 7.2.17 *There are effectively computable functions that are not primitive recursive.*

Proof. Let A be an alphabet and let $f_0, f_1, \dots, f_n, \dots$ be a list of all unary primitive recursive functions on A. Define the function $f : A^* \longrightarrow A^*$ by

$$f(x) = \begin{cases} f_n(a_0^n)a_0 & \text{if } x = a_0^n \in \{a_0\}^* \\ \lambda & \text{otherwise} \end{cases}$$

It is clear that f is effectively computable. However, f is not primitive recursive. Indeed, if f were primitive recursive, f would appear in the above list of primitive recursive functions and we would able to write $f = f_j$ for some $j \in \mathbb{N}$. But, this leads to a contradiction since $f(a_0^j) = f_j(a_0^j) \neq f_j(a_0^j)a_0$. ∎

The proof used in the previous theorem is another example of the technique known as diagonalization first introduced in Section 1.6.

7.3 Primitive Recursive Predicates

To enlarge our collection of primitive recursive functions we introduce the notion of a primitive recursive predicate which we already used in an informal manner. We represent truth values *true* and *false* as two words: a_0 and λ, respectively.

Definition 7.3.1 Let $A = \{a_0, \ldots, a_{n-1}\}$ be an alphabet, where $n \geq 1$. An *m-ary predicate on* A^* is a function $p : (A^*)^m \longrightarrow A^*$ whose range is $\{\lambda, a_0\}$; we assume $m \geq 0$. A function p is a predicate if it is an m-ary predicate for some $m \in \mathbb{N}$.

A *primitive recursive predicate* is a predicate that is a primitive recursive function. □

Example 7.3.2 The unary predicate $\mathsf{isnotnull}$ defined for $x \in A^*$ by

$$\mathsf{isnotnull}(x) = \begin{cases} \lambda & \text{if } x = \lambda \\ a_0 & \text{otherwise} \end{cases}$$

is primitive recursive since we can write

$$\begin{aligned} \mathsf{isnotnull}(\lambda) &= \lambda \\ \mathsf{isnotnull}(xa) &= c_{a_0}(P_0^2(x, \mathsf{isnotnull}(x)), \end{aligned}$$

for $x \in A^*$ and $a \in A$. Similarly, the predicate isnull given for $x \in A^*$ by

$$\mathsf{isnull}(x) = \begin{cases} a_0 & \text{if } x = \lambda \\ \lambda & \text{otherwise} \end{cases}$$

is primitive recursive because

$$\begin{aligned} \mathsf{isnull}(\lambda) &= a_0 \\ \mathsf{isnull}(xa) &= c_{\lambda}(P_0^2(x, \mathsf{isnull}(x)), \end{aligned}$$

for $x \in A^*$ and $a \in A$. □

Example 7.3.3 Let $A = \{a_0, \ldots, a_{n-1}\}$ be an alphabet and end_i be the unary predicate defined by $\mathsf{end}_i(x) = a_0$ if $\mathsf{lastof}(x) = a_i$ for $0 \leq i \leq n-1$. We have

$$\begin{aligned} \mathsf{end}_i(\lambda) &= \lambda \\ \mathsf{end}_i(xa_j) &= h_j(x, \mathsf{end}_i(x)), \end{aligned}$$

for $x \in A^*$, where $h_j(x, y)$ is $c^2_{a_0}$ if $j = i$ and c^2_{λ}, otherwise.

As an example, consider the predicate $\mathsf{samelast}(x, y)$ defined to be true if and only if the last symbol of x is the same as the last symbol of y. Formally, we have

$$\mathsf{samelast}(x, y) = \begin{cases} a_0 & \text{if } \mathsf{lastof}(x) = \mathsf{lastof}(y) \\ \lambda & \text{otherwise,} \end{cases}$$

for $x, y \in A^*$.

The primitive recursiveness of this predicate follows from the following definition by primitive recursion:

$$\begin{aligned} \mathsf{samelast}(x, \lambda) &= \mathsf{isnull}(x) \\ \mathsf{samelast}(x, ya_i) &= \mathsf{end}_i(x), \end{aligned}$$

for $x, y \in A^*$ and $a_i \in A$. □

The standard operations on the truth values are defined by:

x	y	$x \vee y$	$x \wedge y$
a_0	a_0	a_0	a_0
a_0	λ	a_0	λ
λ	a_0	a_0	λ
λ	λ	λ	λ

and

x	$\neg x$
a_0	λ
λ	a_0

Both $\vee$ and $\wedge$ are idempotent, commutative, and associative. In other words, we have

$$
\begin{aligned}
x \vee x &= x, & x \wedge x &= x\\
x \vee y &= y \vee x, & x \wedge y &= y \wedge x\\
x \vee (y \vee z) &= (x \vee y) \vee z, & x \wedge (y \wedge z) &= (x \wedge y) \wedge z,
\end{aligned}
$$

for every $x, y, z \in \{\lambda, a_0\}$. Also, we have the equalities

$$
\begin{aligned}
\neg(x \vee y) &= (\neg x) \wedge (\neg y)\\
\neg(x \wedge y) &= (\neg x) \vee (\neg y)
\end{aligned}
$$

known as the *DeMorgan laws.* We leave to the reader the easy verification of these identities.

These operations allow us to define new predicates. If p, q are both m-ary predicates on A^*, then the predicates $(p \vee q), (p \wedge q), (\neg p)$ are defined by

$$
\begin{aligned}
(p \vee q)(x_0, \ldots, x_{m-1}) &= p(x_0, \ldots, x_{m-1}) \vee q(x_0, \ldots, x_{m-1})\\
(p \wedge q)(x_0, \ldots, x_{m-1}) &= p(x_0, \ldots, x_{m-1}) \wedge q(x_0, \ldots, x_{m-1})\\
(\neg p)(x_0, \ldots, x_{m-1}) &= \neg p(x_0, \ldots, x_{m-1}),
\end{aligned}
$$

for every $x_0, \ldots, x_{m-1} \in A^*$.

Observe that $(p \vee q)(x_0, \ldots, x_{m-1}) = a_0$ if and only if at least one of $p(x_0, \ldots, x_{m-1})$ or $q(x_0, \ldots, x_{m-1})$ equals a_0, while $(p \wedge q)(x_0, \ldots, x_{m-1}) = a_0$ if and only if both $p(x_0, \ldots, x_{m-1})$ and $q(x_0, \ldots, x_{m-1})$ equal a_0.

Theorem 7.3.4 *If p, q are m-ary primitive recursive predicates on A^*, then so are $(p \vee q)$, $(p \wedge q)$ and $(\neg p)$.*

Proof. Note that $(\neg p)(x_0, \ldots, x_{m-1}) = \mathsf{isnull}(p(x_0, \ldots, x_{m-1}))$. Thus, if p is primitive recursive, then so is $(\neg p)$.

To prove that the primitive recursiveness of p, q implies the same property for $(p \wedge q)$ observe that

$$
\begin{aligned}
&(p \wedge q)(x_0, \ldots, x_{m-1})\\
&\quad = \mathsf{isnotnull}(\mathsf{conc}(p(x_0, \ldots, x_{m-1}), q(x_0, \ldots, x_{m-1}))),
\end{aligned}
$$

for $x_0, \ldots, x_{m-1} \in A^*$. On the other hand, we can write

$$
(p \vee q) = \neg((\neg p) \wedge (\neg q)),
$$

which implies the primitive recursiveness of $(p \vee q)$. ∎

Example 7.3.5 Let samelength be defined by $\mathsf{samelength}(x, y) = a_0$ if and only if $|x| = |y|$. Note that $|x| = |y|$ if and only if both $x -_l y = \lambda$ and $y -_l x = \lambda$. Therefore,

$$
\mathsf{samelength}(x, y) = \mathsf{isnull}(x -_l y) \wedge \mathsf{isnull}(y -_l x),
$$

for $x, y \in A^*$. Since both $\mathsf{isnull}(x -_l y)$ and $\mathsf{isnull}(y -_l x)$ are primitive recursive, so is samelength. □

Example 7.3.6 Let $k \in \mathbb{N}$. Consider the following predicates related to the length of words:

$$\begin{array}{ll} \mathsf{length}_{=k}(x) = a_0 & \text{if and only if } |x| = k, \\ \mathsf{length}_{\leq k}(x) = a_0 & \text{if and only if } |x| \leq k, \\ \mathsf{length}_{<k}(x) = a_0 & \text{if and only if } |x| < k, \\ \mathsf{length}_{\geq k}(x) = a_0 & \text{if and only if } |x| \geq k, \\ \mathsf{length}_{>k}(x) = a_0 & \text{if and only if } |x| > k, \end{array}$$

for $x \in A^*$.

It is easy to see that $\mathsf{length}_{=k}$ is primitive recursive for any $k \in \mathbb{N}$ since

$$\mathsf{length}_{=k}(x) = \mathsf{samelength}(x, a_0^k)$$

for $x \in A^*$.

Next, it is possible to prove by induction on k that every predicate $\mathsf{length}_{\leq k}$ is primitive recursive. Note that $\mathsf{length}_{\leq 0} = \mathsf{length}_{=0}$, so the primitive recursiveness of $\mathsf{length}_{\leq 0}$ is established. Suppose that $\mathsf{length}_{\leq k}$ is primitive recursive. Since $\mathsf{length}_{\leq k+1}(x) = \mathsf{length}_{\leq k}(\mathsf{trimlast}(x))$ for $x \in A^*$, it follows that $\mathsf{length}_{\leq k+1}$ is primitive recursive.

The primitive recursiveness of the remaining predicates is a direct consequence of Theorem 7.3.4. □

Theorem 7.3.7 (Definition by Cases) *Let p be an m-ary primitive recursive predicate, where $m \geq 0$, and let $f, g : (A^*)^m \longrightarrow A^*$ be two primitive recursive functions. Then, the function $h : (A^*)^m \longrightarrow A^*$ defined by*

$$h(x_0, \ldots, x_{m-1}) = \begin{cases} f(x_0, \ldots, x_{m-1}) & \text{if } p(x_0, \ldots, x_{m-1}) = a_0 \\ g(x_0, \ldots, x_{m-1}) & \text{otherwise} \end{cases}$$

is primitive recursive.

Proof. Define the function $\mathsf{step} : (A^*)^2 \longrightarrow A^*$ by

$$\mathsf{step}(x, x_1) = \begin{cases} \lambda & \text{if } x = \lambda \\ x_1 & \text{otherwise,} \end{cases}$$

for $x, x_1 \in A^*$. This is a primitive recursive function since we can write

$$\begin{array}{rcccl} \mathsf{step}(\lambda, x_1) & = & \lambda & = & e(x_1) \\ \mathsf{step}(xa_i, x_1) & = & x_1 & = & P_2^3(x, x_1, \mathsf{step}(x, x_1)), \end{array}$$

for $x, x_1 \in A^*$ and $a \in A$.

Note that we can write

$$\begin{array}{rcl} h(x_0, \ldots, x_{m-1}) & = & \mathsf{conc}(\mathsf{step}(p(x_0, \ldots, x_{m-1}), f(x_0, \ldots, x_{m-1})), \\ & & \mathsf{step}(\neg p(x_0, \ldots, x_{m-1}), g(x_0, \ldots, x_{m-1}))), \end{array}$$

which implies that h is primitive recursive. ∎

The definition by cases can be extended as follows. Let $p_0, p_1, \ldots, p_k$ be $k+1$ m-ary predicates on A^* that are *pairwise incompatible*. This means that $(p_i \wedge p_j)(x_0, \ldots, x_{m-1}) = \lambda$ for $0 \leq i, j \leq k$, $i \neq j$ and $x_0, \ldots, x_{m-1} \in A^*$.

Corollary 7.3.8 (Definition by Cases) *Let $p_0, p_1, \ldots, p_{k-1}$ be m-ary recursive predicates and let $f_0, \ldots, f_k : (A^*)^m \longrightarrow A^*$ be $k+1$ primitive recursive functions, where $k \geq 1$. Then, the function $h : (A^*)^m \longrightarrow A^*$ defined by*

$$h(x_0, \ldots, x_{m-1}) = \begin{cases} f_0(x_0, \ldots, x_{m-1}) & \textit{if } p_0(x_0, \ldots, x_{m-1}) = a_0 \\ f_1(x_0, \ldots, x_{m-1}) & \textit{if } p_1(x_0, \ldots, x_{m-1}) = a_0 \\ \vdots & \\ f_{k-1}(x_0, \ldots, x_{m-1}) & \textit{if } p_{k-1}(x_0, \ldots, x_{m-1}) = a_0 \\ f_k(x_0, \ldots, x_{m-1}) & \textit{otherwise} \end{cases}$$

is primitive recursive.

Proof. The argument is by induction on k. The base case, $k = 1$, was proved in Theorem 7.3.7.

Consider the function $h : (A^*)^m \longrightarrow A^*$ given by

$$h(x_0, \ldots, x_{m-1}) = \begin{cases} f_0(x_0, \ldots, x_{m-1}) & \text{if } p_0(x_0, \ldots, x_{m-1}) = a_0 \\ f_1(x_0, \ldots, x_{m-1}) & \text{if } p_1(x_0, \ldots, x_{m-1}) = a_0 \\ \vdots & \\ f_k(x_0, \ldots, x_{m-1}) & \text{if } p_k(x_0, \ldots, x_{m-1}) = a_0 \\ f_{k+1}(x_0, \ldots, x_{m-1}) & \text{otherwise,} \end{cases}$$

for $x_0, \ldots, x_{m-1}$, and let $g : (A^*)^m \longrightarrow A^*$ be the function defined by

$$g(x_0, \ldots, x_{m-1}) = \begin{cases} f_k(x_0, \ldots, x_{m-1}) & \text{if } p_k(x_0, \ldots, x_{m-1}) = a_0 \\ f_{k+1}(x_0, \ldots, x_{m-1}) & \text{otherwise} \end{cases}$$

The function g is primitive recursive by Theorem 7.3.7. We can write:

$$h(x_0, \ldots, x_{m-1}) = \begin{cases} f_0(x_0, \ldots, x_{m-1}) & \text{if } p_0(x_0, \ldots, x_{m-1}) = a_0 \\ f_1(x_0, \ldots, x_{m-1}) & \text{if } p_1(x_0, \ldots, x_{m-1}) = a_0 \\ \vdots & \\ f_{k-1}(x_0, \ldots, x_{m-1}) & \text{if } p_{k-1}(x_0, \ldots, x_{m-1}) = a_0 \\ g(x_0, \ldots, x_{m-1}) & \text{otherwise,} \end{cases}$$

for $x_0, \ldots, x_{m-1}$. By the inductive hypothesis, h is primitive recursive. ∎

The technique introduced by the next definition is referred to as *bounded quantification.* We write $x \leq_{\text{pref}} y$ if and only $x \in \mathsf{PREF}(y)$ and $x <_{\text{pref}} y$ if $x \in \mathsf{PREF}(y)$ and $x \neq y$.

Definition 7.3.9 The m-ary predicate q on A^* is obtained through *bounded existential quantification* from the m-ary predicate p on A^*, where $m \geq 1$ if $q(y, x_1, \ldots, x_{m-1}) = a_0$ if and only if there is an $x \in \mathsf{PREF}(y)$ such that $p(x, x_1, \ldots, x_{m-1}) = a_0$.

The m-ary predicate r on A^* is obtained through *bounded universal quantification* from p if $r(y, x_1, \ldots, x_{m-1}) = a_0$ if and only if for every $x \in \mathsf{PREF}(y)$ we have $p(x, x_1, \ldots, x_{m-1}) = a_0$.

The predicate q is denoted by

$$q(y, x_1, \ldots, x_{m-1}) = (\exists x \leq_{\text{pref}} y) p(x, x_1, \ldots, x_{m-1}),$$

similarly, the predicate r is denoted by

$$r(y, x_1, \ldots, x_{m-1}) = (\forall x \leq_{\text{pref}} y) p(x, x_1, \ldots, x_{m-1}).$$

□

Theorem 7.3.10 *Let p be an m-ary primitive recursive predicate. Both $q = (\exists x \leq_{\text{pref}} y)p$ and $r = (\forall x \leq_{\text{pref}} y)p$ are primitive recursive predicates.*

Proof. Note that $q(\lambda, x_1, \ldots, x_{m-1}) = p(\lambda, x_1, \ldots, x_{m-1})$; also, it is easy to see that $q(xa, x_1, \ldots, x_{m-1}) = a_0$ if and only if $q(x, x_1, \ldots, x_{m-1}) = a_0$ or $p(xa, x_1, \ldots, x_{m-1}) = a_0$.

These observations are formally stated in

$$\begin{aligned} q(\lambda, x_1, \ldots, x_{m-1}) &= p(\lambda, x_1, \ldots, x_{m-1}) \\ q(xa, x_1, \ldots, x_{m-1}) &= \mathsf{isnotnull}(\mathsf{conc}(q(x, x_1, \ldots, x_{m-1}), \\ &\quad p(xa, x_1, \ldots, x_{m-1})), \end{aligned}$$

for $x, x_1, \ldots, x_{m-1} \in A^*$. Thus, q is primitive recursive.

The primitive recursiveness of r follows immediately by observing that

$$(\forall x \leq_{\text{pref}} y) p(x, x_1, \ldots, x_{m-1}) = \neg(\exists x \leq_{\text{pref}} y)(\neg p(x, x_1, \ldots, x_{m-1})),$$

for $x, x_1, \ldots, x_{m-1} \in A^*$ (cf. Exercise 17). ■

Example 7.3.11 Define the predicate $(x = y)$ by

$$(x = y) = \begin{cases} a_0 & \text{if } x \text{ equals } y \\ \lambda & \text{otherwise} \end{cases}$$

for $x, y \in A^*$. The words x, y are equal if and only if they have the same length and both prefixes of length l of x and y end in the same symbol for $0 \leq l \leq |x| = |y|$. If z is a prefix of x, in order to obtain the prefix of the same length of the word y, we reverse y, erase the first $|x| - |z|$ symbols and, then, reverse back the resulting word. In other words,

$$\begin{aligned} (x = y) &= \mathsf{samelength}(x, y) \wedge \\ &\quad (\forall z \leq_{\text{pref}} x)(\mathsf{lastof}(z) = \mathsf{lastof}(\mathsf{rev}(\mathsf{rev}(y) -_l (x -_l z)))), \end{aligned}$$

which allows us to conclude that $(x = y)$ is primitive recursive. This implies immediately that the inequality predicate $(x \neq y)$ is also primitive recursive. □

Example 7.3.12 Let $\mathsf{occ} : (A^*)^2 \longrightarrow A^*$ be the function given by $\mathsf{occ}(x, y) = a_0^n$ if y occurs n times as an infix of x. For example, aa occurs three times in $aaaa$, while ab occurs twice in $abab$. In other words, we have $\mathsf{occ}(aaaa, aa) = 3$ and $\mathsf{occ}(abab, ab) = 2$.

The primitive recursiveness of the equality predicate established in Example 7.3.11 allows us to show that occ is primitive recursive.

It is easy to see that the equalities

$$\begin{aligned} \mathsf{occ}(\lambda, y) &= a_0^0 \\ \mathsf{occ}(xa_i, y) &= \mathsf{conc}((\exists t \leq_{\text{pref}} xa_i)(ty = xa_i), \mathsf{occ}(x, y)) \end{aligned}$$

for $a_i \in A$, constitute a definition of occ by primitive recursion. Thus, occ is primitive recursive. □

Example 7.3.13 Consider the predicate $(x \leq_{\text{pref}} y)$ defined by

$$(x \leq_{\text{pref}} y) = \begin{cases} a_0 & \text{if } x \in \mathsf{PREF}(y) \\ \lambda & \text{otherwise} \end{cases}$$

for $x, y \in A^*$. The primitive recursiveness of $(x \leq_{\text{pref}} y)$ follows from $(x \leq_{\text{pref}} y) = (\exists z \leq_{\text{pref}} y)(x = z)$.

A similar predicate, $x <_{\text{pref}} y$ is given by

$$(x <_{\text{pref}} y) = \begin{cases} a_0 & \text{if } x \in \mathsf{PREFpr}(y) \\ \lambda & \text{otherwise} \end{cases}$$

for $x, y \in A^*$. This predicate is primitive recursive since

$$(x <_{\text{pref}} y) = (x \leq_{\text{pref}} y) \wedge (x \neq y),$$

for $x, y \in A^*$. □

Example 7.3.14 Define the predicate $(x \leq_{\text{infix}} y)$ by $(x \leq_{\text{infix}} y)$ if and only if $x \in \mathsf{INFIX}(y)$. Similarly, $(x <_{\text{infix}} y)$ if and only if $x \in \mathsf{INFIXpr}(y)$. Since

$$(x \leq_{\text{infix}} y) = (\exists z \leq_{\text{pref}} y)(\exists u \leq_{\text{pref}} y)(z = ux)$$

for $x, y \in A^*$ it follows that $(x \leq_{\text{infix}} y)$ is primitive recursive. The primitive recursiveness of $(x <_{\text{infix}} y)$ follows from the equality

$$(x <_{\text{infix}} y) = (x \leq_{\text{infix}} y) \wedge (x \neq y)$$

for $x, y \in A^*$. □

We shall see (in Section 8.5.4) that the bound imposed on z in building a predicate like $(\exists z \leq_{\text{pref}} y)q(x, y)$ is essential.

7.4 Bounded Minimalization

Bounded minimalization gives us a way to construct primitive recursive functions starting with primitive recursive predicates.

Let p be an $(m+1)$-ary predicate on A^*, where $m \geq 0$, and let $y, x_1, \ldots, x_m \in A^*$. If there is a prefix u of y such that $p(u, x_1, \ldots, x_m) = a_0$, let t be the shortest such prefix. Define $(\min u \leq_{\text{pref}} y)p(u, x_1, \ldots, x_m)$ to be that shortest t if t exists; otherwise, that is, if no such prefix exists, define $(\min u \leq_{\text{pref}} y)p(u, x_1, \ldots, x_m) = ya_0$. The function $f : (A^*)^{m+1} \longrightarrow A^*$ given by

$$f(y, x_1, \ldots, x_m) = (\min u \leq_{\text{pref}} y)p(u, x_1, \ldots, x_m),$$

for $y, x_1, \ldots, x_m \in A^*$ is said to be obtained from p by *bounded minimalization.*

We prove that if p is a primitive recursive predicate, then the function obtained from p by bounded minimalization is primitive recursive. To this end we need the following technical result.

Lemma 7.4.1 *Let $g : (A^*)^{m+1} \longrightarrow A^*$ be a primitive recursive function. Then, the function $h : (A^*)^{m+1} \longrightarrow A^*$ defined by*

$$h(y, x_1, \ldots, x_m) = g(y_{0,0}, x_1, \ldots, x_m) g(y_{0,1}, x_1, \ldots, x_m) \cdots g(y_{0,|y|}, x_1, \ldots, x_m)$$

for $y, x_1, \ldots, x_m \in A^*$ is primitive recursive.

Proof. The function h can be defined by primitive recursion as

$$\begin{aligned} h(\lambda, x_1, \ldots, x_m) &= g(\lambda, x_1, \ldots, x_m) \\ h(ya_i, x_1, \ldots, x_m) &= \mathsf{conc}(g(ya_i, x_1, \ldots, x_m), h(y, x_1, \ldots, x_m)), \end{aligned}$$

for $y, x_1, \ldots, x_m \in A^*$ and $a_i \in A$. This shows that h is primitive recursive. ∎

The function h defined above is denoted by

$$h(y, x_1, \ldots, x_m) = \prod_{z \in \mathsf{PREF}(y)} g(z, x_1, \ldots, x_m).$$

Theorem 7.4.2 (Bounded Minimalization Theorem) *Let p be an $(m+1)$-ary primitive recursive predicate. The function $f : (A^*)^{m+1} \longrightarrow A^*$ given by*

$$f(y, x_1, \ldots, x_m) = (\min u \leq_{\text{pref}} y) p(u, x_1, \ldots, x_m),$$

for $y, x_1, \ldots, x_m \in A^*$ is primitive recursive.

Proof. Suppose that there is a prefix u of y such that $p(u, x_1, \ldots, x_m) = a_0$, and let t be the shortest such prefix. Consider the function

$$h(w, x_1, \ldots, x_m) = \prod_{z \in \mathsf{PREF}(w)} p(z, x_1, \ldots, x_m),$$

for $x_1, \ldots, x_m \in A^*$ and $w \in \mathsf{PREF}(y)$. It is easy to see that $h(w, x_1, \ldots, x_m) = \lambda$ if $|w| < |t|$, and $h(w, x_1, \ldots, x_m) \neq \lambda$, otherwise. Consequently, for the function g given by

$$g(y, x_1, \ldots, x_m) = \prod_{w \in \mathsf{PREF}(y)} \mathsf{isnull}(h(w, x_1, \ldots, x_m))$$

for $y, x_1, \ldots, x_m \in A^*$, we have $g(y, x_1, \ldots, x_m) = a_0^{|t|}$, where t is the shortest prefix of y such that $p(t, x_1, \ldots, x_m) = a_0$. Thus,

$$\begin{aligned} &(\min u \leq_{\text{pref}} y) p(y, x_1, \ldots, x_m) \\ &= \begin{cases} y -_r (y -_r g(y, x_1, \ldots, x_m)) \text{ if } (\exists u \leq_{\text{pref}} y) p(u, x_1, \ldots, x_m) \\ ya_0 \text{ otherwise,} \end{cases} \end{aligned}$$

which proves the primitive recursiveness of f. ∎

Example 7.4.3 Define the function $\mathsf{lleftmost}(w, x) = u$ if u is the shortest prefix of w such that $w = uxv$, that is, the word to the left of the leftmost occurrence of x in w.

A related function is $\mathsf{rleftmost}(w, x) = v$ if $u = \mathsf{lleftmost}(w, x)$ and $w = uxv$. In other words, $\mathsf{rleftmost}(w, x)$ gives the suffix of w that begins at the right of the leftmost occurrence of x in w.

The function $\mathsf{lleftmost}$ is primitive recursive since we can write

$$\mathsf{lleftmost}(w, x) = (\min u \leq_{\text{pref}} w)(\mathsf{conc}(u, x) \leq_{\text{pref}} w).$$

The primitive recursiveness of $\mathsf{rleftmost}$ is implied by the equality

$$\mathsf{rleftmost}(w, x) = w -_l \mathsf{conc}(\mathsf{lleftmost}(w, x), x)$$

for $x, w \in A^*$.

Suppose that x, w be two words such that x separates the word w in $k+1$ pieces as in

$$w = w_0 x w_1 x \cdots w_{k-1} x w_k,$$

where x does not occur anywhere else in w. Let $\mathsf{part}(w, x, y)$ be equal to w_m if $|y| = m$. If $|y| \geq k$, then $\mathsf{part}(w, x, y) = \lambda$. The function part is primitive recursive because

$$\begin{aligned} \mathsf{part}(w, x, \lambda) &= \mathsf{lleftmost}(w, x) \\ \mathsf{part}(w, x, ya) &= \mathsf{part}(\mathsf{rleftmost}(w, x), x, y), \end{aligned}$$

for $a \in A$ and $w, x, a \in A^*$.

Finally, let $\mathsf{repl}(x, w, z)$ ($\mathsf{repl}'(x, w, z)$) be the result of replacing the leftmost (the rightmost) occurrence of x in w by z, respectively. Since

$$\mathsf{repl}(x, w, z) = \mathsf{lleftmost}(w, x)\ z\ \mathsf{rleftmost}(w, x)$$

for $x, w, z \in A^*$, we conclude that repl is also primitive recursive.

The equality $\mathsf{repl}'(x, w, z) = \mathsf{rev}(\mathsf{repl}(\mathsf{rev}(x), \mathsf{rev}(w), \mathsf{rev}(z)))$ for $x, w, z \in A^*$, implies that repl' is also a recursive function. □

7.5 Extensions

Primitive recursive functions defined on an alphabet must sometimes be restricted to words that are written using symbols of a subset of the alphabet, or extended to the set of words written on a larger alphabet. In this section we examine extensions of primitive recursive functions that preserve the primitive recursiveness. Restrictions are studied in Section 7.7.

Definition 7.5.1 Let A, B be two alphabets such that $A \subseteq B$, and let $f : (A^*)^k \longrightarrow A^*$ be a primitive recursive function. The *null extension* of f to B is the function $\overline{f} : (B^*)^k \longrightarrow B^*$ defined by

$$\overline{f}(x_0, \ldots, x_{k-1}) = \begin{cases} f(x_0, \ldots, x_{k-1}) & \text{if } (x_0, \ldots, x_{k-1}) \in (A^*)^k \\ \lambda & \text{otherwise} \end{cases}$$

□

Let A, B be two alphabets such that

$$A = \{a_0, \ldots, a_{n-1}\}, B = \{a_0, \ldots, a_{n-1}, \ldots, a_{p-1}\},$$

where $n < p$. It is easy to see that p_{A^*}, the characteristic predicate of A^* is a primitive recursive predicate on B. Indeed, we have

$$\begin{aligned} p_{A^*}(\lambda) &= a_0 \\ p_{A^*}(xa) &= \begin{cases} a_0 & \text{if } p_{A^*}(x) = a_0 \text{ and } a \in A \\ \lambda & \text{otherwise,} \end{cases} \end{aligned}$$

for $x \in B^*$ and $a \in B$. This implies that the characteristic predicate $p_{(A^*)^m}$ is a primitive recursive predicate on B for every $m \in \mathbb{N}$ since

$$p_{(A^*)^m}(x_0, \ldots, x_{m-1}) = p_{A^*}(x_0) \wedge \cdots \wedge p_{A^*}(x_{m-1}),$$

for $x_0, \ldots, x_{m-1} \in B^*$. These observations are used in the proof of the next theorem.

Theorem 7.5.2 (Null Extension Theorem) *Let $A = \{a_0, \ldots, a_{n-1}\}$ and $B = \{a_0, \ldots, a_{n-1}, \ldots, a_{p-1}\}$, where $n < p$. If $f : (A^*)^m \longrightarrow A^*$ is a primitive recursive function on A, then its null extension is a primitive recursive function on B.*

Proof. The argument is by structural induction on the definition of primitive recursive functions. For the base case we need to consider the basic recursive functions on A.

The null extension $\overline{e}$ of the null function e on A is the null function on B, so $\overline{e}$ is obviously primitive recursive.

The null extension $\overline{s_i}$ of a successor function s_i (where $0 \leq i \leq n-1$) is primitive recursive because we can write:

$$\begin{aligned} \overline{s_i}(\lambda) &= a_i \\ \overline{s_i}(xa_j) &= \begin{cases} s_i(xa_j) & \text{if } x \in A^* \text{ and } 0 \leq j \leq n-1 \\ \lambda & \text{otherwise.} \end{cases} \end{aligned}$$

For the projection P_i^m, the last subcase of the base case, we can write:

$$\overline{P_i^m}(x_0, \ldots, x_{m-1}) = \begin{cases} x_i & \text{if } p_{(A^*)^m}(x_0, \ldots, x_{m-1}) \\ \lambda & \text{otherwise,} \end{cases}$$

which allows us to conclude that $\overline{P_i^m}$ is primitive recursive by Theorem 7.3.7.

Suppose now that $f : (A^*)^k \longrightarrow A^*$ is obtained by composition from the primitive recursive functions $h_0, \ldots, h_{m-1}, g$ whose null extensions are primitive recursive functions on B. Since we can write

$$\overline{f}(x_0, \ldots, x_{k-1}) = \begin{cases} \overline{g}(\overline{h_0}(x_0, \ldots, x_{k-1}), \ldots, \overline{h_{m-1}}(x_0, \ldots, x_{k-1})) \\ \quad \text{if } p_{(A^*)^k}(x_0, \ldots, x_{k-1}) \\ \lambda \text{ otherwise,} \end{cases}$$

we conclude that $\overline{f}$ is a primitive recursive function on B.

Finally, suppose that the function $f : (A^*)^m \longrightarrow A^*$ is obtained from the functions g and $h_0, \ldots, h_{n-1}$ by primitive recursion, where the null extensions of the functions g and $h_0, \ldots, h_{n-1}$ are primitive recursive functions on B. It is easy to verify that $\overline{f}$, the null extension of f can be defined by primitive recursion as $\overline{f}(\lambda, x_1, \ldots, x_{m-1}) = \overline{g}(x_1, \ldots, x_{m-1})$, and

$$\begin{aligned}
\overline{f}(xa_0, x_1, \ldots, x_{m-1}) &= \overline{h_0}(x, x_1, \ldots, x_{m-1}, \overline{f}(x, x_1, \ldots, x_{m-1})) \\
&\vdots \\
\overline{f}(xa_{n-1}, x_1, \ldots, x_{m-1}) &= \overline{h_{n-1}}(x, x_1, \ldots, x_{m-1}, \overline{f}(x, x_1, \ldots, x_{m-1})) \\
\overline{f}(xa_n, x_1, \ldots, x_{m-1}) &= c_\lambda^{m+1}(x, x_1, \ldots, x_{m-1}, \overline{f}(x, x_1, \ldots, x_{m-1})) \\
&\vdots \\
\overline{f}(xa_{p-1}, x_1, \ldots, x_{m-1}) &= c_\lambda^{m+1}(x, x_1, \ldots, x_{m-1}, \overline{f}(x, x_1, \ldots, x_{m-1}))
\end{aligned}$$

for every $x, x_1, \ldots, x_{m-1} \in B^*$. By the inductive hypothesis, $\overline{f}$ is indeed primitive recursive. ∎

7.6 Numerical Primitive Recursive Functions

Let $A = \{a_0\}$ be an one-element alphabet. In this section we identify the set A^* with the set $\mathbb{N}$ of natural numbers. In other words, we identify a word a_0^n with the natural number n, and we use the two interchangeably. For example, we identify $\lambda \in \{a_0\}^*$ with 0, and a_0 with 1.

A function $f : (A^*)^m \longrightarrow A^*$ can be naturally regarded as a function $f' : \mathbb{N}^m \longrightarrow \mathbb{N}$ of natural numbers as follows. If $f(a_0^{n_0}, \ldots, a_0^{n_{m-1}}) = a_0^n$, we define $f'(n_0, \ldots, n_{m-1}) = n$ for every $n_0, \ldots, n_{m-1} \in \mathbb{N}$. When there is no risk of confusion, we may write f instead of f'. Similarly, if $p : (\{a_0\}^*)^m \longrightarrow \{a_0\}^*$ is an m-ary predicate over the one-element alphabet $\{a_0\}$, then p can be regarded as a numerical predicate $p' : \mathbb{N}^m \longrightarrow \mathbb{N}$, where $p'(n_0, \ldots, n_{m-1}) = 1$ if $p(a_0^{n_0}, \ldots, a_0^{n_{m-1}}) = a_0$, and $p'(n_0, \ldots, n_{m-1}) = 0$ if $p(a_0^{n_0}, \ldots, a_0^{n_{m-1}}) = \lambda$. When there is no risk of confusion, we may write p rather than p'.

Occasionally, we adopt completely distinct notations for functions defined on natural numbers. The collection of primitive recursive functions and predicates that we built for arbitrary alphabets can be specialized for the case $|A| = 1$ as shown in Figure 7.1.

The two methods that we used to construct primitive recursive functions (composition and primitive recursion) can be specialized for primitive recursive functions on $\mathbb{N}$. The definition of composition remains the same. To examine the primitive recursive functions consider the functions $g : \mathbb{N}^{m-1} \longrightarrow \mathbb{N}$ and $h : \mathbb{N}^{m+1} \longrightarrow \mathbb{N}$.

The function $f : \mathbb{N}^m \longrightarrow \mathbb{N}$ is obtained from g and h by *primitive recursion* if $f(0, x_1, \ldots, x_{m-1}) = g(x_1, \ldots, x_{m-1})$ and $f(x+1, x_1, \ldots, x_{m-1}) = h(x, x_1, \ldots, x_{m-1}, f(x, x_1, \ldots, x_{m-1}))$ for every $x, x_1, \ldots, x_{m-1} \in \mathbb{N}$.

If $m = 1$, $f : \mathbb{N} \longrightarrow \mathbb{N}$ is defined by primitive recursion from h by

$$\begin{aligned}
f(0) &= n_0 \\
f(x+1) &= h(x, f(x)),
\end{aligned}$$

for every $x \in \mathbb{N}$; here n_0 is a number in $\mathbb{N}$.

Example 7.6.1 Let $g : \mathbb{N} \longrightarrow \mathbb{N}$ and $h : \mathbb{N}^3 \longrightarrow \mathbb{N}$ be the functions given by

$$\begin{aligned}
g(x) &= 0 \\
h(x, x_1, x_2) &= x_1 + x_2,
\end{aligned}$$

Function on $\mathbb{N}$	Function on A^*	See
$e(n) = 0$	e	Definition 7.2.1
$s_1(n) = n + 1$	s_i	Definition 7.2.1
$P_i^k(n_0, \ldots, n_{k-1}) = n_i$	P_i^k	Definition 7.2.1
$f(n,p) = n + p$	conc	Example 7.2.7
$c_k(n) = k$	c_w	Example 7.2.9
$n \dot{-} 1 = \begin{cases} n - 1 & \text{if } n > 0 \\ 0 & \text{if } n = 0 \end{cases}$	trimlast	Example 7.2.11
$n \dot{-} p = \begin{cases} n - p & \text{if } n \geq p \\ 0 & \text{if } n < p \end{cases}$ (referred to as the *monus* function)	$x -_l y$	Example 7.2.12
$\text{isnotnull}(n) = \begin{cases} 0 & \text{if } n = 0 \\ 1 & \text{otherwise} \end{cases}$	isnotnull(x)	Example 7.3.2
$n \omega k$, where ω is one of $=, \neq, <, \leq, >, \geq$		Example 7.3.6

Figure 7.1: Numerical Primitive Recursive Functions

for $x, x_1, x_2 \in \mathbb{N}$. The function g is the constant function c_0, so it is a primitive recursive function. The primitive recursiveness of h follows from the equality

$$h(x, x_1, x_2) = P_1^3(x, x_1, x_2) + P_2^3(x, x_1, x_2)$$

for $x, x_1, x_2 \in \mathbb{N}$ since the addition was shown to be primitive recursive (cf. Figure 7.1).

Let $f : \mathbb{N}^2 \longrightarrow \mathbb{N}$ be the function defined by primitive recursion from g and h; we prove, by induction on x, that $f(x, x_1) = x \cdot x_1$ for $x, x_1 \in \mathbb{N}$. The base case, $x = 0$ is immediate. Suppose that the equality holds for x. Then,

$$f(x+1, x_1) = h(x, x_1, f(x, x_1)) = x_1 + f(x, x_1) = x_1 + x x_1 = (x+1)x_1,$$

which concludes the inductive step. □

Example 7.6.2 Consider the functions $g : \mathbb{N} \longrightarrow \mathbb{N}$ and $h : \mathbb{N}^3 \longrightarrow \mathbb{N}$ given by

$$\begin{aligned} g(x) &= 1 \\ h(x, x_1, x_2) &= x_1 \cdot x_2, \end{aligned}$$

for $x, x_1, x_2 \in \mathbb{N}$. The function g is the constant function c_1, so it is a primitive recursive function. The primitive recursiveness of h follows from the equality

$$h(x, x_1, x_2) = P_1^3(x, x_1, x_2) \cdot P_2^3(x, x_1, x_2)$$

for $x, x_1, x_2 \in \mathbb{N}$ and from the primitive recursiveness of multiplication shown in Example 7.6.1.

We leave to the reader (see Exercise 32) to show that the function $f : \mathbb{N}^2 \longrightarrow \mathbb{N}$ defined by primitive recursion from g and h is given by

$$f(x, x_1) = \begin{cases} 1 & \text{if } x = 0 \\ x_1^x & \text{if } x > 0 \end{cases} \tag{7.1}$$

for $x, x_1 \in \mathbb{N}$. So, exponentiation is a primitive recursive function.

Consider the function $\ell : \mathbb{N} \longrightarrow \mathbb{N}$ given by $\ell(x) = 2^x$ for $x \in \mathbb{N}$. If f is the exponentiation function, then

$$\begin{aligned} \ell(0) &= 1 \\ \ell(x) &= f(P_1^1(x), c_2(x)) \end{aligned}$$

for $x \in \mathbb{N}$, so ℓ is primitive recursive. □

Example 7.6.3 The factorial function $f : \mathbb{N} \longrightarrow \mathbb{N}$ given by $f(0) = 1$ and $f(x) = 1 \cdot 2 \cdot \cdots \cdot x$ if $x \geq 1$, is defined by primitive recursion as

$$\begin{aligned} f(0) &= 1 \\ f(x+1) &= s_1(x) \cdot f(x), \end{aligned}$$

for $x \in \mathbb{N}$. This implies the primitive recursiveness of f. □

The next theorem is the numerical counterpart of Lemma 7.4.1.

Theorem 7.6.4 *Let $g : \mathbb{N}^{m+1} \longrightarrow \mathbb{N}$ be a primitive recursive function. Then, the functions $h, h' : \mathbb{N}^{m+1} \longrightarrow \mathbb{N}$ defined by*

$$h(p, q_1, \ldots, q_m) = $$
$$g(0, q_1, \ldots, q_m) + g(1, q_1, \ldots, q_m) + \cdots + g(p, q_1, \ldots, q_m)$$
$$h'(p, q_1, \ldots, q_m) = $$
$$g(0, q_1, \ldots, q_m) \cdot g(1, q_1, \ldots, q_m) \cdot \cdots \cdot g(p, q_1, \ldots, q_m)$$

for $p, q_1, \ldots, q_m \in \mathbb{N}$ are primitive recursive.

Proof. The first part of the theorem follows directly from the lemma mentioned before since concatenation specializes to addition. We leave the second part of the theorem to the reader. ∎

Next, we translate the results involving primitive recursive predicates.

Example 7.6.5 The numerical variant of the predicate isnotnull introduced in Example 7.3.2 is

$$\mathsf{isnotnull}(x) = \begin{cases} 0 & \text{if } x = 0 \\ 1 & \text{otherwise} \end{cases}$$

□

Example 7.6.6 The primitive recursiveness of the predicates

$$x = k, x \leq k, x < k, x \geq k, x > k,$$

follows from the primitive recursiveness of the corresponding predicates given in Example 7.3.6 for every $k \in \mathbb{N}$. Similarly, the binary predicate $(x = y)$ is primitive recursive.

The primitive recursiveness of the predicates $(x \leq y)$ and $(x < y)$ follows from Example 7.3.13. □

Given two n-ary numerical predicates p, q, the predicates $(p \vee q)$, $(p \wedge q)$ and $(\neg p)$ can be redefined now as

$$\begin{aligned}(p \vee q)(x_0, \ldots, x_{m-1}) &= \max\{p(x_0, \ldots, x_{m-1}), q(x_0, \ldots, x_{m-1})\},\\ (p \wedge q)(x_0, \ldots, x_{m-1}) &= \min\{p(x_0, \ldots, x_{m-1}), q(x_0, \ldots, x_{m-1})\},\\ (\neg p)(x_0, \ldots, x_{m-1}) &= 1 - p(x_0, \ldots, x_{m-1}).\end{aligned}$$

The primitive recursiveness of p, q implies immediately the primitive recursiveness of $(p \vee q), (p \wedge q)$ and $(\neg q)$.

If p is an m-ary predicate on $\mathbb{N}$, where $m \geq 1$, then the m-ary predicate q on A^* is obtained through bounded existential quantification from p if $q(y, x_1, \ldots, x_{m-1}) = 1$ if and only if there is $x \in \mathbb{N}$, $x \leq y$ such that $p(x, x_1, \ldots, x_{m-1}) = 1$.

The m-ary predicate r on $\mathbb{N}$ is obtained through bounded universal quantification from p if $r(y, x_1, \ldots, x_{m-1}) = 1$ if and only if for every $x \in \mathbb{N}$, $x \leq y$ we have $p(x, x_1, \ldots, x_{m-1}) = 1$.

The predicate q is denoted by $(\exists x \leq y)p(x, x_1, \ldots, x_{m-1})$; similarly, the predicate r is denoted by $(\forall x \leq y)p(x, x_1, \ldots, x_{m-1})$.

The closure of the collection of primitive recursive predicates under bounded existential and universal quantifications is an immediate consequence of Theorem 7.3.10.

Example 7.6.7 The binary predicate $(y|x)$ that is true if y is a divisor of x is primitive recursive because

$$(y|x) = (\exists u \leq x)(uy = x).$$

This allows us to show that the predicate prime given by

$$\mathsf{prime}(x) = \begin{cases} 1 & \text{if } x \text{ is a prime number} \\ 0 & \text{otherwise,} \end{cases}$$

for $x \in \mathbb{N}$ is primitive recursive because

$$\mathsf{prime}(x) = (x > 1) \wedge (\forall y \leq x)((y = 1) \vee (y = x) \vee (\neg(y|x)))$$

for $x \in \mathbb{N}$. □

Bounded minimalization can be formulated for the special case of numerical functions as follows.

Theorem 7.6.8 *Let p be an $(m+1)$-ary primitive recursive predicate. The function $f : \mathbb{N}^{m+1} \longrightarrow \mathbb{N}$ defined by $f(y, x_1, \ldots, x_m) = t$ if t is the least number that is less than or equal to y such that $p(t, x_1, \ldots, x_m) = 1$ and $f(y, x_1, \ldots, x_m) = y + 1$ if no such t exists, is primitive recursive.*

Proof. This follows immediately from Theorem 7.4.2. ∎

We denote the function f from the previous theorem by

$$f(y, x_1, \ldots, x_m) = (\min u \leq y)p(u, x_1, \ldots, x_m).$$

Example 7.6.9 Let $u, v \in \mathbb{N}$ be two natural numbers. Let $Q(u, v)$ be the quotient of the division of u by v, and let $R(u, v)$ be the remainder. We have

$u = v \cdot Q(u,v) + R(u,v)$, and $0 \leq R(u,v) < v$. Both functions $Q : \mathbb{N}^2 \longrightarrow \mathbb{N}$ and $R : \mathbb{N}^2 \longrightarrow \mathbb{N}$ are primitive recursive because

$$Q(u,v) = (\min t \leq u)((t+1) \cdot v > u),$$

for $u, v \in \mathbb{N}$ and $R(u,v) = u \dot{-} v \cdot Q(u,v)$ for $u, v \in \mathbb{N}$.

The value of $Q(u,v)$ is denoted by u/v. □

Example 7.6.10 Let $\wp : \mathbb{N}^2 \longrightarrow \mathbb{N}$ be the pairing function introduced in Example 1.6.22. Clearly, $\wp$ is a primitive recursive function, and we have $x \leq \wp(x,y)$ and $y \leq \wp(x,y)$ for $x, y \in \mathbb{N}$, as the reader can easily verify. Let $\wp_0 : \mathbb{N} \longrightarrow \mathbb{N}$ $\wp_1 : \mathbb{N} \longrightarrow \mathbb{N}$ be the functions defined by $\wp_0(z) = x$, and $\wp_1(z) = y$, if $z = h(x,y)$. Note that we have both $\wp_0(z) \leq z$ and $\wp_1(z) \leq z$ for $z \in \mathbb{N}$. Thus, we can write

$$\begin{aligned} \wp_0(z) &= (\min x \leq z)(\exists y \leq z)(\wp(x,y) = z) \\ \wp_1(z) &= (\min y \leq z)(\exists x \leq z)(\wp(x,y) = z), \end{aligned}$$

for $z \in \mathbb{N}$, which shows that both $\wp_0$ and $\wp_1$ are primitive recursive functions. □

Example 7.6.11 Let $\mathsf{prn}(i)$ be the ith prime number. Thus, $\mathsf{prn}(0) = 2$, $\mathsf{prn}(1) = 3$, $\mathsf{prn}(2) = 5, \ldots$. To show that prn is primitive recursive, note that $\mathsf{prn}(i+1) \leq \mathsf{prn}(i)! + 1$ for $i \in \mathbb{N}$. Indeed, $\mathsf{prn}(i)! + 1$ is not divisible by any of the numbers $\mathsf{prn}(0), \ldots, \mathsf{prn}(i)$ since the division of $\mathsf{prn}(i)! + 1$ by each of these numbers gives the remainder 1. Therefore, any prime that divides $\mathsf{prn}(i)! + 1$ must be at least equal to $\mathsf{prn}(i+1)$.

Using Example 7.6.7, we see that the function $f : \mathbb{N} \longrightarrow \mathbb{N}$ defined by $f(n) = (\min m \leq n! + 1)(m > n \wedge \mathsf{prime}(m))$. is primitive recursive.

Then prn is primitive recursive because

$$\begin{aligned} \mathsf{prn}(0) &= 2 \\ \mathsf{prn}(i+1) &= f(\mathsf{prn}(i)), \end{aligned}$$

Let $\mathsf{expp}(n,i)$ be the largest power of the ith prime $\mathsf{prn}(i)$ that divides n. For example, $\mathsf{expp}(72,0) = 3$, because the largest power of $\mathsf{prn}(0) = 2$ that divides 72 is 2^3. The function expp is primitive recursive since

$$\mathsf{expp}(n,i) = (\min u \leq n)(\neg(\mathsf{prn}(i)^u | n)) \dot{-} 1.$$

□

Now consider the function $S : \mathbf{Seq}(\mathbb{N}) \longrightarrow \mathbb{N}$ defined by

$$\begin{aligned} S(\lambda) &= 1 \\ S(n_0, n_1, \ldots, n_{m-1}) &= \mathsf{prn}(0)^{n_0+1}\mathsf{prn}(1)^{n_1+1} \cdots \mathsf{prn}(m-1)^{n_{m-1}+1}, \end{aligned}$$

for $(n_0, \ldots, n_1) \in \mathbf{Seq}(\mathbb{N})$ and $m \geq 1$. The uniqueness of the prime decomposition of any natural number implies that S is an injection. We denote $S(n_0, \ldots, n_{m-1})$ by $[n_0, \ldots, n_{m-1}]$, and we sometimes refer to this number as *the code of the sequence* $(n_0, \ldots, n_{m-1})$. If $p = [n_0, \ldots, n_{m-1}]$, then the length of the sequence $(n_0, \ldots, n_{m-1})$ is given by the primitive recursive function

$$\mathsf{length}(n) = (\min k \leq n)(\neg(\mathsf{prn}(k) | n))$$

for $n \in \mathbb{N}$. Using the third part of exercise 33, we see that bounding k by n is sufficient.

Suppose that $n = [n_0, \ldots, n_{m-1}]$. The ith component n_i of the sequence $(n_0, \ldots, n_{m-1})$ is given by $n_i = \mathsf{comp}(n, i) = \mathsf{expp}(n, i) \dot{-} 1$. Clearly, the function comp is primitive recursive. Observe that if $i \geq \mathsf{length}(n)$, then $\mathsf{comp}(n, i) = 0$.

Example 7.6.12 Let $m, n \in \mathbb{N}$. Then,

$$m = [p_0, \ldots, p_{k-1}] \text{ and } n = [q_0, \ldots, q_{l-1}],$$

for some sequences $(p_0, \ldots, p_{k-1})$ and $(q_0, \ldots, q_{l-1})$ in $\mathbf{Seq}(\mathbb{N})$, where $k = \mathsf{length}(m)$ and $l = \mathsf{length}(n)$. Let $\mathsf{concs} : \mathbb{N}^2 \longrightarrow \mathbb{N}$ be the function defined by

$$\mathsf{concs}(m, n) = [p_0, \ldots, p_{k-1}, q_0, \ldots, q_{l-1}].$$

In other words, $\mathsf{concs}(m, n)$ gives the code of the sequence resulting from the concatenation of the sequences whose codes are m and n. The primitive recursiveness of concs follows from the equality

$$\mathsf{concs}(m, n) = m \cdot \prod_{j=0}^{\mathsf{length}(n)-1} \mathsf{prn}(j + \mathsf{length}(m))^{\mathsf{expp}(n, j)}$$

and Theorem 7.6.4. □

Lemma 7.6.13 *Let $f : \mathbb{N}^k \longrightarrow \mathbb{N}$ be a function, where $k \geq 1$. Then, the function $g : \mathbb{N}^k \longrightarrow \mathbb{N}$ given by*

$$g(n, n_1, \ldots, n_{k-1}) =$$
$$[f(0, n_1, \ldots, n_{k-1}), f(1, n_1, \ldots, n_{k-1}), \ldots, f(n-1, n_1, \ldots, n_{k-1})]$$

for $n, n_1, \ldots, n_{k-1} \in \mathbb{N}$ is primitive recursive if and only if f is primitive recursive.

Proof. Suppose that f is primitive recursive. Then, g can be defined by primitive recursion as

$$g(0, n_1, \ldots, n_{k-1}) = 0$$

and

$$g(n+1, n_1, \ldots, n_{k-1}) =$$
$$g(n, n_1, \ldots, n_{k-1}) \cdot \mathsf{prn}(\mathsf{length}(g(n, n_1, \ldots, n_{k-1})))^{f(n, n_1, \ldots, n_{k-1})+1},$$

which shows that g is primitive recursive.

Conversely, if g is primitive recursive, then

$$f(n, n_1, \ldots, n_{k-1}) = \mathsf{comp}(g(n+1, n_1, \ldots, n_{k-1}), n+1),$$

which implies the primitive recursiveness of f. ∎

Lemma 7.6.13 allows us to present a technique for proving the primitive recursiveness of numerical functions whose value $f(n+1, n_1, \ldots, n_k)$ may depend on their entire "course of values":

$$f(0, n_1, \ldots, n_k), f(1, n_1, \ldots, n_k), \ldots, f(n, n_1, \ldots, n_k).$$

Theorem 7.6.14 (Course-of-Values Theorem) *Let $f : \mathbb{N}^k \longrightarrow \mathbb{N}$ be a function such that*

$$f(n, n_1, \ldots, n_{k-1}) = h(n, n_1, \ldots, n_{k-1}, [f(0, n_1, \ldots, n_{k-1}), \ldots, f(n-1, n_1, \ldots, n_{k-1})])$$

for $n, n_1, \ldots, n_{k-1} \in \mathbb{N}$, where $h : \mathbb{N}^{k+1} \longrightarrow \mathbb{N}$ is a primitive recursive function. Then, the function f is primitive recursive.

Proof. Observe that

$$f(n+1, n_1, \ldots, n_{k-1}) = h(n+1, n_1, \ldots, n_{k-1}, g(n, n_1, \ldots, n_{k-1})),$$

where g is the function introduced in Lemma 7.6.13. By the same lemma, it suffices to show that the function g is primitive recursive. Note that we have $g(0, n_1, \ldots, n_{k-1}) = 0$ and

$$\begin{aligned} & g(n+1, n_1, \ldots, n_{k-1}) \\ = \; & g(n, n_1, \ldots, n_{k-1}) \cdot \\ & \mathsf{prn}(\mathsf{length}(g(n, n_1, \ldots, n_{k-1})))^{f(n+1, n_1, \ldots, n_{k-1})+1} \\ = \; & g(n, n_1, \ldots, n_{k-1}) \cdot \\ & \mathsf{prn}(\mathsf{length}(g(n, n_1, \ldots, n_{k-1})))^{h(n+1, n_1, \ldots, n_{k-1}, g(n, n_1, \ldots, n_{k-1}))+1}, \end{aligned}$$

which is a definition of g by primitive recursion, using primitive recursive functions. The primitive recursiveness of g implies the primitive recursiveness of f. ∎

Example 7.6.15 Define the function $\mathsf{fib} : \mathbb{N} \longrightarrow \mathbb{N}$ such that

$$\begin{aligned} \mathsf{fib}(0) &= \mathsf{fib}(1) = 1 \\ \mathsf{fib}(n) &= \mathsf{fib}(n-1) + \mathsf{fib}(n-2) \text{ for } n \geq 2. \end{aligned}$$

It is clear that $\mathsf{fib}(n)$ is the nth Fibonacci number. We claim that the fib is a primitive recursive function.

Define the function $h : \mathbb{N}^2 \longrightarrow \mathbb{N}$ by $h(n, m) = 1$ if $n = 0$ or $n = 1$, and

$$h(n, m) = \mathsf{comp}(m, \mathsf{length}(m) \dot{-} 1) + \mathsf{comp}(m, \mathsf{length}(m) \dot{-} 2)$$

if $n \geq 2$. It is clear that h is primitive recursive. Then, for $n \geq 2$ we have

$$h(n, [\mathsf{fib}(0), \ldots, \mathsf{fib}(n-1)]) = \mathsf{fib}(n-1) + \mathsf{fib}(n-2) = \mathsf{fib}(n).$$

Thus, we obtain $\mathsf{fib}(n) = h(n, [\mathsf{fib}(0), \ldots, \mathsf{fib}(n-1)])$ for $n \in \mathbb{N}$. The course-of-values theorem implies that fib is primitive recursive. □

7.7 Transformations between Alphabets

Now we examine relationships between primitive recursive functions over different alphabets as well as primitive recursive functions over $\mathbb{N}$. In part, this discussion is required because we chose to define primitive recursive functions on words instead of on natural numbers. We then combine translations between words and natural numbers to obtain results about primitive recursive functions on different alphabets.

The main result of this section is Theorem 7.7.16, which addresses the technical difficulties of defining a primitive recursive function $f : (A^*)^n \longrightarrow A^*$ using an enlarged alphabet $B \supseteq A$. Specifically, if the functions used to define f are primitive recursive on B, then when f is restricted to A, it is not a priori clear that f is itself primitive recursive on A.

Let $A = \{a_0, \ldots, a_{n-1}\}$ be an alphabet. The cardinality $n = |A|$ of the alphabet will appear in several expressions used in this section. Recall that in Section 2.2 we defined the bijection $\phi_A : A^* \longrightarrow \mathbb{N}$. Since we identify $\mathbb{N}$ with $\{a_0\}^*$ and $a_0 \in A^*$, this function is primitive recursive over the alphabet A. Indeed, we have the following definition of ϕ_A by primitive recursion:

$$\begin{aligned} \phi_A(\lambda) &= \lambda, \\ \phi_A(xa_i) &= \mathsf{conc}((\phi_A(x))^n, a_0^{i+1}), \end{aligned}$$

for $x \in A^*$ and $a_i \in A$. We denote the inverse of ϕ_A by $\psi_A : \mathbb{N} \longrightarrow A^*$.

Example 7.7.1 Let $A = \{a_0, a_1, a_2\}$. Then, $\psi_A(51) = a_0a_1a_0a_2$, as can be seen from Example 2.2.8. □

If $A' = \{a_0, \ldots, a_{m-1}\}$ is a subset of the alphabet A which includes the symbol a_0, then it is easy to see that the restriction $\phi_A\rceil(A')^*$ is a primitive recursive function on the alphabet A'.

We extend the function $\psi_A : \{a_0\}^* \longrightarrow A^*$ to a function $\psi'_A : A^* \longrightarrow A^*$ by defining $\psi'_A(x) = \psi_A(a_0^{|x|})$ for $x \in A^*$. Of course, this extended function ceases to be a bijection. Nevertheless, we continue to have $\psi'_A(\phi_A(x)) = x$ for every $x \in A^*$ and $\phi_A(\psi'_A(m)) = m$ for every $m \in \mathbb{N}$.

Lemma 7.7.2 *Let $A = \{a_0, \ldots, a_{n-1}\}$ be an alphabet. The extended function ψ'_A is a primitive recursive function over A.*

Proof. We prove that the extended function ψ'_A is primitive recursive by showing that it can be defined by primitive recursion from primitive recursive functions. Note that $\psi'_A(\lambda) = \lambda$.

Define the primitive recursive function $r : A^* \longrightarrow A^*$ by

$$\begin{aligned} r(\lambda) &= \lambda \\ r(xa_i) &= \begin{cases} s_i(x) = xa_i & \text{if } i < n-1 \\ P_0^2(x, r(x)) = x & \text{if } i = n-1 \end{cases} \end{aligned}$$

Thus, $r(x)$ removes all trailing a_{n-1} in the word x.

Another useful primitive recursive function is $q : A^* \longrightarrow A^*$ given by

$$\begin{aligned} q(\lambda) &= a_0 \\ q(xa_i) &= \begin{cases} xa_{i+1} & \text{if } 0 \le i < n-1 \\ xa_{n-1} & \text{if } i = n-1 \end{cases} \end{aligned}$$

for $x \in A^*$. If $\phi_A(x) = a_0^m$ and x does not end in a_{n-1}, then $\phi_A(q(x)) = a_0^{m+1}$.

Observe that the length of the word $\psi'_A(x) -_r r(\psi'_A(x))$ equals the number of symbols a_{n-1} that occur at the end of the word x. Therefore, $l(\psi'_A(x) -_r r(\psi'_A(x)))$ is a word over $\{a_0\}$ whose length is equal to the length of the suffix of trailing a_{n-1}s of x, where l is the function introduced in Example 7.2.8.

Now, the extended function ψ'_A can be defined as

$$\begin{aligned}\psi'_A(\lambda) &= \lambda \\ \psi'_A(xa_i) &= \mathsf{conc}(q(r(\psi'_A(x))), l(\psi'_A(x) - r(\psi'_A(x))))\end{aligned}$$

for $x \in A^*$ and $a_i \in A$, which shows that ψ'_A is primitive recursive. ∎

Lemma 7.7.3 *Let $A = \{a_0, \ldots, a_{n-1}\}$ be an alphabet, and let $f : (\{a_0\}^*)^k \longrightarrow \{a_0\}^*$ be a primitive recursive function over $\{a_0\}$. The function $\hat{f} : (A^*)^k \longrightarrow A^*$ given by*

$$\hat{f}(x_0, \ldots, x_{k-1}) = f(a_0^{|x_0|}, \ldots, a_0^{|x_{k-1}|})$$

for $(x_0, \ldots, x_{k-1}) \in (A^*)^k$ is a primitive recursive function over A.

Proof. By Theorem 7.5.2, the null extension $\overline{f}$ of f to A is a primitive recursive function on A. On the other hand, we proved in Example 7.2.8 that the length function $l : A^* \longrightarrow A^*$ given by $l(x) = a_0^{|x|}$ for $x \in A^*$ is a primitive recursive function on A. Since $\hat{f}(x_0, \ldots, x_{k-1}) = \overline{f}(l(x_0), \ldots, l(x_{k-1}))$ for $(x_0, \ldots, x_{k-1}) \in (A^*)^k$, it follows that $\hat{f}$ is a primitive recursive function on A. ∎

Although f is primitive recursive over $\{a_0\}$, we cannot compose it with l, a primitive recursive functions on A and claim that the result is primitive recursive on A. However, Theorem 7.5.2 allows us to extent f to $\hat{f}$ which is primitive recursive on A and thus, the composition of these functions is itself a primitive recursive function on A, as required. This is a subtle point.

Let $f : (A^*)^k \longrightarrow A^*$ be a function. Define the function $f^+ : \mathbb{N}^k \longrightarrow \mathbb{N}$ by

$$f^+(n_0, \ldots, n_{k-1}) = \phi_A(f(\psi_A(n_0), \ldots, \psi_A(n_{k-1}))),$$

for $(n_0, \ldots, n_{k-1}) \in \mathbb{N}^k$. It is easy to see that

$$f(x_0, \ldots, x_{k-1}) = \psi_A(f^+(\phi_A(x_0), \ldots, \phi_A(x_{k-1}))$$

for $(x_0, \ldots, x_{k-1}) \in (A^*)^k$.

Starting from a function $g : \mathbb{N}^k \longrightarrow \mathbb{N}$, we define the function $g^\#_A : (A^*)^k \longrightarrow A^*$ by

$$g^\#_A(x_0, \ldots, x_{k-1}) = \psi_A(g(\phi_A(x_0), \ldots, \phi_A(x_{k-1}))), \tag{7.2}$$

for $(x_0, \ldots, x_{k-1}) \in (A^*)^k$. As with f and f^+, we have

$$g(n_0, \ldots, n_{k-1}) = \phi_A(g^\#_A(\psi_A(n_0), \ldots, \psi_A(n_{k-1})))$$

for $n_0, \ldots, n_{k-1} \in \mathbb{N}$.

Clearly, we have $(g^\#_A)^+ = g$ for every function $g : \mathbb{N}^k \longrightarrow \mathbb{N}$, and that $(f^+)^\#_A = f$ for every function $f : (A^*)^k \longrightarrow A^*$.

The relationships between f and f^+ and g and $g^\#_A$ are summarized by the commutative diagrams shown in Figure 7.2.

Lemma 7.7.4 *If $g : \mathbb{N}^k \longrightarrow \mathbb{N}$ is primitive recursive, then so is $g^\#_A$.*

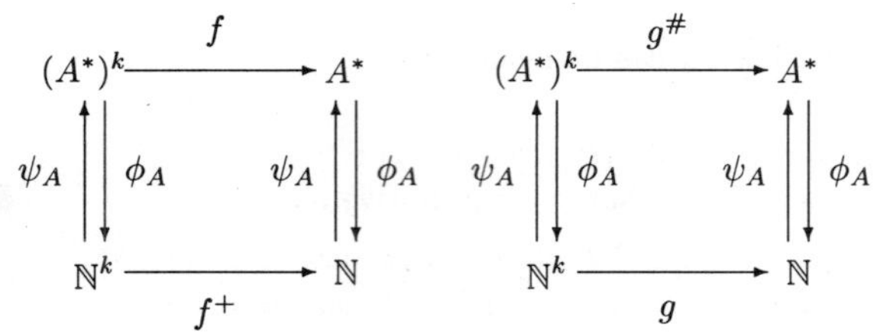

Figure 7.2: The definitions of f^+ and $g_A^\#$

Proof. It is easy to see that we can replace g by $\hat{g}$ and ψ_A by its extension ψ'_A to A in the equality (7.2). By Lemmas 7.7.3 and 7.7.2, respectively, both these functions are primitive recursive functions over A, hence so is $g_A^\#$. ∎

We show next that if $f : (A^*)^k \longrightarrow A^*$ is primitive recursive on A, then the function $f^+ : \mathbb{N}^k \longrightarrow \mathbb{N}$ is primitive recursive on $\mathbb{N}$. To this end, we need to prove this result directly for two simple functions.

Lemma 7.7.5 *The functions* $\mathsf{trimlast}^+$ *and* lastof^+ *are primitive recursive functions on* $\mathbb{N}$.

Proof. Let $A = \{a_0, \ldots, a_{n-1}\}$. Suppose that $m = \phi_A(xa_i)$, where $x \in A^*$ and $a_i \in A$. We have $\mathsf{trimlast}^+(m) = \phi_A(x)$ and $\mathsf{lastof}^+(m) = i$. Note that

$$\mathsf{trimlast}^+(m) = \begin{cases} m/n & \text{if } \neg(n|m) \\ m/n \dot{-} 1 & \text{otherwise} \end{cases}$$

since $\phi_A(xa_i) = n\phi_A(x) + i + 1$. Also, $\mathsf{lastof}(m) = m - n \cdot \mathsf{trimlast}^+(m) - 1$, so both functions are primitive recursive on $\mathbb{N}$. ∎

A useful inequality is $\mathsf{trimlast}^+(m) < m$ for $m > 0$. We leave the proof to the reader (see Exercise 34).

Lemma 7.7.6 *Let* $A = \{a_0, \ldots, a_{n-1}\}$ *be an alphabet. If* $f : (A^*)^k \longrightarrow A^*$ *is primitive recursive on* A, *then the function* $f^+ : \mathbb{N}^n \longrightarrow \mathbb{N}$ *is primitive recursive on* $\mathbb{N}$.

Proof. The argument is by induction on the definition of primitive recursive functions. The basis case consists of verifying that e^+, s_i^+, and $(P_i^k)^+$ are primitive recursive functions. Note that $e^+(m) = 0$, and $s_i^+(m) = nm + i$ for $m \in \mathbb{N}$. Also, $(P_i^k)^+(n_0, \ldots, n_{k-1}) = n_i$ for $(n_0, \ldots, n_{k-1}) \in \mathbb{N}^k$. These three facts show that the statement holds for the basic recursive functions.

If $f : (A^*)^k \longrightarrow A^*$ is obtained by composition using the function $g : (A^*)^p \longrightarrow A^*$ and the functions $h_0, \ldots, h_{p-1} : (A^*)^k \longrightarrow A^*$, where the statement holds for $g, h_0, \ldots, h_{p-1}$, then, since $f^+ = g^+(h_0^+, \ldots, h_{p-1}^+)$, it follows that the statement holds for f as well.

The case when f is obtained by primitive recursion from the functions $g, h_0, \ldots, h_{m-1}$ is more difficult. Suppose that

$$\begin{aligned} f(\lambda, x_1, \ldots, x_{k-1}) &= g(x_1, \ldots, x_{k-1}), \\ f(xa_i, x_1, \ldots, x_{k-1}) &= h_i(x, x_1, \ldots, x_{k-1}, f(x, x_1, \ldots, x_{k-1})), \end{aligned}$$

for $0 \leq i \leq n-1$, $x, x_1, \ldots, x_{k-1} \in A^*$. Assume that the statement holds for the functions $g, h_0, \ldots, h_{n-1}$.

Observe that

$$\begin{aligned} f^+(0, m_1, \ldots, m_{k-1}) &= \phi_A(f(\psi_A(0), \psi_A(m_1), \ldots, \psi_A(m_{k-1}))) \\ &= \phi_A(f(\lambda, \psi_A(m_1), \ldots, \psi_A(m_{k-1}))) \\ &= \phi_A(g(\psi_A(m_1), \ldots, \psi_A(m_{k-1}))) \\ &= g^+(m_1, \ldots, m_{k-1}) \end{aligned}$$

for $m_1, \ldots, m_{k-1} \in \mathbb{N}$.

Define the function $F : \mathbb{N}^k \longrightarrow \mathbb{N}$ by

$$F(m, m_1, \ldots, m_{k-1}) = \qquad (7.3)$$
$$[f^+(0, m_1, \ldots, m_{k-1}), \ldots, f^+(m, m_1, \ldots, m_{k-1})],$$

for $m, m_1, \ldots, m_{k-1} \in \mathbb{N}$.

Since ϕ_A is a bijection, for every $m \in \mathbb{N}$ we can write $m + 1 = \phi_A(xa_i)$ for some $x \in A^*$ and $a_i \in A$. We also have $m_j = \phi_A(x_j)$ for some $x_j \in A^*$, where $0 \leq j \leq k-1$. Then,

$$\begin{aligned} & f^+(m+1, m_1, \ldots, m_{k-1}) \\ &= \phi_A(f(\psi_A(m+1), \psi_A(m_1), \ldots, \psi_A(m_{k-1}))) \\ &= \phi_A(f(xa_i, x_1, \ldots, x_{k-1})) \\ &= \phi_A(h_i(x, x_1, \ldots, x_{k-1}, f(x, x_1, \ldots, x_{k-1}))) \\ &= \phi_A(h_i(\psi_A(\mathsf{trimlast}^+(m+1)), \psi_A(m_1), \ldots, \psi_A(m_{k-1}), \\ &\qquad f(\psi_A(\mathsf{trimlast}^+(m+1)), \psi_A(m_1), \ldots, \psi_A(m_{k-1})))) \\ &= h_i^+(\mathsf{trimlast}^+(m+1), m_1, \ldots, m_{k-1}, \\ &\qquad f^+(\mathsf{trimlast}^+(m+1), m_1, \ldots, m_{k-1})). \end{aligned}$$

Since $\mathsf{trimlast}^+(m+1) \leq m$ for $m \in \mathbb{N}$, the equality (7.3) allows us to write

$$\begin{aligned} & f^+(\mathsf{trimlast}^+(m+1), m_1, \ldots, m_{k-1}) \\ &= \mathsf{comp}(F(m, m_1, \ldots, m_{k-1}), \mathsf{trimlast}^+(m+1)), \end{aligned}$$

for $m, m_1, \ldots, m_{k-1} \in \mathbb{N}$.

Using the definition by cases, consider the primitive recursive function $G : \mathbb{N}^{k+1} \longrightarrow \mathbb{N}$ given by

$$G(0, m_1, \ldots, m_{k-1}, p) = g(m_1, \ldots, m_{k-1}),$$

for $m_1, \ldots, m_{k-1}, p \in \mathbb{N}$ and

$$\begin{aligned} & G(m+1, m_1, \ldots, m_{k-1}, p) \\ &= h_i^+(\mathsf{trimlast}^+(m+1), m_1, \ldots, m_{k-1}, \mathsf{comp}(p, \mathsf{trimlast}^+(m+1))), \end{aligned}$$

if $\mathsf{lastof}^+(m+1) = i$, for $m, m_1, \ldots, m_{k-1}, p \in \mathbb{N}$. Now, we have

$$\begin{aligned} & f^+(m+1, m_1, \ldots, m_{k-1}) \\ &= G(m+1, m_1, \ldots, m_{k-1}, F(m, m_1, \ldots, m_{k-1})), \end{aligned}$$

which is a course-of-values definition of f^+ starting from the primitive recursive function G. Thus, by Theorem 7.6.14, f is primitive recursive. ∎

Theorem 7.7.7 *Let A be an alphabet. The function $f : (A^*)^k \longrightarrow A^*$ is primitive recursive on A if and only if the function $f^+ : \mathbb{N}^k \longrightarrow \mathbb{N}$ is primitive recursive on $\mathbb{N}$.*

Proof. Lemma 7.7.6 shows that the primitive recursiveness of f over A implies the primitive recursiveness of f^+. Conversely, suppose that f^+ is primitive recursive. Since $f = (f^+)^{\#}_A$, Lemma 7.7.4 implies the primitive recursiveness of f over A. ∎

Example 7.7.8 Observe that $\phi_A(\lambda) = 0$ and $\phi_A(a_0) = 1$. Therefore, if p is an m-ary primitive recursive predicate over $\mathbb{N}$, the function $(p)^{\#}_A : (A^*)^m \longrightarrow A^*$ given by

$$p^{\#}(x_0, \ldots, x_{m-1}) = \begin{cases} a_0 & \text{if } p(\phi_A(x_0), \ldots, \phi_A(x_{m-1})) = 1 \\ \lambda & \text{otherwise} \end{cases}$$

is a primitive recursive predicate over A^*. For instance, if p is $(x \leq y)$, then for the corresponding predicate $p^{\#}_A$ we have $p^{\#}(x, y) = a_0$ if and only if $\phi_A(x) \leq \phi_A(y)$. When the alphabet is clear from the context we will denote $p^{\#}_A$ simply by $(x \leq y)$. Similar conventions are followed for other primitive recursive predicates on words $((x < y), (x \geq y)$, etc.) □

In Definition 7.3.9 we introduced the notions of bounded existential quantification $(\exists x \leq_{\text{pref}} y)p(x, x_1, \ldots, x_{m-1})$ and bounded universal quantification $(\forall x \leq_{\text{pref}} y)p(x, x_1, \ldots, x_{m-1})$ for an m-ary predicate p over A^*. In the next definition we introduce yet another type of bounded quantification.

Definition 7.7.9 Let p be an m-ary predicate on A^*, where $m \geq 1$. The m-ary predicate q on A^* is obtained through *numeric bounded existential quantification* from p if $q(y, x_1, \ldots, x_{m-1}) = a_0$ if and only if there is an $x \in A^*$ such that $x \preceq y$ and $p(x, x_1, \ldots, x_{m-1}) = a_0$. The predicate q is denoted by $(\exists x \preceq y)p(x, x_1, \ldots, x_{m-1})$.

If r is an m-ary predicate such that $r(y, x_1, \ldots, x_{m-1}) = a_0$ if and only if for every $x \in A^*$ such that $x \preceq y$ we have $p(x, x_1, \ldots, x_{m-1}) = a_0$, then we say that r is obtained through *numeric bounded universal quantification* from p. In this case, the predicate is denoted by $(\forall x \preceq y)p(x, x_1, \ldots, x_{m-1})$. □

Theorem 7.7.10 *If p is an m-ary primitive recursive predicate on A^*, then the predicates*

$$\begin{aligned} q(y, x_1, \ldots, x_{m-1}) &= (\exists x \preceq y)p(x, x_1, \ldots, x_{m-1}) \\ r(y, x_1, \ldots, x_{m-1}) &= (\forall x \preceq y)p(x, x_1, \ldots, x_{m-1}) \end{aligned}$$

are primitive recursive.

Proof. To prove that q is primitive recursive, note that the predicate p^+ is primitive recursive. Therefore, by the closure of numeric primitive recursive predicates with respect to bounded existential quantification, the predicate p_1 defined by $p_1(k, n_1, \ldots, n_{m-1}) = 1$ if and only if there is $h \in \mathbb{N}$ such that $h \leq k$ and $p^+(h, n_1, \ldots, n_{m-1}) = 1$ is primitive recursive. We claim that $q = p_1^{\#}$. Indeed, $p_1^{\#}(y, x_1, \ldots, x_{m-1}) = a_0$ is equivalent to $p_1(\phi_A(y), \phi_A(x_1), \ldots, \phi_A(x_{m-1})) = 1$, which happens if and only if there is $h \leq \phi_A(y)$ such that

$$p^+(h, \phi_A(x_1), \ldots, \phi_A(x_{m-1})) = 1.$$

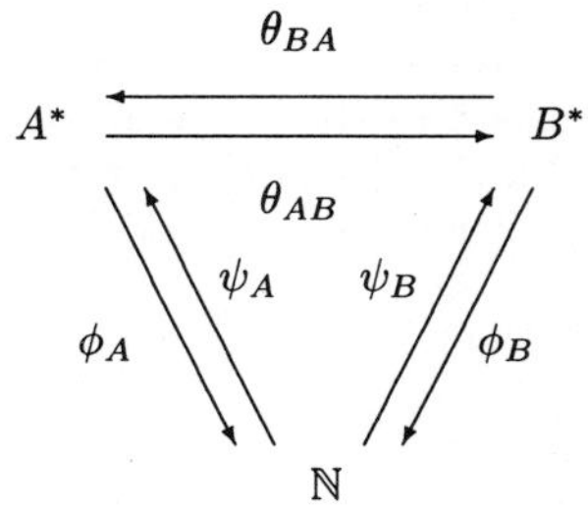

Figure 7.3: Definition of θ_{AB} and θ_{BA}

This is equivalent to

$$\begin{aligned} & p(\psi_A(h), \psi_A(\phi_A(x_1)), \ldots, \psi_A(\phi_A(x_{m-1})) \\ &= p(\psi_A(h), x_1, \ldots, x_{m-1}) \\ &= a_0. \end{aligned}$$

If we denote $x = \psi_A(h)$ (hence, $h = \phi_A(x)$), it is clear that $q = p_1^{\#}$,which means that q is indeed primitive recursive.

A similar argument can be used to prove that the predicate r is primitive recursive. ∎

We now examine the relationships between primitive recursive functions defined over different alphabets.

Let A, B be two alphabets. Define the function $\theta_{AB} : A^* \longrightarrow B^*$ by $\theta_{AB}(x) = \psi_B(\phi_A(x))$ for $x \in A^*$ (see Figure 7.3). Note that

$$\theta_{BA}(\theta_{AB}(x)) = \psi_A(\phi_B(\psi_B(\phi_A(x)))) = x$$

for $x \in A^*$.

Definition 7.7.11 Let A, B be two alphabets and let $f : (A^*)^n \longrightarrow A^*$. The *conjugate function on f over B* is the function $\tilde{f} : (B^*)^n \longrightarrow B^*$ given by

$$\tilde{f}(x_0, \ldots, x_{n-1}) = \theta_{AB} f(\theta_{BA}(x_0), \ldots, \theta_{BA}(x_{n-1})),$$

for $x_0, \ldots, x_{n-1} \in B^*$. □

Corollary 7.7.12 *Let A, B be two alphabets. A function $f : (A^*)^n \longrightarrow A^*$ is primitive recursive over the alphabet A if and only if its conjugate $\tilde{f}$ over the alphabet B is primitive recursive.*

Proof. Note that both f and $\tilde{f}$ have the same conjugate function f^+ over a one-element alphabet (see Exercise 38). Thus, Theorem 7.7.7 implies that f is primitive recursive over A if and only if $\tilde{f}$ is primitive recursive over B. ∎

Lemma 7.7.13 *Let A, B be two alphabets such that $\{a_0\} \subseteq A \subseteq B$. The restriction $\theta_{BA}\lceil A^*$ is a primitive recursive function over the alphabet A.*

Further, the function $\zeta : \mathbb{N} \longrightarrow \mathbb{N}$ given by $\zeta(n) = \phi_B(\psi_A(n))$ for $n \in \mathbb{N}$ is primitive recursive.

Proof. In Lemma 7.7.2 we saw that the extension ψ'_A of ψ_A to A is a primitive recursive function on A. Since the range of ϕ_B is $\{a_0\}^*$, we have $\theta_{BA} = \psi'_A \phi_B$. On the other hand, the restriction $\phi_B \rceil A^*$ is clearly a primitive recursive function on A and, since $\theta_{BA} \rceil A^* = (\phi_B \rceil A^*) \psi'_A$, it follows that $\theta_{BA} \rceil A^*$ is a primitive recursive function on A.

For the second part of the statement note that

$$\zeta^{\#}_A(w) = \psi_A(\zeta(\phi_A(w))) = \psi_A(\phi_B(\psi_A(\phi_A(w)))) = \psi_A(\phi_B(w)) = \theta_{BA}(w),$$

for $w \in A^*$. By the first part of the lemma, $\zeta^{\#}_A$ is a primitive recursive function on A, and by Corollary 7.7.12, we obtain the primitive recursiveness of ζ. ∎

Lemma 7.7.14 *Let A, B be two alphabets such that $\{a_0\} \subseteq A \subseteq B$. The function $\hat{\theta}_{AB} : B^* \longrightarrow B^*$ defined by*

$$\hat{\theta}_{AB}(x) = \begin{cases} \theta_{AB}(x) & \text{if } x \in A^* \\ \lambda & \text{otherwise,} \end{cases}$$

for $x \in B^*$ is a primitive recursive function over the alphabet B.

Proof. Starting from the function $\phi_A : A^* \longrightarrow \{a_0\}^*$, regarded as a primitive recursive function over the alphabet A, consider its null extension $\bar{\phi}_A$ to B which, by Theorem 7.5.2, is a primitive recursive function on B. We have

$$\bar{\phi}_A(x) = \begin{cases} \phi_A(x) & \text{if } x \in A^* \\ \lambda & \text{otherwise,} \end{cases}$$

for $x \in B^*$. If ψ'_B is the extension of ψ_B to a primitive recursive function on B, then we have $\psi'_B(\bar{\phi}_A(x)) = \psi'_B(\phi_A(x)) = \psi_B(\phi_A(x)) = \theta_{AB}(x)$ if $x \in A^*$, and $\psi'_B(\bar{\phi}_A(x)) = \psi'_B(\lambda) = \lambda$, otherwise. In other words, we have $\hat{\theta}_{AB} = \psi'_B \bar{\phi}_A$, which shows that $\hat{\theta}_{AB}$ is a primitive recursive function on B. ∎

Lemma 7.7.15 *Let $A = \{a_0, \ldots, a_{m-1}\}$ and $B = \{a_0, \ldots, a_{n-1}\}$ be two alphabets such that $1 \leq m \leq n$. The function $\theta : A^* \longrightarrow A^*$ given by*

$$\theta(y) = \begin{cases} t & \text{if there is } t \in A^* \text{ such that } \theta_{BA}(t) = y \\ \psi_A(\phi_A(y) + 1) & \text{otherwise,} \end{cases}$$

for $y \in A^*$ is a primitive recursive function on A.

Proof. Let z be a word in $A^* \subseteq B^*$. It is easy to see that $\phi_A(z) \leq \phi_B(z)$ because $|A| \leq |B|$. If $\theta_{BA}(t) = y$, we have $\phi_B(t) = \phi_A(y)$, so $\phi_A(t) \leq \phi_B(t) = \phi_A(y)$.

Let ζ be the primitive recursive function introduced in Lemma 7.7.13; recall that $\zeta(j) = \phi_B(\psi_A(j))$ for $j \in \mathbb{N}$. Now consider the function $f : \mathbb{N}^2 \longrightarrow \mathbb{N}$ given by

$$f(l, m) = (\min j \leq l)(\zeta(j) = m)$$

The primitive recursiveness of ζ implies the primitive recursiveness of f. Therefore, the function $g : \mathbb{N} \longrightarrow \mathbb{N}$ given by $g(m) = f(m, m)$ for $m \in \mathbb{N}$ is clearly primitive recursive.

Note that

$$g(m) = \begin{cases} j & \text{if there is } j \in \mathbb{N} \text{ such that} \\ & j \le m \text{ and } \phi_B(\psi_A(j)) = m \\ m+1 & \text{otherwise,} \end{cases}$$

for $m \in \mathbb{N}$. We shall prove that θ is a primitive recursive function by showing that $\theta^+ = g$. We can write

$$\begin{aligned} \theta^+(m) &= \phi_A(\theta(\psi_A(m))) \\ &= \begin{cases} \phi_A(t) & \text{if there is } t \in A^* \text{ such that } \theta_{BA}(t) = \psi_A(m) \\ m+1 & \text{otherwise} \end{cases} \\ &= \begin{cases} \phi_A(t) & \text{if there is } t \in A^* \text{ such that } \phi_B(t) = m \\ m+1 & \text{otherwise,} \end{cases} \end{aligned}$$

We claim that there is $t \in A^*$ such that $\phi_B(t) = m$ if and only if there is $j \in \mathbb{N}$ such that $j \le m$ and $\phi_B(\psi_A(j)) = m$. In these situations $j = \phi_A(t)$.

Indeed, suppose that there is $t \in A^*$ such that $\phi_B(t) = m$. Define $j = \phi_A(t)$. Then, by our initial comments, $j < m$. Besides, $\phi_B(\psi_A(j)) = \phi_B(\psi_A(\phi_A(t))) = \phi_B(t) = m$.

Conversely, suppose that there is $j \in \mathbb{N}$ such that $j \le m$ and $\phi_B(\psi_A(j)) = m$. Let $t = \psi_A(j) \in A^*$ (which implies $j = \phi_A(t)$). We have immediately $\phi_B(t) = m$. Thus, we may conclude that $\theta^+ = g$ and this implies the primitive recursiveness of θ. ∎

Theorem 7.7.16 *Let A, B be two alphabets such that $A \subseteq B$. If $f : (B^*)^n \longrightarrow B^*$ is a primitive recursive function such that $(x_0, \ldots, x_{n-1}) \in (A^*)^n$ implies $f(x_0, \ldots, x_{n-1}) \in A^*$ for every $(x_0, \ldots, x_{n-1}) \in (B^*)^n$, then its restriction $f' = f\lceil A^*$ is a primitive recursive function on A^*.*

Proof. By Corollary 7.7.12 the conjugate function $\tilde{f} : A^* \longrightarrow A^*$ is primitive recursive and we have $\tilde{f}(x) = \theta_{BA}(f(\theta_{AB}(x)))$ for every $x \in A^*$. We claim that

$$f'(x) = \theta(\tilde{f}(\theta_{BA}\rceil A^*(x))), \tag{7.4}$$

for $x \in A^*$, where θ is the function introduced in Lemma 7.7.15. Observe that if this claim is justified then the proof is completed because θ is a primitive recursive function on A (by Lemma 7.7.15) and $\theta_{BA}\rceil A^*$ is a primitive recursive function on the same alphabet by Lemma 7.7.13.

We have

$$\begin{aligned} &\theta(\tilde{f}(\theta_{BA}\rceil A^*(x))) \\ &\quad = \theta(\theta_{BA}(f(\theta_{AB}(\theta_{BA}\rceil A^*(x))))) \\ &\quad = \theta(\theta_{BA}(f(x))), \end{aligned}$$

for $x \in A^*$.

If $y = \theta_{BA}(f(x))$, then, since $f(x) \in A^*$, by the definition of θ we have $\theta(\theta_{BA}(f(x))) = f(x)$, which shows that equality (7.4) holds. ∎

Theorem 7.7.16 is a very important technical result. It shows that we can construct a primitive recursive function f on an alphabet A using primitive recursive functions on larger alphabets.

As an application we consider an extension of the standard definition of functions by primitive recursion.

Definition 7.7.17 Let $A = \{a_0, \ldots, a_{n-1}\}$ be an alphabet, $g, g' : (A^*)^{m-1} \longrightarrow A^*$, and let $h_i, h'_i : (A^*)^{m+2} \longrightarrow A^*$ for $0 \leq i \leq n-1$ be $2n$ functions of $m+2$ arguments, where $m > 1$.

The functions $f, f' : (A^*)^m \longrightarrow A^*$ are obtained by *simultaneous primitive recursion* from g, g' and $h_0, \ldots, h_{n-1}, h'_0, \ldots, h'_{n-1}$ if $f(\lambda, x_1, \ldots, x_{m-1}) = g(x_1, \ldots, x_{m-1})$, $f'(\lambda, x_1, \ldots, x_{m-1}) = g'(x_1, \ldots, x_{m-1})$ and

$$\begin{aligned}
&f(xa_0, x_1, \ldots, x_{m-1})\\
&\quad = h_0(x, x_1, \ldots, x_{m-1}, f(x, x_1, \ldots, x_{m-1}), f'(x, x_1, \ldots, x_{m-1}))\\
&\quad \vdots\\
&f(xa_{n-1}, x_1, \ldots, x_{m-1})\\
&\quad = h_{n-1}(x, x_1, \ldots, x_{m-1}, f(x, x_1, \ldots, x_{m-1}), f'(x, x_1, \ldots, x_{m-1}))\\
&f'(xa_0, x_1, \ldots, x_{m-1})\\
&\quad = h'_0(x, x_1, \ldots, x_{m-1}, f(x, x_1, \ldots, x_{m-1}), f'(x, x_1, \ldots, x_{m-1}))\\
&\quad \vdots\\
&f'(xa_{n-1}, x_1, \ldots, x_{m-1})\\
&\quad = h'_{n-1}(x, x_1, \ldots, x_{m-1}, f(x, x_1, \ldots, x_{m-1}), f'(x, x_1, \ldots, x_{m-1})),
\end{aligned}$$

for every $x, x_1, \ldots, x_{m-1} \in A^*$. □

Theorem 7.7.18 *Let $A = \{a_0, \ldots, a_{n-1}\}$ be an alphabet. If the functions $f, f' : (A^*)^m \longrightarrow A^*$ are obtained by simultaneous primitive recursion from the primitive recursive functions $g, g', h_0, \ldots, h_{n-1}, h'_0, \ldots, h'_{n-1}$ as in Definition 7.7.17, then they are primitive recursive.*

Proof. To simplify the notation we assume that $m = 2$; the general argument is similar. Let $\sharp$ be a symbol such that $\sharp \notin A$, $B = A \cup \{\sharp\}$. Let $F : (B^*)^2 \longrightarrow B^*$ be the function defined by

$$F(x, x_1) = \begin{cases} f(x, x_1)\sharp f'(x, x_1) & \text{if } x, x_1 \in A^*,\\ \lambda & \text{otherwise} \end{cases}$$

for $x, x_1 \in A^*$. Since

$$\begin{aligned}
f(x, x_1) &= \mathsf{lleftmost}(F(x, x_1), \sharp)\\
f'(x, x_1) &= \mathsf{rleftmost}(F(x, x_1), \sharp),
\end{aligned}$$

for $x, x_1 \in A^*$, by Theorem 7.7.16, it would suffice to show that F is a primitive recursive function on B in order to prove that f and f' are primitive recursive functions on A.

Let $G : B^* \longrightarrow B^*$ be the primitive recursive function given by

$$G(x_1) = \begin{cases} g(x_1)\sharp g'(x_1) & \text{if } x_1 \in A^*\\ \lambda & \text{otherwise,} \end{cases}$$

for $x_1 \in B^*$. It is clear that $F(\lambda, x_1) = G(x_1)$ for $x_1 \in B^*$.

It is easy to see that the predicate p_A defined by $p_A(x, x_1, z) = a_0$ if and only if $x, x_1 \in A^*$ and $z \in A^*\sharp A^*$ is primitive recursive on B. This allows us to introduce the primitive recursive functions $H_0, \ldots, H_{n-1}, H_\sharp$ on B given by

$$\begin{aligned}
H_i(x, x_1, z) \;=\; & h_i(x, x_1, \mathsf{lleftmost}(z, \sharp), \mathsf{rleftmost}(z, \sharp))\sharp\\
& h'_i(x, x_1, \mathsf{lleftmost}(z, \sharp), \mathsf{rleftmost}(z, \sharp))
\end{aligned}$$

if $p_A(x, x_1, z) = a_0$ and $H_i(x, x_1, z) = \lambda$, otherwise, for $0 \leq i \leq n-1$, and $H_\sharp(x, x_1, z) = \lambda$, for $x, x_1, z \in B^*$. Then, it is easy to see that $F(xa_i, x_1) = H_i(x, x_1, F(x, x_1))$ and $F(x\sharp, x_1) = H_\sharp(x, x_1, F(x, x_1))$, which means that F is definable by primitive recursion from $G, H_1, \ldots, H_{n-1}, H_\sharp$, which implies that F is primitive recursive. ■

7.8 Primitive Recursive Languages

In this section we introduce a class of languages closely related to primitive recursive functions.

Definition 7.8.1 Let A be an alphabet such that $a_0 \in A$ and let $L \subseteq A^*$. The *characteristic predicate* of L is the predicate p_L defined by

$$p_L(x) = \begin{cases} a_0 & \text{if } x \in L \\ \lambda & \text{otherwise} \end{cases}$$

for $x \in A^*$.

A language $L \subseteq A^*$ is *primitive recursive on A* if its characteristic predicate p_L is primitive recursive. The class of primitive recursive languages is denoted by $\mathcal{L}_{prec}$. □

Example 7.8.2 Let A, C be two alphabets such that $C \subseteq A$. The language C^* is primitive recursive on A since

$$\begin{aligned} p_{C^*}(\lambda) &= a_0 \\ p_{C^*}(xa_i) &= h_i(x, p_{C^*}(x)), \end{aligned}$$

for $x \in A^*$ and $a_i \in A$, where

$$h_i(x, y) = \begin{cases} y & \text{if } a_i \in C \\ \lambda & \text{otherwise,} \end{cases}$$

for $x, y \in A^*$.

The empty language is clearly primitive recursive because $p_\emptyset = e$. □

Theorem 7.8.3 *Let A be an alphabet. If $K, L \subseteq A^*$ are two primitive recursive languages on A, then $K \cup L$, $K \cap L$, $K - L$, KL, K^*, and K^+ are primitive recursive languages over A.*

Also, every finite language on A is primitive recursive.

Proof. Let $K, L \subseteq A^*$ be two primitive recursive languages on A. Since

$$\begin{aligned} p_{K \cup L} &= p_K \vee p_L \\ p_{K \cap L} &= p_K \wedge p_L \\ p_{K-L} &= p_K \wedge (\neg p_L) \end{aligned}$$

it follows that $K \cup L, K \cap L$ and $K - L$ are primitive recursive languages on A.

Note that every singleton $L_w = \{w\}$ is a primitive recursive language on A since $p_{L_w}(x) = (x = w)$ for $x \in A^*$. If $L = \{w_0, \ldots, w_{n-1}\}$ is a finite language, the first part of the theorem implies that L_w is primitive recursive.

For p_{KL} we have

$$p_{KL}(z) = (\exists u \leq_{\text{pref}} z)(p_K(u) \wedge p_L(z -_l u))$$

for $z \in A^*$, which shows that KL is primitive recursive.

Let $P_K : (A^*)^2 \longrightarrow A^*$ be a predicate defined by

$$\begin{aligned} P_K(x, \lambda) &= \mathsf{isnull}(x) \\ P_K(x, ya) &= (\exists u \leq_{\text{pref}} x)(p_K(u) \wedge P_K(x -_l u, y)) \end{aligned}$$

for $x, y \in A^*$. It is easy to see that $P_K(x, y) = a_0$ if and only if $x \in K^{|y|}$. Note that $x \in K^*$ if and only if there exists $n \in \mathbb{N}$ such that $x \in K^n$ and $n \leq |x|$. Therefore, $p_{K^*}(x) = (\exists z \leq_{\text{pref}} \mathsf{length}(x))P_K(x, z)$ for $x \in A^*$, which shows that K^* is primitive recursive. The primitive recursiveness of K^+ follows from the equality $K^+ = K^*K$. ∎

Theorem 7.8.4 *Let A be an alphabet and let $f : A^* \longrightarrow A^*$ be a primitive recursive function. If $L \subseteq A^*$ is a primitive recursive language, then $f^{-1}(L) = \{x \in A^* \mid f(x) \in L\} \in \mathcal{L}_{prec}$.*

Proof. Let $K = f^{-1}(L)$. Since $x \in K$ if and only if $p_L(f(x)) = a_0$ for every $x \in A^*$, it follows that $p_K = p_L f$. Thus, K is primitive recursive. ∎

We introduce several primitive recursive predicates related to rewriting systems.

Lemma 7.8.5 *Let A be an alphabet and let $\pi : \alpha \to \beta$ be a production on A. The set $D_{\alpha\to\beta} = \{x \Rightarrow y \mid x, y \in A^* \text{ and } x \underset{\pi}{\Rightarrow} y\}$ is a primitive recursive language on the alphabet $A \cup \{\Rightarrow\}$.*

Proof. We have $w = x \Rightarrow y \in D_{\alpha\to\beta}$ if $x = u\alpha v$ and $y = u\beta v$ for some $u, v \in A^*$. Note that in this case we can write $x = \mathsf{lleftmost}(w, \Rightarrow)$ and $y = \mathsf{rleftmost}(w, \Rightarrow)$, $u \leq_{\text{pref}} x$, and $\mathsf{rev}(v) \leq_{\text{pref}} \mathsf{rev}(x)$. Therefore, we have

$$\begin{aligned} & p_{D_{\alpha\to\beta}}(w) \\ &= (\exists u \leq_{\text{pref}} \mathsf{lleftmost}(w, \Rightarrow))(\exists z \leq_{\text{pref}} \mathsf{rev}(\mathsf{lleftmost}(w, \Rightarrow))) \\ & \quad (\mathsf{lleftmost}(w, \Rightarrow) = u\alpha\mathsf{rev}(z) \wedge \mathsf{rleftmost}(w, \Rightarrow) = u\beta\mathsf{rev}(z)), \end{aligned}$$

for $w \in A^*$, which shows that $D_{\alpha\to\beta}$ is indeed primitive recursive on $A \cup \{\Rightarrow\}$. ∎

Theorem 7.8.6 *Let $T = (A, M, P)$ be a semi-Thue system. The language $D_T = \{x \Rightarrow y \mid x, y \in A^* \text{ and } x \underset{\pi}{\Rightarrow} y \text{ for some } \pi \in P\}$ is primitive recursive on the alphabet $A \cup \{\Rightarrow\}$.*

Proof. By Lemma 7.8.5, the primitive recursiveness of the language D_T follows from the fact that $D_T = \bigcup\{D_{\alpha\to\beta} \mid \alpha \to \beta \in P\}$. ∎

Corollary 7.8.7 *Let A be an alphabet and let $\pi : \alpha \to \beta$ be a production on A. The predicate $p_{\alpha\to\beta}$ defined by $p_{\alpha\to\beta}(x, y) = a_0$ if $x \underset{\pi}{\Rightarrow} y$ for $x, y \in A^*$ is a primitive recursive predicate on A.*

Let $T = (A, M, P)$ be a semi-Thue system. The predicate d_T on A defined by $d_T(x, y) = a_0$ if and only if y is obtained from x by a single application of a production of T is primitive recursive.

Proof. The first part of the corollary follows from Theorem 7.8.6 since

$$p_{\alpha\to\beta}(x, y) = p_{D_{\alpha\to\beta}}(x \Rightarrow y).$$

The primitive recursiveness of d_T follows from the primitive recursiveness of D_T. ∎

Definition 7.8.8 Let $T = (A, M, P)$ be a semi-Thue system. The *language of derivations* R_T in T is the language on the alphabet $A \cup \{\Rightarrow\}$ that consists of all words $w_0 \Rightarrow w_1 \cdots \Rightarrow w_{n-1}$ for $n \geq 1$. □

Theorem 7.8.9 *For every semi-Thue system the language R_T is primitive recursive.*

Proof. If w is the word $w_0 \Rightarrow w_1 \cdots \Rightarrow w_{n-1}$, then the length of this derivation is given by $\mathsf{occ}(w, \Rightarrow)$. Note that $w_i = \mathsf{part}(w, \Rightarrow, a_0^i)$ for $0 \leq i \leq n-1$. Therefore, we have

$$\begin{aligned} & p_{R_T}(w) \\ = \; & (\forall a_0^i \leq_{\text{pref}} \mathsf{occ}(w, \Rightarrow)) p_{D_T}(\mathsf{part}(w, \Rightarrow, a_0^i), \mathsf{part}(w, \Rightarrow, a_0^{i+1})) \\ & \vee (\mathsf{occ}(w, \Rightarrow) = \lambda) \end{aligned}$$

for $w \in A^*$, which shows that R_T is a primitive recursive language for every semi-Thue system. ∎

Corollary 7.8.10 *Let G be a grammar. The languages D_G and R_G are primitive recursive on the alphabet $A \cup \{\Rightarrow\}$, where $A = A_N \cup A_T$.*

Proof. This statement follows from Corollary 7.8.7 and from Theorem 7.8.9 since a grammar is a special rewriting system. ∎

In general, the language generated by a semi-Thue system is not primitive recursive, as we shall see in Section 8.6. However, we have the following theorem.

Theorem 7.8.11 *If $T = (A, M, P)$ is a length-increasing semi-Thue system and $B \subseteq A$, then $L_g(T|B)$ is a primitive recursive language.*

Proof. Let $\pi : \alpha \to \beta$ be a length-increasing production in P and suppose that $x \underset{\pi}{\Rightarrow} y$. We have $x = u\alpha v$ and $v \doteq u\beta v$ for some words $u \in A^*$. Therefore, $|x| \leq |y|$, so $\phi_A(x) \leq |A|\phi_A(y) \leq \phi_A(yy)$, by Exercise 29 of Chapter 2.

Let p_α be the predicate defined by $p_\alpha(y, u, v) = a_0$ if and only if $|y| \leq |u|$ and there is a derivation $\alpha \overset{l}{\underset{T}{\Rightarrow}} y$ such that $l \leq |v|$. This predicate is primitive recursive because

$$p_\alpha(y, u, \lambda) = \begin{cases} a_0 & \text{if } y = \alpha \text{ and } |y| \leq |u| \\ \lambda & \text{otherwise} \end{cases}$$

and

$$\begin{aligned} & p_\alpha(y, u, va) \\ = \; & p_\alpha(y, u, v) \vee (((|y| \leq |u|) \wedge (\exists x \leq yy)(p_\alpha(x, u, v) \wedge d_T(x, y)))\,, \end{aligned}$$

for $y, u, v \in A^*$.

Since T is a length-increasing rewriting system, for every derivation of length m

$$\alpha \underset{T}{\Rightarrow} y_1 \underset{T}{\Rightarrow} \cdots y_{m-1} \underset{T}{\Rightarrow} y_m = y$$

we have $|\alpha| \leq |y_1| \leq \cdots \leq |y_m| = |y|$. If $|y| = n$, then there are no more than $(n+1)|A|^n$ distinct words of length less than or equal to n, so there is a derivation of y of length not greater than $(n+1)|A|^n$. Consequently, the characteristic predicate of $L_g(T|B)$ can be written as

$$p_{L_g(T|B)}(y) = p_{B^*}(y) \wedge \bigvee_{\alpha \in M} p_\alpha(y, |y|, (|y|+1) \cdot |A|^{|y|})$$

for $y \in A^*$, which shows that $L_g(T|B)$ is primitive recursive. ∎

Corollary 7.8.12 *The language generated by a length-increasing grammar is primitive recursive.*

Proof. Let $G = (A_N, A_T, S, P)$ be a length-increasing grammar and let $A = A_N \cup A_T$. Suppose initially that $\lambda \notin L(G)$, that is, $S \to \lambda$ is not a production of G. Since $L(G) = L_g(T|A_T)$, where T is the rewriting system $(A_N \cup A_T, \{S\}, P)$, $L(G)$ is primitive recursive by Theorem 7.8.11.

If $\lambda \in L(G)$, let G' be the length-increasing grammar obtained by eliminating $S \to \lambda$ from P. Then, by the previous argument, $L(G')$ is primitive recursive, and thus, $L(G)$ is primitive recursive because $L(G) = L(G') \cup \{\lambda\}$. ∎

7.9 Partial Recursive Functions

The class of primitive recursive functions does not contain every function that is effectively computable, as we saw in Theorem 7.2.17. We begin this section with the definition of an effectively computable function that is not primitive recursive.

Definition 7.9.1 The *Ackermann function* is the function $\mathsf{ack} : \mathbb{N}^2 \longrightarrow \mathbb{N}$ defined by

$$\mathsf{ack}(0, n) = n + 1, \quad (7.5)$$

$$\mathsf{ack}(m+1, 0) = \mathsf{ack}(m, 1) \quad (7.6)$$

$$\mathsf{ack}(m+1, n+1) = \mathsf{ack}(m, \mathsf{ack}(m+1, n)), \quad (7.7)$$

for every $m, n \in \mathbb{N}$. □

It is clear that the function ack can be effectively computed. Indeed, $\mathsf{ack}(0, n)$ is the successor function s_1. Suppose that $\mathsf{ack}(m, n)$ can be effectively evaluated for all n. Then, $\mathsf{ack}(m+1, n)$ can be effectively evaluated by repeatedly using the equality (7.7).

Example 7.9.2 Define the function $\alpha_m : \mathbb{N} \longrightarrow \mathbb{N}$ by $\alpha_m(n) = \mathsf{ack}(m, n)$ for $m, n \in \mathbb{N}$. Clearly, α_0 equals the successor function s_1. For α_1 we can write

$$\alpha_1(0) = \alpha_0(1) = 2,$$

$$\alpha_1(n+1) = \alpha_0(\alpha_1(n)) = \alpha_1(n) + 1,$$

for $n \in \mathbb{N}$. This immediately implies $\alpha_1(n) = n + 2$ for $n \in \mathbb{N}$.

The corresponding recursive definition for α_2 is

$$\alpha_2(0) = \alpha_1(1) = 3,$$

$$\alpha_2(n+1) = \alpha_1(\alpha_2(n)) = \alpha_1(n) + 2,$$

$$
\begin{array}{rcll}
\mathsf{ack}(2,2) & = & \mathsf{ack}(1,\mathsf{ack}(2,1)) & \text{(by Eq. (7.7))} \\
& = & \mathsf{ack}(1,\mathsf{ack}(1,\mathsf{ack}(2,0))) & \text{(by Eq. (7.7))} \\
& = & \mathsf{ack}(1,\mathsf{ack}(1,\mathsf{ack}(1,1))) & \text{(by Eq. (7.6))} \\
& = & \mathsf{ack}(1,\mathsf{ack}(1,\mathsf{ack}(0,\mathsf{ack}(1,0)))) & \text{(by Eq. (7.7))} \\
& = & \mathsf{ack}(1,\mathsf{ack}(1,\mathsf{ack}(0,\mathsf{ack}(0,1)))) & \text{(by Eq. (7.6))} \\
& = & \mathsf{ack}(1,\mathsf{ack}(1,\mathsf{ack}(0,2))) & \text{(by Eq. (7.5))} \\
& = & \mathsf{ack}(1,\mathsf{ack}(1,3)) & \text{(by Eq. (7.5))} \\
& = & \mathsf{ack}(1,\mathsf{ack}(0,\mathsf{ack}(1,2))) & \text{(by Eq. (7.7))} \\
& = & \mathsf{ack}(1,\mathsf{ack}(0,\mathsf{ack}(0,\mathsf{ack}(1,1)))) & \text{(by Eq. (7.7))} \\
& = & \mathsf{ack}(1,\mathsf{ack}(0,\mathsf{ack}(0,\mathsf{ack}(0,\mathsf{ack}(1,0))))) & \text{(by Eq. (7.7))} \\
& = & \mathsf{ack}(1,\mathsf{ack}(0,\mathsf{ack}(0,\mathsf{ack}(0,\mathsf{ack}(0,1))))) & \text{(by Eq. (7.6))} \\
& = & \mathsf{ack}(1,\mathsf{ack}(0,\mathsf{ack}(0,\mathsf{ack}(0,2)))) & \text{(by Eq. (7.5))} \\
& = & \mathsf{ack}(1,\mathsf{ack}(0,\mathsf{ack}(0,3))) & \text{(by Eq. (7.5))} \\
& = & \mathsf{ack}(1,\mathsf{ack}(0,4)) & \text{(by Eq. (7.5))} \\
& = & \mathsf{ack}(1,5) & \text{(by Eq. (7.5))} \\
& = & \mathsf{ack}(0,\mathsf{ack}(1,4)) & \text{(by Eq. (7.7))} \\
& = & \mathsf{ack}(0,\mathsf{ack}(0,\mathsf{ack}(1,3)) & \text{(by Eq. (7.7))} \\
& = & \mathsf{ack}(0,\mathsf{ack}(0,\mathsf{ack}(0,\mathsf{ack}(1,2)))) & \text{(by Eq. (7.7))} \\
& = & \mathsf{ack}(0,\mathsf{ack}(0,\mathsf{ack}(0,\mathsf{ack}(0,\mathsf{ack}(1,1))))) & \text{(by Eq. (7.7))} \\
& = & \mathsf{ack}(0,\mathsf{ack}(0,\mathsf{ack}(0,\mathsf{ack}(0,\mathsf{ack}(0,\mathsf{ack}(1,0)))))) & \text{(by Eq. (7.7))} \\
& = & \mathsf{ack}(0,\mathsf{ack}(0,\mathsf{ack}(0,\mathsf{ack}(0,\mathsf{ack}(0,\mathsf{ack}(0,1)))))) & \text{(by Eq. (7.6))} \\
& = & \mathsf{ack}(0,\mathsf{ack}(0,\mathsf{ack}(0,\mathsf{ack}(0,\mathsf{ack}(0,2))))) & \text{(by Eq. (7.5))} \\
& = & \mathsf{ack}(0,\mathsf{ack}(0,\mathsf{ack}(0,\mathsf{ack}(0,3)))) & \text{(by Eq. (7.5))} \\
& = & \mathsf{ack}(0,\mathsf{ack}(0,\mathsf{ack}(0,4))) & \text{(by Eq. (7.5))} \\
& = & \mathsf{ack}(0,\mathsf{ack}(0,5)) & \text{(by Eq. (7.5))} \\
& = & \mathsf{ack}(0,6) & \text{(by Eq. (7.5))} \\
& = & 7 & \text{(by Eq. (7.5))}
\end{array}
$$

Figure 7.4: Computation of $\mathsf{ack}(2,2)$

which implies $\alpha_2(n) = 2n + 3$ for $n \in \mathbb{N}$. At this point the functions α_n "take off." The next function is an exponential. Indeed, we have

$$
\begin{aligned}
\alpha_3(0) &= \alpha_2(1) = 5, \\
\alpha_3(n+1) &= \alpha_2(\alpha_3(n)) = 2\alpha_3(n) + 3,
\end{aligned}
$$

for $n \in \mathbb{N}$. An elementary computation yields

$$
\begin{aligned}
\alpha_3(n) &= 2^n \cdot 5 + 3 \cdot (2^{n-1} + 2^{n-2} + \cdots + 1) \\
&= 2^n \cdot 5 + 3 \cdot (2^n - 1) \\
&= 2^{n+3} - 3,
\end{aligned}
$$

for $n \in \mathbb{N}$. For the function α_4 we have

$$
\begin{aligned}
\alpha_4(0) &= 13, \\
\alpha_4(n+1) &= \alpha_3(\alpha_4(n)) = 2^{\alpha_4(n)+3} - 3,
\end{aligned}
$$

for $n \in \mathbb{N}$. □

Example 7.9.3 Consider the computation of $\mathsf{ack}(2,2)$ shown in Figure 7.4. Each step has the form

$$\mathsf{ack}(x_0, \mathsf{ack}(x_1, \mathsf{ack}(\cdots, \mathsf{ack}(x_{p-2}, x_{p-1}) \cdots)),$$

and we systematically replace the innermost occurrence $\mathsf{ack}(x_{p-2}, x_{p-1})$ of ack, using one of the equalities (7.5)–(7.7). It is not difficult to see that we can use this technique for computing $\mathsf{ack}(m,n)$ for any $m, n \in \mathbb{N}$. □

Lemma 7.9.4 *The following inequalities hold:*

(i) $\mathsf{ack}(m,n) > n$;

(ii) $\mathsf{ack}(m, n+1) > \mathsf{ack}(m, n)$;
(iii) *if* $n > n'$, *then* $\mathsf{ack}(m, n) > \mathsf{ack}(m, n')$;
(iv) $\mathsf{ack}(m+1, n) \geq \mathsf{ack}(m, n+1)$;
(v) $\mathsf{ack}(m, n) > m$;
(vi) *if* $m > m'$, *then* $\mathsf{ack}(m, n) > \mathsf{ack}(m', n)$;
(vii) $\mathsf{ack}(m+2, n) > \mathsf{ack}(m, 2n)$,

for every $m, n \in \mathbb{N}$.

Proof. The argument for Part (i) is by induction on m. For $m = 0$ the inequality $\mathsf{ack}(0, n) > n$ is immediate since $\mathsf{ack}(0, n) = n + 1$.

Suppose that $\mathsf{ack}(m, n) > n$ for every $n \in \mathbb{N}$. To prove that $\mathsf{ack}(m+1, n) > n$ we use an inductive argument on n.

For $n = 0$ we have $\mathsf{ack}(m+1, 0) = \mathsf{ack}(m, 1) > 1$ (by the "outer" inductive hypothesis), so $\mathsf{ack}(m+1, 0) > 0$. Suppose that $\mathsf{ack}(m+1, n) > n$ (the "inner" inductive hypothesis). Then, $\mathsf{ack}(m+1, n+1) = \mathsf{ack}(m, \mathsf{ack}(m+1, n)) > \mathsf{ack}(m+1, n) > n$, which implies $\mathsf{ack}(m+1, n+1) > n+1$. This concludes the proof of Part (i).

Part (ii) is a simple induction on m and makes use of Part (i). Part (iii) can be shown by induction on $h = n - n' - 1$, using Part (ii). We leave both arguments to the reader.

Part (iv) can be shown by induction on n. For $n = 0$, Part (iv) follows immediately from Equality 7.6. Suppose that the inequality holds for n. Then,

$$\begin{aligned}
\mathsf{ack}(m+1, n+1) &= \mathsf{ack}(m, \mathsf{ack}(m+1, n)) \\
&\quad \text{(by the definition of ack)} \\
&\geq \mathsf{ack}(m, \mathsf{ack}(m, n+1)) \\
&\quad \text{(by ind. hyp. and Part (iii))} \\
&\geq \mathsf{ack}(m, n+2) \\
&\quad \text{(by Part (iii) and Exercise 47).}
\end{aligned}$$

For Part (v), repeated application of Part (iv) gives $\mathsf{ack}(m, n) \geq \mathsf{ack}(0, m+n)$, and by Part (i) $\mathsf{ack}(0, m+n) = m+n+1 > m$.

Part (vi) follows from $\mathsf{ack}(m+1, n) \geq \mathsf{ack}(m, n+1) > \mathsf{ack}(m, n)$, using Parts (iv) and (ii).

Part (vii) can be shown by induction on n. The basis case, $n = 0$, is immediate since $\mathsf{ack}(m+2, 0) > \mathsf{ack}(m, 0)$ by Part (vi). Suppose that $\mathsf{ack}(m+2, n) > \mathsf{ack}(m, 2n)$. We have $\mathsf{ack}(m+2, n+1) = \mathsf{ack}(m+1, \mathsf{ack}(m+2, n)) > \mathsf{ack}(m+1, \mathsf{ack}(m, 2n))$ by Part (iii) and the inductive hypothesis. Therefore, by Part (iv), $\mathsf{ack}(m+2, n+1) > \mathsf{ack}(m, \mathsf{ack}(m, 2n)+1)$. Note that Part (i) implies $\mathsf{ack}(m, 2n) \geq 2n+1$, so $\mathsf{ack}(m+2, n+1) > \mathsf{ack}(m, 2n+2)$, which concludes the inductive argument. ∎

For $x = (x_0, \ldots, x_{n-1}) \in \mathbb{N}^n$ denote $\max\{x_0, \ldots, x_{n-1}\}$ by $\| x \|$.

Theorem 7.9.5 *For each p-ary primitive recursive function* $f : \mathbb{N}^p \longrightarrow \mathbb{N}$, *there is* $k \in \mathbb{N}$ *such that*

$$\mathsf{ack}(k, \| x \|) > f(x_0, \ldots, x_{p-1})$$

for $x = (x_0, \ldots, x_{p-1}) \in \mathbb{N}^p$.

Proof. The argument is by induction on the primitive recursive function f. For the basis case we have the following three subcases:

1. If f is the constant function $e : \mathbb{N} \longrightarrow \mathbb{N}$ given by $e(n) = 0$ for $n \in \mathbb{N}$, then, by taking $k = 0$ we have $\mathsf{ack}(0, \| n \|) = n + 1 > 0 = e(n)$ for $n \in \mathbb{N}$.
2. Let $f = s_1$. In this case, taking $k = 1$ we have $\mathsf{ack}(1, \| n \|) = n+2 > s_1(n)$ for $n \in \mathbb{N}$.
3. If $f = P_i^k$, then $k = 0$ is sufficient because $\mathsf{ack}(0, \| x \|) = \| x \| + 1 > x_i = P_i^k(x_0, \ldots, x_{n-1})$.

For the inductive step assume that the statement holds for all primitive recursive functions that are obtained by using k applications of composition or primitive recursion. There are two subcases to consider.

1. Suppose that $f : (A^*)^p \longrightarrow A^*$ is obtained by composition from the primitive recursive functions $g, h_0, \ldots, h_{m-1}$, where g is an m-ary function and $h_0, \ldots, h_{m-1}$ are p-ary functions. By the inductive hypothesis, there exist $k, k_0, \ldots, k_{m-1} \in \mathbb{N}$ such that
$$\mathsf{ack}(k, \max\{y_0, \ldots, y_{m-1}\}) > g(y_0, \ldots, y_{m-1})$$
for $y_0, \ldots, y_{m-1} \in \mathbb{N}$, and
$$\mathsf{ack}(k_i, \max\{x_0, \ldots, x_{p-1}\}) > h_i(x_0, \ldots, x_{p-1}),$$
for $0 \leq i \leq m - 1$, and $x_0, \ldots, x_{p-1} \in \mathbb{N}$. Then,
$$\begin{aligned} f(x_0, \ldots, x_{p-1}) &= g(h_0(x_0, \ldots, x_{p-1}), \ldots, h_{m-1}(x_0, \ldots, x_{p-1})) \\ &< \mathsf{ack}(k, \max_i\{h_i(x_0, \ldots, x_{p-1})\}). \end{aligned}$$
Let $\bar{k} = \max\{k, k_0, \ldots, k_{m-1}\} + 2$. Since $\bar{k} - 1 > k_i$ we have
$$h_i(x_0, \ldots, x_{p-1}) < \mathsf{ack}(k_i, \| x \|) < \mathsf{ack}(\bar{k} - 1, \| x \|)$$
for $0 \leq i \leq m - 1$, so
$$\begin{aligned} f(x_0, \ldots, x_{p-1}) &< \mathsf{ack}(k, \mathsf{ack}(\bar{k} - 1, \| x \|)) \\ &\leq \mathsf{ack}(\bar{k} - 2, \mathsf{ack}(\bar{k} - 1, \| x \|)) \\ &= \mathsf{ack}(\bar{k} - 1, \| x \|), \end{aligned}$$
which gives the desired inequality for f.
2. If $f : \mathbb{N}^p \longrightarrow \mathbb{N}$ is obtained by primitive recursion from the functions $g : \mathbb{N}^{p-1} \longrightarrow \mathbb{N}$ and $h : \mathbb{N}^{p+1} \longrightarrow \mathbb{N}$, then
$$\begin{aligned} f(0, x_1, \ldots, x_{p-1}) &= g(x_1, \ldots, x_{p-1}), \\ f(x + 1, x_1, \ldots, x_{p-1}) &= h(x, x_1, \ldots, x_{p-1}, f(x, x_1, \ldots, x_{p-1})) \end{aligned}$$
for every $x, x_1, \ldots, x_{p-1} \in \mathbb{N}$. By the inductive hypothesis, there exist $k, k' \in \mathbb{N}$ such that
$$\begin{aligned} g(x_1, \ldots, x_{p-1}) &< \mathsf{ack}(k, \max\{x_1, \ldots, x_{p-1}\}) \\ h(x, x_1, \ldots, x_{p-1}, z) &< \mathsf{ack}(k', \max\{x, x_1, \ldots, x_{p-1}, z\}), \end{aligned}$$
for $x, x_1, \ldots, x_{p-1}, z \in \mathbb{N}$. We claim that if $\bar{k} = \max\{k, k'\} + 3$, then $f(x, x_1, \ldots, x_{p-1}) < \mathsf{ack}(\bar{k}, \max\{x, x_1, \ldots, x_{p-1})$ for $x, x_1, \ldots, x_{p-1} \in \mathbb{N}$. Initially, we prove by induction on y that $f(y, x_1, \ldots, x_{p-1}) < \mathsf{ack}(\bar{k} - 2, y + \max\{x_1, \ldots, x_{p-1})$ for $y, x_1, \ldots, x_{p-1} \in \mathbb{N}$.

For $y = 0$ we have

$$\begin{aligned} f(0, x_1, \ldots, x_{p-1}) &= g(x_1, \ldots, a_{p-1}) \\ &< \mathsf{ack}(k, \max\{x_1, \ldots, x_{p-1}\}) \\ &< \mathsf{ack}(\bar{k} - 2, \max\{x_1, \ldots, x_{p-1}\}). \end{aligned}$$

Suppose that the inequality holds for y. Note that

$$\begin{aligned} &\mathsf{ack}(\bar{k} - 2, y + \max\{x_1, \ldots, x_{p-1}\}) \\ &\quad > \max\{y, x_1, \ldots, x_{p-1}, f(y, x_1, \ldots, x_{p-1})\} \end{aligned}$$

by the inductive hypothesis. Therefore,

$$\begin{aligned} &f(y + 1, x_1, \ldots, x_{p-1}) \\ &\quad = h(y, x_1, \ldots, x_{p-1}, f(y, x_1, \ldots, x_{p-1})) \\ &\quad < \mathsf{ack}(k', \max\{y, x_1, \ldots, x_{p-1}, f(y, x_1, \ldots, x_{p-1})\}) \\ &\quad < \mathsf{ack}(k', \mathsf{ack}(\bar{k} - 2, y + \max\{x_1, \ldots, x_{p-1}\})) \\ &\quad < \mathsf{ack}(\bar{k} - 3, \mathsf{ack}(\bar{k} - 2, y + \max\{x_1, \ldots, x_{p-1}\})) \\ &\quad = \mathsf{ack}(\bar{k} - 2, y + 1 + \max\{x_1, \ldots, x_{p-1}\}). \end{aligned}$$

By Part (vii) of Lemma 7.9.4, we have

$$\begin{aligned} &\mathsf{ack}(\bar{k}, \max\{y, x_1, \ldots, x_{p-1}\}) \\ &\quad > \mathsf{ack}(\bar{k} - 2, 2\max\{y, x_1, \ldots, x_{p-1}\}) \\ &\quad \geq \mathsf{ack}(\bar{k} - 2, y + \max\{x_1, \ldots, x_{p-1}\}) \\ &\quad > f(y, x_1, \ldots, x_{p-1}) \end{aligned}$$

for $y, x_1, \ldots, x_{p-1} \in \mathbb{N}$. ∎

Corollary 7.9.6 *The Ackermann function* ack *is not primitive recursive.*

Proof. Suppose that ack were primitive recursive. Then, by Theorem 7.9.5, we would have a number $k \in \mathbb{N}$ such that $\mathsf{ack}(k, \max\{x_0, x_1\}) > \mathsf{ack}(x_0, x_1)$ for every $x_0, x_1 \in \mathbb{N}$. If we choose $x_0 = x_1 = k$, then we have $\mathsf{ack}(k, k) > \mathsf{ack}(k, k)$, which is a contradiction. Thus, ack is not primitive recursive. ∎

Clearly, ack is computable in some natural sense, even though it is not primitive recursive. Thus, in order to capture the notion of "computable" we have to add a new tool – a new method for obtaining functions from existing functions – that enlarges the class of computable functions to include such functions as ack. The definitions of compositions and primitive recursion remain exactly the same when applied to partial function with the provision that an equality $f(x_0, \ldots, x_{n-1}) = g(x_0, \ldots, x_{n-1})$ means that either both sides are defined and equal, or neither side is defined. In addition, below we introduce the operation of minimalization (not to be confused with the operation of bounded minimalization previously introduced).

Definition 7.9.7 Let A be an alphabet, $a_i \in A$, and let $g : (A^*)^{1+n} \mapsto A^*$ be a partial function. The function $f : (A^*)^n \mapsto A^*$ is obtained from g by *minimalization over* a_i if for all $x_0, \ldots, x_{n-1} \in A^*$ the following conditions are satisfied:

(i) $f(x_0, \ldots, x_{n-1})$ is defined if and only if there exists a $p \in \mathbb{N}$ such that $(a_i^j, x_0, \ldots, x_{n-1}) \in \mathrm{Dom}(g)$, $g(a_i^j, x_0, \ldots, x_{n-1}) \neq \lambda$ for $0 \leq j < p$, and $g(a_i^p, x_0, \ldots, x_{n-1}) = \lambda$;

(ii) if $f(x_0, \ldots, x_{n-1})$ is defined as above, then $f(x_0, \ldots, x_{n-1}) = a_i^p$.

The function f is denoted by $(\min_i u)[g(u, x_0, \ldots, x_{n-1}) = \lambda]$. □

As a special case of the previous definition, if p is an $(1+n)$-ary predicate over A, then we say that f is obtained from p by *minimalization over* a_i if f is obtained by minimalization over a_i of the function $(\neg p)$. In other words, if a predicate is used for constructing the function by minimalization over a_i, then $f(x_0, \ldots, x_{n-1}) = a_i^k$ is the shortest word in $\{a_i\}^*$ such that $p(a_i^k, x_0, \ldots, x_{n-1}) = a_0$; if no such word exists, then $(x_0, \ldots, x_{n-1}) \notin \mathrm{Dom}(f)$. In this case, the function f may be denoted simply as $(\min_i u)p(u, x_0, \ldots, x_{n-1})$.

Example 7.9.8 The partial function $f : A^* \mapsto A^*$ given by

$$f(x) = \begin{cases} \lambda & \text{if } x = \lambda, \\ \text{undefined} & \text{otherwise,} \end{cases}$$

is partial recursive since it can be obtained by minimalization from the primitive recursive function $g(u, x) = ux$ for $u, v \in A^*$. Indeed, we have $f(x) = (\min_0 u)[ux = \lambda]$. □

Definition 7.9.9 The set of *partial recursive functions on the alphabet* A, consists of the following functions:

(i) every basic recursive function is a partial recursive function;

(ii) if $f : (A^*)^p \mapsto A^*$ is obtained by composition from the partial recursive functions $g, h_0, \ldots, h_{m-1}$ then f is partial recursive;

(iii) if f is obtained by primitive recursion from the partial recursive functions g and $h_0, \ldots, h_{n-1}$, then f is partial recursive;

(iv) if f is obtained by minimalization from the partial recursive function g, then f is partial recursive.

We denote this set by $\mathsf{PARREC}(A)$. □

The definition of partial recursive functions immediately implies that every primitive recursive function is also a partial recursive function. There are, of course, partial recursive functions that are totally defined but not primitive recursive. As we shall see in Theorem 7.9.13, Ackermann's function is precisely such a function. We refer to partial recursive functions that are totally defined as *recursive functions.*

The notion of recursive predicate is similar to the notion of primitive recursive predicate. Namely, an *n-ary recursive predicate* is a recursive function $p : (A^*)^n \longrightarrow A^*$ whose range is $\{\lambda, a_0\}$, where $a_0 \in A$.

Note that every primitive recursive function is also partial recursive and many results established for primitive recursive functions and predicates can easily be extended to partial recursive functions and recursive predicates. For example, definition by cases (Theorem 7.3.7) holds if we replace the expressions "primitive recursive predicate" and "primitive recursive function" by "recursive predicate" and "partial recursive function," respectively, as the reader can easily verify.

Theorem 7.7.16 can be extended to partial recursive functions as follows.

Theorem 7.9.10 *Let A, B be two alphabets such that $A \subseteq B$. If $f : (B^*)^n \mapsto B^*$ is a partial recursive function such that $(x_0, \ldots, x_{n-1}) \in (A^*)^n$ implies $f(x_0, \ldots, x_{n-1}) \in A^*$ for every $(x_0, \ldots, x_{n-1}) \in \mathrm{Dom}(f)$, then its restriction $f' = f\lceil A^*$ is a partial recursive function on A^*.*

Proof. The argument follows the same lines as the proof of Theorem 7.7.16. We leave it to the reader as an exercise. ∎

We saw that Ackermann's function is not primitive recursive. Next, we prove that Ackermann's function is partial recursive.

In Example 7.9.3, we noted that there is a computation of the Ackermann function such that each step has the form

$$\mathsf{ack}(x_0, \mathsf{ack}(x_1, \mathsf{ack}(\cdots, \mathsf{ack}(x_{p-2}, x_{p-1}) \cdots))).$$

Now, we systematically replace the innermost occurrence $\mathsf{ack}(x_{p-2}, x_{p-1})$ of ack, using one of the equalities (7.5)–(7.7). Suppose that this is the nth step of the computation, and we represent it as the word w_n on $A = \{a_0, a_1\}$ given by

$$w_n = a_1 a_0^p a_1 a_0^{x_0} a_1 \cdots a_1 a_0^{x_{p-2}} a_1 a_0^{x_{p-1}} a_1,$$

where p is the number of infixes of the form $a_0^{x_i}$ in the word w_n. We refer to w_n as the nth *configuration of the computation of* $\mathsf{ack}(x, y)$. Note that for the first step of the computation of $\mathsf{ack}(x, y)$ we have $w_0 = a_1 a_0^2 a_1 a_0^x a_1 a_0^y a_1$ while for the last step we have $w_n = a_1 a_0^1 a_1 a_0^{\mathsf{ack}(x,y)} a_1$. The computation ends when $h_0(w_n) = a_0^1$.

Lemma 7.9.11 *There exists a primitive recursive function $f : (A^*)^3 \longrightarrow A^*$ such that $f(a_0^n, a_0^x, a_0^y) = w_n$ for every word w_n that represents the nth step in the computation of $\mathsf{ack}(x, y)$.*

Proof. Note that

$$a_0^p = \mathsf{lleftmost}(\mathsf{trimfirst}(w_n), a_1),$$

and

$$\begin{aligned} a_0^{x_{p-2}} &= \mathsf{lleftmost}(\mathsf{rleftmost}(\mathsf{trimfirst}(\mathsf{rev}(w_n)), a_1), a_1) \\ a_0^{x_{p-1}} &= \mathsf{lleftmost}(\mathsf{trimfirst}(\mathsf{rev}(w_n)), a_1). \end{aligned}$$

This suggests considering the primitive recursive functions $h_0, h_1, h_2 : A^* \longrightarrow A^*$ given by

$$\begin{aligned} h_0(z) &= \mathsf{lleftmost}(\mathsf{trimfirst}(z), a_1), \\ h_1(z) &= \mathsf{lleftmost}(\mathsf{rleftmost}(\mathsf{trimfirst}(\mathsf{rev}(z)), a_1), a_1), \\ h_2(z) &= \mathsf{lleftmost}(\mathsf{trimfirst}(\mathsf{rev}(w_n)), a_1), \end{aligned}$$

for $z \in A^*$.

A step in the above computation consists in the application of one of the equalities (7.5)–(7.7), depending on the values x_{p-1} and x_{p-2}.

Define the function $g : (A^*)^3 \longrightarrow A^*$ by

$$g(x, u, v) = \begin{cases} \mathsf{trimfirst}(x) & \text{if } u = \lambda, \\ x & \text{if } u \neq \lambda \text{ and } v = \lambda, \\ x a_0 & \text{if } u \neq \lambda \text{ and } v \neq \lambda, \end{cases}$$

Then, $g(h_0(w_n), h_1(w_n), h_2(w_n)) = a_0^q$, where q gives the number of infixes in w_{n+1} of the form a_0^x; the three cases of the definition of g correspond to the application of the equalities (7.5)–(7.7). Let $g_0 : A^* \longrightarrow A^*$ be the function $g_0(w) = g(h_0(w), h_1(w), h_2(w))$ for $w \in A^*$.

The final part $a_1 a_0^{x_{p-2}} a_1 a_0^{x_{p-1}} = a_1 h_1(w_n) a_1 h_2(w_n) a_1$ of w_n must be replaced by $h(w_n)$, where $h : A^* \longrightarrow A^*$ is given by

$$h(w) = \begin{cases} a_1 a_0 h_2(w) a_1 & \text{if } h_1(w) = \lambda, \\ a_1 \mathsf{trimfirst}(h_1(w)) a_1 a_1 & \text{if } h_1(w) \neq \lambda, h_2(w) = \lambda \\ a_1 \mathsf{trimfirst}(h_1(w)) a_1 h(w) a_1 h_2(w) a_1 & \text{if } h_1(w) \neq \lambda, h_2(w) \neq \lambda. \end{cases}$$

The primitive recursive function $f : A^* \longrightarrow A^*$ such that $f(w_n) = w_{n+1}$ is given by

$$f(w) = \mathsf{repl}'(a_1 h_1(w) a_1 h_2(w) a_1, \mathsf{repl}(a_1 h_0(w) a_1, w, a_1 g_0(w) a_1), h(w)),$$

for $w \in A^*$. ∎

Lemma 7.9.12 *Let $A = \{a_0, a_1\}$. There is a primitive recursive function $F : (A^*)^3 \longrightarrow A^*$ such that $F(a_0^n, a_0^x, a_0^y) = w_n$, where w_n is the nth configuration of the computation of* $\mathsf{ack}(x, y)$.

Proof. The function F can be defined by primitive recursion starting from f by writing:

$$\begin{aligned} F(\lambda, u, v) &= a_1 a_0^1 a_1 a_0^{\mathsf{ack}(|u|,|v|} a_1, \\ F(y a_i, u, v) &= h_i(y, u, v, F(z, u, v)), \end{aligned}$$

where $h_i(y, u, v, z) = f(z)$ for both $i = 0, 1$ and $y, u, v, z \in A^*$. Here f is the primitive recursive function introduced in Lemma 7.9.11. ∎

Theorem 7.9.13 *Ackermann's function* ack *is a partial recursive function.*

Proof. We begin by observing that the number of steps needed to compute $\mathsf{ack}(x, y)$ is given by the partial recursive function t on $A = \{a_0, a_1\}$ defined by

$$t(x, y) = (\min_0 n)[h_0(F(n, x, y)) - 1 = 0].$$

for $x, y \in A^*$. Of course, we really use only values of x and y that have the form $x = a_0^m$ and $y = a_0^k$; however, this definition of t conforms to the definition of partial recursive functions by minimalization. The value $\mathsf{ack}(x, y)$ can be obtained as $\mathsf{ack}(x, y) = h_2(F(t(x, y), x, y))$, where

$$h_2(w) = \mathsf{lleftmost}(\mathsf{trimfirst}(\mathsf{rev}(w_n)), a_1)$$

for $w \in A^*$, is the primitive recursive function introduced in Lemma 7.9.11. Note that when $x, y \in \{a_0\}^*$, then $h_2(F(t(x, y), x, y)) \in \{a_0\}^*$, so, by Theorem 7.9.10, ack is indeed a partial recursive function on $\{a_0\}^*$, that is on $\mathbb{N}$. ∎

Observe that in constructing the definition of ack we used minimalization only once. This is not an accident. We will see later (in Section 8.5.2) that in constructing any partial recursive function we never need to use minimalization more than once.

7.10 Exercises

Primitive Recursive Functions

1. Prove that the set of basic primitive recursive functions is countably infinite.
2. Prove that the function firstof is primitive recursive.
3. ◇ Give two distinct primitive recursive programs $\boldsymbol{p}, \boldsymbol{p}'$ such that $\Phi(\boldsymbol{p}) = \Phi(\boldsymbol{p}') = c_\lambda^n$.
4. ◇ Let $A = \{a_0, \ldots, a_{n-1}\}$ be an alphabet. Prove that the projection function $P_i^k : (A^*)^k \longrightarrow A^*$ can be defined by primitive recursion starting from the functions c_λ^{k-1} and $\{h_i | 0 \leq i \leq k-1\}$, where $h_i : (A^*)^{k+1} \longrightarrow A^*$ is given by $h_i = s_i P_i^{k+1}$ for $0 \leq i \leq n-1$. Conclude that we can eliminate an infinite set of basic functions from the set of basic functions without affecting the set of primitive recursive functions. Can the set of primitive recursive functions be generated by composition and primitive recursion starting from a finite set of basic functions?
5. ◇ Let $A = \{a_0, \ldots, a_{n-1}\}$ be an alphabet.
   (a) Prove that the function $f_p : A^* \longrightarrow A^*$ given by $f_p(x) = x^p$ for $x \in A^*$ is primitive recursive.
   (b) Prove that the function $g : (A^*)^2 \longrightarrow A^*$ given by $g(x, y) = x^{|y|}$ for $x, y \in A^*$ is primitive recursive.
   (c) Part (b) can be generalized as follows. Let $k : \mathbb{N}^{p+1} \longrightarrow \mathbb{N}$ be a primitive recursive function. Prove that the function $g : (A^*)^{p+1} \longrightarrow A^*$ given by
   $$g(x, y_0, \ldots, y_{p-1}) = x^{k(|y_0|, \ldots, |y_{p-1}|)}$$
   for $x, y_0, \ldots, y_{p-1} \in A^*$ is primitive recursive.
6. Let A be an alphabet, and let $i, j \in \mathbb{N}$ be two numbers such that $i \leq j$. Prove that the function $f : A^* \longrightarrow A^*$ given by
   $$f(x) = \begin{cases} x_{i,j} & \text{if } |x| \geq j \\ \lambda & \text{otherwise,} \end{cases}$$
   for $x \in A^*$ is primitive recursive.
7. Let $f : A^* \longrightarrow A^*$ be a primitive recursive function over the alphabet A. For $k \in \mathbb{N}$, define the function $f_k : A^* \longrightarrow A^*$ by
   $$f_k(x) = \begin{cases} \text{the } k^{\text{th}} \text{ symbol of } x & \text{if } |x| \geq k \\ \lambda & \text{otherwise,} \end{cases}$$
   for $x \in A^*$. Prove that f_k is primitive recursive.
8. Let $g : (A^*)^4 \longrightarrow A^*$ be a primitive recursive function. Show that the function $f : (A^*)^2 \longrightarrow A^*$ given by
   $$f(x_0, x_1) = g(x_1, x_0, x_0, x_1)$$
   for $x_0, x_1 \in A^*$ is primitive recursive.

9. $^{\circ\circ}$ Prove the following generalization of Exercise 8 and of Theorem 7.2.6. If $\phi : \{0,\ldots,p-1\} \longrightarrow \{0,\ldots,q-1\}$ is a function, and $g : (A^*)^q \longrightarrow A^*$ is a primitive recursive function, then the function $f : (A^*)^p \longrightarrow A^*$ defined by

$$f(x_0,\ldots,x_{p-1}) = g(x_{\phi(0)},\ldots,x_{\phi(p-1)})$$

for $x_0,\ldots,x_{p-1} \in A^*$ is primitive recursive.

10. Prove that the function $g(x,y) = x -_r y$ for $x, y \in A^*$ (introduced in Example 7.2.12) is primitive recursive.

11. $^{\circ\circ}$ The notion of primitive word, used in this Exercise, was introduced in Section 2.7. Let $p : A^* \longrightarrow A^*$ be the function defined by $p(\lambda) = \lambda$, and $p(x) = y$ if y is the primitive word in A^+ such that $x = y^n$ for some $n \in \mathbb{N}$, $n \geq 1$, where $x \in A^+$. Prove that p is a primitive recursive function.

The notion of primitive recursive function is extended to functions whose values are m-tuples of words by saying that $f : (A^*)^n \longrightarrow (A^*)^m$ is primitive recursive if each function $P_i^m f : (A^*)^n \longrightarrow A^*$ is primitive recursive for $0 \leq i \leq m-1$. If $m = 0$, the unique function $P : (A^*)^n \longrightarrow (A^*)^0$ is primitive recursive.

12. $^{\circ}$ Let $f : (A^*)^n \longrightarrow (A^*)^m$, $g : (A^*)^p \longrightarrow (A^*)^q$ be two primitive recursive functions. Define the function $f \times g : (A^*)^{n+p} \longrightarrow (A^*)^{m+q}$ by

$$\begin{aligned} & f \times g(x_0,\ldots,x_{n-1},x_n,\ldots,x_{n+p-1}) \\ = \; & (y_0,\ldots,y_{m-1},y_m,\ldots,y_{m+q-1}), \end{aligned}$$

where

$$\begin{aligned} f(x_0,\ldots,x_{n-1}) &= (y_0,\ldots,y_{m-1}), \\ g(x_n,\ldots,x_{n+p-1}) &= (y_m,\ldots,y_{m+q-1}), \end{aligned}$$

for $(x_0,\ldots,x_{n-1},x_n,\ldots,x_{n+p-1}) \in (A^*)^{n+p}$. We say that $f \times g$ is obtained from f and g by *combination.*

(a) Prove that the $\times$ operation defined above is associative.

(b) Prove that $P_i^k = \underbrace{P \times \cdots \times P}_{i-1} \times P_0^1 \times \underbrace{P \times \cdots \times P}_{k-i}.$

(c) Show that the functions f, g are primitive recursive if and only if $f \times g$ is primitive recursive.

The operation of primitive recursion can be extended naturally to functions that range over sets of n-tuples. We say that $f : (A^*)^n \longrightarrow (A^*)^m$ is obtained from $g : (A^*)^{n-1} \longrightarrow (A^*)^m$ and $h_0,\ldots,h_{n-1} : (A^*)^{n+m} \longrightarrow (A^*)^m$ by *primitive recursion* if $f(\lambda,x_1,\ldots,x_{n-1}) = g(x_1,\ldots,x_{n-1})$ and

$$\begin{aligned} f(xa_0,x_1,\ldots,x_{n-1}) &= h_0(x,x_1,\ldots,x_{n-1},f(x,x_1,\ldots,x_{n-1})) \\ f(xa_1,x_1,\ldots,x_{n-1}) &= h_1(x,x_1,\ldots,x_{n-1},f(x,x_1,\ldots,x_{n-1})) \\ &\vdots \\ f(xa_{n-1},x_1,\ldots,x_{n-1}) &= h_{n-1}(x,x_1,\ldots,x_{n-1},f(x,x_1,\ldots,x_{n-1})), \end{aligned}$$

for $x, x_1,\ldots,x_{n-1} \in A^*$.

13. $^{\circ}$ Let $A = \{a_0,\ldots,a_{n-1}\}$ be an alphabet. Show that the set of primitive recursive functions on A can be defined starting from the finite set of basic

functions that consists of e, $s_0, \ldots, s_{n-1}$, the identity function P_0^1, and the function P, using the operations of composition, combination, and primitive recursion.

14. $^\diamond$ Let $m, n \in \mathbb{N}$ be two numbers, where $n \geq 1$, $A = \{a_0, \ldots, a_{n-1}\}$ be an alphabet, and $f_i : (A^*)^m \longrightarrow (A^*)^m$ be n functions, where $0 \leq i \leq n-1$. The function $(f_0, \ldots, f_{n-1})^\S : (A^*)^{n+1} \longrightarrow (A^*)^n$ given by
$$(f_0, \ldots, f_{n-1})^\S(x_0, \ldots, x_{n-1}, \lambda) = (x_0, \ldots, x_{n-1})$$
and
$$(f_0, \ldots, f_{n-1})^\S(x_0, \ldots, x_{n-1}, xa_i) = f_i((f_0, \ldots, f_{n-1})^\S(x_0, \ldots, x_{n-1}, x))$$
will be referred to as the *exponential* of the functions $f_0, \ldots, f_{n-1}$.
    (a) Prove that $(s_0, \ldots, s_{n-1})^\S(x, y) = \mathsf{conc}(x, y)$ for $x, y \in A^*$.
    (b) Prove that if $f_0, \ldots, f_{n-1}$ are primitive recursive functions, then $(f_0, \ldots, f_{n-1})^\S$ is a primitive recursive function.

Primitive Recursive Predicates

15. Prove that the unary predicate pal on A^* given by $\mathsf{pal}(x) = a_0$ if and only if x is a palindrome is primitive recursive.
16. $^\diamond$ Let A be an alphabet, $w \in A^*$, and let $S(w)$ be the set of symbols that occur in w. Prove that the predicate $p : (A^*)^2 \longrightarrow A^*$ defined by $p(x, y) = a_0$ if and only if $S(x) = S(y)$ is primitive recursive.
17. $^\diamond$ Prove that for any m-ary predicate p we have
$$(\forall x \leq_{\text{pref}} y)p(x, x_1, \ldots, x_{m-1}) = \neg(\exists x \leq_{\text{pref}} y)(\neg p(x, x_1, \ldots, x_{m-1})),$$
for $x, x_1, \ldots, x_{m-1} \in A^*$.
18. $^\diamond$ Let $f : (A^*)^n \longrightarrow A^*$ be a function, and let p_f be the predicate given by $p_f(x_0, \ldots, x_{n-1}, x_n) = a_0$ if $f(x_0, \ldots, x_{n-1}) = x_n$ for $x_0, \ldots, x_{n-1}, x_n \in A^*$. Prove that if f is primitive recursive, then p_f is a primitive recursive predicate.
19. $^\diamond$ For $x, y \in A^*$ we write $x \leq_{\text{suff}} y$ if and only if $x \in \mathsf{SUFF}(y)$. Define a "suffix variant" of the bounded quantification as follows. The m-ary predicate q on A^* is obtained through *suffix bounded existential quantification* from p if

    $q(y, x_1, \ldots, x_{m-1}) = a_0$ if and only if there is an $x \in \mathsf{SUFF}(y)$ such that $p(x, x_1, \ldots, x_{m-1}) = a_0$.

    The m-ary predicate r on A^* is obtained through *suffix bounded universal quantification* from p if

    $r(y, x_1, \ldots, x_{m-1}) = a_0$ if and only if for every $x \in \mathsf{SUFF}(y)$ we have $p(x, x_1, \ldots, x_{m-1}) = a_0$.

    (a) Prove that if p is a primitive recursive predicate, then both q and r are primitive recursive predicates.
    (b) Similarly, define an infix variant and prove that the class of primitive recursive predicates is closed with respect to the corresponding bounded quantifications.

20. Define the function $\mathsf{lshift} : A^* \longrightarrow A^*$ by

$$\begin{aligned} \mathsf{lshift}(\lambda) &= \lambda \\ \mathsf{lshift}(a_{i_0}a_{i_1}\cdots a_{i_{k-1}}) &= a_{i_1}\cdots a_{i_{k-1}}a_{i_0} \end{aligned}$$

for $k \geq 1$ and $a_{i_0}, \ldots, a_{i_{k-1}} \in A$.
  (a) Prove that lshift is primitive recursive.
  (b) Prove that the function $\mathsf{shift} : (A^*)^2 \longrightarrow A^*$ given by

$$\mathsf{shift}(x, y) = \underbrace{\mathsf{lshift}(\mathsf{lshift}(\cdots \mathsf{lshift}}_{|y| \text{ times}}(x)\cdots))$$

  is primitive recursive.
21. $^\diamond$ Prove that the binary predicate conj defined by $\mathsf{conj}(u, v) = a_0$ if and only if the words u, v are conjugate is primitive recursive.
22. $^\diamond$ Prove that the predicate $p : (A^*)^3 \longrightarrow A^*$ defined by $p(x, y, z) = a_0$ if and only if $z \in \mathsf{shuffle}(\{x\}, \{y\})$ for $x, y, z \in A^*$ is primitive recursive.

Bounded Minimalization

23. Let A be an alphabet, and let $\mathsf{half} : A^* \to A^*$ be the function given by

$$\mathsf{half}(x) = \begin{cases} y & \text{if } x = yy \text{ for some } y \in A^* \\ xa_0 & \text{otherwise.} \end{cases}$$

Prove that half is primitive recursive.
24. $^\diamond$ Let $\gcd(m, n)$ be the greatest common divisor of m, n when at least one of these numbers is greater than 0 and $\gcd(0, 0) = 0$, and $\mathrm{lcm}(m, n)$ be the least common multiple of $m, n \in \mathbb{N}$. Prove that the functions $\gcd : \mathbb{N}^2 \longrightarrow \mathbb{N}$, $\mathrm{lcm} : \mathbb{N}^2 \longrightarrow \mathbb{N}$ are primitive recursive.
25. $^\diamond$ Let $\mathsf{lop}(x, y)$ be the longest common prefix of the words $x, y \in A^*$. Prove that lop is a primitive recursive function. Prove a similar result for the longest common suffix of two words.
26. $^{\diamond\diamond}$ Let p be an $(m+1)$-ary predicate on A, and let $t \in A^*$ be the longest prefix of a word y such that $p(t, x_1, \ldots, x_m) = a_0$. Define $(\max u \leq_{\mathrm{pref}} y)p(u, x_1, \ldots, x_m)$ to be t if such a prefix exists, and ya_0, otherwise. Prove that the function $f : (A^*)^{m+1} \longrightarrow A^*$ given by

$$f(y, x_1, \ldots, x_m) = (\max u \leq_{\mathrm{pref}} y)p(u, x_1, \ldots, x_m),$$

for $y, x_1, \ldots, x_m \in A^*$ is primitive recursive.

Extensions

27. Let A, B, C be three alphabets such that $A \subset B \subset C$. If $f : A^* \longrightarrow A^*$, then show that the null extension of f to C equals the null extension to C of the null extension of f to B.
28. $^\diamond$ Let A, B be two alphabets such that $A \subset B$, $f : (A^*)^n \longrightarrow A^*$ be a primitive recursive function on A, and w be a word in B^*. Prove that the function $g : (B^*)^n \longrightarrow B^*$ given by

$$g(x_0, \ldots, x_{n-1}) = \begin{cases} f(x_0, \ldots, x_{n-1}) & \text{if } (x_0, \ldots, x_{n-1}) \in (A^*)^n \\ w \text{ otherwise} \end{cases}$$

is a primitive recursive function on B.

Primitive Recursive Functions on Natural Numbers

29. $\diamond$ Let $f : \mathbb{N}^{k+1} \longrightarrow \mathbb{N}$ be a primitive recursive function. Prove that the functions $g, h : \mathbb{N}^{k+1} \longrightarrow \mathbb{N}$ given by
$$\begin{aligned} & g(x, x_1, \ldots, x_k) \\ & \quad = \max\{f(0, x_1, \ldots, x_k), f(1, x_1, \ldots, x_k), \ldots f(x, x_1, \ldots, x_k)\} \\ & h(x, x_1, \ldots, x_k) \\ & \quad = \min\{f(0, x_1, \ldots, x_k), f(1, x_1, \ldots, x_k), \ldots f(x, x_1, \ldots, x_k)\} \end{aligned}$$
for $x, x_1, \ldots, x_k \in \mathbb{N}$ are primitive recursive.
30. $\diamond$ Let $f : \mathbb{N} \longrightarrow \mathbb{N}$ be a primitive recursive function. Prove that the function $g : \mathbb{N} \longrightarrow \mathbb{N}$ given by
$$\begin{aligned} g(0) &= 1 \\ g(n+1) &= f(n, g(\lfloor n/2 \rfloor), g(\lfloor n/3 \rfloor)), \end{aligned}$$
for $n \in \mathbb{N}$ is primitive recursive.
31. $\diamond\diamond$ Let $\mathsf{sortseq} : \mathbb{N} \longrightarrow \mathbb{N}$ be the function defined by $\mathsf{sortseq}(n) = m$ if $n = [p_0, \ldots, p_k]$ and $m = [q_0, q_1, \ldots, q_k]$, where $(q_0, \ldots, q_k)$ is a permutation of the sequence $(p_0, \ldots, p_k)$ such that $q_0 \leq \cdots \leq q_{k-1}$. Prove that the function sortseq is primitive recursive.
32. $\diamond$
    (a) Prove the equality 7.1 from Example 7.6.2.
    (b) Let $e : \mathbb{N} \longrightarrow \mathbb{N}$ be the function given by
    $$e(n) = \begin{cases} 1 & \text{if } n = 0 \\ n^n & \text{if } n > 0 \end{cases}$$
    for $n \in \mathbb{N}$. Prove that e is primitive recursive.
33. Prove that:
    (a) if $k \geq 1$, then $\mathsf{prn}(k+1) - \mathsf{prn}(k) \geq 2$;
    (b) $\mathsf{prn}(i) > i$ for every $i \in \mathbb{N}$;
    (c) if $\mathsf{expp}(n, i) > 0$, then $n > i$.
34. Prove that if $n > 0$, then $\mathsf{trimlast}^+(n) < n$ for $n \in \mathbb{N}$.

The notion of pairing function introduced in Section 1.6 can be strengthen as follows. A primitive recursive function $p : \mathbb{N}^2 \longrightarrow \mathbb{N}$ is a *pairing function* if it is a bijection that is strictly monotonic in both its arguments.

35. Prove that the function $p : \mathbb{N}^2 \longrightarrow \mathbb{N}$ given by $p(m, n) = 2^m(2n+1) \dot{-} 1$ is a pairing function.
36. Let p be a pairing function. Define the mappings p_0, p_1 as $p_0(k) = m$ and $p_1(k) = n$ if $p(m, n) = k$ for $k \in \mathbb{N}$. Prove that both p_0 and p_1 are primitive recursive.

Transformations between Alphabets

37. Let $A = \{a_0, a_1, a_2\}$ and $B = \{a_0, a_1, a_2, a_3\}$. Compute $\theta_{AB}(a_2 a_1 a_0)$.
38. $\diamond$ Let A, B, C be three alphabets.

(a) Prove that $\theta_{BC} \circ \theta_{AB} = \theta_{AC}$.

(b) Let $f : (A^*)^n \longrightarrow A^*$ be a function. Prove that f and $\tilde{f}$, the conjugate of f on the alphabet B have the same conjugate over the alphabet C.
Conversely, let $f : (A^*)^n \longrightarrow A^*$ and $g : (B^*)^n \longrightarrow B^*$ be two functions. Show that if both f and g have the same conjugate function over C, then each one is the conjugate of the other.

39. $\diamond$ Prove that if $x \in A^*$ and $|x| > 2$, then $\phi_A(\mathsf{rev}(x)) + \phi_A(x)$ is a multiple of $|A| + 1$.

Primitive Recursive Languages

40. $\diamond$ Prove that if $L \in \mathcal{L}_{prec}$, then $L^R \in \mathcal{L}_{prec}$.

Let $T = (A, M, P)$ be a semi-Thue system on an alphabet A. Define the extended alphabet $\bar{A} = A \cup \{;, \&, \rightarrow, |, :, \Rightarrow\}$. Such a system can be completely specified by the word

$$z_T = \alpha_0; \cdots ; \alpha_{m-1}; \& \beta_0 \rightarrow \gamma_0 | \cdots | \beta_{n-1} \rightarrow \gamma_{n-1}|$$

on the alphabet $\bar{A}$, where $M = \{\alpha_0, \ldots, \alpha_{m-1}\}$ and $P = \{\beta_0 \rightarrow \gamma_0, \ldots, \beta_{n-1} \rightarrow \gamma_{n-1}\}$.

The set of representations of semi-Thue systems on an alphabet A is the regular language $L_{sts} = (A^*;)^* \& (A^* \rightarrow A^*|)^*$; clearly, L_{sts} is primitive recursive.

Consider the function $\mathsf{nax} : \bar{A}^* \longrightarrow \bar{A}^*$ given by $\mathsf{nax}(z) = \mathsf{occ}(z, ;)$ and the function $\mathsf{nprod} : \bar{A}^* \longrightarrow \bar{A}^*$ defined by $\mathsf{nprod}(z) = \mathsf{occ}(z, |)$. For a semi-Thue system T that has m axioms and n productions we have $\mathsf{nax}(z_T) = a_0^m$ and $\mathsf{nprod}(z_T) = a_0^n$.

The primitive recursive functions $\mathsf{stax} : \bar{A}^* \longrightarrow \bar{A}^*$ and $\mathsf{stprod} : \bar{A}^* \longrightarrow \bar{A}^*$ defined by

$$\begin{aligned} \mathsf{stax}(z) &= \mathsf{lleftmost}(z, \&) \\ \mathsf{stprod}(z) &= \mathsf{trimfirst}(\mathsf{rleftmost}(z, \&)) \end{aligned}$$

give the axiom part and the production part of the word $z = z_T$. We have

$$\begin{aligned} \mathsf{stax}(z) &= \alpha_0; \cdots ; \alpha_{m-1}; \\ \mathsf{stprod}(z) &= \beta_0 \rightarrow \gamma_0 | \cdots | \beta_{n-1} \rightarrow \gamma_{n-1}|. \end{aligned}$$

41. $\diamond$ Construct a primitive recursive function $\mathsf{ax} : (\bar{A}^*)^2 \longrightarrow \bar{A}^*$ such that $\mathsf{ax}(z, u) = \alpha_i$ if $|u| = i$ and $\mathsf{stax}(z) = \alpha_0; \cdots ; \alpha_{\mathsf{nax}(w)-1};$ for $0 \leq i \leq \mathsf{nax}(z) - 1$.
Solution. ax is defined by primitive recursion as:

$$\begin{aligned} \mathsf{ax}(z, \lambda) &= \mathsf{lleftmost}(\mathsf{stax}(z), ;) \\ \mathsf{ax}(z, ua) &= \mathsf{lleftmost}(\mathsf{rleftmost}(z, \mathsf{ax}(z, u)), ;) \end{aligned}$$

for $u \in \bar{A}^*$ and $a \in \bar{A}$.

42. Construct a primitive recursive function $\mathsf{prod}(z, u)$ such that $\mathsf{prod}(z, u) = \beta_j \rightarrow \gamma_j$ if $|u| = j$ and

$$\mathsf{stprod}(z) = \beta_0 \rightarrow \gamma_0 | \cdots | \beta_{\mathsf{nprod}(z)-1} \rightarrow \gamma_{\mathsf{nprod}(z)-1}|$$

for $0 \leq j \leq \mathsf{nprod}(z) - 1$.

Starting from the class of semi-Thue systems on an alphabet A we introduce the following languages on the alphabet $\bar{A}$:

$$\begin{aligned} \mathsf{ONESTEPL} &= \{z : x \Rightarrow y \mid x \underset{T,\pi}{\Rightarrow} y \\ &\quad \text{where } \pi \text{ is a production of } T \text{ and } z = z_T\} \\ \mathsf{DERL} &= \{w : x_0 \Rightarrow x_1 \Rightarrow \cdots \Rightarrow x_{n-1} \mid \\ &\quad x_0 \underset{T}{\Rightarrow} x_1 \underset{T}{\Rightarrow} \cdots \underset{T}{\Rightarrow} x_{n-1} \text{ and } z = z_T\}. \end{aligned}$$

43. °° Prove that ONESTEPL and DERL are primitive recursive languages on the alphabet $\bar{A}$.

Solution. Denote the characteristic predicate of the language ONESTEPL by p_s. To have $u = z : x \Rightarrow y \in \mathsf{ONESTEPL}$ the various parts of u:

$$\begin{aligned} z &= \mathsf{lleftmost}(u, :) \\ x &= \mathsf{lleftmost}(\mathsf{rleftmost}(u, :), \Rightarrow) \\ y &= \mathsf{rleftmost}(\mathsf{rleftmost}(u, :), \Rightarrow) \end{aligned}$$

must satisfy the following conditions:

(a) $z = \mathsf{lleftmost}(u, :) \in L_{sts}$;

(b) there exists v such that $|v| < \mathsf{nprod}(z)$, $\mathsf{prod}(z, v) = \beta \rightarrow \gamma$;

(c)

$$\begin{aligned} &(\exists s \leq_{\text{pref}} x)(\exists t \leq_{\text{pref}} \mathsf{rev}(x)) \\ &((x = s\ \mathsf{lleftmost}(\mathsf{prod}(z, v), rw)\ \mathsf{rev}(t)) \wedge \\ &(y = s\ \mathsf{rleftmost}(\mathsf{prod}(z, v), rw)\ \mathsf{rev}(t))). \end{aligned}$$

This shows that ONESTEPL is primitive recursive. If p_d is the characteristic predicate of DERL, then $p_d(u) = a_0$ if $\mathsf{lleftmost}(u, :) \in L_{sts}$, and

$$(\forall a_0^i \leq_{\text{pref}} \mathsf{occ}(\mathsf{rleftmost}(u, :), \Rightarrow))$$

$$p_s(u, \mathsf{part}(\mathsf{rleftmost}(u, :), \Rightarrow, a_0^i), \mathsf{part}(\mathsf{rleftmost}(u, :), \Rightarrow, a_0^{i+1})),$$

or $(\mathsf{occ}(\mathsf{rleftmost}(u, :), \Rightarrow) = \lambda)$. This shows that the language DERL is primitive recursive.

44. °° Prove that there are primitive recursive languages that cannot be generated by length-increasing semi-Thue systems. Conclude that there are primitive-recursive languages that are not context-sensitive.

Solution. Let A be an alphabet that contains at least two symbols a, b, $z_0, z_1, \ldots$ be a list of all words on the alphabet $\bar{A}$ that represent length-increasing semi-Thue systems on the alphabet A, and $L_0, L_1, \ldots$ be a list of all languages on A represented by these systems. The symbols of the alphabet $\bar{A} = A \cup \{;, \&, \rightarrow, |, :, \Rightarrow\}$ can be encoded by the morphism $h : (\bar{A})^* \longrightarrow A^*$ defined by

$$\begin{aligned} h(;) &= aba & h(\&) &= ab^2a \\ h(\rightarrow) &= ab^3a & h(|) &= ab^4a \\ h(:) &= ab^5a & h(\Rightarrow) &= ab^6a \\ h(a) &= ab^7a & h(b) &= ab^8a \\ &\vdots \end{aligned}$$

We leave to the reader to prove that the language H that consists of all words $h(z_T)$, where T is a length-increasing semi-Thue system is primitive recursive.
Define the binary predicate p on A as $p(z,u) = a_0$ if and only if $z = z_T$ for some length-increasing semi-Thue system and $u \in L_g(T|A)$. Let target be the primitive recursive function on B given by

$$\mathsf{target}(v) = \mathsf{part}(v \Rightarrow, \Rightarrow, \mathsf{occ}(v, \Rightarrow))$$

for $v \in B^*$. Using Part (d) of Exercise 8 of Chapter 4 we can write

$$p(z,w) = p_H(z) \wedge (\exists v \leq w^{h(|w|)})(p_d(z:v) \wedge \mathsf{target}(v) = w),$$

for $z, w \in B^*$, where p_d is the characteristic predicate of the language DERL. This shows that p is primitive recursive.
Define the language $K = \{w \in H \mid w \notin L_g(T|A) \text{ and } w = z_T\}$. The language K is primitive recursive because its characteristic predicate can be written as

$$p_K(w) = p_H(w) \wedge (\neg p(w,w)),$$

for $w \in B^*$. On the other hand, K cannot be generated by a length-increasing semi-Thue system. Indeed, suppose that T_0 were a length-increasing semi-Thue system such that $K = L_g(T_0|A)$ and let $w_0 = z_T$. If $w_0 \in K$, this implies $w_0 \in L_g(T_0|A)$, so $w_0 \notin K$. Otherwise, that is, if $w_0 \notin K$, we again obtain a contradiction, because the assumption implies $w_0 \in K$. Thus, K is a primitive recursive language that cannot be generated by a length-increasing semi-Thue system.

Partial Recursive Functions

45. Prove that $\mathsf{ack}(m, n+k) \geq \mathsf{ack}(m,n) + k$ for $m, n, k \in \mathbb{N}$.
46. Prove that $\mathsf{ack}(m+1, 0) \geq 2$ for $m \in \mathbb{N}$.
47. $^\diamond$ Prove that $\mathsf{ack}(m+1, n) \geq n+2$ for $m, n \in \mathbb{N}$.
48. $^\diamond$ Let $A = \{a_0, \ldots, a_{n-1}\}$ be an alphabet. Define $f : (A^*)^2 \longrightarrow A^*$ by
$$\begin{aligned} f(\lambda, y) &= y a_0, \\ f(x a_i, \lambda) &= f(a, a_0), \\ f(x a_i, y a_j) &= f(x, f(x a_i, y)) \end{aligned}$$
for every $x, y \in A^*$ and $a_i, a_j \in A$.
    (a) Suppose that $n \geq 4$. Compute $f(a_1 a_2 a_3, a_1)$.
    (b) Prove that for every $x, y \in A^*$ we have $f(x,y) \in \{a_0\}^*$.
    (c) Prove that f is not primitive recursive.
49. $^\diamond$ Let $\{f_k | k \in \mathbb{N}\}$ be the collection of functions given by $f_k(m) = a(k,m)$ for every $m \in \mathbb{N}$, where a is Ackermann function. Prove that each function f_k is primitive recursive.
50. $^{\diamond\diamond}$ Prove that the language $L = \{a^n b^m c^{\mathsf{ack}(n,m)} \mid n, m \in \mathbb{N}\}$ is context-sensitive.
51. $^\diamond$ Let $f : (A^*)^n \longrightarrow A^*$ be a function and let p_f be the predicate introduced in Exercise 18. Does the primitive recursiveness of p_f imply that f is primitive recursive?

52. $^\diamond$ Let $f : A^* \mapsto A^*$ and $g : A^* \mapsto A^*$ be two partial recursive functions. Prove that the function $h : A^* \mapsto A^*$ defined by

$$h(x) = \begin{cases} \lambda & \text{if } f(x) = \lambda \\ g(x) & \text{otherwise,} \end{cases}$$

for $x \in \text{Dom}(f)$, is a partial recursive function on A.

7.11 Bibliographical Comments

The notion of recursive function originates in the work of R. Dedekind ([1930]), D. Hilbert ([1926]), Ackermann ([1928]) and K. Gödel ([1965a; 1965b]). The term "primitive recursive" was introduced by S. C. Kleene in [1936]. Recursive functions on words were introduced in [Asser, 1960].

The exponentiation of functions discussed in Exercise 14 was introduced in [Eilenberg and Elgot, 1970].

There are many excellent presentations of recursiveness, ranging from a comprehensive reference like [H. Rogers, 1987], to books that have a Computer Science orientation like [Hennie, 1977; Cutland, 1983].

Chapter 8

Recursively Enumerable Languages

8.1 Introduction

In this chapter we present two major models for the notion of effective computation: labeled Markov algorithms and Turing machines. These models can be used for computing functions or for defining classes of languages. We also discuss Church's thesis, the belief that the notion of "effectively computable" is captured precisely by the partial recursive functions. This is an important central principle, but because it is not mathematical — i.e., it cannot be given a formal, precise presentation — there is no way to prove it. There is, however, a long history of showing that various notions of what it means to be "effectively computable" are all equivalent. In other words, any function that can be represented as a partial recursive function can be computed by a Turing machine, by a labeled Markov algorithm, etc.

Turing machines serve as "defining mathematical machines" for the class $\mathcal{L}_0$ of Chomsky's hierarchy, and we discuss capabilities and limitations of these devices. An alternative characterization of the languages in $\mathcal{L}_0$ is presented.

Using labeled Markov algorithms and Turing machines, we exhibit mathematical questions that have no effective solution; i.e., there is no partial recursive function that has the value 1 precisely when the answer to the question is "yes" and the value 0 precisely when the answer is "no." Using these questions, we develop corresponding questions concerning formal languages for which no effective solution can exist.

8.2 Labeled Markov Algorithms

Labeled Markov algorithms are a class of rewriting systems that is used for computing functions on words.

Definition 8.2.1 Let B be an alphabet that does not contain the symbols

$$: \quad \rightarrow \quad / \quad ;$$

A *labeled Markov algorithm* (lMa) on the alphabet B is a pair $\mathcal{A} = (B, P)$, where P is a sequence of productions $P = (\pi_0, \pi_1, \ldots, \pi_{p-1})$, for $p \in \mathbb{N}$.

The ith production π_i of $\mathcal{A}$ has the form $a_0^i : x_i \rightarrow y_i / a_0^{k_i};$, where $x_i, y_i \in B^*$ for $0 \leq i \leq p-1$; a_0^i is *the label of the production* π_i, while $a_0^{k_i}$ is *the goto part of* π_i. □

The application of an lMa $\mathcal{A} = (B, (\pi_0, \ldots, \pi_{p-1}))$ to a word w always begins with the first production π_0.

If $w \in B^*$, and x_i, the left member of the production π_i, is is an infix of w, then the leftmost occurrence of x_i in w is replaced by y_i, the right member of π_i. In this case we say that π_i was *applied to the word* w. The next production to be considered is the production labeled by $a_0^{k_i}$. Otherwise, that is if x_i does not occur in w, w is left unchanged and the algorithm proceeds with the next production π_{i+1}.

The activity of $\mathcal{A}$ ends when there is no next statement in $\mathcal{A}$ with which to continue. This can occur for either of two reasons:

(i) the goto part of the current statement points explicitly to a label that does not exist, or

(ii) none of the x_is that is considered is an infix of w, so the algorithm "runs off the end" of the productions and having consider π_{p-1} would be ready to consider π_p, which does not exist.

If the word v is obtained from the word u by applying the production π_i whose left member is an infix of u, then we write $u \underset{\pi_i}{\Rightarrow} v$. Moreover, if $\pi_{i_0}, \ldots, \pi_{i_{k-1}}$ are k productions of an lMa $\mathcal{A} = (B, P)$ such that $w_\ell \underset{\pi_{i_\ell}}{\Rightarrow} w_{\ell+1}$ for $0 \leq \ell \leq k-1$, we write

$$w_0 \underset{\pi_{i_0}}{\Rightarrow} w_1 \underset{\pi_{i_1}}{\Rightarrow} \cdots \underset{\pi_{i_{k-1}}}{\Rightarrow} w_k,$$

and we refer to the sequence $(w_0, w_1, \ldots, w_k)$ as a *derivation of length k in the algorithm $\mathcal{A}$*. A derivation $(w_0, \ldots, w_k)$ is *terminal* if no production of $\mathcal{A}$ can be applied to w_k.

The relation $\bigcup_{\pi \in P} \underset{\pi}{\Rightarrow}$ will be denoted by $\underset{\mathcal{A}}{\Rightarrow}$, or, when there is no risk of confusion, simply by $\Rightarrow$; its transitive closure will be denoted by $\overset{+}{\underset{\mathcal{A}}{\Rightarrow}}$, or by $\overset{+}{\Rightarrow}$, when the lMa $\mathcal{A}$ is clear from the context.

Example 8.2.2 Let $B = \{a_0, \ldots, a_{n-1}\}$ be an alphabet. Consider the lMa $\mathcal{A} = (B, P)$, where P consists of the following productions:

$$\begin{aligned}
\lambda : a_0 &\to \lambda/\lambda; \\
a_0 : a_1 &\to \lambda/\lambda; \\
a_0a_0 : a_2 &\to \lambda/\lambda; \\
a_0a_0a_0 : a_3 &\to \lambda/\lambda; \\
&\vdots \\
a_0^{n-1} : a_{n-1} &\to \lambda/\lambda;
\end{aligned}$$

We simplify the notation by writing i rather than a_0^i. The formal notation for lMas will be used for theoretical developments; for actual examples we will use the simplified notation. Thus, the previous lMa will be written as

$$\begin{aligned}
&0 : a_0 \to \lambda/0; \\
&1 : a_1 \to \lambda/0; \\
&\vdots \\
&n-1 : a_{n-1} \to \lambda/0;
\end{aligned}$$

This lMa halts only after it erases all symbols of a word $w \in A^*$. For instance, we can write:

$$a_1a_0a_2 \underset{\pi_0}{\Rightarrow} a_1a_2 \underset{\pi_1}{\Rightarrow} a_2 \underset{\pi_2}{\Rightarrow} \lambda \underset{\pi_0}{\Rightarrow} \cdots \underset{\pi_{n-1}}{\Rightarrow} \lambda.$$

□

Example 8.2.3 The lMa $\mathcal{A} = (A, (0 : \lambda \to \lambda/1;))$ always halts and leaves its input unchanged. In contrast, $\mathcal{A}' = (A, (0 : \lambda \to \lambda/0;))$ never halts. □

Example 8.2.4 Let $A = \{a_0, \ldots, a_{n-1}\}$ be an alphabet. Define the lMa $\mathcal{A}_i$ as $\mathcal{A}_i = (A \cup \{X\}, P_i)$, where P_i consists of:

$$\begin{aligned}
&0 : \lambda \to X/1; \\
&1 : Xa_0 \to a_0X/1; \\
&2 : Xa_1 \to a_1X/1; \\
&\vdots \\
&n : Xa_{n-1} \to a_{n-1}X/1; \\
&n+1 : X \to a_i/n+2
\end{aligned}$$

The application of the first production of $\mathcal{A}_i$ to a word w results in Xw, since λ is always an infix of w. Next, X trades places with every symbol of w. When X reaches the end of w only the last production may be applied and X is replaced by a_i; then, the lMa halts. For instance, if $w = a_1a_0a_2$, then the application of $\mathcal{A}_i$ to w results in the following derivation:

$$\begin{aligned} a_1a_0a_2 &\underset{\pi_0}{\Rightarrow} Xa_1a_0a_2 \underset{\pi_2}{\Rightarrow} a_1Xa_0a_2 \\ &\underset{\pi_1}{\Rightarrow} a_1a_0Xa_2 \underset{\pi_3}{\Rightarrow} a_1a_0a_2X \underset{\pi_{n+2}}{\Rightarrow} a_1a_0a_2a_i \end{aligned}$$

We abbreviate the sequence of productions

$$\begin{aligned} &1 : Xa_0 \rightarrow a_0X/1; \\ &2 : Xa_1 \rightarrow a_1X/1; \\ &\vdots \\ &n : Xa_{n-1} \rightarrow a_{n-1}X/1; \end{aligned}$$

as

$$k+1 : Xa_k \rightarrow a_kX/1; \text{ for } 0 \leq k \leq n-1.$$

□

Labeled Markov algorithms can be used to compute functions, as described in the following definition:

Definition 8.2.5 The *function* $\langle \mathcal{A} \rangle : B^* \mapsto B^*$ *computed by the* lMa $\mathcal{A} = (B, P)$ is the partial function defined by $\langle \mathcal{A} \rangle(u) = v$, when there exists a terminal derivation $(w_0, \ldots, w_k)$ such that $u = w_0$ and $w_k = v$. If no such derivation exists, $\langle \mathcal{A} \rangle(u)$ is undefined. □

Example 8.2.6 For the lMa introduced in Example 8.2.2 we have $\langle \mathcal{A} \rangle(x) = \lambda$ for every $x \in A^*$. In other words, the function computed by $\mathcal{A}$ is the null function e. Similarly, the function computed by the algorithm $\mathcal{A}_i$ defined in Example 8.2.4 is given by $\langle \mathcal{A}_i \rangle(x) = xa_i$ for every $x \in A^*$, so $\langle \mathcal{A}_i \rangle = s_i$. □

Definition 8.2.7 The *code* of an *lMa* $\mathcal{A} = (B, P)$ is the word $w_{\mathcal{A}}$ over the alphabet $\hat{B} = B \cup \{:, \rightarrow, /, ;\}$ obtained by concatenating all the productions of P regarded as words over the alphabet $\hat{B}$. □

Example 8.2.8 The code of the lMa $\mathcal{A}$ introduced in Example 8.2.2 is

$$w_{\mathcal{A}} = \lambda : a_0 \rightarrow \lambda/\lambda; a_0^1 : a_1 \rightarrow \lambda/\lambda; \cdots ; a_0^{n-1} : a_{n-1} \rightarrow \lambda/\lambda;$$

□

Given $w_{\mathcal{A}}$, it is easy to dissect various components of $\mathcal{A}$ using primitive recursive functions on words. In all cases we assume that a_0 is a symbol of $\hat{B}$.

Define the primitive recursive function $\mathsf{size} : \hat{B}^* \longrightarrow \hat{B}^*$ as $\mathsf{size}(w) = \mathsf{occ}(w, ;)$. Thus, $\mathsf{size}(w_{\mathcal{A}}) = a_0^\ell$ if the lMa $\mathcal{A}$ has ℓ productions.

The kth production of $\mathcal{A}$ can be extracted using the primitive recursive function $\mathsf{prod} : (\hat{B}^*)^2 \longrightarrow \hat{B}^*$ given by

$$\begin{aligned} \mathsf{prod}(w, \lambda) &= \mathsf{lleftmost}(w, ;) \\ \mathsf{prod}(w, ua) &= \mathsf{lleftmost}(\mathsf{rleftmost}(w, \mathsf{prod}(w, u)), ;), \end{aligned}$$

for every $a \in \hat{B}$. Indeed, this production is given by $\mathsf{prod}(w_{\mathcal{A}}, a_0^k)$ for $0 \leq k|\mathsf{size}(w_{\mathcal{A}})| - 1$.

If π is a production, then its various parts can also be computed using primitive recursive functions. Define the function $\mathsf{label} : \hat{B}^* \longrightarrow \hat{B}^*$ given by $\mathsf{label}(x) = \mathsf{lleftmost}(x, :)$. Then, if π is $a_0^i : x_i \to y_i/a_0^{k_i};$, we have $\mathsf{label}(\pi) = a_0^i$. The left member of the production is given by $\mathsf{leftm}(\pi)$, where $\mathsf{leftm}(x) = \mathsf{rleftmost}(\mathsf{lleftmost}(x, \to), :)$, while its right member $\mathsf{rightm}(\pi)$ can be written as $\mathsf{rightm}(x) = \mathsf{rleftmost}(\mathsf{lleftmost}(x, /), \to)$ for $x \in \hat{B}^*$. Finally, the goto part of π, is given by $\mathsf{goto}(\pi)$, where $\mathsf{goto}(x) = \mathsf{rleftmost}(x, /)$ for $x \in \hat{B}^*$.

Let $\mathsf{nextprod}(w, u, x)$ be the primitive recursive function defined by

$$\mathsf{nextprod}(w, u, x) = \begin{cases} \mathsf{goto}(\mathsf{prod}(w, u)) & \text{if } \mathsf{leftm}(\mathsf{prod}(w, u)) \leq_{\text{pref}} x \\ \mathsf{conc}(u, a_0) & \text{otherwise.} \end{cases}$$

for $w, x, u \in \hat{B}^*$. Then, the label of the next production after the kth production was applied to the word x is given by $\mathsf{nextprod}(w_{\mathcal{A}}, a_0^k, x)$.

Another useful function is $\mathsf{nextword}(w, u, x)$ such that $\mathsf{nextword}(w_{\mathcal{A}}, a_0^k, x)$ is the word obtained by applying the kth production of $\mathcal{A}$ to the word x. This function is given by

$$\begin{aligned} &\mathsf{nextword}(w, u, x) \\ &= \begin{cases} \mathsf{replace}(\mathsf{leftm}(\mathsf{prod}(w_{\mathcal{A}}, u)), x, \mathsf{rightm}(\mathsf{prod}(w_{\mathcal{A}}, u))) \\ \quad \text{if } \mathsf{leftm}(\mathsf{prod}(w, u)) \leq_{\text{pref}} x \\ x \text{ otherwise.} \end{cases} \end{aligned}$$

and, therefore, it is a primitive recursive function.

Our goal is to show that for any lMa $\mathcal{A}$ on an alphabet B the function $\langle \mathcal{A} \rangle$ is a partial recursive function on B. We need the following preliminary result.

Lemma 8.2.9 *There exist two primitive recursive functions* word *and* exec *on the alphabet* $\hat{B}$ *such that for every lMa* $\mathcal{A}$ *on* B, $\mathsf{word}(w_{\mathcal{A}}, t, x)$ *equals the word obtained from* x *after* $|t|$ *steps, and* $\mathsf{exec}(w_{\mathcal{A}}, t, x)$ *gives the label of the production that is about to be executed after* $|t|$ *steps.*

Proof. Starting from the primitive recursive functions nextprod and nextword we can give a simultaneous recursive definition of the functions word and exec as

$$\begin{aligned} \mathsf{word}(w, \lambda, x) &= x \\ \mathsf{exec}(w, \lambda, x) &= \lambda \\ \mathsf{word}(w, ta, x) &= \mathsf{nextword}(w, \mathsf{exec}(w, t, x), \mathsf{word}(w, t, x)) \\ \mathsf{exec}(w, ta, x) &= \mathsf{nextprod}(w, \mathsf{exec}(w, t, x), \mathsf{word}(w, t, x)), \end{aligned}$$

for $w, x, t \in \hat{B}$. Theorem 7.7.18 implies that both word and exec are primitive recursive functions on $\hat{B}$. ∎

Lemma 8.2.10 *There is a primitive recursive predicate* haltsby *on* $\hat{B}$ *such that* $\mathsf{haltsby}(w_{\mathcal{A}}, y, x) = a_0$ *if and only if the lMa* $\mathcal{A}$ *halts in at most* $|y|$ *steps when started with the word* x.

Proof. An lMa $\mathcal{A}$ halts after $|z|$ steps if the next production to be applied, as specified by the function $\mathsf{exec}(w_{\mathcal{A}}, a_0^{|z|})$ is not among the productions of the algorithm. This happens when $\mathsf{exec}(w_{\mathcal{A}}, a_0^{|z|}) \geq \mathsf{size}(w_{\mathcal{A}})$. Therefore, we can define haltsby by bounded existential quantification as

$$\mathsf{haltsby}(w, y, x) = (\exists z \leq_{\text{pref}} y)[\mathsf{exec}(w_{\mathcal{A}}, z, x) \geq \mathsf{size}(w_{\mathcal{A}})],$$

for $w, y, x \in (\hat{B})^*$. This implies the primitive recursiveness of haltsby. ∎

All functions associated so far to lMas were primitive recursive. The function that we are about to introduce is a partial recursive function.

Lemma 8.2.11 *There exists a partial recursive function* time *on the alphabet* $\hat{B}$ *such that for every lMa* $\mathcal{A}$ *on* B, *if* $\mathcal{A}$ *eventually halts when started with the word* x, *then* $\mathsf{time}(w_{\mathcal{A}}, x)$ *equals the number of steps executed by* $\mathcal{A}$.

Proof. We can define time by minimalization as

$$\mathsf{time}(w, x) = (\min_0 y)\mathsf{haltsby}(w, y, x)$$

for $w, x \in \hat{B}$, which shows the partial recursiveness of time. ∎

Theorem 8.2.12 *For every lMa* $\mathcal{A}$ *on an alphabet* B, *the function* $\langle\mathcal{A}\rangle$ *is a partial recursive function.*

Proof. The partial recursiveness of $\langle\mathcal{A}\rangle$ follows from the fact that $\langle\mathcal{A}\rangle(x) = \mathsf{word}(w_{\mathcal{A}}, \mathsf{time}(w_{\mathcal{A}}, x), x)$ whenever $\mathcal{A}$ halts on x; otherwise, $\langle\mathcal{A}\rangle(x)$ is undefined. ∎

To define functions of n arguments computed by lMas we need the following variation of Definition 8.2.5:

Definition 8.2.13 Let $\mathcal{A} = (B, P)$ be an lMa, A be an alphabet such that $A \subseteq B$, $\sqcup$ be a symbol such that $\sqcup \in B - A$, and $n \in \mathbb{N}$.

The *n-ary partial function computed by* $\mathcal{A}$ *on the alphabet* A is the function $f^n_{\mathcal{A},A} : (A^*)^n \leadsto A^*$, defined by $f^n_{\mathcal{A},A}(x_0, \ldots, x_{n-1}) = y$ if and only if $\langle\mathcal{A}\rangle(x_0 \sqcup x_1 \sqcup \cdots \sqcup x_{n-1} \sqcup) = y$.

A partial function $f : (A^*)^n \leadsto A^*$ is *Markov computable* if there exists a lMa $\mathcal{A}$ such that $f = f^n_{\mathcal{A},A}$. □

If f is the n-ary function computed by $\mathcal{A}$, then $(x_0, \ldots, x_{n-1}) \in \mathrm{Dom}(f)$ if and only if $\mathcal{A}$ eventally halts when it is applied to the word $x_0 \sqcup x_1 \sqcup \cdots \sqcup x_{n-1} \sqcup$. Note that an lMa $\mathcal{A}$ computes an n-ary function for every $n \in \mathbb{N}$.

Example 8.2.14 Consider the following lMa obtained from the lMa introduced in Example 8.2.2 by adding the production $n : \sqcup \to \lambda/0$;.

$$\begin{aligned}
&0 : a_0 \to \lambda/0;\\
&1 : a_1 \to \lambda/0;\\
&\vdots\\
&n-1 : a_{n-1} \to \lambda/0;\\
&n : \sqcup \to \lambda/0;
\end{aligned}$$

It is easy to see that for every $n \in \mathbb{N}$ we have $f^n_{\mathcal{A},A}(x_0, \ldots, x_{n-1}) = \lambda$, where $x_0, \ldots, x_{n-1} \in A^*$. □

Example 8.2.15 By modifying the last the production of the lMa defined in Example 8.2.4, adding $a_n = \sqcup$ to the alphabet of this algorithm, and also adding the productions $n+2 : Za_k \to Z/n+2$ for $0 \leq k \leq n$ and the final production

$n+3 : Z \to \lambda/n+4$ we obtain the lMa:

$$\begin{aligned}
&0 : \lambda \to X/1;\\
&i+1 : Xa_i \to a_iX/1; \text{ for } 0 \leq i \leq n-1\\
&n+1 : X\sqcup \to a_iZ/n+2;\\
&n+2 : Za_i \to Z/n+2; \text{ for } 0 \leq i \leq n\\
&n+3 : Z \to \lambda/n+4;
\end{aligned}$$

Using this algorithm a word $x_0 \sqcup x_1 \sqcup \cdots \sqcup x_{\ell-1}$ is transformed into $x_0 a_i$ for every $x_0, \ldots, x_{\ell-1} \in A^*$. Therefore, the function $f^{\ell}_{\mathcal{A},A}$ is

$$f^{\ell}_{\mathcal{A},A}(x_0, x_1, \ldots, x_{\ell-1}) = s_i(x_0)$$

for $x_0, x_1, \ldots, x_{\ell-1} \in A^*$. If $\ell = 1$, then $f^1_{\mathcal{A},A}$ is the successor function s_i. □

Example 8.2.16 Let $\mathcal{A} = (B, P)$ be an lMa and $A = \{a_0, \ldots, a_{m-1}\}$ be an alphabet such that $A \subseteq B$. Assume that $\{Z, c, \sqcup, X\} \cup \{X_a \mid a \in A\} \subseteq B - A$. The following lMa computes the function $\mathsf{rev} : A^* \longrightarrow A^*$:

$$\begin{aligned}
&0 : \lambda \to Z/1;\\
&i+1 : Za_i \to a_iZ/1; \text{ for } 0 \leq i \leq m-1\\
&m+1 : Z\sqcup \to c/m+2;\\
&m+2 : \lambda \to X/m+3;\\
&m+3 : Xc \to \lambda/m^2+3m+4;\\
&m+4 : Xa_0 \to X_0/m+5;\\
&m+5+k : X_0a_k \to a_kX_0/m+5; \text{ for } 0 \leq k \leq m-1\\
&2m+5 : X_0c \to ca_0/m+2;\\
&2m+6 : Xa_1 \to X_1/2m+7;\\
&2m+7+k : X_1a_k \to a_kX_1/2m+7; \text{ for } 0 \leq k \leq m-1\\
&3m+7 : X_1c \to ca_1/m+2;\\
&\vdots\\
&m^2+2m+2 : Xa_{m-1} \to X_{m-1}/m^2+2m+3;\\
&m^2+2m+3+k : X_{m-1}a_k \to a_kX_{m-1}/m^2+2m+3;\\
&\qquad \text{for } 0 \leq k \leq m-1\\
&m^2+3m+3 : X_{m-1}c \to ca_{m-1}/m+2;
\end{aligned}$$

The algorithms is applied to a word $x\sqcup$. The productions

$$\begin{aligned}
&0 : \lambda \to Z/1;\\
&i+1 : Za_i \to a_iZ/1; \text{ for } 0 \leq i \leq m-1\\
&m+1 : Z\sqcup \to c/m+2;
\end{aligned}$$

replace the final $\sqcup$ by the symbol c. Next, the symbol X is appended at the left end of the word. If $x = \lambda$, the word processed by the algorithm is Xc and the application of the production $m+3 : Xc \to \lambda/m^2+3m+4$; yields the word λ and the algorithm halts. Otherwise, that is, if $x \neq \lambda$, the word contains an prefix of the form Xa_i for $0 \leq i \leq m-1$. The group of productions that is applicable in this case is

$$\begin{array}{l} m+4+i(m+2) : Xa_i \rightarrow X_i/m+5+i(m+2); \\ m+5+i(m+2)+k : X_i a_k \rightarrow a_k X_i/m+5+i(m+2); \\ \quad \text{for } 0 \leq k \leq m-1 \\ 2m+5+i(m+2) : X_i c \rightarrow c a_i/m+2; \end{array}$$

and they transform a word $Xa_i \cdots a_j c a_p \cdots a_q$ as follows:

$$\begin{array}{lcl} Xa_i a_l \cdots a_j c a_p \cdots a_q & \Rightarrow & X_i a_l \cdots a_j c a_p \cdots a_q \\ & \Rightarrow & a_l \cdots a_j X_i c a_p \cdots a_q \\ & \Rightarrow & a_l \cdots a_j c a_i a_p \cdots a_q. \end{array}$$

For example, if $x = a_0 a_1 a_2$, then we have

$$\begin{array}{ccccccccc} Xa_0a_1a_2c & \Rightarrow & X_0a_1a_2c & \Rightarrow & a_1X_0a_2c & \Rightarrow & a_1a_2X_0c & \Rightarrow \\ a_1a_2ca_0 & \Rightarrow & Xa_1a_2ca_0 & \Rightarrow & X_1a_2ca_0 & \Rightarrow & a_2X_1ca_0 & \Rightarrow \\ a_2ca_1a_0 & \Rightarrow & Xa_2ca_1a_0 & \Rightarrow & X_2ca_1a_0 & \Rightarrow & ca_2a_1a_0 & \Rightarrow \\ Xca_2a_1a_0 & \Rightarrow & a_2a_1a_0 & & & & & \end{array}$$

□

Theorem 8.2.17 *Let $\mathcal{A}$ be an lMa on an alphabet B, and let A be an alphabet such that $A \subseteq B$ and $\sqcup \in B - A$. The function $f^n_{\mathcal{A},A}$ is a partial recursive on A for any $n \in \mathbb{N}$.*

Proof. Consider the function $k_n : ((A \cup \{\sqcup\})^*)^n \longrightarrow (A \cup \{\sqcup\})^*$ defined by

$$k_n(x_0, \ldots, x_{n-1}) = \begin{cases} x_0 \sqcup \cdots \sqcup x_{n-1} \sqcup \text{ if } x_i \in A^* \\ \text{for } 0 \leq i \leq n-1 \\ \lambda \text{ otherwise} \end{cases}$$

which is clearly a primitive recursive function on the alphabet $A \cup \{\sqcup\}$. Its null extension $\overline{k_n}$ to the alphabet B is also primitive recursive on the alphabet B by Theorem 7.5.2. Therefore, $\langle \mathcal{A} \rangle \overline{k_n}$ is a partial recursive function on B. Since $\mathcal{A}$ computes the function $f^n_{\mathcal{A},A}$, $(x_0, \ldots .x_n) \in (A^*)^n$ implies $\langle \mathcal{A} \rangle \overline{k_n}(x_0, \ldots .x_n) \in A^*$. Therefore, by Theorem 7.9.10, $f^n_{\mathcal{A},A} = \langle \mathcal{A} \rangle \overline{k_n}$ is a partial recursive function on A. ∎

We have seen that in order to compute a function $f : (A*)^n \mapsto A^*$ an lMa $\mathcal{A} = (B, P)$ makes use of a number of auxiliary symbols, that is, symbols in $B - A$. We can limit the number of such symbols to 2 as shown by the next theorem.

Theorem 8.2.18 *Let $\mathcal{A} = (B, P)$ be an lMa and let $A \subseteq B$. There exists an lMa $\mathcal{A}' = (B', P')$ such that $A \cup \{\sqcup\} \subseteq B'$, $|B' - A| = 2$, and $f^n_{\mathcal{A},A} = f^n_{\mathcal{A}',A}$.*

Proof. Let $B' = A \cup \{\sqcup, X\}$ Suppose that $B - A = \{X_0, X_1, \ldots, X_{k-1}\}$, where $\sqcup = X_0$ and define the morphism $h : B^* \longrightarrow (B')^*$ given by $h(a) = a$ for $a \in A \cup \{\sqcup\}$, and $h(X_i) = X \sqcup^i X$ for $1 \leq i \leq k-1$. Let P' be the sequence of productions obtained from P by replacing every rule of the form $a_0^i : x \rightarrow y/a_0^{k_i}$ by $a_0^i : h(x) \rightarrow h(y)/a_0^{k_i}$. It is easy to verify that $u \overset{*}{\underset{A}{\Rightarrow}} v$ if and only if $h(u) \overset{*}{\underset{A'}{\Rightarrow}} h(v)$ for every $u, v \in B^*$. Therefore, $x_0 \sqcup x_1 \sqcup x_{n-1} \sqcup \overset{*}{\underset{A}{\Rightarrow}} y$ for $x_0, x_1, \ldots, x_{n-1}, y \in A^*$ if and only if

$$x_0 \sqcup x_1 \sqcup x_{n-1} \sqcup = h(x_0 \sqcup x_1 \sqcup x_{n-1} \sqcup) \overset{*}{\underset{A'}{\Rightarrow}} h(y) = y$$

which implies $f^n_{A,A} = f^n_{A',A'}$. ∎

8.3 Turing Machines

A Turing machine has the same basic components as a finite automaton (see Section 3.2): an infinite tape divided into cells and a control device with a head that moves along the tape. Two essential enhancements are added:

- the machine may alter the symbol in the cell under the head, and
- at each step the machine may move its head on the tape in either direction or may keep the head on the same cell.

Formally, the tape of a Turing machine is a sequence $(c_0, c_1, \ldots, c_m, \ldots)$ whose components are referred to as *cells*; the cell c_m is the mth cell of the tape. Each cell may contain a symbol from an alphabet that varies from one machine to another. However, the alphabet of any Turing machine contains two special symbols, called the *left marker* and the *blank*, respectively. We write the left marker as $\triangleright$, and the blank symbol as $\sqcup$.

The time scale of the machine is the set $\mathbb{N}$ of natural numbers. The following assumptions are made about the content of the tape of a Turing machine at time $t \in \mathbb{N}$:

1. The cell c_0 always contains the left marker $\triangleright$.
2. The left marker is never in any other cell but c_0.
3. There is $j_t \in \mathbb{N}$ such that if $i > j_t$, then the cell c_i contains the blank symbol. In other words, all cells of the tape with the possible exception of a finite number of initial cells contain the blank symbol.

These considerations are formalized in the next definition.

Definition 8.3.1 A *deterministic Turing machine* (dTm) is a 5-tuple $\mathcal{M} = (A, Q, \delta, q_0, F)$, where A is an alphabet called the *input alphabet*, Q is *the set of states*, $\delta : Q \times A \longrightarrow (Q \cup F) \times A \times \{1, 0, \mathtt{r}\}$ is the *transition function*, q_0 is the *initial state*, and F is the set of final states.

It is assumed that $A \cap (Q \cup F) = \emptyset$, $F \cap Q = \emptyset$, $\delta(q, \triangleright) = (q', a', d)$ implies $a' = \triangleright$ and $d \in \{0, \mathtt{r}\}$, and $\delta(q, a) = (q', \triangleright, d)$ implies $a = \triangleright$ and $d \in \{0, \mathtt{r}\}$ for every $q, q' \in Q$. □

Note an important difference between the definitions of dTms and finite automata: the set of final states is disjoint from the set of the "regular" states Q. Therefore, the transition function δ is not defined on pairs (q, a) when q is a final state.

The read/write head never moves to the left of a cell that contains the left marker, and the symbol in c_0 is never changed to another symbol nor can any other cell be changed to contain the left marker.

If the dTm in state q reads the symbol a at time t and $\delta(q, a) = (q', a', d)$, then, at time $t + 1$, the machine will have assumed the state q', the symbol a will have been replaced by the symbol a', and the read/write head will have moved one cell to the left, rest on the same cell, or move one cell to the right, depending on whether $d = \mathtt{l}$, $d = \mathtt{0}$, or $d = \mathtt{r}$, respectively.

Example 8.3.2 Let $A = \{a_0, \ldots, a_{n-1}\}$ be an alphabet, and let

$$\mathcal{M}_{\text{right}} = (A, \{q_0\}, \delta_r, q_0, \{q_1\})$$

be a dTm such that $\delta_r(q_0, a) = (q_1, a, \mathtt{r})$ for every $a \in A$. $\mathcal{M}_{\text{right}}$ moves its head one cell to the right, and then it stops.

Similarly, the dTm $\mathcal{M}_{\text{left}} = (A, \{q_0\}, \delta_l, q_0, \{q_1\})$, defined by $\delta_l(q_0, a) = (q_1, a, \mathtt{l})$ for $a \in A - \{\triangleright\}$ and by $\delta_1(q_0, \triangleright) = (q_1, \triangleright, \mathtt{0})$, moves its head one cell to the left (when its head is not located on the leftmost cell), and then it halts.

The dTm $\mathcal{M}_0 = (A, \{q_0\}, \delta_0, q_0, \{q_1\})$, where $\delta_0(q_0, a) = (q_1, a, \mathtt{0})$ for $a \in A$ stops on the cell on which it is located without making any moves.

Let b be a symbol from the alphabet A. The dTm $\mathcal{M}_{\text{print } b}$ given by

$$\mathcal{M}_{\text{print } b} = (A, \{q_0\}, \delta, q_0, \{q_1\}),$$

where $\delta(q_0, a) = (q_1, b, \mathtt{0})$ for $a \in A - \{\triangleright\}$ and $\delta(q_0, \triangleright) = (q_1, \triangleright, \mathtt{0})$, writes the symbol b in the cell scanned by the read/write head (unless the cell contains $\triangleright$), and then it halts on the same cell. □

Deterministic Turing machines can be represented by labeled directed multigraphs.

Definition 8.3.3 The *graph of a dTm* $\mathcal{M} = (A, Q, \delta, q_0, F)$ is the marked directed multigraph $\mathcal{G}(\mathcal{M})$, whose set of vertices is the set of all states $Q \cup F$. The set of edges of $\mathcal{G}(\mathcal{M})$ consists of all pairs (q, q') such that there is a transition from q to q'; an edge (q, q') is labeled by $a/a', d$ if $\delta(q, a) = (q', a', d)$.

The initial state q_0 is denoted by an incoming arrow with no source, and the final states are circled. □

Example 8.3.4 The graphs of $\mathcal{M}_{\text{right}}, \mathcal{M}_{\text{left}}, \mathcal{M}_0$ and $\mathcal{M}_{\text{print } b}$ are shown in Figure 8.1a,b,c and d, respectively. □

Definition 8.3.5 Let $\mathcal{M} = (A, Q, \delta, q_0, F)$ be a dTm and let $\star$ be a symbol such that $\star \notin A \cup Q \cup F$. A *configuration of* $\mathcal{M}$ is a word $\mathsf{c} = uqav\star$, where $q \in Q \cup F$, $a \in A$, and $u, v \in A^*$.

$\mathcal{M}$ *is in the configuration* $\mathsf{c} = uqav\star$ if the following conditions are satisfied:

(i) the current state of the machine is q;

(ii) the read/write head is scanning the mth cell of its tape, and that cell contains the symbol a, where $m = |u|$;

(iii) the word $w = uav$ is the shortest word on A that includes $\triangleright$, all non-blank symbols written on the tape, and as many blank symbols to the right of the non-blank symbols as are required to indicate the state and the position of the read/write head.

We denote by $\mathsf{CONFIG}(\mathcal{M})$ the set of all possible configurations of $\mathcal{M}$. □

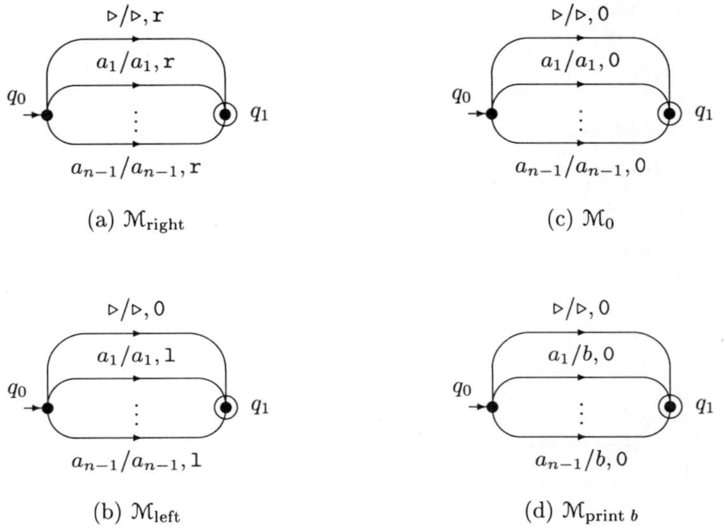

Figure 8.1: Graphs of Four Simple dTms

Every configuration contains exactly one occurrence of each of the symbols $\triangleright$ and $\star$. Also, there is one occurrence of a symbol $q \in Q \cup F$. Therefore, $|\mathsf{c}| \geq 3$ for any $\mathsf{c} \in \mathsf{CONFIG}(\mathcal{M})$.

Theorem 8.3.6 *No configuration of a dTm is a proper prefix or a proper suffix of another configuration of the machine.*

Proof. If c is a configuration of a dTm, then $\star$ may occur only as the last symbol of c, which implies that c may not be a proper prefix of another configuration c′.

Observe that the $\triangleright$ symbol may occur only in the first or second position of c. Thus, if c were a proper suffix of another configuration c′, this would imply $\mathsf{c}' = q \triangleright w$ and $\mathsf{c} = \triangleright w$ for some $w \in A^*$. This is impossible because there is exactly one occurrence of a symbol from $Q \cup F$ in any configuration and, thus, since w contains no occurrence of q, the configuration c would contain no occurrence of a symbol from $Q \cup F$. ∎

Example 8.3.7 Figures 8.2(a)–(d) correspond to four configurations of a dTm, namely, $q_0 \triangleright baba\star$, $\triangleright\sqcup q_1 a\sqcup b\star$, $\triangleright a q_2 \sqcup\star$, and $\triangleright\sqcup\sqcup\sqcup q_3\sqcup\star$, respectively. Note that the last configuration corresponds to a blank tape; the content of the blank tape is $\triangleright$. Since the read/write head is positioned on cell number 4, we need to use the shortest blank extension of $\triangleright$ whose length is at least 5, namely $\triangleright\sqcup^4$. □

Definition 8.3.8 Let $\mathcal{M} = (A, Q, \delta, q_0, F)$ be a dTm. A *terminal configuration* is a configuration $\mathsf{c} = uqav\star$ such that $q \in F$. □

For a dTm $\mathcal{M}$ we introduce the relation $\vdash_{\mathcal{M}}$ on the set $\mathsf{CONFIG}(\mathcal{M})$.

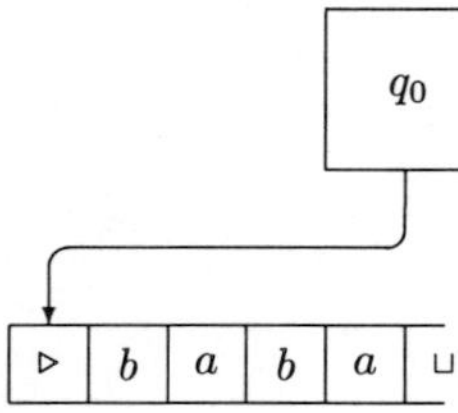

(a) $q_0 \rhd baba\star$

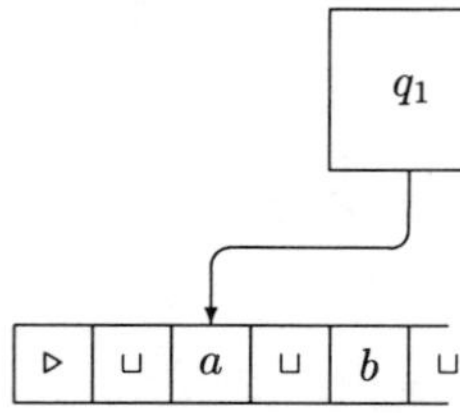

(b) $\rhd\sqcup q_1 a\sqcup b\star$

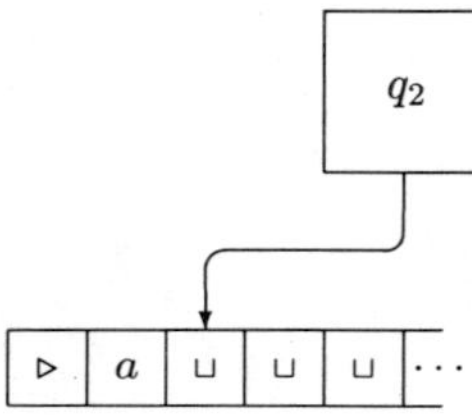

(c) $\rhd a q_2 \sqcup\star$

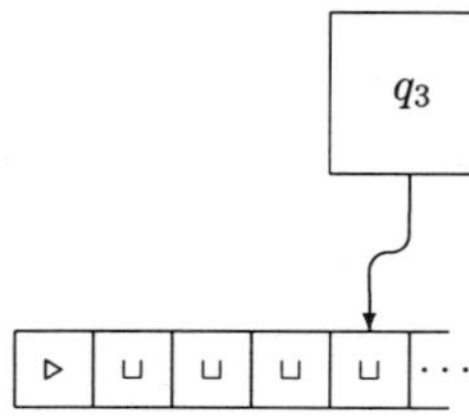

(d) $\rhd\sqcup\sqcup\sqcup q_3\sqcup\star$

Figure 8.2: Turing Machines and Their Configurations

Definition 8.3.9 Let $\mathsf{c}, \mathsf{c}' \in \mathsf{CONFIG}(\mathcal{M})$, where $\mathcal{M} = (A, Q, \delta, q_0, F)$ is a dTm. Define $\mathsf{c} \underset{\mathcal{M}}{\vdash} \mathsf{c}'$ if and only if $\mathsf{c} = uqav\star$, and c' is given by

$$\mathsf{c}' = \begin{cases} ua'q'v\star & \text{if } \delta(q,a) = (q', a', \mathtt{r}) \text{ and } v \neq \lambda \\ ua'q'\sqcup\star & \text{if } \delta(q,a) = (q', a', \mathtt{r}) \text{ and } v = \lambda \\ uqa'v\star & \text{if } \delta(q,a) = (q', a', \mathtt{0}) \\ u_1 q' a_1 a' v\star & \text{if } \delta(q,a) = (q', a', \mathtt{l}), u = u_1 a_1, \text{ and either} \\ & v \neq \lambda \text{ or } a' \neq \sqcup \\ u_1 q' a_1 \star & \text{if } \delta(q,a) = (q', a', \mathtt{l}), u = u_1 a_1, v = \lambda \text{ and } a' = \sqcup. \end{cases}$$

□

In other words, $\mathcal{M}$ changes its configuration from $uqav\star$ to $ua'q'v\star$ when $\mathcal{M}$ switches its state from q to q' by reading the symbol a, replacing a by a' and then, moving its head one cell to the right. The configuration changes from $uqav\star$ to $uqa'v\star$ when the head remains on the same cell after rewriting a into a'. Finally, $\mathcal{M}$ changes its configuration from $u_1a_1qav\star$ to $u_1q'a_1a'v\star$ if the head is moved to the left after rewriting the symbol a into a'. When $\mathcal{M}$ is clear from context we may simply write $\mathsf{c} \vdash \mathsf{c}'$. A certain amount of care must be taken when the head is at the right edge of the tape. Each time it moves further right, a cell with the blank symbol is "added" to the configuration. If it moves to the left, the representation of the cell in the configuration that was read is removed if the cell contains a blank.

It may help to visualize the tape as being infinitely long to the right, with all but an initial segment filled with blanks. In order to write configurations, we display only the minimal amount of the tape to show what is non blank and where the read/write head is located.

Definition 8.3.10 Let $\mathcal{M} = (A, Q, \delta, q_0, F)$ be a dTm. A *run* is a sequence of configurations $\mathsf{r} = (\mathsf{c}_0, \ldots, \mathsf{c}_{k-1})$ such that $\mathsf{c}_i \underset{\mathcal{M}}{\vdash} \mathsf{c}_{i+1}$ for $0 \leq i \leq k-2$ and $k \geq 1$. The number k is the *length of the run* r. □

As we did with other types of machines, starting from the relation "$\underset{\mathcal{M}}{\vdash}$" we denote its nth power by $\overset{n}{\underset{\mathcal{M}}{\vdash}}$, its transitive closure by $\overset{+}{\underset{\mathcal{M}}{\vdash}}$, and its reflexive and transitive closure by $\overset{*}{\underset{\mathcal{M}}{\vdash}}$. Thus, if $\mathsf{c}, \mathsf{c}' \in \mathsf{CONFIG}(\mathcal{M})$ we have $\mathsf{c} \overset{+}{\underset{\mathcal{M}}{\vdash}} \mathsf{c}'$ if and only if there is an $n \geq 1$ such that $\mathsf{c} \overset{n}{\underset{\mathcal{M}}{\vdash}} \mathsf{c}'$, that is, if and only if there exists a run in $\mathcal{M}$ that begins with c and ends with c'. Also, $\mathsf{c} \overset{*}{\underset{\mathcal{M}}{\vdash}} \mathsf{c}'$ if and only if there is an $n \geq 0$ such that $\mathsf{c} \overset{n}{\underset{\mathcal{M}}{\vdash}} \mathsf{c}'$, that is if and only if $\mathsf{c} = \mathsf{c}'$, or there exists a run that begins with c and ends with c'.

Example 8.3.11 Consider the dTm

$$\mathcal{M} = (\{\triangleright, \sqcup, a, b\}, \{q_0, q_1\}, \delta, q_0, \{q_f\}),$$

where δ is defined by the following table:

Input	State	
	q_0	q_1
$\triangleright$	$(q_0, \triangleright, \mathtt{r})$	$(q_f, \triangleright, 0)$
$\sqcup$	$(q_1, \sqcup, \mathtt{l})$	$(q_1, \sqcup, 0)$
a	$(q_0, b, \mathtt{r})$	$(q_1, a, \mathtt{l})$
b	$(q_0, a, \mathtt{r})$	$(q_1, b, \mathtt{l})$

The machine is designed such that if the initial configuration is $\mathsf{c} = q_0 \triangleright w \star$, where $w \in \{a, b\}^*$, then a terminal configuration c' is reached such that $\mathsf{c}' = q_f \triangleright w' \star$, where w' is obtained from w by replacing every a with a b and vice-versa. For instance, we have the following run:

$$\begin{aligned}
& q_0 \triangleright abba \star \underset{\mathcal{M}}{\vdash} \triangleright q_0 abba \star \underset{\mathcal{M}}{\vdash} \triangleright b q_0 bba \star \underset{\mathcal{M}}{\vdash} \triangleright ba q_0 ba \star \\
& \underset{\mathcal{M}}{\vdash} \triangleright baa q_0 a \star \underset{\mathcal{M}}{\vdash} \triangleright baab q_0 \sqcup \star \underset{\mathcal{M}}{\vdash} \triangleright baa q_1 b \star \underset{\mathcal{M}}{\vdash} \triangleright ba q_1 ab \star \\
& \underset{\mathcal{M}}{\vdash} \triangleright b q_1 aab \star \underset{\mathcal{M}}{\vdash} \triangleright q_1 baab \star \underset{\mathcal{M}}{\vdash} q_1 \triangleright baab \star \underset{\mathcal{M}}{\vdash} q_f \triangleright baab \star .
\end{aligned}$$

□

Example 8.3.12 Let A be an alphabet such that $0 \notin A$. The dTm that we discuss shifts a word $x \in (A - \{\triangleright, \sqcup\})^+$ that consists of non-blank symbols (followed by a $\sqcup$) one cell to the right, when started on the leftmost symbol of x.

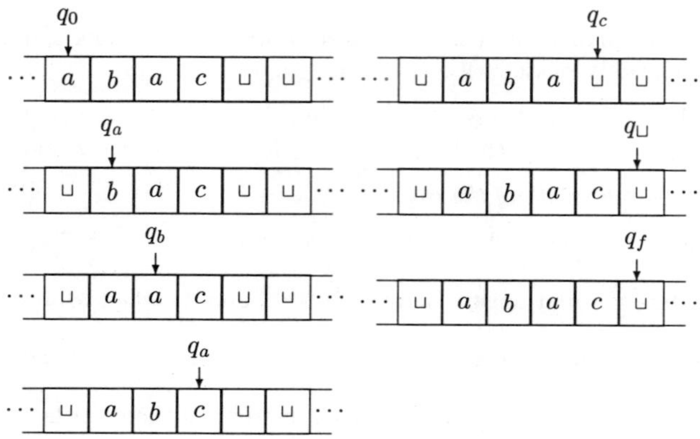

Figure 8.3: Sequence of configurations of $\mathcal{M}_{\text{shift r}}$

Let $\mathcal{M}_{\text{shift r}} = (A, \{q_0\} \cup \{q_a \mid a \in A\}, \delta, q_0, \{q_f\})$, where δ is given by:

$$\begin{aligned}
\delta(q_0, a) &= (q_a, \sqcup, \mathtt{r}) \text{ for } a \in A,\\
\delta(q_c, b) &= (q_b, c, \mathtt{r}) \text{ for } c \in A - \{\triangleright, \sqcup\} \text{ and } b \in A - \{\triangleright\},\\
\delta(q_\sqcup, \sqcup) &= (q_f, \sqcup, 0) \text{ for } b \in A.
\end{aligned}$$

$\mathcal{M}_{\text{shift r}}$ encodes the symbol b currently read from the tape into its state q_b, rewrites this symbol into the symbol previously encoded and moves its head one cell to the right. This process is repeated until a $\sqcup$ is encountered (which means that the end of the word to be shifted was detected). Then, after rewriting this blank, the machine halts on the next cell.

The evolution of $\mathcal{M}_{\text{shift r}}$ that begins with a configuration $\triangleright\sqcup^n q_0 abac\star$ and ends with the configuration $\triangleright\sqcup^{n+1} abaqcq_f\sqcup\star$ is shown in Figure 8.3.

We leave to the reader to design a similar dTm $\mathcal{M}_{\text{shift l}}$ that shifts a non-blank word x one cell to the left. The shift may take place only if the word is preceded by a blank cell. The computation performed by $\mathcal{M}_{\text{shift l}}$ is

$$\triangleright\sqcup^m q_0 x \star \underset{\mathcal{M}_{\text{shift l}}}{\overset{*}{\vdash}} \triangleright \sqcup^{m-1} xq\sqcup\star,$$

for $m \geq 1$ and $x \in (A - \{\triangleright, \sqcup\})^*$. □

8.4 Systems of Deterministic Turing Machines

We now discuss a technique for building complex dTms from a collection of simpler ones.

Renaming the states of a dTm does not affect its functionality. Formally, if $\mathcal{M} = (A, Q, \delta, q_0, F)$ is a dTm and Q', F' are two sets such that there are bijections $f : Q \longrightarrow Q'$ and $g : F \longrightarrow F'$ given by $f(q) = q'$ for $q \in Q$ and $g(r) = r'$ for $r \in F$, then we can replace the sets Q and F in $\mathcal{M}$ by Q' and F'. By defining $\delta'(q', a) = (p', a_1, d)$ when $\delta(q, a) = (p, a_1, d)$ we obtain a dTm $\mathcal{M}' = (A', Q', \delta', q'_0, F')$ that behaves in every respect as $\mathcal{M}$ does. We can choose

Q' and F' such that $Q \cap Q' = F \cap F' = \emptyset$. Thus, when several dTms need to be considered together, we shall be able to assume, without affecting the functionality of these machines, that their sets of states and their sets of final states are pairwise disjoint.

In the next definition we formalize the construction of a dTm that is equivalent to a collection of machines that share the same tape.

Definition 8.4.1 Let A be an alphabet, and let $\mathcal{C}$ be a nonempty, finite collection of dTms such that every machine in $\mathcal{C}$ has A as its input alphabet, and the sets of states and sets of final states of the machines in $\mathcal{C}$ are pairwise disjoint.

A *Turing machine system* (TMS) labeled by the collection $\mathcal{C}$ and by the alphabet A is a labeled directed multigraph $\mathcal{G} = (G, M, \mathsf{m})$, where $M = \mathcal{C} \cup A$ and the labelling function m satisfies the following conditions:

(i) $\mathsf{m}(v) \in \mathcal{C}$ for every vertex v of the graph G;

(ii) $\mathsf{m}(e) \in A$ for every edge of the graph G;

(iii) for every symbol vertex v of the graph G and every symbol $a \in A$ there is at most one edge e emerging from v that is labeled by a.

A special node v_0 of $\mathcal{G}$ is designed as the *initial vertex* and is marked by an incoming arrow with no source. □

All dTms of the collection $\mathcal{C}$ operate on the same tape and at any given moment n we will designate exactly one machine as being *active*. At time 0 the active machine is the dTm that marks the initial vertex. This machine is referred to as the *initial dTm* of $\mathcal{G}$.

Suppose that the dTm $\mathcal{M}$ located at a vertex v is active. If $\mathcal{M}$ enters a halting configuration, the scanned cell contains the symbol a, and G contains an edge labeled by a leading to a vertex marked by $\mathcal{M}'$, then $\mathcal{M}'$ becomes the active machine. The work of $\mathcal{M}'$ begins in its initial state q_0', on the cell on which $\mathcal{M}$ stopped. For example, if the last transition of $\mathcal{M}$ is $\delta(q, a) = (q_f, a', \mathtt{r})$, then $\mathcal{M}'$ reads the cell to the right of the one in which $\mathcal{M}$ just wrote a'.

Definition 8.4.2 Let $\mathcal{G} = (G, M, \mathsf{m})$ be a TMS labeled by the collection $\mathcal{C} = \{\mathcal{M}_0, \ldots, \mathcal{M}_{n-1}\}$ of dTms over the alphabet A, where $\mathcal{M}_i = (A, Q_i, \delta_i, q_{0i}, F_i)$ for $0 \leq i \leq n-1$. Suppose that $p_0, \ldots, p_{n-1}$ are n new states, that is,

$$\{p_0, \ldots, p_{n-1}\} \cap (\bigcup_{i=0}^{n-1} Q_i \cup F_i) = \emptyset.$$

The deterministic Turing machine of $\mathcal{G}$ is the dTm

$$\mathcal{M}(\mathcal{G}) = (A, \bigcup_{i=0}^{n-1} Q_i \cup \{p_0, \ldots, p_{n-1}\}, \delta, q_0, \{q_f\}),$$

where q_0 is the initial state of the initial machine of $\mathcal{G}$, q_f is a unique final state, and δ is defined as follows:

(i) if $q \in Q_i$ and $\delta_i(q, a) = (q', a', d)$, where $q' \notin F_i$, then $\delta(q, a) = (q', a', d)$;

(ii) if $q \in Q_i$, $\delta_i(q, a) = (q', a', d)$, and $q' \in F_i$, then $\delta(q, a) = (p_i, a', d)$;

(iii) if G contains an edge labeled by a symbol $a \in A$ leading from a vertex labeled $\mathcal{M}_i$ to a vertex labeled $\mathcal{M}_j$, then $\delta(p_i, a) = \delta(q_{0j}, a)$ (note that

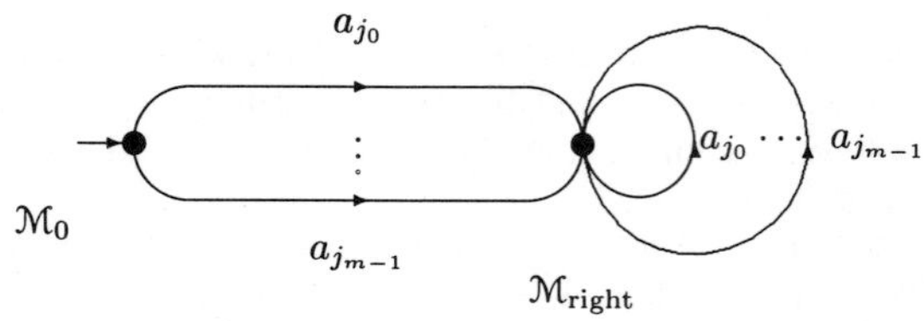

Figure 8.4: Turing Machine System Defining $\mathcal{M}_{\text{right}?C}$

$\delta(q_{0j}, a)$ is already defined from the previous steps); otherwise, $\delta(p_i, a) = (q_f, a, 0)$.

□

Example 8.4.3 Let A be an alphabet, $C \subseteq A - \{\triangleright\}$, where

$$C = \{a_{i_0}, \ldots, a_{i_{\ell-1}}\} \text{ and } A - C = \{a_{j_0}, \ldots, a_{j_{m-1}}\}.$$

The TMS $\mathcal{G}$ shown in Figure 8.4 defines a dTm that moves its head to the right until it encounters a symbol that belongs to the set C.

The dTms that label the vertices of $\mathcal{G}$ are $\mathcal{M}_0$ and $\mathcal{M}_{\text{right}}$. To make their sets of states disjoint we rename the states of $\mathcal{M}_{\text{right}}$ and assume that

$$\begin{aligned} \mathcal{M}_0 &= (A, \{q_0\}, \delta_0, q_0, \{q_1\}) \\ \mathcal{M}_{\text{right}} &= (A, \{q_0'\}, \delta_r, q_0', \{q_1'\}). \end{aligned}$$

Then, the dTm $\mathcal{M}(\mathcal{G})$ is given by

$$\mathcal{M}(\mathcal{G}) = (A, \{q_0, q_0', p_0, p_1\}, \delta, q_0, \{q_f\}),$$

where the transition function is defined by:

$$\begin{aligned} \delta(q_0, a) &= (p_0, a, 0) \text{ for } a \in A \\ \delta(q_0', a) &= (p_1, a, \mathtt{r}) \text{ for } a \in A \\ \delta(p_0, a) &= (q_f, a, 0) \text{ for } a \in C \\ \delta(p_0, a) &= (p_1, a, \mathtt{r}) \text{ for } a \in A - C \\ \delta(p_1, a) &= (q_f, a, 0) \text{ for } a \in C \\ \delta(p_1, a) &= (p_1, a, \mathtt{r}) \text{ for } a \in A - C. \end{aligned}$$

We denote this machine by $\mathcal{M}_{\text{right}?C}$. Similarly, $\mathcal{M}_{\text{left}?C}$ moves to the left until it encounters either a symbol of C or the left marker $\triangleright$. We leave to the reader to design a TMS whose dTm is $\mathcal{M}_{\text{left}?C}$. If $C = \{a\}$, the machines $\mathcal{M}_{\text{right}?\{a\}}$ and $\mathcal{M}_{\text{left}?\{a\}}$ will be denoted by $\mathcal{M}_{\text{right}?a}$ and $\mathcal{M}_{\text{left}?a}$, respectively. Also, if $C = A - \{a\}$ we will denote C simply by $\neq a$, when there is no risk of confusion.

Also, to simplify the notations, a set of edges that share the same source and origin and are marked with every symbol of an alphabet A except a will be replaced in the graph $\mathcal{G}$ by a single edge marked $s \neq a$ (cf. Figure 8.5). □

If there exists an edge from x to y labeled by a for every $a \in A$, then we will join x and y by an unlabeled edge or will simply omit all edges between

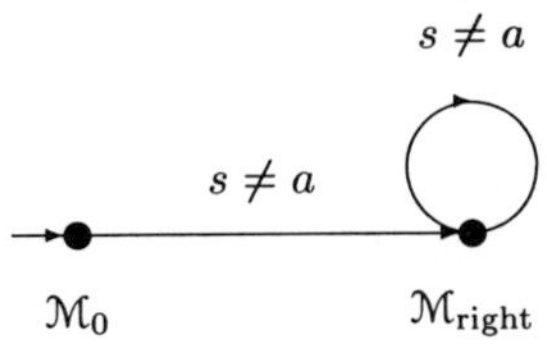

Figure 8.5: Simplified Notation for a Turing Machine System

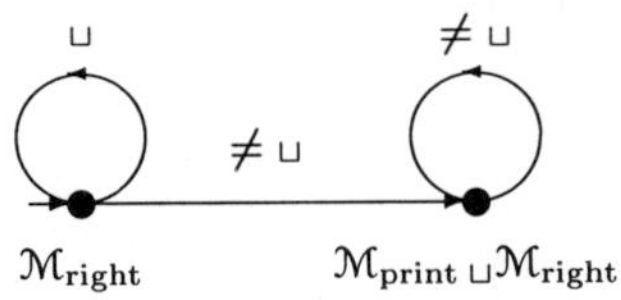

Figure 8.6: The TMS that defines the dTm $\mathcal{M}_{\text{erase}}$

these vertices and collapse x and y into x. In the latter case we mark x with $m(x)m(y)$.

Example 8.4.4 The dTm $\mathcal{M}_{\text{erase}}$ that we design in this example erases the first non-blank segment of the tape and stops on the first blank symbol that follows this segment. The TMS that defines this machine is shown in Figure 8.6. Note that the TMS cycles through the vertex marked $\mathcal{M}_{\text{right}}$ until it encounters a non-blank symbol. At that point, the composite machine $\mathcal{M}_{\text{print }\sqcup}\mathcal{M}_{\text{right}}$ writes a blank and moves to the right. This process is repeated until a blank symbol is encountered. At that point the dTm $\mathcal{M}_{\text{erase}}$ halts. □

Example 8.4.5 Let A, B be two alphabets such that $A \subset B$ and $\{\triangleright, \sqcup\} \cap A = \emptyset$. Assume that the dTm $\mathcal{M}_{\text{dupl},b}$ begins its activity with the word $\triangleright xb$ written on its tape, where $x \in A^*$ and $b \in B - A$. When the machine halts, the content of the tape will be $\triangleright xbx$. In other words, $\mathcal{M}_{\text{dupl},b}$ duplicates every word in A^* written on its tape. Thus, $q_0 \triangleright xb\star \overset{*}{\underset{\mathcal{M}_{\text{dupl},b}}{\vdash}} q \triangleright xbx\star$ for every word $x \in A^*$.

The TMS that defines this dTm is shown in Figure 8.7. □

Example 8.4.6 Let B be an alphabet that does not contain either $\triangleright$ or $\sqcup$. Using the dTm $\mathcal{M}_{\text{shift l}}$ we can design a dTm $\mathcal{M}_{\text{shift l*}}$ that will perform the computation $\triangleright\sqcup^m q_0 x\star \overset{*}{\underset{\mathcal{M}_{\text{shift l*}}}{\vdash}} \triangleright xq\sqcup\star$ for every $m \in \mathbb{N}$ and $x \in B^*$. In other words, $\mathcal{M}_{\text{shift l*}}$ will move the leftmost nonblank portion of its tape as far to the left as possible. The TMS that defines $\mathcal{M}_{\text{shift l*}}$ is given in Figure 8.8. □

Example 8.4.7 Let $x, y \in A^*$ be two words. We will design a dTm $\mathcal{M}_{x\to_l y}$ that will look for the leftmost occurrence of the word x on its tape and replace this occurrence with the word y. If no occurrence of x can be found, the machine

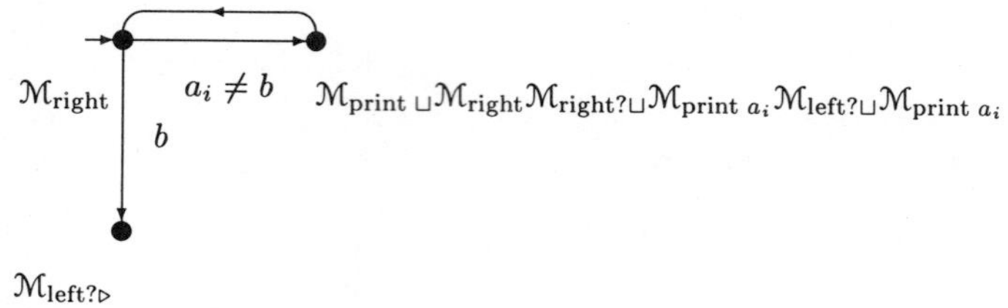

Figure 8.7: Duplicating Turing Machine

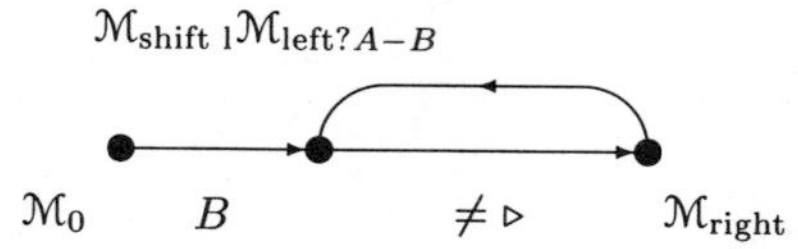

Figure 8.8: TMS that defines the dTm $\mathcal{M}_{\text{shift l*}}$

leaves its tape unchanged. In either case, the head returns on the leftmost cell when $\mathcal{M}_{x \to_l y}$ finishes its work.

We discuss the case when $|x| < |y|$. The other case, $|x| \geq |y|$, is similar and is left to the reader. Suppose that $x = a_0 \cdots a_{k-1}$ and $y = b_0 \cdots b_{m-1}$, where $k < m$. The graph of $\mathcal{M}_{x \to_l y}$ is shown in Figure 8.9. The graph of the TMS consists of two parts. The first detects the leftmost occurrence of x. When this occurrence is detected the aggregate machine $\mathcal{M}' = (\mathcal{M}_{\text{shift r}}\mathcal{M}_{\text{left}}\mathcal{M}_{\text{left?}\sqcup}\mathcal{M}_{\text{right}})^{m-k}\mathcal{M}_{\text{left}}$ shifts the remainder of the tape $m - k$ positions to the right in order to create space for the word y. Then, the word y is written starting with its rightmost symbol and the head returns to the left marker. □

In Figure 8.10 we summarize various dTms introduced so far.

8.5 Church's Thesis

In this section we present arguments that make plausible a fundamental assertion of Computer Science, namely that the class of effectively computable functions coincides with the class of partial recursive functions. This statement is known as *Church's Thesis*, and since it makes use of the non-mathematical concept of "effectively computable function," it cannot be proven within a formal framework. The most compelling argument in its favor is that all successful attempts to formalize the notion of computable function (using Turing machines, Markov algorithms, random access machines, programs in programming languages, etc.) yield exactly the class of partial recursive functions.

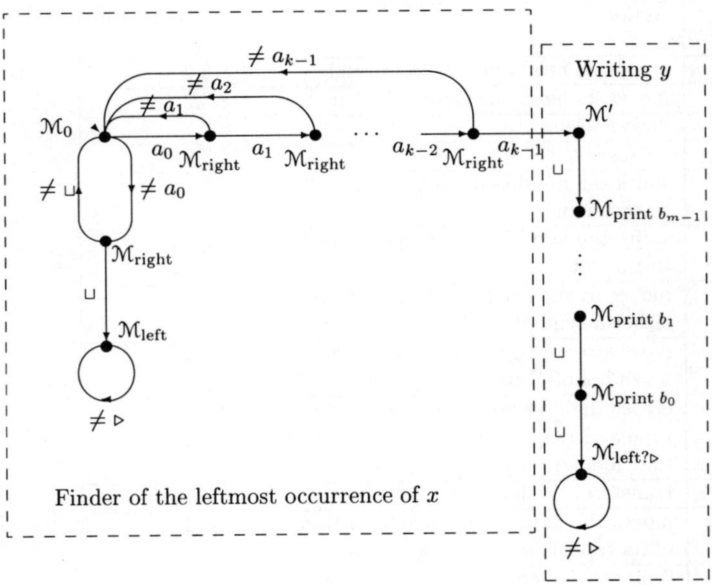

Figure 8.9: The TMS of $\mathcal{M}_{x \to_l y}$

dTm	Action	Introduced in Example
$\mathcal{M}_{\text{right}}$	moves its head one cell to the right	8.3.2
$\mathcal{M}_{\text{left}}$	moves its head one cell to the left	8.3.2
$\mathcal{M}_0$	does nothing	8.3.2
$\mathcal{M}_{\text{print } b}$	writes b	8.3.2
$\mathcal{M}_{\text{shift r}}$	shifts the non-blank portion one cell to the right	8.3.12
$\mathcal{M}_{\text{shift l}}$	shifts the non-blank portion one cell to the left	8.3.12
$\mathcal{M}_{\text{left?}C}$	moves to the left until it encounters either a symbol of C	8.4.3
$\mathcal{M}_{\text{right?}C}$	moves to the right until it encounters a symbol of C or $\triangleright$	8.4.3
$\mathcal{M}_{\text{erase}}$	erases the first non-blank segment of the tape and stops on the first blank symbol that follows	8.4.4
$\mathcal{M}_{\text{dupl},b}$	transforms xb into xbx	8.4.5
$\mathcal{M}_{\text{shift l}*}$	moves the leftmost nonblank portion of its tape as far to the left as possible	8.4.6
$\mathcal{M}_{x \to_l y}$	replaces the leftmost occurrence of x by y	8.4.7

Figure 8.10: List of dTms

8.5.1 Functions Computable by Turing Machines

Definition 8.5.1 Let A be an alphabet and let $\mathcal{M} = (B, Q, \delta, q_0, \{q_f\})$ be a dTm such that $A \subset B$ and $\triangleright, \sqcup \in B - A$.

A *partial function* $f : (A^*)^n \mapsto A^*$ *is computed by* $\mathcal{M}$ if we have

$$q_0 \triangleright x_0 \sqcup x_1 \sqcup \cdots \sqcup x_{n-1} \star \overset{*}{\underset{\mathcal{M}}{\vdash}} q_f \triangleright f(x_0, \dots, x_{n-1})\star,$$

if and only if $(x_0, \dots, x_{n-1}) \in \mathrm{Dom}(f)$.

A partial function f is *Turing computable* if there exists a dTm $\mathcal{M}$ such that f is computed by $\mathcal{M}$. □

In other words, $\mathcal{M}$ computes the function f if

$$q_0 \triangleright x_0 \sqcup x_1 \sqcup \cdots \sqcup x_{n-1} \star \in \mathrm{Dom}(\langle \mathcal{M} \rangle)$$

if and only if $(x_0, \dots, x_{n-1}) \in \mathrm{Dom}(f)$, and

$$\langle \mathcal{M} \rangle (q_0 \triangleright x_0 \sqcup x_1 \sqcup \cdots \sqcup x_{n-1} \star) = q_f \triangleright f(x_0, \dots, x_{n-1})\star,$$

for $(x_0, \dots, x_{n-1}) \in \mathrm{Dom}(f)$.

We shall prove that every partial recursive function is computable by a Turing machine. The argument is by induction on the definition of partial recursive functions. In other words, we prove initially that every basic primitive recursive function is computable by a Turing machine. Next, we prove that any function constructed from functions that are computable by Turing machines by composition, primitive recursion, or minimalization is a partial recursive function.

Lemma 8.5.2 *Let* $A = \{a_0, \dots, a_{n-1}\}$ *be an alphabet. The basic primitive recursive functions in* PRIMREC(A) *are Turing-computable.*

Proof. The Turing machine shown in Figure 8.11 computes the null function $e : A^* \longrightarrow A^*$ since it performs the computation $q_0 \triangleright x_0 \star \overset{*}{\underset{\mathcal{M}}{\vdash}} q_f \triangleright \star$ for every $x_0 \in A^*$.

To compute the successor function s_i, a dTm must perform the computation $q_0 \triangleright x \star \overset{*}{\underset{\mathcal{M}}{\vdash}} q_f \triangleright x a_i \star$. This is accomplished by the dTm give in Figure 8.12.

The dTm that computes a projection functions is technically more complicated. To compute P_i^k a dTM $\mathcal{M}$ must perform the computation

$$q_0 \triangleright x_0 \sqcup x_1 \sqcup \cdots \sqcup x_{k-1} \star \overset{*}{\underset{\mathcal{M}}{\vdash}} q_f \triangleright x_i \star,$$

which may entail the following tasks:

1. erase the words $x_0, \dots, x_{i-1}$;
2. skip over the word x_i;
3. erase the words $x_{i+1}, \dots, x_{k-1}$;
4. shift x_i to the left until its first symbol occupies the cell adjacent to the left marker.

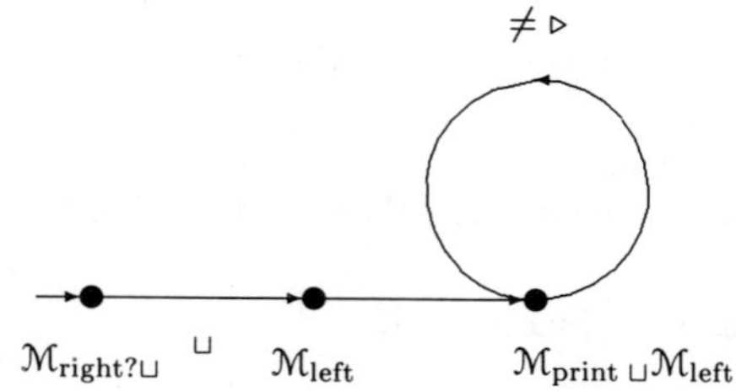

Figure 8.11: A dTm that Computes the Null Function e

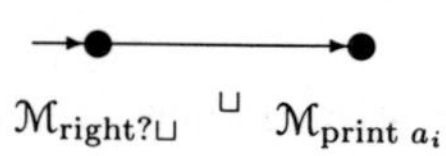

Figure 8.12: A dTm that Computes the Successor Function s_i

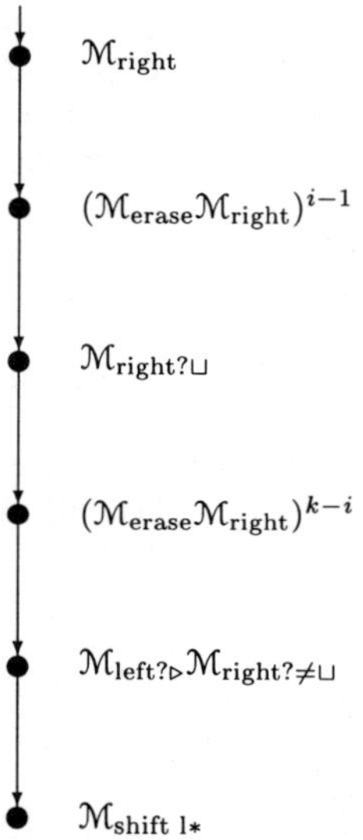

Figure 8.13: A dTm that Computes the Projection Function P_i^k

The design of this dTm is shown in Figure 8.13. ∎

Lemma 8.5.3 *Let $h_i : (A^*)^p \mapsto A^*$ for $0 \leq i \leq m-1$ be m Turing computable functions of p arguments and let $g : (A^*)^m \mapsto A^*$ be a Turing computable function of m arguments. The function $f : (A^*)^p \mapsto A^*$ obtained by composition from the functions $h_0, \ldots, h_{m-1}$ using g is Turing computable.*

Proof. Let $(x_0, \ldots, x_{p-1}) \in \text{Dom}(f)$. This means that $(x_0, \ldots, x_{p-1}) \in \text{Dom}(h_i)$ for $0 \leq i \leq m-1$ and that

$$(h_0(x_0, \ldots, x_{p-1}), \ldots, h_{m-1}(x_0, \ldots, x_{p-1})) \in \text{Dom}(g).$$

Since h_i is Turing computable, there exists a dTm $\mathcal{M}_i$ such that

$$q_{0i} \triangleright x_0 \sqcup x_1 \sqcup \cdots \sqcup x_{p-1} \star \overset{*}{\underset{\mathcal{M}_i}{\vdash}} q_{fi} \triangleright h_i(x_0, \ldots, x_{p-1})\star,$$

for $0 \leq i \leq m-1$. Here q_{0i} is the initial state of $\mathcal{M}_i$ and q_{fi} is its final state. Also, there is a dTm $\mathcal{M}$ (whose initial state is q_0 and final state is q_f) such that

$$q_0 \triangleright y_0 \sqcup y_1 \sqcup \cdots \sqcup y_{m-1} \star \overset{*}{\underset{\mathcal{M}}{\vdash}} q_f \triangleright g(y_0, \ldots, y_{m-1})\star,$$

for $(y_0, \ldots, y_{m-1}) \in \text{Dom}(g)$.

Starting from $\mathcal{M}_0, \ldots, \mathcal{M}_{m-1}, \mathcal{M}$ we construct a TMS such that the composition $f = g(h_0, \ldots, h_{m-1})$ is computed by the dTm $\mathcal{M}$ associated with this system. Modify the dTm $\mathcal{M}_i$ that computes the function h_i into the dTm $\mathcal{M}'_i$ such that a symbol denoted by $\triangleright'$ plays for $\mathcal{M}'_i$ the role played by $\triangleright$ for $\mathcal{M}_i$ for $0 \leq i \leq m-1$.

The main steps in the computation of f are the following:

1. Write the symbol $\triangleright'$ after the last nonblank symbol of the tape to start with the configuration $q_0 \triangleright x_0 \sqcup x_1 \sqcup \cdots \sqcup x_{p-1} \triangleright'$.
2. Copy $x_0 \sqcup x_1 \sqcup \cdots \sqcup x_{p-1}$ immediately after $\triangleright'$ using $\mathcal{M}_{\text{dupl},\triangleright'}$. Move the head until it is located on the symbol $\triangleright'$.
3. The dTm $\mathcal{M}'_0$ computes $h_0(x_0, \ldots, x_{p-1})$ starting its activity on that part of the tape that contains $\triangleright' x_0 \sqcup x_1 \sqcup \cdots \sqcup x_{p-1}$. When $\mathcal{M}'_0$ completes its work, the dTm of the TMS will be in the configuration:
$$\triangleright x_0 \sqcup x_1 \sqcup \cdots \sqcup x_{p-1} q_{f0} \triangleright' h_0(x_0, \ldots, h_{p-1})\star,$$
where q_{f0} is the final state of $\mathcal{M}'_0$. Replace $\triangleright'$ by another special symbol, $\sqcup'$ and move the head to the leftmost position on the tape.
4. Repeat Steps (1) to (3) using the machines $\mathcal{M}'_1, \ldots, \mathcal{M}'_{m-1}$ that are obtained from $\mathcal{M}_1, \ldots, \mathcal{M}_{m-1}$, respectively. At the end of this process, the dTm of the TMS will be in the configuration
$$\begin{array}{l} q_{f\ m-1} \triangleright x_0 \sqcup \cdots \sqcup x_{p-1} \sqcup' \\ h_0(x_0, \ldots, x_{p-1}) \sqcup' \cdots \sqcup' h_{m-1}(x_0, \ldots, x_{p-1}) \star . \end{array}$$
5. Erase the portion of the tape between $\triangleright$ and the first occurrence of $\sqcup'$. Then, replace all occurrences of $\sqcup'$ by $\sqcup$. Shift to the left the content of the tape using $\mathcal{M}_{\text{shift l}*}$. Bring the head to the leftmost cell of the tape. The dTm of the TMS is in the configuration:
$$q \triangleright h_0(x_0, \ldots, x_{p-1}) \sqcup \cdots \sqcup h_{m-1}(x_0, \ldots, x_{p-1}) \star .$$
6. Now apply the dTm $\mathcal{M}$ that computes the function g. At the end of its work the dTm of the TMS will be in the configuration
$$q_f \triangleright g(h_0(x_0, \ldots, x_{p-1}), \ldots, h_{m-1}(x_0, \ldots, x_{p-1})\star,$$
which shows that f is indeed, Turing computable.

∎

Next, we prove that the class of Turing computable functions is closed with respect to primitive recursion. Before reading the proof of Lemma 8.5.4, the reader may wish to work through Example 8.5.5, which provides a specific case of the general construction used in the proof of the lemma.

Lemma 8.5.4 *Let $A = \{a_0, \ldots, a_{n-1}\}$ be an alphabet and let $h_0, \ldots, h_{n-1} : (A^*)^{m+1} \mapsto A^*$ be n Turing computable functions. Also, suppose that $g : (A^*)^{m-1} \mapsto A^*$ is a Turing computable function and that the function $f : (A^*)^m \mapsto A^*$ is obtained from g and $h_0, \ldots, h_{n-1}$ by primitive recursion. Then, f is Turing computable.*

Proof. In this argument we construct a TMS by using determinstic Turing machines whose alphabets contain primed versions of the symbols in A. If $t \in A^*$, then t' is the word obtained from t by replacing its symbols with their primed counterparts.

The preliminary part of this argument involves an elementary but rather tedious construction of a dTm $\mathcal{M}$ whose initial state is q_s and final state is q_s' that is able to perform the computation

$$\begin{aligned} & q_s \triangleright u'v\sqcup x_0 \sqcup \cdots \sqcup x_{m-1} \triangleright' w \star \ \overset{*}{\underset{\mathcal{M}}{\vdash}} \\ & q_s' \triangleright u'v\sqcup x_0 \sqcup \cdots \sqcup x_{m-1} \triangleright' u \sqcup x_0 \sqcup x_1 \sqcup \cdots \sqcup x_{m-1} w \star, \end{aligned}$$

where $u, v, x_0, \ldots, x_{m-1} \in A^*$. In other words, $\mathcal{M}$ copies the marked portion u' of $u'v$ and the word located between the first occurrence of $\sqcup$ and $\triangleright'$ at the right of $\triangleright'$ and, in the process, it shifts the word w to the right. We leave to the reader the construction of this machine.

Another dTm that is needed is $\mathcal{M}_{\text{test}}$. This device checks whether the word located between $\triangleright$ and the first blank contains any unmarked symbol and ends its work on the tape on the cell of the tape following the word $u'v$. The design of $\mathcal{M}_{\text{test}}$ is left to the reader. In addition, we use some of the dTm previously introduced and listed in Figure 8.10.

If no marked symbols exist (that is, if $v = \lambda$) the system enters a final configuration; otherwise, the head is moved to the first cell and control is transferred to $\mathcal{M}$ whose role is to prepare the next stage of the computation.

Let $\mathcal{M}_g, \mathcal{M}_{h_0}, \ldots, \mathcal{M}_{h_{n-1}}$ be the deterministic Turing machines that compute the functions $g, h_0, \ldots, h_{n-1}$, respectively. Let $\mathcal{M}_g', \mathcal{M}_{h_0}', \ldots, \mathcal{M}_{h_{n-1}}'$ be the Turing machines obtained by modifying $\mathcal{M}_g, \mathcal{M}_{h_0}, \ldots, \mathcal{M}_{h_{n-1}}$, respectively, such that a new symbol $\triangleright'$ plays the same role in the modified machine as the symbol $\triangleright$ in the original ones. These machines are used to construct a TMS that defines a machine that computes the function f. This TMS must accomplish the following tasks:

1. The work begins with the configuration

$$q_0 \triangleright x \sqcup x_1 \sqcup \cdots \sqcup x_{m-1} \star .$$

Then, the symbol $\triangleright'$ is written after x_{m-1}.

2. The head is positioned after the first blank; now, using a modified form of the machine $\mathcal{M}_{\text{dupl},\triangleright'}$ the word $x_1 \sqcup \cdots \sqcup x_{m-1}$ is copied after $\triangleright'$. The resulting configuration is

$$\triangleright x \sqcup x_1 \sqcup \cdots \sqcup x_{m-1} q \triangleright' x_1 \sqcup \cdots \sqcup x_{m-1} \star,$$

for some state q. The modified version $\mathcal{M}_g'$ of $\mathcal{M}_g$, is used to compute $g(x_1, \ldots, x_{m-1})$, resulting in the configuration

$$\triangleright x \sqcup x_1 \sqcup \cdots \sqcup x_{m-1} q_g \triangleright' g(x_1, \ldots, x_{m-1}) \star,$$

where q_g is a final state of $\mathcal{M}_g'$.

3. If $x \neq \lambda$, the evolution of the system depends on the symbols contained by x.
   Let u' be the marked portion of x, the first word located between $\triangleright$ and the first occurrence of $\sqcup$, and let v be the unmarked portion of x. Using $\mathcal{M}_{\mathrm{test}}$, the TMS determines whether $v = \lambda$.
   If $v = \lambda$, the portion of the tape that follows $\triangleright$ and ends with $\triangleright'$ is erased, the word that follows $\triangleright'$ is shifted to the left and the computation halts.
   If $v \neq \lambda$, then the TMS uses $\mathcal{M}$ to write the word $u \sqcup x_0 \sqcup x_1 \sqcup \cdots \sqcup x_{m-1}$ at the right of $\triangleright'$ and to shift $f(u, x_1, \ldots, x_{m-1})$ to the right. Next, depending on the leftmost symbol a_i of the unmarked portion of x, the corresponding modified dTm $\mathcal{M}'_i$ is applied, and this leads to the configuration:

$$\triangleright u' a_i \cdots \sqcup x_1 \sqcup \cdots \sqcup x_{m-1} q_{f_i} \triangleright' f(ua_i, x_1, \ldots, x_{m-1}) \star,$$

   where q_{f_i} is a final state of $\mathcal{M}'_i$. Finally, the symbol a_i is replaced by its primed version, yielding the configuration

$$q_s \triangleright u' a'_i \cdots \sqcup x_1 \sqcup \cdots \sqcup x_{m-1} \triangleright' f(ua_i, x_1, \ldots, x_{m-1}) \star,$$

   and the last step is repeated.

∎

Example 8.5.5 To help the reader in following the construction considered in Lemma 8.5.4, consider the alphabet $A = \{a_0, a_1, a_2\}$ and assume that the function $f : (A^*)^3 \mapsto A^*$ is defined by primitive recursion from $g : (A^*)^2 \mapsto A^*$ and the functions $h_0, h_1, h_2 : (A^*)^4 \mapsto A^*$. The values $f(a_0 a_1 a_2, x_1, x_2)$ is obtained through the following steps:

$$\begin{aligned} f(\lambda, x_1, x_2) &= g(x_1, x_2) \\ f(a_0, x_1, x_2) &= h_0(\lambda, x_1, x_2, f(\lambda, x_1, x_2)) \\ f(a_0 a_1, x_1, x_2) &= h_1(a_0, x_1, x_2, f(a_0, x_1, x_2)) \\ f(a_0 a_1 a_2, x_1, x_2) &= h_2(a_0 a_1, x_1, x_2, f(a_0 a_1, x_1, x_2)). \end{aligned}$$

The dTm that corresponds to the TMS begins its computation with the configuration

$$q_0 \triangleright a_0 a_1 a_2 \sqcup x_1 \sqcup x_2 \star .$$

After executing the first step, the configuration becomes

$$q_0 \triangleright a_0 a_1 a_2 \sqcup x_1 \sqcup x_2 \triangleright' \star.$$

In the second step, the machine copies x_1 and x_2 at the right of $\triangleright'$, resulting in the configuration

$$\triangleright a_0 a_1 a_2 \sqcup x_1 \sqcup x_2 q \triangleright' x_1 \sqcup x_2 \star .$$

The application of $\mathcal{M}'_g$ yields the configuration

$$\triangleright a_0 a_1 a_2 \sqcup x_1 \sqcup x_2 q_g \triangleright' g(x_1, x_2) \star .$$

Note that no part of $x = a_0a_1a_2$ is marked now. Applying the third step of the algorithm we obtain the configuration

$$q_s' \triangleright a_0a_1a_2 \sqcup x_1 \sqcup x_2 \triangleright' \sqcup\lambda\sqcup x_1 \sqcup x_2 \sqcup g(x_1, x_2)\star =$$
$$q_s' \triangleright a_0a_1a_2 \sqcup x_1 \sqcup x_2 \triangleright' \sqcup\sqcup x_1 \sqcup x_2 \sqcup f(\lambda, x_1, x_2)\star,$$

where q_s' is the final state of $\mathcal{M}$. Since the leftmost unmarked symbol of x is a_0, the component dTm $\mathcal{M}_{h_0}'$ computes $h_0(\lambda, x_1, x_2, f(\lambda, x_1, x_2))$ acting on the portion of the tape that begins with $\triangleright'$. Thus, the dTm of the system enters the configuration

$$\triangleright a_0a_1a_2 \sqcup x_1 \sqcup x_2 q_{h_0} \triangleright' f(a_0, x_1, x_2)\star,$$

and the symbol a_0 is marked. This leads to the configuration

$$q_s \triangleright a_0'a_1a_2 \sqcup x_1 \sqcup x_2 \triangleright' f(a_0, x_1, x_2) \star .$$

Now the third step is repeated. Using $\mathcal{M}$, the new configuration becomes

$$q_s' \triangleright a_0'a_1a_2 \sqcup x_1 \sqcup x_2 \triangleright' a_0 \sqcup x_1 \sqcup x_2 \sqcup f(a_0, x_1, x_2) \star .$$

The first unmarked symbol of x is a_1, so $\mathcal{M}_{h_1}'$ will be applied resulting in the configuration

$$\triangleright a_0'a_1'a_2 \sqcup x_1 \sqcup x_2 q_{h_1} \triangleright' f(a_0a_1, x_1, x_2) \star .$$

Eventually, we obtain the configuration

$$\triangleright a_0'a_1'a_2' \sqcup x_1 \sqcup x_2 q_{h_2} \triangleright' f(a_0a_1a_2, x_1, x_2) \star .$$

Now, the dTm $\mathcal{M}_{\mathrm{test}}$ decides that there is no unmarked symbol in the portion of the tape between $\triangleright$ and the first $\sqcup$ symbol. The TMS enters the final configuration $\bar{q} \triangleright f(a_0a_1a_2, x_1, x_2)\star$ and the computation halts, where $\bar{q}$ is the final state of the dTm of the TMS. $\square$

Lemma 8.5.6 *Let A be an alphabet, $a_i \in A$, and let $g : (A^*)^{1+n} \mapsto A^*$ be a partial function. If g is Turing computable, then the function $f : (A^*)^n \mapsto A^*$ obtained from g by minimalization over a_i is also Turing computable.*

Proof. Let $\triangleright'$ and $\square$ be two symbols such that $\triangleright', \square \notin A$. If $\mathcal{M}_g$ is the dTm that computes g, let $\mathcal{M}_g'$ be the dTm obtained from $\mathcal{M}_g$ by replacing $\triangleright$ by $\triangleright'$. A TMS that executes the following steps will compute $f(x_0, \ldots, x_{n-1}) = (\min_i u)[g(u, x_0, \ldots, x_{n-1}) = \lambda]$.

1. The initial configuration is $q_0 \triangleright x_0 \sqcup x_1 \sqcup \cdots \sqcup x_{n-1}\star$. Write $\square\triangleright'$ at the end of the non-blank portion of the tape. The portion of the tape located between $\square$ and $\triangleright'$ will contain the word a_i^ℓ, the current argument of the computation of $g(a_i^\ell, x_0, \ldots, x_{n-1})$. At the end of this step the configuration of the TMS is

$$q_1 \triangleright x_0 \sqcup x_1 \sqcup \cdots \sqcup x_{n-1} \square \triangleright' \star,$$

for some state q_1.

2. Write a blank to the right of $\triangleright'$, then copy $x_0 \sqcup x_1 \sqcup \cdots \sqcup$ after that $\sqcup$. Move the head to the cell containing $\triangleright'$. The configuration is now

$$\triangleright x_0 \sqcup x_1 \sqcup \cdots \sqcup x_{n-1} \Box q_{0g} \triangleright' \sqcup x_0 \sqcup x_1 \sqcup \cdots \sqcup x_{n-1} \star,$$

where q_{0g} is the initial state of $\mathcal{M}'_g$.
3. At the beginning of this step the configuration of the TMS is, in general,

$$\triangleright x_0 \sqcup x_1 \sqcup \cdots \sqcup x_{n-1} \Box a_i^k q_{0g} \triangleright' a_i^k \sqcup x_0 \sqcup x_1 \sqcup \cdots \sqcup x_{n-1} \star,$$

Now apply $\mathcal{M}'_g$. If $\mathcal{M}'_g$ halts, the configuration is

$$\triangleright x_0 \sqcup x_1 \sqcup \cdots \sqcup x_{n-1} \Box a_i^k q_{fg} \triangleright' g(a_i^k, x_0, \ldots, x_{n-1}) \star .$$

If $g(a_i^k, x_0, \ldots, x_{n-1}) \neq \lambda$ (that is, if the symbol to the right of $\triangleright'$ is different from $\sqcup$), then erase the portion at the right of $\triangleright'$, insert an extra a_i between $\Box$ and $\triangleright'$ and repeat this step. Otherwise, $\mathcal{M}$ has found the least k such that $g(a_i^k, x_0, \ldots, x_{n-1}) = \lambda$, that is, found the value of $f(x_0, \ldots, x_{n-1})$. In this latter case, erase all symbols located at the right of $\triangleright$ until and including $\Box$, erase $\triangleright'$ and shift a_i^k to the left until it is adjacent to $\triangleright$.

It is clear that the TMS described above computes

$$f(x_0, \ldots, x_{n-1}) = (\min_i u)[g(u, x_0, \ldots, x_{n-1}) = \lambda].$$

∎

Theorem 8.5.7 *Every partial recursive function is Turing computable.*

Proof. This argument, by induction on the definition of partial recursive functions, is a direct application of Lemmas 8.5.2, 8.5.3, 8.5.4, and 8.5.6. ∎

8.5.2 Closing the Circle

We have already shown that every function that is Markov computable is partial recursive (see Theorem 8.2.17). Therefore, to prove that the class of partial recursive functions, the class of functions computed by Turing machines and the class of Markov computable functions coincide, we need to prove only that every Turing computable function is also Markov computable.

Let $\mathcal{M} = (B, Q, \delta, q_0, \{q_f\})$ be a dTm such that $Q = \{q_0, \ldots, q_{n-1}\}$ and $B = \{b_0, \ldots, b_{m-1}\}$, where $n \geq 1$ and $m \geq 2$. The final state q_f will be identified with q_n and the symbol $\star$ will be identified with b_m. We define a sequence of productions $P_{\mathcal{M}}$ of labeled Markov algorithms such that if $\mathsf{c}, \mathsf{c}' \in \mathsf{CONFIG}(\mathcal{M})$ and $\mathsf{c} \vdash_{\mathcal{M}} \mathsf{c}'$, then there is a unique production π in $P_{\mathcal{M}}$ such that $\mathsf{c} \underset{\pi}{\Rightarrow} \mathsf{c}'$.

In $P_{\mathcal{M}}$ we include a sequence of productions for each pair $(q_i, b_j) \in Q \times B$. These productions mirror the definition of $\vdash_{\mathcal{M}}$ (given in Definition 8.3.9). Denote by $p_{i,j}$ the label of the first production of the sequence of productions that corresponds to q_i and b_j.

For each transition $\delta(q_i, b_j) = (q_k, b_l, \mathtt{r})$, include the productions:

$$\begin{array}{rll} p_{i,j}: & q_i b_j b_0 \to b_l q_k b_0 & /p_{k,0} \\ & \vdots & \\ p_{i,j}+m-1: & q_i b_j b_{m-1} \to b_l q_k b_{m-1} & /p_{k,m-1} \\ p_{i,j}+m: & q_i b_j \star \to b_l q_k \sqcup \star & /p_{k,e}, \end{array}$$

where $\sqcup = b_e$.

If $\delta(q_i, b_j) = (q_k, b_l, \mathtt{0})$, then include the production:

$$p_{i,j}: \quad q_i b_j \to q_k b_l \quad /p_{k,l}$$

Finally, if $\delta(q_i, b_j) = (q_k, b_l, \mathtt{l})$ consider the productions

$$\begin{array}{rll} p_{i,j}: & b_0 q_i b_j \to q_k b_0 b_l & /p_{k,0} \\ & \vdots & \\ p_{i,j}+m-1: & b_{m-1} q_i b_j \to q_k b_{m-1} b_l & /p_{k,m-1}. \end{array}$$

At the end of all productions involving q_i add a production:

$$\ell_i : \lambda \to \lambda/\ell_i;$$

so that if none of the above productions is applicable, then the algorithm will enter an infinite loop.

Theorem 8.5.8 *Every Turing computable function is Markov computable.*

Proof. Let $f : (A^*)^n \mapsto A^*$ be a Turing computable partial function. By definition, there is a dTm $\mathcal{M} = (B, Q, \delta, q_0, \{q_f\})$ such that $A \subset B$, $B = \{b_0, \ldots, b_{m-1}\}$, $\triangleright, \sqcup \in B - A$, and

$$q_0 \triangleright x_0 \sqcup x_1 \sqcup \cdots \sqcup x_{n-1} \star \overset{*}{\underset{\mathcal{M}}{\vdash}} q_f \triangleright f(x_0, \ldots, x_{n-1})\star,$$

if and only if $(x_0, \ldots, x_{n-1}) \in \mathrm{Dom}(f)$.

Let $\mathcal{A}_{\mathcal{M}}$ be an lMa whose sequence of productions includes $P_{\mathcal{M}}$ as previously constructed. The activity of the algorithm begins with the word $w_0 = x_0 \sqcup x_1 \sqcup \cdots \sqcup x_{n-1} \sqcup$. The sequence P consists of the following productions:

1. Initial productions that convert the word $x_0 \sqcup x_1 \sqcup \cdots \sqcup x_{n-1} \sqcup$ into the initial configuration c_0 of $\mathcal{M}$, where $\mathsf{c}_0 = q_0 \triangleright x_1 \sqcup x_1 \sqcup \cdots \sqcup x_{n-1}\star$.

   $$\begin{array}{l} 0 : \lambda q_0 \triangleright \to X/1; \\ 1 : Xb \to bX/1; \text{ for every } b \in B \\ m+1 : \sqcup X \to \star/m+2; \end{array}$$

   This sequence contains $m+2$ productions, because $m = |B|$. After the application of the last production we obtain the word c_0. The stage is now prepared for the simulation of the dTm.
2. The next group of productions consists of $P_{\mathcal{M}}$ where we set $p_{0,0} = m+2$. These productions simulate the activity of the dTm. As a result of applying these rules we derive the word $q_f \triangleright f(x_1, \ldots, x_{n-1})\star$ if $(x_1, \ldots, x_{n-1}) \in \mathrm{Dom}(f)$. Let r be the label of the last production in $P_{\mathcal{M}}$.

3. The final group of productions is

$$r+1 : q_f \triangleright \to Z/r+3;$$
$$r+2 : \lambda \to \lambda/r+2;$$
$$r+3 : Zb \to bZ/r+3; \text{ for every } b \in B$$

$$r+2+m : Z\star \to \lambda/r+3+m;$$

The first production of this group is the unique production that has q_f in its left member, and we set to $r+1$ the goto part of all productions of $P_{\mathcal{M}}$ such that $q_k = q_n$. The word produced is $f(x_1, \ldots, x_{n-1})$. The second production "catches" those derivations that do not terminate correctly (that is, with the head on the leftmost symbol) and results into an infinite derivation process. Finally, the last $m+1$ productions of this group erase the $\star$ symbol.

Thus, we have $\langle \mathcal{A} \rangle (x_0 \sqcup x_1 \sqcup \cdots \sqcup x_{n-1} \sqcup) = f(x_0, x_1, \ldots, x_{n-1})$, so f is Markov computable. ∎

Example 8.5.9 Let $A = \{a, b\}$ be an alphabet and let $f : A^* \longrightarrow A^*$ be the function that changes a to b and vice-versa in its argument x. Example 8.3.11 shows that this function is Turing computable. Starting from the dTm $\mathcal{M}$ defined in that example we construct an lMa that computes f. The initial productions are

$$0 : \lambda q_0 \triangleright \to X/1;$$
$$1 : X\triangleright \to \triangleright X/1;$$
$$2 : X\sqcup \to \sqcup X/1;$$
$$3 : Xa \to aX/1;$$
$$4 : Xb \to bX/1;$$
$$5 : \sqcup X \to \star/m+2;$$

The productions in $P_{\mathcal{M}}$ are listed in Figure 8.14.

The final group of productions is

$$37 : q_f \triangleright \to Z/39;$$
$$38 : \lambda \to \lambda/38;$$
$$39 : Z\triangleright \to \triangleright Z/39;$$
$$40 : Z\sqcup \to \sqcup Z/39;$$
$$41 : Za \to aZ/39;$$
$$42 : Zb \to bZ/39;$$
$$43 : Z\star \to \lambda/44;$$

Suppose that lMa begins its work with the word $abba\sqcup$. Using the first group

Transition	Productions
$\delta(q_0, \triangleright) = (q_0, \triangleright, \mathtt{r})$	$6 : q_0 \triangleright \triangleright \rightarrow \triangleright q_0 \triangleright /6;$ $7 : q_0 \triangleright \sqcup \rightarrow \triangleright q_0 \sqcup/11;$ $8 : q_0 \triangleright a \rightarrow \triangleright q_0 a/15;$ $9 : q_0 \triangleright b \rightarrow \triangleright q_0 b/20;$ $10 : q_0 \triangleright \star \rightarrow \triangleright q_0 \sqcup \star /11;$
$\delta(q_0, \sqcup) = (q_1, \sqcup, \mathtt{l})$	$11 : \triangleright q_0 \sqcup \rightarrow q_1 \triangleright \sqcup/26;$ $12 : \sqcup q_0 \sqcup \rightarrow q_1 \sqcup\sqcup/27;$ $13 : a q_0 \sqcup \rightarrow q_1 a \sqcup/28;$ $14 : b q_0 \sqcup \rightarrow q_1 b \sqcup/32;$
$\delta(q_0, a) = (q_0, b, \mathtt{r})$	$15 : q_0 a \triangleright \rightarrow b q_0 \triangleright /6;$ $16 : q_0 a \sqcup \rightarrow b q_0 \sqcup/11;$ $17 : q_0 aa \rightarrow b q_0 a/15;$ $18 : q_0 ab \rightarrow b q_0 b/20;$ $19 : q_0 a\star \rightarrow b q_0 \sqcup \star /11;$
$\delta(q_0, b) = (q_1, a, \mathtt{r})$	$20 : q_0 b \triangleright \rightarrow a q_0 \triangleright /6;$ $21 : q_0 b \sqcup \rightarrow a q_0 \sqcup/11;$ $22 : q_0 ba \rightarrow a q_0 a/15;$ $23 : q_0 bb \rightarrow a q_0 b/20;$ $24 : q_0 b\star \rightarrow a q_0 \sqcup \star /11;$
	$25 : \lambda \rightarrow \lambda/25;$
$\delta(q_1, \triangleright) = (q_f, \triangleright, \mathtt{0})$	$26 : q_1 \triangleright \rightarrow q_f \triangleright /37;$
$\delta(q_1, \sqcup) = (q_1, \sqcup, \mathtt{0})$	$27 : q_1 \sqcup \rightarrow q_f \sqcup/37;$
$\delta(q_1, a) = (q_1, a, \mathtt{l})$	$28 : \triangleright q_1 a \rightarrow q_1 \triangleright a/26;$ $29 : \sqcup q_1 a \rightarrow q_1 \sqcup a/27;$ $30 : a q_1 a \rightarrow q_1 aa/28;$ $31 : b q_1 a \rightarrow q_1 ba/32;$
$\delta(q_1, b) = (q_1, b, \mathtt{l})$	$32 : \triangleright q_1 b \rightarrow q_1 \triangleright b/26;$ $33 : \sqcup q_1 b \rightarrow q_1 \sqcup b/27;$ $34 : a q_1 b \rightarrow q_1 ab/28;$ $35 : b q_1 b \rightarrow q_1 bb/32;$
	$36 : \lambda \rightarrow \lambda; /36$

Figure 8.14: The Sequence of Productions $P_{\mathcal{M}}$

of productions we have the derivation:

$$\begin{array}{lll} ab\,ba\sqcup & \underset{\pi_0}{\Rightarrow} & q_0 \triangleright Xabba\sqcup \\ & \underset{\pi_3}{\Rightarrow} & q_0 \triangleright aXbba\sqcup \\ & \underset{\pi_4}{\Rightarrow} & q_0 \triangleright abXba\sqcup \\ & \underset{\pi_4}{\Rightarrow} & q_0 \triangleright abbXa\sqcup \\ & \underset{\pi_3}{\Rightarrow} & q_0 \triangleright abbaX\sqcup \\ & \underset{\pi_5}{\Rightarrow} & q_0 \triangleright abba\star \end{array}$$

Now the derivation continues as

$$\begin{array}{l} q_0 \triangleright abba \star \underset{\pi_8}{\Rightarrow} \triangleright q_0 abba \star \underset{\pi_{18}}{\Rightarrow} \triangleright bq_0 bba \star \underset{\pi_{23}}{\Rightarrow} \triangleright baq_0 ba\star \\ \underset{\pi_{22}}{\Rightarrow} \triangleright baaq_0 a \star \underset{\pi_{19}}{\Rightarrow} \triangleright baabq_0\sqcup \star \underset{\pi_{14}}{\Rightarrow} \triangleright baaq_1 b \star \underset{\pi_{34}}{\Rightarrow} \triangleright baq_1 ab\star \\ \underset{\pi_{30}}{\Rightarrow} \triangleright bq_1 aab \star \underset{\pi_{31}}{\Rightarrow} \triangleright q_1 baab \star \underset{\pi_{32}}{\Rightarrow} q_1 \triangleright baab \star \underset{\pi_{26}}{\Rightarrow} q_f \triangleright baab \star . \end{array}$$

Finally, the last group of rules yields the derivation:

$$\begin{array}{lll} q_f \triangleright baab\star & \underset{\pi_{37}}{\Rightarrow} & Zbaab\star \\ & \underset{\pi_{42}}{\Rightarrow} & bZaab\star \\ & \underset{\pi_{41}}{\Rightarrow} & baZab\star \\ & \underset{\pi_{41}}{\Rightarrow} & baaZb\star \\ & \underset{\pi_{42}}{\Rightarrow} & baabZ\star \\ & \underset{\pi_{43}}{\Rightarrow} & baab, \end{array}$$

which shows that the algorithm computes indeed $f(abba)$. □

Corollary 8.5.10 *Let A be an alphabet and let $f : (A^*)^n \mapsto A^*$ be a partial function. The following three statements are equivalent:*

(i) *f is a partial recursive function on A;*
(ii) *f is Turing computable;*
(iii) *f is Markov computable.*

Proof. Theorem 8.5.7 shows that (i) implies (ii); (ii) implies (iii) was shown in Theorem 8.5.8. Finally, Theorem 8.2.17 shows that (iii) implies (i). ∎

Corollary 8.5.11 *To construct any partial recursive function the minimalization operation is needed at most once.*

Proof. If f is a primitive recursive function, then no minimalization is needed. Suppose that $f : (A^*)^n \mapsto A^*$ is a partial recursive function. Then, by Corollary 8.5.10, there exists an lMa $\mathcal{A}$ such that $f = f^n_{\mathcal{A},A}$. Therefore, by the argument of Theorem 8.2.17, we have $f = \langle \mathcal{A} \rangle \overline{k_n}$, so

$$\begin{aligned} & f(x_0, \dots, x_{n-1}) \\ & \quad = \mathsf{word}(w_{\mathcal{A}}, \mathsf{time}(w_{\mathcal{A}}, \overline{k_n}(x_0, \dots, x_{n-1})), \overline{k_n}(x_0, \dots, x_{n-1})), \end{aligned}$$

for $(x_0, \dots, x_{n-1}) \in \mathrm{Dom}(f)$, by Theorem 8.2.12. The function word is primitive recursive (cf. Lemma 8.2.9) and the partial recursive function time is built from primitive recursive functions using minimalization just once (see Lemma 8.2.11). Thus, we obtain the statement of the Corollary. ∎

8.5.3 Recursive Languages

Intuitively, a language L is recursive if one can effectively decide the membership problem for that language, i.e., whether for any word w, whether $w \in L$ or $w \notin L$. By Church's thesis, this means that its characteristic predicate must be recursive. This is stated formally in the next definition.

Definition 8.5.12 A language $L \subseteq A^*$ is *recursive* if its characteristic predicate p_L is recursive.

The class of recursive languages is denoted by $\mathfrak{L}_{rec}$. □

Since every primitive recursive predicate is recursive, it is clear that every primitive recursive language is also recursive.

Closure properties for the class of recursive languages can be established in a manner that is completely analogous to the corresponding properties for primitive recursive languages.

Theorem 8.5.13 *Let A be an alphabet. If $K, L \subseteq A^*$ are recursive languages on A, then $K \cup L$, $K \cap L$, $K - L$, KL, K^*, and K^+ are recursive languages over A.*

Proof. See the proof of Theorem 7.8.3. ■

Corollary 8.5.14 *The complement $A^* - L$ of a recursive language L on the alphabet A is a recursive language.*

Proof. This follows directly from Theorem 8.5.13, since A^* is clearly a recursive language. ■

Theorem 8.5.15 *Let A be an alphabet and let $f : A^* \longrightarrow A^*$ be a recursive function. If $L \subseteq A^*$ is a primitive recursive language, then $f^{-1}(L) = \{x \in A^* \mid f(x) \in L\}$ is a recursive language.*

Proof. The argument is similar to the one used in Theorem 7.8.4. ■

To relate recursive languages and Turing machines we need the next definition.

Definition 8.5.16 Let A be an alphabet and $L \subseteq A^*$. The language L is *decidable* if there exists a dTm $\mathcal{M} = (B, Q, \delta, q_0, \{q_{acc}, q_{rej}\})$ such that $A \subseteq B - \{\triangleright, \sqcup\}$ and one of the following two cases occur for every $x \in A^*$:

(i) if $x \in L$, then $q_0 \triangleright x \star \overset{*}{\underset{\mathcal{M}}{\vdash}} q_{acc} \triangleright u\star$ for some $u \in A^*$;

(ii) if $x \in A^* - L$, then $q_0 \triangleright x \star \overset{*}{\underset{\mathcal{M}}{\vdash}} q_{rej} \triangleright u\star$ for some $v \in A^*$.

In the first case we say that x is *accepted* by $\mathcal{M}$; in the second, x is *rejected* by $\mathcal{M}$.

The final state q_{acc}, q_{rej} of $\mathcal{M}$ are referred to as the *the accepting state* and the *rejecting state*, respectively. The dTm $\mathcal{M}$ is said to *decide the language L.* □

Theorem 8.5.17 *Let A be an alphabet. A language $L \subseteq A^*$ is recursive if and only if it is decidable.*

Proof. Let L be a recursive language, $L \subseteq A^*$. Its characteristic predicate is recursive and, therefore, it is Turing computable. Thus, there is a dTm $\mathcal{M}$, $\mathcal{M} = (B, Q, \delta, q_0, \{q_f\})$ such that $q_0 \triangleright x\star \overset{*}{\underset{\mathcal{M}}{\vdash}} q_f \triangleright a_0 \star$ if $x \in L$ and $q_0 \triangleright x \star \overset{*}{\underset{\mathcal{M}}{\vdash}} q_f \triangleright \star$, if

$x \in A^* - L$. Let $\mathcal{M}' = (B, Q \cup \{q_f\}, \delta', q_0, \{q_{acc}, q_{rej}\})$, where $q_{acc}, q_{rej} \notin Q \cup \{q_f\}$ are two new states and δ' is defined by

$$\delta'(q,a) = \begin{cases} \delta(q,a) & \text{if } (q,a) \in Q \times B, \\ (q_f, \triangleright, \mathtt{r}) & \text{if } q = q_f \text{ and } a = \triangleright \\ (q_{acc}, \sqcup, \mathtt{l}) & \text{if } q = q_f \text{ and } a = a_0 \\ (q_{rej}, \sqcup, \mathtt{l}) & \text{if } q = q_f \text{ and } a = \sqcup \end{cases}$$

It is easy to see that $\mathcal{M}'$ decides the language L.

Conversely, suppose that L is decidable. There exists a deterministic Turing machine $\mathcal{M} = (B, Q, \delta, q_0, \{q_{acc}, q_{rej}\})$ that decides L. Based on $\mathcal{M}$ we define a dTm $\mathcal{M}_1$ that calculates the characteristic predicate p_L. Let $\mathcal{M}_1 = (B, Q \cup \{q_{acc}, q_{rej}\}, \delta_1, q_0, \{q_f\})$, where $q_f \notin Q \cup \{q_{acc}, q_{rej}\}$ is a new final state. The transition function δ_1 is given by

$$\delta_1(q,a) = \begin{cases} \delta(q,a) & \text{if } (q,a) \in Q \times B, \\ (q', \triangleright, \mathtt{r}) & \text{if } (q,a) = (q_{acc}, \triangleright) \\ (q'', \triangleright, \mathtt{r}) & \text{if } (q,a) = (q_{rej}, \triangleright) \\ (q'', a_0, \mathtt{r}) & \text{if } q = q' \text{ and } a \in B \\ (q'', \sqcup, \mathtt{r}) & \text{if } q = q'' \text{ and } a \in B - \{\sqcup, \triangleright\} \\ (q''', \sqcup, \mathtt{l}) & \text{if } q = q'' \text{ and } a = \sqcup \\ (q''', a, \mathtt{l}) & \text{if } q = q''' \text{ and } a \in B - \{\triangleright\} \\ (q_f, \triangleright, \mathtt{0}) & \text{if } q = q''' \text{ and } a = \triangleright \end{cases}$$

This dTm simulates $\mathcal{M}$ until it halts, at which time it must be reading the marker $\triangleright$. If $\mathcal{M}$ stops in the state q_{acc}, then $\mathcal{M}_1$ goes into the state q' and moves to the right of $\triangleright$. In the state q_1, $\mathcal{M}_1$ writes a_0 and then enters q'' and erases everything from the cell it starts on and to its right until it encounters a blank cell. It then enters q''', moves left looking for $\triangleright$ and halts in the state q_f on the cell that contains this symbol. If, on the other hand, $\mathcal{M}$ halts in the state q_{rej}, $\mathcal{M}_1$ moves to the right of $\triangleright$ and enters q'' without having written a_0. In state q'' it again behaves as described above. Thus, $\mathcal{M}_1$ calculates the predicate p_L as required. ∎

8.5.4 Universality

The notion of a "universal" lMa is important from both a theoretical and a practical standpoint. Its name derives from that fact that it is a single lMa that can perform the actions of any possible lMa.

The theoretical importance of the existence of a universal lMa comes from the fact that, using it, we can reason about all possible computations that can be performed by any lMa, and this reasoning is "within" the system, because it can be expressed as a statement about the behavior of the universal lMa. This leads to powerful statements about what lMas cannot do.

The practical significance of a universal lMa is that it provides an intellectual basis for modern general purpose computers. In the most elementary terms, the way a universal lMa $\mathcal{A}_{\mathsf{univ}}$ computes what a different lMa $\mathcal{A}$ would have computed is by simulating the behavior of that other lMa. But how does $\mathcal{A}_{\mathsf{univ}}$ know what the lMa $\mathcal{A}$ does? It simply takes the code $w_{\mathcal{A}}$ of the lMa $\mathcal{A}$ and regards it as a program. This is exactly what an interpreter does with a language like Basic, and it is what the hardware of a computer does with the instructions in its memory. We are now so used to this idea that it is hard to imagine that it was once novel, but if we were not familiar with computers and interpreters, universal lMas would appear to be almost magical.

To introduce universal lMas, we examine the possibility of using an alphabet A to encode both the arguments of a partial recursive function and an lMa that computes the function. Then, we prove the existence of an lMa $\mathcal{A}^n_{\mathsf{univ}}$ called the n-ary universal lMa that works as follows. If $\mathcal{A}$ is an lMa that computes a partial function $f : (A^*)^n \mapsto A^*$, and $\mathcal{A}$ is encoded by a word $x \in A^*$, then, when $\mathcal{A}^n_{\mathsf{univ}}$ is provided with $n+1$ arguments, $(x, x_0, \ldots, x_{n-1}) \in (A^*)^{n+1}$, $\mathcal{A}^n_{\mathsf{univ}}$ simulates the work of $\mathcal{A}$ and computes $f(x_0, \ldots, x_{n-1})$.

From Theorem 8.2.18 we know that any function on an alphabet A that can be computed using labeled Markov algorithms can be computed by an lMa that has only two auxiliary symbols, $\sqcup$ and X. Let $B = A \cup \{\sqcup, X\}$, $\hat{B} = B \cup \{:, \rightarrow, /, ;\}$. Let $\theta_{AB} : A^* \longrightarrow (\hat{B})^*$ be the standard bijection introduced in Section 7.7.

The language $S = \{a_0\}^* : B^* \rightarrow B^*/\{a_0\}^*;$ of all statements of lMas on the alphabet $\hat{B}$ is primitive recursive by Theorem 7.8.3. This is useful for proving that the language LMA_B of all lMas over the alphabet B is also a primitive recursive language. A word $\alpha \in (\hat{B})^*$ represents an lMa if the following conditions are satisfied:

1. $\alpha \in S^+$;
2. $\mathsf{label}(\mathsf{prod}(\alpha, u)) = a_0^{|u|}$ for every word u such that $|u| < \mathsf{size}(\alpha)$.

Thus, the characteristic predicate of the language LMA_B can be written as

$$p_{\mathrm{LMA}_B}(\alpha) = p_{S^+}(\alpha) \wedge (\forall u \leq_{\mathrm{pref}} \mathsf{size}(\alpha))(\mathsf{label}(\mathsf{prod}(\alpha, u)) = a_0^{|u|}),$$

for $\alpha \in \hat{B}^*$, which shows that LMA_B is a primitive recursive language on $\hat{B}$.

Our goal is to define a primitive recursive function alg (for algorithm) on the alphabet $\hat{B}$ such that for every lMa $\mathcal{A}$ there is a word $x \in A^*$ such that $\mathsf{alg}(x) = w_{\mathcal{A}}$, the code of the algorithm $\mathcal{A}$. The word x will be regarded as the "program" that corresponds to the algorithm $\mathcal{A}$ and this will allow us to use the same alphabet A for encoding both data and algorithms.

Define $\mathsf{alg} : (\hat{B})^* \longrightarrow (\hat{B})^*$ by

$$\mathsf{alg}(x) = \begin{cases} \hat{\theta}_{A\hat{B}}(x) & \text{if } p_{A^*}(x) = a_0 \text{ and } p_{\mathrm{LMA}_B}(\hat{\theta}_{A\hat{B}}(x)) = a_0 \\ 0 : \lambda \rightarrow \lambda/0; & \text{otherwise,} \end{cases}$$

for $x \in (\hat{B})^*$, where $\hat{\theta}_{A\hat{B}}$ is the primitive recursive function introduced in Lemma 7.7.14.

Since A^* is a primitive recursive language on $\hat{B}$ and $\hat{\theta}_{A\hat{B}}$ is a primitive recursive function on $\hat{B}$, it follows that alg is indeed a primitive recursive function on $\hat{B}$.

Note that for any $x \in A^*$, $\mathsf{alg}(x) = w_{\mathcal{A}}$ for some lMa $\mathcal{A}$. Conversely, if $\mathcal{A}$ is an lMa, then $w_{\mathcal{A}} \in (\hat{B})^*$ and there is $x \in A^*$ such that $\theta_{A\hat{B}}(x) = w_{\mathcal{A}}$, since $\theta_{A\hat{B}}$ is a bijection between A^* and $(\hat{B})^*$. The definition of alg implies that $\mathsf{alg}(x) = w_{\mathcal{A}}$. Observe also that in this case $x = \theta_{\hat{B}A}(w_{\mathcal{A}})$.

Definition 8.5.18 A word $x \in A^*$ is an *index* for the function $f = f^n_{\mathcal{A},A}$ if $w_{\mathcal{A}} = \mathsf{alg}(x)$. □

In general a function has an infinite number of indices. Indeed, note that if $\mathcal{A}$ is an lMa that computes the function f then every lMa $\mathcal{A}_{(k)}$ obtained by padding $\mathcal{A}$ with an initial sequence of "do-nothing" productions

$$\begin{aligned}
&0 : \lambda \rightarrow \lambda/1;\\
&1 : \lambda \rightarrow \lambda/2;\\
&\vdots\\
&k-1 : \lambda \rightarrow \lambda/k;
\end{aligned}$$

and incrementing the labels and goto parts of the productions of $\mathcal{A}$ by k will compute exactly the same function. Every algorithm $\mathcal{A}_{(k)}$ generates a distinct index for f. The function $f^n_{\mathcal{A},A}$ will be denoted by f^n_x, where x is an index for f.

Theorem 8.2.12 shows that $\langle\mathcal{A}\rangle(x) = \mathsf{word}(w_{\mathcal{A}}, \mathsf{time}(w_{\mathcal{A}}, x), x)$ for $x \in B^*$. This allows us to write

$$\begin{aligned}
&\mathsf{f}^n_x(x_0, \ldots, x_{n-1})\\
&\quad = \langle\mathcal{A}\rangle(\overline{k_n}(x_0, \ldots, x_{n-1}))\\
&\quad = \mathsf{word}(w_{\mathcal{A}}, \mathsf{time}(w_{\mathcal{A}}, \overline{k_n}(x_0, \ldots, x_{n-1})), \overline{k_n}(x_0, \ldots, x_{n-1}))\\
&\quad = \mathsf{word}(\mathsf{alg}(x), \mathsf{time}(\mathsf{alg}(x), \overline{k_n}(x_0, \ldots, x_{n-1})), \overline{k_n}(x_0, \ldots, x_{n-1})),
\end{aligned}$$

for $(x_0, \ldots, x_{n-1}) \in \mathrm{Dom}(\mathsf{f}^n_x)$, where $w_{\mathcal{A}} = \mathsf{alg}(x)$.

This suggests considering the partial function $\mathsf{univ}^n : (A^*)^{n+1} \mapsto A^*$ given by

$$\begin{aligned}
&\mathsf{univ}^n(x, x_0, \ldots, x_{n-1})\\
&\quad = \mathsf{word}(\mathsf{alg}(x), \mathsf{time}(\mathsf{alg}(x), \overline{k_n}(x_0, \ldots, x_{n-1})), \overline{k_n}(x_0, \ldots, x_{n-1})),
\end{aligned}$$

for $(x_0, \ldots, x_{n-1}) \in \mathrm{Dom}(\mathsf{f}^n_x)$. By Theorem 7.9.10 we can conclude that univ^n is a partial recursive function on A. We refer to univ^n as the *universal partial recursive function of n arguments* on A. This term is justified by the fact that univ^n is capable of doing the job of any partial recursive function on A. Indeed, if f^n_x is a partial recursive function on A having x as an index, then its value $\mathsf{f}^n_x(x_0, \ldots, x_{n-1})$ can be computed by providing the universal function with the index x (that plays the role of the "program" for f^n_x) and the arguments $x_0, \ldots, x_{n-1}$. We merely take advantage of the equality

$$\mathsf{f}^n_x(x_0, \ldots, x_{n-1}) = \mathsf{univ}^n(x, x_0, \ldots, x_{n-1}),$$

for every $(x_0, \ldots, x_{n-1}) \in \mathrm{Dom}(\mathsf{f}^n_x)$.

A universal function univ^n is a partial recursive function of $n+1$ arguments. Therefore, by Corollary 8.5.10, there exists an lMa $\mathcal{A}^n_{\mathsf{univ}}$ that computes this function. We will refer to $\mathcal{A}^n_{\mathsf{univ}}$ an *n-ary universal lMa on A*. We write f_x rather than f^1_x when $n = 1$; also, the universal function $\mathsf{univ}^1 : (A^*)^2 \mapsto A^*$ will be denoted simply by univ.

The existence of the predicate haltsby introduced in Lemma 8.2.10 allows us to prove the next result.

Theorem 8.5.19 *Let A be an alphabet. There is an $(n+2)$-ary primitive recursive predicate* $\mathsf{haltsby}_A^n$ *on A such that $\mathsf{f}_x^n(x_0, \ldots, x_{n-1})$ is defined if and only if there is $y \in A^*$ such that $\mathsf{haltsby}_A^n(x, y, x_0, \ldots, x_{n-1}) = a_0$.*

Proof. Define the predicate $\mathsf{haltsby}_A^n$ by

$$\mathsf{haltsby}_A^n(x, y, x_0, \ldots, x_{n-1}) = \mathsf{haltsby}(\mathsf{alg}(x), y, \overline{k_n}(x_0, \ldots, x_{n-1})),$$

for $x, y, x_0, \ldots, x_{n-1} \in A^*$. The primitive recursiveness of $\mathsf{haltsby}_A^n$ follows from Theorem 7.7.16. The current statement is a direct consequence of Lemma 8.2.10. ∎

When $A = \{a_0\}$ we denote the predicate $\mathsf{haltsby}_A^n$ simply by $\mathsf{haltsby}_0^n$.

The existence of universal partial recursive functions has many important consequences. For example, it allows us to prove the existence of languages that are not recursive.

Theorem 8.5.20 *The unary predicate p defined by*

$$p(x) = \begin{cases} a_0 & \textit{if } (x,x) \in \mathrm{Dom}(\mathsf{univ}) \\ \lambda & \textit{otherwise} \end{cases}$$

for $x \in A^*$ is not recursive.

Proof. Suppose that p were a recursive predicate. This implies that the function $h : A^* \longrightarrow A^*$ given by

$$h(x) = \begin{cases} \mathsf{f}_x(x)a_0 & \text{if } p(x) = a_0 \\ \lambda & \text{if } p(x) = \lambda, \end{cases}$$

for $x \in A^*$, is recursive. Let z be an index for h, that is $h(x) = \mathsf{univ}(z, x)$ for $x \in A^*$. This leads to a contradiction since $h(z) = \mathsf{f}_z(z)a_0 = \mathsf{univ}(z, z)a_0$ by the definition of h, while on the other hand $h(z) = \mathsf{univ}(z, z)$ by the definition of the universal function. Consequently, p cannot be recursive. ∎

Theorem 8.5.21 *The language $\mathsf{H} = \{x \in A^* \mid x \in \mathrm{Dom}(\mathsf{f}_x)\}$ is not recursive.*

Proof. This follows immediately from Theorem 8.5.20 by noting that p equals p_{H}, the characteristic predicate of the set H. ∎

From Theorem 8.5.19 it follows that p_{H} can also be expressed as

$$p_{\mathsf{H}}(x) = \begin{cases} a_0 & \text{if there is } y \text{ such that } \mathsf{haltsby}(\mathsf{alg}(x), y, x) = a_0 \\ \lambda & \text{otherwise,} \end{cases}$$

for $x \in A^*$. This suggest the usefulness of an *unbounded existential quantifier*. Namely, if $q(x, y)$ is a predicate, let r be the predicate defined by

$$r(x) = \begin{cases} a_0 & \text{if there is } y \text{ such that } q(x,y) = a_0 \\ \lambda & \text{otherwise,} \end{cases}$$

We denote r by $(\exists y)q(x, y)$. The previous comment about p_{H} shows that even if q is a primitive recursive predicate, r is not necessarily recursive.

Corollary 8.5.22 *Let A be an alphabet. The binary predicate q on A given by*

$$q(x,y) = \begin{cases} a_0 & \textit{if } y \in \mathrm{Dom}(\mathsf{f}_x) \\ \lambda & \textit{otherwise,} \end{cases}$$

for $x, y \in A^*$ is not recursive.

Proof. Suppose q were recursive, and let p be the unary predicate introduced in Theorem 8.5.20. Then, since $p(x) = q(x, x)$ for $x \in A^*$, this would imply that p is recursive. ∎

The preceding Corollary shows that there is no algorithm to decide whether an arbitrary lMa halts on an arbitrary input. This fact is known as the *undecidability of the halting problem* and it has important consequences in many areas of Computer Science. It also implies that the similar halting problem for Turing machines is undecidable. To show this we need the following translational result that is the reverse of the translation from dTms to lMas contained in Section 8.5.2.

Theorem 8.5.23 *Starting from an lMa $\mathcal{A} = (A, P)$ one can effectively construct a dTm $\mathcal{M}_{\mathcal{A}} = (B, Q, \delta, q_0, \{q_f\})$ such that $A \subseteq B - \{\triangleright\}$ and $\langle\mathcal{A}\rangle(x) = y$ if and only if $\langle\mathcal{M}_{\mathcal{A}}\rangle(q_0 \triangleright x\star) = q_f \triangleright y\star$ for any $x, y \in A^*$.*

Proof. Let $\mathcal{A} = (A, P)$ be an lMa given by

$$0 : x_0 \to y_0/i_0;$$
$$\vdots$$
$$n-1 : x_{n-1} \to y_{n-1}/i_{n-1};$$

We construct $\mathcal{M}_{\mathcal{A}}$ as a TMS by using a modified form of $\mathcal{M}_{x \to_l y}$ discussed in Example 8.4.7. For each production $k : x_k \to y_k/i_k$ consider a copy of $\mathcal{M}_{x_k \to_l y_k}$, and let v_k be the initial vertex of this copy.

The work of the dTm starts with the configuration $q_0 \triangleright x\star$. If the word x_k does not occur as an infix of the word on the tape, the dTm $\mathcal{M}_{x_k \to_l y_k}$ reaches the vertex $v_k^{not\ found}$ (see Figure 8.9). An arc $(v_k^{not\ found}, v_{k+1})$ is added in order to continue the work by simulating the application of the production $k+1 : x_{k+1} \to y_{k+1}/i_{k+1}$.

If x_k was located on the tape and replaced by y_k, the machine $\mathcal{M}_{x_k \to_l y_k}$ will reach the vertex v_k^{found}. An arc (v_k^{found}, v_{i_k}) will allow the work of the machine to proceed with the application of the production i_k.

If no production i_k exists, then add an arc (v_k^{found}, v^{halt}) to end the activity of the STM; the vertex v^{halt} is labeled by a dTm $\mathcal{M}_0$. Also, connect the vertex $v_{n-1}^{not\ found}$ with v^{halt}. It is clear that the dTm defined by this TMS simulates the work of the lMa and thus satisfies the requirements of the theorem. ∎

Example 8.5.24 Let $A = \{a, b\}$ be an alphabet, and let $\mathcal{A}$ be the lMa:

$$0 : \lambda \to X/1;$$
$$1 : Xa \to aX/1;$$
$$2 : Xb \to bX/1;$$
$$3 : X \to b/4;$$

The application of $\mathcal{A}$ to the word x results in the word xb.

To construct $\mathcal{M}_{\mathcal{A}}$ we need to connect the dTms

$$\mathcal{M}_{\lambda \to_l X}, \mathcal{M}_{Xa \to_l aX}, \mathcal{M}_{Xb \to_l bX}, \mathcal{M}_{X \to_l b}$$

that correspond to the four productions of the lMa. The resulting dTm is shown in Figure 8.15. □

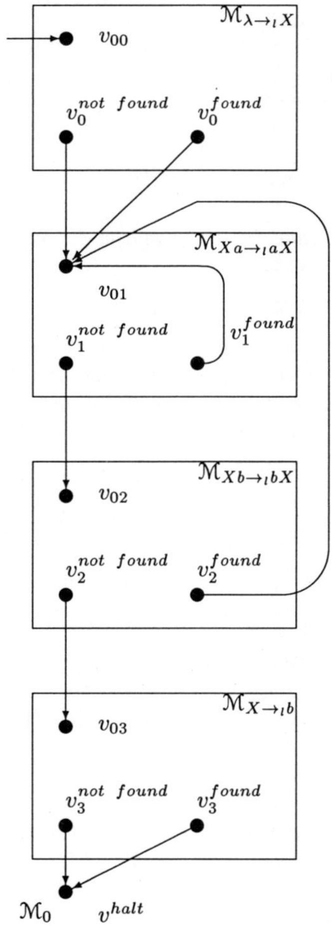

Figure 8.15: TMS that simulates the lMa $\mathcal{A}$

Corollary 8.5.25 *The halting problem for dTms is undecidable.*

Proof. Suppose that we could decide if an arbitrary dTm halts on an arbitrary input. Consider an lMa operating on an alphabet A and an input x. Using the construction outlined in Theorem 8.5.23 construct the dTm $\mathcal{M}_{\mathcal{A}}$. Then, we could decide whether $\mathcal{M}_{\mathcal{A}}$ halts when started on the configuration $q_0 \triangleright x\star$, and this would allow us to decide whether $\mathcal{A}$ halts on input x. ∎

We conclude this section with one of the basic results of computability.

Theorem 8.5.26 *Let f_x^{m+n} be a partial recursive function of $m+n$ arguments on alphabet A. There is a primitive recursive function $h : (A^*)^{1+m} \longrightarrow A^*$ such that*

$$\mathsf{f}_x^{m+n}(x_0, \ldots, x_{m-1}, y_0, \ldots, y_{n-1}) = \mathsf{f}^n_{h(x,x_0,\ldots,x_{m-1})}(y_0, \ldots, y_{n-1}),$$

for $x, x_0, \ldots, x_{m-1}, y_0, \ldots, y_{n-1} \in A^*$.

Proof. Let $\mathcal{A} = (B, P)$ be an lMa such that $f = \mathsf{f}^{m+n}_{\mathcal{A},A}$ and $w_{\mathcal{A}} = \mathsf{alg}(x)$. The input of $\mathcal{A}$ is the word

$$\overline{k_{m+n}}(x_0, \ldots, x_{m-1}, y_0, \ldots, y_{n-1}) = x_0 \sqcup \cdots \sqcup x_{m-1} \sqcup y_0 \sqcup \cdots y_{n-1} \sqcup.$$

We need an lMa $\mathcal{A}'$ that will perform the same computation as $\mathcal{A}$, except that the first m arguments $x_0, \ldots, x_{m-1}$ of $\mathcal{A}$ are fixed. Thus, the input word of $\mathcal{A}'$ must be $y_0 \sqcup \cdots y_{n-1} \sqcup$ and $\mathcal{A}'$ can be obtained from $\mathcal{A}$ by adding a first production that will transform $y_0 \sqcup \cdots y_{n-1} \sqcup$ into

$$x_0 \sqcup \cdots \sqcup x_{m-1} \sqcup y_0 \sqcup \cdots y_{n-1} \sqcup.$$

Of course, this requires all labels and goto parts of the productions in P be incremented by 1. Consider the primitive recursive function $g : (\hat{B}^*) \longrightarrow (\hat{B})^*$ defined by

$$\begin{aligned} g(\lambda, x) &= \lambda : \lambda \to x/a_0; \\ g(wb, x) &= \begin{cases} g(w, x)a_0 b & \text{if } (b =:) \vee (b =;) \\ g(w, x)b & \text{otherwise,} \end{cases} \end{aligned}$$

for $w, x \in (\hat{B})^*$ and $b \in \hat{B}$. It is clear that $w_{\mathcal{A}'} = g(w_{\mathcal{A}}, x_0 \sqcup \cdots \sqcup x_{m-1} \sqcup)$ Let $z \in A^*$ be a word such that $w_{\mathcal{A}'} = \mathsf{alg}(z)$. We have $\theta_{\hat{B}A}(w_{\mathcal{A}'}) = z$. This allows us to define the function h by

$$h(x, x_0, \ldots, x_{m-1}) = \theta_{\hat{B},A}(g(\mathsf{alg}(x), x_0, \ldots, x_{m-1})),$$

for $x, x_0, \ldots, x_{m-1} \in A^*$. Clearly, h is a primitive recursive function on A and we can write:

$$\begin{aligned} & \mathsf{f}^n_{h(x,x_0,\ldots,x_{m-1})}(y_0, \ldots, y_{n-1}) \\ &= \mathsf{f}^n_{\theta_{\hat{B},A}(g(\mathsf{alg}(x),x_0,\ldots,x_{m-1}))}(y_0, \ldots, y_{n-1}) \\ &= \mathsf{f}^n_{\theta_{\hat{B},A}(g(w_{\mathcal{A}},x_0,\ldots,x_{m-1}))}(y_0, \ldots, y_{n-1}) \\ &= \mathsf{f}^n_{\theta_{\hat{B},A}(w_{\mathcal{A}'})}(y_0, \ldots, y_{n-1}) \\ &= \mathsf{f}_z(y_0, \ldots, y_{n-1}) \\ &= f^n_{\mathcal{A}',A}(y_0, \ldots, y_{n-1}) \\ &= f^{m+n}_{\mathcal{A},A}(x_0, \ldots, x_{m-1}, y_0, \ldots, y_{n-1}) \\ &= \mathsf{f}_x^{m+n}(x_0, \ldots, x_{m-1}, y_0, \ldots, y_{n-1}), \end{aligned}$$

which concludes the argument. ∎

A weaker form of Theorem 8.5.26 is known in the computability literature as the *smn* Theorem. The current form, due to Brainerd and Landweber ([1974]), takes advantage of the computing style of lMas to produce the function h that does not depend on n.

8.6 Recursive Enumerable Languages

We saw that $\mathcal{L}_3$, the class of regular languages, is definable using finite automata, while $\mathcal{L}_2$, the class of context-free languages, corresponds to pushdown automata. The goal of this section is to examine the class of languages that can be defined using Turing machines. As we shall see, this class coincides with the $\mathcal{L}_0$ class, the largest class in Chomsky's hierarchy.

We remind the reader that we identify the set of natural numbers $\mathbb{N}$ with the set of words $\{a_0\}^*$. This convention is especially important in this section.

Definition 8.6.1 A set $L \subseteq \mathbb{N}$ is *recursively enumerable* if $L = \emptyset$ or there is a recursive function $f : \mathbb{N} \longrightarrow \mathbb{N}$, called an *enumerating function for* L, such that $L = \{f(0), f(1), \ldots, f(n), \ldots\}$. □

In other words, L is recursively enumerable if it equals the range $\text{Ran}(f)$ of a recursive function $f : \mathbb{N} \longrightarrow \mathbb{N}$. It is important to realize that f may list L in any order — even an apparently random order — and with repetitions. Eventually, though, every element of L will be listed.

Definition 8.6.1 shows that the existence of an enumerating function for a set L allows us to list effectively the elements of the set, albeit with repetitions, in general.

Any recursive set of numbers is recursively enumerable. Indeed, if $L = \emptyset$, then L is recursively enumerable. So, let L be a nonempty, recursive set, and let $n_0 \in L$. Since p_L, the characteristic predicate of L is recursive, the recursive function $f : \mathbb{N} \longrightarrow \mathbb{N}$ given by

$$f(n) = \begin{cases} n & \text{if } p_L(n) = 1, \\ n_0 & \text{otherwise,} \end{cases}$$

for $n \in \mathbb{N}$ is an enumerating function for L. The reverse implication is not true in general: there are recursive enumerable sets that are not recursive, as we shall see later in this section.

While the recursiveness of a set L allows us to decide the membership question "$n \in L$?" for an arbitrary $n \in \mathbb{N}$, recursive enumerability insures only that an affirmative answer can be obtained effectively. Indeed, if L is a recursively enumerable set having the enumerating function f and n is an arbitrary number, then, if $n \in L$, by constructing the list $f(0), f(1), f(2), \ldots$ we will eventually reach a member of this list $f(m)$ such that $f(m) = n$, and we will be able to certify that $n \in L$; however, if $n \notin L$, then the search for a value of f to match n would continue indefinitely.

In Definition 8.6.1, we use one-argument enumerating functions. However, the number of arguments of the enumerating function is immaterial, as shown by the next theorem.

Theorem 8.6.2 *A set $L \subseteq \mathbb{N}$ is recursively enumerable if and only if for every $k \in \mathbb{N}$, $k \geq 1$, there exists a recursive function $f_k : \mathbb{N}^k \longrightarrow \mathbb{N}$, such that $L = \text{Ran}(f_k)$.*

Proof. Assume L is recursively enumerable; then, $L = \text{Ran}(g)$ for some recursive function $g : \mathbb{N} \longrightarrow \mathbb{N}$. Pick $k \in \mathbb{N}$ with $k \geq 1$. Define the function $f : \mathbb{N}^k \longrightarrow \mathbb{N}$ by $f(x_0, x_1, \ldots, x_{k-1}) = g(x_0)$ for $x_0, \ldots, x_{k-1} \in \mathbb{N}$. Since $f = gP_0^k$, it is clear that f is recursive, and that $\text{Ran}(f) = L$.

Conversely, suppose that $L = \text{Ran}(f)$, where $f : \mathbb{N}^k \longrightarrow \mathbb{N}$ is a recursive function and $k \geq 1$. The converse argument is more interesting, and one could proceed by induction on k. We leave the details to the reader, and discuss the case $k = 2$, which makes use of the dovetailing technique mentioned in Section 1.6 and contains the essence of the inductive step.

Let $L = \text{Ran}(f)$, where $f : \mathbb{N}^2 \longrightarrow \mathbb{N}$ is a recursive function. We have $L = \{f(m,n) \mid m,n \in \mathbb{N}\}$. Define the function $g : \mathbb{N} \longrightarrow \mathbb{N}$ by $g(r) = f(\wp_0(r), \wp_1(r))$ for $r \in \mathbb{N}$, where $\wp_0, \wp_1$ are the primitive recursive functions associated to the pairing function $\wp$ in Example 7.6.10. It is obvious that $\text{Ran}(g) \subseteq \text{Ran}(f) = L$. To prove the reverse inclusion, let $t \in L$; then $t = f(m,n)$ for some $m,n \in \mathbb{N}$. If $r = \wp(m,n)$, then $m = \wp_0(r)$, $n = \wp_1(r)$, so $t = f(\wp_0(r), \wp_1(r)) = g(r)$, which shows that $L \subseteq \text{Ran}(g)$. ∎

The notion of recursive enumerability can be generalized to languages on arbitrary alphabets.

Definition 8.6.3 Let A be an alphabet. A language $L \subseteq A^*$ is *recursively enumerable on A* if $L = \emptyset$, or there exists a recursive function $f : A^* \longrightarrow A^*$ such that $L = \{f(x) \mid x \in A^*\}$. The function f will be referred to an *enumerating function.* □

It is easy to see, following the same argument as above, that every recursive language on an arbitrary alphabet is recursively enumerable.

Recursive enumerability is independent of the underlying alphabet in the sense of the next theorem.

Theorem 8.6.4 *If A, B are two alphabets such that $A \subseteq B$ and L is a recursive enumerable language on A, then L is a recursive enumerable language on B.*

Proof. If $L = \emptyset$, it is clear that L is a recursive enumerable language on B. Therefore, suppose that $L \neq \emptyset$, and let $y_0 \in L$. If $L = \{f(x) \mid x \in A^*\}$, where $f : A^* \longrightarrow A^*$ is a recursive function on A, let $\overline{f}$ be the null extension of f to B. Define the function $g : B^* \longrightarrow B^*$ by

$$g(x) = \begin{cases} \overline{f}(x) & \text{if } p_{A^*}(x) = a_0 \\ y_0 & \text{otherwise,} \end{cases}$$

for $x \in B^*$. Then, it is clear that g is a recursive function on B, and $L = \{g(x) \mid x \in B^*\}$, so L is recursively enumerable on B. ∎

The relationship between recursively enumerable languages and recursively enumerable sets of numbers is clarified by the next theorem.

Theorem 8.6.5 *Let A be an alphabet and $L \subseteq A^*$. The language L is recursively enumerable if and only if the set $\phi_A(L)$ is recursively enumerable.*

Proof. Suppose that L is recursively enumerable, and let $g : A^* \longrightarrow A^*$ be a recursive function such that $L = \{g(x) \mid x \in A^*\}$. Then, $\phi_A(L) = \{\phi_A(g(x)) \mid$

$x \in A^*\}$. Since $\psi_A : \mathbb{N} \longrightarrow A^*$ is a bijection, for every $x \in A^*$ there is exactly one $n \in \mathbb{N}$ such that $x = \psi_A(n)$. Thus, we can write $\phi_A(L) = \{\phi_A(g(\psi_A(n))) \mid n \in \mathbb{N}\} = \{g^+(n) \mid n \in \mathbb{N}\}$. This shows that the recursive function g^+ is an enumerating function for $\phi_A(L)$, so $\phi_A(L)$ is recursively enumerable.

Conversely, let $\phi_A(L)$ be recursively enumerable by the enumerating function $f : \mathbb{N} \longrightarrow \mathbb{N}$, that is, $\phi_A(L) = \{f(n) \mid n \in \mathbb{N}\}$. For every $n \in \mathbb{N}$ there is exactly one $x \in A^*$ such that $n = \phi_A(x)$, so $\phi_A(L) = \{f(\phi_A(x)) \mid x \in A^*\}$. Therefore, we have $L = \psi_A(\phi_A(L)) = \{\psi_A(f(\phi_A(x))) \mid x \in A^*\} = \{f^{\#}(x) \mid x \in A^*\}$, so L is recursively enumerable. ∎

As was the case for recursively enumerable languages on a one-symbol alphabet, the number of arguments of the enumerating function is not significant for recursively enumerable languages on arbitrary alphabets.

Theorem 8.6.6 *A set L is the range of a recursive function $f : (A^*)^k \longrightarrow A^*$, if and only if there exists a function $g : A^* \longrightarrow A^*$ such that $L = \text{Ran}(g)$.*

Proof. Let $L = \text{Ran}(f)$. It is easy to verify that $\phi_A(L) = \text{Ran}(f^+)$, where $f^+ : \mathbb{N}^k \longrightarrow \mathbb{N}$. Therefore, by Theorem 8.6.2, $\phi_A(L)$ is recursively enumerable, and so is L, by Theorem 8.6.5.

The reverse implication is straightforward. ∎

In Section 8.5.3 we saw that the class of recursive languages is closed with respect to complementation. Later in this section, we shall see that the class of recursively enumerable languages does not enjoy this property. The next theorem focuses on those recursively enumerable languages whose complements are also recursively enumerable.

Theorem 8.6.7 *Let A be an alphabet. A language $L \subseteq A^*$ is recursive if and only if both L and its complement $A^* - L$ are recursively enumerable.*

Proof. Suppose that $L \subseteq A^*$ is recursive. Since $A^* - L$ is recursive also, both L and $A^* - L$ are recursively enumerable because every recursive language is recursively enumerable.

We begin by proving the converse statement for the case when $A = \{a_0\}$. Suppose that both L and $\mathbb{N} - L$ are recursively enumerable and let f, g be enumerating functions for L and $\mathbb{N} - L$, respectively. Note that a number n is either in the range of f or in the range of g but not both. Then, let h be the recursive function $h : \mathbb{N} \longrightarrow \mathbb{N}$ given by $h(n) = (\min_0 m)((f(m) = n) \vee (g(m) = n))$. If $f(h(n)) = n$ this means that $n \in \text{Ran}(f) = L$; otherwise, that is, if $f(h(n)) \neq n$, then $n \in \text{Ran}(g) = \mathbb{N} - L$. Thus, we can write

$$p_L(n) = \begin{cases} 1 & \text{if } f(h(n)) = n, \\ 0 & \text{otherwise,} \end{cases}$$

for $n \in \mathbb{N}$, so L is recursive.

If $L \subseteq A^*$ is a language on an arbitrary alphabet A such that both L and $A^* - L$ are recursively enumerable, then $\phi_A(L)$ and $\phi_A(A^* - L) = \mathbb{N} - \phi_A(L)$ are recursively enumerable. Thus, $\phi_A(L)$ is recursive, and so is L, by Theorem 8.6.5. ∎

Corollary 8.6.8 *Let $L \subseteq A^*$ be a recursive enumerable language that is not recursive. Then, its complement $A^* - L$ is not recursive enumerable.*

Proof. The statement follows immediately from Theorem 8.6.7. ∎

Definition 8.6.9 Let A be an alphabet and $L \subseteq A^*$. The *partial identity function* of L is the function $\iota_L : A^* \mapsto A^*$, where $\iota_L(x) = x$ if $x \in L$ and $\mathrm{Dom}(\iota_L) = L$. □

Lemma 8.6.10 *Let $L \subseteq \mathbb{N}$. The following statements are equivalent:*

(i) *L is a recursively enumerable set;*

(ii) *L is a finite set, or L is the range of a recursive injective function $f : \mathbb{N} \longrightarrow \mathbb{N}$;*

(iii) *there is a partial recursive function $g : \mathbb{N} \mapsto \mathbb{N}$ such that $L = \mathrm{Dom}(g)$;*

(iv) *the partial identity function ι_L is partial recursive;*

(v) *there is a partial recursive function $h : \mathbb{N} \mapsto \mathbb{N}$ such that $L = \mathrm{Ran}(h)$.*

Proof. If L is infinite we may number the elements of L by the order in which they are first enumerated in $f(0), f(1), \ldots, f(n), \ldots$, giving us e.g. $L = \{x_0, x_1, \ldots, x_n, \ldots\}$. We introduce a function $\mathsf{pl} : \mathbb{N} \longrightarrow \mathbb{N}$ such that $\mathsf{pl}(k)$ is the place where x_k is first enumerated by f, that is, $x_k = f(\mathsf{pl}(k))$ for $k \in \mathbb{N}$. This is accomplished by the following definition by primitive recursion:

$$\begin{aligned} \mathsf{pl}(0) &= 0, \\ \mathsf{pl}(n+1) &= (\min_0 m)(m > \mathsf{pl}(n) \wedge ((\forall \ell \leq \mathsf{pl}(n))(f(m) \neq f(\ell)))), \end{aligned}$$

for $n \in \mathbb{N}$.

The language L is the range of the function $f\mathsf{pl}$. This function is injective for, if $f(\mathsf{pl}(n)) = f(\mathsf{pl}(n'))$ for $n \neq n'$, this would imply $x_n = x'_n$, i.e. that x_n is first introduced into L in two distinct places, which is absurd.

To prove the implication (ii)⇒(iii) suppose initially that L is a finite set, $L = \{m_0, \ldots, m_{e-1}\}$. Let g be the partial recursive function given by

$$g(n) = (\min_0 m)((n = m_0) \vee \cdots (n = m_{e-1})).$$

Clearly, $n \in \mathrm{Dom}(g)$ if and only if $n \in L$, and in such cases, $g(n) = 0$. Thus, $L = \mathrm{Dom}(g)$.

Assume now that L is the range of a recursive injection $f : \mathbb{N} \longrightarrow \mathbb{N}$. The injectivity of f implies that for every n there is at most one m such that $f(m) = n$. Thus, we can define the partial recursive function g by $g(n) = (\min_0 m)(f(m) = n)$. Note that $g(n)$ is defined if and only if $n \in \mathrm{Ran}(f) = L$, so $L = \mathrm{Dom}(g)$.

For the implication (iii)⇒(iv), let L be a set such that $L = \mathrm{Dom}(g)$, where $g : \mathbb{N} \mapsto \mathbb{N}$ is a partial recursive function. Let z be an index for g. Then $n \in \mathrm{Dom}(g)$ if and only if there exists $m \in \mathbb{N}$ such that $\mathsf{haltsby}_0^1(z, m, n) = 1$. Since $\mathsf{haltsby}_0^1$ is a primitive recursive predicate, the function ι_L is a partial recursive function because $\iota_L(n) = n + 0 \cdot (\min_0 m)(\mathsf{haltsby}_0^1(z, m, n) = 1)$ for $n \in \mathbb{N}$.

Part (iv) implies Part (v) because, if ι_L is a partial recursive function, then $L = \mathrm{Ran}(\iota_L)$.

For the implication (v)⇒(i) we again use a dovetailing argument. Suppose that $L \neq \emptyset$ and that $L = \mathrm{Ran}(h)$. Let x be an index for h (that is $h = \mathsf{f}_x$) and let $n_0 \in L$. Define the function $f : \mathbb{N} \longrightarrow \mathbb{N}$ as

$$f(m) = \begin{cases} h(\wp_1(m)) & \text{if } \mathsf{haltsby}_0^1(x, \wp_0(m), \wp_1(m)) = 1, \\ n_0 & \text{if } \mathsf{haltsby}_0^1(x, \wp_0(m), \wp_1(m)) = 0, \end{cases}$$

for $m \in \mathbb{N}$. Since $\mathsf{haltsby}_0^1$ is a primitive recursive predicate, the function f is a recursive function. We claim that $L = \mathrm{Ran}(f)$. Indeed, let $n \in L$. Since $L = \mathrm{Ran}(h) = \mathrm{Ran}(\mathsf{f}_x)$, there are two numbers $n_0, n_1 \in \mathbb{N}$ such that the lMa whose code is x halts in fewer than n_0 steps and produces the output n when the input is n_1, that is, $n = h(n_1)$. Define $m = \wp(n_0, n_1)$, which means $n_0 = \wp_0(m)$ and $n_1 = \wp_1(m)$. The definition of $\mathsf{haltsby}_0^1$ implies that $\mathsf{haltsby}_0^1(x, \wp_0(m), \wp_1(m)) = 1$, so $n == h(\wp_1(m)) = f(m)$. We have shown that $L \subseteq \mathrm{Ran}(f)$.

Conversely, let $n \in \mathrm{Ran}(f)$, that is, $n = f(m)$ for some $m \in \mathbb{N}$. If $\mathsf{haltsby}_0^1(x, \wp_0(m), \wp_1(m)) = 0$, then $n = n_0 \in L$. Otherwise,

$$\mathsf{haltsby}_0^1(x, \wp_0(m), \wp_1(m)) = 1,$$

which implies that the lMa whose code is x eventually halts when started with $\wp_1(m)$ as its input. Thus, $n = h(\wp_1(m))$ and we obtain $\mathrm{Ran}(f) \subseteq L$. ∎

Lemma 8.6.10 is the core of the argument of its generalization contained in the next result.

Theorem 8.6.11 *Let A be a alphabet and let $L \subseteq A^*$. The following statements are equivalent:*

(i) *L is a recursively enumerable language;*
(ii) *L is a finite set, or L is the range of a recursive injective function $f : A^* \longrightarrow A^*$;*
(iii) *there is a partial recursive function $g : A^* \leadsto A^*$ such that $L = \mathrm{Dom}(g)$;*
(iv) *the partial identity function ι_L is partial recursive;*
(v) *there is a partial recursive function $h : A^* \leadsto A^*$ such that $L = \mathrm{Ran}(h)$.*

Proof. Each of the five statements of the theorem about a language $L \subseteq A^*$ is equivalent to the corresponding statement of Lemma 8.6.10 about language $\phi_A(L) \subseteq \mathbb{N}$.

The equivalence of the first statement to the first statement of the lemma is contained in Theorem 8.6.5.

Suppose now that the second statement of the theorem holds, that is, L is a finite set, or L is the range of a recursive injective function $f : A^* \longrightarrow A^*$. Note that L is finite if and only if $\phi_A(L)$ is finite since ϕ_A is a bijection. On the other hand, $L = \mathrm{Ran}(f)$, where f is an injective function, if and only if $\phi_A(L) = \mathrm{Ran}(\phi_A f)$ and it is clear that $\phi_A f$ is injective.

We leave it to the reader to show the remaining equivalences. ∎

Theorem 8.6.12 *Let A be an alphabet. There exists a language $H \subseteq A^*$ such that H is recursively enumerable but not recursive.*

Proof. In Theorem 8.5.21 we proved that the language $\mathsf{H} = \{x \in A^* \mid x \in \mathrm{Dom}(\mathsf{f}_x)\}$ is not recursive. This language is recursively enumerable since H is the domain of the partial recursive function f given by $f(x) = \mathsf{univ}(x, x)$ for $x \in A^*$. ∎

Corollary 8.6.13 *The complement $\bar{\mathsf{H}} = \{x \in A^* \mid x \notin \mathrm{Dom}(\mathsf{f}_x)\}$ is not recursively enumerable.*

Proof. Since H is recursively enumerable but not recursive, by Corollary 8.6.8, the language $\bar{\mathsf{H}}$ is not recursively enumerable. ∎

Turing machines have been used up to this point to compute functions, and we have shown that the class of partial recursive functions equals the class of Turing computable functions. We have also examined the role of dTms in deciding the membership problem for recursive languages. We now consider dTms as acceptors of languages.

Definition 8.6.14 Let A be an alphabet, and let $\mathcal{M} = (B, Q, \delta, q_0, \{q_f\})$ be a dTm such that $A \subseteq B - \{\triangleright, \sqcup\}$. The machine $\mathcal{M}$ *accepts* the language $L \subseteq A^*$ if

$$L = \{x \in A^* \mid q_0 \triangleright x \star \overset{*}{\underset{\mathcal{M}}{\vdash}} q_f \triangleright u\star\}$$

for some $u \in B*$. The dTm $\mathcal{M}$ does not halt when started with the initial configuration $q_0 \triangleright x$ for $x \notin L$.

The language on the alphabet A *accepted* by $\mathcal{M}$ is denoted by $L_A(\mathcal{M})$. If A is clear from context we may denote $L_A(\mathcal{M})$ simply by $L(\mathcal{M})$. □

Theorem 8.6.15 *A language $L \subseteq A^*$ is accepted by a dTm if and only if it is recursively enumerable.*

Proof. We shall prove that L is accepted by a dTm if and only if its partial identity ι_L is a partial recursive function. Then, the statement of the theorem will follow from Theorem 8.6.11.

Suppose that L is accepted by a Turing machine, that is $L = L(\mathcal{M})$, where $\mathcal{M} = (B, Q, \delta, q_0, \{q_f\})$ and $A \subseteq B$. Then, $x \in L$ if and only if $q_0 \triangleright x \star \overset{*}{\underset{\mathcal{M}}{\vdash}} q_f \triangleright u\star$ for some word $u \in B^*$. Starting from the machine $\mathcal{M}$ we can construct a dTm $\mathcal{M}_1$ as a TMS that computes the function ι_L as follows.

Starting from the configuration $q_0 \triangleright x\star$, we apply a dTm $\mathcal{M}_{\text{dupl},\sqcup}$; this results in the configuration $q_1 \triangleright x \sqcup x\star$. Next, replace the $\sqcup$ by $\triangleright'$ and position the head on the symbol $\triangleright'$. Let $\mathcal{M}'$ be the dTm obtained from $\mathcal{M}$ by replacing the symbol $\triangleright$ by $\triangleright'$ and q_f by q'_f. Applying $\mathcal{M}'$, we reach the configuration $\triangleright x q'_f \triangleright' u\star$ for some word u. Finally, the TMS erases the word $\triangleright' u$ and moves the head to the leftmost symbol $\triangleright$. This yields the configuration $q_f \triangleright x\star$, which shows that ι_L is Turing computable and, therefore, a partial recursive function.

Conversely, suppose that ι_L is a partial recursive function. Therefore, ι_L is computable by a dTm $\mathcal{M}$, and we have $q_0 \triangleright x \star \overset{*}{\underset{\mathcal{M}}{\vdash}} q_f \triangleright x\star$ if and only if $x \in \text{Dom}(\iota_L) = L$, which shows that L is accepted by the dTm $\mathcal{M}$. ∎

The relationship between recursively enumerable languages and type-0 languages is discussed next.

Theorem 8.6.16 *For every grammar G, the language $L(G)$ is recursively enumerable.*

Proof. Let $G = (A_N, A_T, S, P)$ be a grammar. In Corollary 7.8.10 we have shown that R_G, the language of derivations in G, is a primitive recursive language on the alphabet $A = A_N \cup A_T \cup \{\Rightarrow\}$, which means that its characteristic predicate p_{R_G} is primitive recursive.

If $L(G) = \emptyset$, then $L(G)$ is clearly recursively enumerable. Therefore, suppose that $L(G) \neq \emptyset$ and let $x_0 \in L(G)$. Define the function $f : A^* \longrightarrow A^*$ by

$$f(z) = \begin{cases} x & \text{if } x \in A_T^* \text{ and } z \text{ is a derivation of } x \text{ in } G \\ x_0 & \text{otherwise,} \end{cases}$$

for $z \in A^*$. Note that if z is a derivation and x is the word produced by this derivation, then $x = \mathsf{target}(z)$, where target is the primitive recursive function on A given by

$$\mathsf{target}(z) = \mathsf{part}(z \Rightarrow, \Rightarrow, \mathsf{occ}(z, \Rightarrow))$$

for $z \in A^*$. It is clear that $L(G)$ is the range of f. Further, this function is recursive since we can write:

$$f(z) = \begin{cases} \mathsf{target}(z) & \text{if } p_{A_T^*}(\mathsf{target}(z)) = a_0 \wedge p_{R_G}(z) = a_0 \\ x_0 & \text{otherwise,} \end{cases}$$

Consequently, $L(G)$ is recursively enumerable. ∎

Theorem 8.6.17 *Let A be an alphabet. If a language $L \subseteq A^*$ is accepted by a dTm, then there exists a grammar G such that $L = L(G)$.*

Proof. Suppose that L is accepted by a dTm $\mathcal{M} = (B, Q, \delta, q_0, \{q_f\})$. We construct a grammar $G = (A_N, A, S, P)$ such that $L(G) = L_A(\mathcal{M})$. The nonterminal alphabet of the grammar G is $A_N = \{S, X\} \cup Q \cup U$, where U is the alphabet

$$U = \{U_{ab} \mid a \in A \cup \{\lambda, \star\}, b \in B \cup \{\lambda, \star\}\}.$$

Define the morphisms $h_0, h_1 : (Q \cup U)^* \longrightarrow B \cup \{\star\}$ by $h_0(U_{ab}) = a$ and $h_1(U_{ab}) = b$ for every $a \in A \cup \{\lambda, \star\}$ and $b \in B \cup \{\star\}$, $h_0(q) = \lambda$, $h_1(q) = q$ for $q \in Q$. If $w \in U^*QU^*$, then $h_0(w)$ gives the word obtained by concatenating the first subscripts of the symbols of w, whereas $h_1(w)$ yields the word obtained by concatenating the second subscripts of the symbols of the same word and leaving intact the state symbols.

Suppose that the tape of $\mathcal{M}$ is the initial configuration $q_0 \rhd x\star$, where $x = a_0 \cdots a_{n-1}$ and that $\mathcal{M}$ reaches the configuration $\mathsf{c} = \rhd b_0 \cdots q b_k \cdots b_{m-1}\star$. Let $\Phi_x : \mathsf{CONFIG}(\mathcal{M}) \longrightarrow U^*QU^*$ be the mapping defined as follows. If $m > n$, then

$$\Phi_x(\mathsf{c}) = U_{\rhd\rhd} U_{a_0 b_0} \cdots U_{a_{k-1} b_{k-1}} q U_{a_k b_k} \cdots U_{\star b_n} U_{\lambda b_{n+1}} \cdots U_{\lambda b_{m-1}} U_{\lambda\star}.$$

When $m < n$, we have

$$\Phi_x(\mathsf{c}) = U_{\rhd\rhd} U_{a_0 b_0} \cdots U_{a_{k-1} b_{k-1}} q U_{a_k b_k} \cdots U_{a_m \star} \cdots U_{a_{n-1}\lambda} U_{\star\lambda}.$$

Finally, when $m = n$,

$$\Phi_x(\mathsf{c}) = U_{\rhd\rhd} U_{a_0 b_0} \cdots U_{a_{k-1} b_{k-1}} q U_{a_k b_k} \cdots U_{a_{n-1} b_{n-1}} U_{\star\star}.$$

It is clear that Φ_x is an one-to-one mapping and that, given $\Phi_x(\mathsf{c})$ we can recover both the configuration c and the initial configuration of $\mathcal{M}$, since $h_0(\Phi_x(\mathsf{c})) = \rhd x\star$ and $h_1(\Phi_x(\mathsf{c})) = \mathsf{c}$.

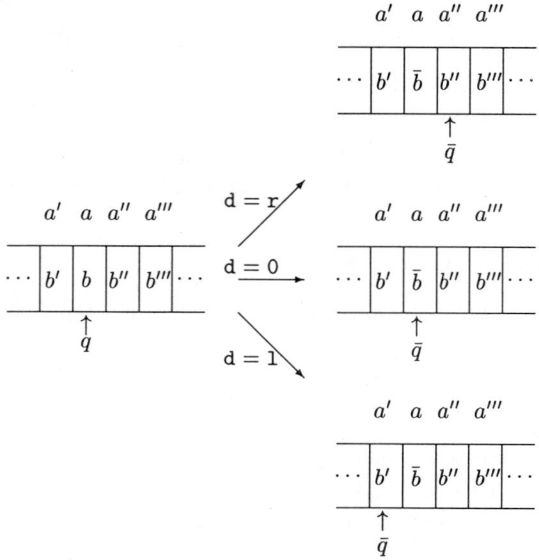

Figure 8.16: Notations Used in the Proof of Theorem 8.6.17

The idea of the construction is to simulate the work of the dTm in the grammar and, at the same time, preserve the initial contents of the tape of the dTm. Then, when $\mathcal{M}$ finishes, remove the dTm's calculations leaving only $a_0 \cdots a_{n-1}$, which is shown to be in $L(G)$. Specifically, the dTm begins its work in the configuration $q_0 \triangleright a_0 \cdots a_{n-1}\star$ and later reaches a configuration $\mathtt{c} = \triangleright b_0 \cdots q b_k \cdots b_{m-1}\star$, if and only if it is possible to generate the word wqw' in the grammar, where $h_0(ww') = \triangleright a_0 \cdots a_{n-1}$, $h_1(w) = \triangleright b_0 \cdots b_{k-1}$, and $h_1(w') = b_k \cdots b_{m-1}\star$.

Initially, the grammar generates the word $q_0 U_{\triangleright\triangleright} U_{a_0 a_0} U_{a_1 a_1} \cdots U_{a_{n-1} a_{n-1}} U_{\star\star}$, using the productions

$$S \to U_{\triangleright\triangleright} X, X \to U_{aa} X \text{ for } a \in A,$$
$$X \to U_{\star\star} Y, U_{aa} Y \to Y U_{aa} \text{ for } a \in A \cup \{\star\},$$
$$Y U_{\triangleright\triangleright} \to q_0 U_{\triangleright\triangleright}.$$

Next, the grammar simulates the work of the dTm. The notations used from now on are based on Figure 8.16, where U_{ab} corresponds to a symbol a above a cell containing b, and qU_{ab} is depicted by placing a q with an arrow pointing to the depiction of U_{ab}. There are several types of productions, depending on the direction of the movement of the head of the dTm, as shown by the table contained in Figure 8.17. We assume that $\delta(q, b) = (\bar{q}, \bar{b}, \mathtt{d})$.

Note that in the set of productions P_{r1}, $a'' \notin \{\star, \lambda\}$ imply that $a''' \neq \sqcup$, i.e. $a''' \in A \cup \{\star\}$.

Finally, once a word $q_f U_{\triangleright\triangleright} \cdots$ is generated by the grammar, we use the

Group	Conditions	Productions
P_{r0}	$\mathtt{d} = \mathtt{r}, b'' \neq \star$	$qU_{ab}U_{a''b''} \to U_{a\bar{b}}\bar{q}U_{a''b''}$ for all $a'' \in A \cup \{\star, \lambda\}, b'' \in A$
P_{r1}	$\mathtt{d} = \mathtt{r}, b'' = \star$ $a'' \neq \star, \lambda$	$qU_{ab}U_{a''\star}U_{a'''\lambda} \to U_{a\bar{b}}\bar{q}U_{a''\sqcup}U_{a'''\star}$ for all $a'' \in A, a''' \in A \cup \{\star\}$
P_{r2}	$\mathtt{d} = \mathtt{r}, b'' = \star,$ $a'' = \star$	$qU_{ab}U_{\star\star} \to U_{a\bar{b}}\bar{q}U_{\star\sqcup}U_{\lambda\star}$
P_{r3}	$\mathtt{d} = \mathtt{r}, b'' = \star,$ $a'' = \lambda$	$qU_{ab}U_{\lambda\star} \to U_{a\bar{b}}\bar{q}U_{\lambda\sqcup}U_{\lambda\star}$
P_{l0}	$\mathtt{d} = \mathtt{l}, \bar{b} \neq \sqcup$	$U_{a'b'}qU_{ab} \to \bar{q}U_{a'b'}U_{a\bar{b}}$ for all $a' \in A \cup \{\star, \lambda\}, b' \in A$
P_{l1}	$\mathtt{d} = \mathtt{l}, \bar{b} = \sqcup,$ $b'' \neq \star$	$U_{a'b'}qU_{ab}U_{a''b''} \to \bar{q}U_{a'b'}U_{a\sqcup}U_{a''b''}$ for all $a'' \in A \cup \{\star, \lambda\}, b'' \in A$
P_{l2}	$\mathtt{d} = \mathtt{l}, \bar{b} = \sqcup,$ $b'' = \star, a'' \neq \lambda$	$U_{a'b'}qU_{ab}U_{a'\star} \to \bar{q}U_{a'b'}U_{a\star}U_{a''\lambda}$ for all $a' \in A \cup \{\star, \lambda\}, a' \in A \cup \{\star\}, b' \in A$
P_{l3}	$\mathtt{d} = \mathtt{l}, \bar{b} = \sqcup,$ $b'' = \star, a'' = \lambda$	$U_{a'b'}qU_{ab}U_{\lambda\star} \to \bar{q}U_{a'b'}U_{a\star}$ for all $a' \in A \cup \{\star, \lambda\}, b' \in A$
P_{00}	$\mathtt{d} = \mathtt{0}$	$qU_{ab} \to \bar{q}U_{a\bar{b}}$

Figure 8.17: Groups of Productions of G

final group of productions to generate the word $a_0 \ldots a_{n-1}$. These productions include

1. $q_f U_{\triangleright\triangleright} \to Z$;
2. $ZU_{ab} \to aZ$ for every $a \in A$ and $b \in B \cup \{\lambda, \star\}$;
3. $ZU_{\star b} \to V$ for every $b \in B \cup \{\lambda, \star\}$;
4. $V \to \lambda$ and $VU_{\lambda b} \to V$ for every $b \in B \cup \{\star\}$,

where Z, V are nonterminal symbols.

We claim that for any configurations c, c', we have $\mathsf{c} \vdash_{\mathcal{M}} \mathsf{c}'$ if and only if $\Phi_x(\mathsf{c}) \underset{G}{\Rightarrow} \Phi_x(\mathsf{c}')$.

Suppose that $\mathsf{c} \vdash_{\mathcal{M}} \mathsf{c}'$, where $\mathsf{c} = \triangleright b_0 \cdots b_{k-1} q b_k b_{k+1} \cdots b_{m-1} \star$. Here we discuss only the situation when $m > n$, where n is the length of the initial word x. The remaining cases are similar and are left to the reader.

We have

$$\begin{aligned}\Phi_x(\mathsf{c}) \;=\; & U_{\triangleright\triangleright} U_{a_0 b_0} \cdots U_{a_{k-1} b_{k-1}} q U_{a_k b_k} U_{a_{k+1} b_{k+1}} \cdots \\ & U_{\star b_n} U_{\lambda b_{n+1}} \cdots U_{\lambda b_{m-1}} U_{\lambda \star}\end{aligned}$$

Depending on the move of the head of $\mathcal{M}$ we need to consider several cases:

1. If the head moves to the right and $k < m-1$, then $b'' = b_{k+1} \neq \star$ and we have

$$\mathsf{c}' = \triangleright b_0 \cdots b_{k-1} \bar{b} \bar{q} b_{k+1} \cdots b_{m-1} \star .$$

There exists a P_{r0}-production $qU_{a_k b_k} U_{a_{k+1} b_{k+1}} \to U_{a_k \bar{b}} \bar{q} U_{a_{k+1} b_{k+1}}$, so we have

$$\begin{aligned}\Phi_x(\mathsf{c}) \;\underset{G}{\Rightarrow}\; & U_{\triangleright\triangleright} U_{a_0 b_0} \cdots U_{a_{k-1} b_{k-1}} U_{a_k \bar{b}} \bar{q} U_{a_{k+1} b_{k+1}} \\ & \cdots U_{\star b_n} U_{\lambda b_{n+1}} \cdots U_{\lambda b_{m-1}} U_{\lambda \star} = \Phi_x(\mathsf{c}').\end{aligned}$$

2. If the head moves to the right, $k = m-1$ (which means that $b'' = \star$), and $a_m = \lambda$ because we assumed $m > n$. The configuration

$$\mathsf{c} = \triangleright b_0 \cdots b_{m-2} q b_{m-1} \star$$

is succeeded by $\mathsf{c}' = \triangleright b_0 \cdots b_{m-2} b_{m-1} \bar{q} \sqcup \star$. Corresponding to c we have:

$$\Phi_x(\mathsf{c}) = U_{\triangleright\triangleright} U_{a_0 b_0} \cdots q U_{a_{m-1} b_{m-1}} U_{\lambda \star}.$$

The existence of the production

$$qU_{a_{m-1} b_{m-1}} U_{\lambda \star} \to U_{a_{m-1} \bar{b}} \bar{q} U_{\lambda \sqcup} U_{\lambda \star}$$

in P_{r3} allows us to write:

$$\Phi_x(\mathsf{c}) \underset{G}{\Rightarrow} U_{\triangleright\triangleright} U_{a_0 b_0} \cdots U_{a_{m-1} \bar{b}} \bar{q} U_{\lambda \sqcup} U_{\lambda \star} = \Phi_x(\mathsf{c}').$$

3. If the head moves to the left and $\bar{b} \neq \sqcup$, then the production

$$U_{a_{k-1} b_{k-1}} q U_{a_k b_k} \to q U_{a_{k-1} b_{k-1}} U_{a_k \bar{b}}$$

exists in P_{l0}. The next configuration is

$$\mathsf{c}' = \triangleright b_0 \cdots \bar{q} b_{k-1} \bar{b} b_{k+1} \cdots b_{m-1} \star$$

and we have

$$\Phi_x(\mathsf{c}) \underset{G}{\Rightarrow} U_{\triangleright\triangleright} U_{a_0 b_0} \cdots \bar{q} U_{a_{k-1} b_{k-1}} U_{a_k \bar{b}} \cdots U_{\lambda\star} = \Phi_x(\mathsf{c}').$$

4. Suppose now that the head moves to the left, $\bar{b} = \sqcup$, and $b_{k+1} \neq \star$, which means that $k < m - 1$; the next configuration is

$$\mathsf{c}' = \triangleright b_0 \cdots \bar{q} b_{k-1} \sqcup b_{k+1} \cdots b_{m-1} \star .$$

The existence of the production

$$U_{a_{k-1} b_{k-1}} q U_{a_k b_k} U_{a_{k+1} b_{k+1}} \rightarrow \bar{q} U_{a_{k-1} b_{k-1}} U_{a_k \sqcup} U_{a_{k+1} b_{k+1}}$$

in P_{l1} allows us to write:

$$\Phi_x(\mathsf{c}) \underset{G}{\Rightarrow} U_{\triangleright\triangleright} U_{a_0 b_0} \cdots \bar{q} U_{a_{k-1} b_{k-1}} U_{a_k \sqcup} \cdots U_{\lambda\star} = \Phi_x(\mathsf{c}').$$

5. If the head moves to the left, $\bar{b} = \sqcup$, $b_{k+1} = \star$ (which means that $k = m-1$), then we have $a_{k+1} = \lambda$ because we assumed that $m > n$. The configuration $\mathsf{c} = \triangleright b_0 \cdots b_{m-2} q b_{m-1} \star$ is succeeded by $\mathsf{c}' = \triangleright b_0 \cdots \bar{q} b_{m-2} \star$. We have the production $U_{a_{m-2} b_{m-2}} q U_{a_{m-1} b_{m-1}} U_{\lambda\star} \rightarrow \bar{q} U_{a_{m-2} b_{m-2}} U_{a_{m-1}\star}$ in P_{l3}, so we can write:

$$\Phi_x(\mathsf{c}) \underset{G}{\Rightarrow} U_{\triangleright\triangleright} U_{a_0 b_0} \cdots \bar{q} U_{a_{m-2} b_{m-2}} U_{a_{m-1}\star} = \Phi_x(\mathsf{c}').$$

6. If the head does not move, we have the production $q U_{a_k b_k} \rightarrow \bar{q} U_{a_k \bar{b}}$ and this allows us to write

$$\Phi_x(\mathsf{c}) \underset{G}{\Rightarrow} U_{\triangleright\triangleright} U_{a_0 b_0} \cdots U_{a_k \bar{b}} \bar{q} \cdots U_{\star b_n} U_{\lambda b_{n+1}} \cdots U_{\lambda b_{m-1}} U_{\lambda\star} = \Phi_x(\mathsf{c}').$$

Conversely, suppose that $\Phi_x(\mathsf{c}) \underset{G}{\Rightarrow} \alpha$ for some $c \in \mathsf{CONFIG}(\mathcal{M})$ using one of the productions listed in the table shown in Figure 8.17. Then, $\alpha = \Phi_x(\mathsf{c}')$ for some $\mathsf{c}' \in \mathsf{CONFIG}(\mathcal{M})$. Since the application of any production of G does not alter the word formed by the first subscripts of the U-symbols it follows that $h_0(\Phi_x(\mathsf{c})) = h_0(\Phi_x(\mathsf{c}')) = \triangleright x\star$. As before, we discuss only the case when $n = |x| < m$ and leave the remaining cases ($n = m$ and $n > m$), which are similar, to the reader. Suppose that

$$\begin{aligned}\Phi_x(\mathsf{c}) &= U_{\triangleright\triangleright} U_{a_0 b_0} \cdots U_{a_{k-1} b_{k-1}} q U_{a_k b_k} U_{a_{k+1} b_{k+1}} \cdots \\ &\quad U_{\star b_n} U_{\lambda b_{n+1}} \cdots U_{\lambda b_{m-1}} U_{\lambda\star}\end{aligned}$$

There are several possible productions that we may apply.

1. If the production applied $q U_{a_k b_k} U_{a_{k+1} b_{k+1}} \rightarrow U_{a_k \bar{b}} \bar{q} U_{a_{k+1} b_{k+1}}$, belongs to P_{r0}, then $b_{k+1} \neq \star$, $k < m - 1$, and $\delta(q, b_k) = (\bar{q}, \bar{b}, \mathtt{r})$. For the next configuration c' we have

$$\Phi_x(\mathsf{c}') = U_{\triangleright\triangleright} U_{a_0 b_0} \cdots U_{a_k \bar{b}} \bar{q} U_{a_{k+1} b_{k+1}} \cdots U_{\star b_n} U_{\lambda b_{n+1}} \cdots U_{\lambda b_{m-1}} U_{\lambda\star}.$$

Therefore, $\mathsf{c}' = \triangleright b_0 \cdots \bar{b} \bar{q} b_{k+1} \cdots b_{m-1} \star$, and $\mathsf{c} \underset{\mathcal{M}}{\vdash} \mathsf{c}'$.

2. If the production applied belongs to P_{r3}, then it must be $qU_{a_k b_k}U_{\lambda\star} \to U_{a_k\bar{b}}\bar{q}U_{\lambda\sqcup}U_{\lambda\star}$, and we have $k = m-1$, $b_m = \star$, and $\delta(q, b_{m-1}) = (\bar{q}, \sqcup, \mathtt{r})$. For $\mathtt{c}'$ we have

$$\Phi_x(\mathtt{c}') = U_{\triangleright\triangleright}U_{a_0 b_0}\cdots U_{a_{m-1}\bar{b}}\bar{q}U_{\lambda\sqcup}U_{\lambda\star}$$

which means that $\mathtt{c}' = \triangleright b_0 \cdots \bar{b}\bar{q}\sqcup\star$. Thus, $\mathtt{c} \underset{\mathcal{M}}{\vdash} \mathtt{c}'$.
Note that no production of P_{r1} or P_{r2} is applicable because we assumed $m > n$.
3. If the production applied $U_{a_{k-1}b_{k-1}}qU_{a_k b_k} \to \bar{q}U_{a_{k-1}b_{k-1}}U_{a_k\bar{b}}$ belongs to P_{l0}, then $\bar{b} \neq \sqcup$, and $\mathtt{d} = \mathtt{l}$, that is $\delta(q, b_k) = (\bar{q}, \bar{b}, \mathtt{l})$. Then,

$$\Phi_x(\mathtt{c}') = U_{\triangleright\triangleright}U_{a_0 b_0}\cdots \bar{q}U_{a_{k-1}b_{k-1}}U_{a_k\bar{b}}\cdots U_{\lambda b_{m-1}}U_{\lambda\star},$$

so $\mathtt{c}' = \triangleright b_0 \cdots \bar{q}b_{k-1}\cdots\star$, which implies $\mathtt{c} \underset{\mathcal{M}}{\vdash} \mathtt{c}'$.
4. If the production applied belongs to P_{l1}, then $\mathtt{d} = \mathtt{l}$, $\bar{b} = \sqcup$, and $b_{k+1} \neq \star$. Then, the production has the form

$$U_{a_{k-1}b_{k-1}}qU_{a_k b_k}U_{a_{k+1}b_{k+1}} \to \bar{q}U_{a_{k-1}b_{k-1}}U_{a_k\sqcup}U_{a_{k+1}b_{k+1}}$$

and

$$\Phi_x(\mathtt{c}') = \triangleright u_{a_0 b_0}\cdots \bar{q}U_{a_{k-1}b_{k-1}}U_{a_k\sqcup}U_{a_{k+1}b_{k+1}}\cdots U_{\lambda\star},$$

which implies $\mathtt{c}' = \triangleright b_0 \cdots \bar{q}b_{k-1}\sqcup\cdots\star$, so $\mathtt{c} \underset{\mathcal{M}}{\vdash} \mathtt{c}'$.
We can exclude the productions of P_{l2} because we assumed that $m > n$.
5. If the production applied belongs to P_{l3}, then $k = m-1$, $\delta(q, b_{m-1}) = (\bar{q}, \sqcup, \mathtt{l})$ and this production can be written

$$U_{a_{m-2}b_{m-2}}qU_{a_{m-1}b_{m-1}}U_{\lambda\star} \to \bar{q}U_{a_{m-2}b_{m-2}}U_{a_{m-1}\star}$$

Therefore, $\Phi_x(\mathtt{c}') = \triangleright U_{a_0 b_0}\cdots \bar{q}U_{a_{m-2}b_{m-2}}U_{a_{m-1}\star}$, so $\mathtt{c}' = \triangleright b_0 \cdots \bar{q}b_{m-2}\star$, which allows us to conclude that $\mathtt{c} \underset{\mathcal{M}}{\vdash} \mathtt{c}'$.
6. We leave to the reader the last case, when the production applied belongs to P_{00}.

Suppose that $x = a_{i_0}\cdots a_{i_{n-1}} \in L_A(\mathcal{M})$. Then, there exists a computation

$$q_0 \triangleright a_{i_0}\cdots a_{i_{n-1}}\star \overset{*}{\underset{\mathcal{M}}{\vdash}} q_f \triangleright b_{j_0}\cdots b_{j_{m-1}}\star.$$

By the previous claim, we obtain the derivation

$$q_0 U_{\triangleright\triangleright}U_{a_{i_0}a_{i_0}}\cdots U_{a_{i_{n-1}}a_{i_{n-1}}}U_{\star\star}$$
$$\overset{*}{\underset{G}{\Rightarrow}} q_f U_{\triangleright\triangleright}U_{a_{i_0}b_{j_0}}\cdots U_{a_{i_{n-1}}b_{j_{n-1}}}U_{\star b_{j_n}}\cdots U_{\lambda\star}$$

The initial set of productions yields the derivation

$$S \overset{*}{\underset{G}{\Rightarrow}} q_0 U_{\triangleright\triangleright}U_{a_{i_0}a_{i_0}}\cdots U_{a_{i_{n-1}}a_{i_{n-1}}}U_{\star\star},$$

while the last group of productions allows us to write

$$\begin{aligned} & q_f U_{\triangleright\triangleright} U_{a_{i_0} b_{j_0}} \cdots U_{a_{i_{n-1}} b_{j_{n-1}}} U_{\star b_{j_n}} \cdots U_{\lambda\star} \\ \underset{G}{\Rightarrow} \quad & Z U_{a_{i_0} b_{j_0}} \cdots U_{a_{i_{n-1}} b_{j_{n-1}}} U_{\star b_{j_n}} \cdots U_{\lambda\star} \\ \underset{G}{\overset{*}{\Rightarrow}} \quad & a_{i_0} \cdots a_{i_{n-1}} Z U_{\star b_{j_n}} \cdots U_{\lambda\star} \\ \underset{G}{\Rightarrow} \quad & a_{i_0} \cdots a_{i_{n-1}} V U_{\lambda b_{j_{n+1}}} \cdots U_{\lambda\star} \\ \underset{G}{\overset{*}{\Rightarrow}} \quad & a_{i_0} \cdots a_{i_{n-1}}. \end{aligned}$$

By putting together the previous three derivations we have $S \underset{G}{\overset{*}{\Rightarrow}} a_{i_0} \cdots a_{i_{n-1}}$, so $a_{i_0} \cdots a_{i_{n-1}} \in L(G)$.

To prove the converse inclusion, suppose that $x = a_{i_0} \cdots a_{i_{n-1}} \in L(G)$, that is, $S \underset{G}{\overset{*}{\Rightarrow}} a_{i_0} \cdots a_{i_{n-1}}$. The definition of the productions of G show that this derivation has necessarily the form

$$\begin{aligned} S \quad \underset{G}{\overset{*}{\Rightarrow}} \quad & q_0 U_{\triangleright\triangleright} U_{a_{i_0} a_{i_0}} \cdots U_{a_{i_{n-1}} a_{i_{n-1}}} U_{\star\star} \\ \underset{G}{\overset{*}{\Rightarrow}} \quad & q_f U_{\triangleright\triangleright} U_{a_{i_0} b_{j_0}} \cdots U_{a_{i_{n-1}} b_{j_{n-1}}} U_{\star b_{j_n}} \cdots U_{\lambda\star} \\ \underset{G}{\overset{*}{\Rightarrow}} \quad & a_{i_0} \cdots a_{i_{n-1}}. \end{aligned}$$

If $\mathsf{c}_0 = q_0 \triangleright a_{i_0} \cdots a_{i_{n-1}} \star$ and $\mathsf{c} = q_f \triangleright b_{j_0} \cdots b_{j_{m-1}} \star$, we can write

$$\begin{aligned} \Phi_x(\mathsf{c}_0) &= q_0 U_{\triangleright\triangleright} U_{a_{i_0} a_{i_0}} \cdots U_{a_{i_{n-1}} a_{i_{n-1}}} U_{\star\star} \\ \Phi_x(\mathsf{c}) &= q_f U_{\triangleright\triangleright} U_{a_{i_0} b_{j_0}} \cdots U_{a_{i_{n-1}} b_{j_{n-1}}} U_{\star b_{j_n}} \cdots U_{\lambda\star} \end{aligned}$$

By the previous claim, we have the computation: $\mathsf{c}_0 \underset{\mathcal{M}}{\overset{*}{\vdash}} \mathsf{c}$, so $x \in L(\mathcal{M})$. ∎

Corollary 8.6.18 *Let A be an alphabet. The following statements about a language $L \subseteq A^*$ are equivalent:*

(i) *L is recursively enumerable;*
(ii) *L is accepted by a dTm;*
(iii) *$L \in \mathcal{L}_0$.*

Proof. The equivalence of the first two statements is contained by Theorem 8.6.15. The second statement implies the third by Theorem 8.6.17. Suppose the third statement holds, that is $L = L(G)$, where G is a grammar. By Theorem 8.6.16, L is a recursively enumerable language. ∎

Theorem 8.6.19 *The membership problem is undecidable for the languages in the class $\mathcal{L}_0$.*

Proof. We saw that the decidability of the membership problem for a language L amounts to the recursiveness of L. Since there are recursively enumerable languages that are not recursive (cf. Theorem 8.6.12), the membership problem is not decidable, in general, for languages in $\mathcal{L}_0$. ∎

The next result deals with certain closure properties of the $\mathcal{L}_0$ class. We already know from Section 4.4 that $\mathcal{L}_0$ is closed under union, product, and the $*$ and $+$-operations.

Theorem 8.6.20 *Let A be an alphabet. If $L, L' \subseteq A^*$, then $L \cap L' \in \mathcal{L}_0$.*

Also, if $f : A^* \longrightarrow A^*$ is a recursive function, then the languages $f(L) = \{y \in A^* \mid y = f(x) \text{ for some } x \in L\}$ and $f^{-1}(L) = \{y \in A^* \mid f(y) \in L\}$ are recursively enumerable.

Proof. Let $L, L' \subseteq A^*$ be two recursively enumerable languages. Since $\iota_L, \iota_{L'}$ are both partial recursive functions, the function $h : A^* \mapsto A^*$ given by $h(x) = \iota_L(x)\iota_{L'}(x)$ is partial recursive and $\text{Dom}(h) = L \cap L'$. Thus, by Theorem 8.6.11, $L \cap L'$ is a recursively enumerable language. In Exercise 24, we suggest a different, constructive argument for proving the same fact.

Suppose that the recursive enumerable language L is the range of a partial recursive function g. Since $f(L)$ is the range of the partial recursive function fg, it follows that $f(L)$ is recursively enumerable.

If L is the domain of the partial recursive function h, then $f^{-1}(L)$ is the domain of the partial recursive function hf, so $f^{-1}(L)$ is recursively enumerable. ∎

Recursively enumerable languages can be represented as homomorphic images of intersections of context-free languages — indeed, of linear, context-free languages.

Theorem 8.6.21 *Every recursively enumerable language L can be expressed as $L = h(K \cap H)$, where h is a morphism and K, H are linear languages.*

Proof. Suppose that $L = L(G)$, where $G = (A_N, A_T, S, P)$,

$$P = \{\pi_0, \ldots, \pi_{m-1}\},$$

and $\pi_i = \beta_i \to \gamma_i$ for $0 \leq i \leq m-1$. Let Δ be a new symbol. The alphabet A'_T consists of primed versions of the symbols of A_T; in other words, $A'_T = \{a' \mid a \in A_T\}$. Let B be the alphabet

$$B = A_N \cup A_T \cup A'_T \cup P \cup \{\Delta\},$$

that contains a symbol π_i for every production $\pi_i \in P$.

Define the morphism $h : B^* \longrightarrow A_T^*$ by

$$h(b) = \begin{cases} a & \text{if } b = a' \in A'_T \\ \lambda & \text{otherwise,} \end{cases}$$

for $b \in B$ and the morphism $h' : A_T^* \longrightarrow (A'_T)^*$, where $h'(a) = a'$ for $a \in A_T$.

Consider the functions

$$t, s : (A_N \cup A_T)^* \times P \times (A_N \cup A_T)^* \longrightarrow (A_N \cup A_T \cup P)^*$$

given by

$$\begin{aligned} t(\alpha, \pi_i, \epsilon) &= \alpha\beta_i\pi_i\epsilon\Delta(\alpha\gamma_i\epsilon)^R\Delta = \alpha\beta_i\pi_i\epsilon\Delta\epsilon^R{\gamma_i}^R\alpha^R\Delta \\ s(\alpha, \pi_i, \epsilon) &= (\alpha\epsilon)^R\Delta\alpha\pi_i\epsilon\Delta = \epsilon^R\alpha^R\Delta\alpha\pi_i\epsilon\Delta, \end{aligned}$$

where $\alpha, \epsilon \in (A_N \cup A_T)^*$ and $0 \leq i \leq m-1$.

Observe that both $\text{Ran}(t)$ and $\text{Ran}(s)$ are linear languages. Indeed, we have $\text{Ran}(t) = L(G_t)$, where G_t is the linear grammar

$$G_t = (\{S, X, Y\}, A_T \cup A_N \cup \{\Delta\} \cup \{\pi_0, \ldots, \pi_{m-1}\}, S, P_t)$$

and

$$\begin{aligned} P_t &= \{S \to X\Delta\} \cup \{X \to aXa \mid a \in V_T\} \\ &\quad \cup \{X \to \beta_i \pi_i Y {\gamma_i}^R \mid 0 \le i \le m-1\} \\ &\quad \cup \{Y \to aYa \mid a \in V_T\} \cup \{Y \to \Delta\}. \end{aligned}$$

Similarly, $\mathrm{Ran}(s) = L(G_s)$, where G_s is the linear grammar

$$G_s = (\{S, X, Y\}, A_T \cup \{\Delta\} \cup \{\pi_0, \ldots, \pi_{m-1}\}, S, P_s),$$

where

$$\begin{aligned} P_s &= \{S \to X\Delta\} \cup \{X \to aXa \mid a \in A_T\} \\ &\quad \cup \{X \to Y\pi_i \mid 0 \le i \le m-1\} \cup \{Y \to aYa \mid a \in A_T\} \\ &\quad \cup \{Y \to \Delta\}. \end{aligned}$$

Thus, the languages

$$\begin{aligned} K &= (\mathrm{Ran}(t))^+ (A'_T)^* \\ H &= \{S\pi_i\Delta \mid 0 \le i \le m-1\}(\mathrm{Ran}(s))^* \{x\Delta h'(x) \mid x \in A_T^*\} \end{aligned}$$

are context-free languages on the alphabet B.

Let $x \in L(G)$. There is a derivation

$$S = \theta_0 \underset{G}{\Rightarrow} \theta_1 \underset{G}{\Rightarrow} \cdots \underset{G}{\Rightarrow} \theta_n = x,$$

where $\theta_i \in (A_N \cup A_T)^*$ for $0 \le i \le n$. Define the function $g : \{0, \ldots, n-1\} \longrightarrow \{0, \ldots, m-1\}$, where $g(i) = j_i$ if the production π_{j_i} is applied at step i. Thus, we can write $\theta_i = \theta_{il}\beta_{g(i)}\theta_{ir}$ and $\theta_{i+1} = \theta_{il}\gamma_{g(i)}\theta_{ir}$ for $0 \le i \le n-1$ and the derivation can be written as

$$\begin{aligned} S &= \theta_0 = \theta_{0l}\beta_{g(0)}\theta_{0r} \underset{G}{\Rightarrow} \theta_{0l}\gamma_{g(0)}\theta_{0r} \\ &= \theta_1 = \theta_{1l}\beta_{g(1)}\theta_{1r} \underset{G}{\Rightarrow} \theta_{1l}\gamma_{g(1)}\theta_{1r} \\ &\ \vdots \\ &= \theta_{n-1} = \theta_{n-1\,l}\beta_{g(n-1)}\theta_{n-1\,r} \underset{G}{\Rightarrow} \theta_{n-1\,l}\gamma_{g(n-1)}\theta_{n-1\,r} \\ &= \theta_n = x. \end{aligned}$$

Denote by $\hat{\theta}_i$ the word obtained from $\theta_i = \theta_{il}\beta_{g(i)}\theta_{ir}$ by replacing $\beta_{g(i)}$ by $\beta_{g(i)}\pi_{g(i)}$ for $0 \le i \le n-1$.

Note that

$$\begin{aligned} t(\theta_{il}, \pi_{g(i)}, \theta_{ir}) &= \theta_{il}\beta_{g(i)}\pi_{g(i)}\theta_{ir}\Delta(\theta_{il}\gamma_{g(i)}\theta_{ir})^R\Delta \\ &= \theta_{il}\beta_{g(i)}\pi_{g(i)}\theta_{ir}\Delta{\theta_{i+1}}^R\Delta \\ &= \hat{\theta}_i\Delta{\theta_{i+1}}^R\Delta, \end{aligned}$$

and

$$\begin{aligned} s(\theta_{il}\beta_g(i), \pi_{g(i)}, \theta_{ir}) &= (\theta_{il}\beta_{g(i)}\theta_{ir})^R\Delta\theta_{il}\beta_{g(i)}\pi_{g(i)}\theta_{ir}\Delta \\ &= {\theta_i}^R\Delta\theta_{il}\beta_{g(i)}\pi_{g(i)}\theta_{ir}\Delta \\ &= {\theta_i}^R\Delta\hat{\theta}_i\Delta. \end{aligned}$$

Let $\eta \in B^*$ be the word

$$\begin{aligned} \eta &= t(\theta_{0l}, \pi_{g(0)}, \theta_{0r})t(\theta_{1l}, \pi_{g(1)}, \theta_{1r}) \cdots t(\theta_{nl}, \pi_{g(n)}, \theta_{nr})h'(x) \\ &\quad \in (\mathrm{Ran}(t))^+(A'_T)^* = K. \end{aligned}$$

The same word can be written as

$$\begin{aligned}\eta &= \hat{\theta}_0\triangle{\theta_1}^R\triangle\hat{\theta}_1\triangle{\theta_2}^R\triangle\cdots\hat{\theta}_{n-1}\triangle{\theta_n}^R\triangle h'(x)\\ &\in \hat{\theta}_0\triangle(\mathrm{Ran}(s))^*{\theta_n}^R\triangle h'(x)\\ &= S\pi_{g(0)}\triangle(\mathrm{Ran}(s))^*x^R\triangle h'(x)\subseteq H.\end{aligned}$$

This allows us to conclude that $\eta \in K\cap H$. Since $x = h(\eta)$, it follows that $L(G)\subseteq h(K\cap H)$.

Conversely, suppose that $x\in h(K\cap H)$. We have $x = h(\eta)$, where $\eta\in K\cap H$, so

$$\eta = u_0\cdots u_p w' = S\pi_j\triangle v_1\cdots v_p y^R\triangle h'(y),$$

because every word in Ran(t) or in Ran(s) contains two occurrences of $\triangle$. We assume here that $u_i\in\mathrm{Ran}(t)$ for $0\le i\le p$, $v_l\in\mathrm{Ran}(s)$ for $1\le l\le p$, $w'\in(A'_T)^*$, and $y\in A_T^*$. Thus, we can write

$$\begin{aligned}u_0 &= \alpha_0\beta_{i_0}\pi_{i_0}\epsilon_0\triangle{\epsilon_0}^R{\gamma_{i_0}}^R{\alpha_0}^R\triangle\\ &\vdots\\ u_p &= \alpha_p\beta_{i_p}\pi_{i_p}\epsilon_p\triangle{\epsilon_p}^R{\gamma_{i_p}}^R{\alpha_p}^R\triangle\\ v_1 &= \bar{\epsilon}_1^R\bar{\alpha}_1^R\triangle\bar{\alpha}_1\pi_{j_1}\bar{\epsilon}_1\triangle\\ &\vdots\\ v_p &= \bar{\epsilon}_p^R\bar{\alpha}_p^R\triangle\bar{\alpha}_p\pi_{j_p}\bar{\epsilon}_p\triangle.\end{aligned}$$

Comparing the words

$$\begin{aligned}&u_0u_1\cdots u_pw'\\ &\quad= \alpha_0\beta_{i_0}\pi_{i_0}\epsilon_0\triangle{\epsilon_0}^R{\gamma_{i_0}}^R{\alpha_0}^R\triangle\alpha_1\beta_{i_1}\pi_{i_1}\epsilon_1\triangle{\epsilon_1}^R{\gamma_{i_1}}^R{\alpha_1}^R\triangle\cdots\\ &\qquad\alpha_p\beta_{i_p}\pi_{i_p}\epsilon_p\triangle{\epsilon_p}^R{\gamma_{i_p}}^R{\alpha_p}^R\triangle w'\end{aligned}$$

and

$$\begin{aligned}&S\pi_i\triangle v_1\cdots v_py^R\triangle h'(y)\\ &\quad= S\pi_i\triangle\bar{\epsilon}_1^R\bar{\alpha}_1^R\triangle\bar{\alpha}_1\pi_{j_1}\bar{\epsilon}_1\triangle\cdots\bar{\epsilon}_p^R\bar{\alpha}_p^R\triangle\bar{\alpha}_p\pi_{j_p}\bar{\epsilon}_p\triangle y^R\triangle h'(y),\end{aligned}$$

using the $\triangle$s as "signposts" it follows that

$$\begin{aligned}\alpha_0\beta_{i_0}\pi_{i_0}\epsilon_0 &= S\pi_i\\ {\epsilon_0}^R{\gamma_{i_0}}^R{\alpha_0}^R &= \bar{\epsilon}_1^R\bar{\alpha}_1^R\\ \alpha_1\beta_{i_1}\pi_{i_1}\epsilon_1 &= \bar{\alpha}_1\pi_{j_1}\bar{\epsilon}_1\\ &\vdots\\ \alpha_p\beta_{i_p}\pi_{i_p}\epsilon_p &= \bar{\alpha}_p\pi_{j_p}\bar{\epsilon}_p\\ {\epsilon_p}^R{\gamma_{i_p}}^R{\alpha_p}^R &= y^R\\ w' &= h'(y).\end{aligned}$$

These equalities imply

$$\begin{aligned}&\alpha_0=\lambda, \beta_{i_0}=S, i=i_0, \epsilon_0=\lambda,\\ &\alpha_\ell\beta_{i_\ell}=\bar{\alpha}_\ell, j_\ell=i_\ell, \epsilon_\ell=\bar{\epsilon}_\ell \text{ for } 1\le\ell\le p\\ &\alpha_\ell\gamma_{i_\ell}\epsilon_\ell=\bar{\alpha}_{\ell+1}\bar{\epsilon}_{\ell+1} \text{ for } 0\le\ell\le p-1\end{aligned}$$

and $x = h(\eta) = h(w') = h(h'(y)) = y$. Thus, we can construct the following derivation in the grammar G:

$$\begin{aligned}
&S = \alpha_0 S \epsilon_0 \underset{G}{\Rightarrow} \alpha_0 \gamma_{i_0} \epsilon_0 = \bar{\alpha}_1 \bar{\epsilon}_1 \\
&= \alpha_1 \beta_{i_1} \epsilon_1 \underset{G}{\Rightarrow} \alpha_1 \gamma_{i_1} \epsilon_1 = \bar{\alpha}_2 \bar{\epsilon}_2 \\
&= \alpha_2 \beta_{i_2} \epsilon_2 \underset{G}{\Rightarrow} \alpha_2 \gamma_{i_2} \epsilon_2 = \bar{\alpha}_3 \bar{\epsilon}_3 = \cdots \\
&= \alpha_{p-1} \beta_{i_{p-1}} \epsilon_{p-1} \underset{G}{\Rightarrow} \alpha_{p-1} \gamma_{i_{p-1}} \epsilon_{p-1} = \bar{\alpha}_p \bar{\epsilon}_p \\
&= \alpha_p \beta_{i_p} \epsilon_p \underset{G}{\Rightarrow} \alpha_p \gamma_{i_p} \epsilon_p = x,
\end{aligned}$$

which shows that $x \in L(G)$. ∎

Another representation result for recursively enumerable languages uses the quotient operation.

Theorem 8.6.22 *Every language $L \in \mathcal{L}_0$ can be written as $L = KH^{-1}$, where K, H are linear context-free languages.*

Proof. Let $L \in \mathcal{L}_0$. Since $\mathcal{L}_0$ is closed with respect to reversal (cf. Theorem 4.3.18), we have $L^R \in \mathcal{L}_0$. Let $G = (A_N, A, S, P)$ be a grammar such that $L(G) = L^R$.

Without loss of generality, we may assume that every word in $L(G)$ has a derivation in G of length at least 2. This can be achieved by adding the production $S \to S$ to P, without changing the language generated by the grammar.

Consider the language K that consists of all words of the form

$$\theta = \theta_{n-1} \triangle \theta_{n-2} \triangle \cdots \triangle \theta_0 \sharp \eta_0 \triangle \cdots \triangle \eta_{n-2} \flat \eta_{n-1},$$

where $\theta_i \underset{G}{\Rightarrow} (\eta_i)^R$, $\theta_i \in (A_N \cup A_T)^*$ for $0 \leq i \leq n-1$, $\eta_i \in (A_N \cup A_T)^*$ for $0 \leq i \leq n-2$, and $\eta_{n-1} \in A_T^*$. Also, consider the language H that consists of all words of the form

$$\sigma = \sigma_{m-1} \triangle \sigma_{m-2} \triangle \cdots \sigma_0 \triangle S \sharp {\sigma_0}^R \triangle \cdots {\sigma_{m-1}}^R \flat,$$

where $m \geq 2$, $\sigma_i \in (A_N \cup A_T)^*$ for $0 \leq i \leq m-1$. We have $\theta = \sigma\gamma$ if and only if

$$\begin{aligned}
&\theta_{n-1} \triangle \theta_{n-2} \triangle \cdots \triangle \theta_0 \sharp \eta_0 \triangle \cdots \triangle \eta_{n-2} \flat \eta_{n-1} \\
&= \sigma_{m-1} \triangle \sigma_{m-2} \triangle \cdots \sigma_0 \triangle S \sharp {\sigma_0}^R \triangle \cdots {\sigma_{m-1}}^R \flat \gamma
\end{aligned}$$

Using the symbols $\triangle, \sharp, \flat$ as signposts (as we did in Theorem 8.6.21), we have $m = n - 1$. Comparison of the words located to the right of the infix $\sharp$ yields the equalities:

$$\theta_0 = S, \theta_1 = \sigma_0, \theta_2 = \sigma_1, \ldots, \theta_{n-1} = \sigma_{n-2}.$$

Similar comparison of the words located between $\sharp$ and $\flat$ yields

$$\eta_0 = {\sigma_0}^R, \eta_1 = {\sigma_1}^R, \ldots, \eta_{n-2} = {\sigma_{n-2}}^R$$

and we also have $\eta_{n-1} = \gamma$ (as the words located beyond $\flat$). Since

$$\theta_i \underset{G}{\Rightarrow} {\eta_i}^R = \sigma_i = \theta_{i+1}$$

for $0 \leq i \leq n-2$, it follows that we have the derivation

$$S \underset{G}{\Rightarrow} \theta_1 \underset{G}{\Rightarrow} \cdots \underset{G}{\Rightarrow} \theta_{n-1} = \gamma \in A_T^*.$$

Conversely, for derivation $S \overset{*}{\underset{G}{\Rightarrow}} \gamma \in A_T^*$ of length at least 2 we can construct $\theta \in K$ and $\sigma \in H$ such that $\theta = \sigma\gamma$. Thus, $L(G) = H^{-1}K$, so $L = L(G)^R = K^R(H^R)^{-1}$. Since the class of linear languages is closed with respect to reversal (cf. Theorem 4.6.5) we must show only that K and H are linear languages. We leave to the reader the construction of linear grammars for K and H. ∎

Theorem 8.6.23 *Let $s : A^* \longrightarrow B^*$ be a substitution. If $s(a)$ is a recursively enumerable language for every $a \in A$ and $L \subseteq A^*$ is a recursively enumerable language, then $s(L)$ is a recursively enumerable language.*

Proof. Suppose that $L = L(G)$, where $G = (A_N, A, S, P)$ is a grammar, and that $s(a)$ is generated by the grammar $G_a = (A_N^a, B, S_a, P_a)$ for $a \in A$. We assume, without loss of generality, that the sets of nonterminal symbols A_N^a are pairwise disjoint. Consider a set of new nonterminal symbols $\{X_a \mid a \in A\}$ and the set of productions $\bar{P}$ obtained from the productions of P by replacing every terminal symbol a by a nonterminal X_a. Define the grammar G' by

$$G' = (\{S_0, Y\} \cup \{X_a \mid a \in A\} \cup A_N \cup \bigcup_{a \in A} A_N^a, B, S_0, P'),$$

where P' consists of the following productions:

- the productions of $\bar{P}$;
- $YX_a \to YS_a$ for $a \in A$ and $Yb \to bY$ for $b \in B$;
- the productions of $\bigcup_{a \in A} P_a$;
- $S_0 \to YS$ and $Y \to \lambda$.

We have $w \in s(x)$ for some $x \in L$ if and only if $x = a_{i_0} \cdots a_{i_{m-1}}$ and $w = w_0 \cdots w_{m-1}$, where $w_k \in s(a_{i_k}) = L(G_{a_{i_k}})$, which is equivalent to $S_{a_{i_k}} \overset{*}{\underset{G_{a_{i_k}}}{\Rightarrow}} w_k$ for $0 \leq k \leq m-1$. Thus, $w \in s(x)$ implies the existence of the derivation:

$$\begin{aligned}
S_0 &\underset{G'}{\Rightarrow} YS \overset{*}{\underset{G'}{\Rightarrow}} YX_{a_{i_0}} \cdots X_{a_{i_{m-1}}} \underset{G'}{\Rightarrow} YS_{a_{i_0}} X_{a_{i_1}} \\
&\cdots X_{a_{i_{m-1}}} \overset{*}{\underset{G'}{\Rightarrow}} Yw_0 X_{a_{i_1}} \cdots X_{a_{i_{m-1}}} \overset{*}{\underset{G'}{\Rightarrow}} w_0 Y X_{a_{i_1}} \cdots X_{a_{i_{m-1}}} \\
&\cdots \\
&\underset{G'}{\Rightarrow} w_0 w_1 \cdots Y X_{a_{i_{m-1}}} \overset{*}{\underset{G'}{\Rightarrow}} w_0 w_1 \cdots Y S_{a_{i_{m-1}}} \overset{*}{\underset{G'}{\Rightarrow}} w_0 w_1 \cdots Y w_{m-1} \\
&\underset{G'}{\Rightarrow} w_0 w_1 \cdots w_{m-1} = w,
\end{aligned} \tag{8.1}$$

which proves that $s(L) \subseteq L(G')$.

Conversely, if $w \in L(G)$, then $S_0 \underset{G'}{\Rightarrow} YS \overset{*}{\underset{G'}{\Rightarrow}} w$. Since the productions of P have been replaced by the productions of $\bar{P}$, the above derivation necessarily has the form

$$S_0 \underset{G'}{\Rightarrow} YS \overset{*}{\underset{G'}{\Rightarrow}} YX_{a_{i_0}} \cdots X_{a_{i_{m-1}}} \overset{*}{\underset{G'}{\Rightarrow}} w$$

The symbols X_a are transformed in the left context of Y into the initial symbols S_a of the grammars G_a for $a \in A$. Note that Y may transform the next symbol $X_{a'}$ only if the derivation of a word $w_a \in L(G_a)$ is complete. This shows that the word w can be written as $w = w_0 w_1 \cdots w_{m-1}$, where $w_k \in s(a_{i_k})$ for $0 \leq k \leq m-1$ and that $a_{i_0} \cdots a_{i_{m-1}} \in L$. Consequently, $L(G') \subseteq s(L)$. ∎

Corollary 8.6.24 *The class $\mathcal{L}_0$ is closed with respect to morphisms.*

Proof. Since a morphism can be regarded as a special type of substitution, the statement follows immediately from Theorem 8.6.23. ∎

8.7 Rice's Theorem

Theorem 8.6.11 shows that if L is a recursively enumerable language on the alphabet A, there exists $x \in A^*$ such that $L = \mathrm{Dom}(\mathsf{f}_x)$.

Definition 8.7.1 Let A be an alphabet and let $L \subseteq A^*$. *An index for the language* L is a word $x \in A^*$ such that $L = \mathrm{Dom}(\mathsf{f}_x)$. □

It is clear that any recursively enumerable language has infinitely many indices since every partial recursive function does. If x is an index for a recursively enumerable language L, then we may denote L by L_x. Thus, $y \in \mathsf{L}_x$ if and only if $y \in \mathrm{Dom}(\mathsf{f}_x)$.

Definition 8.7.2 Two words $x, y \in A^*$ are *equivalent*, written $x \sim y$, if $\mathsf{L}_x = \mathsf{L}_y$. □

It is easy to verify that the relation "$\sim$" is an equivalence on A^*.

Definition 8.7.3 An *index language* on A is a language $I \subseteq A^*$ that is saturated with respect to the equivalence $\sim$. □

In other words, I is an index language if $x \in I$ and $x \sim y$ imply $y \in I$ for every $x, y \in A^*$.

Let $\mathcal{C}$ be a collection of languages. We denote by $I_{\mathcal{C}}$ the language on A that consists of all words that are indices of languages in $\mathcal{C}$.

Theorem 8.7.4 *Let A be an alphabet. A language $I \subseteq A^*$ is an index language if and only if there exists a collection $\mathcal{C}$ of recursively enumerable languages such that $I = I_{\mathcal{C}}$.*

Proof. Suppose that I is an index language and let $\mathcal{C}_I = \{\mathsf{L}_x \mid x \in I\}$. Then, it is immediate that $I_{\mathcal{C}_I} = I$. Conversely, if $I = I_{\mathcal{C}}$, then I is clearly $\sim$-saturated, so it is an index language. ∎

Example 8.7.5 The following languages are index languages:

1. $L_0 = \{x \in A^* \mid \mathsf{L}_x = \emptyset\}$;
2. $L_{fin} = \{x \in A^* \mid \mathsf{L}_x \text{ is finite}\}$;
3. $L_u = \{x \in A^* \mid u \in \mathsf{L}_x\}$, where $u \in A^*$;
4. $L_{reg} = \{x \in A^* \mid \mathsf{L}_x \text{ is regular }\}$;
5. $L_{cf} = \{x \in A^* \mid \mathsf{L}_x \text{ is context free }\}$;
6. $L_{rec} = \{x \in A^* \mid \mathsf{L}_x \text{ is recursive}\}$.

□

Lemma 8.7.6 *The function* $\mathsf{d} : A^* \longrightarrow A^*$ *defined by*

$$\mathsf{d}(x) = \begin{cases} \lambda & \text{if } x \in \mathsf{L}_x \\ \text{undefined} & \text{otherwise,} \end{cases}$$

for $x \in A^*$ *is partial recursive.*

Proof. Note that d can be written as $\mathsf{d}(x) = \mathsf{f}_x(x) -_l \mathsf{f}_x(x)$ because $x \in \mathsf{L}_x = \mathrm{Dom}(\mathsf{f}_x)$ if and only if $\mathsf{f}_x(x) -_l \mathsf{f}_x(x) = \lambda$. Therefore, we can write $\mathsf{d}(x) = \mathsf{univ}(x,x) -_l \mathsf{univ}(x,x)$, which implies the partial recursiveness of d due to the partial recursiveness of univ. ∎

Recall that the language $\mathsf{H} = \{x \in A^* \mid x \in \mathrm{Dom}(\mathsf{f}_x)\}$ defined in Theorem 8.6.12 is recursively enumerable but not recursive. For every $x \in A^*$ we have $\mathsf{d}(x) = \lambda$ if and only if $x \in \mathsf{H}$.

Theorem 8.7.7 (Rice's Theorem) *Let* A *be an alphabet and* $\mathcal{C}$ *be a collection of recursively enumerable languages. If* $\mathcal{C}$ *is a nontrivial collection of type-0 languages, that is, if* $\emptyset \subset \mathcal{C} \subset \mathcal{P}(A^*) \cap \mathcal{L}_0$, *then the language* $I_{\mathcal{C}}$ *is not recursive.*

Proof. We start by observing that if $\bar{\mathcal{C}}$ is the complement of a collection $\mathcal{C}$ of languages, then $I_{\bar{\mathcal{C}}}$ is the complement $A^* - I_{\mathcal{C}}$ of $\mathcal{C}$.

Without loss of generality, we may assume that the empty language $\emptyset$ does not belong to $\mathcal{C}$. Indeed, if $\emptyset \in \mathcal{C}$, we could make the argument for the collection $\bar{\mathcal{C}}$, and the non-recursiveness of $I_{\bar{\mathcal{C}}}$ would imply the non-recursiveness of $I_{\mathcal{C}}$. Since $\mathcal{C} \neq \emptyset$, there is a recursively enumerable language L_{x_0} in $\mathcal{C}$. Let z be an index for the empty language.

Define the partial recursive function $g : (A^*)^2 \mapsto A^*$ by

$$g(x,y) = \mathsf{conc}(\mathsf{univ}(x_0,y), \mathsf{d}(x))$$

for $x, y \in A^*$, where univ is the universal function and d is the function introduced in Lemma 8.7.6. Then, we have

$$g(x,y) = \begin{cases} \mathsf{f}_{x_0}(y) & \text{if } x \in \mathsf{H} \\ \text{undefined} & \text{otherwise,} \end{cases}$$

for $x, y \in A^*$. Applying Theorem 8.5.26, there is a primitive recursive function h on A such that $g(x,y) = \mathsf{f}_{h(x)}(y)$ for $x, y \in A^*$. Thus, we have

$$\mathsf{f}_{h(x)} = \begin{cases} \mathsf{f}_{x_0} & \text{if } x \in \mathsf{H} \\ \emptyset & \text{otherwise,} \end{cases}$$

for $x \in A^*$. In other words, $h(x) \sim x_0$ if $x \in \mathsf{H}$, and $h(x) \sim z$, otherwise. Since $I_{\mathcal{C}}$ is an index language, this means that $h(x) \in I_{\mathcal{C}}$ if and only if $x \in \mathsf{H}$. If $I_{\mathcal{C}}$ were recursive, then H would be recursive. This gives the desired conclusion. ∎

Corollary 8.7.8 *The following languages are not recursive:*

(i) $L_0 = \{x \in A^* \mid \mathsf{L}_x = \emptyset\}$;
(ii) $L_{fin} = \{x \in A^* \mid \mathsf{L}_x \text{ is finite}\}$;
(iii) $L_u = \{x \in A^* \mid u \in \mathsf{L}_x\}$, *where* $u \in A^*$;
(iv) $L_{reg} = \{x \in A^* \mid \mathsf{L}_x \text{ is regular }\}$;
(v) $L_{cf} = \{x \in A^* \mid \mathsf{L}_x \text{ is context free }\}$;

(vi) $L_{rec} = \{x \in A^* \mid \mathsf{L}_x \text{ is recursive}\}$.

Proof. The statements follow immediately from Theorem 8.7.7 by observing that each of the languages involved is an index language for a nontrivial collection of recursively enumerable languages. ∎

8.8 Post Correspondence Problem

In this section we present an undecidable problem originally formulated by Emil Post in [1946] that helps prove that many other problems in formal languages are undecidable.

Definition 8.8.1 Let I be an alphabet, referred to as an *index alphabet*, and let A be an alphabet such that $I \cap A = \emptyset$.

An (I, A)*-instance of the Post Correspondence Problem* (PCP) is a pair of morphisms (g, h), where $g : I^* \longrightarrow A^*$, $h : I^* \longrightarrow A^*$, and $h(i) \neq \lambda$, $g(i) \neq \lambda$ for $i \in I$.

A *solution* of the (I, A)-instance (g, h) of the PCP is a nonnull word $x \in I^+$ such that $g(x) = h(x)$. □

If the alphabets I, A are clear from context we may omit them and we shall refer to (I, A)-instances simply as instances of the PCP.

Example 8.8.2 Let $I = \{0, 1\}$, $A = \{a, b, c\}$ and let $g, h : I^* \longrightarrow A^*$ be the morphisms defined by

$$\begin{array}{lllllllll} g(0) & = & aba, & g(1) & = & ba, & g(2) & = & abac, \\ h(0) & = & abaa, & h(1) & = & b, & h(2) & = & bac. \end{array}$$

The word $x = 0202$ is a solution of the instance (g, h) since $g(0202) = h(0202) = abaabacabaabac$. □

Example 8.8.3 Now consider the alphabets $I = \{0, 1\}$ and $A = \{a, b\}$ and the morphisms (g, h) given by $g(0) = aa, g(1) = b$ and $h(0) = a, h(1) = bb$. We claim that the instance (g, h) has no solution. Indeed, if x were a solution, the number of as in $g(x)$ would be the double of the number of 0s in x, while the number of as in $h(x)$ would equal the number of as in x. This would imply $n_a(x) = 0$. A similar argument would imply $n_b(x) = 0$ and, thus, we would have $x = \lambda$, contradicting the definition of a solution. □

Note that if both x, x' are solutions of an instance of PCP, then xx' is also a solution. Thus, if an instance of the PCP has a solution x, then the set of solutions of this instance is infinite (since it contains all words x^n for $n \in \mathbb{P}$).

Let $x = i_0 i_1 \cdots i_{p-1}$ be a solution of the instance (g, h). Since

$$g(i_0)g(i_1)\cdots g(i_{p-1}) = h(i_0)h(i_1)\cdots h(i_{p-1}),$$

one of the words $g(i_0), h(i_0)$ must be a prefix of the other, and one of the words $g(i_{p-1}), h(i_{p-1})$ must be a suffix of the other. This observation is useful in determining possible "candidates" for the initial and final symbols of solutions of instances of the PCP.

Definition 8.8.4 Let (g, h) be an (I, A)-instance of the PCP. A *primitive solution* of this instance is a solution x such that no proper prefix of x is a solution of the instance. □

Note that if x is a primitive solution of the instance (g, h) and y is a proper prefix of x, then one of the words $g(y), h(y)$ is a proper prefix of the other since $g(y) \neq h(y)$ and both $g(y)$ and $h(y)$ are prefixes of $g(x) = h(x)$.

Example 8.8.5 The solution 0202 of the instance of the PCP considered in Example 8.8.2 is not primitive since we have $g(02) = abaabac = h(02)$ and 02 is a proper prefix of 0202; however, 02 is a primitive solution. □

Note that if $x, y \in I^*$ are two solution of an instance (g, h) such that $x = yz$, then z is also a solution of (g, h) (cf. Exercise 54).

Definition 8.8.6 Let I, A be two alphabets. An (I, A)*-instance of the modified Post correspondence problem* (MPCP) is a quadruple $(g, h, i_{\text{beg}}, i_{\text{end}})$, where $g, h : I^* \longrightarrow A^*$ are morphisms and $i_{\text{beg}}, i_{\text{end}}$ are two symbols in I.

A solution of the (I, A)*-instance of the MPCP* is a word $x \in i_{\text{beg}}(I - \{i_{\text{beg}}, i_{\text{end}}\})^* i_{\text{end}}$ such that $g(x) = h(x)$. □

In other words, a solution of the instance $(g, h, i_{\text{beg}}, i_{\text{end}})$ of the MPCP is a word $x \in I^*$ in which i_{beg} occurs only at the beginning of x and i_{end} occurs only at the end of x. Unlike the case for the PCP, if x is a solution of an instance of an *MPCP*, xx is not a solution of the MPCP.

Theorem 8.8.7 *Let I, A be two alphabets. If (g, h, i_{beg}, i_{end}) is an (I, A)-instance of the MPCP, then there is an (I, A')-instance (g', h') of the PCP such that $A' = A \cup \{\langle, \rangle, \#\}$ and the MPCP instance has a solution if and only if the PCP instance (g', h') has a solution.*

Proof. Starting from the morphisms $g, h : I^* \longrightarrow A^*$ define the morphisms $g', h' : I^* \longrightarrow A'^*$ as:

- if
$$\begin{aligned} g(i_{\text{beg}}) &= a_{i_0} \cdots a_{i_{m-1}} \\ h(i_{\text{beg}}) &= a_{j_0} \cdots a_{j_{p-1}}, \end{aligned}$$
then
$$\begin{aligned} g'(i_{\text{beg}}) &= \langle \# a_{i_0} \# \cdots \# a_{i_{m-1}} \\ h'(i_{\text{beg}}) &= \langle \# a_{j_0} \# \cdots \# a_{j_{p-1}} \# \end{aligned}$$
- if
$$\begin{aligned} g(i) &= a_{k_0} \cdots a_{k_{q-1}} \\ h(i) &= a_{l_0} \cdots a_{l_{n-1}}, \end{aligned}$$
then
$$\begin{aligned} g'(i) &= \# a_{k_0} \cdots \# a_{k_{q-1}}, \\ h'(i) &= a_{l_0} \# \cdots a_{l_{n-1}} \# \end{aligned}$$
- if
$$\begin{aligned} g(i_{\text{end}}) &= a_{d_0} \cdots a_{d_{r-1}} \\ h(i_{\text{end}}) &= a_{e_0} \cdots a_{e_{s-1}}, \end{aligned}$$

then

$$g'(i_{\text{end}}) = \#a_{d_0}\#\cdots\#a_{d_{r-1}}\#\rangle$$
$$h'(i_{\text{end}}) = a_{e_0}\#\cdots a_{e_{s-1}}\#\rangle$$

Suppose that x is a solution of (g', h'). Then, x must begin with i_{beg} since i_{beg} is the unique symbol i in I such that both $g'(i)$ and $h'(i)$ begin with the same character. Similarly, x must end with i_{end} because i_{end} is the only symbol such that both $g'(i)$ and $h'(i)$ end in the same character.

Note that

$$g'(ii_{\text{beg}}) = \#a_{k_0}\cdots\#a_{k_{q-1}}\langle\#a_{i_0}\#\cdots\#a_{i_{m-1}}$$
$$h'(ii_{\text{beg}}) = a_{l_0}\#\cdots a_{l_{n-1}}\#\langle\#a_{j_0}\#\cdots\#a_{j_{p-1}}\#$$

and

$$g'(i_{\text{beg}}i_{\text{beg}}) = \langle\#a_{i_0}\#\cdots\#a_{i_{m-1}}\langle\#a_{i_0}\#\cdots\#a_{i_{m-1}}$$
$$h'(i_{\text{beg}}i_{\text{beg}}) = \langle\#a_{j_0}\#\cdots\#a_{j_{p-1}}\#\langle\#a_{j_0}\#\cdots\#a_{j_{p-1}}\#$$

Therefore, that i_{beg} may not occur in x between an occurrence of i_{beg} and the following occurrence of i_{end}. Indeed, if this would be the case, then $h'(x)$ would contain an infix $\#\langle$ while $g'(x)$ would contain no such infix. Similarly, i_{end} may not occur between an occurrence of i_{beg} and the following occurrence of i_{end}. Consequently, we can write $x = i_{\text{beg}}ui_{\text{end}}i_{\text{beg}}vi_{\text{end}}\cdots i_{\text{beg}}wi_{\text{end}}$, where $i_{\text{beg}}ui_{\text{end}}$, $i_{\text{beg}}vi_{\text{end}}$,...,$i_{\text{beg}}wi_{\text{end}}$ are all primitive solutions to the instance (g', h') of the PCP solution. It is clear that each of them are solutions to the (I, A)-instance of MPCP.

Conversely, suppose that x is a solution of the instance $(g, h, i_{\text{beg}}, i_{\text{end}})$ of MPCP. In other words, we have $x = i_{\text{beg}}zi_{\text{end}}$, for some word $z \in (I - \{i_{\text{beg}}, i_{\text{end}})^*$ and $g(x) = h(x)$. It is easy to verify, by induction on $|z|$ that x is a solution of the instance (g', h') of PCP. ∎

We show initially that the existence of a solution of an instance of the MPCP is undecidable. This result is obtained by proving that for every grammar G there is a MPCP instance such that $\lambda \in L(G)$ if and only if there is a solution to that MPCP instance.

Theorem 8.8.8 *Let $G = (A_N, A_T, S, \{\pi_0, \ldots, \pi_{n-1}\})$ be a grammar, and let \$ be a symbol such that $\$ \notin A_N \cup A_T$. The alphabets I, A are given by:*

$$I = A_N \cup A_T \cup \{\$, i_{beg}, i_{end}\} \cup \{\pi_0, \ldots, \pi_{n-1}\}$$
$$A = A_N \cup A_T \cup \{\$\}.$$

Suppose that the production π_i is $x_i \to y_i$ for $0 \leq i \leq n-1$. Define the morphisms g, h by

s	$a \in A_N \cup A_T$	\$	i_{beg}	i_{end}	π_i
$g(s)$	a	\$	λ	\$	x_i
$h(s)$	a	\$	$\$S$	λ	y_i

The instance (g, h, i_{beg}, i_{end}) of the MPCP has a solution if and only if $\lambda \in L(G)$.

Proof. We claim that if there is a derivation

$$S = w_0 \underset{G}{\Rightarrow} w_1 \underset{G}{\Rightarrow} \cdots \underset{G}{\Rightarrow} w_m = w,$$

where $m \geq 1$, then there is $t \in I^*$ such that

$$g(i_{\text{beg}}t) = \$w_0\$w_1 \cdots \$w_{m-1}$$
$$h(i_{\text{beg}}t) = \$w_0\$w_1 \cdots \$w_{m-1}\$w_m.$$

The argument is by induction on $m \geq 1$. If $m = 1$, we applied a production $\pi_k : S \to y$. By defining $t = \$\pi_k$ we have:

$$g(i_{\text{beg}}\$\pi_k) = \lambda\$S = \$S$$
$$h(i_{\text{beg}}\$\pi_k) = \$S\$y = \$S\$y,$$

which complete the initial step.

For the induction step suppose a word t exists for derivations of length m and let

$$S = w_0 \underset{G}{\Rightarrow} w_1 \underset{G}{\Rightarrow} \cdots \underset{G}{\Rightarrow} w_{m+1} = w,$$

be a derivation of length $m + 1$. Suppose that the production $\pi_\ell : x \to y$ is applied in the last step of this derivation. In other words, we have $w_m = uxv$ and $w_{m+1} = uyv$ for some $u, v \in (A_N \cup A_T)^*$. By the inductive hypothesis, there is $t \in I^*$ such that

$$g(i_{\text{beg}}t) = \$w_0\$w_1 \cdots \$w_{m-1}$$
$$h(i_{\text{beg}}t) = \$w_0\$w_1 \cdots \$w_{m-1}\$uxv.$$

Let $t' = \$u\pi_j v$. Since $g(t') = \$uxv$, and $h(t') = \$uyv$ we have

$$g(i_{\text{beg}}tt') = \$w_0\$w_1 \cdots \$w_{m-1}\$uxv,$$
$$h(i_{\text{beg}}tt') = \$w_0\$w_1 \cdots \$w_{m-1}\$uxv\$uyv,$$

which gives the desired conclusion.

Conversely, we claim that if there is a word $t \in I^*$ such that $g(i_{\text{beg}}t) = \$w_0\$w_1 \cdots \$w_{m-1}$ and $h(i_{\text{beg}}t) = \$w_0\$w_1 \cdots \$w_{m-1}\$w_m$, where $w_i \in (A_N \cup A_T)^*$ for $0 \leq i \leq m$, then $w_i \overset{*}{\underset{G}{\Rightarrow}} w_{i+1}$ for $0 \leq i \leq m - 1$.

Again, the argument is by induction on $m \geq 1$. For $m = 1$, we have

$$g(i_{\text{beg}}t) = \$w_0$$
$$h(i_{\text{beg}}t) = \$w_0\$w_1.$$

Since $g(i_{\text{beg}}) = \lambda$ and $h(i_{\text{beg}}) = \$S$ we have $g(t) = \$w_0$ and $h(t) = \$w_1$. If t contains no symbol π_j, then $w_0 = w_1$; otherwise, $t = \$u_0\pi_{\ell_1}u_1 \cdots \pi_{\ell_{m-1}}u_{m-1}$, $w_0 = u_0x_{\ell_1}u_1 \cdots x_{\ell_{m-1}}u_{m-1}$, $w_1 = u_0y_{\ell_1}u_1 \cdots y_{\ell_{m-1}}u_{m-1}$, so $w_0 \overset{*}{\underset{G}{\Rightarrow}} w_1$. In either case, $w_0 \overset{*}{\underset{G}{\Rightarrow}} w_1$.

Suppose that the statement holds for m and that there is a word t such that $g(i_{\text{beg}}t) = \$w_0\$w_1 \cdots \$w_m$ and $h(i_{\text{beg}}t) = \$w_0\$w_1 \cdots \$w_m\$w_{m+1}$, where $w_i \in (A_N \cup A_T)^*$ for $0 \leq i \leq m+1$. Since $g(\$) = h(\$) = \$$, it follows that we can write $t = \$t_0\$t_1 \cdots \$t_m$, where no word t_i contains a \$, $g(t_i) = w_i$, and $h(t_i) = w_{i+1}$ for $0 \leq i \leq m$. By defining $\bar{t} = \$t_0\$t_1 \cdots \$t_{m-1}$ we can write $t = \bar{t}\$t_m$, where $g(i_{\text{beg}}\bar{t}) = \$w_0\$w_1 \cdots \$w_{m-1}$, $h(i_{\text{beg}}\bar{t}) = \$w_0\$w_1 \cdots \$w_{m-1}\$w_m$, $g(t_m) = w_m$, and $h(t_m) = w_{m+1}$. By the inductive hypothesis, $w_i \overset{*}{\underset{G}{\Rightarrow}} w_{i+1}$ for $0 \leq i \leq m-1$; in addition, it is easy to see that $w_m \overset{*}{\underset{G}{\Rightarrow}} w_{m+1}$, which concludes the argument of the converse implication.

We have shown that there is a word $t \in I^*$ such that

$$\begin{aligned} g(i_{\text{beg}}t) &= \$w_0\$w_1 \cdots \$w_{m-1} \\ h(i_{\text{beg}}t) &= \$w_0\$w_1 \cdots \$w_{m-1}\$w_m. \end{aligned}$$

if and only if

$$w_0 \overset{*}{\underset{G}{\Rightarrow}} w_1 \overset{*}{\underset{G}{\Rightarrow}} \cdots \overset{*}{\underset{G}{\Rightarrow}} w_{m-1} \overset{*}{\underset{G}{\Rightarrow}} w_m,$$

where $w_i \in (A_N \cup A_T)^*$ for $0 \leq i \leq m$,

Suppose that there is a solution $i_{\text{beg}}ti_{\text{end}}$ to the instance $(g, h, i_{\text{beg}}, i_{\text{end}})$ of the MPCP, that is, $g(i_{\text{beg}}ti_{\text{end}}) = h(i_{\text{beg}}ti_{\text{end}})$. By the definition of g, h we have

$$g(i_{\text{beg}}ti_{\text{end}}) = g(t)\$ = h(i_{\text{beg}}ti_{\text{end}}) = \$Sh(t).$$

Therefore, $g(t) = \$Sz$ and $h(t) = z\$$, which implies $g(i_{\text{beg}}t) = \$Sz$ and $h(i_{\text{beg}}t) = \$Sz\$$. By the previous argument this means that $\lambda \in L(G)$.

Conversely, if $\lambda \in L(G)$, there is a derivation

$$S = w_0 \underset{G}{\Rightarrow} w_1 \underset{G}{\Rightarrow} \cdots \underset{G}{\Rightarrow} w_m = \lambda.$$

Thus, there is $t \in I^*$ such that

$$\begin{aligned} g(i_{\text{beg}}t) &= \$w_0\$w_1 \cdots \$w_{m-1} \\ h(i_{\text{beg}}t) &= \$w_0\$w_1 \cdots \$w_{m-1}\$, \end{aligned}$$

which implies

$$g(i_{\text{beg}}ti_{\text{end}}) = \$w_0\$w_1 \cdots \$w_{m-1}\$ = h(i_{\text{beg}}ti_{\text{end}}).$$

Consequently, $i_{\text{beg}}ti_{\text{end}}$ is a solution to the instance $(g, h, i_{\text{beg}}, i_{\text{end}})$ of the MPCP. ∎

Corollary 8.8.9 *The Post correspondence problem is undecidable.*

Proof. Suppose that the PCP were decidable. Theorem 8.8.7 would imply that the MPCP would be decidable and, therefore, by Theorem 8.8.8 we could decide effectively whether $\lambda \in L(G)$ for an arbitrary grammar G. Since we know that this problem is undecidable (by the third part of Corollary 8.7.8), it follows that the PCP is undecidable. ∎

We examine now several undecidability results that follow from the undecidability of the PCP.

Theorem 8.8.10 *It is undecidable whether the intersection of the languages generated by two context-free grammars G, G' is nonempty.*

Proof. Starting from an (I, A)-instance (g, h) of the PCP we construct two grammars G, G' such that $L(G) \cap L(G') \neq \emptyset$ if and only if (g, h) is a solution.

Let

$$\begin{aligned} G &= (\{S\}, I \cup A, S, \{S \to g(i)Si, S \to g(i)i \mid i \in I\}, \\ G' &= (\{S'\}, I \cup A, S, \{S' \to h(i)Si, S' \to h(i)i \mid i \in I\}, \end{aligned}$$

be two context-free grammars. It is easy to see that

$$L(G) = \{g(t)t^R \mid t \in I^+\}$$

$$L(G') = \{h(t)t^R \mid t \in I^+\}.$$

Therefore, $L(G) \cap L(G') \neq \emptyset$ if and only if there is $t \in I^+$ such that $g(t)t^R = h(t)t^R$, that is, if and only if $g(t) = h(t)$, since $I \cap A = \emptyset$. This means that the languages $L(G)$ and $L(G')$ have a nonempty intersection if and only if the (I, A)-instance (g, h) of the PCP has a solution. Since this is undecidable, it follows that the nonemptyness of $L(G) \cap L(G')$ is undecidable. ∎

Theorem 8.8.11 *It is undecidable whether the intersection of the languages generated by two context-sensitive grammars G, G' is nonempty.*

Proof. Note that the grammars G, G' constructed in the proof of Theorem 8.8.10 are also context-sensitive. The result follows immediately. ∎

Theorem 8.8.12 *It is undecidable whether a context-free grammar is ambiguous.*

Proof. Construct the context-free grammars G, G' that correspond to an (I, A)-instance (g, h) of the PCP, as in Theorem 8.8.10 and observe that these grammars are unambiguous.

Let G_0 be the context-free grammar $G_0 = (\{S_0, S, S\}, I \cup A, S_0, P_0)$, where P_0 contains the productions of both G and G' and, also, the productions $S_0 \to S$ and $S_0 \to S'$. Clearly, $L(G_0) = L(G) \cup L(G')$.

We claim that G_0 is ambiguous if and only if $L(G) \cap L(G') \neq \emptyset$.

Indeed, if $t \in L(G) \cap L(G')$, then we have the leftmost derivations $S \overset{+}{\underset{G,\text{left}}{\Rightarrow}} t$ and $S' \overset{+}{\underset{G',\text{left}}{\Rightarrow}} t$ which entail the existence of the leftmost derivations

$$S_0 \underset{G_0,\text{left}}{\Rightarrow} S \overset{+}{\underset{G_0,\text{left}}{\Rightarrow}} t \text{ and } S_0 \underset{G_0,\text{left}}{\Rightarrow} S' \overset{+}{\underset{G_0,\text{left}}{\Rightarrow}} t.$$

Thus, G_0 is ambiguous.

Conversely, if G is ambiguous, then there are two distinct leftmost derivations d, d' of t in G_0. The first production to be applied in a derivation $S \overset{*}{\underset{G_0,\text{left}}{\Rightarrow}} t$ is either $S_0 \to S$ or $S \to S'$. If d, d' were to begin with the application of the same production, say $S_0 \to S$, then both derivations could take place in G, which contradicts the nonambiguity of G. Thus, d and d' must begin with different productions, which means that they have the form:

$$d \ : \ S_0 \underset{G_0,\text{left}}{\Rightarrow} S \overset{*}{\underset{G_0,\text{left}}{\Rightarrow}} t$$

$$d' \ : \ S_0 \underset{G_0,\text{left}}{\Rightarrow} S' \overset{*}{\underset{G_0,\text{left}}{\Rightarrow}} t.$$

Therefore, we have both $S \overset{*}{\underset{G,\text{left}}{\Rightarrow}} t$ and $S' \overset{*}{\underset{G',\text{left}}{\Rightarrow}} t$, so $t \in L(G) \cap L(G')$.

If the ambiguity of context-free grammars were decidable, we could decide whether $L(G_0)$ is ambiguous and, therefore, we could decide whether $L(G) \cap L(G') \neq \emptyset$. Thus, by Theorem 8.8.10, the ambiguity of context-free grammars is undecidable. ∎

8.9 Multitape Turing Machines

Multitape Turing Machines are generalizations of standard dTms, obtained by replacing the single tape of a dTm with k tapes; each tape has a read/write head. It might seem logical that a dTm with k tapes could compute things that a dTm with one tape could not, but while it is easier to express certain algorithms with additional, readily available resources, there is no change in the fundamental capabilities of the machines. One way of formalizing this is to note that any language that can be accepted by a k-tape dTm can also be accepted by an ordinary, one-tape dTm, and this is proven in Theorem 8.9.7. Formally, we have the following definition.

Definition 8.9.1 A k-tape dTm is a is a 5-tuple $\mathcal{M} = (A, Q, \delta, q_0, F)$, where A is an alphabet called the *input alphabet*, Q is *the set of states*, $\delta : Q \times A^k \longrightarrow (Q \cup F) \times A^k \times \{\mathtt{l}, \mathtt{0}, \mathtt{r}\}^k$ is the *transition function*, q_0 is the *initial state*, and F is the set of final states.

As in Definition 8.3.1, we assume that $A \cap (Q \cup F) = \emptyset$, $F \cap Q = \emptyset$. If

$$\delta(q, a_0, \ldots, a_{k-1}) = (q', a'_0, \ldots, a'_{k-1}, d_0, \ldots, d_{k-1}),$$

then $a_i = \triangleright$ implies implies $a'_i = \triangleright$ and $d_i \in \{\mathtt{0}, \mathtt{r}\}$, and $a'_i = \triangleright$ implies $a_i = \triangleright$ and $d_i \in \{\mathtt{0}, \mathtt{r}\}$ for every $q, q' \in Q$ and $0 \leq i \leq k-1$. □

As in the case of single-tape dTms, no read/write head ever moves to the left of a cell that contains the left marker. The symbol in the first cell of any tape is never changed to another symbol nor can any other cell of any tape be changed to contain the left marker.

If the Turing machine in state q reads the symbols $a_0, \ldots, a_{k-1}$ at time t from its tapes (numbered from 0 to $k-1$) and

$$\delta(q, a_0, \ldots, a_{k-1}) = (q', a'_0, \ldots, a'_{k-1}, d_0, \ldots, d_{k-1}),$$

then, at time $t+1$, the machine will have assumed the state q', the symbol a_i on the ith tape will have been replaced by the symbol a'_i, and the read/write head of each tape will have moved one cell to the left, rest on the same cell, or move one cell to the right, depending on whether $d_i = \mathtt{l}$, $d_i = \mathtt{0}$, or $d_i = \mathtt{r}$, respectively. Figure 8.18 shows a k-tape dTm.

Definition 8.9.2 Let $\mathcal{M} = (A, Q, \delta, q_0, F)$ be a k-tape dTm, and let $\star$ be a symbol such that $\star \notin A \cup Q$. A *configuration of* $\mathcal{M}$ is a word

$$\mathsf{c} = u_0 q a_{i_0} v_0 \star u_1 q a_{i_1} v_1 \star \cdots u_{k-1} q a_{i_{k-1}} v_{k-1} \star$$

where $q \in Q \cup F$, $a_{i_0}, \ldots, a_{i_{k-1}} \in A$, and $u_0, \ldots, u_{k-1}, v_0, \ldots, v_{k-1} \in A^*$.

$\mathcal{M}$ *is in the configuration*

$$\mathsf{c} = u_0 q a_{i_0} v_0 \star u_1 q a_{i_1} v_1 \star \cdots u_{k-1} q a_{i_{k-1}} v_{k-1} \star$$

if the following conditions are satisfied:

(i) the current state of the machine is q;
(ii) the jth read/write head is scanning the m_j^{th} cell of the jth tape, and that cell contains the symbol a_{i_j}, where $m_j = |u_j|$;

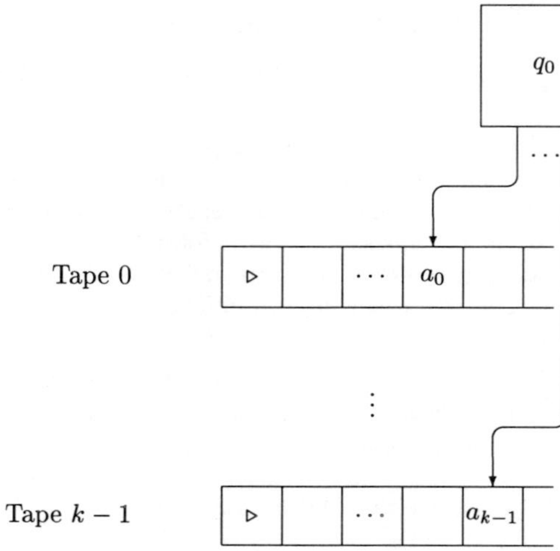

Figure 8.18: A k-tape dTm

(iii) the word $w_j = u_j a_{i_j} v_j$ is the shortest word on A that includes all non-blank symbols written on the jth tape for $0 \leq i \leq k-1$.

□

The set of all configurations of the k-tape dTm $\mathcal{M}$ is denoted by $\mathsf{CONFIG}(\mathcal{M})$.

If

$$\begin{aligned} \mathsf{c} &= u_0 q a_{i_0} v_0 \star u_1 q a_{i_1} v_1 \star \cdots u_{k-1} q a_{i_{k-1}} v_{k-1} \star \\ &= u_0' q' a_{l_0} v_0' \star u_1' q' a_{l_1} v_1' \star \cdots u_{k-1}' q' a_{l_{k-1}} v_{k-1}' \star, \end{aligned}$$

then $q = q'$, $a_{i_m} = a_{l_m}$, $u_m = u_m'$, and $v_m = v_m'$ for $0 \leq m \leq k-1$.

Every configuration of a k-tape dTm contains exactly k occurrences of $\star$. Also, there are k occurrences of a symbol $q \in Q \cup F$, and an equal number of occurrences of $\triangleright$. Therefore, $|\mathsf{c}| \geq 3k$ for any $\mathsf{c} \in \mathsf{CONFIG}(\mathcal{M})$.

Theorem 8.9.3 *No configuration of a k-tape dTm is a proper prefix or a proper suffix of another configuration of the machine.*

Proof. The proof is similar to the argument of Theorem 8.3.6. ∎

The relation $\vdash_{\mathcal{M}}$ on $\mathsf{CONFIG}(\mathcal{M})$ for a k-tape machine is introduced in a manner similar to case of the one-tape machine. Namely, if $\mathcal{M}$ is in the configuration $\mathsf{c} = u_0 q a_{i_0} v_0 \star u_1 q a_{i_1} v_1 \star \cdots u_{k-1} q a_{i_{k-1}} v_{k-1} \star$ and

$$\delta(q, a_{i_0}, \ldots, a_{i_{k-1}}) = (q', a_{j_0}, \ldots, a_{j_{k-1}}, d_0, \ldots, d_{k-1}),$$

then the next configuration c' is

$$\mathsf{c}' = u_0' q' v_0' \star u_1' q' v_1' \star \cdots u_{k-1}' q' a_{j_{k-1}} v_{k-1}' \star,$$

where $u_m' q' v_m'$ satisfies the following conditions:

- if $d_m = \mathtt{r}$, then $u'_m = u_m a_{j_m}$ and

$$v'_m = \begin{cases} v_m & \text{if } v_m \neq \lambda \\ \sqcup & \text{if } v_m = \lambda; \end{cases}$$

- if $d_m = \mathtt{0}$, then $u'_m = u_m$ and $v'_m = a_{j_m} v_m$;
- if $d_m = \mathtt{l}$, $u_m = wa$ for some $w \in A^*$ and $a \in A$, then $u'_m = w$, and

$$v'_m = \begin{cases} a a_{j_m} v_m & \text{if either } a_{j_m} \neq \sqcup \text{ or } v_m \neq \lambda, \\ a & \text{if } a_{j_m} = \sqcup \text{ and } v_m = \lambda, \end{cases}$$

for every m, $0 \leq m \leq k-1$. This is denoted by $\mathrm{c} \vdash_{\mathcal{M}} \mathrm{c}'$. The relations $\overset{n}{\underset{\mathcal{M}}{\vdash}}$, $\overset{+}{\underset{\mathcal{M}}{\vdash}}$, and $\overset{*}{\underset{\mathcal{M}}{\vdash}}$ are introduced in exactly the same manner as the corresponding relations for single-tape deterministic Turing machines.

A word $x \in A^*$ is accepted by a k-tape dTm $\mathcal{M}$ if there exists a run in $\mathcal{M}$ that begins with the word $\triangleright x$ on the first tape and with the remaining $k-1$ tapes empty, and ends in the final state q_f. Formally, we have the following definition.

Definition 8.9.4 Let A be an alphabet and let $\mathcal{M} = (B, Q, \delta, q_0, \{q_f\})$ be a k-tape dTm such that $A \subseteq B - \{\triangleright, \sqcup\}$.

The machine $\mathcal{M}$ *accepts* the language $L \subseteq A^*$ if

$$L = \{x \in A^* \mid q_0 \triangleright x \star \underbrace{q_0 \triangleright \star \cdots q_0 \triangleright \star}_{k-1} \overset{*}{\underset{\mathcal{M}}{\vdash}} q_f \triangleright u \star u_1 q_f a_{l_1} v_1 \star \cdots u_{k-1} q_f a_{l_{k-1}} v_{k-1} \star\}$$

for some $u, u_1, \ldots, u_{k-1}, v_1, \ldots, v_{k-1} \in B*$.

The language over the alphabet A *accepted* by $\mathcal{M}$ is denoted by $L_A(\mathcal{M})$. If A is clear from context we may denote $L_A(\mathcal{M})$ simply by $L(\mathcal{M})$. □

Example 8.9.5 In this example, we design a three-tape dTm,

$$\mathcal{M} = (\{a, b, c, \triangleright, \sqcup\}, \{q_0, q_1, q_2, q_f, q_s\}, \delta, q_0, \{q_f\})$$

to accept the language $L(\mathcal{M}) = \{a^n b^n c^n \mid n \in \mathbb{N}\}$. $\mathcal{M}$ works by copying the first block of *a*s it encounters on its input, tape 0, to tape 1. It then copies the *b*s it encounters onto tape 2. It then matches the *c*s it encounters with the *a*s and the *b*s it copied. At any point in the calculation, if $\mathcal{M}$ encounters an unexpected symbol, it simply goes to a state where it loops forever. The functioning of $\mathcal{M}$ can be understood by examining the following calculation that accepts *aabbcc*:

$$\begin{aligned}
& q_0 \triangleright aabbcc \star q_0 \triangleright \star q_0 \triangleright \star \vdash_{\mathcal{M}} \triangleright q_0 aabbcc \star \triangleright q_0 \sqcup \star \triangleright q_0 \sqcup \star \vdash_{\mathcal{M}} \\
& \triangleright a q_0 abbcc \star \triangleright a q_0 \sqcup \star \triangleright q_0 \sqcup \star \vdash_{\mathcal{M}} \triangleright aa q_0 bbcc \star \triangleright aa q_0 \sqcup \star \triangleright q_0 \sqcup \star \vdash_{\mathcal{M}} \\
& \triangleright aab q_0 bcc \star \triangleright aa q_0 \sqcup \star \triangleright b q_0 \sqcup \star \vdash_{\mathcal{M}} \triangleright aabb q_0 cc \star \triangleright aa q_0 \sqcup \star \triangleright bb q_0 \sqcup \star \vdash_{\mathcal{M}} \\
& \triangleright aabb q_1 cc \star \triangleright a q_1 a \sqcup \star \triangleright b q_1 b \sqcup \star \vdash_{\mathcal{M}} \triangleright aabbc q_1 c \star \triangleright q_1 aa \sqcup \star \triangleright q_1 bb \sqcup \star \vdash_{\mathcal{M}} \\
& \triangleright aabbcc q_1 \sqcup \star q_1 \triangleright aa \sqcup \star q_1 \triangleright bb \sqcup \star \vdash_{\mathcal{M}} \triangleright aabbcc q_2 \sqcup \star q_2 \triangleright aa \sqcup \star q_2 \triangleright bb \sqcup \star \\
& \overset{*}{\underset{\mathcal{M}}{\vdash}} q_2 \triangleright aabbcc \sqcup \star q_2 \triangleright aa \sqcup \star q_2 \triangleright bb \sqcup \star \\
& \vdash_{\mathcal{M}} q_f \triangleright aabbcc \sqcup \star q_f \triangleright aa \sqcup \star q_f \triangleright bb \sqcup \star .
\end{aligned}$$

The transition function is given by the following table:

				$\delta(q,a_0,a_1,a_2)$						
q	a_0	a_1	a_2	q'	a'_0	a'_1	a'_2	d_0	d_1	d_2
q_0	$\triangleright$	$\triangleright$	$\triangleright$	q_0	$\triangleright$	$\triangleright$	$\triangleright$	r	r	r
q_0	a	$\sqcup$	$\sqcup$	q_0	a	a	$\sqcup$	r	r	0
q_0	b	$\sqcup$	$\sqcup$	q_0	b	$\sqcup$	b	r	0	r
q_0	c	$\sqcup$	$\sqcup$	q_1	c	$\sqcup$	$\sqcup$	0	l	l
q_1	c	a	b	q_1	c	a	b	r	l	l
q_1	$\sqcup$	$\triangleright$	$\triangleright$	q_2	$\sqcup$	$\triangleright$	$\triangleright$	l	0	0
q_2	a	$\triangleright$	$\triangleright$	q_2	a	$\triangleright$	$\triangleright$	l	0	0
q_2	b	$\triangleright$	$\triangleright$	q_2	b	$\triangleright$	$\triangleright$	l	0	0
q_2	c	$\triangleright$	$\triangleright$	q_2	c	$\triangleright$	$\triangleright$	l	0	0
q_2	$\triangleright$	$\triangleright$	$\triangleright$	q_f	$\triangleright$	$\triangleright$	$\triangleright$	0	0	0

For those quadruples (q, a_0, a_1, a_2) that do not occur in the table, we have

$$\delta(q, a_0, a_1, a_2) = (q_s, a_0, a_1, a_2, 0, 0, 0).$$

In particular, $\delta(q_s, a_0, a_1, a_2) = (q_s, a_0, a_1, a_2, 0, 0, 0)$, so $\mathcal{M}$ loops forever once it enters state q_s. □

Multi-tape dTms have exactly the same capabilities for accepting languages as single tape dTms. We justify this claim by proving that a k-tape dTm $\mathcal{M}$ can be simulated by a single-tape dTm $\mathcal{M}'$ having a more complex input alphabet. The cells of the tape of $\mathcal{M}'$ contain symbols of both A and of $(A \cup \{\uparrow\})^{2k}$. When a cell or a group of cells contains a $2k$-tuple we can regard that part of the tape as having $2k$ tracks. In this case, the tracks $2j$ and $2j+1$ are used for capturing the content of the jth tape of $\mathcal{M}$ and its corresponding head.

The content of the jth tape of $\mathcal{M}$ is written on the $2j + 1^{\text{st}}$ track of $\mathcal{M}'$; the $2j^{\text{th}}$ track of $\mathcal{M}'$ is blank with the exception of the component that contains the symbol $\uparrow$ that corresponds to the position of the head that scans the jth tape of $\mathcal{M}$ (see Figure 8.19).

Let $\boldsymbol{w} = (w_0, \ldots, w_{k-1}) \in (A^*)^k$ be a k-tuple of words of length m, and $\boldsymbol{p} = (p_0, \ldots, p_{k-1}) \in \mathbb{N}^k$. Denote by $\omega(\boldsymbol{w}, \boldsymbol{p}) \in ((A \cup \{\uparrow\})^{2k})^*$ the word of length m whose n^{th} symbol $\omega(\boldsymbol{w}, \boldsymbol{p})(n)$ is defined by:

$$\omega(\boldsymbol{w}, \boldsymbol{p})(n)_{2\ell+1} = w_\ell(n)$$

$$\omega(\boldsymbol{w}, \boldsymbol{p})(n)_{2\ell} = \begin{cases} \sqcup & \text{if } n \neq p_\ell \\ \uparrow & \text{if } n = p_\ell. \end{cases}$$

for $0 \leq \ell \leq k-1$ and $0 \leq n \leq m-1$.

Suppose that a k-tape dTm $\mathcal{M}$ is in the configuration

$$\mathsf{c} = u_0 q a_{i_0} v_0 \star u_1 q a_{i_1} v_1 \star \cdots u_{k-1} q a_{i_{k-1}} v_{k-1} \star$$

Let $m = \max\{|u_j a_{i_j} v_j| \mid 0 \leq j \leq k-1\}$. Denote by w_j the word of length m obtained from $u_j a_{i_j} v_j$ by adding (when needed) $m - |u_j a_{i_j} v_j|$ blanks at the right. Then, $\Omega(\mathsf{c})$ is the word $\omega(\boldsymbol{w}, \boldsymbol{p})$, where $\boldsymbol{w} = (w_0, \ldots, w_{k-1})$, $\boldsymbol{p} = (p_0, \ldots, p_{k-1})$, and $p_j = |u_j|$ for $0 \leq j \leq k-1$.

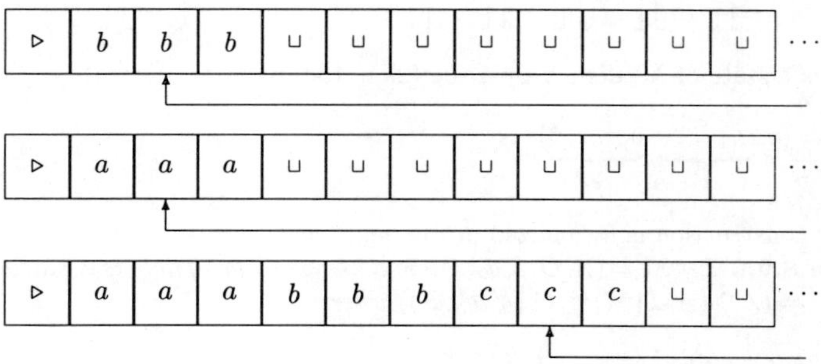

(a) Three-tape dTm $\mathcal{M}$

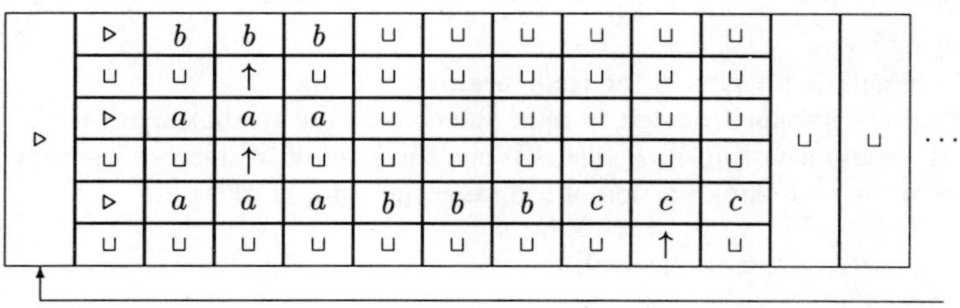

(b) One-tape dTm $\mathcal{M}'$

Figure 8.19: One-tape dTm simulating a 3-tape dTm

For example, the configuration of the three-tape dTm $\mathcal{M}$ shown in Figure 8.19 is $\triangleright bqbb \star \triangleright aqaa \triangleright aaabbbcqcc$, then the corresponding configuration of $\mathcal{M}'$ shown in the same figure is

$$\tilde{q}\triangleright \begin{bmatrix}\triangleright\\ \sqcup\\ \triangleright\\ \sqcup\\ \triangleright\\ \sqcup\end{bmatrix}\begin{bmatrix}b\\ \sqcup\\ a\\ \sqcup\\ a\\ \sqcup\end{bmatrix}\begin{bmatrix}b\\ \uparrow\\ a\\ \uparrow\\ a\\ \sqcup\end{bmatrix}\begin{bmatrix}b\\ \sqcup\\ a\\ \sqcup\\ a\\ \sqcup\end{bmatrix}\begin{bmatrix}\sqcup\\ \sqcup\\ \sqcup\\ \sqcup\\ b\\ \sqcup\end{bmatrix}\begin{bmatrix}\sqcup\\ \sqcup\\ \sqcup\\ \sqcup\\ b\\ \sqcup\end{bmatrix}\begin{bmatrix}\sqcup\\ \sqcup\\ \sqcup\\ \sqcup\\ b\\ \sqcup\end{bmatrix}\begin{bmatrix}\sqcup\\ \sqcup\\ \sqcup\\ \sqcup\\ c\\ \sqcup\end{bmatrix}\begin{bmatrix}\sqcup\\ \sqcup\\ \sqcup\\ \sqcup\\ c\\ \sqcup\end{bmatrix}\begin{bmatrix}\sqcup\\ \sqcup\\ \sqcup\\ \sqcup\\ c\\ \sqcup\end{bmatrix}\star$$

If q is a state of $\mathcal{M}$, denote by $\tilde{q}$ the $(2k+1)$-tuple

$$\tilde{q} = (q, \underbrace{\sqcup, \ldots, \sqcup}_{k}, \underbrace{0, \ldots, 0}_{k}).$$

This construction is formalized in the next lemma.

Lemma 8.9.6 *Let $\mathcal{M} = (A, Q, \delta, q_0, F)$ be a k-tape dTm. There is a single-tape dTm $\mathcal{M}' = (A \cup (A \cup \{\uparrow\})^{2k}, Q', \delta', q_0', F)$, where*

$$Q' = Q \cup (Q \times A^k \times \{\mathtt{l}, 0, \mathtt{r}\}^k),$$

such that $\mathsf{c} \underset{\mathcal{M}}{\vdash} \mathsf{c}'$ *if and only if* $\tilde{q} \triangleright \Omega(\mathsf{c}) \overset{*}{\underset{\mathcal{M}'}{\vdash}} \tilde{q}' \triangleright \Omega(\mathsf{c}')$, *where q, q' are the states that correspond to the configurations c and c', respectively.*

Proof. Each step $\mathsf{c} \underset{\mathcal{M}}{\vdash} \mathsf{c}'$ corresponds to a simulation run in $\mathcal{M}$ that comprizes the following steps:

- The simulation begins in the configuration $\tilde{q} \triangleright \Omega(\mathsf{c})$.
- $\mathcal{M}'$ sweeps its tape from left to right and collects the symbols marked by $\uparrow$ in the components $\tilde{q}(1), \ldots, \tilde{q}(k)$. When the head of $\mathcal{M}'$ reaches the right end of the non-blank portion of the tape, the state of $\mathcal{M}'$ is

  $$(q, a_0, \ldots, a_{k-1}, 0, \ldots, 0).$$

  Now, using the transition function δ, $\mathcal{M}'$ modifies its state to

  $$(q', a_0', \ldots, a_{k-1}', d_0, \ldots, d_{k-1})$$

  if $\delta(q, a_0, \ldots, a_{k-1}) = (q', a_0', \ldots, a_{k-1}', d_0, \ldots, d_{k-1})$.
- In the next phase, the head of $\mathcal{M}'$ sweeps the tape from right to left and, using $a_0', \ldots, a_{k-1}', d_0, \ldots, d_{k-1}$, it adjusts the $2k$-tuples written on the tape to reflect the configuration c'. The movement stops when the head reaches $\triangleright$.
- When the head reaches the left marker, the state becomes $\tilde{q}'$ and the configuration of $\mathcal{M}'$ becomes $\tilde{q}' \triangleright \Omega(\mathsf{c}')$.

∎

Theorem 8.9.7 *Let $\mathcal{M} = (B, Q, \delta, q_0, \{q_f\})$ be a k-tape dTm. There exists a one-tape dTm $\mathcal{M}'$ such that $L_A(\mathcal{M}') = L_A(\mathcal{M})$.*

Proof. Starting from $\mathcal{M}$, construct the dTm $\mathcal{M}'$ to the extent defined by Lemma 8.9.6. The transition function δ' is defined such that the initial configuration $q_0 \triangleright x$ is transformed into the configuration $\tilde{q_0} \triangleright \Omega(\mathsf{c}_0)$, where c_0 is the initial configuration of $\mathcal{M}$. Then, $x \in L_A(\mathcal{M})$ if and only if there exists a run $\mathsf{c}_0 \underset{\mathcal{M}}{\vdash} \cdots \underset{\mathcal{M}}{\vdash} \mathsf{c}_{n-1}$ such that $\mathsf{c}_{n-1} = q_f \triangleright \cdots$. By Lemma 8.9.6 this is equivalent to the existence of a run $\tilde{q_0} \triangleright \Omega(\mathsf{c}_0) \overset{*}{\underset{\mathcal{M}'}{\vdash}} \tilde{q}_f \triangleright \Omega(\mathsf{c}_{n-1})$. When $\mathcal{M}'$ enters the last configuration of the previous run, the state changes to q_f, so $L_A(\mathcal{M}) = L_A(\mathcal{M}')$. ∎

8.10 Nondeterministic Turing Machines

In previous chapters we discussed extensions of finite and pushdown automata that are able to work nondeterministically. The purpose of this section is to introduce nondeterministic Turing machines as extensions of dTms.

Definition 8.10.1 A *nondeterministic Turing machine* (ndTm) is a 5-tuple $\mathcal{M} = (A, Q, \delta, q_0, F)$, where A is an alphabet called the *input alphabet*, Q is *the set of states* , $\delta : Q \times A \longrightarrow \mathcal{P}((Q \cup F) \times A \times \{\mathtt{l}, \mathtt{0}, \mathtt{r}\})$ is the *transition function*, q_0 is the *initial state* , and F is the set of final states.

It is assumed that $A \cap (Q \cup F) = \emptyset$, $F \cap Q = \emptyset$, $(q', a', d) \in \delta(q, \triangleright)$ implies $a' = \triangleright$ and $d \in \{\mathtt{0}, \mathtt{r}\}$, and $(q', \triangleright, d) \in \delta(q, a)$ implies $a = \triangleright$ and $d \in \{\mathtt{0}, \mathtt{r}\}$ for every $q, q' \in Q$.

The number $\max\{|\delta(q, a)| \mid q \in A, a \in A\}$ will be referred to as the *degree of nondeterminism of* $\mathcal{M}$ and will be denoted by $\partial(\mathcal{M})$. □

The relation $\underset{\mathcal{M}}{\vdash}$ is introduced on the set $\mathsf{CONFIG}(\mathcal{M})$ by defining $\mathsf{c} \underset{\mathcal{M}}{\vdash} \mathsf{c}'$ if and only if $\mathsf{c} = uqav\star$, and c' is given by

$$\mathsf{c}' = \begin{cases} ua'q'v\star & \text{if } (q', a', \mathtt{r}) \in \delta(q, a) \text{ and } v \neq \lambda \\ ua'q'\sqcup\star & \text{if } (q', a', \mathtt{r})\delta(q, a) \text{ and } v = \lambda \\ uqa'v\star & \text{if } (q', a', \mathtt{0}) \in \delta(q, a) \\ u_1q'a_1a'v\star & \text{if } (q', a', \mathtt{l}) \in \delta(q, a), u = u_1a_1, \text{ and either} \\ & v \neq \lambda \text{ or } a' \neq \sqcup \\ u_1q'a_1\star & \text{if } (q', a', \mathtt{l}) \in \delta(q, a), u = u_1a_1, v = \lambda \text{ and } a' = \sqcup. \end{cases}$$

The definitions of the relations $\overset{n}{\underset{\mathcal{M}}{\vdash}}$, $\overset{+}{\underset{\mathcal{M}}{\vdash}}$, and $\overset{*}{\underset{\mathcal{M}}{\vdash}}$ are identical to the ones used for dTms.

Nondeterministic Turing machines are generalizations of dTms; namely, if $\mathcal{M} = (A, Q, \delta, q_0, F)$ is a ndTm and $|\delta(q, a)| = 1$ for every $q \in Q$ and $a \in A$, then we regard $\mathcal{M}$ as a dTm.

If $\mathcal{M}$ is a ndTm in a configuration c, then, in general, several possible succeeding configuration may exist. The notion of *run* is defined in a manner similar to Definition 8.3.10. Note that the number of runs of a certain length is limited: there are $(\partial(\mathcal{M}))^p$ runs of length p for $p \geq 1$.

We are interested in nondeterministic Turing machines as devices for defining languages. Formally, the definition of the language accepted by a ndTm is the same as Definition 8.6.14.

Definition 8.10.2 Let A be an alphabet, and let $\mathcal{M} = (B, Q, \delta, q_0, \{q_f\})$ be an ndTm such that $A \subseteq B - \{\triangleright, \sqcup\}$. The machine $\mathcal{M}$ *accepts* the language $L \subseteq A^*$ if

$$L = \{x \in A^* \mid \text{there is a run } q_0 \triangleright x \star \overset{*}{\underset{\mathcal{M}}{\vdash}} q_f \triangleright u\star\}$$

for some $u \in B*$.

The language over the alphabet A *accepted* by $\mathcal{M}$ is denoted by $L_A(\mathcal{M})$. If A is clear from context we may denote $L_A(\mathcal{M})$ simply by $L(\mathcal{M})$. □

A word $x \in A^*$ is accepted if there is a run of $\mathcal{M}$ that begins with the configuration $q_0 \triangleright x\star$ and ends with a configuration $q_f \triangleright u\star$. In other words, in order to have the word x accepted it is not necessary to have every run end in a configuration of the form $q_f \triangleright u\star$; it suffices to have one such run. If x is not accepted, then every run of $\mathcal{M}$ that starts with $q_0 \triangleright x\star$ either loops forever or terminates with $\mathcal{M}$ in a state $q \neq q_f$.

It is clear that every recursive enumerable language is accepted by a nondeterministic Turing machine, since every dTm can be regarded as a special ndTm. However, the nondeterminism does not increase the capability of Turing machines for accepting languages. This is a situation similar to the one encountered for finite automata, but different from the situation of pushdown automata.

Theorem 8.10.3 *If $\mathcal{M} = (B, Q, \delta, q_0, F)$ is a ndTm and A is an alphabet such that $A \subset B$, then $L_A(\mathcal{M})$ is a recursively enumerable language.*

Proof. We will prove initially that the language $L_A(\mathcal{M})$ can be accepted by a three-tape deterministic Turing machine $\mathcal{M}'$. The contents of the tapes of $\mathcal{M}'$ are:

- The first tape (tape 0) contains the input word $x \in A^*$ and is read-only.
- The second tape (tape 1) contains a word $\alpha \in \mathsf{CONFIG}(\mathcal{M})$.
- The third tape (tape 2) contains a word $\alpha \in \{0, 1, \ldots, \partial(\mathcal{M}) - 1\}^*$.

Suppose that $\mathcal{M}$ is in state q and that it is located on a cell that contains a symbol $b \in B$. If

$$\delta(q, b) = \{(q_{i_0}, b_{j_0}, \mathrm{d}_{k_0}), \ldots, (q_{i_{m-1}}, b_{j_{m-1}}, \mathrm{d}_{k_{m-1}})\},$$

then $\mathcal{M}$ can choose any of these m transitions for its next configuration, where $m \leq \partial(\mathcal{M})$. The dTm $\mathcal{M}'$ must check all these choices because the acceptance of a word $x \in A^*$ is determined by the existence of a run that leads to a final configuration. This is assured by the word written on the third tape.

The work of $\mathcal{M}'$ begins in the configuration

$$q_0 \triangleright x \star q_0 \triangleright \star q_0 \triangleright \star$$

Next, using the word x on the first tape, $\mathcal{M}'$ writes the initial configuration of $\mathcal{M}$, $q_0 \triangleright x\star$, on the second tape and positions each head on the first cell of its tape. Then $\mathcal{M}'$ starts simulating the work of $\mathcal{M}$.

Suppose that during the course of the simulation of $\mathcal{M}$ by $\mathcal{M}'$, the head located on the third tape of $\mathcal{M}'$ reads the symbol ℓ, the state of $\mathcal{M}'$ is q and the symbol read on the second tape is b. If $\ell < |\delta(q,b)|$, then $\mathcal{M}'$ modifies the configuration written on the second tape according to the triple $(q_{i_\ell}, b_{j_\ell}, \mathsf{d}_{k_\ell})$ from $\delta(q,b)$ and then moves the head of the third tape one cell to the right. If $\ell \geq |\delta(q,b)|$, then $\mathcal{M}'$ will use the triple $(q_{i_{m-1}}, b_{j_{m-1}}, \mathsf{d}_{k_{m-1}})$, where $m = |\delta(q,b)|$.

The third tape of $\mathcal{M}'$ works like a counter: first the words of length 1 over $\{0,1,\ldots,\partial(\mathcal{M})-1\}$ are generated; they allow $\mathcal{M}'$ to simulate all runs of $\mathcal{M}$ of length 2. Then, words of length 2 over the same alphabet are generated, and so on. In general, a word of length n on this tape allows $\mathcal{M}'$ to simulate a run of length $n+1$ of $\mathcal{M}$. $\mathcal{M}'$ generates the words of $\{0,1,\ldots,\partial(\mathcal{M})-1\}^*$ in lexicographical order on its third tape.

The simulation of $\mathcal{M}$ by $\mathcal{M}'$ involves the following steps:

1. Using the contents of the first tape, the initial configuration of $\mathcal{M}$ is written on the second tape of $\mathcal{M}'$.
2. Using the word written on the third tape, $\mathcal{M}'$ deterministically simulates a run of $\mathcal{M}$. If $\mathcal{M}$ accepts a word x, then $\mathcal{M}'$ will enter its final state and accept. The simulation of the run is completed when the head of the third tape is positioned over a cell containing a blank.
3. If $\mathcal{M}$ did not accept, then the next word on $\{0,1,\ldots,\partial(\mathcal{M})-1\}$ is generated and a new simulation cycle begins.

Thus, we have $L_A(\mathcal{M}) = L_A(\mathcal{M}')$. By Theorem 8.9.7, there is an one tape dTm $\mathcal{M}_1$ such that $L_A(\mathcal{M}') = L_A(\mathcal{M}_1)$, which concludes our argument. ∎

Turing machine systems can be extended to ndTms by dropping the third condition of Definition 8.4.1, as shown in the next definition.

Definition 8.10.4 Let A be an alphabet, and let $\mathcal{C}$ be a nonempty, finite collection of ndTms such that every machine in $\mathcal{C}$ has A as its input alphabet, and the sets of states and sets of final states of the machines in $\mathcal{C}$ are pairwise disjoint.

A *nondeterministic Turing machine system* (NTMS) labeled by the collection $\mathcal{C}$ and by the alphabet A is a labeled directed multigraph $\mathcal{G} = (G, M, \mathsf{m})$, where $M = \mathcal{C} \cup A$ and the labelling function m satisfies the following conditions:

1. $\mathsf{m}(v) \in \mathcal{C}$ for every vertex v of the graph G;
2. $\mathsf{m}(e) \in A$ for every edge of the graph G;

A special node v_0 of $\mathcal{G}$ is designed as the *initial vertex* and is marked by an incoming arrow with no source. □

As was the case with TMSs, all ndTms of $\mathcal{C}$ operate on the same tape and, while operating, one ndTm is active.

Let $\mathcal{G} = (G, M, \mathsf{m})$ be a TMS labeled by the collection $\mathcal{C} = \{\mathcal{M}_0, \ldots, \mathcal{M}_{n-1}\}$ of dTms over the alphabet A, where $\mathcal{M}_i = (A, Q_i, \delta_i, q_{0i}, F_i)$ for $0 \leq i \leq n-1$. Suppose that $p_0, \ldots, p_{n-1}$ are n new states, that is,

$$\{p_0, \ldots, p_{n-1}\} \cap (\bigcup_{i=0}^{n-1} Q_i \cup F_i) = \emptyset.$$

The ndTm of $\mathcal{G}$ is the ndTm

$$\mathcal{M}(\mathcal{G}) = (A, \bigcup_{i=0}^{n-1} Q_i \cup \{p_0, \ldots, p_{n-1}\}, \delta, q_0, \{q_f\}),$$

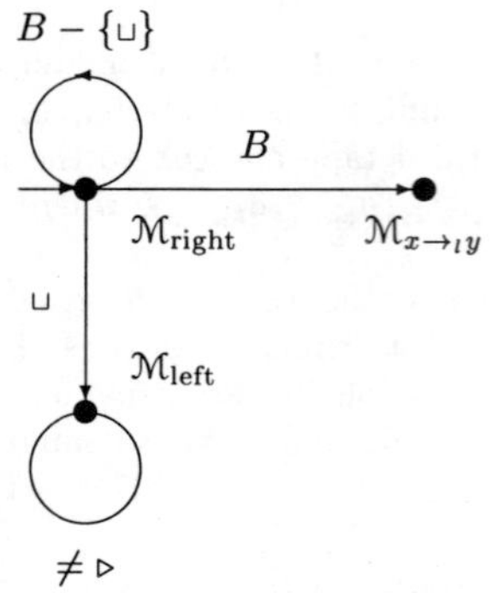

Figure 8.20: The NTMS that defines $\mathcal{M}_{x \to y}$

where q_0 is the initial state of the initial machine of $\mathcal{G}$, q_f is a unique final state, and δ is defined as follows:

1. if $q \in Q_i$, then
$$\begin{aligned} \delta(q, a) &= \delta_i(q, a) - (F_i \times A \times \{\mathtt{l}, 0, \mathtt{r}\}) \\ &\cup \{(p_i, a', d) \mid (q', a', d) \in \delta_i(q, a) \text{ and } q' \in F\}; \end{aligned}$$

2. if G contains an edge labeled by a symbol $a \in A$ leading from a vertex labeled $\mathcal{M}_i$ to a vertex labeled $\mathcal{M}_j$, then $\delta(p_i, a) = \delta(q_{0j}, a)$ (note that $\delta(q_{0j}, a)$ is already defined); otherwise, $\delta(p_i, a) = \{(q_f, a, 0)\}$.

Example 8.10.5 In Example 8.4.7 we introduced the dTm $\mathcal{M}_{x \to_l y}$ which replaces the leftmost occurrence of x by y on its tape if such an occurrence exists; otherwise, $\mathcal{M}_{x \to_l y}$ leaves the content of the tape intact.

Using an NTMS we can define an ndTm $\mathcal{M}_{x \to y}$ that replaces some occurrence of x on its tape by y, but not necessarily the leftmost one. Let B the alphabet whose symbols are written on the tape. The NTMS whose graph is shown in Figure 8.20 defines the ndTm $\mathcal{M}_{x \to y}$. □

8.11 Exercises

Markov Algorithms

1. Construct an lMa $\mathcal{A} = (B, P)$ such that $\langle \mathcal{A} \rangle(x) = x_0$ for every $x \in B^*$, where x_0 is a given word in B^*.
2. Let $A = \{a_0, a_1\}$ and let $\mathcal{A} = (A \cup \{X, Y\}, P)$, where P consists of the

productions

$$\begin{aligned}
&0 : \lambda \to Y/1;\\
&1 : Ya_0 \to a_0Xa_0Y/1;\\
&2 : Ya_1 \to a_1Xa_1Y/1;\\
&3 : Y \to \lambda/4;\\
&4 : a_0a_0X \to a_0Xa_0/4;\\
&5 : a_0a_1X \to a_1Xa_0/4;\\
&6 : a_1a_0X \to a_0Xa_1/4;\\
&7 : a_1a_1X \to a_1Xa_1/4;\\
&8 : X \to \lambda/8;
\end{aligned}$$

Prove that $f^1_{\mathcal{A},A}(x) = xx$ for every $x \in A^*$.

3. Let $A = \{a_0, \ldots, a_{n-1}\}$ be an alphabet and $h : A^* \longrightarrow A^*$ be a morphism. Define the lMa $\mathcal{A} = (A \cup \{X\}, P)$ having the list of productions

$$\begin{aligned}
&0 : \lambda \to X/1;\\
&i+1 : Xa_i \to h(a_i)X/1; \text{ for } 0 \leq i \leq n-1;\\
&n+1 : X \to \lambda;
\end{aligned}$$

Prove that $f^1_{\mathcal{A},A}(x) = h(x)$ for every $x \in A^*$.

4. $\diamond$ Let $\mathcal{M} = (A, Q, \delta, q_0, F)$ be a dfa, where $A = \{a_0, \ldots, a_{n-1}\}$ $Q = \{q_0, \ldots, q_{m-1}\}$, and $F = \{q_{k_0}, \ldots, q_{k_{p-1}}\})$. Define the lMa $\mathcal{A} = (A \cup Q, P)$ having the set of productions

$$\begin{aligned}
&0 : \lambda \to q_0/1;\\
&f(i,j) : q_ia_j \to a_j\delta(q_i, a_j)/1; \text{ for } 0 \leq i \leq n-1\\
&\qquad\qquad\qquad\qquad\qquad \text{and } 0 \leq j \leq m-1\\
&nm : q_{k_0} \to \lambda/nm+p+1;\\
&\vdots\\
&nm+p-1 : q_{k_{p-1}} \to \lambda/nm+p+1;\\
&nm+p : \lambda \to \lambda/nm+p;
\end{aligned}$$

The function f is the bijection defined in Exercise 27.
Prove that $\mathrm{Dom}(f^1_{\mathcal{A},A}) = L(\mathcal{M})$ and that $f^1_{\mathcal{A},A}(x) = x$ for every $x \in L(\mathcal{M})$.

5. $\diamond$ Let $\mathcal{A} = (B, P)$ be an lMa, A an alphabet such that $A \subseteq B$, and let R be a regular language on A. Prove that the partial function $g_{\mathcal{A},A,R}$ given by

$$g_{\mathcal{A},A,R}(x) = \begin{cases} f^1_{\mathcal{A},A}(x) & \text{if } x \in R\\ \text{undefined} & \text{otherwise,}\end{cases}$$

for $x \in A^*$ is computable by an lMa.

6. Let $\mathcal{M} = (A, Z, Q, \delta, q_0, z_0, F)$ be a pda. Design an lMa $\mathcal{A} = (A \cup Q \cup Z, P)$ such that $f^1_{\mathcal{A},A}(x)$ is defined and $f^1_{\mathcal{A},A}(x) = \lambda$ if and only if $x \in N(\mathcal{M})$.

Turing Machines

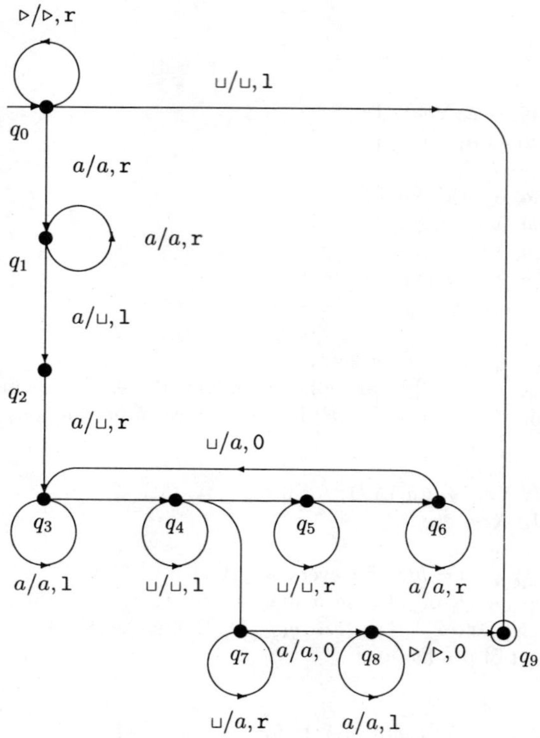

Figure 8.21: The Graph of dTm from Exercise 11

7. Modify the dTm introduced in Example 8.3.12 to work correctly when started on the cell that contains the left marker ▷.
8. Let $\mathcal{M} = (A, Q, \delta, q_0, F)$ be a dTm. How many configurations exist that correspond to a content of the tape of length m?
9. Prove that for every Turing machine $\mathcal{M}$ there is a constant $k_{\mathcal{M}}$ such that at most $k_{\mathcal{M}} + t$ cells are non-blank at any time $t \in \mathbb{N}$.
10. Let A, Q, F be three pairwise disjoint sets such that $|A| = p$, $|Q| = n$, and $|F| = m$. Prove that there are $n(3p(n+m))^{np}$ distinct deterministic Turing machines of the form $\mathcal{M} = (A, Q, \delta, q_0, F)$.
11. Consider the dTm

$$\mathcal{M} = (\{\triangleright, a, \sqcup\}, \{q_0, \ldots, q_{10}\}, \delta, q_0, \{q_9\})$$

whose graph is shown in Figure 8.21. For those transitions not shown on the graph, $\mathcal{M}$ switches to the state q_{10}. Prove that $q_0 \triangleright a^k \star \overset{*}{\underset{\mathcal{M}}{\vdash}} q_9 \triangleright a^{2k} \star$ for every $k \in \mathbb{N}$.

12. Prove that there exists a dTm $\mathcal{M}_n = (A, Q, \delta, q_0, \{q_f\}$ such that $|Q| = n+1$ and

$$q_0 \triangleright \star \overset{*}{\underset{\mathcal{M}_n}{\vdash}} q_f \triangleright a^n \star,$$

where a is a symbol in A.

13. Design a dTm $\mathcal{M}_{\text{shift } 1}$ that shifts a non-blank word one cell to the left by performing the computation

$$\triangleright \sqcup^m q_0 x \star \overset{*}{\underset{\mathcal{M}_{\text{shift } 1}}{\vdash}} \triangleright \sqcup^{m-1} x q \sqcup \star,$$

for $m \geq 1$ and $x \in (A - \{\triangleright, \sqcup\})^*$.

14. Recall that $\ll$ is the lexicographic order on words introduced in Section 2.2. Construct a dTm $\mathcal{M}_{\ll}$ that begins its work in the configuration $q_0 \triangleright x \sqcup y \star$ and ends its work in the configuration $q_f \triangleright 0\star$ if $x \ll y$ and in the configuration $q_f \triangleright 1\star$, otherwise.

15. Construct a dTm $\mathcal{M}$ that shifts cyclically its input. In other words, we have

$$q_0 \triangleright a_{i_0} \cdots a_{i_{n-1}} \star \overset{*}{\underset{\mathcal{M}}{\vdash}} q_f \triangleright a_{i_{n-1}} a_{i_0} \cdots a_{i_{n-2}} \star$$

for every input word $a_{i_0} \cdots a_{i_{n-1}}$.

Systems of Deterministic Turing Machines

16. Design a TMS whose dTm $\mathcal{M}_{\text{left?}B}$ moves its head to the left until it encounters either a symbol of B or the left marker $\triangleright$.

17. $^\diamond$ Let $\beta(n) \in \{0,1\}^*$ be the binary representation of the number $n \in \mathbb{N}$. Using TMSs design a deterministic Turing machines that begin their work with a configuration

$$q_0 \triangleright \beta(p) \sqcup \beta(q) \star,$$

end complete their work in each of the following configurations:
    (a) $q_f \triangleright \beta(p+q)\star$;
    (b) $q_f \triangleright \beta(pq)\star$;
    (c) $q_f \triangleright \beta(p \dot{-} q)\star$.

18. $^\diamond$ Using the dTm $\mathcal{M}_{\ll}$ introduced in Exercise14 construct a TMS that starts with a tape $\triangleright x_0 \sqcup x_1 \sqcup \cdots \sqcup x_n$ and ends in the configuration $q_0 \triangleright 0\star$ if and only if $x_0 \ll x_1 \ll \cdots \ll x_n$.

Church's Thesis

19. Let $A = \{a, b\}$ be an alphabet. For each of the following functions prove that they are Turing-computable by constructing dTms or TMSs:
    (a) $f : A^* \mapsto A^*$, given by $f(x) = x$ if $n_a(x)$ is an even number and undefined otherwise;

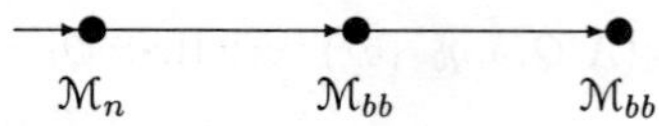

Figure 8.22: The TMS defining the dTm $\mathcal{M}_{bb}$

(b) $g : (A^*)^2 \longrightarrow A^*$, where $g(u, v) = uvu$ for $u, v \in A^*$;

(c) $h : A^* \longrightarrow A^*$, where h is a morphism defined by $h(a) = x$ and $h(b) = y$, for some $x, y \in A^*$.

20. Let $\mathcal{M} = (A, Q, \delta, q_0, \{q_f\})$ be a dTm such that $\{\triangleright, a, \sqcup\} \subseteq A$. The *productivity* of a dTm $\mathcal{M}$ is the number m defined by the computation

$$q_0 \triangleright \star \overset{*}{\underset{\mathcal{M}}{\vdash}} q_f \triangleright a^m \star,$$

if such a computation exists; otherwise, the productivity of $\mathcal{M}$ is 0. Denote by $p(\mathcal{M})$ the productivity of $\mathcal{M}$.
Let $\mathcal{T}_n$ be the class of all dTm of the form

$$\mathcal{M} = (A, Q, \delta, q_0, \{q_f\})$$

such that $\{\triangleright, a, \sqcup\} \subseteq A$ and $|Q| = n$. Define the function $\mathsf{pf} : \mathbb{N} \longrightarrow \mathbb{N}$ by $\mathsf{pf}(n) = \max\{p(\mathcal{M}) \mid \mathcal{M} \in \mathcal{T}_n\}$.

(a) Prove that $\mathsf{pf}(1) = 1$.

(b) Prove that pf is a monotonic function, that is, $n > n'$ implies $\mathsf{pf}(n) > \mathsf{pf}(n')$ for $n, n' \in \mathbb{N}$.

(c) Prove that $\mathsf{pf}(n + 12) \geq 2n$ for $n \in \mathbb{N}$.

21. Prove that the productivity function pf introduced in Exercise 20 is not computable by a dTm (the "busy beaver problem").
Solution. Suppose that pf were computable by a dTm $\mathcal{M}_{bb}$ having k states. Starting from $\mathcal{M}_{bb}$ consider the TMS shown in Figure 8.22, where $\mathcal{M}_n$ is the dTm introduced in Exercise 12. The dTm $\mathcal{M}$ that corresponds to this system has $n + 5 + 2k$ states (since the dTm of a TMS has several extra states) and performs the computation

$$q_0 \triangleright \star \overset{*}{\underset{\mathcal{M}}{\vdash}} q_f \triangleright a^{\mathsf{pf}(\mathsf{pf}(n))} \star .$$

Therefore, $\mathsf{pf}(n + 5 + 2k) \geq \mathsf{pf}(\mathsf{pf}(n))$. The monotonicity of pf implies $n + 5 + 2k \geq \mathsf{pf}(n)$ for $n \in \mathbb{N}$. Replacing n by $n + 12$, by Part (c) of Exercise 20, we obtain $n + 17 + 2k \geq \mathsf{pf}(n + 12) \geq 2n$, so $17 + 2k \geq n$ for $n \in \mathbb{N}$, which is a contradiction. ∎

Recursive Enumerable Languages

22. Let A, B be two alphabets such that $A \subset B$. Prove that the language $B^* - A^*$ is acceptable by a dTm.

23. Let A be an alphabet. Construct a dTm that accepts the set of all words on A that are not palindromes.
24. Prove that the intersection of two languages in $\mathcal{L}_0$ belongs to $\mathcal{L}_0$ by starting from two grammars G_0, G_1 and constructing a grammar G such that $L(G) = L(G_0) \cap L(G_1)$.
25. In Theorem 8.6.23 we proved that the class $\mathcal{L}_0$ is closed under substitution. A similar result was shown for the class $\mathcal{L}_2$ in Theorem 5.6.4 using a simpler construction. Show that this simpler construction will not work for arbitrary grammars.

    Solution. Let $L = \{aa\} \subseteq A^*$, where $A = \{a\}$. Suppose that s is a substitution given by $s(a) = \{b^2\}$, so $K = s(L) = \{b^4\}$. Suppose that L, K are generated by the grammars

    $$\begin{aligned} G &= (\{S\}, A, S, \{S \to a^2\}) \\ G_a &= (\{S_a\}, B, S_a, \{S_a \to b^2, S_aS_a \to b\} \end{aligned}$$

    respectively. The construction applied in Theorem 5.6.4 yields the grammar

    $$G' = (\{S, S_a\}, B, S, \{S \to S_aS_a, S_a \to b^2, S_aS_a \to b\}$$

    and $L(G') = \{b, b^4\} \neq s(L)$. ■
26. Suppose that A, B are two languages such that their symmetric difference $C = A \oplus B$ is recursive. Prove that A is a recursive language if and only if B is a recursive language.

    Does a similar statement hold for recursively enumerable languages? In other words, if C is recursively enumerable is it true that A is recursively enumerable if and only if B is recursively enumerable?
27. $^\diamond$ Prove that the shuffle of two recursively enumerable languages is recursively enumerable.
28. Let $f : A^* \longrightarrow A^*$ be a recursive function. Prove that the language $\{f^{(n)}(x) \mid n \in \mathbb{N}\}$ is recursively enumerable for every $x \in A^*$.
29. $^\diamond$ Let $f : A^* \longrightarrow A^*$ be a partial recursive function and let c be a symbol such that $c \notin A$. Prove that the language $\{xcf(x) \mid x \in \mathrm{Dom}(f)\}$ is recursively enumerable.

A *two-way deterministic finite automaton* (2wdfa) is a dTm $\mathcal{M} = (B, Q, \delta, q_0, F)$ that does not modify the content of its input tape and reads only the nonblank portion of its tape. Formally, this means that $\mathcal{M}$ satisfies the following conditions:

(i) if $\delta(q, a) = (q', a', \mathtt{d})$, then $a = a'$, and

(ii) $\delta(q, \sqcup) = (q', a', \mathtt{d})$ implies $a' = \sqcup$ and $\mathtt{d} = \mathtt{1}$,

for every $q, q' \in Q$ and $a, a' \in A$.

Let $A = B - \{\triangleright, \sqcup\}$. The *language accepted by* $\mathcal{M}$ is the language $L(\mathcal{M})$ given by

$$L(\mathcal{M}) = \{x \in A^* \mid q_0 \triangleright x \star \overset{*}{\underset{\mathcal{M}}{\vdash}} \triangleright xq\sqcup\star\},$$

where q is one of the final states, that is, $q \in F$.

30. $\diamond$ Prove that a language L is accepted by a 2wdfa $\mathcal{M} = (B, Q, \delta, q_0, F)$ if and only if there exists a 2wdfa $\mathcal{M}' = (B, Q', \delta', q_0', \{q_f\})$ such that $L = \{x \in A^* \mid q_0 \rhd x \star \overset{*}{\underset{\mathcal{M}}{\vdash}} q_f \rhd x\star\}$.

31. Let $\mathcal{M} = (A, Q, \delta, q_0, F)$ be a 2wdfa. If $\rhd qx \star \overset{+}{\underset{\mathcal{M}}{\vdash}} \rhd qx\star$, then $\rhd uqx \star \overset{+}{\underset{\mathcal{M}}{\vdash}} \rhd uqx\star$ for every word $u \in A^*$. Is the converse implication true? In other words, does $\rhd uqx \star \overset{+}{\underset{\mathcal{M}}{\vdash}} \rhd uqx\star$ imply $\rhd qx \star \overset{+}{\underset{\mathcal{M}}{\vdash}} \rhd qx\star$.

Suppose that $L = L(\mathcal{M})$, where $\mathcal{M} = (B, Q, \delta, q_0, \{q_f\})$ is a 2wdfa such that $A = B - \{\rhd, \sqcup\}$. Let $\bar{q}$ be a symbol such that $\bar{q} \notin Q$. For $x \in A^*$ define the mapping $t_x : Q \cup \{\bar{q}\} \longrightarrow Q \cup \{\bar{q}\}$ by

$$t_x(q) = \begin{cases} q' & \text{if } \rhd x_1 qa \star \overset{*}{\underset{\mathcal{M}}{\vdash}} \rhd xq'\sqcup\star, \text{ where } x = x_1 a \\ \bar{q} & \text{if no such } q' \text{ exists.} \end{cases}$$

for every $q \in Q$, and

$$t_x(\bar{q}) = \begin{cases} q & \text{if } q_0 \rhd x \star \overset{*}{\underset{\mathcal{M}}{\vdash}} \rhd xq\sqcup\star \\ \bar{q} & \text{if no such } q' \text{ exists.} \end{cases}$$

The mapping t_x is well-defined because, if q' exists, then it is unique.

The equivalence relation $\epsilon_{\mathcal{M}} \subseteq A^* \times A^*$ is defined by

$$\epsilon = \{(\lambda, \lambda)\} \cup \{(x, y) \in A^+ \times A^+ \mid t_x = t_y\}.$$

Define the relation $\overset{+}{\underset{\mathcal{M},min}{\vdash}}$ on $\mathsf{CONFIG}(\mathcal{M})$ by $\mathsf{c} \overset{+}{\underset{\mathcal{M},min}{\vdash}} \mathsf{c}'$ if $\mathsf{c} = \rhd uqv\star$, $\mathsf{c}' = \rhd uq'v\star$ and there is $n \in \mathbb{N}$, with $n > 1$ such that

$$\rhd uqv\star = \rhd u_1 q_1 v_1 \star \underset{\mathcal{M}}{\vdash} \rhd u_2 q_2 v_2 \star \underset{\mathcal{M}}{\vdash} \cdots \underset{\mathcal{M}}{\vdash} \rhd u_n q_n v_n \star = \rhd uq'v\star, \quad (8.2)$$

$u_i v_i = uv$ for $1 \leq i \leq n$, and $u_i \neq u$, $v_i \neq v$ for $1 < i < n$. Thus, if $\rhd uqv \star \overset{+}{\underset{\mathcal{M},min}{\vdash}} \rhd uq'v\star$, then the sequence of configurations shown in (8.2) is a computation that begins and ends at the same place, and it is minimal in that it contains no proper subsequence that ends where this sequence starts. Note that the reading head must move in one direction or the other at the initial step of this computation. If the initial movement of the reading head in this sequence is to the left, then the remaining computation involves only the symbols of u; otherwise, the remaining computation involves only the symbols of v.

32. $^{\circ\circ}$ Let $\mathcal{M} = (B, Q, \delta, q_0, F)$ be a 2wdfa. Prove that if $(x, y) \in \epsilon_{\mathcal{M}}$, then we have $\rhd xqz \star \overset{+}{\underset{\mathcal{M},min}{\vdash}} \rhd xq'z\star$ if and only if $\rhd yqz \star \overset{+}{\underset{\mathcal{M},min}{\vdash}} \rhd yq'z\star$ for every $z \in A^*$ and $q, q' \in Q$.

Solution. If $x = y = \lambda$, the statement is obviously valid. Therefore, assume that $x, y \neq \lambda$, $t_x = t_y$ and $\triangleright xqz \star \overset{+}{\underset{\mathcal{M},min}{\vdash}} \triangleright xq'z\star$, that is

$$\begin{aligned}\triangleright xqz\star &= \triangleright x_0 q_{i_0} z_0 \star \underset{\mathcal{M}}{\vdash} \triangleright x_1 q_{i_1} z_1 \star \\ &\underset{\mathcal{M}}{\vdash} \cdots \underset{\mathcal{M}}{\vdash} \triangleright x_n q_{i_n} z_n \star = \triangleright xq'z\star.\end{aligned}$$

If the first movement of the reading head is to the left, then every x_i is a prefix of x for $1 \leq i \leq n$. If $x = ua$ and $y = vb$, then we have

$$\triangleright xqz\star = \triangleright uaq_{i_0} z_0 \star \underset{\mathcal{M}}{\vdash} \triangleright uq_{i_1} az\star \overset{*}{\underset{\mathcal{M}}{\vdash}} \triangleright uaq'z\star,$$

so $\triangleright uq_{i_1} a\star \overset{*}{\underset{\mathcal{M}}{\vdash}} \triangleright uaq'\sqcup\star$ which implies $t_x(q_{i_1}) = q'$. Thus, $t_y(q_{i_1}) = q'$, so $\triangleright vq_{i_1} b\star \overset{*}{\underset{\mathcal{M}}{\vdash}} \triangleright yq'\sqcup\star$. Also, $\triangleright yqz\star = \triangleright vbqz\star \underset{\mathcal{M}}{\vdash} \triangleright vq_2 bz\star$, because this transition is determined by q and the first symbol of z. Therefore,

$$\triangleright yqz\star = \triangleright vqbz\star \underset{\mathcal{M}}{\vdash} \triangleright vq_{i_1} bz\star \overset{*}{\underset{\mathcal{M},min}{\vdash}} \triangleright yq'z\star.$$

If the first movement of the head is to the right, then we have

$$\triangleright qz\star = \triangleright q_{i_0} z_0 \star \overset{*}{\underset{\mathcal{M},min}{\vdash}} \triangleright q_{i_n} z_n \star = \triangleright q'z\star,$$

so

$$\triangleright yqz\star = \triangleright yq_{i_0} z_0 \star \overset{*}{\underset{\mathcal{M},min}{\vdash}} \triangleright yq_{i_n} z_n \star = \triangleright yq'z\star,$$

which concludes the argument. ■

33. °° Let $\mathcal{M} = (B, Q, \delta, q_0, F)$ be a 2wdfa and let $x, y \in A^*$, where $A = B - \{\triangleright, \star\}$. Prove that if $(x, y) \in \epsilon_{\mathcal{M}}$, then $q_0 \triangleright xz\star \overset{*}{\underset{\mathcal{M}}{\vdash}} \triangleright xqz\star$ if and only if $q_0 \triangleright yz\star \overset{*}{\underset{\mathcal{M}}{\vdash}} \triangleright yqz\star$ for every $z \in A^*$ and $q \in Q$.

Solution. If $x = y = \lambda$, the statement is immediate. Suppose that $x \neq \lambda$, $y \neq \lambda$, $t_x = t_y$, and $q_0 \triangleright xz\star \overset{*}{\underset{\mathcal{M}}{\vdash}} \triangleright xqz\star$. If the reading head does not read any symbol of z, then $q_0 \triangleright x\star \overset{*}{\underset{\mathcal{M}}{\vdash}} \triangleright xq\sqcup\star$ and $t_x(\bar{q}) = q$. Therefore, $t_y(\bar{q}) = q$, which implies $q_0 \triangleright y\star \overset{*}{\underset{\mathcal{M}}{\vdash}} \triangleright yq\sqcup\star$. This, in turn, means that $q_0 \triangleright xz\star \overset{*}{\underset{\mathcal{M}}{\vdash}} \triangleright xqz\star$.

Suppose now that the reading head crosses the boundary into the symbols of z while being in the states $q_{i_1}, \ldots, q_{i_n}$. In other words, we have

$$\begin{aligned}q_0 xz &\overset{*}{\underset{\mathcal{M}}{\vdash}} xq_{i_1} z \overset{*}{\underset{\mathcal{M}}{\vdash}} xq_{i_2} z \overset{*}{\underset{\mathcal{M}}{\vdash}} \cdots \\ &\overset{*}{\underset{\mathcal{M}}{\vdash}} xq_{i_n} z.\end{aligned}$$

Consequently,

$$xq_{i_k}z \overset{*}{\underset{\mathcal{M},min}{\vdash}} xq_{i_{k+1}}z$$

for $1 \leq i \leq n-1$, so $yq_{i_k}z \overset{*}{\underset{\mathcal{M},min}{\vdash}} yq_{i_{k+1}}z$ for $1 \leq i \leq n-1$ by Exercise 32. Since the first time $\mathcal{M}$ crosses into z is when it reaches q_{i_1} we also have

$$q_0 \triangleright x \star \overset{*}{\underset{\mathcal{M}}{\vdash}} \triangleright xq_{i_1} \sqcup\star,$$

so $t_x(\bar{q}) = q_{i_1}$. Therefore, $t_y(\bar{q}) = q_{i_1}$, which implies $q_0 \triangleright y \star \overset{*}{\underset{\mathcal{M}}{\vdash}} \triangleright yq_{i_1}\sqcup\star$ which implies $q_0 \triangleright yz\star \overset{*}{\underset{\mathcal{M}}{\vdash}} \triangleright yq_{i_1}z\star$. This allows us to conclude that

$$q_0 \triangleright yz\star \overset{*}{\underset{\mathcal{M}}{\vdash}} \triangleright yq_{i_1}z\star \overset{*}{\underset{\mathcal{M}}{\vdash}} \triangleright yq_{i_2}z\star \overset{*}{\underset{\mathcal{M}}{\vdash}} \cdots \overset{*}{\underset{\mathcal{M}}{\vdash}} \triangleright yq_{i_n}z\star,$$

so $q_0 \triangleright yz\star \overset{*}{\underset{\mathcal{M}}{\vdash}} \triangleright yqz\star$. The reverse implication can be obtained by interchanging the roles of x and y. ■

34. °° Prove that a language is accepted by a 2wdfa if and only if the language is regular.

Solution. If L is a regular language, then L is accepted by a dfa. Since a dfa can be regarded as a special 2wdfa (whose reading head moves only to the right), it is clear that L is accepted by a 2wdfa.

Conversely, suppose that the language $L \subseteq A^*$ is accepted by the 2wdfa $\mathcal{M} = (B, Q, \delta, q_0, F)$, where $A = B - \{\triangleright, \sqcup\}$. We prove that $(x,y) \in \epsilon_{\mathcal{M}}$ implies $(x,y) \in \nu_L$.

If $x = y = \lambda$, then it is clear that $(x,y) \in \nu_L$.

Suppose that $x \neq \lambda$, $y \neq \lambda$, and $t_x = t_y$. Since $t_x = t_y$, we have either $\mathsf{c} = q_0 \triangleright xz\star \overset{*}{\underset{\mathcal{M}}{\vdash}} \triangleright xq'z\star$ and $\mathsf{c}' = q_0 \triangleright yz\star \overset{*}{\underset{\mathcal{M}}{\vdash}} \triangleright yq'z\star$ for some $q' \in Q$, or no state $p \in Q$ exists such that $q_0 \triangleright xz\star \overset{*}{\underset{\mathcal{M}}{\vdash}} \triangleright xpz\star$ and $\mathsf{c}' = q_0 \triangleright yz\star \overset{*}{\underset{\mathcal{M}}{\vdash}} \triangleright ypz\star$.

If $xz \in L$, then $q_0 \triangleright xz\star \overset{*}{\underset{\mathcal{M}}{\vdash}} \triangleright xzq'\sqcup\star$ for some final state $q' \in F$. Let q be the state entered by the 2wdfa $\mathcal{M}$ the last time it crosses into z. We have $q_0 \triangleright xz\star \overset{*}{\underset{\mathcal{M}}{\vdash}} \triangleright xqz\star \overset{*}{\underset{\mathcal{M}}{\vdash}} \triangleright xzq'\sqcup\star$. This means that $q_0 \triangleright xz\star \overset{*}{\underset{\mathcal{M}}{\vdash}} \triangleright xqz\star$ and $\triangleright xqz \overset{*}{\underset{\mathcal{M}}{\vdash}} \triangleright xzq'\sqcup\star$. The last part of the computation is not influenced by x, so we also have $\triangleright yqz \overset{*}{\underset{\mathcal{M}}{\vdash}} \triangleright yzq'\sqcup\star$.

By Exercise 33 we have $q_0 \triangleright yz\star \overset{*}{\underset{\mathcal{M}}{\vdash}} \triangleright yqz\star$, so $q_0 \triangleright yz\star \overset{*}{\underset{\mathcal{M}}{\vdash}} \triangleright yqz\star \overset{*}{\underset{\mathcal{M}}{\vdash}} \triangleright yzq'\sqcup\star$, which implies $yz \in L$. A symmetric argument shows that $yz \in L$ implies $xz \in L$, so $(x,y) \in \nu_L$.

The previous argument shows that $\epsilon_{\mathcal{M}} \subseteq \nu_L$. Note that all words in a ρ-equivalence class distinct from $[\lambda]_{\epsilon_{\mathcal{M}}}$ define the same mapping t_x. If

$|Q| = n$, then there are $(n+1)^{n+1}$ such mappings, so there are a finite number of $\epsilon_{\mathcal{M}}$-equivalence classes. Since $\epsilon_{\mathcal{M}} \subseteq \nu_L$ we infer that A^*/ν_L is a finite set. Therefore, by Theorem 3.6.7, L is a regular set. ∎

35. Design a 2wdfa that accepts the language $\{0^n 1^m \mid n, m \in \mathbb{N}\}$.
36. ◇ Prove that if $\mathcal{M}$ is a 2wdfa, then there exists a strict 2wdfa $\mathcal{M}_1$ such that $L(\mathcal{M}_1) = L(\mathcal{M})$.

Rice's Theorem

37. Prove that a recursively enumerable language has an infinite number of indices.
38. ◇ Let $\mathsf{L}_x, \mathsf{L}_y \subseteq A^*$ be two recursively enumerable languages. Prove that there exists a primitive recursive function $g : (A^*)^2 \longrightarrow A^*$ such that $\mathsf{L}_x \cap \mathsf{L}_y = \mathsf{L}_{g(x,y)}$.
39. Prove that for every recursively enumerable language $L \subseteq A^*$ there exists a partial recursive function f_{x_0} such that $L = \mathsf{L}_{x_0}$ and $L = \mathrm{Ran}\, \mathsf{f}_{x_0}$.
40. ◇◇ Let $K \subseteq A^*$ be a recursively enumerable language. Prove that the language $\bigcup\{\mathsf{L}_x \mid x \in K\}$ is recursively enumerable language.
Hint. Use a dovetailing argument.
41. ◇◇ Let $K \subseteq A^*$ be a recursively enumerable language. Prove that the language $\bigcap\{\mathsf{L}_x \mid x \in K\}$ is not always recursively enumerable.
42. ◇◇ Let $L, K \subseteq \mathbb{N}$ be two recursively enumerable sets. Prove that there are $L', K' \subseteq \mathbb{N}$ such that both L' and K' are recursively enumerable, $L' \subseteq L$, $K' \subseteq K$, $L' \cup K' = L \cup K$ and $K' \cap L' = \emptyset$.
Using the result obtained above prove a similar statement for recursively enumerable languages over an alphabet A.
43. A language $L \subseteq A^*$ is *productive via the partial recursive function* $f : A^* \mapsto A^*$ if $\mathsf{L}_x \subseteq L$ implies $f(x) \in L - \mathsf{L}_x$. Prove that no productive language is recursively enumerable.
44. A language $L \subseteq A^*$ is *creative* if its complement $A^* - L$ is productive. Prove that every creative language is not recursive.
45. Prove that there is no algorithm to determine whether two recursively enumerable languages are equal.
46. ◇ Let $L, L' \subseteq A^*$ be two languages. L is *reducible* to L' (denoted by $L \preceq L'$) if there exists a partial recursive function $f : A^* \mapsto A^*$ such that $w \in A^*$ if and only if $f(w) \in L'$. Prove that
    (a) if L' is recursive, then L is recursive;
    (b) if L' is recursively enumerable, then so is L.
47. ◇ Prove that the following languages are not recursive:
    (a) $L_{tot} = \{x \in A^* \mid \mathsf{L}_x = A^*\}$;
    (b) $L_{inf} = \{x \in A^* \mid \mathsf{L}_x \text{ is infinite }\}$.
48. Let $\mathsf{H} = \{x \in A^* \mid x \in \mathrm{Dom}(\mathsf{f}_x)\}$ be the recursively enumerable language mentioned in Theorem 8.6.12. Recall that H is not recursive.
Prove that for every recursively enumerable language L we have $L \preceq \mathsf{H}$.
49. Prove that if $L' \preceq L$ and L' is productive, then L is productive.
50. ◇ Let $\mathcal{C}$ be a collection of recursively enumerable languages such that $\emptyset \in \mathcal{C}$ and $\mathcal{C} \subset \mathcal{L}_0$. Prove that the language $I_{\mathcal{C}}$ is not recursively enumerable by

showing that $A^* - \mathsf{H} \preceq I_{\mathcal{C}}$.

51. $^\diamond$ Prove the following generalization of Exercise 50. Let $\mathcal{C}$ be a subclass of $\mathcal{L}_0$ such that there are two recursively enumerable languages L_0, L_1 such that $L_0 \in \mathcal{C}$, $L_1 \notin \mathcal{C}$ and $L_0 \subseteq L_1$. Prove that the language $I_{\mathcal{C}}$ is not recursively enumerable.
52. Applying the result contained in Exercise 51 prove that the languages L_0, L_{fin} defined in Corollary 8.7.8 are not recursively enumerable.
53. $^\diamond$ Let $A = \{a_0, \dots, a_{n-1}\}$ be an alphabet. Prove that there exists a primitive recursive function $f : (A^*)^n \longrightarrow A^*$ such that

$$\mathsf{L}_{f(x_0,\dots,x_{n-1})} = a_0\,\mathsf{L}_{x_0} \cup \cdots a_{n-1}\,\mathsf{L}_{x_{n-1}}$$

for every $(x_0, \dots, x_{n-1}) \in (A^*)^n$.

The Post Correspondence Problem

54. Prove that if $x, y \in I^*$ are two solution of an instance (g, h) such that $x = yz$, then z is also a solution of (g, h).
55. Let A, B be two alphabets and $g, h : A^* \longrightarrow B^*$ be a pair of morphisms. Define the *equalizer of* g, h as the language

$$\mathsf{EQ}(g, h) = \{x \in A^* \mid g(x) = h(x)\}.$$

Prove that the problem "$\mathsf{EQ}(g, h) \in \{\{\lambda\}, \emptyset\}$?" is not decidable.
56. $^\diamond$ Let $A = \{a, b\}$ and let $g, h : A^* \longrightarrow A^*$ be defined by $g(a) = a$, $g(b) = aa$, and $h(a) = aa$, $h(b) = a$. Prove that $\mathsf{EQ}(g, h) = \{x \in A^* \mid n_a(x) = n_b(x)\}$.
57. $^{\diamond\diamond}$ Let A be an alphabet. Prove that for every recursively enumerable language $L \subseteq A^*$ there are two alphabets I, B and three morphisms $f : B^* \longrightarrow A^*$, $g, h : I^* \longrightarrow B^*$ such that $L = f(\mathsf{EQ}(g, h) \cap R)$, where $R \subseteq I^*$ is a regular language.
Solution. Without loss of generality one can assume that L is generated by a grammar whose productions containing terminal symbols have the form $X \to a$. The proof can be obtained by a slight modification of the argument of Theorem 8.8.7. ■
58. $^\diamond$ Prove that for any two morphisms $g, h : A^* \longrightarrow B^*$ there is a language $K \subseteq A^*$ such that $\mathsf{EQ}(g, h) = K^*$.
59. $^\diamond$ Let $I = \{0, 1, 2\}$, $A = \{a, b\}$ and let (g, h) be the instance of the PCP defined by

s	0	1	2
$g(s)$	$aabb$	$aabb$	b
$h(s)$	a	$abba$	$abba$

Prove that $\text{Ran}(g)^+ \cap \text{Ran}(h)^+ = \emptyset$. Can the instance (g, h) of the PCP have a solution?
60. $^{\diamond\diamond}$ Prove that every $(I, \{a\})$-instance of the PCP is decidable.
Solution. Let (g, h) be an $(I, \{a\})$-instance of the PCP. If there is $i \in I$ such that $g(i) = h(i)$, then (g, h) has a solution. Otherwise, a

solution exists if and only if there are $i, j \in I$ such that $|g(i)| \leq |h(i)|$ and $|g(j)| \geq |h(j)|$. Indeed, suppose that there exist two such symbols. Then, the word $w = i^{|g(j)|-|h(j)|} j^{|h(i)|-|g(i)|}$ is a solution because $h(w) = g(w) = a^{|h(i)||g(j)|-|h(j)||g(i)|}$. Conversely, suppose that the PCP (g, h) has a solution and that $g(i) \neq h(i)$ for $i \in I$. If $|g(i)| < |h(i)|$ for every $i \in I$, or if $|g(i)| > |h(i)|$ for every $i \in I$, then it is clear that no solution exists. Thus, there exist $i, j \in I$ such that $|g(i)| \leq |h(i)|$ and $|g(j)| \geq |h(j)|$. ■

61. °° Let $k \in \mathbb{N}$ and let $g, h : A^* \longrightarrow B^*$ be two morphisms. Define the language

$$\mathsf{EQ}_k(g, h) = \{x \in \mathsf{EQ}(g, h) \mid ||g(y)| - |h(y)|| \leq k \text{ for } y \in \mathsf{PREF}(x)\}.$$

Prove that for every $k \in \mathbb{N}$ the language $\mathsf{EQ}_k(g, h)$ is regular.
Solution. If any two morphisms g, h we have either $\mathsf{EQ}_0(g, h) = \{\lambda\}$, or $\mathsf{EQ}_k(g, h) = \{a \in A \mid |h(a)| = |g(a)|\}^*$. Thus, for $k = 0$, $\mathsf{EQ}_k(g, h)$ is regular.
Suppose that $k \geq 1$ and define the dfa $\mathcal{M} = (A, Q, \delta, q_\lambda, \{q_\lambda\})$, where

$$Q = \{q_\lambda, r\} \cup \{q_{+x}, q_{-x} \mid x \in A^+ \text{ and } |x| \leq k\}$$

and the transition function is given by the following table:

State q	Condition	Next State $\delta(q, a)$
q_λ	$g(a) = h(a)$	q_λ
	$g(a) = h(a)x$	q_{+x}
	$h(a) = g(a)x$	q_{-x}
q_{+x}	$h(a) = xg(a)$	q_λ
	$xg(a) = h(a)y$	q_{+y}
	$h(a) = xg(a)y$	q_{-y}
q_{-x}	$g(a) = xh(a)$	q_λ
	$g(a) = xh(a)y$	q_{+y}
	$g(a)y = xh(a)$	q_{-y}

for $x, y \in A^+$, $|x| \leq k$, and $|y| \leq k$. If $\delta(q, a)$ does not occur in this table, then $\delta(q, a) = r$.
We have $\delta^*(q_\lambda, w) = q_{+x}$ if $g(w) = h(w)x$ and $\delta^*(q_\lambda, w) = q_{-x}$ if $h(w) = q(w)x$ for some $x \in A^*$ such that $|x| \leq k$, as the reader can easily verify by induction on $|w|$. Thus, $\mathcal{M}$ reaches q_λ if and only if $g(w) = h(w)$. ■

62. °° Let (g, h) be an (I, A)-instance of the PCP, and let $f : A^* \longrightarrow B^*$ be a morphism.
   (a) Prove that every solution of (g, h) is also a solution of the (I, B)-instance (fg, fh).
   (b) Prove that if f is injective, then the set of solutions of (g, h) and (fg, fh) are equal.
   (c) Use Part (b) to prove that if B is a two-symbol alphabet, then the PCP restricted to (I, B)-instances is undecidable.

63. °° Let A be an alphabet, $(M_{3\times 3}, \cdot, I_3)$ be the monoid of (3×3)-matrices having real entries, and let $h : A^* \times A^* \longrightarrow M_{3\times 3}$ be the mapping defined by

$$h(u,v) = \begin{pmatrix} |A|^{|u|} & |A|^{|v|-|u|} & 0 \\ 0 & |A|^{|v|} & 0 \\ \phi_A(u) & \phi_A(v) - \phi_A(u) & 1 \end{pmatrix}$$

(a) Prove that h is a morphism between the monoids $(A^* \times A^*, \cdot, (\lambda, \lambda))$ and $(M_{3\times 3}, \cdot, I_3)$. In other words, prove that

$$h(\lambda, \lambda) = I_3$$
$$h(u,v)h(u',v') = h(uu', vv'),$$

for every $u, u', v, v' \in A^*$.

(b) A finite set of (3×3)-matrices M is said to be (i,j)-mortal if there is a product of matrices of M, $P = M_{i_0} M_{i_1} \cdots M_{i_{n-1}}$ such that $P_{ij} = 0$. Starting from the PCP prove that (i,j)-mortality of a set of matrices is undecidable.

64. °° Let (g,h) be an (I,A)-instance of the PCP, and let c be a symbol such that $c \notin I \cup A$. Define the languages K_g, K_h by

$$K_g = \{xcg(x^R) \mid x \in I^+\}$$
$$K_h = \{xch(x^R) \mid x \in I^+\}.$$

Prove that the following conditions are equivalent:

(a) $K_g \cap K_h \neq \emptyset$;

(b) $\mathsf{EQ}(g,h) \neq \{\lambda\}$ and $\mathsf{EQ}(g,h) \neq \emptyset$.

(c) $(L - K_g) \cup (L - K_h) = L$ for $L = I^*cA^*$.

Solution. We prove here the equivalence between the first two statements. Suppose that $K_g \cap K_h \neq \emptyset$. Then, there is $xcz \in K_g \cap K_g$, which means that $x \neq \lambda$ and $z = g(x^R) = h(x^R)$. This in turn, implies $g(x) = h(x)$, so $\mathsf{EQ}(g,h) \neq \{\lambda\}$ and $\mathsf{EQ}(g,h) \neq \emptyset$.
Conversely, suppose that $\mathsf{EQ}(g,h) \neq \{\lambda\}$ and $\mathsf{EQ}(g,h) \neq \emptyset$. There is $x \neq \lambda$ such that $g(x) = h(x)$, which implies immediately $g(x^R) = h(x^R)$. Thus, $xcg(x^R) = xch(x^R) \in K_g \cap K_h$. Consequently, $K_g \cap K_h \neq \emptyset$. ∎

65. °° Let $L = I^*cA^*$, and let K_g, K_h be defined as in Exercise 64.

(a) Prove that the language $(L - K_g) \cup (L - K_h)$ is generated by the context-free grammar $G = (\{S_0, \ldots, S_4, X, Y\}, I \cup A \cup \{c\}, S, P)$, where P consists of the following productions

$$S_0 \to X, S_0 \to Y, S_0 \to c, S_0 \to S_4$$
$$X \to iXg(i), X \to S_3a, X \to iS_1w$$
$$\text{for } w \in A^* \text{ such that } |w| < |g(i)|$$
$$Y \to iYh(i), Y \to S_3a, Y \to iS_1w$$
$$\text{for } w \in A^* \text{ such that } |w| < |h(i)|$$
$$X \to iS_2w, \text{ where } w \in A^{|g(i)|} - \{g(i)\}$$
$$Y \to iS_2w, \text{ where } w \in A^{|h(i)|} - \{g(i)\}$$
$$S_1 \to iS_1, S_1 \to c,$$
$$S_2 \to iS_2, S_2 \to S_3,$$
$$S_3 \to S_3a, S_3 \to c,$$
$$S_4 \to iS_4, S_4 \to S_4a$$

(b) Prove that $L = L(G')$, where $G' = (\{S_0, \ldots, S_4, X, Y\}, I \cup A \cup \{c\}, S, P')$, where P' is obtained from P by replacing $S_1 \to c$ and $S_3 \to c$ by $S_4 \to c$.

(c) Let $B = \{S_0, \ldots, S_4, X, Y\} \cup I \cup A \cup \{c\}$. Prove that S_4 is not a productive symbol in G and S_1, S_3 are not productive symbols in G'. Conclude that

$$\{u \in B^* - (I \cup A \cup \{c\})^* \mid S_0 \overset{*}{\underset{G}{\Rightarrow}} u\} =$$
$$\{u \in B^* - (I \cup A \cup \{c\})^* \mid S_0 \overset{*}{\underset{G'}{\Rightarrow}} u\}.$$

(d) Prove that it is undecidable if the sets of sentential forms of two context-free grammars are equal.

66. °° Let A be an alphabet, $c \notin A$, and let $L_0 = \{ucvcwct \mid u, v, w, t \in A^*, u = t^R, v = w^R\}$ be the context-free language on $A \cup \{c\}$ introduced in Exercise 34 of Chapter 5.
In Exercise 64 we defined the languages $K_g, K_h \subseteq (A \cup \{c\})^*$, where (g, h) is an (I, A)-instance of the PCP.
(a) Prove that $H = K_g c (K_h)^R \cap L_0 \neq \emptyset$ if and only if the (g, h) has a solution.
(b) Prove that H is infinite if and only if it is not empty.
(c) Prove that H does not contain any infinite context-free language by using the Pumping Lemma.
(d) Prove that H is either empty or is an infinite, non-context-free language.

67. ° Starting from Exercise 66 prove that it is undecidable whether the intersection of two context-free languages is a context-free language.

68. ° Using Exercise 13 of Chapter 6 give another proof that the problem of the nonemptyness of the intersection of the languages generated by two context-free grammars G, G' is undecidable.

69. ° Let $\mathcal{M} = (A, Q, \delta, q_0, F)$ be a dTm. Show that it is undecidable whether $L(\mathcal{M}) = \emptyset$.

70. ° Prove that if is undecidable whether for a context-free grammar $G = (A_N, A_T, S, P)$ we have $L(G) = A_T^*$.
Solution. Suppose that the problem "$L(G) = A_T^*$?" were decidable for a context-free grammar. Then, if G is an arbitrary grammar, we could decide whether the language $\overline{D(G)}$ defined by second part of Exercise 13 of Chapter 6 equals the set $(A \cup \{\#\})^*$ because this language is context-free. This happens if and only if $D(G) = \emptyset$, which is, in turn, equivalent to $L(G) = \emptyset$. Since the emptyness of languages generated by arbitrary grammars is undecidable, it follows that it is undecidable if the language generated by a context-free grammar equals the language of all words of its terminal alphabet. ∎

71. °° Let $\mathcal{L}$ be a class of language such that for every language $L \in \mathcal{L}$ and $R \in \mathcal{L}_3$ we have $LR, RL \in \mathcal{L}$ and $L \cup R \in \mathcal{L}$. Suppose that the problem "$L = A^*$?" for $L \subseteq A^*$ is undecidable for the languages of $\mathcal{L}$ and for sufficiently large alphabets A.

If $\mathcal{K}$ is a class of languages such that $\mathcal{C} - \mathcal{K} \neq \emptyset$, $\mathcal{L}_3 \subseteq \mathcal{K}$ and $Kx{-}1 \in \mathcal{K}$ for every $K \in \mathcal{K}$, then prove that the problem "$L \in \mathcal{K}$?" is undecidable for the languages of $\mathcal{L}$.

Solution. Suppose that $L_0 \subseteq A^*$ is a language in $\mathcal{L} - \mathcal{K}$ such that A is sufficiently large and the problem "$L = A^*$?" is undecidable. Let c be a symbol such that $c \notin A$ and let $L_1 = L_0cA^* \cup A^*cL$.

If $L = A^*$, then $L_1 = A^*cA^* \in \mathcal{K}$, since $\mathcal{L}_3 \subseteq \mathcal{K}$. If $L \neq A^*$, then there is $x \in A^* - L$, so $L_1(cx)^{-1} = L_0 \notin \mathcal{K}$. Therefore, we have $L = A^*$ if and only if $L_1 \in \mathcal{K}$. If the problem "$L \in \mathcal{K}$?" were decidable for languages of $\mathcal{C}$ we would be able to decide "$L = A^*$?". ■

72. $^\diamond$ Prove that it is undecidable whether a context-free language is regular by applying the results contained in Exercises 71 and 70.
73. $^{\diamond\diamond\diamond}$ Prove that for every recursively enumerable language $L \subseteq B^*$ there is an alphabet A and two morphisms $h, g : A^* \longrightarrow B^*$ such that

$$L = \{x \in B^* \mid x = h(w)^{-1}g(w) \text{ for some } w \in A^*\}.$$

74. $^{\diamond\diamond}$ An (I, A, B)*-instance of the Extended Post Correspondence Problem* (EPCP) is a triple of morphisms $T = (g, h, f)$, where $g : I^* \longrightarrow A^*$, $h : I^* \longrightarrow A^*$, $f : B^* \longrightarrow A^*$ and $h(i) \neq \lambda$, $g(i) \neq \lambda$ for $i \in I$. The language defined by this instance is

$$L_T = \{w \in B^* \mid g(x) = h(x)f(w) \text{ for some } x \in I^*\}.$$

Prove that for every recursive enumerable language there is an instance T of EPCP such that $L = L_T$.

Hint. This is a consequence of the result contained by Exercise 73.
75. $^{\diamond\diamond\diamond}$ Prove that every recursively enumerable language is generated by a grammar having five nonterminal symbols such that all of its productions are context-free, of the form $S \rightarrow \alpha$, where S is the start symbol of the grammar, except two productions $XY \rightarrow \lambda$ and $UV \rightarrow \lambda$.
76. $^{\diamond\diamond\diamond}$ Prove that every recursively enumerable language is generated by a grammar having four nonterminal symbols such that all of its productions are context-free, of the form $S \rightarrow \alpha$, where S is the start symbol of the grammar, except two productions $XY \rightarrow \lambda$ and $UU \rightarrow \lambda$.

Multitape Turing Machines

77. $^\diamond$ Design a two-tape dTm that accepts the language of palindromes.

Let $\mathcal{M} = (B, Q, \delta, q_0, \{q_f\})$ be a k-tape dTm and let $x \in L_A(\mathcal{M})$.

$$q_0 \triangleright x \star \underbrace{q \triangleright \star \cdots q \triangleright \star}_{k-1} \overset{n}{\underset{\mathcal{M}}{\vdash}} q_f \triangleright u \star u_1 q a_{l_1} v_1 \star \cdots u_{k-1} q a_{l_{k-1}} v_{k-1} \star,$$

then *the time required by* $\mathcal{M}$ *on* x is $t_{\mathcal{M}}(x) = n$.

78. $^{\diamond\diamond}$ Prove that if $\mathcal{M}'$ is the one-tape dTm constructed as in Theorem 8.9.7, then there is a number $k \in \mathbb{N}$ such that $t_{\mathcal{M}'}(x) \leq k(t_{\mathcal{M}}(x))^2$ for $x \in L_A(\mathcal{M})$.
79. $^{\diamond}$ Design a multitape dTm $\mathcal{M}$ that accepts the language $\{x \in \{a,b,c\}^* \mid n_a(x) = n_b(x) = n_c(x)\}$.

Nondeterminstic Turing Machines

80. Construct a ndTm that accepts the language

$$\{ab^{n_0}ab^{n_1}a\cdots ab^{n_{p-1}a\,|\,p\geq 1, n_i=n_{i+1}} \text{ for some } {}_{i, 1\leq i\leq p-2}\}.$$

Construct also a dTm that accepts the same language.
81. $^{\diamond}$ Extend the notion of function computable by a dTm to the notion of function computable by a ndTm. Give an example of a function that can be computed more efficiently by an ndTm.
82. $^{\diamond}$ Let L, L' be two languages that are accepted by the dTms $\mathcal{M}$ and $\mathcal{M}'$, respectively.
    (a) Starting from $\mathcal{M}, \mathcal{M}'$ construct a TMS that accepts the language $\mathsf{shuffle}(L, L')$.
    (b) Construct an NTMS that accepts the language $\mathsf{shuffle}(L, L')$.

8.12 Bibliographical Comments

Our treatment of labeled Markov algorithms was inspired by the concept of programmed grammar introduced by D. Rosenkrantz in [1969] and, especially, by approach of Brainerd and Landweber (see [1974]). Turing machine systems were introduced in [Hermes, 1965] as "combinations" of Turing machines.

Theorem 8.6.21 was obtained in [Ginsburg *et al.*, 1967].

Exercise 61 is from [Rozenberg and Salomaa, 1980]. The result contained in Exercise 71 was obtained by S. Greibach in [1968].

The Post Correspondence Problem was formulated in [Post, 1946]. The representation of recursive enumerable languages by quotients of morphisms contained in Exercise 73 was obtained by V. Geffert [1988]. The notion of extended PCP was introduced by the same author in [Geffert, 1991] and was used in the same paper to obtain the normal forms described in Exercises 75 and 76.

Chapter 9

Context-Sensitive Languages

9.1 Introduction

The class of context-sensitive languages has several alternative definitions: as the $\mathcal{L}_1$ class of Chomsky's hierarchy, as the class of languages that can be generated by length-increasing grammars, and (as we prove in Section 9.2) as the class of languages that can be recognized by a special class of nondeterministic Turing machines known as linear-bounded automata. We proved (in Section 4.4) that this class is closed with respect reversal, union, product, and Kleene closure, and we will examine other closure properties of $\mathcal{L}_1$ in Section 9.3. Finally, we will examine normal forms for context-sensitive grammars and the relationships between $\mathcal{L}_1$ and other classes of Chomsky's hierarchy.

9.2 Linear Bounded Automata

Linear bounded automata are nondeterministic Turing machines that use only that portion of the tape originally occupied by the input word. They offer a machine-based characterization of context-sensitive languages.

Definition 9.2.1 A *linear bounded automaton* (lba) is a nondeterministic Turing machine $\mathcal{M} = (B, Q, \delta, q_0, F)$ that satisfies the following conditions:

(i) the input alphabet includes a *right marker* $\triangleleft$;

(ii) if $(q', a', \mathtt{d}) \in \delta(q, \triangleleft)$, then $a' = \triangleleft$ and $\mathtt{d} \in \{\mathtt{0}, \mathtt{r}\}$.

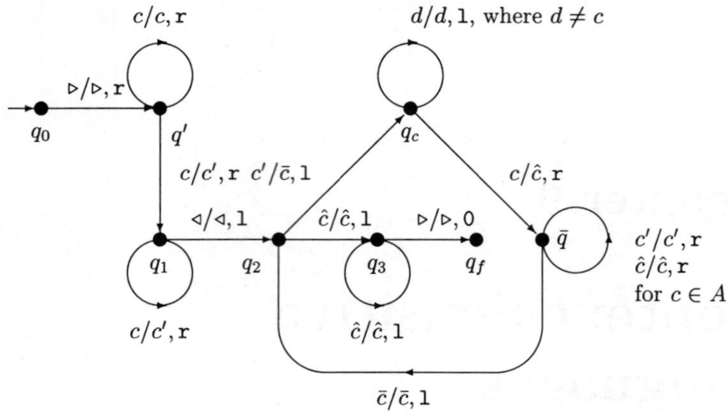

Figure 9.1: Graph of the lba $\mathcal{M}$

□

Definition 9.2.1 implies that the right marker of an lba (like the left marker ▷) cannot be modified; also, the read/write head of the tape cannot move to any cell to the right of the cell that contains ◁.

Every configuration of an lba has the form $\mathsf{c} = \triangleright uqv \triangleleft \star$, so it always ends with the symbols $\triangleleft\star$. Therefore, to simplify the notation, we will simply write c as $\triangleright uqv\triangleleft$.

Definition 9.2.2 Let $\mathcal{M} = (B, Q, \delta, q_0, F)$ be an lba and let A be an alphabet $A \subseteq B$ such that $A \cap \{\triangleright, \triangleleft, \sqcup\} = \emptyset$. The *language* $L_A(\mathcal{M})$ *accepted by* $\mathcal{M}$ is defined by

$$L_A(\mathcal{M}) = \{x \in A^* \mid q_0 \triangleright x \triangleleft \overset{*}{\underset{\mathcal{M}}{\vdash}} q \triangleright w \triangleleft \text{ for some } w \in B^* \text{ and } q \in F\}.$$

□

Example 9.2.3 Let $A = \{a, b\}$ and let $\mathcal{M} = (B, Q, \delta, q_0, \{q_f\})$ be an lba such that

$$B = \{a, b, \bar{a}, \bar{b}, \hat{a}, \hat{b}, \triangleright, \triangleleft, \sqcup\}$$
$$Q = \{q_0, \ldots, q_3\} \cup \{q', \bar{q}, q_a, q_b\}.$$

Denote by $\bar{A}$ and $\hat{A}$ the alphabets $\bar{A} = \{\bar{a}, \bar{b}\}$ and $\hat{A} = \{\hat{a}, \hat{b}\}$. The transition function δ is given by the graph shown in Figure 9.1. For the transitions not shown in the graph we have $\delta(q, a) = \emptyset$.

We claim that

$$L_A(\mathcal{M}) = \{w \in A^* \mid w = uu \text{ for some } u \in A^+\}.$$

A typical computation of $\mathcal{M}$ begins with a configuration $q_0 \triangleright w\triangleleft$ (recall that we omit $\star$), and continues with

$$q_0 \triangleright w \triangleleft \underset{\mathcal{M}}{\vdash} \triangleright q'w \triangleleft \overset{*}{\underset{\mathcal{M}}{\vdash}} \triangleright w_1 q' w_2 \triangleleft,$$

where $w = w_1 w_2$. Somewhere in the computation, q' may switch to the state q_1 and reach the configuration $\rhd u q_1 v \lhd$. From that point all symbols of v are converted to prime versions, so we have $q_0 \rhd w \lhd \overset{*}{\underset{\mathcal{M}}{\vdash}} \rhd uv' q_1 \lhd$. If $w \in L$ and $\mathcal{M}$ guessed correctly, then $v = u$ and we have the configuration $\rhd uu' q_1 \lhd$. Suppose that $u = a_0 \ldots a_{n-1} \in \{a, b\}^*$. The computation continues with

$$\begin{aligned}
&\rhd a_0 \cdots a_{n-1} a'_0 \cdots q_2 a'_{n-1} \lhd \underset{\mathcal{M}}{\vdash} \\
&\rhd a_0 \cdots a_{n-1} a'_0 \cdots q_{a_{n-1}} a'_{n-2} \bar{a}_{n-1} \lhd \overset{*}{\underset{\mathcal{M}}{\vdash}} \\
&\rhd a_0 \cdots q_{a_{n-1}} a_{n-1} a'_0 \cdots a'_{n-2} \bar{a}_{n-1} \lhd \underset{\mathcal{M}}{\vdash} \\
&\rhd a_0 \cdots a_{n-2} \hat{a}_{n-1} \bar{q} a'_0 \cdots a'_{n-2} \bar{a}_{n-1} \lhd \overset{*}{\underset{\mathcal{M}}{\vdash}} \\
&\rhd a_0 \cdots a_{n-2} \hat{a}_{n-1} a'_0 \cdots a'_{n-2} \bar{q} \bar{a}_{n-1} \lhd \underset{\mathcal{M}}{\vdash} \\
&\rhd a_0 \cdots a_{n-2} \hat{a}_{n-1} a'_0 \cdots q_2 a'_{n-2} \bar{a}_{n-1} \lhd \underset{\mathcal{M}}{\vdash} \\
&\rhd a_0 \cdots a_{n-2} \hat{a}_{n-1} a'_0 \cdots q_{a_{n-2}} a'_{n-3} \bar{a}_{n-2} \bar{a}_{n-1} \lhd \overset{*}{\underset{\mathcal{M}}{\vdash}} \cdots
\end{aligned}$$

Eventually, if the machine guessed right when it entered state q_1, then the configuration

$$\rhd \hat{a}_0 \bar{q} \cdots \hat{a}_{n-1} \bar{a}_0 \cdots \bar{a}_{n-1} \lhd$$

will be reached. Then, $\mathcal{M}$ continues as follows:

$$\begin{aligned}
&\rhd \hat{a}_0 \bar{q} \cdots \hat{a}_{n-1} \bar{a}_0 \cdots \bar{a}_{n-1} \lhd \overset{*}{\underset{\mathcal{M}}{\vdash}} \rhd \hat{a}_0 \cdots \hat{a}_{n-1} \bar{q} \bar{a}_0 \cdots \bar{a}_{n-1} \lhd \\
&\underset{\mathcal{M}}{\vdash} \rhd \hat{a}_0 \cdots q_2 \hat{a}_{n-1} \bar{a}_0 \cdots \bar{a}_{n-1} \lhd \overset{*}{\underset{\mathcal{M}}{\vdash}} q_3 \rhd \hat{a}_0 \cdots \hat{a}_{n-1} \bar{a}_0 \cdots \bar{a}_{n-1} \lhd \\
&\underset{\mathcal{M}}{\vdash} q_f \rhd \hat{a}_0 \cdots \hat{a}_{n-1} \bar{a}_0 \cdots \bar{a}_{n-1} \lhd
\end{aligned}$$

If, on the other hand, $\mathcal{M}$ did not make the right guess, or if the first part of w does not match the second, it will impossible for $\mathcal{M}$ to reach the final state q_f. Thus, $L_A(\mathcal{M})$ consists of those words $w \in \{a, b\}^*$ that have the form uu for some $u \in A^*$.

For instance, the accepting computation for the word $abaaba$ is

$$\begin{aligned}
&q_0 \rhd abaaba \lhd \overset{*}{\underset{\mathcal{M}}{\vdash}} \rhd abaq'aba \lhd \overset{*}{\underset{\mathcal{M}}{\vdash}} \rhd abaa'q_1 ba \lhd \\
&\underset{\mathcal{M}}{\vdash} \rhd abaa'b'a'q_1 \lhd \underset{\mathcal{M}}{\vdash} \rhd abaa'b'q_2 a' \lhd \underset{\mathcal{M}}{\vdash} \rhd abaa'q_a b'\bar{a} \lhd \\
&\underset{\mathcal{M}}{\vdash} \rhd abaq_a a'b'\bar{a} \lhd \underset{\mathcal{M}}{\vdash} \rhd abq_a aa'b'\bar{a} \lhd \underset{\mathcal{M}}{\vdash} \rhd ab\hat{a}\bar{q}a'b'\bar{a} \lhd \\
&\overset{*}{\underset{\mathcal{M}}{\vdash}} \rhd ab\hat{a}a'b'\bar{q}\bar{a} \lhd \underset{\mathcal{M}}{\vdash} \rhd ab\hat{a}a'q_2 b'\bar{a} \lhd \underset{\mathcal{M}}{\vdash} \rhd ab\hat{a}q_b a'\bar{b}\bar{a} \lhd \\
&\overset{*}{\underset{\mathcal{M}}{\vdash}} \rhd aq_b b\hat{a}a'\bar{b}\bar{a} \lhd \underset{\mathcal{M}}{\vdash} \rhd a\hat{b}\bar{q}\hat{a}a'\bar{b}\bar{a} \lhd \overset{*}{\underset{\mathcal{M}}{\vdash}} \rhd a\hat{b}\hat{a}a'\bar{q}\bar{b}\bar{a} \lhd \\
&\underset{\mathcal{M}}{\vdash} \rhd a\hat{b}\hat{a}q_2 a'\bar{b}\bar{a} \lhd \underset{\mathcal{M}}{\vdash} \rhd a\hat{b}q_a \hat{a}\bar{a}\bar{b}\bar{a} \lhd \overset{*}{\underset{\mathcal{M}}{\vdash}} \rhd q_a a\hat{b}\hat{a}\bar{a}\bar{b}\bar{a} \lhd \\
&\underset{\mathcal{M}}{\vdash} \rhd \hat{a}\bar{q}\hat{b}\hat{a}\bar{a}\bar{b}\bar{a} \lhd \underset{\mathcal{M}}{\vdash} \rhd \hat{a}\hat{b}\hat{a}\bar{q}\bar{a}\bar{b}\bar{a} \lhd \underset{\mathcal{M}}{\vdash} \rhd \hat{a}\hat{b}q_2 \hat{a}\bar{a}\bar{b}\bar{a} \lhd \\
&\underset{\mathcal{M}}{\vdash} \rhd \hat{a}q_3 \hat{b}\hat{a}\bar{a}\bar{b}\bar{a} \lhd \overset{*}{\underset{\mathcal{M}}{\vdash}} q_3 \rhd \hat{a}\hat{b}\hat{a}\bar{a}\bar{b}\bar{a} \lhd \underset{\mathcal{M}}{\vdash} q_f \rhd \hat{a}\hat{b}\hat{a}\bar{a}\bar{b}\bar{a} \lhd .
\end{aligned}$$

□

Theorem 9.2.4 *Let $\mathcal{M} = (B, Q, \delta, q_0, F)$ be an lba, and let A be an alphabet such that $A \subseteq B$. The language $L_A(\mathcal{M})$ is context-sensitive.*

Proof. The proof is similar to the proof of Theorem 8.6.17, suitably modified to take into account the nondeterminism of $\mathcal{M}$ and the necessity of using length-increasing productions. Suppose initially that $\lambda \notin L_A(\mathcal{M})$.

Consider a finite set U that consists of symbols $U_{b,w}$, where $b \in B$ and $w \in (B \cup Q)^*$ and $|w| \leq 4$. Denote by U_l and U_r the sets

$$\begin{aligned} U_l &= \{U_{a,q\triangleright a} \mid a \in B\} \cup \{U_{a,\triangleright a} \mid a \in A\} \cup \{U_{a,q_0\triangleright a\triangleleft} \mid a \in A\} \\ U_r &= \{U_{a,aq\triangleleft} \mid a \in B\} \cup \{U_{a,a\triangleleft} \mid a \in A\} \cup \{U_{a,q_0\triangleright a\triangleleft} \mid a \in A\}. \end{aligned}$$

Starting from U we construct a length-increasing grammar $G = (\{S, X\} \cup U, A, S, P)$; the set of productions P is defined below.

Suppose that the tape of $\mathcal{M}$ is the initial configuration $q_0 \triangleright x\triangleleft$, where $x = a_0 a_1 \cdots a_{n-1}$. This configuration is represented in the derivation by the word

$$U_{a_0,q_0\triangleright a_0} U_{a_1,a_1} \cdots U_{a_{n-1},a_{n-1}\triangleleft}$$

While leaving unmodified the first subscript of each symbol U, the grammar simulates the work of $\mathcal{M}$ by altering the second subscripts of the symbols U. Observe that the length of the word remains the same for the duration of this simulation. Eventually, assuming that $\mathcal{M}$ reaches a final configuration $q \triangleright w\triangleleft$, the grammar produces the word

$$U_{a_0,q\triangleright b_0} U_{a_1,b_1} \cdots U_{a_{n-1},b_{n-1}\triangleleft}$$

Finally, each symbol $U_{a,w}$ is replaced by a for $a \in A$.

If the initial word consists of one symbol, $\mathcal{M}$ starts with the configuration $q_0 \triangleright a\triangleleft$ and the grammar starts with $U_{a,q_0\triangleright a\triangleleft}$. Thus, we need to consider the following sets of productions for the grammar:

(i) The initialization set consists of the following productions:

$$\begin{aligned} &S \to U_{a,q_0\triangleright a\triangleleft} \\ &S \to U_{a,q_0\triangleright a} X \\ &X \to U_{a,a} X \\ &X \to U_{a,a\triangleleft} \end{aligned}$$

for every $a \in A$.

(ii) The simulation set consists of several rules, depending on the direction of the movement of the read/write head of the lba.

- If $(\bar{q}, \bar{b}, \mathtt{r}) \in \delta(q, b)$, then $b \neq \triangleleft$; in this case include the production $U_{a,qb} \to U_{a,\bar{b}\bar{q}}$ for every $a \in A$.
- If $(\bar{q}, \bar{b}, \mathtt{l}) \in \delta(q, b)$, then $b \neq \triangleright$; in this case include the productions $U_{a'b'} U_{a,qb} \to U_{a',\bar{q}b'} U_{a\bar{b}}$ for every $a, a' \in A$, and $b' \in B$.
- If $(\bar{q}, \bar{b}, \mathtt{0}) \in \delta(q, b)$, then include the production $U_{a,qb} \to U_{a,\bar{q}\bar{b}}$ for every $a \in A$.

(iii) The set of final productions includes:

$U_{\triangleright,q\triangleright a} \to a$ for $a \in A$ and $q \in F$;
$U_{\triangleright,q\triangleright a\triangleleft} \to a$ for $a \in A$ and $q \in F$;
$aU_{a',w} \to aa'$ for $a, a' \in A, w \in B^*$ and $|w| \leq 3$.

Define the morphisms $h_0, h_1 : U^* \longrightarrow (Q \cup B)^*$ by $h_0(U_{b,w}) = b$ and $h_1(U_{b,w}) = w$ for every $U_{b,w} \in U$. We claim that if $\mathcal{M}$ can reach the configuration $\mathsf{c} = \triangleright a_{i_0} a_{i_1} \cdots a_{i_{k-1}} q a_{i_k} \cdots a_{i_{n-1}} \triangleleft$ starting from the initial configuration $\mathsf{c}_0 = q_0 \triangleright a_0 a_1 \cdots a_{n-1} \triangleleft$, then there is a derivation $S \overset{*}{\underset{G}{\Rightarrow}} \alpha \in U_l U^* U_r$ such that $h_0(\alpha) = a_0 a_1 \cdots a_{n-1}$ and $h_1(\alpha) = \mathsf{c}$.

The argument is by induction on the length p of the computation that leads to c. For the basis case, $p = 0$, we have $\mathsf{c} = \mathsf{c}_0$, where $\mathsf{c}_0 = q_0 \triangleright a_0 a_1 \cdots a_{n-1} \triangleleft$ is the initial configuration. In the grammar G we can write

$$\begin{aligned} S &\Rightarrow U_{a_0, q_0 \triangleright a_0} X \Rightarrow U_{a_0, q_0 \triangleright a_0} U_{a_1, a_1} X \Rightarrow \cdots \\ &\Rightarrow U_{a_0, q_0 \triangleright a_0} U_{a_1, a_1} \cdots U_{a_{n-1}, a_{n-1} \triangleleft} = \alpha \end{aligned}$$

It is immediate that $h_0(\alpha)$ and $h_1(\alpha)$ satisfy our claim.

Suppose now that the statement holds for computations of length less than p and let $\mathsf{c}_0 \overset{p-1}{\underset{\mathcal{M}}{\vdash}} \mathsf{c}' \underset{\mathcal{M}}{\vdash} \mathsf{c}$ be a computation of length p. If

$$\mathsf{c}' = \triangleright b_{j_0} \cdots b_{j_{k-1}} q' b_{j_k} \cdots b_{j_{n-1}} \triangleleft,$$

then by the inductive hypothesis there is a derivation $S \overset{*}{\underset{G}{\Rightarrow}} \beta' \in U^*$ such that $\beta' \in U_l U^* U_r$, $h_0(\beta') = a_0 \cdots a_{n-1}$ and $h_1(\beta') = \mathsf{c}'$, which means that

$$\beta' = U_{a_0, \triangleright b_{j_0}} \cdots U_{a_k, q' b_{j_k}} \cdots U_{a_{n-1}, b_{j_{n-1}} \triangleleft}.$$

We need to consider the transition that causes $\mathsf{c}' \underset{\mathcal{M}}{\vdash} \mathsf{c}$. If this transition is $(q, b_l, \mathtt{r}) \in \delta(q', b_{j_k})$, then we have

$$\mathsf{c} = \triangleright b_{j_0} \cdots b_{j_{k-1}} b_l q \cdots b_{j_{m-1}} \triangleleft$$

and P contains the production $U_{a_k, q' b_{j_k}} \to U_{a_k, b_l q}$. Thus, we have the derivation

$$S \overset{*}{\underset{G}{\Rightarrow}} \beta' \underset{G}{\Rightarrow} U_{a_0, \triangleright b_{j_0}} \cdots U_{a_k, b_l q} \cdots U_{a_{n-1}, b_{j_{n-1}} \triangleleft} = \beta.$$

For the word β we clearly have $h_0(\beta) = a_0 a_1 \cdots a_{n-1}$ and $h_1(\beta) = \mathsf{c}$. The subcases that correspond to other transitions ($(q, b_l, \mathtt{l}) \in \delta(q', b_{j_k})$ or $(q, b_l, \mathtt{0}) \in \delta(q', b_{j_k})$) are similar, so we leave them to the reader.

Conversely, if there is a derivation $S \overset{*}{\underset{G}{\Rightarrow}} \alpha \in U_l U^* U_r$ such that $h_0(\alpha) = a_0 a_1 \cdots a_{n-1}$, then we have $q_0 \triangleright a_0 \cdots a_{n-1} \triangleleft \overset{*}{\underset{\mathcal{M}}{\vdash}} h_1(\alpha)$. The argument is by induction on the number p of applications of productions in the simulation set.

For the basis step, $p = 0$, only initialization productions were applied in the derivation $S \overset{*}{\underset{G}{\Rightarrow}} \alpha \in U_l U^* U_r$. Therefore, α has the form

$$\alpha = U_{a_0, q_0 \triangleright a_0} U_{a_1, a_1} \cdots U_{a_{n-1}, a_{n-1} \triangleleft}$$

and we clearly have $h_0(\alpha) = a_0 a_1 \cdots a_{n-1}$ and $h_1(\alpha) = q_0 \triangleright a_0 \cdots a_{n-1}$.

For the induction step, assume that the statement holds for derivations that use productions from the simulation set fewer than q times and let $S \overset{*}{\underset{G}{\Rightarrow}} \alpha \in U_l U^* U_r$ be a derivation that uses such productions q times. There exists a word

$$\gamma = U_{a_0, \rhd b_{j_0}} \cdots U_{a_{k-1}, b_{j_{k-1}}} U_{a_k, q' b_{j_k}} \cdots U_{a_{n-1}, b_{j_{n-1}} \lhd}$$

such that $S \overset{*}{\underset{G}{\Rightarrow}} \gamma \underset{G}{\Rightarrow} \alpha$. Since $\alpha \in U_l U^* U_r$, the production applied in the last step is a simulation production, so in the derivation $S \overset{*}{\underset{G}{\Rightarrow}} \gamma$ the simulation productions were applied $q - 1$ times. By the inductive hypothesis, we have $h_0(\gamma) = a_0 a_1 \cdots a_{n-1}$ and

$$h_1(\gamma) = \rhd b_{j_0} \cdots b_{j_{k-1}} q' b_{j_k} \cdots b_{j_{m-1}} \lhd = \mathsf{c}',$$

where $q_0 \rhd a_0 a_1 \cdots a_{n-1} \lhd \overset{*}{\underset{\mathcal{M}}{\vdash}} \mathsf{c}'$. Assume that the production applied in $\gamma \underset{G}{\Rightarrow} \alpha$ is $U_{a_{k-1}, b_{j_{k-1}}} U_{a_k, q b_{j_k}} \rightarrow U_{a_{k-1}, q b_{j_{k-1}}} U_{a_k, q b_l}$, so

$$\alpha = U_{a_0, \rhd b_{j_0}} \cdots U_{a_{k-1}, q b_{j_{k-1}}} U_{a_k, q b_l} \cdots U_{a_{n-1}, b_{j_{n-1}} \lhd}$$

This production corresponds to a transition $(q, b_l, 1) \in \delta(q', b_{j_k})$, which allows us to write

$$\mathsf{c}' \underset{\mathcal{M}}{\vdash} \rhd b_{j_0} \cdots q b_{j_{k-1}} b_l \cdots b_{j_{m-1}} \lhd = \mathsf{c}$$

Finally, note that $h_1(\alpha) = \mathsf{c}$. The subcases that correspond to the remaining types of simulation productions are left to the reader.

Suppose that $a_0 \cdots a_{n-1} \in L_A(\mathcal{M})$, where $m \geq 1$. Then, there is a computation

$$q_0 \rhd a_0 \cdots a_{n-1} \lhd \overset{*}{\underset{\mathcal{M}}{\vdash}} q \rhd b_{j_0} \cdots b_{j_{n-1}} \lhd$$

for some $b_{j_0} \cdots b_{j_{n-1}} \in B^*$ and $q \in F$. By the previous argument, we have a derivation $S \overset{*}{\underset{G}{\Rightarrow}} \alpha$ such that

$$\begin{aligned} h_0(\alpha) &= a_0 \cdots a_{n-1} \\ h_1(\alpha) &= q \rhd b_{j_0} \cdots b_{j_{n-1}} \lhd \end{aligned}$$

Thus, $\alpha = U_{a_0, q \rhd b_{j_0}} U_{a_1, b_{j_1}} \cdots U_{a_{n-1}, b_{j_{n-1}} \lhd}$. Using productions from the final set we have

$$\begin{aligned} S &\overset{*}{\underset{G}{\Rightarrow}} \alpha \underset{G}{\Rightarrow} a_0 U_{a_1, b_{i_1}} \cdots U_{a_{n-1}, b_{i_{n-1}} \lhd} \\ &\underset{G}{\Rightarrow} a_0 a_1 \cdots U_{a_{n-1}, b_{i_{n-1}} \lhd} \underset{G}{\Rightarrow} \cdots \underset{G}{\Rightarrow} a_0 a_1 \cdots a_{n-1}, \end{aligned}$$

so $L_A(\mathcal{M}) \subseteq L(G)$.

Conversely, suppose that $S \overset{*}{\underset{G}{\Rightarrow}} a_0 a_1 \cdots a_{n-1}$, where $n \geq 1$. Symbols in A are generated in G only as a result of the application of a final production $a U_{a', w} \rightarrow a a'$. Therefore, the derivation has necessarily the form

$$S \overset{*}{\underset{G}{\Rightarrow}} U_{a_0, q \rhd b_{j_0}} U_{a_1, b_{j_1}} \cdots U_{a_{n-1}, b_{j_{n-1}} \lhd} \overset{*}{\underset{G}{\Rightarrow}} a_0 a_1 \cdots a_{n-1},$$

where q is a final state of $\mathcal{M}$.

Let

$$\alpha = U_{a_0,q\triangleright b_{j_0}} U_{a_1,b_{j_1}} \cdots U_{a_{n-1},b_{j_{n-1}}\triangleleft}.$$

It is clear that $h_0(\alpha) = a_0a_1\cdots a_{n-1}$. Since $S \overset{*}{\underset{G}{\Rightarrow}} \alpha$, there exists a configuration c of $\mathcal{M}$ such that $q_0 \triangleright a_0a_1\cdots a_{n-1} \overset{*}{\underset{\mathcal{M}}{\vdash}} \mathsf{c}$ and $h_1(\alpha) = \mathsf{c}$. Thus, $\mathsf{c} = q \triangleright b_{j_0}b_{j_1}\cdots b_{j_{n-1}}\triangleleft$, which implies $\alpha \in L_A(\mathcal{M})$ (because q is a final state of $\mathcal{M}$).

If $\lambda \in L_A(\mathcal{M})$, $L_A(\mathcal{M}) - \{\lambda\}$ is context-sensitive by the above argument. Then, since $\{\lambda\}$ is context-sensitive and $\mathcal{L}_1$ is closed with respect to union, it follows that $L_A(\mathcal{M})$ is context-sensitive. ∎

Theorem 9.2.5 *If $G = (A_N, A_T, S, P)$ is a context-sensitive grammar, then there exists a linear bounded automaton $\mathcal{M} = (B, Q, \delta, q_0, F)$ such that $A_T \subseteq B$ and $L(G) = L_{A_T}(\mathcal{M})$.*

Proof. Let $G = (A_N, A_T, S, P)$ be a length-increasing grammar, where $P = \{\alpha_0 \to \beta_0, \ldots, \alpha_{n-1} \to \beta_{n-1}\}$. Using an NTMS we construct an ndTm $\mathcal{M} = (B, Q, \delta, q_0, F)$ such that $L_{A_T}(\mathcal{M}) = L(G)$, where $A_N \cup A_T \subseteq B$.

Let θ, θ' be two words in B^* such that $|\theta| \geq |\theta'|$. The ndTm $\mathcal{M}_{\theta\to\theta'}$ is an lba that is obtained by modifying the ndTm introduced in Example 8.10.5. Namely, $\mathcal{M}_{\theta\to\theta'}$ may replace some occurrence of θ in the input word γ by an occurrence of θ'; if no occurrence of θ exists in γ, then that input word is left intact, and the head returns to the first cell in the state q_f. In other words, $\mathcal{M}_{\theta\to\theta'}$ is capable of performing the computation

$$q_0 \triangleright \gamma\triangleleft = q_0 \triangleright \gamma'\theta\gamma''\sqcup^k \overset{*}{\vdash} q_f \triangleright \gamma'\theta'\gamma''\sqcup^{|\theta|-|\theta'|+k}\triangleleft$$

for any number $k \in \mathbb{N}$.

Let $\mathcal{M}$ be the ndTm that corresponds to the NTMS $\mathcal{G}$ shown in Figure 9.2. Since each of the ndTms $\mathcal{M}_{\beta_0\to\alpha_0}, \ldots, \mathcal{M}_{\beta_{n-1}\to\alpha_{n-1}}$ is an lba, it is clear that $\mathcal{M}$ is an lba. We assume that $A_N \cup A_T \subseteq B$. Let $\bar{q}_0$ be the initial state and $\bar{q}_f$ be the final state of $\mathcal{M}$.

We claim that if $\gamma \overset{p}{\underset{G}{\Rightarrow}} \eta$, then

$$\bar{q}_0 \triangleright \eta\sqcup^m \triangleleft \overset{*}{\vdash} \bar{q}_0 \triangleright \gamma\sqcup^{m+|\eta|-|\gamma|}\triangleleft$$

for every $m \in \mathbb{N}$.

The proof is by induction on p. For the basis case, $p = 0$, the statement is immediate. Suppose that it holds for derivations of length p, and let $\gamma \overset{p+1}{\underset{G}{\Rightarrow}} \eta$. If the production applied in the last step is $\alpha_k \to \beta_k$, then the derivation can be written as $\gamma \overset{p}{\underset{G}{\Rightarrow}} \eta'\alpha_k\eta'' \underset{G}{\Rightarrow} \eta'\beta_k\eta'' = \eta$. By the inductive hypothesis,

$$\bar{q}_0 \triangleright \eta'\alpha_k\eta''\sqcup^m \triangleleft \overset{*}{\underset{\mathcal{M}}{\vdash}} \bar{q}_0 \triangleright \gamma\sqcup^{m+|\eta'\alpha_k\eta''|-|\gamma|}\triangleleft$$

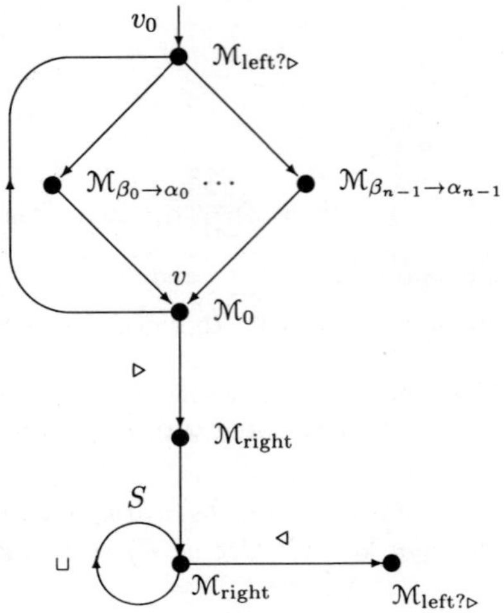

Figure 9.2: NTMS $\mathcal{G}$

for every $m \in \mathbb{N}$. Corresponding to the last step of the derivation we have

$$\begin{aligned} \bar{q}_0 \triangleright \eta \sqcup^l \triangleleft &= \bar{q}_0 \triangleright \eta' \beta_k \eta'' \sqcup^l \triangleleft \\ &\overset{*}{\underset{\mathcal{M}}{\vdash}} \bar{q}_0 \triangleright \eta' \alpha_k \eta'' \sqcup^{l+|\eta|-|\eta'\alpha_k\eta''|} \triangleleft, \end{aligned}$$

for every $l \in \mathbb{N}$. This computation is performed by the component $\mathcal{M}_{\beta_k \to \alpha_k}$ of the NTMS. Choose m and l such that $m = l + |\eta| - |\eta'\alpha_k\eta''|$. Then, combining the last two computations we obtain

$$\bar{q}_0 \triangleright \eta \sqcup^l \triangleleft \overset{*}{\underset{\mathcal{M}}{\vdash}} \bar{q}_0 \triangleright \eta \sqcup^{l+|\eta|-|\gamma|} \triangleleft .$$

Conversely, suppose that we have a computation

$$\bar{q}_0 \triangleright \eta \sqcup^m \triangleleft \overset{n}{\underset{\mathcal{M}}{\vdash}} \bar{q}_0 \triangleright \gamma \sqcup^{m+|\eta|-|\gamma|} \triangleleft \tag{9.1}$$

for $m \in \mathbb{N}$. Note that during the computation (9.1) the lba passes through the vertex v repeatedly, and each time the control returns to v_0. Suppose that v is visited ℓ times. We can prove by induction on ℓ that we have the derivation $\gamma \overset{*}{\underset{G}{\Rightarrow}} \eta$.

For $\ell = 0$, we have $\gamma = \eta$ and the statement is clearly valid. Suppose that the statement holds for computations that pass through v ℓ times and let

$$\bar{q}_0 \triangleright \eta \sqcup^m \triangleleft \overset{n}{\underset{\mathcal{M}}{\vdash}} \bar{q}_0 \triangleright \gamma \sqcup^{m+|\eta|-|\gamma|} \triangleleft$$

be a computation that passes $\ell + 1$ times through v. Let c be the configuration of $\mathcal{M}$ after the first passage through v. We have either $\mathsf{c} = \bar{q}_0 \triangleright \eta \sqcup^m \triangleleft$ if $\mathcal{M}$ has chosen a path through a machine that does not cause any replacement in η, or $\mathsf{c} = \bar{q}_0 \triangleright \eta' \alpha_k \eta'' \sqcup^{m+|\beta_k|-|\alpha_k|} \triangleleft$ if such a replacement took place using the component $\mathcal{M}_{\beta_k \to \alpha_k}$. In the first case, the inductive hypothesis immediately implies the existence of the derivation $\gamma \overset{*}{\underset{G}{\Rightarrow}} \eta$. In the second case, by the inductive hypothesis, we have the derivation $\gamma \overset{*}{\underset{G}{\Rightarrow}} \eta' \alpha_k \eta''$ and the existence of the production $\alpha_k \to \beta_k$ allows us to obtain the derivation

$$\gamma \overset{*}{\underset{G}{\Rightarrow}} \eta' \alpha_k \eta'' \underset{G}{\Rightarrow} \eta' \beta_k \eta'' = \eta.$$

The existence of the derivation $S \overset{*}{\underset{G}{\Rightarrow}} w$, implies the existence of the computation

$$\bar{q}_0 \triangleright w \triangleleft \overset{*}{\underset{\mathcal{M}}{\vdash}} \bar{q}_0 \triangleright S \sqcup^{|w|-1} \triangleleft .$$

Once the configuration $\bar{q}_0 \triangleright S \sqcup^{|w|-1} \triangleleft$ is reached, $\mathcal{M}$ verifies that the contents of the tape has the form $\triangleright S \sqcup^l \triangleleft$ and enters the final state $\bar{q}_f$. Thus, the existence of the derivation $S \overset{*}{\underset{G}{\Rightarrow}} w$ implies the existence of the computation

$$\bar{q}_0 \triangleright w \triangleleft \overset{*}{\underset{\mathcal{M}}{\vdash}} \bar{q}_0 \triangleright S \sqcup^{|w|-1} \triangleleft \overset{*}{\underset{\mathcal{M}}{\vdash}} \bar{q}_f \triangleright S \sqcup^{|w|-1} \triangleleft,$$

which proves that $L(G) \subseteq L_{A_T}(\mathcal{M})$.

Conversely, suppose that $w \in L_{A_T}(\mathcal{M})$. The definition of $\mathcal{M}$ implies that this computation necessarily has the form

$$\bar{q}_0 \triangleright w \triangleleft \overset{*}{\underset{\mathcal{M}}{\vdash}} \bar{q}_0 \triangleright S \sqcup^{|w|-1} \triangleleft \overset{*}{\underset{\mathcal{M}}{\vdash}} \bar{q}_f \triangleright S \sqcup^{|w|-1} \triangleleft .$$

By the previous argument, we obtain the existence of the derivation $S \overset{*}{\underset{G}{\Rightarrow}} w$, which implies $L_{A_T}(\mathcal{M}) \subseteq L(G)$.

This allows us to conclude that for any $x \in A_T^*$, $S \overset{*}{\underset{G}{\Rightarrow}} x$ if and only if $q_0 \triangleright x \triangleleft \overset{*}{\underset{\mathcal{M}}{\vdash}} q_f \triangleright w \triangleleft$ for some $w \in B^*$. Thus, $L(G) = L_A(\mathcal{M})$. ∎

Corollary 9.2.6 *A language $L \subseteq A^*$ is context-sensitive if and only if there exists an lba $\mathcal{M}$ such that $L = L_A(\mathcal{M})$.*

Proof. The statement follows immediately from Theorems 9.2.4 and 9.2.5. ∎

9.3 Closure Properties

In this section we examine several closure and non-closure properties of the class of context-sensitive languages. We saw that $\mathcal{L}_1$ is closed with respect to union,

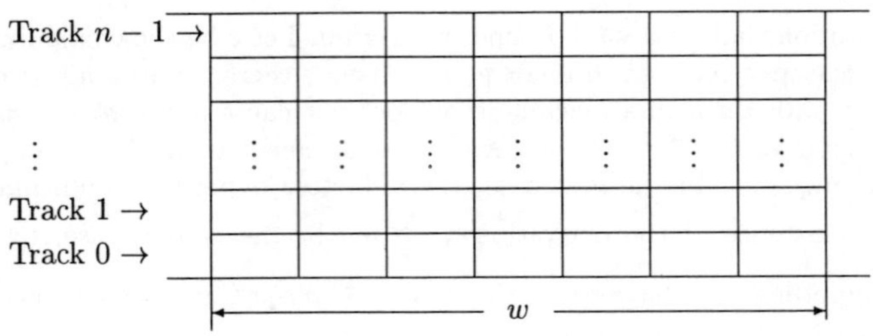

Figure 9.3: Multi-track portion of a tape

product, and Kleene closure. After remaining open for decades, the question of closure under complement of $\mathcal{L}_1$ was solved by N. Immerman[1988] and R. Szelepcsényi[1987].

Theorem 9.3.1 (Immerman-Szelepcsényi Theorem) *Let A be an alphabet. The complement $A^* - L$ of a context-sensitive language $L \subseteq A^*$ is context-sensitive.*

Proof. We assume initially that L is a λ-free language. Since L is context-sensitive language, by Corollary 9.2.6, there is an lba $\mathcal{M} = (B, Q, \delta, q_0, F)$ such that $A \subseteq B$ and $L_A(\mathcal{M}) = L$.

We construct an lba $\mathcal{M}' = (B', Q', \delta', q_0', F')$ such that $q_0' \triangleright x \triangleleft \overset{*}{\underset{\mathcal{M}'}{\vdash}} q_f' \triangleright w \triangleleft$ for some $q_f' \in F'$ and $w \in (B')^*$ if and only if there is no computation

$$q_0 \triangleright x \triangleleft \overset{*}{\underset{\mathcal{M}}{\vdash}} q_f \triangleright w \triangleleft \tag{9.2}$$

with $q_f \in F$ and $w \in B^*$. The difficulty in constructing $\mathcal{M}'$ consists in verifying that there is no computation in $\mathcal{M}$ of the form 9.2 without exceeding the space permitted to an lba.

The tape of $\mathcal{M}'$ is a multitrack one; in other words, its alphabet may contain n-tuples of symbols. Let C be an alphabet. If a cell of a tape contains a n-tuple of symbols $(c_0, \ldots, c_{n-1})$, we will regard this tuple as a single symbol of the alphabet C^n. If a group of m contiguous cells contains a word $w \in (C^n)^*$ we will denote by $(w)_i$ the ith component of the word w for $0 \leq i \leq n-1$ (cf. Figure 9.3) and we will refer to $(w)_i$ as the ith *track component of* w. The word w will be denoted as $[(w)_0, \ldots, (w)_{n-1}]$.

For a word $x \in A^+$, there are no more than $k(x) = |Q|(|x|+2)|B|^{|x|}$ configurations that correspond to words of length $|x|$ on the tape of $\mathcal{M}$. The binary representation of $k(x)$ has $|x| \log_2 |B| + \log_2(|x|+2) + \log_2 |Q|$ bits. Thus, we need $c|x|$ bits for representing the number of these configuration, where c is a constant that does not depend on x, and $k(x)$ can be represented on c tracks of length not exceeding $|x|$ or one one track containing c-tuples of binary digits.

Let B^Q be the alphabet $B^Q = B \cup \{b^q \mid b \in B \text{ and } q \in Q\}$. A configuration $\triangleright b_{i_0} \cdots b_{i_{k-1}} q b_{i_k} \cdots b_{i_{m-1}} \triangleleft$ can be represented as the word

$$\triangleright b_{i_0} \cdots b_{i_{k-1}} b^q_{i_k} \cdots b_{i_{m-1}} \triangleleft$$

on the alphabet B^Q. Thus, every configuration of $\mathcal{M}$ that follows the configuration $q_0 \triangleright x \triangleleft$ can be represented in space $|x|$.

Let $\mathsf{c}_0, \ldots, \mathsf{c}_{k(x)-1}$ be the list of all words that represent configurations of $\mathcal{M}$ of length $|x|$, in lexicographical order.

If $r(x)$ is the number of configurations that can be reached starting from $q_0 \triangleright x \triangleleft$, then $r(x) \leq k(x)$ for every $x \in A^*$.

The core of the proof is the algorithm that computes the number $r(x)$. Let $C_i(x)$ be the set of configurations that $\mathcal{M}$ can reach starting from $q_0 \triangleright x \triangleleft$ in no more than i steps and let $r_i(x) = |C_i(x)|$ for $0 \leq i \leq k(x) - 1$. It is clear that $r_0(x) \leq r_1(x) \leq \cdots \leq r_{k(x)-1}(x)$ and that $r(x) = r_{k(x)-1}(x)$.

Define the function $M(\mathsf{c}, \mathsf{c}')$ that returns 1 if $\mathsf{c} = \mathsf{c}'$ or $\mathsf{c} \underset{\mathcal{M}}{\vdash} \mathsf{c}'$ and returns 0 otherwise. The procedure $\mathtt{REACH}_{\mathcal{M}}(\mathsf{c}, i)$, described next, begins with a configuration c of $\mathcal{M}$ and a number i. This procedure works nondeterministically and may either terminate and return a value of 1 (if c can be reached from $q_0 \triangleright x \triangleleft$ in fewer than i steps) or abort.

procedure $\mathtt{REACH}_{\mathcal{M}}(\mathsf{c}, i)$
    $\hat{\mathsf{c}} = q_0 \triangleright x \triangleleft$;
    for $p = 1$ **to** i **do begin**
        `nondeterministically choose a configuration` c_p;
        $\bar{\mathsf{c}} = \mathsf{c}_p$;
        if $M(\hat{\mathsf{c}}, \bar{\mathsf{c}}) = 0$ **then abort**
          else $\hat{\mathsf{c}} = \bar{\mathsf{c}}$;
    end;
    if $\hat{\mathsf{c}} = \mathsf{c}$ **then return** 1;
    else abort;
end procedure

Due to its nondeterministic character, the procedure $\mathtt{REACH}_{\mathcal{M}}(\mathsf{c}, i)$ may abort even if $\mathsf{c} \in C_i(x)$; what is clear, however, is that if $\mathtt{REACH}_{\mathcal{M}}(\mathsf{c}, i)$ returns 1, then $\mathsf{c} \in C_i(x)$, and that $\mathtt{REACH}_{\mathcal{M}}(\mathsf{c}, i)$ will never return 1 unless $\mathsf{c} \in C_i(x)$. Also, note that $\mathtt{REACH}_{\mathcal{M}}(\mathsf{c}, i)$ makes use of the variables $\hat{\mathsf{c}}, \bar{\mathsf{c}}$ and p, and the values of these variables can be written in space $|x|$.

The procedure $\mathtt{REACH}_{\mathcal{M}}(\mathsf{c}, i)$ is used in a new procedure $R(\mathsf{c}, i, r)$. If $r = r_{i-1}(x)$, then $R(\mathsf{c}, i, r)$ returns 1 if $\mathsf{c} \in C_i(x)$.

procedure $R(\mathsf{c}, i, r)$
    $m = 0$; $\mathsf{ans} = 0$;
    for $q = 1$ **to** $k(x) - 1$ **do begin**
        $\tilde{\mathsf{c}} = \mathsf{c}_q$;
        if $\mathtt{REACH}_{\mathcal{M}}(\tilde{\mathsf{c}}, i - 1) = 1$ **then** $m = m + 1$;
        if $M(\tilde{\mathsf{c}}, \mathsf{c}) = 1$ **then** $\mathsf{ans} = 1$;

```
    end
    if m < r then abort;
    else return ans;
end procedure
```

Note that $R(\mathsf{c}, i, r)$ makes use of the variables $m, q, \tilde{\mathsf{c}}$, whose values can be stored in space $|x|$, and of the variable **ans** that requires constant space.

We have $r_0(x) = 1$ because $C_0(x)$ consists of the initial configuration of $\mathcal{M}$. To compute $r(x) = r_{k(x)-1}(x)$ we use the procedure P that successively retrieves $r_0(x), r_1(x), \ldots, r_{k(x)-1}(x)$:

```
procedure P(x)
    r = 1;
    for i = 1 to k(x) − 1 do begin
            k = 0;
            for l = 0 to k(x) − 1 do begin
                    c̈ = c_l;
                    if R(c̈, i, r) = 1 then k = k + 1;
            end;
        r = k;
        end;
    return r;
end procedure
```

The procedure $P(x)$ uses the variables $r, i, k, l, \ddot{\mathsf{c}}$; each can be stored in space $|x|$.

It is clear that P works nondeterministically. We claim that if P returns a value, then this value equals $r(x)$ and that there exists a successful computation that allows P to do just that.

We claim that for every i, r contains the value $r_{i-1}(x)$ before entering the loop that involves i. Note that initially $r = r_0(x)$ and $i = 1$, so the statement holds. Suppose that the statement holds for l. Then, we test every configuration c_l using $R(\ddot{\mathsf{c}}, i, r)$ to determine whether c_l belongs to $C_i(x)$; if this is the case, there is a computation of $R(\ddot{\mathsf{c}}, i, r)$ that returns 1 and we can increment k. Thus, k will eventually contain $r_i(x)$ and this value is stored in r.

Observe that P directly and indirectly uses fourteen variables c, c' (in procedure M), $\hat{\mathsf{c}}, \bar{\mathsf{c}}$ and p (in procedure $\mathtt{REACH}_{\mathcal{M}}(\mathsf{c}, i)$), $m, q, \tilde{\mathsf{c}}, \mathbf{ans}$ in $R(\mathsf{c}, i, r)$, and $r, i, k, l, \ddot{\mathsf{c}}$ in $P(x)$. This procedure can be implemented as an lba $\mathcal{M}_0$ that has a 20-track tape: the first track is reserved for the input x; the second tape will receive $r(x)$ in binary, 14 tracks will contain the variables mentioned above, and the last four tracks will be used by the next component of the NTMS. There is a computation of $\mathcal{M}_0$ (described by the procedure P) that leaves x intact on track 0 and writes $r(x)$ on track 1.

After the machine $\mathcal{M}_0$ completes its work only the contents of the tracks 0 and 1 are relevant. Control passes to the lba $\mathcal{M}_{test}$.

Let $\mathcal{M}_{test}$ be an ndTm works with a 6 tracks that contain the following pieces of information:

`track 0`: the input word x;

`track 1:` the number $r(x)$, represented in binary;
`track 16:` the value of a looping variable, i, in binary;
`track 17:` the value of a counter variable, count, in binary;
`track 18:` a configuration c of $\mathcal{M}$ that is reachable from the initial configuration $q_0 \triangleright x \triangleleft$ of $\mathcal{M}$;
`track 19:` the current configuration of $\mathcal{M}$, the ndTm being simulated.

The tracks numbered from 2 to 15 are ignored completely by $\mathcal{M}_{test}$.

To conclude that $\mathcal{M}$ does not accept a word x it is necessary to determine that none of the $r(x)$ configurations that can be reached by $\mathcal{M}$ from $q_0 \triangleright x \triangleleft$ is an accepting configuration of $\mathcal{M}$.

At the outset of the work of $\mathcal{M}_{test}$ the track 0 of the tape of $\mathcal{M}$ contains x while the second track contains $r(x)$. $\mathcal{M}_{test}$ performs the following actions:

- Initialize the variable i on track 16 to 0; the maximum value of this variable is $k(x)$.
- Initialize the counter variable count (stored in binary on track 17) to 0.
- $\mathcal{M}_{test}$ simulates a computation of $\mathcal{M}$ (using track 19) that either reaches a configuration c_i (written on track 18) or ends in a blocking configuration.
- If c_i is reached and it is an accepting configuration of $\mathcal{M}$, then $\mathcal{M}_{test}$ enters a halting configuration; otherwise, it increments count.
- After i reaches $k(x)$, we are certain that every configuration of $\mathcal{M}$ that could lead to the acceptance of x by $\mathcal{M}$ has been tested. Determine if count $= r(x)$. If yes, this means that $\mathcal{M}$ did not accept x, so $\mathcal{M}_{test}$ will enter an accepting final state q_f; otherwise, $\mathcal{M}_{test}$ enters a state q_r that leads to a blocking configuration.

The NTMS that consists of the lbas $\mathcal{M}_0$ and $\mathcal{M}_{test}$ is clearly described by an lba $\mathcal{M}'$. The language accepted by $\mathcal{M}'$ is the complement of L. This proves that $A^* - L$ is indeed, context-sensitive.

If $\lambda \in L$ consider the context-sensitive language $K = L - \{\lambda\}$. Since $A^* - L = (A^* - K) - \{\lambda\}$, the context-sensitivity of $A^* - K$ implies the context-sensitivity of $A^* - L$ by Theorem 4.4.3. ∎

Corollary 9.3.2 *The class of context-sensitive languages is closed with respect to intersection.*

Proof. Using DeMorgan's law, this statement follows immediately from the fact that $\mathcal{L}_1$ is closed with respect to union (cf. Theorem 4.4.3) and from Theorem 9.3.1. ∎

We prove that the class $\mathcal{L}_1$ is not closed with respect to arbitrary morphisms. The next lemma contains a preliminary result.

Lemma 9.3.3 *Let $L \subseteq A^*$ be a recursively enumerable language. There is a context-sensitive language $K \subseteq \{a\}^*\#L$, where $a, \#$ are two symbols that do not belong to A, such that for every $x \in L$ we have $a^i\#x \in K$ for some $i \in \mathbb{N}$.*

Proof. Suppose that $L = L(G)$, where $G = (A_N, A, S, P)$ is a grammar. Define the grammar $G' = (A_N \cup \{S', Y\}, A \cup \{a, \#\}, S', P')$, where S', Y are two new nonterminal symbols and P' consists of the following length-increasing productions:

Type	Productions
(A)	$S' \to \#S$, $\#Y \to a\#$
(B)	$sY \to Ys$ for $s \in A_N \cup A$
(C)	$\alpha \to \beta$, where $\alpha \to \beta \in P$ and $\lvert\alpha\rvert \leq \lvert\beta\rvert$
(D)	$\alpha \to Y^{\lvert\alpha\rvert - \lvert\beta\rvert}\beta$, where $\alpha \to \beta \in P$ and $\lvert\alpha\rvert > \lvert\beta\rvert$

Suppose that $S \overset{n}{\underset{G}{\Rightarrow}} \gamma$. We prove by induction on n that there exists a derivation $S' \overset{m}{\underset{G'}{\Rightarrow}} a^i\#\gamma$ for some $m, i \in \mathbb{N}$.

If $n = 0$, we have $\gamma = S$, so $S' \underset{G'}{\Rightarrow} \#S$, which justifies our claim with $m = 1$ and $i = 0$.

Suppose that the statement holds for derivations of length n and let $S \overset{n+1}{\underset{G}{\Rightarrow}} \gamma$. Writing the last step of the derivation explicitly we have $S \overset{n}{\underset{G}{\Rightarrow}} \theta \underset{G}{\Rightarrow} \gamma$. By the inductive hypothesis, there is a derivation $S' \overset{m}{\underset{G}{\Rightarrow}} a^i\#\theta$. If the production applied in the last step was $\alpha \to \beta$ with $|\alpha| \leq |\beta|$, then the same production exists in P', so we obtain $S' \overset{m}{\underset{G}{\Rightarrow}} a^i\#\theta \underset{G'}{\Rightarrow} a^i\#\gamma$. Otherwise, that is if the last production applied was $\alpha \to \beta$ with $|\alpha| > |\beta|$, we have $\theta = \theta_0\alpha\theta_1$, $\gamma = \theta_0\beta\theta_1$, and the production $\alpha \to Y^{|\alpha|-|\beta|}\beta$ belongs to P'. Therefore we have the derivation

$$\begin{aligned} S' & \overset{m}{\underset{G}{\Rightarrow}} a^i\#\theta = a^i\#\theta_0\alpha\theta_1 \\ & \underset{G'}{\Rightarrow} a^i\#\theta_0 Y^{|\alpha|-|\beta|}\beta\theta_1 \\ & \overset{*}{\underset{G'}{\Rightarrow}} a^i\#Y^{|\alpha|-|\beta|}\theta_0\beta\theta_1 \\ & \overset{*}{\underset{G'}{\Rightarrow}} a^i a^{|\alpha|-|\beta|}\#\theta_0\beta\theta_1 = a^{i+|\alpha|-|\beta|}\#\gamma. \end{aligned}$$

Thus, for any $x \in L$, we have $S \overset{*}{\underset{G}{\Rightarrow}} x$, which implies $S' \overset{*}{\underset{G'}{\Rightarrow}} a^i\#x$.

Conversely, let $y \in K$. There is a derivation $S' \underset{G'}{\Rightarrow} \#S \overset{*}{\underset{G'}{\Rightarrow}} y$. The word y has the form $a^i\#z$, so we have $S' \underset{G'}{\Rightarrow} \#S \overset{*}{\underset{G'}{\Rightarrow}} a^i\#z$, which implies the existence of the derivation

$$S' \underset{G'}{\Rightarrow} \#S \overset{*}{\underset{G'}{\Rightarrow}} \#Y^i z. \tag{9.3}$$

Let $h : (A_N \cup A \cup \{Y\})^* \longrightarrow (A_N \cup A)^*$ be the morphism defined by $h(Y) = \lambda$, and $h(s) = s$ for every $s \in A_N \cup A$. We claim that $\#\theta \overset{*}{\underset{G'}{\Rightarrow}} \#\eta$ implies $h(\theta) \overset{*}{\underset{G}{\Rightarrow}} h(\eta)$. The proof is by induction on k, the number of applications of type (D) productions.

The basis case, $k = 0$, is trivial. Suppose that the statement holds for derivations that contain k applications of productions of type (D), and let

$$\#\theta \overset{*}{\underset{G'}{\Rightarrow}} \#\theta_0\alpha\theta_1 \underset{G'}{\Rightarrow} \#\theta_0 Y^m \beta\theta_1 \overset{*}{\underset{\#}{\Rightarrow}} \eta$$

be a derivation that contains $k+1$ applications of productions of type (D), where $\#\theta \overset{*}{\underset{G'}{\Rightarrow}} \#\theta_0\alpha\theta_1$ contains k applications of productions of type (D), and $\#\theta_0 Y^m\beta\theta_1 \overset{*}{\underset{G'}{\Rightarrow}} \#\eta$ contains no applications of such productions. By the inductive hypothesis, we have $h(\theta) \overset{*}{\underset{G}{\Rightarrow}} h(\theta_0)h(\alpha)h(\theta_1)$; by the base case, we have $h(Y^m\theta_0\beta\theta_1) = h(\theta_0)\beta h(\theta_1) \overset{*}{\underset{G}{\Rightarrow}} h(\eta)$ since $h(Y^m\beta) = \beta$. Thus, we obtain $h(\theta) \overset{*}{\underset{G}{\Rightarrow}} h(\eta)$.

The existence of the derivation (9.3) implies the existence of the derivation $S = h(S) \overset{*}{\underset{G}{\Rightarrow}} h(Y^i z) = z$, so $z \in L$, which concludes the argument. ∎

Lemma 9.3.3 allows us to prove that $\mathcal{L}_1$ is not closed with respect to several operations.

Theorem 9.3.4 *The class $\mathcal{L}_1$ is not closed with respect to any of the following: morphisms, substitutions, and quotients with regular languages.*

Proof. Let $L \subseteq A^*$ be a language in $\mathcal{L}_0 - \mathcal{L}_1$. Suppose that $a, \# \notin A$ and let $h : (A \cup \{a, b\})^* \longrightarrow A^*$ be the morphism defined by $h(a) = h(\#) = \lambda$, and $h(s) = s$ for every $s \in A$. If K is the context-sensitive language whose existence is asserted in Lemma 9.3.3, then $h(K) = L$. Therefore, $\mathcal{L}_1$ is not closed with respect to morphisms.

$\mathcal{L}_1$ is not closed with respect to substitutions because morphisms are special cases of substitutions.

Finally, let $R = \{a\}^*\#$. Since $R^{-1}K = L$ it follows that $\mathcal{L}_1$ is not closed with respect to quotient with regular languages. ∎

Morphisms that satisfy certain conditions preserve context-sensitivity. To prove this closure result we introduce the notion of work space of a derivation.

Definition 9.3.5 Let G be an arbitrary grammar and let

$$\gamma_0 \underset{G}{\Rightarrow} \gamma_1 \underset{G}{\Rightarrow} \cdots \underset{G}{\Rightarrow} \gamma_n$$

be a derivation d in G. The number $\max\{|\gamma_i| \mid 0 \leq i \leq n\}$ is the *workspace* of d; we denote it by $\mathsf{ws}_G(d, \gamma_n)$.

If $S \overset{*}{\underset{G}{\Rightarrow}} \gamma$, then the *work space of* γ is the number

$$\mathsf{ws}_G(\gamma) = \max\{\mathsf{ws}_G(d, x) \mid d \text{ is a derivation of } \gamma\}.$$

□

It is clear that if $S \overset{*}{\underset{G}{\Rightarrow}} \gamma$, then $\mathsf{ws}_G(\gamma) \geq |\gamma|$.

Lemma 9.3.6 *Let $G = (A_N, A_T, S, P)$ be an arbitrary grammar. If $\mathsf{ws}_G(x) = |x|$ for every $x \in L(G)$, then $L(G)$ is a context-sensitive language.*

Proof. Note that $\lambda \notin L(G)$ because the condition of the theorem requires $\mathsf{ws}_G(\lambda) = 0$ but $\mathsf{ws}_G(x) \geq 1$ for any $x \in L(G)$. Let Y be a new terminal symbol, $Y \notin A_N$, and let G' be the length-increasing grammar $G' = (A_N \cup \{Y\}, A_T, S, P')$. For each production $\alpha \to \beta$, include in P' the following production:

- if $|\alpha| > |\beta|$, include the production $\alpha \to Y^{|\alpha|-|\beta|}\beta$;
- if $|\alpha| \leq |\beta|$, include the production $Y^j\alpha \to \beta$ for every j such that $0 \leq j \leq |\beta| - |\alpha|$.

Also, the productions $Ys \to sY$ and $sY \to Ys$ are included in P' for every symbol $s \in A_N \cup A_T$.

To prove the context-sensitivity of $L(G)$, by Theorem 4.3.16, it suffices to show that $L(G) = L(G')$.

Let $h : (A_N \cup A_T \cup \{Y\})^* \longrightarrow (A_N \cup A_T)^*$ be the morphism defined by $h(s) = s$ for every $s \in A_N \cup A_T$ and $h(Y) = \lambda$. We leave to the reader the easy argument (by induction on n) that if $S \overset{n}{\underset{G'}{\Rightarrow}} \gamma$, then $S \overset{*}{\underset{G}{\Rightarrow}} h(\gamma)$ for every $\gamma \in (A_N \cup A_T \cup \{Y\})^*$. Therefore, if $x \in L(G')$, then $S \overset{n}{\underset{G'}{\Rightarrow}} x$, which implies $S \overset{n}{\underset{G}{\Rightarrow}} h(x) = x$. Thus, $L(G') \subseteq L(G)$.

To prove the reverse inclusion, we show that if d is the derivation $S \overset{n}{\underset{G}{\Rightarrow}} \gamma$, then $S \overset{*}{\underset{G'}{\Rightarrow}} Y^{\mathsf{ws}_G(d,\gamma)-|\gamma|}\gamma$.

The argument is by induction on n. The base case, $n = 0$, is immediate.

Suppose that the statement holds for derivations of length n and let d' be the derivation $S \overset{n}{\underset{G}{\Rightarrow}} \gamma \underset{G}{\Rightarrow} \gamma'$. Let d be the first part of this derivation, $S \overset{n}{\underset{G}{\Rightarrow}} \gamma$. We have $\gamma = \gamma_0\alpha\gamma_1$, $\gamma' = \gamma_0\beta\gamma_1$, where $\alpha \to \beta$ is a production in G.

If $|\alpha| > |\beta|$, then $|\gamma| > |\gamma'|$, so $\mathsf{ws}_G(d', \gamma') = \mathsf{ws}_G(d, \gamma)$. Then, we can write:

$$\begin{aligned}
S &\overset{*}{\underset{G'}{\Rightarrow}} Y^{\mathsf{ws}_G(d',\gamma')-|\gamma|}\gamma \text{ (by the inductive hypothesis)}\\
&= Y^{\mathsf{ws}_G(d',\gamma')-|\gamma|}\gamma_0\alpha\gamma_1\\
&\underset{G'}{\Rightarrow} Y^{\mathsf{ws}_G(d',\gamma')-|\gamma|}\gamma_0 Y^{|\gamma|-|\gamma'|}\beta\gamma_1\\
&\overset{*}{\underset{G'}{\Rightarrow}} Y^{\mathsf{ws}_G(d',\gamma')-|\gamma|}Y^{|\gamma|-|\gamma'|}\gamma_0\beta\gamma_1\\
&\quad \text{(using the productions of the form } sY \to Ys)\\
&= Y^{\mathsf{ws}_G(d',\gamma')-|\gamma'|}\gamma_0\beta\gamma_1\\
&= Y^{\mathsf{ws}_G(d',\gamma')-|\gamma'|}\gamma'.
\end{aligned}$$

If $|\alpha| \leq |\beta|$ we need to consider two cases:

(i) Suppose $|\gamma'| > \mathsf{ws}_G(d, \gamma)$. In this case, $\mathsf{ws}_G(d', \gamma') = |\gamma'|$. We have

$$\begin{aligned}
S &\overset{*}{\underset{G'}{\Rightarrow}} Y^{\mathsf{ws}_G(d,\gamma)-|\gamma|}\gamma \text{ (by the inductive hypothesis)}\\
&= Y^{\mathsf{ws}_G(d,\gamma)-|\gamma|}\gamma_0\alpha\gamma_1\\
&\overset{*}{\underset{G'}{\Rightarrow}} \gamma_0 Y^{\mathsf{ws}_G(d,\gamma)-|\gamma|}\alpha\gamma_1\\
&\underset{G'}{\Rightarrow} \gamma_0\beta\gamma_1 = \gamma'.
\end{aligned}$$

Note that $0 \leq \mathsf{ws}_G(d,\gamma) - |\gamma| < |\gamma'| - |\gamma|$, so there is a production $Y^{\mathsf{ws}_G(d,\gamma)-|\gamma|}\alpha \rightarrow \beta$ in P'.

(ii) If $|\gamma'| \leq \mathsf{ws}_G(d,\gamma)$, then $\mathsf{ws}_G(d',\gamma') = \mathsf{ws}_G(d,\gamma)$. Now, we can write

$$\begin{aligned} S &\overset{*}{\underset{G'}{\Rightarrow}} Y^{\mathsf{ws}_G(d,\gamma)-|\gamma|}\gamma \\ &= Y^{\mathsf{ws}_G(d,\gamma)-|\gamma|}\gamma_0\alpha\gamma_1 \\ &= Y^{\mathsf{ws}_G(d',\gamma')-|\gamma'|}Y^{|\gamma'|-|\gamma|}\gamma_0\alpha\gamma_1 \\ &\overset{*}{\underset{G'}{\Rightarrow}} Y^{\mathsf{ws}_G(d',\gamma')-|\gamma'|}\gamma_0 Y^{|\gamma'|-|\gamma|}\alpha\gamma_1 \\ &\quad \text{(using productions of the form } Ys \rightarrow sY) \\ &\overset{*}{\underset{G'}{\Rightarrow}} Y^{\mathsf{ws}_G(d',\gamma')-|\gamma'|}\gamma_0 Y^{|\beta|-|\alpha|}\alpha\gamma_1 \\ &\underset{G'}{\Rightarrow} Y^{\mathsf{ws}_G(d',\gamma')-|\gamma'|}\gamma_0\beta\gamma_1 \\ &\underset{G'}{\Rightarrow} Y^{\mathsf{ws}_G(d',\gamma')-|\gamma'|}\gamma', \end{aligned}$$

which gives the desired conclusion.

Now let $x \in L(G)$. There is a derivation d such that $\mathsf{ws}(d,x) = |x|$. Consequently, by the previous argument, we have $S \overset{*}{\underset{G'}{\Rightarrow}} x$, so $L(G) \subseteq L(G')$, which shows that G and G' are equivalent. This implies that $L(G)$ is context-sensitive. ∎

If G is a length-increasing grammar, then $\mathsf{ws}_G(x) = |x|$. An extension of this property to arbitrary grammars is known as the workspace theorem.

Theorem 9.3.7 (Workspace Theorem) *Let $G = (A_N, A_T, S, P)$ be a grammar such that for some $k \in \mathbb{N}$, $k \geq 1$, $\mathsf{ws}_G(x) \leq k|x|$ for every $x \in L(G)$. Then, $L(G)$ is a context-sensitive language.*

Proof. The proof is by induction on k. For $k = 1$, the context-sensitivity of $L(G)$ follows directly from Lemma 9.3.6.

Suppose that the statement holds for $k \geq 1$, and let G be a grammar such that $\mathsf{ws}_G(x) \leq (k+1)|x|$ for every $x \in L(G)$. We may assume without loss of generality that the productions containing terminal symbols have the form $X \rightarrow a$ (cf. Theorem 4.3.13) because the construction given in that theorem does not affect the workspace of the grammar.

We define a grammar $G_1 = (A_N \cup \{S_1, Z\}, A_T \cup \{z\}, S_1, P_1)$, where S_1, Z are new nonterminals, and z is a new terminal symbol such that

(A) if $S_1 \overset{n}{\underset{G_1}{\Rightarrow}} \gamma$ for $n \geq 1$ and $\gamma \in (A_N \cup A_T \cup \{S_1, Z, z\})^*$, then $|\gamma|$ is an even number;

(B) $h(L(G_1)) \subseteq L(G)$, where $h : (A_T \cup \{z\})^* \longrightarrow A_T^*$ is a morphism given by $h(z) = \lambda$ and $h(s) = s$ for $s \in A_T$;

(C) for every derivation d in G given by

$$S \underset{G}{\Rightarrow} \gamma_1 \underset{G}{\Rightarrow} \cdots \underset{G}{\Rightarrow} \gamma_n,$$

where $n \geq 1$, there is a derivation $d_1 : S_1 \overset{*}{\underset{G_1}{\Rightarrow}} \theta$ such that $\theta \in \{\gamma_n, Z\gamma_n\}$ and $\mathsf{ws}_{G_1}(d_1, \theta) \leq \mathsf{ws}(d, \gamma_n) + 1$.

We define the set of productions P_1 of G_1 as follows:

(i) place the production $S_1 \rightarrow ZS$ into P_1;

(ii) for every $s \in A_N \cup A_T$ place the productions $sZ \rightarrow Zs$ and $Zs \rightarrow sZ$ into P_1;

(iii) place $Za \rightarrow za$ for every $a \in A_T$ into P_1;

(iv) if $\alpha \rightarrow \beta \in P$, then include the productions specified by the following table in P_1:

$\|\alpha\|$	$\|\beta\|$	Productions
even	even	$\alpha \rightarrow \beta$
even	odd	$\alpha \rightarrow Z\beta$ $Zs\alpha \rightarrow s\beta$ $Z\alpha s \rightarrow \beta s$ for every $s \in A_N \cup A_T$
odd	even	$Z\alpha \rightarrow \beta$ $\alpha s \rightarrow Z\beta s$ $s\alpha \rightarrow Zs\beta$ for every $s \in A_N \cup A_T$
odd	odd	$\alpha s \rightarrow \beta s$ $s\alpha \rightarrow s\beta$ for every $s \in A_N \cup A_T \cup \{Z\}$

Note that both members of every production of P_1 (with the exception of $S_1 \rightarrow ZS$) have even length. Since S_1 never appears in the right member of any production, this immediately implies property (A).

To prove property (B) define the morphism $h' : (A_N \cup A_T \cup \{Z, z\})^* \longrightarrow (A_N \cup A_T)^*$ is a morphism given by $h(z) = h(Z) = \lambda$ and $h(s) = s$ for $s \in A_N \cup A_T$. It is clear that if $w \in (A_T \cup \{Z, z\})^*$, then $h'(w) = h(w)$. Note that if $\alpha_1 \rightarrow \beta_1 \in P_1$ is one of the productions introduced under (iii), then $h'(\alpha_1) \rightarrow h'(\beta_1)$ is a production of P. Thus, if $\gamma \neq S_1$ and $\gamma \underset{G_1}{\Rightarrow} \gamma'$, then $h(\gamma) \underset{G}{\Rightarrow} h(\gamma')$. A simple induction argument shows that if $\gamma \neq S_1$ and $\gamma \overset{*}{\underset{G_1}{\Rightarrow}} \gamma'$, then $h(\gamma) \overset{*}{\underset{G}{\Rightarrow}} h(\gamma')$.

Now let $w \in L(G_1)$. There is a derivation $S_1 \underset{G_1}{\Rightarrow} ZS \overset{*}{\underset{G_1}{\Rightarrow}} w$. Therefore, we have $h(ZS) = S \overset{*}{\underset{G_1}{\Rightarrow}} h(w)$, which implies $h(w) \in L(G)$. This allows us to conclude that $h(L(G_1)) \subseteq L(G)$.

Statement (C) is proven by induction on n. In the basis case, $n = 1$, we have $S \rightarrow \gamma_1 \in P$. If $|\gamma_1|$ is an odd number, then $ZS \rightarrow Z\gamma_1 \in P_1$ and we have

$$S_1 \underset{G_1}{\Rightarrow} ZS \underset{G_1}{\Rightarrow} Z\gamma_1.$$

If $|\gamma_1|$ is an even number, then $ZS \rightarrow \gamma_1 \in P_1$, and we have the derivation

$$S_1 \underset{G_1}{\Rightarrow} ZS \underset{G_1}{\Rightarrow} \gamma_1.$$

It is clear that in either case the requirements of (C) are satisfied.

Suppose that the statement holds for derivations of length less than n, and let d be a derivation in G given by

$$d : S \underset{G}{\Rightarrow} \gamma_1 \underset{G}{\Rightarrow} \cdots \underset{G}{\Rightarrow} \gamma_n.$$

Consider the derivation

$$d' : S \underset{G}{\Rightarrow} \gamma_1 \underset{G}{\Rightarrow} \cdots \underset{G}{\Rightarrow} \gamma_{n-1}.$$

The inductive hypothesis implies the existence of a derivation

$$d_1' : S_1 \overset{*}{\underset{G_1}{\Rightarrow}} \theta, \text{ where } \theta \in \{\gamma_{n-1}, Z\gamma_{n-1}\}$$

and $\mathsf{ws}_{G_1}(d_1', \theta) \leq \mathsf{ws}_G(d', \gamma_{n-1}) + 1$ Let $\alpha \rightarrow \beta$ be the production applied in $\gamma_{n-1} \underset{G}{\Rightarrow} \gamma_n$; we have $\gamma_{n-1} = \gamma_{n-1}'\alpha\gamma_{n-1}''$ and $\gamma_n = \gamma_{n-1}'\beta\gamma_{n-1}''$.

Suppose that $\theta = \gamma_{n-1}$. If $|\alpha|$ is even, then P_1 contains the productions $\alpha \rightarrow \beta$ if $|\beta|$ is even, or $\alpha \rightarrow Z\beta$, when $|\beta|$ is odd. This allows us to construct the derivation:

$$S \overset{*}{\underset{G_1}{\Rightarrow}} \gamma_{n-1} \underset{G_1}{\Rightarrow} \gamma_n,$$

if $|\beta|$ is even and the derivation

$$\begin{aligned} S_1 &\overset{*}{\underset{G_1}{\Rightarrow}} \gamma_{n-1} = \gamma_{n-1}'\alpha\gamma_{n-1}'' \\ &\underset{G_1}{\Rightarrow} \gamma_{n-1}' Z\beta\gamma_{n-1}'' \\ &\overset{*}{\underset{G_1}{\Rightarrow}} Z\gamma_{n-1}'\beta\gamma_{n-1}'' = Z\gamma_n, \end{aligned}$$

(using the productions $sZ \rightarrow Zs$)

In either case, the workspace of the constructed derivation does not exceed $\mathsf{ws}(d, \gamma_n) + 1$.

Assume now that $\theta = Z\gamma_{n-1}$. By statement (B) $|Z\gamma_{n-1}|$ is even, so $|\gamma_{n-1}|$ is odd. We need to consider several cases:

1. If both $|\alpha|$ and $|\beta|$ are even, then $\alpha \rightarrow \beta \in P_1$, so

$$S_1 \overset{*}{\underset{G_1}{\Rightarrow}} Z\gamma_{n-1} \underset{G_1}{\Rightarrow} Z\gamma_n.$$

2. If $|\alpha|$ is even and $|\beta|$ is odd, then P_1 contains the productions $\alpha \rightarrow Z\beta$, and $Zs\alpha \rightarrow s\beta$, $Z\alpha s \rightarrow \beta s$ for $s \in A_N \cup A_T$. Note that at least one of the words $\gamma_{n-1}', \gamma_{n-1}''$ is not null because $|\gamma_{n-1}|$ is odd and $|\alpha|$ is even. Then, by moving the Z symbol we can apply one of the productions $Zs\alpha \rightarrow s\beta$ or $Z\alpha s \rightarrow \beta s$ and Z will be absorbed; the resulting derivation is

$$S_1 \overset{*}{\underset{G_1}{\Rightarrow}} Z\gamma_{n-1} \overset{*}{\underset{G_1}{\Rightarrow}} \gamma_n.$$

3. If $|\alpha|$ is odd and $|\beta|$ is even, then P_1 contains the productions $Z\alpha \rightarrow \beta$, and $\alpha s \rightarrow Z\beta s$, $\alpha s \rightarrow Zs\beta$ for $s \in A_N \cup A_T$. Now, we have

$$S_1 \overset{*}{\underset{G_1}{\Rightarrow}} Z\gamma_{n-1} \overset{*}{\underset{G_1}{\Rightarrow}} \gamma_{n-1}' Z\alpha\gamma_{n-1}'' \overset{*}{\underset{G_1}{\Rightarrow}} \gamma_{n-1}'\beta\gamma_{n-1}'' = \gamma_n.$$

4. Finally, if both $|\alpha|$ and $|\beta|$ are odd, then P_1 includes the productions $\alpha s \rightarrow \beta s$ and $s\alpha \rightarrow s\beta$ for every $s \in A_N \cup A_T \cup \{Z\}$. In this case, we have:

$$S_1 \overset{*}{\underset{G_1}{\Rightarrow}} Z\gamma_{n-1} \overset{*}{\underset{G_1}{\Rightarrow}} \gamma'_{n-1}Z\alpha\gamma''_{n-1} \overset{*}{\underset{G_1}{\Rightarrow}} \gamma'_{n-1}Z\beta\gamma''_{n-1} = Z\gamma_n.$$

In each case, the workspace condition is satisfied.

Statement (C) implies that for $x \in L(G)$ there is a word $x_1 \in L(G_1)$ such that $\mathsf{ws}_{G_1}(x_1) \leq \mathsf{ws}_G(x) + 1$ and $x_1 \in \{x, zx\}$. Therefore, by statement (B), $h(L(G_1)) = L(G)$.

Now consider the grammar $G' = (A \times A, A_T, (Z,S), P')$, where $A = A_N \cup A_T \cup \{Z, z\}$. The set of productions P' consists of the following:
(i) For every $a, b \in A_T$ include $(a,b) \rightarrow ab$, $(z,a) \rightarrow a$ in P'.
(ii) For every production in P_1 (except $S_1 \rightarrow ZS$) having the form

$$s_0 \cdots s_{2p-1} \rightarrow s'_0 \cdots s'_{2q-1}$$

include the following productions in P'

$$(s_0, s_1) \cdots (s_{2p-2}, s_{2p-1}) \rightarrow (s'_0, s'_1) \cdots (s'_{2q-2}, s'_{2q-1})$$

and

$$(s, s_0)(s_1, s_2) \cdots (s_{2p-1}, s') \rightarrow (s, s'_0)(s'_1, s'_2) \cdots (s'_{2q-1}, s')$$

for every $s, s' \in A$.

Let γ be a word of even length such that $\gamma \in A^*$. Denote by $\hat{\gamma}$ the word on $A \times A$ obtained by grouping two consecutive symbols in one symbol. In other words, if $\gamma = s_0 s_1 \cdots s_{2p-1}$, then $\hat{\gamma} = (s_0, s_1)(s_2, s_3) \cdots (s_{2p-2}, s_{2p-1})$. We claim that $ZS \overset{*}{\underset{G_1}{\Rightarrow}} \gamma$ if and only if $(Z,S) \overset{*}{\underset{G'}{\Rightarrow}} \hat{\gamma}$.

Assume that $ZS \overset{m}{\underset{G_1}{\Rightarrow}} \gamma$. We proceed by induction on m. For $m = 0$ we have $\gamma = ZS$, so $\hat{\gamma} = (Z,S)$ and we obviously have $(Z,S) \overset{*}{\underset{G'}{\Rightarrow}} \hat{\gamma}$.

Suppose now that the statement holds for derivations of length m and let $ZS \overset{m+1}{\underset{G_1}{\Rightarrow}} \gamma$. This derivation can be written as

$$ZS \overset{m}{\underset{G_1}{\Rightarrow}} t_0 \ldots t_{l-1} s_0 \cdots s_{2p-1} t_l \cdots t_{k-1} \underset{G_1}{\Rightarrow} t_0 \cdots t_{l-1} s'_0 \cdots s'_{2q-1} t_l \cdots t_{k-1},$$

where $s_0 \cdots s_{2p-1} \rightarrow s'_0 \cdots s'_{2q-1}$ is the production used in the last step and k is an even number.

There are two cases to consider depending on the parity of l. If l is an even number, then, by the inductive hypothesis, we have

$$\begin{aligned}(Z,S) &\overset{*}{\underset{G'}{\Rightarrow}} (t_0, t_1) \cdots (t_{l-2}, t_{l-1})(s_0, s_1) \cdots \\ &\qquad (s_{2p-2}, s_{2p-1})(t_l, t_{l+1}) \cdots (t_{k-2}, t_{k-1}) \\ &\underset{G'}{\Rightarrow} (t_0, t_1) \cdots (t_{l-2}, t_{l-1})(s'_0, s'_1) \cdots \\ &\qquad (s'_{2q-2}, s'_{2q-1})(t_l, t_{l+1}) \cdots (t_{k-2}, t_{k-1}) = \hat{\gamma}.\end{aligned}$$

If l is an odd number, then, using the inductive hypothesis we have

$$\begin{aligned}(Z,S) &\overset{*}{\underset{G'}{\Rightarrow}} (t_0,t_1)\cdots(t_{l-3},t_{l-2})(t_{l-1},s_0)(s_1,s_2)\cdots \\ &\quad (s_{2p-3},s_{2p-2})(s_{2p-1},t_l)(t_{l+1},t_{l+2})\cdots(t_{k-2},t_{k-1}) \\ &\underset{G'}{\Rightarrow} (t_0,t_1)\cdots(t_{l-3},t_{l-2})(t_{l-1},s'_0)(s'_1,s'_2)\cdots \\ &\quad (s'_{2p-3},s'_{2p-2})(s'_{2q-1},t_l)(t_{l+1},t_{l+2})\cdots(t_{k-2},t_{k-1}) = \hat{\gamma}.\end{aligned}$$

Conversely, assume that $(Z,S) \overset{m}{\underset{G'}{\Rightarrow}} \hat{\gamma}$. We prove, by induction on m, that $ZS \overset{*}{\underset{G_1}{\Rightarrow}} \gamma$. If $m = 0$, then the statement is obvious. Suppose that the statement holds for derivations of length m, and consider the derivation

$$(Z,S) \overset{m+1}{\underset{G'}{\Rightarrow}} \hat{\gamma}. \tag{9.4}$$

If $\gamma = t_0 \cdots t_{l-1}s'_0 \cdots s'_{2q-1}t_l \cdots t_{k-1}$, then $\hat{\gamma}$ is either

$$(t_0,t_1)\cdots(t_{l-2},t_{l-1})(s'_0,s'_1)\cdots(s'_{2q-2},s'_{2q-1})(t_l,t_{l+1})\cdots(t_{k-2},t_{k-1})$$

if l is even, or

$$(t_0,t_1)\cdots(t_{l-1},s_0)(s'_1,s'_2)\cdots(s'_{2q-1},t_l)(t_{l+1},t_{l+2})\cdots(t_{k-2},t_{k-1})$$

if l is odd. In the first case, we used the production

$$(s_0,s_1)\cdots(s_{2p-2},s_{2p-1}) \rightarrow (s'_0,s'_1)\cdots(s_{2q-2},s_{2q-1})$$

while in the second, we used the production

$$(t_{l-1},s_0),(s_1,s_2)\cdots(s_{2p-1},t_l) \rightarrow (t_{l-1},s'_0),(s'_1,s'_2)\cdots(s'_{2q-1},t_l).$$

Both productions correspond to the production $s_0 \cdots s_{2p-1} \rightarrow s'_0 \cdots s_{2q-1}$ in P_1. The word that precedes $\hat{\gamma}$ in the derivation 9.4 is

$$(t_0,t_1)\cdots(t_{l-2},t_{l-1})(s_0,s_1)\cdots(s_{2p-2},s_{2p-1})(t_l,t_{l+1})\cdots(t_{k-2},t_{k-1})$$

if l is even, or

$$(t_0,t_1)\cdots(t_{l-1},s_0)(s_1,s_2)\cdots(s_{2p-1},t_l)(t_{l+1},t_{l+2})\cdots(t_{k-2},t_{k-1})$$

if l is odd. By the inductive hypothesis we have in either case

$$SZ \overset{*}{\underset{G_1}{\Rightarrow}} t_0 \cdots t_{l-1}s_0 \cdots s_{2p-1}t_l \cdots t_{k-1}.$$

By applying the production $s_0 \cdots s_{2p-1} \rightarrow s'_0 \cdots s_{2q-1}$ we obtain the derivation $SZ \overset{*}{\underset{G_1}{\Rightarrow}} \gamma$.

Now we show that $L(G') = L(G)$. Let $x \in L(G')$. There exists a derivation $(Z,X) \overset{*}{\underset{G'}{\Rightarrow}} x$. The terminal symbols of x are produced by applying productions of the form $(a,b) \rightarrow ab$, or $(z,a) \rightarrow a$. Therefore, we may write

$(Z, X) \overset{*}{\underset{G'}{\Rightarrow}} \hat{\gamma} \overset{*}{\underset{G'}{\Rightarrow}} x$, for some $\gamma \in (A_T \cup \{z\})^*$ of even length, where the last part of the derivation makes use of productions of the form $(a, b) \rightarrow ab$, or $(z, a) \rightarrow a$. Thus, γ is a terminal word that differs from x just by occurrences of the symbol z. By the previous argument we have $ZX \overset{*}{\underset{G_1}{\Rightarrow}} \gamma$. Therefore, $S_1 \underset{G_1}{\Rightarrow} ZX \overset{*}{\underset{G_1}{\Rightarrow}} \gamma$ and statement (B) implies $x = h(\gamma) \in L(G)$, so $L(G') \subseteq L(G)$.

Conversely, let $x \in L(G)$. There is a derivation $S \overset{*}{\underset{G}{\Rightarrow}} x$. By statement (C) we have the derivation $S_1 \overset{*}{\underset{G_1}{\Rightarrow}} \theta$, where $\theta \in \{x, Zx\}$. This implies the existence of either the derivation $S_1 \underset{G}{\Rightarrow} ZS \overset{*}{\underset{G_1}{\Rightarrow}} x$ (when $|x|$ is even) or of the derivation $S_1 \underset{G}{\Rightarrow} ZS \overset{*}{\underset{G_1}{\Rightarrow}} Zx$ (when $|x|$ is odd). Thus, we obtain $(Z, S) \overset{*}{\underset{G'}{\Rightarrow}} \hat{x}$, or $(Z, S) \overset{*}{\underset{G'}{\Rightarrow}} \widehat{Zx} \overset{*}{\underset{G'}{\Rightarrow}} zx$, respectively. In either case, using productions of the form $(a, b) \rightarrow ab$ and $(z, a) \rightarrow z$ we have $(Z, S) \overset{*}{\underset{G'}{\Rightarrow}} x$, so $L(G) \subseteq L(G')$.

It is easy to see that for every $x' \in L(G')$ there exists a word $x_1 \in L(G_1)$ such that $\mathsf{ws}_{G_1}(x_1) \leq \mathsf{ws}_G(x) + 1$ and $x_1 = x$ or $x_1 = zx$. Also, we have $\mathsf{ws}_{G'}(x) \leq \max\{|x_1|, \frac{1}{2}\mathsf{ws}_{G_1}(x_1)\}$.

If $\mathsf{ws}_{G'}(x) \leq |x|$, then $L(G')$ is context-sensitive, by Lemma 9.3.6, and so, $L(G)$ is context-sensitive. Otherwise, we can write

$$\mathsf{ws}_{G'}(x) \leq \frac{1}{2}\mathsf{ws}_{G_1}(x_1) \leq \frac{1}{2}(\mathsf{ws}_G(x) + 1) \leq \frac{1}{2}((k+1)|x| + 1) \leq k|x|,$$

which implies, by the inductive hypothesis, that $L(G')$ is context-sensitive. Therefore, $L(G)$ is context-sensitive. ∎

We proved that the classes $\mathcal{L}_2$ and $\mathcal{L}_0$ are closed with respect to substitutions (cf. Theorems 5.6.4 and 8.6.23, respectively). Next, we prove a more limited result for $\mathcal{L}_1$.

Theorem 9.3.8 *The class $\mathcal{L}_1$ is closed with respect to λ-free substitutions.*

Proof. The construction applied in Theorem 8.6.23 works in this case as well because of the workspace theorem. Assume that we use the same notations as in the proof of that theorem and that the languages L and L_a are context-sensitive and that $\lambda \notin L_a$ for $a \in A$. We can assume that the grammars G and G_a (for $a \in A$) are context-sensitive. The workspace of the derivation 8.1 does not exceed $2|w|$, which implies the context-sensitivity of the language $s(L)$. ∎

Corollary 9.3.9 *The class $\mathcal{L}_1$ is closed with respect to λ-free morphisms.*

Proof. This statement follows immediately from Theorem 9.3.8 because every λ-free morphism is a special λ-free substitution. ∎

The workspace theorem allows us to prove that $\mathcal{L}_1$ is closed with respect to morphisms that may erase some symbols provided that the erased portion is limited to a certain fraction of the length of the word.

Definition 9.3.10 Let $L \subseteq A^*$ be a language and let $k \in \mathbb{N}$. A morphism $h : A^* \longrightarrow A^*$ is a *k-linear erasing morphism* on L if $|x| \leq k|h(x)|$ for every $x \in L$. □

Theorem 9.3.11 *Let $L \subseteq A^*$ be a context-sensitive language, and let $h : A^* \longrightarrow A^*$ be a morphism. If h is a k-linear erasing morphism on L for some $k \in \mathbb{N}$, then $h(L) \in \mathcal{L}_1$.*

Proof. If $k = 0$ we have either $L = \emptyset$, or $L = \{\lambda\}$. In either case L is context-sensitive, so we assume that $k \geq 1$.

Without loss of generality, we assume that L is generated by a context-sensitive grammar $G = (A_N, A, S, P)$ such that the productions in P that contain terminal symbols have the form $X \rightarrow a$, where X is a nonterminal and a is a terminal symbol. The language $h(L)$ is generated by the grammar $G' = (A_N, A, S, P')$, where P' is obtained from P by replacing the productions $X \rightarrow a$ by $X \rightarrow h(a)$ for $a \in A$. For the new grammar we can write:

$$\mathsf{ws}_{G'}(h(x)) = \max\{\mathsf{ws}_G(x), |h(x)|\} = \max\{|x|, |h(x)|\} \leq k|h(x)|,$$

for $x \in L$ because $k \geq 1$. Consequently, by Theorem 9.3.7, $h(L)$ is context-sensitive. ∎

Theorem 9.3.12 *Let A, B be two alphabets, and let $L \subseteq B^*$ be a context-sensitive language on B. If $h : A^* \longrightarrow B^*$ is a morphism, then $h^{-1}(L) = \{x \in A^* \mid h(x) \in L\}$ is a context-sensitive language.*

Proof. Suppose initially that $\lambda \notin L$. If $A = \{a_0, \ldots, a_{n-1}\}$, then introduce a new alphabet $C = \{c_0, \ldots, c_{n-1}\}$. Define the λ-free substitution $s : B^* \longrightarrow \mathcal{P}((B \cup C)^*)$ by $s(b) = C^*bC^*$ for $b \in B$.

Let $K = \{c_i h(a_i) \mid 0 \leq i \leq n-1\}$ be a finite language on the alphabet $B \cup C$, and let $H = s(L) \cap K^*$. By Theorem 9.3.8 and Corollary 9.3.2, the language H is context-sensitive. Note that $u \in H$ if and only if $u = c_{i_0} h(a_{i_0}) \cdots c_{i_{m-1}} h(a_{i_{m-1}})$, where $x = a_{i_0} \cdots a_{i_{m-1}} \in L$.

Define the λ-free morphism $g : (B \cup C)^* \longrightarrow (A \cup \{d\})^*$ given by $g(b) = d$ for $b \in B$ and $g(c_i) = a_i$ for $0 \leq i \leq n-1$. By Corollary 9.3.9, $g(H)$ is context-sensitive. If $u = c_{i_0} h(a_{i_0}) \cdots c_{i_{m-1}} h(a_{i_{m-1}}) \in H$, then

$$g(u) = a_{i_0} d^{|h(a_{i_0})|} a_{i_1} \cdots a_{i_{m-1}} d^{|h(a_{i_{m-1}})|}$$

and every word of $g(H)$ has this form for some $a_{i_0} \cdots a_{i_{m-1}} \in L$.

Finally, define a morphism $f : (A \cup \{d\})^* \longrightarrow A^*$ by $f(d) = \lambda$ and $f(a_i) = a_i$ for $0 \leq i \leq n-1$. If $v \in g(H)$ is a word of the form

$$v = a_{i_0} d^{|h(a_{i_0})|} a_{i_1} \cdots a_{i_{m-1}} d^{|h(a_{i_{m-1}})|},$$

then $x = f(v) = a_{i_0} \ldots a_{i_{m-1}} \in L$. Moreover, since L is λ-free, we have $|f(v)| = m + \sum_{0 \leq i \leq m-1} |h(a_i)| \leq m + km = (1+k)|x|$, where $k = \max\{|h(a_i)| \mid 0 \leq i \leq m-1\}$. Thus, f is a $(1+k)$-linear erasing morphism on $g(H)$. Therefore, by Theorem 9.3.11, $f(g(H))$ is context-sensitive.

We claim that $h^{-1}(L) = f(g(H))$. We have $x = a_{i_0} \cdots a_{i_{m-1}} \in h^{-1}(L)$ if and only if $h(a_{i_0}) \cdots h(a_{i_{m-1}}) \in L$ and this happens if and only if

$$a_{i_0} h(a_{i_0}) \cdots a_{i_{m-1}} h(a_{i_{m-1}}) \in H.$$

This is equivalent to $x = a_{i_0} \cdots a_{i_{m-1}} \in f(g(H))$, which justifies the previous equality. We conclude that $h^{-1}(L)$ is context-sensitive.

If $\lambda \in L$, then $L' = L - \{\lambda\}$ is a λ-free context-sensitive language, so $h^{-1}(L')$ is context-sensitive. Note that $h^{-1}(\lambda) = (\{a \in A \mid h(a) = \lambda\})^*$, so $h^{-1}(\lambda)$ is a regular language and, therefore, a context-sensitive language. Since $h^{-1}(L) = h^{-1}(L') \cup h^{-1}(\lambda)$, we obtain the context-sensitivity of L. ∎

9.4 Normal Forms for Context-Sensitive Grammars

In this section we show that we can restrict the productions of context-sensitive grammars without impairing their generative capabilities.

Definition 9.4.1 Let $G = (A_N, A_T, S, P)$ be a grammar. A production $\alpha \to \beta$ is

(i) a *left context-sensitive* if $\alpha = \gamma X$ and $\beta = \gamma\theta$;

(ii) a *right context-sensitive* if $\alpha = X\gamma$ and $\beta = \theta\gamma$;

(iii) a *permutative production* if $\alpha = XY$ and $\beta = YX$,

where $\gamma, \theta \in (A_N \cup A_T)^*$ and $X, Y \in A_N$. □

We begin by introducing a normal form for length-increasing grammars, which we have shown to be equivalent to context-sensitive grammars (cf. Theorem 4.3.16).

Definition 9.4.2 Let $G = (A_N, A_T, S, P)$ be length-increasing grammar. G is in *Kuroda normal form* if each of its production has any of the following forms: $X \to a$, $X \to Y$, $X \to YZ$, or $XY \to ZU$, where $a \in A_T$ and $X, Y, Z, U \in A_N$. □

Theorem 9.4.3 *For every λ-free context-sensitive language L there is an grammar in Kuroda normal form that generates L.*

Proof. Since L is a λ-free context-sensitive language, there exists a length-increasing grammar $G = (A_N, A_T, S, P)$ that generates L and has no erasure production. By Theorem 4.3.13 we can assume that the productions of G that contain terminal symbols have the form $X \to a$.

Let $\alpha \to \beta \in P$, where $2 \leq |\alpha| \leq |\beta|$. All symbols that appear in α or β are nonterminal; thus, we can write $\alpha = X_0 \cdots X_{m-1}$ and $\beta = Y_0 \cdots Y_{n-1}$, where $1 \leq m \leq n$.

Suppose initially that $m \geq 2$ and $n \geq 3$ and let $Z_0, \ldots, Z_{n-3}$ be new nonterminal symbols, that is, $\{Z_0, \ldots, Z_{m-1}\} \cap (A_N \cup A_T) = \emptyset$. Let P' be the set of productions obtained from P by replacing $\alpha \to \beta$ by the set of productions:

$$
\begin{array}{ll}
X_0X_1 \to Y_0Z_0 & Z_{m-2} \to Y_{m-1}Z_{m-1} \\
Z_0X_2 \to Y_1Z_1 & Z_{m-1} \to Y_mZ_m \\
Z_1X_3 \to Y_2Z_2 & Z_m \to Y_{m+1}Z_{m+1} \\
\vdots & \vdots \\
Z_{m-3}X_{m-1} \to Y_{m-2}Z_{m-2} & Z_{n-3} \to Y_{n-2}Y_{n-1}
\end{array}
$$

Let $G' = (A_N \cup \{Z_0, \ldots, Z_{n-3}\}, A_T, S, P'$. The application of the production $\alpha \to \beta$ in G is replaced by the derivation

$$\begin{aligned}
X_0X_1\cdots X_{m-1} &\underset{G'}{\Rightarrow} Y_0Z_0X_2\cdots X_{m-1}\\
&\underset{G'}{\Rightarrow} Y_0Y_1Z_1X_3\cdots X_{m-1}\\
&\underset{G'}{\Rightarrow} Y_0Y_1Y_2Z_2X_4\cdots X_{m-1}\\
&\overset{*}{\underset{G'}{\Rightarrow}} Y_0Y_1Y_2\cdots Y_{m-3}Z_{m-3}X_{m-1}\\
&\underset{G'}{\Rightarrow} Y_0Y_1Y_2\cdots Y_{m-3}Y_{m-2}Z_{m-2}\\
&\underset{G'}{\Rightarrow} Y_0Y_1Y_2\cdots Y_{m-2}Y_{m-1}Z_{m-1}\\
&\underset{G'}{\Rightarrow} Y_0Y_1Y_2\cdots Y_{m-1}Y_mZ_m\\
&\underset{G'}{\Rightarrow} Y_0Y_1Y_2\cdots Y_{m-1}Y_mY_{m+1}Z_{m+1}\\
&\overset{*}{\underset{G'}{\Rightarrow}} Y_0Y_1\cdots Y_{n-3}Z_{n-3}\\
&\underset{G'}{\Rightarrow} Y_0Y_1\cdots Y_{n-3}Y_{n-2}Y_{n-1}.
\end{aligned}$$

Note that the new productions can be applied only in the order specified in the previous derivation, so $L(G') = L(G)$.

By applying the same treatment to every production of the form $\alpha \to \beta$, with $|\alpha| \geq 2$ and $|\beta| \geq 3$ (and introducing new nonterminal symbols each time) we produce a grammar that is equivalent to G and contains productions of the form: $X \to a$, $X \to Y$, $X \to YZ$, $X \to \beta$, where $\beta \geq 3$, or $XY \to ZV$, where X, Y, Z, V are nonterminal symbols and $\beta \in A_N^*$. Finally, observe that the productions of the form $X \to \beta$ can be replaced by productions of the form $U \to VW$, with $U, V, W \in A_N^*$ by using the technique applied in Theorem 5.4.2 to obtain Chomsky normal form. ∎

Starting from a grammar in the Kuroda normal form it is easy to generate an equivalent context-sensitive grammar. Indeed, note that a production of the form $XY \to ZU$ can be replaced by four new context-sensitive productions:

$$XY \to XY', XY' \to X'Y', X'Y' \to X'U, X'U \to ZU,$$

where X' and Y' are new nonterminal symbols. This observation allows yet another proof of Theorem 4.3.16, that is, it provides another construction of a context-sensitive grammar equivalent to a length-increasing grammar.

Observe that the context-sensitive productions introduced here involve both right context-sensitive productions ($XY' \to X'Y'$ and $X'U \to ZU$) and left context-sensitive productions ($XY \to XY'$ and $X'Y' \to X'U$).

Actually, one can further restrict the form of the productions of length-increasing grammars to left context-sensitive and permutative productions, that is, to productions of the form

$$X \to a, X \to Y, X \to YZ, XY \to XZ, \text{ or } XY \to YX,$$

where X, Y, Z are nonterminal symbols and a is a terminal symbol.

9.5 Exercises

Linear Bounded Automata

1. $^\diamond$ Design an lba that accepts the language $\{a^n b^n c^n \mid n \in \mathbb{N}\}$.
2. $^\diamond$ Design an lba that accepts the language $\{x \in \{a,b,c\}^* \mid n_a(x) = n_b(x) = n_c(x)\}$.
3. $^{\diamond\diamond}$ Design lbas that accept the languages $\{a^n \mid n \in \mathbb{N}$ and n is prime$\}$ and $\{a^n \mid n \in \mathbb{N}$ and n is not prime$\}$.
4. $^\diamond$ Prove that for every lba $\mathcal{M}$ there exists an equivalent lba $\mathcal{M}'$ (that is, an lba $\mathcal{M}'$ such that $L(\mathcal{M}') = L(\mathcal{M})$) such that $\mathcal{M}'$ halts on every input.
5. $^{\diamond\diamond}$ Let $\mathcal{M} = (B, Q, \delta, q_0, F)$ be an lba and let $x \in B^*$.
   (a) Prove that the initial configuration $q_0 \triangleright x \triangleleft$ may have at most $k(x) = |Q|(|x| + 2)|B|^{|x|}$ successor configurations.
   (b) Prove that it is decidable whether an arbitrary lba $\mathcal{M}$ halts on an input word x.
6. $^{\diamond\diamond}$ Starting from two lbas $\mathcal{M}_0, \mathcal{M}_1$ give an effective construction of an lba $\mathcal{M}$ such that $L(\mathcal{M}) = L(\mathcal{M}_0) \cap L(\mathcal{M}_1)$.

Closure Properties

7. Let $L_0, \ldots, L_{n-1} \subseteq A^*$ be n context-free languages, where $n \geq 1$. Prove that $\bigcap\{L_i \mid 0 \leq i \leq n-1\}$ is a context-sensitive language.
8. Let $H, K, L \subseteq A^*$ such that $L = H \oplus K$. Prove that if any two of the languages H, K, L is context-sensitive, then the third is also context-sensitive.
9. $^\diamond$ Show that it is undecidable whether the language generated by a context-sensitive grammar is empty.
   Hint. Start from the fact that it is undecidable whether the intersection of the languages generated by two context-sensitive grammars G, G' is nonempty (cf. Theorem 8.8.11) and from Exercise 6.
10. Let G be a type 0 grammar such that $L(G)$ is not context sensitive. Prove that for every $k \in \mathbb{N}$ there is a word $x \in L(G)$ such that $\mathsf{ws}_G(x) > k|x|$.
11. $^{\diamond\diamond}$ Prove that for any two morphisms $g, h : A^* \longrightarrow B^*$ the equalizer $\mathsf{EQ}(g,h)$ is a context-sensitive language. Conclude that every recursive enumerable language is a morphic image of a context-sensitive language.
12. $^{\diamond\diamond}$ Prove that for every polynomial $p(n)$ with coefficients in $\mathbb{N}$ the language $\{a^{p(n)} \mid n \in \mathbb{N}\}$ is context-sensitive,
13. $^{\diamond\diamond}$ Prove that the language $\{a^m b^n c^{\mathsf{ack}(m,n)}\}$ is context-sensitive.
14. $^\diamond$ Let R be a regular language and L be a context-sensitive language. Is the language $\mathsf{shuffle}(R, L)$ context-sensitive?

Normal Forms for Context-Sensitive Grammars

15. $^\diamond$ Give a grammar in Kuroda normal form that generates the language $L = \{a^n b^n c^n \mid n \in \mathbb{N}\}$.
16. $^{\diamond\diamond}$ Let $G = (A_N, A_T, S, P)$ be a length-increasing grammar in Kuroda

normal form, and let $XY \to ZU$ be a production in P. Is the grammar

$$\begin{aligned} G' &= (A_N \cup \{X', Y'\}, A_T, S, P - \{XY \to ZU\} \\ &\cup\{XY \to X'Y, X'Y \to X'U, X'U \to ZU\}) \end{aligned}$$

equivalent to the grammar G?

Solution. G' is not equivalent to G. Indeed, consider the grammar

$$\begin{aligned} G &= (\{S, X, Y, Z, U, V\}, \{a, b\}, S, \{S \to XY, Y \to UV, \\ &XY \to ZU, Z \to b, Y \to a, U \to c\} \end{aligned}$$

and replace the production $XY \to ZU$ as above. We obtain the grammar

$$\begin{aligned} G' &= (\{S, X, Y, Z, U, V\}, \{a, b\}, S, \{S \to XY, Y \to UV, \\ &XY \to X'Y, X'Y \to X'U, X'U \to ZU, \\ &Z \to b, Y \to a, U \to c\}) \end{aligned}$$

We have the derivation

$$\begin{aligned} S &\underset{G'}{\Rightarrow} XY \underset{G'}{\Rightarrow} X'Y \underset{G'}{\Rightarrow} X'UV \\ &\underset{G'}{\Rightarrow} ZUY \overset{*}{\underset{b}{\Rightarrow}} ca, \end{aligned}$$

which is not possible in the grammar G.

17. $^\diamond$ Prove the following extension of Kuroda normal form to arbitrary grammars. Every recursive enumerable language can be generated by a grammar $G = (A_N, A_T, S, P)$ whose productions are of the form

$$X \to a, X \to Y, XY \to XZ, XY \to YX, X \to \lambda,$$

where X, Y, Z are nonterminal and a is some terminal symbol.

18. Using Penttonen's normal form (mentioned in Section 9.6) formulate and prove a stronger version of the statement contained by Exercise 17.

9.6 Bibliographical Comments

Linear bounded automata are due to [Myhill, 1957a] and their relationships with context-sensitive languages was studied by Landweber [1963]. Theorem 9.3.1 was obtained in [Immerman, 1988] and [Szelepcsényi, 1987]. The Workspace Theorem was obtained by N. D. Jones [1966].

Kuroda normal form is described in [Kuroda, 1964]. The normal form that includes left context-sensitive and permutative productions was obtained by G. Révész [1983]. M. Penttonen [1972] proved a stronger result that makes no use of productions of the form $X \to Y$. Moreover, Penttonen [1974] proved that left-context sensitive productions suffice (without permutation productions).

Solution to Exercises 12 and 13 and related results can be found in [Simovici, 1980a; Simovici, 1980b] and [Simovici and Istrail, 1978].

Part IV

Applications

Chapter 10

Codes

10.1 Introduction

In this chapter we present the notion of a code and its properties. The results are relevant both for formal language theory and for a variety of other areas of computer science such as computer networks, data compression, etc.

A *source* can be regarded as a process that produces symbols from a countable set S (cf. [Storer, 1988]). The probabilistic distribution of these symbols is also a part of this process and this suggests the following definition.

Definition 10.1.1 An *information source* (in short, a *source*) is a pair $\mathcal{S} = (S, D)$, where $S = \{s_0, s_1, \ldots\}$ is a nonempty, countable set referred to as the *source set*, and D is is a probability distribution

$$D = \begin{pmatrix} s_0 & s_1 & \cdots \\ p_0 & p_1 & \cdots \end{pmatrix}$$

where $\sum_{i \in \mathbb{N}} p_i = 1$.

If S is a finite set, then we refer to $\mathcal{S} = (S, D)$ as a *finite source*. □

The set S is nonempty but not necessarily finite. Nevertheless, we will refer to the members of $\mathbf{Seq}(S)$ as *words* and will denote the set $\mathbf{Seq}(S)$ by S^*. Note that S^* is a monoid with respect to the concatenation of words and the null word λ.

The symbols generated by the source are encoded as words over an alphabet A, which is, of course, finite, using a morphism $h : S^* \longrightarrow A^*$ referred to as the *encoding morphism*. The encoding of a word $s_0 \cdots s_{m-1}$ generated by the source, $h(s_0) \cdots h(s_{m-1}) \in A^*$, is sent through a communication line to a

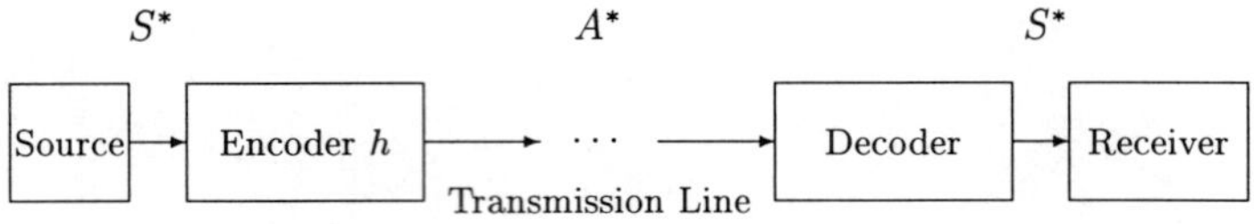

Figure 10.1: General Scheme of Data Transmission

decoder that converts the word $h(s_0)\cdots h(s_{m-1})$ back to a word over the set S (see Figure 10.1).

Different words produced by the source must yield distinct coded messages. This amounts to requiring that h be an injective morphism between S^* and A^*.

Definition 10.1.2 Let A be an alphabet and let $\mathcal{S} = (S, D)$ be a source. A *code* on an alphabet A is a triple $C = (\mathcal{S}, A, h)$, where $h : S^* \longrightarrow A^*$ is an injective morphism.

The *code set* of C is the set $h(S) = \{h(s) \mid s \in S\}$. □

Often, when the source and the alphabet are clear from context we will use the term *code* to refer to either h or the code set $h(S)$.

Example 10.1.3 Let S be a finite source set, A be an alphabet such that $|A| \geq 2$, and $k \in \mathbb{N}$ be a number such that $|S| \leq |A|^k$. Any injective mapping $h : S \longrightarrow A^*$ such that $h(s)$ is a word of length k can be extended to an injective morphism from S^* to A^*. Codes constructed in this manner are known as *block codes of length k*.

For instance, let $S = \{s_0, s_1, s_2\}$ and let $A = \{0, 1\}$. By choosing $k = 2$, we can define a block code of length 2 by $h(s_0) = 00$, $h(s_1) = 01$, and $h(s_2) = 10$. □

If we do not require that $|h(s)| = k$ for each $s \in S$, then even if $h : S \longrightarrow A^*$ is an injective mapping, its extension $h : S^* \longrightarrow A^*$ is not necessarily an injective morphism as shown in the next example.

Example 10.1.4 Let $S = \{s_0, s_1, s_2\}$, $A = \{0, 1\}$, and let $h : S \longrightarrow A^*$ be the injective mapping $h(s_0) = 0$, $h(s_1) = 01$, and $h(s_2) = 10$. Observe that the extension $h : S^* \longrightarrow A^*$ is not injective because $h(s_1 s_0) = h(s_0 s_2) = 010$. □

Also, if L is a code set and $\emptyset \neq L' \subseteq L$, then L' is also a code set (cf. Exercise 2).

10.2 Unique Decipherability

In this section we examine a fundamental characteristic property of code sets: given an encoded word, we can always recover the corresponding source word.

Definition 10.2.1 Let A be an alphabet, and let $L = \{x_0, x_1, \ldots\}$ be a language on A, $L \neq \emptyset$. L is *uniquely decipherable* if the equality

$$x_{i_0} \cdots x_{i_{m-1}} = x_{j_0} \cdots x_{j_{n-1}}$$

implies $m = n$ and $x_{i_\ell} = x_{j_\ell}$, for $0 \leq \ell \leq n-1$. □

Note that if L is a code set, then $\lambda \notin L$. Indeed, if $\lambda \in L$, then we would have $x = \lambda x$ for every $x \in A^*$, which contradicts the uniquely decipherability property.

Theorem 10.2.2 *A language $L \subseteq A^*$ is uniquely decipherable if and only if it is code set.*

Proof. Suppose that $L = \{x_0, \ldots, x_{k-1}, \ldots\}$ is a uniquely decipherable language. Let S be a source set such that S has the same cardinality as L. There exists a bijection $h : S \longrightarrow L$ such that $h(s_i) = x_i$ for every $x_i \in L$. Suppose that $h(s_{i_0} \ldots s_{i_{m-1}}) = h(s_{j_0} \ldots s_{j_{n-1}})$. This is equivalent to $x_{i_0} \cdots x_{i_{m-1}} = x_{j_0} \cdots x_{j_{n-1}}$, so $m = n$ and $x_{i_\ell} = x_{j_\ell}$ for $0 \leq \ell \leq n-1$ by the unique decipherability condition, which, in turn, implies $h(s_{i_\ell}) = h(s_{j_\ell})$ for $0 \leq \ell \leq m-1$. Since $h : S \longrightarrow L$ is a bijection, $s_{i_\ell} = s_{j_\ell}$ for $0 \leq \ell \leq m-1$, which means that $s_{i_0} \ldots s_{i_{m-1}} = s_{j_0} \ldots s_{j_{n-1}}$. This shows that the morphism $h : S^* \longrightarrow A^*$ is injective, so $L = h(S)$ is a code set.

Conversely, suppose that L is a code set, that is, $L = h(S)$, where $h : S \longrightarrow A^*$ is an injective mapping whose extension to S^* is an injective morphism, and that $h(s_i) = x_i$ for every $x_i \in L$. If $x_{i_0}, \ldots, x_{i_{m-1}}, x_{j_0}, \ldots, x_{j_{n-1}}$ are words in L such that $x_{i_0} \cdots x_{i_{m-1}} = x_{j_0} \cdots x_{j_{n-1}}$, then $s_{i_0} \cdots s_{i_{m-1}} = s_{j_0} \cdots s_{j_{n-1}}$, because of the injectivity of the morphism $h : S^* \longrightarrow A^*$. Consequently, $m = n$, $s_{i_\ell} = s_{j_\ell}$ for $0 \leq \ell \leq n-1$, so h is a code, and L is a code set. ∎

Corollary 10.2.3 *A language $L \subseteq A^+$ is not a code set if and only if there exist words $x_{i_0}, \ldots, x_{i_{m-1}}, x_{j_0}, \ldots, x_{j_{n-1}}$ in L such that $x_{i_0} \cdots x_{i_{m-1}} = x_{j_0} \cdots x_{j_{n-1}}$ and x_{i_0} is a proper prefix of x_{j_0}.*

Proof. Suppose that L is not a code set. Then there exist words

$$x_{i_0}, \ldots, x_{i_{m-1}}, x_{j_0}, \ldots, x_{j_{n-1}} \in L$$

such that $x_{i_0} \cdots x_{i_{m-1}} = x_{j_0} \cdots x_{j_{n-1}}$. Suppose that we choose these words such that $\ell = m + n$ is minimal. Then, $x_{i_0} \neq x_{j_0}$ since otherwise, we would have $x_{i_1} \cdots x_{i_{m-1}} = x_{j_1} \cdots x_{j_{n-1}}$ and this would contradict the minimality of ℓ. Therefore, one of the words x_{i_0}, x_{j_0} is a proper prefix of the other.

Conversely, if $x_{i_0} \cdots x_{i_{m-1}} = x_{j_0} \cdots x_{j_{n-1}}$ and x_{i_0} is a proper prefix of x_{j_0} for some words $x_{i_0}, \ldots, x_{i_{m-1}}, x_{j_0}, \ldots, x_{j_{n-1}}$ in L, then L is not uniquely decipherable, so it is not a code set. ∎

Using Theorem 10.2.2 we introduce an important class of codes.

Example 10.2.4 Let A be an alphabet and $L \subseteq A^*$ be a language such that for every $x, y \in L$ with $x \neq y$ we have $x \notin \mathsf{PREF}(y)$. By Corollary 10.2.3 L is a code set. □

This suggests the following definition.

Definition 10.2.5 Let A be an alphabet. A *prefix code* on A is a language $L \subseteq A^*$ such that for every $x, y \in L$ with $x \neq y$ we have $x \notin \mathsf{PREF}(y)$. □

Example 10.2.6 Let $k \in \mathbb{N}$, and let $L_k \subseteq \{a, b\}^*$ be defined by $L_k = \{a^n b \mid 0 \leq n \leq k\}$. Then, L_k is a prefix code, since each code word has exactly one symbol b, which marks its end. □

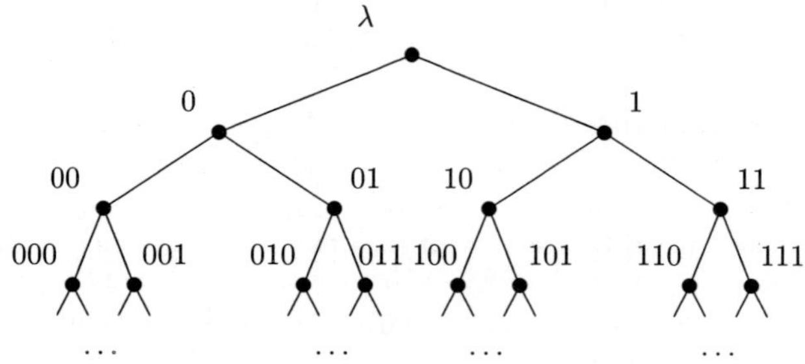

Figure 10.2: The Tree $\mathtt{T}_A$

Prefix codes can be obtained using a labeled ordered tree $\mathtt{T}_A$ as a representation of the set of words over an alphabet A. The root of $\mathtt{T}_A$ is labeled by λ; if $A = \{a_0, \ldots, a_{k-1}\}$, then every node labeled by a word $x \in A^*$ has k successors labeled (from left to right) by the words $xa_0, xa_1, \ldots, xa_{k-1}$.

Example 10.2.7 Let $A = \{0, 1\}$ be an alphabet. The labeled ordered tree $\mathtt{T}_A$ is shown in Figure 10.2. Note that a word u is a prefix of another word v if and only if u is the label of a node that occurs on the path that joins the root with v. Therefore, to obtain a prefix code we need to consider a subtree $\mathtt{T}$ of $\mathtt{T}_A$. The prefix code that corresponds to $\mathtt{T}$ comprises the labels of the leaves of $\mathtt{T}$.

For instance, the prefix code that corresponds to the subtree shown in Figure 10.3 is $\{000, 001, 01, 11\}$. □

To introduce a characterization of code sets we need the next definition.

Definition 10.2.8 A language $L \subseteq A^*$ is *catenatively independent* if $L \cap L^n = \emptyset$ for every $n \geq 2$. □

In other words, L is catenatively independent if no word $w \in L$ can be written as $w = w_0 \cdots w_{n-1}$ where $n \geq 2$ and $w_i \in L$ for $0 \leq i \leq n-1$.

Example 10.2.9 It is easy to see that the language $L = \{a, aba, baba, bb, bbba\}$ over the alphabet $\{a, b\}$ is catenatively independent.

Also, the language $\{x \in A^* \mid |x| = n\}$ is catenatively independent for any n. □

Note that no catenatively independent language may contain λ.

Theorem 10.2.10 (Schützenberger Theorem) *A language L over the alphabet A is a code if and only if L is catenatively independent and $L^*w \cap L^* \neq \emptyset$, $wL^* \cap L^* \neq \emptyset$ for a word $w \in A^*$ imply $w \in L^*$.*

Proof. To prove that the conditions of the theorem are sufficient let $L \subseteq A^*$ be a language that satisfies these conditions. Note that $\lambda \notin L$ because of the catenative independence of L. By Corollary 10.2.3, if L were not a code, we would have words $x_{i_0}, \ldots, x_{i_{n-1}}, x_{j_0}, \ldots, x_{j_{m-1}}$ from L with $x_{i_0} \cdots x_{i_{n-1}} =$

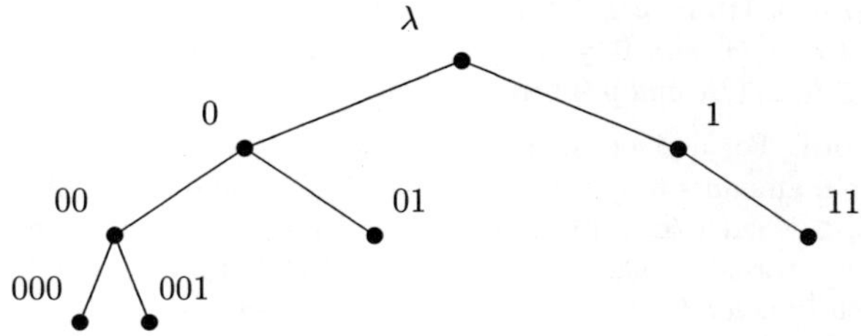

Figure 10.3: The Subtree T of T_A

$x_{j_0} \cdots x_{j_{m-1}}$ and $x_{j_0} = x_{i_0} z$ for some $z \neq \lambda$. Thus, $Lz \cap L \neq \emptyset$, which implies $L^* z \cap L^* \neq \emptyset$. This also gives, by the cancellation property, $x_{i_1} \cdots x_{i_{n-1}} = z x_{j_1} \cdots x_{j_{m-1}}$, so $zL^* \cap L^* \neq \emptyset$; hence, $z \in L^*$ and $z \neq \lambda$. Since $x_{j_0} = x_{i_0} z$, this contradicts the catenative independence of L.

To prove that the conditions are necessary, assume that L is a code. The catenative independence of L is immediate. Suppose that $L^* w \cap L^* \neq \emptyset$ and $wL^* \cap L^* \neq \emptyset$ for a word $w \in A^*$. This means that we have words $x_{i_0}, \ldots, x_{i_{m-1}}, x_{j_0}, \ldots, x_{j_{n-1}}$ and $x_{k_0}, \ldots, x_{k_{p-1}}, x_{l_0}, \ldots, x_{l_{q-1}}$ in L such that

$$\begin{aligned} x_{i_0} \cdots x_{i_{m-1}} w &= x_{j_0} \cdots x_{j_{n-1}}, \\ w x_{k_0} \cdots x_{k_{p-1}} &= x_{l_0} \cdots x_{l_{q-1}}. \end{aligned}$$

Combining the above equalities, we obtain

$$x_{i_0} \cdots x_{i_{m-1}} x_{l_0} \cdots x_{l_{q-1}} = x_{j_0} \cdots x_{j_{n-1}} x_{k_0} \cdots x_{k_{p-1}}.$$

The fact that L is a code implies $m + q = n + p$, and in addition, $x_{i_0} = x_{j_0}, \ldots, x_{l_{q-1}} = x_{k_{p-1}}$.

We must have $m \leq n$, because if $m > n$, then $x_{i_n} \ldots x_{i_{m-1}} w = \lambda$, and this would imply $x_{i_n} = \cdots = x_{i_{m-1}} = w = \lambda$, which contradicts the catenative independence of the language L.

If $m = n$, then $w = \lambda \in L^*$; otherwise, $m < n$, and this implies $w = x_{j_m} \cdots x_{j_{n-1}}$, which gives $w \in L^*$. ∎

Words built by concatenating the words of code sets allow us to reconstruct uniquely the constituent sequence of code words. This is important for molecular biology, data transmission, etc. Thus, the question of whether a language is a code set is of interest. We present an algorithm that allows us to determine whether a finite language L is a code set.

Let $L \subseteq A^+$ be a λ-free language on the alphabet A. Define the sequence of languages $R_0(L), R_1(L), \ldots, R_n(L), \ldots$ by

$$\begin{aligned} R_0(L) &= L^{-1}L - \{\lambda\} \\ R_{n+1}(L) &= L^{-1}R_n(L) \cup R_n(L)^{-1}L \end{aligned}$$

for $n \in \mathbb{N}$.

Lemma 10.2.11 *Let L be a λ-free language on the alphabet A. For all $n \in \mathbb{N}$ and $k \in \mathbb{N}$ with $0 \leq k \leq n$, we have $\lambda \in R_n(L)$ if and only if there exist $w \in R_{n-k}(L)$ and $p, q \in \mathbb{N}$ such that $wL^p \cap L^q \neq \emptyset$ and $p + q = k$.*

Proof. For a given n, the argument is by induction on $k \geq 0$. The basis step, $k = 0$ amounts to proving that $\lambda \in R_n(L)$ if and only if there is $w \in R_n(L)$ and $p, q \in \mathbb{N}$ such that $wL^p \cap L^q \neq \emptyset$ and $p + q = 0$ (which means $p = q = 0$). In other words, we need to show that $\lambda \in R_n(L)$ if and only if there is $w \in R_n(L)$ such that $wL^0 \cap L^0 = w \cap \{\lambda\} \neq \emptyset$. This is clearly the case if we take $w = \lambda$.

For the induction step, suppose that the statement holds for k, that is $\lambda \in R_n(L)$ if and only if there exist $w \in R_{n-k}(L)$ and $p, q \in \mathbb{N}$ such that $wL^p \cap L^q \neq \emptyset$ and $p + q = k$. We need to prove that $\lambda \in R_n(L)$ if and only if there exist $w \in R_{n-k-1}(L)$ and $p', q' \in \mathbb{N}$ such that $wL^{p'} \cap L^{q'} \neq \emptyset$ and $p' + q' = k + 1$. We use the fact that $R_{n-k}(L) = L^{-1}R_{n-k-1}(L) \cup R_{n-k-1}(L)^{-1}L$.

If $\lambda \in R_n(L)$, by the induction hypothesis, there exist $w \in R_{n-k}(L)$ and $p, q \in \mathbb{N}$ such that $wL^p \cap L^q \neq \emptyset$ and $p + q = k$. This implies that $wx = y$ for some $x \in L^p$ and $y \in L^q$. Since $R_{n-k} = L^{-1}R_{n-k-1}(L) \cup R_{n-k-1}(L)^{-1}L$, we need to consider the following cases:

1. either $zw = u \in R_{n-k-1}(L)$, or
2. $vw = z \in R_{n-k-1}$ for some $v \in R_{n-k-1}(L)$,

for some $z \in L$.

In the first case $zy = ux$, so $uL^p \cap L^{q+1} \neq \emptyset$; in the second, $zx = vwx = vy$, so $L^{p+1} \cap vL^q \neq \emptyset$.

Conversely, suppose that there exist $w \in R_{n-k-1}(L)$ and $p', q' \in \mathbb{N}$ such that $wL^{p'} \cap L^{q'} \neq \emptyset$ and $p' + q' = k + 1$. Note that we must have $q > 0$ for, if $q = 0$, then we have $wL^{p'} \cap \{\lambda\} \neq \emptyset$, which means that $\lambda \in wL^{p'}$. Since L is λ-free this is possible only if $p' = 0$, which contradicts the fact that $p' + q' \geq 1$.

Since $q' > 0$, we have

$$wx_{i_0} \cdots x_{i_{p'-1}} = x_{j_0} \cdots x_{j_{q'-1}}$$

for some $x_{i_0}, \ldots, x_{i_{p'-1}}, x_{j_0}, \ldots, x_{j_{q'-1}}$ in L.

We have the following cases:

1. If $|w| > |x_{j_0}|$, then $w = x_{j_0}t$ for some $t \in A^+$. Thus, $t \in L^{-1}R_{n-k-1}(L) \subseteq R_{n-k}(L)$ and
$$tx_{i_0} \cdots x_{i_{p'-1}} = x_{j_1} \cdots x_{j_{q'-1}},$$
which means that $tL^{p'} \cap L^{q'-1} \neq \emptyset$. Since $p' + (q' - 1) = k$, by the inductive hypothesis, $\lambda \in R_n(L)$.
2. If $|w| < |x_{j_0}|$, then $x_{j_0} = wt$ for some $t \in A^+$. In this case, $t \in LR_{n-k-1}(L)^{-1} \subseteq R_{n-k}$ and $x_{i_0} \cdots x_{i_{p'-1}} = tx_{j_1} \cdots x_{j_{q'-1}}$, which amounts to $L^{p'} \cap tL^{q'-1} \neq \emptyset$. By the inductive hypothesis we have again $\lambda \in R_n(L)$.
3. If $|w| = |x_{j_0}|$, then $w = x_{j_0}$, which implies $\lambda \in L^{-1}R_{n-k-1}(L) \subseteq R_{n-k}$. Also, we have $\lambda L^{p'} \cap L^{q'-1} \neq \emptyset$, which implies $\lambda \in R_n(L)$ by the inductive hypothesis.

∎

Theorem 10.2.12 *Let A be an alphabet, and let $L \subseteq A^+$ be a language on A. Define the sequence of sets*

$$R_0(L) = L^{-1}L - \{\lambda\}$$
$$R_{n+1}(L) = L^{-1}R_n(L) \cup R_n(L)^{-1}L$$

for $n \in \mathbb{N}$. Then, L is a code if and only if none of the languages $R_n(L)$ contains λ.

Proof. Suppose that $\lambda \in R_n(L)$. Taking $k = n$ in Lemma 10.2.11, it follows that there is $w \in R_0(L)$ and $p, q \in \mathbb{N}$ such that $wL^p \cap L^q \neq \emptyset$ and $p + q = n$. Since $w \in R_0(L) = L^{-1}L - \{\lambda\}$ we have $w \neq \lambda$, and there exist $x, y \in L$ such that $xw = y$. Since $w \neq \lambda$ we have $x \neq y$.

Since $wL^p \cap L^q \neq \emptyset$ we can write

$$wx_{i_0} \cdots x_{i_{p-1}} = x_{j_0} \cdots x_{j_{q-1}} \tag{10.1}$$

for some $x_{i_0}, \ldots, x_{i_{p-1}}, x_{j_0}, \ldots, x_{j_{q-1}} \in L$. By concatenating x to the left in the equality 10.1 we obtain

$$yx_{i_0} \cdots x_{i_{p-1}} = xx_{j_0} \cdots x_{j_{q-1}},$$

which contradicts the unique decipherability of L.

Conversely, suppose that L is not a code. By Corollary 10.2.3 we have $x_{i_0} \cdots x_{i_{p-1}} = x_{j_0} \cdots x_{j_{q-1}}$ for some words $x_{i_0}, \ldots, x_{i_{p-1}}, x_{j_0}, \ldots, x_{j_{q-1}} \in L$, such that x_{i_0} is a proper prefix of x_{j_0}, so $x_{j_0} = x_{i_0}t$ for some $t \in A^+$. Therefore, we have $t \in R_0(L)$ and also $x_{i_1} \cdots x_{i_{p-1}} = tx_{j_1} \cdots x_{j_{q-1}}$, that is, $L^{p-1} \cap tL^{q-1} \neq \emptyset$. The conditions of Lemma 10.2.11 are thus satisfied for $n = k = p + q - 2$, so $\lambda \in R_n(L)$. ∎

Under certain conditions, Theorem 10.2.12 allows the formulation of an algorithm for deciding whether a language L is a code. Further basis for the algorithm is provided by several preliminary results.

Let $\theta_A \subseteq A^* \times A^*$ be the relation defined by $(x, y) \in \theta_A$ if $x = y = \lambda$, or $x \neq \lambda$ and $y \neq \lambda$. It is easy to see that θ_A is a congruence on A^*. Furthermore, L is a $(\mu_L \cap \theta_A)$-saturated set.

Lemma 10.2.13 *If $L \subseteq A^*$ is a μ-saturated language on A, where μ is a congruence on A^*, then for any language $K \subseteq A^*$, the language $K^{-1}L$ is μ-saturated.*

Proof. We need to prove that if $x \in K^{-1}L$ and $(x, y) \in \mu$, then $y \in K^{-1}L$. If $x \in K^{-1}L$, then $ux = w$ for some $u \in K$ and some $w \in L$. On the other hand, observe that $(ux, uy) = (w, uy) \in \mu$ because μ is a congruence. Since L is μ-saturated, this implies $uy \in L$, so $y \in K^{-1}L$, which shows that $K^{-1}L$ is indeed μ-saturated. ∎

Theorem 10.2.14 *Let L be a λ-free language on the alphabet A. The sets $R_n(L)$, introduced in Theorem 10.2.12, are σ_L-saturated for every $n \in \mathbb{N}$, where σ_L is the congruence on A^* defined by $\sigma_L = \mu_L \cap \theta_A$.*

Proof. If $R_0(L) = \emptyset$, then the result is immediate. So, assume that $R_0(L) \neq \emptyset$. We will prove, by induction on $n \in \mathbb{N}$, that $x \in R_n(L)$ and $(x, y) \in \sigma_L$ implies $y \in R_n(L)$.

For $n = 0$, let $x \in R_0(L) = L^{-1}L - \{\lambda\}$. This means that there are $u, w \in L$ such that $ux = w$ and $x \neq \lambda$. Since $(x, y) \in \mu_L$, we have $y \neq \lambda$, and $uxv \in L$ if and only if $uyx \in L$ for every $u, v \in A^*$. In particular, taking $v = \lambda$, we obtain $uy \in L$ because $ux \in L$. Thus, $y \in L^{-1}L - \{\lambda\}$, which shows that $R_0(L)$ is σ_L-saturated.

Note that L is a σ_L saturated set. Suppose that $R_n(L)$ is σ_L-saturated. By Lemma 10.2.13, both $L^{-1}R_n(L)$ and $R_n(L)^{-1}L$ are σ_L-saturated languages. Therefore, by Theorem 1.2.31, the language $R_{n+1}(L)$ is a σ_L-saturated language. ∎

Corollary 10.2.15 *If $L \subseteq A^*$ is a regular language on the alphabet A, then the collection of languages $\{R_n(L) \mid n \in \mathbb{N}\}$ is finite.*

Proof. Since L is a regular language there are a finite number of μ_L equivalence classes of the congruence μ_L and, therefore, a finite number of equivalence classes of the congruence σ_L. Since each set $R_n(L)$ is a union of such classes, it follows that there are no more than $2^{|A^*/\sigma_L|}$ distinct sets in the collection $\{R_n(L) \mid n \in \mathbb{N}\}$. ∎

Algorithm 10.2.16 (Sardinas-Patterson Algorithm)
Input: A regular language $L \subseteq A^*$.
Output: The decision of whether L is a code.
Method: Compute the sequence of languages $R_0(L), \ldots, R_n(L), \ldots$ defined by

$$\begin{aligned} R_0(L) &= L^{-1}L - \{\lambda\} \\ R_{n+1}(L) &= L^{-1}R_n(L) \cup R_n(L)^{-1}L \end{aligned}$$

for $n \in \mathbb{N}$. Halt the computation when a language $R_n(L)$ equals a previous language $R_p(L)$. L is a code if and only if λ does not occur in any of the languages of this sequence.
Proof of Correctness: The correctness of the algorithm is an immediate consequence of Theorem 10.2.12 and Corollary 10.2.15. ∎

Example 10.2.17 The language $L = \{aa, ab, aab, bbab\}$ on the alphabet $\{a, b\}$ is finite and, therefore, it is regular. The sequence $R_0(L), R_1(L), \ldots$ is given by

$$\begin{aligned} R_0(L) &= \{b\} \\ R_1(L) &= \{bab\} \\ R_2(L) &= \emptyset \\ R_3(L) &= \emptyset. \end{aligned}$$

Since λ does not belong to any of the above sets it follows that L is a code. □

Example 10.2.18 Consider the finite language $L = \{a, ab, baa, bbab\}$. In the process of computing the sequence of languages $R_0(L), R_1(L), \ldots$ we will use the equality 2.4 of Chapter 2. We have:

$$\begin{aligned}
R_0(L) &= \{b\}\\
R_1(L) &= \{aa, bab\}\\
R_2(L) &= \{a\}\\
R_3(L) &= \{\lambda, b\}\\
R_4(L) &= R_3(L) \cup R_1(L)\\
R_5(L) &= R_4(L) \cup R_2(L)\\
R_6(L) &= R_5(L) \cup R_3(L) = R_1(L) \cup R_2(L) \cup R_3(L)\\
R_7(L) &= R_6(L) \cup R_4(L) = R_1(L) \cup R_2(L) \cup R_3(L).
\end{aligned}$$

Since λ belongs to $R_3(L)$ it follows that L is not a code. □

A simple, yet powerful technique for constructing codes is select a set of words such that no word is a prefix of another word. Indeed, if L is a language on the alphabet A that has this property and

$$x_{i_0} x_{i_1} \cdots x_{i_{n-1}} = x_{j_0} x_{j_1} \cdots x_{j_{m-1}}$$

for some words $x_{i_0}, \ldots, x_{i_{n-1}}, x_{j_0}, \ldots x_{j_{m-1}} \in L$, then $n = m$ and $x_{i_l} = x_{j_l}$ for $0 \leq l \leq n$.

10.3 The Kraft-McMillan Inequality

The lengths of the words of a finite prefix code are characterized in the next theorem.

Lemma 10.3.1 (Kraft-McMillan Inequality for Prefix Codes) *Let $A = \{a_0, \ldots, a_{k-1}\}$ be an alphabet. A prefix code L on the alphabet A with word lengths $\ell_0, \cdots, \ell_{m-1}$ exists if and only if*

$$\sum_{i=0}^{m-1} \frac{1}{k^{\ell_i}} \leq 1.$$

Proof. If $m = 1$, all words of L have the same length, so L is a prefix code; therefore, assume that $m > 1$. Suppose that $\ell_0 \leq \cdots \leq \ell_{m-1}$, and consider the complete labeled ordered tree $\mathtt{T}$ of height ℓ_{m-1}. $\mathtt{T}$ has $k^{\ell_{m-1}}$ leaves. If a word of length ℓ_i is included in the code, none of its descendants in $\mathtt{T}$ can be labeled by a word in the code. Thus, a word of length ℓ_i eliminates $k^{\ell_{m-1}-\ell_i}$ leaves. The total number of excluded leaves is $\sum_{i=0}^{m-1} k^{\ell_{m-1}-\ell_i}$ and it cannot exceed $k^{\ell_{m-1}}$. Thus, we have

$$\sum_{i=0}^{m-1} k^{\ell_{m-1}-\ell_i} \leq k^{\ell_{m-1}}$$

or, equivalently,

$$\sum_{i=0}^{m-1} \frac{1}{k^{\ell_i}} \leq 1.$$

Conversely, suppose that we have the nonnegative integers $\ell_0, \ldots, \ell_{m-1}$ such that

$$\sum_{i=0}^{m-1} \frac{1}{k^{\ell_i}} \leq 1.$$

Equivalently, we have

$$\sum_{i=0}^{m-1} k^{\ell_{m-1}-\ell_i} \leq k^{\ell_{m-1}}. \tag{10.2}$$

Select a word x_0 of length ℓ_0 that is the label of a vertex v_0, to include in the code. This corresponds to $k^{\ell_{m-1}-\ell_0}$ leaves in the labeled ordered tree $\mathtt{T}$. Since $m > 1$, the inequality (10.2) gives $k^{\ell_{m-1}-\ell_0} < k^{\ell_{m-1}}$, so $\mathsf{LEAVES}(\mathtt{T}) - \mathsf{LEAVES}(\mathtt{T}_{[v_0]}) \neq \emptyset$. Let w_1 be a leaf in $\mathsf{LEAVES}(\mathtt{T}) - \mathsf{LEAVES}(\mathtt{T}_{[v_0]})$, and let v_1 be a vertex on the path that joins the root to w_1 whose label x_1 is of length ℓ_1. It is clear that neither of the words x_0, x_1 is a prefix of the other. The tree $\mathtt{T}_{[v_1]}$ has $k^{\ell_{m-1}-\ell_1}$ leaves and, if $m \geq 2$, then $k^{\ell_{m-1}-\ell_0} + k^{\ell_{m-1}-\ell_1} < k^{\ell_{m-1}}$, there are leaves of $\mathtt{T}$ that are not included in $\mathsf{LEAVES}(\mathtt{T}_{[v_0]}) \cup \mathsf{LEAVES}(\mathtt{T}_{[v_1]})$, etc. By a repeated application of this technique we construct a prefix code with word lengths $\ell_0, \ell_1, \ldots, \ell_{m-1}$. ∎

Observe that the proof of the lemma contains an algorithm for generating prefix codes that have a prescribed list of word lengths. Since, in general, there are several choices for the words of a given length, the algorithm is nondeterministic.

Example 10.3.2 Let $S = \{s_0, s_1, \ldots, s_7\}$ be the set of symbols of a source and let $A = \{a, b, c\}$ be an alphabet. Suppose that we intend to design a code $h : S^* \longrightarrow A^*$ such that the lengths of the words of the code set $h(S)$ are

s	s_0	s_1	s_2	s_3	s_4	s_5	s_6	s_7
$\lvert h(s)\rvert$	1	2	2	2	3	3	3	3

Since

$$\frac{1}{3} + 3 \cdot \frac{1}{3^2} + 4 \cdot \frac{1}{3^3} = \frac{22}{27} \leq 1,$$

we know that there is a prefix code such that the corresponding code set consists of words having the prescribed length. Applying the construction contained in the proof of Lemma 10.3.1, we can obtain the following prefix code:

s	s_0	s_1	s_2	s_3	s_4	s_5	s_6	s_7
$h(s)$	a	ba	bb	cc	bcb	bcc	cab	cbb

On the other hand, there is no prefix code (and, as we shall see, no code) having as its list of lengths of code words $(1, 1, 2, 2, 2, 3, 3, 3)$ because

$$2 \cdot \frac{1}{3} + 3 \cdot \frac{1}{3^2} + 3 \cdot \frac{1}{3^3} = \frac{10}{9} > 1.$$

□

The Kraft-McMillan inequality can be extended to arbitrary codes.

Theorem 10.3.3 (Kraft-McMillan Inequality) *Let $A = \{a_0, \ldots, a_{k-1}\}$ be an alphabet. A code on the alphabet A with word lengths $\ell_0, \cdots, \ell_{m-1}$ exists if and only if*

$$\sum_{i=0}^{m-1} \frac{1}{k^{\ell_i}} \leq 1.$$

Proof. It is clear that the inequality of the theorem is sufficient since every prefix code is a code.

Conversely, let L be a code that has word lengths $\ell_0, \ell_1, \ldots, \ell_{m-1}$ and let $r = \max\{\ell_i \mid 0 \leq i \leq m-1\}$. Define

$$K = \sum_{i=0}^{m-1} \frac{1}{k^{\ell_i}}.$$

Using the generalized binomial formula We can write

$$K^n = \sum \left\{ \frac{n!}{n_0! \cdots n_{p-1}!} k^{-(n_0\ell_0 + \cdots + n_{p-1}\ell_{p-1})} \mid n_0 + \cdots + n_{p-1} = n \right\},$$

where $n \leq n_0\ell_0 + \cdots + n_{p-1}\ell_{p-1} \leq nr$. If μ_m is the sum of the coefficients c of the terms of the form ck^{-m}, then $K^n = \sum\{\mu_m k^{-m} \mid n \leq m \leq mr\}$. The last equality is obtained by regrouping the sum by collecting coefficients of like powers. Note that μ_m equals the number of solutions in the natural numbers of the equation $x_0\ell_0 + \cdots + x_{p-1}\ell_{p-1} = m$, since each of these solutions corresponds to a word in L^*.

On the other hand, the number of words of length m in L^+ is at least equal to the number of the solutions in the natural numbers of the equation $x_0\ell_0 + \cdots + x_{p-1}\ell_{p-1} = m$ since each each such solution corresponds to a word $x \in L^+$. Since there are at most k^m words of length m in L^+, we have $\mu_m \leq k^m$. This implies

$$\begin{aligned} K^n &= \sum\{\mu_m k^{-m} \mid n \leq m \leq mr\} \\ &\leq \sum\{k^m k^{-m} \mid n \leq m \leq mr\} = mr - m + 1. \end{aligned} \tag{10.3}$$

for $n \in \mathbb{N}$. If $K > 1$, then $\lim_{n\to\infty} K^n = +\infty$, and this would contradict the existence of the upper bound given in (10.3). This implies the Kraft-McMillan inequality. ∎

Corollary 10.3.4 *Let $A = \{a_0, \ldots, a_{k-1}\}$ be an alphabet. A code on the alphabet A with word lengths $\ell_0, \cdots, \ell_{m-1}$ exists if and only if there exists a prefix code that has the same list of word lengths.*

Proof. Suppose that there exists a code on A. By Theorem 10.3.3, its list of lengths $\ell_0, \cdots, \ell_{m-1}$ satisfies the Kraft-McMillan Inequality. Then, by Lemma 10.3.1 there exists a prefix code that has the same list of word lengths.

The reverse implication is obvious. ∎

The Kraft-McMillan inequality does not guarantee that a language L is a code as shown in the next example.

Example 10.3.5 Let $A = \{a, b\}$ and let $L = \{aa, aab, baa\}$. We have $\ell_0 = 2$, and $\ell_1 = \ell_2 = 3$, so

$$\sum_{i=0}^{2} \frac{1}{k^{\ell_i}} = \frac{1}{4} + \frac{1}{8} + \frac{1}{8} = \frac{1}{2}.$$

However, L is not a code since $(aab)(aa) = (aa)(baa)$. □

The Kraft-McMillan inequality suggests the introduction of a numerical characteristic of languages.

Definition 10.3.6 Let A be an alphabet and let L be a language on A. The *code indicator* of a language L is

$$\mathsf{ci}(L) = \sum_{x \in L} \frac{1}{|A|^{|x|}}.$$

□

Now we extend the Kraft-McMillan to arbitrary (not necessarily finite) codes.

Theorem 10.3.7 *If a language $L = \{x_0, x_1, \ldots\}$ on the alphabet A is a code, then* $\mathsf{ci}(L) \leq 1$.

Proof. Suppose that L is a code and $\mathsf{ci}(L) > 1$. There is a finite language K such that $K \subseteq L$ and $\mathsf{ci}(K) > 1$. Since every subset of a code is also a code, this contradicts Theorem 10.3.3. ∎

Definition 10.3.8 A code L on an alphabet A is maximal if $L \cup \{x\}$ is not a code for every $x \in A^+ - L$. □

Corollary 10.3.9 *If L is a finite code on the alphabet L and* $\mathsf{ci}(L) = 1$, *then L is a maximal code.*

Proof. This statement follows immediately from Theorem 10.3.3. ∎

Example 10.3.10 Let A be an alphabet and let L_k be the block code that consists of all words of length k in A^*. Since $\mathsf{ci}(L_k) = 1$, it follows that L_k is a maximal code. □

We discuss next some elementary properties of maximal codes. In Exercise 30 of Chapter 2 we defined an unbordered word on an alphabet A as a word $y \in A^*$ such that $\mathsf{PREFpr}(y) \cap \mathsf{SUFFpr}(y) = \emptyset$. This notion is useful in the next lemma.

Lemma 10.3.11 *If L is a code on an alphabet A and $y \in A^*$ is an unbordered word such that $y \notin \mathsf{INFIX}(L^*)$, then $L \cup \{y\}$ is a code on A.*

Proof. Suppose that

$$x_{i_0} \cdots x_{i_{p-1}} = x_{j_0} \cdots x_{j_{q-1}}, \tag{10.4}$$

where $x_{i_0}, \ldots, x_{i_{p-1}}, x_{j_0}, \ldots, x_{j_{q-1}} \in L \cup \{y\}$ and $x_{i_0} \neq x_{j_0}$. Note that y must occur in both members of equality (10.4). Indeed, if y did not occur in either member, then this would contradict the fact that L is a code. If y were to occur only in one member of the equality, this would imply $y \in \mathsf{INFIX}(L^*)$. There must be a leftmost occurrence of y in each word, so the equality (10.4) can be written as

$$x_{i_0} \cdots x_{i_{k-1}} y \cdots x_{i_{p-1}} = x_{j_0} \cdots x_{j_{l-1}} y \cdots x_{j_{q-1}}, \tag{10.5}$$

where $x_{i_0}, \ldots, x_{i_{k-1}}, x_{j_0}, \ldots, x_{j_{l-1}} \in L$. This shows that either $x_{j_0} \cdots x_{j_{l-1}} y$ is a proper prefix of $x_{i_0} \cdots x_{i_{k-1}} y$, or $x_{i_0} \cdots x_{i_{k-1}} y$ is a proper prefix of $x_{j_0} \cdots x_{j_{l-1}} y$, or $x_{i_0} \cdots x_{i_{k-1}} y = x_{j_0} \cdots x_{j_{l-1}} y$. The last case can be excluded immediately, since it would imply $x_{i_0} \cdots x_{i_{k-1}} = x_{j_0} \cdots x_{j_{l-1}}$, contradicting the fact that L is a code.

Suppose that $x_{i_0} \cdots x_{i_{k-1}} y$ is a proper prefix of $x_{j_0} \cdots x_{j_{l-1}} y$. If

$$|x_{i_0} \cdots x_{i_{k-1}} y| \leq |x_{j_0} \cdots x_{j_{l-1}}|,$$

this means that y is an infix of a word in L^*, which contradicts the definition of y. Otherwise, we have

$$|x_{j_0} \cdots x_{j_{l-1}}| < |x_{i_0} \cdots x_{i_{k-1}} y| < |x_{j_0} \cdots x_{j_{l-1}} y|,$$

and this means that a proper prefix of y equals a proper suffix of y, which contradicts the fact that y is unbordered.

The remaining case can be dealt with in a similar manner. ∎

Theorem 10.3.12 *If L is a maximal code on the alphabet A, then $L^* \cap A^* x A^* \neq \emptyset$ for every $x \in A^*$.*

Proof. Suppose that L is a maximal code and x is a word such that $L^* \cap A^* x A^* = \emptyset$. By Exercise 32 of Chapter 2, there is an unbordered word $z \in A^*$ such that x is a prefix of z. Since x is not an infix of L^* it follows that z is not an infix of L^*. By Lemma 10.3.11, $L \cup \{z\}$ is a code, and this contradicts the fact that L is a maximal code. ∎

Theorem 10.3.12 implies that if L is a maximal code, then every word $x \in A^*$ is an infix of a word in L^*.

The converse of Theorem 10.3.12 is false, in general. Indeed, consider the language $L = \{a^{|x|+1} b x \mid x \in A^*\}$ that is a prefix code on the alphabet $A = \{a, b\}$. It is clear that $L^* \cap A^* x A^* \neq \emptyset$ for every $x \in A^*$. However, L is not maximal, since $L \cup \{b\}$ is also a code.

Let A be an alphabet, $L \subseteq A^*$, and $y \in A^*$. Define the *minimal completion of a word y with respect to L* as the language

$$C_L(y) = \{x \in A^* \mid yx = x_{i_0} \cdots x_{i_{p-1}}, \text{ where } x_{i_0}, \ldots, x_{i_{p-1}} \in L \text{ and } |x| < |x_{i_{p-1}}|\}.$$

It is clear that $C_L(y) \subseteq \mathsf{SUFF}(L)$; consequently, if L is a finite language, then there exist a finite number of languages of the form $C_L(y)$ for $y \in A^*$ because $\mathsf{SUFF}(L)$ is a finite set.

Define the relation ϵ_L on A^* by

$$\epsilon_L = \{(y, y') \mid C_L(y) = C_L(y')\}.$$

Clearly, ϵ_L is an equivalence on A^*. Moreover, ϵ_L is a right congruence on A^*. Indeed, we have $x \in C_L(ya)$ if and only if $yax = x_{i_0} \cdots x_{i_{p-1}}$ and $|x| < |x_{i_{p-1}}|$.

Therefore, we may have either $|ax| < |x_{i_{p-1}}|$, or $|ax| = |x_{i_{p-1}}|$. In the former case we have $ax \in C_L(y)$, while in the latter case we have $yax = x_{i_0} \cdots x_{i_{p-1}}$, and since $ax = x_{i_{p-1}}$, $y = x_{i_0} \cdots x_{i_{p-2}}$. From this, it follows that $\lambda \in C_L(y)$ and $ax = x_{i_{p-1}} \in L$. This allows us to write

$$C_L(ya) = \{x \in A^* \mid ax \in C_L(y) \text{ or } (\lambda \in C_L(y) \text{ and } ax \in L)\},$$

which shows that $C_L(y) = C_L(y')$ implies $C_L(ya) = C_L(y'a)$ for every $y, y' \in A^*$ and $a \in A$, so ϵ_L is a right congruence on A^*. If L is a finite language, then A^*/ϵ_L is a finite set.

Lemma 10.3.13 *Let L be a language on the alphabet A, and let $y, y' \in A^*$. If $C_L(y) = \emptyset$, then $C_L(yy') = \emptyset$.*

Proof. Indeed, if $w \in C_L(yy')$, then $yy'w = x_{i_0} \cdots x_{i_{p-1}}$, and $|w| < |x_{i_{p-1}}|$. Let j be the smallest number such that $|y| < |x_{i_0} \cdots x_{i_{j-1}}|$. Then, if t is the prefix of $y'w$ of length $|x_{i_0} \cdots x_{i_{j-1}}| - |y|$ we have $t \in C_L(y)$, which contradicts the hypothesis. ∎

Lemma 10.3.14 *Let $L \subseteq A^*$ be a finite language such that for every $u \in A^*$ there is $v \in A^*$ such that $uv \notin \mathsf{PREF}(L^*)$. Then, for every language $K \subseteq A^*$ there is a word $z_K \in A^*$ such that for every $y \in K$, $C_L(yz_K) = \emptyset$.*

Proof. We prove a stronger statement, namely that if L is a language that satisfies the previous conditions, then there is a word $z \in A^*$ such that for every $y \in A^*$, $C_L(yz) = \emptyset$. Note that the condition of the lemma implies that for every $u \in A^*$ there is $v \in A^*$ such that $C_L(uv) = \emptyset$.

Let C be an equivalence class of ϵ_L. If $C_L(wv) = \emptyset$ for some $w \in C$ and $v \in A^*$, then for every $w' \in C$ we have $C_L(w'v) = \emptyset$. Let $H = \{w_0, \ldots, w_{p-1}\}$ be a set of representatives of the equivalence classes of A^*/ϵ_L. If $C_L(w_i z) = \emptyset$ for $0 \leq i \leq p-1$, then $C_L(wz) = \emptyset$ for every $w \in A^*$.

The hypothesis of the lemma implies that there is a word $z_0 \in A^*$ such that $C_L(w_0 z_0) = \emptyset$. Next, there is a word $z_1 \in A^*$ such that $C_L(w_1 z_0 z_1) = \emptyset$, and so on. At the ith step, we obtain a word $w_i \in A^*$ such that $C_L(w_i z_0 \cdots z_i) = \emptyset$. Define $z = z_0 \cdots z_{p-1}$. By Lemma 10.3.13 we have $C_L(wz) = \emptyset$ for every $w \in H$, so $C_L(wz) = \emptyset$ for every $w \in A^*$. ∎

Theorem 10.3.15 *If L is a finite maximal code on the alphabet A, then there is a word $y \in A^*$ such that for every $x \in A^*$, $yx \in \mathsf{PREF}(L^*)$.*

Proof. Suppose that for every word $y \in A^*$ there is $x \in A^*$ such that $yx \notin \mathsf{PREF}(L^*)$. By Lemma 10.3.14, there is a word $z \in A^*$ such that for every $y \in A^*$, $C_L(yz) = \emptyset$. On the other hand, by Theorem 10.3.12, $L^* \cap A^*zA^* \neq \emptyset$, which means that there are $y, t \in A^*$ $yzt \in L^*$. This allows us to select a prefix t' of x such that $yzt' = x_{i_0} \cdots x_{i_{p-1}}$ and $|t'| < |x_{i_{p-1}}|$, which shows that $t' \in C_L(yz)$, thus contradicting the emptiness of $C_L(yz)$. ∎

Theorem 10.3.16 *Let L be a λ-free, finite language on the alphabet A. If there is a word $y \in A^*$ such that for every $x \in A^*$ we have $yx \in \mathsf{PREF}(L^*)$, then* $\mathsf{ci}(L) = 1$.

Proof. Let m, M be the minimum and the maximum length of a word in L, respectively. We have $m > 0$ because L is λ-free. Let $y \in A^*$ be a word such that for every $x \in A^*$ we have $yx \in \mathsf{PREF}(L^*)$ and let $n \in \mathbb{N}$ such that $|y| < mn$. This choice for n guarantees that there is $z \in A^*$ such that $yz \in \mathsf{PREF}(L^n)$. Suppose that $C_{L^n}(y) = \{y_0, \ldots, y_{s-1}\}$. We have $|y_i| < nM$ for $0 \leq i \leq s-1$.

If $h > nM$, then every word in A^h will have a word $y_i \in C_{L^n}(y)$ as an infix. Since A^h consists of $|A|^h$ words, we have $\sum_{i=0}^{s-1} |A|^{h-|y_i|} \geq |A|^h$. By multiplying both sides of the inequality by $|A|^{-h-|y|}$ we obtain $\sum_{i=0}^{s-1} |A|^{-|y|-|y_i|} \geq |A|^{-|y|}$, or $\sum_{i=0}^{s-1} |A|^{-|yy_i|} \geq |A|^{-|y|}$. Thus,

$$\mathsf{ci}(L^n) = \sum\{|A|^{-|v|} \mid v \in L^n\} \geq \sum_{i=0}^{s-1} |A|^{-|yy_i|} \geq |A|^{-|y|},$$

which means that for every $n > \frac{|y|}{m}$ we have $\mathsf{ci}(L^n) > |A|^{-|y|}$. If $\mathsf{ci}(L) < 1$, then $\lim_{n\to\infty} \mathsf{ci}(L^n) = 0$, which is a contradiction. Thus, $\mathsf{ci}(L) = 1$. ∎

Corollary 10.3.17 *Let L be a finite code on the alphabet A. Then, L is a maximal code if and only if* $\mathsf{ci}(L) = 1$.

Proof. This statement follows from Corollary 10.3.9, Theorem 10.3.15 and Theorem 10.3.16. ∎

Definition 10.3.18 Let $\mathcal{S} = (S, D)$ be a finite source, where

$$\begin{aligned} S &= \{s_0, \ldots, s_{m-1}\}, \\ D &= \begin{pmatrix} s_0 & s_1 & \cdots & s_{m-1} \\ p_0 & p_1 & \cdots & p_{m-1}, \end{pmatrix} \end{aligned}$$

and $\sum_{i=0}^{m-1} p_i = 1$. If $h : S^* \longrightarrow A^*$ is a coding morphism, then the *average length of the code* is

$$M(h) = \sum_{i=0}^{m-1} p_i |h(s_i)|.$$

□

Note that $M(h)$ depends only on the lengths of the code words. If $\mathcal{S}$ generated ℓ characters, then the expected length of the encoded text will be $M(h)\ell$.

In Exercises 18 and 19 we obtain an important result due to Shannon [1948], by using the Kraft-McMillan Inequality: a lower bound for the average length of a code based on the entropy of the source.

10.4 Huffman Codes and Data Compression

Huffman codes are prefix codes that take the probability distribution of the source into account with the result that they produce optimal length encodings of words.

Suppose that we wish to encode the symbols generated by the source $\mathcal{S}$ as words over the alphabet A using a block code. This requires the use of words of length $\lceil \log_{|A|} m \rceil$, for every symbol s_i, so the total length of the encoded text will be $\lceil \log_{|A|} m \rceil \ell$, for ℓ symbols generated by the source. We can compress this text using codes that are built by taking into account the probabilistic distribution of the source symbols, such that the symbols that are less likely to be generated by the source will be encoded by longer words on A. A class of such codes, known as *Huffman codes* is the main object of this section.

Let $\mathsf{codes}(S, A)$ be the set of codes of the source alphabet S into the alphabet A.

Definition 10.4.1 Let $\mathcal{S} = (S, D)$ be a finite source, and let A be an alphabet. A code $h \in \mathsf{codes}(S, A)$ is $\mathcal{S}$-*optimal* if

$$M(h) = \inf\{M(f) \mid f \in \mathsf{codes}(S, A)\}.$$

□

The next result contains some information on the length of code words for binary optimal prefix codes, i.e., for prefix codes over alphabets that contain two symbols.

Theorem 10.4.2 *Let $\mathcal{S} = (S, D)$ be a finite source, where $S = \{s_0, \ldots, s_{m-1}\}$,*

$$D = \begin{pmatrix} s_0 & s_1 & \cdots & s_{m-1} \\ p_0 & p_1 & \cdots & p_{m-1}, \end{pmatrix}$$

and $\sum_{i=0}^{m-1} p_i = 1$. Suppose that $p_0 \geq p_1 \geq \cdots \geq p_{m-1}$ and that $p_i = p_{i+1} = \cdots = p_{i+k-1}$ implies $|h(s_i)| \leq |h(s_{i+1})| \leq \cdots \leq |h(s_{i+k-1})|$.

The following statements hold:

(i) *If $h : S^* \longrightarrow \{0,1\}^*$ is an optimal prefix code, then $p_j > p_k$ implies $|h(s_j)| \leq |h(s_k)|$ for $0 \leq j, k \leq m-1$.*

(ii) *We have $|h(s_{m-2})| = |h(s_{m-1})|$ and $h(s_{m-2}) = wd$, $h(s_{m-1}) = wd'$, where $\{d, d'\} = \{0, 1\}$.*

Proof. For Part (i) suppose that we have j, k such that $p_j > p_k$ and $|h(s_j)| > |h(s_k)|$. Define the morphism $h' : S^* \longrightarrow A^*$ by

$$h'(s) = \begin{cases} h(s) & \text{if } s \notin \{s_j, s_k\} \\ h(s_k) & \text{if } s = s_j \\ h(s_j) & \text{if } s = s_k. \end{cases}$$

for $s \in S$. Note that h' is also a prefix code and

$$\begin{aligned} M(h) - M(h') &= p_j|h(s_j)| + p_k|h(s_k)| - p_j|h'(s_j)| - p_k|h'(s_k)| \\ &= p_j|h(s_j)| + p_k|h(s_k)| - p_j|h(s_k)| - p_k|h(s_j)| \\ &= (p_j - p_k)(|h(s_j)| - |h(s_k)|) > 0, \end{aligned}$$

which contradicts the optimality of h. Thus, $p_j > p_k$ implies $|h(s_j)| \leq |h(s_k)|$.

For the Part (ii) of the theorem, we claim that $|h(s_{m-2})| \leq |h(s_{m-1})|$. Indeed, we have $p_{m-2} \geq p_{m-1}$. If this inequality is strict, the conclusion follows from the first part of the theorem; otherwise, that is, if $p_{m-2} = p_{m-1}$, we obtain the inequality from the hypothesis of the theorem. However, if $|h(s_{m-2})| > |h(s_{m-1})|$, then the code $\bar{h} : S^* \longrightarrow A^*$ given by

$$\bar{h}(s) = \begin{cases} h(s) & \text{if } s \neq s_{m-1} \\ \mathsf{trimlast}(h(s_{m-1})) & \text{if } s = s_{m-1} \end{cases}$$

for $s \in S$, is also a prefix code and $M(\bar{h}) < M(h)$, thus contradicting the optimality of h. This implies $|h(s_{m-2})| = |h(s_{m-1})|$.

The Part (ii) of this theorem implies that the two longest words of the code set differ only in their last position. This is the case because, otherwise, one could drop the last symbol from $h(s_{m-2})$ and $h(s_{m-1})$ and obtain a prefix code with a smaller average length. ∎

The next result is the basis of a construction of a class of optimal prefix codes, known as *Huffman codes.*

Theorem 10.4.3 *Let $\mathcal{S} = (S, D)$ be a finite source, where $S = \{s_0, \ldots, s_{m-1}\}$, $m \geq 2$,*

$$D = \begin{pmatrix} s_0 & s_1 & \cdots & s_{m-1} \\ p_0 & p_1 & \cdots & p_{m-1}, \end{pmatrix}$$

where $p_0 \geq p_1 \geq \cdots \geq p_{m-1}$ and $\sum_{i=0}^{m-1} p_i = 1$.

Define the source $\mathcal{S}' = (S', D')$, where $S' = \{s_0, \ldots, s_{m-3}, s'_{m-2}\}$,

$$D' = \begin{pmatrix} s_0 & s_1 & \cdots & s_{m-3} & s'_{m-2} \\ p_0 & p_1 & \cdots & p_{m-3} & p_{m-2} + p_{m-1} \end{pmatrix}$$

If $h' : (S')^* \longrightarrow \{0,1\}^*$ is a $\mathcal{S}'$-optimal prefix code, then the code $h : S^* \longrightarrow \{0,1\}^*$ defined by

$$h(s_i) = \begin{cases} h'(s_i) & \text{if } 0 \leq i \leq m-3 \\ h'(s'_{m-2})0 & \text{if } i = m-2 \\ h'(s'_{m-2})1 & \text{if } i = m-1 \end{cases}$$

is an $\mathcal{S}$-optimal prefix code.

Proof. Suppose that h were not an $\mathcal{S}$-optimal code. Then, let $g : S \longrightarrow \{0,1\}^*$ be an $\mathcal{S}$-optimal code. We have $M(h) > M(g)$, that is,

$$\begin{aligned} & p_0|h(s_0)| + \cdots + p_{m-2}|h(s_{m-2})| + p_{m-1}|h(s_{m-1})| \\ & \quad > \; p_0|g(s_0)| + \cdots + p_{m-2}|g(s_{m-2})| + p_{m-1}|g(s_{m-1})|. \end{aligned}$$

The definition of h implies $M(h) = M(h') + p_{m-2} + p_{m-1}$, so

$$\begin{aligned} & M(h') + p_{m-2} + p_{m-1} \\ & \quad > \; p_0|g(s_0)| + \cdots + p_{m-2}|g(s_{m-2})| + p_{m-1}|g(s_{m-1})| = M(g). \end{aligned}$$

By Theorem 10.4.2, $|g(s_{m-2})| = |g(s_{m-1})|$, $g(s_{m-2}) = wd$, and $g(s_{m-1}) = wd'$ for some $w \in \{0,1\}^*$ and $d \neq d'$. Define the prefix code $g' : (S')^* \longrightarrow A^*$ by

$$g'(s) = \begin{cases} g(s) & \text{if } s \in \{s_0, \ldots, s_{m-3}\} \\ w & \text{if } s = s'_{m-2}. \end{cases}$$

We have

$$\begin{aligned} M(g') &= p_0|g'(s_0)| + \cdots + p_{m-3}|g'(s_{m-3})| + (p_{m-2} + p_{m-1})|w| \\ &= p_0|g(s_0)| + \cdots + p_{m-3}|g(s_{m-3})| \\ &\quad + p_{m-2}(|g(s_{m-2})| - 1) + p_{m-1}(|g(s_{m-1})| - 1) \\ &= M(g) - p_{m-2} - p_{m-1} < M(h'), \end{aligned}$$

which contradicts the optimality of h'. Thus, h is optimal. ∎

The information source $\mathcal{S}'$ was obtained from $\mathcal{S}$ by coalescing two of its symbols having the lowest probabilities, s_{m-2} and s_{m-1} into a new symbol

Source	Alphabet	Probability Distribution
$\mathcal{S}_0$	$\{s_0, s_1, s_2, s_3, s_4, s_5\}$	$\begin{pmatrix} s_0 & s_1 & s_2 & s_3 & s_4 & s_5 \\ 0.3 & 0.2 & 0.15 & 0.15 & 0.1 & 0.1 \end{pmatrix}$
$\mathcal{S}_1$	$\{s_0, s_1, s_{45}, s_2, s_3\}$	$\begin{pmatrix} s_0 & s_1 & s_{45} & s_2 & s_3 \\ 0.3 & 0.2 & 0.2 & 0.15 & 0.15 \end{pmatrix}$
$\mathcal{S}_2$	$\{s_0, s_{23}, s_1, s_{45}\}$	$\begin{pmatrix} s_0 & s_{23} & s_1 & s_{45} \\ 0.3 & 0.3 & 0.2 & 0.2 \end{pmatrix}$
$\mathcal{S}_3$	$\{s_{145}, s_0, s_{23}\}$	$\begin{pmatrix} s_{145} & s_0 & s_{23} \\ 0.4 & 0.3 & 0.3 \end{pmatrix}$
$\mathcal{S}_4$	$\{s_{023}, s_{145}\}$	$\begin{pmatrix} s_{023} & s_{145} \\ 0.6 & 0.4 \end{pmatrix}$
$\mathcal{S}_5$	$\{s_{023145}\}$	$\begin{pmatrix} s_{023145} \\ 1 \end{pmatrix}$

Figure 10.4: Recursive Construction of Information Sources

s'_{m-2}. If this symbol is denoted by $s_{m-2\,m-1}$ the probability distribution D' can be written as

$$D' = \begin{pmatrix} s_0 & s_1 & \cdots & s_{m-3} & s_{m-2\,m-1} \\ p_0 & p_1 & \cdots & p_{m-3} & p_{m-2} + p_{m-1} \end{pmatrix}$$

Example 10.4.4 Let $\mathcal{S} = (S, D)$ be the source defined by $S = \{s_i \mid 0 \leq i \leq 5\}$ and

$$D = \begin{pmatrix} s_0 & s_1 & s_2 & s_3 & s_4 & s_5 \\ 0.3 & 0.2 & 0.15 & 0.15 & 0.1 & 0.1 \end{pmatrix}$$

We intend to construct a Huffman code for $\mathcal{S}$. To this end, we construct a sequence of information sources, as shown in Theorem 10.4.3 (see Figure 10.4).

The construction process of the sequence of sources $\mathcal{S}_0, \ldots, \mathcal{S}_5$ is summarized by the binary tree shown in Figure 10.5.

For $\mathcal{S}_5$ the construction of an optimal prefix code is immediate. Indeed, by taking $h_5(s_{023145}) = 0$ we obtain the needed optimal code. Next, an optimal code for $\mathcal{S}_4$ is obtained by taking $h_4(s_{023}) = 0$ and $h_4(145) = 1$. The code for $\mathcal{S}_3$ is given by $h_3(s_0) = 00$, $h_3(s_{23}) = 01$, and $h_{145} = 1$, etc. Eventually, the code for $\mathcal{S}_0$ will be given by

s	s_0	s_1	s_2	s_3	s_4	s_5
$h_0(s)$	00	10	010	011	110	111

Note that if every left edge of the tree shown in Figure 10.5 is labeled by 0 and every right edge by 1, then the code $h_0(s)$ equals the label of the path that joins the root of this tree to the leaf that corresponds to the node s.

The average length of this code is $M(h_0) = 0.3 \cdot 2 + 0.2 \cdot 2 + 0.15 \cdot 3 + 0.15 \cdot 3 + 0.1 \cdot 3 + 0.1 \cdot 3 = 2.5$. Since a binary block code would require three bits

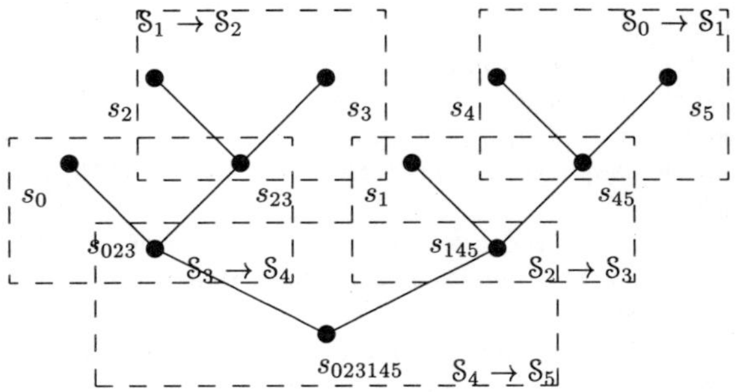

Figure 10.5: Construction of the sequence $\mathcal{S}_0, \ldots, \mathcal{S}_5$

per symbol, the compression achieved by using the Huffman code is in this case 16%. □

10.5 Exercises

Unique Decipherability

1. ◇ We described a sources as a process that produces symbols that belong to a countable set S. How is the definition of codes affected if we drop the countability condition for S?
2. Prove that if L is a code set and $\emptyset \neq L' \subseteq L$, then L' is also a code set.
3. ◇ Let $\mathcal{S} = (S, D)$, and $\mathcal{S}'(A, D')$ be two finite sources such that $C = (\mathcal{S}, A, h)$ is a code on the alphabet A and $C' = (\mathcal{S}', B, g)$ is a code on the alphabet B. Prove that $C'' = (\mathcal{S}, B, gh)$ is a code on the alphabet B.
4. Let $L \subseteq A^*$ be a finite language and let $c \notin A$ be a symbol. Prove that Lc is a code set on $A \cup \{c\}$.
5. ◇ Prove that $L \subseteq A^*$ is a code set if and only if it is catenatively independent and $wL^* \cap L^*w \cap L^* \neq \emptyset$ implies $w \in L^*$.
6. ◇ Prove that $L = \{x, y\} \subseteq A^*$ is not a code if and only $x = z^p$ and $y = z^q$ for some $z \in A^*$ and and two numbers $p, q \in \mathbb{N}$.
7. ◇ Prove that if L and L' are codes, then LL' is not necessarily a code.
8. ◇ Let A be an alphabet. A *prefix language* is a subset $L \subseteq A^*$ such that $L \cap LA^+ = \emptyset$. Show that:
   (a) If L is a prefix language and $\lambda \notin L$, then L is a prefix code.
   (b) If L is a prefix language and $\lambda \in L$, then $L = \{\lambda\}$.
   (c) $K = L - LA^+$ is a prefix language if and only if $\lambda \notin L$.
9. ◇ Let $L \subseteq A^*$ be a prefix-closed language, that is, $\mathsf{PREF}(L) \subseteq L$. Prove that the language $H = LA - L$ is a prefix code.
10. ◇ Prove that if $L, L' \subseteq A^*$ are two prefix languages and $LA^* = L'A^*$, then $L = L'$.
11. Let $\{R_n(L) \mid n \in \mathbb{N}\}$ be the set constructed in the Sardinas-Patterson algorithm, where $L \subseteq A^*$.

(a) Prove that if $L \subseteq A^k$, then $R_0(L) = \emptyset$.
(b) Prove that if $R_n(L) = \emptyset$, then $R_{n+j}(L) = \emptyset$ for $j \in \mathbb{N}$.

12. $^\diamond$ Prove that the language $L = \{a^{|x|+1}bx \mid x \in \{a,b\}^*\}$ is a prefix code on the alphabet $A = \{a,b\}$.
13. $^\diamond$ Prove that the language $L = \{a^{|x|+1}bx \mid x \in \{a,b\}^*\} \cup \{b\}$ is a code on the alphabet $A = \{a,b\}$.
14. $^\diamond$ A language $L \subseteq A^*$ has deciphering delay d if for every $x, y \in L$, $z \in L^d$ and $u \in A^*$, $xzu \in yL^*$ implies $x = y$. Note that if $d = 0$, then L is a prefix code. Prove that:
(a) If L has deciphering delay d and $d \leq d'$, then L also has deciphering delay d'.
(b) If L has deciphering delay d, then L is a code set.
15. $^\diamond$ Give an example of a code set that does not have a finite deciphering delay.
Solution. $L = \{aa, ba, b\}$ is a code that does not have finite deciphering delay.

The Kraft-McMillan Inequality

16. $^{\diamond\diamond}$ Prove that if L is a code, then L^n is a code and $\mathsf{ci}(L^n) = (\mathsf{ci}(L))^n$ for $n \geq 1$.
17. $^{\diamond\diamond}$ Let $L \subseteq A^*$ be a prefix code such that $\mathsf{ci}(L) < 1$. Prove that $L^+ \subset A^+$.

Let $\mathcal{S} = (S, D)$ be a finite source, where $S = \{s_0, \ldots, s_{m-1}\}$ and

$$D = \begin{pmatrix} s_0 & s_1 & \cdots & s_{m-1} \cdots \\ p_0 & p_1 & \cdots & p_{m-1} \end{pmatrix}$$

where $\sum_{0 \leq i \leq m-1} p_i = 1$. The entropy of $\mathcal{S}$ is the number

$$H(\mathcal{S}) = \sum_{0 \leq i \leq m-1} p_i \log_2 \frac{1}{p_i}.$$

18. $^\diamond$ Let $p_0, \ldots, p_{m-1}$ and $q_0, \ldots, q_{m-1}$ two sequences of positive numbers such that $\sum_{0 \leq i \leq m-1} p_i = \sum_{0 \leq i \leq m-1} q_i$. Prove that

$$\sum_{0 \leq i \leq m-1} p_i \log_2 \frac{1}{p_i} \leq \sum_{0 \leq i \leq m-1} p_i \log_2 \frac{1}{q_i}.$$

Moreover, if

$$\sum_{0 \leq i \leq m-1} p_i \log_2 \frac{1}{p_i} = \sum_{0 \leq i \leq m-1} p_i \log_2 \frac{1}{q_i},$$

then $p_i = q_i$ for $0 \leq i \leq m-1$.
Solution. It is easy to verify that if $x > 0$, then $\ln x \leq x - 1$ and that $\ln x = x - 1$ implies $x = 1$ by graphing the function $f(x) = \ln x - x + 1$ for $x \in \mathbb{R}_+$.

Thus, $\ln \frac{q_i}{p_i} \leq \frac{q_i}{p_i} - 1$. Multiplying both sides by p_i yields $p_i \ln \frac{q_i}{p_i} \leq q_i - p_i$. By adding all previous inequalities, we obtain the desired inequality.

19. °° Let $h : S^* \longrightarrow A^*$ be a coding morphism.
 (a) Prove that the average length of the code satisfies the inequality $M(h) \geq \frac{H(\mathcal{S})}{\log_2 |A|}$ (Shannon's Theorem).
 (b) Prove that the equality takes place if and only if $p_i = |A|^{-|h(s_i)|}$ for $0 \leq i \leq m-1$.

Solution. Let

$$q_i = \frac{|A|^{-n_i}}{\sum_{0 \leq i \leq m-1} |A|^{-n_i}}$$

for $0 \leq i \leq m-1$. It is clear that $\sum_{0 \leq i \leq m-1} q_i = 1$. Therefore, by applying the inequality from Exercise 18 we obtain

$$\begin{aligned} H(\mathcal{S}) &\leq \sum_{0 \leq i \leq m-1} p_i \log_2 \frac{\sum_{0 \leq i \leq m-1} |A|^{-n_i}}{|A|^{-n_i}} \\ &= \sum_{0 \leq i \leq m-1} p_i n_i \log_2 |A| + \log_2 \sum_{0 \leq i \leq m-1} |A|^{-n_i}. \end{aligned}$$

Since $\sum_{0 \leq i \leq m-1} |A|^{-n_i} \leq 1$ (by Theorem 10.3.3) we obtain $H(\mathcal{S}) \leq M(h) \log_2 |A|$.

Huffman Codes and Data Compression

20. Let $\mathcal{S} = (\{s_0, s_1, s_2, s_3, s_4\}, D)$ be a source defined by

$$D = \begin{pmatrix} s_0 & s_1 & s_2 & s_3 & s_4 \\ 0.4 & 0.2 & 0.2 & 0.1 & 0.1 \end{pmatrix}$$

Construct a binary Huffman code h for $\mathcal{S}$. What is $M(h)$?

21. ° Prove that if h is a Huffman code for a source $\mathcal{S}$, then $M(h) < H(\mathcal{S}) + 1$.

10.6 Bibliographical Comments

An excellent source for information theory is [Ash, 1965]. The book by Berstel and Perrin [1985] is a comprehensive work on coding theory with a strong algebraic character. A short and elegant introduction can be found in [Salomaa, 1981].

Chapter 11

Biological Applications

11.1 Introduction

In this chapter we examine two areas of applications of formal language theory in biology: the study of development of certain simple organisms and the manipulation of nucleic acids which are the main carriers of genetic information. In both cases, the the formal language theory is relevant due to the fact that simple organisms and nucleic acids too can be described as words over certain alphabets. In turn, the interest in solving biological problems has been very fruitful for formal language theory. The study of L-system and of splicing system opened some of the most active research areas of the theory of formal languages.

11.2 L-Systems

In the rewriting systems introduced so far, only a certain part of a word is rewritten at any given moment. In contrast, in the rewriting mechanism described in this section, productions are applied such that all letters of a word must be rewritten at the same time. This alternative, which is more reflective of the growth processes in living organisms, was introduced in 1968 by Astrid Lindenmayer as a model of plant development, and the generative devices that use this mechanism are thus named *Lindenmayer systems* or, in short, L-systems.

Here we introduce the simplest class of L-systems.

Definition 11.2.1 A *0L-system* is a triple $S = (A, x, s)$, where A is an alphabet, $x \in A^*$ is the *axiom* of S, and $s : A \longrightarrow \mathcal{P}(A^*)$ is a finite substitution.

A *D0L-system* is a triple $S = (A, x, h)$, where A and x are as above, and $h : A^* \longrightarrow A^*$ is a morphism. □

The 0 in the nomenclature used for the *L*-systems refers to the fact that the rewriting of a symbol s is done in a context-free manner, independent of the symbols that surround s; D refers to the fact that the rewriting has a deterministic character.

If we regard morphisms as special cases of finite substitutions, then *D0L*-systems can be regarded is a special *0L*-systems. A $\bar{D}$*0L-system* is a *0L*-system $S = (A, x, s)$, where s is a substitution that is not a morphism.

If $w \in A^*$, then a "successor word" $v \in s(w)$ is obtained by rewriting the symbols of w in parallel. Namely, each symbol a that occurs in w is replaced by a word $u \in s(a)$. In the case of *D0L*-systems, each symbol a of w is replaced by the word $h(a)$ and the successor of a word w is the word $h(w)$.

Let $S = (A, x, s)$ be a *0L*-system. We introduce the relation $\underset{S}{\Rightarrow}$ on A^* by writing $x \underset{S}{\Rightarrow} y$ if $y \in s(x)$. If S is clear from context we may omit the subscript S and simply write $x \Rightarrow y$. As we did for rewriting systems, we introduce the relations $\overset{n}{\underset{S}{\Rightarrow}}$, $\overset{*}{\underset{S}{\Rightarrow}}$, and $\overset{+}{\underset{S}{\Rightarrow}}$ given by:

$$\begin{aligned} \overset{n}{\underset{S}{\Rightarrow}} &= (\underset{S}{\Rightarrow})^n \text{ for } n \in \mathbb{N}, \\ \overset{*}{\underset{S}{\Rightarrow}} &= \bigcup_{n \geq 0} \overset{n}{\underset{S}{\Rightarrow}}, \\ \overset{+}{\underset{S}{\Rightarrow}} &= \bigcup_{n \geq 1} \overset{n}{\underset{S}{\Rightarrow}}. \end{aligned}$$

Thus, $v \in s^{(n)}(u)$ if and only if $u \overset{n}{\underset{S}{\Rightarrow}} v$.

Definition 11.2.2 The *language generated by the 0L-system* $S = (A, x, s)$ is the language $L(S)$ defined by

$$L(S) = \bigcup \{s^{(n)}(x) \mid n \in \mathbb{N}\} = \{u \in A^* \mid x \overset{*}{\underset{S}{\Rightarrow}} u\}.$$

The language generated by a *D0L*-system $S = (A, x, h)$ is

$$L(S) = \{h^{(n)}(x) \mid n \in \mathbb{N}\} = \{u \in A^* \mid x \overset{*}{\underset{S}{\Rightarrow}} u\}.$$

A language L is a *0L*-language (a *D0L*-language) if there exists a *0L*-system (a *D0L*-system) S such that $L = L(S)$.

The classes of *0L*-languages and *D0L*-languages will be denoted by $\mathcal{L}_{0L}$ and $\mathcal{L}_{D0L}$, respectively. □

For any *0L*-system $S = (A, x, s)$ we have $x \in L(S)$ because $x \in s^{(0)}(x)$. By definition, a substitution s satisfies the equality $s(\lambda) = \{\lambda\}$. Consequently, if $S = (A, \lambda, s)$ is a *0L*-system, then $L(S) = \{\lambda\}$. This guarantees that, in all interesting cases, we can assume that the axiom of a *0L*-system is not λ.

In contrast to the situation with other rewriting systems we have examined, the use of symbols outside the derived language is never necessary, as the next theorem shows. This facilitates proofs that certain languages cannot be in $\mathcal{L}_{0L}$.

Theorem 11.2.3 *Let $L \subseteq A^*$ be a language such that $L = L(S)$, where $S = (B, x, s)$ is a 0L-system such that $A \subseteq B$. Then, there is a 0L-system $S' = (A, x, s')$ such that $L = L(S')$.*

Proof. Since $x \in L \subseteq A^*$ it is clear that the axiom x is a word on the alphabet A. Define s' to be the restriction of the substitution s to A. Then, it is easy to show by induction on n that $x \overset{n}{\underset{S}{\Rightarrow}} y$ if and only if $x \overset{n}{\underset{S'}{\Rightarrow}} y$, which shows that $L(S') = L(S) = L$. ∎

Example 11.2.4 Let $L = (\{a, b\}, bab, h)$ be the *D0L*-system defined by $h(a) = \lambda$ and $h(b) = bab$. This *D0L*-system models a filamentous plant that contains two types of cells: b cells that divide in three new cells of types b, a and b, and a cells that die immediately after being generated. Here are a few initial words in $L(S)$:

$$\begin{aligned} x &= bab \\ h(x) &= babbab \\ h^{(2)}(x) &= babbabbabbab \\ h^{(3)}(x) &= babbabbabbabbabbabbabbab \\ &\vdots \\ h^{(n)}(x) &= (bab)^{2^n} \\ &\vdots \end{aligned}$$

Note that the length of the plant grows exponentially with the number of generations. □

Example 11.2.5 The *D0L*-system defined in this example was introduced by Lindenmayer [1968b] as a model of the growth of a red algae, *Callithamnion Roseum* Harvey. *Callithamnion* is a branching filamentous organism that comprises nine types of cells represented by the alphabet $B = \{1, \ldots, 9\}$. A branch is created when a cell of type 8 divides into a cell of type 9 and a cell of type 3 that is the basis of a branch. The new branch is represented by a word enclosed between square brackets. This development mechanism is modeled by the following morphism over the alphabet $B = A \cup \{[,]\}$:

b	1	2	3	4	5	6	7	8	9	[	]
$h(b)$	23	2	24	25	65	7	8	9[3]	9	[	]

The morphism h defines the *D0L*-system $S = (A, 1, h)$ and the first sixteen

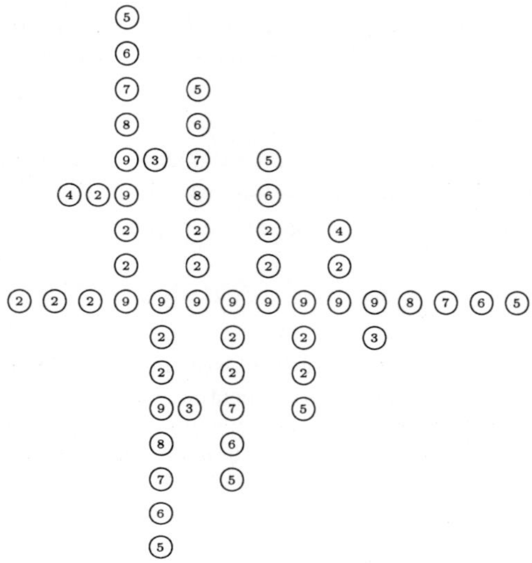

Figure 11.1: Representation of the stage x_{15}

successive development stages $x_i = h^{(i)}(1)$ of the algae are shown below

x_0=1
x_1=23
x_2=224
x_3=2225
x_4=22265
x_5=222765
x_6=2228765
x_8=2229[3]8765
x_9=2229[24]9[3]8765
x_{10}=2229[225]9[24]9[3]8765
x_{11}=2229[2265]9[225]9[24]9[3]8765
x_{12}=2229[22765]9[2265]9[225]9[24]9[3]8765
x_{13}=2229[228765]9[22765]9[2265]9[225]9[24]9[3]8765
x_{14}=2229[229[3]8765]9[228765]9[22765]9[2265]9[225]9[24]9[3]8765
x_{15}=2229[229[24]9[3]8765]9[229[3]8765]9[228765]9[22765]9[2265]9[225]9[24]9[3]8765

The shape described by the word x_{15} is shown in Figure 11.1. The branches that sprout from the main filament are drawn alternately up and down. □

Definition 11.2.6 A *0L*-system $S = (A, x, s)$ is *propagating* (referred to as a *PD0L*-system) if $x \neq \lambda$ and $\lambda \notin s(a)$ for every $a \in A$.

If s is a λ-free morphism we will refer to S as a *PD0L*-system. □

Example 11.2.7 The *D0L*-system introduced in Example 11.2.5 is a *PD0L*-

system, while the system considered in Example 11.2.4 is not a propagating *D0L*-system. □

A common convention used in the theory of *L*-systems is to denote with barred letters those properties of classes of *L*-systems that are lacking. For example, we denoted by $\bar{D}0L$ those *0L*-systems whose substitutions are not morphisms. Similarly, we will refer to the system introduced in Example 11.2.5 as a $D\bar{P}0L$-system.

Example 11.2.8 The following table specifies the *0L*-systems $S_0, \ldots, S_4$ (introduced by Rozenberg and Doucet [1973]) having the form $S_i = (\{a\}, x_i, s_i)$; the languages generated by these systems are also listed.

0L-system	x_i	$s_i(a)$	$L(S_i)$
S_0	a^2	$\{a, a^3\}$	$\{a^{2k} \mid k \geq 1\}$
S_1	a^3	$\{a, a^2\}$	$\{a^k \mid k \geq 3\}$
S_2	a^4	$\{\lambda, a\}$	$\{\lambda, a, a^2, a^3, a^4\}$
S_3	a^3	$\{a^2\}$	$\{a^{3\cdot 2^k} \mid k \geq 0\}$
S_4	a	$\{a^3, a^4\}$	$\{a, a^3, a^4, a^9, \ldots, a^{16}, a^{25}, a^{26}, \ldots\}$

The next table shows three *0L*-systems, S_5, S_6, and S_7 having the form $S_i = (\{a, b\}, x_i, s_i)$ for $5 \leq i \leq 7$:

0L-system	x_i	$s_i(a)$	$s_i(b)$	$L(S_i)$
S_5	ba	$\{a\}$	$\{b, ba\}$	$\{ba^i \mid i \geq 1\}$
S_6	b	$\{a\}$	$\{a^5, a^{15}\}$	$\{b, a^5, a^{15}\}$
S_7	aa	$\{b^2\}$	$\{b^2\}$	$\{a^2\} \cup \{b^{2^k} \mid k \geq 2\}$

□

There are finite languages that cannot be generated by any *0L*-systems as shown by the next example.

Example 11.2.9 The language $L = \{a, a^k\}$ is not a *0L*-language for any $k > 1$. Indeed, suppose that there exists a *0L*-system $S = (\{a\}, x, s)$ such that $L = L(S)$.

Since the axiom x is always in the language, $x = a$ or $x = a^k$. If the axiom of the system were a, then $a^k \in s(a)$, so $a^{k^2} \in s(s(a))$; however, $a^{k^2} \notin L(S)$. If the axiom of the system were a^k, then $a \in L(S)$ would imply that $\lambda \in s(a)$, which, in turn, would yield $\lambda \in L$. These contradictions prove that L is not a *0L*-language.

In fact, it is easy to show that no language $\{a^m, a^k\}$, where $k, m \geq 1$ and $k \neq m$ is a *0L*-language (see Exercise 2). □

The class of *0L*-languages is remarkable in that it fails to be closed with respect to almost all language operations considered so far, as we shall see in Theorem 11.2.10.

Theorem 11.2.10 *The class $\mathcal{L}_{0L}$ is not closed with respect to*

(i) *union;*
(ii) *complement;*
(iii) *intersection;*
(iv) *Kleene closure;*
(v) *+-closure;*
(vi) *morphic image;*
(vii) *inverse image under a morphism;*
(viii) *intersection with regular languages.*

Proof. In this argument we make use of the *0L*-systems $S_0, \ldots, S_7$ from Example 11.2.8.

Part (i): Note that both $\{a\}$ and $\{a^k\}$ (with $k > 1$) belong to $\mathcal{L}_{0L}$; however, $\{a, a^k\} \notin \mathcal{L}_{0L}$, as we saw in Example 11.2.9.

Part (ii): Observe that

$$\{a\}^* - L(S_0) = \{\lambda, a, a^3, a^5, a^7, \ldots\} \notin \mathcal{L}_{0L}.$$

Indeed, suppose that $S = (\{a\}, x, s)$ were a *0L*-system such that $L(S) = \{\lambda, a, a^3, a^5, a^7, \ldots\}$. This would imply $\lambda \in s(a)$ and $a^m \in s(a)$ for some $m > 0$, thus allowing the production of a word of even length. Indeed, by selecting any word $y \in L(S)$, replacing two of its letters by a^m and every other letter by λ we would obtain a word of length $2m$ in $L(S)$. This shows that $\{a\}^* - L(S_0)$ does not belong to $\mathcal{L}_{0L}$.

Part (iii): $\mathcal{L}_{0L}$ is not closed with respect to intersection because $L(S_0) \cap L(S_2) = \{a^2, a^4\} \notin \mathcal{L}_{0L}$, according to Example 11.2.9.

Part (iv): Suppose that the language $L(S_5)^* \in \mathcal{L}_{0L}$, where $L(S_5) = \{ba^i \mid i \geq 1\}$ and that $S = (\{a, b\}, x, s)$ were a *0L*-system such that $L(S) = L(S_5)^*$. Since $L(S_5) \subseteq L(S)$ we must have words of the form ba^n in $L(S)$ for arbitrarily large n.

Note that any word in $L(S_5)^*$ is either λ or of the form $ba^{j_0}ba^{j_1}\cdots ba^{j_{p-1}}$ for $j_0, j_1, \ldots, j_{p-1} \in \mathbb{N}$ and $j_l \geq 1$ for $0 \leq l \leq p-1$. Therefore, the axiom x must contain both the symbol a and the symbol b. From this, is follows that $\lambda \in s(a)$ and $\lambda \in s(b)$. This implies that $s(a) \cap \{a\}^* = \lambda$ because, otherwise, a^m would be in $L(S)$ for some $m \geq 1$. Thus, every $w \in s(a)$ must contain a b symbol. Let $r = \max\{|w| \mid w \in s(a)\}$. The distance between two consecutive symbols b in any word $y \in L(S)$ cannot exceed r, and this would prevent words of the form $ba^{j_0}b^{j_1}$ to belong to $L(S_5)^*$ for sufficiently large j_0. This shows that $L(S) \notin \mathcal{L}_{0L}$.

Part (v): Assume that $S = (\{a, b\}, x, s)$ is a *0L*-system with $L(S) = L(S_7)^+$. Since $\lambda \notin L(S)$, and $a^2 \in L(S)$, we must have $\lambda \notin s(a)$. Similarly, since $b^4 \in L(S)$, $\lambda \notin s(b)$. From this, and the fact that a^2 is the shortest word in $L(S)$ it follows that $x = a^2$ must be the axiom of S. Since $a^4 \in L(S_7)$, we have $a^2 \in s(a)$. Observe that we have neither $a \in s(a)$ nor $a^3 \in s(a)$ since either case would allow words in $L(S_7)^+$ that violate the definition of this language.

Since $b^4 \in L(S)$ we have either $b^4 \in s(a^2)$ or $b^4 \in s(a^4)$. In either case, we must have $s(a) \cap \{b, b^2, b^3\} \neq \emptyset$, which implies $a^2b^k \in L(S)$ for $k \in \{1, 2, 3\}$. This contradicts the assumption that $L(S) = L(S_7)^+$ so no *0L*-system S exists.

`Part (vi):` Let the morphism $h : \{a\}^* \longrightarrow \{a\}^*$ be defined by $h(a) = a^5$. Then, $h(L(S_2)) = \{\lambda, a^5, a^{10}, a^{15}, a^{20}\}$ and this is not a *0L*-language (cf. Exercise 5).

`Part (vii):` Consider again the morphism h defined above. We have $h^{-1}(L(S_6)) = \{a, a^3\}$, and $\{a, a^3\} \notin \mathcal{L}_{0L}$. Therefore, $\mathcal{L}_{0L}$ is not closed with respect to morphic preimages.

`Part (viii):` Finally, consider the regular language $R = a^3\{a\}^*$. Since $L(S_2) \cap R = \{a^3, a^4\}$, it follows that $\mathcal{L}_{0L}$ is not closed with respect to intersection with regular languages. ∎

0L-systems over one-symbol alphabets have received special attention in the literature, since the languages generated by such systems have a nice arithmetic characterization.

Definition 11.2.11 A *unary 0L-system* is a *0L*-system $S = (A, x, s)$ such that $|A| = 1$. We refer to unary *0L*-systems as *U0L*-systems. The class of languages generated by unary *0L*-systems will be denoted by $\mathcal{L}_{U0L}$.

Let $S = (\{a\}, x, s)$ be a *U0L*-system. If $x = a^i$ and $s(a) = \{a^{k_0}, \ldots, a^{k_{m-1}}\}$, where $0 \leq k_0 < k_1 < \cdots < k_{m-1}$, then we refer to the sequence $\mathsf{sch}(S) = (i, k_0, \ldots, k_{m-1})$ as *the schema* of S.

If $S = (\{a\}, x, h)$ is a *DPU0L*-system, then $\mathsf{sch}(S) = (i, k_0)$, where $i \geq 1$ and $k_0 \geq 1$. On the other hand, if S is a $D\bar{P}U0L$-system, then $i = 0$ or $\mathsf{sch}(S) = (i, 0)$.

$S = (\{a\}, x, s)$ is a *growing system* if $i \geq 1$ and $k_0 \geq 2$. The growing property of *U0L*-systems will be specified by the letter G. Thus, for example, if S is a $P\bar{G}U0L$-system then $i \geq 1$ and $k_0 = 1$. □

The next table summarizes some of the notations previously introduced.

Letter	Name	$S = (A, x, s)$
D	Deterministic	s is a morphism
P	Propagating	$x \neq \lambda$ and $\lambda \notin s(a)$ for $a \in A$
U	Unary	$\lvert A\rvert = 1$
G	Growing	$\lvert A\rvert = 1$, $\lvert x\rvert \geq 1$ and $y \in s(a)$ implies $\lvert y\rvert \geq 2$

Let $S = (\{a\}, a^i, s)$ be a *U0L*-system such that $\mathsf{sch}(S) = (i, k_0, \ldots, k_{m-1})$. Define the languages

$$\begin{aligned} L_0(S) &= \{a^i\} \\ L_{n+1}(S) &= \{a^k \mid k = \ell_0 k_0 + \cdots + \ell_{m-1} k_{m-1} \text{ for} \\ &\qquad \ell_0, \ldots, \ell_{m-1} \in \mathbb{N} \text{ and } a^{\ell_0 + \cdots + \ell_{m-1}} \in L_n(G)\}. \end{aligned}$$

Theorem 11.2.12 *We have* $L(S) = \bigcup_{n \in \mathbb{N}} L_n(S)$.

Proof. We begin by proving by induction on n that $L_n(S) \subseteq L(S)$. For $n = 0$ this is immediate because a^i is the axiom of S. Suppose that the inclusion holds for $L_n(S)$, and let $a^k \in L_{n+1}(S)$. Then, there exists $a^\ell \in L_n(S)$ such that $\ell = \ell_0 + \cdots + \ell_{m-1}$ and $k = \ell_0 k_0 + \cdots + \ell_{m-1} k_{m-1}$. By the inductive hypothesis, $a^\ell \in L(S)$. Then, replace each of ℓ_j symbols a in a^ℓ by a^{k_j} for $0 \leq j \leq m-1$. The resulting word belongs to $L(S)$ and by its construction is a^k.

Conversely, suppose that $w \in L(S)$. Then, $x \in s^{(p)}(a^i)$ for some $p \in \mathbb{N}$.

If $p = 0$, we have $x = a^i$, so $x \in L_0(S) \subseteq \bigcup_{n\in\mathbb{N}} L_n(S)$. Suppose that the conclusion holds for words in $s^{(p)}(a^i)$ and let $x \in s^{(p+1)}(a^i)$. Then, $x = s(u)$ for some $u \in s^{(p)}(a^i)$. By inductive hypothesis, $u \in L_n(S)$ for some $n \in \mathbb{N}$. The word x is obtained from u by applying s. If ℓ_j is the number of symbols a in u replaced by a^{k_j} for $0 \leq j \leq m-1$, then $|u| = \ell_0 + \cdots + \ell_{m-1}$ and $|x| = \ell_0 k_0 + \cdots + \ell_{m-1}k_{m-1}$. This implies $x \in L_{n+1}(S)$, and we obtain the reverse inclusion, $L(S) \subseteq \bigcup_{n\in\mathbb{N}} L_n(S)$. ∎

Theorem 11.2.13 *Let $S = (\{a\}, a^i, s)$ be a U0L-system such that $\mathsf{sch}(S) = (i, k_0, \ldots, k_{m-1})$. We have $a^p \in L_{n+1}(S)$ if and only if there are $a^q \in L_n(S)$ and $\ell_1, \ldots, \ell_{m-1} \in \mathbb{N}$ such that $\ell_1 + \cdots + \ell_{m-1} \leq q$, and $p = qk_0 + \sum\{\ell_j(k_j - k_0) \mid 1 \leq j \leq m-1\}$.*

Proof. Suppose that $a^q \in L_n(S)$ and there are $\ell_1, \ldots, \ell_{m-1} \in \mathbb{N}$ such that $\ell_1 + \cdots + \ell_{m-1} \leq q$, and $p = qk_0 + \sum\{\ell_j(k_j - k_0)\}$. Define $\ell_0 = q - (\ell_1 + \cdots + \ell_{m-1})$. Note that

$$\begin{aligned}
p &= qk_0 + \sum\{\ell_j(k_j - k_0) \mid 1 \leq j \leq m-1\} \\
p &= qk_0 + \sum\{\ell_j k_j \mid 1 \leq j \leq m-1\} - \sum\{\ell_j k_0 \mid 1 \leq j \leq m-1\} \\
&= (q - \sum\{\ell_j \mid 1 \leq j \leq m-1\})k_0 + \sum\{\ell_j k_j \mid 1 \leq j \leq m-1\} \\
&= k_0\ell_0 + \sum\{\ell_j k_j \mid 1 \leq j \leq m-1\} \\
&= \sum\{\ell_j k_j \mid 0 \leq j \leq m-1\}.
\end{aligned}$$

Therefore, $a^p \in L_{n+1}(S)$.

Conversely, suppose that $a^p \in L_{n+1}(S)$. By the definition of this language, $p = \ell_0 k_0 + \cdots + \ell_{m-1}k_{m-1}$ for some $\ell_0, \ldots, \ell_{m-1} \in \mathbb{N}$ and $a^{\ell_0 + \cdots + \ell_{m-1}} \in L_n(G)$. Then, if $q = \ell_0 + \cdots + \ell_{m-1}$ we have

$$\begin{aligned}
p &= (q - \ell_1 - \cdots - \ell_{m-1})k_0 + \ell_1 k_1 + \cdots + \ell_{m-1}k_{m-1} \\
&= qk_0 + \sum\{\ell_j(k_j - k_0) \mid 1 \leq j \leq m-1\}.
\end{aligned}$$

It is clear that $\ell_1 + \cdots + \ell_{m-1} = q - \ell_0 \leq q$. ∎

Theorem 11.2.14 *Let $S = (\{a\}, a^i, s)$ be a U0L-system such that $\mathsf{sch}(S) = (i, k_0, \ldots, k_{m-1})$. For each $j \in \mathbb{N}$, if $v \in L_j(S)$, then*

$$|v| = ik_0^j + \sum\{\ell_r(k_r - k_0) \mid \textit{for some } \ell_r \in \mathbb{N}, 1 \leq r \leq m-1\}.$$

Proof. The argument is by induction on j. For $j = 0$, choose $\ell_r = 0$ and the result is immediate. Suppose that the statement holds for j and let $w \in L_{j+1}(S)$. By Theorem 11.2.13, there is $v \in L_j(S)$ such that $|w| = |v|k_0 + \sum\{\ell'_j(k_j - k_0) \mid 1 \leq j \leq m-1\}$ for some numbers $\ell'_j \in \mathbb{N}$. Using the inductive hypothesis we have

$$|w| = ik_0^{j+1} + \sum\{(\ell_r k_0 + \ell'_r)(k_r - k_0) \mid 1 \leq r \leq m-1\},$$

which gives the desired conclusion. ∎

Corollary 11.2.15 (Herman-Rozenberg) *Let $S = (\{a\}, x, s)$ be a 0L-system such that $\mathsf{sch}(S) = (i, k_0, \ldots, k_{m-1})$. We have:*

(i) *If* S *is a DPU0L-system, then* $L(S) = \{a^p \mid p = ik_0^j$ *for* $j \in \mathbb{N}\}$.
(ii) *If* S *is a* $D\bar{P}$*U0L-system, then* $L(S) = \{a^i, \lambda\}$.
(iii) *If* S *is a* $\bar{D}\bar{P}$*U0L-system, then* $L(S) = \{a^i, a^{i-1}, \cdots, \lambda\}$ *whenever* $k_{m-1} = 1$*; otherwise, that is, if* $k_{m-1} > 1$*, then*

$$L(S) = \{a^i\} \cup \{a^{\ell_1 k_1 + \cdots + \ell_{m-1} k_{m-1}} \mid \ell_i \in \mathbb{N} \text{ for } 1 \leq i \leq m-1\}.$$

(iv) *If* S *is a* $\bar{D}P\bar{G}$*U0L-system, then*

$$L(S) = \{a^i\}\{a^{\ell_1 k_1 + \cdots + \ell_{m-1} k_{m-1}} \mid \ell_i \in \mathbb{N} \text{ for } 1 \leq i \leq m-1\}.$$

Proof. For Part (i), note that if is a *DPU0L*-system, the substitution s is a morphism, so $\mathsf{sch}(S) = (i, k_0)$ with $k_0 \geq 1$. Thus, the conclusion follows immediately from Theorem 11.2.14.

If S is a $D\bar{P}$*U0L*-system, then either $i = 0$, which implies $L(S) = \{\lambda\}$, or $\mathsf{sch}(S) = (i, 0)$ which implies $L(S) = \{a^i, \lambda\}$, so Part (ii) follows.

For Part (iii), suppose initially that $k_{m-1} = 1$. In this case, $s(a) = \{\lambda, a\}$, so $L(S) = \{a^i, a^{i-1}, \cdots, \lambda\}$. If $k_{m-1} > 1$, then $\mathsf{sch}(S) = (i, 0, k_1, \ldots, k_{m-1})$. By Theorem 11.2.13, if $n \geq 1$ and $x \in L_n(S)$, then $x = a^{\ell_1 k_1 + \cdots \ell_{m-1} k_{m-1}}$, which implies that $L(S)$ has the desired form.

To prove Part (iv), note that for a $\bar{D}P\bar{G}$*U0L*-system we have $k_0 = 1$ and $k_{m-1} > 1$. Thus, if $v \in L(S)$, then $|v| = i + \sum\{\ell_j(k_j - 1) \mid 1 \leq j \leq m-1\}$. Therefore,

$$L(S) \subseteq \{a^i\}\{a^{\ell_1 k_1 + \cdots + \ell_{m-1} k_{m-1}} \mid \ell_i \in \mathbb{N} \text{ for } 1 \leq i \leq m-1\}.$$

Suppose that the converse inclusion does not hold, and let w be the shortest word in $\{a^i\}\{a^{\ell_1 k_1 + \cdots + \ell_{m-1} k_{m-1}} \mid \ell_i \in \mathbb{N}$ for $1 \leq i \leq m-1\}$ that does not belong to $L(S)$. Since $a^i \in L(S)$, we have $\ell_j > 0$ for at least one j. Let $k = |w| - (k_j - k_0)$. By the definition of w we have $a^k \in L(S)$ and $k \geq i \geq 1$. Then, by Theorem 11.2.13, $w = a^k \cdot a^{k_j - k_0} \in L(S)$, thus contradicting the definition of w. ∎

Corollary 11.2.15 does not include the case of $\bar{D}$*GU0L*-system. This case, which is more complicated than the previous ones, is discussed below.

Let S be a $\bar{D}$*GU0L*-system such that $\mathsf{sch}(S) = (i, k_0, \ldots, k_{m-1})$, and let d be the greatest common divisor of the numbers $k_1 - k_0, \ldots, k_{m-1} - k_0$. Also, let $c_1, \ldots, c_{m-1} \in \mathbb{Z}$ be $m-1$ integers such that $d = c_1(k_1 - k_0) + \cdots + c_{m-1}(k_{m-1} - k_0)$.

Since $k_0 \geq 2$ there is a number j_0 such that

$$ik_0^{j_0} > 2k_{m-1} \sum_{i=1}^{m-1} |c_i|. \tag{11.1}$$

Choose j_0 to be the least such number. Let $s \in \mathbb{R}$ be the number given by

$$s = \frac{k_{m-1}}{d} \sum_{i=1}^{m-1} |c_i|(k_i - k_0).$$

Define the mappings $\mathsf{low}_S, \mathsf{high}_S : \{j \in \mathbb{N} \mid j \geq j_0\} \longrightarrow \mathbb{N}$ by:

$$\begin{aligned} \mathsf{low}_S(j) &= ik_0^j + sd \sum_{n=0}^{j-j_0-1} k_0^n \\ \mathsf{high}_S(j) &= \mathsf{low}_S(j) + d(k_{m-1}^{j-j_0} - 1) \end{aligned}$$

for $j \geq j_0$.

Theorem 11.2.16 *Let S be a $\bar{D}GU0L$-system with* $\mathsf{sch}(S) = (i, k_0, \ldots, k_{m-1})$*. Assume that $ik_0^{j_0} > 2k_{m-1} \sum_{1 \leq i \leq m-1} |c_i|$, as above. If $r, j \in \mathbb{N}$, $j \geq j_0$, $r \equiv ik_0^j$* (mod d)*, and $r \in [\mathsf{low}_S(j), \mathsf{high}_S(j)]$, then $a^r \in L(S)$.*

Proof. Since $r \equiv ik_0^j \pmod{d}$ we can write $r = ik_0^j + ed$ for some $e \in \mathbb{N}$. Therefore, since $\mathsf{low}_S(j) \leq r \leq \mathsf{high}_S(j)$ we have

$$s \sum_{n=0}^{j-j_0-1} k_0^n \leq e \leq s \sum_{n=0}^{j-j_0-1} k_0^n + (k_{m-1}^{j-j_0} - 1)$$

We need to show that for every $j \geq j_0$ and every $e \in \mathbb{N}$ such that

$$0 \leq e - s \sum_{n=0}^{j-j_0-1} k_0^n < k_{m-1}^{j-j_0}$$

we have $a^r = a^{ik_0^j + ed} \in L_j(S)$.

The argument is by induction on $j \geq j_0$. If $j = j_0$, then $e = 0$ and $a^{ik_0^{j_0}} \in L_{j_0}(S)$.

Suppose now that the statement holds for j and let $l \in \mathbb{N}$ be a number such that

$$0 \leq l - s \sum_{n=0}^{j-j_0} k_0^n < k_{m-1}^{j+1-j_0}.$$

We must show that $a^{ik_0^{j+1} + ld} \in L_{j+1}(S)$.

The number l can be written as

$$l = s \sum_{n=0}^{j-j_0} k_0^n + pk_{m-1} + q,$$

where $0 \leq q < k_{m-1}$ and $0 \leq p < k_{m-1}^{j-j_0}$.

The number l' defined by $l' = s \sum_{n=0}^{j-j_0-1} k_0^n + p$ satisfies the inequality

$$0 \leq l' - s \sum_{n=0}^{j-j_0-1} k_0^n < k_{m-1}^{j-j_0},$$

so, by the inductive hypothesis, $a^{ik_0^j + l'd} \in L_j(S)$.

Define the numbers

$$\begin{aligned}\ell_0 &= ik_0^j + sd\sum\{k_0^n \mid 0 \leq n \leq j - j_0 - 1\} \\ &\quad -\sum\{k_{m-1}|c_n| + qc_n \mid 1 \leq n \leq m-1\}, \\ \ell_n &= k_{m-1}|c_n| + qc_n, \\ &\quad \text{for } 1 \leq n \leq m-2,\end{aligned}$$

and

$$\ell_{m-1} = k_{m-1}|c_{m-1}| + qc_{m-1} + pd.$$

Since $0 \leq q < k_{m-1}$, by the Inequality 11.1, we have

$$\sum_{n=1}^{m-1} k_{m-1}|c_n| + qc_n \leq 2k_{m-1}\sum_{n=1}^{m-1} |c_n| \leq ik_0^{j_0} \leq ik_0^j.$$

Thus, we obtain $\ell_n \geq 0$, for $0 \leq n \leq m-1$. Observe that

$$\sum_{n=0}^{m-1} \ell_n = ik_0^j + l'd \in L_j(S),$$

which implies $a^{\ell_0 k_0 + \cdots + \ell_{m-1}k_{m-1}} \in L_{j+1}(S)$. Since $\sum_{n=0}^{m-1} \ell_n k_n = ik_0^{j+1} + ld$, the conclusion follows immediately. ∎

Observe that $\mathsf{low}_S(j)$ grows like k_0^j, while $\mathsf{high}_S(j)$ grows like k_{m-1}^j. Since $k_0 < k_{m-1}$, for any $c \in \mathbb{N}$ we have $\mathsf{low}_S(j+c) < \mathsf{high}_S(j)$ for sufficiently large j.

Corollary 11.2.17 (Herman-Rozenberg) *If S is a $\bar{D}GU0L$-system where $\mathsf{sch}(S) = (i, k_0, \ldots, k_{m-1})$, then one can determine effectively two finite sets $M, P \subseteq \mathbb{N}$ such that*

$$L(S) = \{a^m \mid m \in M\} \cup \{a^{p+\ell d} \mid p \in P \text{ and } \ell \in \mathbb{N}\},$$

where d is the greatest common divisor of the numbers $k_1 - k_0, \ldots, k_{m-1} - k_0$.

Proof. Let $r, r' \in \mathbb{N}$ be the smallest numbers such that $r < r'$ and $ik_0^r \equiv ik_0^{r'} \pmod{d}$. We have $0 < r' - r \leq d$. It is clear that for all $j \in \mathbb{N}$ such that $j \geq j_0$ and $j \geq r$, we have $\mathsf{low}(j) \equiv \mathsf{low}(j + r' - r) \pmod{d}$. According to the observation that precedes this corollary there is $j' \geq j_0$ such that $j \geq j'$ implies $\mathsf{high}(j) \geq \mathsf{low}(j + r' - r)$.

For $r \leq m < r'$, let $p_m = \mathsf{low}(j' + m)$. It follows from Theorem 11.2.16 that for $r \leq m < r'$ and for all $\ell \in \mathbb{N}$ we have $a^{p_m + \ell d} \in L(S)$. Moreover, from Theorem 11.2.14 it follows that all but a finite number of words in L(S) are of the form $a^{p_m + \ell d}$, which gives the statement of the corollary. ∎

Next, we consider one of the few closure results that hold for $\mathcal{L}_{0L}$.

Theorem 11.2.18 *For any language $L \subseteq \{a\}^*$ we have $L^* \in \mathcal{L}_{0L}$.*

Proof. If $L = \emptyset$, or $L = \{\lambda\}$ we have $L^* = \{\lambda\} \in \mathcal{L}_{0L}$.

Assume that v_0 is the shortest non-null word in L. If $v_0 = a$, then $L^* = \{a\}^* \in \mathcal{L}_{0L}$. Now assume that $|v_0| > 1$. For $1 \leq n \leq |v_0| - 1$ let $v_n \in \{a\}^*$ be defined by

$$v_n = \begin{cases} a^i & \text{if } a^i \text{ is the shortest word in } L \\ & \text{such that } i \equiv n \pmod{|v_0|} \\ \lambda & \text{if no such } a^i \text{ exists in } L.\end{cases}$$

Let $H = \{a^\ell \mid \ell = \sum_{0\leq j\leq |v_0|-1} \ell_j|v_j| \text{ and } \ell_j \in \mathbb{N}\}$. It is clear that $H \subseteq L^*$. If $v \in L$, then $|v| = \ell_0|v_0| + n$ for some $\ell_0 \in \mathbb{N}$ and some n, $0 \leq n \leq |v_0| - 1$. Thus, $v \in H$, hence $L \subseteq H$. This implies $L^* \subseteq H^* = H$, so $L^* = H$. ∎

We formulate now the notion of *derivation forest* for *0L*-systems, that is the analog of derivation trees for context-free grammars.

Definition 11.2.19 Let $S = (A, x, s)$ be a *0L*-system. A *derivation forest* for S is a finite sequence of A-labeled ordered trees $\mathtt{F} = (\mathtt{T}_0, \ldots, \mathtt{T}_{p-1})$ defined by the following conditions:

(i) The root of $\mathtt{T}_i$ is labeled by a_i for $0 \leq i \leq p-1$, where $x = a_{i_0} \cdots a_{i_{p-1}}$.

(ii) For every interior vertex v labeled by a symbol a there is a word $t \in s(a)$ such that either $t \neq \lambda$, v has $|t|$ children, and the nodes of $\mathsf{CHILDREN}(v)$ are labeled by the symbols of the word t, or $t = \lambda$ and v has exactly one child that is a leaf and is labeled by λ.

The *height* of a derivation forest is defined as the maximum height of its trees. □

Definition 11.2.20 Let $\mathtt{F} = (\mathtt{T}_0, \ldots, \mathtt{T}_{p-1})$ be a derivation forest of an *0L*-system $S = (A, x, s)$ and $l \in \mathbb{N}$.

The *label of a level* l in $\mathtt{F}$ is a word obtained by concatenating the labels of all vertices located on that level in order from $\mathtt{T}_0$ to $\mathtt{T}_{p-1}$.

The *word spelled by the derivation forest* $\mathtt{F}$ is the word $\mathsf{word}(\mathtt{F})$ obtained by concatenating the labels of the leaves of in order $\mathtt{T}_0, \ldots, \mathtt{T}_{p-1}$. □

Note that if the height of a tree $\mathtt{T}$ is less than l, then the labels of the vertices of $\mathtt{T}$ at level l form the null word λ.

It is clear that if the k-th level of the tree $\mathtt{T}_j$ is labeled by the word u_j, then the next level of the same tree is labeled by a word $v_j \in s(u_j)$ for $0 \leq i \leq p-1$. Thus, if $x = w_0, w_1, \ldots, w_{q-1}$ are the labels of the successive levels of a derivation forest of a *0L*-system S, then

$$w_0 \underset{S}{\Rightarrow} w_1 \underset{S}{\Rightarrow} \cdots \underset{S}{\Rightarrow} w_{q-1}.$$

The derivation $(w_0, w_1, \ldots, w_{q-1})$ is referred to as the *trace* of $\mathtt{F}$. Note that the depth of the derivation forest equals q.

Note also that any vertex of a derivation forest $\mathtt{F}$ labeled by λ is a leaf of one of the trees of $\mathtt{F}$.

Example 11.2.21 Let $S = (\{a, b\}, ab, s)$ be the *0L*-system defined by $s(a) = \{\lambda, b^2\}$ and $s(b) = \{a, \lambda\}$. The derivation forest shown in Figure 11.2 has the trace

$$ab \Rightarrow bba \Rightarrow aabb \Rightarrow bbbba \Rightarrow aabb \Rightarrow bbbbaa$$

□

Let $\mathtt{F} = (\mathtt{T}_0, \ldots, \mathtt{T}_{p-1})$ be a derivation forest of a *0L*-system $S = (A, x, s)$ that has the trace $(w_0, w_1, \ldots, w_{q-1})$. If d is a node in a tree $\mathtt{T}_j$ located on level i, then the subtree $\mathtt{T}_{[d]}$ rooted at d generates a word w that is a subword of the word w_j spelled by the tree $\mathtt{T}_j$. Further, if a is the label of the vertex d, then w belongs to $L(S_d)$, where $S_d = (A, a, s)$. If $w \neq \lambda$, then d has the height $q - 1 - i$

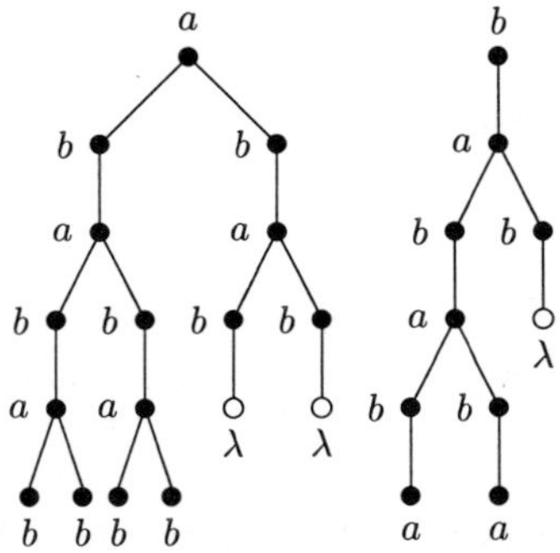

Figure 11.2: Derivation Forest

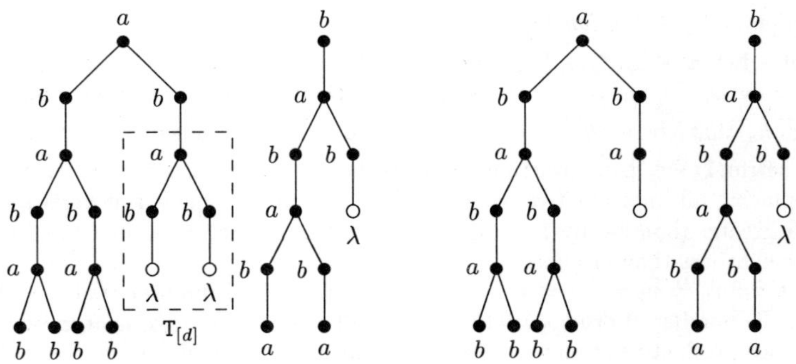

Figure 11.3: Obtaining an Alternative Derivation Forest for b^4a^2

and is referred to as a *productive vertex*; otherwise, that is, if $w = \lambda$, then the height of d is at most $q - 1 - i$ and d is said to be an *improductive vertex*.

Let d be an improductive vertex on level i in a derivation forest F whose trace is $(w_0, \dots, w_{q-1})$. Suppose that d is labeled by a and that (T) is the single-tree derivation forest of an *0L*-system such that the height of T is at most $q - 1 - i$. Then, we may replace $\mathtt{T}_{[d]}$ by T to obtain another derivation forest for the same word w_{q-1}. This observation is illustrated in the next example.

Example 11.2.22 Note that in the *0L*-system introduced in Example 11.2.21 we have the derivation $a \Rightarrow \lambda$ that corresponds to a single-tree derivation forest (T). The height of T is 1 and, by replacing the subtree $\mathtt{T}_{[d]}$ by T we obtain another derivation forest for the word b^4a^2 (cf. Figure 11.3). □

Theorem 11.2.23 *Let $S = (A, x, s)$ be a 0L-system. If $a \in A$ and $a \overset{m}{\underset{S}{\Rightarrow}} \lambda$, then $a \overset{|A|}{\underset{S}{\Rightarrow}} \lambda$.*

Proof. Let $A_i = \{a \in A \mid a \overset{i}{\underset{S}{\Rightarrow}} \lambda\}$ for $i \geq 1$. If $a \in A_i$, then $a \overset{i}{\underset{S}{\Rightarrow}} \lambda \underset{S}{\Rightarrow} \lambda$ because $\lambda \in s(\lambda)$ for every substitution s. Therefore, $A_i \subseteq A_{i+1}$ and this proves that we have an ascending sequence of subsets $A_1 \subseteq A_2 \subseteq \cdots \subseteq A$. Since A is finite, there is a number k such that

$$A_1 \subset A_2 \subset \cdots \subset A_{k-1} \subset A_k = A_{k+1} = \cdots ,$$

which implies $k \leq |A|$. Thus, if $a \overset{m}{\underset{S}{\Rightarrow}} \lambda$, it follows that if $a \overset{k}{\underset{S}{\Rightarrow}} \lambda$, which implies $a \overset{|A|}{\underset{S}{\Rightarrow}} \lambda$. ∎

Theorem 11.2.24 *Let $S = (A, x, s)$ be a 0L-system. There is an integer k_S such that if $w \in L(S) - \{\lambda\}$, then there exists a derivation*

$$x = w_0 \underset{S}{\Rightarrow} w_1 \underset{S}{\Rightarrow} \cdots \underset{S}{\Rightarrow} w_m = w$$

such that $|w_i| \leq k_S|w|$ for $0 \leq i \leq m$.

Proof. Let $w \in L(S) - \{\lambda\}$, and let $\mathtt{F}$ be the derivation forest having the trace $x = w_0 \Rightarrow w_1 \Rightarrow \cdots \Rightarrow w_{p-1} = w$. Denote by $\mathtt{T}_a$ a tree of minimal height h_a that corresponds to a derivation $a \overset{*}{\underset{S}{\Rightarrow}} \lambda$. By Theorem 11.2.23 we have $\mathsf{height}(\mathtt{T}_a) \leq |A|$. Starting from the forest $\mathtt{F}$ construct a new forest $\mathtt{F}'$ by replacing all improductive occurrences of a symbol a located at vertices of height greater than $|A|$ by $\mathtt{T}_a$, respectively. All improductive occurrences in $\mathtt{F}'$ have height less than or equal to $|A|$.

Let $x = v_0 \Rightarrow v_1 \Rightarrow \cdots \Rightarrow v_{p-1} = w$ be the trace of $\mathtt{F}'$. Suppose that $i > |A|$. Then, the number of productive occurrences of symbols in $v_{i-|A|}$ is at most $|w|$ since each productive occurrence contributes at least one symbol to w. Since the descendants of the improductive occurrences in $v_{i-|A|}$ disappear in v_i, we have $|v_i| \leq m^{|A|}|v_{i-|A|}|_{prod} \leq m^{|A|}|w|$, where $|v_{i-|A|}|_{prod}$ is the number of productive occurrences in $v_{i-|A|}$.

If $i \leq |A|$, then we have $|v_i| \leq p$, where $p = \max\{|t| \mid t \in s^{(k)}(x) \text{ for } k \leq |A|\}$. Therefore, $|v|_i \leq \max\{p, m^{|A|}\}|w|$. Choosing $k_S = \max\{p, m^{|A|}\}$ we obtain the desired conclusion. ∎

In order to place $\mathcal{L}_{0L}$ relative to the Chomsky hierarchy observe that the class $\mathcal{L}_{0L}$ is not contained in the class $\mathcal{L}_2$, as the language generated by the *L*-system S_7 from Example 11.2.8 shows. However, we have the following theorem.

Theorem 11.2.25 *Every 0L-language is a context-sensitive language.*

Proof. Let $S = (A, x, s)$ be a *0L*-system. We shall prove that the language $K = L(S) - \{\lambda\}$ is context-sensitive.

Let $w \in L(S) - \{\lambda\}$. By Theorem 11.2.24 there exists a derivation

$$x = w_0 \underset{S}{\Rightarrow} w_1 \underset{S}{\Rightarrow} \cdots \underset{S}{\Rightarrow} w_{m-1} = w \tag{11.2}$$

such that $|w_i| \leq k_S|w|$ for $0 \leq i \leq m - 1$.

Consider a grammar $G = (\{U, X, Y, Z\}, A, U, P)$, where P consists of the productions

$$U \to XxX, X \to \lambda, Xa \to XYa, YX \to ZX, aZ \to Za, XZ \to X$$

for every $a \in A$ and of the productions $Ya \rightarrow yY$ for every $a \in A$ and $y \in s(a)$.

Suppose that $a_{i_0} \cdots a_{i_{p-1}} \underset{S}{\Rightarrow} u$. This implies that u can be written as $u = u_0 \cdots u_{p-1}$, where $u_j \in s(a_{i_j})$ for $0 \leq j \leq p-1$. Then, in G we have the derivation

$$\begin{aligned} Xa_{i_0} \cdots a_{i_{p-1}}X & \underset{G}{\Rightarrow} XYa_{i_0} \cdots a_{i_{p-1}}X \overset{*}{\underset{G}{\Rightarrow}} Xu_0 \cdots u_{p-1}YX \\ & \underset{G}{\Rightarrow} Xu_0 \cdots u_{p-1}ZX \overset{*}{\underset{G}{\Rightarrow}} XZu_0 \cdots u_{p-1}X \\ & \underset{G}{\Rightarrow} Xu_0 \cdots u_{p-1}X = XuX \end{aligned}$$

The work space of this derivation does not exceed $3 + \max\{p, |u|\}$.

Starting from the derivation 11.2, by the above remark, we have the derivation d_w given by

$$U \underset{X}{\Rightarrow} xX \overset{*}{\underset{G}{\Rightarrow}} Xw_1X \overset{*}{\underset{G}{\Rightarrow}} \cdots \overset{*}{\underset{G}{\Rightarrow}} Xw_nX \overset{*}{\underset{G}{\Rightarrow}} w,$$

so $L(S) \subseteq L(G)$. Note that we also have the inverse inclusion because any derivation of the form $U \overset{*}{\underset{G}{\Rightarrow}} w$ has necessarily the form of a simulation of a derivation in the *0L*-system S, so $L(S) = L(G)$.

Observe that $\mathsf{ws}_G(d_w, w) = 3 + \max\{|w_i| \mid 0 \leq i \leq\} \leq 4k_S|w|$ for every $w \in L(G)$. Thus, by Theorem 9.3.7, the language $L(S) - \{\lambda\}$ is context-sensitive. Thus, $L(S)$ is clearly context-sensitive. ∎

In *0L*-systems the rewriting of a symbol (which corresponds to a cell) is independent of its neighbors; thus, a *0L*-system is essentially a context-free and parallel rewriting system. Generalization of *0L*-systems exist where the evolution of the organism is influenced by the communication between cells. This communication may be bilateral, in the case of *2L*-systems, or unilateral, from the left or the right, in the case of *1L*-systems (see Exercises).

11.3 Nucleic Acids

Deoxyribonucleic acid (DNA), the primary carrier of genetic information, is identical in all cells of any individual of any species. The constituents of the DNA are known as *nucleotides.* A nucleotide consists of three parts: a *base*, a sugar and a phosphate (cf. Figure 11.4); nucleotides are generally identified by their base. For DNA, there are four such bases: *adenine* (denoted by A), *guanine* (G), *cytosine* (C), and *thymine* (T).

The five carbon atoms of the sugar are traditionally denoted by (i'), where $1 \leq i \leq 5$.

A molecule of DNA is a long, thin string composed of two strands wound around each other; each strand is a long chain of nucleotides. Each DNA strand has directionality, and its two distinct ends are identified according to the carbon sugar at the end (the $3'$ end and the $5'$ end).

Starting from chemical and physical evidence, Watson and Crick [1953] introduced the *double-helix model* of the DNA. The main features of this model are:

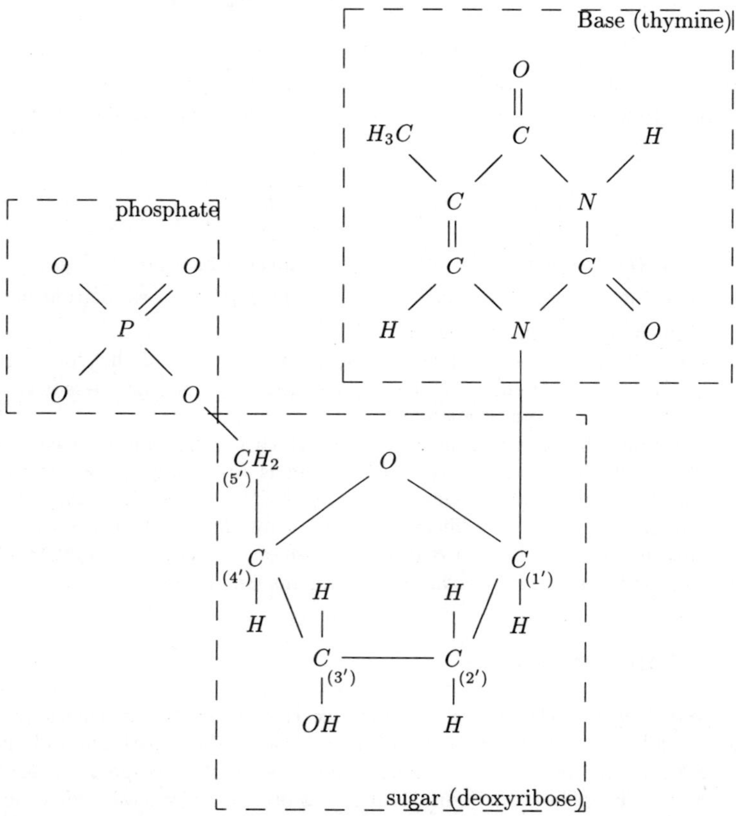

Figure 11.4: The Structure of a Nucleotide

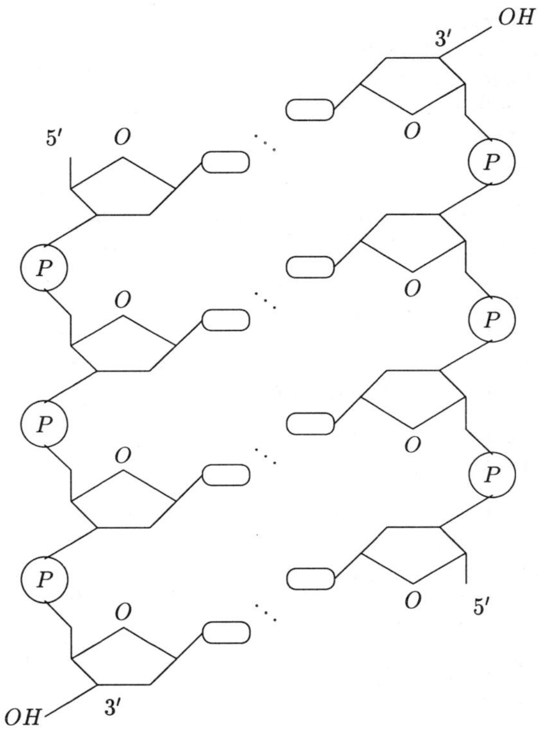

Figure 11.5: A Schematic Representation of the DNA molecule

- The DNA strands are coiled around a central axis, forming a double-helix.
- The two strands run in opposite directions (5′ to 3′, and 3′ to 5′).
- The bases of the nucleotides in both strands are flat structures, positioned perpendicularly to the axis, similar to the steps of a spiral staircase (cf. [Drlica, 1997]).
- The bases of the strands are paired to one another in a specific manner (discussed later in Section 2.4).

The sugar (called *deoxyribose*) and the phosphate form the backbone of the each of the strands of the DNA. A schematic representation of a DNA molecule is shown in Figure 11.5. Thus, the strands of a DNA molecule may be viewed abstractly as a word over the alphabet $A_{\mathbf{DNA}} = \{\mathsf{A}, \mathsf{G}, \mathsf{C}, \mathsf{T}\}$. The length of a DNA molecule can be of the order of millions of nucleotides.

Another important molecule in molecular biology is the *ribonucleic acid* (RNA); RNA can be regarded as a word over the alphabet $A_{\mathbf{RNA}} = \{\mathsf{A}, \mathsf{G}, \mathsf{C}, \mathsf{U}\}$, where the symbol U represents a base called *uracil*. The typical length of an RNA molecule is in the thousands of nucleotides. The are three types of RNA: the *messenger RNA* that is synthesized in the cell nucleus, the *transfer RNA* that is found in the cytoplasm, and the *ribosomal RNA* that is found in the ribosomes, a specialized unit of the cell.

Proteins are macromolecules that are central to the biochemical activity of cells. They can be regarded as words over an alphabet of twenty symbols that correspond to the 20 *amino acids.* The typical length of such words is in the hundreds.

The two strands of a DNA molecule satisfy the *complementary base-pairing rule* that stipulates that the bases of the two strands must fit together in a precise way. Define the very fine morphism $\hbar : A^*_{\mathbf{DNA}} \longrightarrow A^*_{\mathbf{DNA}}$ given by:

b	A	G	C	T
$\hbar(b)$	T	C	G	A

If one of the strands is described by the word x, then its opposite strand is given by $\hbar(x)$. The pairs $(b, \hbar(b))$ are called *base pairs.* For example,

$5'$ end$\cdots$ACAGTAAAT$\cdots 3'$ end
$3'$ end$\cdots$TGTCATTTA$\cdots 5'$ end

are fragments of two complementary strands of a DNA molecule. The word $\hbar(x)$ is referred to as *the complement* of the word x.

The *transcription* process involves the creation of the messenger RNA starting from the blueprint provided by the DNA, using the very fine morphism $k : A^*_{\mathbf{DNA}} \longrightarrow A^*_{\mathbf{RNA}}$ defined by:

b	A	G	C	T
$k(b)$	U	C	G	A

Portions of a DNA molecule unwind, the two strands separate, RNA nucleotides pair with the bases of the DNA and a strand of messenger RNA is formed that is complimentary to the DNA strand. Specifically, if the portion of the DNA that is transcribed is the word x, then the new messenger RNA is $k(x)$.

In turn, the RNA is the blueprint that contains various protein designs.

Specifically, each amino acid is encoded by a three-symbol infix of an RNA strand called a *codon*, and there are several such possible encodings for an amino acid, as specified in the table of Figure 11.6. This table defines a substitution $s : A_{amino} \longrightarrow \mathcal{P}(A^*_{\mathbf{RNA}})$, where A_{amino} is the 20-symbol alphabet of the amino acids. The function of transfer RNA is to carry aminoacid molecules to the ribosomes, the "protein factories" of the cell. A protein $w \in A^*_{amino}$ can be synthesized only if the the transfer RNA is a word $t \in s(w)$. It is important to observe that the substitution described by the previous table has certain properties that are significant from a biological point of view:

1. If $a, a' \in A_{amino}$ and $a \neq a'$, then $s(a) \cap s(a') = \emptyset$. Therefore, each codon corresponds to exactly one amino acid.
2. For every $a \in A_{amino}$ we have $1 \leq s(a) \leq 6$. This property of s is known in biological terms as *degeneracy.*
3. If $|s(a)| = 4$, then $s(a)$ has the form $s(a) = bb'A_{\mathbf{RNA}}$ for some bases b, b'; if $|s(a)| = 6$, then $s(a) = b_0b_1\{b, b'\} \cup b_2b_3A_{\mathbf{RNA}}$, for some bases $b, b', b_0, \ldots, b_3$. This suggests that the third base of the encodings is

Amino Acid	Codon	Amino Acid	Codon
alanine	GCA GCC GCG GCU	leucine	UUA UUG CUA CUC CUG CUU
arginine	AGA AGG CGA CGC CGG CGU	lysine	AAA AAG
asparagine	AAC AAU	methionine	AUG
aspartic acid	GAC GAU	phenylalanine	UUC UUU
cysteine	UGC UGU	proline	CCA CCC CCG CCU
glutamic acid	GAA GAG	serine	AGC AGU UCA UCC UCG UCU
glutamine	CAA CAG	threonine	ACA ACC ACG ACU
glycine	GGA GGC GGG GGU	tryptophan	UGG
histidine	CAC CAU	tyrosine	UAC UAU
isoleucine	AUA AUC AUU	valine	GUA GUC GUG GUU

Figure 11.6: Encoding of Amino Acids

Enzyme	Source	Recognition Site	Cleavage	
EcoRI	Escheria Coli	GAATTC	G	AATTC
		CTTAAG	CTTAA	G
Hind III	Hemophilius Influenzae	AAGCTT	A	AGCTT
		TTCGAA	TTCGA	A
AluI	Arthrobacter luteus	AGCT	AG	CT
		TCGA	TC	GA
Sau3a	Staphilococus Aureus	GATC		GATC
		CTAG	CTAG	
BamHI	Bacillus Amyloliquefaciens	GGATCC	G	GATCC
		CCTAGG	CCTAG	G

Figure 11.7: Recognition Sites for Restriction Enzymes

less important than the first two bases (the *wobble hypothesis* of Crick) (see [Lewin *et al.*, 1997]).

Recombinant DNA refers to the synthetic creation of a new combination of DNA segments that does not occur naturally, by cutting and pasting various fragment of a DNA molecule. The instruments that allow biologists to cut DNA strands are known as *restriction enzymes.* Restriction enzymes are proteins. They typically bear a name derived from the name of the organism from which they were extracted. For example, the enzyme *HindIII* was discovered in *Hemophilius Influenzae*, while *EcoRI* was extracted from *Escheria coli.* Each restriction enzyme has a specific cutting point referred to as a *recognition site.* The patterns resulting from a cut are known as *points of cleavage.* The table contained in Figure 11.7 shows recognition sites and points of cleavage for a few restriction enzymes. Note that some points of cleavage are staggered (e.g. the cleavage caused by EcoRI); others are blunt cuts (e.g. the cut caused by AluI).

The staggered cuts generated by some restriction enzymes can reunite to form weak hydrogen bonds among complementary bases; for this reason, the these staggered ends are sometimes referred to as *sticky ends.* These sticky ends may anneal and allow another enzyme, known as *DNA ligase* to connect the sugar-phosphate backbone of the molecules, resulting in a new DNA molecule.

The main steps in the creation of a recombinant DNA are these:

(i) Using *restriction enzymes*, DNA fragments are generated.

(ii) The fragments produced by restriction enzymes are joined to other DNA fragments that serve as *vectors.* Vectors are transferred to host cells where they replicate, producing copies known as *clones.*

(iii) The clones are extracted from the host cells.

Definition 11.3.1 An infix x of a DNA sequence is *palindromic* if $x = \hbar(x)^R$. □

This means that if x occurs on a DNA strand (read from 5′ to 3′), then its opposite infix (read from 3′ to 5′) equals $\hbar(x)$.

Example 11.3.2 The sequence $w =$ CAGATCTG is palindromic because

$$\hbar(w) = \mathsf{GTCTAGAC}$$

and $\hbar(w)^R = w$. □

For $x \in A^*_{\mathbf{DNA}}$, the word $\hbar(x)^R$ is *the reverse complement* of the word x. Thus, x is palindromic if and only if it coincides with its reverse complement.

In general, the infixes of the DNA that serve as recognition sites for restriction enzymes are *palindromic.* It is easy to see that a word $w \in A^*_{\mathbf{DNA}}$ is palindromic if $w = u\hbar(u)^R$ for some $u \in A^*_{\mathbf{DNA}}$. This property is known as *dyadic symmetry* in molecular biology.

Example 11.3.3 Suppose that we have *in vitro* two DNA molecules:

5′ TAGA[GGATCC]GATA 3′
3′ ATCT[CCTAGG]CTAT 5′

and

5′ GAC[GATC]TC 3′
3′ CTG[CTAG]AG 5′

Note that the first molecule contains the recognition site GGATCC of the restriction enzyme BamHI, while the second contains the recognition site GATC of Sau3a. These sites have been marked by square brackets. In the presence of the restriction enzymes, the two molecules will be cleaved as

5′ TAGA[G 3′   5′ GATCC]GATA 3′
3′ ATCT[CCTAG 5′   3′ G]CTAT 5′

and

5′ GAC 3′   5′ GATC]TC 3′
3′ CTG[CTAG 5′   3′ AG 5′ ,

respectively. Now, if ligase is present, new DNA molecules may be formed using the sticky ends of the participating molecules by splicing the left part of the first molecule with the right part of the second and the left part of the second molecule with the right part of the first.

5′ TAGAGGATCTC 3′
3′ ATCTCCTAGAG 5′

and

5′ GACGATCCGATA 3′
3′ CTGCTAGGCTAT 5′

To simplify the presentation, we have omitted any thermodynamical considerations involving these biochemical reactions.

Since the structure of the DNA is completely determined by either of its strands, the previous examples could be stated using the 5′ to 3′ sequences. In this case, the DNA strands

TAGA[GGATCC]GATA and GAC[GATC]TC

may yield either of the strands:

TAGAGGATCTC or GACGATCCGATA.

Consider the following words on $A_{\mathbf{DNA}}$:

$$\begin{array}{llll} u' = \mathsf{TAGA} & x = \mathsf{G} & x' = \mathsf{GATCC} & u'' = \mathsf{GATA} \\ v' = \mathsf{GAC} & y = \lambda & y' = \mathsf{GATC} & v'' = \mathsf{TC} \end{array}$$

The initial $5' - 3'$ strands can be written as $u'xx'u''$ and $v'yy'v''$, respectively. The new DNA strands are $u'xy'v''$ and $v'yx'u''$. □

The notion of a splicing production is introduced as a model of the splicing operation between words.

Definition 11.3.4 Let A be an alphabet, and let $,# be two symbols such that $\$, \# \not\in A$. A *splicing production on the alphabet* A is a word of the form $x\#x'\$y\#y'$, where $x, x', y, y' \in A^*$.

The words xx' and yy' are referred to as the *splicing sites of the production.*

If $\pi = x\#x'\$y\#y'$ is a splicing production and $u, v \in A^*$, then we write $(u, v) \underset{\pi}{\rightarrow} w$ to denote that

$$u = u'xx'u'', v = v'yy'v'', w = u'xy'v''.$$

for some words $u', u'', v', v'' \in A^*$.

Alternatively, we write $(u, v) \underset{\pi}{\rightarrow} (w, w')$ if u, v, w are as above and $w' = v'yx'u''$. Note that w' can be obtained from u, v and w, so writing it out is not really necessary. In this case, we say that *w and w' are obtained from u and v by splicing.* □

Example 11.3.5 The word

$$\pi = \mathsf{G\#GATCC\$\#GATC}$$

is the splicing production described in Example 11.3.3. □

Definition 11.3.6 Let A be an alphabet and let $\#, \$$ be two symbols such that $\#, \$ \not\in A$. An *$H$-scheme* is a pair $\mathcal{S} = (A, P)$, where $P \subseteq A^*\#A^*\$A^*\#A^*$ is a set of splicing productions. □

In general, an H-scheme is not a finitary object because the set of splicing productions may be infinite. If $P \in \mathcal{L}$, where $\mathcal{L}$ is a family of languages, then we say that $\mathcal{S}$ is *an H-scheme of type $\mathcal{L}$.*

Definition 11.3.7 Let A be an alphabet, $L \subseteq A^*$ be a language, and let $\mathcal{S} = (B, P)$ be an H-scheme, where $A \subseteq B$. The language derived from L by the H-scheme $\mathcal{S}$ is the language $\mathcal{S}(L)$ given by

$$\mathcal{S}(L) = \{w \in A^* \mid (u, v) \underset{\pi}{\rightarrow} w \text{ for some } u, v \in L \text{ and } \pi \in P\}.$$

If $\mathcal{L}, \mathcal{R}$ are two families of languages, the *family of languages* $S(\mathcal{L}, \mathcal{R})$ *obtained by* $\mathcal{R}$*-splicing the languages of* $\mathcal{L}$ consists of all languages $\mathcal{S}(L)$, such that $L \in \mathcal{L}$, and $\mathcal{S} = (A, R)$ is an H-schema for some $R \in \mathcal{R}$. □

For example, if $\mathcal{R} = \mathcal{L}_3$, then $S(\mathcal{L}, \mathcal{R})$ is said to be obtained from $\mathcal{L}$ be *regular splicing.*

If $\mathcal{L} \subseteq \mathcal{L}'$ and $\mathcal{R} \subseteq \mathcal{R}'$, it is easy to see that $S(\mathcal{L}, \mathcal{R}) \subseteq S(\mathcal{L}', \mathcal{R}')$.

Unless we state otherwise, we assume that all families of languages considered from now on contain all finite languages. We begin by presenting a series of technical results following [Head *et al.*, 1997] and [Păun *et al.*, 1998].

Theorem 11.3.8 *Let* $\mathcal{L}$ *is a family of languages such that* $L \in \mathcal{L}$ *implies* $Lc \in \mathcal{L}$ *for every symbol* c. *We have:*

(i) $\mathcal{L} \subseteq S(\mathcal{L}, \mathcal{R})$ *for every family* $\mathcal{R}$.

(ii) *For every* $L, K \in \mathcal{L}$ *we have* $LK^{-1} \in S(\mathcal{L}, \mathcal{L})$.

Proof. Suppose that $L \subseteq A^*$, and let $c \notin A$. The statement follows immediately from the fact that $Lc \in \mathcal{L}$, $\{c\#\lambda\$c\#\lambda\} \in \mathcal{R}$ and $L = \mathcal{S}(Lc)$, where $\mathcal{S} = (A, \{c\#\lambda\$c\#\lambda\})$.

For the second part of the theorem, let $L, K \in \mathcal{L}$. Consider the H-scheme $\mathcal{S} = (A \cup \{c\}, \#Kc\$c\#)$. A production of $\mathcal{S}$ has the form $\pi = \#x'c\$c\#$, where $x' \in K$. Thus, two words $uc, vc \in Lc$ can be spliced using π only if $uc = u'x'c$ and $vc = v'c$. In this case $(uc, vc) \underset{\pi}{\rightarrow} u' \in \mathcal{S}(Lc)$. Since $x'c \in K$, it follows that $u' \in LK^{-1}$, so $\mathcal{S}(Lc) \subseteq LK^{-1}$. The reverse inclusion is left to the reader. Thus, $LK^{-1} \in S(\mathcal{L}, \mathcal{L})$. ∎

Corollary 11.3.9 *Every recursively enumerable set can be obtained by splicing a linear language using a linear set of splicing productions.*

Proof. Since every recursively enumerable language is the quotient of two linear languages (cf. Theorem 8.6.22), the statement follows immediately from Theorem 11.3.8. ∎

Theorem 11.3.10 *If* $\mathcal{L}$ *is a family of languages closed under concatenation, morphisms, inverse morphic images, and intersection with regular languages, then* $S(\mathcal{L}, \mathcal{L}_3) \subseteq \mathcal{L}$. *In other words, in this case,* $\mathcal{L}$ *is closed with respect to regular splicing.*

Proof. Let $L \in \mathcal{L}$ and let $R \subseteq A^*\#A^*\$A^*\#A^*$ be a regular language. We need to prove that $\mathcal{S}(L) \in \mathcal{L}$, where $\mathcal{S} = (A, R)$ is an H-scheme.

Define the regular substitution $s : A \cup \{\#, \$\} \longrightarrow \mathcal{P}((A \cup \{\#, \$\})^*)$ given by $s(a) = \{a\}$ if $a \in A$ and $s(\$) = A^*\$A^*$. Then, by Theorem 3.9.10, the language $R_0 = s(R)$ is regular. This implies the regularity of the language $R_1 = A^*R_0A^*$. Note that $t \in R_1$ if and only if there exists a splicing production $x\#x'\$y\#y' \in R$ such that $t = t_0x\#x't_1\$t_2y\#y't_3$ for some $t_i \in A^*$, $0 \leq i \leq 3$.

Since $\mathcal{L}$ contains all finite languages and is closed with respect to concatenation, we have $L\$L \in \mathcal{L}$. Define the morphism $h : (A \cup \{\#, \$\})^* \longrightarrow (A \cup \{\#, \$\})^*$ by $h(a) = a$ for $a \in A$, $h(\#) = \lambda$, and $h(\$) = \$$. We have $L_1 = h^{-1}(L\$L) \cap R_1 \in \mathcal{L}$ because $\mathcal{L}$ is closed with respect to inverse morphic images and intersection with regular languages. Note that $t \in L_1$ if only if $t = u'x\#x'u''\$v'y\#y'v''$, where $u'xx'u'', v'yy'v'' \in L$ and $x\#x'\$y\#y' \in R$.

Now let $\bar{A}$ be an alphabet that consists of barred versions of symbols of A and let $k : (A \cup \{\#, \$\} \cup \bar{A})^* \longrightarrow (A \cup \{\#, \$\})^*$ be the morphism defined by $k(a) = k(\bar{a}) = a$ for $a \in A$ and $k(\#) = \#$, $k(\$) = \$$. For $w \in A^*$ denote by $\bar{w}$ the word obtained from w by replacing the symbols of A by their barred versions.

The language $L_2 = k^{-1}(L_1) \cap A^*\#(\bar{A})^*\$(\bar{A})^*\#A^*$ belongs to $\mathcal{L}$, and we have $t \in L_2$ if and only if $t = u'x\#\overline{x'u''}\$\overline{v'y}\#y'v''$ for some splicing production $x\#x'\$y\#y' \in R$. Finally, let $g : (A \cup \{\#, \$\} \cup \bar{A})^* \longrightarrow (A \cup \{\#, \$\})^*$ be the morphism defined by $g(a) = a$ for $a \in A \cup \{\#\}$, $g(\bar{a}) = \lambda$ for $\bar{a} \in \bar{A}$, and $g(\$) = \lambda$. It is clear that $g(t) = u'xy'v$ for the word $t \in L_2$. Thus, $g(L_2) = \mathcal{S}(L)$, which implies $\mathcal{S}(L) \in \mathcal{L}$. ∎

There are many interesting properties of families $S(\mathcal{L}, \mathcal{R})$, where $\mathcal{L}, \mathcal{R}$ are various classes of the Chomsky hierarchy and we refer the interested reader to the recent comprehensive monograph on *DNA*-computing [Păun *et al.*, 1998].

Definition 11.3.11 Let $\mathcal{S} = (A, R)$ be an H-schema. The language $\mathcal{S}^n(L)$ is defined inductively by

$$\begin{aligned} \mathcal{S}^0(L) &= L \\ \mathcal{S}^{n+1}(L) &= \mathcal{S}^n(L) \cup \mathcal{S}(\mathcal{S}^n(L)) \end{aligned}$$

for $n \in \mathbb{N}$.

The *language* $\mathcal{S}^*(L)$ *obtained from* L *by* $\mathcal{S}$*-iterated splicing* is given by:

$$\mathcal{S}^*(L) = \bigcup\{\mathcal{S}^n(L) \mid n \in \mathbb{N}\}$$

for every $L \subseteq A^*$. □

Note that $\mathcal{S}^1(L) = L \cup \mathcal{S}(L)$. Also, we have

$$L \subseteq \mathcal{S}^1(L) \subseteq \cdots \subseteq \mathcal{S}^n(L) \subseteq \cdots$$

and $\mathcal{S}(\mathcal{S}^*(L)) = \mathcal{S}^*(L)$ for every $L \subseteq A^*$.

Definition 11.3.12 Let $\mathcal{L}, \mathcal{R}$ be two families of languages. The family of languages obtained from $\mathcal{L}$ by $\mathcal{R}$*-iterated splicing* is given by

$$\mathcal{H}(\mathcal{L}, \mathcal{R}) = \{\mathcal{S}^*(L) \mid L \in \mathcal{L} \text{ and } \mathcal{S} = (A, R), \text{ where } R \in \mathcal{R}\}.$$

□

The next two theorems demonstrate the power of iterated splicing.

Theorem 11.3.13 *Let* $\mathcal{F}$ *be the collection of all finite languages. We have* $\mathcal{H}(\mathcal{L}_3, \mathcal{F}) = \mathcal{L}_3$.

Proof. Let $L \subseteq A^*$ be a regular language, and let $\mathcal{T}$ be a transition system $\mathcal{T} = (A, Q, \theta, Q_0, F)$ such that $L(\mathcal{T}) = L$.

Assume that $\mathcal{S} = (A, R)$, where R is a finite language, that is, a finite collection of splicing productions $R = \{\pi_0, \ldots, \pi_{n-1}\}$, where

$$\pi_j = x_j\#x'_j\$y_j\#y'_j,$$

where $x_jy'_j = a_{j0}a_{j1}\cdots a_{jp_j-1}$ for $0 \leq j \leq n-1$. For each splicing production π_j, consider $p_j + 1$ new states $q_{j0}, q_{j1}, \ldots q_{jp_j-1}, q_{jp_j}$. Let $Q' = \{q_{jl} \mid 0 \leq l \leq p_j, 0 \leq j \leq n-1\}$, and let $\mathcal{T}_0$ be the transition system defined by $\mathcal{T}_0 = (A, Q \cup Q', \theta_0, Q_0, F)$, where $\theta_0 = \theta \cup \{(q_{jl}, a_{jl}, q_{j\,l+1}) \mid 0 \leq l \leq p_j - 1\}$. Next we construct a sequence of transition systems $\mathcal{T}_0, \mathcal{T}_1, \ldots$ beginning with the transition system $\mathcal{T}_0$ introduced above.

Suppose that we have constructed the transition system

$$\mathcal{T}_k = (A, Q \cup Q', \theta_k, Q_0, F).$$

Then, for every splicing production $\pi_j = x_j\#x'_j\$y_j\#y'_j$ and for every pair of states $q, q' \in Q \cup Q'$, add to θ_k the following triples to obtain θ_{k+1}:

- if $(q, \lambda, q_{j0}) \notin \theta_k^*$, then add (q, λ, q_{j0}) if $(q_0, u, q) \in \theta_k^*$, $(q, x_jx'_j, q') \in \theta_k^*$ and $(q', v, q_f) \in \theta_k^*$ for some $u, v \in A^*$, $q_0 \in Q_0$ and $q_f \in F$;
- if $(q_{j,p_j}, \lambda, q') \notin \theta_k^*$, then add (q_{j,p_j}, λ, q') if $(q_0, u, q) \in \theta_k^*$, $(q, y_jy'_j, q') \in \theta_k^*$, $(q', v, q_f) \in \theta_k^*$ for some $u, v \in A^*$, $q_0 \in Q_0$ and $q_f \in F$.

The triples of the first category are called *initial* $(k+1)$*-transitions*, while the triples of the second category are referred to as *final* $(k+1)$*-transitions*.

There are only finitely many triples that can be added to θ_0 and its successors. Consequently, there is a number m such that $\theta_0 \subset \theta_1 \subset \cdots \subset \theta_m = \theta_{m+1} = \cdots$. We prove that $\mathcal{S}^*(L) = L(\mathcal{T}_m)$.

Since $L = L(\mathcal{T})$ and $\theta \subseteq \theta_m$ it is clear that $L \subseteq L(\mathcal{T}_m)$.

We claim that $\mathcal{S}(L(\mathcal{T}_m)) \subseteq L(\mathcal{T}_m)$. Consider a production $x\#x'\$y\#y' \in R$ and $u, v \in A^*$ such that $u = u'xx'u''$, $v = v'yy'v'' \in L(\mathcal{T}_m)$. If $xy' = a_{j0}a_{j1}\cdots a_{jp_j-1}$, then $(q_{j0}, xy', q_{jp_j}) \in \theta^* \subseteq \theta_m^*$.

There are $q_0, q'_0 \in Q_0$, $q_f, q'_f \in F$, and $q, r \in Q \cup Q'$ such that the triples

$$(q_0, u', q), (q, xx'u'', q_f), (q'_0, v'yy', r), (r, v'', q'_f)$$

belong to θ_m^*. The definition of $\mathcal{T}_m$ implies that $(q, \lambda, q_{j0}), (q_{jp_j}, \lambda, r) \in \theta_m^*$. Therefore, we can conclude that $u'xy'v'' \in L(\mathcal{T}_m)$ (cf. Figure 11.8), which proves that $\mathcal{S}(L(\mathcal{T}_m) \subseteq L(\mathcal{T}_m)$. Since $L \subseteq L(\mathcal{T}_m)$, we have $\mathcal{S}^n(L) \subseteq L(\mathcal{T}_m)$ for every $n \in \mathbb{N}$, so $\mathcal{S}^*(L) \subseteq L(\mathcal{T}_m)$.

To prove the converse inclusion, $L(\mathcal{T}_m) \subseteq \mathcal{S}^*(L)$, it suffices to show that if $(q_0, w, q_f) \in \theta_k^*$, then $w \in \mathcal{S}^*(L)$ for $k \in \mathbb{N}$.

The argument is by induction on k. If $k = 0$, then none of the newly introduced states q_{jl} is used (because they are not connected in θ_0 to the states in Q), so $(q_0, w, q_f) \in \theta^*$, which means that $w \in L \subseteq \mathcal{S}^*(L)$.

Suppose that the statement holds for k and let $(q_0, w, q_f) \in \theta_{k+1}^*$. If no $(k+1)$-transitions are used, then $(q_0, w, q_f) \in \theta_{k+1}^*$ and, by the inductive hypothesis, $w \in \mathcal{S}^*(L)$. If l pairs of $(k+1)$-transitions occur on a path (q_0, w, q_f), then w can be written as

$$w = w_0x_{j_1}y'_{j_1}w_1x_{j_2}y'_{j_2}\cdots w_{l-1}x_{j_l}y'_{j_l}w_l$$

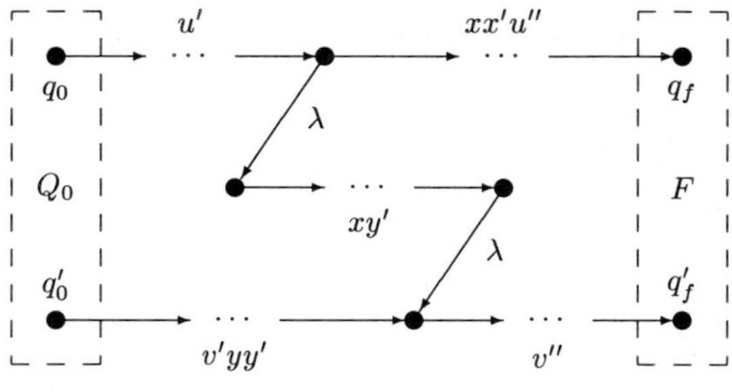

Figure 11.8: Splicing Simulation in $\mathcal{T}_m$

The definition of θ_{k+1} implies the existence of the words

$$\begin{aligned} t_0 &= w_0 x_{j_1} x'_{j_1} u''_1 \\ t_1 &= v'_2 y_{j_1} y'_{j_1} w_1 x_{j_2} x'_{j_2} u''_2 \\ t_2 &= v'_3 y_{j_2} y'_{j_2} w_2 x_{j_3} x'_{j_3} u''_3 \\ &\vdots \\ t_{l-1} &= v'_l y_{j_{l-1}} y'_{j_{l-1}} w_{l-1} x_{j_l} x'_{j_l} u''_l \\ t_l &= v'_{l+1} y_{j_l} y'_{j_l} w_l \end{aligned}$$

such that $(q_{0i}, t_i, q_{fi}) \in \theta^*_k$ for $0 \leq i \leq l$ and the existence of the splicing productions:

$$\pi_1 : x_{j_1} \# x'_{j_1} \$ y_{j_1} \# y'_{j_1}, \ldots, \pi_l : x_{j_l} \# x'_{j_l} \$ y_{j_l} \# y'_{j_l}.$$

By the inductive hypothesis, we have $t_i \in \mathcal{S}^*(L)$ for $0 \leq i \leq l$. Then, we have

$$\begin{aligned} (t_0, t_1) &\underset{\pi_1}{\rightarrow} t_{01} = w_0 x_{j_1} y'_{j_1} w_1 x_{j_2} x'_{j_2} u''_2 \\ (t_{01}, t_2) &\underset{\pi_2}{\rightarrow} t_{012} = w_0 x_{j_1} y'_{j_1} w_1 x_{j_2} y'_{j_2} w_2 x_{j_3} x'_{j_3} u''_3 \\ &\vdots \\ (t_{01\cdots l-1}, t_l) &\underset{\pi_l}{\rightarrow} t_{012\cdots l} = w = w_0 x_{j_1} y'_{j_1} w_1 x_{j_2} y'_{j_2} w_2 \cdots x_{j_l} y'_l w_l \end{aligned}$$

This proves that $w \in \mathcal{S}^*(L)$. This allows us to conclude that $\mathcal{H}(\mathcal{L}_3, \mathcal{F}) \subseteq \mathcal{L}_3$.

The converse inclusion follows immediately from Exercise 22. ∎

Theorem 11.3.14 *For every language $L \in \mathcal{L}_0$ such that $L \subseteq A^*$ there exists a language $K \in \mathcal{H}(\mathcal{F}, \mathcal{L}_3)$ such that $L = K \cap A^*$.*

Proof. Suppose that L is generated by the grammar $G = (A_N, A_T, S, P)$. Let c be a symbol such that $c \notin A_N \cup A_T$, and let $C = A_N \cup A_T \cup \{c\}$.

Consider the alphabet $D = \{X, Y, Z, X'\} \cup \{Y_s \mid s \in C\}$.

Define the H-scheme $\mathcal{S} = (D, R)$, where R is a regular language that consists of the following splicing productions:

(i) the simulation productions:

$$(i)_\pi : X\gamma \# \alpha Y \$ Z \# \beta Y,$$

for every production $\pi : \alpha \to \beta \in P$ and $\gamma \in C^*$;

(ii) the rotation productions:

$$\begin{aligned}(ii)_1 &: X\gamma\#sY\$Z\#Y_s,\\ (ii)_2 &: X's\#Z\$X\#\gamma Y_s,\\ (ii)_3 &: X'\gamma\#Y_s\$Z\#Y,\\ (ii)_4 &: X\#Z\$X'\#\gamma Y\end{aligned}$$

for every $s \in C, \gamma \in C^*$;

(iii) the termination productions:

$$\begin{aligned}(iii)_1 &: \#ZY\$Xc\#xY, \text{ for } x \in A_T^*,\\ (iii)_2 &: \#Y\$XZ\#.\end{aligned}$$

We claim that $L = \mathcal{S}^*(L_0) \cap A_T^*$, where L_0 is the finite language

$$L_0 = \{XcSY, ZY, XZ\} \cup \{Z\beta Y \mid \alpha \to \beta \in P\} \cup \{ZY_s, X'sZ \mid s \in C\}.$$

Note that $L_0 \cap A_T^* = \emptyset$ and every word in L_0 contains an occurrence of Z except the word $XcSY$. All splicing productions involve a word containing Z, which always appears between the two occurrences of $\#$. Therefore, Z never appears in the word obtained by splicing, which means that each splicing operation must involve a word in L_0.

Rotation productions are applied to words of the form $X\gamma sY$ beginning with productions of the form $(ii)_1$, and using $ZY_s \in L_0$ as $(X\gamma sY, ZY_s) \rightarrow X\gamma Y_s$. Next, we can apply only a production of the form $(ii)_2$ using a word $X'sZ \in L_0$: $(X'sZ, X\gamma Y_s) \rightarrow X's\gamma Y_s$. The splicing process may continue only by using a production of the form $(ii)_3$ as $(X's\gamma Y_s, ZY) \rightarrow X's\gamma Y$. The symbol X' can be removed only by an application of a production of the form $(ii)_4$: $(XZ, X's\gamma Y_s) \rightarrow Xs\gamma Y_s$. Observe that the combined effect of the splicing productions of group *(ii)* was to "rotate" the symbol s and the word γ.

We claim that if $S \overset{n}{\underset{G}{\Rightarrow}} \theta$, then $Xc\theta Y \in \mathcal{S}^*(L_0)$. The proof is by induction on $n \in \mathbb{N}$. For $n = 0$ we have $\theta = S$ and $XcSY \in L_0 \subseteq \mathcal{S}^*(L_0)$.

Suppose that the statement holds for all derivations of length n and consider a derivation $S \overset{n+1}{\underset{G}{\Rightarrow}} \theta$, where the production used in the last step is $\alpha \to \theta$. We can write as

$$S \overset{n}{\underset{G}{\Rightarrow}} \theta_0\alpha\theta_1 \underset{G}{\Rightarrow} \theta_0\beta\theta_1 = \theta.$$

By the inductive hypothesis, we have $Xc\theta_0\alpha\theta_1 Y \in \mathcal{S}^*(L_0)$. Using the rotation splicing productions repeatedly we "rotate" the symbols of θ_1 and obtain the word $X\theta_1 c\theta_0\alpha Y$. Now, by use of the splicing production $X\gamma\#\alpha Y\$Z\#\beta Y$ and the fact that $Z\beta Y \in L_0$ we have

$$(X\theta_1 c\theta_0\alpha Y, Z\beta Y) \rightarrow X\theta_1 c\theta_0\beta Y.$$

By repeatedly applying rotation productions, we obtain the word $Xc\theta_0\beta\theta_1 Y = Xc\theta Y$, so $Xc\theta Y \in \mathcal{S}^*(L_0)$.

Conversely, we prove that if $X\theta' c\theta'' Y \in \mathcal{S}^n(L_0)$, then $S \overset{*}{\underset{G}{\Rightarrow}} \theta'\theta''$. The argument is by induction on n.

For $n = 0$, we have $X\theta' c\theta'' Y \in L_0$, and the definition of L_0 implies $\theta' = \lambda$ and $\theta'' = S$, so the statement clearly holds. Suppose that the statement holds for n, and let $X\theta' c\theta'' Y \in \mathcal{S}^{n+1}(L_0) = \mathcal{S}^n(L_0) \cup \mathcal{S}(\mathcal{S}^n(L_0))$. If $X\theta' c\theta'' Y \in \mathcal{S}^n(L_0)$, then the statement holds by the inductive hypothesis. Let $X\theta' c\theta'' Y \in \mathcal{S}(\mathcal{S}^n(L_0))$. This means that $X\theta' c\theta'' Y$ is obtained from the words $\theta_0 \in L_0$ and a word $\eta \in \mathcal{S}^n(L_0)$ by applying a splicing production. Note that θ_0 must contain an occurrence of Z.

Note that the word $X\theta' c\theta'' Y$ contains neither X' nor any Y_s. Therefore, we can assume that $X\theta' c\theta'' Y$ was obtained by applying a simulation production $X\gamma\#\alpha Y\$Z\#\beta Y$, where $\alpha \rightarrow \beta$ is a production of the grammar. Then, we have $\eta = X\gamma\alpha Y$ and $\theta_0 = Z\beta Y$. Note that c must occur in γ, which means that we can write $\gamma = \theta' c\zeta$ and $\zeta\beta = \theta''$. Therefore, $\eta = X\theta' c\zeta\alpha Y$. By the inductive hypothesis, there exists a derivation $S \overset{*}{\underset{G}{\Rightarrow}} \theta'\zeta\alpha$. Using the production $\alpha \rightarrow \beta$ we have $S \overset{*}{\underset{G}{\Rightarrow}} \theta'\zeta\alpha \underset{G}{\Rightarrow} \theta'\zeta\beta = \theta'\theta''$.

Thus, we have proved that $X\theta' c\theta'' Y \in \mathcal{S}^*(L_0)$ if and only if $S \overset{*}{\underset{G}{\Rightarrow}} \theta'\theta''$.

The group of terminal splicing productions allow us to eliminate the extraneous symbols X, c and Y. Note that Xc in a word $XcxY$ can be removed by a splicing production of the form $(iii)_1$ applied to $ZY \in L_0$ and to $XcxY$ for some $x \in A_T^*$. This allows us to write $(ZY, XcxY) \twoheadrightarrow xY$. Finally, using the production $(iii)_2$ we have $(xY, XZ) \twoheadrightarrow x$.

Suppose that $x \in \mathcal{S}^*(L_0) \cap A_T^*$. This can happen only if $XcxY \in \mathcal{S}^*(L_0)$, which, by the previous argument, implies $X \overset{*}{\underset{G}{\Rightarrow}} x$. Thus, $\mathcal{S}^*(L_0) \cap A_T^* \subseteq L$. Conversely, if $x \in L$, then $S \overset{*}{\underset{G}{\Rightarrow}} x$, so $Xx'cx''Y \in \mathcal{S}^*(L_0)$ for some x', x'' such that $x'x'' = x$. Applying terminal splicing productions we obtain $x'x'' \in \mathcal{S}^*(L_0)$, so $x = x'x'' \in \mathcal{S}^*(L_0) \cap A_T^*$. ∎

11.4 Exercises

L-Systems

1. Let $S = (\{a, b, c\}, c, s)$ be the *0L*-system defined by $s(a) = \{a\}$, $s(b) = \{b\}$ and $s(c) = \{aca, bcb\}$. Determine the language $L(S)$.
2. $^\diamond$ Prove that no language $\{a^m, a^k\}$, where $k, m \geq 1$ and $k \neq m$ belongs to $\mathcal{L}_{0L}$.
3. Determine $L(S)$, where $S = (\{a\}, a, h)$ and $h(a) = a^p$.
4. Prove that $\mathcal{L}_{0L}$ is strictly included in $\mathcal{L}_1$.
5. $^\diamond$ Prove that the language $L = \{\lambda, a^5, a^{10}, a^{15}, a^{20}\}$ is not a *0L*-language.
6. $^\diamond$ Let A be an alphabet. Prove that there are languages $L \subseteq A^*$ such that $L \in \mathcal{L}_{0L}$ and $A^+ - L \notin \mathcal{L}_{0L}$.

7. $^{\circ\circ}$ Prove that it is undecidable whether $L(S) = L(S')$, where S, S' are two $0L$-systems.
   Hint. Use the undecidability of the equality of the sets of sentential forms of two context-free grammars (see Exercise 65).

Let $A = \{a_0, \ldots, a_{k-1}\}$ be an alphabet and let $S = (A, x, h)$ be a $D0L$-system. The *growth function* of S is a function $\ell_S : \mathbb{N} \longrightarrow \mathbb{N}$ given by $\ell_S(n) = |h^{(n)}(x)|$. Define the $k \times k$ matrix M_S by $(M_S)_{ij} = n_{a_j}(h(a_i)$ for $0 \leq i, j \leq k-1$. If $\mathsf{pk} : A^* \longrightarrow \mathbb{N}^k$ is the mapping introduced in Definition 5.9.1, then it is easy to verify that $\mathsf{pk}(h(w)) = \mathsf{pk}(w)M_S$. Moreover, since $|w| = \mathsf{pk}\vec{u}^T$, we have $\ell_S(n) = \mathsf{pk}(x)(M_S)^n\vec{u}^T$, where $\vec{u}$ is the $(1 \times k)$-vector $(1, 1, \ldots, 1)$ and $\vec{u}^T$ is its transposed $(k \times 1)$-vector.

8. Let $S = (\{a, b\}, a, h)$ be the $D0L$-system defined by $h(a) = ab$ and $h(b) = a$.
   (a) Prove that $M_S^2 = M_S + I_2$, where
   $$I_2 = \begin{pmatrix} 1 & 0 \\ 0 & 1 \end{pmatrix}$$
   (b) Using Part (a) show that $\ell_S(n+2) = \ell_S(n+1) + \ell_S(n)$ for $n \in \mathbb{N}$.
9. Prove that if $S = (A, x, h)$ is a $D0L$-system, then
   $$\ell_S(n) = \mathsf{pk}(x) M_S^n (1, 1, \ldots, 1)^T$$
   for $n \in \mathbb{N}$.
10. Using Cayley-Hamilton's Theorem prove that if ℓ_S is the growth function of a $D0L$-system $S = (A, x, h)$ satisfies the recurrence
    $$\ell_S(n+k) = c_{k-1}\ell_S(n+k-1) + \cdots + c_0\ell_S(n)$$
    for $n \in \mathbb{N}$, where $k = |A|$ and $c_0, \ldots, c_{k-1} \in \mathbb{N}$.
11. $^{\circ\circ}$ Prove that the growth function of a $D0L$-system is either an exponential or a polynomial.
12. $^{\circ}$ Let $S = (\{a_0, \ldots, a_{k-1}\}, x, h)$ be a $0L$-system such that $n_{a_i}(h(a_i)) = 1$ for $0 \leq i \leq k-1$. Also, assume that if a_j occurs in $h(a_i)$ then $j \geq i$ for $0 \leq i, j \leq k-1$. Prove that $\ell_S(n)$ is a polynomial in n.

The notion of $0L$ system can be extended by allowing the existence of nonterminal symbols. An *extended $0L$-system* ($E0L$-system) is a 4-tuple $E = (A, x, s, B)$, where (A, x, s) is an $0L$-system and $B \subseteq A$ is the *terminal alphabet of* E. The language generated E is

$$L(E) = \{w \in B^* \mid w \in s^{(n)}(x) \text{ for some } n \in \mathbb{N}\}.$$

The symbols in $A - B$ are the *nonterminal symbols of* E.

A language $L \subseteq B^*$ is an $E0L$-language if $L = L(E)$ for some extended $0L$-system E.

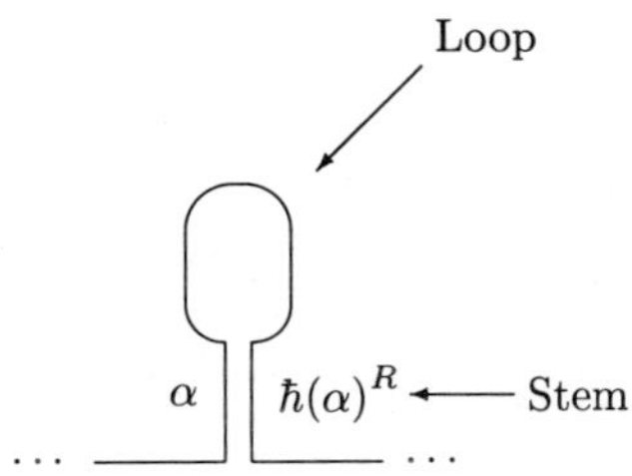

Figure 11.9: Coiling of a Strand of Nucleotides

13. ◇ Prove that every finite language is an *E0L*-language.
14. ◇ An *EOL*-system $E = (A, x, s, B)$ is *synchronized* if for every symbol $b \in B$, $z \in s^{(n)}(b)$ for $n \geq 1$ implies $z \notin B^*$. In other words, E is synchronized if every word word derivable from a terminal word must contain a nonterminal symbol.
   Let S, Z be two symbols such that $S, Z \notin A$. Define the *E0L*-system $E' = (A', S, s', B')$, where $B' = \{b' \mid b \in B\}$, $A' = A \cup B' \cup \{S, Z\}$. For $w \in A^*$ denote by w' the word obtained from w by replacing all symbols in B by their primed versions. The substitution s' is defined by
   $$\begin{aligned} s'(a) &= \{w' \mid w \in s(a)\} \cup s(a) \text{ for } a \in \\ s'(a') &= \{w' \mid w \in s(a)\} \cup s(a) \end{aligned}$$
   Prove that for every *E0L*-system E there exists a synchronized *E0L*-system E' such that $L(E) = L(E')$.

Nucleic Acids

15. ◇ Define the mapping $\ell : A^*_{\mathbf{DNA}} \longrightarrow A^*_{\mathbf{DNA}}$ by $\ell(x) = \hbar(x)^R$ for $x \in A^*_{\mathbf{DNA}}$.
    (a) Prove that ℓ is not a morphism.
    (b) Prove that $\ell^{(2)}(x) = x$ for $x \in A^*_{\mathbf{DNA}}$. This is known as the involutive property of ℓ.
16. ◇ Let $\sigma = \sigma'\alpha\alpha'\sigma''$ and $\theta = \theta'\beta\beta'\theta''$ be two DNA molecules such that $\alpha\alpha'$, $\beta\beta'$ are recognition sites for some restriction enzymes and points of cleavage occur between α and α' in the first molecule and between β and β' in the second molecule. If both restriction sites are palyndromic and $\alpha' -_r \alpha^R = \beta' -_r \beta^R$, show that the resulting fragments may be spliced to form new DNA molecules.
17. The strands of a double-stranded DNA can be separated through a process called *denaturation*. Then, the resulting strands can acquire a *secondary structure* by folding. For example, if a DNA strand contains both a sequence $\alpha \in A^*_{\mathbf{DNA}}$ and its *reverse complement*, $\hbar\alpha^R$, then the strand may coil as shown in Figure 11.9. The formation resulting in dis way displays a *stem* and a *loop*.

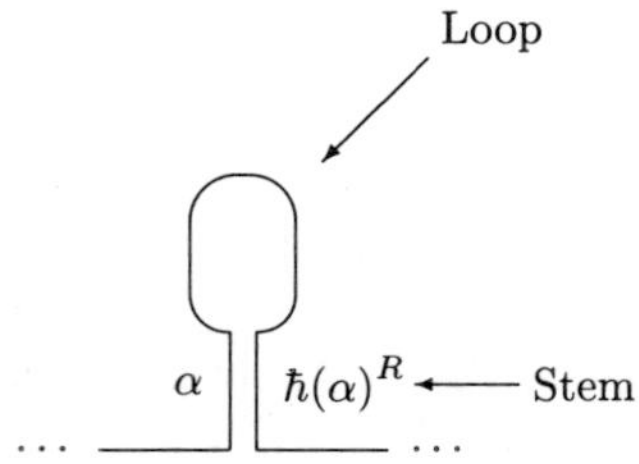

Figure 11.10: Pseudoknot formed by a DNA strand

- Prove that a DNA strand may display this type of coiling if and only if both the strand and its opposite contain an identical infix α.
- Biochemical considerations require that the infixes that form a coil should have a minimal length and they should be located at not too distant sites in the sequence. This is formalized by requiring that the strands that form coils belong to the language

$$L_{p,q} = \{\alpha\beta\hbar(\alpha)^R \mid \alpha, \beta \in A^*_{\mathbf{DNA}}, |\alpha| \geq p, |\beta| \leq q\}.$$

Prove that $L_{p,q}$ is a context-free, non-regular language.

18. $^\diamond$ A DNA may coil to form a *pseudoknot*, as shown in Figure 11.10. Prove that the language

$$L_k = \{\alpha\beta\hbar(\alpha)^R\hbar(\alpha)^R \mid \alpha, \beta \in A^*_{\mathbf{DNA}}\}$$

that describes the pseudoknots is not a context-free language.
Hint. Consider the intersection $L_k \cap \mathsf{G}^+\,\mathsf{A}^+\,\mathsf{C}^+\,\mathsf{T}^+$.

19. $^{\diamond\diamond}$ Consider the operations of duplication, inversion, transposition, and deletion on languages on $A_{\mathbf{DNA}}$ defined by:

$$\begin{aligned} \mathsf{DUP}(L) &= \{xuuy \mid xuy \in L\} \\ \mathsf{INV}(L) &= \{xuvy \mid xvuy \in L\} \\ \mathsf{XPOS}(L) &= \{x \mid \in L\} \\ \mathsf{DEL}(L) &= \{xy \mid xuy \in L\} \end{aligned}$$

for $L \subseteq A^*_{\mathbf{DNA}}$. These operations describe known rearrangements of nucleotide strands. Prove that $\mathcal{L}_2$ is not closed with respect to any of these operations.

20. Prove that if $\mathcal{F}$ is the class of finite languages, then $S(\mathcal{F}, \mathcal{L}_0) = \mathcal{F}$.
21. $^\diamond$ Prove that $S(\mathcal{L}_2, \mathcal{L}_3) = \mathcal{L}_2$.
22. . Prove that for every language $L \subseteq A^*$ there exists an H-schema $\mathcal{S} = (A \cup \{c\}, F)$, where $c \notin A$ and F is a finite set of productions such that $\mathcal{S}^*(L) = L$.
23. $^\diamond$ Prove that $\mathcal{F} \subseteq \mathcal{H}(\mathcal{F}, \mathcal{L}_3) \subseteq \mathcal{L}_3$.

An *insertion-deletion system* (or an *insdel system*)is a semi-Thue system $T = (A, M, P)$ whose productions have one of the following forms:

(i) $\alpha\beta \rightarrow \alpha\theta\beta$ (insertion of θ in the context (α, β);
(ii) $\alpha\theta\beta \rightarrow \alpha\beta$ (deletion of θ in the context (α, β),
where $\alpha, \beta, \theta \in A^*$.

$INS_n^m DEL_p^q$ denotes the class of languages generated by insdel systems that satisfy the following conditions:

$$\begin{aligned}
\max\{|\theta| \mid \alpha\beta \rightarrow \alpha\theta\beta \in P\} &= n, \\
\max\{|\alpha|, |\beta| \mid \alpha\beta \rightarrow \alpha\theta\beta \in P\} &= m, \\
\max\{|\theta| \mid \alpha\theta\beta \rightarrow \alpha\beta \in P\} &= p, \\
\max\{|\alpha|, |\beta| \mid \alpha\theta\beta \rightarrow \alpha\beta \in P\} &= q.
\end{aligned}$$

If $n = 0$, we assume that $m = 0$; also, if $p = 0$, $q = 0$.

Computing based on insertions and deletions can be used for modeling the action of enzymes on DNA sequences.

24. Prove that $INS_n^m DEL_p^q \subseteq \mathfrak{L}_0$ and $INS_n^m DEL_0^0 \subseteq \mathfrak{L}_1$ for $n, m, p, q \in \mathbb{N}$.
25. $\diamond$ Prove that $\mathfrak{L}_0 = INS_3^2 DEL_3^0$.

Solution. By Exercise 24 it is sufficient to prove that $\mathfrak{L}_0 \subseteq INS_3^2 DEL_3^0$. Let $L \in \mathfrak{L}_0$, where L is generated by a grammar $G = (A_N, A_T, S, P)$ in Kuroda normal form (cf. Exercise 17 of Chapter 9). The productions of G are either context-free (of the form $X \rightarrow \theta$, where $|\theta| \leq 1$) or have the form $XY \rightarrow UV$, where X, Y, U, V are nonterminal symbols.

The insdel system $T = (A_N \cup A_T \cup \{K, K', E\}, SEE, P')$ is defined by the following set of insertion productions:

(a) if $X \rightarrow \theta \in P$, then $Xss' \rightarrow XK_1\theta ss' \in P'$;
(b) if $XY \rightarrow UV \in P$, then $XYss' \rightarrow XYK_2UVss'$,

for $s, s' \in A_N \cup A_T \cup \{E\}$. In addition, P' contains the deletion productions $XK_1 \rightarrow \lambda$, $XYK_2 \rightarrow \lambda$, and $EE \rightarrow \lambda$ for $X, Y \in A_N$. It is easy to verify that $\alpha \underset{G}{\Rightarrow} \beta$ implies $\alpha EE \overset{*}{\underset{T}{\Rightarrow}} \beta EE$. Therefore, if $S \overset{*}{\underset{G}{\Rightarrow}} x$, then $SEE \overset{*}{\underset{T}{\Rightarrow}} xEE \underset{G}{\Rightarrow} x$, so $L(G) \subseteq L_g(T|A_T)$.

Conversely, suppose that $SEE \overset{*}{\underset{T}{\Rightarrow}} x$. The key observation is that neither K_1 nor K_2 are part of the right context ss' required for the application of an insertion production of of P'. Thus, the K_1 and its preceeding symbol, and K_2 and the two symbols that precede K_2 remain unaffected by the application of other productions. This allows us to assume that the application of the production $Xss' \rightarrow XK_1\theta ss'$ may be immediately followed by the application of $XK_1 \rightarrow \lambda$, and an application of $XYss' \rightarrow XYK_2UV$ may be immediately followed by an application of $XYK_2 \rightarrow \lambda$. Consequently, if $SEE \overset{*}{\underset{T}{\Rightarrow}} xEE$, then there exists a derivation

$$\begin{aligned}
&SEE = \gamma_0 EE \underset{G}{\Rightarrow} \cdots \gamma_{2k} EE \underset{G}{\Rightarrow} \gamma_{2k+1} EE \underset{G}{\Rightarrow} \gamma_{2k+2} EE \underset{G}{\Rightarrow} \\
&\cdots \underset{G}{\Rightarrow} \gamma_{2n+2} = xEE
\end{aligned}$$

such that the production applied in each step $\gamma_{2k} EE \underset{G}{\Rightarrow} \gamma_{2k+1} EE$ has the form $Xss' \rightarrow XK_1\theta ss'$ or $XYss' \rightarrow XYK_2UVss'$, and the production applied in each step $\gamma_{2k+1}EE \underset{G}{\Rightarrow} \gamma_{2k+2}EE$ is either of the form $XK_1 \rightarrow \lambda$ or $XYK_2 \rightarrow \lambda$, respectively. Correspondingly, there exists a derivation

$$S = \gamma_0 \underset{G}{\Rightarrow} \gamma_2 \underset{G}{\Rightarrow} \cdots \underset{G}{\Rightarrow} \gamma_{2n} = x,$$

which implies $x \in L(G)$.

11.5 Bibliographical Comments

L-systems were introduced in [Lindenmayer, 1968a; Lindenmayer, 1968b]. Theorem 11.2.10 appears in [Rozenberg and Doucet, 1973]. The main references for this area are [Herman and Rozenberg, 1975] and [Rozenberg and Salomaa, 1980]. The characterization of $U0L$-languages contained in Corollary 11.2.15 and its preparatory Theorems 11.2.12– 11.2.14 were obtained in [Herman *et al.*, 1973] and discussed in [Herman and Rozenberg, 1975].

For introductions to molecular biology the reader could consult [Hunter, 1993; Drlica, 1997].

Theorem 11.3.13 was obtained in [Păun *et al.*, 1998]; a stronger result was obtained in [Păun *et al.*, 1996] and is discussed in [Head *et al.*, 1997]. Theorem 11.3.14 is referred to as the "basic universal lemma" in [Păun *et al.*, 1998] and was obtained in a more general form in [Păun, 1996].

Exercises 17–19 are from [Searls, 1993]. Insertion-deletion systems are introduced in [L. Kari, 1996]; the proof included in the solution of Exercise 25 belongs to [Păun *et al.*, 1998] and is much simpler than the original proof; in addition, in [Păun *et al.*, 1998] the reader can find stronger representation results for recursively enumerable languages using insdel systems.

Bibliography

Ackermann, W. [1928]. Zum Hilbertschen Aufbau der reellen Zahlen. *Mathematische Annalen,* **99**, 118–133.

Aho, A. V., and Ullman, J.D. [1972]. *The Theory of Parsing, Translation and Compiling.* Englewood Cliffs, N.J.: Prentice Hall.

Ash, R. B. [1965]. *Information Theory.* New York: Dover Publications.

Asser, G. [1960]. Rekursive Wortfunktionen. *Zeitschrift für Mathematische Logik und Grundlagen der Mathematik,* **6**, 258–278.

Baker, B. S. [1972]. Context-sensitive grammars generating context-free languages. In *Automata, Languages and Programming* (Nivat, M., ed.). Amsterdam: North Holland, pp. 501–506.

Bar-Hillel, Y., Perles, M., and Shamir, E. [1961]. On formal properties of simple phrase structure grammars. *Z. für Phonetik, Sprachwissenschaft und Kommunikationsforschung,,* **14**, 143–172.

Berstel, J., and Perrin, D. [1985]. *Theory of Codes.* New York: Academic Press.

Book, R. V. [1972]. Terminal context in context-sensitive grammars. *SIAM J. Comput.* **1**, 20–30.

Brainerd, W. S., and Landweber, L. H. [1974]. *Theory of Computation.* New York: John Wiley.

Chandra, A.K., Kozen, D.C., and Stockmeyer, L.J. [1981]. Alternation. *J. of ACM,* **28**, 114–133.

Chomsky, N. [1956]. Three models for the description of language. *IRE Trans. on Information Theory,* **2**, 113–124.

Chomsky, N. [1959]. On certain formal properties of grammars. *Information and Control,* **2**, 137–167.

Chomsky, N., and Schützenberger, M. P. [1963]. The algebraic theory of context-free languages. In *Computer Programming and Formal Systems* (Braffort, P., and D.Hirschberg, eds.). Amsterdam: North-Holland, pp. 118–161.

Cummings, L. J., ed. [1983]. *Combinatorics on Words — Progress and Perspectives.* Toronto, New York: Academic Press.

Cutland, N. J. [1983]. *Computability — An Introduction to Recursive Function Theory.* Cambridge: Cambridge University Press.

Davis, M. D., Sigal, R., and Weyuker, E. J. [1994]. *Complexity, Computability and Languages.* Boston: Academic Press, second edition.

Dedekind, R. [1930]. *Gesammelte mathematische Werke* (R. Frieke, ed.). Braunschweig: F. Vieweg and Sohn.

Drlica, K. [1997]. *Understanding DNA and Gene Cloning — A Guide for the Curious.* New York: John Wiley, third edition.

Ehrenfeucht, A., Păun, Gh., and Rozenberg, G. [1997]. Contextual grammars and formal languages. In *Handbook of Formal Languages* (Rozenberg, G., and Salomaa, A., eds.) volume 2. Berlin: Springer-Verlag, pp. 237–293.

Eilenberg, S., and Elgot, C.C. [1970]. *Recursiveness.* New York: Academic Press.

Even, S. [1964]. Rational numbers and regular events. *IEEE Trans. Electronic Comput.* **13**, 740–741.

Fejer, P. A., and Simovici, D. A. [1991]. *Mathematical Foundations of Computer Science*, volume 1. New York: Springer Verlag.

Floyd, R.W., and Beigel, R. [1994]. *The Language of Machines — An Introduction to Computability and Formal Languages.* New York: Computer Science Press.

Gardner, J., Retterath, C., and Gisin, E. [1988]. *MKS LEX & YACC.* Waterloo, Ontario: Mortice Kern Systems, Inc.

Geffert, V. [1988]. A representation of recursively enumerable languages by two momomorphisms and a quotient. *Theoretical Computer Science,* **62**, 235–249.

Geffert, V. [1991]. Normal forms for phrase-structure grammars. *R.A.I.R.O Informatique théorique,* **25**, 473–496.

Ginsburg, S. [1962]. Examples of abstract machines. *IEEE Trans. on Electronic Computers,* **11**, 132–135.

Ginsburg, S. [1966]. *The Mathematical Theory of Context-Free Languages.* New York: McGraw-Hill.

Ginsburg, S. [1975]. *Algebraic and Automata-Theoretic Properties of Formal Languages.* New York: North-Holland/American Elsevier.

Ginsburg, S., and Greibach, S. [1966]. Mappings which preserve context-sensitive languages. *Information and Control,* **9**, 563–582.

Ginsburg, S., Greibach, S., and Harrison, M. [1967]. One-way stack automata. *J. of Assoc. Comput. Mach.* **14**, 389–418.

Ginsburg, S., and Rice, H. G. [1962]. Two families of languages related to ALGOL. *J. of ACM,* **9**, 350–371.

Ginsburg, S., and Rose, G.F. [1963]. Operations which preserve definability in languages. *J. of ACM,* **10**, 175–195.

Ginsburg, S., and Rose, G.F. [1966]. Preservation of languages by transducers. *Information and Control,* **9**, 153–176.

Ginsburg, S., and Spanier, E. H. [1963]. Quotients of context-free languages. *J. of ACM,* **10**, 487–492.

Glaister, I., and Shallit, J. [1996]. A lower bound technique for the size of nondeterministic finite automata. *Information Processing Letters,* **59**, 75–77.

Gödel, K. [1965a]. On formally undecidable propositions of the principia mathematica and related systems, i. In *The Undecidable* (Davis, M., ed.). Hewlett, New York: Raven Press, pp. 5–38.

Gödel, K. [1965b]. On undecidable propositions of formal mathematical systems.

In *The Undecidable* (Davis, M., ed.). Hewlett, New York: Raven Press, pp. 41–74.

Greibach, S. [1968]. A note on undecidable properties of formal languages. *Math. Systems Theory,*, **16**, 1–6.

Greibach, S. A. [1965]. A note on code sets and context free languages. Mathematical Linguistics and Automatic Translation 15, Harvard Univ. Computation Lab. Rept.

H. Rogers, Jr. [1987]. *Theory of Recursive Functions and Effective Computability.* Cambridge, Massachusetts: The MIT Press.

Harrison, M. A. [1978]. *Introduction to Formal Language Theory.* Reading, MA: Addison-Wesley.

Head, T., Păun, Gh., and Pixton, D. [1997]. Language theory and molecular genetics. In *Handbook of Formal Languages* (Rozenberg, G., and Salomaa, A., eds.) volume 2. Berlin: Springer-Verlag, pp. 295–360.

Hennie, F. [1977]. *Introduction to Computability.* Reading, Massachusetts: Addison-Wesley.

Herman, G. T., Lee, K. P., van Leeuwen, J., and Rozenberg, G. [1973]. Characterization of unary developmental languages. *Discrete Mathematics,* **6**, 235–247.

Herman, G. T., and Rozenberg, G. [1975]. *Developmental Systems and Languages.* Amsterdam: North Holland.

Hermes, H. [1965]. *Enumerability, Decidability, Computability.* Berlin, New York: Springer-Verlag and Academic Press.

Hibbard, T. [1966]. *Scan Limited Automata and Context Limited Grammars.* Ph.D. thesis, University of California at Los Angeles.

Hilbert, D. [1926]. Über das Unendliche. *Mathematische Annalen,* **95**, 161–190.

Holcombe, W.M.L. [1982]. *Algebraic Automata Theory.* Cambridge: Cambridge University Press.

Hopcroft, J. E. [1969]. On the equivalence and containment problems for context-free langauges. *Mathematical Systems Theory,* **3**, 119–124.

Hopcroft, J. E., and Ullman, J. D. [1979]. *Introduction to Automata Theory, Languages and Computation.* Reading, MA: Addison-Wesley.

Huffman, D. A. [1954]. The synthesis of sequential switching circuits. *J. Franklin Inst.* **257**, 3–4,161–190,275–303.

Hunt, H. B., and Rosencrantz, D. J. [1978]. Computational parallels between the regular and context-free languages. *SIAM J. of Comput.* **7**, 99–114.

Hunter, L. [1993]. Molecular biology for computer scientists. In *Artificial Intelligence and Molecular Biology* (Hunter, L., ed.). Menlo Park: AAAI Press, pp. 1–46.

Igarashi, Y. [1977]. The tape complexity of some classes of Szilard languages. *SIAM J. of Computing,*, **6**, 460–466.

Immerman, N. [1988]. Nondeterministic space is closed under complementation. *SIAM J. Computing,*, **17**, 935–938.

J. Autebert, J. Berstel, L. Boasson [1997]. Context-free languages and pushdown automata. In *Handbook of Formal Languages* (Rozenberg, G., and Salomaa, A., eds.), volume 1. Berlin: Springer-Verlag, pp. 111–174.

Johnson, S. C., and Lesk, M. E. [1978]. Language development tools. *Bell Sys. Tech. Journal,*, **57**, 2155–2175.

Jones, N. D. [1966]. A survey of formal language theory. Technical Report 3, University of Western Ontario, London, Ontario.

Kleene, S. C. [1936]. General recursive functions of natural numbers. *Mathematische Annalen,* **112**, 727–742.

Kleene, S.C. [1956]. Representation of events in nerve nets and finite automata. In *Automata Studies* (Shannon, C.E., and McCarthy, J., eds.). Princeton: Priceton University, pp. 3–42.

Kozen, D. C. [1981]. On induction vs. $*$-continuity. In *Proc. Workshop on Logics of Programs 1981* (Kozen, D. C., ed.), volume 131 of *Lecture Notes in Computer Science.* New York: Springer-Verlag, pp. 167–176.

Kozen, D. C. [1997]. *Automata and Computability.* New York: Springer-Verlag.

Kuroda, S.Y. [1964]. Classes of languages and linear-bounded automata. *Information and Control,* **7**, 207–233.

L. Kari, G. Thierrin [1996]. Contextual insertion/deletion and computability. *Information and Computation,* **131**, 47–61.

Landweber, P. S. [1963]. Three theorems on phrase structure grammars of type 1. *Information and Control,* **6**, 131–136.

Lewin, B., Siliciano, P., and Klotz, M. [1997]. *Genes VI.* Oxford: Oxford University Press.

Lindenmayer, A. [1968a]. Mathematical models for cellular interactions in development — I. Filaments with one-sided inputs. *J. Theoret. Biology,* **18**, 280–299.

Lindenmayer, A. [1968b]. Mathematical models for cellular interactions in development — II. Simple and branching filaments with two-sided inputs. *J. Theoret. Biology,* **18**, 300–315.

Lothaire, M. [1983]. *Combinatorics on Words.* Encyclopedia of Mathematics and its Applications. Reading, MA: Addison-Wesley.

Marcus, S. [1969]. Contextual grammars. *Rev. Roum. Math. Pures Appl.* **14**, 1525–1534.

McNaughton, R. [1982]. *Elementary Computability, Formal Languages, and Automata.* Englewood Cliffs: Prentice Hall.

Mealy, G. H. [1955]. A method for synthesizing sequential circuits. *Bell Sys. Tech. Journal,* **34**, 1045–1079.

Moore, E. F. [1956]. Gedanken experiments on sequential machines. In *Automata Studies* (Shannon, C.E., and McCarthy, J., eds.). Princeton: Priceton University, pp. 129–153.

Moriya, E. [1973]. Associate languages and derivational complexity of formal grammars and languages. *Inf. and Control,*, **22**, 139–162.

Myhill, J. [1957a]. Finite automata and the representation of events. WADD 57 624, Wright Patterson AFB, Dayton, Ohio.

Myhill, J. [1957b]. Finite automata and the representation of events. Technical Report WADD TR-57-624, Wright Patterson AFB, Ohio.

Nerode, A. [1958]. Linear automaton transformation. *Proc. AMS,* **9**, 541–544.

Oettinger, A. G. [1961]. Automatic syntactic analysis and the pushdown store.

In *Structure of Language and its Mathematical Aspects*, Proc. Symp. Appl. Math., pp. 104–129.

Parikh, R. J. [1961]. Language-generating devices. Quarterly Progress Report 60, Research Laboratory of Electronics, MIT.

Parikh, R. J. [1966]. On context-free languages. *J. of ACM,* **13**, 570–581.

Penttonen, M. [1972]. A normal form for context-sensitive grammars. *Annales Univ. Turkuensis,* **156**, 3–11.

Penttonen, M. [1974]. One-sided and two-sided context in context-sensitive grammars. *Information and Control,* **25**, 371–392.

Perrin, D. [1990]. Finite automata. In *Handbook of Theoretical Computer Science — vol. B.: Formal Models and Semantics* (van Leeuwen, J., ed.). Cambridge, MA: The MIT Press, pp. 3–57.

Post, E. L. [1946]. A variant of a recursively unsolvable problem. *Bull. Am. Math. Soc.*, **52**, 264–268.

Păun, G. [1982]. *Gramatici Contextuale.* Bucharest, Romania: Editura Academiei.

Păun, G., Rozenberg, G., and Salomaa, A. [1996]. Computing by splicing. *Theoretical Computer Science,* **168**, 321–336.

Păun, G., Rozenberg, G., and Salomaa, A. [1998]. *DNA Computing.* Berlin: Springer-Verlag.

Păun, Gh. [1996]. Regular extended h systems are computationally universal. *J. Automata, Languages, Combinatorics,* **1**, 27–36.

Rabin, M. O., and Scott, D. [1959]. Finite automata and their decision problems. *IBM J. Res.* **3**, 115–125.

Raney, G.N. [1958]. Sequential functions. *J. of ACM,* **5**, 177–180.

Révész, G. [1983]. *Introduction to Formal Languages.* New York: McGraw-Hill.

Rosencrantz, D. J. [1967]. Matrix equations and normal forms for context-free grammars. *J. of ACM,* **14**, 501–507.

Rosencrantz, D. J. [1969]. Programmed grammars and classes of formal languages. *J. of ACM,* **16**, 107–131.

Rovan, B. [1981]. A framework for studying grammars. In *Proceedings of the MFCS, 81*, Lecture Notes in Computer Science, 118, pp. 473–482.

Rozenberg, G., and Doucet, P. G. [1973]. On $0L$-languages. *Information and Control,* **19**, 302–318.

Rozenberg, G., and Salomaa, A. [1980]. *The Mathematical Theory of L-Systems.* New York: Academic Press.

Salomaa, A. [1964]. On the reducibility of events represented in automata. *Ann. Acad. Sci. Fennicae,* **353**, 3–16.

Salomaa, A. [1966]. Two complete axiom systems for the algebra of regular events. *J. ACM,* **13**, 158–169.

Salomaa, A. [1973]. *Formal Languages.* New York: Academic Press.

Salomaa, A. [1981]. *Jewels of Formal Language Theory.* Rockville, Maryland: Computer Science Press.

Sankoff, D., and Kruskal, J. B., eds. [1983]. *Time Warps, String Edits, and Macromolecules: The Theory and Practice of Sequence Comparison.* Reading, MA: Addison Wesley.

Schützenberger, M. P. [1963]. Context-free languages and pushdown automata. *Information and Control,* **6**, 246–264.

Schützenberger, M. P. [1965]. On finite monoids having only trivial subgroups. *Information and Control,* **8**, 190–194.

Searls, D. B. [1993]. The computational linguistics of biological sequences. In *Artificial Intelligence and Molecular Biology* (Hunter, L., ed.). Menlo Park: AAAI Press, pp. 47–120.

Shamir, E. [1967]. A representation theorem for algebraic and context-free power series in non-commutating variables. *Information and Control,*, **11**, 239–254.

Shannon, C. E. [1948]. A mathematical theory of communication. *Bell System Tech. J.*, **27**, 379–423,623–656.

Sheperdson, J. C. [1959]. The reduction of two-way automata to one-way automata. *IBM J. Res.*, **3**, 198–200.

Shyr, H. J. [1979]. *Free Monoids and Languages.* Taipei, Taiwan: Soochow University.

Simovici, D. A. [1980a]. Computing of graphs of relations using generative grammars. *R.A.I.R.O Informatique théorique,* **14**, 279–299.

Simovici, D. A. [1980b]. Context-sensitive languages and Ackermann's function. *Foundations of Control Engineering,* **5**, 91–103.

Simovici, D. A., and Istrail, S. [1978]. Computing grammars and context-sensitive languages. *R.A.I.R.O Informatique théorique,* **12**, 33–48.

Smith, D. W., ed. [1994]. *Biocomputing – Informatics and Genome Projects.* San Diego: Academic Press.

Stearns, R. E., and Hartmanis, J. [1963]. Regularity preserving modifications of regular expressions. *Information and Control,* **6**, 55–69.

Storer, J. A. [1988]. *Data Compression — Methods and Theory.* Rockville, Maryland: Computer Science Press.

Szelepcsényi, R. [1987]. The method of forcing for nondeterministic automata. *Bull. of the EATCS,* **33**, 96–100.

Tarjan, R. E. [1981a]. A unified approach to path problems. *J. of ACM,* **28**, 577–593.

Tarjan, R. E. [1981b]. Fast algorithms for solving path problems. *J. of ACM,* **28**, 594–614.

Thompson, K. [1968]. Regular expression search algorithm. *Comm. of ACM,* **11**, 419–422.

Watson, J. D., and Crick, F. H. C. [1953]. Molecular structure of nucleic acids: A structure for deoxyrybose nucleic acid. *Nature,* **171**, 737–738.

Notation Index

A listing of notation in the order in which it is defined.

Topic Index